The Christian Theological Tradition

D0706215

The fourth edition of *The Christian Theological Tradition* provides students with essential theological knowledge of key persons and events of the Bible and the Christian faith, and of Christianity's multifaceted encounter with Western culture.

Historically arranged, the textbook addresses major theological themes such as revelation, God, Jesus Christ, Creation, salvation, and the church. The textbook deals with the entire Christian tradition from an orientation that is both Catholic and ecumenical, with the fourth edition including expanded coverage of modern Protestant Christianity. *The Christian Theological Tradition* has been thoroughly revised and updated with nine new or rewritten chapters, including:

- A new section on the reception of the Second Vatican Council, including the pontificate of Pope Francis.
- A new treatment of contemporary developments in liberation and environmental theology.
- A new examination of the relationship between science and Christianity.
- An entirely rewritten treatment of Islam that focuses on the ways in which the Christian tradition has historically understood and responded to Islam.
- A new discussion of the "New Atheism," with theological responses to this influential movement.
- New textboxes on aspects of religious life, such as liturgy, prayer, art, moral teaching, and social institutions, appropriate to given chapters.

With the assistance of images and maps, key words, and recommended reading, this textbook outlines the methods for Christian theology and demonstrates the relevance of the Christian theological tradition for our contemporary world.

This is an ideal resource for students of theology, biblical studies, or religious studies, and anyone wanting an accessible and comprehensive introduction to the Christian theological tradition.

Mark McInroy received his doctorate from Harvard Divinity School, and after postdoctoral research at the University of Cambridge he joined the Theology Department at the University of St. Thomas, USA, where he is Associate Professor of Theology. He is the author of *Balthasar on the Spiritual Senses: Perceiving Splendour* (2014) for which he received the Manfred Lautenschlaeger Award for Theological Promise in 2015. In addition to his work on Balthasar, he has published examinations of Karl Rahner, Karl Barth, John Henry Newman, Martin Luther, and Origen of Alexandria in journals such as the *International Journal of Systematic Theology*, the *Scottish Journal of Theology*, and *Catholica*, along with several edited volumes. His current projects include co-editing with Anthony Sciglitano and Cyril O'Regan *The Oxford Handbook of Hans Urs von Balthasar* (forthcoming), and with C.A. Strine and Alexis Torrance *Image as Theology: The Power of Art in Shaping Christian Thought, Devotion, and Imagination* (forthcoming). He is presently completing a monograph on the view of deification found in Martin Luther's mature theology.

Michael J. Hollerich is Professor of Theology at the University of St. Thomas, USA. His teaching and academic interests include early Christian exegesis, religion and politics/political theology, modern German Catholic history, and Eastern Christianity. He has articles and chapters in books on all these subjects. His books include *Eusebius of Caesarea's* Commentary on Isaiah*: Christian Exegesis in the Age of Constantine* (1999), partial contribution to *Isaiah: Interpreted by Early Christian and Medieval Commentators*, ed. Robert L. Wilken (2007), and an edition in English of Erik Peterson's *Theological Tractates* (2011). He is currently finishing a book on the reception history of the *Ecclesiastical History* of Eusebius of Caesarea.

PRAISE FOR THE PREVIOUS EDITION

"I think *The Christian Theological Tradition* is the best introduction to the Christian tradition on the market."

Joseph Kroger, *St. Michael's College, Colchester, VT, USA*

ENDORSEMENTS FOR THE FOURTH EDITION

"This superb volume introduces students to the places, forms, and agents of a complex tradition incomprehensible without an accurate version of its historical settings. The new edition is indispensable for instructors and students alike."

Robin Darling Young, *The Catholic University of America, USA*

"This textbook is both thoroughly historical and genuinely theological; it displays the vibrancy and sophistication of Christian attempts to deal with questions of meaning in a way that is accessible to undergraduates and other beginners, whether Christian or not. The text as a whole makes a compelling case that one cannot understand the world today without understanding the Christian tradition. I taught the third edition of this book for many years; this new fourth edition is even better."

William T. Cavanaugh, *DePaul University, USA*

FOURTH EDITION

The Christian Theological Tradition

Edited by

Mark McInroy   **Michael J. Hollerich**

Routledge
Taylor & Francis Group

NEW YORK AND LONDON

Fourth edition published 2020
by Routledge
52 Vanderbilt Avenue, New York, NY 10017

and by Routledge
2 Park Square, Milton Park, Abingdon, Oxon, OX14 4RN

Routledge is an imprint of the Taylor & Francis Group, an informa business

First edition published by Pearson Education, Inc. 2000
Third edition published by Pearson Education, Inc. 2009

Published by Routledge 2016
First issued by Routledge in hardback in 2017

Library of Congress Cataloging-in-Publication Data
Title: The Christian theological tradition / edited by Mark McInroy and Michael J. Hollerich.
Description: Fourth [edition]. | New York : Routledge, 2019. | Includes bibliographical references and index.
Identifiers: LCCN 2018060718 (print) | LCCN 2019021963 (ebook) | ISBN 9781315537627 (eBook) | ISBN 9781138689480 (hardback : alk. paper) | ISBN 9781138689497 (pbk. : alk. paper)
Subjects: LCSH: Theology, Doctrinal–History. | Catholic Church–Doctrines–History. | Christian education–Textbooks for young adults–Catholic.
Classification: LCC BX1751.3 (ebook) | LCC BX1751.3 .C48 2019 (print) | DDC 230/.2–dc23
LC record available at https://lccn.loc.gov/2018060718
ISBN: 978-1-138-68948-0 (hbk)
ISBN: 978-1-138-68949-7 (pbk)
ISBN: 978-1-315-53762-7 (ebk)

Typeset in Bernhard Modern and Baskerville
by Wearset Ltd, Boldon, Tyne and Wear

In Memoriam
Professor Terence Nichols
(1941–2014)
Colleague and Friend

Contents

Figures and Maps

Textboxes

Moral Theology Textboxes
Bernard V. Brady, Amy Levad, Paul J. Wojda

Lived Religion Textboxes
Mary Margaret Hoden

Contributors

Cara Anthony is Associate Professor of Theology at the University of St. Thomas. Her research investigates the nexus of Christian Spirituality, environmental theology, and public life, especially in the practices of pilgrimage, liturgical processions, and faith-based protest marches. Her most recent publication is "Walking as Resistance to Hypermobility: The Camino de Santiago Pilgrimage," in *Spiritus: A Journal of Christian Spirituality* (Spring 2018).

Bernard V. Brady is a moral theologian with a particular interest in Christian social ethics. He is author of several books, including *Christian Love, Essential Catholic Social Thought*, and *Be Good & Do Good*. His articles have appeared in several scholarly journals, including *The Thomist*, the *Journal of Moral Theology*, and the *Journal of Catholic Social Thought*.

Corrine Carvalho has a master's degree from the Graduate Theological Union (Berkeley, CA) and a Ph.D. from Yale University, both in the field of Old Testament/Hebrew Bible. She is Professor in the Theology Department of the University of St. Thomas, and currently serves as Interim Dean of Social Work. Her primary area of research is exilic prophetic literature. She has written two textbooks, *Encountering Ancient Voices*, now in its second edition, and *Primer on Biblical Methods*, both with Anselm Academic. Her most recent book is *Reading Jeremiah* (Smyth & Helwys, 2016).

Richard Cogill teaches in the Theology Department at the University of St. Thomas. In addition, he assists at the Episcopal Parish of St. Andrew in Moose Lake, Minnesota. Prior to his current position, he served as the Dean of Studies for the Anglican archiepiscopal Diocese of Cape Town, and occasionally lectured in the Department of Theology at the University of the Western Cape in Cape Town, South Africa. In addition, he served as the Precentor (chief liturgist) at St. George's Cathedral in Cape Town. He has extensive experience in the NGO sector, having served as a Senior Associate with the Collective Leadership Institute based in Germany, Senior Associate for the Leadership Support and

Development Centre, Director of the Community Healing Network, and Director of the German/South African NGO, Südafrika und AIDS. He completed his bachelor's degree in English Literature at Gustavus Adolphus College (Minnesota), his Master of Divinity at Luther Seminary (Minnesota), and his Master in Sacred Theology at the General Theological Seminary (New York). He is currently a doctoral student at the University of the Western Cape in Cape Town, South Africa. He has taught in the United States, Palestine, South Africa, and South Korea.

David S. Cunningham is Professor of Religion at Hope College (Holland, MI) and Director of the Network for Vocation in Undergraduate Education (NetVUE), a nationwide consortium of more than 225 colleges and universities working to support their students in the work of vocational reflection and discernment. He is the author of five books on various topics in Christian theology and ethics, including *These Three Are One: The Practice of Trinitarian Theology* (Blackwell, 1998), *Friday, Saturday, Sunday: Literary Meditations on Suffering, Death, and New Life* (Westminster/John Knox, 2007), and *Christian Ethics: The End of the Law* (Routledge, 2008). He is also the editor of five books, including a series of three volumes on vocation and calling: *At This Time and In This Place: Vocation and Higher Education*; *Vocation across the Academy: A New Vocabulary for Higher Education*; and *Hearing Vocation Differently: Meaning, Purpose, and Identity in the Multi-Faith Academy* (all Oxford University Press, 2016, 2017, and 2019). He served on the faculty at the University of St. Thomas from 1990 until 1997.

Mark DelCogliano (Ph.D. Emory University, 2009) is Associate Professor of Theology at the University of St. Thomas. His research focuses on patristic doctrinal debates, theological developments, and scriptural exegesis in Late Antiquity. His books include *Basil of Caesarea's Anti-Eunomian Theory of Names: Christian Theology and Late-Antique Philosophy in the Fourth-Century Trinitarian Controversy* (Brill, 2010), as well as several volumes of translations of patristic texts, including *St. Basil of Caesarea: Against Eunomius* with Andrew Radde-Gallwitz (Catholic University of America Press, 2011), *Works on the Spirit: Athanasius the Great and Didymus the Blind* with Andrew Radde-Gallwitz and Lewis Ayres (St. Vladimir's Seminary Press, 2011), *Gregory the Great on the Song of Songs* (Cistercian Publications, 2012), *St. Basil the Great: On Christian Doctrine and Practice* (St. Vladimir's Seminary Press, 2012), and *St. Basil the Great: On Fasting and Feasts* with Susan R. Holman (St. Vladimir's Seminary Press, 2013). He is also one of the four co-editors of *The Cambridge Edition of Early Christian Writings*, a six-volume series offering new translations of a wide range of early Christian writings on the themes of God, Christ, practice, reading, community, and Creation.

Massimo Faggioli is Professor in the Department of Theology and Religious Studies at Villanova University (Philadelphia, PA). He worked in the John XXIII Foundation for Religious Studies in Bologna between 1996 and 2008 and received his Ph.D. from the University of Turin in 2002. His doctoral dissertation discussed the history of the appointment of bishops after the Council of Trent. He was co-chair of the study group "Vatican II Studies" for the American Academy of Religion from 2012 to 2017. His books and articles have been published in eight languages. His scholarly essays focus on Vatican II, on Church history in Italy, on the application of the Council of Trent, on the diplomacy of the Vatican, and on the new Catholic movements. His most recent publications in English include the books *Vatican II: The Battle for Meaning* (Paulist Press, 2012), *True Reform: Liturgy and Ecclesiology in Sacrosanctum Concilium* (Liturgical Press, 2012), *Sorting Out Catholicism: A Brief History of the New Ecclesial Movements* (Liturgical Press, 2014), *The Rising Laity: Ecclesial Movements since Vatican II* (Paulist Press, 2016), and *Catholicism and Citizenship: Political Cultures of the Church in the Twenty-First Century* (Liturgical Press, 2017).

Paul L. Gavrilyuk is an American Orthodox theologian and church historian of Ukrainian descent, who holds the Aquinas Chair in Theology and Philosophy in the Theology Department of the University of St. Thomas. Published in ten languages, his scholarly works include: *The Suffering of the Impassible God: The Dialectics of Patristic Thought* (Oxford University Press, 2004), *Georges Florovsky and the Russian Religious Renaissance* (Oxford University Press, 2013), and *The Spiritual Senses: Perceiving God in Western Christianity*, co-edited with Sarah Coakley (Cambridge University Press, 2012). He is the founding president of the International Orthodox Theological Association (iota-web.org).

Mary Margaret Hoden is a Senior Adjunct Professor in the Theology Department at the University of St. Thomas. She received her B.A. from the University of Minnesota, majoring in journalism and history. Her M.A.T. in Theology was earned at the Saint Paul Seminary School of Divinity. She received her Ph.D. in theology from the University of Notre Dame with a concentration in Liturgical Studies. Her doctoral dissertation was "A Visible Manifestation of the Invisible: The Relationship Between Architecture and Liturgy at Salisbury Cathedral." Dr. Hoden's areas of specialization are liturgy, Christian church architecture, and sacraments. In addition to her academic work, Dr. Hoden serves on her parish Liturgy Commission and was a member of the committee that designed the church's new 200-seat chapel. She has taught in the RCIA program, presented a lecture series, "Theology 101 for Adults," and currently serves as a lector and Eucharistic minister. She is a former member of the Commission on Women for the Archdiocese of St. Paul-Minneapolis, and has lectured at a number of parishes on liturgical topics.

David G. Hunter holds the Cottrill-Rolfes Chair of Catholic Studies at the University of Kentucky. He has published several books and numerous articles on Greek and Latin writers of the early church, among them Augustine, Ambrose, Ambrosiaster, Jerome, and John Chrysostom. His recent monograph, *Marriage, Celibacy, and Heresy in Ancient Christianity: The Jovinianist Controversy* (Oxford University Press, 2007), examined the phenomenon of resistance to asceticism in early Christianity. Co-editor of the *Oxford Handbook of Early Christian Studies* (Oxford University Press, 2008), Hunter is currently director of the Fathers of the Church, a series of translations published by The Catholic University of America Press, and a general editor of the forthcoming *Brill Encyclopedia of Early Christianity*. He is active on the editorial boards of several journals, among them *Vigiliae Christianae*, the *Journal of Early Christian Studies*, the *Journal of Late Antiquity*, *Augustinian Studies*, and *Augustiniana*. His publications have focused primarily on matters relating to marriage and celibacy, most recently on the origins of priestly celibacy.

Fr. (Jan) Michael Joncas, ordained in 1980 as a priest of the Archdiocese of St. Paul-Minneapolis, MN, holds degrees in English from the (then) College of St. Thomas in St. Paul, MN, and in liturgical studies from the University of Notre Dame, Notre Dame, IN, and the Pontificio Istituto Liturgico of the Ateneo S. Anselmo in Rome. He has served as a parochial vicar, a campus minister, and a parochial administrator (pastor). He is the author of six books and more than 250 articles and reviews in journals such as *Worship, Ecclesia Orans,* and *Questions Liturgiques.* He has composed and arranged more than 300 pieces of liturgical music. He is currently Artist in Residence and Research Fellow in Catholic Studies at the University of St. Thomas, St. Paul, Minnesota.

Sherry E. Jordon is Associate Professor of Historical Theology at the University of St. Thomas, specializing in Reformation theology. She received a Ph.D. from Yale University and a Master of Divinity degree from Yale Divinity School. As a result of her research on women in the Reformation, she selected and edited primary texts by women for *A Reformation Reader.* She has had articles on best practices for teaching theology published in the journal *Teaching Theology and Religion.* Her current research is focused on preserving and disseminating the history of the Re-Imagining Community, an influential and ecumenical Christian feminist movement that began with a conference in 1993 to celebrate the World Council of Churches' Ecumenical Decade of Churches in Solidarity with Women.

William Junker is Associate Professor of Catholic Studies at the University of St. Thomas. He has a B.A. in English from the University of Dallas in 2001, an M.A. in philosophy from Notre Dame in 2003, and a Ph.D. from the Committee on Social Thought and the Department of English of the University of Chicago in 2011. His essays and reviews have appeared in *Moreana, Shakespeare Quarterly, ELH, Modern Philology, Marginalia,* and *Religion and Literature.* He is writing a book about Shakespeare, ecclesiology, and historical periodization.

Anne H. King is Professor Emerita of Theology at the University of St. Thomas, where she taught for 32 years before retiring in 2017. Educated at Duke University, she received a B.A. in history before moving to the study of theology first at Duquesne University for her M.A. and then for a Ph.D. from Fordham University. Her research interests have been and continue to be diverse, with most of her writings and her professional papers given in the areas of medieval spirituality and mysticism, the history of mysticism, the theology of the Triune God, and the history of atheism and theism from the seventeenth century to the present. She is currently working on two manuscripts: one on the Trinity, and the other on theism and atheism.

Robert C. Koerpel received his doctorate in historical and systematic theology from the Catholic University of America in Washington, DC. He teaches theology at the University of St. Thomas in St. Paul, Minnesota. He has written articles and reviews on different modern Catholic theologians, the nature and development of tradition, theological aesthetics, and liturgical theology for the *Heythrop Journal: A Quarterly Review of Philosophy and Theology,* the *Journal of Ecumenical Studies, Logos: A Journal of Catholic Thought and Culture,* and *New Blackfriars.* He is co-editor of *Contemplating the Future of Moral Theology* and author of *Maurice*

Blondel: Transforming Catholic Tradition (University of Notre Dame Press, 2018) and *Maurice Blondel and Modern Theology* (forthcoming).

David T. Landry is Professor of Theology at the University of St. Thomas. He earned his Ph.D. in New Testament at Vanderbilt University. He teaches courses on the New Testament, Theology and the Mass Media, and the Bible and American Politics, among others. He has published articles on the Lukan Infancy Narrative, the parables of Jesus, the synoptic problem, and the theological interpretation of film. He was co-editor (with Catherine Cory) of the first two editions of *The Christian Theological Tradition* (Prentice Hall, 1999/2002). His book *Inquiry into the New Testament: Ancient Context to Contemporary Significance* will be published by Anselm Academic Press in 2019.

Amy Levad, a graduate of Emory University in Atlanta, GA, is Associate Professor of Theology at the University of St. Thomas. Her primary discipline is moral theology, with expertise in environmental degradation, restorative justice, mass incarceration, sacramental theology, and Catholic social thought. She has published two books: *Restorative Justice: Theories and Practices of Moral Imagination* and *Redeeming a Prison Society: A Liturgical and Sacramental Response to Mass Incarceration*. Her ongoing research explores faith-based responses to mass incarceration, including education, ministry, and community organizing efforts.

F. Dominic Longo is an accomplished facilitator of interreligious dialogue and scholar of comparative theology and Islamic studies. He has a doctorate in Arabic and Islamic Studies from Harvard University and a master's in comparative theology from Boston College. His principal scholarly interests are in Islamic and Christian religious literature, spirituality, and gender—all of which he explores in his recent book, *Spiritual Grammar: Genre and the Saintly Subject in Islam and Christianity* (Fordham University Press, 2017). From 2015 to 2018, he was director of the Muslim–Christian Dialogue Center and Assistant Professor of Theology at the University of St. Thomas. Dr. Longo has also taught courses in literature, theology, philosophy, Arabic language, and Islamic studies at Harvard, Northeastern University, and the New School in New York City.

Elaine Catherine MacMillan holds the licentiate in systematic theology from Saint Paul University (Ottawa) and the doctorate in systematic theology from the University of St. Michael's College (Regis College, Toronto). She currently teaches at the University of St. Thomas. Her research interests include ecclesiology and feminist and ecumenical theology. She enjoys teaching systematic theology, especially courses about women in the church and interfaith dialogue. She has taught at universities in Canada and the United States. Committed to transcultural learning through study-abroad programs, she has also taught theology and religious studies courses in Europe, North Africa, and Latin America.

John W. Martens is Professor of Theology at University of St. Thomas. He is the author, with Cornelia Horn, of *Let the Little Children Come to Me: Children and Childhood in Early Christianity* (Catholic University of America Press, 2009) and *One God, One Law: Philo of Alexandria on the Mosaic and Greco-Roman Law* (Brill, 2003). For four years, he wrote the popular scripture column at *America Magazine*, "The Word," and these columns are now gathered into three volumes and published as *The Word on the Street, Year A, Year B, Year C* (Liturgical Press, 2016–2018). In addition, his book *Paul, Pastoring God's People (Alive in the Word)* (Little Rock Scripture Study, 2018) has been recently published for use in church Bible studies. He continues to write widely on the lives of children in the ancient world, contributing to numerous academic volumes on children in the earliest churches, and editing, with Kristine Henriksen Garroway, a volume for Brill on the current study of children in the Hebrew Bible and New Testament and the methodologies utilized in such studies of ancient childhood.

Paul Niskanen is Professor of Theology at the University of St. Thomas. He specializes in the study of the Old Testament, with a particular interest in late prophetic and apocalyptic texts from the Second Temple period. Among his publications are *The Human and the Divine in History: Herodotus and the Book of Daniel* (T&T Clark) and *Isaiah 56–66* in the Berit Olam commentary series (Liturgical Press).

David Penchansky is Professor Emeritus of Old Testament at the University of St. Thomas, where he taught in the Theology Department for 29 years. His publications include *Betrayal of God: Ideological Conflict in Job* (Westminster John Knox Press, 1990); *What Rough Beast: Images of God in the Hebrew Bible* (Westminster John Knox Press, 1999); *Twilight of the Gods: Polytheism in the Hebrew Bible* (Westminster John Knox Press, 2005); and *Understanding Wisdom Literature: Conflict and Dissonance in the Hebrew Text* (Eerdmans, 2012). He has contributed articles to journals and reference works. He is currently writing about the Book of Hosea for the *New Jerome Biblical Commentary*, and completing a book about the Qur'an.

Philip Rolnick received his doctorate from Duke University in 1989, and after teaching at Greensboro College, has taught at the University of St. Thomas since 2003. He is Professor of Theology, and has served as chair of the Science and Theology Network (STN), a group that promotes public events and faculty research in science and theology in the Twin Cities. His three major research areas have been: (1) analogy—how words refer to God; (2) what personhood means for Christian faith; and (3) the relation of science and Christian theology. A fourth, recent interest has been the thought of C.S. Lewis. He has been the recipient of the Exemplary Teacher Award of Greensboro College; has received several Templeton Foundation grants; was a North Carolina Humanities Scholar; and received St. Thomas' University Scholars Grant, its highest research award. He has been a member of Notre Dame's Seminar on Human Distinctiveness and Princeton's Center of Theological Inquiry. His books include *Analogical Possibilities: How Words Refer to God* (Scholars Press, 1993); *Person, Grace, and God* (Eerdmans, 2007); and *Origins: God, Evolution, and the Question of the Cosmos* (Baylor University Press, 2015). *Origins*, which has been nominated for three national awards, takes the challenges of contemporary science, including evolutionary theory, and turns them to advantages for faith. He is currently writing a manuscript on faith in a post-Christendom landscape (Baylor University Press, forthcoming).

Robert St. Hilaire earned his doctorate from Harvard Divinity School in 2008. His dissertation examined the relationship between nature and grace as theorized by Pierre Rousselot, S.J. (1878–1915), one of the founding figures of Transcendental

Thomism and a forerunner to *la nouvelle théologie.* Dr. St. Hilaire is currently Associate Professor of Religious Studies at Niagara University in Western New York. His research, publications, and other writings concentrate on the thought of Thomas Aquinas and twentieth-century Thomism, but have also ventured into theological education and how to apply Thomist theology to problems in mental health. He teaches undergraduate courses on the history of Christianity, modern Catholic theology, theological anthropology, Christology, and the development of secularism and atheism.

Gerald W. Schlabach is Professor of Theology and past chair of the Department of Justice and Peace Studies at the University of St. Thomas. Before embarking on graduate studies and receiving his doctorate at the University of Notre Dame, he worked in church-related development and peacebuilding work in Nicaragua and Honduras in the 1980s. He is co-editor with Philip McManus of *Relentless Persistence: Nonviolent Action in Latin America* (New Society, 1991). At the University of St. Thomas, he has continued his interest in global Christianity by developing a course on the subject. He is the editor and lead author of *Just Policing, Not War: An Alternative Response to World Violence* (Liturgical Press, 2007) and co-editor with Margaret Pfeil of *Sharing Peace: Mennonites and Catholics in Conversation* (Liturgical Press, 2013). He is currently completing a book on Catholic peace theology tentatively titled *A Pilgrim People: Becoming a Catholic Peace Church.*

Ry O. Siggelkow (Ph.D., Princeton Theological Seminary) is Adjunct Professor of Theology at the University of St. Thomas and serves as Pastor at Faith Mennonite Church in Minneapolis, MN. His research focuses on twentieth-century theologies of liberation, including the crisis theology of Ernst Käsemann and the black theology of James Cone. With Nancy J. Duff, he is co-editor of the forthcoming volume, *The Revolutionary Gospel: Paul Lehmann and the Direction of Theology Today* (Lexington Books).

Edward Ulrich has been a member of the Theology Department at the University of St. Thomas since 2000. His bachelor's degree is from the University of Minnesota in chemistry, his master's from St. John's University in theology, and his doctorate from the Catholic University of America in comparative religion. He teaches courses in world religions, Hinduism and Buddhism, and Christian theology. In addition, he has led numerous study abroad trips. Four of them were to India and focused on the Hindu, Muslim, and Syriac Christian religions. His writing and research have focused mainly on interreligious dialogue. More recently, Ulrich spent the 2017–2018 academic year in India on a Fulbright Fellowship, researching the issue of violence versus nonviolence in the early stages of India's independence movement. Ulrich has given talks on a variety of topics at Madurai Kamaraja University, Annamalai University, Pondicherry University, Madras University, Jadavpur University, and the University of Mauritius.

Kimberly Vrudny is Professor of Systematic Theology at the University of St. Thomas and author of *Beauty's Vineyard: A Theological Aesthetic of Anguish and Anticipation* (The Liturgical Press, 2016) and *Friars, Scribes, and Corpses: A Marian Confraternal Reading of the Mirror of Human Salvation* (Peeters, 2010). She has lived in South Africa, and visits there almost annually, both to conduct research and to teach courses titled "AIDS, Apartheid, and the Arts of Resistance," as well as "Nazism and Apartheid: Theological Roots." Her academic interests are in the intersections of art, theology, and politics. She is currently investigating the role of seminaries in the transfer of the Nazi/Aryan project to South Africa, c.1933–1948.

Paul J. Wojda, Ph.D., is Associate Professor of Theology at the University of St. Thomas. He received his doctorate in moral theology from the University of Notre Dame in 1993. His areas of academic interest include Catholic health care ethics and political theology. His published essays have appeared in a variety of scholarly journals, including *Word and World*, *Pro Ecclesia*, *Soundings*, *Logos*, and the *Journal of the Society of Christian Ethics*.

Preface

The Christian Theological Tradition is now in its fourth edition as the textbook of the Theology Department of the University of St. Thomas in St. Paul, Minnesota. The book has changed greatly since its first edition in 1996, so it may be useful to readers to understand its history. It was originally intended as a supplement to the foundational course on the "Christian Theological Tradition" that has been taught to all undergraduates at St. Thomas since 1993. That course is the first of three courses required under the rubric of "Faith and the Catholic Tradition." Students subsequently take a second course in a sub-discipline of theology (biblical, historical, moral, or systematic) and then a third chosen from a wide menu of interdisciplinary courses. The foundational course was created by the department in order to meet the changing needs and character of its undergraduate student body. As an urban, Catholic, liberal-arts university, St. Thomas attracts an increasingly diverse body of students. They are drawn to its blend of liberal education and strong career preparation, within the moral and intellectual framework of the Catholic tradition (see the University's Mission Statement at the end of this Preface). Today at least half of our undergraduates come from non-Catholic backgrounds: a large Lutheran minority along with other Protestant denominations, a growing Muslim minority, Hmong students whose families are traditionally animist, and an increasing number of "nones" who profess no religious affiliation. Catholic students themselves are increasingly unversed in their own tradition, since fewer have received their primary and/or secondary education in Catholic schools.

With a mandate to teach students who thus often have little knowledge of the Bible, the major doctrines of Christianity, or the meaning and significance of various forms of Christian worship, the Theology Department therefore designed a foundational course consisting of an elementary introduction to the Bible and to modern methods of biblical interpretation; a broad survey of the Christian tradition focused on key exemplars and creative thinkers; and a selective treatment of modern issues and developments, guided by the documents of the Second Vatican Council. The course is thus intended in part to provide our students with the basic theological literacy necessary to engage in meaningful academic discourse about theological issues that impact their lives.

A second feature of the course is its commitment to teach through reading and analyzing primary texts. Reading a wide range of texts from across the Christian tradition and learning to think critically and write skillfully about these texts develops skills intrinsic to liberal education. A common list of readings is required of all sections of the course, with discretionary choices allowed as well. The substance of the list has changed quite a bit over time. Staple biblical texts have continued to be the opening chapters of Genesis, the call of Abraham, the Exodus story, and the giving of the Law to Moses, prophetic texts from Isaiah, the gospels, and Paul's letters. The list also regularly includes readings from Augustine, Thomas Aquinas, and Martin Luther, with a required reading from one of several texts from women writers. There are also key documents from ecumenical councils, including the Second Vatican Council.

When the Theology Department launched its foundational course in 1993, there was quick recognition of the need for a textbook to supplement and contextualize the primary readings. A number of different books were considered, but none met all of our needs. The department therefore resolved to writing its own, with the following desiderata in mind. We wanted a book sophisticated enough to provide our students with tools to grapple with the course's primary texts, but lucid and accessible enough so that they could read it on their own without a lot of instructor support. We wanted a book comprehensive enough to give instructors flexibility for developing the course as they wished. The book needed to be visually attractive, with an abundance of pedagogical aids. We needed it to be interdisciplinary in its treatment of various topics, since it was a core course for all students and the closest thing to an integrative course that they were likely to take during their entire four years at St. Thomas. Finally, it needed to be thoroughly ecumenical in character, befitting the diversity of our students and the ecumenical mandate for Catholic theology stemming from the Second Vatican Council.

This was an ambitious undertaking, and it is a remarkable tribute to the strong leadership, the wide departmental participation, and the generous institutional support which the project received that within just two years after the initial brainstorming in the summer of 1994, a custom-published volume of 24 chapters was ready for use in the fall of 1996. We wish to acknowledge here the partial support that the first edition received from a major 1993 Bush Foundation grant to St. Thomas for university-wide curriculum revision, and also from St. Thomas' Aquinas Institute, a university grant program for special projects. Credit is due to the editorial vision and strong hand of co-editors Catherine Cory and David Landry, assisted by an editorial board of Terence Nichols, Rev. David Smith, Rev. Jan Michael Joncas, Rev. Thaddeus Posey, OFM Cap., and Michael Hollerich. But it was the generous involvement of a large and diversely talented department that was truly crucial, with most chapters being written by individual authors and others written compositely by multiple contributors. Their varied expertise was invaluable, even as the number of distinct authors tested the editors' ability (blue pencil and patient diplomacy in equal amounts) to keep it all coherent and uniform. That volume established a pattern that has been maintained in all subsequent editions, of crediting authors in the table of contents (by chapter and now, in this fourth edition, by section as well in chapters with multiple authors) but not in the body of the textbook. With rare exceptions, subsequent editions have continued to be the work of current or past members of the Theology Department.

Although this textbook was written in the first instance for use by our students in a course designed for our curriculum, we were pleased to learn that other colleges and universities with programs like ours began asking to use it as well. That led to the first commercially published edition of the book, by Prentice Hall in 1999, followed by a second edition in 2003, both with Catherine Cory and David Landry as co-editors. The book's success, as well as the transformation of the political, religious, and educational landscapes after the tragic events of September 11, 2001, led a new publisher, Pearson/Prentice Hall, to ask for a new and expanded edition, which finally appeared in 2009, with Catherine Cory and Michael Hollerich as co-editors. This third edition was marked by needed updating—the Catholic world had its first new pope in 27 years—and new chapters, most importantly a thoroughly new chapter on Islam in its relation to the Christian tradition.

A decade later, Routledge, our current publisher, has now asked us for a new and substantially expanded edition, which will be marketed internationally. We are pleased, then, to present this fourth edition of *The Christian Theological Tradition*. Almost all chapters have been revised, over half substantially, and nine are new or wholly rewritten, for example, on Thomas Aquinas (Chapter 15, the contribution of Robert St. Hilaire, of Niagara University), on the Renaissance (Chapter 17, the contribution of William Junker, of St. Thomas' Catholic Studies Department), and on the global spread of Christianity (Chapter 21). Like its predecessors, this edition deals with the whole Christian tradition from an orientation that is both Catholic and ecumenical. But there is also expanded coverage of modern Protestant Christianity in wholly new considerations of Christian theology's engagement with modernity and post-modernity (Chapters 22 and 26, respectively), a new section on the reception of the Second Vatican Council including the pontificate of Pope Francis (Chapter 24), a more inclusive and completely rewritten treatment of contemporary developments in liberation and environmental theology (Chapter 27), a new treatment of the relationship between science and Christianity (Chapter 25), and an entirely new treatment of Islam that focuses critically on how the historic Christian tradition has understood and responded to Islam (Chapter 12). A new opening chapter demonstrates the relevance of the Christian theological tradition for our contemporary world, and it also outlines different sources and methods for Christian theology. The overall approach, as before, strives to be both broadly historical—on the assumption that this is the best way to be balanced and inclusive—and genuinely theological.

We thank our colleagues once again for the generous donation of their time and particular expertise. We also thank the many students, now in the thousands, whose feedback over the years, formal and informal, has been a constant stimulus for improvement.

The Theology Department dedicates this fourth edition of *The Christian Theological Tradition* to the memory of the late Professor Terence Nichols (1941–2014). A beloved colleague and former department chair, Terry was a significant contributor to earlier iterations of this book and a figure of unmatched vitality and influence in the life of our department. We miss him still.

Mark McInroy and Michael J. Hollerich
On behalf of the Theology Department
University of St. Thomas
St. Paul, Minnesota

Inspired by Catholic intellectual tradition,
the University of St. Thomas educates students to be morally responsible leaders
who think critically, act wisely and work skillfully
to advance the common good.
(University of St. Thomas Mission Statement)

Chapter

1

INTRODUCTION

Approaching the Christian Theological Tradition

God has been a source of endless fascination for the figures examined in this book. Just as one becomes enthralled with the beauty of the natural world or a masterpiece of art, Christian theologians have been captivated by the object of their study. This intense interest arises from these figures' love for God, to be sure, but it also occurs because of the rich rewards that *thinking* about God offers. Many of these individuals stand out as intellectual giants who have made major contributions to Western civilization. And yet, their towering intellects have been stretched to the limit and ultimately humbled in reflecting on God. To many of them, there is nothing more challenging, nothing more important, and nothing more fulfilling than contemplating God and God's relationship with human beings. After all, the Christian theological tradition offers carefully considered responses to the most profound questions human beings ask: Why are we here? Where does everything come from? What happens after we die? Do the choices we make matter? Does God exist? What does the word "God" mean, anyway?

Christian theology arises in response to wonder at our human condition and the world in which we live. To those who do not naturally marvel at such things, Christian theologians pose provocative questions designed to stir their readers to reflect on the most essential and enigmatic aspects of their existence. Pursuing those questions can be one of the most rewarding enterprises in which human beings engage. It can certainly be challenging; the Christian theological tradition offers exceptionally sophisticated and profound systems of thought. And yet, in spite of its difficulty, exploring Christian theology can be not only rewarding, but indeed an exquisite delight. In fact, to the modern Protestant theologian Karl Barth (1886–1968), it *must* be so. Barth insists, "The theologian who labors without joy is not a theologian at all. Sulky faces, morose thoughts and boring ways of speaking are intolerable in this field" (Barth 1957, 656). Not every theologian has followed Barth's suggestion, but he offers an attractive vision of how theology can and should be done. Joy and wonder lie at the heart of Christian theology.

In the pages of this book, the reader will discover the reasons that many have found Christianity to be so compelling, and also the extensive influence that the Christian theological tradition has had on Western civilization. In an effort at treating these issues briefly at the outset, this Introduction is organized around two questions: First, *why* should one study the Christian theological tradition? Second, *how* should one study the Christian theological tradition? The first section, then, makes a case for the relevance of the Christian theological tradition, and the second section equips the reader with some of the most important tools for examining it.

WHY SHOULD ONE STUDY THE CHRISTIAN THEOLOGICAL TRADITION? UNDERSTANDING OURSELVES, OUR CONTEMPORARY WORLD, AND OUR HISTORY AS A CULTURE

Why should one study the Christian theological tradition? The authors of this book are aware that its value is not self-evident to all readers. However, when it is properly understood, the Christian theological tradition offers a powerful set of resources for understanding ourselves, our world today, and our history as a culture. Or, to put the point differently, it has relevance at the personal, societal, and historical levels.

The first section below, on personal relevance, describes the transformative potential of the Christian theological tradition for those who acquaint themselves with it. After a discussion of the human desire for God as articulated by Christian theologians, the section turns to rival ways of thinking such as nihilism and materialism, each of which stands to diminish the personal relevance of the Christian theological tradition. The section also responds to a number of common caricatures of Christianity, and it offers a series of correctives to those misunderstandings.

The second section, on societal relevance, demonstrates that Christianity exerts enormous influence in our culture today, and it examines the ways in which the Christian theological tradition is currently being used to respond to societal issues such as poverty, climate change, race relations, and education.

The third section, on historical relevance, claims that one cannot understand where we have come from as a culture without knowledge of the Christian theological tradition. This position is advanced by noting the formative influence Christianity has had on Western art, architecture, morality, and even science.

Personal Relevance:
Christian Theology as Transforming One's View of Oneself

Christian theology has a potent ability to transform one's view of oneself and one's place in the world. Many other academic fields examine topics with which one might not be concerned (one can choose, for instance, to be uninterested in astronomy or entomology). Christian theology, by contrast, examines topics in which all human beings have a stake: God, our search for meaning, and the ultimate destiny of humankind. **Augustine of Hippo** (354–430) opens his *Confessions* with the following succinct formulation of these concerns: "You have made us for yourself, O God, and our heart is restless until it rests in you" (Augustine 1998, 3). To Augustine, we go about our lives with a restlessness that cannot be stilled by anything within this world. Desire, then, lies at the very center of who we are as human beings. Although we attempt to satisfy our desire with earthly things, they give us only a temporary respite from our yearnings. Over time, we find that our longings are deep, and our thirst cannot be quenched ultimately by anything within creation. We are never fully at rest. To Augustine, only God can satisfy our searching, restless hearts.

Figure 1–1 Augustine of Hippo (354–430) saw the human heart as aflame with desire for God. Jean-Baptiste de Champaigne (1631–1681).

Along intriguingly similar lines, the modern Protestant theologian **Paul Tillich** (1886–1965) speaks of faith in terms of **ultimate concern**. To Tillich, human beings concern themselves with any number of things in their daily lives, some of which might be trivial, others of which are more significant. The concern that most dominates our thoughts serves as the center around which we organize our existence. For some, it will be career, for others, material possessions, for yet others, family and friends. Every person has a concern that is most significant to him or her, whether that person consciously chooses it or not.

To Tillich, each person's most fundamental concern is, in effect, that person's God. Whatever most occupies our thoughts, whatever we look to in order to give our lives significance, to assuage our fears, or to inspire us, that is the thing in which we place our faith, even if we do not think of it explicitly in those terms. One key implication of this view is that faith is not *optional*; instead, one unavoidably puts faith in something to give one's life meaning and purpose. We all have something that most concerns us.

Tillich holds that the most appropriate object of faith is God, as only God can adequately respond to our *ultimate* concern. To Tillich, we are ultimately concerned about "non-being," or not existing (i.e., death). This concern lies at the root of the human condition. Only God can offer resolution to this deep, persistent preoccupation. Faith in God, then, does not simply affirm the existence of a far-off deity who is uninvolved in our lives. Instead, Tillich maintains that *even now* our existence is sustained and supported over the abyss of nothingness by the unending source of all being. Faith, then, offers a new form of existence in the midst of this world, a new way of life that knows no anxiety or despair, but only the assurance that life with God can offer. This, to Tillich, is what faith is about: the search for relationship with the ultimate ground of our existence.

At its most profound moments, the Christian theological tradition puts forward a vision in which the deepest longings of human beings are fulfilled—and even surpassed. Christian theology offers an understanding of human existence according to which our destiny involves being incorporated into the divine life and ultimately residing with God in that perfected communion. Having this awareness can dramatically transform our perception of ourselves and our place in the world.

Of course, Christian theology is not the only way of thinking that has personal relevance. Other theologies and philosophies clamor for attention in our world today, and a number of them are not terribly friendly to those searching for meaning and value. Although **nihilism** is not often named explicitly, it is a prevalent contemporary philosophy that holds human existence simply has no significance or worth. Nihilists maintain that life is ultimately pointless and any attempt to say otherwise only perpetuates the illusion that we matter at all. If such a view were taken to heart, it most assuredly would affect one's sense of his or her place in the world.

Although the situation is more complex with **materialism,** this way of thinking can also be highly pernicious to assertions of meaning and value. Materialists maintain that the world consists only of physical things; only matter is real, and consciousness or "mind" is simply an ephemeral by-product of the physical. Materialism is a pervasive way of thinking in the natural sciences, although many scientists themselves draw from other disciplines to find meaning and value (even if they are unaware that they do so). In a materialist way of thinking, human beings are simply physical creatures and nothing more. Materialism itself, then, does not offer resources for claiming that human beings have worth, and some hold that materialism directly competes with any such claim. After all, only the physical is real.

To put the issue in its starkest terms, are we just bags of protoplasm, mere collections of chemical processes, or is there something more to us? The natural sciences do not make any comment on the *goodness* of human beings. Do we have inherent value? If so, *where does it come from?*

To be sure, there are a number of ways to meet these challenges, but the Christian theological tradition offers some of the most compelling and intellectually satisfying responses. A number of Christian thinkers claim not only that God created the universe, but that such an assertion provides the necessary foundation for claiming that human beings have value. The contemporary philosopher Alasdair MacIntyre remarks that debates between theists and atheists are not about the number of things in the universe, with theists maintaining that the universe has one more thing (i.e., God) than atheists claim. Instead, the Christian theological tradition describes the nature of the universe itself (MacIntyre 2009). Specifically, Christian theologians hold that the meaning and value of the universe are ultimately grounded in their source, the author of all creation. Furthermore, Christian theologians hold that God is in constant relationship with the world, continually holding it in existence and transforming it such that it reflects more and more fully the glory and goodness of its creator.

Difficulties arise, however, not only because of rival systems of thought that directly oppose Christian claims, as described briefly above, but also because of caricatures of the Christian tradition that misrepresent it to many in our world today. For instance, many people operate under the impression that Christianity consists of sentimental ideas about God that possess little intellectual substance. These individuals see Christianity as simply not credible, which of course compromises its personal relevance. And yet, some of those who reject Christianity for these reasons do so without actually giving the tradition a proper hearing, and their dismissals are often based on misperceptions of the Christian theological tradition. Just as one should not presume that music is inherently dull after only hearing it performed by beginners, one should not allow the most simplistic depictions of Christianity to dictate one's perception of the tradition as a whole.

When the Christian theological tradition is portrayed at its best, and in particular when one receives assurance that one does not need to check one's mind at the door in exploring it, its personal relevance emerges with force. The concept of God stands out as most in need of sophistication. The popular view of God as a large, human-like figure located in the sky remains remarkably prevalent, but the Christian theological tradition offers much more intriguing possibilities. For instance, the medieval Catholic

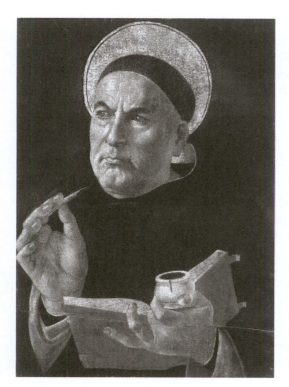

Figure 1–2 Thomas Aquinas (*c*.1225–1274) understood God not as *a* being, but instead as the "act of being," which brings everything into existence and continually keeps it from falling into nothingness. Painting attributed to Sandro Botticelli (1444–1510).

theologian **Thomas Aquinas** (*c*.1225–1274) does not conceive of God as *a* being at all. Instead, to Aquinas, God is *ipsum esse subsistens*, or the "subsistent act of existing" itself. In other words, God to Aquinas is the self-sustaining *act* that brings everything into existence and holds it in being. Like an electric current that must constantly flow to brighten a room with light, God is the continual act that holds all things in existence. Without God's never-ending support, all that exists would fall into nothingness.

Along similar lines, the newcomer to Christian theology easily thinks of faith as "blind." In other words, faith is often seen as an absurd leap into the unknown that has no rational foundations. And yet, Christian theologians frequently regard faith as grounded in reason. To these figures, the claims made within Christian theology are in fact rational. A number of these thinkers also use reason to *refine* the declarations made throughout the Christian tradition in order to advance an intellectually credible version of Christian faith.

At an even deeper level, many Christian theologians challenge the idea of faith as simple belief *that* something is true. According to this prevalent (yet reductive) way of thinking, Christian faith consists of agreeing to propositions; faith is a collection of "beliefs that." Faith is simply believing *that* God exists, believing *that* Jesus Christ is God, believing *that* God is a Trinity, and so on. And yet, numerous Christian theologians emphasize that faith in God consists of something much more holistic; it involves an interpersonal encounter with God from which a different manner of existence follows. The Protestant theologian **Martin Luther** (1483–1546) characterized faith as *trust*, as a willingness to rely completely on God, not on oneself, and to follow wherever God leads. Those who have faith, then, do not merely check items off of a list of things they believe. Rather, in faith they commit themselves to a new way of life, and in so doing dramatically change the very lens through which they view the world. One sees everything anew from the vantage point of faith.

Perhaps the most dominant caricature to overcome concerns the perception that Christianity is obsessed with a highly judgmental morality that will not tolerate the slightest deviation from an extremely restrictive ethical standard. Although this attitude can certainly be found among some Christians today, many teachings of Jesus directly oppose it. For instance, the Parable of the Prodigal Son (Luke 15:11–32) and the Parable of the Pharisee and the Tax Collector (Luke 18:9–14) suggest that God's first response to our failings is not judgment and condemnation, but rather compassion *despite* what we have done wrong. Indeed, as one learns about Jesus' teachings, one is exposed to a radical notion of forgiveness that offers an almost unthinkable

Figure 1–3 *Return of the Prodigal Son.* Painting by Pompeo Girolamo Batoni (1708–1787).

degree of reconciliation with God and one's neighbor. The Christian life, according to these lessons, involves not judging each other on God's behalf, but rather extending to others the same extraordinary generosity that has been offered to us.

In these regards and in many others, the Christian theological tradition can speak directly to contemporary persons about the most important issues in their lives. This ability allows the Christian theological tradition to play a crucial role in a liberal-arts education (the setting in which it takes place at the University of St. Thomas). Such an education aims not only to equip students with various skills, but also to transform them into different people. Study of the Christian theological tradition enables students to understand themselves anew by asking them to articulate and defend their most fundamental convictions in conversation with a host of historical figures, some of whom challenge—and others of whom support—their views. A graduating college senior will be a different person than he or she was when beginning university education, and study of the Christian theological tradition can play a central role in that process of discovery and increased self-understanding. To be clear, the academic study of theology does not require or expect conversion from those who study it, but it does present a wide array of viewpoints that students are invited to probe, question, and—if they are sufficiently persuaded—integrate into their own self-understanding. In many cases, it might be that the Christian theological tradition helps a student to find his or her authentic self.

Societal Relevance:
Christianity as a Decisive Shaper of our Contemporary World

The relevance of the Christian theological tradition extends beyond its importance for understanding ourselves individually; it also plays an enormous role in the broader society in which we live. However, only a few years ago a view known as the **secularization thesis** held that religion would gradually disappear, first from Western cultures, and eventually from the rest of the world. Renowned sociologists such as **Peter Berger** (1929–2017) championed this confident prediction, and it received widespread support from many who study religion. In a number of academic circles, the educated way to think about our future world was to hold that it would be secular, not religious.

And yet, as the twentieth century progressed, religion did not actually fade away, as expected. In the twenty-first century, many religions around the world are alive and well, and Christianity is even thriving in certain parts of the globe. Berger himself has acknowledged the following:

> The world today … is as furiously religious as it ever was, and in some places more so than ever. This means that a whole body of literature by historians and social scientists loosely labeled "secularization theory" is essentially mistaken.
>
> (Berger 1999, 2)

As scholars have largely relinquished the secularization thesis, many now expect that religion will endure in our world—although it is certainly in the midst of seismic shifts around the globe. At present, Christianity has approximately 2.2 billion adherents worldwide, and it is growing particularly quickly in Africa and China. In 1900, there were 7 million Christians in Africa. Today, Africa has more than 400 million Christians. In the 1950s, there were approximately 4 million Christians in China; today 100 million Christians are thought to live there. The post-colonial dynamics of these trends are highly complex (see Chapter 21), but at the very least one cannot simply say that Christianity is dying out.

The United States, too, remains a deeply religious country in spite of the large-scale changes in its religious make-up during the last few decades. A 2014 Pew Research Poll showed that 83 percent of Americans believe in God,[1] and in 2015 more than 70 percent told Pew researchers that they identify as Christian.[2]

In addition to simply being present in our society, Christianity also exerts enormous influence. One sees this impact most clearly in the public sphere, although Christianity clearly influences our culture in other arenas as well. In 2018, 91 percent of the U.S. Congress identified as Christian,[3] and one scholar reports that 90 percent of those members "consult their religious beliefs" before they vote on proposed legislation. One might ask, how do those religious beliefs guide them? Two high-stakes examples will be discussed below.

In 2017, while Congress was in the midst of a debate about health care, Congressman Roger Marshall (R-KS) offered the following rationale for his policy position: "Just like Jesus said, 'The poor will always be with us' … There is a group of people that just don't want health care and aren't going to take care of themselves" (Facher 2017). Although biblical scholars bristle at such a misleading use of this biblical verse (Matthew 26:11), Marshall uses it to suggest that Jesus himself viewed poverty as an intractable feature of human societies that one must simply accept and not hope to eliminate.

Questionable uses of Christianity also play a role in current discussions of climate change. At a town hall meeting in Coldwater, Michigan, in 2017, Representative Tim Walberg (R-MI) insisted, "As a Christian, I believe that there is a creator in God who is much bigger than us … And I'm confident that, if there's a real problem, he can take care of it" (Gajanan 2017). According to the logic of this viewpoint, God is in full control of creation, so much so that God will fix any problem that humans might inflict upon the earth. Ultimately, God's omnipotence outweighs the need to worry about issues such as rising carbon dioxide levels in the atmosphere. Although Christian environmental theologians vigorously oppose such a viewpoint, the suggestion of Walberg's comment is that, if one has faith, one should not be concerned about climate change.

Regardless of where one stands on these controversial issues, they clearly demonstrate that the Christian theological tradition is a powerful force shaping our culture today. Perceptions of Christianity prove to be decisive factors in our policy debates and our elections, and it is no exaggeration to say that the future of our society depends to a remarkable extent on our view of Christianity.

And yet, this highly influential force remains poorly understood. The American historian Stephen Prothero holds that the United States has a religious literacy problem, and he points to some startling statistics to support his view. For instance, although the majority of Americans view themselves as Christian, only *half* can name just one of the four Gospels, and most cannot even name the first book of the Bible (Prothero 2007, 30). Prothero's study reveals that a large portion of Americans profess to be Christian without knowing much at all about the tradition to which they claim to belong. Arguments like those above can be made with relative impunity because knowledge of the Christian tradition is not sufficiently widespread to insist otherwise.

Citizenship, then, requires knowledge of the Christian theological tradition, as a religiously literate electorate can ensure that Christianity not be distorted for political gain by those in positions of public trust. Some members of the previous generation may have thought that the preferable response to objectionable religious views was to presume that religion itself would simply die out with the passing of time. However, given the failure of the secularization thesis, many today hold that questionable religious arguments must be engaged on their own terms. In other words, the most helpful response to Christian attitudes with disturbing implications is not "Christianity is disappearing anyway." Instead, it is "the Christian tradition does not actually say that."

To revisit the example from above concerning Jesus' attitude toward the poor, scholars claim that the biblical verse quoted is actually a directive to the wealthy, not a license for complacency in the face of economic injustice. The verse in question, Matthew 26:11, is typically thought to be an allusion to Deuteronomy 15:11, the first part of which reads, "There will always be poor people in the land." However, the very next sentence in Deuteronomy goes on to insist, "Therefore I command you to be openhanded toward your neighbors who are poor and needy in your land" (Deuteronomy 15:11). At minimum, therefore, the presence of poverty should inspire generosity, not result in unresponsive resignation. Even more hopeful is a verse from the same chapter in Deuteronomy that reads,

> There need be no poor people among you, for in the land the Lord your God is giving you to possess as your inheritance, he will richly bless you, if only you fully obey the Lord your God and are careful to follow all these commands I am giving you today.
>
> (Deuteronomy 15:4–5)

According to this section of the text, poverty can indeed be eliminated, if one but follows God's commands.

Other portions of the Bible portray Jesus as intensely concerned with poverty in his ministry, thus further challenging the notion that the Christian tradition allows indifference to the poor. In the Gospel of Luke, Jesus frames his work as bringing "good news to the poor" (Luke 4:18–19), and he delivers clear imperatives to his followers regarding poverty:

> When you give a luncheon or a dinner, do not invite your friends or your brothers or your relatives or rich neighbors, in case they may invite you in return, and you would be repaid. But when you give a banquet, invite the poor, the crippled, the lame, and the blind. And you will be blessed.
>
> (Luke 14:12–14)

In direct opposition to the hoarding of wealth by the rich, Jesus tells the Parable of the Rich Fool:

> The land of a rich man produced abundantly. And he thought to himself, "What should I do, for I have no place to store my crops?" Then he said, "I will do this: I will pull down my barns and build larger ones, and there I will store all my grain and my goods. And I will say to my soul, Soul, you have ample goods laid up for many years; relax, eat, drink, be merry." But God said to him, "You fool! This very night your life is being demanded of you. And the things you have prepared, whose will they be?" So it is with those who store up treasures for themselves but are not rich toward God.
>
> (Luke 12:16–21)

Here and elsewhere, Jesus passionately preaches against accumulating wealth so as to harm the poor (see, for instance, Mark 10:17–21).

These biblical passages and others serve as key resources for Catholic social teaching, which develops their broader societal implications. One of the most well-known features of this influential way of thinking concerns the fundamental **option for the poor**, which the United States Conference of Catholic Bishops describes as follows:

> As followers of Christ, we are challenged to make a fundamental "option for the poor"— to speak for the voiceless, to defend the defenseless, to assess life styles, policies, and social institutions in terms of their impact on the poor. This "option for the poor" does not mean pitting one group against another, but rather, strengthening the whole community by assisting those who are the most vulnerable. As Christians, we are called to respond to the needs of all our brothers and sisters, but those with the greatest needs require the greatest response. ... Decisions must be judged in light of what they do for the poor, what they do to the poor, and what they enable the poor to do for themselves. The fundamental moral criterion for all economic decisions, policies, and institutions is this: They must be at the service of all people, especially the poor.
>
> (United States Conference of Catholic Bishops 1986, §§ 16, 24)

According to the Catholic bishops who authored this document, concern for the poor should be a key consideration not just in individual acts of charity, but in economic policy decisions as well.

Most visibly, perhaps, Pope Francis has recently placed care for the poor at the very center of his pontificate (he chose the name "Francis" in honor of Francis of Assisi and his ministry to the poor). In his encyclical *Evangelii Gaudium* (The Joy of the Gospel), the pope insists that addressing poverty is a necessary component of Christian faith:

> We have to state, without mincing words, that there is an inseparable bond between our faith and the poor. May we never abandon them. ... How can it be that it is not a news item when an elderly homeless person dies of exposure, but it is news when the stock market loses two points?
>
> (*Evangelii Gaudium*, §§ 43, 55)

Additionally, in his message on the first World Day of the Poor (November 17, 2017), Francis remarks, "We are called ... to draw near to the poor, to encounter them, to meet their gaze, to embrace them and to let them feel the warmth of love that breaks through their solitude" (Francis 2017, §3). At both a broad, societal level, and an intimate, interpersonal level, Christians are called to keep the poor at the center of their lives. Many more voices could be added to those mentioned here to make the point that the Christian tradition explicitly disallows neglecting poverty in our world today.

Concerning climate change, a number of contemporary theologians see care for the environment as central to the Christian faith (see Chapter 27). Many of these figures insist that the Creation story in Genesis does not simply grant human beings license to dominate the earth and its inhabitants. Instead, the text charges human beings with the obligations of being good stewards of creation. The story, after all, says that Adam must "till and keep" the earth (Genesis 2:15). Close reading of the Bible, then, reveals that the world is not ours to use and abuse as we like; instead, we must watch over creation as responsible caretakers.

Furthermore, although care for the environment frequently aligns with a progressive political agenda, Catholic theologians such as Christopher Thompson insist that *traditional* Christian theology leads directly to environmental concerns. Thompson advocates a school of thought known as "Green Thomism," which uses the traditional thought of Thomas Aquinas "to place ecology (the study and care of living organisms and their surroundings) where it belongs: at the forefront of Catholic concerns" (Thompson 2017, xxii).

Similarly, Pope Francis' widely acclaimed encyclical *Laudato Si': On Care for our Common Home* casts environmental concerns as inextricably connected to Christian faith:

> Climate change is a global problem with grave implications: environmental, social, economic, political and for the distribution of goods. It represents one of the principal challenges facing humanity in our day. ... Some committed and prayerful Christians, with the excuse of realism and pragmatism, tend to ridicule expressions of concern for the environment. ... What they all need is an "ecological conversion," whereby the effects of their encounter with Jesus Christ become evident in their relationship with the world around them. Living our vocation to be protectors of God's handiwork is essential to a life of virtue; it is not an optional or a secondary aspect of our Christian experience.
>
> (Francis 2015, §§ 25, 217)

Francis places environmentalism in a central position in Catholic social teaching. Particularly striking is the way in which the pope connects care for the environment with care for the poor, as the poor are most affected by environmental degradation.

Another misuse of the Christian theological tradition can be found among those who have questionably deployed it in their efforts at subjugating ethnic minorities (see Chapters 21, 23, and 27). And yet, the commitment to justice in Christianity has served as a powerful resource for those seeking equal treatment under the law. After all, the Civil Rights Movement of the 1960s began in the church, and many of its leaders were Christian ministers who drew from their tradition in order to combat discrimination. Most memorably, perhaps, the evocative speeches of **Martin Luther King, Jr.** (1929–1968) are permeated with references to the Bible. In particular, King made frequent use of Old Testament prophets such as Amos, who proclaims, "Let justice roll down like waters, and righteousness like an ever-flowing stream" (Amos 5:24).

Figure 1–4 Pope Francis (b. 1936).

Figure 1–5 Martin Luther King, Jr. (1929–1968).

In the contemporary setting, too, Christians find resources in their tradition as they fight the modern-day slave trade of human trafficking. In fact, their efforts have been called the "New Christian Abolition Movement." Organizations such as Abolition Now and World Relief work to rescue victims of trafficking and forced prostitution. These contemporary abolitionists see their work as grounded in the Christian view that each and every person has dignity and worth. As a member of World Relief puts it, "I don't think I'm any different than anyone I work with, in vulnerability or dignity … I really believe that Christ saw everyone equally" (Marrapodi 2012).

For good and for ill, then, the Christian theological tradition is continually pressed into service for a wide range of causes in our world today. Some of these efforts directly follow from the central claims of Christianity; others seem to be dangerous distortions of Christian theology. In order to determine which is which, one needs knowledge of the Christian theological tradition.

The above treatment points to the relevance of the Christian theological tradition for *education* in our society today. One of the principal arguments for liberal-arts education is that it fosters an educated citizenry, which serves as the necessary foundation for democratic forms of government. Particularly important is the ability to assess the soundness of arguments advanced by those in positions of public trust. As John Alexander Smith famously puts this point, "If you work hard and intelligently you should be able to detect when a man is talking rot, and that, in my view, is the main, if not the sole, purpose of education" (quoted in Delbanco 2014, 29). Although detecting "rot" (or poor argumentation) might at first seem like a fairly minimal achievement, it turns out to be a remarkably frequent exercise that demands considerable intellectual resources. An electorate that cannot identify specious reasoning will be easily swayed by fear-mongering, demagoguery, and other forms of manipulation.

Knowledge of the Christian theological tradition, then, is crucial not only for equipping citizens with resources to object to questionable uses of Christianity, but also to advance a different vision of the Christian tradition that stands against the caricatures and distortions often displayed in the public sphere. Even those who do not themselves subscribe to Christian views are frequently asked to vote for candidates who represent, among other things, some version of Christianity. Such representatives should be held accountable for their characterizations of the Christian faith, but this can be done only if their constituencies have a basic competency in Christianity.

Of course, one should study theology for other reasons besides its usefulness for objecting to dangerous distortions of Christianity. The Christian theological tradition has contributed historically to the fabric of our society in numerous ways, as outlined in the next section. For now, the role to appreciate concerns the function of Christian theology in the university. Figures such as the English Catholic convert

Figure 1–6 John Henry Newman (1801–1890).

John Henry Newman (1801–1890) argue that theology occupies an indispensable position in the university in that: (1) it offers a perspective not given by other academic disciplines; and (2) it functions to integrate the findings of other disciplines into a coherent, unified world-view.

Concerning the first point, Newman observes that the academic disciplines pursued in the university each gives only a *partial* view of any given subject. For instance, the human being can be studied from the perspective of biology, anthropology, sociology, psychology, literature, art, and even economics and political science. Each discipline has its own methodology that produces results distinct from those of the other disciplines, even though the subject is the same. Therefore, any single discipline will not produce exhaustive or complete knowledge of the subjects it investigates; other disciplines are needed to complement the findings of any given academic field.

According to this view, theology should be part of a university curriculum because it presents a perspective not offered by any other academic discipline. It has its own methodology that yields results distinct from those of other fields of study. In order to make as complete as possible one's understanding of the human being, one should consider theological treatments of humanity in addition to biological, sociological, psychological, and other assessments. Conversely, to remove theology from the university would be to truncate one's knowledge by depriving the university and those who learn there of a crucial perspective. Furthermore, as Newman astutely observed, the vacuum created by such a loss would be filled by other disciplines ill-equipped to handle the issues best addressed through theological methods (topics such as the nature of the universe, our ultimate origin and destiny, the meaning of human existence, etc.). This is the case with other disciplines as well. For instance, if ethics were removed from a university curriculum, fields such as economics and political science would attempt to answer, on their own, questions about the good and human flourishing. In so doing, they would overstep their disciplinary boundaries. Or, as MacIntyre has observed, natural scientists have often transgressed these disciplinary boundaries by pretending to possess a competence for matters that are ultimately metaphysical or theological (MacIntyre 2009, 146). Theology, then, has a necessary presence in the university because it enables the "circle of knowledge," as Newman called it, to be complete.

A yet stronger case can be made for theology in the university. Theology is more than just one field of study alongside other fields. Newman's second point is that theology *integrates* the partial perspectives offered by other disciplines into a single, coherent account of reality. It is called upon to perform this function because investigation of our universe does not stop at the natural world, but instead pushes right up to its limit, and indeed inquires beyond it. The order we find in the natural world begs questions about the source of that order; the freedom that human beings exercise begs questions about the source of that freedom; the moral intuitions that guide human behavior beg questions about the source of those moral intuitions. Contemporary scientist and theologian John Polkinghorne claims that the natural world alone is insufficient for adequately explaining these phenomena. A purely naturalistic view of the world's order posits that such order all came about purely by chance; it posits that freedom arose from necessity; it posits that moral intuitions arose from an otherwise amoral cosmos. Conversely, a theological view of the universe holds that the best way to make sense of the order, freedom, and morality in our world is to see them as echoes or imitations of the divine mind behind all things, of the God in whom all things participate. To Polkinghorne, this means that:

> a theological faculty is a necessary presence in a true university because the search for knowledge is incomplete if it does not include in its aim gaining knowledge of the Creator as well as gaining knowledge of creatures. The unity of knowledge is fractured if theology is excluded.
>
> (Polkinghorne 2008, 5)

Just as the study of a masterpiece of literature would arguably be incomplete without an attempt to understand its author, Newman, MacIntyre, Polkinghorne, and others insist that the study of our world in fields as diverse as physics, anthropology, and economics remains incomplete without knowledge of the author of all creation. If scholars were to pursue research in their disciplines without consideration of the ultimate source of their subjects, they would neglect their subjects' deepest, most significant aspect. As Newman memorably puts it,

> Admit a God and you introduce among the subjects of your knowledge, a fact encompassing, closing in upon, absorbing every other fact conceivable. How can we investigate any part of any order of Knowledge, and stop short of that which enters into every order? All true principles run over with it, all phenomena converge to it; it is truly the First and the Last.
>
> (Newman 1982, 19)

To be clear, we should state that theology does not *interfere* with the methods of other academic fields of study. Biologists, physicists, and sociologists conduct their inquiries using discipline-specific methodologies that allow independence to those areas of study. However, theology does ask, at the end of the day, after those disciplines have reached their conclusions, where it all comes from and what it is all for; it asks why one would engage in such pursuits in the first place. Theology, in other words, examines the ultimate source of meaning and value from which other disciplines are derived and toward which they are directed.

Historical Relevance: Christianity as Crucial for Understanding our Past

In addition to informing our understanding of ourselves and our contemporary world, studying the Christian theological tradition illuminates the history of Western culture in profound ways. In fact, fields of study that examine our past actually *require* some knowledge of the Christian theological tradition in order to be conducted adequately. Christian ideas saturated pre-modern Western societies; there was no secular world, and every facet of life bore the imprint of Christianity. If one is to understand where we have come from as a civilization, one needs a grasp of the Christian theological tradition.

One vividly sees the impact of the Christian theological tradition in the history of art and architecture. Flip through a book devoted to Western art, and the images there will consist of one religious subject after another. Masterpieces such as Leonardo DaVinci's *The Last Supper*, Michelangelo's *Pietà*, Johann Sebastian Bach's *Mass in B Minor*, Dante's *Divine Comedy*, and Chartres Cathedral each arose from a society that had God at its center, and the artistic genius of these works is inextricably tied to their religious aspects. To choose one more example, the works of Shakespeare alone contain approximately 1,300 allusions to the Bible. In order to appreciate these and other towering contributions to Western art, one needs knowledge of the Christian theological tradition.

The influence of Christianity can be observed in other aspects of our history as well. Our most central values as a culture are grounded in the Christian theological tradition. A number of historians emphasize this point by noting the challenge that Christianity presented to attitudes pervasive in the Roman Empire in which Christianity took root. Pre-Christian Rome was an unabashedly hierarchical society in which some individuals quite explicitly had more worth than others. Slaves, in particular, had no status or rights whatsoever. Dignity was not something that one had simply by being human.

Christianity brought about nothing less than a moral revolution in the Roman Empire, and it was initially viewed as utterly preposterous, in part because of the value it placed on each and every person. In his ministry, Jesus again and again lifted up those who were marginalized in his society: women, children, lepers, Samaritans, etc. In his Letter to the Galatians, Paul advanced a radical message that sought to break down divisions among people on the basis of their ethnicity, social class, and gender: "There is no longer Jew or Greek, there is no longer slave or free, there is no longer male and female; for all of you are one in Christ Jesus" (Galatians 3:28). Most incredibly, early Christians spread the message that, in the person of Jesus Christ, God actually "took the form of a slave" (Philippians 2:7), suggesting that God had taken on and inhabited the lowliest form of humanity known in that time. In short, Christianity introduced an understanding of human beings according to which *all* people, even the lowliest, have dignity and value.

The modern German philosopher Friedrich Nietzsche (1844–1900) criticized Christianity in ways that theologians resist (see Chapter 22), but many agree that he saw its concern for the disadvantaged with remarkable clarity. To Nietzsche, Christianity propagated a "slave morality," as he called it, which endorsed care for the weak. This slave morality replaced a previous moral system that placed value on might and vitality. Nietzsche lamented the Christian revolt against the established morality of its day, and he called for a return to pre-Christian values. The virulence of Nietzsche's attack bespeaks the enormous influence that Christian morality has had in shaping Western culture, and also the fact that *things could have been otherwise*. In other words, attitudes that we today might take for granted, such as the equality of all persons, do not in fact arise inevitably. Instead, they are highly contingent ways of thinking that, in case of Western culture, happened to be shaped by Christianity through its compassion for the disadvantaged and downtrodden.

To be sure, the audacious egalitarianism found in portions of the New Testament has had difficulty in coming to full fruition during the last 2,000 years. However, the Christian emphasis on care for the weak has served as a powerful

Figure 1–7 *The Last Supper*, by Leonardo DaVinci (1452–1519).

moral imperative; it has animated the creation of hospitals, orphanages, charities, and other institutions that attend to the needs of the sick and disadvantaged. As one scholar puts it,

> Christian teaching, from the first, placed charity at the center of the spiritual life as no pagan cult ever had, and raised the care of widows, orphans, the sick, the imprisoned, and the poor to the level of the highest of religious obligations ... To follow Christ, one must love the poor and give to them without reserve or preference.

(Hart 2009, 164)

Figure 1–8 *Pietà*, by Michelangelo (1475–1564).

The Christian emphasis on the dignity of all persons has manifested itself in a wide variety of ways throughout the history of Western civilization. One of the most noteworthy is the abolitionist movement. Although portions of scripture were used for centuries to claim that slavery is a legitimate institution (especially Genesis 9:25), at the beginning of the eighteenth century, Christian abolitionist arguments against slavery began to exert influence. In 1700, the Massachusetts Puritan Samuel Sewall (after some moral failings for which he would repent) published *The Selling of Joseph*, an abolitionist pamphlet that drew attention especially to Exodus 21:16, which reads "He who kidnaps a man and sells him ... shall surely be put to death" (MacCulloch 2009, 868). In nineteenth-century England,

Figure 1–9 Chartres Cathedral, France.

Evangelical Christians inveighed against slavery and ultimately prevailed. Among these, William Wilberforce was especially influential. Wilberforce devoted much of his career as a member of British Parliament to abolishing slavery. Among his anti-slavery publications is *An Appeal to the Religion, Justice and Humanity of the Inhabitants of the British Empire in Behalf of the Negro Slaves in the West Indies*, which opens with a quotation from Jeremiah: "Woe unto him that buildeth his house by unrighteousness, and his chambers by wrong; that useth his neighbour's service without wages, and giveth him not for his work" (Jeremiah 22:13). Elsewhere in the book, Wilberforce insists in no uncertain terms that the institution of slavery is "immoral, inhuman, and unjust" (Wilberforce 1823, xix). His efforts in Parliament resulted in the Slave Trade Act of 1807, which abolished the slave trade in the British Empire. Just three days before his death in 1833, Parliament passed the Slavery Abolition Act, which outlawed not just the trade of slaves, but the institution itself throughout the British Empire.

In addition to having a transformative effect on our values, the Christian theological tradition has deeply influenced our attempts to understand the natural world. In fact, historians of science such as Stanley Jaki hold that Christianity supplied the underlying view of the cosmos necessary for science to begin in the first place. Such a claim will be surprising to those familiar with the idea that science and Christianity conflict with each other. However, as discussed in Chapter 25, Christian theology and science are highly compatible in many ways. Jaki goes so far as to claim that science actually *needed* a Christian world-view in order to get off the ground. Specifically, by holding that God brought order out of disorder in the act of creation, Christian theologians described a world that functions with law-like regularity. This view of the cosmos was *not* first established through rigorous empirical testing; rather, the viewpoint was simply a logical consequence of the idea that an all-powerful God subdued chaotic elements in God's creation. Equipped with what was initially an *assumption* about the orderliness of the universe, scientists had the confidence to examine it closely and find that it does indeed follow certain patterns. By contrast, many other cosmologies, such as that of Greek philosophy, understood the universe itself as eternal, and therefore as having no creator. As a result of being creator-less, the universe was seen as unpredictable and ultimately indecipherable, which did not encourage scientific inquiry (Stark 2006, 15).

One further sees the intellectual contribution made by Christianity in the university itself, which arose out of Christian monasteries in the early medieval period. For centuries, monasteries had functioned as centers of learning; their libraries preserved many of the most important manuscripts in Western civilization. Both monastic schools and "cathedral schools" (schools organized by bishops and connected to their churches) offered instruction in the seven liberal arts: grammar, rhetoric, logic, arithmetic, geometry, astronomy, and music. In the thirteenth century, the cathedral schools in Paris, Oxford, and Bologna were transformed into the first universities. The method of instruction offered was one in which close scrutiny was brought to bear on aspects of the Christian tradition in an effort at resolving any seeming inconsistencies that might be found there (see Chapter 15). Various "disputed questions," as they were called, were posed, and scholars advanced arguments for and against the question at hand. This application of logical rigor, along with the university system as a whole, stands out as one of the most culturally significant legacies of the Christian theological tradition.

With all of this said, the reader should understand that the Christian theological tradition is not just important for studying our past as something *removed* from us and our contemporary concerns. The past is not simply "back there" in time, wholly unrelated to our present. Instead, history influences us all the time, and studying it informs enormously the issues of personal relevance raised earlier in this chapter. Most importantly, the study of history exposes just how restricted our current age can be, and it offers liberation from the view that present ways of thinking are the only ways of thinking. Lord Acton puts the point this way: "History must be our deliverer not only from the undue influence of other times, but from the undue influence of our own, from the tyranny of environment and the pressure of the air we breathe" (quoted in Pelikan 1992, 131).

It is not just that those who do not know their history are doomed to repeat it, as the saying goes. Those who do not know their history are destined to reproduce unimaginatively the thoughts of their own generation, but no other. They are actually *captives* to the present. The study of history allows one to move beyond the prejudices and blind spots of one's age and to engage with different perspectives on their own terms.

When it comes to thinking about God, one runs into limitations very quickly in our contemporary world. The less one knows about the history of Christian theology, the more limited one's ideas about God will be. This is true for both the Christian and the atheist. The atheist can reject any number of ideas of God without actually touching the heart of the Christian tradition. To choose an obvious example, if the atheist does not believe that there is a big man in the sky who grants us wishes, he or she has rejected one idea about God, but by no means has he or she satisfactorily dismissed the sophisticated views of Aquinas or Augustine. The atheist needs to know what he or she is rejecting.

The Christian, too, benefits from understanding that his or her ideas are not simply his or her own, as authentically as they might be held. Views of God do not develop in a vacuum, but instead draw from a history of such ideas, whether one is aware of that history or not. Saying something about God, then, inevitably involves learning what others have said about God. To study the Christian theological tradition is to expand one's imagination beyond the narrow confines of the present. It is to stand on the shoulders of giants, and to see farther than one ever could on one's own.

Ultimately, many of the figures examined in these pages would say that one should study Christian theology because it is its own end. In other words, it does not have only instrumental value, that is, value *for* something; instead, it is a good and a delight that is independent of any purpose to which it might be put. With this sense of the multifaceted relevance of the Christian theological tradition in place, we turn to a treatment of how one should study it.

HOW SHOULD ONE STUDY THE CHRISTIAN THEOLOGICAL TRADITION? TOOLS FOR THE APPROACH

Like any academic field of study, Christian theology uses tools specific to the discipline. What are the best tools with which to study the Christian theological tradition? This section examines a number of key issues that should be kept in mind throughout the pages of this book.

Does One Have to Be Christian to Study Christian Theology? Insider–Outsider Issues

The short answer is "no," but a lively conversation today centers around "insider–outsider" issues in the study of Christian theology. The key question is: Which person has the more insightful perspective on Christianity, the insider, who is committed to the Christian faith, or the outsider, who is not Christian and who strives to maintain a disinterested stance? Those who see the outsider's perspective as superior examine Christianity through a neutral approach, also called a **"religious-studies"** model. Those who view the insider's perspective as more insightful examine Christianity through a **confessional approach**, also called a "theological" model.

Advocates of the neutral approach hold that one must be detached from the object of one's study in order to understand it best. This person worries that being committed to Christianity biases one in favor of it, and that as a result one will not take seriously the problems that it might have. If one is to be *objective*, according to this way of thinking, one must not commit.

How does one gain knowledge of Christianity through this method? The neutral approach borrows tools from the social sciences in order to investigate Christian beliefs and practices. In other words, it studies Christian rituals like an anthropologist; it inquires into an individual's motivations for belief like a psychologist; it looks at contemporary Christian communities like a sociologist. In every case, however, this approach insists that the scholar remain *outside* of the beliefs of the Christian community. Anthropologists are cautioned against adopting the views of their subjects for themselves, lest they compromise their objectivity. Similarly, the neutral approach insists that the scholar remain removed from Christian systems of belief.

The neutral approach, then, requires considerable discipline and self-awareness on the part of the scholar. Why go to such trouble? Supporters hold that standing outside the Christian tradition frees one such that he or she can ask tough, critical questions of it. In other words, the advocate of the neutral approach worries that being committed to a set of beliefs causes one to shy away from rigorously questioning that belief. One might not be motivated to bite the hand that feeds him or her.

Additionally, outside observers often notice behaviors or beliefs that are unusual, and asking why such things are done or believed can result in greater insight into a tradition. Anyone who has ever attended a friend's church, synagogue, mosque, or temple may have thought that certain portions of the service stood out as unexpected or strange. Asking questions about why different things happen at key points in worship can lead to better understanding.

With that said, however, many who study Christian theology do so through the confessional approach as Christians themselves. These scholars claim that being committed to a Christian viewpoint actually helps them to understand Christian theology *better*, with greater depth than the person merely looking in from the outside. To these figures, there is no substitute for first-hand experience, and one acquires such an exposure to Christianity only if one actively participates in it. To use an instructive analogy, one could describe in great detail all of the ingredients that make up a meal, but in order to understand how the food actually tastes, one will need to enjoy the meal for oneself. Similarly, advocates of commitment insist that one needs to occupy a position *within* Christianity in order to understand best the claims it makes about God.

Such persons often emphasize that Christianity does not simply consist of knowledge *about* God. Instead, Christianity involves *relationship* with the object of its study. Just as one could not be in a meaningful relationship with another person if one constantly withheld commitment to him or her, one who is not in relationship with God cannot understand the full depth of what theology is about.

Furthermore, some who endorse the confessional approach to Christian theology insist that the alternative operates under an illusion; the religious-studies approach errs in thinking that anything like neutrality can actually be achieved. Whether we like it or not, we are all biased in one way or another. There simply is no purely "neutral" stance. Pretending that the outsider's stance is neutral perpetuates a myth of scholarly objectivity that does not in fact stand up to scrutiny. Each and every scholar is situated in a particular historical and geographical location that unavoidably influences what he or she regards as credible and not credible.

As an additional point concerning the issue of bias, it should be said that, if something is *true*, and one is in favor of it, that person should not exactly be called "biased." The term "bias" suggests a narrow assessment of the facts that prevents a person from arriving at the real truth of an issue. However, to choose an obvious example, if one strongly believes that genocide is wrong, and that person resists those who would enact genocide, it would not be quite right to say that he or she has a "bias" against genocide. Instead, impassioned commitment to a world without genocide could be seen as *right*. Similarly, if it is true that there is a God who seeks to transform humanity so as to eliminate everything that stands in the way of perfect communion with the divine, and the committed believer thinks that this is indeed the case, advocates of the theological approach would insist that the believer is not *biased*, but instead accurately perceives the true state of affairs.

Last, advocates of the confessional approach are eager to remind their counterparts that religious-studies scholars do not have a monopoly on asking critical questions about Christianity. Instead, the history of Christian theology demonstrates that some of its most noteworthy proponents have asked extremely challenging questions of their faith. In something of the same way that one is hardest on one's home team, or on members of one's own family whom one deeply loves, Christian theologians have often demanded that Christian claims stand up to critical scrutiny. After all, Christianity reflects on them personally. Augustine had no shortage of criticisms of Christian theology, even after his famous conversion to the faith. Similarly, the *Summa Theologiae* of Thomas Aquinas manifests countless questions that are asked of the Christian tradition. Critical engagement with theological claims is *internal* to the Christian tradition, not simply imposed on it from outside.

In regard to these critical questions, the academic study of Christian theology differs from some forms of catechesis in which many students are shaped before beginning their university education. Although that type of Christian instruction often communicates the basic claims made within the Christian tradition, critical questions are not always encouraged. In the academic study of theology, however, such questions are not only welcomed; they are actually required.

With regard to the question with which we began, one does not need to be Christian to study Christian theology, and in fact something of a middle attitude can be adopted. According to this approach, even if one is not Christian, one can read texts within the Christian tradition with empathy, entering into the world they are describing and taking their viewpoints on their own terms. Indeed, one value of studying the Christian theological tradition is that it asks one to attend to the other, and in so doing to move beyond the self.

What Sources Does Christian Theology Use?
Scripture, Tradition, Reason, and Experience

The Christian theological tradition draws from four distinct sources in developing ideas about God and God's relationship with human beings: scripture, tradition, reason, and experience. Each of these sources presents important claims about God, and each of them comes with its own methodological complexities. One sees an intricate relationship among the four sources, as tensions sometimes arise between one source and another. Although negotiating these tensions can be difficult, Christian theology is ultimately made richer and more resilient by having multiple sources for its claims.

How Should One Read the Bible?
Biblical Interpretation and the Issue of Inspiration

The next six chapters of this book examine the Bible, which Christian theologians typically view as the most significant source for Christian theology. It not only records God's interactions with human beings throughout history, it also discloses God's character to its readers, and it serves as a guide for Christians today. The Bible is a key medium through which God's self-revelation has taken place, and it has an authoritative status to many Christians.

To say that the Bible is authoritative, however, is not to say that it goes unquestioned, nor is it to say that it is only taken literally. The view that every single word of the Bible is literally true has *not* been the stance of the church for most of its history, and even today only a small number of churches (which are typically called **fundamentalist**) occupy this position. Fundamentalist Christians uphold biblical inerrancy, meaning that to them the Bible is without error in every sense. According to this view, scripture is completely accurate not only in what it says about God, but also in its scientific and historical claims. When fundamentalists maintain that the Bible is "inspired," they mean that God kept the authors of the Bible from making any mistakes whatsoever. It is crucial to understand that this view only begins in the modern period, and it can actually be seen as an attempt on the part of biblical interpreters to imitate the natural sciences, which privilege straightforward, literal truth claims (see Chapter 22).

This view is not only an outlier in the Christian theological tradition, it also encounters considerable difficulties upon further examination. First, it requires that one support the literal meaning of scripture over contemporary scientific views of the world. Most infamously, the fundamentalist approach insists that God created the world in six days, and it requires that one reject the modern scientific viewpoint that the universe is billions of years old. Second, biblical inerrancy has a very difficult time explaining those portions of scripture that stand in tension with one another. For instance, the opening chapters of Genesis contain two distinct creation stories that convey different sequences of events. In the first creation story, God makes Adam and Eve simultaneously (Genesis 1:27); in the second story, God first makes Adam (Genesis 2:7), then makes Eve some time later (Genesis 2:22). How could both stories be *literally* true?

Difficulties such as these drove ancient interpreters of the Bible to a complex view of the meaning contained within scripture, and this interpretive approach has been the dominant one throughout the centuries of the Christian theological tradition. Down to the present day, Roman Catholic, Eastern Orthodox, and many Protestant churches view scripture as containing not merely one, literal meaning. Instead, to such readers the Bible is an intricate, multi-layered text that has many different levels of meaning. To ancient Christian theologians such as Origen of Alexandria (*c.*184–*c.*253), when two or more portions of scripture conflict with each other (or, for that matter, when the literal meaning leads to questionable conclusions), the reader should look for the deeper, *allegorical* meaning of the text (see Chapter 8). Such an approach allowed highly influential early Christian theologians such as Origen, Basil of Caesarea (330–379), Gregory of Nyssa (335–394), and Augustine of Hippo (354–430) to adopt a non-literal view of the creation story in Genesis. From a very early date, Christian theologians knew better than to look to the Bible as a scientific textbook.

And yet, these Christian theologians and countless others hold that the Bible is *inspired*. This term, however, means something different to most Christians than what it means for fundamentalists. According to this understanding, inspiration does not indicate that God preserves human authors from any error whatsoever; instead, it means that God communicates to human beings, who then record in the books of the Bible various ideas about God and the world according to their necessarily *limited*, often all-too-human ways of thinking. The Bible, then, reliably reveals God's character and the crucial things for human beings to know about salvation, but it does so according to ways of thinking that often belong to previous historical eras. Ancient Israelites did not understand the Big Bang; early Christians did not understand quantum physics. One should not expect that God would reveal God's self in a manner that would be utterly incomprehensible to those who beheld that revelation. Instead, God *accommodated* God's revelation to the culturally available thought-forms of the time period in which God disclosed God's self. Those ancient views might be outdated when it comes to their science, but the scientific elements of the stories were never the core of God's message to humanity to begin with, and the truth about God's character can still be found in the Bible.

The academic study of theology acknowledges these interpretive difficulties and creatively engages with them in order to advance durable, intellectually sound interpretations of the Bible for our contemporary world. It does so, however, not based on the Bible alone, but instead through a complex engagement with tradition, reason, and experience. To the next of these topics we now turn.

How Should One View Tradition?
Is It Just a Depository for Old Ideas, or Something More?

The Bible leaves its readers with an enormous number of questions. For all of its capacity to reveal God's character to its readers, one still emerges from its pages with a sense of unfinished business. Tensions and ambiguities remain. To choose one of the most important interpretive difficulties, at certain moments, the Bible seems to present Jesus Christ as a human being. He grows tired, suffers, and even dies. However, at other moments, the Bible seems to present Jesus Christ as God. He performs miracles, he is worshipped, and he is present as "the Word" at the creation of the world. At first glance, there seems to be tension, to say the least, between these two aspects of scripture.

Tradition can be viewed as the centuries-long effort at clarifying this and other ambiguities within the Bible. Christian theologians have collectively attempted to find harmony and coherence between those portions of scripture that seem to contradict one another. They seek to resolve tensions and to make into a coherent whole the difficulties contained within scripture.

Some today have a negative reaction to the idea of tradition. As children of modernity, many view tradition as an irrelevant depository of antiquated ideas, and even as a hostile force that shackles free thinking (see Chapter 22). However, the description of tradition offered here characterizes it as a map of sorts that enables one to navigate theological topics with greater ease than one would be able to do through scripture alone. Tradition, in other words, can serve as a *resource* for thinking through theological problems. The tradition of reflection on these topics can help one to understand where a line of theological argument goes, and it can illuminate implications that would otherwise remain unseen.

In fact, many in the early church viewed tradition as a tool for resisting incorrect interpretations of the Bible. This problem became especially pronounced during the second and third centuries as Christians encountered new currents of thought throughout the Roman Empire. One of the most influential of these movements was the group of views known as Gnosticism (see Chapter 8). Gnostics presented highly innovative interpretations of the Bible that stood at odds with the tradition of the early church. For instance, some Gnostic texts insisted that Jesus did not actually have a body at all, and that he was instead merely an apparition of sorts. In the effort at resisting such interpretations, the early Christian theologian **Irenaeus of Lyons** (130–202) invoked tradition as a key guide. To Irenaeus, the church had passed down correct Christian teaching from the earliest followers of Jesus to the present day. This "apostolic tradition" is preserved in the bishops of the church, who stand in a living chain that reaches back to the apostles themselves. Any new ideas that the church encounters must, to figures such as Irenaeus, be evaluated based on the tradition of the church.

As much as tradition can serve as a bulwark against misleading interpretations of Christianity, it does nevertheless manifest *change* in response to historical events. In his classic work, *An Essay on the Development of Christian Doctrine* (1845), John

Henry Newman acknowledges a fact that must be taken seriously in modern treatments of Christian theology: doctrine *develops*. The church has not simply proclaimed the exact same set of teachings since its founding. Instead, as the church encountered new ways of thinking in the various cultures in which it took root, Christian theologians were faced with new questions that had not been previously considered. In responding to these provocations, Christian theologians were pushed to elicit from the original idea of Christianity aspects of Christian doctrine that had not yet been expressed. To Newman, these creative responses to unanticipated historical circumstances could result in legitimate outworkings of original Christian claims. In other words, change could occur *in continuity* with the original gospel. Just as the development of a living organism displays continuity even as it changes into a more mature creature, Christian doctrine can remain true to its inner principles even as it develops.

Newman's view of development gestures toward a facet of tradition that should be made explicit, namely, that the Christian theological tradition is a *living* tradition. It does not consist of pat answers that have been given once and for all. Instead, the Christian theological tradition creatively responds to the new discoveries and new questions that emerge in every era. Christian theology is a dynamic field of study engaged in the ongoing project of continually rearticulating the Christian faith in each new historical setting. In this effort, it draws from other academic disciplines, including mathematics, physics, biology, anthropology, sociology, literary studies, and art history. Ultimately, it has the confidence to engage in this rather audacious task because of the underlying belief that, even today, God continues to be in relationship with the church, constantly informing and guiding it through history.

Is Christian Faith Rational? The Role of Reason

The newcomer to the Christian theological tradition may be surprised to discover that reason plays a crucial role for many of its most influential theologians. In fact, reason is seen by some as a God-given tool that can be used to understand God and God's creation. In describing this feature of the Christian theological tradition, Pope John Paul II (1920–2005) memorably opens his encyclical *Fides et Ratio* (Faith and Reason) with the following: "Faith and reason are like two wings on which the human spirit rises to the contemplation of truth." Later in the same document, he insists, "The Church remains profoundly convinced that faith and reason 'mutually support each other'; each influences the other, as they offer to each other a purifying critique and a stimulus to pursue the search for deeper understanding" (John Paul II 1998, 100). Here and at many other points in the Christian theological tradition, one finds a high regard for reason.

Of course, the term "reason" can mean different things. Some Christian theologians hold that reason can be used to prove the existence of God (see Chapters 15 and 25). For example, the so-called "cosmological argument" uses reason to investigate the world, ultimately to ask how the universe began (in contemporary terms, it asks what happened *before* the Big Bang). According to the argument, the universe cannot have come from sheer nothingness, for nothingness does not create anything; nothingness does not do anything at all. What must be the case, then, is that a necessary being (God) created the universe. Such a use of reason seeks to prove God's existence through reason alone in the interest of building other Christian claims atop that rationally established foundation.

The cosmological argument and similar efforts are part of an academic discipline known as **philosophical theology**, which develops ideas about God through reason, often without particular recourse to scripture. It is from philosophical theology that we get ideas about God such as omniscience. Some insist that these terms as such do not appear in scripture, and in fact philosophical theology often presents understandings of God that stand in some tension with the portrayal of God found in the Bible. For instance, the "God of philosophy," as it is sometimes called, is immutable, or unchanging. In contrast to the continual flux found in the world, God remains the same. However, God in the Bible seems to change considerably at a number of moments, for instance in those portions of the narrative in which God changes God's mind in response to human actions.

And yet, there are also occasions when harmony can be achieved between philosophical theology and biblical theology. The term "omniscience" itself might not occur in the Bible, but God certainly does come across as knowing a great deal at many points throughout the text. Negotiating the tension between philosophical theology and its biblical counterpart stands out as an important task for Christian theologians.

Thus far we have spoken of reason as having considerable power. However, not everyone today holds that reason can do things like indubitably prove that God exists. Nevertheless, many theologians maintain that Christian faith is still *rational*, and that the life of faith has a logic to it. Such figures often highlight the large number of things that we believe without absolute proof. If something is highly likely, but not proved beyond a doubt, is it still rational to think it? Many Christian theologians say yes, and that the existence of God is one of those things. The rational investigation of our world begs enormous questions—about, for instance, how the natural world came to be so intricately ordered—and many Christian theologians hold that positing the existence of God offers the best explanation of these phenomena. In this view, the rationality of a way of thinking is measured by its ability to make sense of our experience.

With this said, many Christian theologians acknowledge that human reason is capable of comprehending only a *part* of reality, not its entirety. In particular, there are aspects of God that will always escape our attempts at understanding, despite our best efforts. Christian theologians typically insist that some dimensions of faith are simply *above* human reason (they are "supra-rational"). Two classic examples from this category are the Incarnation and the Trinity, which claim respectively that the eternal, infinite God became incarnate in a human being, and that the one God is three distinct persons: Father, Son, and Holy Spirit. Crucially, according to many Christian theologians, these aspects of faith do not run *contrary* to reason; they are not

Figure 1–10 Pope John Paul II (1920–2005).

irrational. Instead, they simply surpass reason's best efforts at understanding; they are ultimately beyond our ability to comprehend.

More broadly, reason often serves a refining function in Christian theology, as expressed in John Paul II's notion above that faith and reason offer each other a "purifying critique." That is, Christian theologians frequently use reason in order to sift through the various claims made within the Christian theological tradition in order to advance an intellectually durable version of the Christian faith. Although the use of reason might pose difficult questions to the claims made throughout the Christian tradition, Christian theology ultimately benefits from the rigor that reason brings to theological reflection.

Most fundamentally, the emphasis on reason signals that logic and argumentation play crucial roles in Christian theology. Reason assesses the various claims that are made in scripture and tradition. Some students who come to Christian theology, especially those who focus on the sciences in their studies, are often struck by how "fuzzy" Christian theology seems to them. Such students typically take objective facts seriously, but everything that cannot be *proved* they see as merely subjective opinion. Much could be said about the historical circumstances that have given rise to this quintessentially modern way of thinking (see the treatment of René Descartes in Chapter 22). For the moment, the point to emphasize is that a large number of academic disciplines do not actually provide the kind of absolute certainty that some might like. Within political science and economics, just to provide two examples, one will never encounter completely definitive, once-and-for-all "proof" that a particular political or economic system is superior to its rivals. There is no laboratory in which all extraneous variables could be eliminated so as to offer a neutral environment for testing such ideas. And yet, the views of political scientists and economists are not merely subjective opinions. Instead, scholars in these fields present *arguments* for their views, and they respond to the arguments of others. Similarly, the history of Christian theology displays arguments for different theological viewpoints, and some of those arguments are better than others. Securing a place for reason in theological discourse ensures that competition between different Christian claims will not degenerate into a mere clash of subjective opinions or a brute exertion of power by one group on the other.

Experience as a Source for Christian Theology

Experience offers something distinctive to Christian theology. Christian reflection on God does not consist simply of statements about a reality that is *external* to human beings. Instead, Christian theological themes often resonate deeply with the experiences of those who encounter them. Many of these individuals view Christianity as authentic not simply because the Bible says so (and perhaps because tradition has refined scriptural claims with the help of reason), but because they have experienced the claims of Christianity *firsthand.*

This experiential awareness of God—a portion of which is sometimes characterized as mystical experience—is portrayed in varying degrees of intensity throughout the Christian theological tradition. For some, these experiences take place at a low volume, so to speak, in otherwise mundane aspects of life such as doing laundry, watering plants, and eating meals. God is the "still small voice" (1 Kings 19:12) that is continually present, but easily overlooked. For others, the presence of God is so overwhelming that it stops them in their tracks and commands a complete change of life in response. Paul's experience on the road to Damascus is one dramatic example of the experience of God resulting in a complete reversal of course (see Chapter 7). Paul had persecuted Christians for a period of time, but while traveling to Damascus he had an encounter with the risen Christ that knocked him off of his horse, left him blind for days, and ultimately drove him to advocate for the church with unmatched zeal. Others who have tasted of the heights of mystical experience report a profound sense of union with God, being transported beyond themselves, and feeling flooded with absolute love. Some of these encounters are described as intoxicating, and in fact erotic terminology is often used: the soul is characterized as aflame with a passionate love for God.

Although the experiences of God reported by some mystics frequently confirm established Christian claims, they have also been used to destabilize traditional theological views. Julian of Norwich (1342–1416), for instance, had a mystical experience after which she often spoke of God as Mother in addition to Father (see Chapter 20), which has served as a provocation to reconsider exclusively male language for God (see Chapter 27). In this instance and many others, experience introduces tensions with tradition.

Even when not overturning established theological views, experience often serves as a reminder of lost emphases within the Christian theological tradition. Christian theology regularly enters periods of dryness during which its experiential dimension is neglected. For instance, much Christian theology became highly rationalistic during the seventeenth and eighteenth centuries (see Chapter 22), and a number of theologians appealed to authority to the exclusion of experience in the late nineteenth and early twentieth centuries (see Chapter 24). In both cases, experience was eventually used to correct these overly arid theological schemes. Appeals to experience, then, often re-emphasize the intimacy with which God relates to human beings.

In all of this, however, there is a danger, namely, that the individual Christian will use experience as the *only* measure for the truth of Christian claims. An over-reliance on experience can result in theological musings that are completely unmoored from any other source that would hold those reflections to a more rigorous standard. This can become especially dangerous when one's own personal experience narrows the realm of possibility for understanding God. That is to say, God will always be bigger than any human experience, and one runs the risk of reducing the magnificent, transcendent God to human ways of thinking, if one relies on experience alone. For this reason, the modern Catholic theologian **Hans Urs von Balthasar** (1905–1988) turns to the experience of beauty as an instructive analogy for the experience of God. To Balthasar, profound experiences of beauty do two different things. On the one hand, they connect with the human being and resonate with deep aspects of his or her person. To experience something as beautiful is to be *moved* by it. And yet, when beholding truly arresting beauty, the human being does not simply get what he or she expects. Instead, the experience *surprises*, it pushes one beyond oneself into a new realm of possibility, a new understanding of what one is capable of experiencing in the first place. Beauty *astonishes*. In a similar fashion, Balthasar holds that the experience of God resonates with the individual Christian, but it also does not simply give what is expected. Instead, the experience of God drives one to new vantage points from which to behold previously unseen—indeed previously *unimaginable*—aspects of God.

Looking at the four sources of Christian theology together, one is struck by the need for balance among them. An exclusive reliance on scripture can result in a theology that is not rationally grounded and is driven solely by authority. Excessive dependence on tradition can lead to theologies that are excessively rigid. Over-reliance on reason can result in rationalistic views of God that do not allow sufficient mystery. An exclusive appeal to experience can lead to egocentric ideas about God that are disconnected from anything outside of oneself. Through the correctives that the four sources make on one another, Christian theology is strengthened and held accountable to multiple standards in its efforts at describing God and God's relationship with human beings.

This introduction has offered reflections on the personal, societal, and historical relevance of the Christian theological tradition, and it has also presented some tools for approaching the Christian theological tradition. With this understanding in place, we now turn to the Bible in order to gain a more detailed grasp of this key source for Christian theology.

Key Terms

Thomas Aquinas
Augustine
Peter Berger
confessional approach
fundamentalism
Irenaeus of Lyons
Martin Luther

Martin Luther King, Jr.
materialism
John Henry Newman
nihilism
option for the poor
philosophical
    theology

religious-studies
    approach
secularization thesis
Paul Tillich
ultimate concern
Hans Urs von Balthasar

Questions for Reading

1. What does Paul Tillich mean by "ultimate concern," and how is it relevant to contemporary persons?

2. What is the current thinking concerning the secularization thesis? To sociologists such as Peter Berger, is religion disappearing around the world?

3. When Jesus said, "The poor will always be with you," what was his point, according to scholars of Christianity?

4. What does the Christian theological tradition have to say about care for the environment, according to contemporary theologians?

5. In what ways has the Christian theological tradition been used to address issues concerning race?

6. According to John Henry Newman, what functions does theology serve in the university?

7. In what ways did Christianity overturn the values that were prevalent in the pre-Christian Roman Empire?

8. Why do figures such as Stanley Jaki see Christianity as important for the development of science?

9. How do the "religious-studies approach" and the "confessional approach" to examining Christianity differ from one another?

10. Why is fundamentalism often viewed as unsatisfying by many Christian theologians? What are its shortcomings?

11. What different meanings for scripture being "inspired" can be found in the Christian theological tradition?

12. What are some of the different ways in which reason is used in the Christian theological tradition?

13. For what reasons does Hans Urs von Balthasar turn to the experience of beauty in describing the experience of God? Why is the experience of beauty instructive?

Notes

1. See "Belief in God," Pew Research Center, www.pewforum.org/religious-landscape-study/belief-in-god/.
2. See "America's Changing Religious Landscape," Pew Research Center, May 12, 2015, www.pewforum.org/2015/05/12/americas-changing-religious-landscape/.
3. See Aleksandra Sandstrom, "Faith on the Hill: The Religious Composition of the 115th Congress," Pew Research Center, January 3, 2017, www.pewforum.org/2017/01/03/faith-on-the-hill-115/.

Works Consulted/Recommended Reading

Augustine. 1998. *Confessions.* Translated by Henry Chadwick. Oxford: Oxford University Press.

Balthasar, Hans Urs von. 1982–1989. *The Glory of the Lord: A Theological Aesthetics.* 7 volumes. Translated by Erasmo Leiva-Merikakis et al. San Francisco, CA: Ignatius Press.

Barth, Karl. 1957. *Church Dogmatics II/1: The Doctrine of God.* Translated by T.H.L. Parker et al. Edinburgh: T&T Clark.

Berger, Peter. 1999. "The Desecularization of the World: A Global Overview." In *The Desecularization of the World: Resurgent Religion and World Politics.* Edited by Peter Berger, 1–18. Washington, DC: Ethics and Public Policy Center; Grand Rapids, MI: Eerdmans.

Delbanco, Andrew. 2014. *College: What It Was, Is, and Should Be.* Princeton, NJ: Princeton University Press.

Facher, Lev. 2017. "Two Months Ago, This Doctor was Delivering Babies. Now he's at the Nexus of the Obamacare Fight." *Stat News,* March 3. www.statnews.com/2017/03/03/roger-marshall-kansas-obamacare/.

Francis. 2013. *Evangelii Gaudium.* https://w2.vatican.va/content/francesco/en/apost_exhortations/documents/papa-francesco_esortazione-ap_20131124_evangelii-gaudium.html.

Francis. 2015. *Laudato Si': On Care for our Common Home.* http://w2.vatican.va/content/francesco/en/encyclicals/documents/papa-francesco_20150524_enciclica-laudato-si.html.

Francis. 2017. "Let us Love, not with Words but with Deeds: Message on the First World Day of the Poor." https://w2.vatican.va/content/francesco/en/messages/poveri/documents/papa-francesco_20170613_messaggio-i-giornatamondiale-poveri-2017.html.

Gajanan, Mahita. 2017. "Republican Congressman Says God Will 'Take Care Of' Climate Change." *Time Magazine,* May 31. http://time.com/4800000/tim-walberg-god-climate-change/.

Hart, David Bentley. 2009. *Atheist Delusions: The Christian Revolution and Its Fashionable Enemies.* New Haven, CT: Yale University Press.

Jaki, Stanley L. 1986. *Science and Creation: From Eternal Cycles to an Oscillating Universe.* Edinburgh: Scottish Academic Press.

John Paul II. 1998. *Fides et Ratio.* http://w2.vatican.va/content/john-paul-ii/en/encyclicals/documents/hf_jp-ii_enc_14091998_fides-et-ratio.html.

MacCulloch, Diarmaid. 2009. *Christianity: The First Three Thousand Years.* New York: Penguin.

MacIntyre, Alasdair. 2009. *God, Philosophy, Universities: A Selective History of the Catholic Philosophical Tradition.* Lanham, MD: Sheed and Ward Book/Rowman & Littlefield Publishers.

Marrapodi, Eric. 2012. "The New Christian Abolition Movement." *CNN Belief Blog,* February 5. http://religion.blogs.cnn.com/2012/02/05/the-new-christian-abolition-movement/.

Newman, John Henry. 1982. *The Idea of a University.* Notre Dame, IN: University of Notre Dame Press.

Newman, John Henry. 1989 (1845). *An Essay on the Development of Christian Doctrine.* Notre Dame, IN: University of Notre Dame Press.

Pelikan, Jaroslav. 1992. *The Idea of a University: A Reexamination.* New Haven, CT: Yale University Press.

Polkinghorne, John. 2008. *Faith, Science, and Understanding.* New Haven, CT: Yale University Press.

Prothero, Stephen. 2007. *Religious Literacy: What Every American Needs to Know—And Doesn't.* San Francisco, CA: HarperCollins.

Stark, Rodney. 2006. *The Victory of Reason: How Christianity Led to Freedom, Capitalism, and Western Success.* New York: Random House.

Thompson, Christopher. 2017. *The Joyful Mystery: Field Notes Toward a Green Thomism.* Steubenville, OH: Emmaus Road.

United States Conference of Catholic Bishops. 1986. *Economic Justice for All: Pastoral Letter on Catholic Social Teaching and the U.S. Economy.* www.usccb.org/upload/economic_justice_for_all.pdf.

Wilberforce, William. 1823. *An Appeal to the Religion, Justice, and Humanity of the Inhabitants of the British Empire in Behalf of the Negro Slaves in the West Indies.* London: J. Hatchard and Son.

PART

I

THE OLD TESTAMENT

An examination of the Christian theological tradition begins with the Bible, because the Bible comprises the sacred texts (or scriptures) of Christianity and hence is the foundation upon which Christianity and much of its theology is built. All Christian churches regard the Bible as "revealed" or "inspired" by God, declaring that God is its author, though, as we saw in the introduction to this book, not everyone agrees on the manner in which it is inspired. The word **Bible** is from a Greek word that is actually a plural and means "the books," which is also why the Bible is sometimes called "the Scriptures." It consists of two major sections, which are traditionally called the *Old Testament* and the *New Testament*. Within each section are a number of shorter documents called books, although the oldest texts were individual scrolls. The Bible can be likened to a library of sacred texts for Christian believers.

The list of books contained in the Bible is called a **canon**, which literally means "rule" or "measuring stick." Therefore, the books of the Bible are a measure of faith insofar as they are regarded as authoritative for Christian belief and practice. All Christians refer to their canon of sacred books as the Bible, but as we shall see, Christian churches do not all agree on how many books should be included in the canon. How did these different canons originate? Who are the major characters of the Old Testament and what is the significance of the events that it narrates? What other kinds of literature are contained in the Old Testament? These are some of the questions that will be addressed in Part I of our book. The section introducing Chapters 6 and 7 discusses similar topics related to the New Testament.

WHAT'S IN A NAME?

It was not until the third century C.E. that Christians began using the terms "Old Testament" and "New Testament" to describe the two major parts of the Bible, though there was already considerable agreement about which books now included in the Old and New Testaments were to be regarded as "scripture." The word **testament** is a synonym for the word covenant, which we can define provisionally as a sacred or formal agreement between two parties (in this case between God and human beings).

31

Thus, use of the terms *Old Testament* and *New Testament* reflect the Christian belief that God made an earlier covenant with the Jews, which is described in the Old Testament, and a "new" covenant with the followers of Jesus Christ, which is described in the New Testament.

However, this terminology can be problematic, because some people might conclude that the books of the Old Testament proclaim an *old* covenant that is no longer valid or has somehow been nullified. This view is incorrect for at least two reasons. First, God's covenants are always eternal; therefore the "old" covenant with the Jews based on these books remains in effect. Second, although individual Christian churches might come to different conclusions about the meaning of particular biblical texts, all would agree that the books of the Old Testament enjoy the same status within the Bible as do those of the New Testament. They are neither less authoritative than the books of the New Testament nor do they constitute a lesser canon.

Various names have been offered for these two parts of the Bible: Hebrew Scriptures and Christian Scriptures, First and Second Testament, etc. None of these designations completely solves the problems. The motive for seeking alternative descriptions of the Old and New Testaments is a positive one: respect for Judaism as the elder brother or sister of Christianity. This textbook will use the terms "Old Testament," "Hebrew Scriptures," and "Hebrew Bible" more or less interchangeably, recognizing that whatever terminology is used will have its limitations. We should also note that the terms "Old Testament" and "New Testament" need not be problematic so long as we remember that these are distinctively Christian designations and that they represent a Christian perspective on the interpretation of the first testament of the Bible. However, these terms should not be used to deny or downplay the unique and privileged status of God's covenant with Israel, manifested as it is in Judaism today.

HOW THE HEBREW BIBLE CAME TO BE

In large part, the Old Testament was the scripture of the Jews before it became part of the scripture of the Christians. Christianity is an outgrowth of Judaism, and when Christians parted ways with Judaism, one of the things that they retained was their acceptance of the sacred literature that later came to be known as the Old Testament. Of course, Jews do not call it the "Old Testament," because for Judaism there is no New Testament to supplement or perhaps supplant it. The Jewish name for these texts is **Tanakh**, which is an acronym for the three parts of the Jewish scriptures: the **Torah** (the Law), the Nevi'im (the Prophets), and the Khetuvim (the Writings). The Tanakh is also known as the Hebrew Bible.

Most biblical scholars think that the Torah—also called the Law or the **Pentateuch**, meaning "five scrolls"—was the first of these three parts of the Jewish scriptures to be developed. Further, they believe that the writing of the Torah took place over a relatively long period of time, beginning with stories and traditions that were passed on orally, some as early as the twelfth century B.C.E., and only much later committed to writing. By approximately 400 B.C.E., the Law apparently had been accepted as sacred scripture, though we do not know exactly what form it took or what was contained in it. Eventually the books of the Law became the first five books of the Bible: Genesis, Exodus, Leviticus, Numbers, and Deuteronomy. These books cover the history of Israel from Creation until the death of Moses. The narratives focus on the traditions related to Israel's founders: Abraham, Isaac, and Jacob in Genesis and Moses in Exodus through Deuteronomy.

Calendar Designations B.C.E. and C.E

The abbreviations B.C.E. and C.E. are part of a system of dating frequently used among biblical scholars. For the period "before Christ," for which the traditional abbreviation has been "B.C.," we substitute "B.C.E.," meaning "before the Common Era." For the period "after Christ," for which the traditional abbreviation has been "A.D." (from the Latin *Anno Domini*, meaning "Year of the Lord"), we substitute "C.E.," meaning "the Common Era." The new system of dating is an attempt to be sensitive to Jews, Muslims, and other non-Christians who do not believe in the divinity of Jesus Christ and naturally would not want to have such belief inscribed in their dating system. On the other hand, some theologians argue that since they are doing *Christian* theology, a specifically Christian system of dating is more appropriate. To honor both concerns, this textbook will use "B.C.E." and "C.E." in the chapters devoted to biblical literature, and "B.C." and "A.D." for the remainder of the chapters.

The second of the three parts of the Hebrew Bible, the Prophets, underwent a similarly lengthy process of development. Jewish tradition divides the Prophets into two sections: the Former Prophets and the Latter Prophets. The collection called the **Former Prophets**, today also known as Deuteronomistic History (see Chapter 4), includes Joshua, Judges, 1–2 Samuel, and 1–2 Kings. **Deuteronomic History** books tell the stories of legendary early prophets like Samuel, Nathan, Elijah, and Elisha, and of those famous (and sometimes infamous) kings like Saul and David. Biblical scholars think that this body of literature was completed some time between 600 and 440 B.C.E. The collection called the **Latter Prophets** is often further divided into the Major Prophets (Isaiah, Jeremiah, and Ezekiel) and the Minor Prophets (Hosea, Joel, Amos, Obadiah, Jonah, Micah, Nahum, Habakkuk, Zephaniah, Haggai, Zechariah, and Malachi), also called the Book of the Twelve.

For the most part, the books of the Latter Prophets were put together by disciples of the prophets who began with traditional stories and remembered speeches of the prophets and then added their own or other people's interpretations of the prophets' teachings as well as historical narratives that provide a context for the prophets' teachings. The earliest of these books was written in approximately 750 B.C.E., while the last was written in approximately 300 B.C.E. About a century later, when the books of the prophets were beginning to be accepted as sacred scripture, they are mentioned alongside the Law, described by the phrase "the Law and the Prophets" (2 Maccabees 15:9). However, we have no way of knowing whether this collection is exactly the same as the list of prophetic books that comprise today's Bible.

The Writings, the third major section of the Hebrew Bible, is a miscellaneous collection of books that were committed to writing sometime between the sixth and second centuries B.C.E., though many of the prayers and proverbs contained in these books might go back as early as the tenth century B.C.E. The author of the Prologue to the Book of Sirach calls them "the other books of our ancestors." Today, the Writings include Psalms, Proverbs, Job, a collection of books called the five Megilloth (Song of Songs, Ruth, Lamentations, Ecclesiastes, and Esther), Daniel, Ezra/Nehemiah, and 1–2 Chronicles. However, most biblical scholars agree that the list of books designated as belonging to the Writings was not fixed until the second century C.E. Thus, Jesus and his disciples, who were first-century Jews, would have understood their scriptures to include the Law and the Prophets. They probably also knew some of the literature that would eventually make up the Writings—the Psalms, for example—but the Tanakh would not take its final form until after many of the books of the New Testament had already been written.

How did the Jewish people decide which books should be included in the Tanakh and which should not? Biblical scholars have proposed a few theories, but the biblical books themselves do not provide many clues, nor do other Jewish writers of the time, except perhaps for one—a Jewish historian of the late first century C.E. named Josephus. In his *Against Apion*, he writes that their sacred books contain the "records of all the past times" and are "justly believed to be divine" in origin. He adds that they were viewed with such authority that people would hold fast to their teachings even to the point of death (*Against Apion* 1.8; trans. Whiston). Using more contemporary language, we might say that Josephus considered these sacred texts to be canonical because they were inspired of God. They were authoritative insofar as their stories reminded the Jewish people of who they were, and their teachings showed them how they ought to live as God's chosen people.

The People: Hebrews, Israelites, and Jews

The people who wrote and collected the books of the Old Testament are known alternately as **Hebrews**, **Israelites**, and **Jews**. This people emerged as an identifiable group around 1200 B.C.E. Over time, they described themselves as both a religious and a national entity. They inhabited the land now known as Israel, they worshipped a God they named **YHWH** (usually pronounced "Yahweh"), and they told stories about their distant origin from a family of Mesopotamian semi-nomads (Abraham and his descendants). In the Bible, the word "Hebrew" was first used to refer to Abraham (Genesis 14:13), but it was more widely used in relation to the history of Israel in Egypt, (Genesis 37–50; Exodus 1–15; see Chapter 3). However, with only a few exceptions, it is a term used by outsiders; this people usually referred to itself as "Israel" or as the "Israelites." The term "Israel" is said to derive from a name given to Jacob, whom the biblical narrative describes as the grandson of Abraham (Genesis 25:19–35:29). He, together with his 12 sons, became known as the tribal ancestors of the Israelite people. The term "Israeli" is reserved today for a citizen of the State of Israel.

The terms "Jew" and "Jewish" had a later development. When the kingdom of Israel divided in 922 B.C.E., the Northern Kingdom was called Israel and the Southern Kingdom was called Judah, after the Israelite tribe that dominated that region. Two centuries later, the Northern Kingdom was destroyed, and all that was left was the Southern Kingdom, Judah, which in turn was destroyed in 587 B.C.E. and its people taken into exile in Babylon (see Chapter 3). During the exile, this people gradually established a religious identity apart from the land of their ancestors and, by the end of the exile, their religion had evolved into new forms. This new expression of the Israelite religion is what scholars today call early Judaism. It is part of the same family of words as "Jew" and "Jewish," which refer to followers of Judaism and/or members of the ethnic group from which Judaism originated, and which derive from Judah, the name of their kingdom of origin.

WHICH BIBLE ARE YOU READING?

Anyone who has visited a bookstore to purchase a Christian Bible has probably noticed that there are at least two different versions of the Bible, sometimes designated as the Catholic Bible and the Protestant Bible. The history of the development of the Bible is lengthy and extremely complex, but the difference between these versions can be summarized in the question: "What books shall we include in the Old Testament?"

Canons of the Old Testament

Roman Catholic Bible	Protestant Bible	Hebrew Bible (Tanakh)
1. Genesis	1. Genesis	1. Genesis "in the beginning" (Bereshith)
2. Exodus	2. Exodus	2. Exodus "Names" (Shemoth)
3. Leviticus	3. Leviticus	3. Leviticus "And he called" (Wayiqra)
4. Numbers	4. Numbers	4. Numbers "In the wilderness" (Bemidbar)
5. Deuteronomy	5. Deuteronomy	5. Deuteronomy "Words" (Debarim)
6. Joshua	6. Joshua	6. Joshua (Yehoshua)
7. Judges	7. Judges	7. "Judges" (Shofetim)
8. Ruth	8. Ruth	17. Ruth
9–10. 1 and 2 Samuel	9–10. 1 and 2 Samuel	8. Shemuel
11–12. 1 and 2 Kings	11–12. 1 and 2 Kings	9. "Kings" (Melakim)
13–14. 1 and 2 Chronicles	13–14. 1 and 2 Chronicles	24. "Chronicles" (Dibre Hayamim)
15–16. Ezra and Nehemiah	15–16. Ezra and Nehemiah	23. Ezrah-Nehemyah
17. Tobit	Apocryphal	Noncanonical
18. Judith	Apocryphal	Noncanonical
19. Esther	17. Esther	21. Esther
20. 1 Maccabees	Apocryphal	Noncanonical
21. 2 Maccabees	Apocryphal	Noncanonical
22. Job	18. Job	15. Job (Iyyob)
23. Psalms	19. Psalms	14. Psalms "Praises" (Tehillim)
24. Proverbs	20. Proverbs	16. "Proverbs of" (Mishle)
25. Ecclesiastes	21. Ecclesiastes	19. Ecclesiastes "Preacher" (Qoheleth)
26. Song of Solomon	22. Song of Solomon	18. "Song of Songs" (Shir Hashirim)
27. Wisdom of Solomon	Apocryphal	Noncanonical
28. Sirach (Ecclesiasticus)	Apocryphal	Noncanonical
29. Isaiah	23. Isaiah	10. Isaiah (Yeshayahu)
30. Jeremiah	24. Jeremiah	11. Jeremiah (Yirmeyahu)
31. Lamentations	25. Lamentations	20. Lamentations "How" (Ekah)
32. Baruch	Apocryphal	Noncanonical
33. Ezekiel	26. Ezekiel	12. Ezekiel (Yehezaqel)
34. Daniel	27. Daniel	22. Daniel
35. Hosea	28. Hosea	13. "Twelve" (Tere Asar)
36. Joel	29. Joel	" "
37. Amos	30. Amos	" "
38. Obadiah	31. Obadiah	" "
39. Jonah	32. Jonah	" "
40. Micah	33. Micah	" "
41. Nahum	34. Nahum	" "
42. Habakkuk	35. Habakkuk	" "
43. Zephaniah	36. Zephaniah	" "
44. Haggai	37. Haggai	" "
45. Zechariah	38. Zechariah	" "
46. Malachi	39. Malachi	" "

Figure I–1 Canons of the Old Testament.

The collection that Christians call the Old Testament includes a short list of 39 books written in Hebrew (with some in Aramaic). Some Christians—Catholics and several Orthodox churches, for example—include an additional seven books, which until recently were thought to have been distinguished from the others by the fact that they were written in Greek and not in Hebrew or Aramaic, the sacred languages of Judaism. Today, we know that most of these books also were originally composed in Hebrew and Aramaic. Christians who do not accept these books as part of their canon call them the **Apocrypha** (literally, "hidden" books, but generally understood as religious writings that have religious value but that are not authoritative for Christian faith and practice). Christians who do accept these books as canon call them **deuterocanonical**. This does not mean that they constitute a secondary or lesser canon. Rather, the term acknowledges their disputed status over time: not all Christians have always accepted them as canonical.

To understand how this situation came to be, we need to go back to the period of the early church. Early Christians adopted a Greek translation of the Jewish scriptures, called the **Septuagint**, as their sacred writings even before there was a New Testament. But the Septuagint included several books that did not become part of the Hebrew Bible, namely, Tobit, Judith, 1 and 2 Maccabees, Wisdom, Sirach (also known as Ecclesiasticus), Baruch, and parts of Esther and Daniel. These are the apocryphal or deuterocanonical books. During the Protestant Reformation in the sixteenth century A.D., the reformers favored the shorter list of books that included in the Tanakh and chose not to retain the deuterocanonical writings. However, because these disputed books had been read in the churches for a long time, the reformers were not always eager to exclude them altogether. Today, Protestants are accustomed to finding the Apocrypha grouped together at the end of the Old Testament. However, the Roman Catholic Church and those Orthodox Christian churches that accept the deuterocanonical books as sacred scripture have them interspersed throughout the Old Testament in the locations found in the Septuagint.

Thus, it is the canonical status of these seven books and parts of books—variously known as apocryphal or deuterocanonical books—that comes into question when we talk about differences between Catholic and Protestant Bibles. These differences can be summarized as follows:

We have already mentioned that some Orthodox Christian churches (see Chapter 11) accept the deuterocanonical books as part of their canon and others do not. In fact, each has its own rich and complex history when it comes to the development of its specific canon. Some Orthodox churches have canons that go beyond the Hebrew Bible and the deuterocanonical books. Ethiopian Christians, for example, include Jubilees, 1 Enoch, and 4 Ezra, and Pseudo-Josephus (Josippon). The Greek Orthodox Church includes 2 Esdras and 3 Maccabees. If you would like to read any of these books, they are available at http://wesley.nnu.edu/biblical_studies/noncanon/pseudepigrapha.htm. They are also published in collections of Old Testament Apocrypha such as James Charlesworth's two-volume work, *Old Testament Pseudepigrapha* (Garden City, NY: Doubleday, 1983–1985).

Key Terms

Apocrypha	Former Prophets	Pentateuch
Bible	Hebrews	Septuagint
biblical inerrancy	Jews	Tanakh
canon	Israelites	testament
deuterocanonical	Latter Prophets	Torah

Chapter

2

ISRAEL'S STORY OF THE CREATION OF THE WORLD

The introduction to the Old Testament defined the Bible as "a collection of ancient texts considered authoritative by communities of faith." The discussion in this chapter will apply this definition to a specific **pericope**, Genesis 1–11. First the discussion will examine models for how this text, which reflects its ancient cultural context, came together. Then the focus will turn to its role as part of the biblical canon, followed by a brief discussion of the ways these chapters have influenced theological discourse across the centuries.

GENESIS 1–11: THE PRIMEVAL HISTORY

Genesis 1–11 covers the history of the world from its creation until the birth of Abraham. Its outline follows one found in other Near Eastern creation texts: a deity creates the world; there is a series of threats to that creation; the deity's response to those threats results in the world as the authors knew it. In some Mesopotamian creation stories, such as the account in a text called *Gilgamesh*, the creator god sends a flood so that he can start over, but a trickster god manages to save a single human household along with various animals, which become the basis for the contemporary world order. In other texts, such as the Babylonian liturgical text *Enuma Elish*, the creator god fights a chaos monster in order to secure the world as an ordered and thriving entity.

Creation stories use narratives to explain why the world is like it is. For the peoples of the **Fertile Crescent**, these narratives often addressed the difficulties that the society as a whole faced: the quest for economic security, the reason for the separation between humans and animals, the perennial problem of human violence, and the desire for tranquility in the household. Behind many of these narratives lurks the uneasy feeling that, since mere humans can imagine a better world, why was that not the one that the great gods created?

In the Fertile Crescent, creation was not a single act in the past, but an ongoing activity of the creator god. This need for ongoing renewal of the natural order reflects the experience that life is fragile and threatened. In these narratives, when

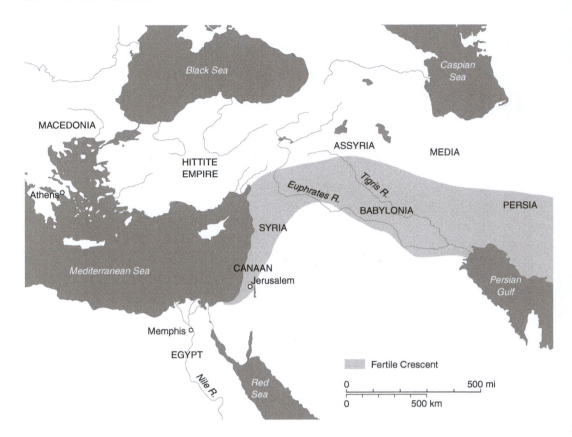

Figure 2–1 The Ancient Near East.

the gods first created the world, the divides between deities–humans–animals were porous and unclear; the authors could imagine a world where gods, humans, and animals could converse, interact, and live in peace. Human actions threatened this order, however, and so the gods had to create impassable boundaries between the three realms.

Water in Creation

Many of the creation stories use water as a metaphor for both creation and its opposite, chaos. In the ancient world, access to fresh water was essential for survival, yet in many of these hot and arid lands, it was often hard to come by. Fresh water in the form of springs, rivers, and rain came to represent creation as a dynamic, ongoing event. Salt water, on the other hand, killed, especially crops and landscape. Salt water, often embodied in a sea monster, represented the forces that oppose abundant life. In addition, the mixture of salt and fresh water represented chaos because only a deity was able to separate them.

The Israelite authors also used narrative to represent their experience of the world in which they lived. Like other peoples that surrounded them, they had different creation narratives to explain different aspects of their world. These were not viewed as being incompatible or competing narratives, since none of them aimed to present scientific explanations for the world. Each narrative tradition functioned in varying social contexts and used metaphors that fit that context.

Babylonian priests recited *Enuma Elish* in a liturgical context, their week-long New Year's festival, because it represented new beginnings and the restoration of order. In this text, the Babylonian head god, Marduk, defeats a chaos monster, Tiamat (along with her minions), and is enthroned as king of the inhabitable world. Genesis 1:1–2:3 displays a similar pattern. The repetitious language of the text suggests that priests recited it in a liturgical context. The text stresses God's deliberate imposition of order over chaotic elements (called *tehom* in Hebrew, echoing the name of the Babylonian chaos monster). God separates light from darkness, chaos water from fresh water, and the heavens from earth, so that humans can be fruitful, multiply, and worship God, who now rests from this divine work.

This creation account focuses on the orderliness of creation, but even more on its goodness. The story of each day culminates in the declaration of that day's creative act as "good," almost like a refrain that builds to the cry that the whole creation (literally, "everything that God made" [Genesis 1:31]) is "very good." The culmination of this creation account is not the creation of humans, but rather the ongoing worship of the God who has created this excellent, well-ordered world. All humans, signified by the merism "male and female" (a merism is when an author combines two contrasting words to refer to an entirety) are created in the "image and likeness" of God, a phrase in the ancient Near East that means they have responsibility for the world as God's representatives. This does not make humans a substitute for God, however, but rather God's servants. Their service allows God to rest while all creation worships the creator.

An alternative creation account follows in Genesis 2:4–3:24, this one focused on the relationships between God, humans, animals, and the earth. While some people read this version as an expansion of the sixth day of creation in Genesis 1:24–31, the ancient authors made no attempt to reconcile the two accounts. In fact, throughout the Fertile Crescent (see Figure 2–1), societies preserved and used varying creation accounts depending on the occasion. Each narrative of creation had a different purpose.

The creation account in Genesis 2:4–3:24 echoes the pattern of creation found in a Mesopotamian text titled *Atrahasis*. In that text, the gods create humans as slaves who do hard labor, after some minor deities refuse to do the work. While the humans do not rebel, they proliferate at an astonishing rate and make so much noise that the gods cannot sleep. They decide to wipe out the humans with a series of disasters, culminating in a flood, but some survive. The gods then set a

Figure 2–2 *Ancient of Days,* by William Blake (1757–1827). Frontispiece for Blake's *Europe: A Prophecy* (1794).

clearer divide between the human and divine realms in order to maintain the proper order. The Mesopotamian version of this creation narrative stresses the lowly status of humans compared to gods, and explains why the gods seem so distant.

Issues in Moral Theology: Israel's Story of the Creation of the World

Creation and Fall in Moral Theology: "Dominion" and the Care of Creation

At the core of moral theology are questions about who God is and who human beings are. Our theologies and anthropologies shape our evaluation of good character and action. In the Christian tradition, creation stories are a primary source for answering these questions, and interpretations of them have shifted in new contexts throughout the tradition, influencing understanding of morality.

Today, our context is marked by what Pope Francis calls "the rapid pace of change and degradation" of the Earth and its inhabitants (*Laudato Si'* §61). As a result, important questions about the interpretation of Genesis 1–3 have arisen. Traditional interpretations of these creation stories have sometimes been accused of justifying human domination of nature and thereby contributing to our current crisis.

In contrast, Pope Francis maintains that "a correct interpretation" of Genesis 1–3 cannot support "the unbridled exploitation of nature" (§67). Against anthropocentrism (seeing everything centered on human beings), Francis argues that the biblical text offers a view of God as creator of a "very good" universe in which human beings, as bearers of God's image, have "the duty to protect the earth and to ensure its fruitfulness for coming generations" (*Laudato Si'* §61).

This debate about the interpretation of Genesis 1–3 indicates several features of moral theology. First, new contexts (such as the environmental crisis) present new challenges for interpreting the Bible, and new meanings of the text can be seen when a new cultural situation calls for them. Second, an ongoing challenge in theology is to discern how to interpret these texts correctly. Finally, interpreting these texts is crucial if we are to reach an adequate understanding of who God is and who human beings are, which will then influence how we relate to God, neighbor, and creation (for more on theology and the environment, see Chapter 27).

One of the most common means of interpreting scripture for approximately its first 1,700 years was uncovering multiple meanings in the text. In the Patristic period, scholars often read Old Testament texts in particular as allegories, a reading strategy which Greek and Roman philosophers had developed in order to find hidden meanings in poetry and mythology. In an allegory, the literal meaning of a word or a narrative is only superficial, with its deeper and truer meaning available only to skilled interpreters. Paul's letter to the Galatians says that Sarah and Hagar from the book of Genesis (Sarah is Abraham's wife and Hagar her slave) should be understood allegorically and that they really stand for Christians and Jews (Galatians 4:14–24). For someone like the Christian theologian Origen of Alexandria (see Chapter 8), the Holy Spirit had inspired biblical texts with two levels of meaning: a literal meaning (what the words on the paper stated) and a spiritual or allegorical meaning (what those passages symbolized or represented).

If the literal meaning seemed erroneous or objectionable, Origen held that was a signal from the Holy Spirit to dig more deeply for possible hidden meanings. By the Middle Ages, this twofold meaning (or "sense") developed into the principle of the fourfold senses: the literal meaning, and three spiritual meanings (its allegorical meaning, its moral meaning, and its "heavenly" or eschatological meaning).

The Israelite version also focuses on the relationships between humans, God, animals, and nature, first describing a pristine state of creation where all live in harmony in God's garden, Eden. Human transgression of the one boundary set by God (not to eat from the tree of knowledge of good and evil) led to a revision of the original created order by establishing a wall between humans and God. This divide also ruins the harmonious relationship humans had with animals and nature. Because the creation account in Genesis 2–3 is more story-like, with rising tension and final resolution, it has captured the imagination of readers for millennia. Each element of the narrative is significant, from the proper names (the Lord, Eden, Adam and Eve) to the configuration of space in the narrative (garden, trees, rivers, and eventually a wall).

Names

Israelite names were not just conglomerations of random sounds; they were nouns or sentences that expressed something significant about that person. The name "Adam" is simply the Hebrew word for "human being," and does not mean "male." In fact, the female form of the word means "ground" or "dirt," and not woman. Eve's name comes from the Hebrew verb "to live," and thus is connected to her role as mother of all humans, that is, the one who gives them life. God's proper name, "the Lord," comes from the verb "to be," connecting God (the one who causes things to be) to both God's presence as well as creation depending on how it was pronounced. In traditional usage, in the Hebrew Bible, the divine name was not pronounced and a polite substitute was used—"Adonai," meaning "the/my Lord"—a practice followed in many modern English biblical translations. God's personal name will be revealed and explained in the book of Exodus.

While it is not clear in what contexts this creation narrative would have been recited or performed, the account clearly focuses on human experience. Chapter 3, in particular, tells the story from the perspective of the two humans. They eat fruit from a tree they should not harvest, they hide from God, and they receive the divine sentences for their transgressions: curses and expulsion.

The Lord's curses reveal what this account attempts to explain. God levies the first curse against the serpent. In the ancient Near Eastern myths, serpents represented a variety of concepts, including healing and eternal life (because ancients thought they gave birth to themselves), the sun (in Egyptian iconography, where serpents bear the sun across the sky each day), wisdom, and death/chaos. Chaos monsters like Leviathan in Job and Rahab in Psalm 89 are serpent-like creations, often associated with the sea. God's curse reduces the cosmic serpent to a hostile animal that even a woman can defeat.

The curse on the woman demonstrates the difficulty of childbirth in the ancient world (as well as in many places in the world still today). The life expectancy of women in ancient Israel was around 30 years (40 for men) because of the high rate of death in childbirth. Because of the high infant mortality rate as well as death from childhood diseases, it would take on average five to six pregnancies for a couple to have one adult surviving son. Adult males were needed for work and to carry on the family heritage. The references to the "pains" of childbirth (v. 16, perhaps better translated as "agonies") express the mortal threat childbirth posed for women. So why would women not avoid pregnancy? Because they will "desire" their husbands (a euphemism for lust), and, even if they do not, husbands have the right to demand intercourse ("he will rule over you").

The curse on Adam reflects the economic reality of ancient Israel. As a people who depended on subsistence farming (i.e., farming by a household used to feed that household with little left over), crops formed their economic base. The lack of large freshwater rivers in that area of the Levant rendered Israel's economic status precarious. This meant that hard labor was required to dig cisterns to gather the meager rainfall and create terraces on hills so that topsoil would not completely erode in times of heavy rains. Yet even if crops took hold, weeds would equally thrive. God curses Adam with hard work for few results.

Ancient Israel was primarily an oral culture. The production of physical texts required economic resources that were scarce in a subsistence economy. The book form had not yet been invented, so each text was written on a scroll made of either papyrus or leather by a specially trained scribe. As a result, scrolls were a specialized item, probably found primarily in temples and royal treasuries. People had contact with these texts through various types of oral performance. Those reciting the text in a public setting probably did so from memory and not by reading a text that was opened before them. The scrolls assisted the oral proclamation, serving as part archive and part reference work. Therefore, the presence of two different creation narratives at the start of a scroll, that aims to preserve traditions about the history of the world, makes perfect sense.

This model for how the textual version of these narratives came together also explains similar variations throughout Genesis 1–11 (and, we will see, throughout the first five books of the Old Testament). The story of the Flood clearly weaves together two different accounts. One refers to the divine being as God, has Noah take a pair of each ritually unclean animal but seven pairs of ritually clean animals, and ends with sacrifice of some clean animals; another refers to God as the LORD, has Noah take two of every animal on board, and has no sacrifice at the end. The Flood

Figure 2–3 *The Garden of Eden*, the Limbourg brothers (active 1385–1416). This painting depicts different points in the Genesis narrative. At the right is the expulsion of Adam and Eve from the Garden.

separates humans and God even further. Before the Flood, humans could have intercourse with heavenly beings (Genesis 6:1–4), but after it humans were so cut off from contact with God, they tried to build a tower to reach heaven (Genesis 11:1–9). Before the Flood, humans lived extraordinarily long lives, a narrative signal that humans were semi-divine or at least more like the gods. But at the start of the Flood narrative, God limits human life to 120 years (Genesis 6:3) (that is, although tying this age limit to the Flood occurs in only one of the versions of the narrative).

The final divide takes place in the story of the Tower of Babel. This narrative starts with something that looks good: the ability of people to come together to attain a mutual goal. The problem lies in the purpose of that unified goal: the attempt to once again transgress the boundary between heaven and earth. While the story contains an explicit polemic against the Babylonian practice of building ziggurats (stair-step towers) in their temples, the function of the story in its current setting is to explain the final divide of creation: the divide within the human race itself. This narrative depicts human miscommunication and cultural separation as a divinely decreed punishment, because the only thing that unites these groups is their capacity for evil.

The genealogies that link each of these narrative islands serve three functions. First, they preserve oral traditions about groups' ancestors. Although the oral preservation of genealogies sounds strange to contemporary ears, it is a common practice in oral societies, ancient and modern. Second, the lists demonstrate the ongoing orderliness of creation, for good or ill. They record the first cities, the first metalworker, the first farmer, as well as the first murderer and the first clemency law. Third, they record the founding of various groups that existed in the ancient world. For example, the genealogies at the end of the Noah accounts trace the founders of the nations surrounding Israel: from Asia, to Africa, to Europe.

As a result, the book of Genesis begins with the textual preservation of Israel's narratives about its place in the world. While the bulk of the story will focus on Israel's own history (from Genesis 12 forward), the story starts with various pictures of God's deliberate ordering of the world. It commences with two ideal visions of order and harmony, but then deals with the reality of human existence then and now. While humanity has made material advances that make life more livable, divides still remain between humans and God, humans and nature, and, ultimately, among humans themselves.

Genesis 1–11 as a Canonical Text

As seen above, the development of the scroll of Genesis took place very organically over a period of time. At some point, an unknown person or persons gathered the narratives of creation together in the form that we now have and placed them at the beginning of the narratives of Israel's own founders (which will be the topic of Chapter 3). Some of these traditions did not stop with creation but continued onward to preserve traditions about Abraham's household (Genesis 12–50), as well as about Israel's origins in Egypt (Exodus 1–20) and eventual arrival at a place God had promised to them (Exodus 21–Deuteronomy 34).

This reconstruction of the history of these texts' production can raise questions about how we understand inspiration and canonicity. In the Middle Ages, Thomas Aquinas (see Chapter 15) described inspiration as a kind of prophetic experience. Although Aquinas himself asserts a very subtle view of the process of inspiration, his definition was interpreted as follows: an individual author received a prophetic-like revelation from God that the person then recorded. The ascription of biblical authorship to prophetic individuals stems from this model, including the assumption that Moses wrote the book of Genesis.

In most Christian communities, however, the canonicity of a text does not depend on the identity of the author, single or collective. In Catholic terms, God cooperates with human authors in whatever ways they produce texts. Whether the final form of Genesis 1–11 was created by a group of priests deciding which texts to include or by a single editor working for the royal palace to create a unified history of the nation does not affect the canonical status of the text.

Then, if Genesis 1–11 was created in a manner similar to *Enuma Elish*, what makes it different or distinct? For Christians, what makes it distinct is that communities of faith going back well before the time of Jesus experienced this text as a reliable and authoritative source of who and what God is, and how humans should respond to this God. The view of God captured in Genesis 1–11 does not have to be a unique view of God to be authoritative; it does not matter if other religions also experience God as an intentional creator of a good world. What matters is that this is what Christians and Jews believe based on their reliable sources of divine revelation, including scripture.

This model of the text's production also shows that the meaning of a text changes, sometimes becoming narrower, sometimes expanding, when it is placed in a new literary context. While Genesis 1 may have had meaning within a New Year's ritual at the temple of Jerusalem, it takes on added meaning as the opening of Israel's history, which makes a more explicit connection with the configuration of the social and political world of its writers. The simple connection of Genesis 1:1–2:3 with Genesis 2:4–3:16 invites readers to think about the relationship of the two narratives, one of which focuses on God's complete command over the acts of creation and their inherent goodness, the other of which highlights human failure and disappointment. Although the accounts are not reconciled, their meanings result in a conversation between two particular narratives about human and divine nature.

Other Jewish texts also contain reflexes of these texts, which leads to the creation of another literary context for them. For example, Wisdom 2:21–24, a first-century B.C.E. Jewish text that is canonical for Catholic and Orthodox Christians, refers to the serpent of Genesis 3:1 as the devil, an identification that has had a significant impact on the way the story has been understood by subsequent audiences. The same passage from Wisdom also appears to adopt the Greek doctrine of the immortality of the soul as the meaning of being in the image of God (Wisdom 2:23). Ezekiel 47, which describes a vision of the ideal temple, includes images of an abundant garden watered by a river coming from beneath God's throne, an image that contains parallels with the description of Eden.

For Christians, uses of the story in the New Testament also add to the meaning of the canonical text. The description of Jesus as the new Adam in Paul's letter to the Romans locates the origin of sin with Adam (Romans 5:12–21), and its ultimate recompense in Christ. First Timothy 2:13–15 identifies Eve as the first sinner, and on that basis limits women's authority in the church. The imagery of the woman and the dragon in Revelation 12 reverberates with echoes of Eve, the serpent, and Mary, again connecting creation and Christ.

Such inner-biblical allusions provided fertile sources for both Jewish and Christian interpreters to play with the possible interactions of these diverse texts. Within Jewish tradition, the literary practice of **midrash** provided a deliberate vehicle for playing with these connections. For Christians, the relationships between Jesus and Adam, God and Christ led to a vibrant tradition of theology based on Genesis 1–11.

Genesis 1–3 in the Christian Tradition

Interpretations of Genesis 1–3 have played a foundational role in Christian theological discussions across the ages. The narrative depictions of God's creation of humanity address fundamental questions about the nature of human beings and their relationship with God. The fact that these chapters have functioned for centuries as fertile ground for theological reflection highlights the profundity of this ancient Israelite text. While it is impossible to write a complete history of the text's interpretation, this final section will highlight interpretations related to other theological figures and movements mentioned in this textbook. The discussion here introduces topics that will be covered in more detail later.

In the first two centuries after the death of Jesus, early Christians had intense debates about the nature of the creator God and whether the Jewish scriptures remained authoritative for Christians. For example, there were certain radical Christian groups who believed in two divine beings, one evil and one good. For them, the world was created by an evil god who sought to trap spirits (which were good) in material bodies (which were bad). With the help of Greek philosophy, a growing institutional structure, and eventually Christianity's establishment as a state religion, core Christian beliefs on such issues will be defined (see Chapters 8 and 9).

The contemporary Christian understanding of original sin came out of these debates. Augustine's writings reflect the fullest development of the Western Christian interpretation of Genesis 1–3, but his views were not unique. In the first book of his autobiography, the *Confessions*, his presentation of the newborn infant as already sinful echoes his description of the human person as inherently flawed (see Chapter 10). Original sin, then, refers to the gap between divine perfection and human imperfection, a gap for which humans themselves are responsible, and which manifests itself in human inclination to sin and evil. For theologians of the early church, the depiction of humans disobeying the one command that God had given them—not to eat of the tree of the knowledge of good and evil—illustrated the fact that all humans sin; Augustine's narrative of his own sin in Book 2 of the *Confessions* recasts his adolescent sins in terms of Genesis 2–3.

Many of the stories attached to the creation account in popular tradition come from an early retelling of the story which scholars refer to collectively as "The Life of Adam and Eve." This fascinating text is not part of the biblical canon but builds on material from the canonical narratives to produce yet more narratives. "The Life of Adam and Eve" tells what happened to Adam and Eve after they were banished from Eden. It also contains the narrative of the fall of the angels, and depicts Satan as actively tempting people to sin. The story was widely popular; fragments in a variety of languages have been found across the ancient world, lasting well into the Middle Ages. Many people mistakenly assume that these stories are in the Bible, which demonstrates the influence they have exercised in the history of Christian interpretation of this text.

The Fourfold Sense of Jerusalem

In medieval biblical interpretation, "Jerusalem" was a favorite word for illustrating what became the classic fourfold senses of meaning in the Bible. The literal meaning of "Jerusalem" was the actual city of Jerusalem. Its allegorical meaning was the church. Its moral meaning was the way of life appropriate for residents of Jerusalem. And its final or eschatological meaning was the heavenly Jerusalem toward which the saved were traveling.

Throughout the Patristic period and the Middle Ages, theologians speculated on the pre-Fall and post-Fall status of humans, a discussion that reflects concern about humans in their own perfected state versus the reality of an imperfect worldly existence. For example, the question of whether Adam and Eve would have had intercourse in the garden gives voice to questions about human sexuality and sexual pleasure within God's creative plan. Theologians speculated on whether Adam and Eve could have avoided sinning or if God's foreknowledge of their fate meant they were predestined to sin. These debates played out in the Reformation when Christians split into distinct groups based in part on various answers to these questions (see Chapters 18, 19, and 20).

Even though much of the theological discussion has pertained to the interpretation of Genesis 2–3, Genesis 1 also played an important role. Jews interpreted God's statement to the first humans to be fruitful, multiply, and fill the earth as the first divine command; within Jewish traditions celibacy rarely was viewed as a virtue. In the late medieval and early Reformation periods, as explorers from Christian countries in Western Europe had new and more extensive interactions with people in sub-Saharan Africa as well as the Americas, questions arose about the status of these people in God's creative plan. While many Christians viewed these groups as somehow less than human (did they have a soul, for instance, or were they cursed by God in Genesis 9?), others, such as Bartolomé de las Casas, argued for their full human dignity, basing their position in large part on Genesis 1 (see Chapter 21).

It was also during this period that conflicts between the biblical account of creation and the scientific understanding of the world came to the fore. Perhaps the best-known such clash concerns the Catholic Church's condemnation in 1616 of the theory of **heliocentrism** (the sun as the center of the solar system) and the condemnation in 1633 of Galileo subscribing to the theory. It was not until 1983 that the Catholic Church officially rescinded that censure (see Chapter 25). This was not the only clash between scientific conclusions and Scriptural interpretation. The controversies provoked by Darwin's theories of evolution and natural selection, which contradict literal interpretations of Genesis 1–3, are still going on. The rise of the historical method questioned whether Moses wrote the Pentateuch (or whether David wrote the Psalms).

Perhaps the most influential and compelling scientific advances that changed the way many Christians interpret the Bible were in the field of archaeology. Modern archaeology of the Fertile Crescent began with Napoleon's invasion of Egypt in 1798. As European nations began to colonize parts of the Middle East and North Africa in the nineteenth century, archaeological excavations of ancient sites increased, blossoming during the twentieth century. The discovery of King Tutankhamen's tomb in 1922 was front-page news. Many of these discoveries had a direct impact on biblical studies. Twelfth-century B.C.E. texts in a city named Ugarit, located in modern Lebanon, provided direct insight into Canaanite religion. The discovery near Qumran overlooking the Dead Sea of 11 jars containing scrolls written in the Hellenistic period provided the earliest versions of many Old Testament texts. The huge cache of Mesopotamian texts discovered in the twentieth century provided an unprecedented number of parallels to biblical traditions, while also providing more social context to the use of these ancient narratives.

While many of the discoveries added to the historical analysis of biblical texts, some directly challenged long-held assumptions about the veracity of biblical historical accounts. Excavations in modern Israel, such as those at Jericho and Bethel, revealed contrary evidence to the biblical accounts of those same sites, for example.

Knowledge of Persian history called into question the unity of the book of Isaiah. Mesopotamian accounts of creation mentioned earlier with direct parallels to biblical accounts challenged the "uniqueness" of the biblical testimony.

Today, many Jewish and Christian biblical scholars no longer hold to the factual veracity of this ancient collection, and instead focus on the theological meanings of these texts. Although not returning to the fourfold method of biblical interpretation, scholars today recognize the literary qualities of the texts, and interpret them within those literary conventions. As the Vatican II text *Dei Verbum* states, recognition of the conventions of ancient literary genres is essential for beginning to understand the meaning intended by the human author (see Chapter 24). Only when we grasp how creation stories functioned in the ancient world before can we ask what they mean in the world of today.

Key terms

clean/unclean	heliocentrism	pericope
Fertile Crescent	midrash	

Questions for Reading

1. What evidence do many modern biblical scholars use to argue for the presence of two separate creation stories in Genesis 1–3?

2. What do the curses at the end of Genesis 3 tell us about the problems the ancient audience faced?

3. What are some of the separations that occur throughout Genesis 1–11? What is the final separation?

4. How have later Jewish and Christian interpretations of Genesis 1–3 shaped contemporary assumptions about the content and meaning of the biblical stories of creation?

Works Consulted/Recommended Reading

Carvalho, Corrine L., ed. 2014. *Anselm Companion to the Old Testament.* Winona, MN: Anselm Academic.

Clifford, Richard J., SJ. 1994. *Creation Accounts in the Ancient Near East and in the Bible.* Catholic Biblical Monographs 26. Washington, DC: Catholic Biblical Association.

Tromp, Johannes. 2005. *The Life of Adam and Eve in Greek: A Critical Edition.* Pseudepigrapha Veteris Testamenti Graece 6. Leiden: Brill.

3

THE PENTATEUCH

TIMELINE

3000–2000 B.C.E.	Beginnings of civilization in Mesopotamia (Sumer, Babylonia, and Assyria) and in the areas of Syria and Canaan.
c.1850–1750? B.C.E.	Abraham migrates to Canaan. Beginnings of the patriarchal period.
c.1700 B.C.E.	The *Enuma Elish* is circulated in Babylonian culture.
c.1300–1250 B.C.E.	Moses delivers God's people from Egypt in the Exodus. God's covenant people journey to the promised land.

The methods of biblical interpretation demonstrated in Chapter 2 on Genesis 1–11 apply to other biblical material as well. The first five books of the Bible constitute a section called the **Pentateuch**. Jewish tradition refers to this material as the **Torah**, which is a Hebrew noun meaning "teaching." The books in this section are Genesis, Exodus, Leviticus, Numbers, and Deuteronomy. Jews began to view these books as authoritative texts starting in the Persian period, some 300–400 years before the birth of Jesus. This collection marks not only the beginning of the formation of the Bible, but it is also the one part of the Bible that all Jews and Christians agree upon. This makes these books theologically foundational.

This chapter will present a survey of the contents of these five books, discuss possible models for how they developed as a collection, and then examine the central roles of Abraham, Jacob, and Moses within these narratives. The chapter will conclude with a brief discussion of how these biblical figures were engaged in later Jewish and Christian traditions.

The Narrative Arc of the Pentateuch

Reduced to their simplest form, Genesis through Deuteronomy tell the history of Israel from the creation of the world until the death of Moses. After the narrations of the creation in Genesis 1–11, the books turn their focus to the history of the people of Israel. Genesis 12–50 contains narratives about Abraham, Isaac, Jacob, and his 12 sons, referred to collectively as the **Patriarchs**, who are presented as the founders of Israel and its 12 tribes. These Patriarchs are semi-nomads and displaced peoples. At the beginning of these stories, Abraham moves out of Mesopotamia into the land that will eventually become Israel. At the end of the book, this large kinship group moves on to Egypt, now as economic refugees.

The fragility of life as a marginalized people, deemed permanently "foreign" by a host culture, drives the narrative structures of the book of Exodus. When this book begins some 430 years after the death of Jacob (Exodus 12:40), the Hebrews have become forced laborers who have no safety or security. God responds to their suffering, and delivers them from this unjust situation. The book of Exodus highlights the role that Moses plays in that deliverance. The account in Chapters 1–20 reads like a great adventure, a contest between good and evil fought on both the human and the divine planes. Once God delivers them safely, the people are given divinely revealed laws that define what it means to live as the people of the Lord.

Issues in Moral Theology: The Pentateuch

The Liberating God of Exodus

The Pentateuch offers additional insight into a key question of moral theology: *Who is God?* By narrowing the focus of the story to Israel, these texts answer not only the anthropological question of who human beings are, but more specifically, the communal question: *Who are the people of Israel as a community?* For Jews and Christians, exploring these questions in light of the Pentateuch helps to define how their communities ought to relate to God and neighbor, thus shaping morality.

The stories of the Pentateuch portray God as one who chooses enslaved people, wanderers in the desert, refugees. God walks amongst marginalized people, delivers people from injustice, and forms a covenant with them to create a just community. The reminder that God liberates frequently punctuates the Pentateuch, inspiring the moral response of the liberated. For example, Deuteronomy 23 calls the people to be just and merciful, as God has been just and merciful: "Do not oppress a foreigner; you yourselves know how it feels to be foreigners, because you were foreigners in Egypt" (Deuteronomy 23:9).

Christians continue to interpret the Pentateuch in response to emerging challenges. The Exodus in particular has shaped the moral identities of communities experiencing poverty, oppression, and injustice. As enslaved Africans adopted Christianity in the Americas, for example, the liberating God of Exodus spoke to their oppression, as we see in spirituals such as "Go Down, Moses!" or in the moniker given to Harriet Tubman, who was called "Black Moses." It continues to influence contemporary Black theology. The Exodus story is also fundamental to Latin American liberation theology (see Chapter 27). Peruvian theologian Gustavo Gutiérrez has said that the Exodus experience is paradigmatic for confronting oppression.

The stories of the Pentateuch thus remain fruitful sources for moral theological reflection today, as Christians seek to discern what God requires in the midst of injustice.

The bulk of the material from Exodus 21 through to the end of Deuteronomy is a collection of laws, punctuated by occasional accounts of life in the wilderness between Egypt and the Levant (historic Syria and Palestine). These narratives depict the people as a collection of nomads who continually search for a permanent, settled existence promised to them by their God. The storyline takes a back seat, since the Law forms the bulk of the material in these books. The Law outlines such things as the calendar of religious festivals, the duties of the priests, punishments for crimes, dietary restrictions, and how to conduct a war.

The book of Deuteronomy closes off this section of Israel's history. It opens with this nomadic group about to cross the Jordan River and enter the land where they will settle. It has been 40 years since the Hebrews had left Egypt, and only three people who were adults when that happened are still alive: Joshua, Caleb, and Moses. God has told Moses, however, that he will not enter that land, so Moses knows he is about to die. The book of Deuteronomy is his last speech to this community, in which he reminds them of the Law that they should observe once they have settled, built cities, and determined a king. At the end of that speech, God takes Moses to Mount Nebo in Moab, across the Jordan River, and shows him the **Promised Land** but tells him he will not enter it. In a poignant scene, Deuteronomy, and the Pentateuch, ends with God burying Moses, and the text comments laconically, "But no man knows the place of his burial to this day" (Deuteronomy 34:6). Later Jewish and Christian tradition will develop a rich tradition about Moses, such as the reference in the New Testament's letter of Jude to the archangel Michael contending with Satan over the body of Moses (Jude 9).

The Formation of the Pentateuch

While the narrative summary provided above gives a linear account of the events described in these books, the kinds of variations seen in Genesis 1–11 continue throughout the rest of the Pentateuch. Some stories are repeated with subtle differences, suggesting that the compiler(s) of these books had multiple accounts of some events. Other times, narratives contradict one another and different names are used for God. Readers experience the impact of these variations most explicitly in the legal material, which contains multiple laws on the same subject that cannot be reconciled with one another.

Variations in Slavery Laws

There are three major discussions of slavery in the Pentateuch: Exodus 21:1–11; Leviticus 25:39–55; and Deuteronomy 15:12–18. While these laws have some similarities, they also contain variations. This is seen in the treatment of female debt slaves, who are permanent slaves in Exodus but are redeemed in the seventh year in Deuteronomy.

Starting in the eighteenth century, biblical scholars began proposing different models that would account for these variations. At first, this effort proceeded as an examination of the sources Moses would have used to write the Pentateuch, but gradually it became clear that no one would write a history of Israel until there actually was an entity called "Israel." The dating of this compilation, then, got pushed back to the rise of the United Monarchy under David (*c.*1000 B.C.E.) at the earliest.

In the twentieth century, the most influential reconstruction of the composition of the Pentateuch was that of Julius Wellhausen, who published his reconstruction in the 1890s. Wellhausen proposed that a final editor or redactor had four distinct written sources for this early period of Israel's history that the compiler wove together to form the text as we know it now. In his model, these four written documents had reached such a status of authority that the redactor was not free to choose what to include or leave out, resulting in an uneven final text. Later scholars conjectured that this collection was formed under Persian rule in the fourth century B.C.E. in response to Persian practice of gathering the ancient traditions and laws of the peoples that they conquered.

The Four Sources of the Pentateuch

The following chart provides a brief outline of Wellhausen's sources.

NAME OF THE SOURCE	APPROXIMATE DATE	LOCATION OF THE AUTHOR	DISTINGUISHING FEATURES
Yahwist	United Monarchy (900 B.C.E.)	South in or around Jerusalem	• Calls God "Yahweh" in Genesis • God depicted with human-like characteristics • Lively storyteller
Elohist	Early Divided Monarchy (800 B.C.E.)	North	• Does not use Yahweh for God in Genesis, but does use it after that • Lively storytelling

Deuteronomist	Late Divided Monarchy/Judah Alone (600)	South but includes northern traditions	• Found primarily in the book of Deuteronomy • Characterized by sermon-like speeches • Characteristic focus on law as covenant
Priestly Source	Persian Period (500)	South	• Uses only Elohim for God in Genesis, but both names after that • Very transcendent God • Focused on purity and ritual

While Wellhausen's model assumes written traditions, another scholar, Hermann Gunkel, examined evidence of oral traditions in these texts, evidence he called a "form." Engaging contemporary studies of folklore, Gunkel's approach focused on the social settings for the oral delivery of the material, for example, laws developed in legal settings, ritual traditions reflecting the work of temple personnel, stories featuring the sanctity of a place like Bethel stemmed from a setting in Bethel, etc. While the models proposed by Wellhausen and Gunkel were not immediately compatible, subsequent biblical scholars smoothed out the differences, conjecturing both oral and written developments of the material in these books.

The scholarly consensus on these models began to fade in the late twentieth century, however, for a variety of reasons. For example, archaeological excavations suggest that Israelite society was not stable or economically rich enough to have produced some of the texts that Wellhausen's model requires. Other scholars note that the development of complex prose appears in the ancient world only in the late Persian and early Hellenistic period. Scholars have also lost confidence in identifying four complete separate streams within these five books; Wellhausen's theory oversimplifies the variety of material. Most recently, the model of copying and pasting on which Wellhausen's theory depends does not work for scrolls, especially in a primarily oral culture.

Today, most scholars of the Pentateuch agree on the existence of two major traditions in the final texts: one that represents the concerns and expertise of the priests (Wellhausen's Priestly source) and another, which is called, for the sake of convenience, the Deuteronomist. While this source is found primarily in the book of Deuteronomy, there are also reflexes in Exodus especially. There is currently no consensus, however, on the dates of this material (even broadly speaking), the social location of the Deuteronomists (Levites? Northerners? Post-exilic scribes?), or the unity of the material now deemed non-D and non-P. Some scholars continue to promote a Yahwistic source, especially in Genesis, but the presence of an "Elohist" has far fewer advocates.

As a result, what can be said about the formation or authorship of the Pentateuch at this point? First, the models of its formation arise from the character of the texts themselves. Was Ishmael a baby when Hagar set him under a bush to die in Genesis 21:15, or was he a teenager, as the chronology suggests (Abraham was 86 when Ishmael was born in Genesis 16:15, but 100 when Isaac was born; Ishmael is banished after Isaac is weaned, probably three to five years later)? Did God limit human lives to 120 years (Genesis 6:3) before the Flood, in light of Abraham's death at age 175 (Genesis 25:7) and Sarah's death at the age of 127 (Genesis 23:1)? Which Passover law was obligatory in ancient Israel? These questions have led scholars to recognize that even Wellhausen's model of composition cannot explain the production of such a complex collection.

Second, the history of these texts' production is probably far more complicated than any single model can account for. The recorded traditions were handed down both orally and in written form over centuries within contexts that continued to shape their transmission. This complexity witnesses to the texts' continued theological and cultural impact across many different periods and settings.

Third, at some point, the development of the traditions slowed down and eventually stopped, but that does not mean that it stopped at the same time in every place. The form of the scrolls used at the Second Temple of Jerusalem may have become more stable earlier than the transmission of traditions among diaspora communities in Mesopotamia, Egypt, and eventually southern Europe. Even within the Levant, Jews continued to tell these stories in new forms, such as the non-canonical book of Jubilees that retells the stories of the patriarchs, and the Temple Scroll (one of the longest of the Dead Sea Scrolls), which presents another set of laws given to Moses on Mount Sinai.

Finally, the authoritative status of these particular texts developed organically among people of faith (here, various Jewish communities) and was not based on either the decisions of a committee or requirements about how they were produced or who wrote them. For many Jews and Christians, their function as authoritative revelation from God is actualized within the worshipping community as a whole.

The Patriarchs and Matriarchs

Genesis 12–50 contains Israel's descriptions of its own beginnings. While the narratives have a particular historical setting, the stories transcend that setting. They function as stories about origins, and, as stories of origin like the creation accounts, they express Israel's view of itself and its relation to God. The stories about Jacob, for instance, are not historical archives; instead, the characterization of Jacob embodies the collective identity of Israel.

These narratives highlight the kinship relationships between the founders of the tribes of Israel. Genealogies become the latticework that connects various episodes. The story tracks not only paternity, but also the identity of the various mothers. In this book, Israel is stripped down to its basic components as a kinship group or household. Each person knows his or her role and fulfills his or her function within that social structure. This is not a romanticized view of family, however; within this collective group, people behave badly. Husbands sell off their wives, wives beat slaves, and siblings try to kill each other.

Family in Ancient Israel

Ancient Israelite families had a distinctly different social configuration than contemporary Christian families. Perhaps the most obvious difference is the practice of polygamy evident in the stories in Genesis. Polygamy was legal throughout Israel's history. Because of the harsh conditions of the ancient world that affected women more than men, polygamy both provided a way for more women to have the protection of a male head of household and increased the chances for a man to sire male children who would reach adulthood. The word sometimes translated as "concubine" in the Bible simply means a wife of lower social status. While in contemporary parlance, the word "family" usually refers to one set of parents and their children, in the ancient world "family" was a multi-generational group, which included several sets of related parents and their children. The oldest male among this kinship group held the place of honor, and dissent by other adult males in the group constituted "dishonor" of the "father."

The household also included anyone economically dependent on this group. This would include the family's slaves, as well as free workers contracted as retainers to the family. When the patriarchs moved about with their families in the book of Genesis, the group included the kinship group and all of these servants and slaves. In the stories of Abraham, Sarah is a primary wife, while Hagar is Sarah's female slave. In the Jewish scripture, since Sarah gives Hagar to Abraham to father a child for her, Hagar acts as a surrogate mother and Ishmael is the legal son of Sarah and Abraham. The status of Hagar and Ishmael changes when Abraham banishes them. Then they become foreigners or resident aliens who cannot own land.

The accounts of Abraham feature God's role in directing the action. Abraham moves from Ur to Haran to the land of Canaan because God tells him to. God enters into a covenant agreement with Abraham, an agreement that the Lord must repeat and further specify two more times (Chapters 12, 15, and 17). This Abrahamic covenant focuses on land ownership: God will "give" Abraham land, as well as male progeny to inherit this land right. The sign of the covenant, circumcision, marks the male body part through which the covenant will carry forward. Even though the covenant agreement requires Abraham's complete obedience, God can freely opt out. This is demonstrated when God commands Abraham to offer up Isaac as a burnt offering, which would have resulted in the nullification of the covenant.

Although in some of these stories Abraham does what is required and immediately obeys, this is not always the case. In Genesis 12, directly after God has made the covenant with Abraham for the first time, Abraham leaves the inherited land because of drought and contracts with Pharaoh to marry Sarai. Either the abandonment of the land or the attempt to disavow his wife would have resulted in Abraham's rejection of the covenant. The covenant remains in effect only because God intervenes and reinstates it.

Similar accounts of human foibles and divine rescue punctuate the stories of the patriarchs and matriarchs. Isaac designates the wrong son as his heir. Jacob deceives his brother-in-law, and Jacob's ten oldest sons conspire to kill their younger brother. The covenant remains intact through its repetition in the book, and through God's involvement in their lives. Even though these patriarchs seem deeply flawed, the contemporary audience needs to remember that these stories are the Israelites' own testimony to who they are as a people and what their relationship with God is like.

Within the Israelite tradition, Jacob was the most important patriarch. There are very few references to Abraham outside of the book of Genesis, but there are

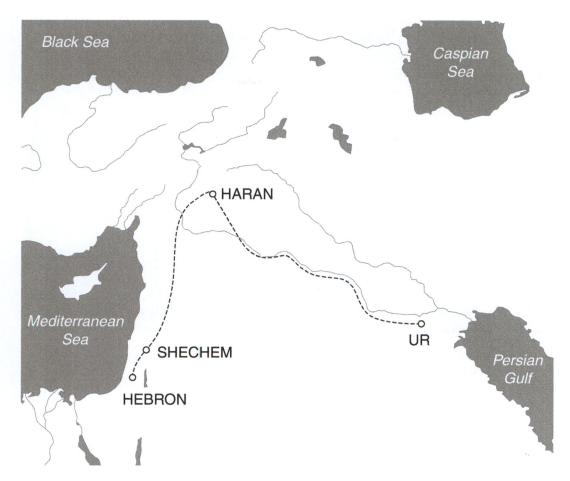

Figure 3–1 The Journey of Abraham from Ur to Canaan.

numerous references to Jacob. In Genesis, Jacob is the character whose name is changed to Israel, a very explicit indication of the role that the Jacob traditions played within Israelite society. Genesis contrasts the weak, effeminate, trickster Jacob with his brother, the ruddy, brutish Esau. While Jacob becomes Israel, Esau is renamed Edom, the country just to the south and east of ancient Israel. The stories of the brothers capture Israel's recognition that they were superior to the Edomites not because they were stronger or better at war, but because they were smarter and had the right deity on their side.

While the figure of Jacob embodies the group identity of Israel as a whole, the accounts of Jacob's 12 sons represent the variation in character of the 12 tribes of Israel (defined as descendants of each of these sons). Although the book of Genesis does not preserve very many individual traditions connected to the tribal patriarchs, here and there variations peek through. This is especially true for Judah in Genesis 39, and for Benjamin and Joseph, the two sons of Rachel, who are presented as the youngest and most favored offspring. It is not surprising that the final form of the book of Genesis preserves traditions related to the primary tribes in the later nation of Israel (Judah, Benjamin, and Joseph's sons, Ephraim and Manasseh).

Figure 3–2 Mosaic in San Vitale, Ravenna. The illustration in the center depicts the scene in which three visitors come to Abraham at the oak of Mamre to announce Isaac's birth. The illustration on the right depicts the scene of Abraham's near-sacrifice of Isaac (see Genesis 18:1–15 and 22:1–19).

The book of Genesis ends in a surprising way: with the family residing in Egypt. The stories move from the area east of the Levant (Eden, Babel, and Ur) into the Levant (Sodom, Bethel, and Shechem) and then back out of the land, this time to the south and west (Egypt). Scholars debate the significance of these locations, but what is clear is that the book ends with the family of Israel still outside the land. They survive only through the assistance of Joseph, the very brother they tried to kill. The story ends up valorizing the outsiders and marginalized, not because they are more noble than the elite or those in power, but simply because God has chosen them.

THE BOOKS OF EXODUS, LEVITICUS, NUMBERS, AND DEUTERONOMY

The material in the Pentateuch that follows Genesis centers around the figure of Moses; Exodus begins with his birth and Deuteronomy closes with his death. The narrative slows down to recount a few important episodes in his life. This begins with the account of his birth in Exodus 1–2. The mortal threat that baby Moses faced marks him as an important, fated figure. The fact that Moses' deliverer was the Pharaoh's own daughter undercuts this unnamed Pharaoh's claim to power.

These two chapters stand as a prelude to the real contest that unfolds in Chapters 3–15. God appears to the fugitive Moses, and tells him to deliver the Hebrews (who do not even know this deity's name) out of slavery. In this account, the Hebrews name their God as the deity of their ancestors (the God of Abraham, Isaac, and Jacob), but at the burning bush, this God provides the name YHWH. This name is actually a form of the Hebrew word for "to be," and depending on how it is vocalized, it means either "the one who is" or "the one who creates." The narrative of the deliverance of the Hebrew slaves is told in epic fashion. While the dialogues focus on the interaction between Moses and Pharaoh, the real contest involves the Lord's repudiation of Pharaoh's claims to be semi-divine. This narrative focus is achieved not only by the delaying tactic of the Ten Plagues that demonstrate the Lord's control over nature in Egypt, but even more by God's ability to manipulate Pharaoh, exemplified by the phrase "hardening his heart." While logically it does not make sense to extend the Hebrew suffering by God's changing Pharaoh's mind to release them (Exodus 10), it makes perfect narrative sense to undercut Pharaoh's claims to power.

The narrative slows down even more with its depiction of the last plague, the slaying of the firstborn of the Egyptians, which leads directly into the Israelites' escape and crossing of the Red Sea. The passage almost grinds to a halt with the instructions of how to celebrate **Passover** in Chapter 12–13, but this material highlights the liturgical function of the story in ancient Israel, and still today.

Chapters 11–15 focus less on the interaction between God and Pharaoh as individuals and more on the contrast between the heavily militarized Egyptians and the helpless Hebrew slaves. The story plays with ironic twists. The Israelites "plunder" the Egyptians even before the battle begins (Exodus 12:36). The military might of the Egyptians literally bogs them down in the mud of the river, allowing the slaves to escape (Exodus 14:25). The greatest irony involves the plague itself. While Pharaoh had tried to kill the firstborn of the Hebrews in Chapter 1, the Lord succeeds in killing the firstborn of the Egyptians in Exodus 12:25.

Passover

The Jewish festival of Passover celebrates the night the Hebrews were delivered from slavery in Egypt, when the angel of death passed over the houses of the Israelites. Passover is mentioned 24 times in the Pentateuch, including descriptions of how the ritual should be celebrated, notably in Exodus 12, Leviticus 23, Numbers 9, and Deuteronomy 16. Some of these passages describe sacrifices that take place at the Temple of Jerusalem, while others present it as primarily a household-based ritual. It was the domestic version of the ritual that became prominent in Judaism after the destruction of the Second Temple when sacrificial rituals were no longer possible. Today, the Jewish observation of the Passover follows the rituals laid out in the rabbinic text, *The Passover Haggadah*, which identifies symbolic foods that represent different elements of the Passover event. The Gospel writers focus on the proximity of Jesus' death to the festival of Passover in their accounts of his last days. While they differ on the exact timing of Jesus' arrest vis-à-vis Passover, they all see a meaningful connection between the death of Jesus and the sacrifice of the Passover lamb, which symbolized God's gift of freedom.

The material from Exodus 15 through to the end of Deuteronomy covers Israel's 40-year migration through the wilderness of the Sinai Peninsula. The story slows down again in Chapters 19 and 20 to describe the revelation of the Torah to Moses at Mount Sinai (also called Horeb by the Deuteronomist). While many Christians think that only the Ten Commandments are revealed, the narratives place the origin of all of Israel's laws in this location. The bulk of laws makes the narrative flow difficult to follow, but one thing becomes clear. In spite of their miraculous deliverance and the

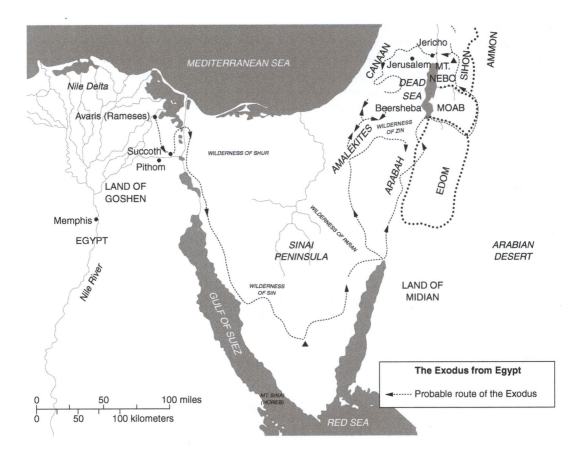

Figure 3–3 The traditional route of the Exodus.

gift of divinely revealed laws, the Hebrews continue to complain. They rebel against Moses' authority and even occasionally wish they were back in Egypt. Moses himself becomes increasingly frustrated and angry, while the next generation, represented by Joshua and Caleb, are the ones to carry the hope forward.

Moses and the Exodus

Moses casts the greatest shadow across the pages of the Old Testament, more than any other biblical figure. The narratives set during his lifetime span four biblical books. Direct references and indirect allusions to him can be found in every section of the Old Testament canon. As an ad hoc leader, he brings the Hebrews out of slavery in Egypt and provides them with divinely revealed laws. As a prophet, he sees God in visible form. As a religious leader, he establishes the priesthood and builds the Tabernacle, which foreshadows the temple in Jerusalem. Moses is the superhero of the Old Testament.

Within the Pentateuch, different texts stress different aspects of his leadership, evidence that traditions about this important biblical figure circulated in a variety of forms throughout Israelite society and history. While some of these were less influential (e.g., how he used a bronze serpent to ward off snake attacks [Numbers 21:1–9]),

Figure 3–4 Moses at the Burning Bush. Icon from Saint Catherine's Monastery, Sinai.

others come to prominence, not only in the Pentateuch but throughout the biblical canon. This section will provide a summary of a few of the pertinent texts.

First, Moses is a prophet. While most Christians might regard his deliverance of the Hebrews from Egypt as his most important deed, his role as prophet comes first. While prophecy will be covered more extensively in Chapter 4, it is important to note this characteristic of Moses here. God, in the form of a burning bush, calls him to be a prophet, a call Moses tries to avoid. Within ancient society, Moses' reticence displays honorable humility and deference, not defiance to a divine command. God's promise to remain with Moses rewards him for this attitude of respect. As a result, the Pentateuch presents Moses as the greatest prophet (Deuteronomy 34:10; Exodus 33:11; Numbers 12:7–8).

Second, Moses does deliver the Hebrews from Egypt, a feat for which he is celebrated. He functions as a heroic liberator, and within this paradigm, his reluctance at the burning bush indicates the magnitude of what God asks him to do. Several of the texts in Exodus stress the size of Pharaoh's army and contrast that with the unarmed vulnerability of the fleeing slaves. References to Moses and Aaron as deliverers can be found in a variety of biblical books, such as 1 Samuel 12:6, Psalm 77, and Micah 6:4 (which adds Miriam). It also sits at the heart of the celebration of Passover within both ancient and modern Judaism.

Third, Moses is the lawgiver. His mediation of the divinely revealed Torah, which forms ancient Jewish identity, especially in periods of exile, colonization, and diaspora, makes him the true founder of fully formed Judaism. In this function, the characterization of Moses does not embody the characterization of Israel, as the depictions of Abraham and Jacob do. Instead, he functions more as a righteous royal figure. This lawgiving aspect of Mosaic identity informs the portrayal of Josiah in 2 Kings, as well as Ezra in the book of Ezra. In the New Testament, Jesus' Sermon on the Mount in Matthew 5–7 engages this aspect of Moses, as Jesus gives an authoritative interpretation of the Law.

The Ten Commandments

The book of Exodus connects God's revelation of the Ten Commandments to the giving of the Law, even though the Commandments are not technically laws. Instead, they are prohibitions of categories of sin, such as murder, lying, and adultery. The laws that follow them flesh out the specifics of these categories with specific laws. The Commandments appear twice in the Pentateuch (Exodus 20:1–17

Figure 3–5 *Moses descending from Mount Sinai with tablets of stone,* by Gustave Doré (1832–1883).

and Deuteronomy 5:6–21) with slight variations. The numbering varies among religious traditions. Jews, Eastern Orthodox Christians, and Protestants aside from Lutherans divide the two "tables of the Law" between first four and the last six commandments. Catholics and Lutherans divide them between the first three and the last seven. The first table of the Law deals with the relationship between humans and God. These include the requirement to worship this single deity and to observe the **Sabbath** as a weekly enactment of that exclusive relationship. The second table of the Law, although numbered differently in Exodus and Deuteronomy, extends the effects of the relationship with God to the Israelites' relationships to each other. It begins with the household (treat the male and female heads of that household with honor) and then moves out into the community. It ends with the relationship between households, one of mutual respect of family and property.

Fourth, related to this legal function, Moses is the founder of Israelite religious practices. At the center of Israelite religion were the rituals performed at the temple. These rituals were rooted in the Laws preserved in the Pentateuch. Although Moses' brother, Aaron, is the founder of the hereditary priesthood, Moses is the one who appoints him to serve in this role. The shared leadership of Moses and Aaron foreshadows the ideal relationship between king and priests in ancient Israel. In the post-biblical period, Moses will even be celebrated by Jewish scholars like Philo of Alexandria, and by Christians as well, as a philosopher.

The Theology of the Pentateuch

A major theme in the Pentateuch is that of covenant. The Hebrew word for "covenant" is also used for treaties and other legally binding relationships. In the ancient world, covenants were used for a variety of purposes, including the sealing of treaties and contracts between kings and their subjects. Simply stated, a **covenant** is a solemn agreement between two parties (individuals or groups) listing their respective rights and responsibilities in the relationship. Because they were sealed with an oath, ancient covenants carried a religious significance—a sense of being guaranteed by God. In the book of Genesis, the Lord is described as confirming a divine promise to Abraham and his descendants by "making a covenant" with Abraham.

There are several covenants between God and the people in the Hebrew Bible/ Old Testament. God makes a permanent covenant with Noah in Genesis 9, not to flood the earth again. The Lord will make a covenant with David in 2 Samuel 7 focused on the security of the Davidic dynasty. The two major covenants in the Pentateuch involved first Abraham and then Moses. The Abrahamic covenant focused on inheritable land. God grants Abraham and his progeny the rights to the land in the Southern Levant, and guarantees that there will be offspring to inherit the land.

The other major covenant in the Pentateuch consists in the Law as revealed to Moses on the mountain. This Law focuses on the conditional nature of God's covenant. Attached to the Law, most explicitly in Deuteronomy 28, are blessings if the people obey it and curses if they do not. Most of the emphasis falls upon political stability, which is threatened by economic disaster, catastrophic natural disasters, and military takeover. The prophets tend to use the Israelites' refusal to follow the Law as an explanation for national disasters.

This notion of covenant has become a major theme in both Jewish and Christian theology, but in each tradition covenant came to mean a variety of things. For example, the biblical book called the Wisdom of Ben Sirach contains a much longer hymn of praise for Aaron and his son than it does for Moses. For Christians, the death and resurrection of Jesus marked the end of the old covenant that relied on human action and the beginning of a new covenant based on God's grace. Because Abraham's covenant precedes the revelation of the Law, which shaped Jewish identity, Paul engages the traditions about Abraham to argue that God deems people as righteous who do not follow the Pentateuchal laws because they did not yet exist.

Ibrahim and Hagar in Islam

While the Jewish scriptures contain narratives about Abraham, Sarah, and Hagar, Islamic traditions pass on narratives of these same figures but with some notable differences. For example, in some Islamic traditions, the child that Ibrahim almost sacrifices, although unnamed in the Qur'an, is Ishmael, and the place of the sacrifice is in modern-day Jerusalem at the Dome of the Rock (where the Jewish temple had stood). In other traditions, Hajar, as she is called, is not banished at Sarah's insistence, but stays in the desert with her son willingly, which exemplifies both her and Ibrahim's faith in God. Ibrahim leaves them in the area that later became Mecca, and the Islamic pilgrimage, required at least once in every male's life, commemorates these traditions with various rituals. Ishmael is the child promised by God, and the prophet Muhammad traces his lineage back to Ishmael.

Key Terms

Covenant	Pentateuch	Torah
Passover	Promised Land	
Patriarchs	Sabbath	

Study Questions

1. What are some of the reasons that biblical scholars believe that the final form of the Pentateuch incorporates earlier written and oral traditions?

2. Why is it important to recognize that the Patriarchs were the founders of later Israel? How does this affect how the stories are read?

3. What are some of the roles that Moses takes on from Exodus through Deuteronomy?

4. What is a covenant, and what are some of the covenants found in the Old Testament?

Sources Consulted and Recommended Reading

Baden, Joel S. 2012. *The Composition of the Pentateuch: Renewing the Documentary Hypothesis.* Anchor Yale Bible Reference. New Haven, CT: Yale University Press.

Kaminsky, Joel S., and Joel N. Lohr. 2011. *The Torah: A Beginner's Guide.* Oxford: One World.

Meyers, Carol. 2013. *Rediscovering Eve: Ancient Israelite Women in Context.* New York: Oxford University Press.

Rousseau, Philip, and Janet Timbie, eds. 2019. *The Christian Moses: From Philo to the Qur'an.* Washington, DC: Catholic University of America.

Chapter

ISRAEL IN THE LAND

Settlement, Exile, Return

TIMELINE

*c.*1250–1020 B.C.E.	Joshua and the Israelites enter Canaan. The period of the Judges.
*c.*1020–1000 B.C.E.	Saul reigns as king of the Israelite people.
*c.*1000–961 B.C.E.	David is king of Israel and establishes Jerusalem as its capital.
*c.*961–922 B.C.E.	Solomon reigns as king of united Israel and builds the Temple in Jerusalem.
922 B.C.E.	Solomon's kingdom is divided in two: the Northern Kingdom (Israel) and the Southern Kingdom (Judah).
*c.*750–745 B.C.E.	The prophets Amos and Hosea preach in the Northern Kingdom of Israel. Assyria becomes a world power.
*c.*742–700 B.C.E.	The prophet Isaiah preaches in the Southern Kingdom of Judah.
721 B.C.E.	The Northern Kingdom of Israel is defeated by the Assyrians.
*c.*626–587 B.C.E.	The prophet Jeremiah preaches in the Southern Kingdom of Judah. Babylon becomes a world power.
597 B.C.E.	Judah is defeated by Babylon. The Babylonian exile begins.
597–573 B.C.E.	The prophet Ezekiel preaches in exile in Babylon.
587–586 B.C.E.	The Jerusalem Temple is destroyed.
*c.*540 B.C.E.	The prophet known as Second Isaiah preaches during the exile; Persia becomes a world power.
538 B.C.E.	King Cyrus of Persia issues a decree allowing the people of Judah to return to their homes.
*c.*520 B.C.E.	Ezra and Nehemiah begin a religious reform of Judaism. The Temple in Jerusalem is rebuilt.

JOSHUA AND JUDGES

At the end of the book of Exodus, God forbids Moses to enter the land promised to the Israelites. He is buried on the top of a mountain overlooking the land, and the Israelites are on the edge of their inheritance (Numbers 34:1–8). God promised this land first to the patriarch Abraham (Genesis 12). The two books of Joshua and Judges both describe the Israelite possession of this land, the land of Canaan. However, there are two distinct versions promoted by the two books. Joshua describes a lightning conquest and destruction of the indigenous people. In Judges, the settlement is more gradual. In the book of Joshua, Moses' second-in-command took the Israelites through the center of Canaan, dividing the country in half. Then they went toward the north, picking off the Canaanite city-states one by one, then they conquered the southern ones.

These are stories that the Israelites told one another, hundreds of years after the events were supposed to have happened. It therefore becomes difficult to determine which of these accounts are historical—that is, which actually happened—and which ones acquired a kind of legendary status. The existence of more than one version of the "historical" event, which is a frequent occurrence, compounds the problem. The books of Joshua and Judges view the Israelite entrance into Canaan quite differently.

The Canaanites, as portrayed in Joshua and Judges, did not organize a centralized government. Rather, they gathered in agrarian communities living together as satellite villages around walled cities governed by a king. The surrounding villages would provide food and workers for the king, and in return, in times of crisis, the king would protect the villages, sometimes bringing the population and livestock behind the protective walls of the city. These city-state kings constantly warred against one another. Therefore, Joshua and the Israelite armies were able to overwhelm the cities one by one and exterminate them in an "ethnic cleansing" of entire populations. The Israelites regarded the Canaanites as aliens who could not coexist with the Israelite population.

The discipline in Joshua's company of religious warriors was intense, and the punishment for disloyalty was extremely severe, for example, when one soldier concealed in his tent things he stole from the Canaanites, he and all his family were stoned to death. God told the Israelites that their war was a holy war because they fought on behalf of the Israelite God YHWH (Deuteronomy 20; Joshua 7). Therefore, all the spoils of war were dedicated to YHWH. This conflict over the land has spilled over to contemporary events, where factions in the modern State of Israel claim sovereignty over territory because of their understanding that God promised it to them.

In the book of Judges, the picture changes. Instead of a lightning-fast conquest, here the Israelites must fit themselves into a complex society, not displacing the native peoples, but rather living alongside them. The Israelites settled on the mountainous spine that runs up the center of the country. They lived there because the other peoples occupied all the good places. The Canaanites inhabited the fertile valleys. The Philistines, who would give their name to "Palestine," lived on the coast. Even the city of Jerusalem, which would become King David's capital and remain the capital for the duration of his dynasty, even Jerusalem was a Canaanite stronghold until David conquered it.

According to the book of Judges, the Israelites faced two challenges. First, they had to coexist with peoples who were wedded to the agricultural cycles of the land and worshipped the various Canaanite gods and goddesses. They resisted against

Canaanite influence, as they sought to maintain their own distinct identity as Israelites and worshippers of YHWH. Second, the Israelites struggled against being dominated and even occupied by some of the city-states in their territory.

Bronze Age to Iron Age

This period was a time of great technological change. Historians often date periods by the dominant technology of the time. The first human cultures lived in the "Stone Age." Stone, the first material used for tools, is easy to find and a relatively simple technique gives certain stones a sharp edge. However, that edge chips easily and must be constantly re-sharpened. The next technological age is called the "Bronze Age." Bronze (copper mixed with other metals) took more skill to refine into a pure and useful form. Bronze held an edge much better than stone and replaced it. Finally, there is the "Iron Age." Iron must be heated to thousands of degrees in order to be shaped into usable form. The only way to do that is with some kind of a forge-bellows system. Those who operate such a system cannot use wood, but must manufacture and employ charcoal to attain the needed temperature. It is more difficult to mine iron, but it is much stronger than bronze and keeps a sharper edge. During the period from Judges to 1 Kings, the region transitioned from the Bronze to the Iron Age. For much of this time, the Philistines had the technological advantage because they knew how to work with iron while the Israelites did not. Furthermore, with the invention of the spoked wheel, the chariot became a terrifying battle platform. According to Judges, the Canaanites employed "iron chariots" to great effect. Most likely, the iron only banded the wheels so they could run over rocky terrain without shattering. On the chariot were two people, one driving the horses and the other in the back, wielding a spear or a bow and arrows.

The book of Deuteronomy describes Moses' gathering all the Israelite tribes together to renew the covenant that YHWH had made with them on Mount Sinai. The book of Joshua ends with a second renewal of the covenant, as they take possession of the land promised to them by God. The Israelites promise in sacred ceremony to follow the Law that God gave to Moses on the mountain.

The two books, Joshua and Judges, both describe a two-layered political organization by which the Israelite tribes organized themselves. First, one finds a loose tribal confederation—each tribe governed by elders who ruled their individual tribes independently from the other tribes. In the wars of conquest and defense, Israelite soldiers were volunteers. Ideally, the tribes would band together to turn aside any threat to one of their members. Any concerted action taken against a foreign enemy required a general call to arms. In Judges, the various wars fought were regional, involving one, two, or at the most three tribes. The other tribes remained uninvolved. In this organization, certain shared beliefs unified the disparate tribes. All the tribes shared the narrative of their liberation from Egypt and Mount Sinai when Moses received the Law. Additionally, each of the tribes recognized the same central shrine. During the time of Joshua and Judges, the shrine was located at Shiloh. This shared tribal shrine housed the **Ark of the Covenant**. The Ark represented the presence of YHWH. It was a wooden box, overlaid with gold, that contained relics from the time of the Exodus.

A second system of government also operated in Israel. It emerged only in times of national emergency. Moses and Joshua, for instance, were not tribal leaders, but the tribes recognized them as God's chosen leaders of the entire company. They ruled by virtue of the recognition of God's choice. The later figures who fulfilled this intertribal role were called "**judges**." Although the Hebrew word might legitimately be translated as "one who judges," these figures did not decide legal cases. Rather, they led the tribes into battle against their enemies like chieftains or warlords. The structure of the book of Judges follows a certain pattern with regard to these judges. Every time the Israelites face a crisis, God "raises up" a deliverer who leads the people and becomes their "judge." The authority of the judges did not stem from tribal loyalty, but rather from their loyalty to YHWH. Therefore, they had the ability to gather and motivate more than one tribe to action.

A single author assembled these stories of judges, and later of the kings, collecting them and arranging them to make a specific theological point. We call this author the "**Deuteronomic Historian**," or the "Deuteronomist," because the work reflects the theology of the book of Deuteronomy regarding the responsibilities of the Israelites to the covenant, and their destiny. The Deuteronomic History includes the books of Joshua, Judges, 1 and 2 Samuel, and 1 and 2 Kings. Deuteronomic History demonstrates that when the Israelites obeyed YHWH and kept his covenant, they prospered. If they disobeyed his covenant by following after other gods, they would suffer wars and famine. The Deuteronomist wrote at a later time, when destruction threatened the entire Israelite community. It was vitally important that the surviving population come to the correct theological conclusion regarding their setbacks. It was not that YHWH had failed them—rather, they had failed to keep the covenant, and as a result, they suffered a disaster.

Underlying the Deuteronomistic idea is the theological assertion that God always rewards righteousness and punishes evil *in this life*. According to the Deuteronomist, people always get what they deserve, and God rules the world with justice. This raises the problem of the innocent who suffer. Other Israelite writers, most particularly in the wisdom and prophetic traditions, challenged the Deuteronomic position. They claimed that God does not resolve unfairness in this life. Even in the New Testament, Jesus' disciples asked, "Rabbi, who sinned, this man or his parents, that he was born blind?" (John 9:1).

Worship in Judges

Worship in Judges did not take place in a centralized shrine, as would be true later in Israelite history. Rather, there were many regional sites, each with its own priest and altar, where people came with their sacrifice and, overseen by the priest, ritually slaughtered their animals. They commonly linked these sites with some great event in Israel's memory, such as a time at which Abraham or Jacob had encountered God. Alternatively, they located their shrines next to an impressive geographical feature such as a mountain or a grove of tall trees. They associated these places with the cycles of nature; for instance, the special days for liturgical celebrations were the equinox and solstice, or key moments in the agricultural calendar, such as planting, harvest, and the rainy season.

The Beginnings of Monarchy: 1 and 2 Samuel

Divination as a Means of Determining God's Will

Ancient peoples often determined the will of the deity through various forms of divination, or discerning divine messages in the random patterns of nature. Samuel determined that God had chosen David to be king by means of dice-like stones called Urim and Thummim. When cast, they gave answers to yes–no questions. Sometimes the answer came up "maybe," or "no answer."

The prophet Samuel appointed Saul as the first king of united Israel. The tribes approved of Saul because he came from a relatively weak tribe with little territory, and so did not threaten the independence of the other tribes. The Philistine presence, Saul's personal weaknesses, and the opposition of Samuel all contributed to the failure of Saul's reign. In the end, Saul and his sons died fighting against the Philistines in the Battle of Gilboa.

A rising charismatic star in Saul's court, David immediately became king in southern Israel, the territory of Judah. A short time later, the northern tribes declared their loyalty to David. The new king expanded the territory of Israel through conquest and established the Israelite capital as Jerusalem. David had a court prophet named Nathan, who promised him, speaking for YHWH, that his kingdom and his dynasty would endure forever (2 Samuel 7:16). This meant that no matter what happened, there would always be a descendant of David on the throne in Jerusalem. Later inhabitants of Jerusalem and supporters of David's dynastic successors believed this made them invulnerable to enemy attack.

The latter half of David's reign did not go well. David lost control over his family and the kingdom partly because it became known that he had murdered the husband of his lover and future wife, Bathsheba, as told in 2 Samuel. David's career, as reported by the Deuteronomist, was decidedly mixed. However, in later biblical writings, including the New Testament and post-biblical Christian tradition, David looms large as a symbol. In the stories of later kings, Israel's image of David becomes the standard by which they are judged. A king is good insofar as he follows the example of his ancestor David, who was "a man after God's heart," that is, especially beloved by God. Later tradition connects King David with the Psalms. The Psalms served as Israel's songbook and liturgy for worship. The Deuteronomist records David as writer of many psalms, one of which he quotes in full (Psalm 18). Some of the Psalms contain a superscription (annotation), "A Psalm of David," and a few of these superscriptions even mention events in David's life connected with the particular psalm.

Issues in Moral Theology: Monarchy and Prophecy

When addressing the key theological, anthropological, and communal questions of moral theology, a specific concern develops about the use and arrangement of power in and by the covenant community. What ought to be the relationship of people in covenant with God to power? How ought power to be wielded? Who ought to have power?

The Deuteronomic History conveys how Israelites sorted out these questions for themselves—often in contrary ways. While the stories here may not offer

Figure 4–1 *David*, by Michelangelo (1475–1564).

direct analogies to contemporary questions of power for Christians, they illustrate some possible responses. For example, the Israelites dispute whether they ought to have a monarch. On one hand, monarchical governments can temper the chaos and violence created when "people did what was right in their own eyes" (Judges 21:25). By analogy, Christians today might maintain the importance of strong government for maintaining "law and order."

On the other hand, monarchs present the danger of tyranny, with the centralization of power leading to exploitation of people who are geographically, economically, and politically on the margins. If YHWH liberates the marginalized, this arrangement of power violates the expectations of how Israelites are to be a community in covenant with God. Problems with monarchical power are apparent in 1 Samuel 8, where YHWH instructs Samuel to give the people a king, although in requesting a king, the people "have rejected me [YHWH] from being king over them" (1 Samuel 8:7). In this view, the recognition of the ultimate power of God ought to temper the power of rulers. This perspective highlights the danger even in our contemporary context of idolatrizing power and those who wield it.

Prophets offer a third perspective on the relationship of followers of God to power. Rather than wielding official political power as rulers, prophets "speak truth to power." By recalling the requirements of the covenant, they demand that the powerful of Israelite society worship YHWH correctly through just and merciful action that upholds the flourishing of marginalized people in the community. In this view, Christians might find that their appropriate relationship to power in society is to hold those who have power accountable to norms of right relationship and human flourishing for all.

When Israel ceased to be a monarchy (see After the Babylonian Exile section below), the prophets foretold the coming of a leader from David's ancestral line, to restore the monarchy. This expected figure, the one anointed by God to lead Israel and free it from captivity, the Messiah (the anointed one), the Israelites regarded as "the son of David." The New Testament writers connect Jesus with David. The genealogies at the beginning of Matthew and Luke trace Jesus' lineage through David, and the Gospel writers link him to Davidic prophecies. David thus becomes a prefiguration of the Messiah or Christ ("anointed one" in Greek).

King Solomon and the End of the United Kingdom

David appointed his son Solomon to rule after him. Solomon was his son by Bathsheba, the woman whose husband David had murdered, who had become his favorite wife. Solomon is known for his great wisdom, his wealth, his many wives and concubines, and most importantly, for building a magnificent temple to YHWH in Jerusalem, his father's capital city. A number of later biblical books are ascribed in whole or in part to Solomon, because of his reputation for wisdom, poetry, and romance. The Deuteronomist describes him as the writer of many proverbs. He is therefore connected to the biblical books of Proverbs and the Wisdom of Solomon. A collection of love poetry in the Bible called the Song of Solomon or the Song of Songs suggests that he is the author and leading actor. Although the great king likely did not write these texts, linking him to them gave the writings added authority and credibility.

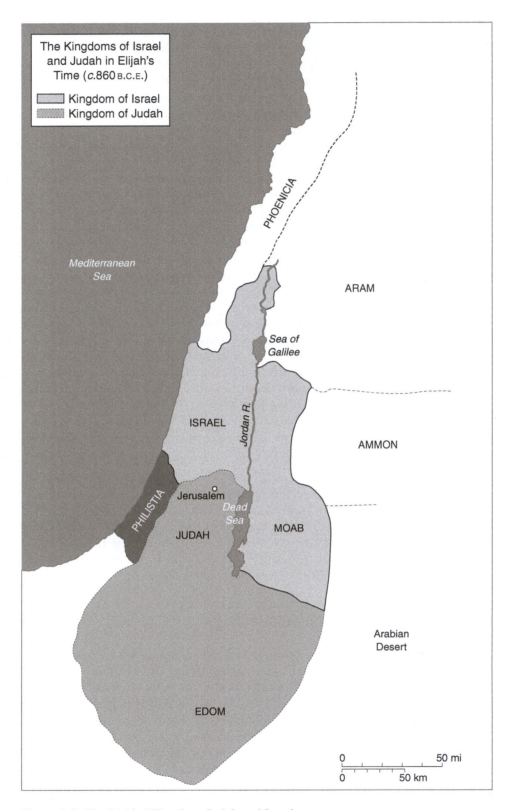

Figure 4–2 The Divided Kingdom, Judah and Israel.

Tensions within Solomon's domain led to a split after his death. The northern territories seceded, but the southern region, consisting of Judah, the tribe to which David belonged, and the tiny tribe of Benjamin, remained loyal to Solomon and his dynasty. Henceforth, the territories that seceded formed the Northern Kingdom which would retain the traditional name "Israel." The Southern Kingdom, which remained loyal to David's dynasty, would be called Judah.

The Ark, Tabernacle, and Temple

The **Ark of the Covenant** was a wooden box overlaid with gold, with two golden statues of cherubim on the top, wings outstretched and meeting in the center. It was supposed to carry a jar of manna, the miraculous bread that fed the Israelites in the wilderness, and the stone copies of the Ten Commandments that God carved on Mount Sinai. The Ark was regarded as the throne of YHWH. The Israelites believed that YHWH ruled Israel as king, sitting on his throne between the cherubim, sphynx-like figures with a lion's body, eagle's wings, and a human's head. "Tabernacle" is an old English word for "tent" and serves as the translation of the sacred tent erected in the wilderness to house the Ark. The Hebrew word for "temple" is the same as the word for "palace." If it houses a king, we translate it as "palace." If it houses a god, we call it "temple." When King Solomon built the temple, he put the Ark in the "holiest place," a chamber inside the building.

The Institution of the Prophet

Prophets began to emerge in Israel at about the same time as the monarchy. As the leadership in Israel became more and more institutionalized and less charismatic, the prophets provided an outlet for the Spirit, for God to speak from outside the institutions of power. Prophets provided no credentials beyond their claim to speak for God. In the Bible, they are typically portrayed as being called by God (and anxious about the responsibility and the risks), not as having nominated themselves for the role. There were court prophets in the hire of the king—they would usually prophesy whatever the king wanted to hear. There were marginal prophets who did not depend upon the king for employment but worked in some other sphere. Because of their independence, they were more free to speak truth to power. Offending the king could end in arrest and execution. Prophets did not primarily speak about the future, although they did that at times. For the most part, they offered what they believed was God's perspective on the current issues of the day. They were "forthtellers," rather than "foretellers."

The Role of the Priest

Ancient peoples regarded it as dangerous to approach deity. Therefore, elaborate rituals developed that would minimize the danger to the worshippers by making the encounter more predictable and reliable. The persons responsible for overseeing the activity were the priests, who mediated between the people and God, led the people in prayer, and taught the people the sacred texts. Most importantly, they led the sacrificial rituals. In Israel, the recognized priests were from the Israelite tribe of Levi, although King David incorporated some Canaanite priests into the guild.

Jeroboam, now king in the north, established sanctuaries/temples to compete with the Temple built by Solomon in Jerusalem. The country became religiously divided. The people of Judah, the Southern Kingdom, believed that YHWH had chosen David and his family to be king forever, ruling from Jerusalem (2 Samuel 7:16). The people of the Northern Kingdom of Israel believed that they followed the ancient Mosaic laws and tribal codes, although they too had become a monarchy like Judah.

The Divided Kingdom and the Assyrian Crisis

The two nations lived in uneasy coexistence until a significant threat from Assyria arose in the eighth century B.C.E. Assyria, located in northern Mesopotamia (modern Iraq), had become the superpower of its day. All the little nations in the region, including Israel and Judah, had to make a choice. They could submit to the Assyrians, who were kinder to those who surrendered than to those who resisted. Or they could resist and hope that their alliance would be powerful enough to halt Assyrian expansion. They could also hope to receive aid from the Egyptians, Assyria's chief rival. Israel and Syria decided to form an alliance and raise up a military response to Assyria. They asked and then demanded that Judah join forces with them. The

Figure 4–3 This portion of the Black Obelisk of Shalmaneser III (King of Assyria from 859–825 B.C.E.) depicts the conquered Jehu, King of Israel, prostrating before the Assyrian King.

prophet Isaiah served as advisor to Ahaz, king of Judah. In the long prophetic book named after Isaiah, we read how Isaiah advised Ahaz to refuse to join the alliance (Chapter 7 of the book of Isaiah; Chapter 6 describes Isaiah's call to be a prophet). In retaliation, the combined forces of Israel and Syria attacked Judah. At that point, the king of Judah made a serious move that would have far-reaching consequences in the region. He asked Assyria to aid him in defense against Syria and Israel. With this occasion to intervene, in 722 B.C.E. the Assyrians proceeded to destroy both Syria and Israel, taking their inhabitants captive and forcibly resettling them in other conquered territories. This marked the end of Israel, the Northern Kingdom. The captured Israelites lost their identity and history never hears from them again, a disappearance that would lead to legends and speculation about "the Ten Lost Tribes."

In spite of the king of Judah's goodwill toward the Assyrians, the Assyrian army continued its sweep southward and devastated the Judean countryside. It came to the walls of **Jerusalem** and laid siege to it, but after a few months, the siege was broken. The Judeans came to believe that YHWH had protected them from the Assyrian invasion. Because God had chosen David to be king, and his descendants after him, and because Solomon had dedicated his temple to YHWH, they believed God would never allow Jerusalem to fall to invaders. The prophet Isaiah assured a succession of Judean kings that Jerusalem and the temple on Mount Zion would always be safe.

Judah Alone and the Babylonian Crisis

Now only Judah remained. Assyrian garrisons occupied the former territory of Israel, which was now populated with resettled foreign peoples whom later biblical tradition called "Samaritans," after the city of Samaria, a capital of the now destroyed Northern Kingdom (the newcomers would eventually adopt the first five books of the Bible, the Torah, with their own temple on Mount Gerizim, but would never be accepted by Jews). The Judeans believed themselves divinely protected. In peaceful times, when Assyria was less aggressive, Judean kings would assert their independence. Most notably, King Josiah (r. c.640–609 B.C.E.) cleansed Solomon's temple of Assyrian images and deities, and centralized Judean worship in the Temple in Jerusalem. He closed down the local shrines because he saw them as hopelessly compromised and vulnerable to syncretism, that is, the combining of elements of different religions. Now all animals had to be sacrificed in Jerusalem. As a result, worshippers came to the holy city on feast days, bringing their sacrificial animals. At other times, when Assyria was in ascendancy, Judean kings had to submit to their Assyrian overlords. Ultimately, in the late seventh century, the Assyrians were conquered and overthrown by the other Mesopotamian power, Babylon.

In the waning years of the Davidic dynasty, the Judeans struggled with the burgeoning power of the Babylonian emperor. Finally, Babylon moved south and laid siege to Jerusalem, as the Assyrians had done a century and a half earlier. Many in Jerusalem were confident that YHWH would once again protect their sacred city from invasion. The prophet Jeremiah stood at the entrance to the Temple and declared that they were not safe as long as they violated the divine covenant. He declared that YHWH would treat them just as he had treated their northern cousins. For his efforts in warning the inhabitants of Jerusalem, the Judean king imprisoned and tortured Jeremiah. Things became increasingly desperate inside the city. Finally, King Zechariah, the last king of Judah, broke through the city walls in the middle of the night and tried to escape with his family. He was caught and brought before Nebuchadnezzar, the Babylonian emperor. The emperor killed Zechariah's sons before his eyes. Then the king was blinded and carried in chains to Babylon, along with most of the leadership and wealthy in the city. The Temple was destroyed and its treasures hauled off as booty.

This disaster marked the end of the Davidic dynasty. From 1000 B.C.E. to 587 B.C.E., almost half a millennium, a descendant of David had ruled on the throne in Jerusalem. The promise that the prophet Nathan had made to David that his throne and kingdom would last forever now seemed null and void. From the Exodus, people had believed that YHWH was a powerful warrior god who would defeat Israel's enemies, as he destroyed the Egyptian army. In the south, they believed that as long as they had a descendant of David on the throne in Jerusalem, and as long as the Temple of Solomon stood on Mount Zion in Jerusalem, they were safe. The Babylonians exposed the emptiness of this illusion. In the view of the Deuteronomist, the Judeans and Israelites brought this on themselves by their religious unfaithfulness and their failure to keep the covenant that YHWH had made with the nation. After this point in biblical history, the focus of the biblical text rested on the community sent into exile in Babylon. Although some prophets proclaimed that the captivity would be short-lived, the great prophet Jeremiah told the community to settle in, because their exile in a foreign land would endure for generations.

AFTER THE BABYLONIAN EXILE

SECOND ISAIAH

Toward the end of the Babylonian Exile, a new prophetic voice arose among the exiles of Judah. The words of this otherwise anonymous prophet appear in the latter part of the book of Isaiah (Isaiah 40–66). A careful examination of the material in these chapters reveals that we are no longer hearing the words that Isaiah of Jerusalem spoke at the end of the eighth century (*c.*742–700 B.C.E.), but rather words addressed to Jewish exiles shortly before their liberation at the hands of Cyrus of Persia in 538 B.C.E. Why then is this material part of the book of Isaiah instead of a new book bearing this exilic prophet's name? The most likely answer is that the exilic author considered his work a continuation or application of Isaiah's message in a new historical moment. What Isaiah of Jerusalem had prophesied about God's salvation for a remnant of Judah and the future restoration and glorification of the holy city Jerusalem was now taking shape in a new way 200 years later.

Among the new developments one finds in Second Isaiah (also known as Deutero-Isaiah) is a message of unmitigated mercy and consolation. Especially in Isaiah 40–55, which seems to date before 538 B.C.E. (Isaiah 56–66, from a slightly later period, is often called Third Isaiah), some of the most beautifully comforting passages in all of scripture are to be found. One example is the comparison of God's love and care for his people to that of a mother for her baby (Isaiah 49:15). The warnings and accusations of the pre-exilic prophets are entirely absent. The message of hope and comfort seeks to renew a people who have already suffered for their sins and more (Isaiah 40:1–2).

The Servant of YHWH

Another significant development in Second Isaiah is the appearance of a figure known as the Servant of YHWH (Servant of the Lord). In four main passages (Isaiah 42:1–4; 49:1–6; 50:4–11; 52:13–53:12), the prophet speaks of this Servant who, endowed with God's spirit, brings teaching and salvation to the nations, and bears insult, injury, and death to save and heal God's people. These texts are among the most significant in the Old Testament for the Christian understanding of Jesus and his mission. Each is quoted or alluded to in the New Testament with reference to Jesus (Matthew 12:17–21; Luke 2:31; Mark 15:19; Acts 8:32–33). The redemptive suffering that the Servant endures is especially highlighted in Isaiah 52:13–53:12, which explains why this text is read in the church's liturgy on Good Friday and why this figure is often called "the Suffering Servant."

While the Christological interpretation of these passages is significant, the Servant of YHWH was understood in various ways in its original historical context. Isaiah 49:3 would identify the Servant with Israel, while Isaiah 50:4–6 seems to be referring to the prophet himself. Even in the New Testament, these Servant passages are not always applied exclusively to Jesus, but sometimes to his followers as well (Acts 13:47). This is quite typical of prophetic imagery. The use of imagery invites continual reappropriation and actualization of the prophetic word, so that it is never simply a dead word in the past, but a living word to each new generation.

POST-EXILIC PROPHECY AND APOCALYPTIC LITERATURE

Post-exilic prophecy continues the earlier prophetic calls to worship YHWH not by mere ritual but through practicing justice and mercy (Isaiah 58). However, one also finds exhortations to rebuild the Temple (Haggai 1–2) and to renew the cultic life (Malachi 3:3–4) and national identity (Isaiah 62) of the returned exiles. Prophecy in this new era also focuses on the fulfillment of messianic expectations, not only in David's heir, but in priestly (Zechariah 3–4) and prophetic (Isaiah 61) figures as well. Post-exilic prophecy evolves into what has come to be called **apocalyptic** literature. The word "apocalyptic" comes from a Greek word meaning "to reveal" or "to uncover," referring to revelations of the heavenly realms and the destiny of this world. Much of apocalyptic literature is pseudonymous, written as if by an ancient figure. This gives it an air of authority since scripture—the written word from the past—had by this time taken precedence over the spoken words of contemporary prophets. Perhaps most significantly, apocalyptic literature is densely symbolic and therefore extremely difficult to interpret without knowledge of the meanings of Jewish symbols and numbers as well as the historical events to which these texts frequently allude. The puzzling nature of these writings has often led to fanciful misinterpretations, often associating the texts with literal prophecies about the end of the world. In reality, they are not road maps to the end of the world but rather texts of faith and hope, affirming God's plan and providence in human history during moments of tribulation.

Apocalyptic literature is often distinguished by a heightened eschatology in which the dramatic events of the present are seen as a turning point in history. It is frequently found in moments of crisis, especially war or persecution, and flourishes from the second century B.C.E. to the second century C.E. During this period, apocalyptic literature will be inspired by events such as the persecution of the Syrian king Antiochus IV, the Jewish–Roman Wars, and the earliest Roman persecutions of Christians. In apocalyptic scenarios, this present evil age is to be replaced by God's kingdom and his triumph over evil, which will soon take place. In many apocalypses, the force of evil is personified in the form of Satan or the Devil, though some, like Daniel, personify evil in oppressors of the Jews. After evil is conquered, both the wicked and the righteous are resurrected. At this point, a final judgment takes place, in which the righteous receive their final reward, eternal life, and the wicked receive eternal punishment.

THE BOOK OF DANIEL

The book of Daniel is our main Old Testament exemplar of apocalyptic literature. Written in three languages (Aramaic, Hebrew, and Greek), Daniel shows evidence of being a composite work, incorporating material from various hands in the post-exilic period. The final form of the book can be dated to the second century B.C.E. due to the many historical allusions in Chapters 7–12. This makes Daniel one of the latest Old Testament writings. In it, we find late theological developments such as belief in a resurrection from the dead and final judgment (Daniel 12). As a collection of diverse material, Daniel is a difficult book to classify. Chapters 1–6 are mostly folktales about the wise hero Daniel; thus it is fitting that Daniel is located among the Writings of the Tanakh. Chapters 7–12 are the more properly apocalyptic visions of Daniel (similar to the prophetic visions of Ezekiel and Zechariah); hence Daniel is situated among the prophets in Christian Bibles. Chapters 13 and 14, found in the Greek translation of the Hebrew Bible known as the Septuagint, also fit into the genre of folktales.

One Like a Son of Man

One of the most famous and significant visions appears in Daniel 7: a vision of four beasts followed by a human-like figure. The four beasts are symbolic of four world kingdoms that dominated the Jewish people, starting with Babylon and ending with the Greeks. The description of the final beast has many allusions to the Syrian king Antiochus IV (of the Seleucid dynasty that followed Alexander the Great in Syria) and his persecution of the Jews from 167 to 164 B.C.E. But the vision does not end there. A final figure appears "like a son of man with the clouds of heaven" (Daniel 7:13). This figure is described as receiving an everlasting kingship that will never be destroyed (Daniel 7:14). Like the beasts earlier in the vision, this human figure is symbolic. Just as the beasts represented a succession of earthly kingdoms, the more elevated imagery of a human-like figure represents a more lofty kingdom—God's everlasting rule. This passage is pivotal for understanding Jesus' self-designation as the "son of man" in the Gospels. While the term in itself in Aramaic simply means a human being, the reality that it symbolizes is God's kingdom breaking into the world. The connection between the Gospels' usage of son of man (usually capitalized Son of Man in translations of the Gospels, to indicate it has apparently become an actual title) and the vision in Daniel 7 is made most explicit in Jesus' response to the high priest in Mark 14:62. Jesus' reference to himself as the son of man also ties in to the good news he proclaimed: "the time is fulfilled, and the kingdom of God is at hand" (Mark 1:15).

Key Terms

apocalyptic	Deuteronomic Historian	prophet
Ark of the Covenant	judges	

Study Questions

1. What is the significance of the different versions of the conquest of Canaan in the books of Joshua and Judges?
2. How did the Israelites govern themselves in the books of Joshua and Judges? How does it compare with the government under the kings?
3. What were the special roles of prophets?
4. How did the Ark of the Covenant function in the Israelite community?
5. What was the Deuteronomist's philosophy of history? Do you agree that history works this way? Why or why not?
6. How would you characterize David's reign and Solomon's reign?
7. How did the rise of Assyria and Babylon affect the Israelite and Judean territories?
8. How has Isaiah's figure of the Servant of YHWH been variously understood and interpreted in the Jewish and Christian traditions?
9. What are some of the prominent features of apocalyptic literature, and when does this literature appear and flourish?

Works Consulted/Recommended Reading

Campbell, Antony F., and James W. Flanagan. 1990. "1–2 Samuel." *New Jerome Biblical Commentary*. Edited by Raymond Brown. New York: Prentice Hall.

Collins, John J. 2016. *The Apocalyptic Imagination: An Introduction to Jewish Apocalyptic Literature.* 3rd edn. Grand Rapids, MI: Eerdmans.

Edelman, Diana V. "Saul." 1992. *Anchor Bible Dictionary*. Vol. 5. Edited by David Noel Freedman, 989–999. New York: Doubleday.

Howard, David M. Jr. "David." 1992. *Anchor Bible Dictionary*. Vol. 2. Edited by David Noel Freedman, 41–49. New York: Doubleday.

McKenzie, Steven L. 1992. "Deuteronomic History." *Anchor Bible Dictionary*. Vol. 2. Edited by David Noel Freedman, 160–168. New York: Doubleday.

Penchansky, David. n.d. "Ehud and Eglon: A Video on Deuteronomic History." www.youtube.com/watch?v=tAGwcnKAlBE.

Seow, C.L. 2003. *Daniel.* Louisville, KY: Westminster John Knox Press.

Sweeney, Marvin A. 2016. *Isaiah 40–66.* Grand Rapids, MI: Eerdmans.

Walsh, Jerome T., and Christopher T. Begg. 1990. "1–2 Kings." *New Jerome Biblical Commentary*. Edited by Raymond Brown. New York: Prentice Hall.

SECOND TEMPLE JUDAISM (520 B.C.E. to 70 C.E.)

TIMELINE

332 B.C.E.	Alexander the Great conquers the Near East and begins the process of hellenization.
167 B.C.E.	The Maccabeans revolt against the Seleucid king Antiochus IV.
164 B.C.E.	Rededication of the Temple in Jerusalem, commemorated in the festival of Hanukkah.
c.145 B.C.E.	Beginnings of the Qumran Community.
63 B.C.E.	The Romans conquer Palestine.
70 C.E.	The Destruction of the Jerusalem Temple.

After the Persians under Cyrus defeated the Babylonians, the Jews who were exiled to Babylon were allowed to return to Palestine (as the biblical land of Israel would come to be called). Some Jews remained in Babylon, however. Thus, a distinction is made between Jews who lived in Palestine and Jews who lived outside of Palestine in the **Diaspora** (meaning "dispersion" and referring to those Jews who were "dispersed" through historical circumstances outside the traditional Jewish homeland). The religious practices of these Palestinian Jews and Diaspora Jews developed in somewhat different ways. For example, Diaspora Judaism centered more on the Torah and the synagogue than on the Temple and its sacrifices. Synagogues were buildings where Jews gathered to read and discuss their written scriptures. The increasing importance of following the Law in one's daily life gradually led to the establishment of a synagogue in every town or city with a significant Jewish population. Although being far from the Temple probably forced Diaspora Jews to place more stress on the Torah and the synagogue, the development of the synagogue changed Judaism both inside and outside Palestine.

MAJOR ELEMENTS OF JEWISH FAITH IN THE SECOND TEMPLE PERIOD

Those Jews who did return to Palestine after the Babylonian Exile soon set about rebuilding the Temple in Jerusalem, which had been destroyed in 587/6 B.C.E. This version of the Temple is distinguished from Solomon's Temple and is called the **Second Temple**. Although Judaism in Palestine after the Exile continued to be practiced in many ways that are similar to the pre-exilic period, there are distinctive elements as well, and so the Judaism of this period is referred to as Second Temple Judaism. Temple sacrifice continued to be a major element of this religion, but in the Second Temple period obedience to the written Law (or Torah) took on increased importance, as did Jewish belief in a figure called the **messiah**, meaning "anointed one," especially as it develops in the matrix of ideas known as apocalyptic thought. This chapter will begin with a closer look at the Temple, the Torah, messiah, apocalyptic thought, and the Land of Israel.

Temple

The major way of relating to God in the Jewish religion was through sacrifice. In fact, sacrifice was an important part of almost every ancient religion. Some of these religions offered sacrifices of animals and grain because their practitioners felt that they needed to "feed" their hungry gods. It was considered the priest's job to provide this service to the gods to appease them and prevent disaster from befalling the people. However, there is little evidence that the Jews understood their sacrifice as food for YHWH.

The Hebrew Bible gives several reasons for sacrifice. Some sacrifices were understood as "gifts" to YHWH, in thanksgiving for what he had provided, or as part of a petition for further divine help. Thus, farmers or shepherds would give a portion of their crops and livestock back to God in recognition of the fact that God had given them all that they had. A person who desired some favor from God could also offer a sacrifice. Another purpose of sacrifice was purification or atonement. Those who had sinned against God or their neighbor could "atone" (make up) for their sin through a sacrifice.

Figure 5–1 Replica of the Jerusalem Temple (after the renovations of Herod the Great). Israel Museum, Jerusalem.

Sacrifices offered by Jews involved grain, incense, and animals. These sacrifices were sometimes burned on an altar. In the case of animal sacrifices, more often the animal would be killed and the blood would be poured out on the foot of the altar. This was particularly the case in sacrifices offered to atone for sins, since the blood was thought to "wash away" the defilement caused by the sin.

There were many elaborate rules for performing sacrifices. These can be reduced to four essential requirements. First, sacrifices had to be done by the right people, namely the **priests**. The Jews believed that God had set aside a portion of the people of Israel to specialize in making proper sacrifices. Thus, the primary responsibility of the priesthood in Judaism did not involve conducting weekly worship services, but making sacrifices. The priesthood in Judaism was hereditary, traced through the male line, and priests could only marry daughters of other priests. One could not choose to become a priest; one had to be born into the priesthood. There was one priest who exercised leadership over the other priests and was, in fact, the religious leader of the Israelite nation as a whole—the high priest.

Second, sacrifices had to be offered at the right time. Although it was true that sacrifices went on almost continually in the Temple, certain times and seasons required particular sacrifices. For example, special sacrifices were always offered on the Sabbath, since this was a day set aside for God. In addition, there were three pilgrimage festivals during the year during which Jewish men were supposed to journey to Jerusalem to make sacrifices. One of these festivals was **Passover**, which commemorated God's rescue of the Israelites from slavery in Egypt, when the angel of death "passed over" the homes of the Israelites that had been marked with lamb's blood and killed the firstborn sons of the Egyptians. At Passover (which corresponded to the spring barley harvest), the people of Israel would sacrifice a lamb in commemoration of this event. The other pilgrimage festivals were **Pentecost** (which corresponded to the spring wheat harvest) and Booths (which corresponded to the autumn olive and fruit harvest). Another day set aside for sacrifice, but not requiring the attendance of all male Jews, was the Day of Atonement, or **Yom Kippur**. On this day each year, the high priest would offer a sacrifice for the sins of the nation as a whole.

Third, sacrifices had to be done with the correct offering. There were certain animals that one could sacrifice (bulls, lambs, pigeons, and turtledoves—animals that were considered "clean" and whose sacrifice was dictated in the book of Leviticus) and other animals that one could not sacrifice (pigs, snakes—animals that were considered "unclean"). Moreover, one could not sacrifice just any bull or lamb, but only the firstborn and only an unblemished animal, one without defect. It was also mandatory to sacrifice the firstborn offspring of an animal. The firstborns, whether animal or human, were already thought to belong to God, but human offspring (and more valuable animals) could be redeemed or "bought back" from God by substituting a different offering. Another term for this redemption was "ransom."

Finally, sacrifices had to be done at the right place. In Israel's early history, there were a number of altars and shrines at which sacrifices were done. After the building of Solomon's Temple in Jerusalem, however, a king named Josiah eventually centralized all sacrifice in this one location. After Solomon's Temple was destroyed, the Jews set about the long, gradual process of rebuilding. At first, the Second Temple was a modest building, not approaching the magnificent structure erected by Solomon. However, in the first century B.C.E., Herod the Great (r. 37–4 B.C.E.), who had been appointed by the Romans, began a major renovation and expansion of the Temple, which (when completed around 66 C.E.) re-established the Temple in Jerusalem as one of the greatest structures in the ancient world.

The site of the Temple was considered the most sacred ground in the world to Jews. It was here that the divine realm and the human realm intersected. The innermost part of the Temple contained the **Holy of Holies**, where the Ark of the Covenant had been kept and God's presence dwelled. No one ever entered the Holy of Holies except once each year, when the high priest would enter to offer a sacrifice on the Day of Atonement. On the outside of the Temple was a series of courts where people could assemble in order of their "rank" in holiness according to Judaism, with priests at the top of the hierarchy, followed by Israelite men, Israelite women, and then Gentiles. The area between the first court—the court of priests—and the Holy of Holies housed the altar where all other sacrifices were conducted. It was a place of intersection between God and Israel, where the priests gave God his animal sacrifices, grain, and incense.

Torah

When Israel was exiled to Babylon and the Temple was destroyed (587/6 B.C.E.), the Jewish leaders struggled to explain to themselves why God had allowed these terrible disasters to occur. The explanation, given to them by God through the prophets, was that they had sinned gravely and thus violated the terms of the covenant. Israel had always believed that God made certain ethical and ritual demands on them as part of the covenant and that the reason for the Exile was their failure to live up to those demands. The answer to the problems of the Jewish people, then, was obvious: a renewed commitment to the terms of the covenant. The Jews in exile rededicated themselves to obedience to God's commands. Part of this effort involved a new emphasis on putting God's laws *in writing* and disseminating knowledge of the divine statutes and applying them properly to the common people of Israel.

This emphasis continued after the Exile was over. It was during the Second Temple period that Israel truly established its scriptures, or sacred books. At first, these consisted of only the five scrolls of the Law, or the Pentateuch. The Jewish word for "law" is Torah, and this word can refer to these five books alone. Eventually, some other books were accepted, at least by some Jews, as sacred scripture as well, and thus the word "Torah" can also refer in a more general sense to all of the books accepted as scripture by Israel. Gradually, the books of the Prophets were included as a second major "section" of the Jewish scriptures, although subordinate in importance to the Law. A third major section, called the Writings, was the last to be written and included in the Jewish canon. This section includes books of prayers and wisdom teachings such as Psalms and Proverbs, and stories with theological themes such as the book of Job. Although Jews did not wholly agree about the limits of the canon, all Jews felt themselves to be bound by God's demands as they are expressed in the Torah. Thus, obedience to the Torah took its place alongside Temple sacrifice as the main ways that Jews expressed themselves religiously. In order to be a Jew one needed to be circumcised (if you were male), sacrifice in the Temple at the prescribed times, and follow the Torah in one's daily life (which included following both the ethical guidelines and the special Jewish dietary restrictions called "keeping **kosher**").

Messiah

The Jews believed that they had a covenant relationship with God whereby, if they followed the Torah and performed their sacrifices, God would fulfill certain promises to them. God had promised Abraham that his descendants would be numerous, that they would possess the land of Canaan (or Palestine), and that they would form a great nation. For most of their history, it appears that these promises were not fulfilled. Israelite historians spoke fondly of the reigns of King David and King Josiah as a kind of "golden age." However, most of the kings of Israel and Judah presided over societies that were beset by the worship of false gods, social injustice, internal conflict, and threats from rival kingdoms. Even David's rule was far from perfect. After David, the kingdom was eventually split in two, and the Israelites were conquered successively by the Assyrians, the Babylonians, the Persians, the Greeks, and, finally, the Romans. God's chosen people often suffered terribly under the rule of these foreign powers.

The Jewish explanation for these disasters was always the same. They believed that they must have sinned against the Lord and broken the covenant, which caused God to withdraw his protection and thus expose the Jews to oppression by foreign powers. The Jews always blamed themselves, not God, for breakdowns in the proper functioning of the covenant. In this way of thinking, the solution was equally clear. The way to regain God's favor and release themselves from bondage to their enemies was to repent of their sins and begin adhering more precisely to the terms of the covenant.

During these times of oppression, some of the later Jewish prophets and seers began to predict that God would send someone to rescue the Jews from their affliction, just as God had sent Moses to deliver them from slavery in Egypt, the judges to rescue them from the Philistines, and the prophets themselves to deliver God's messages. The most common and recent of these manifestations of God's will were the prophets, but there seems to have been a decline in prophecy starting in the fourth century B.C.E. Thus, Israel began to hope for a different sort of divine agent. The figure around whom the Jewish hopes coalesced came to be called the messiah. The word "messiah" means "anointed one." The great leaders of Israel's past succeeded, the Jews believed, because they had been *chosen* by God, and God's election of them was symbolized by the process of anointing with oil. Thus, by using the term messiah, the Jews were simply expressing their belief that God would raise up a chosen leader from among the people to save them.

Exactly how God was going to intervene in history to rescue the Jews was a matter of some disagreement, however. Some believed in a political sort of messiah, a righteous king. They interpreted 2 Samuel 7 to mean that God promised to raise up a descendant of David and re-establish him on the throne of Israel so that David's dynasty would last forever (2 Samuel 7:13). God would be like a father to him and he would be like a son to God (2 Samuel 7:14). Some of the Psalms of the Hebrew Bible carry similar themes. In Psalm 89, for example, the psalmist reminds God of his promise to David and his descendants:

> You said, "I have made a covenant with my chosen one,
>   I have sworn to my servant David:
> 'I will establish your descendants forever,
>   and build your throne for all generations.'" (Psalm 89:3–4; see also Psalm 132:11–12)

Similarly, Psalm 2 describes God as having said about his "anointed," that is, the Davidic monarch, "You are my son; today I have begotten you" (Psalm 2:7). The psalmist also suggests that the descendants of the Davidic dynasty will rule over all the earth, not simply over Israel (Psalm 2:8–9). This promise and the themes associated with it became the foundation for Jewish belief in a future messiah who would restore David's dynasty and who would be known (metaphorically) as a son of God.

There are other passages in the Torah that seem to speak of yet another kind of messiah, although the meaning of these passages is controversial. They are the Servant Songs of the book of Isaiah (Isaiah 42:1–4; 49:1–6; 50:4–9; 52:13–53:12). The most famous is the fourth Servant Song (Isaiah 52:13–53:12), which speaks of a **Suffering Servant**, one who takes the sins of other people onto himself and wins forgiveness for them through his suffering. Other Jews, however, anticipated an **apocalyptic** sort of messiah, which brings us to the broader complex of ideas known as apocalyptic thought, in which this conception of the messiah will be discussed. Christians today tend to overemphasize the significance of the messiah in Jewish faith, when in fact the level of belief in the messiah varied widely from one Jewish group to another. Some Jews were waiting for the restoration of God's reign on earth, others did not believe in a messiah or messianic age at all, and still others may have been familiar with one or more of these messianic expectations but were mostly unaffected by them in their daily lives.

Apocalyptic Thought and Literature

For those Jews who awaited an apocalyptic messiah, the coming of the messiah was associated with the apocalyptic ideas introduced in Chapter 4 and with the pseudonymous and symbolic literature that expressed them: a terrible and final crisis in which God triumphs over the forces of evil and the suffering righteous are vindicated. In the book of **Daniel**, they are rewarded with resurrection from the dead and eternal life in a new world, while the wicked are punished forever. While Daniel is the only example of apocalyptic literature in the Hebrew Bible, many other examples of Jewish apocalyptic literature, such as 1 Enoch and some of the Dead Sea Scrolls, were also written during this period and influenced groups such as the Essenes, the Pharisees, and the Christians. The apocalyptic messiah is God's agent in that triumph. According to Daniel, God would send a heavenly emissary, "one like a son of man," (Daniel 7:13) to purge the world of evil and rescue the righteous. Another Jewish religious text called the Similitudes of Enoch (1 Enoch 37–71) describes a similar scene in which the Righteous One, who is also called the Elect One and the Messiah, will judge the wicked and rescue God's holy ones:

> When the secrets of the Righteous One are revealed,
>   He shall judge the sinners;
> And the wicked ones will be driven from the presence of the righteous and the elect,
>   And from that time, those who possess the earth will neither be rulers nor princes,
> They shall not be able to behold the faces of the holy ones,
>   For the light of the Lord of the Spirits has shined
> Upon the face of the holy, the righteous, and the elect. (1 Enoch 38.3–4; Charlesworth, 1983: 30)

Yet another Jewish text, the Testament of Levi, describes a messiah who would serve as a priest in God's heavenly temple and have kingly authority over all the earth. At least one Jewish group expected more than one messiah. The *Rule of the Community*, one of the **Dead Sea Scrolls**, the collection of Jewish religious writings and biblical texts that were preserved at Qumran and discovered only in the mid-twentieth century (1947–1960), speaks of two messiahs—the Messiah of Aaron is a priestly figure (recalling Aaron, the brother of Moses), and the Messiah of Israel is a kingly figure—and an end-time prophet (see Essenes on page 92).

Satan

The growth of apocalyptic thought in some sectors of Second Temple Judaism led to important changes in the figure of Satan and in conceptions of life after death. In earlier parts of the Hebrew Bible, "the Satan" (Hebrew *ha-Satan*), meaning "the Accuser," was a heavenly being who reported on human misdeeds to God. Our word "devil" comes ultimately from the Greek word *diabolos*, also meaning "accuser." He evolved from being a reporter into a tempter, and finally into a rebellious angelic being who rebels against God and is expelled from heaven along with his allies. The rebel angels, now become demons, rule with Satan over the realm of Hell, from which they continue their war against God and humanity, whom they try to recruit for their cause. When and how God will win the final victory over them is a central concern of apocalyptic thought.

The Afterlife

A comparable change occurs in conceptions of the afterlife. The traditional view in the Hebrew Bible is that all dead human beings have a single destination in "Sheol," "the land of the dead." There they are but shadows or shades without strength or personality (Psalm 87:5), knowledge or feeling (Job 14:13). It is a place of silence (Psalms 87:13, 94:17), gloom, and darkness (Job 10:21–22). Some groups, like the Pharisees, came to see this as a sleeping condition from which the dead bodies would be awakened at the end of time to face a final judgment and an eternal destiny (Daniel 12:2). It is possible that the suffering and death experienced in the Maccabean Revolt stimulated growth in such radical hopes. Previously, God's justice was realized in this world in the form of health, prosperity, and offspring. Now, Jews who died for their faith came to be regarded as **martyrs**, and might expect God's justice for them in a new world to come. Greek-influenced concepts of the immortality of the soul may also have played a role in this shift.

Jewish Life and Practice in the Land

Because of the loss of the land of Palestine, the forced deportation of many of the Jewish people during the Babylonian destruction and exile, and continuing foreign occupation even after the Persians allowed the Jews to return home to the land, the relationship with the land of Palestine became a complex reality for the Jewish people. Since Israel was the holy land, chosen by God for the people, the role that the land played in the religious hopes of all Jews could never be cast aside, only imagined and reimagined. Continuing foreign oppression did not lead the Jews to place all of their hopes in the lands of the Diaspora or abandon hope in God's covenant promise of the land. While a renewed focus on Torah and the development of the synagogue made living in the Diaspora much easier religiously, the need to rebuild the Temple in Jerusalem spoke not just to religious needs, but to the political and community aspirations of the Jewish people to live according to the Torah in the land that God gave them. Jerusalem was the place where the temple had to be located, but it was only the holiest site in the land, not the only holy site. Jews considered all of the land holy.

But while all Jews wished to live free of foreign oppression, some sought to create that reality through military means, like the Maccabees fighting against the foreign oppressors, which was a military response that would continue to inspire Jewish warriors into the time of Jesus with the Zealots. Apocalyptic groups, as noted above, hoped for a messiah to establish God's kingdom over the whole world, whether that would take place in a renewed earthly realm or in a world to come. Whether the Jews felt that it was up to them to reclaim their land militarily or wait on God to establish the kingdom for them, hope in the holy land never waned.

JUDAISM IN THE HELLENISTIC AGE

In 336 B.C.E., a young Greek named Alexander took over the throne of Macedonia (in antiquity, the northern part of Greece) and immediately set about an ambitious program of conquest. Ten years later, Alexander the Great had conquered a substantial part of the known world, including Asia Minor, Syria, Israel, Egypt, and Persia. Alexander's armies reached India before finally refusing to follow him any further. Alexander's plans for the people that he conquered included a program of cultural transformation called **hellenization**. The Greeks' name for their own country is "Hellas," and "to hellenize" meant to spread Greek culture or to attempt to turn people into "Greeks." Alexander saw Greek culture as superior to that of other peoples, and his goal was to impose Greek culture on his entire empire, such that people would speak Greek, attend Greek schools, and worship the Greek gods.

This program of hellenization created a dilemma for the Jews. On the one hand, some Jews were enthusiastic about the Greek culture and saw this as a way to "blend into" the new empire, take advantage of its prestige and opportunities, and avoid further suffering. On the other hand, many Jews were proud of their culture and religion and felt that adopting Greek ways would force them to abandon the true path of Judaism, which would bring God's wrath down upon them even more harshly.

Alexander did not force people to adopt Greek culture, however, and so it was possible for these two groups of Jews to coexist for a time under Greek rule. This changed in 175 B.C.E., when a new Greek king named Antiochus IV ascended to power and began an effort to force the Jews to become hellenized. Antiochus prohibited the observance of the Torah and ordered that sacrifices in the Temple be made to the Greek god Zeus instead of YHWH. These actions enraged the Jews, and, under the leadership of a family called the **Maccabees**, they revolted against Antiochus IV. The Maccabean Revolt began in 167 B.C.E., and by 164 B.C.E. the Jews had retaken Jerusalem and rededicated the Temple to YHWH. Eventually, the Maccabees were able to re-establish an independent Jewish state. The holiday that celebrates the consecration of the Temple following this victory is called **Hanukkah**, or the Festival of Lights. Although many Jews celebrated the stunning victory of the Maccabees over the powerful Greeks, some Jews did not think that the Maccabees should be controlling the Temple and the Jewish state, and they went off into the desert to await God's wrath. They were convinced that the world had become so corrupt that God would surely bring an end to it—an example of the apocalyptic way of thinking described above.

JUDAISM IN NEW TESTAMENT TIMES

By the middle of the first century B.C.E., the Jews had been conquered again, this time by the Romans, a domination which would continue for several centuries. Judaism at the turn of the millennium was diverse, comprising a number of different Jewish groups that had rather different beliefs. Although all Jews agreed on the basic points of Judaism, such as Temple sacrifice and obedience to the Torah, different groups of Jews during the first century disagreed on points of emphasis involving Temple, Torah, messiah, apocalyptic thought, and the role the land of Palestine played in their theology.

Figure 5–2 The Empire of Alexander the Great.

Sadducees

Although the **Sadducees** are mentioned in several historical documents of the Second Temple period, our knowledge of them is limited. We know at least that the Sadducees were part of the ruling classes: the priests, the landed nobility, and the major property owners. Because of the Roman policy of allowing local aristocrats to rule their own regions of the empire, the Sadducees occupied some of the major roles of leadership in Judea and Jerusalem, including management of the Temple. Thus, they were both the religious and the political leaders of Judaism. The Sadducees also dominated the highest Jewish council in Jerusalem, which was known as the **Sanhedrin**. According to the Gospels, which consistently refer to the Sadducees as "chief priests," Jesus was put on trial before this body.

As members of the ruling aristocracy, the Sadducees were conservative in outlook. They wanted to preserve their power and maintain the status quo, and so they tried to avoid change or reform. To preserve their property and influence, the Sadducees pursued close and cordial ties with the Romans. By contrast, other Jews resented the presence of the Romans in their homeland, and some actively sought to overthrow the Romans through violent revolution. The Sadducees negotiated certain special privileges for the Jewish people, such as exemption from making sacrifices to the emperor as a god or military service in the Roman legions, privileges that enabled them (in the Sadducees' view) to continue practicing authentic Judaism.

Temple. For the Sadducees, Temple sacrifice was the most important aspect of Judaism. This is not surprising, since the Temple was the source of both wealth and power for the priests who ran it. However, the Sadducees did not support the Temple for purely selfish reasons. All Jews believed that sacrifice was a primary means of relating to God. The Sadducees simply emphasized Temple sacrifice more than any other group. This, too, is not surprising, when we consider that the Sadducees had close associations with the chief priests of the Jerusalem Temple and the captain of the Temple guard (see Acts 4:1; 5:17).

Torah. The Torah was essential to all Jewish groups, and the Sadducees were no exception. It was in the Torah, after all, that God's demands for sacrifices were set forth. However, in contrast with the Pharisees (see Pharisees below), the Sadducees did not accept as authoritative the collections of traditional (oral) interpretations and legal rulings that had evolved over centuries of studying the Torah. Only the written traditions of the Law, that is, the first five books of the Hebrew Bible, were considered to be authoritative as scripture. The Law was most important to them, since it is in the Law that the rules for sacrifice are laid out. Most scholars believe that the Sadducees did not accept the Prophets or the Writings as part of the canon, although the sources are not perfectly clear on this point. Second, they interpreted the Law conservatively and were opposed to newer interpretations that appeared to deviate from the literal sense of the Law. One could not add anything to what was in the written text.

Messiah. There is no evidence that the Sadducees believed in a messiah, unless understood as a simple earthly king. Although there are no clear reasons for this, it is true that belief in a messiah tends to be more popular among the disenfranchised lower classes than among the ruling upper classes. Belief in the messiah during this period also tended to be associated with apocalyptic thought. While Jews did not see the messiah as a divine figure prior to the Christian development of understanding about Jesus, apocalyptic groups often saw the messiah as an agent of God sent to earth either to restore or to establish God's kingdom. The Sadducees do not seem to have shared any of these beliefs or placed any hope in a messianic figure.

Apocalyptic Thought. There is also no evidence that the Sadducees accepted any of the other apocalyptic ideas of this time. Since the Sadducees did not find some of the more "recent" Jewish ideas in the Torah, such as the notion that the soul survives the body after death, resurrection of the dead and judgment after death, the existence of angels and spirits, and the coming of a spiritual or otherworldly messiah, they did not give those ideas any credence.

The Land. The Sadducees were grounded in this world, not in the hope of the world to come. Specifically, they focused on Jerusalem and the Jerusalem Temple as the most important places on earth; not only was the Temple holy in itself, but the Holy of Holies was the most sacred place on earth. As a result, though the Sadducees certainly would have preferred that the Jews not be under the thumb of foreign oppressors such as the Romans, as long as they were able to control and operate the Temple according to the Torah, they could make common political cause with the Romans to keep the peace.

Pharisees

The **Pharisees** were also religious leaders, but they were not priests. Rather, they were scholars of the Torah, experts on the written Law and its interpretation. Their practice was rooted not in the Temple but in the synagogue, where the teachers (or **rabbis**) read from the Torah and presided over subsequent arguments about its meaning and application to present problems and situations. The Pharisees believed strongly that the Torah affected the entirety of human existence, and they sought to develop rules for every area of human life based on the Torah.

Because of their emphasis on living in strict accordance with the rules of the Torah, the Pharisees were known for pious living (alms, tithing, prayer, and fasting). The Pharisees also believed that the rules for ritual purity that operated in the Temple should be applied to everyday existence, and so they tried to avoid contact with anything that would make them "unclean." This is why Pharisees did not eat with or associate with tax collectors, prostitutes, or sinners. Some biblical scholars think that the name Pharisees (which means "separated ones") derives from the desire of this group not to be contaminated by the uncleanness of others.

Temple. The Pharisees believed in Temple sacrifice, since it is prescribed in the Torah, which they revered. Likewise, they would have participated in the pilgrimage feasts that brought large crowds to Jerusalem at various times of the year. However, by all estimates, the Pharisees were small in number. Being well educated, they probably were among the social elite, but they did not have the political connections that the Sadducees had. As a consequence, they had little influence on the operations of the Temple or relations with Israel's Roman occupiers.

Torah. By training and occupation, the Pharisees were interpreters of the Torah, so it obviously was very important to them. They apparently accepted all three parts of the Hebrew Bible, including the Writings, which were still not universally accepted as sacred scripture in the first century C.E. Since the Pharisees were strict interpreters of the Law, they tried to apply the Torah to all aspects of daily life. Occasionally, they would discover apparently contradictory regulations, or they would encounter laws whose application was ambiguous. Sometimes, they would even come across a situation or problem for which there was no answer in the written Torah. The experts among the Pharisees (later called rabbis after the Hebrew word which means "teacher") would attempt to determine how the Law should be interpreted in these particular cases or what regulations should be added to the Law to ensure that the Torah was properly observed. The teachings of the great rabbis on such matters were circulated in oral form from one rabbinic school to another and from one generation to another. Eventually, this oral Torah acquired much the same status as the written Torah, and (after some centuries) these teachings of the great rabbis were written down. The books called the Mishnah and the Talmud, which are still read, studied, and followed by Jews today, are examples of the practice of preserving the teachings, interpretations, and oral traditions of the great rabbis.

Messiah. The evidence suggests that the Pharisees believed in a messiah and that the kind of messiah they were expecting was a royal messiah. Some passages in the Torah suggest that God will send a leader like King David to rescue the Jewish people. This leader would unite the Jewish people, lead them to victory over their oppressors, establish Israel as an independent nation, and assume the role of the nation's king. For the Pharisees, and indeed for most Jews who awaited a messiah, the common expectation was of a military/political messiah.

Apocalyptic Thought. Compared to the Sadducees, the Pharisees were more progressive in their theology, accepting less traditional teachings on a variety of topics, such as immortality of the soul, resurrection of the dead, the spiritual world of angels, and the role of fate in people's lives. Combined with their belief in a royal messiah, it seems that they maintained the basic beliefs of apocalyptic thought, including the judgment of all people and a general resurrection at the end of time.

The Land. The Pharisees revered the Temple and the land of Palestine, but their focus was not on reclaiming the land from the Romans. The Pharisees had as their goal the piety of the Jewish people through teaching and the broad acceptance of their interpretation of Torah, which would bring holiness by means of ritual purity to the Jewish people. As a result, although the land of Israel was especially holy, they could bring their teaching regarding the holiness of people to the synagogues, including in the Diaspora, in order to prepare the people for the establishment of God's kingdom through the coming of the messiah.

Lived Religion: Liturgy in the Synagogue in New Testament Times: Shabbat Service

During the historical period shortly before and after the birth of Jesus Christ, people outside Jerusalem worshipped in synagogues. On the Sabbath, the entire village gathered at sundown in the small building with stone seats along three walls. On the fourth wall, facing Jerusalem, was the bema, a low platform. It contained the seat of Moses, a chair for the service leader, the reading desk, and a niche or ark for the Torah scrolls, covered by a veil with a seven-branched menorah nearby.

The opening prayer was the *Shema,* made up of three sections from the Torah (Deuteronomy 4:6–9; 11:13–21; Numbers 15:37–41). This prayer, commanded by the Torah, was said morning and evening. It was followed by two introductory benedictions and the reading of the Ten Commandments. Next were other benedictions called the Amidah because they were said standing. These prayers profess belief in one God, thanksgiving for all God has done, including abundant crops, healing, forgiveness of sin, and peace for Israel. The congregation responded to each blessing with "Amen."

There was also a litany, a series of prayers blessing God for His love. This was followed by a confession of God's faithfulness and humankind's sin. After the prayers, there was a reading from the Torah and one from the Prophets. This was commanded in Deuteronomy 31:10–13, in which Moses required the priests to read the Torah to the people every seven years. The entire Torah was to be read in one year, although some synagogues did it differently. The reading from the Prophets was chosen to correspond to the Torah reading. In Galilee, most of the readings came from Isaiah, especially Chapters 40–66, which speak of the coming messiah. The service concluded with a sermon that explained the scripture reading, and then a final blessing.

Essenes

The **Essenes** are nowhere mentioned in the New Testament, but biblical scholars know of them from other sources, like the first-century Jewish historian Flavius Josephus and the first-century Jewish philosopher Philo of Alexandria, and from archeological evidence. Apparently, there were two kinds of Essenes. The monastic community at Qumran near the Dead Sea is the one with which most people are familiar, because of the Dead Sea Scrolls. This community was thought to consist of Jewish males who shared all property in common, took vows of celibacy, and lived an ascetic lifestyle of fasting and meditation. Smaller groups of Essenes lived outside of the Qumran community in the cities and villages of Palestine. According to Josephus, they allowed marriage, but only for the purpose of having children. They owned their own property, but they were also obligated to provide hospitality to fellow Essenes traveling through their village, so perhaps, in some ways, they were like a commune. Both groups, but especially the monastic community, were concerned about ritual purity and strict observance of community rules.

No one knows exactly how the Essenes originated, but they are often traced back to the Hasideans, a group of pious Jews who supported the Maccabean Revolt in 166 B.C.E. and opposed Jonathan's ascent to the position of High Priest in Jerusalem (152 B.C.E.). Their leader was called the "Teacher of Righteousness." Some Qumran scholars think that he had been a priest of the Jerusalem Temple and that he established this community as a protest movement after he had been ousted from his position in the Temple. After the Jewish War and the destruction of the Jerusalem Temple, the Essenes disappeared from history without a trace, believed to have been destroyed by the Roman army.

Temple. The Temple was crucially important to the Essenes, but they did not attend its pilgrimage feasts or participate in its sacrifices. They thought that the Temple and its leadership were corrupt and not following the proper religious calendar and, as a consequence, that the sacrifices currently being offered in Jerusalem were illegitimate and not acceptable to God. Therefore, they developed their own strict purity regulations and religious rituals, which they performed in the wilderness at Qumran as a protest against the activities of the Jerusalem Temple. Some of these regulations have been preserved in the *Rule of the Community*, one of the Dead Sea Scrolls. The Essenes awaited the time when the priestly messiah would come and purify the Temple and thus allow the members of the Essenes to perform their duties as priests in the Temple.

Torah. Included among the Dead Sea Scrolls are fragments of every book of the Bible except the book of Esther. Therefore, scholars are quite certain that the Essenes accepted all three parts of the Hebrew Bible (Law, Prophets, and Writings) as scripture. They were strict interpreters of the scriptures, adhering to the demands of the Torah as thoroughly as possible in their daily lives, though they also made additions to a variety of biblical texts as suited their community's needs and seem to have accepted additional texts as scriptural, including texts that were written within their own community. They believed that in order to survive the coming apocalypse, they needed to be as pure and holy as possible. This is why they followed the Law so strictly and probably also why they withdrew into the desert, to avoid contact with people and things that would make them ritually unclean.

Messiah. Because of their apocalyptic world-view and their perception that the Jerusalem Temple was corrupt, the Essenes had developed some unique views about the coming of the messiah. Essentially, they believed in two messiahs. The first was a royal messiah who would lead the children of light into battle with the children of darkness and then establish himself as king after the forces of good had vanquished the forces of evil. The second was a priestly messiah who would cleanse the Temple of the illegitimate priests, re-establish the Essenes as the correct priests, and install himself as the new high priest.

Apocalyptic Thought. The Essenes were apocalyptic not just in their thinking, but in their behavior as a community. They believed that the end time was imminent and that it included a cataclysmic destruction of the present world order and the triumph of God's holy ones. The document called the *War Scroll* shows how the Essenes organized themselves for the coming final battle between God and the forces of evil. The Essenes also believed that the two messiahs would emerge from their own remnant community at the end of time and lead them to victory.

The Land. The Essenes organized their small community according to the priestly orders of the Temple and the 12 tribes of Israel. They believed that after the glorious final battle, they would take control of the holy land of Israel and establish God's kingdom in Israel and throughout the world. It would be no ordinary political kingdom, but God's true kingdom here on earth. Because the Essenes saw themselves as the chosen "remnant," it would be the members of their community, not all Israel, who would inherit the land after the final apocalyptic battle.

Scribes

The word "scribe" denotes an occupation based upon the knowledge of reading and writing. Since most people could not read or write, they relied upon **scribes** to do these things for them. Scribes performed such functions as writing out contracts for people, advising rulers, keeping official records, and taking care of correspondence. Scribes are often associated with the Jewish Law as copyists and sometimes as legal experts themselves. They functioned as a professional class rather than as an organized group with a consistent point of view like the Essenes, Pharisees, or Sadducees. As trained writers, though, they could be found within most of these groups. Pharisees who interpreted the Torah, for example, must also have been scribes, and some scholars believe that the Pharisees themselves originally emerged from the scribal class.

"People of the Land"

It should be noted that the majority of Jews did not belong to any these various "parties." Most members of these groups belonged to the upper classes, constituting possibly as few as 3 to 5 percent of the population. The remaining 97 to 95 percent were called **People of the Land** (*am ha'aretz*), meaning "commoners" or "people of the countryside." Often the term was used in a derogatory manner to refer to the uneducated lower classes. The vast majority of the People of the Land were peasant farmers, though a small number were artisans, while others belonged to the unclean class (those who performed distasteful tasks, such as mining and tanning) and the "expendable" class (the homeless of Jewish society, who survived by begging or stealing).

These people usually did not have the time or the means to concern themselves with the specifics of the interpretation of the Torah, the composition of the priesthood, or the operations of the Temple. Very little is known about them except that the elite among the Jewish people often avoided them or treated them with disdain because they could not or would not adhere to the "rules" of Judaism as strictly as these groups felt they should. A notable exception to this elitism is the Jesus Movement, which was known for welcoming all sorts of "undesirable" people into its ranks. It should be noted, however, that this kind of class discrimination was hardly unique to Jewish people but was common throughout the first-century Mediterranean world.

The Jesus Movement

Although much more will be said about the development of Christianity in the next chapters, it is important to realize that the first followers of Jesus can be understood as members of another group within Judaism, not unlike the Sadducees, Pharisees, and Essenes. In its early decades, Christianity was not a religion separate from Judaism. Early "Christians" (they were not actually called by this name until a few decades after the death of Jesus) still considered themselves Jews, and they continued to observe the religious practices of Judaism—sacrificing in the Temple, obeying the rules of the Torah, being circumcised, and keeping kosher. Christians did have some distinctive attitudes, however, about the Temple, the Torah, and especially the messiah.

Temple. There is evidence in the Gospels to suggest that Jesus and his followers (like the Essenes) were upset about how the Temple was being run. For example, some biblical scholars think that the gospel scene in which Jesus overturns the moneychangers' tables in the Temple and drives out those who are selling animals for sacrifice (Mark 11:15–19 and parallels) indicates that early Christians believed that the Temple would be destroyed because it had become corrupt. However, this did not mean that the Christians abandoned their Jewish roots. The Gospels show Jesus as their exemplar: he participated in synagogue services and traveled to Jerusalem for the Temple pilgrimage festivals, as Jewish men were required to do, and in other ways was an observant Jew. The New Testament also presents Jesus' disciples as continuing to teach and preach in the Temple precincts after his death. It seems that what Jesus desired was an apocalyptic restoration of the Temple, not its removal altogether. Thus, Christians, like other Jews, struggled to make sense of the destruction of the Temple in 70 c.e., and the Gospels are in many ways a theological response to this tragic event.

Torah. Like other Jews, the earliest Christians believed that the Torah was a gift from God. In fact, it was their only scripture for the first decades of their existence. These Jesus followers were not required to abandon observance of the rules and regulations of the Torah. In fact, the author of Matthew's Gospel describes Jesus' mission in this way: "Do not think that I have come to abolish the law or the prophets; I have come not to abolish but to fulfill" (Matthew 5:17). Like the Essenes and the Pharisees, Christians accepted all three parts of the Torah (Law, Prophets, and Writings). On the question of interpreting Torah, the Gospels present Jesus as developing case law in much the same way as the Pharisees did. Thus, like the Pharisees, the Christians believed that the written law must be interpreted or supplemented. However, their "supplements" did not include the legal judgments of the Pharisees, but the teachings of Jesus. For example, divorce and certain forms of violence or retribution, which were allowed according to the Jewish Law, were strongly frowned upon in early Christianity due to Jesus' teaching. Another example is the Gospels' presentation of Jesus occasionally breaking the law about not working on the Sabbath when he encountered someone who was ill or disabled. Rabbinic teachers cite the principle "Great is human dignity" to allow for such exceptions, but the Gospels also associate Jesus' Sabbath healings with the coming reign of God. Matthew's Gospel describes early Christians' view of Sabbath observance this way: "But if you had known what this means, 'I desire mercy and not sacrifice,' you would not have condemned the guiltless. For the Son of Man is lord of the Sabbath" (Matthew 12:7–8; cf. Hosea 6:6).

Messiah. Where Christians disagreed most with their counterparts in other Jewish groups was in their belief that the messiah had already come and that this messiah was Jesus of Nazareth. This is the single most important distinguishing feature of early Christianity: the Christians thought that the messiah had already arrived, while (most) other Jewish groups were still waiting for the messiah. Christians supported their claims that Jesus was the messiah by pointing out how the events of his life fulfilled prophecies in the Torah, how he spoke with great wisdom and could perform miracles, and most important of all, how he rose from the dead after being crucified, appeared to his disciples, and ascended to the right hand of God the Father.

Just *what kind* of a messiah Jesus became was a matter of some disagreement among various groups of Christians, but it is clear at least that Jesus did not fit the mold of a political/military messiah that the Pharisees and many other Jews were expecting, including some of Jesus' earliest disciples. There are other ideas about the messiah expressed in the Torah, and the Christians began to explore them to try to discover who Jesus was and to find evidence to convince their fellow Jews that Jesus was in fact the messiah.

Apocalyptic Thought. While the understanding of Jesus underwent some significant changes during the first decades of Christianity, one view that emerges from Jesus' teachings in the Gospels and Paul's letters is that Jesus is an apocalyptic messiah. The early Christians believed that Jesus had come to gather a community, a people of God (*qahal* in Hebrew; *ekklesia* in Greek), to prepare for the final apocalyptic battle and the coming reign of God. Although these events did not occur in Jesus' lifetime, as a number of disciples hoped that they would, Jesus' resurrection and ascension convinced them that the establishment of God's kingdom was only "delayed" and that Jesus would come again soon (the *parousia* or "second coming") to inaugurate God's kingdom. As time went on and Jesus did not return, Christians modified their beliefs about the nearness of the end of the world, but not their hope that Jesus would return to establish God's kingdom.

The Land. Jesus seemed to maintain the understanding found in some of the prophetic books, such as Isaiah and Zechariah, that at the end of time the Gentiles would come to the Temple in Jerusalem to worship God. In Matthew 8:11, Jesus says, "I tell you, many will come from east and west and will eat with Abraham and Isaac and Jacob in the kingdom of heaven." The centrality of the land of Palestine and the Temple is seen in this saying of Jesus, but as Christianity grew, the apostles and other disciples came to believe that their task was to take the Gospel to the world, not have the world come to Jerusalem. The end of Matthew contains the "Great Commission," in which Jesus says, "Go therefore and make disciples of all nations, baptizing them in the name of the Father and of the Son and of the Holy Spirit" (Matthew 28:19). This same impetus to take the message to the world is seen in Acts of the Apostles, where the movement of the gospel is from Jerusalem and the Temple to Samaria, and then to "the ends of the earth." The diminished centrality of the land is also found in the spiritualization of the Jerusalem Temple in Jesus' encounter with the Samaritan woman in the Gospel of John. The Samaritan woman says, "Our ancestors worshipped on this mountain, but you say that the place where people must worship is in Jerusalem" (John 4:20). In response, Jesus claims that "the hour is coming when you will worship the Father neither on this mountain nor in Jerusalem" (John 4:21). The centrality of the land of Palestine is replaced with a focus on the whole world as "mission" field and the spiritualization of religious worship, which could be carried out anywhere.

THE JEWISH WAR (66–70 C.E.)

The various Jewish groups coexisted more or less peacefully in Palestine until 66 C.E., when war broke out between the Jews and the Romans. Almost all Jews strongly resented the Roman presence in Palestine, and some Jews advocated violent revolt. Minor rebellions had broken out several times before. However, a series of events led to the development of a full-blown revolution in 66 C.E., a revolution that was to prove disastrous for the Jewish people.

The revolt was led by the **Zealots**, a group of radical Jews who believed that once the war started, YHWH would enter it on the side of the Jews and help them defeat the vastly more powerful Romans. Their hopes were not realized and the Romans eventually crushed the Jewish rebellion. Thousands of Jews were killed and their leaders crucified. The worst disaster, however, came in 70 C.E., when Jerusalem was destroyed and the Temple burned to the ground. This time the Temple was never rebuilt.

This war proved fateful for most of the various groups within Judaism. Toward the end of it, a large group of Essenes was discovered by the Romans in the desert and massacred. Without the Temple, the Sadducees had lost the source of their wealth and power, and for all practical purposes they ceased to exist. The only groups to survive the Jewish War relatively intact were the Pharisees and the Christians. With the Temple gone, however, the Pharisees needed to undertake some major renovations in the Jewish religion. By the end of the first century, the Pharisees had reimagined a Judaism that relied solely on the Torah and eliminated the practice of sacrifice. This came to be called rabbinic Judaism, and it is this version of Judaism that survives in various forms today.

Figure 5–3 Depiction of Roman armies carrying off spoils from the Second Temple in Jerusalem after its destruction. Arch of Titus. Rome, Italy. Constructed in 82 C.E. by Emperor Domitian to commemorate Titus's victories.

Key Terms

am ha'aretz	kosher	rabbis
apocalyptic	Maccabees	Sadducees
Daniel	martyr	Sanhedrin
Dead Sea Scrolls	messiah	Scribes
Diaspora	*parousia*	Second Temple
dualism	Passover	Suffering Servant
ekklesia	Pentecost	Synagogue
Essenes	People of the Land	Yom Kippur
Hanukkah	Pharisees	Zealots
hellenization	priests	
Holy of Holies	*qahal*	

Questions for Reading

1. What was the purpose of sacrifice? What kinds of rules did the Jews have about the sacrifices that they conducted?

2. What did the Jewish scriptures consist of? How did these scriptures develop?

3. Explain the development of the concept of the messiah in Jewish thinking and distinguish between the different kinds of messiahs that Jews believed in.

4. What was "hellenization," and how did Jews of the time react to it?

5. Compare and contrast the Sadducees, Pharisees, Essenes, and Christians in terms of their beliefs about the Temple, Torah, messiah, apocalyptic thought, and land.

6. What happened to each of the Jewish groups following the Jewish War of 66–70 C.E.?

Works Consulted/Recommended Reading

Baumgarten, A.I. 1997. "The Flourishing of Jewish Sects in the Maccabean Era: An Interpretation." Supplements to the *Journal for the Study of Judaism*, 55. Leiden: Brill.

Boyarin, Daniel. 2006. *Border Lines: The Partition of Judaeo-Christianity*. Philadelphia, PA: University of Pennsylvania Press.

Charlesworth, James H. ed. 1983. *The Old Testament Pseudepigrapha*. Vol. 1: *Apocalyptic Literature & Testaments*. New York: Doubleday.

Cohen, Shaye, J.D. 2006. *From the Maccabees to the Mishnah*. Louisville, KY: Westminster John Knox Press.

Collins, J.J. 2016. *The Apocalyptic Imagination: An Introduction to Jewish Apocalyptic Literature*. Grand Rapids, MI: William B. Eerdmans.

Jaffee, Martin S. 2006. *Early Judaism. Religious Worlds of the First Judaic Millennium*. Bethesda, MD: University Press of Maryland.

Murphy, Frederick J. 1991. *The Religious World of Jesus: An Introduction to Second Temple Palestinian Judaism*. Nashville, TN: Abingdon Press.

Perrin, Norman, and Dennis C. Duling. 1982. *The New Testament: An Introduction*, 2nd edn. San Diego, CA: Harcourt Brace Jovanovich.

VanderKam, James C. 2010. *The Dead Sea Scrolls Today*. Grand Rapids, MI: William B. Eerdmans.

PART II
THE NEW TESTAMENT

The second major section of the Bible is the New Testament. The New Testament has been the single most important text for Christians throughout the centuries because it provides the basis for articulating the Christian community's identity and for formulating much of its theology and moral principles. Christians call this section the New Testament because it proclaims the new covenant between God and human beings made possible by the coming of Jesus Christ, as distinct from the "old" covenant between God and Israel described in the Hebrew scriptures.

Like the Old Testament or Hebrew Bible, the New Testament is not always an easy document to read and interpret because it is an ancient piece of literature from a culture and historical period vastly different from modernity. At the same time, Christians treat it as a timeless document that has authority to direct and guide their lives. The challenge, then, is to learn how to read and interpret biblical texts as their human authors intended, utilizing the wide range of methods of historical and literary analysis that are available today, while also appreciating their enduring character as documents of faith. However, even before beginning that work, familiarity with the content and organization of the New Testament is required. What kinds of books are contained in the New Testament? How were these books collected into this larger document we call the New Testament?

DIVISIONS OF THE NEW TESTAMENT

The New Testament is usually divided into four sections or subdivisions. The first subdivision consists of four Gospels. They are listed here with their most commonly accepted dates of composition. Although the Gospels are placed first in the order of the books of the New Testament, they were not the first to be written. Paul's letters, which eventually became part of the New Testament, were written approximately 10 to 20 years before the earliest New Testament gospel.

Mark (*c*.65–70 C.E.)
Matthew (*c*.80–90 C.E.)

Luke (c.80–125 c.e.)
John (c.90–100 c.e.)

The Gospels tell the story of the life of Jesus and in that sense they are historical and biographical documents. However, unlike modern histories or biographies, which are supposed to strive for objectivity and documented verifiability, the Gospels are more appropriately understood as proclamations of faith. The word gospel comes from the Anglo-Saxon god-spell, which means "good tidings." The Greek word for gospel is *euangelion*, which means "good news." The writers of the Gospels are called evangelists, that is, "preachers of the good news." The Gospels proclaim early Christian communities' faith experience of Jesus as the messiah of God. Chapter 6 explains the distinctive character of each of the four Gospels.

The second subdivision of the New Testament includes only one book, the Acts of the Apostles. This book is a continuation of Luke's Gospel and it is written by the same author. Acts tells the story of the spread of the gospel of Jesus Christ and the development of early Christian communities from shortly after the death and resurrection of Jesus until the time of Paul's preaching in Rome—the period covering approximately 30–64 c.e. Most biblical scholars think this book was written in the last quarter of the first century, after the destruction of Jerusalem and the Temple (70 c.e.), perhaps even later. Although it is "historical" in tone and structure, the Acts of the Apostles is like the Gospels in that it is not a neutral and objective retelling of the beginnings of Christianity. Rather, it provides a theological interpretation of the events that eventually led to Christianity's separation from Judaism and the spread of this new religion throughout the Mediterranean world. In the process, it presents a somewhat idealized version of Christianity's earliest decades.

The third subdivision of the New Testament consists of 21 letters addressed to a variety of Christian churches and individual Christians of the first and early second century c.e. Although 13 of these letters are attributed to the missionary Paul, perhaps only seven were actually written by him: Romans, 1–2 Corinthians, Galatians, Philippians, 1 Thessalonians, and Philemon. Biblical scholars agree that these letters were written between 50 and 60 c.e. The others were likely written by anonymous authors, perhaps by surviving associates of Paul who felt entitled by their status as the trustees of the "Pauline school" to continue to write in his name. These books are called "deutero-Pauline" letters (the word "deutero" means "secondary") and include 2 Thessalonians, Ephesians, Colossians, 1–2 Timothy, and Titus. Seven more letters are attributed to other apostles and early church leaders: James, 1–2 Peter, 1–3 John, and Jude. One remaining document that bears the title "to the Hebrews" is not really a letter but, because it has traditionally been included with the letters, is included in this grouping. Biblical scholars believe that these non-Pauline documents were written at various points in the second half of the first century or in the first part of the second century c.e.

The book of Revelation (also known as the Apocalypse of John) makes up the fourth and last subdivision of the New Testament. This book, probably written between 90 and 100 c.e., is an apocalyptic account of a divine revelation to a Christian prophet named John of Patmos. Like other apocalyptic writings, it is marked by highly symbolic language—communicated by an angel or other heavenly being—that reveals in coded language secrets about the coming end of all things. Its prediction of the imminent return of Christ and the establishment of God's kingdom in a renewed earth has inspired Christians ever since, sometimes for endurance during persecution, other times for revolutionary action.

THE QUESTION OF CANON

How did these particular 27 books end up being included in the New Testament? Early Christian communities in the first and second centuries C.E. were reading other religious literature besides the books that eventually found their way into the New Testament. The question of how and why some gospels were classified as "scripture" and others were denied that status is answered in the history of the formation of the canon. The formation of the Christian canon also took several centuries and was characterized by a robust debate before the issue was settled, and the canon was "closed," in the late fourth century C.E.

At the earliest stages of Christianity, there was no New Testament. For Jesus and his disciples, as well as for the early missionaries of the gospel like Paul and his co-workers, "scriptures" simply meant Jewish scriptures. By the latter part of the first century and the beginning of the second, Christians began to put together their own distinctive scriptures in stages.

First Stage: The Letters of Paul Attain "Canonical" Status

The earliest collections of Christian texts did not include the Gospels, but they probably consisted of some of the letters of Paul. In the Second Letter of Peter (*c.*100 to 125 C.E.), the author says:

> So also our beloved brother Paul wrote to you according to the wisdom given him, speaking of this as he does in all his letters. There are some things in them hard to understand, which the ignorant and unstable twist to their own destruction, as they do the other scriptures.
>
> (2 Peter 3:16)

This tells us both that Christians were beginning to create their own canon and that some Christians, at least, regarded the letters of Paul as having an authority comparable to the scriptures of Judaism.

Second Stage: The Selection of Gospels

The Gospels of Matthew, Mark, Luke, and John were not the only gospels being written and read in the first and early second centuries C.E. From early church writers like Clement of Alexandria (wrote 180–220), Origen (d. 253/254), and Eusebius of Caesarea (d. 339/340), we know of the Gospel to the Hebrews, the Gospel of the Egyptians, the Gospel of the Ebionites, the Gospel of Peter, and the Gospel of Thomas, to name a few. There were thus many so-called gospels in the early years of the church, but only four obtained the status of sacred scripture.

Our earliest evidence for this canonization process comes from Justin Martyr, writing in the middle of the second century. Commenting on the Christian celebration of the Eucharist, Justin mentions that the "memoirs of the apostles" or the writings of the prophets were being read (*Apology* 1.67). The phrase "memoirs of the apostles" most likely refers to the Gospels, and Justin appears to be giving them the same status as the books of the prophets.

Irenaeus, bishop of Lyons, writing *c.*180, was apparently the first Christian writer to single out as authoritative the four gospels that would later become part of the New Testament (*Against Heresies* 3.11.8). He also provides evidence that, already in the late second century C.E., people were beginning to distinguish between orthodox and heretical gospels. For example, he dismisses the Gospel of Truth because it "agrees in nothing with the gospels of the apostles" (*Against Heresies* 3.11.9) and he condemns the Gospel of Judas as a "fictitious history" (*Against Heresies* 1.31.1). Likewise, in the fourth century, Eusebius tells us that the Gospel of Peter was banned in Antioch by the end of the second century because it was considered to contain false teaching about Jesus (*Ecclesiastical History* 6.12).

Third Stage: Proposals for a Complete Listing of Christian Scriptures

Paradoxically, Marcion (*c.*140 C.E.), a Christian preacher in Rome eventually condemned as a heretic, was responsible for the first canon of the New Testament. Christians of his time had inherited the scriptures of Judaism as their sacred writings, but Marcion was troubled by their apparent internal contradictions, which he could not resolve. Likewise, he struggled with what he saw as the Old Testament's portrayal of God as a violent and vengeful God in contrast with his own (Christian) understanding of God as benevolent and merciful. Further, he understood Jesus Christ to be the Son of the God of goodness and not the messiah of the Jewish God of justice. Thus, he created a very restrictive canon of Christian scriptures that excluded all of the Old Testament scriptures. He also rejected much Christian literature that had Jewish overtones, accepting as his canon only a single unattributed gospel (which appears to have been either an early or an altered version of the Gospel of Luke) and ten of the letters attributed to Paul. In effect, any text with positive references to Judaism was edited or excluded.

The dominant group within early Christianity—which scholars have dubbed the "proto-orthodox" group—rejected both Marcion's fierce anti-Judaism and his restrictive understanding of the Christian scriptures. But Marcion's canon did have the effect of prompting other church leaders to form their own canons or lists of approved books. The earliest surviving example of a "proto-orthodox" canon is the Muratorian fragment (named for its eighteenth-century discoverer), which is usually dated to the latter part of the second century. It included the four Gospels of Matthew, Mark, Luke, and John, the Acts of the Apostles, 13 letters attributed to Paul (excluding Hebrews), Jude, 1 John, 2 John, the Wisdom of Solomon (today included in the Old Testament Apocrypha or deuterocanonical books), Revelation, and the Apocalypse of Peter (today included among New Testament Apocrypha). So this list had 24 books total, including 22 of the books that would eventually be included in the New Testament. Other lists or partial lists can be found in the writings of Origen, Tertullian (d. 220?), and Eusebius of Caesarea (*Ecclesiastical History* 3.25), among others.

The consistent elements in all of the lists that had been compiled in response to Marcion's canon were the four Gospels, Acts of the Apostles, Paul's letters (either 13 or 14, depending on whether Hebrews was included), and the first letter of John. So there was broad consensus about 19 books. There were eight books that eventually made it into the New Testament, but had either been excluded or listed as "doubtful" or "disputed" prior to their ultimate inclusion: 2 and 3 John, 1 and 2 Peter, James, Jude, Hebrews, and Revelation. Bishop Athanasius of Alexandria, in his *Festal Letter* of

367 C.E., was the first to propose a list of the 27 books that ended up forming the New Testament canon. Athanasius' list was subsequently used by Jerome as the basis for the Vulgate (a Latin translation of the Old and New Testaments) later in the fourth century, and the extraordinary and enduring popularity of the Vulgate had the effect of cementing into place the list of 27 books that Athanasius had proposed. For all intents and purposes, the Christian canon was "closed" in the late fourth century, although there was no official proclamation to this effect. It was not until the Council of Trent in 1546 that the Catholic Church made an official statement listing the books that constitute the canon of the Bible. Such a statement was only necessitated by the fact that the reformer Martin Luther had recently reopened the debate over the canon.

THE CRITERIA FOR CANONICITY

Why exactly did these 27 books make it into the New Testament while others did not? Because so little evidence survives, modern biblical scholars cannot fully reconstruct the history of the development of the canon. Yet certain criteria seem to have been operative, as we can infer from the standards to which the early writers themselves appealed.

One criterion that appears to have been used among the early Christian churches was "apostolic origin," meaning that the book could be attributed to an apostle or to an associate of an apostle. If there were doubts about whether a book was written by an apostle or an "apostolic man," then the book might be excluded from the canon. The anonymous Letter to the Hebrews is an example of a book that aroused such doubts. Similarities to the Pauline corpus made Paul a possible candidate in the eyes of some, though other Christian writers disputed it. Or, to take another example, the book of Revelation identifies its author as "John of Patmos." But was this the same John who was among the 12 apostles, the brother of James and the son of Zebedee? Or did he just happen to share his name? Uncertainties about authorship help explain why prominent Christian writers assembling a canon listed letters such as 2 and 3 John and 1 and 2 Peter as "doubtful" or "disputed."

A second criterion involved the book's content. To be included, a book needed to conform broadly to proto-orthodox doctrine. This did not mean that every book needed to agree precisely with every element of orthodoxy as it assumed its officially defined form over the course of the first five centuries. But a book could not be seen as *contradicting* some important belief that was already regarded on the basis of preaching and oral tradition as central and fundamental. An example of this criterion in action is provided by early church writers' discussions of the Gospel of Peter, mentioned above. The fragment that is still available to modern readers tells the story of the trial, death, and resurrection of Jesus. It is a strange gospel, complete with enormous angels and a cross that talks. However, the early church historian Eusebius recounts that Bishop Serapion of Antioch (*c.*190) forbade Christians to read it not because it was historically inaccurate but because some of those who held it as sacred were led into heresy (wrong teaching) by its words. The wrong teaching to which Serapion referred was "docetism," which held that Jesus did not really suffer and die but merely seemed to have done these things. Such a view denied Jesus' true humanity in favor of an understanding of him as an essentially spiritual being whose body was only apparent but not real. This contradicted the emerging orthodox view that Jesus was both divine and human. The Gospel of Peter's exclusion from the canon of the New

Testament appears to have been at least in part a question of conformity to proto-orthodox doctrine.

A third criterion seems to have been wide distribution and familiarity and use in the liturgy, as we saw above in Justin's reference to the "memoirs of the apostles" that were read, along with the prophets, at celebrations of the Eucharist. A book preserved by only a few communities and not already sanctioned by use in worship would not have won inclusion in canonical lists.

Chapter 6

JESUS AND THE GOSPELS

TIMELINE

37–4 B.C.E.	Herod the Great is king of Palestine. During his kingship, Herod initiates a major renovation of the Jerusalem Temple.
6–4 B.C.E.	Jesus of Nazareth is born.
26–36 C.E.	Pontius Pilate is procurator in Judea and Samaria.
c.30 C.E.	The death and resurrection of Jesus.
66–70 C.E.	The Jewish war against Rome.
70 C.E.	The Romans capture Jerusalem and destroy the Temple.
65–70 C.E.	The Gospel of Mark is written.
80–90 C.E.	The Gospel of Matthew is written.
80–125 C.E.	The Gospel of Luke is written.
90–100 C.E.	The Gospel of John is written.

Figure 6–1 *The Holy Face*, by Georges Rouault (1871–1958).

In the early part of the first century C.E., a man named Jesus emerged from the small village of Nazareth in Galilee. This Jesus of Nazareth was a teacher and a miracle worker, and many were drawn to follow him. He began his ministry by proclaiming the nearness of God's kingdom to his Jewish brothers and sisters, and those who became his followers understood him to be the long-awaited Jewish messiah. By all accounts, he was an observant Jew: he attended synagogue, went to the pilgrimage festivals in Jerusalem, and otherwise obeyed Torah law. However, some were offended by the sometimes radical nature of his teachings and his controversial interpretations of Jewish Law.

Then one year, near the Passover feast, Jesus was arrested in Jerusalem. Charges were made against him and he was quickly handed over to the Roman authorities for execution. He was crucified and those who had him arrested probably thought that would be the end of his movement. His disciples would scatter, and his other supporters would lose whatever hopes they had for him. However, some women from among his followers began to spread the news that he had been raised from the dead. As Jesus' disciples continued to proclaim the message of Jesus Christ after his death and resurrection, a reform movement was born within Judaism that later spread outward into the Gentile, or non-Jewish, world. This Jesus Movement came to be known as Christianity.

In order to learn more about the Jesus Movement, it is customary to start with the Gospels of the New Testament. It is important to note that, among the books of the New Testament, the Gospels were not the first to be written. In fact, all of the authentic letters of Paul were written before the first Gospel, Mark, was written. Likewise, many of the other books of the New Testament were written by the time the last Gospel, John, was written. Why begin with the Gospels? Why not read Paul's letters first? Paul and other New Testament authors like him seem to have assumed that their readers already knew the stories about Jesus' words and deeds, most likely from the preaching and oral traditions that led to their initial conversion. Hence, Paul's letters and most of the other New Testament books say very little about the teaching and life of Jesus, with the notable exception of his crucifixion and resurrection. But when the first generation of preachers and eyewitnesses passed away, people decided to preserve the stories about Jesus and his teachings in writing. The result was the Gospels.

HOW THE GOSPELS CAME TO BE

The Greek word for gospel, *euangelion*, means "good news." As their name suggests, the Gospels are proclamations of faith concerning Jesus of Nazareth, whom his followers believed was the messiah of God. Although they have individuals' names attached to them—Matthew, Mark, Luke, and John in the case of the New Testament—they were not authored in the same way as books are written today. Instead, they are the result of a somewhat lengthy process of collecting, passing on, recording, and editing the stories and sayings of Jesus into a coherent narrative.

The stages of composition of the Gospels can be described briefly as follows: (1) Shortly after the death and resurrection of Jesus, those who had once traveled with him and others who had become preachers of the "good news" began to hand on by word of mouth stories and sayings concerning Jesus' ministry and teachings. (2) Early Christian communities used these stories and sayings in worship and teaching, in preparation for Baptism, to encourage and console the believers, to resolve controversies, and to admonish the wrongdoers. Gradually, some Christians began to write down these stories about Jesus, compiling collections of sayings and miracle stories, as well as the narrative of Jesus' **passion**—the events surrounding Jesus' betrayal and arrest, trials, crucifixion, and resurrection. However, as yet, there were no "complete" written gospels, at least in the sense of books that covered Jesus' ministry from beginning to end. (3) Eventually, the gospel writers began to collect these oral and written traditions, arranging them into a coherent narrative or story of the life, death, and resurrection of Jesus Christ. The authors of the gospels selected and arranged these stories and sayings, with special attention to the particular situation of the communities for which they were writing and to the proclamation of faith that they wanted to make concerning Jesus.

The composition of gospels did not bring an immediate halt to the use of oral tradition. Stories about Jesus continued to circulate orally throughout the decades in which the canonical gospels were written and even beyond. There is no doubt that there were stories of the sayings and deeds of Jesus that were never recorded in a gospel, and it is in fact likely that some of the oral traditions that did not make it into a canonical gospel were preserved in the non-canonical gospels. The non-canonical gospel that biblical scholars believe is most likely to contain some authentic "quotes" from Jesus that are otherwise unknown to history is the *Coptic Gospel of Thomas*.

When the canonical gospels were first written, they circulated anonymously. The earliest quotations of the gospels in other literature do not contain any attribution of the quote to an individually named evangelist. Early Christians attached the titles "Matthew," "Mark," "Luke," and "John" to the New Testament Gospels at some point in the second century C.E. However, the case for attributing any of the four to the person whose name is now attached to it is slender at best. Scholars today generally agree that their actual authors are mostly unknown to us. The majority would say that the Gospel of Mark was written between 65 and 70 C.E. by a Gentile (non-Jewish) Christian. The strong apocalyptic mood of the Gospel suggests that the community was enduring some kind of persecution. Concerning the Gospel of Matthew, most say that it was written between 80 and 90 C.E. by an anonymous Jewish-Christian author and for a Jewish-Christian audience. Evidence cited includes the large number of references to important Jewish figures and to symbols of the Jewish faith as well as numerous quotations from the Jewish scriptures. Luke's Gospel is more difficult to date with precision, although most scholars argue that it was written between 80 and 90 C.E. by a Gentile Christian. Some other scholars date it to the early or mid-second century. In the introduction to his Gospel, the author of the third Gospel indicates that he was not an eyewitness to Jesus' life, but that he had access to traditions, oral or written, from eyewitnesses, and he was aware that others had attempted to write the gospel story of Jesus before him (Luke 1:1–4). Finally, the Fourth Gospel—known as the Gospel of John—appears to have been written approximately 90–100 C.E. by a Jewish-Christian author and for a community that was suffering persecution at the hands of its Jewish neighbors.

Questions of authorship aside, Christians profess that the Gospels reveal the truth about Jesus Christ. As inspired texts, the Gospels are believed to be the Word of God, but they are written in the words of their human authors. Therefore, they should be read with an awareness of the historical and political environments in which they were written, the needs of the people for whom they were written, and the literary expressions and cultural practices of the time.

The Synoptic Gospels

The Gospels of the New Testament provide its readers with four distinctive portraits of Jesus. However, three of these Gospels—Matthew, Mark, and Luke—are similar insofar as they tell the same general story of the life and teachings of Jesus Christ, and they contain a large number of passages that resemble one another nearly word for word. For this reason, they are called **synoptic gospels**, from the Greek word *synoptikos*, which means "seeing the whole together." Biblical scholars frequently employ a tool called a synopsis that places these texts side by side in parallel columns for ease of comparison. Any such comparison yields the inevitable conclusion that the only way these Gospels could have such a high degree of similarity in content and wording is if there was some copying done among them. This is called the **synoptic problem**.

The three Gospel versions of the Jewish authorities challenging Jesus' authority provide an excellent example of the synoptic problem.

Matthew 21:23–27

And when he entered the temple, the chief priests and the elders of the people came up to him as he was teaching, and said, "By what authority are you doing these things, and who gave you this authority?"

Jesus answered them, "I also will ask you a question; and if you tell me the answer, then I also will tell you by what authority I do these things. The baptism of John, whence was it? From heaven or from men?"

And they argued with one another, "If we say, 'From heaven,' he will say to us, 'Why then did you not believe him?' But if we say, 'From men,' we are afraid of the people, for all hold that John was a prophet."

So they answered Jesus, "We do not know." And he said to them, "Neither will I tell you by what authority I do these things."

Mark 11:27–33

And they came again to Jerusalem. And as he was walking in the temple, the chief priests and the scribes and the elders came to him, and they said to him, "By what authority are you doing these things, or who gave you this authority to do them?"

Jesus said to them, "I will ask you a question: answer me, and I will tell you by what authority I do these things. Was the baptism of John from heaven or from men? Answer me."

And they argued with one another, "If we say, 'From heaven,' he will say, 'Why then did you not believe him.' But shall we say, 'From men?'—they were afraid of the people, for all held that John was a real prophet."

So they answered Jesus, "We do not know." And Jesus said to them, "Neither will I tell you by what authority I do these things."

Luke 20:1–8

One day, as he was teaching the people in the temple and preaching the gospel, the chief priests and the scribes with the elders came up and said to him, "Tell us by what authority you do these things, or who it is that gave you this authority."

He answered them, "I also will ask you a question; now tell me. Was the baptism of John from heaven or from men?"

And they discussed it with one another, saying, "If we say, 'From heaven,' he will say, 'Why did you not believe him?' But if we say, 'From men,' all the people will stone us; for they are convinced that John was a prophet."

So they answered that they did not know whence it was. And Jesus said to them, "Neither will I tell you by what authority I do these things."

The literary similarities among the three versions of the story are obvious, and they include word-for-word similarity in both the quotations and the narration.

The synoptic gospels contain many, many examples of this kind of literary dependence. During the eighteenth century, biblical scholars set to work trying to discover which of the three synoptic gospels was the earliest and, potentially, the source for the other two. At first, the goal of this was to determine which gospel was the earliest and hence (presumably) the most historically reliable. Later another goal would be pursued: to learn how these later gospel writers had redacted (edited) their sources and what their redaction process tells us about the gospel writers' world-view and theological perspectives on the life and teachings of Jesus Christ.

Proposed Solutions to the Synoptic Problem

Biblical scholars have investigated a number of solutions to the synoptic problem. Although scholars disagree about certain aspects of the data, one theory that has gained almost universal acceptance is Markan Priority. This theory posits that Mark was written first, and was used as a source by both Matthew and Luke, each of whom adopted both its overall structure and almost all of its individual episodes. While the more traditional view that Matthew was the first Gospel written prevailed for much of Christian history and accounts for Matthew's placement as the first Gospel in the order of the canon, modern scholars have developed a large number of convincing arguments that Mark came earlier. For example, Mark is the shortest Gospel overall, only about 60 percent as long as Matthew and Luke. It is more likely that Matthew and Luke expanded upon Mark than that Mark came later and produced a "short-ened" Gospel. This is especially evident when one considers the material Mark would have supposedly omitted if he was the later writer and had access to Matthew or Luke: the virgin birth, the Sermon on the Mount/Plain, the Lord's Prayer, many of Jesus' best-known parables, and appearances by the risen Jesus to his followers. If Mark had wanted to produce an abbreviated version of Matthew and/or Luke, it is highly unlikely that he would have omitted all of these crucial passages. Some other arguments for Markan Priority include the fact that Mark contains the most instances of erroneous or inelegant grammar, syntax, and style. Most of these instances appear to have been "corrected" by Matthew and Luke. Mark is somewhat akin to a rough draft, while the drafts of Matthew and Luke are more polished. This is true in terms of theology as well. Mark has a number of passages that are difficult, puzzling, or problematic from a theological point of view. The theology found in Matthew and Luke is more refined and developed.

By itself, however, Markan Priority cannot completely solve the synoptic problem. There are a large number of passages—mostly sayings of Jesus—that are found in Matthew and Luke but not in Mark. Hence, Mark cannot have been the source for Matthew and Luke for this material. One possible explanation for this is that Luke had access not only to Mark but to Matthew as well, and copied stories and sayings from both of these sources. However, it is also possible that both Matthew and Luke had access to another source, one that they each used independent of the other. Biblical scholars have named this hypothetical source **Q**, for the German word *Quelle* ("source"). There have been a number of attempts to reconstruct Q, but no actual copies exist today, and some biblical scholars question whether it ever existed.

The **Two-Source Hypothesis** combines the theory of Markan Priority with the theory about Q and solves the synoptic problem by proposing that the writers of the Gospels of Matthew and Luke composed their gospels by drawing from two early sources, the Gospel of Mark and Q, and then incorporating other stories from oral or written sources that were exclusive to them. Matthew's famous Sermon on the Mount (Matthew 5:1–7:29) and its parallel Sermon on the Plain from Luke's Gospel (Luke 6:17–49) are examples of the material that supposedly belonged to Q. Matthew's story about the guards posted outside Jesus' tomb to prevent anyone from stealing the body and faking the resurrection (Matthew 27:62–66; 28:11–15) is one of the many stories that are unique to Matthew's Gospel. Similarly, stories like the parables of the Prodigal Son (Luke 15:11–32) and the Good Samaritan (Luke 10:25–37) were recorded only in Luke's Gospel. The Two-Source Hypothesis can be diagrammed as follows:

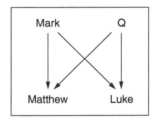

Although the Two-Source Hypothesis is the most widely accepted solution to the synoptic problem, it is not universally accepted. Therefore, biblical scholars have continued to experiment with alternative theories to describe the literary dependence of the synoptic gospels. These theories are often a prominent part of academic courses dedicated exclusively to the New Testament.

The Gospel of John

The Gospel of John is different from the synoptic gospels in a number of ways. Instead of parables and individual sayings or collections of sayings of Jesus like those found in the synoptic gospels, the Gospel of John contains long discourses or speeches delivered by Jesus in a style that is distinctive to this evangelist. Both the Gospel of John and the synoptic gospels contain miracle stories, but John appears to

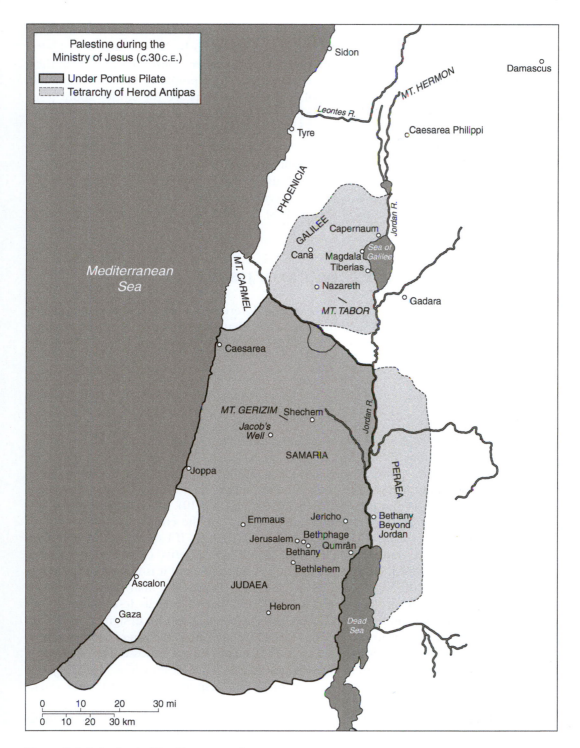

Figure 6–2 Palestine in New Testament times.

have known only a few of the same miracle stories found in the synoptic gospels. Two examples are Jesus multiplying loaves and fishes (John 6:1–15; cf. Matthew 14:13–21; Mark 6:32–44; Luke 9:10–17) and Jesus walking on water (John 6:16–21; cf. Matthew 14:22–27; Mark 6:45–51). At the same time, John incorporates a number of miracle stories that are unique to this gospel. The most famous are the stories about Jesus turning the water to wine at Cana (John 2:1–10) and the raising of Lazarus from the dead (John 11:1–44). Finally, some of the important characters in John's Gospel—most notably, Nicodemus, the Samaritan woman, and the mysterious "disciple whom Jesus loved"—are absent from the synoptic gospels.

Differences such as these have led most biblical scholars to conclude that the author of John's Gospel may have had access to some of the same oral traditions as those known to the synoptic gospel writers, but that he did not have knowledge of their gospels.

COMMON THEMES IN THE TEACHING OF JESUS

While the Gospels do have many fascinating differences and each has its unique elements, there are some overarching similarities that should not be overlooked. What follows is an analysis of some of the most important themes in the teaching and example of Jesus.

Compassion

Jesus taught the importance of compassion and demonstrated empathy, concern, and kindness throughout his ministry. Jesus' many miracles are first and foremost a demonstration of his divine power, but equally important is the fact that they are motivated by Jesus' compassion for those who are suffering, hungry, and in need. When Jesus feeds 5,000 (Mark 6:30–44 and parallels) and 4,000 (Mark 8:1–10), he is concerned to alleviate the hunger of the crowds. "I have compassion for the crowd, because they have been with me now for three days and have nothing to eat. If I send them away hungry to their homes, they will faint on the way" (Mark 8:2–3). Jesus' cleansing of the leper (Mark 1:40–45) follows the afflicted man's plea for help, and it is noted that Jesus was "moved with pity." In addition to the terrible skin disease, the man would have been considered an unclean outcast, and it is this suffering that elicits Jesus' empathy. In addition to healing and feeding miracles, Jesus' exorcisms are also designed to alleviate the suffering of those who had been possessed by demons. The father of the man with the epileptic child (Mark 9:14–29) tells Jesus that the demon in possession of his son's body "has often cast him into the fire and into the water, to destroy him." He asks Jesus, "If you are able to do anything, have pity on us and help us" (Mark 9:22). Jesus apparently did feel pity for the members of this family, for he does help them.

Jesus also demanded compassion from his followers, and commended those who demonstrated this quality. When his disciples showed a lack of compassion by speaking sternly to the children who came to Jesus, he rebuked them: "Let the little children come to me; do not stop them. For it is to such as these that the kingdom of God belongs" (Mark 10:14). In a famous passage called "the Great Judgment" (Matthew 25:31–46), Jesus foretells that when he returns from heaven as the Son of Man, he will separate the righteous from the wicked as a shepherd separates the sheep from the goats. And he will say to the saved that they will inherit the kingdom prepared for them from the foundation of the world,

> For I was hungry and you gave me food, I was thirsty and you gave me something to drink, I was a stranger and you welcomed me, I was naked and you gave me clothing, I was sick and you took care of me, I was in prison and you visited me.
>
> (Matthew 25:34–36)

When the righteous ask when they did these things for Jesus, he will answer, "Truly I tell you, just as you did it to one of the least of these who are members of my family, you did it to me" (Matthew 25:40). Similarly, he explains to the damned that their condemnation is a result of their failure to show compassion to those in need. Those who are selfish and concerned only with themselves are frequent targets of Jesus' ire, as in the parables of the Rich Fool (Luke 12:15–21) and the Rich Man and Lazarus (Luke 16:19–31). By contrast, the Good Samaritan (Luke 10:25–37) shows tremendous compassion and care to a stranger (probably Jewish) who was beaten by robbers and left half-dead, even though Jews and Samaritans were sworn enemies. Jesus tells his audience to "go and do likewise" (Luke 10:37).

Jesus' greatest act of compassion, according to the Gospels, was to take the sins of humanity on himself and "give his life as a ransom for many" (Mark 10:45). More will be said about this below, but the idea is perhaps best summarized in the King James translation of John 15:13—"Greater love hath no man than this, that he lay down his life for his friends."

Repentance and Forgiveness

The predecessor of Jesus was John the Baptist. John preached a "baptism of repentance for the forgiveness of sin" (Mark 1:4), encouraging people to engage in a ritual in which their sins were symbolically washed away; their old sinful selves "died" and they emerged as new and better persons. John's condemnation of sinners was stern and angry—he called the unrighteous a "brood of vipers" and warned them that "even now the axe is laid to the root of the trees; every tree therefore that does not bear good fruit is cut down and thrown into the fire" (Luke 3:7, 9). He instructed people to be more generous ("He who has two coats, let him share with him who has none; and he who has food, let him do likewise") and ordered tax collectors and soldiers to practice their professions in ways that did not create suffering and misery for others (Luke 3:10–14).

Like his predecessor, Jesus had an acute sense of human sinfulness, and of humans' need to recognize their wrongdoing, to commit to acting differently, and to seek and receive forgiveness from those they have offended, both divine and human. Jesus famously said, "Judge not, lest you be judged" (Matthew 7:1), but he himself frequently pronounced judgment upon others, insisting that before there can be forgiveness there must be acknowledgment of wrongdoing. Jesus was aware that humans are notoriously resistant to the idea they have done wrong, and some of his strongest criticism is reserved for those "who trusted in themselves that they were righteous and despised others" (Luke 18:9), refusing to admit the possibility that they too were transgressors and that their sins grieved the eternal God. It did not matter whether a person's sins were lesser than their neighbors (as in the case of the Pharisee and the woman who was a sinner in Luke 7:36–51 or the Pharisee and the tax collector in Luke 18:9–14) or exceeded the sins of those whom they held in disdain. In Paul's

Figure 6–3 *The Return of the Prodigal Son*, by Rembrandt van Rijn (1606–1669).

words, "All have sinned and fallen short of the glory of God" (Romans 3:23).

Jesus reserved his most strident condemnation for the scribes and Pharisees whose sanctimony, self-righteousness, and false piety aroused his anger (Mark 3:1–6, 7:1–13). He particularly excoriated them for hypocrisy: pretending to be holy and pious when their actions were often far from pure (Matthew 23:1–39). But he did not spare his own followers, whom he criticized for jealousy and internal squabbles (Mark 9:33–39, 10:35–45), failures of fellowship (Mark 14:32–33, 37–42), and a host of other transgressions. However, Jesus engaged in this criticism not to berate and demoralize his hearers, but in order to spark in them a moment of self-reflection and a corresponding sense of shame or remorse, and to call them to **repentance**. The Greek word for "repentance" is *metanoia*, which literally means to "think differently after." In both the Jewish and Christian traditions, the word refers to a radical turn from one way of thinking to another, specifically from a stance of self-love and self-assertion that leads to sin to a stance of surrender and obedience to God's will. True repentance requires an acknowledgment of guilt, a sincere commitment not to repeat the offense, and an attempt to restore what has been broken or damaged by one's wrongdoing to a status of wholeness and integrity.

If these conditions are met, then the result can be forgiveness. Jesus emphasizes God's justice, but this justice is always tempered with mercy. One of the best examples of Jesus' teaching in this regard is the famous parable of the Prodigal Son (Luke 15:11–32), in which a man's younger son disrespects him by demanding his inheritance prior to his father's death, and then leaves home to a dissolute life in which he squanders his fortune on prostitutes. He finds himself in abject poverty, struggling not to starve, when he begins to think that his father might allow him to return home, almost certainly not as a son but perhaps as a hired hand. When the father sees that his son has returned (and repented), he is overjoyed and welcomes him home—not as a hired hand but *as a son*. In this parable, Jesus is comparing the father's remarkable capacity for love and mercy to that of God, and assuring his followers that to receive forgiveness they have only to ask for it in a way that is true and sincere. The theme of forgiveness also plays a central role in the Lord's Prayer, in which the capacity to receive forgiveness is linked to one's willingness to forgive others: "Forgive us our debts, as we have forgiven our debtors" and "For if you forgive others their trespasses, your Heavenly Father will also forgive you" (Matthew 6:12, 14).

Conflict with Jewish Authorities

A significant number of the stories in the Gospels show Jesus sparring with various kinds of Jewish authorities—scribes, Pharisees, and chief priests (Sadducees). In the three synoptic gospels, these disagreements have a great deal to do with the Law and its interpretation. In John, the conflict is less about Torah and more about Jesus' identity—whether he is "from God" (John 9:16, 33) or a "sinner" (John 9:24) who is a Samaritan and possessed by a demon (John 8:48). In all four Gospels, this clash leads eventually to Jesus' death, a killing that the Gospels characterize clearly as a murder motivated by religious jealousy. One cannot speak of the content of the Gospels without reckoning with Jesus' conflict with the Jewish authorities.

In many of the synoptic stories, the scribes and Pharisees are portrayed as advocates of a kind of narrow **legalism** with respect to the Jewish Law or Torah. This means that they adhered to the letter of the law rather than its spirit, were unwilling to consider the circumstances that led ordinary people to be out of compliance with their strict and rigid codes, and took excessive pride in their own superficial righteousness while being disdainful toward those who were less observant. They also placed great importance on the maintenance of ritual purity through the avoidance of unclean foods and unclean persons like lepers, tax collectors, and anyone who was bleeding. This is an aspect of Judaism that Jesus is said in the Gospels to have completely rejected (see Mark 1:40–45, 2:15–17, 5:24–34, 7:1–20). As Chapter 5 indicates, it is true that the Pharisees were known for their love of Torah and their advocacy of personal piety, but whether they were "legalistic" as the term is defined above is disputed by many Jewish and Christian scholars today. Nonetheless, this term would be an accurate characterization of how the Jewish authorities are often *portrayed* in the Gospels.

Many of the conflicts between Jesus and the scribes and Pharisees involve the Sabbath, which Jesus had a tendency to interpret more loosely than his Jewish opponents. For example, in Mark 2:23–28, the scribes and Pharisees accuse Jesus' disciples of violating the prohibition against work on the Sabbath when they are seen plucking heads of grain on the holy day of rest. Jesus' response indicates that the disciples are not truly engaged in the "work" of harvest, but merely plucking heads of grain in order to give themselves something to eat, for they were hungry. He concludes by saying, "The sabbath was made for humankind, and not humankind for the sabbath" (Mark 2:27). Here Jesus suggests that to interpret the Torah correctly one must look behind the law itself and understand the purpose behind it. The purpose of the Sabbath, in Jesus' understanding, is to *benefit* human beings, not to harm them. The Pharisees' interpretation suggests that God would be more pleased if Jesus' disciples went hungry, in order to adhere to the letter of the law. They permitted work to be performed on the Sabbath only in order to save a person's life. Jesus does not agree that God's laws should cause suffering, nor does he think that they should allow suffering to continue. Hence, Jesus also performed healings on the Sabbath (as in Mark 3:1–6 and John 9:1–7), arguing that it should be lawful to "do good" on the Sabbath whether a life was at stake or not (Mark 3:4).

The Pharisees' refusal to engage in debate with Jesus on this question of whether any good action should be permitted on the Sabbath made him "angry" and "he was grieved at their hardness of heart" (Mark 3:5). The concept of a hardened heart should be familiar to readers of the Bible from the story of Exodus, where God hardens Pharaoh's heart so that he does not release the Israelites until all ten plagues have been unleashed. In the Gospels, God is not understood to be hardening the hearts of the scribes and Pharisees; they are hardening their own hearts. The implication, though, is that the Jewish authorities are no more able to be convinced by Jesus that he is truly God's representative than Pharaoh is to release the children of Israel from bondage. The phrase "hardened hearts" suggests that Jesus' enemies are incapable of persuasion, immune to any kind of evidence Jesus might supply, and stubbornly determined to oppose him no matter what.

The reason for this implacable opposition, the Gospels hint, is jealousy. Toward the end of the Gospel, the Roman governor Pontius Pilate correctly perceives that the Jewish authorities have trumped up false charges against Jesus and are seeking his death because of jealousy (Mark 15:10). But this envy has its origins in the beginning of the story. Jesus creates a sensation from his very first appearance on the public stage, dazzling audiences with his teaching and miracles. The people see their current leaders as poor substitutes for a genuine man of God—"He taught them as one having authority, and not as the scribes" (Mark 1:22). Jesus and the scribes/Pharisees are clearly fighting over the same patch of turf—each claimed religious authority and each was competing for the loyalty and allegiance of the people. Jesus' spectacular successes made him immensely popular, and every follower he gained came at the expense of the scribes and Pharisees. They saw him as a threat to their positions of power and privilege. And they feared him with good reason, apparently, for Jesus attracted such crowds that he could not go into a town without being mobbed (Mark 1:45), and when he entered a house, people could not even get near the door, but had to take the roof off of the house to lower a paralyzed man down to meet with Jesus (Mark 2:2–4).

The Jewish authorities initially seek merely to discredit Jesus, to show the people that he associated with the wrong people (Mark 2:15–17), or was sloppy in keeping his disciples on the path of piety and righteousness (Mark 2:18–22), and hence was unworthy of their adulation and allegiance. They followed him from place to place, waiting for him to make a mistake they could pounce on with an accusation of wrong-doing that would reverse the exodus of followers from their sphere of influence to that of Jesus. But they were unsuccessful in every attempted accusation, and Jesus emerged with his reputation intact and his followers growing: "They were all amazed and glorified God, saying, 'We have never seen anything like this!'" (Mark 2:12). Hence the scribes and Pharisees decided that the only way to preserve their positions was to have Jesus killed. They resolve in Mark 3:6 "to destroy" Jesus, despite his many good works and the fact that he had committed what were, at worst, only minor infractions against the Law as they understood it.

The plot to have Jesus killed gains steam when Jesus travels to Jerusalem and "cleanses" the Temple (Mark 11:15–19). Jesus completely disrupts the business of the Temple—overturning the tables of the moneychangers and driving out those selling animals—and he accuses the chief priests who run the Temple of corruption, of turning what should have been a house of prayer into a "den of robbers." This incendiary act earns Jesus a new and powerful set of enemies: the Sadducees, whose wealth, power, and influence with the Romans could obviously lead to his doom. Nonetheless, Jesus forges ahead bravely, continuing his attack on the Jewish authorities with the blistering parable of the Wicked Tenants (Mark 12:1–12). However, shortly thereafter, he is betrayed and arrested by the Jewish police. He is quickly tried and convicted of blasphemy in a trial noteworthy for its unfairness. The judges are biased against him and the witnesses against him all give false testimony (Mark 14:55–59). He is then sent on to the Roman governor of Judea for final sentencing, although Jesus was now being accused of treason against Rome rather than blasphemy. Jesus is charged with claiming to be the "king of the Jews," an assertion he never made and to which he does not admit. Despite his manifest innocence, he is convicted and condemned to die on a cross.

Although there is no question historically that the Romans found Jesus guilty of treason and executed him—crucifixion was a Roman punishment, not a Jewish one—all of the Gospels do their best to shift as much of the blame for this from the Romans to the Jews. Each of the Gospels portrays Pontius Pilate, the man who actually

Figure 6–4 *Christ before Pilate*, by Jacopo Tintoretto (1518–1594).

sent Jesus to his death, as a fair judge who thought Jesus was innocent and tried to release him, only to be overwhelmed by the demands of the Jews that Jesus be crucified. There were no doubt political reasons for assigning as much guilt for Jesus' murder to the Jews and as little to the Romans as possible by the late first century when the Gospels were written. Christians were already being persecuted by the Romans and may have sought to relieve some of the pressure by portraying the Romans favorably. The rupture between Judaism and Christianity was also nearing completion and becoming increasingly bitter. There was everything to gain and little to lose by blaming the Jews and exonerating the Romans, or so it must have appeared at the time. Unfortunately, this decision would prove tragic, as it resulted in centuries of Christian persecution of Jews motivated in large part by the accusation that they were "Christ-killers" and the belief that later generations of Jews bore as much guilt for this murder as their ancestors. The conflict between Jesus and the Jewish authorities is too well attested not to have been real. But whether the Jews were as responsible for Jesus' death as the Gospels indicate is very much an open question in modern biblical scholarship.

Peace and Nonviolence

Jesus was well known as an advocate of peace and nonviolence, even in the early Church. It was not for no reason that so many early Christian leaders preached pacifism, insisting that a good Christian could not kill or take up arms against others. An example is the early third-century document called *The Apostolic Tradition* attributed to Hippolytus of Rome, which proclaimed:

> A soldier of the civil authority must be taught not to kill men and to refuse to do so if he is commanded, and to refuse to take an oath. If he is unwilling to comply, he must be rejected for baptism.
>
> (Apostolic Tradition 16:11)

The biblical evidence for this stance is not voluminous, but to many early Christians the teaching of Jesus in the Gospels was clear and decisive. For example, included among the beatitudes is "Blessed are the peacemakers, for they will be called children of God" (Matthew 5:9). Jesus also commands his followers to love their enemies (Matthew 5:44). When someone sought to defend him from unwarranted arrest with violence, Jesus demanded that he stop, saying, "Put your sword back into its place, for all who take the sword will perish by the sword" (Matthew

26:52). Jesus thus taught that violence was self-defeating, that it cannot truly resolve conflicts but will merely exacerbate and prolong them indefinitely. Some modern theologians have called this the "spiral of violence." Whether an initial injury is inflicted by an individual or by a larger group or system, the one harmed will lash out, seeking to "even the score" and "teach a lesson" to the oppressor. But such lessons are seldom if ever learned, because the initial offender is either unaware of the injustice of his actions or convinced that his treatment of the other was justified in some way. For this reason, the counter-violence tends only to provoke further repression, which in turn produces more counter-violence, and then still more repression *ad infinitum*. Killing one's opponents might bring an end to a conflict, but that does not mean the conflict was truly resolved.

The key passage in the minds of most proponents of Christian peacemaking is Jesus' teaching against retaliation. The law of Moses allowed an injured party to take revenge upon an attacker, but restricted the retribution to the imposition of an equal measure of harm. This is known as the *lex talionis* (law of retaliation), and it is summed up in the phrase from the Old Testament: "If any harm follows, then you shall give life for life, eye for eye, tooth for tooth, hand for hand, foot for foot, burn for burn, wound for wound, stripe for stripe" (Exodus 21:23–25). But Jesus appears to explicitly reject this teaching in the Sermon on the Mount/Plain, saying,

> You have heard that it was said, "An eye for an eye and a tooth for a tooth." But I say to you, Do not resist an evildoer. But if anyone strikes you on the right cheek, turn the other also.
>
> (Matthew 5:38–39)

To many people, this seems like the most impractical and unrealistic of Jesus' teachings, a recipe for being bulldozed by one's opponents. But there are many who believe that Jesus was not advocating passive acceptance of injustice and evil but advocating a form of active nonviolent resistance. A person struck on the cheek will usually fight back or run away. Both of those choices often lead to disaster. If you choose not to run but to fight back, you may defeat your opponent, but he may come back at you another time with even greater force. Jesus seems to be suggesting that there is a third option: to stand your ground—to say that you will not submit, but neither will you be turned away. This requires courage; it is not the way of a coward. Sometimes such a stance will cause your opponent to gain respect for you. Other times you might take a beating. But even taking a beating has the potential to produce good results in a way that fighting back does not. Some interpreters believe Jesus was saying that accepting a blow, or even many blows, can awaken something in the human nature of your opponent that will cause his hatred for you to decrease and his respect for you to increase. In other words, unearned suffering can be redemptive.

This certainly appears to have been Jesus' stance with respect to his own situation. He never advocated violent revolution against Rome even though it was an extremely repressive government. He marched to his own crucifixion without complaining or fighting back, apparently confident in the belief that his unearned suffering would have an effect on those who saw it and heard about it. It is interesting that after Jesus breathes his last, a Roman centurion (officer)—probably one of those who flogged Jesus, mocked him with a crown of thorns, and supervised his humiliating, torturous execution—says, "Truly this was the son of God" (Mark 15:39). Apparently, something about the nature of Jesus' death pricked the conscience of this Roman soldier and caused him to reconsider his opinion of Jesus.

The End of the World and the Kingdom of God

The popularity of apocalypticism in late Second Temple Judaism is well attested, as Chapters 4 and 5 indicate. Early Christians evidently agreed with those Jews who eagerly awaited the end of the world and were convinced that it was coming very soon. Paul's letters show that he definitely expected the return of Jesus from heaven and the consummation of history to occur within his lifetime (1 Thessalonians 4:15–17), and he was by no means alone in this hope. Readers of the synoptic gospels would have been encouraged to believe this as well, because these three gospels (excluding John, in which the end of the world does not play any role in Jesus' teaching) show Jesus frequently teaching that the end was near.

One strain of Jesus' teaching in this regard shows that he regarded the end of the world not as a personal or spiritual transformation but as a cataclysmic event of cosmic significance that would occur in the near future. Of particular importance in this regard is Jesus' "apocalyptic discourse"—a long speech in which he outlines the warning signs and the sequence of events, hints about the timing and the criteria for rescue or salvation from the destruction that would accompany the apocalypse (Mark 13, Matthew 24, Luke 21). The sequence of events includes: (1) the "birth pangs" (a dramatic increase in wars, famine, and natural disaster; see Mark 13:5–8); (2) the outbreak of a severe persecution of Christians (Mark 13:9–13); (3) the "desolating sacrilege set up where it ought not to be" (an apparent reference to false gods being worshipped in the Temple; see Mark 13:14); (4) cosmic collapse, wherein the sun and moon will not give their light, and the stars will fall from the sky (Mark 13:24–25); and (5) the second coming of Christ with armies of angels who will rescue the faithful and spare them from the destruction to which unbelievers will be subjected (Mark 13:26–27). The road to the end will be difficult for believers, Jesus warns, but "the one who endures to the end will be saved" (Mark 13:13). The exact cause of the descent of God's wrath on the world is not specified in the apocalyptic discourse, but elsewhere Jesus indicates that the cause is simply God's anger over human wickedness and his refusal to allow a terrible situation to continue indefinitely. The parable of the Wicked Tenants (Mark 12:1–12) illustrates this point clearly—the tenants: (1) refuse to pay their rent; (2) ignore, beat, and kill the vineyard owner's servants when they are sent to remind the tenants of what is owing; and (3) murder the owner's beloved son when he gives them one final chance to change their ways and show some respect. The parable suggests that the imminent destruction of such wicked tenants is truly well deserved and probably long overdue. "What then will the owner of the vineyard do? He will destroy those tenants and give the vineyard to others" (Mark 12:9).

While there is a very definite future element to Jesus' teaching about the apocalypse, there is also a present element that is best understood by looking at Jesus' statements about the **kingdom of God**. All four New Testament Gospels mention the notion of God's kingdom, but again it is especially prominent in the synoptic gospels. In Mark, for example, Jesus' first words of preaching are about the kingdom: "The time is fulfilled, and the kingdom of God is at hand" (Mark 1:15; cf. Matthew 3:2). There are also a great many parables that are explicitly designed to illuminate some aspect of the kingdom of God. Many of these parables begin with the heading, "The kingdom of God is like…" (see, e.g., Mark 4:26, 30 and Matthew 13:24, 31, 33). The meaning of the term "kingdom of God" (or "kingdom of heaven," as Matthew prefers) is not entirely clear in the Gospels. Some texts seem to suggest that the kingdom of God is a place, that it is a kind of perfect human society that will begin after certain events have occurred; other texts suggest that it is a state of mind possessed by individuals and groups independent of the occurrence of any specific future events. An example of the latter can be found in the Gospel of Luke. Asked by the Pharisees when the kingdom of God would come, Jesus said in reply, "The coming of the kingdom of God cannot be observed, and no one will announce, 'Look, here it is,' or, 'There it is.' For behold, the kingdom of God is among you [or within you]" (Luke 17:20–21).

These apparent contradictions can be resolved if one thinks of the term as referring to the idea of God's kingly rule, where God is truly sovereign and his people live in peace, justice, and obedience. In this sense, an individual or group can commit to thinking and acting as if God is their king in the here and now, but might also hope that there will come a time and a place when "all flesh" will acknowledge God's sovereign rule together and the kingdom will be fully realized. The Gospels describe the reign of God as something that is manifested in the coming of the Son and in the conviction that God's grace is greater than all the powers of evil in the world. Jesus' miracles, especially his healings, feedings, and exorcisms, are thought to show how the kingdom of God was already breaking into the present reality, even if it would only be fully consummated in the future. In the kingdom of God, it was thought that there would be no hunger, no poverty, no suffering or disease, and no demonic forces. Jesus was already making this a reality for those he encountered in his earthly ministry, and he was giving them a taste of what glorious future awaited them. The kingdom of God signifies a situation in which, by the power of God, good has triumphed over evil and a new world order has been established.

Wealth and Poverty

Roman society was characterized by a huge gap between rich and poor. The great majority of people were desperately poor. There was very little economic opportunity as well and therefore little social mobility. Most wealth was inherited, so there was not a strong sense that the wealthy had *earned* their fortunes and were thus entitled to them. These fortunes were often gained originally—and then augmented by—conquest, land theft, and the exploitation of labor. Of course, slavery was the ultimate form of exploitation, but even those who were not enslaved were paid low wages, worked long hours, endured dangerous working conditions, and always had to worry about food scarcity, indebtedness, high taxation, and the threat of displacement.

All of the Gospels show Jesus identifying himself with the poor and speaking on their behalf. Two Gospels (Matthew and Luke) show Jesus blessing the poor in the beatitudes. Three Gospels (Matthew, Mark, and Luke) include the story of the rich man/ruler whose wealth prevents him from following Jesus. But the one Gospel that does the most to elucidate Jesus' teachings on wealth and poverty is Luke. The Gospel of Luke includes a series of unique passages in which Jesus articulates both his criticisms of the rich and his hopes for their salvation. One is the parable of the Rich Fool (Luke 12:15–21). Jesus prefaces the parable by saying, "Be on your guard against all kinds of greed, for one's life does not consist in the abundance of possessions." He then proceeds to tell of a wealthy man whose land produces abundantly. He now has so much grain that he has nowhere to store it, for his barns are already full. He decides to tear down his barns and build larger ones, and thus to keep everything he has gained for himself. He congratulates himself for his wisdom in a rather strange soliloquy: "Soul, you have ample good laid up for many years; relax, eat, drink, and be merry." But God's voice intervenes and proclaims, "You fool! This very night your life is being demanded of you. And the things you have prepared, whose will they be?" Jesus then concludes: "So it is with those who store up treasures for themselves but are not rich toward God."

What is "foolish" about the rich man's behavior here? On the one hand, he seems to be unaware of his own mortality, and is undoubtedly taken by surprise when he dies sooner than he expects. He has focused on the material dimension of life ("storing up treasures" for himself) but has neglected the spiritual dimension of life (he is not "rich toward God"). His confusion about these two dimensions is partially illustrated by the fact that he addresses his "soul" and tells it to "eat, drink, and be merry." It is the body, not the soul, that needs to eat and drink. The spirit needs a different kind of nourishment. His neglect of the spiritual dimension of life is also manifested in his selfishness and greed. The parable emphasizes that he *already has far more than he could ever need* (he is a rich man, and his barns are already full of grain). Despite this, when he receives an additional windfall, he never even considers doing anything but keeping it all for himself, even though in every part of the Roman Empire there were people who were starving.

The lack of compassion toward the needy is *implicit* in the parable of the Rich Fool, but it becomes *explicit* in the parable of the Rich Man and Lazarus (Luke 16:19–31). The parable begins by emphasizing how the rich man lives a life of incredible luxury. He wears the finest clothing and feasts sumptuously every day. This luxury is contrasted with the abject poverty of Lazarus, who lies sick and starving at the rich man's very gate. Lazarus longed to eat even the crumbs that fell from the rich man's table, but the rich man apparently gives him nothing. Both men die, and Lazarus finds himself in heaven, in the bosom of father Abraham, while the rich man is being tormented in hell. In an ironic twist, the rich man asks father Abraham to send Lazarus—to whom he had never shown an ounce of concern in life—down to dip the tip of his finger in some cool water and place it on his tongue, because he is in agony in the flames. He somehow expects to receive the kindness that he never was willing to give when he had the opportunity. Father Abraham refuses, for "between you and us a great chasm has been fixed, so that those who might want to pass from here to you cannot do so, and no one can cross from there to us." Greed and a lack of compassion for the less fortunate were *serious* sins deserving of permanent damnation. This is the only parable Jesus tells in which a man ends up in hell. And it is about a selfish rich man, not a murderer or a rapist.

The story of the Rich Ruler is found in all three synoptic gospels. But it fits in especially well with Luke's other warnings about the danger of riches. A rich man approaches Jesus and asks him what he must do to attain eternal life. Jesus tells him to follow the Commandments, and the man tells him that he has kept them from his youth. Jesus tells him that he lacks one thing: he must sell all of his possessions and give the money to the poor, and then "come, follow me." The man leaves disheartened and sorrowful. He is unable to submit to Jesus' demand because he has many possessions and is apparently quite *attached* to them. The story seems to suggest that riches have a corrupting influence on people. Once something is gained, it is difficult to part with it. Wealth does not make people more generous, but less so. Jesus concludes by proclaiming:

> How difficult it will be for those who have wealth to enter the kingdom of God! … It is easier for a camel to pass through the eye of a needle than for a rich person to enter the kingdom of God.

> (Luke 18:23, 25)

The fact that salvation for the rich is not impossible is illustrated by the inclusion in the Gospel of Luke of the story of Zacchaeus (Luke 19:1–10). Zacchaeus was a chief tax collector, and very rich. When Jesus came to his town and was swarmed by the crowds, Zacchaeus showed his interest by climbing a tree to get a glimpse of Jesus. When Jesus saw him, he told Zacchaeus that he wished to stay at his house that night. Knowing that Zacchaeus was a tax collector, people began to grumble: "He has gone to the house of one who is a sinner." But without a word from Jesus, Zacchaeus redeems himself: "Look, half of my possessions, Lord, I will give to the poor; and if I have defrauded anyone of anything, I will pay back four times as much." After this, Jesus proclaims that "salvation has come to this house." Despite his riches and his sinful occupation, Zacchaeus is saved.

To gain this status, Zacchaeus depends on the mercy and grace of God, but he also demonstrates four qualities that Luke's Gospel seems to suggest many of his fellow rich men lack. The first is *compassion*. When Zacchaeus declares his willingness to donate money to the poor, and to repay the poor wretches he defrauded (most likely by overcharging them on their taxes), he shows that his empathy has been awakened, and with it, his sense of solidarity with other human beings.

The second quality is *generosity*. Zacchaeus does not give a small percentage of his wealth to the less fortunate, leaving a huge sum for himself. He gives fully half of his fortune to the poor, and repays those he has defrauded four times over. But the Torah only requires a person wanting to atone for defrauding another to repay him *twice* as much. Given how much of a tax collector's profits came from overcharging, this repayment will probably consume most of the remaining half of Zacchaeus' fortune. Unlike the rich people in Luke 21:1–4 who put their gifts into the treasury "out of their abundance" (i.e., apparently still leaving themselves with large fortunes), Zacchaeus is more like the poor widow who put in two copper coins, which represented "all she had to live on." Zacchaeus also implies that he will no longer defraud people as a tax collector. Zacchaeus demonstrates the third quality that the Gospel of Luke suggests can lead to salvation for the rich: a *commitment to earning an honest living*. The idea that it matters how a person earns his/her money is not unprecedented in the Gospel of Luke. In Luke 3:10–13, John the Baptist gives advice to sinners wanting to turn their lives around. His advice to tax collectors is not to quit their jobs, but to do those jobs honestly: "Collect no more than the amount prescribed for you" (Luke 3:13). When soldiers appeal to him as well, he does not tell them that they cannot serve in the military but commands them not to resort to immoral means of making more money: "Do not extort money from anyone by threats of false accusations, and be satisfied with your wages" (Luke 3:14).

Lastly, and perhaps most unusually, Zacchaeus demonstrates the quality of *non-attachment*. Zacchaeus is that rare bird who is not excessively attached to his wealth. He gives away what is almost certainly at least 90 percent of his fortune, voluntarily and without prompting.

In the end, the Gospels do not seem to argue that wealth itself is evil. Rather, Jesus' attitude as it is presented by the evangelists seems to be similar to that of the author of 1 Timothy, who did not write (as is often mistakenly assumed) that money itself is the root of all evil but rather that "the *love* of money is the root of all evil" (1 Timothy 6:10). The gospel example of Jesus suggests that there are two good purposes for money, namely, to spend it and to give it away. Only by accumulating it for its own sake and denying others the benefits that might be gained from it does one become sinful and earn Jesus' strongest disapproval.

FOUR PORTRAITS OF JESUS

An important feature and distinguishing mark of each Gospel is its **Christology**, or teaching about Jesus as the messiah or "Christ." Each Gospel paints a somewhat different portrait of Jesus and therefore has its own distinctive Christology. One of the key elements involved in Christology is whether more emphasis is placed on Jesus' humanity or divinity. There were in fact early Christian groups that denied that Jesus was in any way a god, claiming instead that he was born as an ordinary human and later "adopted" as God's son when he was chosen to be the messiah. Other groups took the opposite position and claimed that Jesus was not at all human, but was in fact purely divine. This led them to claim that Jesus was a spirit who did not have a body that could suffer or corrupt and die. Both of these extreme positions, known as **Adoptionism** and **Docetism**, were eventually proclaimed as heresies by the orthodox Church. None of the canonical gospels espouse these extreme views. However, there are passages that seem to emphasize Jesus' humanity and hence to suggest that he was something less than fully divine and equal or identical to God, such as "The Father is greater than myself" (John 14:28) and "Why do you call me good? No one is good but God alone" (Mark 10:18). There are also passages that suggest that there was no distinction between Jesus and God, such as "The Father and I are one" (John 10:30). All of the canonical gospels portray Jesus as both human and divine, although they do so to different degrees and in different ways.

Mark's Christology

The opening line of Mark's Gospel identifies Jesus as the messiah ("The beginning of the gospel of Jesus Christ the son of God"). But what does this term mean? Chapter 5 reviews the various concepts of the messiah or Christ that were in circulation at the time of Jesus. Some thought of the messiah as a prophetic figure, perhaps someone like Moses or Elijah. Others thought that the messiah would inaugurate the apocalypse and judge the living and the dead at the end of time. But the most common view was that the messiah would be a political and military leader who would bring together great armies, overthrow the oppressors of Israel, and re-establish an independent Jewish kingdom.

Mark's Gospel in some ways draws upon these expectations, in some ways repudiates them, and in other ways *redefines* the term "messiah." Jesus does act very much like a prophet in Mark, performing healing and feeding miracles as did the prophets Elijah and Elisha (Mark 1:40–45, 3:1–6, 5:21–43, 6:30–44, etc.), proclaiming God's judgment on sinners as did so many of the prophets of Judah and Israel (Mark 9:43–48, 10:24–25, 11:12–25), and offering up authoritative legal pronouncements in the vein of Moses (Mark 2:27, 3:4, 7:14–20, 10:2–12, etc.). Jesus' preaching also has an apocalyptic element. He begins his ministry by proclaiming, "The time is fulfilled, and the kingdom of God is at hand; repent and believe in the gospel" (Mark 1:15). In Mark 13, Jesus foretells the events surrounding the end of the world and marks out a key role for the "Son of Man," who will come with armies of angels to rescue the faithful from the destruction engulfing the world. Jesus consistently refers to himself in the Gospel as the "Son of Man" (Mark 2:10, 2:27, 8:31, etc.), and hence the Gospel expects Jesus to fulfill the apocalyptic task of the messiah when he returns at the Second Coming. However, Jesus never embraces any political or military role for himself, and consistently dampens the hopes and expectations of his various followers in this regard. Instead, Mark insists that Jesus will be a *suffering* messiah. This understanding does not draw upon any existing Jewish conception of the messiah but is a Christian innovation and a redefinition of the term.

Mark's Gospel tells a story that is traditionally called Peter's Confession, in which Jesus asks his disciples what people were saying about who he was (Mark 8:27–38). Peter answers that most believe him to be a prophet, or Elijah returned from heaven, or John the Baptist raised from the dead. But when Jesus asks, "Who do you say that I am?," Peter responds to Jesus' query with the words, "You are the Messiah" (Mark 8:29). Jesus goes on to say, in a passage known as the "First Passion Prediction," that "the Son of Man must undergo great suffering, and be rejected by the elders, the chief priests, and the scribes, and be killed, and after three days rise again" (Mark 8:31). Twice more, in the next two chapters, Jesus predicts that he will not lead an army to any glorious victory but will be arrested, mocked, flogged, and killed before rising again from the dead (Mark 9:30–32, 10:32–34).

From this point onward in the Gospel, Mark is consistent in his presentation of Jesus as the suffering messiah. At the conclusion of the story about the two disciples who wanted places of authority in Jesus' coming kingdom (Mark 10:35–45), Jesus declares, "For the Son of Man also came not to be served but to serve, and to give his life as a ransom for many" (Mark 10:45).

Matthew's Christology

Matthew's Gospel contains a rather different and more multifaceted portrait of Jesus as the Christ. First, Matthew uses imagery associated with David, the greatest king of Israel, to describe Jesus as the fulfillment of God's promise to establish an everlasting kingdom through his heir (see 2 Samuel 7). Thus, in the genealogy that introduces the Gospel, Jesus is proclaimed as "the messiah, son of David, son of Abraham" (Matthew 1:1). Likewise, Matthew's infancy narrative (the story of Jesus' birth and childhood) describes Jesus as having been born in Bethlehem, David's city, in fulfillment of a prophecy about a ruler who would arise to shepherd God's people, Israel (Matthew 2:5–6; cf. Micah 5:2).

Second, Matthew uses a variety of images and scripture quotations associated with the Exodus to portray Jesus as a great prophet like Moses. His infancy narratives include a story about how Jesus' family had to flee to Egypt to avoid Herod Antipas, who was trying to kill the child Jesus—reminders of the story about the infant Moses' amazing escape from death at the hands of the Egyptian Pharaoh (Matthew 2:13–15; cf. Exodus 2:1–10). Another Matthean story that is reminiscent of the Exodus is Jesus' stay in the wilderness before he begins his teaching ministry. Unlike the Israelites who failed their test in the desert and grumbled against God, Matthew describes how Jesus succeeded, having defeated the devil in a scripture-based debate in the middle of the wilderness (Matthew 4:1–11; cf. Exodus 32:1–35).

Again using imagery associated with Moses, Matthew portrays Jesus as the new lawgiver who makes perfect the Law and provides ethical teachings to guide the lives of his followers. This point is demonstrated most clearly in the Sermon on the Mount (Matthew 5:1–7:29), the first of five long discourses, which some biblical scholars think were intended to correspond with the five books of the Torah. Beginning with the **beatitudes** (statements that start with the phrase "Blessed are they..." or "Blessed are you..."), Matthew describes Jesus as teaching a new and more perfect way of keeping the Commandments and fulfilling the covenant relationship that had already existed for centuries between God and Moses and the Israelite people.

Matthew also has a "higher" christology than that found in Mark, meaning that he emphasized Jesus' divinity and resisted the idea that Jesus' humanity extended to the point where he exhibited qualities that were less than God-like. In Mark, Jesus admits that he does not know certain things (Mark 5:30–32, 13:32), and his power (while great) seems to be limited (Mark 6:5, 8:22–25). In Matthew, these passages are either absent or told in such a way that Jesus does not profess ignorance and his power is never constrained. In Mark, the disciples and others tend to address Jesus as "Teacher" (Mark 4:38, 5:35, 9:17, etc.), while in Matthew, the disciples typically refer to him as "Lord" (Matthew 8:25, 14:28, etc.)—a "loftier" title that implies Jesus was divine and not merely a man of unusual wisdom.

Luke's Christology

Luke's Gospel has a keen interest in proclaiming God's plan of salvation for all people, especially the poor and dispossessed. Luke's Gospel also stresses the essential continuity between Judaism and Christianity by presenting Jesus as the fulfillment of all the promises that God made to Abraham and the Jews in the Old Testament. He also explains the difficulty of a crucified messiah by arguing that the Old Testament prophecies testify to the fact that the messiah was destined to suffer.

What is the best way to describe Luke's distinctive portrait of Jesus? A scene from the Gospel that describes the beginning of Jesus' ministry is perhaps the most revealing. Luke says that Jesus, filled with the Holy Spirit, was teaching in the synagogues of Galilee (Luke 4:14–15). When he came to his hometown of Nazareth, he went to the synagogue on the Sabbath (Luke 4:16). When he stood up to do the reading, he was given the book of Isaiah to read. This is what follows:

> He unrolled the scroll and found the place where it was written:
> The Spirit of the Lord is upon me,
> because he has anointed me to bring good news to the poor.
> He has sent me to proclaim release to the captives
> and recovery of sight to the blind, to let the oppressed go free,
> to proclaim the year of the Lord's favor.
> And he rolled up the scroll, gave it back to the attendant, and sat down. The eyes of all in the synagogue were fixed on him. Then he began to say to them, "Today this scripture has been fulfilled in your hearing" (Luke 4:17–21; cf. Isaiah 61:1, 58:6, 61:2).

Thus Luke introduces Jesus, at the beginning of his ministry, as the prophet par excellence, specifically as the "prophet like Moses" foretold in Deuteronomy 18:15–19, whose coming would prove decisive for the salvation of the people. In Luke, Jesus is filled with the Holy Spirit and anointed by God to proclaim the good news to the poor and disadvantaged. His ministry is one of compassion for people who are marginalized from society and otherwise disenfranchised.

As Luke develops the plot of his Gospel, he continues to highlight this portrait of Jesus. In Luke's Sermon on the Plain (Luke 6:20–49), Jesus blesses the poor and the hungry, but he also curses those who are rich and comfortable. Further, Luke shows Jesus' special concern for the lowest segments of society by incorporating stories that highlight Jesus' compassion for those whom society has rejected. He depicts Jesus going out of his way to associate with tax collectors and sinners. For example, there is the story about Zacchaeus being invited down from his perch in the sycamore tree to meet Jesus (Luke 19:1–10). Luke also portrays Jesus as allowing women to take an active part in his ministry (Luke 8:1–3) and serve in roles traditionally reserved for men (Luke 10:38–42). In sum, Luke presents Jesus, the messiah, as the prophet of justice and compassion.

John's Christology

The portrait of Jesus found in the Gospel of John is very different from those of the synoptic gospels. In its prologue, Jesus is presented as the Word—the Greek term is *logos*—who came down from the Father to dwell among humanity (John 1:1–18).

What does it mean to describe Jesus as the Word of God? In addition to its many ordinary and popular meanings—in Greek, *logos* means "word," "book," "speech," "mind," and "reason/rationality," among other things—*logos* is a technical term used in Greek (Stoic) philosophy. It describes the unifying principle of all creation, the power that underlies all of creation, and the principle of order in the universe. For the Stoics, the *logos* represented the mind of God; they also believed that the human soul contained a spark of the divine *logos*.

By describing Jesus as the "speech" or "mind" of God, the author of John is expressing his central conviction that Jesus is the one who makes the Father known to us (John 1:18). The event in which the divine Word came down from God and took on flesh is called, in theological terms, the **incarnation** (meaning "enfleshment"). This kind of Christology, which describes Jesus as the *logos* who comes down from heaven to dwell with humankind, is sometimes called high Christology, because it focuses primarily on the divinity of Christ, in contrast to low christologies that focus first on the humanity of Jesus. John's Gospel is also called a three-stage Christology, as the diagram below illustrates.

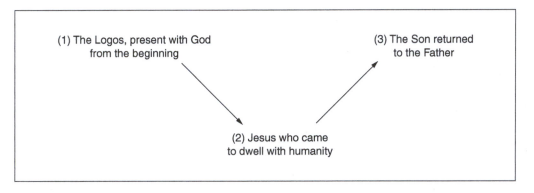

(1) The Logos, present with God from the beginning

(3) The Son returned to the Father

(2) Jesus who came to dwell with humanity

THE DEATH AND RESURRECTION OF JESUS

Among all of the events recorded in the Gospels, the death and resurrection of Jesus continue to be the touchstone of the Christian faith. Each of the four canonical gospels tells how Jesus was crucified and later raised from the dead. The evidence that the gospel writers provide for Jesus' resurrection varies from one gospel to another, but all include the empty tomb. They also tell of a messenger or messengers sent by God to testify to the fact that Jesus had been raised. Three of the gospels contain stories about the risen Jesus appearing to his followers shortly after his death.

The earliest Christians saw Jesus' resurrection from the dead as God's glorious act of vindicating Jesus after his shameful death by crucifixion. However, within contemporary Judaism, resurrection of the dead was thought to happen only in the end

Figure 6–5 *The Crucifixion,* by Andrea Mantegna (1431–1506).

Figure 6–6 *The Resurrection of Christ,* by Piero Della Francesca (*c.*1416–1492).

time. Hence, the earliest Christians thought that Jesus' resurrection marked the beginning of the end time. Just as God raised Jesus from the dead, God would soon rescue the rest of God's righteous ones. They needed only to wait for the glorious return of the messiah, at which time the kingdom of God would be fully established for the righteous, while the wicked would be consigned to eternal damnation. Thus, belief in the Second Coming of Christ—the technical term is *parousia*—became an important feature of early Christianity. Indeed, most of the earliest Jesus followers believed that he would return within their lifetimes. Most Christians today still believe in the *parousia,* though some think it will come soon, while others view it as something that will not occur until the distant future.

Key Terms

Adoptionism	kingdom of God	Q
beatitudes	legalism	repentance
Christology	*logos*	synoptic gospels
Docetism	parousia	synoptic problem
Incarnation	passion	Two-Source Hypothesis

Questions for Reading

1. Briefly describe the three-stage process that led to the development of the Gospels. What distinguishes each stage from the other?

2. What is the synoptic problem and how does the Two-Source Hypothesis provide a possible answer to this problem?

3. Which teachings of Jesus illustrate the importance of compassion and empathy? How did Jesus exemplify these qualities in his own life, according to the Gospels?

4. What was the teaching of John the Baptist on repentance and forgiveness? How did Jesus both continue the themes preached by John and develop them further?

5. What was the nature of the conflict between Jesus and the Jewish authorities? What issues did they argue about? How did the opposition of the Jewish authorities toward Jesus grow as his ministry progressed, and what were some of the key moments in this development?

6. What were Jesus' views about the end of the world? How does the concept of the kingdom of God relate to both the coming apocalypse and life in the present?

7. What features of Roman economic life and the characteristic behavior of the rich at that time drew Jesus' ire? What qualities do the Gospels suggest a rich person needs to possess in order to gain salvation?

8. Although all four Gospels tell the story of Jesus' life, each provides a somewhat different portrait of Jesus. For each Gospel, select one key idea that you think best describes its Christology.

9. Explain some of the reasons why the death and resurrection of Jesus was an important event for early Christians and how they made it a central part of their theological reflection on the Christian faith.

Works Consulted/Recommended Reading

Brown, Raymond E. 1997. *An Introduction to the New Testament.* New York: Doubleday.

Duling, Dennis C., and Norman Perrin. 1994. *The New Testament: Proclamation and Parenesis, Myth and History,* 3rd edn. Fort Worth, TX: Harcourt Brace.

Eusebius. 1990. *Ecclesiastical History.* Translated by Isaac Boyle. Grand Rapids, MI: Baker Book House.

Metzger, Bruce, and Roland Murphy, eds. 1991. *The New Oxford Annotated Bible with Apocrypha, New Revised Standard Version.* New York: Oxford University Press.

Powell, Mark Allan. 1998. *Fortress Introduction to the Gospels.* Minneapolis, MN: Fortress.

Raisanen, Heikki. 1990. *The "Messianic Secret" in Mark.* Translated by Christopher Tuckett. Edinburgh: T&T Clark.

Chapter

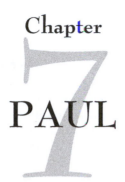

PAUL

TIMELINE

*c.*4–6 C.E.	Birth of Paul.
30? C.E.	Death of Jesus.
32–33? C.E.	Paul's conversion on the road to Damascus.
37–40 C.E.	A Christian church is established at Antioch.
49 or 50 C.E.	Jerusalem Conference meets to decide whether Gentile converts must observe Jewish Torah regulations.
49 C.E.	A Christian church already established at Rome.
49–50 C.E.	Paul establishes a church at Corinth.
50–60 C.E.	Paul writes his letters to churches he founded during his missionary journeys.
58–60 C.E.	Paul is arrested in Jerusalem.
60–61 C.E.	Paul is tried in Jerusalem and sent to Rome.
62–64 C.E.	Paul is probably killed by the Roman emperor Nero.
70 C.E.	Destruction of Second Temple during Jewish revolt.
*c.*90 C.E.	Expulsion of Christian Jews from synagogues.

Although Christians were still a tiny minority in the Roman Empire in 100 c.e., the seeds of Christianity's emergence as the dominant religion in the Mediterranean world were sown by the success of first-century missionaries who spread the word about the crucified and risen Jesus. By the end of the first century, Christian churches thrived in most of the major cities of the Roman Empire. However, because Christianity grew so rapidly in its first decades and with so little institutional control, the religion quickly began to mean different things to different people. The result was that Christianity in the first century was an extremely diverse religious phenomenon, with all sorts of people calling themselves "Christians" but having some very different beliefs and practices.

In spite of the diversity of beliefs and practices among first-century Christian churches, it is possible to see traces of three unifying forces that will manifest themselves in later centuries. (1) Already, from the beginning, the apostles and first followers of Jesus held a place of authority within the churches as teachers and spiritual guides for the Christian communities. Some Christian communities gave to Peter a special status as the first of the apostles. Later, the "bishops" and leaders of the church would trace the source of their teaching authority back to Peter and the apostles (see Chapter 8). (2) The early churches also proclaimed the same basic message, namely, that Jesus was the messiah and Son of God, the one who was crucified, but also raised from the dead by God's power, so that all who believe might have eternal life. Later, the leaders of these churches used this message to formulate and refine "doctrine" (teaching) concerning the nature of God, the relationship between God and Jesus, and a variety of other issues that divided the churches. In addition, Christian communities had an intense belief in the power of the Holy Spirit acting in their midst as comforter, inspiration, and guide in the Christian life. (3) Finally, it was during this early period that the books that will later be known as the New Testament were being written. In the centuries that followed, they would become known as the "canon" or list of religious documents that are authoritative for defining the Christian faith and governing its way of life.

The Apostle Paul

The most prolific of the first generation of Christian missionaries was **Paul**. His importance for the spread of early Christianity is demonstrated by the amount of space in the New Testament that is devoted to him: Fourteen of the 27 books in the New Testament were included because they were believed to have been written by Paul. Another New Testament book, the Acts of the Apostles, devotes a majority of its pages to describing Paul's missionary activities. These books are the main sources for our understanding of Paul's life and message. Paul's centrality in what became the New Testament has given him an enormous importance in the Christian tradition. That is why we give him so much attention here. But it must be remembered that he was only one of many such missionaries, even if our knowledge of others is often fragmentary and preserved in sometimes legendary elaborations.

Who is Paul?

Paul was reportedly born in the city of Tarsus, in Asia Minor (modern-day Turkey), into a Jewish family that belonged to the party of the Pharisees. Paul's membership in this

Figure 7–1 *St. Paul,* by Pompeo Girolamo Batoni (1708–1787).

group meant that he was known for pious behavior and spent a great deal of time studying the Torah. In fact, Paul claims that he surpassed even the other Pharisees in his devotion to the Law, as he says in one of his letters: "I advanced in Judaism beyond many among my people of the same age, for I was far more zealous for the traditions of my ancestors" (Galatians 1:14). Although Paul apparently received an outstanding education in the ways of Judaism, his letters also show that he gained a broad knowledge of the Greek language and culture. It is this combination of Judaism and Hellenism in his background that enabled Paul to assume the leadership of Christianity when it was beginning to make the transition from a small Jewish sect to a major world religion.

Little is known of Paul's life prior to his becoming a follower of Jesus, although some scholars theorize that he was a Jewish missionary. In Paul's time, there were many Gentiles who were interested in Judaism, which was attractive to them in large part because of its monotheism and strict ethical code. In Acts of the Apostles, people who were attracted to Judaism but uncertain whether to become fully Jewish (perhaps because of other Jewish requirements, such as circumcision and the kosher dietary restrictions) are called **God-fearers** (e.g., Acts 10:1–2). They would often attend the synagogue and listen to the readings of the Torah and debates over the Jewish Law. They also participated in certain Jewish feasts and other aspects of Jewish life where Gentiles were permitted. Biblical scholars think that the first Gentile Christians came from among these God-fearers. They would have already known the stories of Israel's salvation history, and they would have understood the significance of the feasts, which Christianity eventually expropriated for its own.

We do not know in what capacity Paul first encountered the message about Jesus Christ. However, since the early Jesus Movement was a reform movement within Judaism, it is possible that he learned of it in the synagogues where Jewish-Christian missionaries might have gone to spread their belief that Jesus was the messiah. We also do not know exactly how Paul first received this message, except to say that he was not positively disposed. From the Acts of the Apostles, we learn that he was present as a witness to the killing of a Christian leader named **Stephen**, who was accused of speaking against the Temple and against Jewish Law (Acts 6:13). Later, we learn that he was harassing Jesus' followers, breaking into their homes and hauling them off to prison (Acts 8:3). He even solicited a letter from the high priest of the Jerusalem Temple to authorize him to arrest any among the members of the synagogues in Damascus who "belonged to the Way" (Acts 9:1–2).

It was while he was on his way to Damascus that Paul became a follower of Jesus Christ. Paul himself never describes the conversion experience in any detail (see Galatians 1:13–17), but the Acts of the Apostles tells us that Paul was blinded by a bright light and heard a voice from heaven that said, "Saul, Saul, [Paul's Jewish name] why do you persecute me?" Paul answered, "Who are you, Lord?" The voice replied, "I am Jesus, whom you are persecuting" (Acts 9:4–5; cf. Acts 22:4–16, 26:9–18). This experience convinced Paul that Jesus was in fact the messiah. He was led into Damascus, where his blindness was cured, he received the Holy Spirit, and he was baptized as a Christian by a man named Ananias (Acts 9:8–19).

Figure 7–2 *The Conversion of Saint Paul,* by Nicolas Bernard Lépicié (1735–1784).

Evidence for the Events of Paul's Life

Our evidence for certain events in Paul's life, such as the details of Paul's conversion, his participation in the martyrdom of Stephen, and his final arrest and trials, is found only in the Acts of the Apostles. It must be said that the interests of the author of the Acts of the Apostles (also the author of the Gospel of Luke) were more theological than historical. What this means is that Acts is not universally regarded as being a completely reliable source for historical information about Paul or other figures and events in early Christian history. Paul's letters themselves are usually regarded by historians as a more reliable source. Hence, in this overview of Paul's life, we rely more on Paul's letters than on Acts, and we attempt to acknowledge those places in which evidence is used from the Acts of the Apostles.

What Did Paul Believe?

After this revelation, Paul immediately redirected his missionary zeal toward the Christian message. His first journeys were to Arabia (not what is now called Saudi Arabia, but instead the land southeast of the Dead Sea, also known in antiquity as Nabataea) and Damascus (Galatians 1:17), then to Jerusalem to meet Peter and James (Galatians 1:18–19), and later to Damascus (again) and Cilicia (Galatians 1:21). There is no record of Paul having any great successes in these areas or writing letters to Christian groups in these areas. At some point, Barnabas, a Jewish-Christian missionary, brought Paul to Antioch in Syria, where Paul taught along with a group of Christian prophets and teachers. After some time in Antioch, as they prayed, the Holy Spirit spoke, saying, "Set apart for me Barnabas and Saul for the work to which I have called them" (Acts 13:3), and so they were sent off to preach the message of Jesus Christ. As they traveled to various cities throughout the Mediterranean, they first went to the synagogue, where their message met with mixed success among Jews but was enthusiastically received by the Gentile God-fearers (Acts 13:13–14:28).

As large numbers of Gentiles began to accept the message of Jesus, the question arose as to whether these Gentiles must first become Jews in order to convert to Christianity. Up to this point, as far as we know, the Christian movement had retained all of the requirements of Judaism. Did these Gentiles then also need to become circumcised, follow the Torah, sacrifice in the Temple, and keep "kosher" (meaning following Jewish dietary laws)? Or was it enough that they believed in Jesus Christ, without taking on the other requirements of the Jewish faith? Paul and Barnabas thought that faith in Jesus Christ was enough and that Gentiles were not required to do such things as become circumcised and follow the Jewish Law. However, this position created a storm of controversy among Christian Jews who believed strongly that there could be no compromise about keeping the core elements of Judaism.

In 49 or 50 C.E., a conference was called to discuss the question of whether Gentiles needed to become Jews in order to convert to Christianity. This meeting is called the **Jerusalem Conference**. Paul and Barnabas attended the conference and defended the position that the Gentiles did not need to follow the Law and become circumcised (Acts 15:2–3, 12; Galatians 2:1–3, 5, 7–8). Opposed to them was a group of conservative Jewish Christians who supported requiring all Christians to keep the

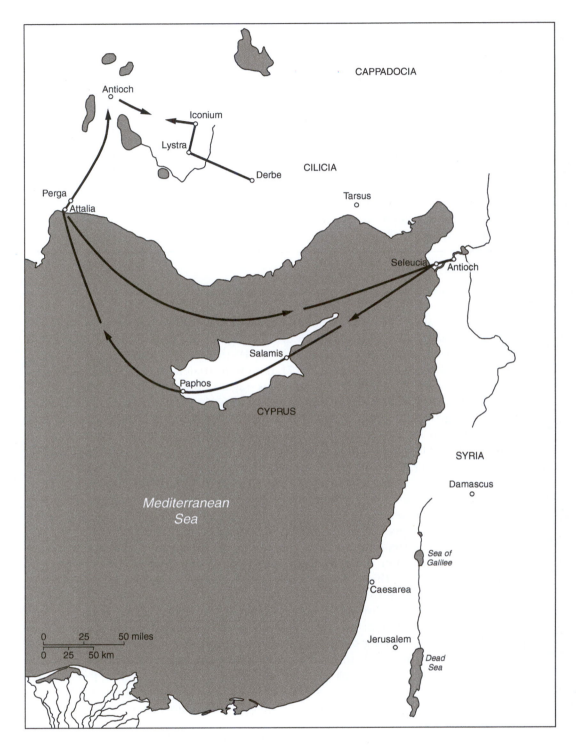

Figure 7–3 Paul's First Missionary Journey.

requirements of Judaism (Acts 15:5; Galatians 2:4–5). The leaders who were convened to decide the question were the Jerusalem apostles, led by Peter, John, and James, the last of whom Paul calls "the brother of the Lord."

Exactly what happened at the Jerusalem Conference is a matter of some dispute. Paul records that the conference ended with the Jerusalem apostles completely vindicating his Gospel and approving unconditionally that he be allowed to preach the message of Jesus Christ to the Gentiles without obligating them to become Jews (Galatians 2:9–10). The Acts of the Apostles (Acts 15:1–35) records more of a compromise proposed by James, who headed the church in Jerusalem itself. According to Acts, those at the conference agreed that Gentile converts could be released from the obligation of circumcision, but nevertheless must avoid meat sacrificed to idols and sexual behaviors outside of marriage (*porneia*) (Acts 15:19–21), and must abstain from "blood," meaning meat from which the blood had not been drained, in keeping with God's permission to eat meat after the Flood in the book of Genesis (Genesis 9:4). Apparently, the issue was not decided once and for all, however, as Paul continued to have difficulty with conservative Jewish Christians who often tried to undermine his subsequent missionary efforts. Sometimes Paul was even forced to confront the same Jerusalem apostles who had given approval for his activities, as in his serious

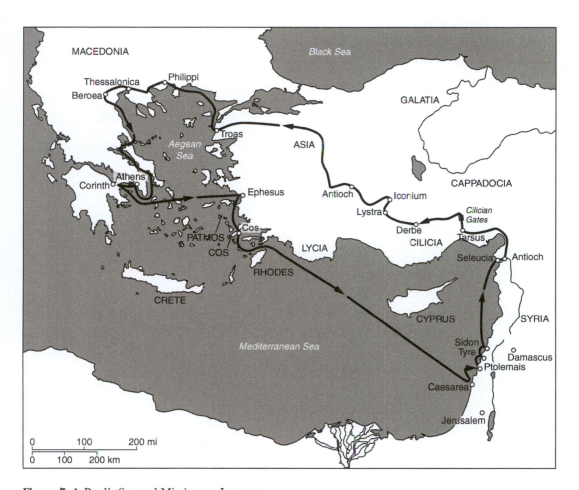

Figure 7–4 Paul's Second Missionary Journey.

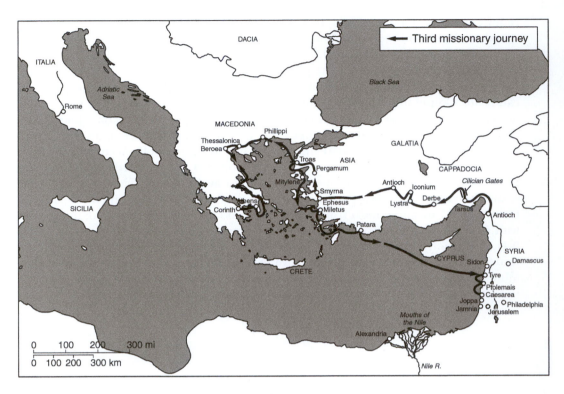

Figure 7–5 Paul's Third Missionary Journey.

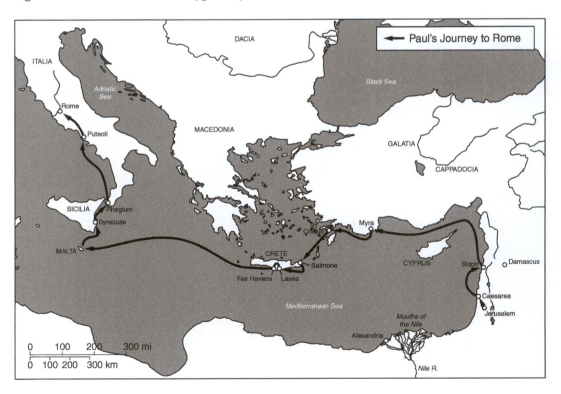

Figure 7–6 Paul's Journey to Rome.

confrontation with Peter in Antioch over Jewish and Gentile Christian table fellow-ship (see Galatians 2:11–14).

Whatever the precise outcome of the Jerusalem Conference, Paul felt that he had been given a mandate by God to preach a gospel without the Law and circumcision to the Gentiles. After the conference, he began a series of ambitious missionary journeys, which included travels to Cyprus, Asia Minor, Macedonia, and Greece. These journeys were a stunning success. Paul founded numerous churches and made thousands of converts, so that later Christian tradition will often call him simply "the Apostle," without further description.

Why Did Paul Write Letters?

Except for the Pastoral letters (1 and 2 Timothy, and Titus), which most scholars do not believe are written by Paul, the letters of Paul found in the New Testament are all written to churches or communities of believers. Among those, all except the letter to the Romans are written to churches that he himself founded, and they all contain Paul's specific responses to the questions, needs, and problems of that particular church. For this reason, Paul's letters are known as "occasional" or "situational" letters, since they respond to unique situations or occasions within a community. After Paul left a community—either because he wanted to continue his missionary work elsewhere or because he was forced by persecution to leave—he would communicate with the church he left behind through the mail, especially if he heard that there was some problem or crisis facing the community. Some of these letters survived and were eventually included in the canon of the New Testament.

While Paul might not have ever considered that he was writing "scripture," there is no question that Paul wrote letters to take the place of his authoritative apostolic presence, and he expected that the Christian communities would accept them as authoritative. Paul presented himself in a number of his letters as the spiritual "father" of his churches who desired that his spiritual "children" imitate him and obey his teachings (1 Corinthians 4:14–17; 1 Thessalonians 2:11–12). His letters, therefore, offer advice and instruction in a number of ways. Paul attempts to settle concrete pastoral problems, such as a man living with his stepmother (1 Corinthians 5:1–5), he exhorts his communities to moral Christian living (1 Thessalonians 4:1–12), and he instructs his churches on complex theological questions (Galatians 3–4; 1 Corinthians 15; Romans 9–11).

Paul's Authentic Letters and the Question of Pseudonymity

It must be acknowledged that not all of the letters traditionally ascribed to Paul are thought to have been written by him. One of them (the letter to the Hebrews) does not actually have Paul's name attached to it. Only seven of the other 13 letters are universally believed by scholars to have been written by Paul (1 Thessalonians, 1 and 2 Corinthians, Galatians, Philippians, Philemon, and Romans). Authorship of the other six letters (2 Thessalonians, Colossians, Ephesians, 1 and 2 Timothy, and Titus) is disputed to varying degrees. Many scholars believe that these letters were written by disciples of Paul in their master's name. The practice of writing a document with a false name attached is called **pseudonymity**. Today, we might be inclined to view pseudonymous works as somehow suspicious or deceptive. However, in the ancient world, and especially when it came to religious literature, writing under a pseudonym was an important way to honor a great and holy person and also to continue his legacy. Therefore, we should not consider the possibility that the New Testament contains pseudonymous letters of Paul as a challenge to their authoritative status. Rather, they are testimony to the success of Paul's work and the acclaim he had earned in the early decades of Christianity.

Paul's missionary activity, including his letter writing, came to an end when he had journeyed to Jerusalem to deliver a collection he had been taking up to support the Jerusalem church, which was undergoing some sort of persecution or financial difficulty (see Acts 11:29–30, 24:17; Romans 15:26; 1 Corinthians 16:1–3; 2 Corinthians 8:1–15). At first, he was greeted warmly, but then he was accused of telling Jews who lived among Gentiles that they were not required to obey Mosaic law, circumcise their children, or keep other Jewish customs (Acts 21:17–22). Soon a huge riot erupted in the Temple precincts, and Paul was seized by the crowd. As they were trying to kill him, a Roman military tribune noticed what was going on and rescued Paul by arresting him and throwing him in jail (Acts 21:27–38). Eventually, he was taken to Rome, where church tradition has it that he was executed by the Roman emperor Nero in approximately 62–64 C.E.

The Authority of Paul as an Apostle

In almost every one of Paul's letters, he identifies himself as an **apostle**. The word "apostle" comes from the Greek word *apostello*, which means, "to send out." An apostle, then, is "one who is sent out." For early Christians, the term meant "one who is sent out by Jesus to preach the word about him." Thus, an apostle is distinct from a **disciple**. The word "disciple" refers simply to a learner or a follower. One could be both a disciple and an apostle (like Peter and John, who both followed Jesus during his lifetime and were sent out by him to preach the word to others), but one could be a disciple without being an apostle. That is, it was quite possible to have been a follower of Jesus but not specifically sent out by him to preach the word. It was presumed by many early Christians that in order to be an apostle, one must have known Jesus and had been sent out by him to preach during his lifetime (see Acts 2:21–26).

By this definition, it would be impossible for Paul to be an apostle, because he never knew Jesus during his lifetime. However, Paul claimed that he was an apostle (e.g., Romans 1:1; Galatians 1:1) because he had been sent out by Jesus to preach the word. How was Paul's apostleship different from that of Peter or the others who walked with Jesus? Paul's mission was not given to him during Jesus' lifetime, but in a revelation that took place after Jesus' death and resurrection.

Paul's revelation-based claim to be an apostle was eventually accepted by the church as a whole, as is attested by the inclusion of Paul's letters in the canon of the New Testament. However, the fact is that Paul often struggled to be accepted as an apostle during his lifetime. Indeed, much of the controversy that dogged Paul throughout his career can be attributed to the question of whether or not he was a "real" apostle like Peter and John. Many people were skeptical about his claim to have had a revelation and felt more comfortable with the leadership of those people who had been among Jesus' original 12 apostles and whose apostleship was not in dispute.

Lived Religion: Ministry in the Bible

The New Testament, especially the Epistles, tell us about early Christian ministry. In Matthew 16:18, Jesus commissions Peter, telling Peter he is the rock on which the Church will be built, with the authority to bind and loose in heaven and on earth.

In the Acts of the Apostles, Matthias is chosen to replace Judas in ministry by drawing lots after a prayer for discernment (Acts 1:25–26). Later in Acts, we see the selection of seven men to be deacons, freeing the apostles for preaching. The seven were presented to the apostles "who first prayed over them and then imposed hands on them" (Acts 6:6), an act that will become central to ordination.

One ministry mentioned is the bishop. The first letter to Timothy provides a job description for bishops and deacons (1 Timothy 3:8–10), and the letter to Titus does the same for bishops and presbyters (Titus 1:7–9). Bishops are to be men of good character, married once, good teachers, sensible, gentle, and good managers of their households (1 Timothy 3:2–7). The ministry of the bishop includes presiding at liturgies, and serving as a prophet by speaking God's word to the community.

Deacons and presbyters are described in much the same way, being honest, sober, and not greedy for money. Some early churches recognized women as deaconesses, like Phoebe at Cenchreae (Romans 16:1) and Prisca at Ephesus (Acts 18:25). Deaconesses assisted women at Baptism and ministered to women who were ill, to orphans and the imprisoned, as did the male deacons. All the ministries were meant to spread the gospel, manage the community, and assist those in need. Each minister was called on to serve, using the charisms or gifts God has given for the benefit of all (2 Corinthians 3:6).

An Overview of Paul's Message

It is no easy matter to summarize Paul's message. His letters are often difficult to understand because they were not written to satisfy the curiosity of future generations, but instead to meet the concrete needs of particular first-century communities, and we are no longer aware of all of the situations that precipitated his letters. Nonetheless, Paul's letters are important for describing a number of important themes in Christian theology.

Many scholars today locate the "center" of Paul's theology in the Christocentric nature of his teaching since Paul believes that Jesus' life, death, and resurrection have reoriented the world and placed Christ at the center of human destiny. As a result, Paul calls upon people to become members of the Body of Christ and to shape their lives in the cruciform model of Christ, which means living life according to the Gospel, even if that choice results in suffering or dying for Christ. The reason for this is not only to live a life worthy of God's calling, as Paul says, but to prepare for the return of Christ and entry into God's kingdom.

Paul believes that God's grace has been poured out on believers in order to enable them to live out the life in Christ. In fact, one scholar has noted that Paul describes a number of "effects" of the Christ-event that define what Christ's life, death, and resurrection have gained for humanity. Although the tendency since the Reformation has been to focus on "justification" in Paul's letters, in fact Paul describes what Christ has done for humanity by using a number of images, such as "new creation," "reconciliation," "redemption," "transformation," **sanctification**," and "glorification."

Justification

The principle of **justification** is prominent in the letter to the Galatians and in the letter to the Romans. In both of these letters, Paul argues that one cannot be justified by the works of the Law, but only through faith in Jesus Christ. What does Paul mean by this? Justification originally referred to "justice" and the results of justice that had been delivered—a just verdict—in a court of law. In this use, it has a legal sense of being acquitted. In its use in Judaism, in the Septuagint, it came also to mean "righteousness," especially as it related to the keeping of God's law. Paul's use of this group of words takes us in a new direction, though obviously related to its previous use in Greek and Jewish settings.

Both Judaism and Christianity teach that human beings sin against God and this sin creates distance between ourselves and God. What can repair this relationship? Paul believes that it is only through Christ's passion, death, and resurrection, and our participation in it through Baptism and a life of holiness that we become "justified." As a result, those who have been baptized into Christ stand before God acquitted or innocent (Romans 4:25). Paul seemed to come to this conclusion after his revelatory experience of the risen Jesus. But an issue then emerged for this devout Jew: why did God give the Jews the Torah if justification comes through faith in Christ?

It is in trying to make sense of justification through faith in Jesus that Paul argues that the "works of the Law" cannot justify a person.

Jews did not believe that they earned salvation, but that God had given them a covenant which they were called upon to obey in order to remain in covenantal relationship with God. First, the Law of Moses was intended to help the Jewish people avoid sin. Second, when people did sin, one could atone for sin by performing sacrifices, fasting, praying, or giving alms (donating money to the poor). These are the works or good deeds prescribed by the Law. For Israel, keeping the covenant—that is, staying in right relation with God—meant keeping the Law.

It is in light of Paul's experience of Christ that he begins to question the role of the Law. In the words of one Pauline scholar, "the solution preceded the problem," that is, only after Paul experienced salvation in Jesus Christ did he begin to question the purpose of the Law of Moses. Paul believes that people cannot be justified by works of the Law because it is impossible for human beings to successfully avoid all sin or to "make up" for sins with good deeds. Even more, though, Paul believes the Law of Moses was not intended to save, but only to function as "guardian" (*paidagogos*) until Christ came. Since the Law was only intended for a limited time, after Christ came its function was fulfilled in Christ and following the Law was not necessary for those who follow Christ (Galatians 5:14; Romans 10:4).

Paul says that justification is not based upon one's one observance of the Law of Moses, but by a participation in God's righteousness through faith in Christ. Perhaps the two meanings of the Greek verb *dikaioun* ("to justify") can help us understand why Paul argues that a person can only be justified by faith. One meaning of the word *dikaioun* is "to acquit," as in a court of law. When Paul says that we cannot be justified by our works, he means that if human beings were judged on the merits of their case, according to what we really deserved, no one would be justified. The only way we can be acquitted is if God simply gives it to us as a free gift, in spite of the fact that we do not deserve it. This idea of God's bestowal of a free gift is what theologians mean by **grace**.

The other meaning of *dikaioun* is "to make upright." For Paul, Jesus' death on the cross functions as a sacrifice that makes us upright and allows us to stand before God in right relationship. This understanding of the purpose of Jesus' death—that Jesus died for our sins—is called **sacrificial atonement**. The death of Jesus constitutes, for Paul, God's offer of salvation to human beings. We cannot bridge the gulf between God and ourselves through our own efforts, but we can allow God to bridge this gulf for us. We respond in trust, believing that it is true. But this trust does not mean that the Christian sits back and does nothing. For Paul, faith is *active* trust, or trust that manifests itself in the way the believer lives his or her life. He describes it as "faith working through love" (Galatians 5:6).

Paul's teaching on justification might appear to be fairly straightforward and unambiguous, but the action whereby God "justifies" the sinner has been the subject of much debate. Since the Protestant Reformation, Lutherans and other Protestants have argued that "justification by faith" means that we add nothing to what God through Christ has gained for us. In legal terms, we are called "just," but in fact this language is only "forensic," which means that there is no change in our ability to be just or to participate in this event. Catholics claim also that what Christ has done for believers is "by grace as a gift" and that there is nothing that can be done to earn this gift gained "through faith in Christ." However, Catholics also claim that when we are justified, it is a "transformative" event, allowing Christians to participate in their justification and grow in holiness.

In fact, the teaching on justification has been an important point of discussion in Lutheran and Roman Catholic ecumenical dialogue for many years. In 1999, the Lutheran World Federation and the Catholic Church published the *Joint Declaration on the Doctrine of Justification*, which identifies areas of common understanding and explains the differences that still remain in their interpretations of the doctrine of justification by faith. The document notes that they were able to come to these common understandings by using the insights of modern biblical studies and research into the history of the development of doctrine (§2). It is a good example of how communities of faith can come together in dialogue on a matter that they once thought divided them irreparably. But while the image of justification is most frequently used to explain what Christ has done for humanity, there are many other images Paul uses that describe the results of the Christ event.

Other Effects of the Christ Event

In both Galatians 6:15 and 2 Corinthians 5:17, Paul states that those who are in Christ are a "new creation." Paul seems to indicate by this that as Jesus is the "new Adam," the head of a new humanity, his followers share in the new life that the resurrected Jesus brings. Paul also claims that Jesus has brought "reconciliation" (2 Corinthians 5:18–19; Romans 5:10–11), thereby reconciling sinful humanity to God—and not only humanity but all of creation, which Paul says has been "groaning in travail until now" (Romans 8:22). Another effect of the Christ event is "redemption" (Romans 3:24), an image which might be taken from the world of hellenistic slavery in which slaves were redeemed from bondage or, more particularly, an image which describes the act of God who in the Hebrew Bible redeems his people Israel (e.g., Deuteronomy 6:6–8). Paul also speaks of "transformation," especially in 2 Corinthians 3:18, where Paul describes Christians being "transformed into a likeness" of God. This passage has been particularly influential in Orthodox Christian churches and in their understanding of the process of *theosis* (or "deification"), by which Christians are transformed to become like God more and more. Christians, according to Paul, also share in "glorification" (Romans 8:30), a foretaste already of the glory which Christians will share for eternity with God. Finally, Paul speaks of "sanctification," or "becoming holy," a term which appears more often in Paul's letters to describe Christians than any other—except for "brothers" and "sisters." Sanctification is the status to which Christians have been called to be set apart from the world in their behavior. It is important to note that the word used for "sanctification" in Greek is the same root word which underlies the English words "saints" and "holiness," so this concept is more abundant than might first appear when reading Paul's letters. Paul, for instance, says that the Christians in Corinth have been "sanctified in Christ Jesus, called to be saints" (1 Corinthians 1:2). In 1 Thessalonians 4, Paul says that "this is the will of God, your sanctification" (4:3) and that "God did not call us to impurity but in holiness" (4:7). There are other terms that Paul uses as well to outline what Christ has gained for his disciples ("salvation," "expiation," and "freedom," for instance), but these give a sense of the many images used by Paul to describe the impact of the Christ-event.

Life in Christ

Although Paul's major focus seems to be on justification and the other effects of the Christ event, all of his letters together reveal an equal concern for how persons are to live as Christians. But if living the good Christian life does not earn one salvation in Paul's view, a moral life is the expected response to God's grace in Christ Jesus. Why? "I have been crucified with Christ; and it is no longer I who live, but it is Christ who lives in me" (Galatians 2:19–20). The "life in Christ" could be outlined in many ways in Paul's letters, but the following examples will suffice: (1) freedom and love; (2) the activity of the Holy Spirit; (3) church as the Body of Christ; (4) sacrament and worship in the Pauline churches; (5) social concerns; and (6) preparing for the coming of Christ.

Freedom and Love

Paul writes at some length about freedom in his letter to the Romans and his letter to the Galatians. In our contemporary Western culture, we tend to think of freedom as a person's right to do whatever he or she wishes without limitation, except perhaps the constraint of not harming another. Paul's "freedom from the Law" can sound quite similar. Apparently, some people in the church at Corinth thought so too, because it seems that they had written to him saying, "All things are lawful for us" (1 Corinthians 6:12, 10:23). In his response to the Corinthian church, he corrects their wrong thinking about freedom by adding, "but not all things are beneficial" (1 Corinthians 6:12, 10:23). Elsewhere, he writes about freedom "in regard to righteousness" (Romans 6:20) and freedom from the power of sin, which brings death (Romans 6:7, 22–23).

Paul talks about both *freedom from* and *freedom for*. They are like two sides of the same coin: those who are justified are freed from slavery to sin so that they can be freed for slavery (or committed service) to God (Romans 6:16–18, 20–22). The imagery is reminiscent of God's covenant with Moses and the Israelites which placed on its recipients certain obligations, namely, the Law. Paul believes that, when God justified humanity through the death and resurrection of Jesus, he restored the covenant relationship as a free gift for all who believe (trust) in his name (Romans 3:24).

The proper response to God's gift of freedom, says Paul, is "faith working through love" (Galatians 5:6). Furthermore, he exhorts his communities with these words: "For you were called to freedom, brothers and sisters; only do not use your freedom as an opportunity for self-indulgence, but through love become slaves to one another" (Galatians 5:13). Paul says that this love should be genuine, patient and kind, not be hurtful or boastful, and it should always rejoice in the truth (1 Corinthians 13:4–7). Furthermore, the community should be known by their mutual regard for one another, living in harmony, holding up the weak, providing for the needs of those who have less, and giving hospitality to strangers (Romans 12:9–16). If they love one another, then they have fulfilled the whole of the Law (Romans 13:8–10; Galatians 5:14).

The Activity of the Holy Spirit

Paul's first letter to the Corinthians was written to address numerous issues troubling the community there. The Christian community at Corinth enjoyed and promoted certain gifts of the Holy Spirit such as *glossolalia* (speaking in tongues), but some Corinthians also considered themselves to be more spiritual than others because they possessed such gifts (1 Corinthians 14:1–12; see also 1 Corinthians 3:1–3, 4:6–7).

Paul certainly values the gifts of the Holy Spirit. He tells his communities that it is through the Spirit that they have become children of God (Romans 8:14–17) and that the Spirit helps them in their need and intercedes for them (Romans 8:26–27). He also attributes the various ministries in the community—being an apostle, teacher, prophet, and other kinds of leaders—to the work of the Holy Spirit (1 Corinthians 12:8–11, 27–31). However, he cautions the Christian community at Corinth about the use of glossolalia. The gifts of the Spirit are intended for the common good (1 Corinthians 12:7), but speaking in tongues does not benefit the community unless there is someone present who can interpret the strange words. Indeed, those who have the gift of tongues might be tempted to use it to build up themselves instead of the "upbuilding and encouragement and consolation" of the church as do those who prophesy (1 Corinthians 14:1–5).

In general, Paul urges those who are eager for the spiritual gifts to "strive to excel in them for the building up of the church" (1 Corinthians 14:12). And how does a person discern what is the activity of the Holy Spirit and what is not? Paul identifies these virtues as the fruits of the Holy Spirit: love, joy, peace, patience, kindness, generosity, faithfulness, gentleness, and self-control (Galatians 5:22–23). Whatever manifests itself in contrary ways does not belong to the Holy Spirit (see, e.g., Galatians 5:19–21), and the Christian community that manifests the fruits of the Spirit knows that it lives in Christ.

Church as the Body of Christ

For Paul, God's grace-filled gift, which is effected through Christ's death and resurrection, both reconciles sinners to God and unites all baptized Christians with Christ and with each other to form Christ's body. The source of this unity, Paul believes, is the Spirit of God dwelling in them:

> For just as the body is one and has many members, and all the members of the body, though many, are one body, so it is with Christ. For in the one Spirit we were all baptized into one body—Jews or Greeks, slaves or free—and we were all made to drink of one Spirit.
>
> (1 Corinthians 12:12–13)

How does the Spirit make the church into the one body of Christ? As Paul sees it, the members of the Christian community are not simply committed to one another through friendship or church affiliation. Rather, they are each individually united with Christ through Baptism, making their bond to one another of the highest order—they share the same Holy Spirit. Different members have different gifts, according to God's grace, all for the common good (Romans 12:3–8; 1 Corinthians 12:4–11). However, no member of the body is more important than the others, and no member of the body is less honorable, and when one member of the community suffers they all suffer (Romans 12:3; 1 Corinthians 12:22–24). They are all one body, and they must demonstrate the "same care for one another" (1 Corinthians 12:25). In other words, this notion of the church as the Body of Christ is not simply a theoretical concept that captures the imagination of theologians. Rather, it has profound ethical implications for how the Christian community ought to live in the world.

Sacrament and Worship in the Pauline Churches

Life in Christ expresses itself ritually and sacramentally in Baptism and the Eucharist. Paul taught that in Baptism the believer was incorporated into Christ. The baptized went down into the water in order to be baptized into Christ's death and to be buried with him so that, just as he was raised from the dead, they could walk in the new life of a Christian (Romans 6:1–4). Similarly, Paul saw the Eucharist as a way in which Christians participated in the body of Christ (1 Corinthians 10:16). Thus, the Eucharist ought to be the source of their unity with other Christians. If it is not celebrated in a way that demonstrates their unity—if the wealthy and privileged of the community do not wait for the poor and allow them to share equally of the Eucharistic table—then eating the bread and drinking the cup of the Lord will be their condemnation (1 Corinthians 11:17–34).

We are not certain of exactly how worship in Paul's churches was carried out. For the most part, it initially took place in people's homes, though Paul gives us some scattered clues. It seems that worship was more informal and inclusive of all members than modern Christians might be used to experiencing, and it was also more *charismatic*, that is, guided by the Holy Spirit. In 1 Corinthians 14:26, Paul writes, "When you come together, each one has a hymn, a lesson, a revelation, a tongue, or an interpretation. Let all things be done for building up." Apart from this, Paul speaks of prophecy and prayer in his churches, in addition to the practice of the Eucharist, which at this time seems to have been carried out in the context of a larger community meal (1 Corinthians 11:17–22).

The organization of these early Pauline house churches is not clear from Paul's letters. Paul himself functions as the authority among his brothers and sisters in Christ as an apostle, yet he also speaks on occasion of others who have authoritative roles in the community, mentioning "those who labor among you, and have charge of you in the Lord and admonish you" (1 Thessalonians 5:12), and stating that "God has appointed in the church first apostles, second prophets, third teachers; then deeds of power, then gifts of healing, forms of assistance, forms of leadership, various kinds of tongues" (1 Corinthians 12:28). Apart from these roles, Paul mentions at the beginning of Philippians the "bishops and deacons" in Philippi, though he gives no additional information about their roles within the community. These charismatic early Christian communities stand at the beginning of a process that would lead to a more formalized worship structure and hierarchy within the church.

Social Concerns

Paul understands the "life in Christ" to have implications for how Christians were to live in the world with others, not just within the Christian community. However, these social concerns are not often well developed due to his understanding that the world in its present form is soon to end with the coming of Christ. Paul's most significant statement on dealing with political authorities comes in Romans 13:1–7, in which he says that every Christian ought to "be subject to the governing authorities; for there is no authority except from God, and those authorities that exist have been instituted by God" (Romans 13:1). In this passage, Paul argues for Christian obedience to government authorities because the government is "the servant of God" to punish the wrongdoer. Paul never answers, though, what the position of the Christian to an unjust government ought to be and when God's laws ought to be followed instead of those of the State. Paul himself would later lose his life to this same government.

These same issues arise in his treatment of slavery, a legal institution in the Roman Empire. Paul nowhere condemns slavery outright, though he does write a letter asking a Christian slave-owner Philemon to release his slave Onesimus who had become a Christian while with Paul (Philemon 1–25). Paul writes in 1 Corinthians 7:21 that if people were slaves when they became Christians, they ought "not be concerned about it. Even if you can gain your freedom, make use of your present condition now more than ever." It is obvious that Paul is concerned more with spiritual freedom than legal freedom in this world, as he says in Galatians 3:28 that "there is no longer Jew or Greek, there is no longer slave or free, there is no longer male and female; for all of you are one in Christ Jesus," but the reality is that a Roman slave's life could be harsh, subject to backbreaking working conditions, corporal (and even capital) punishment, and sexual abuse. Some later passages from letters attributed to Paul (Colossians 3:21–25; Ephesians 6:5–9) even assert that slaves should put up with whatever treatment was meted out to them, since their masters will have to account for their behavior in the world to come. For the slave in this world, though, this stance might have provided little comfort.

Another area in which Paul's spiritual teachings affected the social world was in the realm of sexuality and marriage. Because Paul understood this world to be passing away, he suggested that the best path was not to be married and to remain celibate like him (1 Corinthians 7). In this long chapter, Paul states that even those who are married to unbelievers ought to remain married, but if the non-Christian partner wants to separate, "let it be so" (1 Corinthians 7:15). He also notes that those who were married ought to remain sexually active within marriage (1 Corinthians 7:2–6). Paul's preference, though, is that people remain celibate and unmarried if possible, a social innovation that would alter the Roman Empire in the decades and centuries to come. The real-world impact of such decisions would alter the life courses of boys and girls throughout the empire. Since it was no longer necessary to be married, choices for monasticism and consecrated virginity could be made by either the young people in question or their parents for them.

Issues in Moral Theology: Paul and the Community Setting of Moral Teaching

A wide variety of moral advice can be found scattered throughout the 14 New Testament letters traditionally ascribed to Paul. This is hardly surprising, as moral controversies within the churches addressed by these letters are often what prompted Paul (or in the case of the seven "disputed" letters, disciples of Paul) to write them in the first place. In almost every instance, these moral controversies threatened the unity, and thus the very existence, of these early Christian communities.

In Corinth, for example, the community was divided by disagreement over issues having to do with marriage and sexual morality. Some members were claiming that the "new life" conferred by Baptism freed the Christian from all moral rules regarding sex, and went so far as to quote Paul's own words in their defense: "for me everything is permissible" (1 Corinthians 6:12). Others drew the opposite conclusion: life in Christ required the renunciation of sex and marriage altogether (Paul, himself single, seemed more inclined to this position, though not entirely). In Rome, some seemed to believe that being a Christian meant that one no longer was obliged to pay taxes or obey the imperial authorities (Romans 13:1–7) (not so, writes Paul). In Thessalonika, some church members felt they didn't need to work at all (2 Thessalonians 3:10–12) (such as these, Paul writes, should not expect to partake equally at community meals!). And in Colossae, the good order of many a household was being vexed by anger, back-biting, and grudge-keeping between its members: husbands and wives, parents and children, masters and slaves ("Bear with one another," Paul writes, "the Lord has forgiven you; now you must do the same" [Colossians 3:14]).

As this last response makes clear, Paul's moral advice, which in substance would have been approved by many hellenistic Jewish writers and even some pagan authors of his day, was nevertheless distinguished by Paul's abiding conviction that the capacity of the Christian faithful to "do the right thing," and of the Christian community to live together peaceably, was the work of divine love reconciling all humanity to God. By the gift of the Spirit, opened up by the resurrected Christ, this love was mysteriously alive in the church (1 Corinthians 13:1–13), whose visible unity was but the foretaste of a far grander renewal yet to come (Romans 8:22).

It is important to note that Paul's moral advice does not constitute an unchanging rulebook for Christian behavior, much less a fully developed moral theology. Rather, it is best seen as a kind of *casuistry*, or "case-based" form of moral reasoning, drawing on what was an already established and growing tradition. In some cases, Paul was clearly transmitting what he understood to be the moral teaching of Jesus himself (Romans 13:8–10; 1 Corinthians 7:10). In other cases, he (or one of his disciples) was drawing what he took to be reasonable conclusions from that teaching, but appealing to his own authority, not Jesus' (1 Corinthians 7:12). The inclusion of Paul's letters in the canon of the New Testament meant, of course, that Paul's letters quickly became authoritative moral voices in their own right. However, whether and to what extent these letters' more specific judgments remain authoritative for Christians *today*, especially on hotly contested questions of sex, economics, politics, etc., is much disputed.

Preparing for the Coming of Christ

All of Paul's teaching regarding the place of Christians in the world must be understood in the context of Paul's goal as a missionary of Christ to gather as many people as possible to prepare for Jesus' return and the establishment of God's kingdom. In Paul's earliest extant letter, 1 Thessalonians, he tells the community that they have turned away from idolatry to the true, living God in order "to wait for his Son from heaven, whom he raised from the dead—Jesus, who rescues us from the wrath that is coming" (1:10). In 1 Corinthians, Paul explains his ethics regarding marriage and the preference for celibacy in the context of the end which is coming soon (1 Corinthians 7:26–34). Indeed, Paul's tour de force on the resurrection in 1 Corinthians 15 states, "If for this life only we have hoped in Christ, we are of all people most to be pitied" (15:19).

This is the reason Paul sees his suffering for Christ as meaningful and encourages his churches to suffer willingly for the faith—it is not the end of the story. Indeed, this present-day suffering is grounded in the hope of resurrection and eternal life. As Paul writes, "our citizenship is in heaven, and it is from there that we are expecting a Savior, the Lord Jesus Christ" (Philippians 3:20). Not only that, but Christian hope is a part of the redemption of the entire world as Paul outlines in Romans 8. There he says, "I consider that the sufferings of this present time are not worth comparing with the glory about to be revealed to us" (Romans 8:18). It is this glory that is the goal of the life in Christ for Paul, a goal that leads us from present-day suffering to eternal life spent in the presence of God.

The Delay of Christ's Return

Paul expresses in his letters on numerous occasions his understanding and hope that Christ would return soon. Indeed, his urgency in his missionary travels and letter writing comes from his sense that we have only a little time before Christ's glorious return. The earliest Christians believed that Christ's resurrection was a sign of the beginning of the end of time, which would be completed very soon when Christ returned in glory. However, when the first generation of Christians began to die, those who were left had to deal with the unexpected delay. It became necessary to ensure the safe transmission of their tradition for the interim period, however long that might be. Moreover, some Christians thought that the second coming was delayed because the church had not completed the task that Christ had given to it: to spread the gospel to the whole world. They therefore took the risen Christ's commission to preach the gospel to all nations (Matthew 28:19) and turned the movement outwards to the larger **pagan** (meaning everyone that was neither Christian nor Jewish) world of the Roman Empire and beyond, especially to the east, into territory ruled by Persia, Rome's great superpower rival. Despite Paul's prominence in the sources enshrined in the New Testament canon, Paul was scarcely the only such evangelizer. "Mission," in the sense of bringing in all of humanity, seems to have been a driving force from the time of the Resurrection, even if the terms of entrance had to be resolved by debate and experiment. Chapter 8 will consider how the movement gradually separated from its Jewish matrix and defined the governance structures, the doctrines, and the ways of life that, over time, became normative.

Key Terms

apostle
disciple
glossolalia
God-fearers
grace

Jerusalem Conference
justification
pagan
Paul
pseudonymity

sacrificial atonement
sanctification
Stephen

Questions for Reading

1. Why was there so much diversity in early Christian beliefs and practice? What elements of early Christianity would later be used to unify the church?

2. Give an account of Paul's activities prior to his becoming a follower of Jesus Christ, and explain how he eventually came to follow Jesus.

3. What was the issue addressed at the Jerusalem Conference, and how was it resolved?

4. Define the term "apostle" (distinguishing it from the term "disciple") and explain why Paul had difficulty being accepted as an apostle in his lifetime. Is he currently recognized as an apostle by the church?

5. Explain Paul's understanding of justification and why Paul believes justification comes through faith and not by works.

6. Explain Paul's understanding of the church as the Body of Christ.

7. Explain how Paul's expectation about the end sheds light on his views of the state, of slavery, and of marriage.

Works Consulted/Recommended Reading

Boccaccini, Gabriele, Carlos A. Segovia, and Cameron J. Doody. 2016. *Paul the Jew: Rereading the Apostle as a Figure of Second Temple Judaism.* Minneapolis, MN: Fortress Press.

Bornkamm, Gunther. 1971. *Paul.* New York: Harper & Row.

Brown, Raymond E., Joseph A. Fitzmyer, Roland E. Murphy, and Carlo Maria Cardinal Martini. 1990. *The New Jerome Biblical Commentary.* Englewood Cliffs, NJ: Prentice-Hall.

Cousar, Charles. 1996. *The Letters of Paul.* Nashville, TN: Abingdon Press.

Daniélou, Jean, and Henri Marrou. 1964. *The First Six Hundred Years: The Christian Centuries.* Vol. 1. New York: Paulist Press.

Di Berardino, Angelo, ed. 1992. *Encyclopedia of Early Christianity.* Translated by Adrian Walford. New York: Oxford University Press.

Fitzmyer, Joseph A. 1990. "Pauline Theology." In *The New Jerome Biblical Commentary.* Edited by Raymond E. Brown, Joseph A. Fitzmyer, Roland E. Murphy, and Carlo Maria Cardinal Martini, 1382–1416. Englewood Cliffs, NJ: Prentice-Hall.

Gorman, Michael J. 2017. *Apostle of the Crucified Lord: A Theological Introduction to Paul and His Letters.* Grand Rapids, MI: Eerdmans.

Hurtado, Larry W. 2016. *Destroyer of the Gods: Early Christian Distinctiveness in the Roman World.* Waco, TX: Baylor University Press.

Malina, Bruce, and Pilch, John. 2006. *Social-Science Commentary on the Letters of Paul.* Minneapolis, MN: Fortress Press.

Metzger, Bruce, and Roland Murphy, eds. 1991. *The New Oxford Annotated Bible with Apocrypha,* New Revised Standard Version. New York: Oxford University Press.

Official Dialogue Commission of the Lutheran World Federation and the Vatican. 1998. "Joint Declaration on the Doctrine of Justification." *Origins* 28: 120–127.

Perrin, Norman, and Dennis C. Duling. 1982. *The New Testament: An Introduction,* 2nd edn. San Diego, CA: Harcourt Brace Jovanovich.

Roetzel, Calvin. 1998. *The Letters of Paul: Conversations in Context.* Louisville, KY: Westminster John Knox Press.

Sanders, E.P. 1983. *Paul, the Law, and the Jewish People.* Philadelphia, PA: Fortress Press.

Ziesler, J.A. 1990. *Pauline Christianity.* Oxford: Oxford University Press.

PART

THE HISTORY OF CHRISTIANITY

SCRIPTURE AND TRADITION

Christianity is first of all based on belief in a person, Jesus Christ, rather than on belief in a book. The priority of the person to the book was vividly stated already in the early second century in a letter written by Ignatius, bishop of Antioch:

> When I heard some people say, "If I don't find it in the original documents [*meaning the Jewish scriptures that Christians would eventually call the Old Testament*], I don't believe it in the gospel," and when I said in response to them, "But it *is* written," they answered me, "That begs the question." But as far as I am concerned, *Jesus Christ* is the original "documents," his cross and death and resurrection are the inviolable "documents," and the faith which comes through him.
>
> (*Letter to the Philadelphians* 8:2, trans. M.J. Hollerich)

Ignatius meant that it was faith in Jesus Christ, as passed on by tradition, which allowed for the proper understanding of "the original documents," meaning the scriptures Christians inherited from Judaism.

There is an important sense, however, in which Christianity, like Judaism before it and Islam after it, can also be called a "religion of the book." Parts I and II of this textbook have explored the character of the Christian sacred book, the Bible. All Christian churches accept the Bible as the revealed word of God, even if they do not agree on the precise list of books included in the Old Testament. During the second and third centuries, Christians gradually came to agree that God's public revelation in Christ ended with the death of the apostolic generation. Sometime during the late fourth century, the canon was therefore considered "closed," and no further books were considered for inclusion in the New Testament. The biblical canon of Old and New Testaments has remained the only universally accepted standard for defining the character of Christianity.

With the passage of time, a religion with a fixed canon must deal with problems and issues not addressed in the sacred texts. The canonical texts will need interpretation if they are to speak to these new circumstances. Conflict in interpretation will in turn

151

require some sort of criterion or authority outside of the canonical text to resolve disagreement. Moreover, even if there were no gaps in the answers provided by the canonical texts, they must still be made to live in the lives of the faithful. Human creativity will never to cease to find ways to do that—by inventing new symbols, new literary forms, new prayers and ceremonies, new role models for living out the faith, new ways of organizing the community, and innovations of many other kinds to nurture and refresh the religion. This is as true of Islam and Judaism as it is of Christianity. For Christianity, the doctrine of the Holy Spirit serves as the source and ultimate arbiter of the validity of such innovation.

There is thus a need to supplement the original revelation with **tradition**, which effectively mediates or communicates the written revelation to later generations. Tradition here will refer broadly to the accumulated wisdom through which the faith derived from the scriptures, contained in the creeds, expressed in the liturgy, and lived out in practice is passed on and interpreted anew for contemporary believers. This book's textboxes on moral theology and on religious practices (i.e., "lived religion") are meant to illustrate such adaptation in Christianity.

All Christian churches employ tradition in at least some sense of the word, but they do not agree on the status and authority of tradition. The most serious division is between Catholic and Orthodox churches, on the one hand, and Protestant churches on the other. Catholics and Orthodox hold that scripture and tradition are in *continuity* with one another, and hence that tradition is also an authoritative guide for answering Christians asking questions about behavior and belief. Protestant forms of Christianity relativize the authority of tradition and make a more rigid distinction between the written revelation in the Bible and post-Biblical tradition. In actual practice, Protestant churches too end up relying on some type of tradition as a normative supplement to scripture, and their different ways of doing so is a major cause of the variety in Protestant Christianity.

The rest of this book surveys the history of Christianity from the time of Christ up to the present. As Chapter 1 explains, there are multiple ways to present the Christian tradition. This book has chosen a historical approach for three reasons. First, narrative (the telling of stories) is typical of the Bible's own approach to revelation. Second, especially since the conversion of the Roman Empire, Christianity has been an inseparable element of the history of Western civilization, understood in the broadest sense though, as we will see, Christianity also has a rich history outside the West as well. The globalization of Christianity in the modern period will require Christians to rethink their historic ties to Western civilization. Finally, a historical approach seems the fairest and most efficient way to illustrate both the continuity and the diversity of Christianity.

The Divisions of Christian History

It is customary to divide the history of Christianity into three different periods, each of which has been marked by the differentiation of new types of Christianity. The Introduction to Part IV, the Modern Period, will give an important critique of this traditional three-period or tripartite division of history.

The Early Christian or "Patristic" Period (Second to Fifth Centuries)

During its early years, Christianity grew away from its Jewish roots and spread throughout the Roman Empire. Christianity developed the institutions, doctrines, and practices that gave it its classic shape. During the fourth century, the church underwent a momentous change—from a persecuted minority to the established religion of the state. Theological disagreements and cultural divisions with their roots in the councils of the fourth and fifth centuries would eventually lead several Christian churches in the Middle East to separate from the rest of the Christian tradition. The history of this period is covered in Chapters 8–11.

The Medieval Period (Sixth to Fifteenth Centuries)

This period is marked by major geographical shifts in the Christian map. In the fifth century, the Roman Empire in the west was replaced by a series of Germanic kingdoms, and Western Christianity, led by the pope of Rome, shouldered the burden of rebuilding civilization on a Christian foundation. After the seventh century, the spread of Islam, the third great monotheistic faith, caused Christianity to lose most of North Africa, the Middle East, and even parts of Europe. The Christianity that had existed in the eastern (Greek) and western (Latin) halves of the Roman Empire split permanently into Orthodox and Catholic versions of Christianity. The medieval period came to a close with Catholic Christianity locked in crisis and seeking to reform itself. At the same time, the cultural movement of the Renaissance was renewing European culture and moving it toward a new stage of human self-awareness. The history of this period is found in Chapters 11–16.

The Modern Period (Sixteenth to Twenty-First Centuries)

The modern period is broken down into two phases. The first embraces the sixteenth to mid-seventeenth centuries and is nowadays named "Early Modernity." It includes the European Renaissance, the roots of which go back into the medieval period and the Protestant Reformation. The second phase embraces the mid-seventeenth century to the present.

1. Early Modernity (sixteenth to mid-seventeenth centuries): Frustrated late medieval tensions for reform finally split Western Christianity into Roman Catholicism and the various types of Protestant Christianity. The result was the destruction of the old internationalist ideal of Christianity ("Christendom") and its replacement by nationalized state churches. The Protestant reforming vanguard was led by Martin Luther in Germany and Ulrich Zwingli and John Calvin in Switzerland. They became the architects of the Lutheran and the Reformed types of Protestantism, respectively. In England, King Henry VIII withdrew the English (Anglican) church from communion with the pope; this began a turbulent century and a half, during which English monarchs tried unsuccessfully to impose a single version of Christianity. On the continent, smaller numbers of Christians sought an even more radical reform by withdrawing altogether from participation in the state and returning to the voluntary status of Christianity prior to Constantine. Catholicism itself engaged in a renewal movement known as the Catholic Reformation, partly in response to the challenges posed by the Protestant reform movements.

    The early modern period also sees the beginning of Christianity's globalization, as it moved out of its medieval home in European Christendom. Already in the fifteenth century, Catholic Christianity began to migrate by conquest and by persuasion westward to the Americas and eastward to India and the Far East. In the seventeenth century, European Protestantism joined this global expansion. Chapters 17 to 20 (with part of Chapter 21) cover the early modern phase of the modern period.

2. Mid-seventeenth century to the present: along with Christianity's continuing global expansion, these centuries are marked by developments that are conventionally thought of as modern, such as the scientific revolution, the Enlightenment, the sovereign territorial nation-state, the separation of church and state and other forms of secularization, movements of social emancipation and equal rights, democratic political systems, urbanization and industrialization, globalization through trade, communication, and migration, and first the spread and then the rollback of European colonialism around the globe. Christianity is intimately involved in all of these developments, which are dealt with in Chapters 21–28.

The Genealogy of Christianity

The following chart is a highly schematic genealogy of Christianity from the early church up to the modern period. It highlights the major forks in the road and indicates the genetic affiliation of the main branches of the Christian family tree. The chart ends with the eighteenth century, when the secularization of Christian states got underway, beginning in post-revolutionary America. The separation of church and state was a constitutional deregulation of religion that led to intense religious competition, the rise of many new churches, and the virtual commodification of Christianity (see Chapter 23).

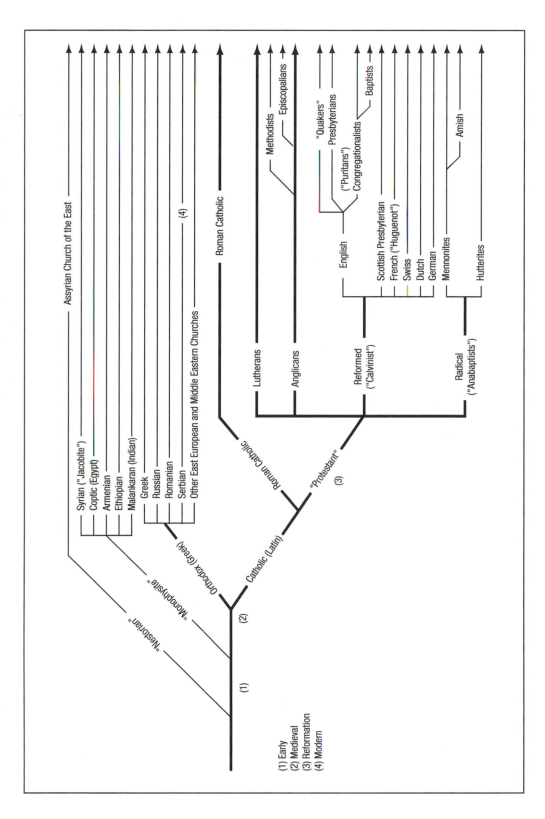

Figure III-1 The Genealogy of Christianity up to 1800.

Chapter

CHRISTIANITY AFTER THE APOSTLES

Breaking history into periods is somewhat arbitrary. "Early Christianity" could be thought of as the period from Jesus to Muhammad (d. A.D. 632). Today, historians tend to speak of "late antiquity" as the long period straddling the end of the ancient Roman Empire and the rise of the medieval world of eastern and western Christianity and what Muslims call the *dar al-Islam*, the realm of Islam (see Chapters 11, 12, and 13)—perhaps from *c.* A.D. 200 to 800. This book will follow an older practice of limiting "early Christianity" to the time between the writing of what will become the New Testament (up to *c.*a.d. 100)—and the Council of Chalcedon, which met in A.D. 451, the fifth century marking the beginning of what are still permanent divisions in the Christian tradition. This period is also called the **patristic** era, because the major orthodox writers of the time are known as the Fathers (*patres* in Latin) of the church, a term whose gender specificity is today rather on the defensive. In several branches of the Christian tradition (mainly Catholic, Orthodox, and Anglican), the patristic writings have a special prestige because of their formative role in shaping the Christian tradition.

During the patristic period, Christianity assumed many of the classical features that mark it as a distinct religion separate from Judaism: its biblical canon, with a Christian New Testament that complemented the Jewish scriptures, now known as the Old Testament; its fundamental doctrines of God and of Jesus Christ; and its basic organizational structure, especially the office of the **bishop**. The fact that the early period really created the set of books we call the Christian Bible should remind us not to create a false wall between the New Testament and the early Church. This chapter will present developments prior to the conversion of Constantine, when Christianity finally gained legal toleration. Chapter 9 will study Christianity's experience under Christian Roman emperors.

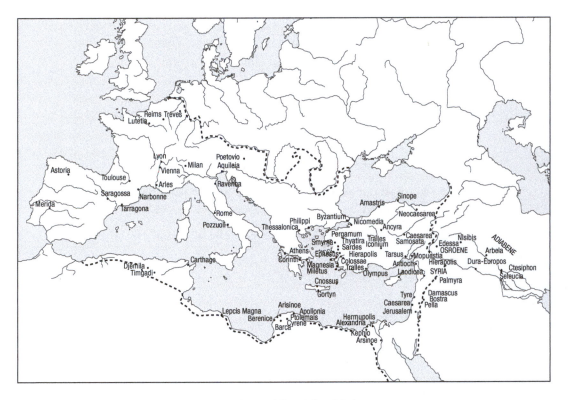

Figure 8–1 The spread of Christianity by the middle of the third century.

THE SPREAD OF CHRISTIANITY IN THE PATRISTIC ERA

During the second and third centuries, Christianity developed its distinctive identity. Three circumstances shaped this development: the gradual break with Judaism; the delay in Christ's return; and Christianity's encounter with the Greco-Roman world.

Christianity's Break with Judaism

The earliest followers of Jesus did not see Christianity as a separate religion but as a sect or reform movement within Judaism. Judaism in the first century A.D. accommodated quite a bit of diversity within itself. Christians saw themselves as distinct from other Jews because they believed that Jesus was the long-awaited Messiah. The status of Jesus' followers within Judaism began to change after the failure of the great Jewish Revolt of A.D. 66–70. During the Romans' capture of Jerusalem in A.D. 70, the Temple was destroyed. It was never rebuilt. Since the Temple was the only place where valid sacrifices could be offered, the destruction of the Temple meant the end of the sacrificial cult and the decline of the priestly class, which had maintained the Temple liturgy. Groups like the Sadducees and the Essenes gradually disappeared from Jewish life: the Sadducees because of their link with the Temple and its priesthood, the Essenes because the Romans destroyed their major community at Qumran. The role of the Pharisees was gradually taken over by rabbis who set in motion a redefinition of Judaism that eventually produced the Mishnah (interpretations of Jewish scripture) and the Talmud (discussions of the Mishnah and case law related to interpretations of the Torah), both of which came to form a kind of secondary Jewish canon.

The redefinition of Judaism tightened its boundaries, leading to an apparent expulsion of Christian Jews from Jewish community life sometime in the 90s. Perceived by the Roman state as rebels against their own religious tradition, Christians lost the legal toleration that Judaism had traditionally enjoyed and became vulnerable to persecution. At the same time, the increase of Gentile conversions meant that Jewish Christians were gradually outnumbered in a movement they themselves had started. Christians began to think of Jews as "other" and of themselves as "the true Israel." Probably by the middle of the second century, we can speak of "Judaism" and "Christianity" as distinct and opposed religions. But even then, the Christian teacher Justin Martyr admitted that Christians who observed Mosaic practice could be saved, so long as they did not insist that other Christians also observe it (Justin, *Dialogue with Trypho* 47).

The Delay of Christ's Return

The earliest Christians believed that Christ's resurrection was a sign of the beginning of the end of time, which would be completed very soon when Christ returned in glory. When the first generation of Christians began to die, those who were left had to deal with the unexpected delay. It became necessary to ensure the safe transmission of their tradition for the interim period, however long that might be. Moreover, some Christians thought that the second coming (*parousia*) was delayed because the church had not completed the task that Christ had given to it: to spread the gospel to the whole world. The delay therefore led Christians to pursue their missionary activities with great zeal. They took the risen Christ's commission to preach the gospel to all nations (Matthew 28:19) and turned the movement outwards to the larger **pagan** (meaning everyone who was neither Christian nor Jewish) world of the Roman Empire. There, Christians encountered significant challenges, such as the intellectual tradition of Greek philosophy, the opposition of the Roman state, and the rich diversity of the empire's many religions.

The Move into the Greco-Roman World

The risk of persecution did not keep Christians from spreading their message and winning converts. By the end of the third century, Christian communities existed from Spain in the West to Mesopotamia in the East, and even as far as Persia, beyond the Roman Empire's eastern frontier. This geographic spread covered three main linguistic environments: Latin in the western Roman world; Greek in most of the eastern Roman world; and Syriac in scattered parts of the East. Although Greek was the dominant language, each of these geographic areas eventually produced its own Christian literature, beginning with translations of the Bible. This chapter looks mainly at the Greek Christian tradition, though readers must understand that there was a vigorous Latin-speaking Christianity in Roman North Africa, with its center in Carthage, the home of important Latin Christian writers like the layman Tertullian (*c.*160–*c.*220) and Cyprian, bishop of Carthage from 248 to his martyrdom in 258.

The Christian message circulated by word of mouth, household connections, street corner preaching, public lectures, and the spectacular form of witnessing known as martyrdom. Roman cities were highly competitive religious "free markets," in which many cults and religions contended for attention and support. There were the official cults of the cities, devoted to the traditional Olympian gods and to local deities who were identified with them. There were the tribal and national gods of the many ethnic groups absorbed into the empire. For those who sought answers for more personal needs, there were shrines and oracles which offered healing and divine counseling for the insecurity and grief of daily life: worries about health, love, fertility, money, work, and the like. The huge popularity of magic and also of astrology seems to reflect a widespread fear that powerful spiritual forces ultimately dictated human destiny.

Another form of more personal religious experience was the **mystery religions**, so called because they relied on initiating converts into secret rituals and mysteries (the word comes from Greek *mystês*, meaning "initiate") about a particular god or goddess. The mystery religions deserve special mention because of features which they shared in common with Christianity: initiation and purification rituals that symbolically expressed death and rebirth, intense emotional experiences, divine revelations, membership in a privileged group, sacred meals, professional priesthoods and grades of membership, and personal devotion to a single deity. To name several examples: Mithraism was inspired by the ancient Persian god Mithra. The cult, practiced in caves or underground chambers, was open only to men and was especially popular in the Roman army. Mithras, to use his Roman name, was closely identified with the sun, either as his divine companion or actually as the same divine person; both of them were called *Invictus* ("Unconquered"), and the god's birthday on December 25, the Roman winter solstice, made that date an appealing choice when Christians were establishing an anniversary for the birth of Christ, the "Sun of Righteousness" (cf. the book of Malachi 4:2). The mysteries of the goddess Isis spread devotion to her far beyond her homeland in Egypt, as evidenced by the many poems written in praise of her virtues. In this example she is credited with a universal authority, with the establishment of human culture, and even with creation itself (thus absorbing functions traditionally claimed by other divinities):

I am Isis, the mistress of the whole land ... I am she who discovered fruit on behalf of human beings ... I am she who separated the earth from heaven ... I discovered navigation ... I have shown mortals the initiations [*mysteries*]. I have taught them to honor the images of the gods ... I have established language for Greeks and for barbarians ... I am she who is called the legislator.

(Cited in Klauck 2000, 132)

Images of Isis nursing her infant son Horus resemble later Christian representations of the Mother of God nursing the child Jesus. The wild rites—"orgies" was the term that was used—associated with the mysteries of Dionysus, the Greek god of wine and fertility, have given us the word *bacchanalia,* from "Bacchus," Dionysus' alternative name. Wall paintings of what appear to be Dionysian ceremonies were discovered in a villa at Pompeii, the Italian city buried by the eruption of Mt. Vesuvius in A.D. 79. The mysteries of the goddess Demeter and her daughter Persephone were celebrated at Eleusis, outside Athens, the only mystery religion that did not "travel" but was restricted to a single site.

Despite the superficial resemblances between Christianity and the mysteries, there were even more notable differences: the Christian clergy were an actual confederation which linked communities all over the empire; the Christian rituals required a more rigorous moral discipline than the pagan mysteries; the Christian sacramental enactment of death and rebirth was based on events that had happened in recent historical time, not in some distant mythic time; and most importantly, the Christian deity required exclusive loyalty ("no man can serve two masters," as Jesus had said in the Sermon on the Mount, Matthew 6:24) that forbade participation in any other cult. Pagan religions in general had no such prohibition against multiple memberships.

Sometimes the mystery religions disclosed the prospect of an afterlife. Mithraism, for example, appears to have taught the ascent of the soul through the heavenly spheres, and the Eleusinian mysteries, which spoke of Persephone's annual return from her months of captivity in the underworld (originally reflecting vegetation myths and rituals), seem to have held out the hope of a better destiny beyond the grave ("the Elysian fields"). But it is difficult to tell how literally we should understand the language of "rebirth" in accounts of the mysteries. Did rebirth merely entail an enlarged emotional experience and insight into life here and now? Or was it really believed to pave the way for personal existence after death? In general, it seems that the pagan world was skeptical or vague about a personal afterlife. An important exception was those who had been educated in the Platonic philosophical tradition.

Christian converts seem to have been seeking the same things that drew people to other religions and cults: the desire for healing from physical and spiritual ills; the need for advice and counsel; the promise of fellowship and mutual support; and the desire to know one's destiny in a mysterious and threatening universe. Christianity answered these various needs in a potent and comprehensive way. Christians were known and admired for helping and supporting each other in their community life. They were also known for their single-minded devotion to Jesus Christ as savior and Son of God, an exclusive loyalty that was a prime mover behind the persecutions. A chief sign of Christians' zeal was the extravagant courage with which their martyrs faced death, based on their belief in the resurrection of Jesus. As opposed to the cosmic determinism that many ancient people felt looming over them, early Christianity stressed human free will, responsibility, and ultimate redemption, not just for a few initiates or philosophical supermen, but for all men and women, however humble their station, who embraced Jesus' way of life and the church's sacramental rebirth.

Portrayals of Christ in Christian Art

Despite the focus of Christian faith on the person of Jesus, no actual likeness of him survives. Christians at first were reluctant to use paintings or statues of any kind, for fear of committing the sin of idolatry. This reluctance began to disappear in the fourth and fifth centuries, as more and more people became Christians. However, even before that time, Christians used paintings to decorate walls of tombs and house churches. Likenesses of Jesus were first adopted from generic pagan models that were compatible with Christian ideas about Jesus, the Good Shepherd and the philosopher-teacher being favorite types.

Late in the fourth century, the first depictions of Jesus with long hair and a beard begin to appear. After A.D. 500, in the Greek-speaking East, Jesus is always represented with a beard, though in the West, the youthful unbearded type survived for centuries. Also in the fourth century, Jesus is shown more frequently as reigning in heavenly majesty, either giving the Law to his earthly representative, St. Peter, or receiving honor from the angels and saints. Representations of Christ on the cross are not found until the fifth century. Before that time, Christians tended to use a bare cross.

Figure 8–2 Christ as a seated philosopher, dated mid-fourth century. He is often represented in Christian art as a philosopher teaching the true philosophy of Christianity to his disciples.

ROMAN ATTITUDES TOWARD CHRISTIANITY

The Roman Empire did not have an official "state" religion in the sense of one single faith to which everyone had to belong, even though many of the cults, temples, and priesthoods received public funding and support. It should be remembered that "paganism" was not a religion per se but a catch-all term for all Greco-Roman religions that were neither Jewish nor Christian. The Roman policy toward religion was inclusive and pragmatic: to tolerate as many gods as possible, so that at all times someone, somewhere was paying the worship which a particular deity wanted—otherwise, gods who were ignored might inflict their wrath on the empire. "Religion" was primarily a pattern of ritual interaction between human beings and the invisible powers that actually governed the world. But religion was also crucial for shaping personal and social behavior, and a diversity of religions fit the diversity of the

Figure 8–3 Christ as the good shepherd, from a late third-century sarcophagus.

Figure 8–4 Sixth-century San Vitale in Ravenna shows Jesus sitting on the orb of the world, attended by angels and receiving the martyr's crown from St. Vitalis. The figure on the right is the bishop who built the church.

Roman Empire's approximately 60 million inhabitants. Religious myths, beliefs, rituals, and symbols were embedded in every aspect of the empire's public life, from its art, architecture, and literature to its economics and politics: anyone who refused to recognize the empire's gods in some form or other was undercutting, not just belief in the gods, but a broad consensus underlying politics and culture as well. They instantly made themselves outcasts. Even at that, persecution was usually a last resort. The empire did not have the police force or the bureaucracy to indulge casually in religious manhunts.

One apparent exception to this generally tolerant posture was the **imperial cult**, or worship of the emperor. But even that was in principle voluntary, and it was certainly not exclusive. The imperial cult was both genuinely political, being a public demonstration of loyalty to the emperor, and genuinely religious, since it consisted of temples, feast days, sacrifices, and priesthoods. The extent to which people really thought of the emperor as a divinity on earth is unclear. Technically, a reigning emperor was "a son of a god" in the sense that he had been adopted by his predecessor, who in turn had been declared *divus* (divine) by decree of the Senate after his death. Most often, the imperial cult represented worship not of the emperor in his own person but of his *genius* or *tychê* (Greek for "fortune"), a guiding and protecting spirit rather like what Christians call a guardian angel. But no doubt many did think of the emperor as a kind of earthly god, since the pagan world recognized various levels or degrees of divinity. Jews were not expected to participate in the imperial cult and were allowed instead to offer prayers on the emperor's behalf in their synagogues (and sacrifices in the Temple when the Temple still existed). Judaism's and the Jewish people's antiquity earned the Romans' reluctant respect and toleration. Christians on the other hand gained no such respect. Having split off from the Jews, they were seen as rebels against the traditions of their ancestors—a serious charge in a culture that prized tradition, the *mos maiorum* ("the ways of the ancestors"), as the surest benchmark of truth. Nor did it help that their founder was known to have been executed by the Roman government. Once the Empire decided that Christians deserved punishment, participation in the imperial cult was used to test an accused person's loyalties.

Prior to the third century, persecutions were sporadic and local affairs mainly inspired by popular prejudice against Christians, though they were no less bloody for being occasional, as documents such as *The Martyrdom of Perpetua and Felicity* graphically illustrate). This changed in A.D. 250, when the Emperor Decius (249–251) targeted the Christian church for the first truly universal persecution. His motive is uncertain, but he probably wanted to return the empire to traditional beliefs and customs as a way of unifying the empire and pleasing the gods at a time when the empire was under great stress. Under the emperor's orders, local examining boards issued certificates to all Roman citizens to verify that they had offered sacrifice to the emperor's image. Christians who died for their faith rather than offer sacrifice were called **martyrs** (Greek for "witnesses"). Their bodily remains were venerated as holy **relics** and the anniversaries of their deaths were celebrated annually (the origin of saints' feast days). Those who were arrested and stood firm but were not put to death were called **confessors** for having confessed their faith publicly; they enjoyed great prestige in the churches and sometimes claimed the right to forgive sins. Those Christians who did offer sacrifice in the persecution of A.D. 250 created a crisis afterwards when they regretted their sin of **apostasy** (falling away from the faith) and pleaded to be readmitted to communion with their Christian brothers and sisters. The bishops and their clergy were hard pressed to find a middle way between the "rigorists" (very strict Christians), who wanted to deny any forgiveness to those who had lapsed into apostasy, and those, like some of the confessors, who wanted to extend forgiveness immediately and to do so on their own authority, not that of the bishop.

Figure 8–5 A second-century pagan graffito of a Christian worshipping a crucified ass. The inscription reads, "Alexamenos worships god."

According to Christian authors, the most frequent Roman charge against Christians was *atheism*. The accusation did not mean that Christians denied the existence of God as such, but rather that they denied everyone else's gods except their own. Christians said publicly that the gods were demonic deceptions and that worshipping them was idolatry. That undercut Roman religious policy, which depended on a broad consensus about religion, morality, and the state.

Pagans, especially pagan intellectuals, had other objections to Christianity. They resented the claim (made of course by Jews as well) that God had revealed himself uniquely in the history of a particular people, the people of Israel. Such a concept of revelation seemed narrow and bigoted. Furthermore, Christianity claimed that this special relationship with one people culminated in God's appearance in human form, as a man who had been subjected to a shameful death as a criminal. While some pagan critics admired Jesus personally, they were offended by the Christian belief that he was divine. The first Roman eyewitness to Christianity that we have—the Roman official Pliny the Younger's celebrated letter to the Emperor Trajan, written around A.D. 112—says that they "sang hymns to Christ as to a god." Enlightened pagans believed in a single supreme being who existed at the top of a pyramid of lower divinities, the many gods of polytheism, who acted as his subordinates in the divine government of the universe. A quasi-monotheism of this sort was compatible with polytheism. But belief in the divinity of Jesus implied that there could be two such supreme gods. Furthermore, the very idea of a divine incarnation (God taking on human flesh) was thought to be unworthy of God. Pagan thinkers influenced by the philosophy of Plato believed that the spiritual was inherently superior to the material, so they found the doctrines of incarnation and resurrection unbelievable and even offensive. Christians were regarded as gullible because they emphasized "faith" more than "knowledge." They were also accused of political irresponsibility for refusing to hold office or to serve in the military. Christians' refusal to kill even in war seemed dangerous and foolish to an empire with enemies on its borders.

THE APOLOGISTS AND THE DEFENSE OF CHRISTIANITY

Christian writers called the **Apologists** (the word means "defenders") tried to respond to Roman criticisms of Christianity. They insisted that Christians were loyal citizens who prayed for the emperor when he engaged in just wars, even though they themselves refused to fight in them (cf. Origen, *Against Celsus* 8.73–75). They also attempted to explain, in imagery and terminology that made sense to pagans, what it was that Christians believed and how they lived their lives.

The most important accomplishment of the Apologists of the second and third centuries was the development of the *Logos* theology, by which the Apologists established a link between pagan philosophy and Christian theology. The Greek word *logos* has many meanings, but two in particular: (1) spoken or written word, and (2) internal reason or mind. As spoken or written word, the Logos could stand for God's Word in the scriptures and in their proclamation. As reason or mind, the Logos could also be identified as the divine Mind, which Greek philosophers like Plotinus (A.D. 204–270) saw as a secondary divine principle that contained God's "thoughts," the Ideas that were the eternal patterns of everything that exists (in his book *Confessions*, St. Augustine will recognize the parallels, but also the profound differences, between Plotinus and the Christian doctrine of God—see Chapter 10 in this book and *Confessions* 5.9). Christians identified this divine Logos with Jesus, who according to the Gospel of John was with God in the beginning as God's agent in creation (John 1:1–3), was the true light who enlightens everyone (John 1:9), and became human and dwelt among us (John 1:14). The Apologists saw the pagan acceptance of the Logos principle as a preparation for receiving the message about Jesus Christ. Since Jesus was divine Reason incarnate, the Apologists could argue that the Christian life was based on reason, and all who lived according to reason already had a limited knowledge of God. In the words of Justin, a second-century Christian philosopher (often called "Justin Martyr" because he was executed by the Roman state in 165):

> We have been taught that Christ is the first-born of God [*Colossians 1:15*], and we have already mentioned that he is the Logos of which the entire human race has a share and in whom they participate. Those who lived according to reason are Christians, even though they were regarded as atheists. Examples of these among the Greeks include Socrates, Heraclitus, and others like them. Among the barbarians they include Abraham, and Hananiah, Azariah, and Mishael [*Daniel 1:6–7*], and Elijah, and many others whose names and deeds it would take too long to list. Those who existed before the time of Christ and who did not live according to reason could therefore be called non-Christian and hostile to Christ, and the murderers of those who do live according to reason; those who in the past lived according to reason and those who do so now are Christians, with a right to live free from fear and disturbance.
>
> (*First Apology* 46.2–4, trans. M.J. Hollerich)

THE DEVELOPMENT OF CHRISTIAN DOCTRINE

The history of Christianity has been preoccupied with debates about **orthodoxy** (correct doctrine). The factors that guided the development of orthodox Christian doctrine were many: the church's preaching, its biblical interpretation, its standards of discipleship, its communal life and ministry, its central rituals of Baptism and the Eucharist, and its prayers and hymns. These different aspects of Christian life all served as carriers of the faith in Jesus as Savior and Son of God. They made up a tradition that Christians believed was the work and witness of the Spirit of God, poured out through Jesus' death and resurrection. The early Christian period was especially concerned with establishing the orthodox doctrines of the Trinity and the Incarnation.

A look at the early development of the doctrine of the Trinity (according to which the one God exists as three distinct "persons," the Father, the Son, and the Holy Spirit) shows how orthodox doctrine was determined by factors such as evidence from the Bible and from assumptions inherent in Christian rituals. Christians saw that the New Testament speaks of the God of Israel, whom Jesus called "Father"; Jesus himself, who is both Son of God, the Word made flesh (John 1:14), and the Son of Man who died as a ransom for many (Mark 10:45); and the Spirit, who is God's powerful presence among believers after Jesus' ascension (Acts 2). The baptismal formula also revealed the threefold character of God, because the Christian was baptized (initiated) in the name of the Father, the Son, and the Holy Spirit (Matthew 28:19). Early Christian **creeds** (short summaries of belief), which originated as baptismal instructions, were therefore usually divided into three sets of clauses dealing with the Father, the Son, and the Spirit. The fourth-century Christian Church would formally define the Trinity as three persons equally sharing one divine nature (see Chapter 9).

The doctrine of the Incarnation (meaning "taking on flesh") is concerned with the belief that Jesus Christ is the eternal Son of God who took on flesh for our sake. Christians always believed that Jesus was in some sense both human and divine. But they disagreed about precisely *how* he was both human and divine. It may surprise us to know that many Christians probably found it easier to grasp his spiritual and divine aspect than his fleshly and human one. The sacrament of the Eucharist helped ensure that Christians did not lose sight of the reality of Jesus' human embodiment. That is because Christians were taught to believe that they became truly united with Jesus in the Eucharistic bread and wine. Early descriptions of the Eucharist can be startlingly realistic in the way they equate the elements of bread and wine with the flesh and blood of Christ. Already around the year 110, Ignatius of Antioch had called the Eucharistic bread "the medicine of immortality" (*Letter to the Ephesians* 20.2), meaning that it was food that nourished eternal life in the believer. Here is how Justin Martyr described it in a famous passage from his *First Apology*, written in the mid-second century:

> Among us this food is called *eucharist* ... [W]e do not receive it as if it were ordinary bread or ordinary drink. But just as Jesus Christ our Savior, when he was made flesh by the Word of God, took on flesh and blood for the sake of our salvation, in the same way, so we have been taught, this food, once it has been consecrated by the word of prayer that comes from him, and which nourishes our flesh and blood by digestion, is also the flesh and blood of that Jesus who was himself made flesh.
>
> (*First Apology* 66.1–2, trans. M.J. Hollerich)

Early Christianity, especially in its first 150 years, exhibited considerable diversity. There were various approaches as to how communities should be organized, how Christians ought to live, what biblical books they should accept, and what they ought to believe. The diversity perhaps reflected the speed with which Christianity spread, the new challenges awaiting the movement once it outgrew its Jewish matrix, and the adjustment to the delay in Christ's return. In such unsettled conditions, we should not be surprised that there was a degree of trial and error.

By the end of the second century, this diversity was giving way to a greater uniformity, as the main standards of **catholic** (the word simply means "universal") Christianity became recognized: (1) agreement on the core books of the New Testament and on the necessity of retaining the Jewish scriptures; (2) the development of short summaries of beliefs called creeds, which were used to instruct candidates for Baptism; and (3) the universal acceptance of the office of the bishop as the leader of the local Christian community. To these we may add (4) the sacramental life of Christianity (see previous paragraphs on the doctrinal implications of Baptism and the Eucharist). These four elements—canon, creed, **episcopacy** (government by bishops), and liturgy—consolidated Christianity's identity in a compact and durable form that would enable it to survive the eventual collapse of the whole ancient world in which it had come into being.

THE GNOSTIC CHALLENGE

The opposite of orthodoxy is **heresy** (false teaching). The word comes from a Greek word that means "choice" or "faction." Originally, it applied to either political factions or the various schools or sects of ancient Greek philosophy that a student could choose to join. Christianity too had its separate schools and teachers. During the second-century shakeout of belief and practice, teachers and bishops had to distinguish differences of opinion that were acceptable from those they rejected as heretical.

During the second and third centuries, an important factor in the shaping of orthodoxy was a spiritual and intellectual movement that moderns have called **Gnosticism**. It takes its name from the Greek word *gnosis*, meaning "knowledge," because its adherents claimed to possess a special secret knowledge that was known only to them. In the Bible, "faith," meaning trust and belief in God, matters more than "knowledge," and Abraham would be an exemplary figure. But as we saw above, knowledge and reason are what counted in the classical philosophical tradition, in which Socrates is the ideal type. Christians who were attracted to Gnosticism were often those who wished for more satisfying answers to questions about the origin of evil and the imperfections of the material world and of the human body in comparison to the spiritual world—topics that mattered especially to anyone conversant with Plato's philosophy. Gnosticism also appealed to those who were critical of various aspects of the Bible: the sometimes crude and capricious ways in which God is represented as acting, his changeability of mood, the uneven moral behavior of many prominent figures in the Bible, and, perhaps most of all, the differences between the Old Testament and the New (problems like these will crop up again when Augustine explains the appeal that the Gnostic-like religion of the Manichees had for him—see Chapter 10).

It is not easy to describe accurately the confusing variety of teachers, books, and ideas that ancient and modern observers think of as "Gnostic." Older descriptions of the movement had to rely largely on what the orthodox opponents of the Gnostics said about them. A more direct understanding of Gnosticism became possible after a collection of ancient treatises, most of them Gnostic in character, was discovered in Egypt in 1945. The books were written in Coptic (the popular language of Egypt) but are believed to be translations of writings originally in Greek. In their present form, they are dated to the late fourth century A.D., though many of the Greek originals may go back to the second century A.D.

The "knowledge" of the human situation claimed by the Gnostic is expressed in this often-quoted second-century statement: "[It is] the knowledge of who we were, what we have become; where we were, where we have been thrown; where we are hastening, from where we are redeemed; what birth is, what rebirth is" (preserved in Clement of Alexandria, *Excerpts from Theodotus* 78.2, trans. M.J. Hollerich). According to one recent study (Markschies 2003, 16–17), a catalog of the knowledge thus claimed typically included elements such as the following:

- the extreme other-worldliness of God, who is unknown to us;
- the existence of a whole series of intermediary semi-divine principles (often called "aeons" in Gnostic texts) who separate God from the rest of reality;
- the experience of the created world as evil and wretched, and of the misery of human life in it;
- the introduction of a different and inferior deity, thought of as ignorant or even as evil, who is the actual creator of our world and is equated with the creator God of the Old Testament;
- the blaming of the chain of events that creates our world on some kind of fault or fall in the heavenly realm itself (thus, in the Gnostic scenario, the biblical sequence of "creation and fall" is actually reversed and becomes fall-and-creation);
- the fall of some of the divine substance from the heavenly world into one particular class of human beings in this world, in whom alone it slumbers and from whom it must be liberated;
- and the need for a heavenly messenger who brings the needed awakening and knowledge that enables the liberation, and who then returns to the heavenly realm.

Gnosticism was thus typically marked by a strong *dualism*: two divine beings, two realities (spiritual and material), and two classes of human beings (those with the divine spark and those without it).

For orthodox Christians, there were obvious problems with such a set of beliefs, above all the rejection of the creator God of the Old Testament as a different divine being from the God of Jesus. Orthodox Christians also could not accept the common corollary that Jesus Christ himself was not truly human but a purely spiritual being who only used a body that was not to be identified with himself. The doctrine that Jesus only appeared to be human and to suffer and die is called **docetism** (from a Greek word that means "appearance"). Some Gnostic texts regard the suffering as real, but still seem to separate the person who suffers from the Christ who is the actual heavenly messenger (the closer that Gnostic texts come to mainstream Christianity, the more they tend to take the reality of Jesus' suffering and death seriously). Gnostic denial of Jesus' real embodiment also entailed doubts about his resurrection: because it was the spirit that mattered, not the body, the Resurrection was understood symbolically as the Gnostic's rebirth. Finally, Gnostic speculation divided the human race into two predetermined classes of people, those who would be saved and those incapable of salvation (versions of Gnosticism associated with the Christian Gnostic teacher Valentinus added a third category, those human beings who might be saved, but only for a lower order of salvation).

Sometime around A.D. 180, **Irenaeus of Lyons**, bishop of the Christian community in Lyons in southern Gaul (modern-day France), wrote a lengthy work called *Against Heresies*, primarily in response to Gnosticism. Irenaeus is our foremost witness to mainstream Christianity in the second century. His defense of orthodox teaching—he called it "the apostolic tradition"—focused on the fourfold elements of catholic (i.e., universal) Christianity mentioned above: canon, creed, episcopate, and liturgy. Irenaeus was the first early Christian writer to mention all four canonical gospels as a set. Besides written scriptures, he also stressed the oral tradition of apostolic teaching. He called it "the rule of truth," and in his descriptions it sounds like a type of creed used to prepare people for Baptism (see, e.g., *Against Heresies* 1.9.4, 1.22.1, 3.2.1, 3.11.1, etc.). Irenaeus understood this creed to be a measure by which orthodoxy is determined. Thus, he made an explicit contrast between the rule of truth, which is public and everywhere the same, and the teachings of the Gnostics, which are esoteric and contradictory.

Irenaeus pointed to the bishops as the authorized preservers of the apostolic tradition, because they stood in a living chain that went back to Jesus' first followers. This claim, he said, was open to verification by anyone who wished to examine it. All they had to do was trace the succession of the bishops of a given church back to the apostles. Interestingly, he singled out the church in Rome ("greatest and oldest," he called it) as a special reference point for the apostolic tradition, because of its "foundation" by two apostles, Peter and Paul (by which he meant the fact that they were buried in Rome). In a passage whose exact meaning has been debated, he appears to say that every authentic church must be in agreement with the apostolic tradition as preserved in Rome (Irenaeus, *Against Heresies* 3.3.2), though any church with an apostolic foundation will also have the same apostolic tradition (e.g., Ephesus in Asia Minor, where the apostle John lived).

Against Gnostic dualism, Irenaeus consistently emphasized *unity*. Creator and Redeemer were one: the God who created the world is the same God who redeems it, instead of positing two opposed gods. Jesus Christ was one person, both human and divine, rather than a disembodied spiritual messenger who only appeared to take on flesh. The human race was one: fallen in Adam and redeemed in Christ, not divided into those who can be saved and those who cannot. The Old and the New Testaments were a single Bible, in which God's plan for redemption—what Irenaeus called God's "dispensations" or his "economy" of salvation—was disclosed progressively by degrees. Irenaeus was so convinced of the goodness of the created though fallen world, including our bodies, that he interpreted "heaven" as a transformed earth: in language that somewhat embarrassed Christians more inclined to Plato's ideas about the superiority of the spiritual realm, Irenaeus talked about the restored and renewed world in highly materialistic terms (e.g., *Against Heresies* 5.33.3–4). Even the gap between God and humanity was now bridged: When Irenaeus asked, "How could humanity cross over to God, if God had not crossed over to humanity?" (*Against Heresies* 4.33.4, trans. M.J. Hollerich), he was laying the basis for the Christian doctrine of the "divinization" of humanity, or *theôsis* in Greek, which has been important in the Eastern Christian tradition (see Chapter 11). For Irenaeus, the redemption won by Jesus was really a **recapitulation**, a repetition or "doing-over" of all that had gone wrong in human history beginning with the Fall, a history that was now going to return to the pure condition in which it had begun.

THE BIRTH OF THEOLOGY

We have thus far spoken about doctrine or teaching more than about theology as such. The word "theology" literally means "discourse or talk about God." Its origin is in Greek philosophy. The Platonic tradition saw theology as a *mythic* way of talking about the gods and their relation to the world, understanding "myth" in the sense of symbolic stories that should not be taken literally. Aristotle saw theology as the *rational* knowledge of God and a branch of metaphysics (in Aristotle's philosophy, "metaphysics" is the understanding of first principles or ultimate reality). The Stoics gave the most prominent attention to theology, which they divided into three sub-categories: "mythic" (by which they meant the traditional stories about the gods as found in classical literature); "physical" or "natural" (meaning rational knowledge about the divine as known from the character of the world); and "political" (meaning the knowledge of the gods mandated by the city and preserved by the priests and the public cult).

Christian authors were slow to adopt the word for themselves. In Christian usage to "theologize" meant first of all to ascribe divinity to the Son and the Holy Spirit; second, it meant describing the descent of divinity to our world in the Incarnation. Then it was extended to mean *praise* of God, as in the liturgy, or mystical knowledge of God, as in the search for union with God—in this sense, theology meant something more like prayer than reflection or argument. The people who "did" theology were originally Christian teachers, often lay people, especially if they had had some training in philosophy and rhetoric. Such teachers were sometimes independent practitioners who functioned like what we might call consultants. After Christianity was legalized in the fourth and fifth centuries, theology came more under the control of the institutional church and its clergy. At the same time, the rise of the monastic movement (see Chapter 9) would provide a setting for theology different from that of the bishops and their priests.

Early Christian theological literature was devoted in the first instance to commentary and preaching on God's revelation in the Bible. Other subjects that were treated included the defense of the faith against both pagans and Jews, and doctrinal controversies within the church. Most early Christian literature, however, was written to meet various practical needs of Christian life and scarcely qualifies as "theology." The manuals modern scholars call *church orders*, the oldest of which is the **Didache** or "The Teaching of the Twelve Apostles" (parts of it probably go back to the end of the first century), dealt with issues of church government, worship, and discipline. Christians liked to read inspirational stories about the first generation of Christians, which led to the production of apocryphal (non-canonical) acts of Peter, Andrew, John, Thomas, Paul (who is described as traveling with a woman companion named Thecla), and others, on the analogy of the New Testament's Acts of the Apostles. Hagiography, or the writing of the lives of saints, began with the acts of Christian martyrs, some of which, like the *Martyrdom of Perpetua and Felicity*, have a historical foundation. There was instructional literature to prepare people for Baptism. Beginning with Athanasius' *Life of Antony*, the monastic movement of the fourth and fifth centuries would produce a rich literature of spiritual advice avidly read by lay people as well as monks.

Theology, in the sense of a reasoned examination of revelation, required a philosophical education that few early Christians before the fourth century were able to acquire. In the second and third centuries, Christian intellectual leadership was to be found in Alexandria in Egypt, for long the ancient world's greatest center of scholarship. It was the home of the Library, with its enormous book collection, and the Museum, a center for study and lecturing. If Christians in Alexandria were to compete with pagans on an equal footing, they, like the Jewish community that preceded them, could not afford to ignore the role of study and learning in theology. It is not an accident that many of the Christian Gnostics of whom we have knowledge originally came from Alexandria.

Christian scholarship in Alexandria began with freelance teachers and with catechetical instruction of candidates for Baptism. Such work may have led in the third century to a more structured program that involved baptismal preparation and higher learning in philosophy and related disciplines. Two of the most important and creative early Christian theologians, Clement of Alexandria (mid-second century– *c.*215) and **Origen of Alexandria** (*c.*185–*c.*253), were active in Alexandria. Clement, who was very well read in Greek philosophy and Greek literature in general, said that philosophy was the Greeks' preparation for the Gospel, just as the Law had been for the Jews. Origen achieved extraordinary fame for his teaching, his intellectual brilliance, and his holiness. The Christian historian Eusebius of Caesarea reports that even pagan rulers wished to meet him—Julia Mamaea, mother of the Roman Emperor Severus Alexander (222–235), invited Origen to visit her in Antioch. Pagan intellectuals read his books and attended his lectures. Christian bishops allowed him to preach in their presence, even though he was not ordained (but see below), and enlisted him as a theological expert to cross-examine bishops whose orthodoxy was in question. He inspired a generation of students who went on to become missionaries, bishops, and theologians in their own right. We still have an oration attributed to Gregory Thaumaturgus, who came from what is now northeast Turkey, that explains Origen's educational program and honors his teaching. Wealthy lay people generously supported his scholarly labors. He taught and wrote in Alexandria until 231, when he had a falling out with Demetrius, the bishop of Alexandria, because bishops in Palestine had ordained Origen a priest without Demetrius' permission. As a result, Origen spent the last two decades of his life in Caesarea in Palestine. It has been estimated that his *Hexapla* was the longest book ever written in the ancient world. It consisted of the Old Testament written out in six parallel columns (hence the name, meaning "sixfold"): the Hebrew original, the Hebrew written in Greek letters (presumably so that it could be pronounced by someone who didn't know Hebrew), the Septuagint (the Greek translation of the Hebrew Bible that had become the church's Old Testament), and at least three other Greek translations. The purpose of this mammoth work was to correct mistakes which had crept into the church's biblical manuscripts, and to give access to the Hebrew original for Christian scholars and for debates with Jews.

Origen believed that the theologian had a calling from the Holy Spirit. Though everyone was obliged to accept what apostolic tradition taught, he believed that theologians were called to investigate subjects that apostolic tradition had not already defined. In this way, members of the church who were endowed with intellectual talent and had advanced in personal holiness could arrive at a deeper understanding of the church's faith beyond that held by simple believers. Origen left the Christian tradition with a massive intellectual and spiritual legacy. In the area of biblical interpretation, he pioneered the writing of line-by-line biblical commentaries. His use of the **allegorical** method (looking for hidden spiritual meanings beneath the bare literal meaning of the text) was especially influential, and would eventually help Augustine get around some of his objections to the Bible (see *Confessions* 5.14.24). Likewise, his homilies were copied and circulated everywhere. Works of spirituality such as *On Prayer* and his commentary on the Song of Songs from the Bible have exerted a permanent influence on Christian teaching about the soul and its relationship with God.

Two of Origen's works deserve special mention. His *Against Celsus*, written late in his life, is a lengthy response to the first serious non-Christian critique of Christianity of which we have a record. Along with Augustine's *On the City of God*, it is one of the two most important apologies from the early Christian period. Indeed, of early Christian authors only Augustine can match Origen for his lasting influence on the whole scope and breadth of the Christian tradition—and unlike Augustine, Origen shaped both eastern and western branches of the tradition. The other book is a product of Origen's youth, the treatise called *On First Principles*, a bold exposition of Christian doctrine that could be called the first Christian systematic theology. The original version of the book is partially lost because some of Origen's ideas (such as the pre-existence of souls, the idea that human souls existed in heaven before they were born into bodies, which had been an acceptable hypothesis in Origen's own time) were condemned as heretical long after his death. Enough survives in Latin translation and from the Greek original to give a good idea of its contents. It was a highly creative interpretation of Christian teaching, with the help of Platonic philosophy, for the purpose of defending scripture and apostolic tradition and addressing the questions of educated Christians.

CHRISTIAN LIFE AND COMMUNITY

Standards of membership in the early Christian churches were at first very high because the church was thought of as an ark of the saved, the only refuge in a drowning world. The *Didache*, for example, is an excellent witness to the Christian commitment to high moral standards and the expectation that the church would be a community of saints—though even then, in the early second century, we can see evidence that the community that kept the *Didache* had to worry about prophets who were quick to ask for money, and about people who were taking advantage of Christian almsgiving (charity). A prospective convert underwent years of preparation before being judged fit for Baptism. Certain occupations were forbidden, especially if they involved bloodshed (such as being a gladiator), illicit sexual activity, and pagan religious ceremonies. There was also a prohibition against careers in teaching, because the myths about the gods were taught in school. As noted above, military service was consistently frowned on because of the Christian rejection of bloodshed and the oath of loyalty taken by soldiers. In some Christian sources, such as the third-century church manual known as the *Apostolic Tradition* and traditionally attributed to Hippolytus of Rome (d. 235), military service was regarded as a disqualification for Baptism:

> A soldier in command must be told not to kill people; if he is ordered to do so, he shall not carry it out. Nor should he take the oath. If he will not agree, he should be rejected. Anyone who has the power of the sword, or is a civil magistrate wearing the purple, he should desist, or he should be rejected. If a catechumen or a believer wishes to become a soldier, they should be rejected, for they have despised God.
>
> (*Apostolic Tradition* 16:8–10, trans. A. Stewart-Sykes)

Despite such an explicit prohibition, it is clear that Christians were already serving in the Roman army. The rationale for this change is uncertain, but it may have been based on Christian respect for the Empire's role as protector and peacekeeper. Christians would eventually find justification in New Testament passages such as John the Baptist's words to soldiers, "Be content with your wages" (Luke 3:14—the point is that he did not tell them to resign their commission), Peter's Baptism of the Roman centurion Cornelius (Acts 10), or Paul's description of the one who bears the sword as "the servant of God to execute his wrath on the wrongdoer" (Romans 13:4).

Lived Religion: Liturgy in the Early Church (A.D. 100–300): Initiation

In the earliest days of Christianity, worship usually took place in private homes. This was especially true before Christianity became a tolerated faith when Constantine issued the Edict of Milan in A.D. 313.

Since Christianity was an illegal faith, those who desired to join the community were brought to the teachers and were asked why they wanted to hear the Word of God. They had to be presented by a community member who vouched for their good character. They were asked about their lives, and those in certain professions like astrologers, idol makers, or gladiators could not "hear," as it was put—that is, hear the Word of God. Those possessed by demons could not hear until they had been exorcized.

Those who were accepted were called catechumens, meaning "ones under instruction." They heard the Word for three years, but some entered in less time, if they learned quickly. The hearers met weekly for prayer, instruction, and exorcisms to drive out demons. When they were ready for Baptism, the catechumens, now called the Elect, prayed, fasted, and were exorcized one final time by the bishop before their initiation.

On the evening before Easter, each person was anointed with blessed chrism and he or she made a statement of Christian faith before entering the baptismal pool. Children were baptized first, followed by the men and then the women. Water was poured over them three times by the presbyter as he baptized them in the name of the Father, the Son, and the Holy Spirit.

After their Baptism, the new Christians were dressed in white to signify that their sins were forgiven, they had received the Holy Spirit, and they were now part of the body of Christ, the Church. Then, they joined the faithful for the first time to receive the Eucharist. It was a time of great rejoicing as the Church celebrated the Resurrection of Christ and welcomed new members.

By the third century, the growing number of Christians seems to have caused a decline in standards. Origen complained about this decline, and the large number of lapsed Christians (those guilty of apostasy) in the Decian persecution (A.D. 250) confirms his pessimism. There were heated debates over what to do with those who failed to live up to the promises of their Baptism. Some Christians went so far as to deny that the church had the right to forgive serious sins after Baptism; they thought their severity was justified by the New Testament itself (cf. Hebrews 6:4–6). The most common practice seems to have been to allow repentant sinners a one-time chance for forgiveness for serious sin after Baptism. By the fourth century, after the conversion of the Roman emperor Constantine, the problem of diluted standards would become even greater.

The fellowship of the bishops was the chief institutional expression of the churches' catholicity or universality. At the same time, the bishop was the overseer of a local church or group of churches. The blend of local and universal was symbolized by the fact that the bishop was elected locally by the board of priests or presbyters (elders), with the consent of the laity, but could not be consecrated as a bishop without the cooperation of several other bishops. Bishops were regarded in principle as equal, all being successors of the apostles, but bishops in larger cities naturally carried more weight than those in small towns. A few bishops, chiefly Rome, Alexandria, and Antioch, enjoyed exceptional influence and prestige.

The bishops exercised primary control over the teaching and governing aspects of the church. They also presided at the Eucharist. However, they did not enjoy a complete monopoly of authority. By virtue of their Baptism, all Christians were thought eligible to enjoy the gifts of the Spirit, such as prophecy. Although prophecy gradually waned as a force in community life, it probably lasted longest in North Africa. The *Didache* shows a very early state of affairs when traveling prophets, teachers, and "apostles" outranked local bishops and deacons. Likewise, the charismatic authority (meaning authority freely granted by the Spirit) of martyrs and confessors was a powerful force in church life, as we can see in *The Martyrdom of Perpetua and Felicity*. According to Origen, Christian teachers also possessed a charismatic authority based on the gifts of wisdom and holiness.

Christian churches kept in touch through official letters called "letters of peace," through the travels of business people and other folk, and through regular meetings with neighboring churches on matters of common interest. As the church's organization grew, it took on the character of a state within the state. The churches were strengthened by the belief that they were the earthly extension of a community that existed in heaven as well; as St. Paul wrote, "Our commonwealth is in heaven" (Philippians 3:20). Besides the communion they shared with their sister churches around the Roman world, Christian churches were thus linked spiritually to the angels and martyred saints who praised God in heaven. This "communion of saints," as it was called in early Christian creeds, was experienced in the liturgy and in prayer, with the angels being thought of as individual protectors and co-worshippers with the church on earth. When persecution failed to crush this alternative society, the way was open in the fourth century for the Roman Empire to win over Christianity by merging with it rather than by trying to destroy it.

Key Terms

allegorical	docetism	mystery religions
Apologists	dualism	Origen of Alexandria
apostasy	episcopacy	orthodoxy pagan
bishops	Gnosticism	pagan
catholic	heresy	*parousia*
confessors	imperial cult	patristic era
creeds	Irenaeus of Lyons	recapitulation
Didache	martyrs	relics

Questions for Reading

1. What effect did the Fall of Jerusalem in A.D. 70 have on the Christian movement?

2. What sorts of motives seem to have attracted converts to Christianity during the second and third centuries?

3. Why did the Roman Empire persecute Christians? What kinds of objections did pagans raise against Christianity?

4. How did the Logos theology help the Apologists defend Christianity?

5. What were the most important factors in the formation of orthodox Christian doctrine? (Illustrate with specific reference to Baptism and the Eucharist.)

6. By the end of the second century, a universal (catholic) Christian consensus was beginning to take shape. What were the four main elements that helped to consolidate Christianity's identity?

7. What are the doctrines about God, creation, humanity, and redemption that are regarded as broadly typical of Gnosticism?

8. How did the theology of Ireneaus of Lyons respond to Gnostic dualism?

9. According to Irenaeus, how are we able to identify and know what apostolic tradition is?

10. How did Origen of Alexandria see the calling of the theologian, in relation to the apostolic tradition of the church? List some of Origen's lasting contributions to the Christian tradition.

11. The bishop played the key role in the life of the local Christian community and also served as the main link to Christian communities elsewhere. What were his local responsibilities? What other types of authority existed in Christian communities?

Works Consulted/Recommended Reading

Bauer, Walter. 1971. *Orthodoxy and Heresy in Earliest Christianity.* 2nd edn. Translated by Georg Strecker. Philadelphia, PA: Fortress Press.

Brakke, David. 2011. *The Gnostics: Myth, Ritual, and Diversity in Early Christianity.* Cambridge, MA: Harvard University Press.

Crouzel, Henri. 1989. *Origen: The Life and Thought of the First Great Theologian.* Translated by A.S. Worrall. San Francisco, CA: Harper & Row.

Daniélou, Jean. 1960. *From Shadows to Reality: Studies in the Biblical Typology of the Fathers.* Translated by Dom Wulstan Hibberd. Westminster, MD: Newman Press.

Daniélou, Jean. 1964–1977. *A History of Early Christian Doctrine before the Council of Nicaea.* 3 vols. Translated by John A. Baker. London: Darton, Longman, & Todd.

Eusebius of Caesarea. 1990. *The History of the Church: from Christ to Constantine.* Translated by G.A. Williamson. Revised edn., Andrew Louth. London: Penguin Classics.

Grafton, Anthony, and Megan Williams. 2006. *Christianity and the Transformation of the Book: Origen, Eusebius, and the Library of Caesarea.* Cambridge, MA: Harvard University Press.

Grant, Robert M. 2004. *Augustus to Constantine: The Rise and Triumph of Christianity in the Roman World.* Louisville, KY: Westminster John Knox Press.

Gregory Thaumaturgus [Wonderworker]. n.d. *Oration and Panegyric Addressed to Origen.* www.newadvent.org/fathers/0604.htm.

Hippolytus. 2001. *On the Apostolic Tradition.* Translated, Introduction, and Commentary by Alistair Stewart-Sykes. Crestwood, NJ: St. Vladimir's Seminary Press.

Jensen, Robin M. 2017. *The Cross: History, Art, and Controversy*. Cambridge, MA: Harvard University Press.

Jensen, Robin M. 2005. *Face to Face: Portraits of the Divine in Early Christianity*. Minneapolis, MN: Fortress.

Jensen, Robin M. 2000. *Understanding Early Christian Art*. London: Routledge.

Kelly, J.N.D. 1972. *Early Christian Creeds*. 3rd edn. New York: Longman.

Klauck, Hans-Josef. 2000. *The Religious Context of Early Christianity: A Guide to Graeco-Roman Religions*. Translated by Brian McNeil. Edinburgh: T.&T. Clark.

Lampe, Peter. 2003. *From Paul to Valentinus: Christians at Rome in the First Two Centuries*. Minneapolis, MN: Fortress.

Lane Fox, Robin. 1987. *Pagans and Christians*. New York: Alfred A. Knopf.

Markschies, Christoph. 2003. *Gnosis: An Introduction*. Translated by John Bowden. London: T.&T. Clark.

Mitchell, Margaret M., and Frances M. Young, eds. 2006. *Origins to Constantine*. Vol. 1. *The Cambridge History of Christianity*. Cambridge: Cambridge University Press.

Origen. 1986. *Contra Celsum*. Introduction, Notes, and Translated by Henry Chadwick. Cambridge: Cambridge University Press.

Robinson, James M., ed. 1996. *The Nag Hammadi Library in English*. 4th rev. edn. Leiden: Brill.

Sanders, E.P., ed. 1980. *The Shaping of Christianity in the Second and Third Centuries. Jewish and Christian Self-Definition*. Vol. 1. Philadelphia, PA: Fortress Press.

Swift, Louis J. 1983. *The Early Fathers on War and Military Service*. Message of the Fathers of the Church, 19. Wilmington, DE: Michael Glazier.

Trigg, Joseph Wilson. 1983. *Origen: The Bible and Philosophy in the Third-Century Church*. Atlanta, GA: John Knox Press.

Wilken, Robert L. 1984. *The Christians as the Romans Saw Them*. New Haven, CT: Yale University Press.

Young, Frances M. 2002. *Biblical Exegesis and the Making of Christian Culture*. Peabody, MA: Hendrickson.

Chapter

THE AGE OF THE IMPERIAL CHURCH

During the course of the fourth century, Christianity underwent a great reversal in its relationship with the Roman Empire. From 303 to 313, it endured the last and most prolonged of the persecutions. But shortly after this, the conversion of the emperor **Constantine** (r. 306–337) inaugurated a new era in which Christianity won legal toleration and eventual establishment as the empire's official religion. Christianity had begun as a Jewish movement looking forward to Jesus' Second Coming and the full realization of the Kingdom of God. Now it embarked on its long career as an established religion approved and promoted by the state. The union of church and state profoundly influenced Christianity. This chapter discusses Constantine's conversion and the transformation of Christianity into an "imperial church" (the church of the Roman Empire), the church councils and doctrinal developments of the period, and important trends in Christian life. Chapter 10 will be devoted entirely to St. Augustine of Hippo (354–430), the theologian whose ideas most fully reflected Christianity's transition to becoming a state church.

CONSTANTINE AND HIS LEGACY

Rise to Power and Religious Policies

Constantine came to power at a time when the Roman Empire was divided into sections ruled by an imperial board or college. This system was invented by the emperor Diocletian (r. 284–305), who restored the empire to stability after it almost collapsed in the late third century A.D. In 303, Diocletian inflicted a brutal persecution on Christianity. He did so because he wanted to make the empire's peoples return to traditional Roman values, to secure the good will of the gods, and to ensure the loyalty of the army (despite the church's prohibitions against bloodshed mentioned in Chapter 8, Christians were serving in the Roman army by the third century). Although the persecution failed, it left the churches bitterly divided over what to do with those who had lapsed in their faith during the persecution, just as had happened in the third-century persecutions (see Chapter 8). Schisms broke out in Egypt and in North Africa; in the latter area, Christians in the Donatist movement refused to accept sacraments from Catholic clergy whom they accused of betraying the faith during the persecution (see Chapter 10).

Constantine's father had been one of three co-rulers with Diocletian. When his father died in 306, Constantine succeeded him. For the next six years, he fought for control of the Western half of the empire. The crucial battle came in 312, when he defeated his last Western rival at the Milvian Bridge outside of the city of Rome. Before the battle, he became convinced that he would achieve victory with the help of the Christian God. According to the earliest account, he had a dream in which he was told to place the "heavenly sign of God" on the shields of the soldiers. The "sign" was probably the cross, though it has also been construed as the "Chi-Rho," a monogram consisting of the first two letters of the Greek spelling of Christ's name (the Greek letters *chi* and *rho*, which look like our "x" and "p," superimposed on one another; it was later featured on Constantine's standards and on his battle helmet).

Figure 9–1 The Chi-Rho, a monogram for the name of Christ, which Emperor Constantine used on his royal standards and battle gear.

A later account by his biographer, the church historian Eusebius of Caesarea (*c.*260–339), says that he had a daytime vision of a cross of light above the sun, with the words "By this, conquer," followed by a dream in which Christ told him to put the sign he had seen as a protection in battle (Eusebius, *Life of Constantine* 1.28–32). In the following year, he and his Eastern counterpart, the emperor Licinius, agreed to announce universal religious toleration and the restoration of seized property to the Christian churches, a decision traditionally known as the "Edict of Milan" (313), though it is more correctly seen as a letter of instruction from the emperors to governors of provinces. Constantine later went to war with Licinius and defeated him in 324, thus uniting the whole empire under his sole rule until his death in 337.

Modern historians have argued about whether Constantine was really a Christian. During the decade after 312, the evidence of his official coins (a traditional way for emperors to advertise their allegiances) is ambiguous. Some coins represent him under the sponsorship of the "Unconquered Sun," a pagan form of monotheism especially popular in the army—but also a religion less offensive to Christianity than polytheism. Nevertheless, after 312, Constantine produced a constant flow of letters and decrees that demonstrate his deep involvement in the affairs of the Christian church, even though he was not baptized until just before he died. He called church councils and enforced their decisions by exiling dissenters and burning condemned books. He subsidized the construction of new churches, especially in Palestine, which became a Christian "holy land" from this time forward. He gave large grants of money to the churches for their charitable work. He made his new eastern capital of Constantinople, founded on the site of the ancient city of Byzantium, into an explicitly Christian city.

Christianity represented for Constantine, above all, a divine guarantee of victory over evil. That is why he adopted the Chi-Rho and the cross as imperial symbols. He believed that God had chosen him for a special mission to bring the Roman Empire to Christianity, in return for which God would bless his reign and give the empire peace and prosperity.

Constantine saw the Christian church as providing heavenly support for the Roman Empire through the prayers of its clergy, and a common religion to hold its diverse peoples together, even though Christians were still just a small proportion of the population. To realize these goals, he gave the clergy important benefits, such as tax exemption and the power to act as judges in civil lawsuits. To a certain extent, Christian values influenced his laws, though an enactment like making Sunday ("the day of the Sun") a day of rest was the kind of ambiguous act that could please both Christians and non-Christians. He confiscated the wealth of pagan temples to finance construction of Constantinople, ended their state subsidies, and imposed certain restrictions on Jews. Nonetheless, he never revoked the toleration embodied in the "Edict of Milan." It was his successors, especially **Theodosius I** (r. 379–395), who made Christianity the sole legal religion of the empire.

Constantine's Impact on the Development of Christianity

The reign of Constantine affected Christianity in fundamental ways. Constantine established the practice of calling an **ecumenical** or **general council** (a universal gathering of Christian bishops) to resolve urgent issues affecting the whole church, and also set the precedent that it was Christian emperors—not popes or patriarchs—who summoned and enforced them. These councils and their decrees were crucial to the development of Christianity from the fourth century on. Constantine's conversion and his policies as emperor greatly increased the rate of conversion to Christianity, although contemporary observers like Eusebius admitted that many of these conversions were politically motivated. Constantine founded the city of **Constantinople**, which can be seen as a symbolic beginning of the Byzantine Empire, the name that historians give to the continuation of the Roman Empire in the East. The Byzantine Empire lasted for over 1,000 years until the Ottoman Turks (adherents of Islam) finally captured Constantinople in 1453. This Christianized Eastern Roman Empire became the center of what we now call Eastern Orthodox Christianity (Chapter 11).

Moreover, Constantine inaugurated a model of Christian kingship in which the king receives his authority to rule directly from God, not from an institution such as the church. According to Eusebius, the emperor once said to him, "You are bishops of those within the Church, but I am perhaps a bishop appointed by God over those outside [the church]" (*Life of Constantine* 4.24). Constantine was making an analogy between the bishops' oversight of the church—the word *bishop* means "overseer"— and his own divinely ordained oversight of the empire as a whole. In his view, the emperor was not supposed to take over the spiritual work proper to the church, but to enable the church to perform its divine tasks rightly. This type of Christian kingship was imitated by Byzantine emperors, by many Western kings and emperors in the medieval period and, in some cases, even into the modern period.

Finally, Constantine inspired the growth of a Christian devotion to the Roman state as an institution willed by God. Henceforth, Christians demonstrated their patriotism by holding public office and serving in the army. This Christian patriotism can be seen in both a positive and a negative light. In a positive sense, it reflected a deepened awareness of civic responsibility. To Christians like Eusebius, it seemed logical that Christians should not flee from the world but should seek to exercise power on behalf of the church and the gospel. He is the first Christian writer to describe two codes of conduct, a higher and a lower, and two classes of Christians, as permanent features of Christian life. Eusebius went so far as to describe the Roman Empire and its monarchical government as an image of the one God's heavenly government (see his *Oration in Praise of Constantine*, given on the 30th anniversary of Constantine's reign). This new patriotism and civic involvement provided an answer to pagan critics, who had accused Christians of shirking their public duties while enjoying the benefits and protection of the Roman Empire.

To justify the duty to defend the state, Christians could appeal to many texts in the Bible, such as Romans 13:1–7 ("Those authorities that exist have been instituted by God …"), which recognized that all earthly power is under God's direction and is answerable to God. Some Christian writers, such as St. Augustine, distinguished individual killing from the publicly authorized use of the sword on behalf of the community (see *On the City of God* 1.21 and 19.7). Augustine and St. Ambrose, archbishop of Milan from 374 to 397, helped to form a Christian version of "just war theory" by adapting traditional Roman criteria for deciding when and how to wage war justly.

On the negative side, Christianity's alliance with the state created some problems, too. Emperors were always tempted to overstep their limits and intervene in church affairs. Moral responsibility for the actions of a supposedly Christian state exposed Christians to new tests of their consciences. Hadn't Jesus said to Pontius Pilate, "My kingdom is not from this world" (John 18:36)? Was the abandonment of Jesus' prohibition of bloodshed actually justified? In later centuries, some Christian churches like the Mennonites and the Quakers would reject Christian participation in war as incompatible with the teachings of Jesus in the Sermon on the Mount.

Another issue was the possible corruption of the church. Wealth and political influence threatened the integrity of the church's government. Bishops were tempted to switch from one city to another in the hope of increasing their power and influence, and church laws against this practice were widely ignored. There was also a growing tendency to equate Christianity with the civilization of the Roman Empire, when in fact many Christians already lived outside of the empire. Constantine's conversion, for instance, exposed Persian Christians across the eastern border to the threat of persecution as disloyal subjects. Finally, there was the beginning of religious coercion, as the institutional church used its privileged position within the state to persecute heretics and unbelievers. Under the Christian emperors, Jews would gradually lose many of the legal protections and exemptions they had enjoyed earlier under the pagan emperors.

DOCTRINAL DEVELOPMENT: TRINITY AND INCARNATION

The most significant theological achievement of the fourth and fifth centuries is the formal defining of the doctrines of the Trinity and the Incarnation, which are complementary Christian teachings about God and Christ that distinguish Christianity from all other religions. The doctrine of the Trinity reconciles biblical monotheism with the scriptural testimony to the Father, Son, and Holy Spirit. Similarly, the doctrine of the Incarnation explains how the one Jesus Christ can be simultaneously human and divine. Why were these important doctrines not fully articulated until centuries after Jesus' death, even though the followers of Jesus seem to have paid him divine honors from not long after the Resurrection (e.g., Philippians 2:6–11)? For the most part, Christians of the early centuries preferred to state their beliefs in a minimalist manner that kept to the language of the Bible. But arguments with Jews and pagans alike, as well as disagreements within the Christian movement, made more precise definition unavoidable. So did growing acquaintance with the ideas and methods of Greek philosophy, especially philosophical conceptions of God and sophisticated ways of reading texts, including biblical texts. The influence of rhetoric (the art of persuasion and argumentation) sharpened a taste for aggressive debate. Finally, the Christianization of the Roman state brought the government into theological debate: disagreement and disunion had legal and political consequences, because rulers believed that divine protection of the empire depended on unity in the Church.

Controversy over doctrine thus became acute. Beginning with Constantine, ecumenical ("world-wide") church councils were instituted to resolve these disputes. Of the councils that were held in the fourth and fifth centuries, those which Catholics, Eastern Orthodox, and most mainstream Protestants accept are the ones that met at Nicaea (325), Constantinople (381), Ephesus (431), and Chalcedon (451).

Nicaea (325) and Constantinople (381)

In around 320, in Alexandria, Egypt, a priest named **Arius** and his bishop **Alexander** had a dispute over the Trinity. The core theological issue was the relation of Jesus Christ as divine to God himself—in other words, between God the Father and his Son or Word (*Logos*), as he is called in the Gospel of John. Jesus stood in some way between God and humanity—"the one Mediator between God and human beings, the man Jesus Christ" (1 Timothy 2:5)—but how was this intermediary status to be explained? Expressing it in words became even more challenging insofar as philosophically educated Christian theologians had already taken on board the doctrines of divine simplicity (that God is by definition one and indivisible) and divine incorporeality (that God is immaterial). The scriptural flashpoint was a passage from the Old Testament book of Proverbs 8:22–31, in which God's Wisdom is personified and gives a speech to God: "As the beginning of his ways, he [God] made me [God's Wisdom] for his works, before the ages he established me in the beginning" (Proverbs 8:22–23 Septuagint).

Alexander taught that the Father and Son were co-eternal on account of the Father's eternal generation of the Son; that is, if God exists eternally as Father, then the Son must also exist eternally in order for God to be called "Father" in a meaningful way. But Arius construed texts like Proverbs 8 to mean that God pre-existed, so to speak, the generation of the Son. To Arius, it seemed as if Alexander's theology implied two beings who were "ungenerated," that is, two first principles, thereby imperiling monotheism and veering into ditheism (belief in two gods). The philosophical term "ungenerated" (*agenētos*) had long been used in Christianity to signify that God was the uncreated, unoriginated source of all. Thus, when Alexander taught that both the Father and the Son were eternal, Arius saw this as saying that there were two unoriginated sources of all. Arius also thought that Alexander's insistence on the co-eternity of the Father and Son ignored the hierarchy inherent in "Father–Son" language. Accordingly, Arius stressed the Son's inferiority to the Father. He held that God had not always been Father, but only became Father when he brought the Son into existence. Arius argued that only God the Father could be called God in the fullest sense, since he alone was ungenerated; all else was generated, including the Son. The Son was a "second-class" god who was necessary in order to be the link between the truly transcendent God and the rest of the universe.

The controversy sparked by Arius spread and in 325 Constantine convened a council of bishops at Nicaea to resolve it. They ratified a creed, or statement of beliefs, now called the **Nicene Creed**, designed to exclude the theology of Arius as a viable option by saying that the Father and Son were "same-in-substance" (*homoousios*). Arius was excommunicated and exiled; thereafter, he was marginal. But the controversy he started continued regardless. Christians could not agree what sort of divinity should be ascribed to the Son, and whether one could speak of degrees of divinity (as Arius did)—indeed, there was no agreement on what the nature of divinity itself was. It was also unclear what "Father–Son" language implied, and in what sense Father and Son were "one." The word that the Nicene Creed used to express that oneness, *homoousios*, could be misunderstood in a materialist sense, as if God were "stuff" that could be divided, or even taken to mean that Father and Son were simply the same being. Besides being philosophically suspect in the eyes of many educated bishops, the word also did not come from the Bible, a departure from the preference for biblical language and images. On top of that, the word had previously been found mostly among Gnostic writers. The term *homoousios* would prove to be a sticking point for decades. (In this early stage of the Trinitarian controversy, there was relatively little reflection as yet by anyone on the divinity of the Holy Spirit or the Spirit's relation to the Father and Son, a deferred aspect of the Trinity that would not be resolved until the second ecumenical council at Constantinople.)

Athanasius of Alexandria, who succeeded Alexander as bishop in 328, became a controversial and forceful defender of the Nicene Creed. Much like Alexander, Athanasius stressed God's eternal Fatherhood, which implies the Son's co-eternity with the Father. In his manifesto *Orations against the Arians*, Athanasius emphasized that the Father, like any father, begets a Son that is of the same nature; in other words, just as a human father does not give birth to a different sort of creature, such as a horse, so too does the Father beget a Son who is the same as he in substance. Athanasius asserted this "genetic" understanding of "Father–Son" language against those who seemed to reduce the Father to a kind of producer of a product that is different in nature, similar to a potter making a pot. Athanasius repeatedly affirmed that the Son is "proper to the Father's substance"; in other words, the Son's existence is intrinsic to the Father's nature. For Athanasius, the Father and Son were one in virtue of the single divine nature they shared.

The decades after Nicaea were marked by turbulent debates over the question of the Son's divinity and relation to the Father. Numerous councils of bishops met. All failed to gain widespread acceptance. Radical heirs of Arius directly contradicted the notion that Father and Son shared the same substance by saying that the Father's being "ungenerated" meant that Father and Son were actually different in substance. More moderate thinkers recoiled at that assertion and began to band together to create a broad alliance in support of the Nicene Creed and its language of "same-in-substance" (*homoousios*), if it was supplemented by a clear affirmation of the full divinity of the Spirit as well. Central to this movement were **Basil of Caesarea** (*c.*330–378), **Gregory of Nyssa** (*c.*335–after 394), and **Gregory of Nazianzus** (*c.*330–390), all from Cappadocia in central Asia Minor, hence known collectively as "the Cappadocian Fathers." They have remained paramount as benchmark Trinitarian theologians in most Christian traditions. A key contribution of the Cappadocians was making a conceptual distinction between "nature" or "substance" on the one hand, and "person" on the other: henceforth Christians would hold that there was only one divine substance or nature, but existing in three distinct and equally divine persons.

The pro-Nicene position won the support of **Theodosius I** (emperor 379–395), who convened the **Council of Constantinople** in 381, which has been received by the Christian tradition as the Second Ecumenical Council. The Nicene Creed was confirmed and expanded; the new creed was not intended to replace the creed of 325, but to restate the faith contained therein in new circumstances. This amended form of the Nicene Creed, more properly known as the Nicene-Constantinopolitan Creed, has become the most universally accepted benchmark of the Christian faith outside of the Bible itself. With the exception of the dispute between Western and Eastern Christians over the "procession" of the Holy Spirit from the Father (see Chapter 11), this is essentially the wording of the Creed as it is recited in churches today:

> We believe in one God, Father, almighty, maker of heaven and earth, of all things both seen and unseen.
>
> And in one Lord, Jesus Christ, the Son of God, the only-begotten, who was begotten from the Father before all ages, light from light, true God from true God, begotten, not made, same-in-substance with the Father, through whom all things came to be, who for us humans and for our salvation came down from the heavens, and became incarnate of the Holy Spirit and Mary the virgin, and became human, and was crucified for our sake under Pontius Pilate, and suffered and was buried, and rose again on the third day in accordance with the scriptures, and ascended into the heavens, and is seated at the right hand of the Father, and is coming again with glory to judge the living and the dead, whose kingdom will have no end.
>
> And in the Holy Spirit, the Lord and giver of life, who proceeds from the Father, who with Father and Son is worshiped and glorified, who has spoken through the prophets.
>
> In one, holy, catholic, and apostolic church. We confess one baptism for the forgiveness of sins. We await the resurrection of the dead, and the life of the age to come. Amen.
>
> (Trans. Mark DelCogliano, in Radde-Gallwitz 2017, 268–9)

Pro-Nicene Trinitarian theology can be summed up as follows:

- *The person-nature distinction.* Whatever it is that God is, there is *one* of it, and the Father, Son, and Spirit share it equally. All possess the fullness of whatever it is to be God. At the same time, the Father, Son, and Spirit are distinct, equal, irreducible, and perfect individuals or "persons" existing eternally together. Each person of the Trinity has distinctive qualities that distinguish it from the other two and indicate the manner in which it is God: the Father is unbegotten, the Son is begotten of the Father, and the Spirit proceeds from the Father. One person of the Trinity is not "more God" than another.
- *The eternal generation of the Son.* The Father and Son are co-eternal even as the Father has begotten the Son from his own essence. This act of divine begetting occurs eternally within the unitary and simple divine nature. The "genetic" understanding of "Father–Son" language also predominates among pro-Nicene thinkers, such that the Father and Son are held to be the same-in-substance (*homoousios*).
- *Inseparable operations.* Any divine action is the work of Father, Son, and Spirit together, as they always operate inseparably from one another. Because the one God is simple and indivisible, the three divine persons cannot operate in a divided manner as three human beings do. Rather, each of the three divine persons is fully present and active at every moment in every divine activity, whether creating, sanctifying, or saving.
- *Theology and knowledge of God.* God is ultimately incomprehensible; the divine essence cannot be grasped by human intellects. However, we can have meaningful knowledge of God, even if it falls short of full comprehension, through the contemplation of God's saving acts as revealed in scripture, the variety of titles and images by which God is presented in the scriptures, and so forth. We progress in such knowledge to the degree that we grow in love of God through ascetical disciplines and religious practices that refashion the mind and reorient the heart.

Theodosius I also made the pro-Nicene doctrine of the Trinity the law of the empire and enacted a sweeping edict against paganism in 391. His reign was thus the time when Christianity really became the official religion of the empire.

Ephesus (431) and Chalcedon (451)

While Christians had always confessed Jesus Christ to be both human and divine, the fourth-century debates over the Trinity made the need for greater precision more urgent. The Nicene-Constantinopolitan Creed stated that the Son "became incarnate [literally, "became flesh"; cf. John 1:14] of the Holy Spirit and Mary the virgin, and became human," but these formulations were ambiguous. In the 370s, the pro-Nicene theologian **Apollinarius of Laodicaea** (*c.*310–390) provided one interpretation of what it meant for the Son to become incarnate. He understood the Incarnation to consist of the union of the Logos or Son with a human body but not with a human soul. In other words, the Logos took the place of Christ's human soul. This view of the Incarnation made it easier to see how divine and human could be joined in one person. But it also suggested that Christ's human flesh was all that he had in common with other human beings.

Pro-Nicene theologians repudiated Apollinarius because they believed that Christ had redeemed *all* of human nature. Gregory of Nazianzus gave a classic expression to the doctrine that Christ took on a complete human nature when he said, "For that which Christ has not assumed, he has not healed, but what is united with God is saved" (*First Letter to Cledonius*). Humanity's sinfulness was not a function of the flesh alone but of the whole person, soul and body, and so it was the whole of human nature that Christ had come to save. Henceforth, Christological reflection was conducted in an anti-Apollinarian framework that affirmed Christ's full divinity and full humanity.

Yet it remained difficult for theologians to see how a fully divine nature and a fully human nature could coexist in a single person. One problem in particular was reconciling divine *impassibility* (that God cannot suffer or change) with the fact that the one true God had taken on flesh and suffered and died for human beings, a central aspect of Christ's saving work. Fourth- and fifth-century pro-Nicene theologians accepted the idea of divine impassibility because they understood suffering to involve implicit change and lack of stability, characteristics inherent to created things, which tend to decay and die. But God, by definition, was above such things. Accordingly, in explaining the Incarnation, theologians sought to preserve the impassibility of the Word, while respecting the gospel testimonies to Jesus' full humanity, particularly his suffering and death.

One approach is associated with **Nestorius** (patriarch of Constantinople 428–431, d. 451). He sought to protect the integrity of Christ's divinity and humanity by keeping them separate, as it were, free from real contact with each other. He spoke as though the Word had assumed a complete human being, or of the Word's "indwelling" of Christ's human nature as if "in a temple," suggesting that whatever happens on the outside (to the human Jesus) does not affect what is inside (the divine Word). This made the Incarnation seem more like a divine–human partnership rather than a true unity of subject. Critics charged Nestorius with implying that there were "two Sons" or "two Christs," two separate realities, indeed two persons, one human and one divine.

To press his point, Nestorius began to preach that it was inappropriate to call Mary the Mother of God (in Greek, *Theotokos*, "the Godbearer"), since God could not be said to have been born as it implied suffering and change. Rather, Mary was at best the Mother of Christ, meaning of his humanity. To Cyril, patriarch of Alexandria (r. 412–444), Nestorius' denial of Mary's divine motherhood implied that Christ is dual and that his divinity did not participate in experiences like being born and suffering, in which only the humanity is implicated. This would have suggested to Cyril that Nestorius held that there was something akin to two persons in Christ, as mentioned above.

For Cyril, the divine–human fact of the Incarnation was the proper starting point for Christological reflection. From the instant of his conception, Jesus had been both God and human. Divinity and humanity were so indissolubly united that they could only be distinguished in thought, but not as separately existing realities. The real subject of all the actions reported of Jesus in the Gospels was the Word of God, but the Word *incarnate*, that is, personally united with a human nature in a single reality, or in language he sometimes used, "the one incarnate nature of the Word." Christ's human nature was indeed complete so far as soul and body were concerned. But it lacked a human personal "identity," to use modern language. All of Jesus' human experiences were truly human; but they were referred to the Word, who claimed them as "his own." Cyril held that was possible because of the "hypostatic union," meaning that Christ's human and divine natures are indissolubly united at the level of the person or *hypostasis*, to use the Greek word. In the Incarnation, the person of the Word assumed humanity, body, and soul.

At the **Council of Ephesus** in 431, Mary was declared to be the Mother of God, and Nestorius was deposed for heresy. Cyril's *Second Letter to Nestorius* was endorsed as a model expression of orthodox Christology. But some of Cyril's refutations of Nestorius had gone too far, particularly the so-called "Twelve Anathemas" appended to his *Third Letter to Nestorius*, which alienated important bishops led by John of Antioch and Theodoret of Cyrrhus. The rift was healed only in 433, when Cyril penned the *Formula of Reunion*, one of the clearest expositions of his Christology.

That did not end controversy. In 448, **Eutyches**, a supporter of Cyril, was condemned for denying that Christ was same-in-substance as other human beings according to his humanity, and therefore refused to acknowledge two natures in Christ after the Incarnation, exaggerating Cyril's language of "one incarnate nature of the Word." Eutyches made it seem that Christ's human nature was somehow absorbed by his divine nature and had ceased to be fully human.

Eutyches' supporters managed to get him exonerated at a second council of Ephesus (Ephesus II) held in 449 and presided over by Cyril's successor, Dioscorus of Alexandria. The Twelve Anathemas of Cyril's *Third Letter to Nestorius* were all but accepted as an expression of Christological orthodoxy, and a powerful protest submitted by Pope **Leo I**, known as the *Tome* of Leo, was ignored.

But the **Council of Chalcedon**, held just two years later in 451, overruled it, and so Ephesus II has not been received by the Christian tradition as an ecumenical council. At Chalcedon the condemnation of Eutyches was affirmed, the *Tome* of Leo was accepted, and a new definition of the faith was produced, known as the *Chalcedonian Definition*. It was called a "definition" rather than an actual creed, so that it did not seem to replace the Nicene-Constantinopolitan Creed, which was declared final, once and for all (that is why the Definition, unlike the Creed, is never recited in the liturgy). The Definition was supported by Cyril's *Second Letter to Nestorius* and the *Formula of Reunion*, and the *Tome* of Leo. Here is the key passage:

> For [the council] is arrayed against those who attempt to tear apart the mystery of the economy into a duality of sons, ... stands opposed to those who concoct a mixture or confusion in the case of the two natures of Christ, ... and anathematizes those who make up a story of two natures of the Lord before the union but imagine one after the union. Following, then, the holy fathers [of the Councils of Nicaea, Constantinople, and Ephesus], all of us in unison teach the confession of one and the same Son, our Lord Jesus Christ; the same perfect in divinity and the same perfect in humanity; the same truly God and truly a human being consisting of a rational soul and a body; same-in-substance with the Father according to his divinity and the same same-in-substance with us according to his humanity, like us in every respect except for sin, begotten before the ages from the Father according to his divinity and in the last days the same for us and for our salvation from the virgin Mary the *Theotokos* according to his humanity; one and the same Christ, Son, Lord, Only-Begotten, acknowledged in two natures unconfusedly, unchangeably, undividedly, inseparably, the difference of the natures being in no way destroyed because of the union but instead the distinctive feature of each nature being preserved and coming together into one person and one *hypostasis*; not separated or divided into two persons but one and the same Son, Only-Begotten, God, Word, Lord, Jesus Christ, just as the prophets from the beginning taught about him and the Lord Jesus Christ himself instructed us and the symbol of the fathers handed it down to us.
>
> (Trans. Mark DelCogliano, in DelCogliano 2019)

In this balanced and minimalist statement of Christological belief, the bishops set out the boundaries of acceptable orthodox discourse on the subject, largely by endorsing the Christology of Cyril and ruling out the views associated with Nestorius and Euty-ches. For example, the Definition affirms against Nestorius that Christ is the incar-nate Son of God, one person, one *hypostasis*, a "single subject," and against Eutyches that Christ is fully divine and fully human, with a humanity just like ours (except for sin). Even after the Incarnation, Christ is "acknowledged in two natures unconfus-edly, unchangeably, undividedly, inseparably"—the first two adverbs are directed against Eutyches and the last two against Nestorius.

The council failed to satisfy everyone. The Chalcedonian Definition's phrase "acknowledged in two natures" seemed to some of the supporters of Cyril as a rever-sion to Nestorianism. They feared the phrase meant a continuing of two separate realities that was tantamount to two persons. They conceded that Christ was "from" or "out of" two natures, but after his incarnation, they insisted on speaking of only "one nature," meaning "nature" in the sense of a single, concrete reality. Growing dissent against Chalcedon and hostility to the Empire's efforts to coerce its accept-ance, would lead to the creation of permanently separate Christian churches in the Middle East and North Africa, one group stigmatized as "Monophysites" (holders of only one nature) and the other as "Nestorians" (see Chapter 11).

The Chalcedonian doctrine of the Incarnation in summary:

- There is a single "subject" in Christ, not two.
- There are two complete natures, one fully human, the other fully divine. Each nature retains the qualities that belong to it.
- The Word assumed a human nature, not a human person ("hypostatic union").
- Each of the natures is intact but "shares" its qualities with the other, because only one person is involved.
- The Definition attempts to describe a *mystery* that will always escape full human understanding.

CHRISTIAN LIFE IN THE IMPERIAL CHURCH

The fourth and fifth centuries saw important developments in other areas besides politics and theology. We will discuss three: the consolidation of the church's uni-versal government; the rise of monasticism; and trends in liturgy and church design.

Church Government

Until the fourth century, Christianity had consisted of a confederation of local churches linked by a common faith and the fellowship of the bishops. In theory, all bishops were equal successors of the apostles, but in reality the bishops of the larger cities dominated. The Council of Nicaea recognized regional spheres of interest cen-tered in Rome, Alexandria, and Antioch (the largest cities in the empire), with Jeru-salem enjoying an honorary status as the historic mother church of Christianity. To these four was soon added Constantinople, the new Eastern capital. Four of these cities were located in the eastern part of the Roman Empire (Antioch, Alexandria, Jerusalem, and Constantinople), with only one in the West (Rome). The bishops of these cities eventually gained the honorary title of **patriarch**. The idea later developed

Figure 9–2 A relief on a sarcophagus, or a stone casket, which has the very common artistic theme of Christ handing Peter the Law in the form of a scroll; Peter is holding a cross, a portion of which has been broken off at the top, in token of Christ's prediction in John 21:18–19 that Peter would die a martyr's death. From the Alyscamps Cemetery, Arles, Provence, France.

in the Eastern churches that the five patriarchs should share spiritual jurisdiction as a committee or college. Such a system never got much beyond the level of theory, however, mainly because of rivalry among the patriarchs.

The Roman church represented a special case in that it was the only church with a convincing claim to *primacy* (literally, being first). Rome's unique prestige was based mainly on its possession of the tombs of both Peter and Paul, and on its location in the capital of the empire. Moreover, the Roman church and its bishop had always shown a strong sense of responsibility for the Christian churches as a whole. In the fourth century, Eastern bishops and theologians looking for support abroad often went to Rome as a refuge and a court of appeal, although the Easterners never accepted that the bishop of Rome had the right to intervene in their affairs without being asked first. The bishop of Rome eventually came to be called the **pope** (the word comes from the Latin *papa*, meaning "father," and originally could be applied to other bishops as well; the head of the Coptic Orthodox Church in Egypt still claims it as a title). A major concern for the bishop of Rome was the growing ambition of the church of Constantinople; according to certain conciliar canons (statements issued by church councils), which the Roman church has never accepted, Constantinople possessed an authority second only to that of Rome's. This claim to authority was made on the frankly secular and political ground that, as the Eastern capital, it was the "new Rome."

The sermons, letters, and decrees of Pope Leo I (r. 440–461) expressed many of the ideas that have remained basic to the **papacy** (the government of the pope) ever since: Peter was the chief or prince of the apostles; he was divinely commissioned to rule the church at the center of the empire; the pope is the direct successor of Peter, "the doorkeeper of the kingdom of heaven," as Leo called him (see Matthew 16:15–19); and the pope's authority is grounded not in his personal merit but in the merits of Peter.

Peter's Confession according to Matthew 16:15–19

[Jesus] said to them, "But who do you say that I am?" Simon Peter answered, "You are the Messiah, the Son of the living God." And Jesus answered him, "Blessed are you, Simon son of Jonah! For flesh and blood has not revealed this to you, but my Father in heaven. And I tell you, you are Peter, and on this rock I will build my church, and the gates of Hades will not prevail against it. I will give you the keys of the kingdom of heaven, and whatever you bind on earth will be bound in heaven, and whatever you loose on earth will be loosed in heaven."

These ideas concerning papal primacy would not be fully applied even in the West until the Germanic invasions and the conquests of Islam radically reshaped the Christian map and left the papacy largely in a world of its own. But they were never fully accepted in the East. Although Eastern Christians did not view the primacy of Rome the same way that Westerners did, the acceptance of Leo's *Tome* at the Council of Chalcedon testifies to the regard in which the Eastern bishops held the Roman church: "Peter has spoken through Leo," they cried. They did not mean that Leo's teaching was true just because it was Leo who had said it; rather that in their judgment Leo had correctly expressed the faith that they too held, for they also shouted out, "Cyril [of Alexandria] so taught … Leo and Cyril taught the same thing." In the Christian East (but also in the West), a common interpretation of Peter's confession of faith in Matthew 16:16–19 was that the "rock" on which Jesus founds the church was not so much the *person* of Peter as his faith in Christ, which was professed by all. Eastern Christianity has traditionally seen the Roman bishop as, at best, "the first among equals," meaning that he has a unique spiritual prestige, a primacy of honor, but not a right of command or jurisdiction over other patriarchs.

Monasticism and the Ascetical Movement

While ascetical practices had always been part of Christianity, the fourth century saw the rise of asceticism as a distinct way of life in the church, called monasticism. **Asceticism** is the training or discipline of the passions and the appetites through corporeal and spiritual practices. **Monasticism** refers to the way of life of monks. The word **monk** comes from the Greek word *monachos*, meaning "a single or a solitary person." It began to be used in the fourth century as a name for men and women who dedicated their lives to asceticism, prayer, and other spiritual disciplines. Most monks were convinced that they needed to live differently from mainstream society and even from ordinary Christians in order to achieve salvation. It is probably not a coincidence that monasticism emerged as Christianity was winning acceptance by the Roman Empire. The monastic life replaced martyrdom as the model of Christian perfection.

Pre-monastic ascetics lived as solitaries or in groups of varying sizes, typically in urban centers or on their edges, with different degrees of participation in the local

Christian church and wider society. Their lives were marked by renunciation and withdrawal. Renunciation is the voluntary sacrifice of something considered good in itself for the sake of spiritual gain, such as food or marriage and family. Withdrawal refers to the breaking of ties, whether ethical, familial, social, or physical. Ascetics practiced some form of withdrawal from ordinary social conventions and lifestyles as well as from family. Monks did the same, but also *physically* and *spatially* separated themselves from cities and villages, to which they nevertheless remained bound socially and economically, since they aspired to support themselves and thus participated in local economies and social networks.

Monasticism's roots are in Eastern Christianity. Some monks lived as hermits (also called "anchorites"). The most famous of these early hermits was **Antony of Egypt** (251–356).

Initially practicing renunciation in his village, Antony innovated by withdrawing from his village to live by himself in the desert. He set the pattern of physical and spatial separation. As early as the 330s, monastic centers developed in Lower Egypt in Scetis, Nitria, and the Cells, where "desert fathers" and "desert mothers" lived as hermits in separate huts (or cells) in configurations ranging from isolated anchorites to loose communities. Here they pursued "stillness" (*hesychia*), a state of inner and outer calm and quiet that they cultivated to pray continually in the presence of God. The collections of *Apophthegmata* or "sayings" of the desert fathers and mothers that have come down to us witness to these Egyptian monks' simple lifestyle, humble virtue, and pithy wisdom.

There were also communal forms of monasticism. In Tabennesi, in Upper Egypt, **Pachomius** (290–346) became a pioneer in the development of **cenobitic monasticism** (from the Greek words for "common life"). Such organized communities lived in a monastery and were governed by a spiritual leader called an **abbot** (from the Aramaic word for "father"). They usually followed a written rule and a routine of manual labor, public and private prayer, and community meetings for instruction by the abbot. These rules and routines—along with the separation from society—were designed not only to help monks avoid sin but also to focus continually on God. Near Akhmim, in Upper Egypt, **Shenoute of Atripe** (*c.*348–*c.*464) presided over the White Monastery, a cenobitic institution which housed more than 2,000 men and women. An authoritarian figure, Shenoute's influence went far beyond the walls of the monastery. He acted as a patron for Christians in the surrounding areas, defending the poor against the powerful, welcoming refugees, and feeding the hungry. In Cappadocia, **Basil of Caesarea** formulated a rule for cenobitic monasticism that stressed mutual service and works of charity. If you live alone, he asked, whose feet will you wash? (the reference is to Jesus' washing of his disciples' feet at the Last Supper in the Gospel of John). Basil saw hospitality for society's marginalized as a special mark of the monastic vocation, and so his monks lived in buildings close to cities and villages where the monastic community could provide various forms of social service: caring for the sick, raising orphans, providing food and clothing for the poor, and offering employment for the destitute. A set of monastic rules is attributed to Basil—really, numerous questions put to him by monks and his responses—which became central in Byzantine Christianity. Monasticism also flourished in Syria, independent of developments in Egypt. Syrian monasticism was notable for its extreme forms of physical self-denial, such as that of the pillar saints like Symeon the Stylite (*c.*390–459). Monasticism also took root in Palestine, near the holy sites in Jerusalem and Bethlehem, but also in the Judean desert and in Gaza. A distinctive form of monastic living was developed in Palestine, the *laura*, in which hermits and cenobites lived in a single community under the authority of an abbot.

There were non-Christian analogues to the monastic movement, but it is hard to gauge their impact. In Judaism, there was the Essene community of Qumran, where celibacy for some and community ownership of goods were practiced, and the communities of Jewish contemplatives in Egypt described by Philo of Alexandria. There were pagan ascetics, too, influenced by philosophical ideas of the superiority of the spiritual realm over the material, for the ascetical life appealed to high-minded pagans as well as to Christians. But when Christian writers presented monastic life to readers, they used biblical precedents and language, much as they had done when formulating doctrine.

The first such literary production is the *Life of Antony* by Athanasius of Alexandria, written soon after Antony's death. Athanasius wrote that Antony chose to change his life when he heard the gospel story of Christ's counsel to the rich young man: "If you wish to be perfect, go, sell your possessions and give the money to the poor ... then come, follow me" (Matthew 19:21). His basic motive was thus the full discipleship of Christ and his command to be perfect (Matthew 5:48). The *Life of Antony* became a "best-seller" in the fourth century, rooting the monastic life in the scriptures and providing a pattern that would inspire many. In his *Confessions* (Book 8.6.14–15), Augustine, who had never heard of Christian monks, is amazed to learn of men who had been converted to an ascetical life by reading the *Life of Antony*. The primary model for the monastic life came to be seen as Jesus himself, who had no family but his followers (Mark 3:33–35). Other biblical models included the prophets of Israel, the ascetical preacher John the Baptist, and Saint Paul, who seems not to have been married and who recommended celibacy as superior to marriage (1 Corinthians 7:8). Another biblical inspiration was the communal sharing of property in the Jerusalem church (Acts 2:44–45). The monastic goal was to anticipate the "angelic life": "For in the resurrection, they neither marry nor are given in marriage, but are like angels in heaven" (Matthew 22:30).

Evagrius of Pontus (345–399) articulated the most influential account of the monastic life. A cleric from Cappadocia, he spent the last 17 years of his life among the desert fathers at Nitria and the Cells. In his writings, he systematized their teachings by providing the monastic life with a theoretical framework. He divided it into two stages, each with a set of ascetical disciplines and specific goals. First is "practice," which is devoted to the struggle to subdue human appetites and passions of all kinds. Evagrius identified eight principal passions or "thoughts" (harmful psychological tendencies) that cause spiritual illness and thereby keep the monk from truly loving God and neighbor: gluttony, lust, love of money, sadness, anger, *acēdia* (a term hard to translate, but expressing a combination of boredom, restlessness, listlessness, discouragement, and despondency), vanity, and pride. His writings helped monks recognize these passions and overcome them, often by conceptualizing the struggle against them as battle with demons. The goal of "practice" was *apatheia*, or freedom from the passions, understood as a state of spiritual health and acquisition of virtues. This was not an end in itself, but a stepping-stone to unimpeded love of God and neighbor and the higher stages of the monastic life. The second stage was "knowledge," in which the monk initially strives to gain insight into God by contemplating the inner essence of natures created by God, and then the spiritual meaning of the scriptures. Evagrius calls the highest level of knowledge "theology," in which the monk experiences the vision of God and gains intimate knowledge of the Trinity. The spiritual practice most associated with this second stage is "pure prayer," namely, prayer that is imageless, wordless, and unceasing. Evagrius' scheme of the monastic life, his catalogue of the principal passions, and other aspects of his theories became singularly influential in all branches of Christianity. For example, his list of the eight passions is the origin of the later "seven deadly sins" in Western Christianity.

Monasticism became popular in the Latin West too, starting in the late fourth century, inspired by accounts of monastic theory and practice coming from the East. Yet Western monasticism developed its own unique approach, as it was largely animated by clerics and bishops in urban centers and cenobitic in orientation, in contrast to Eastern monasticism's lay movements of anchorites in the desert. Athanasius' *Life of Antony* was twice translated into Latin by 370, contributing much to the spread of monasticism in the West. The numerous writings of the priest Jerome (*c.*347–420), who lived as a monk in Bethlehem, popularized monasticism and ascetical ideals, particularly his *Lives* of the hermits and letters on monastic topics. He also translated some Pachomian literature into Latin. The *Life* of the monk-bishop Martin of Tours (d. 397) written by Sulpicius Severus did the same. Augustine established a cenobitic monastery of clerics in his episcopal residence in Hippo, for whom he compiled a set of *Rules*; a number of his letters and treatises also deal with monastic topics, such as *On the Work of Monks*, written on the value of monastic labor against monks who refused to work in order to devote more time to reading the scriptures.

The most important early monastic writer in the Latin West is the transplanted Easterner **John Cassian** (360–435). After ascetic training in both Bethlehem and Egypt, Cassian organized monasteries for monks, both male and female, in southeastern France. In his writings, he took the ideals of Eastern monasticism, and in particular the teachings of Evagrius, and adapted them for Westerners. For example, Cassian translated the Evagrian concept *apatheia* with the more biblical expression *puritas cordis*, or "purity of heart" (see Matthew 5:8). In *The Institutes*, he described the basic pattern of genuine cenobitic living and prescribed practical methods of overcoming the eight principal passions. In *The Conferences*, he outlined the progressive stages of the spiritual life and delved into key monastic topics such as prayer, spiritual knowledge, and friendship, as he had come to understand them from personal experience and from conversation with famous Eastern spiritual guides. The works of Cassian would have tremendous influence on the direction of Western monasticism, praised, for example, in the Rule of St. Benedict (see Chapter 13).

Monks often remained close enough to towns and villages to serve as advocates for those in need, to proclaim Christ's message to the high and the mighty, to heal the sick and counsel the troubled, and above all to serve as an example to others. Ordinary Christians saw them as living links to heaven, and often they traveled great distances to visit monks in remote locations to seek their advice and prayers. Their graves became pilgrimage centers. Christian asceticism was not a condemnation of the world as such but a personal struggle against the reign of sin and of the demons in the soul. It did not condemn Christians who continued to live in the world nor did it protest against the conversion of the empire to Christianity. In time, the writings produced during monasticism's formative period—lives of the desert fathers and mothers, their sayings, rules, letters, treatises, and so forth—would become central texts in the spiritual literature of the Christian tradition, and thus monasticism came to play a crucial role in the development of all branches of Christianity.

Religious Life and Church Architecture

The newly won support of the Roman emperors and the rapid growth of the church affected the worship life of Christians. This is shown most visibly in the development of church architecture. For the first three centuries, Christians met for the weekly Eucharist and for other activities in private homes adapted for worship. Of these "house churches," the best example is a mid-third century house church discovered in the Syrian town of Dura-Europas, on the Roman frontier with Persia. The town was abandoned by the Romans when the Persians attacked it in 256. As a result, it was not built over by later churches the way other house churches must have been. Only a short distance away, archaeologists found a Jewish synagogue. The house church consisted of an assembly hall, with a raised podium (presumably for the bishop), which had room for about 65 to 75 people. A smaller room had been altered into a baptistery (a place for Baptism), with a step-up basin covered by a canopy and arches. The baptistery's walls were decorated with frescoes (wall paintings) of subjects such as Adam and Eve, the Good Shepherd, the Samaritan Woman at the Well, David and Goliath, and Peter with Jesus, who was walking on the water.

Publicly identifiable Christian churches began to appear already during the reign of the pagan emperor Diocletian (284–305). The historian Eusebius says there was a Christian church directly across the street from Diocletian's palace, hinting at the security the Christian community enjoyed prior to the unexpected trauma of the Great Persecution. After the rise of Constantine, church construction mushroomed, with the help of imperial subsidies, in order to accommodate the crowds of new converts and to celebrate the church's new status.

Figure 9–3 Church of Santa Sabina in Rome, early fifth century, showing the basilica plan.

These new buildings were of three types. The most common is called a **basilica** (from the Greek word for "royal") because it was an adaptation of the standard rectangular layout of royal audience halls and public buildings in Roman cities. The Christian version of a basilica was an audience hall for Christ, the heavenly king. It consisted of a long rectangular building, often with two or even four side aisles along the central hall, which was called the *nave*. In larger churches, a shorter cross-section called a *transept* was often built at the end or partway down the nave. A rounded extension called an *apse* was usually found at the east end of the nave, in the direction of Jerusalem. The bishop's chair, his *cathedra* (a bishop's church is therefore known as a **cathedral**), was on the back wall of the apse, where he sat with his priests in a semicircle around him. Sermons were given from this chair, the symbol of his teaching authority.

The basilica served the weekly liturgy of the Eucharist. The east end of the nave, where the apse was located, was called the *sanctuary* ("holy place") and was set off from the rest of the church by a screen or a rail, reflecting the distinction between the clergy and the laity. The *altar*, where the bread and wine of the Eucharist were consecrated, was a removable table placed in the nave. The only other furniture was a raised pulpit for reading the scriptures. There were no pews or kneelers; the congregation stood for the service. The interiors of large churches were richly decorated with hanging curtains, marble, lamps, gold inlay, and *mosaics* (pictures made of small fragments of colored glass) on the walls of the apse and sanctuary. Scholars have often noted the contrast between the plain exterior of the buildings, usually unadorned brick, and the rich ornamentation of the interior: believers entered a place where the worship service, or *liturgy* (literally, "the people's work"), was a participation in the worship of the angels in the heavenly Jerusalem.

Figure 9–4 Sanctuary of the Church of Santa Sabina in Rome.

A quite different design from the long axis of the basilica was the centered structure of a type of church called a *memoria*, built to honor the tomb of a saint or martyr, or a holy site such as the tomb in Jerusalem where Christ was thought to have been laid after the Crucifixion. A *memoria* could be octagonal or cruciform in shape,

Figure 9–5 Baptistery of the Orthodox in Ravenna, late fourth/fifth centuries.

or even circular, in which case it was called a *rotunda*. The lines of vision oriented the visitor to the middle of the building, where the shrine or tomb lay. The *memoriae* are important witnesses to the growing Christian devotion to the physical remains of the dead and to the belief in the spiritual power of the saints, both in heaven and on earth. In the case of pilgrimage sites in Palestine, memorial churches testify to the growing desire to experience salvation in connection with the physical location of the saving events of Jesus' life.

A third type of Christian structure was the baptistery, where at Easter new Christians were initiated into the faith. A **baptistery**, like a *memoria*, had a centered design. Instead of a tomb, the focus was on the baptismal font into which the candidate stepped. The association with a tomb was intentional, since Christian Baptism was understood as an identification with Christ's death, burial, and resurrection. Baptisteries could be either freestanding or attached to churches.

Lived Religion: Liturgy in the Age of the Imperial Church
Christian Architecture—Basilicas

On May 9, A.D. 549, the basilica of Sant' Apollinare in Classe was dedicated in Ravenna, Italy. The new basilica was named for Ravenna's first bishop, Saint Apollinaris, who was martyred by the Emperor Valens.

The church was built in the style of the Roman administrative buildings that were given to the church by the emperor Constantine. It was an open rectangular space with a curved apse at one end and two side aisles. The apse that originally contained the seat of the Roman administrator was modified to contain the bishop's chair and the altar, built above the site of Apollinaris' martyrdom. The open space originally used for business accommodated the congregation, and the aisles were used for the procession of the clergy. The flat wooden ceiling supported by 24 marble columns, the windows high up in the walls, and the brick exterior were similar to the public building design, but the interior was decorated with Christian images.

The walls of the nave and the arch above the apse were covered with colorful mosaics. The most magnificent image in the apse depicted Christ surrounded by symbols of the four evangelists. Below them were the 12 apostles, palms which represented justice, and the archangels Michael and Gabriel. In the center of the apse was the Crux Gemmata or Jeweled Cross and the face of Christ, floating in a starry sky. In the lower section were precious gems from which 12 lambs emerge, representing the 12 apostles. Between the windows were the four bishops who founded Ravenna's basilicas, each holding a book. The choice of these images was meant to fight Arianism, a heresy that denied the divinity of Christ. The beauty of the basilica gave glory to God, taught orthodox Christian doctrine, and brought honor to the city of Ravenna.

The religious life of ordinary Christians was oriented around the sacraments of Baptism and the Eucharist. In the fourth century, Baptism for adults was still common, with many people intentionally deferring their Baptism until adulthood. Infant Baptism did not become the norm, apparently, until the fifth century. Most lay people received the Eucharist each week, unless they were **catechumens** (candidates for Baptism who were undergoing instruction in the Christian religion) or **penitents** (people who were denied Communion because of serious sin such as murder, adultery, or apostasy), both

Figure 9–6 The apse of Sant' Apollinare, Ravenna.

of whom had to leave the liturgy after the biblical readings and the sermon. Penitents for serious sin usually performed a lengthy public **penance** (a penalty) before they could be readmitted to Communion. Postbaptismal forgiveness for serious sin was generally extended just once, after public confession to the bishop and his clergy. Otherwise, fasting, works of charity, and prayers, such as the Our Father (Matthew 6:9–13), were recommended as the normal means of forgiveness for less serious sins.

The familiar year-long cycle of Christian religious feasts began to take shape during the fourth century, anchored by Easter and its season of penitential preparation called **Lent**. Following Easter came the season of **Pentecost** (commemorating the day on which the Holy Spirit descended upon the apostles), a time of joy and also of further instruction for the newly baptized. Christ's birth (Christmas) was celebrated in the West on December 25, previously the pagan feast of the Unconquered Sun. The feast days of the martyrs' deaths were also becoming more prominent points in the calendar, and sometimes the occasion of riotous celebration—to the consternation of the bishops, who realized that some of the enthusiasm was a carry-over of pagan habits of feasting at the graveside of deceased family members.

Key Terms

abbot
Alexander
Antony of Egypt
   monasticism
Apollinarius of Laodicaea
Arius
asceticism
Athanasius
baptistery
Basil of Caesarea
Basilica
cenobitic monasticism
Constantinople
Cappadocian Fathers
catechumens

cathedral
Constantine
Council of Nicaea
Council of
   Constantinople
Council of Ephesus
Council of Chalcedon
ecumenical council
Eutyches
Evagrius of Pontus
homoousios
Gregory of Nazianzus
Gregory of Nyssa
John Cassian
Lent

memoria
monk
Monophysite
Nestorius
Nicene Creed
Pachomius
papacy
patriarch
penance
penitent
Pentecost
pope
Shenoute of Atripe
Theodosius I
Theotokos

Questions for Reading

1. In what ways did Constantine affect the long-term development of the Christian tradition? Assess both the positive and the negative aspects of the new partnership between Christianity and the state.

2. In rejecting Arius' teachings, the Council of Nicaea ruled that the Son was "same-in-substance" with the Father. What did Arius teach, and why did Christians like Alexander and Athanasius oppose his teaching?

3. How did the Cappadocians contribute toward the definition of the Trinity as this doctrine was declared at the Council of Constantinople? What are the distinctive features of pro-Nicene Trinitarian theology?

4. Contrast the different concerns and emphases in understanding the union of divine and human in the Incarnation as we find them in Nestorius and Cyril. Explain how each preserves the impassibility of the Word.

5. What was the teaching of the Council of Chalcedon on the union of divine and human in the Incarnation? How is this teaching indebted to Cyril, and how does it reject the teachings of Nestorius and Eutyches? Why did many Eastern Christians refuse to accept the council's definition?

6. During the period of the fourth and fifth centuries, what was the status of the pope, the bishop of Rome, in the universal church? Describe this both from the Roman point of view, as seen in the writings of Pope Leo I, and from the point of view of Eastern bishops.

7. What was the historical circumstance in which monasticism arose? What was the monastic movement's basic motive and biblical models?

8. Describe how Athanasius, Evagrius of Pontus, and John Cassian contributed to the dissemination of the monastic teachings to ordinary Christians.

9. How did the floor plan of the church design called the basilica reflect the distinction between laity and clergy in the church?

Works Consulted/Recommended Reading

Athanasius of Alexandria. 1980. *Life of Antony and the Letter to Marcellinus.* Translated and Introduction by Robert C. Gregg. New York: Paulist Press.

Ayres, Lewis. 2004. *Nicaea and its Legacy: An Approach to Fourth-Century Trinitarian Theology.* Oxford: Oxford University Press.

Barnes, T.D. 1981. *Constantine and Eusebius.* Cambridge, MA: Harvard University Press.

Barnes, T.D. 2010. *Early Christian Hagiography and Roman History.* Tübingen: Mohr Siebeck.

Barnes, T.D. 2011. *Constantine: Dynasty, Religion, and Power in the Later Roman Empire.* Chichester: Wiley-Blackwell.

Baynes, Norman H. 1955. "Eusebius and the Christian Empire." In *Byzantine Studies and Other Essays,* 168–72. London: Athalone Press.

Brown, Peter. 1981. *The Cult of the Saints: Its Rise and Function in Latin Christianity.* Chicago, IL: University of Chicago Press.

Brown, Peter. 1988. *The Body and Society: Men, Women, and Sexual Renunciation in Early Christianity.* New York: Columbia University Press.

Brown, Peter. 2012. *Through the Eye of a Needle: Wealth, the Fall of Rome, and the Making of Christianity in the West, 350–550 AD.* Princeton, NJ: Princeton University Press.

Chitty, Derwas. 1966. *The Desert a City: An Introduction to the Study of Egyptian and Palestinian Monasticism under the Christian Empire.* Crestwood, NY: St. Vladimir's Seminary Press.

Clément, Olivier. 2003. *You Are Peter: An Orthodox Theologian's Reflection on the Exercise of Papal Primacy.* Hyde Park, NY: New City Press.

DelCogliano, Mark, ed. 2019. *The Cambridge Edition of Early Christian Writings.* Vol. 3, *Christ.* Cambridge: Cambridge University Press.

Drake, H.A. 1976. *In Praise of Constantine: A Historical Study and New Translation of Eusebius' Tricennial Orations.* Berkeley, CA: University of California Press.

Eusebius of Caesarea. 1999. *Life of Constantine.* Translated with Introduction and Commentary by Averil Cameron and Stuart G. Hall. Oxford: Clarendon Press.

Evagrius of Pontus. 2003. *The Greek Ascetic Corpus.* Translated and Introduction by Robert E. Sinkewicz. Oxford: Oxford University Press.

Hanson, R.P.C. 1988. *The Search for the Christian Doctrine of God: The Arian Controversy 318–381.* Edinburgh: T&T Clark.

Harmless, William. 2004. *Desert Christians: An Introduction to the Literature of Early Monasticism.* Oxford: Oxford University Press.

Jensen, Robin Margaret. 2000. *Understanding Early Christian Art.* London: Routledge.

Jones, Christopher P. 2014. *Between Pagans and Christians.* Cambridge, MA: Harvard University Press.

Kelly, J. N.D. 1972. *Early Christian Creeds.* 3rd edn. New York: Longman.

MacMullen, Ramsay. 1984. *Christianizing the Roman Empire (A.D. 100–400).* New Haven, CT: Yale University Press.

MacMullen, Ramsay. 2006. *Voting about God in Early Church Councils.* New Haven, CT: Yale University Press.

Mathews, Thomas. 1993. *The Clash of the Gods: A Reinterpretation of Early Christian Art.* Princeton, NJ: Princeton University Press.

McGuckin, John A. 1994. *St. Cyril of Alexandria: The Christological Controversy, Its History, Theology, and Texts.* Leiden: E.J. Brill.

Meer, F. van der, and Christine Mohrmann. 1958. *Atlas of the Early Christian World.* Translated and edited by Mary F. Nelson and H.H. Rowley. London: Nelson.

Radde-Gallwitz, Andrew, ed. 2017. *The Cambridge Edition of Early Christian Writings.* Vol. 1. *God.* Cambridge: Cambridge University Press.

Tsafrir, Yoram, ed. 1993. *Ancient Churches Revealed.* Washington, DC: Israel Exploration Society and Biblical Archaeological Society.

Weitzmann, Kurt, ed. 1979. *Age of Spirituality: Late Antique and Early Christian Art, Third to Seventh Century.* New York: Metropolitan Museum of Art.

Wilken, Robert L. 2003. *The Spirit of Early Christian Thought: Seeking the Face of God.* New Haven, CT: Yale University Press.

Chapter

10

AUGUSTINE OF HIPPO

TIMELINE

A.D. 311	Beginnings of the Donatist schism.
A.D. 354	Augustine is born in Thagaste in North Africa.
c.A.D. 374	Augustine joins the dualistic religion of the Manichees.
A.D. 384	Augustine arrives in Milan and meets Ambrose.
A.D. 387	Augustine is baptized by Bishop Ambrose.
c.A.D. 388	Pelagius comes to Rome to teach.
A.D. 391	Augustine is ordained a presbyter.
A.D. 396	Augustine becomes bishop of Hippo in North Africa.
A.D. 397–401?	Augustine writes the *Confessions*.
c.A.D. 410	Caelestius, one of Pelagius' disciples, begins to teach Pelagian doctrines in North Africa.
A.D. 410	Sack of Rome by the Visigoths; two years later Augustine begins to write *On the City of God* in response to the disaster.
A.D. 411	State-mandated conference in Carthage tries for definitive resolution of Donatist schism.
A.D. 418	The teachings of Pelagius are condemned by the bishop of Rome, and Pelagius and Caelestius are banished by the emperor.
A.D. 430	Augustine's death.

Among Western Christian thinkers in the early church, **Augustine of Hippo** was surely the greatest and the most influential (Origen of Alexandria has that honor among Eastern Christian thinkers). The sheer extent of his work is staggering. Augustine wrote hundreds of treatises and sermons, ranging from philosophical discussions of the nature of good and evil, to moral essays on marriage and celibacy, to commentaries on the books of the Old and New Testaments, to speculative theological treatises on the Trinity, and much more. Western Christian notions of original sin and grace received their distinctive character from Augustine's teaching. Catholic understandings of the sacraments and the nature of the church were also definitively shaped by his work. Augustine's thinking even affected Christian views on the relation between the church and the wider political and social world.

One of the remarkable things about Augustine in contrast to most ancient people is that we do actually know a lot about his life. Not only has he been blessed with gifted biographers (ancient and modern), but Augustine himself, in his *Confessions*, also narrated in some detail the course of his first 33 years. Although the *Confessions* is carefully constructed to convey Augustine's later theological understanding and interpretation of his life, nonetheless the basic accuracy of the events that he describes is not disputed.

HISTORICAL SITUATION

Augustine was born in the year 354 in the small backwater town of Thagaste in the Roman province of North Africa (modern-day Algeria). Barely 40 years had passed since the first Roman emperor had embraced the Christian faith, and it would take some time before Christianity became the official religion of the Roman Empire. The first 50 years of Augustine's life saw a dramatic change in the character of the church and society, which in many ways mirrored his own life and concerns.

The rise of Constantine marked the end of nearly 300 years of intermittent persecution by the Roman authorities; the age of the martyrs had come to an end. The Christian church could now look forward to an unparalleled period of growth and development. Large numbers flocked to the Christian communities, encouraged by the imperial favor now bestowed on the Christian religion. Needless to say, these converts did not always reflect high standards of morality, and Christian preachers in the late fourth century A.D. often expressed their frustration at those who did not cease to be "pagan" when they entered the church doors. Some Christian teachers even looked back with nostalgia to the age of persecutions, when (so they claimed) the threat of death had produced more authentic Christians.

The question of how to be an authentic Christian was one that troubled many Christians in the late fourth century, and it hovers persistently over Augustine's *Confessions*. The monastic movement, the origins of which were discussed in Chapter 9, had posed the question in the starkest possible way: Is it necessary to abandon the city, to leave all that bound one to "the world" (sex, marriage, career, family) in order to follow Christ faithfully? The words of Jesus from Matthew's Gospel were echoed again and again in the stories of the lives and deeds of the holy men and women who had given up the glamour and risks of secular society for monastic seclusion: "If you wish to be perfect, go, sell your possessions, and give the money to the poor ... then come, follow me" (Matthew 19:21, cited in Athanasius, *Life of Antony* 2).

The ascetic rejection of sex, marriage, property, and career became associated in the minds of many Christians with the path of perfection. The story of Augustine's

Figure 10–1 *Augustine of Hippo* (354–430), by Sandro Botticelli (1444–1510).

own life, as he narrated it in the first nine books of his *Confessions*, presupposes this understanding of Christian holiness. Augustine's decision to accept the Christian faith and to be baptized at the age of 33 was intimately connected with his decision to renounce marriage and a successful career. Judging from his account in the *Confessions*, being a married Christian seemed like a pale approximation of authentic Christianity.

If the conversion of the emperor Constantine and a widespread optimism about the new possibilities of a Christian Roman Empire characterized Christian hopes in the first half of Augustine's life, the opening decades of the fifth century brought profound disillusionment. In the year 410, the city of Rome was attacked and sacked by the Gothic chief Alaric (an Arian Christian). Twenty years later, as Augustine lay dying at Hippo, another northern people, the Vandals, were consolidating their control over Roman North Africa. The sack of Rome provoked Augustine to write *On the City of God*, his greatest book and the culmination of early Christian apologetics against paganism. Pagan critics blamed Christianity for Rome's decline. They said that when the empire ceased to worship the gods, the gods in turn had ceased to protect the empire. They also said that a perfectionist religion like Christianity was too other-worldly to be the religion of a great empire. Augustine responded by saying that Rome had largely been built on the lust for power (*libido dominandi*), and that the gods had never kept Rome safe from disaster. God was not supposed to be worshipped merely for the sake of this-worldly advantage—God would use all empires and kingdoms, Christian and non-Christian alike, for his own purposes, which were often hidden from us; in this world, as Jesus had said, "your heavenly Father sends his sun and his rain on the just and on the unjust alike" (Matthew 5:45), a text Augustine was fond of quoting. The church, composed of saints and sinners alike, was the City of God on pilgrimage to the heavenly City of God. In the meantime, Christians were obliged to contribute to the peace of the earthly city, even though that earthly city should never be confused with the Kingdom of God.

Early Life and Conversion of Augustine

Augustine came from a family of modest means, not impoverished, but not excessively wealthy. His father does not seem to have had any serious religious affiliation until he became a Christian late in life. Augustine's mother, **Monica**, on the other hand, was a devout Christian who prayed eagerly for her son to embrace the faith and who, as time went on, exerted a great influence upon him. At a young age, Augustine was enrolled as a catechumen (literally "a person undergoing instruction") in the church. But for someone of Augustine's depth and complexity, there was to be no easy entrance into the Christian religion.

Part of the difficulty stemmed from Augustine's own acute and restless intellect. He excelled in school, especially in the study of Latin rhetoric, or public speaking. After studying in his hometown of Thagaste, in nearby Madaurus, and later in the capital Carthage, Augustine became a teacher of Latin rhetoric. In an effort to escape horrendous teaching conditions and rowdy students, Augustine traveled from Carthage to Rome to Milan, where he received a distinguished post as professor of rhetoric.

But Augustine's love of ancient Latin literature drew him further and further from the Christianity of his mother. At the age of 19, Augustine read a philosophical work of Cicero, called the *Hortensius*, which included a review and critique of the various schools of ancient philosophy. The treatise filled him with a desire to "love and see and pursue and hold fast and strongly embrace wisdom itself, wherever found" (*Confessions* III.iv.8). When he dipped into the scriptures to see how they compared with the wisdom of Cicero, Augustine found them "unworthy in comparison," that is, inferior in literary style. More than ten years were to pass before Augustine could read the Bible again and take it seriously.

The other significant aspect of Augustine's life at this time was his discovery of the pleasures of sex. As he described it in the *Confessions*, the "bubbling impulses of puberty befogged and obscured my heart so that it could not see the difference between love's serenity and lust's darkness" (II.ii.2). After what may have been an initial period of promiscuity, Augustine settled down into a monogamous relationship, known to the Romans as "**concubinage**" (literally, "sleeping together"). Such liaisons were common, especially between upwardly mobile young men and women of slave or lower-class backgrounds. Augustine seems always to have regarded the relationship as a temporary one, a sexual convenience until it was time to contract a marriage with a woman of wealth and proper standing. Nonetheless, he loved the woman deeply and with her had a son, whom they named **Adeodatus** (literally, "gift of God"). One of the most poignant passages in the *Confessions* is Augustine's description of the pain he felt when he and his partner finally separated after 13 years together: "My heart which was deeply attached was cut and wounded, and left a trail of blood. She had returned to Africa vowing that she would never go with another man" (*Confessions* VI.xv.25). Nowhere, however, in all his voluminous works, does Augustine ever tell us her name.

At around this time (*c.*374), when Augustine was about 20 years old, he became involved with a new religion called **Manicheism**. It derives its name from its founder Mani, a prophet and visionary who lived in the third century A.D. in Mesopotamia. Mani was born into a baptist religious sect that lived on the margins of Judaism and Christianity. As a result of his reading and visionary experiences, he believed he was inspired to found a new universal religion that would supersede all previously existing religions: Christianity, Judaism, Buddhism, and Zoroastrianism (the official religion of the Persian Empire, in which Mani was born). At the heart of Mani's teaching was the notion that from the beginning of time there have existed two fundamental realities: a principle or power of good (the kingdom of Light) and a power of evil (the kingdom of Darkness). The kingdom of Light basically consisted of spirit, and the kingdom of Darkness consisted of matter and the dark elements, such as smoke. These two powers, according to the Manichees, were co-eternal and co-equal.

Because of its inherent restlessness and desire for conquest, the kingdom of Darkness invaded the kingdom of Light and succeeded in swallowing up a large chunk of it. By generating an elaborate series of spiritual beings, the kingdom of Light defended itself and managed to produce a created world, though part of that world (the material part) was considered to be evil. The aim of this creation was to liberate the elements of spiritual light that were still trapped in evil matter. The waxing and waning of the moon for the Manichees signaled special times when light was being returned to its source. One special place for the liberation of spirit from matter was the bodies of the Manichean leaders (the **Elect**). When these special persons, who were celibate and vegetarian, ate selected fruits and vegetables, their digestive organs were thought to facilitate the escape of the light from darkness. To engage in sex or to partake of meat, the Manichees believed, was to perpetuate the enslavement of spirit in matter. Although both of these activities were allowed to those on the fringes of the sect (the **Hearers**), they were forbidden to the Elect.

Augustine remained a Hearer in the Manichean sect for nine years. He was attracted by their clear answer to a question that would long exercise his mind: Where does evil come from? Since the Manichees believed (like some of the second-century Gnostics) that the God of the Old Testament was a vicious demon, their criticisms of the Hebrew scriptures appealed to Augustine's sense that the Bible was a document unworthy of a philosopher. For example, the Manichees mocked the polygamy (multiple wives) of the patriarchs in Genesis as sexual degeneracy.

Most of all, Augustine was persuaded by the Manichees' dualistic conception of the human person. The Manichees could explain why it was that Augustine felt himself torn between his intellectual desire for truth and wisdom, on the one hand, and his craving for sexual delight and worldly success, on the other hand. Their answer was that Augustine's spirit belonged to the kingdom of Light, but his body belonged to the kingdom of Darkness. In other words, Manichean dualism helped explain Augustine to himself and, significantly, absolved him of responsibility for the actions of his "wicked" half. When Augustine finally did come to reject the views of the Manichees, an important aspect of his conversion away from Manicheism and toward orthodox Christianity came through a recognition that the human person is a unity and that this unity implies moral accountability.

During most of his 20s, Augustine remained attached to the Manichees. However, as he tells the story in the *Confessions*, he was growing increasingly skeptical and critical of Manichean theology. In these years, Augustine became interested in astrology and discovered the disconcerting fact that astrologers generally had more reliable scientific data (e.g., for predicting eclipses of the sun and moon) than did the Manichees. This rational failure of the Manichees' science was troubling (see *Confessions* V.iii.6–v.9), and Augustine soon realized that even the most authoritative Manichean teachers were unable to answer his questions. Even more dissatisfying to someone as philosophically minded as Augustine was the Manichees' view of God (the kingdom of Light) as fundamentally weak and vulnerable to invasion by evil. Augustine came to see that even though the Manichees believed in a so-called "spiritual" world (light, goodness) in conflict with a "material" world (darkness, evil), their idea of God was really modeled on a kind of material substance. Such a God, Augustine came to hold, was not worth believing in (see *Confessions*, Book VII).

By the time that Augustine arrived in Milan, in autumn 384, he had virtually abandoned the Manichees but had not yet found a persuasive alternative. Augustine now encountered certain ideas and individuals who were to lead him back to the Christianity of his youth. He began to attend the sermons of **Ambrose of Milan**, a learned Christian bishop and former provincial governor. Ambrose was just the sort of eloquent, educated Christian that the young Augustine could admire. Furthermore, Ambrose was skilled in the allegorical method of biblical interpretation, which he had learned from Greek Christian writers, such as Origen of Alexandria. Ambrose taught Augustine that the embarrassing aspects of the Old Testament, which the Manichees had held up to ridicule, could be interpreted nonliterally, that is, as symbols of moral or spiritual truths.

Even more significant, at the urging of Simplicianus, a priest of Milan who had begun to serve as mentor to the young professor, Augustine began to read certain "books of the Platonists," namely, the writings of the third-century A.D. philosopher Plotinus, as recorded by his disciple Porphyry. In these writings, Augustine found a version of Plato's philosophy, now called "Neoplatonism," which gave him a new way to think about God, the world, and evil that enabled him finally to break with the harsh dualism of the Manichees. Neoplatonism also was to serve as a sort of intellectual bridge that would lead Augustine ultimately to Christianity.

In the teaching of Plotinus, God was a reality that surpassed all human categories of knowing or describing. In fact, rather than use the name "God," Plotinus preferred to speak of the supreme Being simply as "the One," to characterize its primary quality of pure simplicity or oneness. While the One could not be comprehended or grasped in its essence or entirety by the human mind (whose knowledge is always partial and fragmentary), nonetheless the Neoplatonists taught that this One produced a succession of other realities or substances from itself: Intellect, Soul, and, finally, Matter. Each level of being proceeds from the higher one and depends on the higher level for its life and order, just as in a human being one might say that the mind or soul serves to organize the physical functions of the body. Even Matter, Plotinus taught, was capable of being formed and directed toward the good, although left on its own it tended to disorder, corruption, and non-being. Only in this limited and non-moral sense did the Neoplatonists speak of Matter as "evil."

Augustine found Neoplatonism an exhilarating alternative to the views of the Manichees. Here was a vision of God as truly supreme, the source of all being, goodness, and beauty; God was Being itself, the "I am who I am" of Exodus 3:14. If God and all that came from God was truly good, Augustine reasoned, then evil itself cannot be a substance in the sense that the Manichees taught. Evil (in the non-moral sense) must be the tendency in the lowest level of creation toward disorder, corruption, and non-being, and this is the very opposite of the order, life, and being that come from God. But Plotinus also taught that there is evil in the moral sense, when rational creatures freely choose to turn toward the lower goods rather than toward the One who is their source. As Augustine describes it in the *Confessions*: "I inquired what wickedness is; and I did not find a substance but a perversity of will twisted away from the highest substance, you O God, toward inferior things, rejecting its own inner life and swelling with external matter" (VII. xvi.22).

Neoplatonism, Augustine tells us, seemed to be profoundly compatible with what he knew of Christianity, especially as it was being preached by Bishop Ambrose. Its views of God, creation, and evil could easily be assimilated; the Christian elements that were missing from Neoplatonism (Augustine tells us in hindsight) were the doctrine of divine incarnation and the notion of divine grace (*Confessions* VII.ix, xviii–xxi). The *Confessions* says little about what led Augustine at this time to move toward an intellectual acceptance of Christian teachings, but we are well informed about the moral dimensions of his struggle to embrace Christianity fully. In the eighth book of the *Confessions*, Augustine describes in vivid detail the emotional turmoil he experienced as he tried to bring himself to the point of making a decision to be baptized.

The basic problem was that Augustine saw his conversion to Christianity as entailing a conversion to the monastic or ascetic way of life; to be a serious Christian meant that Augustine would have to abandon his career and his desire for sex, marriage, and family. After more than fifteen years of sexual activity, Augustine found himself subject to a habit that he no longer had the power to break:

> I ... was bound not by an iron imposed by anyone else but by the iron of my own choice.... The consequence of a distorted will is passion. By servitude to passion, habit is formed, and habit to which there is no resistance becomes necessity.
>
> (*Confessions* VIII.v.10)

Augustine felt himself torn between two "wills," between two competing desires, neither of which was strong enough to overcome the other, and he found the internal division devastating.

In the famous garden scene in book eight of the *Confessions*, Augustine describes the moment when he finally decided to entrust himself into the hands of God. Looking back on his decision ten years later, as he wrote the *Confessions*, Augustine saw the key to his conversion as his allowing God to produce in him the work of "continence" (that is, self-control in the face of tempting desires, which in this case meant abstention from sex), which he was unable to will on his own. As the figure of Lady Continence says in the paragraph preceding the garden scene:

> Why are you relying on yourself, only to find yourself unreliable? Cast yourself upon him, do not be afraid. He will not withdraw himself so that you fall. Make the leap without anxiety; he will catch you and heal you.
>
> (*Confessions* VIII.xi.27)

Only after experiencing himself as powerless and after reading the passage from Paul (Romans 13:14: "put on the Lord Jesus Christ and make no provision for the flesh in its lusts") did Augustine find the division within himself healed: "it was as if a light of relief from all anxiety flooded into my heart. All the shadows of doubt were dispelled" (*Confessions* VIII.xii.29).

Augustine's experience of his own conversion and his subsequent reflection on it were to prove foundational for the development of his theological vision. Central to this vision was Augustine's notion that human beings are impelled to their actions by their own deepest desires, by their "love." "A body by its weight tends to move towards its proper place .... My weight is my love. Wherever I am carried, my love is carrying me." After the first sin of Adam and Eve, Augustine believed, all human beings are born with an inherent tendency to a pernicious form of self-love, a tendency to love the lower goods of the world rather than the God who is their source.

Figure 10–2 *The Conversion of St. Augustine*, by Fra Angelico (1395–1455).

Only the grace of God, the power of the Holy Spirit, can heal the damaged human will and transform it into a will that loves God and self properly: "By your gift we are set on fire and carried upwards: we grow red hot and ascend ... Lit by your fire, your good fire, we grow red-hot and ascend, as we move upwards 'to the peace of Jerusalem'" (*Confessions* XIII.ix.10).

Augustine and the Ordering of our Loves

The most important concept in St. Augustine's view of morality is love. As he says, "For when we ask how good a person is, we do not ask what he believes or what he hopes for, but what he loves." For Augustine, love is a movement of the soul toward something we perceive to be good. There are three important points to understand here. First, love is fundamentally a passion or a desire. A basic feature of being human is the experience of wanting things and being drawn toward things and other people. This fundamental instinct is in itself natural and in the abstract, morally neutral.

A second point is that we are capable of directing our loves. We are not creatures who are simply driven by our desires. Augustine holds that persons have a certain freedom to choose particular loves on which to act. We have a will, as he famously discusses in book eight of *Confessions*. We have the intellectual ability to perceive and acknowledge the goodness of things and persons.

A third point considers our ability to perceive and to act on what is good in the objective order of reality. Knowing and doing what is good is not easy. Since the Fall of Adam and Eve, humans experience not only multiple loves, but we experience some loves more strongly than others, namely, the loves that give us temporary pleasure. He calls this form of love "cupidity." Pursuing these loves gives us little lasting fulfillment. Indeed, they soon leave us "empty" and wanting more.

This third point is morality, properly speaking. The good person is marked by "rightly ordered love." There is an objective and hierarchical order in the goodness of creation: some things are "better" than others, though every being is good in its own way. The highest good, the good that gives goodness to everything else that exists, is God. Augustine holds that we must love God first of all, for God's own sake; and everything else proportionately. Morality, then, consists in developing the intellectual ability to "see" the relative goodness in all things and then to direct one's love accordingly.

AUGUSTINE THE BISHOP

In spring 387, Augustine was baptized by Bishop Ambrose at the Easter vigil. He returned to Africa in the following year, shortly after the death of his mother in Italy. Augustine had originally hoped to live quietly in a monastic community with some devoted friends, but a man of his talents was much needed in the North African church. By the year 391, he had been ordained presbyter (literally "elder" or priest) of the seaport town of Hippo Regius, and by 396 he had become bishop. Though he was now tossed into an active life, he remained supportive of the monastic movement and even formulated guidelines for the communal living of monks and nuns (*The Rule of St. Augustine*), which became very influential in the Middle Ages.

From this point onward, during the final three decades of his life, Augustine was to be preoccupied with preaching, pastoral concerns, and the writing of numerous theological and polemical treatises against the pagans, the Manichees, and other Christian heretics. Among the controversies that absorbed his attention, the debates with the Donatists and the Pelagians were most bitter and the most consequential for later Christian theology.

The Donatist Schism

The North Africa to which Augustine returned in 388 was deeply divided in a schism that had already lasted for nearly a century. During the last persecution (*c.*303), the emperor Diocletian had issued an edict directing Christian clergy to hand over all copies of the scriptures to be burned. Some bishops had cooperated with the authorities, and others had pretended to do so by handing over copies of heretical writings instead. In North Africa, where the spirit of the martyrs had long been strong, opposition to any collaboration with the persecutors was especially fierce. Those who handed over the scriptures were dubbed *traditores* ("traitors") and were judged guilty of apostasy (renunciation of one's religious faith); many Christians refused to acknowledge that these bishops or priests had any authority in the church.

In 311, when Caecilian, a new bishop of Carthage, was elected, great opposition arose. One of the bishops who had consecrated Caecilian, it was claimed, had been a *traditor.* Furthermore, Caecilian himself had had a dubious record during the recent persecution. A large number of bishops in North Africa refused to recognize the legitimacy of Caecilian and soon a rival bishop of Carthage was elected in his place. The opponents of Caecilian, soon to be called **Donatists** (from Donatus, the name of one of the early rival bishops of Carthage), appealed to the emperor Constantine. After consulting with the bishop of Rome and a Western council, the emperor decided against the Donatists. From this point onward, the Donatists regarded all non-Donatist Christians as illegitimate; Donatism in their view represented the true Christian church, and outside of that church there was no salvation.

Throughout the fourth century, Donatism thrived in North Africa, especially in the countryside where hostility to Roman rule had always run high. In some places, roving gangs armed with clubs—called "Circumcellions" because of their association with rural shrines and altars—tried to enforce Donatism with violence. Some scholars have seen the movement as grounded in the social protest of the poor and disenfranchised against the power of wealthy landowners. But there was a serious theological side to Donatism as well. The Donatists saw themselves as the true continuation of the church of the martyrs. They emphasized that the church must be pure and holy and set apart from the world. As long as a bishop remained allied with the (false) church of Caecilian and his successors, the Donatists argued, he remained tainted by sin and unable to bestow the grace of God in any way. Donatists believed, therefore, that sacraments administered in the non-Donatist churches (e.g., Baptism) were invalid because those churches did not possess the power of the Holy Spirit.

In the 390s, when Augustine began his priesthood and episcopacy, Donatist Christians probably outnumbered Catholics in North Africa. Augustine immediately began to engage the Donatists in debate and to write polemical treatises against the sect. He challenged them on a variety of grounds. First, he questioned whether their historical facts were correct. He cited the evidence of investigations showing not only that Caecilian and his consecrators had not been *traditores,* but also that certain Donatist bishops had been. But Augustine's most significant arguments were theological ones. Whatever holiness the Donatists might have possessed, he argued, was now destroyed by their schism. Unity is a primary characteristic of the church, and to violate that unity, Augustine taught, is to violate the essentials of Christian charity.

Furthermore, Augustine maintained, universality or catholicity was another distinguishing feature of the church. Both the promise made to Abraham (Genesis 12:3), which St. Paul had recalled (Galatians 3:8), and Jesus' own command to his disciples after the Resurrection (Acts 1:8), were prophecies of the worldwide spread of Christianity. The Donatist claim to represent the faithful remnant, the only pure and holy church, was as arrogant as it was unfounded. The true church, Augustine argues, is the catholic church, that is, the church of Christians united throughout the world. The holiness of the church is the holiness of Christ, not the holiness of human beings. In this life, good and bad persons are mixed together within the one body of the church. In fact, Augustine notes, in this life all people are stained by sin and that is why the church itself in all its members prays the words of the Lord's Prayer, "Forgive us our trespasses..."

In response to the Donatist notion that the sacraments administered by a sinful priest or bishop (that is, a *traditor*) were invalid, Augustine answered that Jesus Christ is the source of any grace conveyed in sacramental actions. Therefore, even when a minister is guilty of the gravest sins, the effectiveness of the sacraments themselves remains unchanged. A guilty priest brings greater guilt upon himself by his actions, Augustine argued, but the sacraments themselves remain effective. Augustine could even recognize the validity of the Baptisms conveyed by Donatist clergy, since they had been carried out in the proper form. Augustine's notion of the character of the sacraments, as well as his idea of the universality or catholicity of the church, were to become standard aspects of Catholic teaching from this point onward.

The Pelagian Controversy

It is ironic that Augustine's last and greatest opponents were to come from the very group that had so attracted him to orthodox Christianity: the monks and ascetics of Rome. Augustine's initial conversion to Christianity was very much a conversion to the life of ascetic renunciation and monastic seclusion. But in the decade or so after his conversion, leading up to his writing of the *Confessions* (*c.*397), Augustine's thought had begun to turn in a fundamentally different direction than that of most of the leaders of the ascetic movement. By the time he wrote the *Confessions*, Augustine had developed two distinctive notions that deeply troubled many of his contemporaries. One is his view that sin, in particular the **original sin** of Adam and Eve, has thoroughly damaged human nature. Even the newborn baby is not innocent of the tendency toward greed and envy, which is the sign of a distorted will in the human person (*Confessions* I.vii.11). The other distinctively "Augustinian" idea is that God's grace, the gift of charity bestowed by the Holy Spirit, is absolutely necessary to change the orientation of the human will and to direct the human heart toward God.

Before the time of Augustine, there had not been any extensive discussion among Christians about the effects of sin on the human will or the nature of the grace that saves humanity. If anything, in response to the fatalism and pessimism of Gnostics and Manichees, most Christians, especially among the Greek fathers of the church, taught that human nature remained fundamentally sound. Original sin, however real and pernicious it may have been, did not deprive human beings of the two great gifts that represented the divine image in humans: freedom and reason.

Especially in the monastic movement of the fourth century, we find Christian thinkers emphasizing that it is entirely within the power of human beings to free themselves from evil habits and to conform themselves to the precepts of Christ.

Pelagius was a monk from Britain who came to Rome probably about the same time as Augustine's last sojourn there (388). For more than 20 years, Pelagius taught and gave spiritual advice to Christians at Rome who were interested in pursuing the ascetic way of life. Like Augustine, Pelagius was a bitter opponent of the Manichees, and he attempted to undermine their influence among Christians. However, he was also a Christian reformer who sought to convince the wealthy and worldly Christians of Rome that they could be authentic Christians by turning away from sin and by living in simplicity and monastic rigor. In the process of developing this spiritual teaching, Pelagius also expressed views about sin, grace, and human nature that led to a serious conflict with Augustine.

The core of Pelagius' teaching, which he may have derived from Eastern Christian theologians, was that God has given human beings the power to know right from wrong (reason) and the ability to choose to do either (free will). To deny either of these, Pelagius reasoned, was to question the goodness of God's creation and to make nonsense of the Christian belief concerning the justice of rewards and punishments in the afterlife. God would be unjust to punish us for sins that we could not avoid. True, there is sin in the world, especially in the social customs of the non-Christian world, and sin can sometimes create habits that become almost second nature. Nevertheless, Pelagius argued, with sufficient effort and help from the grace of God (that is, the Jewish Law, the teachings of Christ, and the forgiveness of sins), human beings are capable of overcoming the power of sin, and they can live holy lives. The proof of the basic integrity of human nature, according to Pelagius, could be seen in the many examples of those who lived virtuously even before the coming of Christ.

Pelagius' teaching appears to have caused no complaints during the decades when he taught in Rome. However, in the wake of Alaric's sack of Rome in 410, Pelagius and some followers left the city and fled to North Africa and eventually to Jerusalem. While visiting Carthage, one of Pelagius' less diplomatic disciples, Caelestius, began to teach Pelagian doctrines in an extreme form that shocked the North African bishops, Augustine among them. Caelestius denied that the sin of Adam and Eve caused harm to anyone but themselves. Newborn infants were born in exactly the same state in which Adam and Eve were originally created, that is, in innocence. The condemnation of Caelestius by a synod of African bishops (411) marks the beginning of the Pelagian controversy. For the next 20 years, Augustine actively attacked traces of Pelagian views wherever he found them. Ultimately, the theology of Augustine and the North African bishops was to triumph, at least in the West. In the year 418, the teachings of Pelagius were condemned by the bishop of Rome, and Pelagius and Caelestius were banished by the emperor.

At stake in the Pelagian controversy, as Augustine saw it, was the very notion of Christian salvation. If, as Pelagius claimed, human nature had been left fundamentally undamaged by original sin, then there was no need for Christ's saving death or the action of God's grace. The test case was the Baptism of newborn children: If it is appropriate to baptize infants (both Pelagius and Augustine agreed on this point), then the infants must have inherited from their parents some sin that needed to be washed away in Baptism. Augustine found further justification for his understanding of inherited guilt in Paul's letter to the Romans 5:12–21; Augustine's text of Romans 5:12, in the Old Latin translation, read, "*in whom* [i.e., Adam] all have sinned," whereas the Greek original merely said, "*inasmuch as* all have sinned"—the Old Latin version more explicitly implicated all humans in responsibility for Adam's sin. Augustine's view was also based on the notion that God's grace is necessary throughout human life in order to create in human beings the love that oriented them toward God. Whereas Pelagius had insisted on human freedom in order to urge people to take responsibility for their actions, Augustine saw this emphasis on human self-sufficiency as leading to pride. Human beings can take no credit for any good action, according to Augustine, since even the very will to do good has been created in them by the grace of God.

In the long run, Western Christian tradition was to side with the teaching of Augustine. Pelagianism was ultimately seen as too naive and optimistic a view of human nature after the Fall. On the other hand, there were also elements in Augustine's theology that the church did not embrace in their totality. One of these is the idea that God has decided beforehand that some people would be saved and others damned (**predestination**). In the course of the Pelagian controversy, Augustine eventually argued that, since salvation depends entirely on the will of God, God's grace must be completely effective and even irresistible; in other words, by not giving some people the grace to be saved, God was effectively choosing to condemn them.

Throughout the fifth century, especially in the monasteries of southern Gaul (modern-day France), some Christian monks and bishops questioned whether Augustine had gone too far in denying any role to the human will. While agreeing with Augustine on original sin and the absolute necessity of grace, these thinkers—who have come to be called, inaccurately, "semi-Pelagians"—argued that there must be cooperation between God and the person being saved, perhaps even a prior good disposition. If no human freedom was involved, they reasoned, there would be no point in preaching the gospel or offering correction to one's fellow monks. In a definition of faith issued at the Synod of Orange (529), the bishops of Gaul repeated the Augustinian teaching that God "first inspires in us both faith and love of himself, so that we will faithfully seek the sacrament of Baptism and then with his help be able to fulfill the things which please him after Baptism." Nonetheless, the bishops also emphasized that once grace has been received, the individual Christian must labor faithfully and cooperate with God's grace. There is no divine predestination to evil.

The questions raised in the Pelagian controversy were to be opened once again in the sixteenth century. When the Protestant reformers challenged the Roman Catholic practice of linking salvation with the performance of certain good works, they appealed to the authority of Augustine who had stressed the utter priority of God's grace before any human action. The Catholics responded by noting Augustine's teaching that God's grace creates in human beings a will transformed by love, which then desires to do good works. Both sides could appeal with some legitimacy to certain aspects of Augustine's teaching. Despite the divergences that developed between Protestant and Roman Catholic forms of Christianity, both sides still share Augustine's conviction that all human beings have lost their innocence in the sin of Adam and Eve and that the grace of the Holy Spirit must be given to move people toward God.

Another aspect of Augustine's teaching on original sin that was to have a great impact on the later Christian tradition was his understanding of the "**concupiscence**" or "lust of the flesh" and its effect on human sexuality. In one of his later writings, *The Literal Commentary on Genesis*, composed in the decade after the *Confessions*, Augustine attempted to deal in detail with the Genesis stories about human origins. As Augustine interpreted it, God had originally instructed human beings to "increase and multiply," but Adam and Eve had sinned before they had a chance to fulfill the divine command. One result of their eating of the tree of the knowledge of good and evil was a disruption within their own bodies: the presence of sexual desires that seemed to run contrary to the mind or will; it was the presence of this "animal impulse" (*bestialis motus*) that caused the first human beings to feel shame about their naked bodies (cf. Genesis 3:7). In addition to the other penalties for their sin (mortality, pain in childbirth, and difficulty in farming the earth), therefore, Augustine believed that a loss of control over sexual functions was a direct result and symptom of the first sin.

Augustine's "sexualized" interpretation of original sin provided a theological grounding for the popularity of ascetic behavior and especially of celibacy, but not all Christians agreed with Augustine on this point. The Italian bishop Julian of Eclanum, who was a supporter of Pelagius, argued that Augustine's teaching ended up portraying sex and marriage as inherently sinful and was essentially "Manichaean." The last decade of Augustine's life was spent in bitter debate with Julian, who had suffered exile for his support of Pelagius in 418. Augustine responded to Julian by pointing to his earlier writings on marriage and celibacy (e.g., *De bono coniugali* or *The Good of Marriage*). There he had insisted that marriage was something genuinely good, though inferior to celibacy. The goodness of marriage was threefold, Augustine had argued; it consisted in the good of procreation, the good of mutual faithfulness, and the good of permanence or indissolubility (the latter Augustine called its "sacrament," by which he meant its symbolism of Christ and the church). Augustine remained convinced that his teaching on the "three goods" of marriage could be reconciled with his equally firm belief in the evil of the "concupiscence of the flesh." As he put it, Christian spouses could make "a good use of a bad thing" when their marital intercourse was directed to procreation or to the support of marital fidelity. Augustine's arguments on behalf of the goods of marriage and the dangers of concupiscence eventually became central to the Western Christian tradition and still influence contemporary Catholic teaching.

Key Terms

Adeotatus	Donatists	original sin
Ambrose of Milan	Elect	Pelagius
Augustine	Hearers	predestination
concubinage	Manicheism	
concupiscence	Monica	

Questions for Reading

1. How did the rise of the monastic movement affect Augustine's thinking about marriage in his *Confessions*?
2. What were the conditions that led Augustine to compose *On the City of God*?
3. What were some of the main ideas of the Manichees? What made these ideas attractive to the young Augustine?
4. What were the main ideas of the Neoplatonists? How did Neoplatonism help to free Augustine from the Manichees?
5. What was the problem of the "two wills" (or the "divided will") that Augustine experienced prior to becoming Christian? How did the advice of Lady Continence help to resolve this problem?

6. How did the Donatist schism begin? What were the Donatists' main theological ideas?

7. What were Augustine's primary theological arguments against the Donatists?

8. What were the main ideas of the monk Pelagius? What were Augustine's primary theological arguments against Pelagianism?

9. How did Augustine's ideas about sin and grace lead to the notion of "predestination"? How did the Synod of Orange respond to this view of Augustine?

10. What were the positive and the negative effects of Augustine's teaching on marriage?

Works Consulted/Recommended Reading

Athanasius of Alexandria. 1980. *Life of Antony and the Letter to Marcellinus*. Translation and Introduction by Robert C. Gregg. New York: Paulist Press.

Bonner, G. 2002. *St. Augustine of Hippo. Life and Controversies*, 3rd edn. Norwich: Canterbury Press.

Bonner, G. 2007. *Freedom and Necessity: St. Augustine's Teaching on Divine Power and Human Freedom.* Washington, DC: The Catholic University of America Press.

Brown, Peter. 2000. *Augustine of Hippo: A Biography. A New Edition with an Epilogue*. Berkeley, CA: University of California Press.

Burns, J. Patout, and Robin M. Jensen. 2014. *Christianity in Roman North Africa: The Development of its Practices and Beliefs*. Grand Rapids, MI: William B. Eerdmans.

Chadwick, H. 1986. *Augustine*. Oxford: Oxford University Press.

Cooper, Stephen A. 2002. *Augustine for Armchair Theologians*. Louisville, KY: Westminster John Knox Press.

Dodaro, Robert. 2004. *Christ and the Just Society in the Thought of Augustine*. Cambridge: Cambridge University Press.

Dodaro, Robert, and George Lawless, eds. 2000. *Augustine and his Critics: Essays in Honour of Gerald Bonner*. London: Routledge.

Harrison, Carol. 2000. *Augustine: Christian Truth and Fractured Humanity*. Oxford: Oxford University Press.

Harrison, Carol. 2006. *Rethinking Augustine's Early Theology: An Argument for Continuity*. Oxford: Oxford University Press.

Hunter, David. 2002. "Augustine, Sermon 354A: Its Place in his Thought on Marriage and Sexuality." *Augustinian Studies* 33: 39–60.

Hunter, David. 2007. *Marriage, Celibacy, and Heresy in the Early Church: The Jovinianist Controversy*. Oxford: Oxford University Press.

Hunter, David, ed. 2018. *Marriage and Sexuality in Early Christianity*. Minneapolis, MN: Fortress Press.

Markus, R.A. 1989. *Conversion and Disenchantment in Augustine's Spiritual Career*. Villanova, PA: Villanova University.

Meilaender, Gilbert. 2006. *The Way that Leads There: Augustinian Reflections on the Christian Life*. Grand Rapids, MI: Wm. B. Eerdmans.

O'Donnell, James J. 1992. *Augustine: Confessions*. 3 vols. Oxford: Clarendon Press.

O'Donnell, James J. 2005. *Augustine: A New Biography*. New York: Ecco/HarperCollins.

Paffenroth, Kim, and Robert P. Kennedy. 2003. *A Reader's Companion to Augustine's Confessions*. Louisville, KY: Westminster/John Knox.

Rombs, Ronnie. 2006. *Saint Augustine and the Fall of the Soul: Beyond O'Connell and his Critics*. Washington, DC: The Catholic University of America Press.

TeSelle, Eugene. 1970. *Augustine the Theologian*. New York: Herder.

TeSelle, Eugene. 2006. *Augustine*. Abingdon Pillars of Theology. Nashville, TN: Abingdon.

Wetzel, James. 1992. *Augustine and the Limits of Virtue*. Cambridge: Cambridge University Press.

Chapter
11
EASTERN CHRISTIANITY

TIMELINE

A.D. 410	The Assyrian Church of the East gains administrative independence as the Christian church in Persian territory.
A.D. 451	In the century after the Council of Chalcedon, dissent against the council leads to the creation of non-Chalcedonian Eastern Christian churches in Armenia, Syria, Egypt, Ethiopia, Eritrea, and India.
A.D. 527–565	Reign of Justinian, greatest Byzantine (Eastern Roman) emperor. Partial and temporary recovery of lost Western territory.
A.D. 538	Justinian rebuilds Hagia Sophia ("Church of Holy Wisdom").
A.D. 635	Chinese emperor authorizes Chinese translation of Bible, brought to China by Nestorian missionaries.
A.D. 787	Second Council of Nicaea decides in favor of the veneration of icons.
A.D. 863	Traditional date for the beginning of the mission of Cyril and Methodius to the Slavs.
A.D. 867	Photius, patriarch of Constantinople, issues a letter condemning the Roman Church's use of the *filioque* clause in the Nicene Creed.
A.D. 1054	Traditional date for the definitive separation of Eastern and Western Christianity. Pope Leo IX and Michael Cerularius, patriarch of Constantinople, excommunicate each other.
A.D. 1204	Knights of the Fourth Crusade launch an attack against Constantinople.
A.D. 1296–1359	Life span of Gregory Palamas. He defends the *hesychasts* in his work known as *The Triads*.
A.D. 1439	Council of Florence attempts to reunite the Church of Rome and the Church of Constantinople.
A.D. 1453	Ottoman Turks capture Constantinople; end of Byzantine Empire.
A.D. 1965	Ecumenical Patriarch Athenagoras I and Pope Paul VI withdraw individual excommunications of 1054.

Many North Americans view Christianity primarily as a Western religion and are familiar only with its Catholic and Protestant expressions, which have dominated the Western world. Such a view runs against the fact that Christianity emerged in the eastern part of the Roman Empire and had a distinct history in a non-Western world. While this chapter focuses on the distinctive features of Eastern Christianity, it is also important to emphasize that the history of Eastern Christianity, particularly in the first millennium, is closely intertwined with the history of Western Christianity. For example, monasticism emerged in the East and very soon spread to the West. The Ecumenical Councils of the first millennium were held in the East, yet included delegates from all parts of the Roman Empire. The canon of scripture, the structure of the liturgy, and the threefold pattern of church leadership involving bishop, priest, and deacon are complex developments that also belong to a mutual heritage of East and West. While these shared aspects of the Christian theological tradition could serve as a common ground, they have also functioned as causes of divisions.

After a brief introduction on how Christianity came to be divided into East and West, we will consider four categories of Eastern Christian churches, all claiming historic continuity with apostolic Christianity, but now separated by their acceptance or rejection of the teachings of various ecumenical councils. We will first discuss the Eastern Orthodox churches, which accept the teachings of seven ecumenical councils. We will then sketch two other forms of Eastern Christianity: the Assyrian Church of the East and the non-Chalcedonian churches. We will conclude with an introduction to the Eastern Catholic churches.

THE BYZANTINE CONTEXT

The development of Eastern churches, separate from their Western counterparts, was in part a consequence of the division of the Roman Empire into two halves, eastern and western. The division was a gradual process. In the latter part of the third century, the emperor Diocletian (r. 284–305) attempted to strengthen his empire by dividing it between himself and a co-emperor, each with separate royal bureaucracies. When Diocletian went to live in the east, the balance of power and the empire's resources also shifted to the richer and more populous eastern part of the empire. Later, the emperor Constantine attempted to bring the empire back together again. In order to better position himself to lead the united Roman Empire, Constantine moved its capital from Rome in the western part of the empire to **Constantinople** (formerly known as "Byzantium") in the east. After his death in 337, however, his three sons redivided the empire.

In the fifth century, the western half of the divided empire collapsed under the pressure of war and invasion, mostly by Germanic tribes pushed west by invading Huns from central Asia. But the empire survived in the east for about another 1,000 years. From the emperor **Justinian** (r. 527–565) onward, historians are accustomed to call what was left of the Roman Empire the Byzantine Empire, from the former name for the city of Constantinople. Although the language was Greek (Latin survived for a while as the language of the law), the empire considered itself authentically Roman, and the patriarchate of Constantinople always styled itself "New Rome." The Byzantine Empire survived as a Christian bulwark in the Balkans, Asia Minor, and the eastern Mediterranean until its conquest in 1453 by the Ottoman Turks, who were Muslim in religion (Syria, Palestine, and Egypt had already been lost in the seventh-

Figure 11–1 Interior of Hagia Sophia in Constantinople. This great Christian church was converted into a mosque after the Muslim conquest of Constantinople in 1453.

century Arab conquests—see Chapter 12). Unlike in the west, then, the eastern empire did not fall until the very end of the Middle Ages, and the civilization of the ancient world continued without a break. Eastern and Western Christianity thus had very different histories and developed in different ways as a result.

THE EASTERN ORTHODOX CHRISTIAN CHURCHES

The primary form of Christianity that emerged in the eastern part of the Roman Empire is today known as Eastern Orthodoxy. The term **orthodox** is formed from two Greek words meaning "right praise" and "right belief." Orthodox Christians consider themselves to be one church in the sense that they share a single faith and the same Byzantine liturgical, canonical, and spiritual heritage. However, at the level of church government, Orthodoxy is a communion of churches. The bishops of these churches gather at a council or regional synod to resolve theological questions or questions related to worship. Historically, these churches were led by the four ancient patriarchates of Constantinople, Alexandria, Antioch, and Jerusalem. Headed by the archbishops, and later by the patriarchs, the four churches maintained a certain degree of self-governance, gathering together for councils in order to decide on matters of universal importance. From the ninth century onward, Byzantine missionaries established local churches among various ethnic groups outside the empire's borders, most importantly by converting the Slavic peoples of Kievan Rus' in 988. Their initiatives produced Orthodox churches on the territories of present-day Ukraine, Russia, Romania, Greece, Serbia, Bulgaria, Georgia, Cyprus, Poland, Albania, and Slovakia, among others. Members of nearly all of these Orthodox churches currently reside in North America, although the greatest number are representatives of Russian and Greek Orthodoxy.

While cultural expressions of the Orthodox faith are diverse, the churches mentioned share core beliefs and practices. First, we will look at the Orthodox theory of church–state relations, that is, its understanding of the relationship between the emperor and the patriarch of the Orthodox Christian churches. Second, we will review the teachings of the (first) seven ecumenical councils in order to describe the distinctive doctrinal position of Orthodox Christian churches. Third, we will examine some characteristics of the worship and spirituality of this kind of Christianity: veneration of icons, Byzantine liturgy, and hesychast spirituality. Finally, we will examine some of the reasons for the enduring split between the Eastern churches and the Western Roman Catholic Church.

Church and State in Byzantine Theory

Bishop **Eusebius of Caesarea** (*c.*260–339), the Christian scholar and Apologist who celebrated Constantine's reign in several of his writings, formulated the fundamental principle of Byzantine imperial theory: "as in heaven, so on earth." According to this theory, the Byzantine emperor serves as God's deputy on earth, acting as the living representative of Christ. The emperor's rule on earth mirrors the rule of God in heaven. Byzantine social order, the harmonious activity of humankind in a Christian state under the emperor's absolute rule, parallels God's celestial order, the harmonious arrangement of all created things under divine sovereignty.

The fact that in the East (more than in the West) the emperor played a major role in religious as well as political affairs can be illustrated by two actions of the

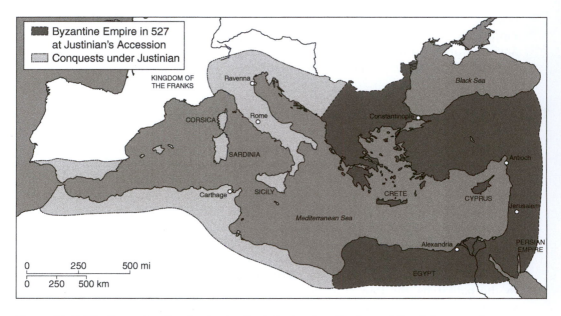

Figure 11–2 The Byzantine Empire during Justinian's reign. By the middle of the seventh century, much of the territory depicted here would be lost.

emperor **Justinian** (527–565). First, Justinian produced a monumental compilation of Roman law titled the *Codex Juris Civilis* (Code of Civil Law), which combined the legal wisdom of Roman civilization, the moral principles of Christianity, and the heritage of Greek philosophy. Second, in 538, Justinian rebuilt the great **Hagia Sophia** (Church of Holy Wisdom) in Constantinople as the image of the harmonious working together (*symphonia*) of empire and church for the common good. When the emperor entered the sanctuary of Hagia Sophia to offer to the patriarch and clergy the bread and wine to be transformed during the divine liturgy, he stood as a representative of an empire under God.

Given the Byzantine emperor's role as the guardian of the Orthodox faith, his relationship with the patriarch of Constantinople was complex. The emperors not only safeguarded the decisions of the church leaders, but often sought to influence those decisions. When disagreements between the emperor and the ruling patriarch arose, the latter was often replaced with a church leader who was more obedient to the emperor's wishes. Religious dissent within the Byzantine Empire was often treated as an expression of disloyalty to the emperor and was accordingly punished by the state.

In the territories of the Byzantine Empire that fell under the control of the Muslim Arabs in the seventh century, such as Armenia, Syria, and Egypt, the Christian church leaders faced different political circumstances. On the one hand, their Christian communities were sometimes pressured to convert to Islam by various forms of discrimination, such as taxation. On the other hand, their Muslim overlords generally meddled less in their internal religious affairs than was the case with the Byzantine Christian emperors. Whatever the vicissitudes of coexistence with the Muslim rulers, first the Arabs and then the Ottomans, Christianity in the East has outlived the empires and continued into the present, although its survival is quite precarious in many parts of the Middle East. Their situation has become even more uncertain since the destabilization following the American invasion of Iraq in 2003. By contrast, the circumstances of Eastern Orthodox churches in Russia and the Balkans have improved since the fall of Communist dictatorships and the rise of regimes that are more sympathetic to Orthodox concerns.

Teachings of the (First) Seven Ecumenical Councils

The Orthodox Church is committed to the teaching of the seven ecumenical councils that were held between 325 and 787. The topics treated by these seven councils that define the faith of Orthodox churches fall into three categories: the nature of the Trinity, the proper understanding of Jesus, and the use of icons. As discussed in Chapter 9, the doctrine of the Trinity was defined at the Councils of Nicaea (325) and Constantinople (381). The doctrine of the Incarnation was worked out at the Councils of Ephesus (431), which also defined Mary's status as *theotokos* or Mother of God, and Chalcedon (451). The definition of the Incarnation involved explaining, in part, what Jesus Christ, as the Word made flesh, was *not*: the Chalcedonian Definition further states that the union of divine and human natures in Christ is "without confusion, without change, without division, without separation." These four qualifications (the phrases are negative adverbs in the original Greek) define the union of Christ's two natures by stating what it is *not* rather than what it *is*. Similarly, the Nicene Creed, when describing the generation of the Son from the Father, states that the Son is "begotten, *not* made." In other words, generation is primarily defined by what it is *not*—namely, it is not creation. The theological language that deploys negations in order to rule out misconceptions about God and in order to express a more general fact that God infinitely surpasses everything in the created order is called "negative" or **apophatic theology**. In contrast, the theological language that deploys affirmations is called "positive" or **cataphatic theology**.

The distinction between cataphatic and apophatic theology was classically formulated by the sixth-century Byzantine theologian known as Pseudo-Dionysius the Areopagite ("pseudo," because he worked under the pseudonym of the Apostle Paul's convert in Athens, mentioned in Acts 17:34):

> Since [God] is the Cause of all beings, we should posit and ascribe to it all the affirmations we make in regard to beings, and, more appropriately, we should negate all these affirmations, since it surpasses all being. Now we should not conclude that the negations are simply the opposites of the affirmations, but rather that the cause of all is considerably prior to this, beyond privations, beyond every denial, beyond every assertion.
>
> (*Mystical Theology*, trans. Colm Luibheid)

Pseudo-Dionysius' point may be illustrated using the above-mentioned example from the Nicene Creed. When the creed speaks of the Son as "begotten, *not* made" it negates the claim that the Son is "made" or "created." This negation is not a mere privation of the property of being; in other words, the predicate "uncreated" does not mean "non-existent." Rather, this negation indicates that the Son surpasses all finite created beings, or that the Son does not belong to the same order of being as creatures. As the transcendent creator, God is beyond affirmations and negations because God surpasses everything in creation.

Pseudo-Dionysius insists—and his insistence has found resonance in the Western theological tradition—that apophatic theology is the most fitting way to speak about God. While the apophatic attitude respects the mystery of God, apophatic

Figure 11–3 Apse of Hagia Irene in Constantinople.

theology should not be confused with agnosticism or pious ignorance. On the contrary, apophatic theology is just as concerned with doctrinal precision as cataphatic theology is. The proper use of theological language requires a balance of affirmation and negation, exhibited by the Nicene Creed and the Chalcedonian Definition. Two additional councils were held in Constantinople, in 553 and 681, respectively, which further clarified the teaching of Chalcedon on the understanding of Christ as one person comprising two natures.

The third issue to receive attention during the era of the seven ecumenical councils was triggered by controversies over icons. An **icon** is a visual representation of Christ or the saints. Icons are most commonly painted on wood but also appear as mosaics or frescoes affixed to church walls, or as portraits in metal. In 730, the Byzantine emperor Leo III issued a ban on all religious imagery and proceeded to destroy the images displayed in public places and frescoes on the walls of the churches. The emperor's immediate reasons are obscure and controversial. It is possible that Leo III was concerned about the loss of the Eastern provinces of the Byzantine Empire, including Syria and Egypt, to the Muslim Arabs, whose religion rejected the use of anthropomorphic depictions of God. It is also possible that the emperor wished to weaken the power of the monastic institutions, which relied on religions images as a means of maintaining their authority and popularity. In 754, Leo's son and successor, Emperor Constantine V, summoned a council in Constantinople that rejected the use of icons.

The opponents of icons (**iconoclasts**) marshaled two main arguments against the use of images. The first was biblical and relied on the Second Commandment of the Decalogue:

You shall not make for yourself an idol, whether in the form of anything that is in heaven above, or that is on the earth beneath, or that is in the water under the earth. You shall not bow down to them and worship them.

(Exodus 20:4–5)

For the iconoclasts, any depiction of God was a form of idolatry. The alleged threat of idolatry was also believed to weaken the empire politically and militarily by provoking divine displeasure.

The second argument was more philosophical and started with the premise that God is uncreated, invisible, and infinite. The implication was that any created, visible, and finite representation of God was bound to be a failure or a misrepresentation. It was simply impossible to make a material image of God, who was immaterial. Hence, the use of icons was at best a superstition and at worst idolatry.

In 787, with the support of the empress Irene, another council gathered in Nicaea to reopen the case concerning the icons. The council bishops addressed the biblical objection against the use of icons by introducing a distinction between worship, which belongs to God alone, and veneration or honor, which is appropriate for the icons, holy objects, relics, the book of scripture, and humans, who are made in the image of God. The council declared, quoting Basil of Caesarea, that "the honor rendered to an image passes on to its prototype"—in other words, that by paying respect to religious images, the believers are able to acknowledge those who are represented by the images—namely, Christ and the saints. The defenders of the icons were therefore called **iconodules**, because they venerated (but did not worship) icons.

More significantly, the council bishops saw this controversy as a continuation of the earlier Christological debates. The material depiction of God was possible, they argued, because God, who is immaterial and invisible, became visible and assumed human nature in Jesus Christ. The divine Incarnation provided the main rationale for the use of icons. The representations of Christ bore witness to the fact that the Son's humanity was not merely apparent, but real. The iconoclasts could still object that since only the human nature of Christ could be depicted, while the divine nature could not, the production of an icon amounted to the separation of Christ's divine and human natures and hence indirectly supported a form of Nestorianism, which was condemned at the Council of Ephesus. The iconodules responded that the subject being depicted was neither the divine nature nor the human nature, but one undivided person of God incarnate. To refuse to portray Christ visually was in effect to deny the reality of his human nature and the inseparable union of the divine and human natures in one person.

Thus, the council declared in promoting the veneration of icons:

This is the faith of the apostles,
This is the faith of the fathers,
This is the faith of the Orthodox,
This faith has made firm the whole world.

After a brief revival of iconoclasm in the early ninth century, the position of the iconodules was vindicated and the council of 787 was acknowledged as the Seventh Ecumenical Council.

Figure 11–4 Virgin of Tenderness. Benaki Museum of Greek Civilization.

Veneration of Icons

Icons play a central role in all Orthodox worship: incense is burned before them, candles are lit to honor them, worshippers bear them in procession, prostrate themselves before them, and/or kiss them. An important feature of Orthodox churches is the **iconostasis** ("icon screen"), a wall bearing icons arranged in a prescribed order, which divides sanctuary from nave. Icons also adorn private homes and are even carried by faithful individuals as devotional aids, much as a Roman Catholic might wear a crucifix. In late antiquity, icons were considered to be "the Bible for the illiterate." In our time, the icons contribute to theological literacy by serving as powerful means of remembrance of all that God has done throughout human history.

The most important function of religious images can be explained by the analogy with the function of the icons on a computer screen. Computer icons serve as a portal into the hidden realm of a particular application, which remains hidden from sight until you click on the icon. In a similar manner, the religious icon serves as a portal into the invisible realm of the divine reality, when the believers direct their gaze toward them. By contemplating an icon, an Orthodox believer passes into sacred space and sacred time, effectively encountering the person or mystery depicted. As a means of communion between heaven and earth, icons play a sacramental role in Orthodoxy.

Unlike many Western visual representations of biblical scenes or church legends, an icon does not attempt to provide a snapshot of a historical event or a psychological portrait of a historical person, but a symbolic representation of humanity transformed by divine grace. This difference could easily be illustrated by the contrasting treatment of the light source in post-medieval Western religious painting and in Eastern iconography. In the Western pieces, the artist indicates "natural" light sources such as the sun, moon, candles, and the like, by carefully depicting shadows. But in an icon there are no shadows; the light sources lie "behind" or "within" the art piece, inviting the observer to enter into its radiant world. Icons also employ a fixed color scheme and method of depicting subjects. The world without shadows intimates the transfiguration of human persons by the light of Christ. For believers, the icons are intended to serve as windows into the kingdom of heaven.

Byzantine Liturgy

If icons represent the most characteristic visual artifacts of Orthodoxy, the Byzantine liturgy represents its most characteristic ceremonial creativity. Produced by a fusion of the monastic practices of Syria, Cappadocia, and Constantinople with the public worship of the imperial church, the Byzantine Eucharistic liturgy takes three characteristic forms: the Liturgy of St. John Chrysostom (the most common form), the Liturgy of St. Basil, and the Liturgy of the Presanctified Gifts. Only the Liturgy of St. John Chrysostom will be outlined here.

The Liturgy of John Chrysostom begins with the *Enarxis* (Opening) consisting of prayers, hymns, and responses. The *Monogenes* (Only-begotten) chant, a stirring and powerful expression of Orthodox faith in Christ as "one person in two natures," appears as part of the second hymn, sung by the assembled worshippers (or by the choir on their behalf):

> Only begotten Son and Word of God, immortal One, who humbled Yourself for our salvation taking flesh by the Theotokos and ever-virgin Mary, You became man without change; and were crucified, O Christ our God, conquering death by death; being one of the Holy Trinity, together glorified with the Father and the Holy Spirit: save us!

The liturgy continues with the part of the service devoted to readings from scripture, begun with the Little Entrance (a procession of clergy and ministers through the body of the church bearing a decorated book of scriptural readings) and the *Trisagion* hymn (another powerful expression of Orthodox Trinitarian faith sung by the assembly or the choir):

> Holy God, Holy Mighty One, Holy Immortal One, have mercy on us! (Three times)
> Glory to the Father and to the Son and to the Holy Spirit now and forevermore. Amen.
> Holy Immortal One, have mercy on us.
> Holy God, Holy Mighty One, Holy Immortal One,
> have mercy on us!

This service of the Word continues with two readings: an Epistle (usually taken from one of the New Testament letters) and a Gospel. Preaching may follow at this point.

The ritual high point of the Orthodox liturgy then takes place: the Great Entrance. This is another procession of clergy and ministers through the body of the church, but this time they carry liturgical fans, incense, and the bread and wine, which will be consecrated later in the service. During the Great Entrance, which is popularly understood as a dramatic re-enactment of either Jesus' triumphal entrance into Jerusalem or his funeral cortege, the congregation and/or choir accompanies the procession with the singing of the *Cherubic Hymn*:

> We, who mystically represent the Cherubim [an order of angels] and sing the thrice-holy hymn to the life-giving Trinity, let us set aside the cares of life that we may receive the King of all invisibly escorted by the Angelic Hosts. Alleluia!

After another prayer and the recitation of the Creed, the presiding priest prays the Eucharistic Prayer (*Anaphora*) and the congregation and/or choir perform some sung interventions. The characteristic mode of Byzantine worship is wonderfully expressed in the opening of the *Anaphora* (the equivalent of the Preface in the Roman Catholic Mass). First, the priest and people exchange the dialogue: "The grace of our Lord Jesus Christ and the love of God the Father and the communion of the Holy Spirit be with you all"/"And with your spirit"/"Let us lift up our hearts"/"We lift them up to the Lord"/"Let us thank the Lord"/"It is proper and right." Then the priest rhapsodically exults in the mystery of God's interaction with humanity:

> It is right and proper to praise, bless, glorify, thank and worship You in all places of Your dominion; for You are God ineffable, beyond comprehension, invisible, beyond understanding, ever-existing and always the same, You and Your only-begotten Son, and Your Holy Spirit. You have brought us from non-being into being, and when we fell You raised us up again, and You have not ceased doing everything to lead us into heaven and grant us Your Kingdom to come. For all these we thank You, and Your only-begotten Son, and Your Holy Spirit; for blessings of which we know and of which we do not know; for benefits apparent and non-apparent that have been bestowed upon us. We also thank you for this Liturgy which You have condescended to accept from our hands, even though You are surrounded by thousands of Archangels and myriads of Angels, by the Cherubim and Seraphim, six-winged, many-eyed, borne aloft and singing the victory song, proclaiming, heralding, and saying: (with congregation and/or choir) Holy, Holy, Holy, Lord of Angelic Hosts, heaven and earth are full of your glory. Hosanna in the highest! Blessed is He who comes in the name of the Lord! Hosanna in the highest!

The consecration of the bread and wine is followed by another prayer and group recitation of the Lord's Prayer. After Communion, the priest blesses the assembly with the remaining consecrated bread and wine while the congregation and/or choir sings:

> We have seen the true Light; we have received the heavenly Spirit; we have found the true faith, worshipping the undivided Trinity; for this has saved us.

Further prayers and blessings conclude the service.

While this description of the liturgy and these few texts may suggest something of the other-worldly character of Orthodox worship, they cannot convey the complexity of the ceremony, its impact on all the senses, and its profoundly popular yet theologically sophisticated character.

Hesychast Spirituality

Another characteristic of Orthodox Christianity is its *hesychast spirituality*, especially associated with the fourteenth-century theologian **Gregory Palamas** (1296–1359), a monk of Mount Athos in Greece. *Hesychia* means "inner stillness" or "silence of the heart." A hesychast is one who seeks *hesychia* through various ascetic disciplines, most notably the use of the **Jesus Prayer**. This is a very brief prayer (usually "Lord Jesus Christ, Son of the living God, have mercy on me, a sinner"), which the person repeats in rhythm, usually coordinated with his or her breathing and/or heartbeat. The goal of reciting the prayer in this manner is to have the prayer "descend from the mind into the heart," allowing the believer to enter into meditation, an experiential union with God. This Christian prayer technique might be compared to the *mantras* of certain non-Christian religions.

Barlaam the Calabrian, a South Italian monk and Neoplatonist philosopher living in Constantinople in the fourteenth century, attacked the hesychast movement as gross superstition. Did not scripture itself forbid "vain repetition" in prayer? Were not the physical techniques a form of self-hypnosis or an attempt to manipulate God through magic? Worst of all, was not the hesychasts' claim to experience God unmediated in the here-and-now a blasphemous denial of God's utter transcendence and unknowability? In response to Barlaam, Gregory Palamas defended the hesychasts' practice in his work commonly known as *The Triads*. Gregory here distinguished between God's essence, which remains inaccessible to humans in this life and the next, and God's energies, which communicate God to creation. God is known through his works and is experientially accessible through his energies. In this ontology, there is no separation between the natural order and grace because everything in nature is sustained and penetrated by the divine energies. Gregory's teaching on the energies of God was confirmed by three local councils held in Constantinople in 1341, 1347, and 1351: The hesychast movement was vindicated.

The hesychast spirituality provided a concrete experiential backing and theological framework for the understanding of salvation as deification. The doctrine of deification is a corollary of the doctrine of the Incarnation: God became man so that humans could be deified, a doctrine already anticipated by Irenaeus of Lyons, as seen in Chapter 8. According to the Orthodox understanding, deification assumes a process of life-long transformation that reaches its fulfillment beyond this life. Deification includes not only the transformation of human beings, but the eventual eschatological transfiguration of the whole cosmos, when God will be "all in all" (1 Corinthians 15:28). Deification conceives of salvation in terms of healing of the human condition and participation in the life of God. This therapeutic and ontological emphasis differentiates deification from the understandings of salvation that draw on sacrificial, juridical, and transactional categories. While deification is foundational in Orthodox theology, the importance of this doctrine is also increasingly appreciated by Christian theologians in the West.

The Separation of Christian East and West

A number of issues led to the division of Christianity into Eastern (Byzantine) and Western churches. Political tensions were heightened in A.D. 800, when Pope Leo III crowned the Frankish king Charlemagne as emperor of a restored Roman Empire in the West (see Chapter 13). By this act, the papacy severed its historic political allegiance to the Roman Empire in the East, and claimed the right to transfer the imperial title to the West. There were also considerable cultural differences between East and West, evidenced in the fact that the West was Latin-speaking while the East was Greek-speaking. Consequently, Eastern Christianity developed a spirituality and worship style that was more mystical in orientation than Western churches.

While these differences are significant, they need not have led to the separation of Christianity into Eastern Orthodoxy and Roman Catholicism. In fact, it is difficult to name one particular event that brought about the separation. Instead, we will consider several situations that gradually led to the split between these two churches. One of the most decisive events was the **Fourth Crusade** in 1204. The crusades created considerable tension between East and West, as knights from the West marched through the Eastern empire, conquering lands that had been taken over by Muslims and then declining to return control of them to their original Byzantine rulers. More importantly, Greek Orthodox Christians have never been able to forget how the knights of the Fourth Crusade, having become enmeshed in Byzantine court politics, besieged, conquered, and looted the city of Constantinople itself. Pope Innocent III, despite opposing the Western attack but eager to end a schism that had begun in 1054, acquiesced in the election of a Latin (Western) bishop as the new patriarch of Constantinople, and hoped (in vain, as it turned out) to bring the Greek church into line with Latin practices. Even today, Greek Orthodox Christians have not forgiven the Catholic Church for this disastrous chain of events, which weakened the Byzantine Empire in its defense against the Turkish military threat. In his 2001 visit to Athens, Pope John Paul II apologized to the Greek church for past and present Catholic sins against Orthodox Christians and expressed deep regret for the sack of Constantinople.

Another major issue that brought about the eventual separation of Eastern and Western Christians concerns the doctrine about the relationship of the Holy Spirit to the Father and the Son. Both Eastern and Western Christians believe that the Holy Spirit is personal, in the same way that the Father and Son are persons of the Trinity, and that the Spirit is fully divine. Orthodox Christians also believe that the Father is the sole source of being in the Trinity, as stated in the original form of the Nicene-Constantinople Creed: "We believe in the Holy Spirit who proceeds from the Father." However, as early as the sixth century, some Christian churches in the West began adding the phrase "and the Son" to the creed, declaring that the Holy Spirit proceeded from the Father *and from the Son*. In Latin, the additional phrase is *filioque*. Orthodox Christians opposed this addition, because it denies to the Father what is distinctive to the person of the Father, namely, that he is the source of the other two persons of the Trinity.

The addition of the *filioque* to the creed was not formally accepted by the church at Rome itself until the eleventh century. When it was accepted, it was done without the consent of Eastern Christian leadership. Orthodox Christians consider the first seven ecumenical councils, from which the Nicene-Constantinople Creed originated, to be one of the highest expressions of God's continued presence in the church. Therefore, they argued that no one has the right to tamper with the contents of the creed. Moreover, the Orthodox claimed, everyone had agreed at the Second Council of Nicaea (787), the last of the early ecumenical councils, that tradition ought to be preserved intact: "We take away nothing and we add nothing ... We preserve without change or innovation all the ecclesiastical traditions that have been handed down to us, whether written or unwritten." The *filioque* clause continues to be a major issue of separation between Eastern Orthodox and Roman Catholics today.

The *filioque* controversy is related to another issue that gradually separated Orthodox and Catholic Christians—namely, **papal primacy**. In Eastern Christianity, church leadership is understood to be conciliar (working together in council), rather than monarchial (having a single ruler over all). Orthodox Christians honor the pope as the first and elder brother among the bishops of the churches throughout the world. However, they do not give him any special power or jurisdiction over the churches of the East nor do they attribute to him any spiritual gifts beyond those of other bishops. When it comes to speaking God's word to the world, neither the pope nor any other patriarch or bishop has highest authority, but only the whole Church in an ecumenical council.

Two situations in the history of the relationship between Eastern Orthodoxy and the Roman Catholic Church will help to illustrate the difficulties that arose over papal primacy. The first concerns Pope Nicholas I (r. 858–867) and Photius, patriarch of Constantinople in 861. Nicholas disagreed with the appointment of Photius to the position of patriarch and reinstated his predecessor. Although the Eastern Orthodox churches simply ignored Nicholas' order, they resented his interference. Later, in 867, Photius issued a letter condemning the Roman Church's use of the *filioque* clause. In the same year, a council in Constantinople decided to excommunicate Pope Nicholas.

The second situation is sometimes called the Great Schism of 1054. The surface issues had to do with long-standing disciplinary and liturgical differences, which the

Byzantines chose to complain about in 1053. Beneath the surface was ecclesiastical competition for control of territory where the pope's and the patriarch's jurisdictions confronted one another in southern Italy and in the Balkans. But the really fundamental disagreement had to do with different views of papal primacy, on which East and West had long differed (see Chapter 9). This was a particularly unfortunate time for the question of the pope's place in the universal church to become a hot issue, since both Michael Cerularius, the patriarch of Constantinople, and the papal delegate to Constantinople, Cardinal Humbert, were intolerant and overbearing. This was also a time when the papacy was gathering momentum in the great church renewal movement called the Gregorian Reform (see Chapter 13); Easterners were not prepared to listen to Pope Leo IX (r. 1049–1054) when he proudly claimed in a letter hand-delivered by Humbert that the Roman church was "mother and head of all churches." When the discussions between Cerularius and Cardinal Humbert got out of hand, the pope's delegate excommunicated the patriarch and his close associates. In response, a synod of Constantinople excommunicated Humbert, whom they accused of forging the pope's letter. No one at the time imagined that the controversy would harden into a definitive separation—prior ruptures had always been resolved—and the excommunications were personal, not applying to whole churches; furthermore, the pope and the Byzantine emperor remained on good terms and had a common political enemy in the aggressive Norman settlers in southern Italy. Nevertheless, under the influence of subsequent disasters like the Fourth Crusade, this did indeed harden and become permanent. The excommunications were mutually withdrawn only recently, in 1965, but full communion between the churches has yet to be restored.

The churches of East and West differed on a number of other issues: rules about fasting, regulations concerning celibacy among clergy (Eastern Orthodox churches allow priests to marry, although their bishops must be unmarried and are therefore usually elected out of monasteries; precisely at the time of the 1054 schism, the papacy was trying to make old laws on celibacy apply universally to priests as well—see Chapter 13), the use of leavened or unleavened bread at Eucharist, circumstances in which divorce and remarriage might be permitted, teachings about purgatory, and the proper way to celebrate the sacrament of Confirmation. Today, as Orthodox and Roman Catholic Christians gather together in dialogue, perhaps reconciliation will eventually be possible. As the Second Vatican Council was drawing to a close, on December 7, 1965, Pope Paul VI and Ecumenical Patriarch Athenagoras I withdrew the individual excommunications of 1054, as a first step toward reconciliation. The late Pope John Paul II, the first pope ever from Eastern Europe, made such reconciliation a prime goal of his reign as pope, as may be seen in his encyclical letter *Ut Unum Sint* (That They May Be One, 1995) and his apostolic letter, *Orientale Lumen* (Eastern Light, 1995). His hopes were disappointed, in spite of the changed political situation created by the fall of communism. In particular, the Russian Orthodox Church, the largest in the Eastern Orthodox communion of churches, has been very cautious and even suspicious of Western efforts, Protestant as well as Catholic, to be part of Christianity's revival in Russia. Nevertheless, an authoritative endorsement of the importance of ecumenical dialogue was made at the Holy and Great Council of the Orthodox Church, which took place on the island of Crete in 2016.

OTHER EASTERN CHRISTIANITIES

The Assyrian Church of the East

This ancient Eastern Christian church has traditionally been known as the "Nestorian" Church, but, like so many Christian church names, it was pinned on them by their ecclesiastical enemies and is rejected by the church itself. Its proper name, the Assyrian Church of the East, reflects its status as ancient Christianity's easternmost expansion, and its historic heartland in Assyria, in the northern part of Mesopotamia (modern-day Iraq). Christianity spread into Mesopotamia no later than the mid-second century. By the early third century, Christian communities had been founded in Persian territory, outside the Roman Empire altogether. During the fifth century, Persian Christianity organized as a separate church no longer in communion with Roman Christianity, for political and doctrinal reasons: as Rome's great imperial rival, Persia expected loyalty from its Christian subjects. And Persian Christianity favored a doctrine of Christ's two natures that was condemned at the Council of Ephesus in 431 as a "Nestorian" division of Christ into two distinct persons. Though never a majority in Persia, the Church of the East nonetheless grew to be quite large in the Middle Ages, spreading as far east as China and as far south as the southern tip of India. A celebrated monument to the Church of the East's evangelization of China is a ten-foot-high, black marble block, inscribed in Chinese characters and Syriac script (Syriac, a dialect of Aramaic, is the church's liturgical language), dated to the year 781. It was discovered probably in 1625 and is now kept in His-an-fu, in northern China. The Syriac inscription records the preaching of the Christian faith to the emperors of China, who are said to have authorized the translation of the Christian Bible into Chinese in 635. The church has suffered a drastic decline in its numbers since the thirteenth century, thanks to waves of invasion and persecution that culminated in massacres at the hands of Turks and Kurds in the wake of World War I. Today, its numbers have been reduced to a few hundred thousand in the Middle East and in scattered diasporas around the world. They still cling to their home territory in Iraq, despite the most recent persecution from the Islamic State (ISIS), and their head, Catholicos-Patriarch Mar Gewargis III Sliva, resides in Erbil, in the Kurdish-controlled portion of northeastern Iraq.

Eighth-Century Nestorian Inscription from China

The following is an excerpt from a long inscription written in Chinese in A.D. 781 in the name of the Christian monk Jingjing, or "Adam, bishop and priest," as he identifies himself in Syriac. It tells of the emperor T'ai-tsung's authorization of the preaching of Christianity, which the writer calls "the luminous teaching," and includes an exposition of Christianity and the names in Syriac of Christian monks and clergy from the Church of the East. This translation is by Dr. L. Eccles and Prof. Sam Lieu and is used by permission.

§6. The way of the true constant is mysterious, and it is difficult to give it a name, but its merits are manifest, impelling us to call it the Luminous (or Illustrious) Teaching (Jingjiao, i.e., Christianity). If it is only a way and is not holy, then it is limited. If it is holy but is not the way, then it is not great. When the way and holiness match each other, then the world will be enlightened.

§7. When Emperor Taizong's reign (627–649 C.E.) began, he was wise in his relations with the people. In Syria, there was a man of great virtue (bishop), known as Aluoben, who detected the intent of heaven and conveyed the true scripture here. He observed the way the winds blew in order to travel through difficulties and perils, and in the ninth year of the Zhenguang reign (635 C.E.), he reached Chang'an. The emperor dispatched an official, Duke Fang Xuan-ling, as an envoy to the western outskirts to welcome the visitor, who translated the scriptures in the library. [The emperor] examined the doctrines in his apartments and reached a profound understanding of their truth. He specially ordered that they be promulgated. In Autumn, in the seventh month of the twelfth year of the Zhenguang reign (638 C.E.), the emperor proclaimed:

§8. "The way does not have a constant name, and the holy does not have a constant form. Teachings are established according to the locality, and their mysteries aid mankind. Aluoben, the virtuous man of Da Qin [= Rome], has brought scriptures and images from afar and presented them at the capital. He has explained the doctrines, so that there is nothing left obscure. We have observed its basic teachings. They set forth the most important things for living, their words are not complicated, and their principles, once learnt, can be easily retained. Everything in them benefits man. It is appropriate that it should spread throughout the empire."

The Assyrian Church of the East recognizes seven sacraments, though what counts as a sacrament, beyond Baptism, Eucharist, Marriage, and Holy Orders (ordination), seems to vary. Priests are married, but bishops must be celibate. Until very recently, the patriarchs came from the same family, descending from uncle to nephew. The last two have been elected. A recent schism has produced a parallel patriarchate. Icons are rejected in both churches and homes. The only church decoration is a simple cross, not a crucifix (i.e., there is no body on the cross), placed on the church building and over the altar. Despite the church's rejection of all but the first two ecumenical councils, in 1994, Patriarch Mar Dinkha IV signed a "Common Christological Agreement" with Pope John Paul II and the Catholic Church. It recognized that the differences of the past were due "in large part to misunderstandings":

The controversies of the past led to anathemas, bearing on persons and on formulas. The Lord's Spirit permits us to understand better today that the divisions brought about

in this way were due in large part to misunderstandings. Whatever our christological divergences have been, we experience ourselves united in the confession of the same faith in the Son of God who became man so that we might become children of God by his grace. We wish from now on to witness together to this faith in the One who is the Way, the Truth and the Life, proclaiming it in appropriate ways to our contemporaries, so that the world may believe in the Gospel of salvation … Living by this faith and these sacraments, it follows as a consequence that the particular Catholic churches and the particular Assyrian churches can recognise each other as sister Churches.

(Atiya 1968)

The churches also agreed to cooperate in such areas as education and priestly formation.

Figure 11–5 Stone monument erected in 781 by Assyrian Christian missionaries to China. The monument is currently located at Xi'an, China.

The Non-Chalcedonian Eastern Christian Churches

Several other ancient Eastern Christian churches originated in the fallout from the Council of Chalcedon (451): the Armenian Apostolic Church; the Coptic Orthodox Church in Egypt; the Ethiopian Orthodox Church, with a separate Orthodox church in the newly independent country of Eritrea; the Syriac Orthodox Church in Syria; and the Malankara Orthodox Syrian Church in India. Although they are completely independent of one another juridically, with different liturgical traditions and widely diverse histories, they share in

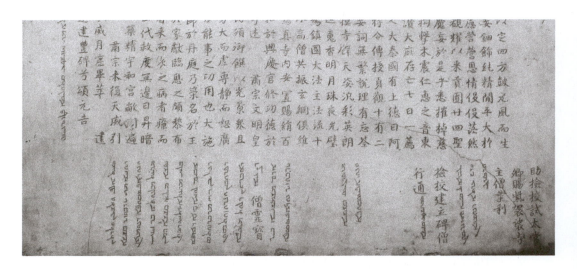

Figure 11–6 Detail of Assyrian Christian monument showing Chinese and Syriac.

common a rejection of Chalcedon's definition that Jesus Christ is "one person recognized in two natures, undivided and unconfused." Today, they are sometimes called collectively the Oriental Orthodox Churches, to distinguish them from churches in communion with Constantinople, since they too are "Eastern" and claim the name "Orthodox." Since the members of these churches originally believed that Chalcedon's definition compromised the unity of Christ's person by focusing too much on distinctions concerning his humanity and divinity, they preferred the formula proposed by Cyril of Alexandria, "one nature of the incarnate Son of God" (see Chapter 9). Although they clearly rejected the belief that the humanity of Christ had been absorbed into a single divine nature, these churches have often been erroneously called "Monophysite" (from the Greek words for "of a single nature").

In the fifth century, these dissenters against Chalcedon represented a large segment of Christians along the eastern rim of the Roman Empire and beyond it, in Armenia, Syria, Egypt, and Ethiopia. In Egypt, the Coptic Orthodox Church, under its pope Tawadros II (r. 2012–), is estimated to include at least 10 percent of the country's population. In Armenia, the Armenian Apostolic Church has been the carrier of Armenian national identity for centuries ever since the conversion of King Trdat in 314. In Ethiopia, Christianity took root by the late fourth century, under the tutelage of the Egyptian church, and Ethiopia remains to this day a majority Christian nation. In India, the Malankara Orthodox Syrian Church claims continuity with "Nestorian" communities that settled in the south of India no later than the sixth century. Today, the numbers of some of these churches are greatly reduced due to conversions to Islam and to persecution under modern dictatorships. Nevertheless, even in their diminished state, they represent a historic continuity with Christianity's ancient roots in the Middle East, and in the case of those with Syriac liturgical traditions, even with the Aramaic language of Jesus and his first followers. The contemporary resurgence of Islam, along with the heightened tensions with the West, has made them even more vulnerable by magnifying religious differences between them and their Muslim neighbors and fellow citizens. Those who can emigrate often choose to do so. As a result, in recent decades, they have sought to improve relations with Catholic and Eastern Orthodox churches. Under Pope John Paul II, the Catholic Church has reached formal Christological agreements, resembling the one quoted above with the Assyrian Church of the East, with the Coptic Orthodox Church in 1988, and with the Syriac Orthodox Church in 1984, that the doctrinal differences which historically divided the Catholic Church from their non-Chalcedonian Eastern churches have more to do with the verbal formulations of the faith rather than with the substance of the faith itself, and originated mainly in linguistic and political differences.

The Eastern Catholic Churches

The split between the Eastern and Western Christian churches, symbolized by the mutual excommunications of the bishops of Rome and Constantinople in 1054, became definitive in the minds of the common people of the East after the Crusades and the sacking of Constantinople by Western Christians in 1204. Both the Second Council of Lyons (1274) and the Council of Florence (1439) attempted to reunify Eastern and Western Christianity, but neither was successful. Over time, however, individual segments of the various Eastern churches have re-established communion (formal ties) with Rome by accepting papal primacy. The first to do so were the

Maronite Christians of Lebanon, named for their ancient center in the monastery of St. Maroun in the mountains of Lebanon. At the time of the Crusades, the Maronites re-entered into communion with Rome (1182), although they claim never to have actually been out of communion, just isolated from other Christian churches since the spread of Islam in the seventh century. Today there are about 21 such Eastern Catholic churches, most of them rather small. Sometimes they are called "Eastern rite" churches because, as part of their reunion with Roman Catholicism and their acceptance of the pope's primacy, they were allowed to retain many of their traditional customs, such as their non-Roman rite liturgies and elements of church law (most controversially, this usually included their custom of allowing priests to marry).

Orthodox Christians generally reject these Eastern Catholic churches and view them as an obstacle to Catholic–Orthodox reunion. They feel that their very existence is a denial of the reality of the Orthodox churches, that these unions were efforts to split local Eastern Christian communities, and that Eastern Catholics are really Orthodox who were forcibly seized from their mother churches. Since the collapse of communism in Eastern Europe, Orthodox resentment of these Eastern Catholic Churches has grown even stronger. This is particularly true of the situation in Ukraine, where the Ukrainian Greek Catholic Church (UGCC; "Greek" because it uses the Byzantine liturgy of John Chrysostom), the largest of the Eastern Catholic Churches, came into being in 1596 when some Eastern Orthodox bishops, fearful of losing their people to the Protestant Reformation (see Chapters 18–19), agreed to reunion with Rome. After its brutal suppression under communism in 1946, the UGCC came back to life when Ukraine became independent in 1991. Ukrainian Catholics are trying to build bridges to the several groups of Orthodox Christians in Ukraine, but must work hard to defuse Orthodox anxieties that they are merely a Catholic vanguard to claim all of Ukraine for Catholicism.

The Decree on Eastern Catholic Churches, one of the documents of the Second Vatican Council (see Chapter 24), presents current official Catholic teaching on these churches. It affirmed their equality with Western Roman Catholics. It also called Eastern Catholics to a rediscovery of their own traditions and affirmed that they have a special vocation to foster ecumenical relations with non-Catholic Eastern Christians. Recent developments hold out hope that these and other ecumenical efforts may finally bear fruit and that at least some non-Catholic Eastern Christians may eventually be reunited with their Catholic brothers and sisters in the East and the West. An outstanding example of progress is the agreement in 2001 between the Assyrian Church of the East and the Catholic Church to allow sharing of the Eucharist between Assyrian Christians and members of the Chaldean Catholic Church, as the Assyrians' Eastern Catholic opposite number is known—Chaldean Catholics are the largest Christian communion in Iraq, though much depleted since the American invasion in 2003. The agreement builds on the good faith created by the 1994 Common Christological Declaration mentioned above. It was inspired by the pastoral situation in war-torn Iraq and in the worldwide diaspora of Iraqi Christians, Chaldean and Assyrian alike, who cannot always find a priest of their own communion from whom to receive the Eucharist. In such situations, it is now possible for them to receive the Eucharist from a priest of the other church.

Key Terms

apophatic theology
cataphatic theology
Constantinople
Eusebius of Caesarea
filioque
Fourth Crusade

Gregory Palamas
Hagia Sophia
hesychia
icon
iconoclast
iconodule

iconostasis
Jesus Prayer
Justinian
Orthodox
papal primacy

Questions for Reading

1. Who governs the Eastern Orthodox churches? To what degree was the Byzantine emperor involved in the government of this church during the period in which the Byzantine Empire existed? What principle justified the emperor's involvement in the church?

2. Formulate the distinction between apophatic and cataphatic theology. In what sense might we say that the definition of the Incarnation adopted in the first four ecumenical councils was "negative"?

3. What is an icon? What arguments were made for and against the veneration of icons, and how was the dispute over icons finally resolved? What function do icons serve in the Eastern Orthodox Church? Do all Eastern churches accept the veneration of icons?

4. What is *hesychia*? How does one achieve it? What arguments were made for and against *hesychia*, and how was the dispute over it finally resolved?

5. What events or circumstances led to the separation of Eastern Orthodox and Roman Catholic Christians?

6. What is the doctrinal issue that historically caused the separation of "non-Chalcedonian" or Oriental Orthodox Christian churches from churches that accepted Chalcedon? How does that doctrinal difference tend to be negotiated today, with the agreements reached with the Catholic Church under Pope John Paul II as examples?

7. What are "Eastern *Catholic* churches," and how do they differ from *Roman* Catholic churches?

Works Consulted/Recommended Reading

Atiya, Aziz S., ed. 1968. *A History of Eastern Christianity*. London: Methuen and Company.

Atiya, Aziz S., ed. 2010 (1991). *The Coptic Encyclopedia*. 8 vols. New York: Macmillan. Reprinted Gorgias Press.

Common Christological Declaration between the Catholic Church and the Assyrian Church of the East. www.vatican.va/roman_curia/pontifical_councils/chrstuni/documents/rc_pc_chrstuni_doc_11111994_assyrian-church_en.html.

Constantelos, D. 1982. *Understanding the Greek Orthodox Church: Its Faith, History, and Practice*. New York: Seabury.

First Non-Official Consultation on Dialogue within the Syriac Tradition: Vienna, June 1994. 1994. Syriac Dialogue, 1. Vienna: Pro Oriente.

Griffith, Sidney H. 2008. *The Church in the Shadow of the Mosque: Christians and Muslims in the World of Islam*. Princeton, NJ: Princeton University Press.

Hussey, J.M. 1986. *The Orthodox Church in the Byzantine Empire.* Oxford: Clarendon Press.

Lossky, Vladimir. 1957. *The Mystical Theology of the Eastern Church.* Cambridge: James Clarke and Company.

Louth, Andrew. 2013. *Introducing Eastern Orthodox Theology.* Downers Grove, IL: IVP Academic.

McGuckin, John A. 2011. *The Orthodox Church: An Introduction to Its History, Doctrine, and Spiritual Culture.* Oxford: Wiley-Blackwell.

Meyedorff, J. 2001. *The Byzantine Legacy in the Orthodox Church.* Crestwood, NY: St. Vladimir's Seminary Press.

Papadakis, Aristeides, and John Meyendorff. 1994. *The Christian East and the Rise of the Papacy: The Church 1071–1453 A.D.* Crestwood, NY: St. Vladimir's Seminary Press.

Parry, Ken, ed. 2010. *The Blackwell Companion to Eastern Christianity.* Oxford: Wiley-Blackwell.

Pelikan, J. 1974. *The Christian Tradition: A History of the Development of Doctrine.* Vol. 2. *The Spirit of Eastern Christendom (600–1700).* Chicago, IL: University of Chicago Press.

Pseudo-Dionysius the Areopagite. 1987. *The Complete Works.* Translated by Colm Luibheid. Mahwah, NJ: Paulist Press.

Roberson, Ronald G. 2010. *The Eastern Christian Churches: A Brief Survey.* 7th rev. edn. Rome: Pontifical Institute of Oriental Studies.

Schmemann, Alexander. 1973. *For the Life of the World.* Crestwood, NY: St. Vladimir's Seminary Press.

Schulz, H. 1986. *The Byzantine Liturgy: Symbolic Structure and Faith Expression.* New York: Pueblo.

Spidlik, T. 1986. *The Spirituality of the Christian East: A Systematic Handbook.* Cistercian Studies, 79. Kalamazoo, MI: Cistercian Publications.

Vatican Statement on Dialogue with Oriental Orthodox. 2009. www.vatican.va/roman_curia/pontifical_councils/chrstuni/anc-orient-ch-docs/rc_pc_christuni_doc_20090129_mission-church_en.html.

Ware, K. 1984. *The Orthodox Church.* New York: Penguin Books.

Ware, K. 1992. "Eastern Christendom." In *The Oxford Illustrated History of Christianity.* Edited by John McManners, 123–162. Oxford: Oxford University Press.

Chapter

12
ISLAM AS SEEN IN THE CHRISTIAN TRADITION

Since their first encounters with Christians, Muslims have presented a challenge for Christian theologians. Indeed, Muslims have played an extremely important role in the history of Christian theology. Muslims have not only been powerful political adversaries and military enemies, but also religious rivals. The purpose of this chapter is to elucidate the historical significance for Christian theology of Muslims and their beliefs, especially in the Christian theology written in the geographical regions most central to Christian history, namely, the lands around the Mediterranean basin. While tracing the outlines of the role of Islam and Muslims in this history, this chapter will also provide a basic account of Islamic religious history on its own terms. How the Christian theological tradition has made sense of foreigners and religious others will thus become clearer, as will certain aspects of how Christian theology has related to political and military power, especially the power of Christian and Islamic empires. This background on Islam and how Christian theologians have made sense of it is the legacy inherited by those today who seek greater Muslim–Christian understanding through dialogue.

The Qur'an, the Prophet Muhammad, and His Successors

At the heart of the religious tradition that came to be called "Islam" is the Qur'an. It is an extraordinary text in its literary form, content, and style as well as in its significance.

The Arabic word *qur'an* means "recitations," an apt name for this fundamentally oral text. For those who worship the One God in accord with the religious tradition inaugurated by Qur'an, this collection of recitations is the word of God revealed to the Prophet Muhammad. For anyone who speaks or studies the Arabic language, this extraordinary text is also of unsurpassable significance for its place in the history of the Arabic language and Arabic literature. From the first hearers of the Qur'an up to today, Muslim and non-Muslim Arabic speakers, authors, and scholars recognize the uniqueness of the Qur'an as compelling verbal expression.

At the same time, approaching the Qur'an as if it were like the Bible or some modern book makes for confusion or even frustration. The place of the Qur'an within Islamic history, religion, and theology is by no means the same as the place of the

237

Bible in the Christian tradition. Unlike the Bible, the Qur'an is not an anthology of diverse writings from various eras, in different languages. The Qur'an is also not chronological or linear in structure. Moreover, it is an oral text, meant for recitation aloud, not for being read silently. In numerous ways, the Qur'an defies contemporary expectations of what a book is supposed to be. Clearing these assumptions and expectations is necessary for entering into the world of the Qur'an and the religious tradition of those believers who call themselves *muslims*, meaning those who submit to the One God.

Although the Qur'an is quite different from the Bible, it places itself in the religious tradition of the Bible in multiple ways. The Qur'an takes for granted its listeners' familiarity with a long list of characters from the book of Genesis, whose names are given here also in Arabic form, such as Adam, Eve (Hawa'), Cain (Qabil), Abel (Habil), Abraham (Ibrahim), Noah (Nuh), Lot (Lut), and Joseph (Yusuf). David (Dawud), Moses (Musa), Mary (Miriam), and Jesus ('Isa) also figure quite prominently.

The view of religious history presented in the Qur'an is of God sending again and again a multiplicity of prophets, who remind humanity of God and the path of God that we are meant to follow. The prophetic message thus centers on the oneness or unicity of God—a central concept known in the Islamic theological tradition as *tawhid*—and the call for humanity to live justly. The Qur'an presents Muhammad as a prophet (*nabi*) in this line of prophets, and it regards scriptural texts by other prophets as divinely revealed. For example, the Qur'an refers to the Torah of Moses, the Psalms of David, and the Gospel of Jesus. Muhammad is also called "*rasul Allah*" meaning the "messenger" or "apostle" sent by God to call people to know, worship, and obey God.

The Qur'an portrays remembering God (*dhikr Allah*) and God's path as true knowledge (*'ilm*) in contrast to forgetting God. It also portrays how God wants humanity to live in justice. ***Jahiliyya***, meaning ignorance, is thus the name for the cultural and historical period into which the Qur'an was revealed. Although the Qur'an is universal in its overall significance for Muslims, it is written in the Arabic language, and in the first instance it called the nomadic and settled peoples of the Arabian Peninsula in the time of Muhammad (*c.*570–632 c.e.) to "remember God."

The first word revealed to Muhammad (in *c.*610 c.e.) was "iqra'," which we can translate as "Read!" or "Recite!" In the original Arabic, *iqra'* is the imperative form from the same three-letter root as the word "*qur'an*," which came to be the name for the entire set of "recitations" that God commanded Muhammad to say aloud. This command came to Muhammad while he was on a spiritual retreat, praying and practicing seclusion in the mountain cave of Hira. Muhammad came to understand the angel Gabriel to be the agent of God revealing God's word for Muhammad to recite. This first experience of revelation was extremely disturbing to Muhammad, so he left the cave to go tell his wife, Khadija, about it. She consoled him, believing the experience to be from God, and thereafter played an important part in Muhammad coming to understand his role as a prophet.

Just as with traditional Christian accounts of the life of Jesus of Nazareth, the biographical information and narratives about Muhammad that have been passed down through the Islamic tradition are primarily religious in nature, not historical in the modern, scientific sense. The search for the "historical Muhammad," like the twentieth century search for the "historical Jesus," can access little material that has not been crafted by authors and editors with agendas that were devotional, hagiographical, polemical, spiritual, theological, or the like. Just as the Gospels were crafted by authors who believed in the resurrected Christ and whose purpose in writing was to bring the "good news" to others, so the Islamic sources related to the Prophet were crafted by authors who held to the basic Islamic declaration of faith that "There is no God but

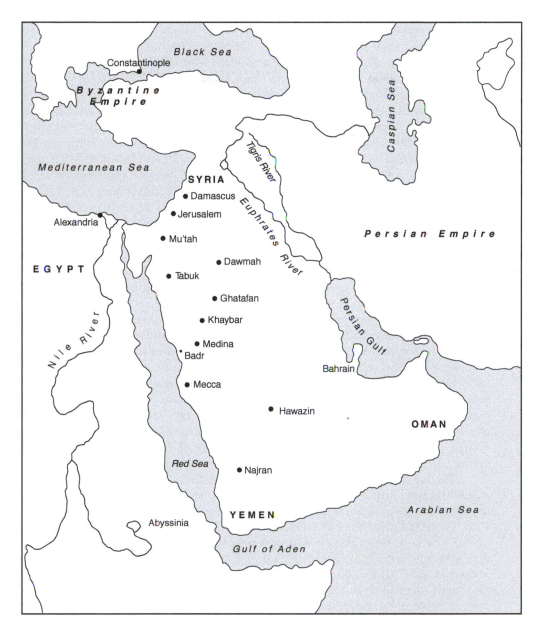

Figure 12–1 Arabia in Muhammad's time.

God, and Muhammad is the messenger of God." In the service of presenting an introduction to Islam and its significance for the Christian theological tradition, the present chapter thus relies on Islamic sources and modern, critical historical, scholarly treatments of them that were written by authors of a variety of religious orientations.

Muhammad ibn ʿAbdullah ibn ʿAbd al-Muttalib and **Khadija bint Khuwaylid** lived in Mecca, in a desert region called the Hijaz, on the west side of the Arabian Peninsula, near the Red Sea. He was an orphan in that his father ʿAbdullah died before he was born and his mother Amina died when he was six years old. Muhammad's paternal uncle, Abu Talib, raised him with his own sons, including **ʿAli ibn Abi**

Talib. Though never becoming a Muslim, Abu Talib gave his nephew powerful protection until his death. According to traditional Islamic accounts, Khadija was a wealthy widow engaged in commerce and trade when she employed him to supervise her caravan trading between Mecca and Syria. When she was 40 years old and Muhammad was 25, she proposed marriage to him, which he accepted. For 25 years after that, until Khadija's death at age 65, she remained his only spouse. They had two sons who died young and four daughters, including Fatima, who eventually married her first cousin, Abu Talib's famous son, 'Ali. Besides building up Muhammad's confidence as he made sense of his experience of revelation and began preaching to others, Khadija with her wealth also made it possible for Muhammad not to work year-round but rather to devote himself to spiritual practices in seclusion, such as contemplation and prayer, which prepared him for the revelation of the Qur'an.

The city where Khadija and Muhammad lived, Mecca, had religious significance before the Qur'an began to be revealed there to Muhammad. By one important tradition, it was a settlement established by Abraham, Hajar (the biblical Haggar), and their son Isma'il (the biblical Ishmael). Abraham and his son were said to have built the ancient shrine known as the Ka'ba to be the center for worshipping the one true God. Before Muhammad's birth, Mecca was already a site for pilgrimage, as well as a center for trade. Muhammad's tribe, the Quraysh, ruled Mecca and were devoted to the Ka'ba. They protected it and the pilgrims who came to it during certain months that were deemed holy.

In the society of pre-Islamic Arabia, oasis sanctuaries like Mecca were important places for rest and refuge, as well as ritual and culture. People would come to an oasis sanctuary in order to resolve disputes, consult soothsayers, find spouses, and enjoy listening to recited poetry, which was the hallmark of pre-Islamic cultural life. No one could bring weapons or do violence in any sanctuary, and all warfare ceased during the holy months when tribes from all over Arabia came to Mecca. The Quraysh safeguarded this environment of exchange and worship by providing hospitality to pilgrims, while also hosting profitable trade fairs and special poetry contests.

The religious observances at the Ka'ba were diverse, including a ritual walk around the Ka'ba, ancestor veneration, animal sacrifice, and the use of idols. Some Meccans sought *al-hanifiyya*, the pure religion of Abraham centered on the worship of the one true God. These Meccans thus eschewed idol veneration and the meat sacrificed to them.

Christians, Jews, and Zoroastrians were all parts of the cultural context of sixth- and seventh-century Arabia. For example, the city of Yathrib, which came to be known as Medina, was home to several Jewish tribes. Some Meccans were Christian, and many more lived not far away in Najran and Yemen. Because of the great importance of trade in the economic life of the Arabian tribes, the Quraysh and others living in Arabia, which was a geopolitical backwater, were exposed to the three great empires surrounding the region, namely, the Sassanian Persian, the Byzantine Roman, and the Abyssinian or Ethiopian. Indeed each of these three empires had certain Arab tribes that were under their specific cultural and political influence. Meanwhile, the pastoral nomads known as Bedouin were called the *'arab* and seen by Arabian townsfolk as the true bearers of authentic Arab culture and language.

Besides Mecca and Medina, Jerusalem—whose very name in Arabic is **al-Quds**, meaning "the Holy"—was also a holy city for the Prophet Muhammad and the Muslim community from very early in Islamic history. For a time during the life of the Prophet, Muslims even faced the city of Jerusalem for their daily ritual prayers. Jerusalem remains a very important site for Muslims today.

In Muslim understandings of the history of God's revelation for humanity, the holiness of the city of Jerusalem has a basis in events that preceded the revelation of

Qur'an. The Qur'an takes for granted that at numerous points throughout history God has sent to humanity a number of prophets with revelations for how to live in accord with God's will. As mentioned previously, a first basis for the holiness of the city of Mecca for Muslims lies in Abraham's worship there of the One True God. Similarly, Muslims recognize Jesus as a prophet who brought the revelation of the Gospel, and Moses as a prophet who brought the revelation of the Torah. Jerusalem was already a holy city for the Prophet Muhammad because of its significance in the life of Jesus and other Jews. This religious context is relevant for understanding an extremely important mystical experience of the Prophet Muhammad in which Jerusalem played a special part.

The seventeenth sura of the Qur'an is named for this mystical "night journey," which transported the Prophet from the great mosque of Mecca to "the farthest mosque."

> Glory to (Allah) Who did take His servant for a Journey by night from the Sacred Mosque to the farthest Mosque [al-Masjid al-Aqsa], whose precincts We did bless, in order that We might show him some of Our Signs: for He is the One Who heareth and seeth (all things).
>
> (Q.17.1 "Al-Isra, The Night Journey")

Early Islamic sources, including Ibn Ishaq's (d. 768 C.E.) authoritative biography of the Prophet, locate this "farthest mosque" in Jerusalem. This mystical journey from Mecca to Jerusalem is also connected in the Islamic tradition to a "heavenly ascent" by the Prophet. The angel Gabriel is the Prophet's guide for this journey, and a tall white animal called Buraq is the vehicle. Early Islamic sources recount Muhammad's stops along this journey to meet Abraham, Moses, Jesus, and to visit other holy sites. Islamic art, poetry, and religious literature have reflected on this extremely important episode in the extraordinary life of the Prophet Muhammad.

This background is important for understanding the cultural context of Qur'anic language, the occasions of revelation for specific Qur'anic verses, and the broader scene in which Muhammad and those who believed in his prophethood came to influence.

Muhammad continued to receive Qur'anic revelations for the remaining years of his life up to his death in 632 C.E. Many of his family members, starting with Khadija and then his first cousin 'Ali ibn Abi Talib, came to believe in the veracity of the Qur'anic revelation and Muhammad's claim to prophethood. The Muslim community or *ummah* grew as more and more people came to heed the Prophet Muhammad's message. They would listen to the Prophet recite the Qur'an and recite it themselves in turn as an important part of their ritual practice and worship of God.

As the *ummah* grew in number, the interests of the Quraysh tribe were threatened. For example, the tribe profited from the Meccan pilgrimage in its current form, which included the use of idols, which the Qur'an condemned. Several powerful leaders of the Quraysh tribe opposed Muhammad and the Muslim community. Indeed, one of Muhammad's own uncles, named Abu Lahab, was one such enemy of the *ummah*; another was named Abu Sufyan. These opponents began persecuting the converts to this new religious faith. To pressure the Muslims, the Quraysh eventually organized a commercial boycott of the two clans of the tribe that were most closely associated with Muhammad. The situation of Muhammad and the *ummah* worsened still further when, in a single year, both Khadija and Abu Talib died. The Prophet thus lost two people who were among the most important in his life and most powerful sources of support and strength. He went on to marry other women, including the daughters of several of his Companions and allies, such as Abu Bakr's daughter, 'Aisha, and Omar ibn al-Khattab's daughter, Hafsa.

The persecution of the early Muslim community even went so far as martyrdom. Some slaves who became Muslim were tortured and killed by their owners. The first such martyr or *shahid* (literally meaning "witness") was a slave woman named Sumayya. Another slave, an African named Bilal, was being tortured by his owner until purchased and freed by Abu Bakr.

In the year 622 C.E., accompanied by Abu Bakr and others, the Prophet left Mecca for Yathrib, where a small group of residents had already become Muslim. This emigration or *hijra* is such a momentous event in Islamic history, that it became the basis for a new "*hijri*" calendar used till today by the Muslim community. Yathrib became known as Medina, meaning the "city" of the Prophet, because there Muhammad and the other Muslims began to apply Qur'anic values for a just social order. The parts of the Qur'an, called *suras*, are also categorized as either Meccan or Medinan, depending on whether they were revealed before or after the Prophet's *hijra* or emigration to Medina.

The Meccan period of Qur'anic revelation lasted around 13 years, and the Medinan period about ten years, from the *hijra* in 622 C.E. until the Prophet's death in 632 C.E. In these approximately 23 years, more than 6,000 verses were revealed. These *ayat*, or verses, are organized into 114 suras, the shortest of which ("Al-Kawthar," Q.108) is only three verses while the longest ("Al-Baqara," Q.2) is 286 verses.

Each sura is preceded by a phrase called the *basmala*, which Michael Sells has rendered into English as "In the name of God the Compassionate the Caring." Sells' book, *Approaching the Qur'an*, contains particularly masterful English renditions of the early Meccan suras, which he describes as "hymnic." Sells successfully conveys the two most striking aspects of the divine voice in the Qur'anic text, which are intimacy and awesomeness. The Qur'an is dizzying in content as well as style. The thematic content of the Qur'anic revelations includes such elements as eschatology, moral principles, divine speech about God's own nature, specific prescriptions and proscriptions, narrative, parable, divine responses to particular episodes in the life of Muhammad, divine responses to public affairs in the life of the *ummah* in Medina, and literary and historical allusions to elements familiar in seventh-century Arabian culture, including biblical prophets and Jesus Christ.

Qur'anic Passage (Translated by Michael Sells)

"The Most High" (Q.87)
In the Name of God the Compassionate the Caring
Holy be the name of your lord most high
Who created then gave form
Who determined then gave guidance
Who made the meadow pasture grow
then turned it to a darkened flood-swept remnant
We will make you recite. You will not forget except what the will of God allows
He knows what is declared and what lies hidden
He will ease you to the life of ease
So remind them if reminder will succeed

Those who know awe will be brought to remember
He who is hard in wrong will turn away
He will be put to the fire
neither dying in it nor living
He who makes himself pure will flourish
who remembers the name of his lord and performs the prayer
But no. They prefer the lower life
Better is the life ultimate, the life that endures
As is set down in the scrolls of the ancients
the scrolls of Ibrahim and Musa.

Recitation of Qur'an is central to Muslims' prayer and devotion. They often use the *basmala* to invoke God's blessing at the start of an undertaking, whether a meal, or a speech, or a journey. Reciting memorized Qur'anic suras is an important part of *salah*, the ritual prayer that Muslims traditionally perform at certain times of the day. During Ramadan, which commemorates the revelation of Qur'an to the Prophet Muhammad, special recitations take place in mosques so as to take the community through the entire Qur'anic text during the course of the holy month.

The fact that the Qur'an includes relatively little narrative (with the notable exception of "Yusuf," Sura 12) is another illustration of how different its place in Islamic tradition is from the place of the New Testament in the Christian tradition. The Qur'an does not tell the story of Muhammad. It does not describe in a narrative how the Prophet lived or spoke or touched the lives of those around him. At the same time, the occasions for the revelation of various verses are often some incident or another in the life of Muhammad or the Muslim community. God responded to various situations by revealing certain verses to the Prophet. Although the Islamic tradition regards the Qur'an as having universal import, the specific contexts in which different verses were revealed are crucial for their interpretation.

Other texts from the Islamic tradition provide the biographical information, historical context, and other background material that Muslims use to understand Qur'anic revelations in context. **Hadith** are the reports of the words and deeds of the Prophet Muhammad and his Companions. These customs and practices are called the **sunna,** from which the adjective Sunni comes, a term that is used to describe the largest sect of Muslims today. Genealogical and biographical dictionaries are an extremely important and voluminous kind of Islamic literature covering the Prophet, his relatives and Companions, and many other cultural, religious, political, and intellectual figures. Another biographical field called *sira* literature focuses fully on the life of the Prophet. *Tafsir* is the term for exegetical writings that interpret the Qur'anic text in light of linguistic, cultural, biographical, historical, philosophical, theological, spiritual, and other concerns.

Upon the death of the Prophet Muhammad in 632 C.E., the *ummah* faced multiple new challenges. For one, the Qur'anic revelation was definitively complete. No new revelations would come to the Prophet to give the *ummah* guidance for how to respond to any new situation that arose. The Qur'an would require preservation as those reciters who learned it directly from the Prophet also began to die. A great many developments in the Arabic linguistic sciences would take place in the ensuing centuries including the creation of a uniform writing system, the first dictionaries, grammatical texts, and studies of Arabic dialects, which, for example, affected how Qur'anic reciters pronounced various words of the revelations somewhat differently.

The problem of succession was an even more urgent issue. Because of his close relationship with Muhammad and the confidence that the Prophet showed in him, 'Ali ibn Abi Talib was a clear contender to succeed the Prophet as leader of the *ummah*. However, Abu Bakr emerged as the first caliph or successor, and he stayed two years in this role. After Abu Bakr's death, Omar ibn al-Khattab became "caliph" (which means "successor") for ten years (634–644 C.E.). Omar is remembered for his successful military expeditions which expanded what came to be known in the later tradition of Islamic jurisprudence as **dar al-islam** (literally, "the abode of Islam"), meaning the earthly domain where people worship only God and govern their affairs in accord with divine teaching.

After Omar's death, a six-member council of Muslim elders elected one of their number, 'Uthman of the prominent Umayyad clan from Mecca. He was the Prophet's son-in-law, having married in succession two of the Prophet's daughters from Khadija, first Ruqayya and then (upon her death) Umm Kulthum. A significant number of Muslims had thought since the Prophet's death that 'Ali ibn Abi Talib, who was another member of this council of elders, should have been the caliph or successor. After this third election of a caliph other than 'Ali, the tensions between his partisans (which in Arabic is **shi'a**) and others in the *ummah* continued to increase, leading to the murder of 'Uthman 12 years into his reign, in 656 C.E. 'Ali then became caliph, though some in the *ummah* never recognized him as such. In the midst of this tension, 'Ali fled Medina for a city in Iraq called Kufa. A relative of the slain 'Uthman named Mu'awiya, who was governor of Syria, led the military opposition against 'Ali and his partisans, the *shi'a*. Following numerous battles and an arbitration, Mu'awiya

Figure 12–2 The Expansion of Islam up to 750.

ibn Abi Sufyan proclaimed himself caliph in 660 and six months later, in 661, at the entrance of a mosque in Kufa, 'Ali was assassinated.

The caliphate of Mu'awiya, with its capital in Damascus, was the first of the Umayyad dynasty of Islamic rule, which lasted until 750 C.E. Many other Islamic states and empires followed over the ensuing centuries. The split between the partisans of 'Ali and other Muslims continues in what we now call the Shiite and Sunni sects of Islam.

The Islamic tradition, with its many layers of intellectual, artistic, cultural, literary, philosophical, scientific, spiritual, and theological production, all begins with the Qur'an, the Prophet Muhammad, and the life of the early Muslim community. The learned elite of classical Islamic civilization, known as the *ulama*, reflected on the Qur'an and the model of the Prophet, while also integrating and advancing knowledge inherited from ancient Greek civilization, for example, in medicine, mathematics, and philosophy. The wealthy ruling class of Islamic societies supported the development of institutions such as mosques and madrasas to be centers for prayer, Qur'an recitation, and study.

The so-called "**five pillars of Islam**" came to be important reference points for Muslims' ritual practice. First among these is the previously mentioned declaration of faith or *shahada* that "There is no god but God, and Muhammad is the Messenger of God." The other four pillars are *salah* (prayer), fasting dawn to dusk during the month of Ramadan, almsgiving, and *hajj*, which is a pilgrimage to the cities central to the Prophet's life, Mecca and Medina.

This rudimentary sketch of the beginnings of the Islamic tradition lays a few building blocks for understanding something of the significance of Islam and Muslims for the Christian theological tradition, to which we now turn our attention.

Christian Theological Responses to Islam

The hallmarks of Christian theological responses to Muslims for most of their history have been opposition, antagonism, and enmity. Christian theologians framed their writings about Muslims in the broader context of experiences of people who were different from themselves. The classical civilization of Greece and Rome had fostered a sense of cultural superiority over neighboring peoples. From classical philosophy, Christian theologians adopted the tools of logic and rhetoric for doctrinal debate. The biblical doctrine of election was taken over by Christians and applied to themselves as the new Israel. The Bible's teaching of a single creator God who was directing human history to its providential end was also adopted by Christians. With the conversion of the Roman Empire to Christianity, Christians like the historian Eusebius of Caesarea (d. 339 C.E.) found it tempting to think that the Christianized Roman Empire, by now called the Byzantine Empire (see Chapter 11), enjoyed God's favor as the political means by which the world should be governed. Christian experiences of religious "others" in pre-Islamic Christian history principally had meant pagans, Jews, and Christian heretics. When Christians first encountered Muslims, they thus tried to fit these new religious "others" into one of these three categories. Some saw them as new Jews because of their rejection of Jesus' divinity, their practice of circumcision, and their hostility to the cross and to images in general. Others tried to frame Muslim monotheism and rejection of idols as a return to the pre-Mosaic monotheism of Abraham, and to claim that Muhammad had taken his teaching from prior acquaintance with the Bible.

The interpretive tools and categories that scholars, popes, monks, and other Christians developed starting with their first encounters with Muslims would have a long history, continuing in some respects up to our own time. Christian writings about Muslims have mainly been quite polemical, fueled by fear and marked by prejudice. Among their ideas were that God allows Muslims to gain power to punish Christians for their sins; that Muslims are brutal, barbaric, and sexually depraved pagans; that Muslims are heretics; that Muslims are diabolical or collaborators with Satan; and that Muhammad is a false prophet or an "antichrist" harkening the apocalypse or end of the world. Christian ideas about Muslim carnality reflected the Muslim practice of polygamy, including by Muhammad, whom Christians compared to Jesus, who never married at all. The apocalyptic assertions grew out of a conventional Christian idea that the four beasts of the biblical book of Daniel 7:1–14 stood for four kingdoms, of which the last and final one was the Roman Empire, which would never pass away (Daniel 2:44). To this political interpretation, Christian theologians joined New Testament passages about an antichrist, a false Messiah, who would seize power until defeated by the return of Jesus Christ at the end of time.

In line with the view of history as under God's providence was an understanding that the Holy Spirit guided the Christian Church's decisions regarding the canon of the Bible and the doctrinal definitions of the ecumenical councils (see Chapter 9). The Council of Chalcedon (451 c.e.) had defined the dogma of the Incarnation of Christ, according to which there was a complete divine nature and a complete human nature joined without separation or confusion in a single person, the Word of God made flesh. Since Chalcedon and other early church councils concerned the nature of Jesus Christ, the fact that Muslim belief aligned with certain Christian understandings of Christ but not with others disposed Christian theologians to regard Muslims as heretics. For some theologians, heretics were "antichrists," like the ones referred to in the first letter of John in the New Testament:

> Children, it is the last hour! As you have heard that antichrist is coming, so now many antichrists have come. From this we know that it is the last hour. They went out from us, but they did not belong to us; for if they had belonged to us, they would have remained with us. ... Who is the liar but the one who denies that Jesus is the Christ? This is the antichrist, the one who denies the Father and the Son. No one who denies the Son has the Father; everyone who confesses the Son has the Father also.
>
> (1 John 2:18–19, 22–23)

Scriptural passages such as this one thus gave rise to the idea of Muhammad as an Antichrist and a harbinger of the Apocalypse, as did scriptural references to "false prophets" and "false messiahs," for example, in the Gospels of Mark and Matthew (Mark 13:22; Matthew 24:24).

After their dramatic victories over both the Byzantine Empire and the Persian Empire, Muslims organized themselves into a more and more powerful and effective society across an expanding geographic domain. They rapidly became civilizational and religious rivals to Christians in the historic heartlands of Christendom, on every side of the Mediterranean basin. Some Christians found themselves living under Muslim rule, and only gradually recognized that this situation would not be temporary.

"Saracens, Ishmaelites, Muhammadans"

Christians were not sure what to call these new political, military, and religious rivals coming out of Arabia. From their first encounters in the seventh century, they drew on pre-Islamic Roman and Jewish understandings of the people of Arabia. From the Genesis accounts of Abraham and his concubine Hagar, who gave birth to Ishmael, came names used by Christians for Muslims such as "Ishmaelites" and "Hagarenes." The name "Saracens" was very commonly used, often interchangeably with "Arabs." Of uncertain etymology, "Saracens" became, for many medieval Europeans, also interchangeable with "pagans." Besides these ethnic terms, Christians also called Muslims "Muhammadans," on the model of the term "Christians," coming from the name of the most important and charismatic figure in the religious tradition.

As Muslims came forth from Arabia and took over Syria and Palestine, the responses of the different groups of Christians in the Eastern Mediterranean to Muslim governance varied according to their relationship to their previous rulers (see Chapter 11). Syria, Palestine, Egypt, and part of Armenia had been ruled by the Byzantine Empire before the Muslim conquest. Christians of the region who aligned with Byzantine rule and supported the decisions of the Council of Chalcedon were thus called Melkites ("royalists"). Melkite Christians lost power and privilege with the Muslim conquest. They accordingly explained it as divine retribution for Christians' sins, with apocalyptic undertones, and described the Arabs as barbarians in contrast to the civilized Byzantines.

Christians in Egypt, Syria, and Armenia who rejected Chalcedon's two-natures doctrine (and were therefore called "Monophysites") hated imperial persecution. As a result, they were at first more open to Arab rule. For them it was easier than it was for the Melkites to substitute the Arabs for the Romans as the fourth world kingdom of Daniel.

Still another Christian group was the Church of the East, sometimes called "Nestorians." They had been expelled from the Christianized Roman Empire long before and had settled in Persia, governed by the Sasanian dynasty. Their sources tell of the suffering and deaths during the conquests but are notably unhostile toward Arab rule.

Bishops and theologians of the Monophysite and Nestorian communities, which had not been faring particularly well under Byzantine rule, wrote affirmingly of how the Muslims worshipped the God of Abraham, knew the law of Moses, respected priests and saints, and aided churches and monasteries. Such theological perspectives were based in their positive experiences of Islamic conquest. Only under Muslim rule were Nestorians, for example, able to build monasteries in Palestine for the first time.

In these contrasting cases of Christians in the Eastern Mediterranean who were among the first Christians to encounter Muslims, the Christian theological interpretations of Muslims were determined, to a great extent, by the political positions of the Christians writing them. This phenomenon remains apparent throughout the succeeding centuries of Muslim–Christian encounter.

St. John of Damascus (d. 749) was a Syrian monk who is a revered figure in the Eastern Orthodox tradition, especially because of his defense of the veneration of images. He was also a pioneer in Christian theological treatment of Islam. Named for his native city, which was the capital of the Ummayad Empire, John had firsthand knowledge of and experience with Muslims. In fact, before becoming a monk at Mar Saba, near Jerusalem, John, like his father, was a tax official in the court of the Umayyad caliph in Damascus. Accordingly, John describes this religion of the "Ishmaelites" as the prevailing religion, which indeed in his context it was.

John's treatise *On Heresies* treats 100 heretical sects, the last of which is Islam. There John gives an abbreviated account of selected Islamic theological teachings before providing responses to Muslim attacks on Christian belief. John's account of the history of Islam is that a false prophet named Mamed (i.e., Muhammad) invented his heretical book (i.e., the Qur'an) from picking and choosing bits from the Bible and from speaking with a monk aligned with the Arian heresy. This false prophet pretended that his heresy was divinely inspired and convinced misguided people to believe in it. Among the Islamic theological ideas that John somewhat accurately represents are that God is One, the creator of all. John also describes Islamic Christology as holding that Christ is called "word of God" and "spirit of God," was born of the Virgin Mary, and was eventually assumed into heaven. Muslims likewise believe that Christ was not crucified and did not die. From there, John responds to Muslim theological attacks on Christians, such as the charge that Christians are idolaters since they worship the cross. Among his responses are to turn the accusation of idolatry around and accuse Muslims of worshipping the Ka'ba. He also more or less accurately names specific suras of the Qur'an: Women (Q.4), The Table (Q.5), and The Cow (Q.2), and inaccurately refers to a sura that he calls "The Camel of God."

In this treatise, John thus combines what he knows first hand about Islamic thought and the Qur'an along with slanderous representations of Muhammad in order to provide Eastern Christians with material to use in their debates with Muslims.

As more and more Christians converted to Islam in both the Eastern and Western Mediterranean, later Christian theologians also felt the need to address the religious particularities of Islam. **Peter the Venerable**, Abbot of Cluny (d. 1156), is one of the most important medieval Western Christian figures who did so. He saw himself as refuting the diabolical heresy of the Saracens. To support this project, Peter assembled a team of Arabic–Latin translators to give him access to Islamic texts, including the first Latin version of the Qur'an, indeed the first in any European language. Twelfth-century readers of this Latin adaptation wrote notes in its margins that illustrate their attitudes about the Qur'anic text. These annotations call some suras "diabolical" and others "stupid, vain, and impious." They ridicule as lies and silly fables any Qur'anic narratives that differ from biblical accounts of such characters as Cain and Abel, Joseph and Potiphar from the book of Genesis, Mary, and, above all, Jesus.

Peter the Venerable used this Latin version of the Qur'an and other Islamic material to compose his own anti-Muslim tracts in which he urged his readers to preach to heretics and infidels in a spirit of Christian love, then, if unsuccessful, to use violence and military power to oppose them. In contrast to his calling Jews irrational beasts in an earlier anti-Jewish tract, Peter is capable of praising Muslims as learned and rational because of their achievements in philosophy and the sciences. They should, therefore, be open to his rational refutation of their errors about religious truth. But, at the same time, he also regards Muslims primarily as heretics, and slanders Muhammad as base, conniving, and in cahoots with Satan, because Muslims deny the divinity of Christ and also that Christ really died, though Peter also acknowledges the Muslim teaching that Christ returned to heaven.

The work of Peter the Venerable and of other Christian Apologists was influential in motivating and justifying the armed pilgrimages to Jerusalem that came to be known (in the mid-thirteenth century) as the **Crusades**, which were one of the most important Christian responses to Islam in the medieval period. These were wars called by popes and justified by preachers. The enemy that the Crusaders set out to defeat in Jerusalem were the "Saracens," and the standard stated objective was to win back the "Holy Land."

The theological arguments crafted by Christian clergy to build support for these military expeditions in foreign lands made use of the material generated in the previous centuries of Christian discourse about Islam. In 1095, Pope Urban II (r. 1088–1099) made a call to action that successfully moved many to set out on an expedition of war and conquest in Palestine that we now call the First Crusade (1096–1099). In a speech to clergy and nobles at a church council in France, Pope Urban called on his listeners to mount a rescue operation for their Christian "brethren" in Byzantine territory conquered by "the Turks and Arabs," and promised the full and immediate remission (forgiveness) of sins of those who died en route to do battle with those he called "infidels" and "a vile race."

Urban II's call was wildly successful. Tens of thousands of Christians, including women, children, and the elderly, embarked on this journey of holy war and blessed conquest. This journey was an armed pilgrimage. The Christian militants conquered Jerusalem in 1099. The first Crusaders set up there the "Kingdom of Jerusalem" to rule over the land they conquered, and they held it for almost 100 years until 1187. Other military campaigns in the following centuries were waged with papal support as crusades. For example, the pope accorded a special indulgence, or remission for the penalties of sin, to those undertaking war expeditions against Muslims in Spain. This admixture of spiritual and religious meaning in a military struggle against the Saracens has overshadowed Muslim–Christian relations ever since.

Following the period of the Crusades, towering figures of the Christian theological tradition such as Thomas Aquinas and Martin Luther replicated in their own writings the anti-Muslim polemics and slurs generated by earlier Christian thinkers.

Thomas Aquinas (d. 1274), for example, appears to have depended on Christian predecessors like John of Damascus and Peter the Venerable for his knowledge of Islam rather than read a Latin translation of the Qur'an for himself. He repeats familiar themes such as Islam as the sum of all heresies in his *Summa contra Gentiles* (*Summa against Non-Believers*, not to be confused with his *Summa Theologiae*) and his *Reasons for the Faith against the Saracens*. For example, at the beginning of his apologetic work *Reasons for the Faith against the Saracens*, Thomas notes Muslims' objections to the ideas that Jesus Christ is God; that God is three persons in one God; and that Christ was crucified for the salvation of humankind. Thomas also recounts the accusation from Muslims' anti-Christian polemics that Christians "eat their God on the altar." Besides his theological opposition to Islam, Thomas, like many other Christian scholars in the medieval Scholastic period, gained much from Muslim scholars such as Ibn Sina (d. 1037, "**Avicenna**" in Latin), who carried out important philosophical and scientific work that advanced from the contributions of classical Greek civilization. The so-called Dark Ages of Christian Europe were a "Golden Age" for Islamic thought.

Martin Luther (d. 1546) similarly reproduced medieval Christian polemic against Muslims, in the service of the agenda of the Protestant Reformation. Luther's insult for Muslims was to call them "black devils." He likened them to the Pope, as antichrists, signaling the coming of the Apocalypse. Like Thomas Aquinas, Luther was thoughtful and scholarly in his reflection on Islam, as he was on so many other topics. To learn what he could about this rival religion, Luther actually read the

Qur'an. Yet this great theologian was also filled with a certain dread of Islam, which he put to use in advancing his agenda against the Roman Catholic Church. He constructed an image of the evil "Turks" as a rival threat, parallel to Luther's primary foe, the pope. The powerful Turkish hordes threatened Christendom, and Luther used Europeans' fear of the Muslim Turks in service of his hostility to the Catholic Church. They were both in Luther's-rhetoric "enemies of Christ." As he wrote in his *Military Sermon against the Turks*, "If we fall under the Turk, we go to the Devil; if we remain under the pope, we go to hell."

Starting in the sixteenth and seventeenth centuries, members of the Catholic religious order the Society of Jesus, known as the Jesuits, played an important role in Christian engagement with Muslims. Ignatius of Loyola (d. 1556), founder of the Jesuits, himself established a "House of Catechumens" in Rome to instruct Jewish and Muslim converts to Christianity. He also had Jesuits study the Qur'an, which Ignatius Lomelini (d. 1645) later translated into Italian for use in Jesuit colleges. Arabic-speaking Jesuit communities were established in two cities of Sicily, Messina and Monreale, and later in Istanbul (1582) and Cairo (1697). Mughal Emperor Akbar famously invited the Jesuits in Goa to his court at Fatehpur Sikri (which became the city of Lahore, Pakistan) for religious discussions with Muslim counterparts. Following the end of the Ottoman siege of Vienna in 1683, Jesuits wrote a number of treatises about Muslims and Islam in the tradition that we have traced in this section. For example, Thyrso Gonzales wrote an 866-page *Guide to the Conversion of Mohammedans* (1689) and Nicolò Pallavicino wrote *The Modern Prosperity of the Catholic Church against Mohammedanism* (1688).

European Colonization, Christian Missionaries, and Muslims

The image of Christopher Columbus "discovering" in 1492 what for Europeans at that time was a "New World" is a convenient starting point not only for the American patriotic narrative but also for the history of European colonization (see Chapter 21). As capitalism developed, the economic needs and commercial interests of Spanish, Portuguese, French, Dutch, English and other European polities drove the movement of foreign quest symbolized in the American imagination by Columbus. European nations built empires for themselves that by the early twentieth century covered 85 percent of the earth's land surface. By 1800, Muslims were almost everywhere ruled by others. In the historic heartlands of Islam, Western powers had an enormous impact and eventually drew the maps of the modern Middle East, most famously in the Sykes–Picot Agreement of 1916. This age of European colonial empires lasted until the 1960s.

A number of ideas familiar from Christian theological interpretations of Islam and Muslims in previous centuries became useful in the construction of European colonial ideology: a sense of superiority over other "races"; a sense of "mission" to bring civilization to peoples whom they regarded as primitive and barbaric; and a missionary impulse to evangelize the heathen and convert them to Christianity. The French, for example, famously invoked their *la mission civilisatrice* (literally, "civilizing mission") as justification for taking over places with Muslim majorities such as Algeria and much of West Africa.

The European colonial project of conquering an empire to serve capitalist needs afforded new opportunities for Christian missionaries to propagate their faith and for scholars to produce new knowledge. At the same time, the relationship between these missionaries and scholars, on the one hand, and imperial authorities, on the other, was complex. Some were complicit collaborators with the colonial project; others saw themselves as anti-imperialist.

Meanwhile, the Protestant Reformation instigated a splintering of the Western church into multiple denominations and an ongoing rivalry between them and the Roman Catholic Church. In 1622, the Catholic Church, for example, founded the Sacred Congregation for the Propagation of the Faith in part out of concern that British and Dutch colonial efforts would lead to Protestant conversions in the New World.

Overlapping with the European "Age of Discovery," the fourteenth to sixteenth centuries were the period when Islam spread in Asia. Traders and itinerant Sufis brought their religion to northern India, western China, Southeast Asia, and Bangladesh. Islam had its own "New World" in, for example, the vast Malay archipelago, versus its "Old World" of Egypt, Syria, Palestine, Iraq, and the Hijaz.

Turning our attention to the British Empire in particular, by the nineteenth century, it ruled over tremendous swaths of the Muslim world, from India to Africa to the Middle East. Nineteenth-century British missionaries were moved by eschatological anticipation. Anglicans saw the waning (e.g., the Ottomans) or gaining (e.g., in Africa) power of Islam and the Vatican's loss of the papal states in 1870 as "signs of the times" indicating the impending rapture. Like their medieval forebears, these missionaries hoped that rational disputation would be effective in converting Muslims. Some of them also regarded Eastern Christians as heretics who should be converted to Anglicanism. In 1841, the Church of England established the bishopric of Jerusalem for these purposes, and its missionaries were also very active in Cairo, Egypt and Khartoum, Sudan. Some saw the expansion of the British Empire in India as especially portentous, for there these Protestant missionaries could evangelize both Hindus and Muslims. Others believed that returning Jews to the land of Israel would precede their conversion to Christianity along with that of Muslims and Hindus to usher in a millennium of paradise on earth and the Second Coming of Jesus Christ. As an example of this kind of colonial Christian interpretation of Islam, at a prayer meeting of the Christian Missionary Society in 1881, the vicar of Fareham, England declared, "Certainly it is a sign of the times that the Crescent is waning before the Cross, that though Mohammedanism as a religion is not worn out, Mohammedan nations have come under the power or the influence of Christian rulers" (Porter 2004, 215–16).

Orientalism

Besides missionary work, scholarly endeavor has constituted another important way in which European Christians engaged with Muslims and Islam in recent centuries. Napoleon, for example, invaded Egypt in 1798. He brought with him a large team of scholars who documented and studied all that they found, from the flora and fauna to the art and architecture left from ancient pharaonic civilization. The British came to dominate Egypt for the following 150 years, but the French effectively invented the field of knowledge called Egyptology.

Orientalism refers to the European project of studying the languages, literature, cultures, and art of the "Orient," which encompassed many Muslim peoples. The Arabic language began being taught regularly at European universities from the late sixteenth century. Some Orientalists focused on philological projects, such as editing manuscripts and analyzing linguistic structures of ancient or medieval texts. Others performed archaeological excavations or collected art for exhibition and interpretation. Like Christian missionaries, scholars in the field of Orientalism had a complex relationship with imperial power. Racial ideology and a sense of religious superiority often imbued Orientalists' study, as did earnest curiosity, intellectual rigor, and—for some scholars—great erudition.

Around the turn of the twentieth century, a new generation of Orientalist scholars began to take a new approach to their work on Islam. Mastering important Islamic languages such as Persian, Turkish, and Arabic, scholars such as David Samuel Margoliouth (d. 1940), Duncan Black Macdonald (d. 1943), Louis Massignon (d. 1962), and W. Montgomery Watt (d. 2006) were also ordained Christian ministers and had extensive interactions with Muslim counterparts. Many of these twentieth-century Orientalist scholars contributed to missionary and colonial projects like their forebears. Christians were by no means the only ones who contributed to Orientalist scholarship in the West. One seminal figure was Ignaz Goldziher (d. 1921), secretary of the Jewish community of Budapest.

Edward Said (d. 2003), a Palestinian American from a Greek Orthodox Christian family, is the most influential critic of this scholarly tradition and its concomitant ideology. Born in Jerusalem in 1920 (under British colonial rule), raised there and in Cairo, and educated at Princeton and Harvard, Said spent most of his life as a professor of English at Columbia University in New York City. In his famous book *Orientalism* (1978), Said defines Orientalism as:

> the corporate institution for dealing with the Orient—dealing with it by making statements about it, authorizing views of it, describing it, by teaching it, settling it, ruling over it: in short, Orientalism [is] a Western style for dominating, restructuring, and having authority over the Orient.
>
> (Said 1978, 11)

He assigned the beginning of Orientalism to Napoleon's expedition to Egypt, but as we have seen in this chapter, Orientalism has significant roots in Christian theological treatments of "Saracens" throughout the entire history of Muslim–Christian encounter. Said's critique of Orientalism has been enormously important in the field of post-colonial studies, which critically examines the legacy of imperialism.

Muslims in America

Muslims have been part of every era of American history, from the colonial period to the present day. Estimates by the Pew Research Center suggest that today approximately 3.3 million Muslims live in America. African Americans make up around 28 percent of this number and Asians (i.e., from China, Southeast Asia, and the Indian subcontinent) make up an equivalent portion. People from the Middle East and others considered by the U.S. Census Bureau as "White" are estimated to be 38 percent of the Muslim population in the U.S.A. (rounded out by 4 percent Latino and 3 percent "Other").

The story of American Muslims begins in Africa, where in the earliest times of Islam, in the 600s, the faith spread across North Africa. From there, Berber traders brought Islam through their trade relationships to people in West Africa. By the tenth and eleventh centuries, prominent leaders in the region, including Ghana, became Muslim. Traders and rulers were often the first to convert to Islam in a given region, followed by more common agrarian people.

The life journeys of two remarkable men can serve to illustrate the history of Muslim slaves connecting Africa and America. Abd al-Rahman Ibrahima was a noble leader and warrior of the Fulani ethnic group living in the city of Timbo in what today is the West African country of Guinea. He was learned in Arabic and spoke several West African languages. In 1788, he was captured by a rival ethnic group and sold to European slave traders, who transported him to the West Indies, then New Orleans, then Mississippi, where he was purchased and put to work in the fields, and also told to take care of his owner's livestock.

Abd al-Rahman married, had eight children, and grew his own produce to sell. In 1807, a white man named John Coates Cox, who had traveled in West Africa, saw Abd al-Rahman and said he recognized him from Timbo. Cox appealed unsuccessfully to the Mississippi governor to try to free Abd al-Rahman. In 1826, Abd al-Rahman wrote a letter in Arabic requesting freedom. That letter was passed from a U.S. Senator to the U.S. consul in Morocco and then to the U.S. Secretary of State, Henry Clay, who with the support of President John Quincy Adams, agreed to Abd al-Rahman's request and offered for the U.S. government to pay for the man's transportation back to his homeland in West Africa. To raise funds to buy the freedom of his wife and children, Abd al-Rahman went on a high-profile tour of the East Coast of the United States speaking of his plight. He met prominent Congressmen, abolitionists, cultural figures, and other civic leaders, including Francis Scott Key, who wrote "The Star Spangled Banner." By 1829, he raised $3,400, which was enough to buy back his family. Abd al-Rahman's story ends with him arriving that year in Monrovia, Liberia and dying shortly thereafter of illness.

Abd al-Rahman was one of many African Muslims enslaved and brought to the New World. Another Fulani Muslim, Omar ibn Sayyid, documented his life story. From him we have the only autobiography of a North American slave written in the Arabic language. Omar ibn Sayyid was educated in Qur'an and *hadith* before being captured and sold, then transported to America, arriving in 1807 in Charleston, South Carolina. He begins his text in the traditional Islamic way, with a *basmala*: "In the name of God, the merciful the gracious. God grant his blessing upon our Prophet Mohammed. Blessed be He in whose hands is the kingdom and who is Almighty; who created death and life…" Omar ibn Sayyid goes on to tell the story of his Islamic education and enslavement by Christians:

> My birthplace was Fut Tur, between the two rivers. I sought knowledge under the instruction of a Sheikh called Mohammed Seid, my own brother, and Sheikh Soleiman Kembeh, and Sheikh Gabriel Abdal. I continued my studies twenty-five years, and then returned to my home where I remained six years. Then there came to our place a large army, who killed many men, and took me, and brought me to the great sea, and sold me into the hands of the Christians, who bound me and sent me on board a great ship and we sailed upon the great sea a month and a half, when we came to a place called Charleston in the Christian language. There they sold me to a small, weak, and wicked man called Johnson, a complete infidel, who had no fear of God at all.
>
> (Curtis 2009, 23–24)

Other Muslims came to America of their own accord. For example, Muslim (and even more Christian) emigrants from territories of the Ottoman Empire came, especially between 1880 and World War I, settling in the Dakotas and elsewhere. From British India, Bengali Muslims who came as sailors would sometimes desert their ships in

New Orleans or New York to settle in the United States, where the government would classify them as "Negro" or "colored." Other men from the Punjab region of India came to Imperial Valley, California and married Mexican Americans. Attracted in part by jobs in the automobile industry, many Muslims from Syria and Lebanon settled in Detroit and Dearborn, Michigan. The Immigration Act of 1924 imposed quotas based on national origins that placed sharp limits on non-white immigration. These racist policies greatly affected the immigration of Muslims to the United States, until 1965, when President Lyndon B. Johnson signed the Hart–Celler Act that banned racially discriminatory quotas for immigration visas.

The Civil Rights Movement is another important chapter in the history of Muslims in America, as exemplified by the extraordinary figure, **Malcolm X**. Born Malcolm Little in Omaha, Nebraska in 1925 as the son of a Baptist minister, Malcolm X is among the most noteworthy Muslim Americans and civil rights leaders. Part of the zoot suit generation, Malcolm X converted to Islam while in prison after a phase of life in which he danced, drank, and made money in New York City as a "hustler," to use his word for the chapter of his life of petty crime that landed him in prison. Paroled in 1952, Malcolm X became a prominent member of the Nation of Islam, a Muslim organization and heterodox sect led at that time by Elijah Muhammad. In 1964, Malcolm publicly affiliated himself with more mainstream Sunni Islam, under the influence of Islamist missionaries. He also went on *hajj* to the Hijaz, where he was hosted by the Saudi royal family. No American civil rights leader more powerfully criticized racism from a Muslim perspective.

Quoting from Dr. Martin Luther King, Jr., Malcolm X wrote in his *Autobiography*: "[T]he very man [i.e., King] whose name symbolizes non-violence here today has stated: 'Our nation was born in genocide when it embraced the doctrine that the original American, the Indian, was an inferior race'" (X and Haley 1965, 375). Malcolm X went beyond American colonial history to indict Christianity more widely as infected with white racism from the time it became a predominantly European religion and was joined with colonialism.

Islam and "Modernity"

Besides Orientalism, another important development in Western thought that has had a major influence on Western interpretations of Islam in modern times is the post-Enlightenment invention of the study of religion. As part of the Enlightenment project to relegate the church and especially clergy to a diminished role in society, scholars developed a particular concept of "religion" to be the opposite of the "secular." "Religion" applied to parts of human life that were not verifiable in empirical terms. It also presumed that features like a church, a scripture, creeds, laws, and an authoritative clergy were standard aspects of what counted as "religion." "Religion" was further defined by personal and communal subjection to a higher power, especially through ritual piety and worship.

Defined thus, religion was allowed to hold sway in the space of church and individual conscience, while the public spaces of society were to be "secular." To be "modern" came to require having "religion" along these lines. Orientalists applied this concept to the cultures and societies of the "East," and elites in those societies to a great degree likewise remade themselves as "moderns" as defined by their imperial masters. Islam thus came to be conceptualized as a "religion," on the model of how post-Enlightenment Europeans conceptualized Christianity, despite significant differences.

While proponents of modernity developed this notion of "religion" to minimize its power and allow secularism to dominate, others reacted against modernity by becoming religious in new ways. **Fundamentalism** as a religious category originated among conservative Christians in the United States (see Chapter 23). It has since been appropriated by scholars of religion to refer to a communitarian response to modernity that nostalgically creates a mythical past and endeavors to (re-)create that myth in the present. As such, the term can and has been applied to anti-modernist movements in all religions. Muslims who call themselves *salafi* fit into this anti-modernist religious phenomenon. They strive to imitate the *salaf*, who were the earliest Muslims and Companions of the Prophet. *Salafis*, such as Wahhabi Muslims in Saudi Arabia, see much of the Islamic tradition as unauthorized innovation in religion. Wahhabis are so named because of the influence of Muhammad ibn 'Abd al-Wahhab (d. 1792), who saw the need to return to a "pure" Islam in order to reverse the political demise of the great Muslim political powers. At its root, Islamic fundamentalism developed as a response to the loss of sovereignty by Muslims to European colonial powers.

Still another response to the political and economic conditions of the world, especially in the last several decades, is so-called "terrorism," that is, indiscriminate violence directed at civilians for ideological or political purposes. While most *salafi* Muslims do not participate in or support terrorism, in a range of political contexts some groups and individuals have developed Islamic ideologies that support indiscriminate violence aimed to intimidate. The 9/11 attacks using airplanes arriving in the United States gave rise to the term "Islamic terrorist" and to the ongoing "War on Terror" by the American government.

In this context, many concepts and rhetorical strategies developed by Christian theologians over the centuries to describe and demonize Muslims have found new utility. In fact, a small number of figures in the U.S. context today make their living in what has been called "professional Islamophobia." One important study of professional Islamophobia in the United States is called *Fear, Inc.: The Roots of the Islamophobia Network in America* (2011).

Understanding Muslims and Islam has become an urgent issue in the West today. While professional Islamophobes trade in the hostile and slanderous discourse that dates back to the earliest Christian writings on Islam, other actors in the West today have charted a strikingly new course. *Christian Lives Given to the Study of Islam* (2012) profiles a generation of Christian theologians and other scholars in the post-colonial era after Vatican II who have pioneered this new path of understanding between Muslims and Christians. Among those profiled are David Burrell, Kenneth Cragg, Daniel Madigan, Jane McAuliffe, Thomas Michel, Christiaan van Nispen tot Sevenaer, and Giuseppe Scattolin. Many are members of religious orders, such as the Jesuits, Dominicans, Comboni missionaries, and the Society of Missionaries of Africa. Many have worked at such institutions as the Pontifical Institute for the Study of Islam and Arabic and centers for Muslim–Christian dialogue at Catholic universities, such as the Al-Waleed Center at Georgetown University.

While the Vatican II *Declaration on the Relation of the Church to Non-Christian Religions*, known by its first two words in the Latin original, *Nostra Aetate*, has had a very positive impact on Muslim–Christian relations, other Christian theological developments that recognized the dignity of the human person in new ways also contributed to the emergence of very different Christian approaches to Muslims and Islam. Many of the pioneers of this new approach mastered important languages of Islamic discourse, such as Arabic, Persian, Turkish, Urdu, and Indonesian, through academic study and living in places where these are the spoken idioms of everyday life. Some have helped rethink the nature and purpose of Christian missionary work. All of them entered into deep and multi-layered relationships with Muslims. Indeed, long-term friendship with Muslims is perhaps the most distinctive characteristic of the lives of these Christians who have pioneered an approach to Muslims and Islam that veers far from the anti-Muslim polemic of the Christian theological tradition.

Christian Zionism

Zionism refers to the nineteenth- and twentieth-century Jewish movement to create a state for Jews, defined ethnically and religiously. Christian Zionism refers to faith-based Christian political action "to promote or preserve Jewish control over the geographic area now comprising Israel and Palestine." Christian Zionism has been an important factor undergirding Western support for the State of Israel that has taken shape in Palestine since Zionists declared its existence in 1948.

For many Muslims, the creation of the State of Israel is highly significant and deeply problematic. The native inhabitants of this territory are predominantly Muslim, with a sizeable Christian community. When the United Nations Relief and Works Agency for Palestine Refugees in the Near East (UNRWA) was established in 1950, it addressed the needs of around 750,000 people who were displaced by the newly established State of Israel. Today, UNRWA counts 5 million people as eligible for its services. Beyond the humanitarian crisis of Palestinian refugees, many Muslims were and are also troubled by Israeli sovereignty over the city of Jerusalem which, after Mecca and Medina, is the most religiously significant city for Muslims.

For these and other reasons, Christian Zionism is thus for Muslims a significant and problematic aspect of recent Christian theology. Given their historical memory of the medieval Crusades that established a "Kingdom of Jerusalem" and the more recent colonial domination of Palestine, the Levant, and the rest of the historic heartlands of Islam, many Muslims regard Israel as the most recent European colony in the Middle East.

Christian Zionism is often considered an Anglo-American phenomenon. Both the British and Americans have seen themselves as "elect," like the idea of Jews as the "chosen people" of God. The British Empire and the American took pleasure in seeing God at work in their conquest of new territories. In nineteenth-century American political discourse, the slogan of "Manifest Destiny" meant that Providence had given the entire continent to the United States. One important Christian Zionist was Anthony Ashley-Cooper, Lord Shaftesbury (d. 1885). He was a restorationist, meaning that he believed that the "restoration" of Jews to their biblical homeland was a necessary step to the Second Coming of Jesus Christ. For Shaftesbury and others, restorationism was part of a millennialist vision in which Christ will rule over a Paradise on Earth for 1,000 years before the final judgment (see Chapter 23). From this Christian theological perspective, Lord Shaftesbury devoted his adult life to advocating for British imperial support for bringing Jews to Palestine. He was also instrumental in creating the Anglican bishopric of Jerusalem, since he foresaw the Jews becoming (Anglican) Christians.

Key Terms

ʿAli ibn Abi Talib	*jahiliyya*	Saracens
Avicenna	Khadija bint Khuwaylid	*shahada*
Crusades	Malcolm X	*shiʿa*
dar al-Islam	Orientalism	St. John of Damascus
five pillars of Islam	Peter the Venerable	*sunna*
fundamentalism	*al-Quds*	*suras*
hadith	*salaf*	*ulama*
hijra	*salah*	*ummah*

Questions for Reading

1. What is the role of the Qurʾan in Islamic history and religious practice?

2. Who were the Companions of the Prophet and why are they important?

3. Before Christians first encountered Muslims, who were the religiously different groups they knew? How did these categories for religious "others" affect Christian interpretations of Muslims?

4. What were the Crusades? What is their significance in the history of Christian theological interpretations of Muslims and Islam?

5. What is Orientalism? On what basis did Edward Said critique it?

6. What is the post-Enlightenment concept of "religion"? What purposes did it serve in Western history? What is its role in defining modernity?

7. What role has eschatological anticipation of the Second Coming of Christ played in the history of Christian theological reflections on Muslims and Islam?

Works Consulted/Recommended Reading

Ahmed, Shahab. 2016. *What is Islam? The Importance of Being Islamic.* Princeton, NJ: Princeton University Press.

Ali, Kecia. 2014. *Lives of Muhammad.* Cambridge, MA: Harvard University Press.

Bowersock, Glen. 2017. *The Crucible of Islam.* Cambridge, MA: Harvard University Press.

Brady, Thomas A. 2009. *German Histories in the Age of Reformation.* New York: Columbia University Press.

Curtis, Edward. 2009. *Muslims in America: A Short History.* Oxford: Oxford University Press.

Fletcher, Richard. 2004. *The Cross and the Crescent: Christianity and Islam from Muhammad to the Reformation.* New York: Viking.

Green, Todd H. 2015. *The Fear of Islam: An Introduction to Islamophobia in the West.* Minneapolis, MN: Fortress Press.

Gunner, Goran, and Robert O. Smith, eds. 2014. *Comprehending Christian Zionism: Perspectives in Comparison.* Minneapolis, MN: Augsburg Fortress.

Hoyland, Robert G. 1997. *Seeing Islam as Others Saw It: A Survey and Evaluation of Christian, Jewish, and Zoroastrian Writings on Early Islam.* Studies in Late Antiquity and Early Islam, 13. Princeton, NJ: Darwin Press.

Lockman, Zachary. 2010. *Contending Visions of the Middle East: The History and Politics of Orientalism.* Cambridge: Cambridge University Press.

Loewen, Harry. 2015. *Ink Against the Devil: Luther and His Opponents*. Waterloo, ON: Wilfred Laurier University Press.

Mattson, Ingrid. 2013. *The Story of the Qur'an: Its History and Place in Muslim Life*. Chichester: Wiley-Blackwell.

Michel, Thomas. 2010. *A Christian View of Islam: Essays on Dialogue*. Maryknoll, NY: Orbis.

Pew Research Center. n.d. "Religious Landscape Study." www.pewforum.org/religious-landscape-study/religious-tradition/muslim.

Porter, Andrew. 2004. *Religion Versus Empire? British Protestant Missionaries and Overseas Expansion, 1700–1914*. Manchester: Manchester University Press.

Quinn, Frederick. 2008. *The Sum of All Heresy: The Image of Islam in Western Thought*. Oxford: Oxford University Press.

Ryan, James D., ed. 2013. *The Spiritual Expansion of Medieval Latin Christendom: The Asian Missions*. Farnham: Ashgate.

Said, Edward. 1978. *Orientalism*. New York: Pantheon Books.

Sells, Michael. 2007 (1999). *Approaching the Qur'an: The Early Revelations*. Ashland, OR: White Cloud Press.

Southern, Richard William. 1962. *Western Views of Islam in the Middle Ages*. Cambridge, MA: Harvard University Press.

Tolan, John Victor, ed. 1996. *Medieval Christian Perceptions of Islam: A Book of Essays*. New York: Garland.

Tolan, John Victor. 2002. *Saracens: Islam in the Medieval European Imagination*. New York: Columbia University Press.

Tolan, John Victor. 2008. *Sons of Ishmael: Muslims Through European Eyes in the Middle Ages*. Gainesville, FL: University Press of Florida.

Troll, Christian W., and C.T.R. Hewer, eds. 2012. *Christian Lives Given to the Study of Islam*. New York: Fordham University Press.

Volf, Miroslav. 2011. *Allah: A Christian Response*. New York: HarperOne.

Wajahat, Ali, et al., eds. 2011. *Fear, Inc.: The Roots of the Islamophobia Network in America*. Center for American Progress. www.americanprogress.org/issues/religion/reports/2011/08/26/10165/fear-inc/.

X, Malcolm, and Alex Haley. 1965. *The Autobiography of Malcolm X*. New York: One World.

Chapter

CHRISTIANITY IN THE EARLY MEDIEVAL PERIOD

TIMELINE

A.D. 480–547	Life span of Benedict of Nursia, the founder of Benedictine monasticism.
A.D. 590	Gregory I, also known as Gregory the Great, elected pope.
A.D. 597	Mission of Augustine of Canterbury sent by Pope Gregory I to England to convert the Anglo-Saxons.
A.D. 732	Battle of Tours, maximum point of Arab advance in Western Europe.
A.D. 754	"Donation of Pippin" to the papacy inaugurates the papacy's temporal kingdom.
c.A.D. 785	The Roman Rite, the primary form of liturgy for the Roman Catholic Church, is established.
A.D. 800	Charlemagne is crowned "Emperor of the Romans" by Pope Leo III, thus restoring the imperial title in the West.
A.D. 910	Founding of new Benedictine monastery at Cluny. Beginning of the Cluniac reform movement.
A.D. 942–1022	Life span of Symeon the New Theologian.
A.D. 1033–1109	Life span of Anselm of Canterbury.
A.D. 1073	Pope Gregory VII is elected pope. The "Gregorian Reform" takes its name from him.
A.D. 1075	Gregory VII drafts his *Dictatus Papae* asserting the primacy of the pope.
A.D. 1077	Emperor Henry IV does penance to have Gregory VII lift his excommunication.

Chapter 13 is the first of four chapters dealing with the Western Christian tradition during the Middle Ages, meaning the roughly 1,000 years between the fall of the Roman Empire in the West (476) and the Renaissance and the Protestant Reformation of the sixteenth century. They are deemed "middle" according to a common division of history into three phases: ancient, medieval (from the Latin word for "middle age"), and modern, in which "modernity" was understood to begin with the Renaissance and the Reformation. As the Introduction to Part IV will explain, this conventional threefold division of time is an unsatisfactory solution to the problem of giving shape to historical time. Not only does it simplify a millennium of complex developments, but it fosters false notions of a clean and sharp break between periods, and uncritical notions of "progress."

This chapter will cover the early medieval period, the sixth through the eleventh centuries. In the popular imagination, this era is frequently termed the "Dark Ages" because of the steep decline in the standard of living amidst waves of invasions and population movement in the centuries following the end of the Roman Empire in the West. The decline was long lasting and affected all areas of life: culture, population, economy, law, government, technology, and so on. But the decline also marked a beginning: the "birth of Europe," understanding Europe as a new cultural synthesis of classical antiquity, Christianity, and the cultures of the newly converted and civilized peoples, from Ireland to Russia, and from Scandinavia to Spain. Europe was "born," so to speak, during the great, though short-lived cultural revival known as the Carolingian Renaissance. (Contemporary debates in Europe about European "identity" are sometimes debates about whether Europe's Christian roots are merely historical or should be regarded as still valid today.)

This chapter explores several features of early medieval Christianity: the fall of the Roman Empire in the West and its restoration by the popes as the "Holy Roman Empire"; the further development of monasticism; and the evolution of the papacy. We will also explore some of the cultural contributions of this period and some of its major theological figures.

THE HOLY ROMAN EMPIRE

The end of the ancient Roman Empire in the West was marked by great movements of peoples. Historians term these movements as "migrations" or "invasions", depending on whether they are considered circumstantial accompaniments to the fall of the empire or its cause. Some of these newcomers were already Christian, such as the Visigoths and the Ostrogoths, who had been converted in the fourth century by missionaries from Constantinople (ironically, because Arian ideas had been dominant at Constantinople at that time, the Goths received an Arian version of Christianity). Others would become Christian because of missionary efforts launched primarily by Celtic and Anglo-Saxon monks. Conversion usually took place as a top-down affair, beginning with the king and queen, followed by the people subject to them. The history of Christianity among these newly converted peoples is memorably recorded in the historical accounts written by the Benedictine monk Bede (c.672–735) in his *Ecclesiastical History of the English People*, and the Frankish clergyman Gregory of Tours (c.538–c.594) in his *Histories* (often inaccurately called *History of the Franks*).

After the last resident Western emperor was deposed in 476, a Frankish warrior chieftain named Clovis, who converted to Christianity and was baptized perhaps in 508, collaborated with the remaining Romans to establish a Christian dynasty north of the Alps, in ancient Gaul (modern-day France). Clovis' dynasty is identified as the

Merovingian kingdom, named after his grandfather Merowig. The Frankish peoples controlled considerable territory in Europe at this time, but their organizational structure was mostly tribal, with local chieftains governing smaller autonomous regions. Although the Merovingian kings attempted to create a centralized government, they were never successful in doing so. Severely weakened during the seventh century in a series of internal power struggles, the Merovingian kings finally ceded power to a leader of the major landowners in the region, Charles Martel.

Charles Martel gave his name to the Merovingians' successor dynasty, the Carolingians. He is best known for his military victory in 732–733 over the Arabs of 'Abd ar-Rahman who were approaching Tours (in southern France) on a looting raid of the wealthy shrine of St. Martin there—a battle which marked the westernmost advance of Muslim armies. Charles also led a series of campaigns in Burgundy and Aquitaine, extending Frankish dominion beyond northern Gaul. A significant feature of the Carolingian dynasty was its relationship with the Catholic Church. With the approval of Pope Zachary (r. 741–752), Charles Martel's son, Pippin III, forced the last of the Merovingian kings into a monastery, and in 751 was acclaimed king by the Frankish nobility and anointed by St. Boniface (see "Pope Gregory I," in The Evolution of the Papacy, below), acting as the pope's legate or representative.

The papacy's role in the deposing of the Merovingians implicitly acknowledged its right to arbitrate in political struggles. The anointing of the king with oil also implied the king's quasi-priestly character and connoted divine approval of his coronation. Later, at the request of Zachary's successor, Pope Stephen II (r. 752–757), the Carolingian kings became the political protectors of the papacy as replacements for the ineffective Byzantine governor in Ravenna in northeastern Italy. Pippin made good on this agreement in 754 and again in 756 when he invaded Italy to restrain the Lombards from menacing the pope. On the second trip, he donated conquered Lombard land in central and northeastern Italy to St. Peter (Peter was thoroughly identified with his tomb as though he were still alive, and the Pope was regarded as his vicar or spokesman); this "Donation of Pippin" was the beginning of the Papal States, the territory which the popes governed as their own state up until the final unification of Italy as a single nation-state in 1870 (since signing a treaty with the Italian state in 1929, the popes have received the one square mile area in Rome called "Vatican City" as their sovereign territory).

Pippin's son, Karolus, known to history as **Charlemagne** ("Karolus the Great"), became the most famous of the Carolingian rulers. During his long reign (768–814), he had significant impact on the development of Christian worship by imposing the liturgical practices of Rome throughout his empire. He also made important contributions to the development of culture by establishing a scholarly brain trust at his court and raising the educational standards of his clerics and courtiers. The so-called "Carolingian Renaissance" produced a group of scholars whose work in poetry, history, textual criticism, theology, and philosophy represented the major creative achievement of the early medieval period, and whose manuscript preservation projects transmitted much of the classical Greco-Roman heritage to the later Middle Ages.

On Christmas Day 800, Pope Leo III crowned Charlemagne, who had already styled himself "king of the Franks and of the Lombards," as "emperor of the Romans," thereby restoring the Roman imperial title in the West, despite the strong disapproval of the Byzantines. By the time of his death in 814, Charlemagne had created a Christian empire stretching from the border between modern-day Spain and France to the edge of Germany, and from northern Italy to the English Channel. His empire would come to be known as the "*Holy* Roman Empire," because of its close association with the church. During its turbulent 1,000-year history until its dissolution by Napoleon in 1806 (it was the original "thousand-year Reich"), the **Holy Roman Empire** would be the primary carrier of the medieval Catholic ideal of a single universal Christian state long after it had any real ambition or capability to be such a thing.

Charlemagne's son and heir, Louis the Pious, sponsored continued church reform, most notably imposing the *Rule* of Benedict (see Celtic and Benedictine Monasticism, below) as the sole organizational blueprint for all monks and nuns in the empire. However, from the late 820s through Louis' death in 840, he was in continual conflict with one or more of his sons and a bitter civil war broke out at Louis' death. By the treaty of Verdun in 843, the Carolingian Empire was split into several different parts. It remained divided and weakened through the latter part of the ninth century and into the early part of the tenth century.

The Holy Roman Empire experienced a revival under the leadership of Henry I (919–936) and Otto I (936–973), the founders of the Ottonian dynasty, whose power lay in what is now Germany. Otto I proved himself a strong supporter of the church, appointing clerics to positions of responsibility, sponsoring missionary encounters in Eastern Europe, and even responding to a papal request for military assistance. In gratitude for Otto's services, Pope John XII anointed and crowned him emperor, a title and position conferred in turn on Otto's son and grandsons. The yoking of papal and imperial power in the Ottonian dynasty eventually led to numerous conflicts over control of the church. These conflicts would reach their climax in the eleventh century in a dramatic confrontation between Pope Gregory VII and Emperor Henry IV (see Pope Gregory VII, below).

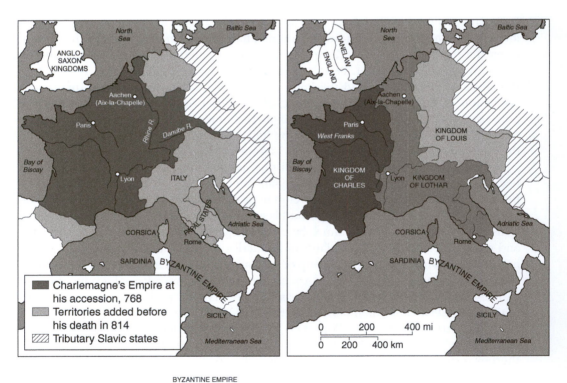

Figure 13–1 The Carolingian Empire at the Treaty of Verdun, 843. At his death, Louis the Pious' empire was divided among his three children: Charles the Bald, Lothar, and Louis the German. Lothar retained the title "Holy Roman Emperor."

CELTIC AND BENEDICTINE MONASTICISM

Christian monasticism originated in the early Christian period after persecution ended and the Roman Empire became Christian (see Chapter 9). In the early medieval period, monasticism in the West developed in new ways to meet the changed circumstances created by the end of Roman rule and the influx of new peoples who did not share the classical heritage of the ancient world. In a rather ironic development, monks, who had begun as a movement by separating themselves from the world, became almost by default the protectors of learning and the builders of a new social order.

We have already discussed how the monastic writer **John Cassian** transmitted Eastern monastic teaching and practices to the western part of the Roman Empire, where they had been largely unknown. Two rather different types of monasticism spread throughout the West, and northwards as well, among the recently converted or still pagan peoples of the British Isles and northern Europe. Celtic monasticism originated at some point near the end of the fifth century or the beginning of the sixth century. Its two emphases were to have a strong impact on the rebirth of civilization in the Early Middle Ages. The first was the love of scholarship. Although other monastic communities gave rudimentary education to their members, Irish monks developed more highly specialized monastic schools, placing high priority on literacy, preservation and transmission of knowledge, and on the production of manuscripts. The greatest monument to Irish monastic manuscript production is the ninth-century illuminated book of the four Gospels known as the *Book of Kells*, with its elaborate initial letters, geometrical patterns, and human and animal illustrations, including a full-page decorated version of the Chi-Rho symbol made famous by Constantine's use. The second legacy of Celtic monasticism was the penitential practice of self-imposed exile from the monastery. This Irish monastic practice sent monk-missionaries throughout vast stretches of northern Europe to preach the gospel message. The combination of scholarship and missionary activity made Irish monks important sources of social and cultural transformation in northern Europe. The Irish monk Columbanus (543–615) pioneered the tradition by founding monasteries such as Luxeuil (590) in Burgundy (eastern France near Switzerland) and Bobbio (613) in the Appenine Mountains of northern Italy, both of which became early medieval centers of spirituality and learning.

What became the standardized form of Western monasticism first appeared in the *Rule for Monasteries* of **Benedict of Nursia** (480–547). Little is known of Benedict's life other than his Roman ancestry, his life as a hermit in a cave, and his establishment of a monastic community at Monte Cassino, south of Rome. Monks who followed Benedict's *Rule* took vows of poverty, chastity, obedience, and stability (permanent commitment to a particular community of monks). They gathered eight times a day for community prayer. Lauds (Morning Prayer at dawn), Vespers (Evening Prayer at sunset) and Matins (a lengthy vigil prayed in the dead of night) were the hinges of the *Opus Dei* ("work of God"). Shorter prayers interrupted the workday (Tierce, Sext, and None). Other prayers were prescribed for the dormitory at rising (Prime) or before sleep (Compline). Each monk had particular work responsibilities assigned him by his monastic superiors. They ate their meals together in silence or accompanied by spiritual readings. Although the ascetic practices outlined in Benedict's *Rule* were quite moderate and balanced by comparison to other monastic rules, the monks still fasted for a significant proportion of the year. Thus, the essence of Benedict's *Rule* can be summed up in a Latin motto: *Ora et labora* ("Pray and work").

Lived Religion: Liturgy in the Early Middle Ages 800–1150
Liturgy of the Hours

Daily prayer has been a part of Christian practice from its beginnings. Over time, however, the frequency of daily prayer increased, culminating in the daily cycle of monasticism, known as the divine office or liturgy of the hours.

Monastic communities gathered eight times a day for prayer as directed first in the Rule of St. Benedict. They sat in stalls facing each other across the aisle of the choir, the section of the church in front of the high altar reserved for the monks. The daily office was usually led by the abbot or another senior monk, but anyone could lead prayer; a priest was not needed.

The cycle began with evening prayer, or Vespers, which was done at dusk. It started with a verse from Psalm 69, sung by the leader with a response from the community. Next, those assembled prayed "Glory to the Father, and to the Son and to the Holy Spirit…" followed by "Alleluia," then they sang four psalms with an antiphon (a short text from scripture). This was followed by a hymn, a verse and a response for that day, and then the *Magnificat*, the song of Mary from Luke 1:46–55. They finished with the *Kyrie*, or "Lord have mercy," the Lord's Prayer, a Collect, or prayer of the day, and a blessing. All of this took about half an hour.

Saying the daily office could be a complicated matter, since the number of psalms, the hymns, and the prayers varied depending on the day of the week, the time of year, and the feast day that was being celebrated. It could be confusing at first, but it soon became familiar, especially the psalms, since all 150 of them were sung every week. By gathering for prayer about every three hours around the clock, the monks fulfilled the command in 1 Thessalonians 5:17 that we should "pray without ceasing."

Benedictine monasticism eventually became the primary style of monastic life in the West. Its dominance was so complete that historians have sometimes called the sixth through eleventh centuries "the Benedictine centuries." The self-sufficiency of Benedict's communities made them well suited for the reduced conditions in the West after the fall of the Empire. As urban life disappeared along with the institutions associated with cities (schools, learning, government, trade, health care, etc.), monasteries slowly took on many of these functions by default. And as they were endowed with lands by the wealthy classes who wanted monks and nuns to pray for their souls after death, monasteries became significant economic institutions. By the ninth and tenth centuries, Benedictine monasteries, far from being the withdrawn communities that Benedict had envisioned, were essential pillars of the early medieval world.

This degree of worldly involvement created problems. Secular rulers and wealthy nobility naturally wanted to exploit the resources of prosperous monasteries and did everything they could to increase their control over them. In some ways, this was beneficial for monasteries, because they depended upon powerful benefactors to be their protectors and financial supporters in time of need. In other ways, monasteries suffered under this influence. When wealthy landlords deeded the monks' land to build their monasteries, the monastery became, for all practical purposes, part of the **feudal system**. Their abbot was now a vassal of the lord, owing the lord certain services like military assistance against his enemies, and the monastery now needed serfs or peasants to help farm the land. The monastery, in turn, was responsible for providing the serfs with the basic necessities of life.

Monasteries lost even more independence through **lay investiture**. According to this practice, the emperor and secular leaders took upon themselves the right to appoint bishops, abbots, and other church officials. Their appointees were not necessarily holy men, nor were they necessarily trained in spiritual matters. Rather, they were given appointments because of their family connections. Sometimes they obtained their appointments through **simony** (the buying and selling of spiritual things, including church leadership positions). All of these factors contributed to the gradual decline of the spiritual focus of the monastery.

The decline of monasticism began to change when William the Pious founded a new Benedictine monastery at Cluny in A.D. 910. This monastery committed itself to a reform of monasticism by demanding the strictest observance of Benedict's *Rule of Monasteries* and renewed dedication to the liturgical (worship) practices of monastic life. The Cluniac reform movement, under the direction of the monasteries' abbots, was determined to maintain the spiritual character of the church. The abbots spoke out against secular leaders who attempted to wield control over bishops and other clergy. Cluny's great innovation was to sponsor the creation of new monastic communities without allowing them to have their own abbots; instead, the new daughter communities were enrolled as affiliates of Cluny in a kind of federation (before this time Benedictine communities had been essentially free-standing operations), which increased their political leverage. They taught that the pope in Rome was the only one who ought to have authority over the clergy, and they put the whole Cluniac federation under the pope's special protection.

The monastic reformers also spoke out against **concubinage**. Although celibacy was required of monks, it was not universally required of "secular" clergy, that is, what today would be called parish priests: clergy who did not belong to a monastery and who lived in the cities and villages, ministering to the people there. As a result, some of these "secular" clergy maintained concubines in a relationship something like marriage. The Cluny reformers denounced this practice, arguing that the clergy ought to be celibate so that the church might be their spouse and so that the Eucharist might be offered by pure hands unsullied by sexual contact. The position of the reformers eventually won the day, and Roman Catholicism has continued to require celibacy of its bishops and priests to the present day.

THE EVOLUTION OF THE PAPACY

The relationship between the emperor and church leadership developed differently in the eastern and western halves of the Roman Empire. In the East, the emperor had authority over the patriarchs even to the point of calling councils and prescribing solutions to doctrinal issues in the church. In the West, the pope and other bishops maintained their independence a little more successfully, though strong rulers like the emperor Justinian I (r. 527–565) were able to bend even popes to their will.

The pope's prestige in the early church had been connected with Rome's importance as the site of the tombs of Saints Peter and Paul, and also as the capital of the Empire. Although the city's political importance waned with the decline of the Western Roman Empire in the fifth and sixth centuries, its significance as a pilgrimage center only increased. In addition, the decline of civil authorities in the West worked to the advantage of the popes, who, by default as much as by design, began to take on purely secular duties as the de facto rulers of the city and the surrounding territory.

The early medieval period saw three further highly significant developments in the history of the papacy: the conversion of the peoples of northern Europe, which the popes actively supported; the eighth-century alliance with the kings of the Franks and the creation of the popes' own state; and the papal supremacy promoted by the eleventh-century **Gregorian Reform**. The histories of two popes from this era, Pope Gregory I at the beginning and Pope Gregory VII at the end, demonstrate the first and third of these developments in action; the second has already been discussed above.

Pope Gregory I

Pope **Gregory I** (*c.*540–604) is so notable a figure that tradition recognizes him as "Gregory the Great." The son of a Roman nobleman, Gregory spent his young adulthood in civic service, so that eventually he occupied the office of prefect of the city of Rome. By around 574, Gregory retired from public life, sold his inherited possessions, and used the proceeds to care for the poor. He established several monasteries and lived the monastic life himself, following the *Rule* of Benedict with such intensity that he damaged his physical health. Eventually, he was called out of the monastery to serve as a church leader, first as a regional deacon, charged with care for the physical and spiritual needs of the city's destitute, and later as an ambassador to Constantinople. After another interlude in the monastic life, Gregory was elected pope in 590.

The 14 years that Gregory served as pope were notable for his missionary outreach. Gregory himself sought to evangelize the Lombards in Italy itself. His most important accomplishment was to direct Augustine of Canterbury in 597 to undertake a missionary journey to the British Isles to preach the Christian message to the pagan Anglo-Saxons, who had migrated there from northern Germany. Later popes imitated Gregory's initiative by sponsoring similar missionary efforts, such as Pope Gregory II (r. 715–731), who renamed the Anglo-Saxon monk Winfrid (*c.*672–754) as "Boniface" when he commissioned him in 719 to bring Christianity to the Germanic peoples east of the Rhine River. In 754, Boniface was murdered by pagan Frisians near the mouth of the Rhine and today is venerated as "the Apostle of Germany." Sponsoring such missions helped to promote a strong sense of loyalty between these newly converted peoples and the papacy in Rome.

Gregory the Great accomplished his missionary outreach while maintaining cordial relations with the Byzantine emperors, keeping up communication with the Christian communities in the surviving urban areas of the West, and overseeing the day-to-day functioning of the city of Rome. More than 850 of Gregory's letters are preserved, addressed to emperors, patriarchs, bishops, subdeacons, and notables, revealing a man of prodigious energy, convinced that the future of Christianity lay with the Germanic peoples north of the Alps and not simply in the Christian East. He was the first to style the pope as *servus servorum Dei* ("servant of the servants of God").

Pope Gregory VII

Gregory VII (*c.*1020–1085) was elected pope nearly 500 years after Gregory I's pontificate (reign as pope). The reign of Pope Gregory VII demonstrates how the institution of the papacy developed into a European political power in addition to its role as a religious center. His given name was Hildebrand and he had committed himself at an early age to the life of a monk. For over 20 years, he had served as secretary to five popes and was firmly convinced of the need for a strong church independent of lay political control if its spiritual life was to be reformed. Hildebrand was a person of passionate moral uprightness—his friend Peter Damian once described him as a "holy Satan." He is so closely associated with the reform movement that historians have named it the "Gregorian Reform," even though it was well underway before he became its leader.

From the time of his election in 1073, Gregory VII vigorously attacked three issues: simony, clerical concubinage, and lay investiture. Why were these so important to him? The ultimate goal of the reform movement was "the freedom of the church" (*libertas ecclesiae* became almost a political slogan), meaning the liberation of the priestly structure of the church from control by powerful lay people, in order to make the church the effective spiritual conscience and controller of a Christian society. In the process, he differentiated "lay" from "clerical" more radically than had any before him; from this time on, "the Church" without qualification meant essentially the ordained clergy (i.e., bishops, priests, and deacons).

The clergy themselves were to take on the style of a new type of worldly monk, an activist monasticism as it were. Celibacy was thought to be necessary for two distinct reasons. An unmarried priesthood was bound more tightly to the clerical structure of the church: since clerical dynasties were in theory now impossible, it was harder for powerful local families to get control of the church's property and to keep it in the family. A second reason for requiring clerical celibacy was a widespread belief that sexual intercourse was intrinsically impure and therefore inappropriate for someone who offered the sacrifice of the Mass. The same desire to hold priests to a higher standard was behind the Gregorian reformers' demand that the clergy not carry weapons and shed blood. And rooting out simony meant returning control of the church to its rightful owners, the monks and clergy, who should be able freely to elect their abbots and bishops. It would also rid the church of the further worldly taint of money.

All of this would have been explosive enough on its own terms. But Gregory incorporated one further ambition that made his reforms downright revolutionary: the elimination of "lay investiture," so called because of the practice in which a nobleman or king would "invest" a prospective abbot or bishop with the spiritual symbols of his office as part of the ceremony in which the candidate in return made feudal homage to his temporal lord as his vassal. In 1075, the Holy Roman Emperor Henry IV touched off a controversy over lay investiture when he appointed three bishops to *sees* (a bishop's official seat or center of authority) in Italy. All of the *sees* which were under the pope's ecclesiastical jurisdiction, but in imperial territory. Gregory VII responded by excommunicating Henry and calling on Henry's subjects to force him to recant.

In 1077, Henry did public penance, standing for three days in the snow outside of Gregory's castle retreat at Canossa, and was temporarily reconciled with the pope. But in 1080, the breach reopened. Gregory again excommunicated Henry, and, in response, Henry appointed and installed his own anti-pope (a pope regarded as having been elected illegally is called an "anti-pope"), Clement III. The stakes were heightened by Gregory's unprecedented claim that an excommunicated ruler was also deposed from his office and his subjects absolved of their oath of obedience to him. This was a potentially revolutionary claim. It remained the papacy's political trump card throughout the Middle Ages, until it was used for the last time (in vain) by Pope Pius V in 1570 against the Protestant queen of England, Elizabeth I.

The "investiture conflict," as it is called, was not just an institutional struggle but a battle for public opinion. It was not settled until 1122, long after Henry and Gregory were dead, with the compromise known as the Concordat (treaty) of Worms. The emperor renounced his claim to appoint bishops, who would now be elected freely by the clergy. But he retained the right to be present at such elections and to receive feudal homage (the ceremony in which a vassal pledged himself to his lord) for whatever lands the new bishop received as a vassal of the emperor. Both of these concessions gave the emperor ways to influence the choice of candidates.

The long-term significance of Gregory's reform program lay in his twin effort to detach the clerical order from lay and local control and to incorporate it in an international hierarchy with the papacy at the top. The effect was to radically distinguish what we now call "church" and "state" in an unprecedented way. While there was still a single Christian society (see discussion of "Christendom" in Chapter 14), more clearly than ever there were now two heads. It was unlikely that there would be another Constantine, another Justinian, or even another Charlemagne, who had regarded the pope as a sort of court chaplain. The ruler would no longer be considered "sacred" in the same way; royal anointing would continue as a ceremony, but its religious significance was greatly weakened—even though centuries later Shakespeare's Richard II would protest, "Not all the water in the rough rude sea can wash the balm from an anointed king" (*Richard II*, Act III, Scene 2). Nonetheless, the first, very tentative steps, toward the secularization of the state had been taken.

Gregory's program is famously expressed in a short set of 27 theses called the *Dictatus Papae* ("Statements of the Pope") probably written in 1075, perhaps as the table of contents for a collection of church laws in support of his program. They proclaim that the pope, as supreme judge under God alone, holds supreme power over all Christian souls; all bishops and abbots are subject to him and he alone holds absolute powers of absolution (the power to forgive sins) and excommunication (the power to exclude someone from membership in the church). It also proclaims the pope's right to depose princes (§22). The history of the papacy in the High Middle Ages will witness the effort to realize these claims.

Figure 13–2 Christ Enthroned in Majesty. Illumination from a tenth-century French manuscript, an example of the artistic contributions of the Carolingian period.

CULTURAL CONTRIBUTIONS OF THE EARLY MEDIEVAL PERIOD

A number of remarkable and significant cultural developments took place in the Western Roman Empire during the early medieval period, especially during the so-called Carolingian Renaissance. We will consider three expressions of this cultural creativity: the forging of the Romano-Frankish liturgy (the

Roman Rite), the creation of Romano-Frankish (Gregorian) chant, and the development of Romanesque architecture.

Before the Carolingian period, Christian worship in the West was conducted in Latin, but otherwise there was no standardized form of service. Prestigious cities such as Milan, Braga, Lyons, and Paris developed texts and ceremonies as well as calendars of feasts and occasions that were particular to their own location. In an attempt to unify his empire, Charlemagne directed that the Christian worship practices of the city of Rome should become the norm throughout his territories. To this end, Charlemagne sent one of his scholar-courtiers to ask Pope Hadrian I for a "pure Gregorian" **sacramentary** (a book of the prayers needed by a priest to celebrate the Eucharist) popularly believed to have been composed by Pope Gregory I. Around 784–785, Hadrian sent such a book to the imperial court at Aachen, where it was deposited in the palace library to serve as the exemplar for all copies of sacramentaries to be used in Charlemagne's empire. However, the book was incomplete, and as a result it was supplemented with texts and ceremonies familiar to Frankish worshippers. This fusion of sober, classical Roman prayer with the dramatic, exuberant Frankish prayer forms the core of the **Roman Rite**, the primary form of liturgy for the Roman Catholic Church.

Issues in Moral Theology: The Penitentials
Auricular Confession and the Penitential Handbooks

The early middle ages witnessed the widespread adoption within the church of a practice known as "auricular confession," that is, the private confession of one's sins to a priest. Auricular confession would come to have an enormous influence on how Christians, especially in the West, understood the nature of both sin and salvation. After listening to a person's private confession, the confessor (a priest or monk) formally declared the person's sins forgiven and then assigned him or her a "penance," that is, some act or acts intended as restitution for the damages done by the sin.

It was important that the confessor assign a "fitting" penance, neither too harsh nor too lenient, and to do so he would often consult books written especially for this purpose. These books, the Handbooks of Penance (Latin *Libri Poenitentiales*), were organized according to the Seven Capital Sins (better known as the seven "deadly" or "cardinal" sins): in ascending order of moral gravity, they are gluttony, lust, avarice, wrath, despair, sloth, and pride. This organization suggests a more "medicinal" than legal approach to sin. Gluttons, for example, should fast from food and/or drink for an appropriate time period; idlers should be given more strenuous work to do; one who seriously injures another in a quarrel should cover the victim's medical costs and do his work until he heals, etc. The aim of the practice, in other words, was to restore the penitent to full "moral health," where health (salvation) is understood in terms of the virtues—above all charity—of which the seven deadly sins were the corruption.

The content of these handbooks, and their organizing principle of the seven deadly sins, would later be incorporated into the more formal "manuals" of moral theology that became standard textbooks for the training of priests from the later Middle Ages until Vatican II (1962–1965). However, after the sixteenth-century Reformation, these manuals tended increasingly to be organized according to the Ten Commandments, taking a correspondingly more juridical approach to morality. In a nod to this long tradition, the section dedicated to morality in the current *Catechism of the Catholic Church* (1997) combines both virtues/vices and Commandments.

This attempt to standardize worship throughout the Carolingian empire encouraged much artistic activity. The prayer texts themselves had to be copied into volumes intended for liturgical use. These manuscripts were often decorated with intricate designs or devotional pictures. The ceremonial clothing worn by the clergy during public worship demanded the skills of weavers, dyers, and embroiderers. Workers in precious metals and stones produced covers for the liturgical books and vessels for housing saints' relics, burning incense, and serving Holy Communion.

In conformity with his unification policy, Charlemagne's *General Admonition of 780* mandated, among other reforms, the use of Roman music at worship services throughout the empire. The **Gregorian chant** that was created for Roman Rite worship seems to be a fusion of chants used in the city of Rome together with the native chants of the Frankish churches. These chants were sung in unison, and they varied in complexity from simple recitation tones (which allowed biblical texts to be heard by worshipping assemblies prior to the invention of microphones) to melismatic melodies in which 50 or more notes might decorate a single syllable. This chant repertoire is one of the richest expressions of Christian spirituality in the early medieval period.

Figure 13–3 Charlemagne's palace chapel at Aix-la-Chapelle.

By the ninth century, some worship centers (bishops' churches and major monasteries) developed liturgical music in which more than one melody was sounded. Music of such complexity demanded the development of notational systems which were developed in the ninth century. By the eleventh century, notation had become so accurate that one could learn a new chant directly from a written page without the guidance of a singer who already knew the piece. The development of notation in turn led to further advances in musical art.

Another important cultural development of this period was Romanesque architecture. Strictly speaking, **Romanesque architecture** refers to the style of buildings constructed in Western Europe between the end of the eleventh century and the rise of the Gothic style in the middle part of the twelfth century, but we will use it to refer to the buildings developed during the Carolingian and Ottonian dynasties. Romanesque was an adaptation of ancient Roman architectural practices to the changed circumstances of the Early Middle Ages. The outstanding achievement of Romanesque architects was the development of stone vaulted buildings that would replace the highly flammable wooden roofs of pre-Romanesque buildings. Introducing vaulting (especially in "barrel" or "tunnel" form) led to the erection of heavy walls and piers in place of the light walls and columns that had been used to support wooden roofs. These thick-walled buildings usually had only small openings for light, creating a fortress-like impression. Churches built in this style probably symbolized safety and security in the turbulent society of the tenth and eleventh centuries. A fascinating example of the transition into Romanesque architecture is Charlemagne's palace chapel at Aachen built between 792 and 805. On the one hand, its polygonal, domed shape is reminiscent of Byzantine architecture; on the other, its massive walls, narrow windows, and vaulting all look forward to later developments.

Churches in the early medieval period underwent a number of artistic and architectural changes. Carolingian architects created what was termed *westworks*, a multistoried façade usually flanked by bell towers before the entrance of the church building. Monastic communities developed churches with multiple chapels and altars for the devotional practices of individuals or groups, thus transforming the earlier patristic principle of "one people gathered around one altar in one church building." Churches at major shrines developed special walkways called *ambulatories* that allowed visitors access to the saints' relics even when services were being held in the main body of the church. Façades, doors, and windows of Romanesque churches were often decorated with carvings and sculptures that served to teach people the Bible stories and other elements of their faith through the medium of art.

Figure 13–4 Charlemagne's throne, palace chapel at Aix-la-Chapelle.

MAJOR THEOLOGICAL FIGURES IN THE EARLY MEDIEVAL PERIOD

The scholars of the early medieval period suggest that this era provided us with rather few great popes or theologians. While this may be generally correct, particular theologians of eminence still grace this epoch, indicating that critical reflection upon the reality of God and the beliefs and practices of the Christian religion did, in fact, take place in the early medieval period. We will consider one representative from the Eastern and two from the Western theological tradition.

An Eastern theologian who is representative of the early medieval period is **Symeon the New Theologian** (942–1022). Born into the Byzantine Empire, Symeon was a monk, abbot, theologian, and poet—one of the most Spirit-centered of all Christian writers. Anticipating the claims of twentieth-century charismatic Christians, Symeon asserted that it was possible for every baptized Christian to attain direct, conscious experience of the Holy Spirit even in this life. The spiritual experience in which a person achieves direct communion with the divine is called **mysticism**. His *Hymn 25* communicates both mystical insight and theological precision in a rapturous outpouring of language:

> —But, Oh, what intoxication of light, Oh, what movements of fire!
> Oh, what swirlings of the flame in me, miserable one that I am,
> coming from You and Your glory!
> The glory I know it and I say it is Your Holy Spirit,
> who has the same nature with You and the same honor, O Word;
> He is of the same race, of the same glory,
> of the same essence, He alone with Your Father
> and with You, O Christ, O God of the universe!
> I fall down in adoration before You.
> I thank You that You have made me worthy to know, however little it may be,
> the power of Your divinity.
> I thank You that You, even when I was sitting in darkness,
> revealed Yourself to me, You enlightened me,
> You granted me to see the light of Your countenance
> that is unbearable to all.
> I remained seated in the middle of the darkness, I know,
> but, while I was there surrounded by darkness,
> You appeared as light, illuminating me completely from Your total light.
> And I became light in the night, I who was found in the midst of darkness.
> Neither the darkness extinguished Your light completely,
> nor did the light dissipate the visible darkness,
> but they were together, yet completely separate,
> without confusion, far from each other, surely not at all mixed,
> except in the same spot where they filled everything.
> So I am in the light, yet I am found in the middle of the darkness.
> So I am in the darkness, yet still I am in the middle of the light.
> —How can darkness receive within itself a light and, without being dissipated by the light,
> it still remains in the middle of the light?
> O awesome wonder which I see doubly,
> with my two sets of eyes, of the body and of the soul!
>
> (Symeon the New Theologian, *The Discourses*, 24–25)

The first representative of Western early medieval theology has already appeared in our discussion on the evolution of the papacy. Pope Gregory I was not only a statesman and an important church leader, he was also a noted pastoral theologian. His *Homilies on Ezechiel* and his *Homilies on the Gospels* are filled with exegetical insights applied to the life situation of his hearers. His *Dialogues* is a delightful collection of anecdotes about the saintly ascetics and wonder-workers of Italy. More importantly, in his *Pastoral Rule* and *Moral Teachings from Job*, Gregory created the earliest manuals of moral and ascetic theology. In the following passage from the *Moral Teachings from Job*, Gregory discusses a core issue of soteriology (doctrine about salvation): why Jesus had to be sacrificed for humanity.

> [T]he Devil himself, tripping us up radically in our first parents, held man bound in his captivity in a seemingly just way—man, who, created with a free choice, consented, under his persuasion, to what was unjust. For man, created unto life in the freedom of his own will, was, of his own accord, made the debtor of death. This fault, therefore, had to be taken away; but it could not be taken away except through sacrifice. A sacrifice, then, was to be sought; but what kind of a sacrifice would be discovered that would suffice for the absolving of men? It would not be just that victims from among brute animals should be slain on behalf of rational man.... If the victim was to be rational, a man would have to be offered; and if it was to cleanse men of sin, the victim must be a man without sin. But how should a man be without sin, if he were the offspring of a sinful heritage? That is why the Son of God came, for man's sake, into the womb of the Virgin, where, on our behalf, He was made Man. From mankind He took its nature, but not its fault. He made a sacrifice on our behalf. For the sake of the sinner He delivered up His body as a Victim without sin, a Victim who would be able both to die in respect to His humanity and to cleanse us in respect to justice.
>
> (Cited in Jurgens 1979, 316)

Another Western theologian who is representative of the early medieval period is **Anselm of Canterbury** (1033–1109), who could equally well be considered a figure transitional to the High Middle Ages. Anselm was a Benedictine monk who eventually rose to the position of Archbishop of Canterbury. Anselm made several great contributions to the Christian understanding of God, two of which will be described here. First, in his *Cur Deus Homo* ("Why Did God Become Man?"), Anselm constructed a "debt-satisfaction" theory of the atonement, arguing that the sin of Adam could only be forgiven if sufficient satisfaction for that sin were offered to the Father. But only a divine person could adequately resolve the debt incurred by human sin. Therefore, God had to become human if humanity was to be restored to God's friendship. However, Anselm's most original theological contribution appears in his so-called "ontological" (having to do with the being or essence of something) argument for the existence of God. In his *Proslogion*, Anselm argued that God, understood as "a being than which nothing greater can be thought," must necessarily exist, since if that being existed only in thought, one could conceive of that being also existing in reality, which would be greater.

To conclude this section, three things can be said about the theological developments of the early medieval period. First, in an era of great social and political turmoil, theologians took great pains to preserve the heritage of patristic thought (i.e., the thought of the early Church Fathers). They did this by means of compilations of early Christian literature: collections of ancient Christian sermons, extracts from patristic writings, "chains" of patristic commentary on the Bible, systematized lists of citations on a particular topic, and canonical collections (in which patristic teaching on Christian living and church discipline appeared). Second, monasteries were primarily responsible for developing a theology aimed at helping Christians attain sanctification. The writers of these texts consciously employed images and symbols in an attempt to evoke an experience of God for their readers. These images and symbols dealt with archetypal human experiences of fear, anxiety, humiliation, sickness, hope, joy, confidence, and friendship. Thus, theology was never simply intellectual speculation but a response of the whole person to the divine mystery (e.g., Symeon the New Theologian's *Hymn 25*). Third, toward the end of the period, theologians evinced an ever-more-confident trust in human reason and developed new forms of systematic inquiry (e.g., Anselm of Canterbury's *Proslogion*) that would bear fruit in the high medieval Scholastic period.

Key Terms

alienation of property
Anselm of Canterbury
Benedict of Nursia
Charlemagne
concubinage
feudal system
Gregorian chant

Gregorian reform
Gregory I
Gregory VII
Holy Roman Empire
John Cassian
lay investiture
mysticism

Romanesque architecture
Roman Rite
sacramentary
simony
Symeon the New
    Theologian

Questions for Reading

1. How did the special relationship between the Carolingian dynasty and the papacy come into being in the eighth century?

2. What were the two major contributions of Celtic monasticism to the development of the early medieval Western Christian tradition?

3. What was the Cluniac Reform Movement? Where did it originate? What abuses was it addressing?

4. Who was Gregory I? What role did Gregory play in spreading the Christian message?

5. Who was Gregory VII? What was the most radical feature of the theses expounded in Gregory's *Dictatus Papae*?

6. Charlemagne had a passion to bring "Roman" elements into the religious life of his Frankish kingdom. Describe how this affected the development of the liturgy in his domain.

7. What was distinctive about the theological approach to the Holy Spirit by the early medieval Eastern theologian Symeon the New Theologian?

8. Describe one major theological contribution of two Western theologians of the early medieval period, Pope Gregory I and Anselm of Canterbury.

Works Consulted/Recommended Reading

Bede. 1990. *Ecclesiastical History of the English People.* Translated by Leo Sherley-Price. Revised edn. R.E. Latham. London: Penguin.

Cowdrey, Herbert Edward John. 1970. *The Cluniacs and the Gregorian Reform.* Oxford: Clarendon Press.

Fichtenau, Heinrich. 1963/1965. *The Carolingian Empire.* Translated by Peter Munz. New York: Harper & Row.

Gregory of Tours. 1974. *History of the Franks.* Translated and Introduction by Lewis Thorpe. London: Penguin.

Hillgarth, J.N. 1986. *Christianity and Paganism, 350–750: The Conversion of Western Europe.* Revised edn. Philadelphia, PA: University of Pennsylvania Press.

Hunter Blair, Peter. 1971. *The World of Bede.* New York: St. Martin's Press.

Jurgens, W.A. 1979. *The Faith of the Early Fathers.* Vol. 3. Collegeville, MN: The Liturgical Press.

Kantorowicz, Ernst Hartwig. 1957. *The King's Two Bodies: A Study in Mediaeval Political Theology.* Princeton, NJ: Princeton University Press.

Lawrence, Clifford Hugh. 1989. *Medieval Monasticism: Forms of Religious Life in Western Europe in the Middle Ages.* 2nd edn. London: Longman.

Leyser, Karl J. 1979. *Rule and Conflict in an Early Medieval Society: Ottonian Saxony.* Bloomington, IN: Indiana University Press.

McKitterick, Rosamund. 1977. *The Frankish Church and the Carolingian Reform 789–895.* London: Longman.

Meehan, Bernard. 2012. *The Book of Kells.* New York: Thames and Hudson.

Noble, Thomas F.X. 1984. *The Republic of Saint Peter: The Birth of the Papal State, 680–825.* Philadelphia, PA: University of Pennsylvania Press.

Riché, Pierre. 1976. *Education and Culture in the Barbarian West, Sixth through Eighth Centuries.* Translated by John J. Contreni. Columbia, SC: University of South Carolina Press.

Richter, Michael. 2008. *Bobbio in the Early Middle Ages: The Abiding Legacy of Columbanus.* Portland, OR: Four Courts Press.

Southern, Richard William. 1990. *Saint Anselm: A Portrait in a Landscape.* Cambridge: Cambridge University Press.

Symeon the New Theologian. 1980. *The Discourses.* Translated by C.J. DeCatanzaro. Classics of Western Spirituality. New York: Paulist Press.

Tellenbach, Gerd. 1993. *The Church in Western Europe from the Tenth to the Early Twelfth Century.* Translated by Timothy Reuter. Cambridge Medieval Textbooks. Cambridge: Cambridge University Press.

Ullmann, Walter. 1972. *A Short History of the Papacy in the Middle Ages.* London: Methuen.

Wallace-Hadrill, John Michael. 1983. *The Frankish Church.* Oxford: Clarendon Press-Oxford University Press.

Chapter

CHRISTIANITY IN THE HIGH MIDDLE AGES

TIMELINE

A.D. 1097–1291	Beginning and end of Western Christian states recovered from Islam in Syria and Palestine.
A.D. 1098	The Cistercian order is founded to restore Benedictine life to its original form.
A.D. 1184	The Council of Verona condemns the Waldensians as heretics.
A.D. 1198–1216	Reign of Pope Innocent III.
A.D. 1209	Francis of Assisi founds the mendicant order known as the Franciscans.
A.D. 1215	Fourth Lateran Council institutes some reforms of the clergy and defines the dogma of transubstantiation.
A.D. 1220–1221	Dominic Guzman founds the mendicant order known as the Dominicans.
A.D. 1232	Emperor Frederick II issues an edict permitting the hunting of heretics. The period of the inquisitions formally begins.
A.D. 1294–1303	Reign of Pope Boniface VIII.
A.D. 1302	Pope Boniface VIII issues bull *Unam Sanctam*, an extreme statement of church authority over temporal power.

The late eleventh, twelfth, and thirteenth centuries are often called the High Middle Ages in order to distinguish them from the prior period (approximately 500 to 1050, when Western Europe reorganized itself after the fall of the Roman Empire in the West) and from the one that followed (see Chapter 16), which led up to the Protestant Reformation. These centuries are also "high" in the sense that they mark numerous peak developments and events of lasting importance in the Christian tradition. During this period of tremendous ferment, Christianity became thoroughly identified with European culture and society. The medieval church ran schools, licensed universities, owned and farmed land, tried to control fighting and violence and bring stability and discipline to economic life, rebuked kings and emperors, engaged in its own diplomacy and politics, cared for the poor and the sick, and exercised legal control over issues relating to marriage, family, and inheritance. Modern historians have given the name of **Christendom** to this unprecedented merging of Christianity and culture.

This chapter describes trends in the practices, doctrines, and institutions of Catholic Christianity. The following topics are examined: the spirit of creativity and innovation found in religious reform movements, both within and outside of the institutional church; the papacy and its emerging role as spiritual head of Christendom; devotional practice and religious life in the medieval period; the spread of the Gothic style in church architecture; and Christendom's relations with non-Christians. Theology and the medieval universities will be treated in Chapter 15.

THE FOREIGN POLICY OF CHRISTENDOM: PAGANS, JEWS, AND MUSLIMS

The Latin word *Christianitas*, not meaning "Christianity" as a religion but "Christendom" in the sense of a closed and totally Christian society and territory, became widespread around the time of the First Crusade (1095). From this time, European Christians began to think of their society as defined by its religious identity, in conscious opposition to groups that did not share that identity: pagans, Jews, and Muslims.

Paganism on the Margins

By the end of the eleventh century, almost all of Europe had become nominally Christian. Scandinavia, central Europe, and part of Eastern Europe, especially the Poles and Hungarians, had accepted Latin Christianity and communion with Rome. The eastern Slavic peoples living in what is now Russia, Belarus, and Ukraine, and most of the peoples of the Balkans, were in the cultural and political orbit of the Byzantine Empire and therefore became Orthodox.

The last large concentration of pagan peoples lay along the Baltic seacoast in northeastern Europe. Their incorporation into Christendom occurred only after two and a half centuries of warfare and colonization. Prior to the twelfth century, conversion generally occurred in the manner traditional since the first Germanic tribes became Christian in the waning days of the Roman Empire: the king or noble elite became Christian and brought their people along with them. Charlemagne's decades-long conquest of the Saxons (772–804) was marked by unprecedented use of forced conversion—what a late ninth-century writer called "preaching with an iron tongue." A further turn to conversion by conquest began in 1147, when a new type of religious warfare, the *crusade* (see Medieval Christianity and Islam: Holy Wars, below), was authorized against a Slavic people called the Wends in central and eastern Germany. The Wendish crusade offered a religious justification for German and Danish armed expansion. When St. Bernard of Clairvaux (see Monastic Renewal: the Cisterians, below) predicted a stark alternative of Baptism or death for the pagan Wends, he was not justifying forced conversion of individuals but stating the blunt fact that the survival of the historic identity of pagan peoples depended on their conversion. Nevertheless, his call to arm the faithful "with the Holy Cross of Christ against the enemies of the Cross of Christ" (cited in Tyerman 2006, 679) helped to sanction what amounted to glorified land-grabbing. Although normal church teaching opposed the use of armed force to baptize large numbers of people, involuntary Baptism became part of a pattern of militarized expansion in the late medieval period. The early Christian understanding that Baptism must be free was undercut by efforts to distinguish absolutely forced conversion from conversion induced by threats and intimidation—after which, coercion could be used to enforce the newly Christian identity—recall Augustine's defense of coercive incentives against the Donatists (see Chapter 10). Thus, in 1209, Pope Innocent III urged the Danish king Valdemar II to pursue "the war of the Lord ... to drag the barbarians into the net of orthodoxy" (cited in Tyerman 2006, 683). The brutal culmination of this policy was the 100 years and more during which the military crusading order of the Teutonic Knights fought to conquer, convert, and govern Prussia and Livonia (modern-day Latvia), in the process also "Germanizing" these areas until the massive population and border changes after World War I and World War II. The order would also have annexed Lithuania, home of the last pagan holdouts, had not the crusading impetus petered out after the Lithuanians made a diplomatic conversion to Christianity in 1386 (under Polish influence rather than pressure from the Teutonic Knights).

Jews in Christian Society

In Christendom, the Jews were the only "outsiders" who remained. Medieval Jews suffered from numerous injustices. They were restricted to their own quarter of the city (the original *ghetto*) and made to wear identifying signs on their clothing. They could not appear in public at Eastertime. They were prohibited from owning Christian slaves, exercising dominance over Christians (which kept them out of local government), and acquiring land. In addition, they were occasionally subjected to violent and bloody persecution, and their goods were liable to seizure. Sometimes, they were forced by law to attend Christian services, where attempts were made to convert them. Eventually, they were expelled altogether from the western parts of Europe: England (1290), France (1306), and, at the very end of the medieval period, from the newly unified kingdom of Spain (1492), and from Portugal (1497).

Why were Jews singled out for such treatment? There appear to have been two major sources of medieval anti-Judaism: popular prejudice and bigotry against Jews; and traditional Christian teaching that Christianity had superseded Judaism. Some of the popular prejudice was based on economic resentment. Jews first prospered as artisans and traders of goods. Since church law forbade Christians to loan money at interest to other Christians, civil authorities allowed Jews to move into money-lending and to perform the banking services that were so important to the economic recovery of medieval Europe. This is the context in which the traditional hostile stereotypes of Jews as grasping and greedy originated. The Jews were also vulnerable targets for mass resentment in turbulent or troubling times. Rumors about Jews killing Christians and using their blood to make bread for their festivals, what came to be called "the blood libel," began to spread in the twelfth century, as did stories about Jews desecrating the Eucharistic host. During the fourteenth-century plague known as the Black Death, Jews were accused of causing the disease by poisoning wells. Pogroms (massacres) of Jews also frequently broke out in the wake of the crusading movement.

Another source of medieval anti-Judaism was the traditional Christian teaching that the Christian church was the true Israel, and the belief that the Jews inherited a collective punishment for the murder of Jesus ("His blood be on us and on our children," Matthew 27:25). Such teaching was not the primary cause of medieval anti-Judaism, but it certainly contributed to people's fears and prejudices once these began to appear. To their credit, the popes regularly condemned persecutions and forced Baptisms of Jews, and tried to discourage popular prejudices about ritual murder and well poisoning. However, they also firmly supported the legalized subordination of Jews to Christians, and from the thirteenth century increased efforts to convert Jews.

The prejudice and persecution experienced by medieval Jews is not the whole story, for Jewish and Christian interaction in the medieval period was rich and many-sided. Jewish and Christian scholars and theologians, for example, made constructive contacts over the study of the Bible. The great Jewish scholar Rashi wrote biblical commentaries that were also used by Christian scholars. At St. Victor's abbey in Paris, the twelfth-century theologians known as the Victorines learned Hebrew and consulted Jewish biblical experts in their study of the sacred scriptures. In general, Christian scholars gradually recognized that they had much to learn from Jewish biblical interpretation, especially where the original Hebrew text was concerned.

Medieval Christianity and Islam: Holy Wars

Medieval Christianity's relations with Islam are characterized most famously by the **Crusades**, the Christian holy wars that, beginning in the late eleventh century, the medieval church launched against unbelievers, especially Muslims, and heretics. Prior to the Crusades, the church had made serious efforts to curb the violence that was ingrained in feudal society. In movements such as the Peace of God and the Truce of God, bishops had tried to limit both the victims of knightly violence and the times and seasons in which war could be conducted. With the rise of crusading, some of that violence was exported outside Christendom.

Since the conversion of the Roman Empire, Christianity had qualified its initial opposition to shedding blood by the gradual adoption of the concept of a just war (see Chapter 9). The Crusades represented a further stage in the Christianizing of military service—and the militarizing of Christianity—by adopting the biblical concept of a *holy war*, a war willed by God himself. The chief promoters of holy war and the inventors of the crusading movement were the popes of the Gregorian Reform (see Chapter 13). Because the reformers forbade the clergy to shed blood themselves, they delegated this division of social labor to the laity. Here is the

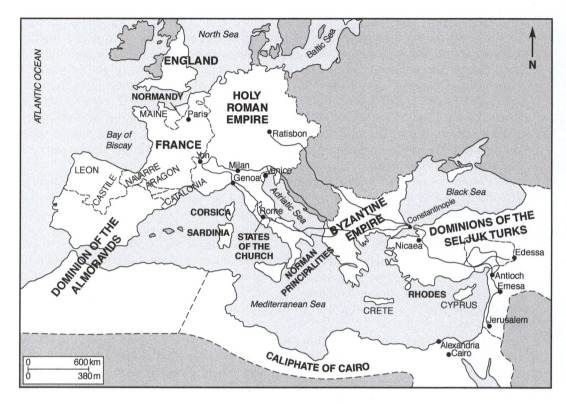

Figure 14–1 Boundaries between Christianity and Islam at the time of the First Crusade.

somewhat condescending way in which a monastic writer described the layman's new vocation in his history of the First Crusade:

> God has instituted in our time holy wars, so that the order of knights and the crowd running in their wake, who following the example of ancient pagans have been engaged in slaughtering one another, might find a new way of gaining salvation. And so they are not forced to abandon secular affairs completely by choosing the monastic life or any religious profession, as used to be the custom, but can attain in some measure God's grace while pursuing their own careers, with the liberty and in the dress to which they are accustomed.
>
> (Guibert of Nogent, *The Deeds of God through the Franks,* cited in Riley-Smith 1987, 9)

The church had long encouraged the faithful to fight for Christendom and had even promised eternal life to those who died in battle defending it against unbelievers. In 1074, Pope Gregory VII announced his intention to lead in person a military expedition that would aid Greek Christians against the Turks (in 1071, the Byzantines had lost a major battle to the Turks) and would continue on to Christ's Holy Sepulchre in Jerusalem, which a Muslim caliph had destroyed in 1009. That hope went unfilled until Pope Urban II launched what became the First Crusade (1096–1099). According to later accounts of Urban's speech in 1095 at a council at Clermont in southern France, the pope promised a plenary indulgence (performance of penance and complete remission of sin) to all who took the crusading oath to aid Eastern Christians and free the holy places from their oppressors. Normally pilgrims were forbidden to carry arms, but these new-style pilgrims were "an army of God." In the past, soldiers who had killed even in a just war had to do penance for the bloodshed; now killing itself was conceived as an act of penance. The novelty of crusading was its character as an armed penitential pilgrimage.

The response to Urban's appeal was overwhelming. Within four years Western armies had reconquered Jerusalem and established a network of Latin states in Syria and Palestine which lasted for almost two centuries. These Christian invaders were no doubt motivated in part by greed for land and booty, but crusading was too risky and expensive to have been driven by just economic motives. Idealistic and spiritual motives were at work as well. Doing penance for one's sins was a powerful spiritual factor. Another was the old Germanic warrior ideal of loyalty to the lord of one's warband: just as the oath of allegiance required one to avenge wrongs that were done to one's lord, so crusading could be seen as avenging wrongs done to Christ. An especially powerful motive was the religious aura of Jerusalem, which for centuries had been a popular pilgrimage site for Christians. Jerusalem exercised a profound fascination on the religious imagination of medieval Christians, particularly as Christians became interested in imitation of the earthly life of Jesus during the High Middle Ages. The church guaranteed the crusader the same traditional privileges as the pilgrim, such as the protection of his land and family in his absence. He made a vow when he "took the cross," which was worn as his symbol. His slogan, chanted loudly at Clermont, was "God wills it."

The ultimate expression of warfare in the service of the gospel was the rise of the hybrid institution of the *military order*. These were originally religious orders of knights who took monastic vows to defend pilgrims and the holy places. The most famous military orders were the Teutonic Knights, already mentioned, who from 1245 had a papally granted right to perpetual crusade in their own state along the Baltic coast; the Knights Templar, so called from their headquarters in Jerusalem; and the Knights of St. John or "Hospitallers," so called because their original work was the maintenance of the Hospital of St. John in Jerusalem. The military orders were always controversial. Some critics were scandalized by the union of the sword and monastic vows and the orders' often brutal activities, but others were simply jealous of their power and independence.

Although the First Crusade did succeed in recapturing Jerusalem in 1099, within less than 100 years Jerusalem—a holy city for Muslims as well—was again in Muslim hands. The last crusader state in the Middle East fell in 1291. During the two centuries of Western settlement in "Outremer," as medieval French writers called it ("The Land beyond the Sea"), Christians and Muslims practiced an uneasy coexistence. Intermarriage was not common. Western interaction was mainly with local non-Catholic Christians more than with Muslims—Arabic-speaking Middle Eastern Christians played a role as go-betweens. Muslims received roughly the same measure of disdainful tolerance they had extended to conquered Christian populations. The victories of "the Franks," as Western Christians were called collectively, did inspire a Muslim military revival and successful *jihad*.

Seen in a longer historical perspective, the Crusades' overall military threat to Islam was virtually nil, although that has not kept their memory from being any less bitter, as contemporary experience is revealing once again. Crusader states elsewhere were gradually secularized, although the Hospitallers held onto the island of Malta until Napoleon's arrival in 1798. In Europe, crusading can claim partial credit for the recovery of Spain and Sicily from Islam. In the early modern period, when Turkish expansion again threatened Christendom with Muslim invasion, Europe had papally inspired Holy Leagues, which were essentially *defensive* crusades, to thank for stopping the Turkish advance, which in 1683 had reached as far as Vienna in central Europe. Since the eighteenth century, the concept of "holy war" has gradually been discredited among most Christians, though in times of crisis it can still be a tempting invocation. Secularization has forced Christianity to think in less territorial terms than in the medieval period. Today, Christian moral reflection on war tends to move between the poles of just-war theory and updated versions of early Christian pacifism.

It would be misleading to characterize medieval Christianity's relations with Islam exclusively in terms of warfare. In areas like Spain and Sicily, where Christians and Muslims lived close to one another, commercial and cultural relations were rich and varied. The large medieval intellectual debt to Islam is discussed in Chapter 15. Peaceful if ineffective efforts were made to convert Muslims to Christianity. By the twelfth century, the Qur'an had been translated into Latin so that Western Christians could read it. The new religious orders of the Franciscans and Dominicans (see The Mendicant Orders: Dominicans and Franciscans, below) both saw it as part of their mission to preach the gospel to unbelievers, chiefly Muslims. A famous episode in the life of St. Francis of Assisi was his audience before the sultan of Egypt in 1219. In the middle of the Fifth Crusade, which had gone to Egypt rather than to Palestine or Syria, Francis risked his life by walking unprotected into the Muslim camp in order to preach to the sultan and his court. The sultan, Malik al-Kamil (1180–1238), resisted advice to have Francis executed immediately and allowed him to preach. Although he failed to convert al-Kamil, Francis made a powerful impression with his courage and integrity.

THE PRIMACY OF THE PAPACY

In the early medieval period, Pope Gregory VII had envisioned the pope as the spiritual head of a single Christian society. His successors came close enough to realizing this vision that the High Middle Ages are sometimes called the period of the papal monarchy. This does not mean that popes tried to replace kings and emperors as rulers of nations, but that kings and emperors were now subjected to the moral and religious scrutiny of the popes in ways that previous kings had not experienced.

The increasing power of the papacy was accompanied by a growing church bureaucracy in Rome. The twelfth century saw the rise of the papal court, or **curia**, staffed by the College of Cardinals. The term "cardinal" originally was an honorary title for certain ordained clergy who assisted the pope in his liturgical and administrative tasks in the city of Rome. In 1059, a papal decree granted these "cardinal" clergy the exclusive right to elect the pope. The popes then began to extend the title to important churchmen outside of Rome. The College of Cardinals thus came to assist the pope in governing the universal church, particularly through their management of the Curia, which handled official correspondence, finances, record keeping, and legal business. Training in canon law became a virtual requirement for the papal office, as the papacy became a popular court of appeal for litigants from all over Europe. At the same time, friendly critics pleaded with the popes not to let their spiritual mission get swallowed up in bureaucratic routine. Pope Innocent III and Pope Boniface VIII are two popes of the High Middle Ages whose reigns coincide with the height of papal power and the beginning of its decline.

Pope Innocent III and the Zenith of Papal Power

Innocent III (r. 1198–1216) became pope at the age of 37, the youngest person ever to hold the office. He is perhaps best known for his political involvements. Besides being ruler of the Papal States, the popes' own realm in central Italy, Innocent also had special feudal rights over Poland, Hungary, Aragon (in Spain), and Sicily. He believed he could intervene in political affairs when moral or religious issues were involved. The church could and did claim competence in affairs and transactions that might seem personal but were inevitably public and political as well. One example is the centrality of personal oaths in feudal political relations. Another is marriage and reproduction: the church's power to determine marital legitimacy could affect dynastic successions and diplomacy, which was often based on marital alliances.

Oath of Peter II, King of Aragon, made to Pope Innocent III

"I will defend the catholic faith; I will persecute heresy; I will respect the liberties and immunities of the churches and protect their rights. Throughout all of the territory submitted to my power I will strive to maintain peace and justice."

An example of Innocent III's power over kings is his disciplining of the king of England in a dispute over who would be appointed archbishop of Canterbury. When the king objected to the canonically elected archbishop, Innocent III excommunicated the king and put all of England under interdict for five years. An **interdict** is a kind of "strike" in which the church shuts down the sacramental system (Eucharist, Baptism, Penance, etc.). Most English clergy seem to have honored the interdict. Eventually, the king of England surrendered and even gave England to the papacy as a feudal holding (meaning that the king presented himself as the pope's vassal, though this more a symbolic relationship than a legal one).

Innocent always denied that he was taking over the legitimate rights of kings. His decrees and letters say plainly that he recognized the distinction between the two public authorities, civil and ecclesiastical, of the one Christian society. However, he was capable of speaking in very bold terms about the pope's unique authority:

> To me is said in the person of the prophet [Jeremiah], "I have set thee over nations and over kingdoms, to root up and to pull down, and to waste and destroy, and to build and to plant' (Jeremiah 1:10) … thus the others were called to a part of the care but Peter alone assumed the plenitude [fullness] of power. You see then who is this servant set over the household, truly the vicar [substitute] of Jesus Christ, successor of Peter, anointed of the Lord, a God of Pharaoh, set between God and man, lower than God but higher than man, who judges all, and is judged by no one…
>
> (Cited in Tierney 1964, 131–132)

Some of Innocent's policies failed badly. The crusade that he called against the Albigensian or Cathar heretics in southern France (see discussion of Catharism below) backfired when nobility and clergy from northern France used the war as an opportunity for conquest and exploitation. Twenty years of war (1209–1229) that began as a crusade to eliminate heresy had as its main result the French monarchy's political annexation of a large part of what is now southern France. The Fourth Crusade, which he first proclaimed in 1198, never even got to the Holy Land. Instead, the crusaders, desperately short of money, were forced to hire out their services, first to

Venetian merchant-princes and then to a discontented Byzantine prince, who hired them to put him and his deposed father back on the imperial throne in Constantinople. When they didn't get the money they were promised, the crusaders sacked the city in 1204 and elected one of their own leaders to become emperor. They also made a Western priest the patriarch of Constantinople. This Latin empire and Latin patriarchate lasted until 1261. The experience embittered Orthodox Christians so much that reunion under any terms became unthinkable, even when the Muslim Turks finally destroyed the Byzantine Empire in 1453. Disillusioned Orthodox Christians are reported to have said, "Better the turban of the sultan than the tiara [crown] of the pope."

Innocent's most fateful political decision may have been his sponsorship of the youthful Frederick II (r. 1212–1250), heir of the Hohenstaufen dynasty of the Holy Roman Empire, as the rightful claimant to the imperial throne. In return for his support, Innocent made Frederick promise not to unite the empire, which controlled the north of Italy, with the kingdom of Sicily in the south. The medieval popes' greatest security fear was that the same ruler would control both the northern and southern borders of the Papal States. Unfortunately, Frederick reneged on the agreement after Innocent died. The papacy eventually triumphed in the long and ferocious war that followed, but the struggle sapped its financial strength and its spiritual prestige. The war was an important turning point in the later medieval papacy's declining sense of spiritual mission.

The climax of Innocent's reign was the **Fourth Lateran Council** (1215). The council pressured the clergy to fulfill their pastoral duties of preaching, saying Mass, and hearing confession (clergy, especially at higher levels, were often "absentee" because governments siphoned off church salaries and personnel for government service; universities were another drain on clerical talent and resources). To keep lay people in contact with the sacramental system (see Seven Sacraments, under Medieval Religious Life, below), the council instituted the "Easter duty" (still in force among Catholics), which required all Christians to go to confession and to receive Communion at least once a year. It also defined the dogma of **transubstantiation** concerning the reality of Christ's real presence in the Eucharist. According to this teaching, the bread and wine are transformed by God's power in the action of a properly ordained priest, so that the body and blood of Jesus Christ are truly present in the Eucharist, albeit under the "species" (appearance) of bread and wine.

Figure 14–2 *The Dream of Pope Innocent*, by Giotto di Bondone (1266–1337), in which Francis shores up a collapsing church building, which happens to be the basilica of St. John Lateran, the home church of the pope as bishop of Rome.

Innocent's greatest service to the church may have been his endorsement of St. Francis of Assisi and his order of friars. Innocent prevented Francis' movement from suffering the fate of similar movements like the Waldensians by approving its rule and keeping it within the institutional system of religious orders, despite its unique character. Perhaps he recognized that it could provide the institutional church with desperately needed religious vitality and inspiration.

Pope Boniface VIII: The Papacy and National Kingdoms

The pontificate of **Boniface VIII** (r. 1294–1303) demonstrates the real-world limits of papal power in the High Middle Ages. Emerging national dynasties like those in England and France were growing in power. By the beginning of the fourteenth century, the old ideal of an international Christian empire was all but dead: it suffered a mortal wound with the papally inspired execution in 1254 of the last of the Hohenstaufen rulers of the Holy Roman Empire. During the late Middle Ages, the church would find itself steadily subjected to the political demands of national kingdoms. Boniface VIII twice collided with the powerful French king Philip IV, and twice he lost. The first conflict involved the right of kings to tax the clergy of their realm, and the second the pope's jurisdiction over the French bishops. In the latter struggle, he failed to win the obedience of the French clergy, more than half of whom supported their king over their pope—a forecast of the future trend toward the nationalization of Christianity. In retaliation, Boniface issued the bull *Unam Sanctam* (1302), probably the most famous medieval statement on church and state. Its teachings have often been cited as reasons for seeing Catholicism and the papacy as a threat to the stability of the political order. Boniface and the papacy paid a price for his boldness. Several months after *Unam Sanctam* appeared, Philip's agents arrested him. He died soon afterwards, perhaps of injuries suffered from his brutal treatment. Within two years, a French pope, Clement V (1305–1314), moved the papacy from Rome to Avignon in southern France, where it remained for much of the fourteenth century.

Pope Boniface VIII in *Unam Sanctam*

We are taught by the words of the Gospel that in this church and in her power are two swords, a spiritual and a temporal one.... But the one is exercised for the church, the other by the church, the one by the hand of the priest, the other by the hand of kings and soldiers, though at the will and sufferance of the priest ... if the earthly power errs it shall be judged by the spiritual power.... Therefore we declare, state, define, and pronounce that it is altogether necessary for salvation for every human creature to be subject to the Roman pontiff.

(Cited in Tierney 1964, 188–189)

REFORM WITHIN THE SYSTEM: NEW RELIGIOUS ORDERS

After the eleventh century, the institutional church struggled to keep control of the religious zeal and creative energies unleashed by the Gregorian Reform. At first, enthusiasm for reform stayed mainly within the bounds of the institutional church and produced a variety of new religious movements.

Monastic Renewal: The Cistercians

The *Rule* of St. Benedict inspired several new monastic orders. The most successful of these new orders was the **Cistercians**, the name of which is taken from their first house at Cîteaux in France. The Cistercians sought to restore the original simplicity of Benedictine monasticism by emphasizing a highly austere way of life, which included manual labor and economic self-support. They departed from the *Rule* in not accepting children into the monastery, in developing a strong governmental system that united all the houses of the order under a centralized authority (in contrast to the Benedictines' decentralized model), and in sponsoring a second order of lay brothers, the *conversi* (literally, "converts"), who took care of most of the day-to-day activities involved in running a monastery. The Cistercians built their monasteries in marginal and unsettled areas, significantly expanding the amount of European land under cultivation. Their numbers grew rapidly, partly because of the prestige brought to the order by **Bernard of Clairvaux** (1090–1153), whose writing, preaching, and fiery temperament made him the dominant religious figure in the twelfth century. Ironically, their success eventually led to some of the same temptations of wealth and comfort that had plagued the Benedictine communities from which the Cistercians had split.

The Mendicant Orders: Franciscans and Dominicans

The most innovative orders were those of the **mendicants** (from a Latin word for "begging") or **friars** (from Latin *frater*, "brother"). The mendicants grew out of a widespread popular religious movement called the *vita apostolica*, which sought to restore the "apostolic life" of Christ and his first followers, above all by imitating Christ's poverty. At first, the mendicants avoided priestly ordination. Their founders located their communities in towns and cities rather than in monastic isolation in the countryside. The cities were home both to the uprooted poor and the newly prosperous middle class. Bringing the ideals of Christ and his apostles home to these people meant leaving the monastic cloister for the city street. The two most important founders of mendicant orders in the High Middle Ages were St. Francis of Assisi and St. Dominic.

Francis of Assisi (*c.*1182–1226) was born into a merchant family in Assisi (central Italy). As a young man, he chose, rather like Antony of Egypt, to heed the gospel by abandoning his wealth and adopting a life of poverty. Unlike Antony, Francis gathered followers around him and commissioned them to preach the gospel and to witness to it in action. His new community became known as the Order of Friars Minor ("the lesser brothers") or **Franciscans**. Francis taught the renunciation of the goods of this world for the sake of the gospel, but also the affirmation of the world's goodness. He sang nature's praises in poetry and popularized the use of the Christmas crèche (the stable setting of Jesus' birth) to show how God humbled Himself for our sake by being born into the world. Francis sought to bring back to life the radicalism of Jesus' preaching in the Sermon on the Mount. For him, that meant avoiding anything resembling an institutionalized religious life (income, property, books, houses, etc.). At the same time, he required his movement to be totally loyal to the church's clerical leadership.

The Franciscan movement became enormously popular. However, its popularity proved the undoing of its founder's vision. The institutional church, hungry for dedicated preachers and confessors, and for talented teachers in the new universities, tried to shape the order along more conventional lines. Eventually, a conflict broke out between a radical minority party called the Spirituals, who were fanatically faithful to Francis' ideal of absolute poverty, and a majority party called the Conventuals, who were willing to make compromises for the sake of a broader mission. The Spirituals wanted to withdraw for the sake of preserving Francis' vision in all its purity. However, Francis' vision had also included the obligation to obey the church. When the church took the Conventuals' side by endorsing compromises in the observance of poverty, the Spirituals were forced to choose. At the Council of Vienne (1311–1312), Pope Clement V rejected both the Spirituals' insistence on real, practical poverty and their petition to secede from the order. Many of the Spirituals chose to reject the pope and the council, and thus became heretics in the eyes of the church.

Dominic Guzman (d. 1221) was a Spanish contemporary of Francis' who founded an order of a similar character, marked by a commitment to a life of communal poverty and public preaching. The mendicant orientation may have come from contact with Francis' movement. Unlike the Franciscans, the **Dominicans** at least allowed the acceptance of money. They also developed a strong organizational structure (again quite unlike the Franciscans) based on the principle of representative government. The Dominicans were further distinguished by the emphasis on preaching against heresy, which led them more quickly to the new universities and to a mission more directly identified with study. For this reason, they are called the Order of Preachers. St. Thomas Aquinas (1225–74), who is featured in Chapter 15, belonged to the Dominicans and became their most accomplished theologian.

The Beguines: Independent Lay Communities for Women

This period saw a rise in communities of sisters or nuns who were sponsored by orders of friars and monks and who adopted their rules. For example, the Franciscans sponsored the Poor Clares, who lived by a rule that Francis had given to Clare of Assisi. The enthusiasm for preaching and living the apostolic life (imitating the life of the early church communities) also led to the formation of independent communities of laywomen known as **Beguines**. These groups had no rule or permanent religious vows but shared some form of common life and were either engaged in contemplative prayer or in ministries of caring for the sick and the poor. They were not obliged to renounce property, though many did, nor were they bound to a lifetime commitment to the community. There was no centralized structure beyond the local community. Because of the flexibility and openness of these new religious movements, whether they were communities of men or women, they became vital sources of renewal and devotion, but also of dissent and heresy.

DISSENT AND HERESY

With rare exceptions, medieval heresy did not involve questions about beliefs and doctrines as much as debate over practical issues of worship, discipleship, and ministry. Lay reform movements that failed to gain acceptance by the institutional church often became intensely "anticlerical" (critical of the church's clergy). The clergy left themselves open to criticism when they failed to live up to the high standards and expectations set for them by the Gregorian Reform of the eleventh century (see Chapter 13). Anticlericalism also led to criticism of the sacraments of the church because it was the clergy's duty to administer the sacramental system. People who held anti-sacramental views rejected the church's control of the forgiveness of sin, the doctrine of the real presence of Christ in the Eucharist, and the practice of praying for the dead (praying for the dead was opposed because private masses for the dead were an important source of clerical income).

The Poor Men of Lyons or **Waldensians**, named for their founder Valdes, are the best example of an apostolic movement that was forced into dissent and subsequently took up anticlerical and anti-sacramental heresy. Valdes studied the Bible and preached and practiced voluntary poverty, but he and his movement were denied official permission to preach, principally because they were using unapproved translations of the Bible. When they persisted, they were condemned at the Council of Verona in 1184. The condemnation hardened his group's resistance and turned them into an underground alternative church.

The **Cathars** (from the Greek word for "the pure ones"), who appeared in the mid-twelfth century, were rooted in the same soil of popular disenchantment with the clergy and the sacramental system. However, their critique was far more radical, for the Cathars taught a thoroughgoing dualism between a good god and an evil god (note the similarities to the Manichean dualism that originally attracted Augustine). The world and the flesh were the work of the evil god. Marriage and reproduction were therefore rejected, as was eating any food that originated in animal intercourse, such as meat and dairy products. All forms of killing and violence were also rejected. Catharism's organization mimicked that of Catholicism, with an ordained male clergy of bishops and deacons; a spiritual elite called the "perfect," who blended priestly and ascetical functions and could be male or female; and a rank and file of laity, who were called "believers." Only the perfects were required to adopt the full ascetical discipline of the Cathars, and only they could administer the Cathar sacrament of the *consolamentum*, a "laying on of hands" that prepared the recipient on his deathbed for birth into eternal life. Catharism was appealing to lay Christians in part because of the spiritual superiority of the perfects as compared to many of the Catholic clergy. One reason the popes promoted the friars was to present a convincing Catholic alternative to the spirituality of the Cathars. Catharism was most widespread in southern France, where the town of Albi gave rise to the name by which they were also known, the **Albigensians**.

To deal with such heretical movements, the medieval church developed a two-pronged strategy: it promoted the good example and preaching of the mendicants; and it instituted the machinery of religious repression known as the **Inquisition**. In 1184, bishops were authorized to conduct investigations, or inquisitions, into accusations of heresy. At first, the accused had the traditional protections of Roman law, which required accusations to be made in the form of sworn testimony. The accused were examined and if found guilty given a chance to repent. The unrepentant were excommunicated and imprisoned by the secular authorities. After 1231, the papacy began to license teams of investigators who traveled around and collected testimony wherever they could find it. It became customary to rely on anonymous accusations and to deny the accused the right to call witnesses on their behalf. After 1252, torture was used to get confessions. In rare cases, unrepentant heretics were executed—one study of hundreds of penalties imposed in mid-thirteenth-century investigations of Catharism in southern France estimated death sentences at 1 percent and imprisonment at 10 to 11 percent, with the rest being given lesser penances such as the compulsory wearing of a cross (Tyerman 2006, 602). The worst abuses occurred in the fourteenth and fifteenth centuries, when secular governments used the inquisition as an instrument of political control.

MEDIEVAL RELIGIOUS LIFE: THE MEDIATION OF GRACE

Religious life in the High Middle Ages was characterized by increased attention to the sacraments, devotions to Mary and the saints, and a variety of religious practices that appealed to ordinary lay Christians whose experience of Christianity had become increasingly different from that of the clerics and nobility.

The Seven Sacraments

For much of its history up to this time, Christianity did not have a rigidly defined list of the rituals called **sacraments**. For example, the ritual for anointing a king at his coronation was often considered a sacrament. In the twelfth century, the number of the sacraments was fixed definitively at seven. Each sacrament had a symbolic ritual consisting of words and visible gestures or material substances (bread, wine, water, oil, etc.). When properly performed for a recipient who was open to its action, the sacrament became the visible means of transmitting the invisible reality called "grace," God's gift of his own presence. The sacrament caused God's grace in the soul *ex opere operato*, "by the very performance of the action," so that the effectiveness of the sacrament was not dependent on the worthiness of the one who administered it, a principle established long ago by Augustine in his controversy with the Donatists (see Chapter 10).

The seven sacraments embraced all the significant moments of a Christian's life from birth to death. *Baptism* brought the newborn Christian into the new life of grace. *Extreme Unction* (from the Latin words for "last anointing"), the sacrament today called the Anointing of the Sick, was given at life's end. *Confirmation*, the sealing in the Holy Spirit, was originally part of Baptism, as it still is in the Orthodox churches. But in the Latin West, Confirmation became a rite distinct from Baptism because it required the presence of a bishop, who would not have been available every time Baptisms were performed. *Matrimony* (Christian marriage) developed as a means of sanctifying the life of the laity. Its distinctive marks were its permanence and its foundation in the consent of the married couple. *Holy Orders*, the rite of priestly ordination, set a man apart from the laity and enrolled him in the international priestly class that governed the church. The Gregorian program of priestly celibacy was intended to detach the clergy from their local connections to family and property and to bind them to a higher calling as the ritually pure gatekeepers of the sacramental system.

The *Eucharist*—at which Christians ate bread and drank wine that had been transformed into the body and blood of Jesus—was the fundamental sacrament. The bread was eaten in the form of a white wafer called a *host*, made with unleavened bread in memory of Jesus' Last Supper—which the synoptic gospels describe as a Passover meal—when Jesus instituted the Eucharist. The reality of the presence of Christ's body and blood in the bread and wine was taken with the utmost seriousness, to the point that tales were told about hosts that bled or visions of the child Jesus in the hands of the priest. Mention has already been made of the formal definition of "transubstantiation" as the way in which the change in the bread and wine was to be understood. Respect for the Eucharist was so powerful that people frequently avoided receiving it, out of fear of receiving it unworthily. By this time, lay people were no longer allowed the Eucharistic wine at all, which was reserved to the clergy. Though the frequency of reception declined, devotion to the Eucharist actually intensified. At the consecration of the Mass, bells were rung as the host and cup were raised for viewing. During the ceremony known as "benediction" and in public processions, the host was shown for veneration in ornate display cases called "monstrances." In the churches, a lit candle signaled the presence of the host in the tabernacle, or storage chamber, on the altar, toward which respect was shown by "genuflection" (bending the knee, as would a vassal before his lord). The Eucharist even received its own day in the calendar, the feast of *Corpus Christi* ("Body of Christ"), established by the pope in 1264 in response to popular demand, especially from Beguine communities. Corpus Christi was observed at the end of May or in June and became a hugely popular feast day, marked by public processions, dramatic performances, and fairs.

The sacrament of *Penance* also held a predominant place in the life of the Christian. Its three elements were defined as sorrow for sin, confession, and penance. The term penance comes from Latin *poena*, "penalty" or "punishment," and reflects the practice of the early church, when sinners who had been expelled from the community for their sins had to perform penitential works of "satisfaction" before being readmitted. The period of penitential rehabilitation could last for years. In the Early Middle Ages, it became customary to accept substitutes, such as reciting prayers, giving alms, or going on pilgrimage in lieu of the long periods of penance. At the same time, it also became normal to grant absolution (forgiveness) for sin *before* the penance was completed. On special occasions, the church granted cancellations called **indulgences** for penance not yet performed. A *plenary* indulgence (a kind of "blanket pardon," where punishment for all of an individual's sins was canceled) was first granted by the pope to those who pledged to go on the First Crusade (1095).

Applying such cancellations to those who had already died represented a significant extension of indulgences. The extension was justified on the basis of the traditional practice of praying for the dead, and of the doctrines of vicarious satisfaction and of the communion of saints: just as Christians could pray to the saints for intercession, so could they perform works of satisfaction on behalf of all the faithful departed, not merely those recognized as saints. Integral to this change was the development of the doctrine of **purgatory**. Early Christianity had held various notions of a transitional state of the soul after the body's death, as the *Martyrdom of Perpetua* showed already at the beginning of the third century. In the medieval period, these notions crystallized around the doctrine of purgatory as a place or temporary state in which the soul was purified before its admission to heaven. This temporary stage of purification was only open to those who had not died in mortal sin. The feast of All Souls Day (November 2) was instituted in 998, specifically to pray for those who had died with unperformed penances. By the fourteenth century, the church took the further step of applying indulgences (as well as works of satisfaction like prayers and alms) to benefit the souls of the dead who might still be in purgatory. Eventually, the bishops and the papacy, pressed for revenue, began to license traveling preachers in effect to sell such indulgences. Although they were not supposed to claim that they could release the souls of the dead from purgatory, many did so anyway. That was the system in place in 1517, when it would arouse the ire of Martin Luther and lead ultimately to the Protestant Reformation (see Chapters 18 and 19).

Human Mediators: Christ, Mary, and the Saints

From the beginning, Christianity had seen Jesus Christ as "the judge of the living and the dead." In the book of Revelation, he is the King of Kings, who will sit on the throne of judgment at the end of the world. Christians of the Middle Ages were fascinated with this picture of Christ as king and judge. However, a powerful new devotion to Christ's suffering humanity also came into being during this period. Earlier representations of Christ on the cross showed him in a stiff, heroic, victorious pose. By the end of the medieval period, the crucified Christ was rendered so graphically as to border on the fantastic. Bernard of Clairvaux and other mystics fostered this devotion to Christ's human suffering. This shift in focus was due in part to medieval Christians' enthusiasm for the "apostolic life," based on a desire to imitate Jesus' earthly life as fully as possible. The Stations of the Cross (a 14-step pattern of prayer in remembrance of the events of Christ's passion and death) became a popular devotion, as did the veneration of the Five Wounds of Christ on the cross. No one preached and lived the imitation of Christ more convincingly than St. Francis. In an apparently miraculous occurrence, he became the first person to manifest the mystical phenomenon of the *stigmata*, bleeding wounds in hands, feet, and side.

Figure 14–3 Mary Seated with Child, tympanum of west right-hand door of Chartres Cathedral. This pose became known as the *Sedes Sapientiae*, "Seat of Wisdom," because the Divine Wisdom of the *Logos* became incarnate in Mary. To symbolize the medieval conviction that classical and Christian learning could be harmonized because they came from the same divine source, the seven liberal arts and seven Greek and Roman masters are sculpted in the archivolts (the semicircular archway). Chartres cathedral was built 1194–1250 and is a fine example of Gothic architecture. It was declared a UNESCO World Heritage Site in 1979.

Mary also received enormous devotion from medieval Christians. Her popularity as Mother of God and as the Blessed Virgin goes back to the early church, but the new attention to the humanity of Christ gave devotion to Mary a further boost. Traditionally, she had been represented as seated with the child in her lap. In the medieval period, these representations of mother and son evolved toward more realistic poses in the same way that images of the crucifixion changed. Eventually these led to a set of standard artistic representations of mother and son, such as the laughing child, the child playing with an apple or ball, the caressing child, and the nursing child. Pictures of Mary without the child also became popular, especially representations of her enthroned in heaven. Toward the end of the medieval period, she appears frequently as the *mater dolorosa* (the mother of sorrows), holding the body of Christ after it was taken down from the cross, and as mother of mercy and pity.

The Cistercians, the Franciscans, and the Beguines were especially devoted to Mary. All Cistercian monasteries were under her protection, and it was the Cistercians who popularized the use of the prayer called the "Hail Mary." The "rosary" (the recitation of 50 "Hail Marys" along with other prayers, usually using a set of beads to help count the prayers) also came into use at this time. A number of feasts that commemorated events in her life were added to the year's cycle of worship. From the twelfth century, literary collections with titles like *Miracles of the Virgin* were made that celebrated the favors she had granted to those who honored her. These stories typically show her as the dispenser of undeserved mercies that soften or even subvert the normal workings of justice.

A certain thief called Ebbo was devoted to the Virgin, and was in the habit of saluting her even on his marauding expeditions. He was caught and hanged, but the Virgin held him up for two days, and when his executioners tried to fix the rope more tightly, she put her hands on his throat and prevented them. Finally, he was released.

(Cited in Southern 1970, 247)

Medieval Christians greatly desired human mediators in their relationship with God, in part because they viewed God as utterly transcendent. As mother of Christ, Mary had access to God, but as a human mother, Christian believers could have access to Mary and thus have access to God.

Another expression of the medieval desire for human mediators with God was the veneration of saints, a practice still observed in Catholic and Orthodox churches. It originated in the early church's belief concerning the "communion of saints": the worship of the church on earth was a participation in the heavenly liturgy of the angels and the souls of the righteous. Since Christian martyrs were guaranteed a place in this company, it became customary to pray to them to intercede with God and to recommend them as role models for believers attempting to live the Christian life. These two functions of "intercession" and "imitation" became the foundation of the veneration of the saints. Neither intercession nor imitation were seen as a devaluing of Christ's status as mediator or as example. Rather, the saints were thought of as "grafted on" to Christ in a corporate identity in which all Christians were called to participate.

The medieval veneration of saints yielded a rich harvest of religious devotion, along with more than a little commercialism, legend, and sometimes outright fraud. Devotion to the saints ranged from the sublime case of St. Francis to the curious cult of St. Cunefort, venerated as a healer of children, who was originally a dog that died while rescuing a child (as the very name reveals: "brave dog"). In earlier centuries, the process of declaring someone a saint tended to focus on local church communities. By the twelfth century, when responsibility for approval of saints was placed in the hands of the papacy, **canonization** (the process of nomination and approval for sainthood) became more centralized and more bureaucratic. Though fewer saints were recognized officially, popular piety continued to nominate them at the local level.

The Religion of Lay People

The nobility practiced their religion with the help of priests who lived on their estates, or through monasteries that they founded and supported financially. Elaborately illustrated prayer books, called "books of hours" (so called because they adapted the monastic routine of daily prayer for lay use), helped their devotional life. By contrast, ordinary lay people depended on the parish system that had spread almost everywhere by now as a kind of "branch office" of the bishop's cathedral. Lay people could not understand the Latin Mass, but they heard the scriptures read in translation and were taught the commandments and basic prayers like the Our Father, the Creed, and the Hail Mary. Pictures, statues, and religious plays were also used for instruction. Preaching was more the work of the friars than of parish priests, who often lacked education and sometimes could not themselves understand Latin, since seminaries (special schools for the education of the clergy) were not established until the sixteenth century.

Germanic and Slavic paganism left its mark on the religious practice of lay people. Folkloric religion merged with Christianity so thoroughly that the two are sometimes hard to distinguish; take, for example, the rural belief in holy wells and woodlands and the widespread practice of blessing animals, crops, houses, or weapons. Blessed objects called "sacramentals" (a term coined by medieval theologians, who distinguished them from sacraments by saying that the former dealt with sanctifying *things* while the latter sanctified *people*) became and have remained popular features of Catholic life. Holy water is an excellent example. The blessed water used in Baptism was kept near the church door, and people dipped their fingers and made the sign of the cross over themselves when entering the church. They might also take some home to protect their houses and families.

Expressions of religious life among lay people could be found in a variety of places. Groups called *confraternities* or *guilds* offered lay people an opportunity for fellowship and support because they were based on common interests such as a profession or trade. A prime religious function of such groups was to pay for prayers and private masses for their deceased members. Pilgrimages to shrines near and far were another expression of lay piety. The most popular sites were Jerusalem and Rome, followed by Compostella in Spain, where St. James was believed to be buried. Compostella was so popular that medieval art always represents James in the travelling garb of a pilgrim. Other major destinations were the church of Mary Magdalene at Vézelay in France and the tomb of Thomas Becket in the Cathedral of Canterbury in England.

Christian shrines were another major attraction, principally because of their relics (physical remains, articles of clothing, or possessions thought to have come from Christ, Mary, or the saints). Relics were prized for protection and healing, but they were also a major source of revenue. Churches, towns, and monasteries sought them eagerly because of their spiritual power and because they attracted travelers and donations. Their profit potential was so ironclad that they were used as collateral in loans. Theft of relics was common and expeditions were even mounted to seize them by force. In 1087, seafaring residents of Bari in southern Italy stopped in Myra in Asia Minor and liberated the relics of a fourth-century bishop, St. Nicholas of Myra, thus inaugurating his long and gradual transformation into the secular cult of Santa Claus. However, the greatest seizure of relics came when the Fourth Crusade sacked Constantinople in 1204 and took home great quantities of Byzantine relics.

CHURCH ARCHITECTURE: THE GOTHIC STYLE

To a modern observer, the most dramatic testimony to the spirit of Christianity in the High Middle Ages is the Gothic cathedral, "the mind of the Middle Ages made visible," as a modern scholar has said of the cathedral of Chartres. From its homeland in central and northern France, Gothic architecture spread to neighboring countries and gradually displaced the previously dominant Romanesque style. The chief technical advance that led to the new style was the perfection of the groined or ribbed vault, in place of the older barrel or dome vaulting, and the replacement of the rounded arch by the pointed arch. These developments made it possible to raise the height of the building while reducing the amount of stone needed to bear the load. Buttresses were added outside the building to further distribute the weight. Walls became less massive and ponderous, allowing the extensive use of stained glass windows and greatly increasing the amount of light that shone into the nave of the church. As a result, the visual lines of a Gothic cathedral were strikingly vertical, the whole building seeming to soar and to direct the eye upward. The use of light and material decorations was meant to raise the minds of worshippers to the incorporeal light of God and to Christ, the true Light of the World. The careful geometrical calculations and balanced ratios that underlie Gothic architecture have led people to compare it with the grand design and careful structure of medieval theology.

Gothic cathedrals served many purposes besides spiritual inspiration and aesthetic beauty. With their stained-glass windows and abundant statuary—Chartres is said to contain as many as 6,000 painted or sculpted personages—they became instruments

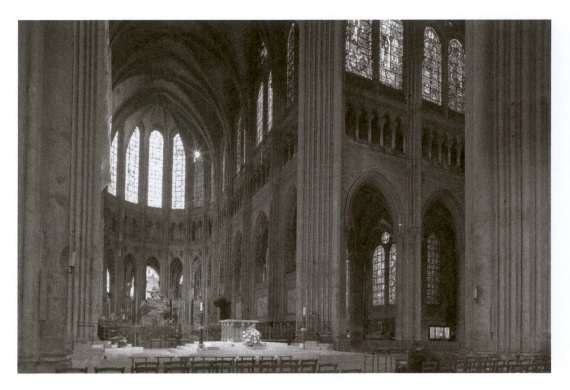

Figure 14–4 The interior of Chartres Cathedral, illustrating both the verticality of the design and the abundant light of the Gothic style of architecture.

of instruction for those who could not read. They were also powerful expressions of the social fabric of medieval Europe: contemporary sources tell of entire populations, from the nobility to the peasantry, working voluntarily to build them. Financing such massive projects came from voluntary donations, from conquest, and from the profits of saints' shrines in the church precincts. Adjacent to the great churches, a host of related businesses flourished.

Lived Religion: Liturgy in the High Middle Ages
Art in a Gothic Cathedral

Salisbury Cathedral in southwest England is a marvel in many ways. A Gothic structure, it was built in a remarkable 46 years, all in one architectural style, on a virgin site where nothing else had ever been constructed. It is also known for the beauty of its interior decoration, particularly the Old Testament prophets and the Labors of the Months in the space above the choir.

The design above the choir stalls, closest to the nave, depicts 24 prophets from the Old Testament. Each one is seated, bearing a scroll with a quotation predicting the coming of the Messiah. Just east of the prophets, above the high altar, is Christ seated in majesty. On one side the four Evangelists are at his feet, each holding his Gospel, with the Apostles arranged on the other three sides. These images are surrounded by angels, representing God's heavenly court. Farther east, inside the ambulatory or aisle around the choir, are the Labors of the Year, one for each month of the year.

The subjects of the paintings and their arrangement is deliberate. The canons were intended to meditate on the words of the prophets regarding the coming of Christ during their daily prayers; this represents anticipation in the Old Testament. Clergy were meant to contemplate the presence of Christ in the Gospel and the Eucharist as they said Mass beneath the images of Christ and the Evangelists; the future fulfillment of the promise found in the New Testament. The common folk who worshipped in the cathedral were meant to be inspired to honest work and Christian living by pondering the labors intended for each month of the year, representing the present. The decorative scheme in the choir at Salisbury demonstrates the purpose of medieval Christian art: to be educational and inspiring as well as beautiful.

The massive size of the great cathedrals was not meant so much to accommodate large congregations at Mass, but to allow space for public processions and crowds of pilgrims coming to see the collections of relics and to pray at shrines. The liturgical de-emphasis is reflected in the displacement of the bishop's seat from its old central position in the apse, looking out to the congregation, to a side wing in the crossing, in order to make room for shrines containing relics. Walkways called *ambulatories* were added behind the apse to ease the traffic flow. Side altars were built along the ambulatories for the saying of private Masses. Thus, the building was actually more of a cluster of buildings, segmented for several distinct functions. The separation between clergy and laity, which became more pronounced at this time, was symbolically represented by the wall or screen, called a *rood screen* (from a Saxon word for "cross," since an image of the crucified Christ was always placed at the top of the screen), which separated the congregation of lay people in the nave from the clergy, who celebrated Mass in the sanctuary.

Figure 14–5 The interior of Salisbury Cathedral, England.

Key Terms

Albigensians	curia	Inquisition
Beguines	Dominic Guzman	interdict
Bernard of Clairvaux	Dominicans	mendicants
Boniface VIII	Fourth Lateran Council	purgatory
canonization	Francis of Assisi	sacramental
Cathars	Franciscans	sacraments
Christendom	Friars	transubstantiation
Cistercians	indulgences	Waldensians
Crusades	Innocent III	

Questions for Reading

1. Describe the relationship between Christians and Jews during the High Middle Ages. What were the conditions that brought about discrimination against the Jews and occasional persecution in this period?

2. What various motives inspired the military campaigns called the Crusades? Who started the movement? Against whom were they directed?

3. On what basis did medieval popes like Innocent III claim to intervene in secular affairs? Why was Pope Boniface VIII less successful than Innocent III had been in his efforts to deal with Christian rulers?

4. How did the new mendicant religious orders of the High Middle Ages differ from the already established monastic orders? Explain the main issue in the struggle that broke out within the Franciscan order over the meaning of Francis' vision. Which party eventually triumphed, and why?

5. What was *anticlericalism*, and why was it often a factor in medieval heresy?

6. How did the medieval church officially define the Real Presence of Christ in the Eucharist? Describe some of the beliefs and practices that illustrate the centrality of the Eucharist in medieval Christian life.

7. What is the relationship between the medieval form of the sacrament of Penance and the developing doctrine of purgatory? (Include an account of indulgences in your answer.)

8. What basic shifts occur in artistic representations of both Jesus and Mary during the High Middle Ages?

9. Describe how the Gothic style of church architecture differed from the previously dominant Romanesque style. How does this shift relate to Christians' understanding of God and God's relationship to humanity?

Works Consulted/Recommended Reading

Bredero, Adrian H. 1994. *Christendom and Christianity in the Middle Ages.* Translated by Reinder Bruynsma. Grand Rapids, MI: Eerdmans.

Brooke, Christopher N.L. 1989. *The Medieval Idea of Marriage.* Oxford: Oxford University Press.

Chazan, Robert. 2006. *The Jews of Medieval Western Christendom 1000–1500.* Cambridge: Cambridge University Press.

Colish, Marcia L. 2014. *Faith, Fiction, and Force: Medieval Debates on Baptism.* Washington, DC: Catholic University of America.

Duffy, Eamon. 1992. *The Stripping of the Altars.* New Haven, CT: Yale University Press.

France, John. 2005. *The Crusades and the Expansion of Catholic Christendom 1000–1714.* London: Routledge.

Jacobus de Voragine. 1993. *The Golden Legend: Readings on the Saints.* 2 vols. Translated by William Granger Ryan. Princeton, NJ: Princeton University Press.

Jones, Charles W. 1979. *St. Nicholas of Myra, Bari, and Manhattan: Biography of a Legend.* Chicago, IL: University of Chicago Press.

Katzenellenbogen, Adolf. 1959. *The Sculptural Programs of Chartres Cathedral.* Baltimore, MD: Johns Hopkins Press.

Lambert, Malcolm. 2002. *Medieval Heresy: Popular Movements from Bogomil to Hus.* 3rd edn. New York: Blackwell Publishing.

Le Goff, Jacques. 1981. *The Birth of Purgatory.* Translated by Arthur Goldhammer. Chicago, IL: University of Chicago Press.

Le Goff, Jacques. 2014. *In Search of Sacred Time: Jacobus de Voragine and the* Golden Legend. Translated by Lydia G. Cochrane. Princeton, NJ: Princeton University Press.

McGinn, Bernard. 1979. *Visions of the End: Apocalyptic Traditions in the Middle Ages.* New York: Columbia University Press.

Morris, Colin. 1989. *The Papal Monarchy: The Western Church from 1050 to 1250.* Oxford: Clarendon Press.

Reeves, Marjorie. 1969. *The Influence of Prophecy in the Later Middle Ages: A Study in Joachimism.* Oxford: Oxford University Press.

Riley-Smith, Jonathan. 1987. *The Crusades: A Short History.* New Haven, CT: Yale University Press.

Rubin, Miri. 1991. *Corpus Christi: The Eucharist in Late Medieval Culture.* Cambridge: Cambridge University Press.

Schimmelpfennig, Bernhard. 1992. *The Papacy.* Translated by James Sievert. New York: Columbia University Press.

Simson, Otto von. 1962. *The Gothic Cathedral: Origins of Gothic Architecture and the Medieval Concept of Order.* 2nd edn. Bollingen Series, 48. Princeton, NJ: Princeton University Press.

Smalley, Beryl. 1964. *The Study of the Bible in the Middle Ages.* Notre Dame, IN: University of Notre Dame Press.

Southern, R.W. 1953. *The Making of the Middle Ages.* New Haven, CT: Yale University Press.

Southern, R.W. 1970. *Western Society and the Church in the Middle Ages.* Pelican History of the Church. Vol. 2. Baltimore, MD: Penguin Books.

Stow, Kenneth. 2007. "The Church and the Jews: St. Paul to Pius IX." In Kenneth Stow, *Popes, Church, and Jews in the Middle Ages: Confrontation and Response.* Variorum Collected Studies, 1–70. Burlington, VT: Ashgate.

Tierney, Brian, ed. 1964. *The Crisis of Church and State 1050–1300.* Upper Saddle River, NJ: Prentice Hall.

Tyerman, Christopher. 2006. *God's War: A New History of the Crusades.* Cambridge, MA: Harvard University Press.

Chapter

15

THOMAS AQUINAS

Figure 15–1 *Thomas Aquinas (c.1225–1274),* attributed to Sandro Botticelli (1444–1510).

St. Thomas Aquinas (*c.*1225–74) ranks among the intellectual giants in the history of Christian theology. In the West, apart from the biblical authors, his influence is perhaps second only to Augustine. His teachings, furthermore, are foundational to much of modern Catholic thought.

LIFE

Thomas was born to members of a noble family at their castle in Roccasecca in southern Italy, between Rome and Naples. From the beginning, his parents had plans for him to become a Benedictine monk and eventually take charge of a local monastery. Early in his schooling, however, he encountered friars from the newly established **Order of Preachers**, commonly called the **Dominicans**. Founded by St. Dominic (Domingo de Guzmán, 1170–1221), the Dominicans were mendicants or "beggars," embracing poverty and rejecting ownership of private property. In addition, they were deeply committed to study, instruction, and preaching. Drawn to these ideals, Thomas joined the order at about 18 years old. At first, his family disapproved strongly, even going so far as to capture him and keep him under house arrest for a year (and perhaps much longer) to force him to change his mind. Eventually, however, they relented and allowed Thomas to choose his own path.

After his basic education and then advanced training in scripture and theology, Thomas led a career dedicated to contemplation, writing, preaching, and teaching. He held positions in a number of cities in Western Europe, including Paris, Naples, and Rome.

In regard to his personality, Thomas was often very quiet and reserved. While he was a student, because he was also tall and bulky, his peers nicknamed him "the dumb ox." Despite his tendency toward silence, however, many of Thomas' contemporaries noticed his powerful intelligence and memory. According to one story, his most famous teacher, **Albert the Great** (*c.*1200–1280), after witnessing Thomas at work on a particularly thorny theological problem, declared, "We call this one the dumb ox, but one day he will give such a bellowing in teaching that it will sound throughout the whole world!"

Thomas also had the habit of becoming lost in thought. There is an anecdote about this happening to him while at a banquet hosted by King Louis IX of France. Emerging from his reflections, Thomas suddenly brought the festivities to a halt by pounding his fist on the table and shouting his victory over his religious opponents. He even called for his assistant, who was absent, to begin writing. Later, in explaining the disruption, Thomas confessed he had forgotten where he was, believing he was still in his study.

An especially well-known incident took place near the end of Thomas' life. While celebrating Mass, he had an experience that might be described as a religious or mystical vision, some sort of physical trauma (such as a stroke), or both. Whatever its cause, the event was for him profoundly spiritual and transformative. From that point forward, he refused to write ever again. When questioned why, he remarked that all he had previously authored now seemed to him as straw (*omnia quae scripsi videntur michi palee*).

After that episode, his health deteriorated. A few months later, while journeying to the Second Council of Lyons, he suffered an accident, striking his head on a tree branch. He was eventually taken to the nearby Cistercian monastery of Fossanova, where he died.

It was not long before reports surfaced of Thomas' holiness and even miraculous deeds and interactions. From a modern historical perspective, it is difficult to judge such accounts, yet it is indisputable that Thomas was an outstanding representative of the Christian life. He was canonized (named a saint) in 1323. In recognition of the profound impact of his teachings, Pope Pius V officially gave him the highly honorific title of "Doctor of the Church" in 1567.

SCHOLASTICISM

Thomas' thought cannot be adequately understood apart from the social and cultural movement in the Middle Ages known as **Scholasticism**. At its heart, Scholasticism is an approach to theology as an independent and comprehensive academic discipline. In this regard, theology is treated as on equal footing with philosophy, mathematics, or any other organized area of study, as opposed to being merely a spiritual exercise or personal expression of belief. In addition to detailed analysis and the rigorous use of logic, one of the fundamental goals of Scholastic thinkers was to reconcile apparently conflicting statements on the faith from scripture, the Church Fathers, councils, and other authorities.

A leading contributor to this medieval project was the archbishop **Anselm of Canterbury** (*c.*1033–1109), nicknamed the "Father of Scholasticism." His theological method is perhaps best summed up by his often-quoted phrase "faith seeking under-standing" (*fides quaerens intellectum*). For him, the job of theology is to take up Chris-tian doctrines and examine them rationally in order to show their depths and comprehensibility and to resolve any apparent contradictions. At moments, Anselm shows tremendous confidence in the capacity of the intellect to explore the divine mysteries and offer proofs that even nonbelievers would be compelled to accept. This sort of intimate interplay between faith and reason, cast in varying fashions, would become one of Scholasticism's hallmarks.

Another key figure in the development of Scholasticism was the theologian **Peter Abelard** (1079–1142). In his *Sic et Non* (*Yes and No*), he exposes seeming incon-sistencies among the teachings of the Church Fathers. In doing so, he urges a closer and more thoughtful engagement with the traditional sources of the Christian faith.

The growth of Scholasticism went hand in hand with the rise of universities in the thirteenth century. The very word "Scholasticism" derives from Greek and Latin roots that mean having to do with schooling. Before long, these academic institutions would become the main centers of theological activity in Western Europe. When Thomas began his education, formal instructional programs and defined curricula were already in place. A chief requirement for the highest degree in theology was the completion of a commentary on the *Four Books of Sentences* by **Peter Lombard** (*c.*1095–1160). Composed in the previous century and partly inspired by Abelard, the *Sentences* gathers together conflicting statements from scripture and the Church Fathers under various headings and seeks to harmonize them.

Thomas' own achievements within Scholasticism are numerous, but two deserve mention here. The first was the prominence he gave to the philosophy of **Aristotle** (384–322 B.C.E.). Certainly, before Thomas' day, Aristotle had been known in Western Europe. Attention, however, had been limited mostly to his treatment of logic. In fact, his other works were often regarded with suspicion in part because some of his conclusions were at odds with basic Christian doctrines. For instance, he held that the universe existed from eternity, in contrast to the Christian belief that God created it at a distinct moment in the past. By the middle of the thirteenth century, however, new translations of Aristotle's writings had brought greater familiarity with both the impressiveness of his philosophy and the recognition of its potential for Christian theology and culture. As a student under the guidance of Albert and others, Thomas was exposed to Aristotle's metaphysics, ethics, and other aspects of his thought. In his own work, Thomas made Aristotle central. The reasons for this decision are compli-cated, but in short Thomas found in this philosophy an effective vehicle for carrying forward his own theological endeavors. Like other Scholastic theologians, he often referred to Aristotle simply as "the Philosopher." Given both the novelty and reputa-tion of Aristotelianism in the West in Thomas' time, his preference for it was con-sidered both innovative and controversial. It would also prove profoundly influential to the later Scholastic thinkers who would follow Thomas' lead.

Thomas' second noteworthy accomplishment was his broad synthesis or bring-ing together of different sources. As has already been suggested, Thomas, like other Scholastic theologians, did not operate in a vacuum, but drew upon a variety of reli-gious and intellectual traditions with the aim of integrating them into a rational, coherent whole. For Christian teachings, Thomas relied heavily on his own Western heritage as represented by the Latin Church Fathers, especially Augustine. Yet he also appealed routinely to the Eastern or Greek Church Fathers, too, such as the widely influential Pseudo-Dionysius the Areopagite, a mystic who probably lived in Syria sometime in the late fifth or early sixth century. For philosophy, while Thomas' primary resource was Aristotle, he often turned to schools of thought deriving from Plato as well as other Greco-Roman philosophers. Finally, Thomas was informed by Jewish and Muslim thinkers, too. In describing the relationship between God and creation, for example, he borrows from the highly respected Jewish rabbi Moses Maimonides (1135–1204), and Thomas' reading of Aristotle was profoundly shaped by the commentaries of the Muslim scholars **Avicenna** (Ibn Sina, 980–1037) and **Averroes** (Ibn Rushd, 1126–1198). It seems fair to claim that, among the Scholastics, Thomas' ability to systemize was unsurpassed in its depth, range, and creativity.

WRITINGS

The collection of Thomas' writings is enormous. In addition to his commentary on Lombard's *Sentences*, his numerous compositions include commentaries on scripture and the works of Aristotle, philosophical and theological treatises, letters, sermons, and "Disputed Questions" (*Quaestiones Disputatae*). A standard genre of Scholasticism, a Disputed Question is a rigorous treatment of select topics stemming from classroom debates. One well-known example is Thomas' *Disputed Questions on Truth*, which discusses not only truth, but also knowledge, goodness, grace, and still other issues.

Summa Contra Gentiles

Among Thomas' works, two are typically highlighted. The first is his *Book on the Truth of the Catholic Faith against the Errors of Unbelievers*. More commonly, it is called the **Summa contra gentiles** or "Summary against the Gentiles." In the Middle Ages, a *Summa* was a genre employed by theology and other disciplines (such as philosophy, law, and medicine) to treat a topic in an especially thorough and systematic manner.

Intended most likely for missionaries preparing to engage Jews, Muslims, and other non-Christians, the *Summa contra gentiles* aims, as Thomas asserts, to demonstrate the truth of Catholic teachings and refute the errors opposing them. It is divided into four books. Books I through III (on God, creation, and divine governance of creation, respectively) cover doctrines that, according to Thomas, can be established by reason alone. Book IV, on the other hand, deals with the Trinity, the Incarnation, and other matters of faith beyond rational proof.

Summa Theologiae

Of all his works, Thomas' most renowned is his masterpiece, the **Summa theologiae** or "Summary of Theology." It is massive, although Thomas himself never finished it, having composed 512 Questions containing 2,668 Articles before he died. Its intended purpose was most probably for the training of young Dominicans to preach and hear confessions. In its opening, Thomas describes it as for "beginners."

In terms of organization, the *Summa theologiae* has three main divisions or parts. The First Part (*Prima Pars*) examines God and creation. The Second Part contains Thomas' moral theology. It is itself divided in two. The First Part of the Second Part (*Prima Secundae Partis*) discusses human actions in general, beginning with the goal of happiness and God as its fulfillment and then moving on to the forces that determine behavior (such as the will, emotions, sinfulness, and grace). The Second Part of the

Second Part (*Secunda Secundae Partis*), the longest of all four sections, explores particular human actions, mainly according to virtues and vices (that is, good and bad habits). Finally, the Third Part (*Tertia Pars*) addresses Christ and the sacraments. Thomas originally planned to include here also treatments of the Resurrection, Last Judgment, Heaven, and Hell.

Each of these parts has questions that investigate particular topics. For instance, in the First Part, Question 14 deals with God's knowledge. Under each question are articles on the related sub-topics. For Question 14, Article 9 inquires into whether or not God's knowledge extends even to non-existing things.

The standard layout of each article is as follows.

- At the start, the phrase "*it seems that*" (*videntur quod*) introduces the subject under discussion.
- The *objections* immediately come next, which are challenges to the opinion Thomas will defend. Objections and their corresponding replies (see below) reflect the back-and-forth reasoning that is the backbone of Scholastic methods and teaching practices.
- With the phrase, "*on the other hand*" (*sed contra*), the article turns. Against the objections, Thomas proposes his position, supporting it with an authoritative quotation, say, from scripture or one of the Church Fathers.
- In the *response* (*responsio*), Thomas presents his argument. This is the main portion or body of the article.
- Finally, the *replies to the objections* answer one by one the initial opposing claims.

As a rule, citations of the *Summa theologiae* begin with *ST* and then identify the part, question, and article. For the article on God's knowledge of non-existing things, the reference would appear as *ST* I q. 14. a. 9 (or a similar variant). Each of the sections within the article can also be specified. Thus, to cite in this same article the reply to the second objection, one could note it as *ST* I q. 14 a. 9 ad 2.

TEACHINGS

The scope of Thomas' theology is far too expansive even to summarize here. What follows, then, are merely selections from his most familiar and distinctive teachings.

Theology

Perhaps the best place to begin is with Thomas' notion of theology itself, which he spells out with care in Question 1 of the First Part of the *Summa theologiae*. When discussing theology, Thomas prefers the terminology of "sacred doctrine" or "holy teaching" (**sacra doctrina**). The meaning of this phrase, however, extends well beyond that of the English word "theology" to include not only rational reflection on the faith, but also all the ways in which God's truth is conveyed to believers. It signifies first and foremost—and indeed is sometimes synonymous with—what God reveals in scripture. Yet it can also refer to the writings of the Church Fathers, the pronouncements of Church councils, and the claims of other Christian authorities. Furthermore, in addition to its sources, sacred doctrine also indicates the manner in which the faith is passed on to others through informed examination and teaching.

Thomas calls sacred doctrine a science (*scientia*). He does not use the term "science" in the modern sense, but rather one deriving from Aristotle's definition. For Thomas, what makes theological reasoning "scientific" is, first, that it starts with sure and reliable principles: what Christians believe, the articles of faith given by God and found in scripture, such as those of the Trinity and the Incarnation. Second, from these principles, reason then goes on to demonstrate other truths. For instance, from God's creation of the universe out of nothing, which is a matter of faith, one could argue the further point that God has total power over the universe. Thomas himself often favors the example of how the Apostle Paul shows from the fact of Christ's Resurrection that all the children of God will one day be raised from the dead (see 1 Corinthians 15). In such theological argumentation, sometimes the conclusion follows from the premise necessarily; at others, only with a degree of probability.

One reason Thomas classifies sacred doctrine as a science is to give it legitimacy as a field of study and thereby justify its place in the university. Nevertheless, he acknowledges that as a science it has a somewhat unusual character. Part of what distinguishes sacred doctrine is that its fundamental principles, the articles of faith, are beyond human knowledge. One may reflect upon the mystery of the Trinity, but in the end it can only be believed, not understood. Such is not the case, say, for mathematics. It is perfectly possible for an intelligent person to comprehend the rules of addition, subtraction, multiplication, and division. Thomas stresses that while the articles of faith do indeed escape the grasp of reason, this in no way compromises their trustworthiness. On the contrary, because these truths come directly from God, they are more certain than truths discovered by human reason on its own.

All that said, as much as Thomas defends its status as a science, he does not view sacred doctrine as a science merely, but also as wisdom (*sapientia*), for it is the wise person who "orders and judges" everything according to God.

The Five Ways

Among Thomas' teachings, probably the most famous is his set of proofs for the existence of God known as **the Five Ways** (*Quinque Viae*), which appears in Question 2, Article 3 of the First Part of the *Summa theologiae*.

For many of us today, any attempt to prove God's existence can seem strange and even foolish. Our secular culture tends to be mistrustful of philosophy or religion to give us hard facts or objective truths, at least not without the support of chemistry, astronomy, biology, or the other experimental sciences. Whether or not God is real is often taken to be a question of faith or even personal preference—an "opinion," as is sometimes (imprecisely) said—not an issue that can be decided with evidence or argument.

Thomas, however, shaped by his medieval world-view as well as the Scholasticism of his era, does not share these same modern assumptions. He recognizes, of course, that there are many truths about God that cannot be proven. As discussed above, the articles of faith (Trinity, Incarnation, Resurrection, etc.) are beyond comprehension, which also means they cannot be proved, only believed. Thomas does not count the existence of God, however, as one of the articles of faith. Rather, he considers it to be a "preamble" (*praeambulum*) to the faith. That is, it is a truth presumed or presupposed by the faith, but it is itself open to human discovery. On Thomas' view, then, God's existence can indeed be proven as an objective fact, specifically through philosophical reasoning, and he staunchly disagrees with those who assert otherwise. He concedes, however, that most people are not actually in a position to understand abstract rational demonstrations, whether through lack of education, intelligence, or opportunity for reflection. Therefore, as a practical issue, it is permissible to accept God's existence on faith alone, even though this truth is in principle within reason's reach (see *ST* I q.2. a.2 ad 1).

As distinctive as each of the Five Ways is, what all these proofs have in common is the same general method adopted from Aristotle. They take as their starting point the kind of phenomena we encounter in the world every day: growth and transformation, birth and death, generation and destruction, and things, in all their enormous variety, moving, developing, and interacting with each other in recurring and consistent fashions. From these observable effects, Thomas tries to show that the only explanation for them is an Ultimate Cause that he identifies as God.

The arguments of the Five Ways are extraordinarily sophisticated. To explain them fully, each one would require an entire chapter of its own. Their basic strategies, however, can be briefly summarized as follows.

- The First Way begins from change or what Thomas calls motion (*motus*). An example he gives is wood being heated (i.e., changing from cold to hot). Thomas traces the cause of this type of movement back to an unchanging agent or Unmoved Mover (God). To express the logic here in another fashion, this Unmoved Mover, which itself does not change, must be the primary source of all the changes we witness taking place in the universe.
- The Second Way is based on "efficient causality." This is a notion of causality resembling that of modern science, which occurs when one thing brings another thing into existence or produces some transformation—a rock shattering a window or green leaves turning sunlight into energy. From these causal interactions, Thomas argues to a First Efficient Cause (God). Similar to the Unmoved Mover, this First Efficient Cause is not itself caused—it does not "come from" anything else—but is the origin of all other efficient causes.
- The Third Way focuses on the fact that things come in and out of existence. We observe this happening for both living creatures and inanimate objects. For such things to exist at all, Thomas reasons, they must have as their cause a Being whose existence is absolutely necessary, that is, a Being that could not *not* exist (God). In other words, on Thomas' reckoning, a Necessary Being is in the long run the only way to account for the existence of unnecessary beings.
- The Fourth Way calls attention to the varying degrees of being in the universe, such as lesser or greater amounts of goodness, truth, beauty, or related qualities. Today, when we describe something as, say, "more beautiful" or "less beautiful," we assume this judgment to be a matter of opinion or perspective. Thomas, however, following a philosophical heritage stretching back to Plato, regards such differences as objective realities. From these sorts of gradations of being or perfection among things, Thomas deduces a Perfect Being (God) as their source. Just as fire causes differing levels of heat, he holds, so does the Perfect Being cause differing levels of perfection.
- The Fifth Way concerns the regular, repeated movements of things. Although there are some crucial differences, Thomas' assumptions here are somewhat akin to those of modern science, which takes for granted that things in nature move according to fixed rules or "laws." From these patterns, Thomas concludes

there must be a Supreme Intelligence (God) that directs them, keeping the universe running in its orderly and predictable manner.

The Five Ways have long been a matter of debate, and philosophers and theologians remain today divided on how to interpret and evaluate them. Two common points of confusion, however, are worth clearing up here. The first is the alleged incompleteness of the proofs. Critics sometimes claim that when Thomas at the end of the First Way concludes there must be an Unmoved Mover, he makes a mistake in calling it "God." Thomas never demonstrates, so this accusation goes, that this Unmoved Mover has any of the other characteristics Christianity typically ascribes to God, such as omnipotence (being all-powerful), omniscience (being all-knowing), and omnibenevolence (being all-good). Thomas is said to be too hasty, then, in claiming he proves the existence of God (even if he manages successfully to prove an Unmoved Mover—the two are not necessarily the same). These critics further contend that Thomas commits parallel errors in the other Ways, too.

This objection, however, fails to consider Thomas' proofs in their full context in the *Summa theologiae*. After the Five Ways in Question 2 demonstrate in their varying fashions an Ultimate Cause (Unmoved Mover, First Efficient Cause, etc.), Questions 3 to 11 go on to prove, step by step, a number of divine characteristics that necessarily belong to this Cause, such as goodness, infinity, and eternity, among others. When all these characteristics are taken together, they do indeed describe the Christian God. Therefore, by the finish of Question 11, it becomes clear that the name "God" in each of the Five Ways is perfectly appropriate as long as it is used with an eye to the later part of the discussion. This is, in fact, how Thomas uses it. In short, the proofs for God's existence should not be read in isolation from the larger argument. When Thomas says "God," he is merely anticipating the rest of what he means to show.

The second common misunderstanding of the Five Ways concerns the so-called problem of infinite regress. Let us go back to the First Way. In it, Thomas asserts that change cannot depend on a string of causes that stretches on endlessly. As he states,

> Everything that is moved must be moved by another. If that by which something is moved is itself moved, then this, too, must be moved by another. If that other is also moved, it must be moved by still another. This, however, cannot continue infinitely…

According to Thomas, instead of causes going on forever in this manner, there must eventually be a starting point that is itself not caused by something else. He makes essentially the same claim regarding efficient causality in the Second and Third Ways, too. Here, Thomas is sometimes charged with making an error in logic. Why cannot a series of causes "keep going back" without ever stopping? Whenever we identify some cause, can we not always ask what came before *that*? Why must a series of causes have a beginning at all?

The issues raised here are fair. One significant problem, however, is that such criticisms usually come with false assumptions about the kind of causality Thomas actually has in mind, at least according to most scholars today. When reading the Five Ways, it is easy to make the mistake of imagining that Thomas is referring to what are called temporal or "horizontal" causal chains, which are ones whose cause and effects are separated by time. Think, for example, of a row of dominoes falling one after the other or several generations of fathers and sons (a man is "caused" by his father, who was caused by his father, who was caused by his father, and so on). In a temporal causal series, for any effect, the causation runs backward into the past. This is not the category of causality, however, that Thomas addresses. Rather, what he deals with are simultaneous or "vertical" causal chains in which causes and effects occur in the same instant. In the First Way, Thomas gives the example of a staff being moved by a hand, but this could also be illustrated by a tower of interconnected gears: when the top gear turns, all the rest turn with it. Thomas' larger point in the Five Ways is that there are some lines of causality that happen *all at once*, and that these cannot stretch out infinitely, or else they would not exist at all (see also *ST* I q. 46 a. 2). For this reason, he deduces that there must exist an original, starting Cause that is not itself caused. Now whether this conclusion is demanded by logic (or modern physics) is a complex matter that remains open to dispute.

Analogy

Another of Thomas' most influential teachings is that of **analogy**, which is part of his theory of theological language (how language applies to God). He explains this doctrine and some of its underlying principles in Questions 12 and 13 of the First Part of the *Summa theologiae*.

According to Thomas, there is a fundamental incongruity or gap between human ideas or concepts, on the one hand, and God, on the other. In forming concepts, our minds depend on information perceived through the senses. We can only properly understand things that we can see, hear, taste, smell, and touch. God, however, does not have a physical body; there is nothing about God that our senses can detect. Therefore, it follows that we are unable to form any genuine concept or have any adequate comprehension of God. If we cannot sensibly perceive God, then we cannot know God (at least, not in any natural mode of knowing). Furthermore, if language is an expression of our concepts, which Thomas thinks is the case, then we should also expect that it, too, will always fall short of God. In other words, because God is beyond our knowledge, then it seems that God is entirely beyond our language as well.

Yet Christians do talk about God. At times, they avoid the limitations of our concepts by simply using **negative theological language**. That is, they do not say what God is, but rather deny something of God or say what God is not. For instance, God is described as "unchanging" (*not* changing) or as "immortal" (*not* mortal, *not* subject to death). At other times, however, believers move beyond mere negation and employ **positive** (or affirmative) **theological language**. They mean to say something true and definitive about God, as when they call God "wise." Yet, if the term "wise" reflects our merely human concept of wisdom, formed from what we perceive in the world (perhaps the wise people we encounter in our lives), can it really be rightly applied to God? Would it not be better to acknowledge the shortcomings of our conceptual knowledge and say nothing affirmative about God at all?

Despite this difficulty, Thomas holds that it is indeed appropriate to use positive theological language of God. His doctrine of analogy is intended to explain why this is so. In order to appreciate his viewpoint here, let us take as an example another affirmative term: "good." As Thomas recognizes, Christians apply this adjective to God as well as, say, sunshine. For him, it is a perfectly acceptable use of the word in both instances. Furthermore, the phrases *God is good* and *sunshine is good* are quite true in the literal (and not some metaphorical) meaning.

Yet, in each case, language functions differently. When it comes to sunshine, "good" expresses a quality we sense and grasp from experience. We feel its warmth on our faces, blink our eyes in its brightness, understand that it makes plants and trees grow. With God, however, the quality that "good" signifies, the divine goodness, entirely surpasses in excellence the goodness of sunshine or any other perceptible thing. According to Thomas, God, as Creator, is the cause of all goodness in creation. More than that, God *is* goodness, Goodness itself (we will return to this point in the next section). In this regard, "good" actually applies *better* to God than to any created thing. At the same time, however, as real as it is, we have no proper comprehension of such supreme goodness. It is outside the perception of our senses. Thus, in calling God good, language and concepts separate, leaving us with only the barest hint of what we mean. Of course, in speaking about divine goodness, we cannot help but use "good" in the same manner we would of the good things that we are familiar with (in keeping with the rules of grammar, for example), but this is no indication that we can adequately conceive what such extreme goodness is.

Thomas' notion of analogy includes all the above relations. In defining analogical language, he locates it between **univocity** and **equivocity**. To speak univocally is to give language consistent meaning, as in using the word "hot" to describe both water just poured from the kettle for tea and fresh embers from a campfire. To speak equivocally, on the other hand, is for the same language to have different meanings, as the word "off" in the sentence, *This morning, right after the alarm clock went off, she turned it off* (in this case, the meanings of "off" do not merely differ, but are the exact opposite). Analogy, then, refers to language with meanings that are neither entirely the same nor entirely distinct. In calling God and sunshine good, "good" is analogical insofar as what it signifies in the two cases are not equivalent (God's goodness far excels in proportion the sunshine's goodness, to the point of incomprehensibility), but neither are they entirely different (both God and sunshine are genuinely good).

God and Creation

Thomas' teaching on analogy ultimately depends on his broader views of reality. Throughout his writings, he offers a sweeping vision of the cosmos, one which includes God, angels, demons, human beings, and purely physical or material things. It would be impossible in this short chapter to cover all of Thomas' metaphysics (philosophy of existence and existing things). Some of its major themes, however, are represented in how he construes the basic relationship between God and creation.

As mentioned earlier, echoing the Christian tradition before him, Thomas holds that God created the universe out of nothing. Contrary to Aristotle, then, the universe did not exist from all eternity, but had a beginning in time. This does not mean, however, that God's creative activity is confined to a single moment in the past. Rather, according to Thomas, in addition to fashioning creation in the first place, God also upholds or sustains it, constantly preserving it in existence. If God were ever to withdraw, then the universe would immediately return to the nothingness from which it came.

We come, then, to one of the primary differences between God and creation: whereas the Being of God is absolutely necessary—recall the Third Way—the being of created things depends utterly on God's loving will and power.

To specify further this distinction between God and created things, Thomas turns to the categories of *essence* (*essentia*) and *existence* (*esse*). For any given thing, we can distinguish *what* a thing is from *the fact that* it is. To see this difference, imagine a unicorn. It is perfectly possible to describe this or any other unicorn in vivid detail, even to come up with a precise definition for unicorns, without ever addressing whether or not unicorns actually exist. *What* a unicorn is differs from *whether or not* a unicorn is. The same distinction applies to every other thing we can conceive. Thomas calls the what-ness of a thing its essence, and the actuality (or that-ness) of a thing its existence.

Yet while the distinction between essence and existence holds true for all created things, this is not so for God. Rather, God's essence is identical to God's existence. In other words, it is of God's very essence to be; as stated earlier, God cannot *not* be. For this reason, Thomas identifies God as Subsistent Being Itself (*Ipsum Esse Subsistens*).

This brings us to the notion of **God's simplicity** (**divine simplicity**). We should not misunderstand this doctrine as a claim that God is somehow easy to understand. On the contrary, as discussed previously, Thomas considers God to be beyond human concepts and knowledge. Thomas maintains that while reason can prove *that* God exists, it cannot comprehend *what* God is—the divine essence entirely escapes it.

Rather than God being understandable, when Thomas speaks of divine simplicity, he means to deny within God any metaphysical composition or "parts." One example, as we have just seen, is the lack of distinction between essence and existence. No other such distinctions belong to the divine essence either. In God, everything is one: essence, existence, goodness, wisdom, understanding, and all other attributes and powers. To express this in another way: God *is* Existence, *is* Goodness, *is* Wisdom, etc., with no differences among these characteristics. By comparison, human beings can have the qualities of, say, goodness and wisdom, but they can never be *identical* to goodness and wisdom. Such a state of existence, in fact, is not even comprehensible. The radical simplicity of the divine essence marks yet another fundamental distinction between God and created things.

Yet as much as Thomas insists on their differences, he nevertheless points out similarities or likenesses between God and creation, too. Among them is the mere fact of existence. Simply by virtue of bringing things into reality, God imparts to them a share in existence, which makes them like God, who is Existence itself. Another similarity is in the diversity of created things. According to Thomas, the enormous variety of created things that make up the universe, when taken all together, mirror in some small degree the divine goodness. Finally, Thomas mentions that humans are specially made in the image and likeness of God (see Genesis 1:26–27). Still, despite these and other similarities, Thomas insists that it is not proper to say that God is like created things, but rather that created things are like God, just as a statue can be said to be like a man, but not a man like a statue. For every similarity between God and creation, the difference is all the greater.

Nature and Grace

In addressing God and creation, Thomas not only compares their respective manners of existence. He also distinguishes two general arrangements of relations between them, what can be called more precisely dispensations or orders. The first is the **order of nature** (or the **natural order**). To understand what this is, we must first appreciate that for Thomas the qualities and capacities of any given thing are determined by the specific kind of thing that it is—by its essence or what is also called its "nature." Take, for example, human beings. Part of what it means to be human (at least, as a rule) is to be able to laugh. We can say, therefore, that *it belongs to human nature* to laugh or that humans laugh *by nature*. There are, of course, many other activities and characteristics that fall within the range of human nature, too. Some of them are exclusive to humans, such as the power to reason or to make art. Others are shared with animals (eating, reproduction), and still others with inanimate physical objects (occupying space, having shape and size). Now just as the human being is defined and determined by its own proper nature, so is every other variety of being in creation—asteroids, tree sap, dust, anything one can name—as well as creation as a whole. All the principles and properties that belong to created things according to their natures constitute the natural order.

It is important to emphasize here the relationship of the natural order to God. Thomas holds that while God generates and sustains their existence, created things nevertheless are given a relative independence and integrity. Each thing has its own being and nature, as opposed to, say, constituting some aspect of God's Being. This insistence on the limited autonomy of creation allows Thomas to use to the extent he does the philosophy of Aristotle, which takes for granted the independent being of things.

The second arrangement of relations between God and creation is the **order of grace** or the supernatural ("above the natural") order. This refers to the various ways God elevates things beyond the capacities of their natures to become more God-like or closely united to God. If we limit ourselves to humans only, the order of grace includes all of God's interventions in history, in the church, and in the lives of individuals that make possible the forgiveness of sin, holiness, and eternal salvation. At the center of the supernatural order are the life, death, and Resurrection of Christ.

The distinction between the order of nature and the order of grace touches almost every aspect of Thomas' thought. The reasons for it are complex, but in short, it allows him to maintain the Christian doctrine, shaped largely by Augustine, that forgiveness and salvation are not owed to or earned by humans in any fashion, but are rather free gifts from God. Yet while Thomas regards these two orders as each operating according to its own distinctive logic, he does not characterize them as in conflict or opposition. On the contrary, for him grace presupposes and perfects nature.

We see something of this delicate relationship of the two orders in Thomas' approach to how humans know God. According to Thomas, there are certain divine truths that humans must accept in order to attain salvation. Some can be reached by the natural power of reason alone—reason operating with its innate capacities given to it according to the order of nature. One such truth, as we have seen previously, is God's existence. Other divine truths, however, surpass natural reason. These are the articles of faith, such as the mystery of the Trinity or the Incarnation. Belonging to the order of grace, these truths can only be discovered through God's revelation. Both categories of truths, however, are contained in scripture so that all believers, whether educated enough or not to understand advanced philosophical proofs, can come to eternal life.

We see a similar interplay of natural and supernatural orders in Thomas' moral theology. In his view, there are some virtuous behaviors that humans can acquire and develop by nature that lead to a certain natural goodness of character (despite the corruptive influence of sin). Chief examples of such virtues are prudence, justice, temperance, and fortitude. Yet these same virtues become elevated and perfected when infused into the person by God through grace along with the "theological" virtues of faith, hope, and charity, which are the habits that define a holy life.

The above distinction in morality corresponds with different kinds of happiness, the goal of the moral life. Thomas ties natural virtues to a kind of natural happiness, although it is necessarily incomplete and not entirely satisfying to human beings even at its most ideal. Supernatural virtues, however, lead to the perfect happiness that can only be found in the eternal vision of God.

As critical as the division between natural and supernatural orders is for Thomas, it can be difficult to determine where one ends and the other begins, or even if there is always a firm line between them at all. Consider the Five Ways. On the surface, they seem to be strictly rational exercises, using reason's natural abilities to demonstrate God's existence. It seems, then, that reason limits itself here to its own natural sphere. Some contemporary scholars, however, have challenged this view. They argue that in this and related sections of the *Summa theologiae,* reason does not actually operate in a space free of Christian assumptions, but rather relies at key points on revelation to prove God's existence. They add that Thomas seems to imply that there is something deficient in the knowledge of God that comes by reason alone and not through faith (*ST* II-II q. 2 a. 2 ad 3). Thus, so this line of argument goes, the Five Ways are not in fact an exercise of the natural capacities of reason only, but rather are situated in the context of faith and grace.

What is said about the Five Ways can also be said about the human being in general. At times, Thomas seems to be willing to describe human beings hypothetically in terms of their nature alone, completely apart from any considerations of sin, grace, salvation, and the desire for the heavenly vision of God—what can be called "pure nature." At other times, however, Thomas seems to deny that human beings can be properly defined without considering their deepest inner orientation to God, which implies a certain expectation of grace. In such instances, Thomas seems to align himself with Augustine, who sees human beings as made precisely for union with God. If so, then for Thomas humanity itself must be regarded as a mystery, both natural and supernatural at once. On this view, no strictly rational investigation could ever yield a complete picture of what it means to be human, even on the level of nature.

Whatever the proper way to read Thomas here, it is beyond question that his treatment of human beings, and indeed all of creation, is in service to his foundational conviction that God calls humanity to salvation and eternal life with God.

Issues in Moral Theology: Thomas Aquinas

Few figures in the Christian theological tradition have been as influential as Thomas Aquinas in the development of the disciplined and systematic study of morality, otherwise known as "moral theology" or "Christian ethics." Aquinas' importance lies chiefly in his synthesis of an already long but relatively unorganized tradition of Christian moral teaching (found mostly in the sermons and biblical commentaries of many early Church bishop-theologians, especially St. Augustine of Hippo, d. A.D. 430) with the more systematic insights of the ancient Greek philosopher Aristotle (d. 322 B.C.). Many of Aristotle's works, recently translated into Latin, were just then attracting the attention of scholars in newly established European universities such as Oxford, Paris, and Naples (Aquinas' *alma mater*).

For many of Aquinas' contemporaries, the prospect of using Aristotle's moral philosophy to articulate the basic principles, underlying dynamic, and overarching vision of the Christian moral life did not seem promising. Unlike the more mystical and ascetically inclined philosophies of Plato and the Stoics, which had informed Christian morality for generations, Aristotle's ethical thought appeared mundane, pragmatic, and without obvious need of religion, even if it was not openly hostile to it.

Like all classical thinkers, Aristotle assumed that ethics was fundamentally reflection about what constituted "the good life" (*eudaimonia*). But for Aristotle, the essential features of that life, and how to achieve it, could be known by careful observation of human experience, without need of reference to a sacred text, revealed doctrine, or an inspired figure. What experience shows us, argues Aristotle, is that the best sort of life is a shared life, one that allows the fullest and freest exercise of those capacities uniquely latent in human beings, above all the capacity for reasoned discourse about the nature and aims of that shared life.

It is precisely this emphasis on *virtue* and *friendship* that is at the heart of Aquinas' reading of Aristotle's ethics. In that reading, Aquinas' experience of both the delights and demands of Dominican fellowship doubtlessly played a role; however, for Aquinas, much of what Aristotle wrote on virtue and friendship also allowed the scriptural character of the Christian life to be expressed with great clarity and force. "I no longer call you slaves," Jesus tells his disciples, "because a slave does not know what his master is doing. I have called you friends, because I have told you everything I have heard from my Father" (John 15:15 NAB).

For Aquinas, the Christian life is fundamentally a sharing in God's own Trinitarian life, made fully possible only by God's gift of the Spirit through the life, death, and resurrection of Jesus Christ. Participation in that life requires the acquisition and cultivation of those capacities that permit the ever greater, and freer, enjoyment of God's friendship: pre-eminently faith, hope, and love. But here Aquinas, even while using Aristotle, goes beyond him. For Aristotle, it was an essential characteristic of all virtue that it is achieved by human action. For Aquinas, on the other hand, these three virtues, virtues par excellence, cannot be achieved by human effort, but are rather the result in and on us of *divine* action.

As this one example illustrates (there are many more), Aquinas' synthesis of traditional Christian moral thought with Aristotle's ethics involved a transformation not only of the Christian tradition, but in the interpretation of Aristotle's texts. This is sometimes obscured by a long-standing caricature of Aquinas as a "natural law" thinker when it comes to ethics, that is, as someone primarily interested in constructing a system of universally binding moral principles and rules (laws) based on an account of human nature alone. One of the major fruits of the renewal in Catholic moral theology since the Second Vatican Council has been a rediscovery of the complexity of Aquinas' moral thought, its essentially theological character, and a renewed appreciation for the subtlety of his interpretation of the thinker he more often than not refers to as simply "the Philosopher."

THOMAS AQUINAS IN HISTORY

Thomas undoubtedly represents the high point of Scholasticism. His impact, however, is hardly confined to the Middle Ages. The general term **Thomism** is applied to the wide variety of philosophies and theologies that have arisen directly from his work beginning from his time until now.

Thomism

Thomism through the start of the modern period has a long and complicated history. Just a few of its milestones are as follows.

- Although Thomas' thought would eventually become widely known and respected, immediately after his death, it met controversy. The bishops of Paris and Oxford condemned a number of his teachings in 1277 out of concern that they compromised the role of faith by giving too dominant a place to philosophy (and Aristotle) in theology. Such worries subsided quickly, however, after his canonization.
- Much of the work of pre-modern Thomism was carried forth in often detailed and sophisticated commentaries on Thomas' writings. John Capreolus (c.1380–1444), called the "Prince of Thomists," a Dominican at the University of Paris, stands at the forefront of this tradition. Among Thomas' commentators, the Italian Dominican Thomas de Vio (1468–1534), better known as Cajetan, deserves special mention. The influence of his commentary on the *Summa theologiae* is hard to overestimate.
- Thomism did not remain exclusively with Thomas' fellow Dominicans, but spread to other religious orders and thinkers, too. For instance, after founding the Society of Jesus (the Jesuits), Ignatius of Loyola (1491–1556) made the teachings of Thomas a requirement for the education of its members. This decision reflects the widespread success Thomism had managed to achieve throughout Western Europe in the sixteenth century. The Jesuit Francisco Suárez (1548–1617) stands among the great Thomist commentators.
- During the Catholic Reformation, Thomas' thought played a significant role at the Council of Trent (1545–1563), particularly in regard to the theological problem of justification or righteousness before God, a central area of dispute between Catholics and Protestants (see Chapters 18 and 19).

Neo-Thomism

In the nineteenth century, Thomism took a dramatic turn. Over the previous few centuries, the disciples of Thomas had worked in increasing isolation from modern thought. Their focus, moreover, gravitated toward technical or arcane questions of minimal interest to non-Thomists. The major philosophers of the Enlightenment, such as René Descartes (1596–1650), John Locke (1632–1704), and Immanuel Kant (1724–1804), paid little to no attention to Thomas or the legacy of Scholasticism more generally.

The attitude among Thomists, however, began to change in light of the tremendous social and cultural developments of modernity that seemed to threaten

Christianity, including the loss of many traditional forms of religion and the challenges to the political authority of the Catholic Church sparked by the French Revolution of 1789. More narrowly, Thomists perceived dangers in the philosophies of Descartes and Kant that called into question the ability of reason to prove the existence of God or discover other metaphysical truths. In response, Thomists launched an organized campaign to expose the errors of modern thought and defend Thomas' philosophy as a viable alternative. This movement is now called **Neo-Thomism** or sometimes "Neo-Scholasticism," as Thomas' teachings were not always carefully distinguished from those of other Scholastic theologians. Two major Thomists associated with Neo-Thomism were the Jesuits Matteo Liberatore (1810–1892) and Joseph Kleutgen (1811–1883).

Neo-Thomism reached its zenith when **Pope Leo XIII** (1810–1903) endorsed the philosophy of Thomas in 1879 in his encyclical *Aeterni Patris*. This document was just the leading edge of an aggressive program to spread Thomism throughout the church. In 1880, the Leonine Commission was established in order to produce critical editions of all of Thomas' works (a task still in progress today). In 1914, the Sacred Congregation of Studies established what it considered to be essential doctrines in Thomas' philosophical thought. Lastly, in 1917, the Code of Canon Law held that Thomas must be central to the education of clergy.

The Twentieth Century, the Second Vatican Council, and Today

In the early decades of the twentieth century, there were thinkers who continued to carry forward the Neo-Thomist project enthusiastically. One of the most prominent was the Dominican Reginald Garrigou-Lagrange (1877–1964), whose most famous student was Karol Wojtyła (1920–2005), later to become Pope John Paul II.

At the same time, however, inspired by *Aeterni Patris*, a flurry of new interpretive approaches to Thomas began to emerge. Many of them were critical of Neo-Thomism, sometimes harshly so. Among their objections was that Neo-Thomists, in emphasizing Thomas' philosophy, neglected his theology, forgetting that he was not just an interpreter of Aristotle, but also a devout and pious Christian. They further complained that the Neo-Thomists failed to recognize the unique genius of Thomas' thought, overlooked the historical circumstances in which it arose, and relied far too much on the tradition of commentaries instead of Thomas' writings directly. Among the new interpreters was the Dominican Marie-Dominique Chenu (1895–1990), whose widely influential historical work sought to present Thomas' teachings in their own medieval and theological context. The Jesuits Karl Rahner (1904–1984) and Bernard Lonergan (1904–1984) turned to Thomas, especially his theory of knowledge, to engage less defensively and more appreciatively the philosophy of Kant. Finally, the lay historian Étienne Gilson (1884–1978) and theologian Jacques Maritain (1882–1973) aimed to recover Thomas' rich philosophy of being. This is just a small sampling of the many novel investigations into Thomas' thought that arose during this period.

These new interpretations preceded yet another shift that would happen with the Second Vatican Council (1962–1965). The spirit of the council was one of Catholic renewal. There was not only a new openness to the modern world, but also a return to Patristic and biblical sources. Certainly, Thomas played a role at this council, but his thought was hardly exclusive to it, and he was not used for the heavily defensive purposes to which he had been put since the nineteenth century. The council, then, signaled the end of Neo-Thomism as a movement authoritatively endorsed by the church and singularly dominant in Catholic philosophy and theology.

Since the council, despite the loss of its previous status, Thomism goes on. In fact, in light of the tremendous variety and depth of scholarship, it is arguably flourishing now more than ever. Some Thomists operate in conscious connection with the commentarial tradition and continue to draw inspiration from the era of Neo-Thomism; others follow the lines of interpretation that began in the early twentieth-century; and still others have more original approaches. Thomism, moreover, is not limited to just Catholics, but also Protestants and some Orthodox theologians, too. Finally, many interpreters of Thomas do not formally consider themselves Thomists, but instead draw inspiration from his work in a piecemeal fashion. Thomas' teachings remain today part of the mainstream of Christian theological discourse.

Key Terms

Peter Abelard
Aeterni Patris
Albert the Great
analogical, univocal, and equivocal language
Anselm of Canterbury
Aristotle
Averroes
Avicenna
divine simplicity
The Five Ways

negative theological language
Neo-Thomism
order of grace (supernatural order)
order of nature (natural order)
order of preachers (Dominicans)
Pope Leo XIII

positive (affirmative) theological language
sacra doctrina
Scholasticism
Summa contra gentiles
Summa theologiae (including its organization)
Thomism

Questions for Reading

1. What is Scholasticism? Describe one way that Thomas Aquinas contributed to it.
2. According to Thomas, in what manner is sacred doctrine a science? How does it differ from other sciences?
3. Consider the Five Ways. Do you believe it is possible to prove the existence of God based on observations of the world around us?
4. Compare analogical language with both univocal and equivocal language.
5. In Thomas' view, what is one way in which God differs from created things?
6. Describe how the distinction between natural and supernatural orders shapes one area of Thomas' thought.
7. What are some key features of Neo-Thomism? What are some criticisms of it?
8. Do you think any of Thomas' teachings have special relevance for Christians today?

Works Consulted/Recommended Reading

Bauerschmidt, Frederick Christian. 2013. *Thomas Aquinas: Faith, Reason, and Following Christ.* Oxford: Oxford University Press.

Boyle, Leonard E., O.P. 1982. *The Setting of the Summa theologiae of Saint Thomas.* Toronto: Pontifical Institute of Mediaeval Studies.

Cessario, Romanus, O.P. and Cajetan Cuddy, O.P. 2017. *Thomas and the Thomists: The Achievement of Thomas Aquinas and His Interpreters.* Minneapolis, MN: Fortress Press.

Chenu, M.-D., O.P. 1963. *Toward Understanding Saint Thomas.* Translated by A.-M. Landry, O.P. and D. Hughes. Chicago, IL: Henry Regnery Company.

Chesterton, G.K. 1933. *Saint Thomas Aquinas: "The Dumb Ox."* New York: Sheed & Ward.

Davies, Brian, O.P. 2002. *Aquinas.* New York: Continuum.

Davies, Brian, and Eleonore Stump, eds. 2012. *The Oxford Handbook of Aquinas.* Oxford: Oxford University Press.

Kenny, Anthony. 1969. *The Five Ways: St. Thomas Aquinas' Proofs of God's Existence.* London: Routledge & Kegan Paul.

Kerr, Fergus. 2002. *After Aquinas: Versions of Thomism.* Malden, MA: Blackwell Publishing.

Kretzman, Norman, and Eleonore Stump, eds. 1993. *The Cambridge Companion to Aquinas.* Cambridge: Cambridge University Press.

Leinsle, Ulrich G. 2010. *Introduction to Scholastic Theology.* Translated by Michael J. Miller. Washington, DC: The Catholic University of America Press.

McCool, Gerald A., S.J. 1994. *The Neo-Thomists.* Milwaukee, WI: Marquette University Press.

McGinn, Bernard. 2014. *Thomas Aquinas's Summa Theologiae: A Biography.* Princeton, NJ: Princeton University Press.

McInerny, Ralph. 1996. *Aquinas and Analogy.* Washington, DC: The Catholic University of America Press.

Nichols, Aidan, O.P. 2002. *Discovering Aquinas: An Introduction to His Life, Work, and Influence.* Grand Rapids, MI: William B. Eerdmans.

O'Meara, Thomas F., O.P. 1997. *Thomas Aquinas, Theologian.* Notre Dame, IN: Notre Dame Press.

Pope, Stephen J., ed. 2002. *The Ethics of Aquinas.* Washington, DC: Georgetown University Press.

Swafford, Andrew Dean. 2014. *Nature and Grace: A New Approach to Thomistic Ressourcement.* Eugene, OR: Pickwick Publications.

Torrell, Jean-Pierre, O.P. 2003. *Saint Thomas Aquinas.* Vol. 2: *Spiritual Master.* Translated by Robert Royal. Revised edn. Washington, DC: The Catholic University of America Press.

Torrell, Jean-Pierre, O.P. 2005. *Aquinas's Summa: Background, Structure, & Reception.* Translated by Benedict M. Guevin, O.S.B. Washington, DC: The Catholic University of America Press.

Torrell, Jean-Pierre, O.P. 2005. *Saint Thomas Aquinas.* Vol. 1: *The Person and His Work.* Translated by Robert Royal. Revised edn. Washington, DC: The Catholic University of America Press.

Van Nieuwenhove, Rik, and Joseph Wawrykow, eds. 2005. *The Theology of Thomas Aquinas.* Notre Dame, IN: University of Notre Dame Press.

Wippel, John F. 2000. *The Metaphysical Thought of Thomas Aquinas: From Finite Being to Uncreated Being.* Washington, DC: The Catholic University of America Press.

16
CHRISTIANITY IN THE LATE MEDIEVAL PERIOD

TIMELINE

c.A.D. 1285–1347	Life span of William of Ockham, famous for the nominalist principle known as Ockham's Razor.
A.D. 1309–1377	The period of the Avignon Papacy, when the pope moves the papal residence to Avignon, France.
c.A.D. 1342–1413	Life span of Julian of Norwich, an English mystic who records her visions in *Showings*.
A.D. 1347–1351	The bubonic plague, also known as the Black Death, strikes Europe, resulting in enormous loss of life.
c.A.D. 1347–1380	Life span of Catherine of Siena, religious mystic and prominent writer.
c.A.D. 1375	John Wycliffe begins spreading his teachings of reform within the church.
A.D. 1381	The Peasants' Revolt.
A.D. 1378–1417	The Great Schism in the papacy: The church had first two, then three popes at the same time.
A.D. 1415	John Hus is put to death as a heretic.
A.D. 1414–1418	The Council of Constance asserts the authority of conciliarism to end the Great Schism and condemns the teachings of John Wycliffe.

The late medieval period (c.1300–1500) is often seen as a time of decline, disinteg- ration, conflict, and upheaval. Weather conditions in Europe were appalling, causing widespread drought and starvation. The bubonic plague, or Black Death, was ravaging Europe, destroying nearly one-third of its population in some areas (1348–1350). The European economy was in shambles, and its social institutions were crumbling as well. The church hierarchy, on which people had come to depend as a source of safety and security, had become a source of scandal. And France and England were engaged in an extended conflict that would come to be known as the Hundred Years' War (1337–1453). In spite of all these difficulties, this was also a time of great creativity that paved the way for later accomplishments in the Renaissance period.

The disintegration and the creativity of this period resulted in a number of very real challenges and opportunities for Christian faith and life. First, shifts in the intel- lectual climate of the late medieval period gave rise to nominalism, a development within Scholasticism that would have a radical impact on theological inquiry. Second, there was the scandal of the Avignon papacy, the Great Schism, and the responses of reformers who sought to bring the church back to holiness. Third, the Black Death had a profound impact on the Christian imagination, specifically its art and liter- ature. Finally, the late medieval period saw a new rise of mysticism, a spiritual phe- nomenon that provided people with direct experiences of humanity's deeply personal and intimate relationship with God.

SCHOLASTICISM AND NOMINALISM

In the High Middle Ages, education was greatly influenced by the Scholastic method (see Chapter 15). Its assumption was that truth was already available to the learner, whether in the writings of ancient authorities, in scripture, or in church teachings. One only needed to organize it properly, explain it clearly, and defend it appropri- ately. As a result, logic became an important part of the educational endeavor. The primary emphasis of Scholasticism was debating important texts and speculating about the conclusions that might be drawn from these texts. In the area of theology, the "Schoolmen" tried to take the truths uncovered by the philosophers and show how they were compatible with elements of Christian faith, which depended on divine revelation. They tried to show how human reason could deepen one's under- standing of what one believed on God's authority.

The impact of Scholasticism on theology was profound, as we can see from Thomas Aquinas' *Summa Theologiae*. However, in the late medieval period, there was a development within Scholasticism called **nominalism**. The person most often associ- ated with nominalism is William of Ockham (c.1285–1347). He argued that only indi- vidual things exist. Universal natures or essences, such as human nature, existed only as general concepts in the mind; they did not exist outside of the mind or in God. Universal or general terms like *human nature* were merely linguistic constructions necessary for communication. A consequence of this view was that one could not know anything about God by reason alone. Aquinas had argued that we could under- stand something about God's goodness and wisdom by using the analogy of human goodness and wisdom: Divine goodness and wisdom were like human goodness and wisdom but freed from every limitation and hence infinitely more perfect. For Ockham, on the other hand, wisdom and goodness were concepts, not universal natures or qualities. Hence, according to Ockham, we can only know about God through revelation, accepted in faith, not through reason. Faith, not reason, is the basis for our relationship with God.

Some scholars suggest that nominalism was a particularly appropriate philosophy for this period because of its focus on the individual and its pessimism about one's ability to reason about God. It was an important movement because it would set the stage for several later developments. In particular, William of Ockham's nominalism, with its conviction that God could be known only through revelation, accepted by faith, would prepare the way for sixteenth-century Reformation theology and its emphasis on justification by faith. Likewise, nominalism's concern about acquiring knowledge through the experience of particular occurrences would lay the foundation for the development of the natural sciences in the later eighteenth-century Age of Enlightenment.

THE AVIGNON PAPACY AND THE GREAT SCHISM

Throughout most of the Middle Ages, the Roman church was a dominant force for the preservation and development of the Western world. In the late medieval period, however, the church, or more accurately, the papacy, became a source of disunity and scandal. Once seen as the spiritual center of Europe, the activities taking place in Rome became increasingly confusing to the average Christian. Likewise, the pope, once seen as a bulwark of authority in both the religious and political spheres of influence, became little more than a pawn of the emerging national kingdoms. Two related incidents that characterize the extent of the crisis facing the church of the fourteenth century are the Avignon Papacy and the Great Schism.

The Avignon Papacy

In 1309, the newly elected French Pope Clement V moved the papal court from Rome to Avignon in southeastern France. There were many circumstances that contributed to this move to Avignon. Rome had become a rather dangerous place to live because of some disturbing political and religious fighting going on there—the consequence of a nasty fight between Clement's predecessor, Pope Boniface VIII (1294–1303), and the French king, Philip IV. Philip may even have pressured Clement into the move, since he had just recently been elected pope under Philip's influence. Some have suggested that the move was made because the climate was more conducive to the health of the pope and his court. In fact, Clement himself, as pope, had the right to move the seat of the papacy anywhere he wished. However, the move, which appeared at first to be temporary, lasted well past Clement's lifetime, through six more popes, until 1377. The period of the **Avignon Papacy** would later be referred to derisively as "the Babylonian Captivity," taking its name from the original captivity of Jews in Babylon in the sixth century B.C.E.

The Avignon Papacy was compared to the Babylonian Captivity with good reason. The papacy at Avignon was under French influence, if not under France's complete control. While the papacy was centered in Rome it had a particular status, because of the authority of tradition which associated St. Peter and the apostolic succession with Rome. This disturbed both the allies and enemies of France. Both feared that, with the "captivity" of the pope, the French could control all of European affairs from Avignon. To make matters worse, the pope lived richly in Avignon, and the luxuries of the papal court were paid for in part by practices that many considered contrary to Christian faith and church law. These practices included the selling of church offices (simony), the selling of indulgences (a pardon for punishment due as a result of a person's sin) to support the financial obligations of the Avignon papacy, and **nepotism** (making exceptions to church laws for the advancement of one's relatives).

The problems of the Avignon papacy were made worse by the emergence of national kingdoms. While the Late Middle Ages still had a feudal social structure, national identities and interests were beginning to develop, supported by developments in particular languages, a rising merchant class, and the acceleration of trade. The pope was supposed to represent the universality of the church and the Christian faith. Instead, during the Avignon Papacy, the people had a pope seemingly under the control of one nation and one king. This would inevitably lead to a weakening of the authority and power of the papacy. Questions about the pope's role as a temporal and spiritual leader also eventually poisoned Christian thinking about the meaning and importance of the notion of a universal church.

The Great Schism

By the middle of the fourteenth century, there was growing pressure from different circles for the pope to return to Rome. However, the Avignon controversy would not be settled quickly or easily. Pope Gregory XI moved the papal court back to Rome in 1377, only to die the following year. When the new pope Urban VI announced that he planned a reform of the curia (College of Cardinals), a large faction of cardinals, most of them French, protested by calling for a return of the papacy to Avignon. Claiming that they had been pressured into a hasty election, they withdrew their vote and elected a substitute, who took the name of Clement VII. Urban VI stayed in Rome, while Clement VII returned to Avignon. Thus began the era in papal history known as the **Great Schism**. For almost 40 years, the church would have two, and ultimately three, popes at the same time. This period is not to be confused with the separation of Eastern and Western Christianity (1054), which is also known as the Great Schism.

During the Great Schism (1378–1417) of the papacy, the problem of identifying the legitimate pope was, in the end, a contest between the emerging nations and city-states of Europe for control of the papacy and the power that was thought to go with it. France and its allies (Scotland, Navarre, Castile, and Naples) sided with the pope in Avignon, calling the pope in Rome the antipope. England and its allies (Scandinavia, northern Italy, Ireland, and Portugal) declared for the pope in Rome, calling the pope in Avignon the antipope. While some were motivated by purely political goals, many declared for one pope or the other because they authentically believed, on theological grounds, that the pope they supported was the proper successor of St. Peter.

After scandalizing the Christian world and being condemned by holy persons and saints, the schism was finally healed by a series of councils held in the early fifteenth century. The Council of Pisa (1409) elected a new pope, presumably to replace the two currently reigning popes, but they refused to abdicate. As a result, there were three popes competing for support. Five years later, a renewed effort was made to solve the schism at the Council of Constance (1414–1418). The participants at Constance defended the legitimacy of their meeting, which had only shaky papal support, by appealing to the principles of **conciliarism**, a theory of the church which had become popular among some theologians. The decree known as *Haec Sancta*, adopted by the Council of Constance on April 6, 1415, reads: "First, it [the Council] declares that, legitimately assembled in the Holy Spirit, constituting a general council, and representing the catholic church militant, it has power immediately from Christ"; therefore, everyone, including the pope, must be obedient to its authority. On this basis, the council deposed all *three* popes and elected Martin V (r. 1417–1431) to replace them. Because Martin's legitimacy was eventually recognized, Constance could be said to have successfully ended the schism, though the Catholic Church has only accepted the decrees of the council from the time of Martin's election (1417).

Later, the Council of Basel (1431–1449) also appealed to the principles of conciliarism in discussing the reform of the church. When Basel invoked Constance's doctrine that a council was superior to a pope, Pope Eugene IV in 1437 withdrew his support from the Basel meeting and moved the council to Ferrara in Italy. In 1460, Pope Pius II condemned conciliarism insofar as it taught that a council was superior to a pope. In that sense, the papacy survived the crisis of the fourteenth and fifteenth centuries. But grave damage had already been done to papal prestige and authority. It was more and more difficult to see the church, under papal leadership, as a universal reality that could overcome the boundaries of class and nation, of feudal obligation and responsibility. The movement toward national and territorial churches would not be stopped.

THE BLACK DEATH AND THE CHRISTIAN IMAGINATION

Because of the Black Death, it must have seemed to the population of Europe that the world was about to come to an end from 1347 to 1351. Traveling from the Middle East, ships returning to Europe carried rats and fleas, which spread two virulent forms of bubonic plague: one spread by contact with the blood of its victims, the other by respiration as a form of pneumonia. We must bear in mind as the story unfolds that the ancient and medieval worlds were accustomed to periodic ravages by famine, plague, and illness. However, they had never experienced anything quite like this plague. It caused widespread panic and a belief that perhaps the biblical plagues of the book of Revelation had finally come upon them.

Bubonic plague, which still exists in small pockets today, was especially devastating to late medieval Europe for a variety of reasons. One was the speed with which it killed. While the first form of this plague could take up to five days for the victim to die, the second spread so quickly that the healthy could become ill and die in a night. Another was the horror of the disease itself. It was familiarly known as the Black Death, because black growths and pustules appeared on the victim's body. These would burst, and gradually the entire body would swell, discolor, and decay. Yet another reason for its devastation was the mystery of its transmission. Although doctors of the time did not know much about how diseases were transmitted, they usually learned by process of elimination how to protect others from their spread. The fact that the plague was spread in two forms by two hosts made it virtually impossible to understand how it was being transmitted, and, since both fleas and rats were a fact of life in the medieval world, they were not suspected. This pestilence, or "the pest" as it was called, knew and respected none of the trappings of wealth, influence, or status. It seemed to strike at random, killing rich and poor, in cities and in the countryside, sinners and holy people. It simply did not discriminate.

Perhaps the greatest effects of the plague were on the Christian imagination. Panic increased as the disease spread and as others abandoned the suffering victims. Many could not receive the last rites (the sacrament of Anointing of the Sick), because a priest was not available or because he would not come out of fear of contamination. Special dispensations were given for lay persons to hear the last confessions of the dying to reassure them that God would not forget them but forgive them at the end. A new kind of religious piety (devotional practice) also began to emerge, as some Christians chose to identify with the suffering of victims and families by increasingly meditating on the sufferings of the crucified Christ. Processions of flagellants (people who beat themselves as an act of penance) began to appear in the streets, praying for God's intervention in ending the plague. Tragically, some Christians made the Jews the scapegoats for the plague, and in some cities pogroms (organized massacres) erupted against them.

The Black Death produced several indelible artistic images that reflect the sentiments of the times. The first is a gruesome representation of death as a grinning skeleton holding the traditional scythe (a tool for gathering in the harvest), hovering over the dead and decaying, and showing the healthy and prosperous where their futures lie. The second is the bloody portrayal of Christ on the cross, with discolored flesh and weeping wounds. These artistic representations of Christ's crucifixion were meant to warn people that this world was passing away. However, they also gave hope to Christians, because they believed that, by Christ's redemptive death on the cross, better things awaited those who experienced great suffering as Christ had suffered. The third artistic representation typical of this time was the figure of the **pietà**, in which Mary mourns over her crucified son. It encouraged Christians to identify their suffering and death with that of Christ and to wonder at the amazing love of God present even in life's most difficult moments.

While many Christians fled from the infected (contemporaries observed that "charity was dead"), others helped the ill and dying, ministering to them despite great risk to themselves. Many were clergy and religious; others were devout lay persons. Among them were two saints named Catherine: Catherine of Siena, who will be discussed in a later section of this chapter, and Catherine of Genoa.

Catherine of Genoa (1447–1510) chose to live amid the plague victims and people suffering from other diseases, establishing a hospital for all the needy. Her husband later joined her, and together they pledged their lives to chastity and to the service of the poor. Her most lyrical and important work is the *Purgation and Purgatory*, which speaks of

Figure 16–1 The so-called Röttgen Pietà, Western Germany, early fourteenth century, Rheinisches Landesmuseum, Bonn, Germany.

the cleansing given to us by God, a cleansing that will leave us shining brightly, as gold is refined in the fire. Her attitude is characteristic of many devout Christians of the late medieval period who decided that, in solidarity with those who suffer, they wanted to be like Christ in the world, working and caring for others through God's strengthening spirit.

In this selection from her works, Catherine describes the process of God loving and cleansing the souls here and in purgatory:

> Not that those souls dwell on their suffering;
> they dwell rather on the resistance they feel in themselves
> against the will of God,
> against His intense and pure love bent on nothing
> but drawing them up to him.
> And I see rays of lightning
> darting from that divine love to the creature,
> so intense and fiery as to annihilate not the body alone,
> but, were it possible, the soul.
> These rays purify and then annihilate.
> The soul becomes like gold that becomes purer as it is fired,
> all dross being cast out.
>
> (Catherina of Genoa 1979, 79)

The importance of the Black Death cannot be underestimated. Its toll was devastating not only in the depletion of Europe's population, but also in the loss of a sense of certainty about life, in the breakdown of social organization, and in radical changes in Christian attitudes and lifestyle. In addition, the enormous number of clergy and religious who died during the great pestilence left a vacuum that needed desperately to be filled. Priests were ordained as quickly as possible so as to have the sacraments available once more to the populace, but many were uneducated and unlettered. Some were probably not morally suited to priesthood either. Abuses were on the rise, whether from ignorance, misinformation, or deliberate callousness. Thus, preachers arose who rallied the people against the abuses of a corrupt church, suggesting that these abuses were the cause of God's wrath upon the people. We now turn to these figures and the religious and social unrest caused in large part by the plague.

Lived Religion: Liturgy in the Later Middle Ages (1200–1450)
Feast of Corpus Christi

During the Middle Ages, numerous popular worship practices or devotions developed that were distinct from Sunday liturgy. One such devotion was the Feast of Corpus Christi, which began in 1246 in Liège, France and ultimately became a universal feast of the church.

Corpus Christi was celebrated every year on the Thursday following Trinity Sunday. A feast to honor the body and blood of Christ in the Eucharist, it began when a holy woman, Juliana of Cornillon, had a vision of the moon with a small part missing. Christ later revealed to her that this meant the church was missing a feast day to honor Him in the Eucharist.

On that day, special prayers and readings were included in the Mass, and the monks of the five city monasteries had special prayers in their daily liturgy. There was also a colorful procession that included the trade guilds, the city officials, the students at the local colleges, and the clergy, all carrying candles. Most important was the bishop, in beautiful vestments, carrying the Eucharist under a canopy in a golden vessel called a monstrance. All the church bells rang, alms were distributed to the poor, and sermons were given that explained the importance of the Eucharist as a source of grace, virtue, and strength, and as a way to contemplate Christ's love for humanity.

The celebration was organized by the fraternities of the city, which were dedicated to the Eucharist. They helped their sick members, provided for their funerals, and cared for a chapel in the cathedral where they held their annual meeting. They also took the Eucharist to the dying and engaged in charitable works for the whole community. This feast was a way to show civic pride as well as devotion to Christ.

REVOLTS AGAINST CHURCH AND STATE

As the legitimacy of the Avignon Papacy weakened, the monarchies of France, England, and Germany attempted to put controls on the church's leadership and on its ability to raise taxes to support its projects. Opposition was not limited to the political arena, however. Lay religious movements were beginning to emerge as critics of church corruption and religious superstition. Two reformers of the late medieval period, John Wycliffe and Jan Hus, are often mentioned together and seen as forerunners of the Protestant Reformation. In reality, Wycliffe and Hus lived in different places at different times and left legacies that are distinct from one another.

John Wycliffe

John Wycliffe (*c.*1330–1384) was a highly controversial figure in the Late Middle Ages, a man of quick temper and incisive thought. He was well educated and an ordained priest. Indeed, Wycliffe even had a patron who supported his work financially and a steady church post in England. In the early phase of his preaching, Wycliffe appealed not only to Christians scandalized by the Avignon Papacy, but also to advocates of English nationalism. He believed that the clergy ought to live a life of poverty, without ownership of property, somewhat like the mendicant orders, and therefore he began to preach against the wealth and power of the clergy and the Avignon Papacy. He also believed that the English kings ought to have the right to appoint candidates to key church positions and to collect taxes in their own land. Both practices at that time belonged to the authority of the pope, but Wycliffe saw them as sources of corruption in the church.

Wycliffe also challenged or denied several widely held church doctrines. For example, he held that it was not the "visible" church represented by the church of Rome that counted, but the "invisible" church of the saved. The trappings of the external church and its claims to be the source of salvation for Christians were both wrong and dangerous. Those whom God had predestined for salvation were chosen by God alone. He also taught that personal holiness ought to be the basis of religious authority in the church, not one's ecclesiastical rank or ordination. Wycliffe also attacked the doctrine of transubstantiation and the notion of the real presence of Christ in the Eucharist. If the bread and wine became in substance Christ's body and blood, then bread and wine must be destroyed in order to become Christ's body and blood. This destruction seemed to Wycliffe to have no place in the image of the loving God who had created universal realities in the first place. He called his doctrine one of "remaining." Christ was present in the Eucharist in a spiritual way, but the bread remained bread.

Wycliffe advocated a translation of the Bible into English. In fact, two translations were begun under his commission between 1380 and 1381, although neither was completed. He also wanted to found a group of poor followers who would preach as he did and represent a contrast to the corrupt clergy and religious orders. His ideal of a community of the poor eventually materialized in a group known as the Lollards, who implemented his ideas in a more radical way than Wycliffe probably intended. They were preachers but were much more active politically than Wycliffe was. They advocated clerical poverty and confiscation of church property. They also distributed vernacular translations (in the language of the people) of the Bible and preached a return to the simple, scripture-based Christianity of the early church. Whether or not Wycliffe was actually involved in the founding of the Lollard movement in England is a matter of dispute. However, they certainly spread his ideas and kept his legacy alive. They were active in several social uprisings, and as a result many were put to death.

Jan Hus

Jan Hus (*c.*1372–1415) was born in Bohemia (in the modern-day Czech Republic) shortly before the death of John Wycliffe. Like Wycliffe, he was well educated and an ordained priest. The figure of Wycliffe was to be a powerful one in his life because they shared a number of common concerns about church reform. In fact, many of his teachings were taken directly from the writings of Wycliffe. For example, Hus accepted Wycliffe's teaching about the authority of scripture as the source of doctrine. However, he did not accept Wycliffe's doctrine of "remaining" in the Eucharist. What prompted him to begin preaching reform was the Great Schism. Appalled by the Schism, yet part of it (since Bohemia supported one of the antipopes), he refused to support any of the various popes' actions. He was completely scandalized by the intention of one of the antipopes to send a crusading force against Christians in Naples. He railed against this move and against the corrupt practice of selling indulgences. This put him in jeopardy with the king of Bohemia, who profited from these practices. He preached widely in Czech and wrote on the Ten Commandments and the Lord's Prayer. His most important work was *De ecclesia* (On the Church). In it he described the church as "the body of Christ," with Christ as its only head.

Hus was finally ordered by the pope to appear at the Council of Constance (1414–1418). The king of Bohemia, who had been protecting Hus against his opponents, released him under safe conduct to attend. Although Hus denied the allegations brought against him, especially concerning the Eucharist, the council did not believe him. They claimed that, like Wycliffe, Hus taught the doctrine of "remaining." When asked to recant (take back his radical beliefs), he protested that he could not take back what he never had believed in the first place. In the end, the council decided that Hus was a dangerous heretic spreading the ideas of Wycliffe. He was stripped of his priesthood, condemned, and turned over to the secular authorities to be put to death. His execution served to increase the devotion of his followers who considered him a martyr. In Bohemia and among its close neighbors, his death resulted in the establishment of a Czech national church known as the Hussites in 1420, a century before the Reformation.

The Peasants' Revolt

Although the Peasants' Revolt of 1381 was confined to England, it is a powerful symbol of the social and political unrest engendered by the plague. In large part, the revolt was caused by the farm labor shortage resulting from the plague. The shortage was made even worse by the fact that peasants who had been farmers were leaving the farms for more interesting jobs as artisans. The large landowners were not pleased about their loss of income and the higher wages they had to pay the workers who remained in farming. In order to recoup their losses and stop the flow of peasants off the land, the landowners shifted to wool production and other more profitable, less labor-intensive crops. They also managed to get extremely repressive legislation passed to keep peasants on their farms. They froze farm wages at very low levels and exacted very high taxes from the peasants.

The Peasants' Revolt came about because of the mistreatment and overworking and overtaxing of the peasantry. The preaching of the Lollards also inflamed an increasingly discontented populace. While the unrest in England proved serious, it did not threaten the social fabric for long. Within a year, the revolt was extinguished with deadly force. Yet this revolt and others like it would mark the beginning of the end of a workable feudal economy.

MYSTICISM IN THE LATE MIDDLE AGES

Although mysticism had been part of Christianity from its beginnings, it burst forth again with particular force in the fourteenth century. **Mysticism** is a particular spiritual phenomenon that expresses itself in direct, intense experiences of union and oneness with God. The mystical journey at its simplest consists of three phases: purgation (cleansing from sin); illumination (an attraction to all the things of God, especially scripture and the divine office, the official prayer of the church); and finally, union (the state of oneness with God). The experience of union might be momentary, but it has lasting effects on the mystic, leaving him or her with an assurance of God's constant presence. Perhaps the reason that mysticism flourished in the fourteenth century was that the passionate and prophetic character of the mystic was sorely needed in a time when the church and the Christian people were wondering if they had indeed been abandoned by God, or if they were victims of God's wrath. In such troubled times, when the world seemed to be falling to pieces, people needed the guidance of the mystics.

Although mystics throughout the ages share certain characteristics in common, they also differ from one another. Some mystics were primarily visionaries, whose union with God produced visions which taught them about faith and often called them to prophecy or to service. Others were so overcome by the presence of God that they would experience ecstasies (from *ek-stasis*, "standing outside"). While in ecstasy, they experienced supernatural phenomena of various sorts: raptures, trances, and various types of transformation (levitation, changes in appearance, and miraculous events). Still others did not see visions or have raptures but felt drawn closer to God in an experience of the "divine darkness" where they realized just how little God can be understood or perceived. Yet, whatever the differences in their experiences of God, mystics maintained that the most important quality of their extraordinary gifts was the love and union with God that these experiences brought about.

The church in general has always been somewhat suspicious of mysticism for a variety of reasons. Some persons claimed to have revelations from God but did not. These people simply used the claim for their own purposes (e.g., status, recognition, or special favors). Another factor that influenced the church's reluctance to endorse mystical experiences was the number of women who had such experiences. Their claims of authority from God were a threat to the medieval understanding of woman's traditional role. In fact, mystics came from all social classes and levels of education, from many walks of life (they were not always clergy or religious), and from the ranks of both men and women. Some, whether their mystical experiences were genuine or not, held strange or possibly heretical ideas about God, Christ, or salvation. Mystics were usually judged during and after their lifetimes by their fidelity to the doctrines of the church, their accurate expression of Christian faith, their service to others, and their conformity to some known pattern of mystical growth.

In looking at Catherine of Siena and Julian of Norwich, two important mystics of the fourteenth century, and in referring back to Catherine of Genoa, we can see the similarities and the differences of mystical experience in its immediacy and in the way it inspired those who experienced God in this way to participate in the world and to act on its behalf.

Catherine of Siena

Born Caterina Benincasa, **Catherine of Siena** (*c.*1347–1380) was the daughter of a large family of lower rank in Siena. From an early age, she saw herself as dedicated to Christ alone. Her opposition to marriage infuriated her parents, who confined her to their home, where she decided to serve them lovingly. Her parents reluctantly accepted her choice when Catherine began having powerful prayer experiences, visions, and raptures. She continued to live at home and she devoted herself to contemplation. Catherine's prayer life had led her into a vision of mystical marriage to Christ. Her visions were often of the nourishing and cleansing blood of the sacrifice of Christ on the cross. Her emphasis on the blood of Christ may be due both to her Eucharistic devotion and to the suffering caused by the presence of plague among the populace. Yet, she was destined for more than contemplation in her short lifetime. In 1363, she became a Dominican tertiary (member of the lay third order) dedicated to serving and especially to feeding the poor. She would give up her own meals to feed others, convinced that she could live on the substance of the Eucharist alone. Many sought Catherine's help, advice, or counsel because of her closeness to God and her saintly reputation. Before long, she became a local celebrity of sorts.

Living during the time of the Avignon controversy, Catherine criticized and implored the church to heal itself of scandal and abuse. She wrote letters to influential church figures all over Europe, including the popes, calling them back to the ways of God and God's church. Her greatest desire was to see an end to the captivity of the papacy in Avignon, and she lived long enough to help bring it about, only to see it fall into the situation of the Great Schism. Catherine also wrote of her experiences of God, not as autobiography, but as a way to inspire other Christians to be faithful to the church despite its abuses. Her most famous work is *The Dialogue.* God is speaking in this excerpt:

So the memory, all imperfect past, is filled at this breast
because it has remembered and held
without itself my blessings. Understanding receives the light.
Gazing into the memory,
it comes to know the truth and shedding the blindness of selfish
love, it remains in the
sunlight of Christ crucified in whom it knows both God and
humanity. Beyond this knowledge,
because of the union [with me] that she has realized, the soul
rises to a light
acquired not by nature nor by her own practice of virtue but by
the grace of my gentle Truth
who does not scorn any eager longing or labors offered to me.

(Catherine of Siena 1980, 178–179)

Because of her deep spirituality, her thoughtful theology, and her devotion to the church, Catherine was declared a saint in 1461. Later, in the twentieth century, she was proclaimed a Doctor of the Church, an honor reserved for those whose teaching and scholarship have reflected Catholic Christian beliefs and those who have been important in the lives and faith of others.

Figure 16–2 Julian of Norwich (*c.*1342–1417).

Julian of Norwich

We know very little about **Julian of Norwich** (*c.*1342–after 1417), except from her own writings and those of Margery Kempe, a contemporary of Julian. Like Catherine, Julian had mystical experiences. Unlike Catherine, her mystical experiences were limited to one overwhelming set of visions during a brief period of illness. She spent the remainder of her life contemplating and interpreting these visions (which are called "shewings" or "showings"), in order to achieve a greater theological understanding of their meaning. Her mystical experiences are recorded in both a short text and a long text. One hypothesis, generally accepted, is that the short text was written immediately after her mystical experience, and the long text provides the reflection, thought, prayer, and theological explanation of the original visions.

We do not know whether or not Julian had already chosen her vocation at the time of her "showings," but we do know that before, or shortly after, she chose to live the life of an **anchoress** (a recluse who lived in solitude). Anchorites, male or female, were

Figure 16–3 The anchorage at the Church of St. Julian in Norwich, England.

common in this period. They pledged to spend their entire lives in prayer and contemplation, and when they entered the anchorhold (their private rooms attached to a church) they were enclosed as if they were being buried. The symbolism was that of dying to the world outside and devoting one's life to God in silence and prayer. When enclosed, they took on the name of the church to which they were related. Thus, we do not know Julian's birth name or history. Julian was the anchoress of the church of St. Julian at Norwich, England. Julian would have had one or two rooms in which to live, she would have had a single servant who took care of tasks in the outside world such as shopping for food, and she would have been permitted a pet for company. She would also have had two windows in her enclosure: one looked into the church, so that she could hear the Mass and participate in the Eucharist; the other looked out to a small room where those seeking her wisdom and advice could come during certain hours of the day. These hours were limited so as not to disturb prayer but were considered essential as a way of being of service to God's people. In many ways, anchorites acted as the spiritual counselors of their time.

Although not entirely unique to her, Julian speaks in her *Showings* of the Motherhood of God and the Motherhood of Christ. Her use of gender references is fluid, moving easily from masculine to feminine and back, when speaking of God. In this way, she both incorporates and transcends gender limitations when imaging God. Also in her visions, she is especially aware of the suffering Christ who redeems all. Her reflections on that mystical experience show that she spent her life dealing with the tumult of plague and disorder in Norwich. She speculates on the meaning of sin and struggles with the question of why God allows sin and evil to exist. Thus, her assertion, "All will be well," is not empty optimism, but thoughtful and prayerful conviction.

CONCLUDING REMARKS

The problems of the papacy and the occurrence of the Black Death were devastating to people's beliefs about divine order in Christendom. Each alone would have produced major shifts in Christian thought and practice, and together they changed the landscape of the Christian imagination. This unrest led people to pay attention to charismatic figures who seemed to have answers to the difficult problems of life, whether heretical preachers, orthodox mystics, or teachers and educators of the nominalist school. Later in the fifteenth century, the fall of Constantinople, the invention of the printing press, and the Spanish Reconquest, which drove the Muslims and Jews out of Spain, would lead to other new and dramatic changes. In Chapter 17, we look at some of those dramatic changes in the movement that would come to be called the Renaissance.

Key Terms

anchoress	Jan Hus	pietà
Avignon Papacy	Julian of Norwich	Scholasticism
Catherine of Siena	mysticism	John Wycliffe
conciliarism	nepotism	
Great Schism	nominalism	

Questions for Reading

1. Why do we speak of the fourteenth century as one of change and crisis?

2. What is nominalism? How does it differ from the Scholasticism of the Middle Ages and why does this matter?

3. To what situation does the Avignon Papacy refer? Why is it sometimes called the "Babylonian Captivity"? How does the Avignon Papacy relate to the Great Schism, and what was the effect of these two situations on the church of the time?

4. What was the Black Death, and how did this plague get its name? Discuss with others what it would have been like to live in a time of uncertainties: plague and schism in particular.

5. What was the impact of the Black Death on religious art and literature and on the social structure of Europe at the time?

6. Who were John Wycliffe and Jan Hus? What were their concerns and why do they surface in this time period? What were the religious teachings that brought them into conflict with the authorities?

7. What exactly is mysticism, and why was it considered an essential part of the spirituality of the Late Middle Ages? What are the stages of mystical experience?

8. How does Julian of Norwich resemble Catherine of Siena in her mystical experience? How is she different?

9. Think about how the desire for the Bible in one's own language and the close relationship with God described in mysticism are appealing in this century. Are they still important to religious understanding today?

Works Consulted/Recommended Reading

Bynum, Caroline Walker. 1982. *Jesus as Mother: Studies in the Spirituality of the High Middle Ages.* Berkeley, CA: University of California Press.

Catherine of Genoa. 1979. *Purgation and Purgatory, The Spiritual Dialogue.* Translated by S. Hughes. New York: Paulist Press.

Catherine of Siena. 1980. *The Dialogue.* Translated by S. Noffke. New York: Paulist Press.

Chadwick, Owen. 1964. *The Reformation.* Baltimore, MD: Penguin.

Copelston, Frederick. 1963. *History of Philosophy.* Vol. 3. New York: Doubleday.

Egan, Harvey. 1992. *Christian Mysticism.* Collegeville, MN: Liturgical Press.

Huizinga, Johan. 1985. *The Waning of the Middle Ages.* New York: St. Martin's Press.

Jantzen, Grace. 1988. *Julian of Norwich, Mystic and Theologian.* New York: Paulist Press.

Julian of Norwich. 1978. *Showings.* Edited by Edmund Colledge and James Walsh. New York: Paulist Press.

Kelly, John. 2006. *The Great Mortality: An Intimate History of the Black Death, The Most Devastating Plague of All Time.* New York: Harper Perennial.

McGinn, Bernard. 1998. *The Flowering of Mysticism: Men and Women in the New Mysticism 1200–1350. The Presence of God, Book 3.* New York: The Crossroad Publishing Company.

Pelphrey, Brant. 1989. *Julian of Norwich: Christ our Mother.* Collegeville, MN: Liturgical Press.

Tanner, Norman P., ed. 1990. *Decrees of the Ecumenical Councils.* 2 vols. Washington, DC: Georgetown University Press.

Tuchman, Barbara. 1978. *A Distant Mirror: The Calamitous 14th Century.* New York: Ballantine.

Ullman, Walter. 1972. *The Short History of the Papacy in the Middle Ages.* London: Methuen.

Zeigler, Philip. 1969. *The Black Death.* New York: A. Knopf.

PART

IV

THE MODERN PERIOD

Chapter 16 of this book marks the end of the historical period known as the Middle Ages. The Middle Ages, as was noted in the introduction to Chapter 13, refers to the roughly 1,000 years between the fall of the Roman Empire in the West (476) and the Renaissance and the Protestant Reformation of the sixteenth century. With the Renaissance and the Protestant Reformation, then, we enter into a new period of history: the modern period, or "modernity," as it is often called. But the modern period, we have also learned, is itself made up of two overlapping stages (see Introduction to Part III). The first stage of modernity extends over the sixteenth and seventeenth centuries—over the Renaissance and Protestant Reformation, in other words—and is usually referred to as "the early modern period" or "early modernity." The second stage of modernity begins in the seventeenth century and extends all the way into our own present. These two stages of modernity explain why our textbook introduces the modern period twice, first in this section, and then a second time in Chapter 22.

This may seem an odd way to proceed, but there is nothing strange about it. By proceeding in this way, this textbook is simply following the established conventions of historical periodization. This really means something like "the standard rules for carving up the past into meaningful bite-sized chunks." These rules tell us to divide history into three main periods—ancient, medieval, and modern—and to further divide the modern period into two overlapping stages, and so this is what this book does—and not just this book but other standard historical introductions to theology, or philosophy, or literature, indeed the very academic curriculum itself and the disciplines it embodies. They are all likely organized in accordance with the same conventions of historical periodization—the same rules for carving up the past—that inform this book.

But nearly universal use does not explain why these conventions (and not others) were adopted in the first place. One may reasonably ask why one should divide history into periods at all. And if so, why just three, and not four or five? In fact, the present book does engage in such further subdivisions of individual periods, such as dividing the Middle Ages into three distinct periods, "Early," "High," and "Late." Why are these three parts of one period, and not three distinct periods?

This is a legitimate question. It points to a real difficulty in how history is taught in the twenty-first century. The difficulty is that the way we *talk* about history today does not reflect what we *know* about history today. When we talk about history, we use a vocabulary and set of distinctions that originated in the eighteenth century. Before that time, nobody carved up the past into three distinct periods called "ancient," "medieval," and "modern," or used labels like "The Middle Ages," "The Renaissance," or "The Protestant Reformation." It was the work of eighteenth-century historians to invent and popularize this way of talking, and they were quite successful in doing so. For this is how we have talked about history ever since.

When eighteenth-century historians first invented this way of talking, they did so with a definite purpose in mind. They wanted to tell a new story about European civilization, and they designed their new historical terms and categories in order to help them do so. The story they ended up telling was simple, compelling, and extremely influential. But it was also, we now know, seriously inadequate. It gives an image of the past that is as distorted as an image in a fun-house mirror. The problem, however, is that historians have not agreed upon a way of talking about the past except in the terms this same story provides.

This creates a dilemma for a book of this kind, which seeks to present a complex religious tradition like Christianity in historical terms, as explained in Chapter 1 and in the Introduction to Part III. The book tries to deal with the dilemma by retaining the conventional periodization, while correcting, for example, the eighteenth-century category of "The Middle Ages" in at least two ways. First, the book does not describe the period in the very negative language preferred by eighteenth-century scholars, for whom "The Middle Ages" was a period of "darkness and confusion," to quote the great historian Edward Gibbon's *History of the Decline and Fall of the Roman Empire*. We now know that a description like this of 1,000 years of history is not only wildly inaccurate, but also very self-interested: eighteenth-century historians benefited by making the "medieval" period look bad in order to make their own time, the "modern" period, look good. Second, as noted, this book carves up the Middle Ages into three smaller parts—the "early medieval," "High Middle Ages," and "late medieval." This reflects our increased appreciation for the complexity and variety of the period itself, which requires a more finely grained analysis than the originally uniform "The Middle Ages" allows.

But qualifications of this sort are not adequate to deal with the inevitable implication that the beginning of a new period means the end and supersession of the previous one, and the illusion of a fresh start, a reboot, in a new one. No matter how respectful and sophisticated our treatment of the Middle Ages, the period must still come to an "end" at the moment the modern period begins. As a result, there has always been a strong temptation to introduce (early) modernity in a way that exaggerates and distorts its differences with the (now superseded) Middle Ages. Indeed, for a long time it was the common practice among historians to present both "The Renaissance" and "The Protestant Reformation" as marking a kind of rupture with the Middle Ages. But this was a serious misrepresentation of historical reality. There are many ways in which the Renaissance of the fifteenth and sixteenth centuries represents not a break with but the continuation of "medieval" political and intellectual developments, and the same is true of the Reformation. The notion that either of these "modern" movements can be clearly differentiated from (what we now call) the High or Late Middle Ages is an illusion created by our own categories and labels, and it is important to admit as much.

This introduction to Part IV, then, recognizes fully the serious shortcomings and distortions of the conventional periodization. Nevertheless, we will honor the convention by having four chapters on the Renaissance (Chapter 17), the Protestant Reformation (Chapters 18 and 19), and the Catholic response to the Reformation (Chapter 20), followed by chapters on the globalization of Christianity since the medieval period (Chapter 21), the distinctively modern challenges to Christianity (Chapter 22), Christianity in the United States (Chapter 23), modern Catholic theology centered on the Second Vatican Council (Chapter 24), Christianity and science (Chapter 25), Christianity in the contemporary setting (Chapter 26), theologies of liberation that treat global Christianity (Chapter 27), and Christianity in dialogue with world religions (Chapter 28).

Chapter

THE RENAISSANCE

The Renaissance refers to a complex and many-sided cultural movement beginning in Italy in the fourteenth century and spreading gradually northward across the whole of Europe during the next two centuries. This chapter provides a selective introduction to the Renaissance in four parts. The first part will trace the historical roots of the Renaissance to the unique social and political environment of twelfth-century Italian city-states like Florence and Pisa. The second part will look at the origins and development of what we now call "Renaissance humanism," a far-reaching educational and scholarly movement organized around the *studia humanitatis*, or "the study of the humanities." The third part discusses the central dynamic that animated the Renaissance as a whole and was summed up in the Latin phrase *ad fontes!*—Back to the sources! The fourth part will examine how this dynamic led to the development and revitalization of theology during the Renaissance. The chapter concludes by offering some general observations about how the Renaissance relates to the Reformation.

ORIGINS OF THE RENAISSANCE

Unlike most other places in Europe, the regions of central and northern Italy had never been unified under a single government or kingdom after the sixth-century fall of the Roman Empire in the West. Rather, these regions had developed as a patchwork of independent city-states, including Florence, Pisa, Padua, Verona, and a few others. These city-states were self-governing fortified communes that possessed their own territories and were responsible for their own defense. They had been able to retain their independence on account of their geographic location. Pinned between the Holy Roman Empire in the north and the Roman Papacy in the south, they were able to take advantage of the competing interests of these larger and more powerful political entities, neither of whom wanted to see northern Italy fall into the hands of the other. The location of these city-states was beneficial in another way as well. Most of them were situated on the Mediterranean trade routes connecting transalpine Europe with Africa, Arabia, and Asia. As a result, city-states like Florence and others gave rise to an increasingly wealthy, literate, and powerful merchant class, and by 1300 or so they had become some of the most populous cities in Europe.

The independence, prosperity, and size of these city-states led to the formation of a unique kind of political culture. At a time when most political structures in Europe were monarchical, Florence, Pisa, and other city-states were organized as oligarchic republics. This meant that they were ruled not by a single leader, but by a council made up of the city's wealthiest and most established citizens. Over time, these active and politically engaged citizens came to view their own form of life as an echo of ancient Roman republicanism. As this feeling grew and developed among the literate elite of northern Italy, so did their enthusiasm for the texts and authors of classical Rome.

The writings of Cicero were especially important to them. **Cicero**, a Roman orator from the first century B.C., had been a fierce champion of the Roman republican ideal. Several of Cicero's works had been transmitted in uninterrupted fashion through the schools and universities of Europe for hundreds of years, but they began to be read in a different light during the time of the Renaissance. They were studied not merely as a record of the past, but as a living model for the present. Cicero's vision of politics, citizenship, and education increasingly became the standard against which contemporary practices and institutions were judged.

The enthusiasm for Cicero among the ruling elite led to attempts to recover the writings of other ancient Roman authors as well. Fourteenth-century scholars like Francesco Petrarch (1304–1374) and Giovanni Boccaccio (1313–1375) collated, copied, and edited newly discovered manuscripts of Cicero, the Roman poet Propertius (56–15 B.C.), and the Roman historians Livy (64 B.C.–A.D. 12) and Tacitus (A.D. 56–120). Most of these manuscripts were found hidden away in monastic libraries scattered throughout Europe. Some had been preserved by copyists hundreds of years earlier, but had not been disseminated and were not widely known. All this changed in the course of one century. By 1400, European scholars had access to twice as many classical Roman texts as they had 100 years before.

THE *STUDIA HUMANITATIS* AND RENAISSANCE HUMANISM

One of the texts discovered by Petrarch was an oration by Cicero titled *Pro Archia*, or "In defense of Archias." In this oration, Cicero argues that the *studia humanitatis* ("the studies of humanity" or "humane studies," what we today call "the humanities") are essential to living a free and self-determining human life. For Cicero, to live a free and self-determining human life was to live as a citizen of Rome, actively contributing to the political life of the republic. Roman citizens did not take their directions from leaders, but rather collectively deliberated their own course of action—to pass this law or not, to negotiate a treaty or go to war, to reform this institution or that one, and so on. To succeed at this kind of life, as an individual and as a body politic, required plenty of practice, a great deal of skill, and the right kind of knowledge.

The purpose of education in a republic like Rome was to impart this knowledge to the next generation of citizens. As such, it was humanistically oriented, which is to say that it took as its focus the social and political life of human beings. Its curriculum included poetry, history, rhetoric, and ethical and political philosophy. As Cicero explained in *Pro Archia*, each of these disciplines has "some link which binds it to another," and together they form a kind of whole. Rhetoric teaches the future citizen how to speak persuasively and convincingly in the public arena. History instructs him or her in the lessons learned from the past, so that he or she is able to act with political prudence in the present. Philosophy instructs the citizen in ethical virtue, and teaches him or her to analyze and identify the strengths and weaknesses of different political regimes.

Cicero's account of the *studia humanitatis* came to exercise a strong influence upon a large number of fifteenth- and sixteenth-century scholars, giving rise to the movement known as "Renaissance humanism." Like Cicero, later Renaissance humanist scholars emphasized the importance of the humanities and sought to revitalize these disciplines through their own educational programs and scholarship. They did so through both the study of classical authors and the creation of new work modeled on the prior achievements of the ancients. Over time, Renaissance humanists affected most aspects of learning and culture in contemporary Europe. In the main, they were unified less by any coherent set of political or theological beliefs (though nearly all humanists were Christians) than by a general orientation or style which stressed the direct engagement with primary sources and texts whenever possible. The direct encounter with the sources could have serious practical consequences, because it encouraged scholars to try harder to read their texts without preconceived ideas of what they meant. A famous example of the critical potential of humanist scholarship was the successful effort of the Italian humanist Lorenzo Valla (*c.*1401–1457) to prove that "the Donation of Constantine," the document believed to record the emperor Constantine's grant of imperial power to Pope Sylvester of Rome (r. 314–335), could not be genuine because the vocabulary and style of its text did not match the Latin used in Constantine's own time but that of a much later period (see Chapter 13 on the papacy and the restoration of the imperial title in the West).

AD FONTES

If there is one metaphor that captures the general spirit of what we have come to call the Renaissance, it is that of the *fontes*, a Latin word meaning sources or wellsprings. The Renaissance called for a return to the sources: **Ad fontes!**—"Back to the wellsprings!" In this metaphor, the historical transmission of knowledge is imagined as a river that flows down into the present from its wellsprings in the ancient past. The further this river journeys from its source, the muddier its water becomes, losing its original clarity and freshness. During the Renaissance, painters, sculptors, poets, and scholars exhorted each other to go back to the river's pure and undiluted source—to the artists, philosophers, and historians of classical Greece and Rome—and to drink directly from their works and writings. In this way, the fullness of their ancient wisdom could give life to one's culture in the present.

The centrality of this metaphor for the Renaissance derives from its ability to unify and explain the work of otherwise very different thinkers and movements between the fourteenth and sixteenth centuries. For example, consider the two figures of **Dante Alighieri** (1265–1321) and Niccolò Machiavelli (1469–1527). In many ways, these two men could not be more different. Dante was a poet, self-trained theologian, and philosopher of the early fourteenth century. Machiavelli was a historian, political theorist, and playwright of the early sixteenth century. Dante's most famous work, *The Comedy* (1314–1320), depicts the poet's trek through the three realms of Hell, Purgatory, and Paradise, and concludes with a mystical vision of the Incarnate God; Machiavelli's most famous work, *The Prince* (1516), presents itself as a strategic manual for current and prospective political rulers, and it offers a strikingly realist—some would say amoral—vision of politics. Dante's poem prophetically denounces the money-grubbing Roman papacy; Machiavelli's treatise cynically analyzes its use of religion for temporal gain. Dante thinks the Roman Empire was providentially ordained; Machiavelli thinks it was the corrupt devolution of the Roman republic. At the time of Dante's death, the printing press had not been invented, Europeans had not yet arrived in the "New World" of the Americas, and the Avignon Papacy (see Chapter 16) had just begun. By the time of Machiavelli, two centuries later, all these things had changed. The printing press had come into use between 1440 and 1450, the course to the "New World" had recently been charted by Columbus in 1492, and the Reformation was about to begin.

Despite their many differences, however, Dante and Machiavelli are unified by a shared commitment to the ideal of *ad fontes*. Both men regard ancient texts and authors as sources of light and nobility in an otherwise dark and drab world. Both depict their reading of these authors as a conversation between distant friends and equals. Dante presents himself in his *Comedy* as speaking directly with the ancient poets Homer, Virgil, and Ovid. Machiavelli similarly describes himself as "received with affection" by the ancient historians and statesmen; he is "not ashamed to speak with them and to ask them the reasons for their actions," and they "in their kindness answer [him]." And yet neither Dante nor Machiavelli reads the ancients simply as a means of escaping the realities of their present. Instead, the study of the ancients is what enables both men to understand and intervene in these realities. Both Dante and Machiavelli go back to the ancients in order to contribute to their own contemporary cultures. Dante's *Comedy* and Machiavelli's *Prince* are the results of this process; both texts witness to the power and range of the results produced by the Renaissance return *ad fontes*.

RENAISSANCE THEOLOGY

The reform and development of theology during the Renaissance similarly involved a return to ancient sources. A growing number of humanists, beginning in Italy and then spreading northward through Europe, began to advocate for a return to what Dante called the "evangelical doctrine" of the Gospels and the writings of patristic authors, the "Church Fathers" from the early Christian period (see Chapters 8 and 9). Humanist reformers such as Dante, Petrarch, and many others believed that the Roman Church's pursuit of temporal power and wealth had led to the harmful prioritization of papal decretals (legal decisions) over much richer biblical and patristic sources of spiritual inspiration. In a scathing letter addressed to the cardinals in Rome, Dante laments the contemporary Roman Church's self-interested abandonment of its own ancient authorities: "Gregory the Great lies among the cobwebs; Ambrose lies on the neglected shelves of the clergy; Augustine lies forgotten; and Dionysius, Damascene, and Bede have been thrown aside" for the sake of papal power and wealth.

In the life of the Church, then, the movement *ad fontes* registered the desire for political, ecclesial, and spiritual renewal—first in Italy, and soon after across the rest of Europe.

The first generations of Christian humanists focused on the study and recovery of Latin authors, as Greek texts were still largely unavailable, as was the knowledge of the language itself. By the early fifteenth century, however, this began to change. Aided by the financial and institutional support of Cosimo de Medici (1389–1464), the powerful ruler of Florence, Greek manuscripts that had been lost to the West for centuries were imported from Byzantine libraries, as were professional teachers and scholars of the Greek language. Within just a few decades, the Florentine monk Ambrogio Traversari (1386–1439) and the doctor-priest **Marsilio Ficino** (1433–1499) had become teachers and scholars of that ancient language. Traversari and Ficino soon began to publish critical editions and Latin translations of the works of Plato and Plotinus (the third-century Neoplatonist philosopher whose teachings had influenced Augustine and other Church Fathers), and the writings of the Greek fathers Clement of Alexandria, Athanasius, and John Chrysostom. Ficino also translated a number of mystical and pseudonymous texts (i.e., texts written under a pen name) from late antiquity, such as the *Hermetic Corpus*. The third-century *Hermetic Corpus* is a compilation of dialogues between the mythical Egyptian priest-king Hermes Trismegistus and one of his disciples about the nature of God and the stages of the human being's spiritual ascent.

The recovery of these Greek works inflected the already robust movement *ad fontes* toward a renewed Christian Platonism, which over the next two centuries would develop in a variety of different directions. In addition, by the end of the century, Christian humanists like Pico della Mirandola (1463–1494) and Johann Reuchlin (1455–1522) had learned Hebrew from Jewish scholars and rabbis and had begun to take an interest in the esoteric interpretation of the Hebrew scriptures known as the *kabbalah*. The recovery of Greek and Hebrew spurred further interest in biblical scholarship and motivated sixteenth-century scholars like Erasmus to produce more accurate translations and editions of biblical texts.

Erasmus (1469–1536)—Catholic priest, humanist, and reformer—was the first literary celebrity of the printed age. His extremely productive and illustrious career exemplifies the success of the *ad fontes* movement within theology and biblical studies. His scholarly works included no less than ten editions of the Church Fathers—among them Jerome, Ambrose, Augustine, Origen, and Basil of Caesarea—and the first ever printed edition of the Greek text of the New Testament, which he published in 1516. Erasmus' New Testament was also notable because it printed the original Greek text of the New Testament alongside Erasmus' new Latin translation. Offering a new translation based on a better edition of the Greek helped to "defamiliarize" the biblical text and encourage new insights into the meaning of the New Testament. Erasmus' rehabilitation of the works of the Fathers, combined with his attempt to publish an accurate version of the Greek New Testament text, was decisive in influencing the next two centuries of biblical scholarship, Christian piety, and theological controversy.

Like the Church Fathers, Erasmus' approach to theology was scriptural, literary, and somewhat open-ended. Indeed, instead of "theology," Erasmus preferred to speak of "the philosophy of Christ," a patristic phrase he rehabilitated for his own times. This "philosophy" was to be found primarily in the Gospels and Epistles of the New Testament, and its study was to lead to the reader's own spiritual transformation, her coming to share in the freedom and peace of Christ himself. While Erasmus held the great theologians of the thirteenth century in high esteem, he believed that later developments in Scholastic theology had ignored and neglected the philosophy of Christ. The Scholastic theologians of his own day, he thought, were obsessed with "thorny abstractions" that had little to do with Christ. For this reason, Erasmus was convinced that a return to the study of scripture by both laypersons and clergy alike was the "chiefest hope for the restoration and rebuilding of the Christian religion."

The increasing familiarity with these patristic writings among sixteenth-century

Catholic humanists like Erasmus, his friend Thomas More, and Juan de Vives, led to an evangelical and patristic vision of Catholicism. These Christian humanists avoided Scholastic formulations and de-emphasized popular "traditions" that had begun to be abused by clergy and lay alike, such as pilgrimages and the veneration of the saints. What is more, they did so by appeal to the authority of scripture and the writings of the Church Fathers in addition to using the tools of ancient rhetoric to mock and lampoon superstitions.

REFORMATION

The relationship between the Renaissance and the Reformation is a complicated one. On the one hand, the Reformation inherits from the Renaissance an emphasis on evangelical doctrine as the source and measure of Christian theology. It also inherits the reformist and anti-papal spirit of this return *ad fontes.* Yet the Reformation emphasis on the scriptural letter quickly hardens into a rigid dogmatism about its meaning in a way that is foreign to the pluralistic and open-ended approach of the earlier Christian humanists. Likewise, the anti-papal spirituality that was the common inheritance of most scholars worth reading between the fourteenth and the sixteenth century becomes, with the political portioning of Germany at the Diet of Speyer in 1526, an overtly political program—one tied up in developing notions of sovereignty and the nation-state. In general, it is fair to say that by the end of the sixteenth century, the competing theologies of the Protestant Reformers and the Roman Church had led to a more dogmatic, confessional, and therefore more combative approach to theology than that which had marked the prior two centuries of theological thought.

The insights of the Renaissance humanists were thus embraced by the Reformation only in part. The thought of Martin Luther (1483–1546), for example, represents a marriage between the scriptural focus of Renaissance Christian humanists and the Scholastic theology of the *via moderna* that these same humanists had rejected (see Chapter 16). The Reformers Ulrich Zwingli (1484–1531) and John Calvin (1509–1564), likewise, owe much to Erasmus' spiritual understanding of Christian thought and practice (see Chapter 19). But where Erasmus is happy to allow for a range of more and less imperfect practices within one church (so long as those with less pure belief are encouraged to purify their faith as much as they can), such is not the case for Zwingli and Calvin. They tend to insist that every member of the church must understand and practice the faith at the level that, on Erasmus' understanding, could only be expected of the spiritually mature. The Roman Church, likewise, attempted to harden its own lines of differentiation from the Protestant churches; by doing so it unfortunately turned its back on many of the most insightful and important ideas of the Renaissance humanists. The Roman Church will arguably not return to pick up and develop these ideas for another 400 years, when another "return to the sources" movement will renew Roman Catholicism at the Second Vatican Council (see Chapter 24).

Key Terms

ad fontes	Dante Alighieri	Marsilio Ficino
Cicero	Erasmus	*studia humanitatis*

Study Questions

1. The homeland of the Renaissance was north Italian city-states like Florence and Pisa. How did their distinctive political culture come to be, and why was that a favorable soil for what became the Renaissance?

2. "Renaissance humanism" is rooted in the ideal of "humane studies" popularized in ancient Rome by Cicero. Why did Cicero think the *studia humanitatis* were so important?

3. Dante and Machiavelli were writers and thinkers of very different outlooks. Exactly how did they differ? What does this chapter try to emphasize that they also had *in common*?

4. The "return to the sources" (*ad fontes*) began with a recovery of classical Latin literature. What other two ancient languages were also recovered, and what were their respective attractions?

5. Erasmus, Zwingli, and Calvin were all "humanists" and religious reformers. How did Zwingli's and Calvin's understanding of reform differ from that of Erasmus?

Works Consulted/Recommended Reading

Eire, Carlos M.N. 2016. *Reformations: The Early Modern World, 1450–1650*. New Haven, CT: Yale University Press.

Nauert, Charles G. 2006. *Humanism and the Culture of Renaissance Europe*. New York: Cambridge University Press.

Stinger, Charles. 1977. *Humanism and the Church Fathers: Ambrogio Traversari (1386–1439) and Christian Antiquity in the Italian Renaissance*. Albany, NY: State University of New York Press.

Wind, Edgar. 1967. *Pagan Mysteries in the Renaissance*. Revised edn. New York: W.W. Norton.

Chapter

18

MARTIN LUTHER

TIMELINE

1483	Martin Luther is born in Eisleben, Germany.
1504–1505	Luther enters a monastery and is ordained a priest.
1512	Luther begins his career as professor of biblical studies at the University of Wittenberg.
1517	Luther posts his *95 Theses* on the door of the Wittenberg Castle Church calling for a debate on the issue of indulgences.
1519	Luther and John Eck debate at Leipzig and Luther publicly denies the authority of the pope.
1520	Luther writes several documents, including *On the Babylonian Captivity of the Church* and *Christian Liberty*, which summarize his theology and describe his call to reform.
1521	Luther is formally excommunicated by the pope.
1521	The Holy Roman Emperor Charles V issues the Edict of Worms, declaring Luther an outlaw.
1524–1525	The Peasants' Revolt.
1525	Luther marries Katharina von Bora.
1529	Six Lutheran princes protest the agreements made at the Second Diet of Speyer and thereby acquire the name *Protestant*.
1530	The *Augsburg Confession* is signed.
1546	Luther dies in Eisleben, the place of his birth.

Why are some Christians today known as Catholics and others identified as Protestants? To answer this question we need to look at the life of Martin Luther, a sixteenth-century monk and university professor. Luther's life was shaped by his struggle with a central question: How are humans saved? He believed he found the answer to that question in his reading and study of the Bible. However, the answer to this question became explosive when it led him to criticize the theology and practices of the church.

The call for reform has been—and continues to be—a constant element in the history of the church. We have already seen the spirit of reform working in the medieval monastic communities and the friar movement. In the sixteenth century, however, efforts at reform led to the fragmentation of the Roman church and the establishment of the Lutheran church (among others). This was a consequence Luther himself had neither intended nor foreseen. Although Luther called for change and reform, he did not see himself as a religious innovator, introducing new ideas and practices into the Christian tradition. He understood his criticisms as an attempt to "re-form" the church in accordance with the beliefs and practices of the early church.

Who was this person? Why did he have such a powerful effect on the church and society at large? This chapter will focus on Martin Luther. The following chapters will examine other reform movements, both Catholic and Protestant, which occurred during and immediately following Luther's life.

LUTHER'S EARLY LIFE

Luther was born on November 10, 1483, in the town of Eisleben, today located in northeastern Germany. At the time Luther was born, Germany did not yet exist and Eisleben was in Saxony, one of the many territorial states that formed the Holy Roman Empire. Luther's father, Hans, was from a family of peasants, but he turned to the mining business and eventually owned his own mine shafts and copper smelters. Hans had high hopes for his son and was very pleased when Martin received his master's degree from the University of Erfurt. Hans assumed his son would now prepare for a career in law. However, Martin's plans suddenly and unexpectedly changed. Luther was returning to the University of Erfurt after a visit with his parents when he was caught in a violent thunderstorm. A bolt of lightning threw him to the ground, and Luther cried out to the patron saint of miners: "Help me, St. Anne! I will become a monk!" A few weeks later, at the age of 21, Luther entered an order of the Observant Augustinians.

This decision may not have been as sudden and unexpected as it appears. When Luther was caught in the thunderstorm, he was returning to the university from a leave of absence, taken just one month after beginning his law studies. He vowed to become a monk, a holy vocation that he believed would most nearly assure his salvation, at a significant crossroads in his life. When his father reacted with fury at his decision, Luther reminded him that he could do much more for his family with his prayers as a monk than he could ever do with his wealth and position as a lawyer. As with many others in his day and time, Luther had chosen the holiest life one could lead in order to secure salvation for himself and others.

Luther took his vow seriously and appears to have been a very conscientious and dedicated monk. Only one year after entering the monastery, Luther was ordained as a priest. Shortly thereafter the leader of his order, John von Staupitz, selected him for

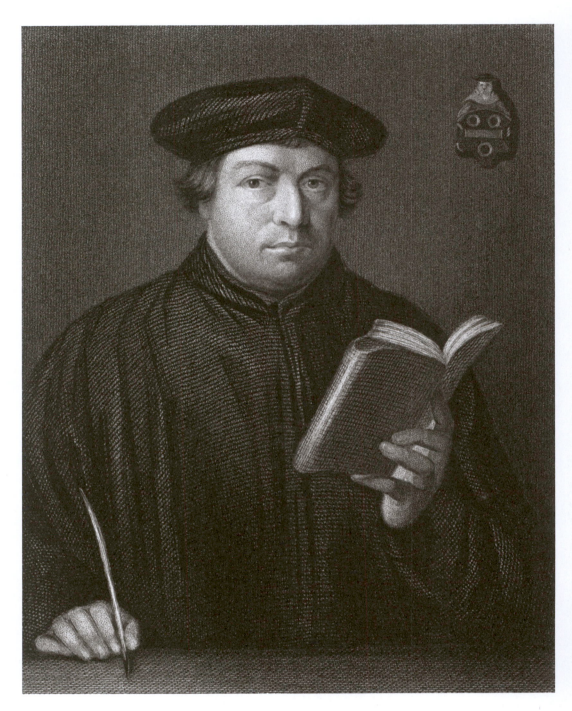

Figure 18–1 Martin Luther (1483–1546).

further education and a teaching career. Many years later, Luther declared, "If anyone could have gained heaven as a monk, then I would indeed have been among them" (WA 38,143). However, Luther's dedication to the holy life of a monk did not bring him the assurance of salvation he was seeking.

Some of Luther's doubts and questions can be traced to the nominalist theology he learned at the University of Erfurt. Nominalist theology saw salvation in terms of a contract between humans and God. If humans fulfilled their part of the contract by doing their best, then God would fulfill God's part by giving them grace. This was summed up in the phrase, "God will not refuse grace to those who do what is within them." Humans could not achieve salvation on their own, but if they did their best, God would graciously grant them the grace they needed to be saved. This understanding of salvation caused Luther incredible anguish and despair. He constantly wondered whether he had done his best. He saw himself as a poor, miserable sinner and God as a holy and righteous God. How could he ever do enough to earn the grace he needed to be saved?

The church offered grace and hope to sinners in the sacrament of Penance. As a monk, Luther confessed his sins daily, but this did not bring him peace. Grace was offered in the sacrament, but had he done his best? Had he confessed all his sins? Was he truly sorry for his sins? Tormented by these questions, Luther came dangerously close to the unforgivable sin of despair. His confessor was finally driven to say, "God is not angry with you, but you are angry with God" (LW 54:15; WATr 1,47).

JUSTIFICATION BY GRACE THROUGH FAITH

Luther finally found peace with God through his study of the Bible. In 1512, Luther began his career as professor of biblical studies at the University of Wittenberg, a new school with only a few hundred students. His lectures during the next few years (on the Psalms, Romans, Galatians, and Hebrews) indicate that Luther experienced a gradual change in his understanding of God and God's relationship to humanity. This new view can be summed up in the phrase *justification by grace through faith*. It may be helpful to look at each element of this phrase in detail.

Justification means "to be put right with God." This was Luther's central question: How can miserable, sinful humans "be put right with" a holy, righteous God? Years later, he said that he found the answer to that question through a new understanding of the righteousness of God. The righteousness of God originally terrified him because he understood it to refer to the holiness and perfection of God, and he hated this righteous God who punishes unrighteous sinners. As he studied Paul's letter to the Romans, however, he came across the phrase, "The one who is righteous will live by faith" (Romans 1:17). Luther said that righteousness here does not refer to a quality that God possesses in order to judge people but to a gift God gives in order to save people. Luther later referred to this as **passive** or **alien righteousness** because it is *God's* righteousness (and not their own) that justifies people before God. Salvation does not depend on their own goodness or righteousness, but on God's righteousness, freely and lovingly given to sinners (LW 34:336–7; WA 54,185–6).

Justification is therefore *by grace*; it is a free gift from God. As sinners, humans do not deserve it, and they can do absolutely nothing to earn it. Luther rejected nominalist theology with its call to "do what is within you," and he responded that justification is by grace *alone*. Humans do nothing to justify themselves before God. How, then, does God justify sinners? Through faith in Christ. Humans are saved by what God has done for them in Christ, not by what they do themselves. If people continue to bring their works before God, seeking to be saved by them, then they really do not have faith in what God has done for them in Christ. They need to depend completely and entirely on Christ, not on what they do.

Luther argued that even faith in Christ is not something people do. In other words, faith does not come because people try as hard as they can to believe. Luther described faith as a response to the Word of God, and that response is a gift from God. Luther understood the Word of God as pre-eminently Christ himself (John 1:1), but he also used this phrase to refer to preaching about Christ or to the Bible as a written testimony to Christ. However, Luther did not understand faith in Christ as assent to certain ideas or propositions about Jesus. It is much more than that. Thus, faith might better be translated as trust, the willingness to risk anything and everything for Christ. For Luther, the central question was no longer, "Have I done what is within me?" Luther now asks: "Where do I place my ultimate faith and trust? In myself? Or in Christ?"

THE INDULGENCE CONTROVERSY

Luther may have found the answer to his religious dilemma, but this does not explain how this brilliant but relatively obscure professor became a man known to popes and princes in his own day and acknowledged for his influence today, 500 years later. His fame stems from his attack on the sale of indulgences, a practice associated with the sacrament of Penance. Penance was composed of several elements: **contrition** (sorrow for sin), confession of sin to a priest, **absolution** (forgiveness for the guilt associated with sin), and **works of satisfaction** (to remove the penalties or consequences of sin). These works might involve special prayers, fasting, pilgrimages, or giving alms (money) to the poor. They were called works of satisfaction because they were intended to provide satisfaction or compensation for sin. If these penalties were not paid in this life, then they would be in the next—in purgatory. Purgatory is a place or state following death in which sinners destined for heaven undergo the punishment still remaining for forgiven sins and thereby are purged in order to be made ready for heaven.

According to the theology of the church, indulgences were only applied to the last stage in Penance, works of satisfaction. This meant that the sinner should still feel sorrow for sin, confess the sin, and receive forgiveness for the guilt associated with the sin. Indulgences released people from the penalties or works of satisfaction they still owed by drawing on the surplus good works of the saints and of Christ. These good works formed a **treasury of merit** under the control of the pope. When an indulgence was granted, the pope transferred these excess merits to the repentant sinner. Thus, for example, a sinner might receive an indulgence to offer prayers and alms instead of a pilgrimage as her work of satisfaction, and the merits of Christ and the saints would make up the deficiency.

Unfortunately, this practice of granting indulgences became vulnerable to abuse, especially as a means of raising funds. In 1517, Pope Leo X authorized Archbishop Albrecht of Mainz to sell a special indulgence throughout much of northern Germany. The proceeds for this indulgence were to be used to build St. Peter's Basilica in Rome and to pay the debts Albrecht had accumulated in acquiring the office of archbishop. In his instructions to the indulgence sellers, Albrecht claimed that the indulgences would remove guilt as well as punishment, persons already in purgatory could be released, and those who contributed money on their behalf need not be contrite or confessed.

The *95 Theses*

Luther became involved in the issue of indulgences because a Dominican friar named Johann Tetzel was selling this special indulgence just across the border of Saxony, and some of Luther's own parishioners were purchasing it. As a professor and priest, Luther decided to address this issue by calling for a discussion of indulgences in a public university debate. On October 31, 1517, Luther followed the usual practice for announcing public debates and posted his *95 Theses* on the door of the Wittenberg Castle Church. These theses were written in Latin, the language of the educated class, and were intended for an academic audience. The academic character of this debate changed when Luther's *95 Theses* were translated into German, the vernacular, and were rapidly disseminated by means of the printing press. Soon his *95 Theses* were being discussed and debated by people throughout the Holy Roman Empire and beyond.

Why did the *95 Theses* have such an impact? Luther clearly and powerfully expressed the reservations and questions that many others had regarding indulgences. He attacked the practice of selling indulgences on both theological and moral grounds, as indicated by the following examples:

> Thesis 36: Any truly repentant Christian has a right to full remission of penalty and guilt, even without indulgence letters.
> Thesis 43: Christians are to be taught that the one who gives to the poor or lends to the needy does a better deed than the one who buys indulgences.
> Thesis 82: Why does not the pope empty purgatory for the sake of holy love and the dire need of the souls that are there if he redeems an infinite number of souls for the sake of miserable money with which to build a church?
> Thesis 86: Why does not the pope, whose wealth is today greater than the wealth of the richest king, build this one basilica of St. Peter with his own money rather than with the money of poor believers?
> (LW 31:25–33 [some changes in translation]; WA 1:233–238)

Luther identified the last two questions as questions that were being asked by ordinary lay people. They would certainly have received hearty approval from those Germans who felt resentment and anger because the pope was taking money from them to build a church in Rome. Whereas strong central governments had developed in England, France, and Spain, the Holy Roman Empire was an empire in name only. It was actually a loose union of many independent states, unable to resist the financial demands of the Renaissance popes who needed to raise money for their building projects and art collections. However, Luther's criticisms about the church went deeper than German complaints about the pope's financial demands. He began by raising theological and moral questions about the current practice of selling indulgences, but soon he would raise more challenging questions about the authority of the pope himself.

The Leipzig Debate

In summer 1519, Luther was engaged in a heated debate with John Eck, a fellow professor and theologian. Representatives of the church had already challenged Luther's criticism of indulgences by appealing to the authority of the pope. Luther therefore prepared for this debate by studying the decrees establishing the authority of the papacy. This research led him to question the pre-eminence and infallibility of the pope. In the course of the debate, Eck confronted Luther with the traditional arguments for the authority of the pope and then declared that anyone who denied this authority agreed with Jan Hus, the reformer who had been burned at the stake for heresy by the Council of Constance in 1415.

   Luther initially denied that he was a Hussite, but during a break in the proceedings he read Hus' statements on the church and was surprised to discover that he agreed with him. Luther returned to state that many of Hus' declarations were not heretical and that he should not have been condemned by the Council of Constance. Eck thus succeeded in having Luther publicly deny not only the authority of the pope but also the authority of the councils of the church. Thus, the controversy over indulgences, a specific practice of the church, had become a controversy over church authority.

Luther's Excommunication

John Eck traveled to Rome with notes on the Leipzig Debate and condemnations of Luther by the universities of Cologne and Louvain. In June 1520, a **papal bull**, a formal document issued by the pope, was published in Rome. This bull gave Luther 60 days to recant (formally deny his statements) or be excommunicated along with his followers. The bull, according to custom, called for the burning of Luther's books. Students and faculty at the University of Wittenberg responded by burning books of church law and Scholastic theology. In an act of defiance, Luther also threw the papal bull that had condemned him into the flames. In January 1521, Luther was formally excommunicated by the pope.

Writings of 1520

Throughout these events, Luther continued to write, composing three very significant works in the year 1520. In his *Address to the Christian Nobility of the German Nation,* he called on the German princes and rulers to enact the reforms that church officials refused to undertake. He defended their right to do so by outlining his doctrine of the priesthood of all believers. In this doctrine, Luther said that all Christians are made priests by Baptism, faith, and the gospel, but not all are called to exercise that office in the church. If church officials fail to reform the church, however, then Christian princes have the right to do so by virtue of their Baptism.

   In his next treatise, *On the Babylonian Captivity of the Church,* Luther argued that the sacraments, especially the Eucharist, were being held "captive" by the church. Luther accepted the teaching about the real presence of Christ in the Eucharist (as opposed to a spiritual or figurative presence) because Jesus referred to the bread and wine as his body and blood. Luther, however, denied **transubstantiation**, the transformation of the bread and wine into the body and blood of Christ. This doctrine used concepts from the philosophy of Aristotle to describe how the bread and wine can continue to look, taste, and feel the same even after this change has occurred. According to the doctrine of transubstantiation, the substance (underlying reality) of the bread and wine changes into the substance of the body and blood of Christ, while the accidents (outer appearance) remain the same. Luther rejected this on the grounds that it is not biblical and that it relies on Scholastic philosophy. Luther concluded that one should simply accept Jesus' words in faith and not attempt to use philosophy to describe or explain them. This agreed with Luther's general understanding of the sacraments in terms of the Word and faith; a Word of promise is offered in the sacrament and accepted by faith.

At first glance, Luther's understanding of sacraments appears to conflict with the practice of infant Baptism. How can an infant hear and accept the Word in faith? If faith is so important, would it not make more sense to baptize believing adults? Luther rejected this argument, in part because the church had been baptizing infants for centuries. He was a conservative reformer who believed that the tradition of the church should be preserved unless it was contradicted by the Bible. In Luther's view, infant Baptism not only did not contradict the Bible, but it also proclaimed the central message of justification by grace through faith. The infant is given faith by God, completely apart from its own efforts and abilities. Faith is a gift, and nowhere is this seen more clearly than in the Baptism of an infant.

Many of Luther's contemporaries, including Erasmus, saw *On the Babylonian Captivity* as his most radical work to date, for in it Luther criticized the very heart of the church, its theology and practice of the sacraments. Of the seven sacraments of the church, Luther retained only two: Baptism and the Eucharist. At the beginning of his treatise, Luther still referred to Penance as a sacrament (because it was instituted by Christ and carries a Word of promise), but by the end of the treatise, he concluded that it is not a sacrament because it lacks a "visible sign" (like the water of Baptism or the bread and wine of the Eucharist). He continued, however, to regard private confession as a useful practice in the life of the Christian.

In Luther's third treatise, *Christian Liberty*, he described his theology of justification by grace through faith and outlined its consequences for living a Christian life. He posed the question: If justification is by faith alone, are Christians then free to live immoral lives? Luther answered this question by defining Christian freedom and describing the proper relationship between faith and works in the life of a Christian.

Diet of Worms

While Luther continued to write, his immediate political superior, Frederick the Wise of Saxony, was trying to negotiate a hearing for Luther before the princes and rulers of the Holy Roman Empire. Frederick had supported the election of the current emperor and persuaded him to promise that Luther would not be condemned without a hearing. Emperor Charles V therefore invited Luther to attend the next formal meeting, or **diet**, of the Holy Roman Empire of the German Nation. The emperor soon withdrew his invitation, however, when the pope's representative pointed out that Luther had already been condemned by the church and should not be granted a hearing by the laity. The tide changed yet again when the diet convened at Worms in 1521, and the rulers of various states and cities called on the emperor to bring Luther before them. They claimed that Luther's teaching had become so influential that condemnation without a hearing might lead to rebellion. The emperor once again invited Luther to attend the diet.

This political maneuvering would become commonplace in the years to come and was a significant factor in the success of the Lutheran Reformation. Although Charles V had inherited the right to rule over a substantial portion of Western Europe (Spain, Austria–Hungary, parts of Italy, and the Netherlands), he was strongly opposed by the other European powers, especially the popes and the king of France. The Ottoman Turks also presented a significant military threat as they pressed up the Danube and into Charles' Austrian lands. Faced with the daunting task of ruling an extensive empire without the benefit of modern communication or transportation, Charles was forced to compromise with the German princes again and again. His pre-occupation with other threats meant that Charles could never fully devote himself to the religious and political divisions developing within the Holy Roman Empire.

These divisions would soon become apparent when Luther arrived at the Diet of Worms. Luther was hoping for an opportunity to present and defend his views, but those hopes were quickly dashed. As he stood before the assembly, a representative of the archbishop of Trier pointed to a pile of books and asked Luther two questions: Had he written these books? Was there a part of them he would now choose to recant? Momentarily taken aback, Luther asked for some time to consider his answer. He appeared before the imperial diet on the following day and this time his answer was clear and unequivocal:

> Unless I am convinced by the testimony of the Scriptures or by clear reason (for I do not trust either in the pope or in councils alone, since it is well known that they have often erred and contradicted themselves), I am bound by the Scriptures I have quoted and my conscience is captive to the Word of God. I cannot and will not retract anything, since it is neither safe nor right to go against conscience. May God help me! Amen.
>
> (LW 32:112–3; WA 7,838)

Figure 18–2 *Luther at the Diet of Worms*, engraving based on painting by Émile Delperée (1850–1896).

Luther's declaration that he would not recant was followed by several days of unsuccessful meetings and negotiations. He finally left the city, and soon after the emperor issued the **Edict of Worms**, declaring Luther an outlaw and subject to capital punishment. Luther the monk and professor was now a heretic and outlaw. At the Leipzig Debate, Eck had compared Luther to Jan Hus, the reformer condemned and killed by the Council of Constance. How would Luther avoid meeting the same fate?

EXILE AND RETURN

On his way home from the Diet of Worms, Luther's wagon traveled down an empty road in the woods. Suddenly, armed horsemen attacked the wagon, his companions fled, and he was dragged away by his assailants. As word of his capture spread, many thought that they had heard the last of Luther. However, Luther's "kidnapping" had been arranged by his ally and ruler, Frederick the Wise of Saxony. To prevent discovery, Luther grew a beard, exchanged his monk's habit for the attire of a knight, and adopted the name Junker Jörg (Sir George). The protection Luther received from some of the German princes, especially Frederick of Saxony, ensured his continued survival. He would spend the next ten months hidden at Elector Frederick's castle, the Wartburg.

Wartburg Castle

Luther struggled with ill health and depression during his exile at Wartburg Castle and yet these were some of the most productive months of his life. In addition to publishing over a dozen books, Luther translated Erasmus' Greek text of the New Testament into German. This translation was so influential and widely read that it helped to create the modern German language. Luther translated the New Testament into German because he believed that scripture was the sole authority in matters of faith and that all Christians should be able to read it in their own tongue.

In his Preface to the New Testament, Luther offered guidance on the proper way to read and interpret scripture. He admonished Christians to properly distinguish between the law (the Commandments of God) and the gospel (the promises of God). The law (which is found throughout the Bible, including the New Testament) condemns people, shows them their sin, and prepares them to receive the good news of the gospel. Keeping in mind that distinction between law and gospel, Luther emphasized once again that people are not saved by doing the works of the law but by trusting the promises of the gospel.

Issues in Moral Theology: Martin Luther

Luther on Morality

Martin Luther's theology led him to rethink the nature of Christian morality. His call for "scripture alone" rejected a morality based on reason alone in favor of a morality based on the divine commands found in the Bible. His call for "faith alone" rejected the notion that we become good by doing good acts. Rather, we are "made right" by grace through faith.

Three points stand out in Luther's moral doctrine. First, it is oriented to the individual, who is utterly fallen and in the grip of powers beyond one's control.

When we have faith, we recognize our impotence and entrust ourselves to God. The experience of God's undeserved grace frees us in gratitude to serve others, without exception. The love we have for others comes from God, not from ourselves.

Second, since all are fallen and saved apart from their merits, there is no value in one way of life over another. Celibacy is not a higher or holier way of life than marriage. Luther's affirmation of "the priesthood of all believers" was therefore, according to philosopher Charles Taylor, "an affirmation of ordinary life." When Luther declared that all "callings" were equal, he took the concept of a religious vocation out of the monastery and into people's homes and work lives. Your work, whatever it is, is a calling to serve your neighbor (perhaps paradoxically, discrediting celibacy to the benefit of marriage had an unintended effect of depriving women of the opportunity for education, leadership, and writing that the convent offered, and restricted them to the roles of wife and mother).

Third, Luther taught that God authorized social institutions, such as the state and the family, in order to curb and limit human sinfulness. Obedience is therefore owed to those in governmental authority, and those who exercise authority should see their work as a sacred vocation within the secular order.

Return from Exile

As Luther continued to write and translate at Wartburg Castle, he heard disturbing reports of violence and upheaval in Wittenberg. Some of his friends and colleagues, in particular a fellow professor and priest named Carlstadt, had begun implementing Luther's reforms, creating considerable unrest in the process. On Christmas Day 1521, Carlstadt celebrated the Mass without wearing the traditional robes and vestments, delivered parts of the liturgy in German instead of Latin, and distributed both bread and wine to the assembled worshippers, instead of bread alone. Luther agreed with these reforms, at least in principle, but he was disturbed by the coercive manner in which they were carried out. He was especially troubled by episodes of **iconoclasm**, or image breaking, in which statues, stained glass, and paintings were forcibly destroyed or removed from churches. He was also concerned that others were implementing reforms without consulting him and without regard for proper order and authority.

The town council of Wittenberg, seeking leadership and guidance, invited Luther to return. When he informed Frederick the Wise of the council's request, Frederick responded that he could not protect Luther if he came out of hiding. Luther returned to Wittenberg despite the warning and preached a series of sermons declaring that reform should be accomplished by persuasion and love, not by violence and force. He argued that faith must come freely, without compulsion, and that reform inevitably will follow when the Word of God is preached and believed. His call for moderation and patience was heeded, and order was restored in Wittenberg.

The Peasants' Revolt

A few years later, another group tried to push Luther's call for reform in a more radical direction. In 1524 and 1525, a group of peasants in southern Germany appealed to Luther's ideas in their call for economic and social justice. The princes had consolidated their power by imposing greater taxes and services on the peasants and displacing local law codes, which guaranteed common land, in favor of Roman Law, which acknowledged only private property. In one of the most widely circulated lists of peasant demands, *The Twelve Articles*, the authors used Luther's language and ideas to prove the justice of their cause.

Luther responded with his own tract titled *An Admonition to Peace*. In this tract, Luther condemned the princes and lords for their unjust treatment of the peasants and declared that they were bringing revolt on themselves. Luther then addressed the peasants, and although he acknowledged the justice of many of their demands, he rejected their call for rebellion and violence. Luther stated that even unjust and cruel rulers are ordained by God and Christians are required to obey them. Christians may only disobey the proper authorities when the gospel is in jeopardy. Luther did not believe that was the case here, and so he objected to the peasants' appeal to the gospel and Christian freedom to support their social and economic demands. He concluded that there was nothing specifically Christian at stake in this revolt and called on the princes and peasants to negotiate a peaceful resolution.

Luther traveled about the countryside, admonishing the peasants to maintain the peace, but he was met with jeers and threats. Luther responded to the peasants' continued rebellion with his infamous treatise *Against the Robbing and Murdering Hordes of Peasants*. In this work, he called on the princes to give the peasants one last chance to negotiate. If the peasants did not lay down their arms, Luther proposed the following measures:

> Therefore let everyone who can, smite, slay, and stab, secretly or openly, remembering that nothing can be more poisonous, hurtful, or devilish than a rebel. It is just as when one must kill a mad dog; if you do not strike him, he will strike you, and a whole land with you.
>
> (LW 46:50; WA 18,358)

This tract was published just as the princes were killing the peasants by the thousands, even those who had surrendered or been taken prisoner. Luther was criticized for this treatise in his own day, but he maintained his position against rebels, especially those who claim the Word of God to justify their rebellion. Luther's response to the Peasants' Revolt clearly demonstrated that he did not equate social, political, or economic reform with his call for religious renewal.

LUTHER'S MARRIAGE

In 1525, at the peak of the Peasants' Revolt, Luther took the sudden and unexpected step of marrying a former nun. Although Luther had taught for several years that celibacy and monastic asceticism were contrary to the Bible and that priests, monks, and nuns should be free to marry, he had not indicated any desire to do so himself. His change of heart was precipitated by the plight of Katharina von Bora, one of several nuns he had helped smuggle out of a Cistercian convent two years earlier. By 1525, Luther had found homes or husbands for all of the women but Katharina. At the age of 26, Katharina's chances for marriage were slim, and after several potential suitors proved unacceptable, she offered to marry Luther himself. Luther accepted her offer

Figure 18–3 Portraits of Martin Luther and Katharina von Bora, Lucas Cranach the Elder (1472–1553).

in order to provide his father with grandchildren, to spite the pope who forbade clerical marriage, and to witness to his convictions before his martyrdom.

Luther's anticipated martyrdom never occurred, and the marriage he entered into at the age of 42 would last until his death two decades later. Although Luther declared that he felt neither "passionate love" nor the "burning" of desire when he married, genuine affection and love developed between husband and wife (LW 49:117; WABr 3,541). Luther and Katharina had six children, four of whom survived into adulthood. Katharina managed the household, which included several relatives, student boarders, and frequent guests. Money was a constant concern, especially given Luther's reckless generosity. Katharina took charge of the family's finances and proved to be a shrewd businesswoman who supplemented the family's income by farming, brewing beer, breeding pigs, and taking in lodgers.

THE PROTESTANTS

In the years following Luther's marriage, the division between those who accepted his reforms and those who did not continued to widen. In 1526, the First Diet of Speyer decided that until a council could be held to discuss recent religious developments, each German prince was free to act as he saw fit before God and the emperor. Some princes supported Luther while others remained loyal to the

Roman church. This compromise was challenged three years later when the majority of princes at the Second Diet of Speyer declared that Lutheranism would be tolerated only in those areas where it could not be suppressed without violence. The diet further decided that religious liberty must be extended to Catholics in Lutheran lands, but the same liberty would not be given to Lutherans in Catholic lands. Six Lutheran princes protested this arrangement and thereby acquired the name **Protestant.** This attempt to re-establish Catholic faith and practice throughout Germany failed and Germany was divided into two camps: Catholic and Protestant.

Emperor Charles V came to Germany in the following year (1530) to preside over the Diet of Augsburg, a meeting of German rulers summoned for the purpose of resolving the religious question. Luther was not permitted to attend this meeting since the Edict of Worms was in effect, and he was still considered an outlaw. His friend and colleague Philip Melanchthon represented the Lutheran position and drafted a statement of faith known as the *Augsburg Confession.* Melanchthon hoped for a reconciliation between Catholics and Protestants, and thus he stressed their common ground. The differences between the two parties were too deep to be resolved in this way, however, and the *Augsburg Confession* was rejected not only by Catholics but also by certain Protestants. The Protestants of Switzerland and the south German cities submitted their own statements of faith, while the Lutherans signed the *Augsburg Confession.* To this day, the *Augsburg Confession* remains an important statement of Lutheran doctrine.

At the conclusion of the diet, Charles V ordered all Protestant territories to return to traditional religious practices by the following year or prepare for war. He was not able to act on his threat when the year ended, but eventually he did engage the Protestant princes in battle. Neither side achieved a decisive victory, and finally they were forced to reach a compromise.

In 1555, after 25 years of conflict, the Peace of Augsburg established the principle that each prince was free to choose either the Roman Catholic or the Lutheran tradition. This was not religious freedom in the modern sense, however, for all the subjects of the prince were expected to follow the religion of their ruler. Those who did not share the religion of their prince were permitted, after selling their property, to migrate to another territory. As a result of this agreement, most of southern Germany remained Catholic while northern Germany adopted Lutheranism. The Lutheran faith eventually spread beyond Germany to Scandinavia, where it displaced Catholicism as the established church.

THE LUTHERAN CHURCH

Although the most dramatic events of his life were behind him after 1525, Luther spent the next 20 years working with his supporters to form the Lutheran church. What structure or organization should this new church have? Luther was inclined to locate power in local, independent congregations, but he concluded that they did not have the resources to deal with the problems facing the reform movement. He was unable to maintain the traditional episcopal structure in which bishops exercise authority, in part because the bishops had generally remained loyal to the Roman church. In addition, he was persuaded that the term *bishop* in the New Testament did not refer to a distinct office but to every pastor. Luther finally called on the princes to function as "emergency bishops" and assume responsibility for the work of reorganizing the church. However, Luther did not live to see the Peace of Augsburg and the establishment of the Lutheran church in Germany and Scandinavia.

Luther was primarily concerned with the preaching and worship life of the new church, not its structure. He believed the true church was found where the Word was truly preached and the sacraments rightly administered. He did not think he was establishing this church for the first time or even re-establishing it after years of neglect. On the contrary, he believed that the true Christian church had existed without interruption from the time of the apostles to his own day. Thus, despite his criticisms of the Roman church, Luther held that God had preserved the true church—through the preaching of the gospel and the administration of the sacraments—even under a church structure that had erred in many ways. Luther did not identify the church with a particular structure or organization but with a community of believers called by God. Those who responded to the Word in faith were the true but hidden church.

Luther believed, however, that the true preaching of the Word and the proper administration of the sacraments were being obscured by the current practices and structures of the Roman church. He concluded that the Lutheran church required a good translation of the Bible, a catechism to instruct the young, a reformed liturgy to correct abuses in worship, and a hymnbook to inspire and instruct the people. Luther himself would fulfill each of these requirements (Bainton 1983).

The Bible

Luther translated the New Testament into German during his exile at Wartburg Castle and started his translation of the Old Testament after his return to Wittenberg. A translation of the entire Bible was not printed until 1534 and he continued to revise this translation until his death. Luther believed the church must be founded on the Word of God and this Word should be accessible to all believers in their own language.

The Catechisms of 1529

Luther thought that Christians also required instruction in the doctrines and practices of the church. To determine the current state of Christian belief and practice, Luther asked his new prince, Elector John of Saxony, to organize a formal visitation of churches in his territory. Appalled by the results of the visitations, especially the lack of religious knowledge among the common people, Luther composed two **catechisms** (manuals of Christian doctrine) to instruct believers. Luther was following an ancient tradition in doing so, for catechisms can be traced to the earliest days of the Christian church. Luther organized his catechisms around five elements: the Ten Commandments, the Apostles' Creed, the Lord's Prayer, Baptism, and the Eucharist. Luther wrote a *Large Catechism* for adults but his *Small Catechism*, written for children, had the greatest influence. Many Lutheran churches encouraged the practice of committing the *Small Catechism* to memory—a practice that still continues today.

Liturgy

Luther was a conservative reformer, inclined to maintain the status quo except where he felt it contradicted the gospel. This is evident in his reform of the liturgy. In the Mass, the priest offers the body and blood of Christ as a sacrifice to God. Luther objected to this on the grounds that it makes the Mass into a good work that humans perform for God. To emphasize the Word of promise that God offers in the sacrament, he changed the traditional Eucharistic prayer (with its reference to sacrifice) to a simple reading of the account of the Last Supper. However, since the prayers of the Mass were still in Latin, Luther feared that most worshippers would not understand the significance of the change. As a consequence, he translated the liturgy of the Mass into German. Luther maintained many of the traditional elements of the liturgy, but he emphasized proclamation of the Word and religious instruction through the sermon.

Lived Religion: Liturgy in the Early Reformation, 1540–1650

In 1526, Martin Luther composed the *Deutsche Messe* (German Mass) to replace the pre-Reformation Catholic liturgy. The new liturgy caused major changes in worship and belief, but not everything was different. Many of the prayers like the Collect, the *Kyrie* (Lord have mercy), the *Sanctus* (Holy, Holy, Holy), and the *Agnus Dei* (Lamb of God) were still there in their usual places. The priest wore vestments in the familiar seasonal colors, there were candles on the altar, and the order of the service was much the same, but now the Creed was sung as well.

Some things were different, however. Instead of worshipping in Latin, the whole service was in German, although some places still used Latin if the people there spoke that language. For the average person, German was preferable, so the entire service, including the readings from the scriptures and the sermon, was proclaimed in German. Hymns were sung by the entire congregation using familiar tunes. The use of music was very important to Luther, who was a fine singer and composed numerous hymns. Perhaps his most famous hymn is "A Mighty Fortress Is Our God" which is still sung today. Eucharist was celebrated every Sunday, blessing the bread and wine using the words of Jesus at the Last Supper. Both the bread and wine were given to the people, while previously they only received the bread.

Churches began to look different, too. Many of the statues and images were removed, and the altar was longer on the far wall, but was moved forward so that the priest faced the people and they could see and hear him clearly. Hard wooden pews were replaced by cushioned seats so the congregation was comfortable when listening to the sermon, which was preached from a large pulpit that was sometimes situated in the aisle so the preaching could be heard clearly.

Hymnbook

One of the most significant changes Luther made in the service was the active involvement of the congregation in the singing of hymns. The first German hymnal was published in 1524, containing four hymns written by Luther himself. Luther continued to write the words and occasionally the music for many other hymns, drawing on portions of scriptures (especially the Psalms) and Latin liturgical chants for inspiration.

In his most famous hymn, "A Mighty Fortress Is Our God," Luther adapted Psalm 46 to express his faith in the midst of struggle:

> God's Word forever shall abide,
> No thanks to foes, who fear it;
> For God himself fights by our side
> With weapons of the Spirit.
> Were they to take our house,
> Goods, honor, child, or spouse,
> Though life be wrenched away,
> They cannot win the day.
> The Kingdom's ours forever.

> (*Lutheran Book of Worship*, Hymn 229)

LUTHER'S DEATH AND LEGACY

In 1546, Luther traveled to Eisleben, the place of his birth, to settle a feud between the local rulers. Luther was 62 years old and had struggled with ill health throughout his life. He fell ill during this visit to his hometown and died of heart failure on February 18. A slip of paper found in his pocket summed up his central conviction that people are saved by grace alone: "We are beggars. That is true" (LW 54:476; WATr 5,318).

Luther's new understanding of justification by grace through faith and his efforts to reform the Catholic Church led to the division of the church in the west and centuries of conflict. During the twentieth-century ecumenical movement, however, representatives of the Catholic Church and Lutheran Churches met to discuss the theological issues that continued to divide them. This led to a historic document in 1999, the ***Joint Declaration on the Doctrine of Justification***, issued by the Lutheran World Federation (which includes the Evangelical Lutheran Church in America) and the Catholic Church (the Pontifical Council for Promoting Christian Unity in collaboration with the Congregation for the Doctrine of the Faith). In this document, the Lutheran World Federation and the Catholic Church acknowledged that they have not resolved everything that either church teaches about justification and that other issues still need further clarification (including ecclesiology, ministry, and the sacraments). However, they affirmed that they have reached "a consensus on basic truths of the doctrine of justification" and that the mutual condemnations of former times do not apply to the Catholic and Lutheran doctrines of justification as they are presented in the *Joint Declaration* (paragraphs 5, 13, 43). They affirmed a common understanding of justification:

> Together we confess: By grace alone, in faith in Christ's saving work and not because of any merit on our part, we are accepted by God and receive the Holy Spirit, who renews our hearts while equipping and calling us to good works.

> (para. 15)

Although some of those who participated in the proceedings disagreed with the formulation of justification in the *Joint Declaration*, the document has nevertheless advanced efforts at achieving unity between Catholics and Lutherans on this important matter.

Luther's influence is still felt today in his theological and biblical writings, his hymns, and the catechism he wrote to instruct children. His ideas and convictions have left their mark on the church that bears his name. Five hundred years after he posted his *95 Theses* and sparked the Protestant Reformation, Lutherans across the globe continue to be inspired by his commitment to scripture, faith in Christ, and God's grace.

Key Terms

absolution	iconoclasm	Protestant
Augsburg Confession	*Joint Declaration on the*	transubstantiation
catechism	*Doctrine of Justification*	treasury of merit
contrition	papal bull	works of satisfaction
diet	passive or alien	
Edict of Worms	righteousness	

Questions for Reading

1. Why did nominalist theology cause problems for Luther?

2. Why was Luther initially concerned about his salvation? What did Luther mean by justification by grace through faith and how did it resolve his questions about salvation? What are the implications of this doctrine today?

3. What did Luther mean by *justification by faith*? How did he come to this idea?

4. What was the indulgence controversy and how did it become a controversy over church authority?

5. How did Luther's *95 Theses* relate to the controversy over indulgences? How did this controversy become a controversy over church authority?

6. What was Luther's general understanding of a sacrament? How did this affect his views on Eucharist and Baptism? How would you respond to his description of the sacraments?

7. What do the events of Luther's life (the Diet of Worms, his exile at Wartburg Castle and return to Wittenberg, the Peasant's Revolt, and his marriage) tell you about his beliefs and his understanding of reform?

8. What is the origin of the word *Protestant*?

9. How did Luther define the true church? When and where does it exist?

10. What innovations did Luther make with respect to the Bible, the catechism, the liturgy, and the hymnbook? Why did he consider these changes necessary?

Works Consulted/Recommended Reading

Atkinson, James. 1968. *Martin Luther and the Birth of Protestantism*. Atlanta, GA: John Knox.

Bainton, Roland H. 1983. *Here I Stand: A Life of Martin Luther*. Nashville, TN: Abingdon.

Brecht, Martin. 1990. *Martin Luther: Shaping and Defining the Reformation 1521–1532*. Translated by James L. Schaaf. Minneapolis, MN: Fortress.

Edwards, Mark, and George Tavard. 1983. *Luther: A Reformer for the Churches*. Philadelphia, PA: Fortress.

Inter-Lutheran Commission on Worship. 1978. *Lutheran Book of Worship*. Minneapolis, MN: Augsburg.

Joint Declaration on the Doctrine of Justification. 1999. www.vatican.va/roman_curia/pontifical_councils/chrstuni/documents/rc_pc_chrstuni_doc_31101999_cath-luth-joint-declaration_en.html.

Kittelson, James M. 1986. *Luther the Reformer: The Story of the Man and His Career*. Minneapolis, MN: Augsburg.

Loewenich, Walther von. 1982. *Martin Luther: The Man and His Work*. Minneapolis, MN: Augsburg.

Luther, Martin. 1955–1986. *Luther's Works*. Edited by Jaroslav Pelikan and Helmut T. Lehmann. 56 vols. Philadelphia, PA: Fortress Press; St. Louis: Concordia Publishing House (LW above).

Luther, Martin. 1883–2009. *D. Martin Luthers Werke: kritische Gesamtausgabe*. Weimar: Hermann Böhlau (WA above).

Metzger, Bruce, and Roland Murphy, eds. 1991. *The New Oxford Annotated Bible with Apocrypha, New Revised Standard Version*. New York: Oxford University.

Nestingen, James Arne. 1982. *Martin Luther: His Life and Teachings*. Philadelphia, PA: Fortress.

Oberman, Heiko A. 1989. *Luther: Man between God and the Devil*. Translated by Eileen Walliser-Schwarzbart. New Haven, CT: Yale University.

Ozment, Steven. 1980. *The Age of Reform 1250–1550: An Intellectual and Religious History of Late Medieval and Reformation Europe*. New Haven, CT: Yale University.

Spitz, Lewis W. 1985. *The Protestant Reformation 1517–1559*. New York: Harper and Row.

Chapter

OTHER PROTESTANT REFORMERS

TIMELINE

1484	Ulrich Zwingli is born in the Swiss canton of St. Gall.
1509	John Calvin is born in Noyon, France.
1519	After successful preaching in several small parishes, Zwingli comes to preach at a major church in Zurich. This marks the beginning of his reform preaching.
1524–1525	German Peasants War.
1525	Public debate between Ulrich Zwingli and Conrad Grebel over the issue of infant baptism. Conrad Grebel and Felix Manz baptize George Blaurock and others upon a public confession of faith, marking the emergence of the Radical Reformation or Anabaptist movement.
1525	The theological leader of the Peasants' Uprising, Thomas Münzter, is tortured and executed.
1527	The Schleitheim Confession is drafted and endorsed by a group of Swiss Anabaptists.
1527	William Tyndale publishes a translation of large portions of the Bible in English.
1529	Zwingli and Luther debate their differences regarding theology and church reform at Marburg.
1531	Zwingli dies at the battle of Kappel, a conflict that broke out when an incident of iconoclasm got out of hand.

1533–1553	Thomas Cranmer, Archbishop of Canterbury, provides a stabilizing force for the English reform movement.
1534	King Henry VIII declares himself head of the church in England.
1534	John of Leiden takes power in Münster, leading to the establishment of a proto-communist theocratic community.
1535	Calvin begins his involvement in the Reformation and moves to Geneva.
1536	Menno Simons (namesake of the Mennonites) joins the Anabaptists.
1539	Calvin writes his famous Reply to Sadoleto in which he defended the principles of the Reformation.
1553	Queen Mary attempts to reverse England's reform movement and return the church to its pre-Reformation state.
1558	Queen Elizabeth I resumes the course of English reform and establishes the Church of England as it is known today.
1564	Death of John Calvin.
1670	Philipp Jakob Spener publishes *Heartfelt Desire for a God-pleasing Reform of the True Protestant Church*, an important text for Pietism.
1693	Jakob Ammann (namesake and founder of the Amish) leads an effort to reform the Mennonite church in Switzerland and South Germany.
1727	Count Nikolaus Ludwig Zinzendorf organizes the political and religious community of Herrnhut, which began as a settlement of persecuted Bohemian Brethren, or Moravians.
1732	Johann Conrad Beissel founds the Ephrata Cloister, a Protestant monastic community, in Lancaster County, Pennsylvania.
1738	John Wesley has his "Evangelical Conversion," a religious experience during which he reports feeling his "heart strangely warmed." The event is celebrated as "Aldersgate Day" in the Methodist Church.
1833	The Oxford Movement begins in the Church of England.

The Protestant Reformation involved more than Martin Luther, and Lutherans constitute only a portion of Protestant Christians today. Indeed, during the Reformation, a host of other figures played influential roles in reforming the church (often in ways distinct from Luther), and their efforts have resulted in Protestant denominations such as the Reformed, Presbyterian, Anglican, Episcopal, Methodist, and Baptist churches, just to name a few.

What are the differences among these Protestant Christians, and how did those differences come about? This chapter examines the Reformation beyond Luther in an attempt at answering this question. The chapter begins with "Reformed Christianity," which took a different shape from Lutheranism not only because of the distinct theological concerns of its leaders (Ulrich Zwingli and John Calvin), but also because it unfolded in a different political environment, namely, the Swiss Confederation (a precursor to modern-day Switzerland). From Reformed Christianity the chapter moves to the so-called "Radical Reformation," which as the name suggests involved those who sought to push reforming efforts to a radical extreme. This movement gave rise to Baptist, Mennonite, Amish, and Quaker churches, among others. The next section, on Pietism, similarly examines figures who sought to reform the church further than either the Lutheran or Reformed churches would. A final section on the English Reformation examines the distinctive manner in which reform took place in England.

THE SWISS REFORMATION

The Reformation in Switzerland was led by Ulrich Zwingli and John Calvin. In the sixteenth century, the Swiss Confederation, the precursor to modern-day Switzerland, was composed of 13 independent cantons without a central governing authority or a common language. Each canton, and even individual cities and towns, were governed by several elected councils (although not all citizens were eligible to vote). This political situation affected religious reform; while Luther looked to princes in the Holy Roman Empire for support, Zwingli and Calvin negotiated with city councils in Zurich and Geneva to achieve their reforms.

Ulrich Zwingli

Figure 19–1 Ulrich Zwingli (1484–1531).

Ulrich Zwingli was born on January 1, 1484 in the Swiss village of Wildhaus to a prosperous peasant family. He was prepared for the priesthood from a young age and educated in Scholastic theology and humanism at Bern, the University of Vienna, and the University of Basel. Renaissance humanism, with its emphasis on studying texts in the original languages, was a major influence on Zwingli and his study of the Bible. The humanist Erasmus produced a Greek New Testament which was used by both Zwingli and Luther. Zwingli was also influenced by Erasmus' understanding of the Christian faith as simple worship based on scripture and morality modeled on the life of Jesus. Erasmus' Neoplatonism, with its sharp separation of the spiritual and the material, would shape Zwingli's views on the Eucharist and his rejection of images.

Zwingli was ordained at the age of 22 and served as priest in Glarus and Einsiedeln. He continued to read and study the Greek and Latin classics, as well as the Bible and the writings of theologians such as Augustine and John Chrysostom. In 1519, he was called as a priest at the Great Minster (or major church) in Zurich. He began by preaching a series on the Gospel of Matthew, a departure from the usual practice of focusing on appointed texts using commentaries, and an innovation which reflected his biblical and humanist studies. He attacked practices which he regarded as unbiblical: indulgences, pilgrimages, clerical celibacy, and the honoring of saints. The implications of his preaching became clear in 1522 with the "Affair of the Sausages," when a printer and his workers broke the Lenten fast by eating sausages, a violation of both church and civic authority. Zwingli defended the men in a sermon, arguing that the Bible does not prohibit eating meat during Lent and Christians are free to fast or not as they choose. The town council agreed and established the precedent that the Bible alone would determine religious practices in Zurich. This was followed by a petition by Zwingli and other clergy in the Swiss Confederation calling for the bishop of Constance to end clerical celibacy, arguing that it was both unscriptural and widely ignored. Several of them, including Zwingli, were already married. When the bishop not surprisingly refused to do so, Zwingli publicly rejected his authority.

In 1523, the Zurich government sided with Zwingli by calling for a public disputation on religious reform. By insisting that the Bible and not tradition would be the only authority, and by claiming that town councils rather than a council of bishops could decide theological issues, they had already decided the question in Zwingli's favor. Zwingli's Sixty-Seven Articles of faith were accepted and the clergy in Zurich were required to preach from the Bible alone. However, the role of images in worship remained a contentious issue and there were several incidents of iconoclasm (the violent removal of sacred images). Zwingli supported the iconoclasts, based on the biblical commandment, "You shall not make for yourself an idol" (Exodus 20:4) and Neoplatonist philosophy which made a sharp distinction between spirit and matter. Zwingli understood this to mean that material objects (like images) would not help people to worship spiritually and in fact would become idols. In 1524, the city council called for the removal of all sacred images and ritual objects. By the following year, the Mass had been abolished, replaced by a simple meal of bread and wine that served to remember Christ's sacrifice.

Differing attitudes toward the Eucharist not only divided Catholics from Protestants, but also separated Protestant reformers from one another. This became clear in 1529 when Philip of Hesse tried to unite the various reform movements against Charles V, the Roman Catholic emperor of the Holy Roman Empire. He realized that a military alliance would depend on agreement on articles of faith, so he brought Swiss and German reformers together at his castle in Marburg. This led to a confrontation between Luther and Zwingli on the meaning of the Eucharist. Luther insisted that the body and blood of Christ were physically present "in, with, and under" the bread and wine, citing Jesus' words at the Last Supper: "This **is** my body." Zwingli countered that "is" should be understood as "signifies," offering as evidence the verse in John's Gospel: "It is the spirit that gives life; the flesh is useless" (John 6:63). Zwingli's biblical interpretation and his Neoplatonic conviction that the material cannot communicate the spiritual led him to affirm that Christ is not present in the bread and wine on the altar but in the hearts of the believers. Thus, Zwingli rejected the traditional doctrine of the "real presence" of Christ in the Eucharist, because Christ's risen body was present with the Father in heaven. Following Christ's words at the Last

Figure 19–2 Depiction of the Marburg Colloquy, in which Luther and Zwingli debate the Real Presence in the Lord's Supper, from Walter Hutchinson, *History of the Nations.*

Supper, "Do this in remembrance of me," Zwingli described the Eucharist as a memorial meal and a remembrance of Christ's sacrifice on the cross. Although the Marburg Colloquy ended with the reformers agreeing to 14 of 15 articles, their inability to come to a consensus on the Eucharist reflected larger theological disagreements and ultimately led to two distinct branches of the Protestant tradition: Lutheran and Reformed.

Zwingli was able to form alliances with other Protestants, however, including several Swiss cantons and some south German cities. In opposition to this, five of the Catholic cantons formed a "defense league," allied to both the pope and the Holy Roman Empire. Eventually, full-scale war broke out and Zwingli died on the battlefield at Kappel in 1531, defending the city which was inextricably tied to his vision of reform. Reformation in Switzerland continued after his death, most notably under the leadership of Heinrich Bullinger, Zwingli's successor in Zurich, and later under the guidance of John Calvin, the French reformer in Geneva.

John Calvin's Life

John Calvin was a second-generation reformer; he was only eight years old when Martin Luther posted his *95 Theses* in 1517. Calvin was therefore influenced by other

Figure 19–3 *John Calvin* (1509–1564), engraving by John Sartain, based on a painting by Hans Holbein the Younger.

Protestant reformers as well as humanism. However, Calvin created a theology, worship, and understanding of the Christian life that was uniquely his own and that had a major impact on a variety of Christian denominations as well as Western society.

Calvin was born in Noyon, France on July 10, 1509. His father was an administrator for the cathedral chapter (a group of clergy who assist the bishop) and his mother died when he was a child. His father originally intended a career in the church for Calvin and therefore he began studying philosophy in preparation for further study in theology. However, after a conflict with church authorities, his father changed his mind and decided that his son should pursue a more lucrative career in law. Calvin completed his legal studies in obedience to his father but after his father's death, he returned to the philosophical, literary, and biblical studies that he preferred.

At the University of Paris, Calvin studied the Greco-Roman classics, the Bible, the Church Fathers, and Luther. His friend Nicholas Cop was appointed rector of the university in 1533 and preached a sermon influenced by humanism and Lutheran theology. Given his association with Cop, and under suspicion that he was involved in writing the sermon, Calvin was forced to flee Paris in 1533. As persecution continued under the Catholic king Francis I, Calvin eventually had to leave France, never to return.

Calvin traveled to Basel and wrote the first edition of his theological masterpiece, the **Institutes of the Christian Religion**, published in 1536. It was intended to present clear instruction in the Christian faith, as well as to inspire devotion and piety. Calvin would revise and expand this work for the rest of his life, producing multiple editions in both Latin and French.

Leaving Basel, Calvin hoped to pursue a quiet, scholarly life in the reformed city of Strasbourg but he was forced to make a detour to the Swiss city of Geneva because of fighting between France and the Holy Roman Empire. What began as a brief stopover became his home for most of his life. Shortly before Calvin arrived, the city had voted to become a reformed city, expelled the Catholic bishop, and renounced control by neighboring Savoy. This was a declaration of both religious and political independence. Geneva's government was now under the control of four syndics (or mayors) and several councils elected by citizens. One of the key reformers in the city, William Farel, recognized Calvin as the author of the *Institutes* and convinced him that staying to reform Geneva was God's will. Calvin reluctantly agreed and as professor of Holy Scripture began the work of establishing the theology and practices that would guide the city. He wrote a catechism, a confession of faith, and a church ordinance that established rules for conduct. This soon brought him into conflict with the councils that governed the city and culminated in a dispute over who had the power to determine how and when the Eucharist should be distributed. The councils claimed that right for themselves and when Calvin and Farel asserted that the pastors had that authority instead, the Genevan city councils expelled them from the city.

In 1538, Calvin resumed his interrupted trip to Strasbourg and spent several happy years there, serving as pastor to the French refugees and marrying a widow named Idelette de Bure. However, Geneva was struggling without Calvin and when city councilors sympathetic to Calvin were elected, he was invited to return. Despite his sentiment "that there is no place under heaven of which I can have a greater dread," in 1541, Calvin returned to Geneva to continue the work that God had called him to do (Letter to Viret, March 1, 1541).

One of Calvin's first actions was to have the city councils approve his new church ordinance (or constitution) to govern faith and life in Geneva. He established a church structure that he believed was based on the New Testament and included four offices: pastors (who preached and performed the sacraments), teachers (who provided religious instruction), elders (lay people who helped to establish discipline in the community), and deacons (who cared for the sick and poor). The elders and pastors were members of the Consistory, an administrative body to oversee the spiritual and moral discipline of Geneva. He also wrote a catechism to teach the fundamentals of the Christian faith and a handbook for worship. These innovations reflected Calvin's deep conviction that purity of doctrine must be connected to purity of life.

As preacher and teacher, Calvin's influence in the city depended on his ability to educate, to persuade, and to establish the rules and organization for the city. His efforts to establish a biblical and godly community were often met with fierce opposition from the councils and residents of the city. Many native residents of Geneva also resented the influx of foreigners fleeing persecution for their Protestant beliefs and drawn to the city by Calvin's writings and reform. However, these refugees, many from France, helped Calvin to succeed and to make Geneva a model and inspiration for reform. He founded the Geneva Academy in 1559, which attracted students from all over Europe, many of whom became pastors and professors who spread the Reformed faith.

Calvin died on May 27, 1564, at age 55. He had asked to be buried in an unmarked grave so his burial site would not become a place of pilgrimage or honor. In death, as in life, his primary goal was to give glory to God.

John Calvin's Theology

Calvin's theology had several elements in common with Luther and Zwingli: the primacy of scripture, justification by grace through faith, and the two sacraments of Baptism and Eucharist. In order to understand the distinctive character of Calvin's theology, it will be helpful to refer to the comprehensive statement of his theology in the *Institutes of the Christian Religion*. The final 1559 edition of the *Institutes* consists of four books based on the Apostles' Creed: God the Father, Jesus Christ the Son, the Holy Spirit, and the Church.

Book One on "The Knowledge of God the Creator" begins with the assertion that knowledge of God and of ourselves are intimately related (I,i,1). It is only when humans know the wisdom, strength, and holiness of God that they can know their own folly, weakness, and corruption. He compares this to a person who thinks he or she knows light from looking only at earthly objects. This person does not really know what light is until he or she looks up at the brilliance of the sun. This sad state of affairs is not God's fault, but rather the result of Adam and Eve's sin. Adam (who represented all of humanity) was created good and in the image of God but he freely chose against God, implicating all of humanity in his sin. Thus, to know God is to know ourselves as both created good and fallen into sin. It is also to trust and honor the God who made us and who continues to provide and care for us.

But how does one gain this knowledge of God? Calvin argues that this knowledge is implanted in the human mind and displayed in the universe but it has been distorted by sin. All humans have some awareness of God but it has been corrupted into superstition and idolatry. So God has given us a teacher and guide in scripture, which Calvin compares to a pair of glasses that correct our blurry vision.

How are humans saved from sin? Book Two, on "The Knowledge of God the Redeemer in Christ," begins with a discussion of original sin and its effects. Calvin says that the root of Adam's sin was unfaithfulness or lack of trust in God's Word, and this led to pride and disobedience. The consequences of this first sin include the almost total obliteration of the image of God and original sin as the inherited corruption of the good nature created by God. As a result, humans no longer have the freedom of choice that Adam possessed, but only the freedom to sin. By recognizing the depths of our sinful condition, we are able to acknowledge with gratitude the salvation offered in Christ. Following Paul, Calvin describes Christ as the Second Adam. Since the root of Adam's sin was lack of faith in God's Word, salvation is found through faith in Christ, the Word of God. Adam's disobedience is corrected by Christ's obedience. The corruption of original sin is undone by **sanctification**, or being made holy. Thus, in Christ, God restores human nature and our creation in the image of God.

How does this restoration in Christ occur? Calvin addresses this question in Book III titled "The Way in Which We Receive the Grace of Christ." The answer is through the gift of the Holy Spirit, which unites us to Christ and by which we receive the benefits of all he has done for the salvation of humanity. The principal work of the Holy Spirit is faith in Christ which justifies or puts humans right with God. As with Luther, justification is by grace through faith and therefore a free gift. More than Luther, however, Calvin emphasizes the work of the Spirit in sanctification or making humans holy. He describes this in terms of rebirth or regeneration, a process that continues throughout life and brings the believer closer to the image of God.

It is in this context that Calvin discusses his famous (or infamous) doctrine of double predestination: the belief that God has chosen some for salvation (the elect) and others for damnation (the reprobate). It is important to note that Calvin did not invent predestination; Augustine developed this in his controversy with the Pelagians and versions of it can be found in most Western theologians after him, including Aquinas and Luther. Like Augustine, Calvin also believed predestination was found in scripture, in God's choice of Israel and specific individuals within Israel (e.g., Abraham, Isaac, and Jacob). Calvin appealed to other biblical references, especially "[God] chose us in Christ before the foundation of the world to be holy and blameless before him in love" (Ephesians 1:4). He therefore claimed that the goal or purpose of election was to be made holy (or sanctified) by the Holy Spirit. For Calvin and many of his followers, the doctrine of predestination was hopeful and reassuring. It affirmed that salvation was due to God's grace, it emphasized **God's sovereignty** or rule, and it inspired gratitude to God and love toward neighbor. Both in Calvin's day and since, criticism of this doctrine has focused on several issues, including the fact that Calvin went beyond single predestination (God chooses some to save) to argue for double predestination (God also chooses some to damn). His critics argued that this creates the terrible image of a God who creates people (the reprobate) only to damn them and the charge that it makes God the author of sin and a tyrant. In defending predestination, Calvin argued that it is revealed in scripture and that it affirms God's power and glory.

In Book IV, Calvin moves from the internal experience of grace in the individual to its external manifestation in the church, the sacraments, and the state. He makes a distinction between the invisible church of the elect and the visible church which includes the reprobate as well. The visible church is known by "the Word of God purely preached and heard, and the sacraments administered according to Christ's institution" (*Institutes*, IV.i.9). As seen in Geneva, Calvin also regarded discipline as crucial to the church in order to hold the members together and to bring sinners to repentance and restoration.

Calvin, Luther, and Zwingli all based their understanding of the Eucharist on Christ's words at the Last Supper: "This is my body, given for you; do this in remembrance of me," but they interpreted it differently. Luther emphasized "this **is** my body" and thus the real, physical presence of Christ's body; Zwingli emphasized "do this is remembrance of me" and thus a meal of remembrance and fellowship; while Calvin focused on "given for you" and thus the benefits of the meal for the believer. Calvin describes the Eucharist as a "spiritual banquet" where the bread and wine feed the bodies of believers while their souls are nourished by body and blood of Christ. Like Zwingli, he interpreted the words of the Apostles' Creed that Christ "sits at the right hand of the Father" to mean that Christ's body cannot be present everywhere. Calvin declared that in the Lord's Supper Christ's body is not "dragged from heaven" but the soul is united to Christ by the Holy Spirit and lifted up to heaven (*Institutes*, IV.xvii.31).

Calvin ends the *Institutes* by distinguishing between spiritual and civil government and declaring that both are given by God. The purpose of civil government is to protect the church and true religion while keeping peace among sinful humans. He says that rulers are representatives of God on earth and Christians owe even unjust ones obedience, but he does allow the possibility that God may raise up leaders (appointed officials or magistrates) to resist an ungodly king or prince.

John Calvin's Legacy

The reform movement led by Calvin quickly spread beyond Geneva, far surpassing the earlier Lutheran movement which was largely confined to the German territories and Scandinavia. Some of its success was due to its organizational structure, which did not depend on the support of a political leader. In his struggles with the city councils of Geneva, Calvin devised a church structure that could function independently and could survive even in countries (like France) where it faced persecution.

The spread of Calvinism had major implications for the development of modern Western society. In fact, it is often credited with contributing to the development of representative democracy and capitalism, although the nature and extent of its influence is hotly debated. In *The Protestant Ethic and the Spirit of Capitalism*, the sociologist Max Weber articulated his thesis that Calvin's emphasis on the doctrine of predestination led his followers to seek to demonstrate evidence of their election through worldly success and thus contributed to the development of capitalism. This thesis has been criticized, but Weber's book has influenced scholars trying to explain why

Figure 19–4 Plain church interiors became common in those portions of northern Europe influenced by Calvin and Zwingli. St. Pieter's Church, Utrecht, the Netherlands, Pieter Jansz Saenredam (1597–1665).

so many merchants and entrepreneurs were Calvinists. Some have pointed to Calvin's acceptance of loaning money at interest (a practice criticized by medieval Christian theology), his emphasis on the value of work in the world and social responsibility, or his concern for holy living and therefore the virtues of hard work and self-denial.

Calvin's influence on the development of representative democracy is also a major topic of discussion and debate. Calvin's views on civil government as well as his experience of working with elected city councils in Geneva influenced later Calvinists. In Geneva, Calvin sought to maintain a balance between the civil government (composed of several city councils and elected officials) and the church. His ideal government was a mixture of aristocracy and democracy in which a number of people, rather than one ruler, exercise power. However, he regarded the rulers as God's chosen representatives and therefore argued that only duly appointed officials could resist a ruler and then only when he demanded disobedience to God. His followers, especially those experiencing persecution, expanded the right of rebellion to all people against unjust and tyrannical rulers.

Calvin's impact on America can be traced to the Puritans, who were seventeenth-century English Calvinists. Their conviction that they were the chosen people of God is reflected in a 1630 sermon by the Puritan John Winthrop when he described the new Massachusetts Bay Colony as "a city upon a hill" (Matthew 5:14) and a model to the world. This phrase and the conviction behind it has contributed to "American exceptionalism," or the belief that the United States has a special (and often superior) history and mission in the world (see Chapter 23).

Calvin's most direct legacy can be found in the many Reformed denominations that look to his theology for inspiration and guidance. The Reformed movement began with Ulrich Zwingli and continued under the able leadership of Heinrich Bullinger, his successor in Zurich. In 1549, Calvin reached a formal agreement on the Eucharist with Bullinger, laying the foundation for a common Reformed tradition. This agreement adopts Zwingli's language of sign and remembrance but also affirms Calvin's understanding that the Eucharist communicates spiritual gifts to the elect by God's grace. Today, that tradition includes a variety of Presbyterian and Reformed denominations in the United States, including the Presbyterian Church (U.S.A.), the Presbyterian Church in America (P.C.A.), the United Church of Christ, the Christian Reformed Church in North America, and the Reformed Church in America. These denominations do not share a common confessional statement or church structure, and they differ widely on how closely they adhere to Calvin's theology. However, they share some typical characteristics including an emphasis on scripture, education, lay involvement in governing the church, and the motto *Ecclesia reformata, semper reformanda* (the church reformed, always reforming), meaning that reform is never completed once and for all, but is instead an ongoing project for the church.

Lived Religion: Liturgy in the Later Reformation 1650–1750

Martin Luther began the Reformation, but many other reformers developed liturgies as well. One such reformer was John Knox, who wrote the liturgy for the Presbyterian Church in Scotland.

Worship began with a confession of sin, and a prayer for pardon and absolution read by the minister. A metrical psalm using no instruments was sung, followed by a prayer for illumination, that God may open our hearts and show us mercy. This was followed by a reading from the Gospels; one chapter was usually read each Sunday. Next was the sermon, the longest and most important part of the service, in which the minister explained the Gospel.

Following the sermon, offerings were collected, followed by a prayer of thanksgiving, prayers of intercession for the ministers and for those in need. This part of the service concluded with the recitation of the Lord's Prayer by the entire community.

On the four Sundays of the year when the Lord's Supper was celebrated, the bread and wine were prepared while the Apostles' Creed was sung. The minister then said the words of institution, based on Jesus' prayer at the Last Supper, followed by a prayer thanking God for creation and redemption, and an exhortation that the community should make themselves worthy to receive. The Presbyterian Church did not believe the bread and wine were changed to the real body and blood of Christ. Instead, they celebrated the grace we have received in this life and the life we anticipate in Heaven. The community distributed the bread and wine among themselves, sitting around a table placed at the front of the church where the altar used to be. As the people received, the history of Christ's passion was read to them.

Following Communion, there was another prayer of thanksgiving, followed by Psalm 113 and the Aaronic blessing from Numbers 6:24–26.

THE RADICAL REFORMATION

Although the Reformation is dominated by figures such as Luther, Calvin, and Zwingli, it would not have had such significance and scope were it not for the hundreds of smaller, grass-roots movements that spread like wildfire throughout sixteenth-century Europe. Because these groups were many and various, often decentralized and without a single theological leader, we should use caution when grouping them all under the single heading of "the Radical Reformation." To this day, there is no consensus regarding the origins of the Radical Reformation, with the majority of scholars opting for a multiple-origin thesis ("polygenesis") rather than viewing the Radical Reformation as emerging from a single origin ("monogenesis"). The differences among them could be quite substantial, which often led to debates and divisions and even outright hostility toward one another. For example, there were radicals who objected to any form of violence, maintaining a doctrine of non-resistance, and radicals who supported violent revolutionary uprisings, believing with apocalyptic fervor that Christ was due to return to earth at any moment to judge the ungodly and to transform the world. There were also spiritualist radicals, who emphasized the mystical elements of the faith and inner transformation.

The Radical Reformers are so called because they sought to radicalize the theology and practice of the better-known Protestant Reformers. The word *radicalize* suggests that these reformers pushed certain Reformation claims to their logical conclusions; they often went "one up" on reformers such as Luther, Zwingli, and Calvin by extending their teachings and urging for more thoroughgoing theological and ecclesiological reforms. For example, some groups went further than Luther in their sole reliance on the Bible as the Word of God and their eschewal of established church traditions. Others went further than Zwingli in their rejection of traditional claims about the Eucharist and other sacraments. Still others went further than Calvin in their claims about divine election and the need for a strict code of conduct. While most of the Radical Reformers sought to radicalize the theology and practice of the major Protestant Reformers, some sought to retrieve certain forms of piety more characteristic of popular lay movements within medieval Catholicism, which has led some scholars to question whether the term "Radical" is even an appropriate characterization of this diverse group.

Four Distinctive Elements

What holds these diverse Radicals together? Four distinctive elements unite most (though not all) of the movements generally associated with the Radical Reformation. First and foremost was their agreement about the significance of **voluntary discipleship**—that is, most Radicals insisted that becoming a Christian or a follower of Christ requires an active decision of voluntary faith. For the Radical Reformers, one's geographical location or familial heritage could never serve as the basis of discipleship or membership in the church. Instead, discipleship of Christ must be *freely* chosen, not coerced, by the individual as a response to God's grace and call. Thus, the church, in the perspective of the Radical Reformers, is always the "gathered" church, in which members voluntarily join with others in a community of faith. Such a perspective stood in opposition to the parish system (common in Roman Catholic, Lutheran, and some Reformed denominations), in which a person simply attended the church of one's own town or region.

This voluntarist understanding of discipleship and church membership is rooted in the Radical Reformers' views of Baptism. Almost all of them had doubts about the appropriateness of the practice of infant Baptism, and many were explicitly hostile toward it. They agreed that Baptism was a cleansing from sin and a dying and rising with Christ. But they maintained that a faithful reading of the scriptural text indicates that Baptism is to be understood as a visible marker of the new life given in Christ, which must include a new way of living in faith within the context of a community of believers. Baptism required a positive, active belief on the part of the person who would be baptized. Thus, they argued, only adults who were old enough to make such a decision of faith could be baptized. This is usually referred to as **believer's Baptism**. Because many of the first generation of Radical Reformers had been baptized as infants, their critics sometimes called them Anabaptists, which means "re-baptizers." Although they argued that only adult Baptism counted, the name stuck with them, and today the term applies to a number of churches, including the Mennonites, Amish, Hutterites, and the Church of the Brethren. Believer's Baptism continues to be practiced today in these churches and other bodies of Christians who are not generally called Anabaptist, and whose historical and theological genealogies differ, in some respects, from those of the Radical Reformation, for example, certain Baptist denominations, Pentecostals, and the Christian Church (Disciples of Christ).

Second, the Radical Reformers were not interested in making minor modifications in the church; instead they advocated for radical reform in the church, seeking to take seriously in theology and practice what the other reformers called the "**priesthood of the laity**." Many groups sought to reconstitute the theology and practice of the earliest Christian communities in which, they maintained, every baptized Christian was a minister of the gospel. Some groups sought a return to the church as described in the New Testament book of the Acts of the Apostles, in which members of the congregation held property and possessions in common; others looked forward to a future return of Christ that would restore the church with power. In either case, most groups were highly committed to basing their beliefs and actions and polity upon a literal interpretation and application of scripture. Some—the Hutterites, for example—argued against the ownership of private property, noting that the earliest Christians would "sell their possessions and goods and distribute the proceeds to all, as any had need" (Acts 2:45, 4:32–35). Others turned to the teachings of the Sermon on the Mount, in which they were urged to strive toward perfection (Matthew 5:48).

While many Protestant denominations espouse some degree of ecclesiological **resto-rationism**, which is the idea that the contemporary church should model its way of life after the early church as described in the New Testament, very few have been as wholly committed to the idea as those traditions that stem from the Radical Reforma-tion. The emphasis on the church as the "priesthood of the laity" has meant that the churches of the Radical Reformation have often retained a degree of suspicion about, for example, the sacrament of ordination, which would seem to place some indi-viduals above others. Indeed, many of the Radical Reformers of the sixteenth century were explicitly, and often polemically, anticlerical in orientation. The church is viewed as that community of believers in which *all* members are gifted with charisms or gifts of the Holy Spirit. By way of an alternative to the mainstream of the Christian tradition, they have generally sought after non-hierarchical modes of church polity, even while the history of these denominations often reveals operations of hierarchi-cal power and authority that exclude minority voices.

Third, the Radicals were **Christocentric** in orientation, both in matters of faith and practice. A commitment to church tradition and doctrine was viewed as secondary to a commitment to the way of Jesus Christ, which included following his life and his teachings. For example, many Radicals committed themselves to love of enemy, accord-ing to the teachings of the Sermon on the Mount. Such a commitment meant that participation in violence—specifically in the military—was often viewed as contrary to the call of discipleship, and even cause for excommunication from the community, which they generally called "the ban." For the Radicals, faith was never viewed as merely intellectual assent to certain doctrinal propositions, but was to be proven on the path of lived discipleship, specifically the way of the cross. Thus, the way of the Christian dis-ciple was to be visibly different than the ways of the world, which often led to violent confrontation with other mainstream or "magisterial" Reformers. The Radicals were usually, though not always, at the receiving end of this violence, often under attack by both Catholics and magisterial Reformers. In this sense, for many of the Radical Reformers justification and sanctification (being made right by God's gracious act in Christ and being made "holy" by the transforming power of the Spirit) were of one piece. For the Radicals, faith in Christ always means a *faith-in-action*, the fruits of which visibly distinguish the baptized disciple from the non-baptized.

Finally, the Radical Reformers believed that conformity (or obedience) to Christ invariably meant **nonconformity** to what the New Testament writers call "the world." Violently persecuted by both Catholics and the "magisterial" Protestants, they often had no choice but to live in separation from the rest of society, sometimes in wholly isolated communities. But separation and nonconformity were also a direct consequence of the theology of the Radicals, who tended to view their own com-munities as expressions of the "true church," in contrast to the Catholic Church and many of the churches that emerged around the magisterial Protestant reformers. Most refused to hold public office, swear oaths, or fight in wars, and many were icon-oclasts who strongly contested the legitimacy of religious icons in the Christian com-munity. Most interpreted the Sermon on the Mount (Matthew 5–7) as normative for Christian practice, in which Jesus prohibits his followers from activities that the civil government (or the culture) often encourages and even requires—such as using people, taking oaths, protecting one's property, judging others, and hating one's enemies. Most of the Radical Reformers believed that the laws of government should be obeyed, but only as long as they did not conflict with the call of discipleship.

While most of the Radical Reformers refused to participate in earthly govern-ment, they were expected to serve the Christian community and those outside the community. Congregations tended to manage their own affairs, enforcing their own rules of conduct and choosing their own pastors, which again signals differences in polity, or church governance, with the mainstream Reformation. This required a stronger commitment to the life of the Christian community than is commonly practiced today. Nevertheless, it can still be seen in some Amish communities, where long-standing Christian traditions take precedence over the changing practices of society. For example, the Amish refuse to use electricity in their homes or travel in automobiles, using horse and buggy instead, in order to maintain their principle of separation and nonconformity to the world. Other groups retain at least some aspects of this separation from society, but this is expressed in different ways, for example, in the Mennonite commitment to pacifism, active nonviolence, and social justice.

Isolation and Persecution

The distinctive practices of the Radical Reformers often put them at odds with more powerful forces in society. They were persecuted from all directions—not only by Catholics, but also by mainstream Reformers. Luther, in particular, was so distraught by many of their practices that he considered reincorporating many Catholic elements into his theology. Zwingli described the advocates of believer's Baptism as heretics and had them drowned. The Radicals were also persecuted by secular society, since many of their practices put them outside the mainstream of culture and sometimes even outside the civil law.

The unremitting persecution, which they experienced from all sides, created in the Radicals something of a siege mentality, and their own rhetoric sometimes became very fiery and dramatic—not an uncommon occurrence when a person or group feels cornered or surrounded. Here, for example, are the words of Melchior Hoffman, written in 1530:

> Infant Baptism is absolutely not from God but rather is practiced, out of willfulness, by Antichrists and the satanic crowd, in opposition to God and all his commandments, will, and desire. Verily, it is an eternal abomination to him. Woe, woe to all such blind leaders who willfully publish lies for the truth ... their inheritance and portion is eternal damnation.
>
> (Cited in Williams and Mergal, translation emended, 1957, 193)

Overall, sixteenth-century theological debates were highly polemical and all sides used harsh and often condemnatory language at times, though many of the Radical Reformers were confident in the righteousness of their cause and the injustice of their persecution. Consider these words by a Dutch woman who advocated believer's Baptism, written just before her execution and addressed to her infant daughter:

> There are many in this world who are enemies of the cross [of Christ], who seek to be free from it among the world, and to escape it. But, my dear child, if we could with Christ seek and inherit salvation, we must also help bear His cross; and this is the cross which He would have us bear; to follow His footsteps, and to help bear his reproach. ... He himself went before us in this way of reproach, and left us an example, that we should follow His steps; for, for His sake, all must be forsaken, father, mother, sister, brother, husband, child, yea, one's own life.
>
> (Cited in Hillerbrand 1968, 148)

These two passages provide enough contrast to remind us that, even though we are here describing the Radical Reformers as one group, they also varied greatly from one another. But they were certainly united in the persecution they suffered, which has led many to view the faith of the Radical Reformation from the perspective of martyrdom. As an example of the continued prevalence of this tradition of martyrdom, Mennonites, in particular, hold up the *Martyrs Mirror*—a massive volume that documents the lives and deaths of thousands of Christian martyrs since the time of Christ—as an important piece of their theological legacy.

Many Christian groups of the Radical Reformation eventually settled in American colonies, primarily in an attempt to escape religious persecution in Europe. Their conviction that they should be able to worship without fear of persecution and their commitment to voluntary faith and separation from society may have contributed to the development of the notion of the separation of church and state found in the U.S. Constitution.

In terms of sheer numbers, the largest heirs of the Radical Reformation today are Mennonites, who are no longer predominantly of European origins. In recent times, much work has been done to document the long and significant history of Latino/a Mennonites in the Americas, African and African-American Mennonites, American Indian Mennonites, and LGBTQ Mennonites, among others. Mennonites of European descent, in particular, have been forced to confront their complicity in the ongoing history of Western colonialism and land theft, their active and passive assimilation to a global culture of White supremacy, and the ways in which their long-standing commitment to peace, nonviolence, and nonconformity has often covered up other pernicious forms of violence. Throughout the twentieth century and into the twenty-first century, Mennonites and other Anabaptists have wrestled with questions of Christian practice concerning nonviolence and violence, resistance and non-resistance, often struggling to make sense of their place in modern nation-states that often demand allegiance in a variety of ways as well as the distinctiveness and faithfulness of their "peace witness" in global struggles for justice and liberation.

PIETISM

Pietism has often been described as a "Reformation within the Reformation" because it encompasses a variety of spiritual movements within Protestantism that sought to renew the church. It developed among both Reformed (or Calvinist) and Lutheran Christians during the mid- to late seventeenth century, but its origins can be traced to earlier movements that emphasized inner renewal and church reform, especially English, French, and Dutch Calvinists as well as German Anabaptists, Spiritualists, and mystics. The term "Pietism" was originally a derogatory name given to them by their opponents to ridicule their emphasis on piety or religious devotion. They preferred to call themselves "children of God" or "friends of truth." The various Pietist groups are often divided into churchly, radical, and Moravian branches, but they all shared an emphasis on an experience of rebirth or conversion, holy living, small group Bible study, a belief that they were living in the "end times," and a strong commitment to missions and social reform. Pietism was very significant in the later development of Protestantism, including the evangelical movement in Europe and the United States.

Churchly Pietism

One branch of Pietism has been named "churchly" because its adherents wanted to remain within the church as they reformed it. A German Lutheran pastor, **Philipp Jakob Spener** (1635–1705), is generally considered the founder of churchly Pietism. He believed that the sixteenth-century Reformation had accomplished a reform of doctrine, but a reform of life was still needed. In part, this was a reaction against the focus on reason and correct doctrine in the Lutheran Orthodoxy or Scholasticism of his day. Spener accepted Luther's doctrine of justification but he believed that in his day there needed to be a greater emphasis on sanctification (becoming holy) as the completion of justification. He therefore focused on the role of the Holy Spirit in an experience of spiritual rebirth and a commitment to a more godly life. In 1670, he established a small group within his congregation to encourage religious devotion through prayer, bible study, and the sharing of religious experiences. These **conventicles**, or "little churches within the church," would play a central role in the Pietist movement and its efforts to bring about both individual renewal and church reform. Five years later, Spener wrote a foundational Pietist text, the *Pia Desideria* or *Heartfelt Desire for a God-pleasing Reform of the True Protestant Church.* In this text, he described six proposals for reforming the church: individual study of the Bible; a greater role for lay people; the importance of good works; prayer and love in controversy; better training of pastors; and preaching that would inspire greater devotion. He also expressed his belief that these reforms would be part of a millennarian or 1,000-year reign of God on earth, prior to the end of the world.

Spener's reform was carried forward by his protégé and fellow Lutheran pastor **August Hermann Francke**, who became a professor at the new University of Halle in 1692. Like Spener, he emphasized the importance of a new birth but based on his own dramatic experience, he interpreted the rebirth experience as a struggle for repentance followed by a sudden conversion. This would become a distinctive characteristic of Halle Pietism. Inspired by the Pietist belief that they could help to build God's reign or kingdom on earth, Francke established several institutions in Halle that supported education, missions, and social reform. These included an orphanage, schools to train teachers and pastors, soup kitchens, a mission society, a pharmacy, and a publishing house. Pietism was responsible for the first Lutheran missions outside Europe, beginning in 1706 with missionaries from Halle sent to India. Orphanages and schools based on the Halle model were established around the world, including Denmark, Hungary, England, North America, and India. Pietist publications helped to communicate their beliefs and inspire reform through inexpensive Bibles, hymns, prayer books, and devotional works.

The spread of Pietism was viewed with suspicion by some Lutheran theologians, especially among the Orthodox or Scholastics. They were concerned that the Pietist emphasis on sanctification was another form of the "works righteousness" that Luther condemned and their concern for spiritual rebirth encouraged an emotional and individualistic religion. Conventicles were seen as both a religious and political threat by state churches and laws were issued against them. Spener, Francke, and other churchly Pietists responded that they were remaining faithful to Luther's theology and seeking to reform the church in accordance with the Bible and the early church.

Radical Pietism

Another branch of Pietism has been labeled radical or separatist and it encompasses a wide variety of individuals and groups. In *An Introduction to German Pietism*, Douglas Shantz identifies seven characteristics these groups had in common: the language of personal and cosmic renewal found in Jakob Böhme and Johann Arndt; hopes for Christ's coming kingdom on earth; a migratory lifestyle; an eclecticism that draws from mystical, alchemical, and Radical Reformation traditions; a willingness to downplay differences across confessional traditions; involvement in—as well as critique of—state churches; and an openness to women leaders and prophets (Shantz 2013, 158). Some of these same influences and characteristics can also be found in churchly pietism. In fact, radical pietism and churchly pietism were intertwined from the very beginning, and the lines between them remained fluid. For example, although Spener and other churchly Pietists intended the conventicles as an addition to regular Sunday worship, some of the members eventually became disillusioned with the church and left. This included Johann Jakob Schütz, a member of Spener's congregation who was instrumental in organizing the first conventicle there but left the Lutheran church to form his own community.

One of the most important influences on pietism, and radical pietism in particular, was the German mystical writer Jakob Böhme. He believed that true knowledge of God is found in the inner person, in the light of God in the soul. He emphasized new birth, inward transformation through Christ, and the coming age of the Spirit which will bring the final restoration of the church. This view of a spiritual church, defined by mystical union with Christ, was taken up by radical Pietists to assert that they were the true followers of Christ. Radical Pietist and Lutheran theologian Gottfried Arnold developed this theme in his *Impartial History of the Church and Heretics* (published 1699–1700). In this text, Arnold reverses the usual categories and identifies the institutional church with heresy and the true church with those who were inspired by the Holy Spirit and persecuted by the established church. Radical Pietists identified themselves with the true, spiritual church being persecuted by the state churches.

Some Radical Pietists responded to this persecution by immigrating to North America and establishing their own communities. An example of this can be found in the Ephrata Cloister, a Protestant monastic community founded by Johann Conrad Beissel in Lancaster County, Pennsylvania in 1732. Although some families were included, most of the members took vows of celibacy, wore habits, fasted, and prayed throughout the day. Their religious life was shaped by a belief that Beissel had inherited from Jakob Böhme, namely, that Sophia (the biblical term for wisdom) represented the female dimension of God and spiritual rebirth occurred through marriage with heavenly Sophia. The community supported itself through farming and a variety of industries, including a saw mill and a paper mill. It flourished until the late eighteenth century and during that time it had a vibrant cultural life, producing an impressive collection of theological treatises, poetry, art, handcrafts, and music.

Another expression of Radical Pietism can be found in the movement known as Philadelphianism, founded in England by Jane Leade and brought to Germany by a married couple, Johann Wilhelm Petersen and Johanna Eleonora Petersen. Inspired by Böhme's writings, Jane Leade founded the London Philadelphian Society in 1694. Philadelphia is one of the "seven churches" referred to in the book of Revelation (3:7–12) and the Greek word means "brotherly love." This group abandoned denominational churches in expectation of Christ's coming kingdom on earth and the establishment of a church of love and peace. Leade taught that at the end of time, all of creation will be saved by God, including the devil and the fallen angels. The Petersens spread Leade's doctrine of universal reconciliation by extensive travels throughout Germany, often at the invitation of powerful church and city officials, and through their many popular writings.

Moravians

A third branch of Pietism has been traced to Count **Nikolaus Ludwig Zinzendorf** and the Moravians. Zinzendorf was influenced by Pietism from an early age. He was a godson of Spener, raised by a devout Pietist grandmother, and attended Francke's preparatory school from age 10 to 16. Although he wanted to become a Lutheran minister, his aristocratic family insisted that he study law and he became a judicial counselor to the court in Dresden. In 1722, he welcomed a group of persecuted Bohemian Brethren, also known as Moravians, to settle on his land. These spiritual descendants of the fifteenth-century Hussites named their settlement Herrnhut, meaning "the Lord's Watch," both to honor God's watch over them and their desire to watch for God. A variety of religious refugees fled to the settlement over the next several years which led to controversy and strife. In 1727, Zinzendorf left his position in Dresden and organized Herrnhut as a political and religious community. In order to prevent persecution from German authorities, the group was officially placed under the authority of a Lutheran parish but the rules and statutes retained the worship and discipline of the Moravian Brethren. A communion service on August 13, 1727 is regarded as the beginning of the Renewed Unitas Fratrum ("Unity of Brethren") or the current Moravian Church. After the celebration of Communion, many of the participants were so moved by the service that they were reluctant to leave, so Count Zinzendorf sent them food and they continued to pray and sing hymns. This event was understood as a return to the meals celebrated by the early Christians before Communion and it developed into the Moravian lovefeast, a service of song accompanied by a simple meal, often of coffee and rolls.

The early years of the Herrnhut settlement developed many of the distinctive characteristics of the Moravian Church: the division of the community into small groups to promote religious devotion, a strong communal life, a rich musical tradition, and a deep concern for foreign missions. The influence of Zinzendorf's Pietism can be seen in the Moravian emphasis on spiritual rebirth and in particular on his understanding of it as a joyful experience rather than Francke's emphasis on sorrow for sin and a struggle for repentance. Zinzendorf's piety was also characterized by a mystical devotion to the blood and wounds of Christ and a deeply personal encounter with Jesus, often described in terms of the soul's marriage to Christ. He believed that all denominations, including the Moravians, helped to lead people to faith but none of them were the final "true church." His efforts to unite Christians, particularly the German-speaking Protestants of America, ultimately failed.

The Moravians were successful, however, spreading out from Herrnhut across Germany to other areas of Europe and beyond, including the colonies of Georgia and Pennsylvania. In addition to establishing their own settlements, the Moravians greatly influenced John Wesley, the founder of Methodism. He and his brother Charles first encountered Moravians on a ship traveling to America. During a storm at sea, Wesley was impressed by the calm faith of the Moravians in contrast to the terror that he and other passengers experienced. As an Anglican rector in Georgia, he was in constant contact with the Moravian settlers and admired their worship and their mission to Native Americans. When he returned to England, Wesley was in despair over the failure of his ministry in Georgia and he turned to a Moravian, Peter Böhler, for advice and spiritual help. On May 24, 1738, Wesley experienced conversion and an assurance of salvation when he attended a Moravian meeting on Aldersgate Street in London (see John Wesley and Methodism in the English Reformation, below). He would later visit Halle and Herrnhut and meet with Count Zinzendorf. Although Wesley eventually disagreed with aspects of Moravian piety, it deeply shaped his own religious faith and Methodism shares their emphasis on conversion, sanctification, and small groups for spiritual growth.

Legacy

Pietism has been one of the major influences on modern Protestantism, particularly in North America. Many of the German and Scandinavian immigrants to the "New

World" in the eighteenth and nineteenth centuries brought their Pietism with them. The father of American Lutheranism, Henry Melchoir Mühlenberg, was a Pietist who was sent by Halle in 1742 to minister to the German Lutherans in Pennsylvania. A variety of radical Pietist groups emigrated to America to avoid persecution by state churches and founded their own communities, including the Ephrata community, the Community of True Inspiration (also known as the Amana Colonies), and a group called the Society of the Woman in the Wilderness (based on Revelation 12:6). Radical Pietism influenced a host of Protestant denominations, including the Church of the Brethren, the Mennonite Brethren, German and Swedish Baptists, the Evangelical Free Church, and the Evangelical Covenant Church.

Pietism was a major influence on the most important Protestant theologian of the nineteenth century, Friedrich Schleiermacher. It contributed to nineteenth-century revivalism and twentieth-century Evangelicalism with its emphasis on being "born again" and having a personal relationship with Jesus Christ. At times, this concern for heartfelt conversion led to an overemphasis on individual subjective experience, anti-intellectualism, and sectarian fragmentation. For example, the Pietist practice of lay people reading the Bible for devotional purposes led some followers to rely exclusively on the Holy Spirit and reject serious study of the text. On the other hand, Spener and Francke's commitment to careful study of the bible in the original languages contributed to the development of the historical critical approach to scripture. Although Pietism has had varied and at times even contradictory effects on modern Protestantism, it has profoundly influenced it through its Bible study, hymnody, social reform, ecumenism, lay involvement, and missionary zeal.

THE ENGLISH REFORMATION

Figure 19–5 *Henry VIII* (1491–1547), by Hans Holbein the Younger (1497–1543).

The English Reformation differed in an important way from other efforts at reforming the church in the sixteenth century (be they Lutheran, Reformed, Radical, or Pietist). The distinguishing feature of church reform in England is that its instigator was none other than the King of England himself, **Henry VIII** (1491–1547). Those who led other reforming movements in continental Europe had to persuade government officials to support their cause—and in some cases their pleas fell on deaf ears, forcing them to oppose the authorities entirely. Reform of the Church of England, however, began at the very top of the government itself. This decisive role of the crown meant, as we will see below, that the fortunes of reforming efforts would change dramatically depending on who sat on the English throne.

Why Did England Break with Rome?

Precisely because of the central role of the monarch in the English Reformation, an analysis of its causes must examine the attitude toward reform held by the king. A multitude of considerations shaped Henry's mind, but *doctrinal* reform of the Catholic

Church in England was not among them. In other words, whereas reformers such as Martin Luther and John Calvin were animated by convictions about Christian *doctrine*, such as the Christian being saved purely by grace, Henry did not display any desire to change church teaching. In fact, shortly after the Reformation broke out on the Continent, the king turned to scholars at the universities of Oxford and Cambridge to formulate arguments to refute Luther's claims. He even offered a defense of the traditional Catholic teaching on the sacraments, which was published under his name as *Assertio Septem Sacramentorum* or Defense of the Seven Sacraments (1521) and earned him the title "Defender of the Faith" from Pope Leo X.

However, with time a number of concerns began to change Henry's mind, among them his widely known desire for an annulment of his marriage to Catherine of Aragon (1485–1536). Henry and Catherine had been unable to have a male heir who lived into adulthood (all of their children except their daughter Mary had died in infancy), and Henry eventually came to the conclusion that he would try to have a male heir by another wife. Henry's lengthy efforts to secure an annulment became known as his "great matter," and it consumed him and many of his top advisors. Despite his efforts, Pope Leo X would not grant Henry the annulment he sought (in part because of the fact that Catherine's nephew, Holy Roman Emperor Charles V [1500–1558], had his troops stationed in Rome at the time).

A change in marital status, however, was not the king's only consideration as he watched the Reformation unfold. Renaissance humanism informed Protestant theology in certain ways (see Chapter 17), and Henry was warm to some humanist learning. Additionally, in the early sixteenth century, it was not at all obvious that the Catholic Church would successfully push back against Protestant advances, especially in northern Europe, and Protestantism looked to many at this time like the wave of the future. A new day was dawning in Europe, and it presented an opportunity for independence from Rome. At Henry's behest, Thomas Cromwell (1485–1540) was able to pass a series of acts of legislation through the English Parliament that culminated in the Act of Supremacy (1534), which declared England's king to be "the only supreme head in earth of the Church of England" (Haugaard 1998, 6). This was the stroke that formally separated the Church of England from the Roman Catholic Church, as it made Henry, not the pope, the head of the English church. Wielding his new authority, Henry dissolved the English monasteries, a move that transferred their wealth to the crown so that it might be used for "the public good," however that might be determined by the king. In practical terms, by dissolving the monasteries, Henry secured financial self-sufficiency for his new national church.

The reader will note, as mentioned briefly above, the lack of interest in reforming church *teaching* throughout these maneuverings, and in fact one of the acts of Parliament explicitly declared that no variance from the Catholic faith would be sought. Instead, Henry's primary goals seem to have centered around achieving ecclesial autonomy, which resolved his "great matter" by affording him the right to have his marriage annulled (and to marry Anne Boleyn, by whom Elizabeth was born), but which also granted him a much broader authority to determine to an unprecedented degree the future course of the Church of England. How would he shape his English church? In an important sense, the church that Henry established was not actually a Protestant church. Instead, the Church of England continued to be Catholic in its doctrine and liturgy. The difference was that it was a Catholic Church without the pope as its head.

Although this characterization is for the most part accurate, it should be said that influential figures in Henry's church had Protestant inclinations of various

Figure 19–6 *Thomas Cranmer* (1489–1556), by Gerlach Flicke (1495–1558).

sorts. Most importantly, perhaps, Henry appointed as Archbishop of Canterbury **Thomas Cranmer** (1489–1556), who had been influenced significantly by Protestant ideas (a fact that would become clear under Henry's successor). Additionally, the Church of England at this time did display a small number of Protestant characteristics, even though its dominant features were Catholic. For instance, in 1539, an English edition of the Bible was published (called the "Great Bible"), which made scripture accessible to those who did not have facility with the ancient languages in which it was written. Protestant reformers such as Luther had appealed directly to scripture itself in order to overcome Catholic interpretations of the Bible, and the English scholar William Tyndale (1494–1536) had been inspired by Luther to render the Bible in English. His version was published in 1527 (in what was at that time Roman Catholic England), and he endured persecution for his efforts. The 1539 Great Bible can be viewed as a continuation of this characteristically Protestant desire to make scripture accessible.

Although some sought to reform the Church of England further so as to bring it into doctrinal alignment with Protestant movements unfolding in continental Europe, during Henry's reign, they were unable to act on their convictions in a comprehensive manner. However, after Henry's death in 1547, many of these figures saw their opportunity to make the Church of England truly Protestant.

A Protestant Church of England: The Reign of Edward VI

Edward VI (1537–1553), known as the "Boy King," ascended the throne at a mere nine years old (he was the only male heir of Henry VIII). As a result, the actual governing of England was done by a council of regency rather than the young king himself. Edward's uncle, the Duke of Somerset, headed the council, and with Thomas Cranmer and others, he was able to enact much more significant reforms of the Church of England than anything witnessed during Henry's reign. After the Duke of Somerset was replaced in 1550 by John Dudley (who accepted the title Duke of Northumberland the next year), those reforms intensified and, in turn, encountered significant resistance from many. As Eamon Duffy has demonstrated with considerable force, religious life in late medieval England was not decadent and crying out for reform (Duffy 1992). Quite the contrary, the practice of Catholicism in England in the fifteenth and sixteenth centuries displayed a vitality that bespeaks just how deeply cherished it was at this time. The Reformation was not welcome in many segments of English society, a fact which became clear during the tumultuous 1550s.

Two key works illustrate just how Protestant the Church of England became during Edward's reign: *The Book of Common Prayer* and the *Articles of Religion*. In 1549, Parliament authorized the first *Book of Common Prayer*, assembled by Cranmer, which replaced the Latin Mass with English-language liturgies. The second edition (published in 1552) is often regarded as more Protestant than its predecessor, and it contained palpably Calvinist and Zwinglian (i.e., Reformed) sentiments. For instance, the 1552 *Book of Common Prayer* elevates to a central position the notion that Communion is a *memorial* of Christ's death and resurrection, as Zwingli emphasized, rather than an event at which the bread and wine actually become the body and blood of Christ, as upheld by the Catholic Church. Additionally, a number of characteristically Catholic practices were dropped in the 1552 edition, such as adoration of the Eucharist, and vestments for clergy were minimized, with only the surplice being authorized.

Cranmer's *Forty-Two Articles* are often viewed as the apex of Protestant influence on the Church of England. The *Articles of Religion* were first composed in 1536, during Henry VIII's reign, as a description of the beliefs held by the Church of England. Ten articles were initially put forward in 1536, and they would be periodically revised for decades to come. Their number changed with each iteration, as did the theological stance they espoused. In 1553, Cranmer published the *Forty-Two Articles*, which aligned the Church of England with Protestant Christianity. Clergy and others responsible for religious instruction in England were required to adhere to them.

The Church of England, then, became recognizably and unambiguously Protestant during Edward's reign. Bishops, priests, and deacons were allowed to marry. Most visibly, perhaps, iconoclasts during Edward's reign thoroughly stripped English churches of their religious images. They thus continued the destruction of images that had begun under the leadership of Zwingli and others during the Swiss Reformation. However, as emboldened as Protestants were in the early 1550s, the future of their reforming efforts became doubtful when Edward was diagnosed with tuberculosis and died of his illness in 1553. Protestant hopes were utterly dashed when Edward's Catholic half-sister Mary (daughter of Catherine of Aragon) ascended the throne, as she had a strong antipathy toward Protestant reforms.

England Returns to Roman Catholicism: Mary I

Mary I (1516–1558) ruled as queen for only five years, but during her brief reign, she dramatically reinstated Roman Catholicism in England. Shortly after she was crowned, Parliament repealed the legislation passed by Edward VI and Henry VIII, returning the Church of England to Rome. A complication arose surrounding the monasteries, as a number of wealthy English had purchased the properties from the crown, and they were not eager to see them go back to the Roman Catholic Church. Mary succeeded in forging an agreement with Pope Julius III according to which the properties would remain in the possession of their new owners, but the episode demonstrates that her efforts at reintroducing Roman influence in England were not received warmly among a number of influential figures.

Nevertheless, she was successful in reinstating Roman Catholicism. Clerical celibacy was once again required, and the 1552 *Book of Common Prayer* disappeared during her reign. The Latin Mass was restored, and Christian worship took a decidedly Catholic shape. Neither the "Great Bible" nor any other English translation was used. Crucially, too, in 1555, Mary brought back the Heresy Acts, which allowed her to convict and execute hundreds of figures who had advocated Protestant reforms, among them

Thomas Cranmer, who was burned at the stake in 1556. Many Protestants with means fled to continental Europe to avoid death in England. Mary's zealous efforts to eliminate Protestantism earned her the appellation "Bloody Mary," and stoked considerable anti-Catholic sentiment in England. When she died in 1558 (perhaps of uterine or ovarian cancer), she left an England that was weary of conflict and unclear of the path to religious and political stability.

The Elizabethan Settlement

In the 11 years before **Elizabeth I** (1533–1603) ascended the throne in 1558, England had tacked hard in the direction of Protestant reform, only to return with equal force to traditional Roman Catholicism. The events that had transpired since the death of Henry VIII exposed the wide range of religious views in England in the mid-sixteenth century, and the unenviable task of achieving steadiness for church and state fell to Elizabeth. She did so by returning the Church of England to its course of Protestant reform, but in a moderate fashion that allowed a range of different theological views to coexist within the same church. Her lasting success has been termed the "Elizabethan Settlement," and it determined much of the distinctive character of the Church of England, as will be discussed below.

Protestants who had lived in exile during Mary's reign returned to England eager to continue their forceful reforms of the Church of England, but Elizabeth moderated their expectations shortly after their arrival. She allowed many outward features of Catholic devotion to continue, such as vestments and religious images, even though she ultimately viewed the Church of England as Protestant. In 1559, a third edition of the *Book of Common Prayer* was published, and it displays Elizabeth's willingness to accommodate a range of theological views. For instance, at the administration of Communion, the 1559 *Book of Common Prayer* contains the words "Take, eat, in *remembrance* of me," as had the 1552 version, but this new edition also has words from the 1549 prayer book, "the *Body* of our Lord Jesus Christ." To many interpreters, the Zwinglian focus on remembrance (i.e., the notion that Communion is a memorial) combines here with language suggesting that Christ is truly present in the bread and wine, thus including aspects of both Protestant and Catholic views of the Eucharist.

The version of the *Articles of Religion* published in 1563 similarly demonstrates the broad, accommodating theological stance of Elizabeth's church. The *Thirty-Nine Articles*, as they are called, were published in their final version in 1571, and they remain an important document for the Church of England down to the present day. In them, one finds that certain positions are ruled

Figure 19–7 Elizabeth I (1553–1603) in her coronation robes, 1558.

out, but in many cases they allow a range of interpretations of important theological topics.

As successful as Elizabeth was in establishing long-term stability for the Church of England, a minority remained discontent with the direction taken by the English church during her reign. They wanted more significant Protestant reform along the lines of that which had begun under Edward VI, but Elizabeth resisted the attempts of these "Puritans," as they later came to be called. Eventually, many Puritans would quit England and look to the New World for the opportunity to structure the church and society in accord with their views (see Chapter 23).

The Distinctive Character of "Anglicanism"

The events described above, especially those that took place during Elizabeth's reign, have given the Church of England a character not found among other Protestant churches, and it is rightly said that "Anglicanism" lies closest to Catholicism along the spectrum of Protestant positions. As a whole, the Church of England has a warmer attitude toward tradition and historical continuity than those Protestant churches that insist on *sola scriptura*, and worship services in the Church of England are often virtually indistinguishable from their Roman Catholic counterparts. Although the term *via media* (middle way) would not appear for some time after Elizabeth's death, it has been used to describe the distinctive position of the Church of England as somewhere "in the middle" between Catholicism and Protestantism.

On a related point, from a very early date, Anglicans were called upon to remain united as one church in spite of the different religious views of its members, and as a result the Church of England has had significant experience living with diversity. As Fredrica Thompsett puts this point:

> Anglicans have inherited from … Elizabeth I a preference both for moderation and breadth in theology along with a reluctance to define the mysteries of salvation too closely. One way of describing this stance has been to refer to Anglican theology as a *via media*, or middle way, between Roman Catholic and Protestant theologies. … We could interpret the Elizabethan Settlement and its struggle for religious identity and stability as a success story about living with controversy, and in many ways this is correct.
>
> (Thompsett 1999, 108–109)

In certain respects, this feature of Anglicanism has equipped it with resources for responding to the so-called "postmodern condition," which places enormous value on diversity, as we will see in Chapter 26.

Later Developments: The Emergence of Methodism

One of the most noteworthy movements to emerge from the Church of England is **Methodism**, which began with **John Wesley** (1703–1791) in the eighteenth century. Wesley was an Anglican priest who became convinced that the somewhat rigid church of his time needed to be enlivened through an increase in energetic worship and personal piety. Although Wesley himself regarded Methodism as a movement that belonged *within* the Church of England, after his death, the **Methodist Church** became a separate denomination within Protestant Christianity.

Figure 19–8 *John Wesley* (1703–1791), engraving by Alexander Hay Ritchie, from painting by John Jackson (1778–1831).

When he was 34 years old, Wesley had an experience that changed his life forever. After hearing Martin Luther's Preface to the Epistle to the Romans in a church service, Wesley reported the following:

> I felt my heart strangely warmed. I felt I did trust in Christ, Christ alone for salvation, and an assurance was given me that he had taken away my sins, even mine, and saved me from the law of sin and death.
>
> (Wesley 1827, 194)

This event is celebrated as Wesley's "Evangelical Conversion" (Aldersgate Day in the Methodist Church), and it signals the strong emphasis on personal experience for Wesley and Methodism more broadly. To Wesley, salvation was a matter between the individual Christian and God; no one could stand in for the Christian and determine his or her relationship with God. Wesley rejected the Calvinist doctrine of predestination that had risen to prominence in England at the time, and he instead held that the individual human being could choose to accept God's grace, which was available to all.

Wesley's view of what happens *after* one accepts God's grace stands out as the most significant feature of his theology. To Wesley, after one accepts God's grace, he or she is not only *justified* before God, as other Protestants would say; that person should also expect to be "entirely sanctified," as Wesley put it. By this notion of "entire sanctification," Wesley meant that God's grace can eliminate all sin so that the Christian actually lives in a state of *perfection*. Controversial though this idea was in its time (and today), it does have scriptural precedent: 1 Thessalonians 5:23 reads, "May the God of peace himself sanctify you entirely; and may your spirit and soul and body be kept sound and blameless at the coming of our Lord Jesus Christ." Wesley often spoke of complete sanctification as a state of perfect love that knows no pride, anger, or selfishness. It should be said that Wesley does not hold that the individual Christian attains this perfection on his or her own. Instead, it is a gift of God's *grace*, which preserves the Christian from falling into sin.

The intensity of Wesley's devotion to God and neighbor is captured especially powerfully in the music of the Methodist Church. John Wesley's brother Charles (1707–1788) wrote over 6,000 hymns during his lifetime, including "Hark! The Herald Angels Sing," "Love Divine, All Loves Excelling," and "Christ the Lord is Risen Today." Methodist music remains one of its strongest legacies down to the present day.

The Nineteenth Century

In the nineteenth century, prominent leaders within the Church of England determined that it was once again due for reform. Most of these leaders were parish priests

Figure 19–9 John Henry Newman (1801–1890).

connected with Oxford University; as a result, their efforts at renewing the church came to be called the **"Oxford Movement."** Figures such as **John Henry Newman** (1801–1890), John Keble (1792–1866), and Edward Pusey (1800–1882) sought to retrieve the Catholic heritage of the Church of England, and they developed a view of the English church that would redefine its self-understanding. A similar "Catholic Revival" was underway in the United States, begun by John Henry Hobart (1775–1830), and in parts of the British Empire, so the movement came to impact many parts of the **Anglican Communion** down to the present day.

Beginning in 1833, Newman, Keble, Pusey, and others published a series of tracts, or short pamphlets, that offered a new interpretation of the Church of England. The "Tractarians," as they were called, insisted that there was in fact *continuity* between the Church of England and the Roman Catholic Church from which it had diverged during the English Reformation. This position challenged the perception of the Church of England as a Protestant institution, and the Tractarians inspired many members of the Church of England to view themselves as "Anglo-Catholic," that is, as Catholic, even though they remained within the Church of England.

In order to persuade their contemporaries to their point of view, the Tractarians rewrote the history of the Church of England. They focused in particular on a group of English theologians and priests who had resisted the Puritan (sometimes called "ultra-Protestant") influence on the church in the sixteenth and seventeenth centuries. The Tractarians used these figures to argue that the Church of England had been opposed to Protestantism from its early days. Based on these claims, the Oxford Movement developed the so-called "branch theory" of the church, which claimed that the "one, holy, catholic, and apostolic church" mentioned in the Nicene Creed (see Chapter 8) could be found in three distinct branches: Eastern Orthodoxy, Roman Catholicism, and Anglicanism. This move brought the Church of England close to Catholicism and Orthodoxy, but distanced it from Protestant Christianity.

The Tractarians also examined the ancient church, with Newman taking an interest in the fourth century in general and Athanasius in particular (see Chapter 8). For a time, Newman held that the best representation of that ancient church was found in the Church of England. Therefore, although Tractarians viewed the Orthodox, Catholic, and Anglican Churches as three branches from the same tree, so to speak, they were not all equal. Newman argued that Anglicanism best preserved the church's ancient heritage.

A number of liturgical and devotional changes followed from this conception of the Anglican Church. Precisely because it had been redefined as standing in continuity with Catholicism, practices that had been previously perceived as too "Romish" for the Church of England became prevalent. Anglo-Catholic liturgies developed into elaborate services with ornate vestments, incense, and bells. One of the most visible legacies of the Oxford Movement can be observed in the "high church" tradition it inspired.

In 1839, Newman began having doubts about the view of Anglicanism that he had developed just a few years earlier. In his studies of the Monophysites of the early church (see Chapter 9), he saw a parallel between the disobedience of those ancient theologians to Rome and the Anglican Church's ongoing disobedience. In studying another ancient heresy, Donatism, he came to understand the need for an international authority above the regional bishops, as Donatist bishops had not been able to protect their churches from error. His concerns worked on him for a period of years until finally he was received into the Roman Catholic Church in 1845.

The Oxford Movement did not collapse after Newman's departure. Only a small number of priests (about 40) joined him in converting to Roman Catholicism. Likewise, although the disastrous intervention by a secular English court in the interpretation of church doctrine drove another 56 to convert (1850–1854), including the future Cardinal Manning, most of them were junior priests. Pusey led the Oxford Movement and continued a dialogue with the future Cardinal Newman about doctrines concerning the Blessed Virgin Mary and papal infallibility.

The Oxford Movement left a considerable legacy to Anglicanism. In the first place, it made church buildings and worship in the worldwide Anglican Communion look more like Catholic churches. Additionally, the Oxford Movement solidified the identity of the Anglican Church as more than simply a "big tent" under which many diverse views can be found; Newman and others gave Anglicanism an identity as the *via media* that preserves the heritage of the ancient church, and such a self-understanding endures in the contemporary setting. Last, by appealing to the Church Fathers as a guide for contemporary theology, the Oxford Movement modeled a theology of retrieval (or *ressourcement*) from which Catholic theologians would draw in renewing the Roman Catholic Church in the twentieth century, as we will see in Chapter 24.

The Worldwide Influence of Anglicanism

As the British Empire grew to dominate the globe, the reach of the Church of England expanded with it, and as a result Anglicanism has shaped Christian theology and worship far beyond the island on which it began in the sixteenth century. Although the Church of England would often change subtly as it took root in various parts of the world, its different versions are all a part of the "Anglican Communion," which is a worldwide body of churches that stand in the tradition of the Church of England. The **Episcopal Church** is the American component of the Anglican Communion, and 43 other churches compose it worldwide. At roughly 80 million members, it is one of the largest Christian communions in the world today.

Having examined a wide array of figures and movements within Protestant Christianity, we turn in Chapter 20 to reforming efforts within Roman Catholicism, both before and after the Protestant Reformation began in the early sixteenth century.

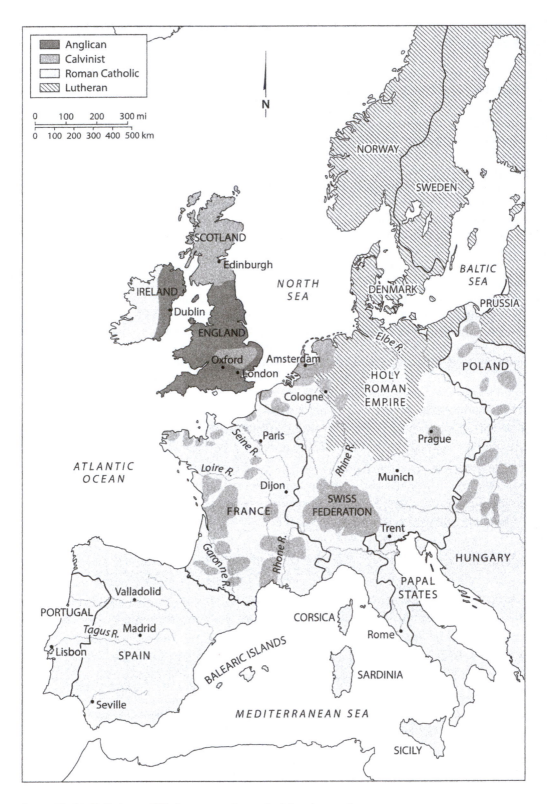

Figure 19–10 Religious affiliations near the end of the sixteenth century.

Key Terms

Anglican Communion
believer's Baptism
John Calvin
Christocentric
Churchly Pietism
Conventicles
Thomas Cranmer
double predestination
Elizabeth I
Episcopal Church
August Hermann Francke

Henry VIII
Institutes of the Christian Religion
Marburg Colloquy
Methodism
Methodist Church
Moravians
Oxford Movement
John Henry Newman
nonconformity
priesthood of the laity

Radical Pietism
Restorationism
sanctification
sovereignty of God
Philipp Jakob Spener
voluntary discipleship
John Wesley
Nikolaus Ludwig Zinzendorf
Ulrich Zwingli

Questions for Reading

1. Describe Zwingli's central beliefs and why he held them.
2. Give specific examples of how Zwingli and Calvin's need to cooperate with city councils affected their reforms.
3. Describe Calvin's central beliefs as found in his *Institutes*. How would you evaluate their strengths and weaknesses?
4. How does Calvin's understanding of the Eucharist differ from that of Luther and Zwingli? Which (if any) of these views do you find most persuasive and why?
5. How would you describe and evaluate Calvin's legacy?
6. What are the four distinctive elements that unite most of the Radical Reformers?
7. In what sense(s) can the Radical Reformers be considered "radical?"
8. The Radical Reformers emphasized Christocentrism and have often sought to follow the life and teachings of Jesus on nonviolence and enemy-love. In what ways does this differ from other Christian traditions?
9. Why do you think the Radical Reformers were viewed as such a serious threat to both the magisterial Protestants and the Catholics?
10. What was Pietism and how did it try to reform and renew Protestant churches?
11. What did all three branches of Pietism (churchly, radical, and Moravian) have in common? How were they different?
12. Why was Pietism seen as threatening to other Protestants? How did Pietists survive persecution and spread their beliefs?
13. How has Pietism affected Protestantism today? How would you evaluate its legacy?
14. List the three monarchs who followed Henry VIII, and summarize the religious policy of each.
15. List the chief contributions of Thomas Cranmer to the English Reformation.
16. In what ways is Anglicanism distinctive?
17. For what is John Wesley most well known?
18. What was the Oxford Movement?

Works Consulted/Recommended Reading

Bach, Jeffrey. 2010. "Pietism." *Encyclopedia of Religion in America*. Vol. 3. Edited by Charles H. Lippy and Peter W. Williams, 1656–1662. Washington, DC: CQ Press.

Bromiley, G.W., ed. 1953. *Zwingli and Bullinger*. Library of Christian Classics. Louisville, KY: The Westminster Press.

Brown, Dale. 1978. *Understanding Pietism*. Grand Rapids, MI: William B. Eerdmans.

Calvin, John. 1960. *Institutes of the Christian Religion*. Library of Christian Classics. Vols. 20 and 21. Edited by John T. McNeill. Translated by Ford Lewis Battles. Philadelphia, PA: The Westminster Press.

Calvin, John. 1858. "LXI.—To Viret." *Letters of John Calvin*. Edited and translated by Jules Bonnet. Presbyterian Board of Publication. www.gutenberg.org/files/45423/45423-h/45423-h.htm.

Dickens, A.G. 1967. *The English Reformation*. Glasgow: William Collins and Sons, Fontana.

Dickens, A.G., and Dorothy Carr, eds. 1967. *The Reformation in England to the Accession of Elizabeth I. Documents of Modern History*. London: Edward Arnold.

Duffy, Eamon. 1992. *The Stripping of the Altars: Traditional Religion in England 1400–1580*. New Haven, CT: Yale University Press.

Durnbaugh, Donald F. 2003. *The Believer's Church: The History and Character of Radical Protestantism*. Eugene, OR: Wipf & Stock.

Eire, Carlos M. 2016. *Reformations: The Early Modern World, 1450–1650*. New Haven, CT: Yale University Press.

Elwood, Christopher. 2002. *Calvin for Armchair Theologians*. Louisville, KY: Westminster John Knox Press.

Erb, Peter C., ed. 1983. *Pietists: Selected Writings*. The Classics of Western Spirituality. Paulist Press.

Ganoczy, Alexandre. 2005. "Calvin, John." *The Oxford Encyclopedia of the Reformation*. Oxford: Oxford University Press.

Gleixner, Ulrike. n.d. "Pietism." *The Oxford Handbook of the Protestant Denominations*. Edited by Ulinka Rublack. Oxford Handbooks Online. DOI: 10.1093/oxfordhb/9780199646920.013.34.

Goertz, Hans-Jürgen. 1982. *Profiles of Radical Reformers: Biographical Sketches from Thomas Müntzer to Paracelsus*. Scottdale, PA: Herald Press.

Granquist, Mark A., ed. 2015. *Scandinavian Pietists*. The Classics of Western Spirituality. Mahwah, NJ: Paulist Press.

Grell, Ole Peter, and A.I.C. Heron. 2005. "Calvinism." *The Oxford Encyclopedia of the Reformation*. Oxford: Oxford University Press.

Haugaard, William P. 1998. "From the Reformation to the Eighteenth Century." In *The Study of Anglicanism*. Edited by Stephen Sykes, John Booty, and Jonathan Knight, 3–30. Minneapolis, MN: Fortress Press, .

Herring, George. 2016. *The Oxford Movement in Practice: The Tractarian Parochial World from the 1830s to the 1870s*. Oxford: Clarendon Press.

Hillerbrand, Hans J., ed. 1968. *The Protestant Reformation*. New York: Harper Books.

Hillerbrand, Hans J., ed. 2007. *The Division of Christendom: Christianity in the Sixteenth Century*. Louisville, KY: Westminster John Knox Press.

Johnson, William Stacy. 2009. *John Calvin: Reformer for the 21st Century*. Louisville, KY: Westminster John Knox Press.

Lindberg, Carter. 2010. *The European Reformations*. 2nd edn. Oxford: Wiley-Blackwell,.

MacCulloch, Diarmaid. 2004. *The Reformation: A History*. New York: Viking Penguin.

McNeill, John T. 1954. *The History and Character of Calvinism*. Oxford: Oxford University Press.

Metzger, Bruce, and Roland Murphy, eds. 1991. *The New Oxford Annotated Bible with Apocrypha, New Revised Standard Version*. New York: Oxford University Press.

Mullett, Michael. 1994. *Calvin*. London: Routledge.

Parker, T.H.L. 1975. *John Calvin: A Biography*. Tring: Lion Publishing.

Potter, G.R. 1976. *Zwingli*. Cambridge: Cambridge University Press.

Potter, G.R., ed. 1978. *Huldrych Zwingli*. Documents of Modern History. London: Edward Arnold.

Potter, G.R., and M. Greengrass, eds. 1983. *John Calvin*. Documents of Modern History. London: Edward Arnold.

Roth, John, and James M. Stayer, eds. 2006. *A Companion to Anabaptism and Spiritualism (1521–1700)*. Leiden: Brill.

Shantz, Douglas H. 2013. *An Introduction to German Pietism: Protestant Renewal at the Dawn of Modern Europe*. Baltimore, MD: Johns Hopkins University Press.

Spijker, W. van 't. 2009. *Calvin: A Brief Guide to His Life and Thought*. Translated by Lyle D. Bierma. Louisville, KY: Westminster John Knox Press.

Stayer, James M. 2002. *Anabaptists and the Sword*. Eugene, OR: Wipf & Stock.

Stoeffler, F. Ernest. 1976. *Colonial Pietism and Early American Christianity*. Grand Rapids, MI: William B. Eerdmans,.

Strom, Jonathan, Hartmut Lehmann, and James Van Horn Melton, eds. 2009. *Pietism in Germany and North America 1680–1820*. Burlington, VT: Ashgate.

Stroup, George W. 2009. *Calvin*. Abingdon Pillars of Theology. Nashville, TN: Abingdon Press.

Ward, W.R. 1992. *The Protestant Evangelical Awakening*. Cambridge: Cambridge University Press.

Williams, George H. 2000. *The Radical Reformation*. Kirksville, MO: Truman State University Press.

Williams, George H., and Angel M. Mergal, eds. 1957. *Spiritual and Anabaptist Writers*. Library of Christian Classics. Vol. 25. Philadelphia, PA: Westminster Press.

Wesley, John. 1827. *The Works of the Rev. John Wesley*, Vol. 1. New York: J&J Harper.

"Zwingli, Huldrych." 2005. *The Oxford Encyclopedia of the Reformation*. Oxford: Oxford University Press.

Chapter

THE CATHOLIC REFORMATION

20

TIMELINE

A.D. 1495–1517	Cardinal Ximenes leads Catholic reform activities in Spain.
A.D. 1517	The Oratory of Divine Love is founded in Rome.
A.D. 1529	The Capuchins, a reform branch of the Franciscans, is officially recognized by the pope.
A.D. 1540	Ignatius of Loyola founds the Society of Jesus, also known as the Jesuits.
A.D. 1534–1549	Pope Paul III institutes a limited number of reforms prior to the Council of Trent.
A.D. 1545–1547	First session of the Council of Trent.
A.D. 1551–1552	Second session of the Council of Trent.
A.D. 1562	Teresa of Avila founds her first house of reformed Carmelites.
A.D. 1562–1563	Third session of the Council of Trent.
A.D. 1580	Discalced Carmelites are given legal status and receive their own province.
A.D. 1593	Discalced Carmelites make final break with Carmelites, forming their own order.

The Roman Catholic Church responded to the Protestant Reformation with two overlapping yet distinct movements. One is called the **Counter-Reformation** and the other is called the **Catholic Reformation.** The Counter-Reformation, as its name implies, refers to the efforts of those who were loyal to the pope and supportive of the customary practices of the Roman Catholic Church to counter (go against) the teachings and practices of the Protestant reformers. Because it was a movement designed to aggressively stop Protestant teachings, ideas, and practices, it was polemical and negative in its form. In contrast, the Catholic Reformation refers to the efforts of those who wanted to bring about the internal rebirth of Catholic sensibility—in theology, spirituality, religious piety, and morality.

Although the Catholic Reformation is often studied in relationship to the Protestant Reformation, it is not a movement that simply reacted to the Protestant Reformation. In fact, it began before the initial crises of the Protestant Reformation and continued even after the Reformation had resulted in the establishment of distinctive Protestant churches. Many of the figures belonging to the Catholic Reformation were as critical of the corrupt practices of the church as any of the Protestant reformers were. Rather than leaving the church, these Catholic reformers saw the abuses as an opportunity to call the church back to godly ways by reclaiming the traditions it had ignored or forgotten.

This chapter will focus on the Catholic reform movements prior to, during, and immediately following the Council of Trent (1545–1563). The Council of Trent is an important event in Catholic reform because one of its functions was to respond to the Protestant Reformation. Another function was to initiate an internal reform and spiritual reawakening based upon a re-evaluation of doctrinal issues that affected the lives of sixteenth-century Catholics. It is vital to understand that **conciliar** reform was a tradition in the Catholic Church that was used to clearly define doctrines and practice. The Council of Trent is often seen only in terms of the Counter-Reformation, whereas it stands in continuity with previous conciliar reforms. This chapter will look at the major movements of the Catholic Reformation, which includes the Council of Trent, the standardization of Catholic doctrine and practice, and the new spiritual awakening in Catholicism expressed both in the founding of religious orders and in the art of the period.

PRE-TRIDENTINE REFORM

Even before the Protestant reformers entered the scene, there were several early indications that Catholics were indeed ready for widespread reform and revival. Looking back at previous chapters, we can see that the call for reform councils is not new: this is especially significant in the Council of Constance (1414–1418), which had to address the Great Schism and the challenge of John Hus. Constance used the phrase "reform in head and members" to indicate that universal councils included the entire body of bishops as well as the Pope (the Bishop of Rome). Moreover, the "members" included all of the members of the church: in its widest sense, it was inclusive of every member, laity and clergy alike.

The Catholic reform movements that took place immediately before the Council of Trent are sometimes called pre-Tridentine reforms. Foremost among these was the reform that took place in Spain under Cardinal Ximenes (1495–1517). After the Spanish *reconquista* ("reconquest"), Spain became an ardently Christian country. Monks and friars were required to make reforms consistent with their vow of poverty. Religious houses that did not comply with approved standards of behavior were dissolved, their revenues going to the education of children, hospitals, and the poor.

Cardinal Ximenes also created a university at Alcala that encouraged the study of Hebrew and Greek for the training of Scholastic theologians and the encouragement of scholarly thought. A group of scholars under the cardinal's direction produced a critical edition of the Bible in Hebrew, Greek, and Latin, with commentaries. The Spanish Inquisition would later destroy many of these **polyglot Bibles** (containing several languages) along with the scriptures and numerous spiritual writings that had been translated into the vernacular (common speech) of the country. This was, in part, a Counter-Reformation movement directed against Protestant reformers who encouraged the common people to read the Bible and who spread their reform ideas through literature written in the vernacular. These Bibles appear also to have encouraged the Council of Trent's decision to declare that only one particular Latin translation of the Bible, the Vulgate, was the authoritative Bible of the Catholic Church.

During this time, many new religious orders were founded to revitalize the church, some coming out of this early Spanish reform. One of the most interesting developments of the pre-Tridentine period was a series of groups called **oratories**. These oratories were groups of clergy who banded together for the purpose of prayer, meditation, and mutual support as they participated in discussions about how they might reform the church. The most famous of these was the Oratory of Divine Love, which was founded in Rome *c.*1517. Likewise, a new religious order known as the Theatines was founded in 1524 by two members of the Oratory of Divine Love for the purpose of combating the abuses and scandals that corrupted the church at that time by training reform-minded clergy for positions of leadership in the church.

Other religious orders dedicated to reform include the Congregation of the Mission founded by St. Vincent de Paul in 1625 and the Ursulines founded in 1535. The Congregation of the Mission (also known as the Lazarists or the Vincentians) contributed to the Catholic Reformation by preaching missions (renewal retreats for lay people) and by preparing young men for ordination to the priesthood. One of the reasons the Catholic Church suffered so much abuse and corruption was that many of its priests had little education and were poorly trained for the priesthood. The Ursulines were the first religious order of women to dedicate themselves to teaching. These new orders represent what we call the "active" life. They did not withdraw from the world, as monks and nuns had done for centuries before. Rather, their entire mission was directed outwardly in ministry to those in need. They lived an ascetic lifestyle and devoted themselves to serving others in hospitals, orphanages, and schools for children. They also placed great emphasis on living a life of charity, a life lived for others that was socially responsible and Christian in its inspiration.

Perhaps the most influential of these new orders was the **Society of Jesus** or the Jesuits, founded by **Ignatius of Loyola** (1491–1556) in 1540. The small band that joined together with Ignatius was first called "the Company of Jesus." Like the mendicant orders, they lived a simple lifestyle, relying on alms for their livelihood. Ignatius intended for the Society to minister to the poor and to unbelievers, in particular, and to work with children and those who could not read or write. His interest in converting unbelievers would anticipate one of the results of the Catholic Reformation, namely, a trend of missionary expansion into newly discovered lands. He was also committed to the reform of the church and to the education of its members. Thus, the order became renowned for its achievements in education, especially higher education, including the education of members of the upper classes and the training of clergy. Their establishment as professors in the university system enabled the Jesuits to use their study of theology not only to serve the pastoral needs of the church, but also in disputes with the Protestant scholars of their times. The Jesuits viewed the Protestant reformers as disobedient to the church, whereas the Jesuits themselves took a vow of absolute obedience to the pope. They vowed to go without question and without delay wherever the pope might order them for the salvation of souls and the spreading of the true faith.

Ignatius of Loyola, the founder of the Jesuits, could not have seemed a more unlikely candidate for the religious life and sainthood. He was a Spaniard trained as a knight, shaped by a military background and way of thinking. His life before his conversion was not an exemplary one. He was even arrested once and accused of crimes in Pamplona, Spain, although we do not know the nature of the charges brought against him. His conversion came during a long convalescence, after he was gravely injured during a battle. He had been reading devotional books, including a life of Christ and lives of the saints—the only books that were available to him. Inspired by these stories, he decided that he would become a soldier for Christ. Shortly afterward, he went to a monastery and dedicated himself to prayer and meditation. He discovered—as did Luther—that he was tortured by his sins and by scruples. He was finally commanded by a confessor to stop punishing himself through excessive penance.

He obeyed, and it is in this story of his life that we can see the great importance he would place on obedience in his new order.

During his stay in the village of Manresa, Ignatius also drafted the first sketch of his **Spiritual Exercises**, which would become the tool of spiritual formation for those who joined him in his quest. It is a month-long examination and participation of the individual in the drama of sin and salvation, leading to a turning over of everything, especially the will, to obedience to one's religious superior and to the teachings of the church and its traditions. With his band of followers, Ignatius set off to offer himself to the pope for whatever service the church might need. Despite the papacy's resistance to the establishment of new religious orders, the Jesuits were officially recognized in 1540. Their motto sums up the Ignatian approach nicely: *Ad majorem Dei gloriam* ("To the greater glory of God").

In addition to these new religious orders, significant reforms resulted in new branches of already existing orders. These include the **Capuchins,** a reform branch of the Franciscan movement, and the Discalced ("without shoes") Carmelites, a reform branch of the Carmelite order. Both of these reforms met with great success but

Figure 20–1 *Ignatius of Loyola* (1491–1556), by Peter Paul Rubens (1577–1640).

were at times in great peril. The Capuchins, whose influence and preaching would be vital to the Catholic reform movement, were almost condemned when their superior (and popular preacher) Bernardino Ochino converted to the Protestant cause. This scandal, plus the unwavering opposition of the Observant Franciscans to this new branch of the order, almost led to their suppression. They weathered the crisis, however, and the Capuchins were recognized by the pope in 1529, getting their name from the unique four-pointed hood, which they wore with their brown habit. They were perhaps the most successful of the movements to reconstruct the spirit of an older order, and much of the credit for this goes to their founder Matteo da Bascio.

There were papal reforms, as well. Pope Paul III (r. 1534–1549) was elected pope upon the recommendation of the previous pope, who had attempted reform but was unable to carry it out. Although he was very much a Renaissance pope—enjoying the comforts of wealth and the power of his office—he was also intent on internal reform of the church. He appointed a number of reformers to the **College of Cardinals** (advisors to the pope and second in line of authority after the pope), all of whom had been members of the Oratory of Divine Love. He also appointed a reform commission to recommend changes in the way the church was run. Their report revealed some very serious problems: the papal office had become too secular; the cardinals needed to be less infatuated with the power and wealth of the world and more concerned about spiritual matters; and abuses such as the selling of church offices and indulgences needed to be stopped. Pope Paul III instituted a few reforms immediately as the result of this commission, but many others would have to wait for the Council of Trent.

THE COUNCIL OF TRENT AND CATHOLIC REFORM

It is difficult to neatly untangle the threads of the Catholic Reformation into those reforms that occurred before the important **Council of Trent** and those that took place afterwards. Additionally, reading conciliar documents is difficult: they sum up in statements the crucial issues of Christian faith and practice in a very dense form. It is necessary to know which issues were brought to the Council of Trent in order to understand fully the impact of these statements. In general, Catholics agreed on the need for an official council to either reconcile with the reformers, especially Luther, or to refute them and inaugurate reform from within the church itself. They had many concerns, among which were the scriptures, the **Eucharist**, the process of justification, the role of sin and grace, and the education of the clergy. Already in 1535, Pope Paul III had announced his intention to call a council, but the council did not actually take place until 1545. There were a number of factors that led to this delay.

First, there was a problem about its location. The cardinals insisted it be in Rome, and the Holy Roman Emperor, Charles V, insisted it be in Germany. Second, Charles V was pressuring Pope Paul III to call the council, but the emperor wanted the council to deal with the Lutherans who were causing political havoc in his territories. More specifically, he wanted some quick practical religious compromises to defuse the tension. The pope and the bishops, however, wanted to hold a doctrinal council rather than a practical one. They wanted to come to grips with the basic teachings of the church and then initiate an internal reform that would flow from this doctrinal clarification. Third, some church leaders wanted to avoid a council altogether. Those with pure motives doubted whether it was possible to convene a general (ecumenical) council that would include all Christendom. Some opposed the council because of political motives. The French king was often at war with Germany, and a council held in Germany would offend French church leaders. Others opposed it out of fear. They were not certain that the pope would be able to maintain control of the council and its proceedings.

When the Council of Trent was finally convened in 1545, its location was something of a compromise. The city of Trent, located in the Italian Alps and situated between southern German and northern Italian regions, was barely inside Charles' domain, yet it offered easy access to Italy. The council was made up of three separate sessions, which spanned 18 years and the reigns of four different popes. The first session (1545–1547) was largely controlled by representatives of the pope and so dealt with doctrinal definitions. The second session (1551–1552) dealt with a mixture of doctrinal and practical matters. The third and final session (1562–1563) concentrated mainly on disciplinary correction and means of regulating church activities in the future. Some meetings were poorly attended, the first session having only 28 delegates. A number of Protestants were present at the second session, but discussions between the two sides broke down without coming to any mutual understandings. Italian church leaders attended in the greatest numbers; French church leaders were noticeably absent. Some sessions had huge delegations from Spain and Portugal. Others did not. Yet, despite all its difficulties, the Council of Trent was successful in initiating reform within the Catholic Church. The council addressed a number of doctrinal issues that had relevance for the Protestant Reformation. In response to the Protestant reformers, who said that a person was justified by faith alone, the delegates of the council made a distinction between **justification** and salvation, asserting that a person is justified by faith, that faith is a gift, and that faith is the first stage of human salvation. When a person is justified, he or she is infused with faith, hope, and charity, all of which are necessary for the person to be united to Christ.

This link between justification and salvation emphasized the process of growth through God's gift of grace and the ability of human beings to assent to and cooperate with God's grace. This process of growth is called sanctification, and it follows justification. The fathers of the council were careful here to incorporate the insights of different theological schools, which stressed faith (Augustinian), feeling (Scotist), and action (Thomistic) working together in the relationship between God's grace and human nature. Luther's views were strictly Augustininian: God's grace, given in faith, was irresistible and could not be lost, as it is God's action alone. The council asserted that just as God's grace could allow for human cooperation, it also left the free will to deny that gift of grace, such as in apostasy. The contrast between the position of the Reformers and Trent on grace is linked to their interpretation of the nature and consequences of original sin. Luther and other Protestant reformers maintained that our human nature had been so severely damaged by the Fall that we had been made incapable, apart from the grace of God, of doing anything good in this life except through our justification in grace, which is the work of God alone. Although the council fathers agreed that our nature had disordered and remained so even after Baptism as the Protestant reformers asserted, they disagreed that our nature had been utterly destroyed. To the council fathers, human beings were capable of cooperating with God's grace in the life of the faithful. They therefore asserted that a "natural" cooperation with the "supernatural" grace of God was possible in human life and action.

Confronted by the Protestant reformers' appeal to the Bible as the sole authority, the council stated that unwritten tradition of the church must also be received with reverence, since it too contains the word of God, having its origins in the teaching of the apostles. The sacraments were reasserted as essential to the Christian life. The number of sacraments was fixed at seven: Baptism, Confirmation, Eucharist, Matrimony, Holy Orders, Penance, and Extreme Unction (Anointing of the Sick). They also developed the notion of *sacramentals*, those religious objects or devotions that convey spiritual benefits, though they do not have the full efficacy and centrality of the seven official sacraments. Holy water, as it is traditionally called, is an example of such a sacramental.

Luther and other reformers had attacked the traditional idea that the Mass (the Eucharist) was a re-enactment of Christ's sacrifice (see Chapter 18). For Luther, the concept of justification and of the "sacrifice" of the Mass were intertwined. He saw the emphasis on Mass as a sacrifice of *works* to appease God rather than a recollection of the grace of justification gained in *grace* due only to Christ. The Council of Trent recognized that Christ died once and for all for sin, but said that the Mass was a re-presentation of that one sacrifice.

The reality of Christ's presence in the Eucharist was an ancient Christian tradition, but the precise nature of the reality of this presence was debated over the centuries. Many Protestant Reformers took the position that Christ was spiritually present in the Lord's Supper, but not physically present. The Council of Trent, in response, asserts clearly that the elements of the bread and wine in the Mass were transformed into the body and blood of Christ in reality, officially adopting the Scholastic explanation of a change of substance (reality) but not of accident (appearance).

The council also defined the order and shape of the liturgy in a more uniform way than before. This ended many local variations and created the fixed form of the Mass as Catholics were to know it until the Second Vatican Council (see Chapter 24). The **Vulgate** (a Latin translation of the Bible widely in use in the West at least from the sixth century and containing the books of the Apocrypha) was declared to be the only authoritative translation of the Bible. At the time of the Council of Trent, Latin was still the recognized, official language of the universities and the educated. However, it had already begun to fall into disuse among the common people. In response to this cultural change, Protestant reformers had been commissioning vernacular translations of the Bible. However, because of certain doctrinal issues that were of concern to the reformers, they had been using versions of the Bible that did not contain the apocryphal books for their vernacular translations. Thus, Catholics and Protestants emerged from the Reformation with two different canons of scripture.

Although the Council of Trent had addressed a number of doctrinal issues, it was also a pastoral council dedicated to eliminating abuses and inspiring holiness among the church's clergy. To correct abuses, the fathers abolished the office of seller of indulgences. Bishops were given the power of supervision in their dioceses. Simony (the selling of church positions) and nepotism (the giving of church positions to relatives) were abolished; penalties were imposed for blasphemy and violation of celibacy. Luxurious dress and affluent lifestyles were discouraged among all Christians. Clerics who had previously worn the ordinary clothes of the time now had to wear special clerical garb. The **breviary** (prayer book containing the liturgy of the hours, the official prayer of priests and monks) was reformed to make it clearer and simpler to use, and it included more prayers and readings from scripture.

The Council of Trent also exhorted the clergy to be devout shepherds of souls, and to that end, it called for reforms that included education of clergy. Bishops were instructed to send their candidates for ordination to the university, or if there were no universities in the diocese, they should establish a **seminary** for their training. The Jesuit order was especially influential in implementing this aspect of the reforms. It greatly improved the clergy's ability to preach the Word, one of the principal reasons that many of the people had abandoned the Catholic Church for the preachers of the Protestant reformation. Bishops and clergy were now to be preachers and teachers of their flock. Therefore, after the council was concluded, a short summary of what had been upheld by Trent was put together to provide clergy with uniform instruction on doctrine and religious practice. This document was called the Roman Catechism, though it was not a catechism in the usual sense of the word because it was intended for the instruction of clergy.

As had been the case in the Protestant Reformation, the Catholic Reformation produced a large number of catechisms for the instruction of lay people. These catechisms usually contained summary teaching on the Apostles' Creed, the Lord's Prayer and the Hail Mary, the Ten Commandments, the commandments of the church, the sacraments, and the virtues and vices. Perhaps the most respected and widely read Catholic catechism was *Summa Doctrinae Christianae* (1554) written by Peter Canisius, a Jesuit. This catechism was admired by many, even by Protestant preachers, for its clarity and persuasiveness. Another important figure in Catholic religious education was Charles Borromeo, who established the Confraternity of Christian Doctrine (1566) for the instruction of children.

THE REVIVAL OF MYSTICISM IN SPAIN

Although many new religious orders were founded and older orders were reformed in the period immediately preceding the Council of Trent, others were being established or reformed during and immediately following the council. Some of these were vital to the conciliar process and its implementation; all of them were important because of the spiritual fervor with which they led the people to a greater understanding of church doctrine and practice, involving a variety of church members. In particular, Spain was experiencing a reform of the Carmelite order and the revival of mysticism in the persons of Teresa of Avila and John of the Cross.

Teresa of Avila (1515–1582) had spent much of her life in a struggle between worldly comforts and the interior life of prayer. At the age of 40, she experienced such a profound conversion, accompanied by ecstasies and visions, that she felt called to return to the simpler, harsher rule of the Carmelite founders. Thus, Teresa and her protégé and follower, **John of the Cross** (1542–1591), established the Discalced Carmelites. The term *discalced* means "unshod," referring to the spiritual practice of going barefoot in order to fulfill Jesus' mandate to provide oneself with nothing for the journey, not even sandals (Matthew 10:9–10). Teresa's primary calling was to poverty and prayer. The "barefoot" Carmelites were to rely only on charity and the providence of God to support them. Teresa's first foundation was made in Avila in secret, for she knew the opposition her reforms would face. She ultimately made 17 separate foundations during her lifetime, traveling widely throughout Spain to do so. These foundations were made up of sisters who followed her example and teaching. However, there was no official recognition of these foundations or the Carmelite reform movement until 1580, when permission finally was granted for them to form a separate province within the Carmelite order. Later, in 1598, the order of **Discalced Carmelites** received its own superior and became a separate order. Teresa's combination of common sense, political acumen, and profound spirituality enabled her to establish her foundations against opposition from other Carmelite branches and in spite of the suspicions of the Spanish Inquisition.

We have many of Teresa's writings because the priests who served as her confidantes and advisors insisted that she write down her life and her method of prayer as a means of convincing the inquisitors that she was not a heretic. The most famous of these are her *Life*, an autobiographical account, and the *Interior Castle*, a description of her method of prayer. We also have a number of the writings of John of the Cross, including his exquisitely written poems in the *Ascent of Mount Carmel* and his *Dark Night of the Soul*. Teresa and John's contemplation of God and their life lived from the center of that contemplation was one of the great contributions of the Carmelite reform movement. The simple beauty of their prayer of the heart and their focus on the love of God can be seen in these brief excerpts from their writings.

> The important thing is not to think much but to love much;
> and so do that which best stirs you to love.
>
> (Teresa of Avila 1979, 70)

> To come to the knowledge of all desire,
> the knowledge of nothing ...
> To come to the knowledge you have not
> you must go by a way you know not.
>
> (John of the Cross 1987, 137)

> Let nothing upset you,
> Let nothing startle you,
> All things pass;
> God does not change.
> Patience wins all it seeks.
> Whoever has God lacks nothing;
> God alone is enough.
>   (*Prayer of St. Teresa*, written on the inside of her prayer book; Teresa of Avila 1996, 33)

> How gently and lovingly
> You awake in my heart,
> Where in secret You dwell alone;
> And in your sweet breathing,
> Filled with good and glory,
> How tenderly You swell my heart with love.
>   (John of the Cross, "The Living Flame of Love," in Adels 1987, 203)

Both John of the Cross and Teresa of Avila are saints and Doctors of the Church. Teresa is one of only two women to have been awarded this title.

ART AS A REFLECTION OF THE REFORMATION PERIOD

The art of the Reformation period, both Catholic and Protestant, reflects a number of theological issues. When Protestant Reformation communities, particularly those associated with the later reformers, built new churches, they built them with a simplicity and austerity that did not exist in churches dating from the Middle Ages or before. Most often, however, older churches were merely taken over and the ornamentation removed. The walls were whitewashed to cover paintings and elaborate decorations on the walls and to bring a greater sensation of light and simplicity into the worship space. They stripped churches of their statues and ornamentation in order to concentrate on the centrality of the Word. On occasion, these churches would even be stripped of their furniture so that only a pulpit (preaching stand) remained in a central place in the church. This stripping of ornamentation was consistent with their ban on the use of images. Lutheran churches, which tended to be more moderate in their reforms, often retained the ornamentation of pre-Reformation churches.

The art of the Renaissance movement is recognizable for its realism. This realism was especially evident in the subject matter portrayed by artists of the Protestant Reformation. Although some depicted actual scenes from the Bible, others focused on everyday life situations that could be used as visual metaphors for preaching and teaching about the moral life. In particular, the Dutch artists of the late sixteenth and early seventeenth centuries sought to depict in portraits, landscapes, and other types of art a variety of ordinary circumstances of life illustrating the beauty of creation, the positive and negative sides of human nature, the vanity of striving for power, and the human need for salvation. Germany did not produce any famous Protestant artists during the Reformation. However, it did create new kinds of music designed for the participation of large congregations of lay people. The hymns were sung in the vernacular (rather than Latin). Some of our most well-known Christian hymns, including several new arrangements by Johann Sebastian Bach, date back to the time of the Reformation.

In contrast with their Protestant counterparts, Catholics not only preserved the architecture of the medieval churches whenever possible but also commissioned new ornamentation and art which would dramatically illustrate the truths of Catholic orthodoxy. The style begun in this period is termed the **Baroque**. While it had been influenced by the realism of the Renaissance, Baroque art and architecture added the dimension of light and darkness, suggesting that the division between this world and the heavenly realm is penetrable, at least through the mediation of the Virgin Mary and the saints. In Figure 20–2, we have a scene in which Paul experiences his conversion on the road to Damascus. What is uniquely different is the perspective of the scene: the artist is clearly trying to personally involve the observer, who looks up at the horse and sky as if he or she is lying on the ground with St. Paul. The artists attempted to involve the worshippers, appealing to their feelings and engaging them in the movement of faith. Observers, as believers, were invited to put themselves into the story, to see the conversion as St. Paul experienced it. Note also the use of light to express the drama of the event.

Baroque art also sought to impress its viewers with awesome displays of riches and to evoke in the viewer a sense of awe. Baroque churches were filled with rich and

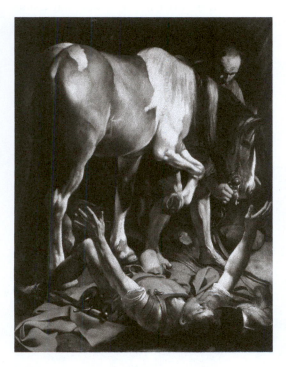

Figure 20–2 This famous painting of Paul's conversion on the way to Damascus is by Caravaggio, *c.*1601, and typifies Baroque art. Cerasi Chapel, Santa Maria del Popolo, Rome.

Figure 20–3 *St. Teresa in Ecstasy,* by Bernini, 1646 (1598–1680). Santa Maria della Vittoria, Rome. This statue portrays the piercing of the heart that Teresa reports in the *Life,* 29:13–14.

ornate illustrations of the great events of the Bible and church history. They would overwhelm the visitor with dramatic representations of the avenues of salvation available to the believer: Mary, the saints and relics, the crucified Christ, and symbols of the Eucharist.

In Figure 20–3, the observer looks up at Bernini's famous statue *St. Teresa in Ecstasy.* This statue conveys to the observer complex devotional and erotic overtones as it portrays the saint caught up into the divine realm as her heart is pierced. The church is small and dark; the statue offers a glance into the realms of heavenly light in which the human and the divine meet and are joined in bliss.

Figure 20–4 sums up many of the themes of this chapter and draws together the many strands of the Catholic Reformation. It shows a processional float, honoring a saint by bringing the presence of the art and ornamentation out of the church itself and into the everyday settings and lives of the people. As an art form, it was the intention of the Baroque to bring immediacy of experience, to appeal to the feelings and the emotional side of faith, and to illustrate doctrine in a way that made pastoral sense and yet was compelling religiously

Figure 20–4 A typical processional reflecting the Baroque Catholic sense of bringing the sacred out of the church and to the people.

and artistically. In a new way, this continues the tradition of "sacramentals," as procession was also a way of bringing the holy into the everyday places and things which people encountered. This presents God as everywhere, and not confined only to the inside of the churches, but in all experience.

CONCLUDING REFLECTIONS

The Reformation period was a turbulent time for both Catholics and Protestants. Yet from this age of turmoil emerged a clearer understanding of Christianity. Despite the scandal of disunity, Christians were now more apt to know what they believed and why. They were more informed participants in worship, and they had more powerful and inspiring preaching available to them. For Catholics, there was the additional result of the new spiritual awareness of the traditions of the church, their valuing of the sacraments, and the desire to express their faith through charity and actions for the salvation of souls. Forced by crisis to define itself at the Council of Trent, Catholicism began to express in new ways what it held to be true. Through the council, the catechism, the new and reformed religious orders, and the artistic and popular revivals of spiritual devotions, the Catholic Church found its way both to an inner reform and to a new place in the world.

Key Terms

Baroque	Counter-Reformation	seminary
breviary	Discalced Carmelites	Society of Jesus
Capuchins	Eucharist	*Spiritual Exercises*
Catholic Reformation	Ignatius of Loyola	Teresa of Avila
College of Cardinals	John of the Cross	transubstantiation
conciliar	justification	Vulgate
Council of Trent	polyglot Bible	

Questions for Reading

1. What is the difference between the Counter-Reformation and the Catholic Reformation?

2. What signs of reform were present in the Catholic Church even before the challenge of Luther and other Protestant reformers?

3. Who was Ignatius of Loyola, and how did he shape the movement he founded? Why did this movement become so important to the effort of Catholic reform?

4. For what purpose was the Council of Trent called? What difficulties did it encounter?

5. What were the *doctrinal* issues addressed by the Council of Trent, and what is their importance for Christian theology?

6. What were the *disciplinary* or *practical* reforms made by the Council of Trent?

7. What are the seven "official" sacraments? What is a sacramental? What is the difference between the two?

8. Name three of the new orders founded during the Catholic Reformation. How are they different from previous religious orders?

9. Contrast the worship styles and decoration of churches in the Protestant and Catholic traditions during the Reformation period. What is the Baroque style of art, and how is it representative of the Catholic Reformation?

Works Consulted/Recommended Reading

Adels, Jill Haak, ed. 1987. *The Wisdom of the Saints: An Anthology.* New York: Oxford University.

Chadwick, Owen. 1965. *The Reformation.* Baltimore, MD: Penguin Books.

Dupre, Louis, and James Wiseman, eds. 1988. *Light from Light: An Anthology of Christian Mysticism.* New York: Paulist Press.

Egan, Harvey. 1991a. *An Anthology of Christian Mysticism.* Collegeville, MN: Liturgical Press.

Egan, Harvey. 1991b. *Ignatius of Loyola the Mystic.* Collegeville, MN: Liturgical Press.

Hempel, Eberhard. 1965. *Baroque Art and Architecture in Central Europe.* Baltimore, MD: Penguin.

Iserloh, Erwin, Josef Glazik, and Hubert Jedin. 1980–1982. *History of the Church.* Vol. 5. *Reformation and Counter Reformation.* Translated by Anselm Biggs and Peter W. Becker. New York: Seabury.

John of the Cross. 1976. *Collected Works.* Translated by Kieran Kavanaugh and Otilio Rodriguez. Washington, DC: ICS Publications.

John of the Cross. 1987a. *Ascent of Mount Carmel and The Dark Night of the Soul.* Translated by Kiernan Kavanaugh. New York: Paulist Press.

John of the Cross. 1987b. *Selected Writings: John of the Cross.* Translated by Kieran Kavanaugh and Otilio Rodriguez. New York: Paulist Press.

McNally, Robert. 1970. *The Council of Trent, the Spiritual Exercises, and the Catholic Reform.* New York: Fortress.

Mullet, Michael. 1999. *The Catholic Reformation.* London: Routledge.

Olin, John. 1990. *The Catholic Reform: From Cardinal Ximenes to the Council of Trent, 1495–1563.* New York: Fordham University.

O'Malley, John W. 2013. *Trent: What Happened at the Council.* Cambridge, MA: Harvard University Press.

Sheldrake, Philip. 1992. *Spirituality and History.* New York: Crossroad.

Short, William S. 1989. *The Franciscans.* Collegeville, MN: Liturgical Press/Michael Glazier.

Teresa of Avila. 1976. *Collected Works.* Vol. I. Translated by Kieran Kavanaugh and Otilio Rodriguez. Washington, DC: ICS Publications.

Teresa of Avila. 1979. *The Interior Castle.* Translated by Kieran Kavanaugh and Otilio Rodriguez. New York: Paulist Press.

Teresa of Avila. 1996. *The Complete Poetry of St. Teresa of Avila: A Bilingual Edition.* Edited and translated by Eric W. Vogt. New Orleans, LA: University Press of the South.

Wisch, Barbara, and Susan Scott Munshower, eds. 1990. *"All the World's a Stage—": Art and Pageantry in the Renaissance and Baroque.* University Park, PA: Penn State University.

Chapter

THE COMING OF GLOBAL CHRISTIANITY

Mission, Empire, and Post-Colonialism

TIMELINE

1493	Pope Alexander VI issues *Inter caetera* and divides newly discovered lands between Spain and Portugal.
1550–1551	Bartolomé de Las Casas and Juan Ginés de Sepúlveda debate rights of indigenous peoples at Council of Valladolid in Spain.
1583	Matteo Ricci arrives in China to begin the Jesuit mission there.
1742	Congregation for the Propagation of the Faith condemns the "Chinese rites."
1906	A prolonged "revival" on Azusa Street in Los Angeles brings national and international attention, helping to launch the Pentecostal movement.
1921	Believed to be a prophet by his followers, Simon Kimbangu begins a ministry in the Belgian Congo that launches one of the largest of many African Initiated Churches.
1962	Pope John XXIII offers prayers for "a new Pentecost" as he opens the Second Vatican Council.
1975	Cardinal Léon-Joseph Suenens wins Vatican approval for the Catholic Charismatic Renewal movement, which had been growing since the late 1960s, and conducts a Charismatic mass at St. Peter's Square in Rome.
c.2000	More Christians in the world start to live in the Global South than in the Global North.

Between the seventh-century Arab conquests and the Reformation of the sixteenth century, the map of the Christian world grew significantly smaller. Losses were only partially offset by the late ancient and medieval conversion of non-Romanized, northern portions of Europe. As noted in Chapters 13 and 14, the world of the "Middle" Ages between antiquity and modernity had been marked by Christianity's creation of a distinctively Christian culture that built upon the classical culture of antiquity. Christianity took on a distinctively geographical and territorial character as "Christendom." The very concept of "Europe" as Christian territory came into being at this time, thanks to the Carolingian renaissance (see Chapter 13).

Christianity's identification with Europe became even more marked after the gradual occupation of the Byzantine Empire's Asian territories by the Ottoman Turks, who finally captured Constantinople in 1453 and destroyed the Byzantine Empire altogether. Christianity's medieval expansion to Central Asia, China, and India under the Church of the East (often called "Nestorians") had ended and largely been reversed by the Mongol invasions of the thirteenth and fourteenth centuries. Small communities did survive in the south of India. African Christianity was limited to Ethiopia, which converted in the fourth century and remained a Christian kingdom until the twentieth century. Nubia (southern Egypt and central Sudan) had been converted either from Alexandria to the north or Aksum (Ethiopia) to the east, sometime between the late fourth to late fifth centuries, but nearly 1,000 years of Nubian Christianity came to an end at about this time. Both Nubian and Ethiopian Christianity were isolated from the rest of "Christendom" because of the spread of Islam and by their refusal to accept the Council of Chalcedon (see Chapter 11). Christians also survived, in considerable though declining numbers, under Muslim governance in the *dar al-Islam*, the Muslim territorial equivalent of Christendom.

Christianity began to break out of its European shell well before the Reformation permanently fragmented Western Christianity. At the same time that Catholicism was losing its European domination, it began a massive new expansion with the era of world exploration and colonization, led by the Catholic monarchies of Portugal and Spain. Portuguese ships had been exploring the west and then the east coast of Africa throughout the fifteenth century, culminating in Vasco da Gama's voyage to the southwest coast of India in 1497–1499. Meanwhile, Christopher Columbus had already claimed what he insisted were "the Indies" in the name of King Fernando and Queen Isabela of Spain. To resolve conflicting claims, in 1493 Pope Alexander VI's bull *Inter caetera* ("Among other [works]") established a dividing line in the Atlantic, from the North Pole to the South Pole, that granted Portugal ownership of newly discovered lands to the east of the line and to Spain lands to the west of it. The pope's global partitioning was further defined by a treaty between Spain and Portugal in 1494, and another treaty in 1524 that extended the boundary to the east in the Pacific Ocean and also gave Portugal what is now Brazil. Before long, Catholic France, Protestant England, and the Protestant Netherlands would join in, and their conquests, along with Portuguese and Spanish decline, would eventually make the global demarcation lines irrelevant.

The first part of Chapter 21 considers Christianity's global expansion from the fifteenth to the twentieth centuries by focusing on several developments or episodes that seemed especially valuable for illustrating the difficulty of fulfilling Jesus' gospel command to teach all nations (Matthew 28:19) in tandem with European conquest and colonization. The second part of the chapter discusses how Christianity since the mid-twentieth century has learned to live without colonial sponsorship in a post-colonial world. Subsequent chapters will focus on Christianity's responses to the conditions of the modern (post-Enlightenment) world and to globalization.

CHRISTIANITY IN THE AGE OF GLOBAL EXPLORATION
CONVERSION, CONQUEST, AND COLONIALISM

After the Fall of the Roman Empire in the West, Christianity had spread in two different ways. In societies less developed than that of classical civilization, especially in lands to the north and the south, Christianity came top-down after the elites of those societies were converted either by official deputations from Rome or Constantinople, or by wandering Celtic or Benedictine monkish evangelists. But it also spread in more personal and entrepreneurial fashion via commercial routes, especially to the East, where Christians encountered equally advanced civilizations in Persia, India, and China. Top-down conversion continued, heavily aided now by military conquest, beginning with the Portuguese explorations in Africa. There the papacy conceded to the crown via the *padroado real* ("royal patronage"), the control of church appointments and revenues, an arrangement mirrored in the papal grant of the similar *patronato real* to the Spanish crown in its newly acquired territories. But the tradition of courageous individual operators also continued, usually in the wake of exploration and conquest. The new Catholic religious order called the Jesuits (see Chapter 20) brought Christianity to indigenous peoples in French-occupied North America and to peoples in ancient civilizations like India, China, and Japan.

Whether by individual initiative or as an adjunct of colonial occupation, conversion to Christianity could come at great human and cultural cost, aspects of which were apparent to at least some observers at the time, others of which have only been acknowledged with the benefit of hindsight: the horrific demographic effects of diseases brought by Europeans to peoples who had never been exposed to them (deadly smallpox may have spread from Hispaniola [today Haiti and the Dominican Republic] to Cuba, Mexico, Yucatán, and Peru in less than 20 years); the de facto imposition of Christian faith by conquest; the destruction of indigenous cultures, often in the name of incompatibility with Christian doctrine or morality; and ruthless economic exploitation, including forced labor and slavery. That sensitive consciences among both clergy and lay people tried at times to counteract these lamentable trends cannot make up for the damage done, often in the name of fidelity to the gospel of Jesus Christ.

413

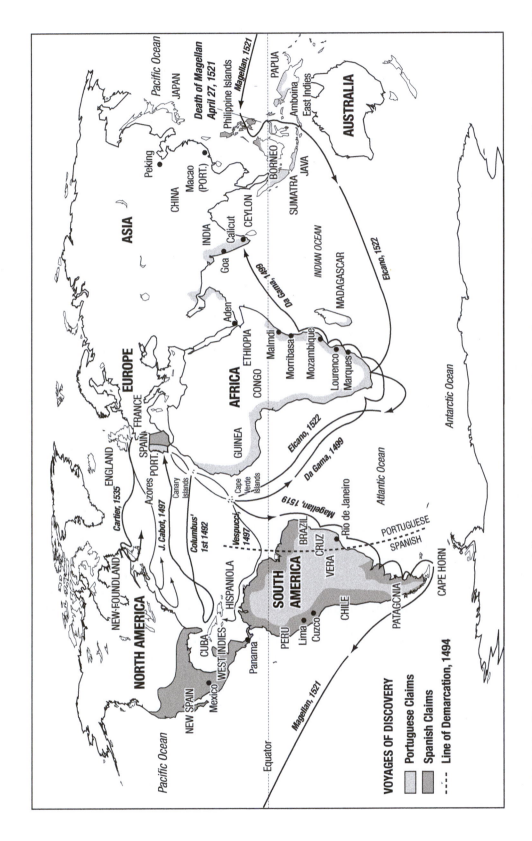

Figure 21–1 Map illustrating European voyages of discovery during the fifteenth and sixteenth centuries and the colonial claims of Spain and Portugal.

Preaching the Gospel in the New World: Bartolomé de Las Casas and the Rights of Indigenous Peoples

Pope Alexander VI's partitioning of the globe had called on the Spanish and Portuguese monarchs to bring the inhabitants of the new lands into the Catholic faith. The papal mandate raised fundamental questions. The pope had said that the inhabitants were to be brought into Christianity "in charity." Was military conquest compatible with that evangelizing mission, or was it supposed to happen quite apart from Spanish and Portuguese arms? What rights did the inhabitants have simply as human beings, a status that not all were willing to grant? Could they be conquered and enslaved if they refused to accept the Christian message? What were their rights even *if* they accepted Christianity? These questions were raised almost immediately after Columbus' voyages to the Caribbean islands. Their early answers laid down some basic principles for the exploration and conquests that followed. Indian slavery was forbidden for Indians who were subjects of the Spanish crown. But an important exception was the class of islanders called "Caribs," whose supposed cannibalism made them fit objects of attack in a just war, and traditional war doctrine accepted enslavement of defeated enemies as compensation for a just war. It helped too that the definition of who was and who was not a Carib was essentially arbitrary.

The "Laws of Burgos," adopted in 1512 after debate in the presence of the king, were an early attempt to settle policy. The Laws declared that Indians were to be treated as free beings, but they could nevertheless be forced to listen to instruction in the Catholic faith. They could also be forced to work in return for clothes and housing, an imposition that was justified by using the involuntary nature of taxation as an example. One-third of Indians were expected to work in gold mines. Pregnant women would not be required to do manual labor. The Laws thus enfranchised the labor system called the *encomienda*, which gave landowners grants of Indians to work their land. A "Clarification" one year later offered further protection to children, who could learn trades. Indians would be required to work for nine months and to have three months to work on their own farms. A sinister supplement was the *Requerimiento* ("Requirement"), a public pronouncement *in Spanish* that would henceforth be made whenever Spaniards encountered new indigenous peoples, who were to be told that God had given the new lands to the king of Spain, that they must hand over their lands to him, and listen to the declaration of the Catholic faith. If they accepted it, they could become the king's vassals. If they rejected it, they would be attacked and enslaved and their property would be seized.

The religious order of the Dominicans led a protest against the Laws of Burgos, most prominently a latecomer to the order named **Bartolomé de Las Casas** (1484–1566), originally a secular priest (not a member of a religious order) in Hispaniola and a commercial entrepreneur with his own Indian workers. Las Casas had participated willingly in the conquest of Cuba in 1512–1514. But the atrocities that he saw disillusioned him with war as a means of gaining new territory for Christianity. He renounced his *encomienda* and in 1518 began to preach against the injustice of wars of conquest. Four years later, he joined the Dominicans and became a tireless advocate for the non-coercive preaching of the gospel. As he later argued in a treatise on evangelizing methods, *On the Only Way of Converting* (1539), written against Franciscan methods that favored mass conversions and mass Baptisms, the gospel must be presented in a non-coercive way, with full and free understanding and indoctrination. Any other way was both wrong and futile. He also asked for restitution of what had been taken from the Indians.

His first effort to realize his ideal was a colonization program, with peasants from Spain, on the South American mainland in what is now Venezuela. It failed badly. To get a royal concession for his colony, Las Casas had to secure investors and was never able to make the venture profitable. Indian attacks, some in reprisal for Spanish slaving expeditions, forced the colony to end in 1522. To deal with the problem of a reliable labor supply, in 1518, he endorsed African slavery as an alternative to Indians or Spanish peasants. Many years later, in his three-volume *History of the Indies*, he regretted that position and conceded that African slavery was no more legitimate than Indian slavery. His most ambitious and successful experiment to implement his program was the Dominican-governed territory in what is now Guatemala. In 1537, he secured a contract from the governor of Guatemala to enter unconquered land until then dominated by fierce and war-like Indians, hence its name of Tuzulutlán, "Land of War," and to pacify it and turn it to the king's service using friars alone and no soldiers. A condition was that no *encomienda* would be granted nor Spaniards permitted to enter for five years. The results were sufficiently successful that in 1547 the emperor Charles V recognized the new name of Tuzulutlán as *Verapaz* ("True Peace"). Despite occasional violent episodes, including one in 1555 in which Christian Indians attacked other Indians in reprisal for the deaths of two Dominican missionaries and their followers, with a total death toll of 300, the mission survived and its territory remained closed to soldiers and under Dominican jurisdiction for nearly the next three centuries.

Las Casas himself was not in Guatemala for long. To recruit more Dominicans, he traveled back to Spain in 1540, where he was an influential voice in the adoption of the "New Laws of 1542," which once again forbade the enslavement of Indians (the earlier prohibition had been overturned in 1530) and set the *encomienda* system on the way to eventual elimination by restricting it to those currently alive who already held it. To promote his case for an immediate end of the *encomienda*, he composed an account of the brutality of the early years of Spanish conquest, especially in Hispaniola, that was published a decade later as his celebrated *Brief Account of the Destruction of the Indies* (1552), the book that would make him famous—or in some quarters notorious. Settlers and even many clergy strongly resented the New Laws of 1542. As their supposed author, Las Casas became the lightning rod for their resentment. Appointed bishop of Chiapa in 1545, he faced near rebellion when he made a condition of the 1545 Easter duty (the Catholic obligation to have one's confession heard once a year) the freeing of all Indian slaves.

Issues in Moral Theology: Francisco de Vitoria and the Rights of the Indigenous Peoples

The travels of Columbus and the subsequent Spanish conquest of "undiscovered" lands created a dramatic challenge to medieval Christianity and its moral system. Commonly held moral restraints were destroyed during the Spanish Conquistadors' brutal attacks on the Native American "barbarians" and seizure of their property. The violence attracted the attention of many in Spain, including a prominent Dominican priest and scholar, Francisco de Vitoria (1483–1546). Vitoria defended the Indians and their rights to property and self-governance, using a primitive human rights argument. All persons, he said, whether barbarian, heretic, or Christian, have a common rational faculty, a universal human characteristic based on the "possession of the image of God." This faculty enables humans to have dominion over their actions and thus dominion over temporal goods as well. Just as it was wrong for the Spanish to unjustly attack, steal from, or enslave non-Catholic Europeans, it was equally wrong to bring such harm on the Indians.

Vitoria noted the Indians' use of reason. They possessed an orderly social system that included marriage, governing authorities, a system of economic exchange, and "a kind of religion." Natural reason and morality dictated that they were entitled to the same treatment as Europeans.

A further contribution of Vitoria was his application of the doctrine of a just war, as Augustine and Thomas Aquinas had developed it. According to that doctrine, war was not moral except as a defense against aggression or to correct a grave evil. Wars against other religions or against people who refused to convert were not moral. The doctrine applied in the New World just as it did in the Old. More interesting, Vitoria argued that Christians must examine the justice of particular wars. If there is no just cause, the killing of the others is immoral. He writes:

> But in the case before us the enemy is innocent. Therefore they may not be killed. Again, a prince sins when he commences a war in such a case … Therefore soldiers are not excused when they fight in bad faith.

Continuing agitation over the New Laws culminated in 1550–1551, when Charles V authorized a public debate in Valladolid in Spain between Las Casas and the prominent theologian and humanist Juan Ginés de Sepúlveda (1494–1573), on the justice of wars of conquest and on the rights and nature of the indigenous peoples. The debate has become famous as one of the earliest public discussions of what are now called human rights. Though conducted in theoretical terms, the debate had urgent contemporary implications. Sepúlveda argued mainly in terms of natural law, saying that war could and should justly be waged against peoples guilty of crimes against nature like human sacrifice, cannibalism, and sodomy. Such peoples did not seem able to govern themselves in a civilized way and therefore needed pacification, and some of them were a violent threat to weaker Indians. Also, the papacy's mandate entailed conquest in the name of spreading the true faith. Las Casas' replies consisted of denying Sepúlveda's premises about Indian incapacity for self-government, saying that there was no evidence that they were of the sort whom Aristotle had described as "slaves by nature"; that Christian tradition forbade conversion by force; and that biblical injunctions to wage war against idolatry could only apply to the Canaanites and others named in the Bible (he was thinking of the institution of holy war in the biblical book of Joshua) and not to people generally. He also said it was better to tolerate the lesser evil of human sacrifice than the greater evil of indiscriminate war.

The jurists and theologians in attendance argued for months but could not reach agreement about who won the debate. In practical terms, perhaps, Las Casas lost. The Franciscans continued to accept armed escorts in their missionary work. The *encomienda* survived as a labor system, though Las Casas could claim victory in Peru in a ten-year struggle throughout the 1550s to keep the crown from making *encomiendas* "perpetual" with the descendants of the current holder—instead, they would end with the death of the current holder. Despite his failures and his rather difficult personality, posterity has hailed him as a true prophet of human rights, and a latter-day Jeremiah for the Spaniards, in the words of Helen Rand Parish. Besides his tireless advocacy on behalf of the Indians, there are his invaluable historical and ethnographic books. The Dominican order began a cause for his canonization in 1976, and the Catholic Church initiated a process for his beatification in 2002. His impact on Latin American liberation theology has been recognized by Gustavo Gutiérrez (see Chapter 27).

The Jesuit Missions to the Far East: Inculturation and the Rites Controversy

The Jesuits, befitting their origin as a kind of rapid deployment evangelizing team, were well suited for the ambitious missionary enterprises launched not long after their founding by Ignatius Loyola in 1534. Their bold experimentation with linguistic, cultural, and ceremonial adaptation to local conditions make their work of great historical and theological interest. Long before **inculturation** was coined as a theological concept, the Jesuits were pushing the proverbial envelope by shaping their presentation of the Christian faith to the cultural conditions of proud and long-established religions and civilizations. In 1542, Francis Xavier (1506–1552) went first to India, to the western port of Goa where the Portuguese were long established, and then in 1549 to Japan. The challenge for such missionaries would be breaking free of the governmental control, the *padroado*, exercised by the Portuguese crown. Decades later, in 1605, Italian Jesuit Roberto de Nobili came first to Goa and then traveled inland to the Indian town of Madura, where he presented himself as a *sannyasi*, a Hindu holy man, dressed in a saffron robe, wearing wooden clogs, and keeping a vegetarian diet. Eventually he won acceptance into upper castes and over a lifetime made several thousand converts. Despite constant opposition from Catholic rivals in other religious orders, de Nobili ultimately succeeded in getting official permission for Brahmin converts to retain features emblematic of their status, such as the three

Figure 21–2 The upper level of this print depicts Fr. Matteo Ricci (1552–1610) and two other missionaries, along with symbols of the sciences for which the Jesuits in China became famous. The lower level depicts two Chinese converts to Christianity making their profession of faith.

threads of white cotton from the left shoulder, or the single plait of hair called the *kudumi*, on the grounds that they were civil, not religious designations.

Xavier had tried and failed to enter China just before his death in 1552. It would be another generation before two Italian Jesuits, including scientist and missionary **Matteo Ricci** (1552–1610), secured invitations to enter in 1583, but only after learning the language and dressing first as Buddhist monks. Ricci later donned the square bonnet and silk robes of a Confucian scholar in order to get access to the Mandarin (imperial government) bureaucracy. He was able to use his training in mathematics and astronomy, and his skills with clocks, map projections, and the like to gain admission to the imperial capital of Beijing in 1598. A great accomplishment was his world map, "Great Map of Ten Thousand Countries," which positioned China accurately relative to global dimensions. His religious treatise *T'ien-chu shih-i* (The True Meaning of the Lord of Heaven) was his most important apologetic work. For his contributions to Chinese culture, he became known as the "Doctor from the Great Western Ocean," with the Chinese name of Li Mat'ou. At his death in 1610, he was buried in a plot outside the city given by the emperor and honored with an imperial consecration.

The success of the Jesuits in India and China was always controversial, not only with local non-Christians but also with rival Christian groups. The authorities in Rome were constantly being lobbied to crack down on Jesuit adaptations of Christian motifs to local conditions. Controversy began while Ricci was still alive and burned on for more than a century. It came to be known as the **Rites controversy** because of Jesuit adaptations to such Confucian rituals as prayers, prostrations, and offerings to ancestors at family tombs, as well as the cult of Confucius himself, who was regarded as the "ancestor" of magistrates and scholars. There was also criticism of the Jesuits' adoption of the Chinese character meaning "Heaven" as a substitute for "God," because "Lord of Heaven" was more familiar to Chinese as a reference to divinity. The defenders of such adjustments always argued that Confucian practices were chiefly civil and not religious. Despite much back-and-forth from Rome, the ultimate resolution in 1742 forbade all participation in Confucian rites. That meant the virtual end of the Catholic mission to China. It would take another 200 years before the papacy would concede the legitimacy of the civil-not-religious distinction. In 1942, the Vatican department in charge of missions, the Congregation for the Propagation of the Faith, finally reversed its earlier condemnation, partly in response to Japanese Catholics in the 1930s who were under pressure to salute Japanese war dead at a Shinto shrine (among other things, the history of the controversy shows the difficulty of defining what is properly "religious" and what is not).

The Jesuit Reductions in Paraguay

An altogether different kind of Jesuit mission was the one carried out over a period of about 150 years in Spanish-governed Paraguay, among the indigenous people called the Guarani, who lived in a region adjoining what is today Paraguay, Uruguay, northeastern Argentina, and the southern portion of Portuguese-governed Brazil. The missions, which were called "**reductions**," were based on the Jesuits' desire to keep the Guarani safe from slave traders and other forms of exploitation in a secure environment in which they could be trained in the Catholic faith. The basic model was that of the Spanish mission system, with a pastor and at least one other priest, *caciques* (native chieftains), and a *cabildo* or town council, whose members served one-year terms and were elected by the outgoing council, with a chief magistrate chosen by the governor. Families lived in long houses with separate apartments. The economy was a mix of private and collective, with communally farmed property but individual family gardens. Products such as painting and sculptures were sold to buy necessities that could not be made on site. The people were educated and taught Christian doctrine, how to read, play musical instruments, and so on. Europeans were banned from the settlements. At the system's peak, in the 1730s, there were more than 100,000 people spread out among about 30 settlements, in sizes ranging from 1,000 to 8,000.

The reductions eventually came to grief as a consequence of a 1750 treaty between Portugal and Spain that required some of the missions to be moved. Resistance to the move had to be put down by armed force. The reductions' final end came in 1773 when Catholic monarchies forced the papacy to suppress the Jesuit order altogether. The reductions have ever since exercised an understandable fascination, with older Catholic literature describing them as an Indian utopia under benign Jesuit guidance. A powerful 1986 movie *The Mission*, with big-name stars, portrayed the tragic end of the reductions in lurid colors that to some extent played off contemporary 1980s debates over the role of violence in liberation theology (see Chapter 27). A different vein of criticism has seen the reductions as the ultimate exercise in white European paternalism, though a contrary scholarly opinion has responded that the Guarani were neither passive victims nor innocent, dependent children, but active agents in their own destiny. The whole experiment, as broadly based as it was and over such a long period of time, represents a very different approach to the encounter of civilizations that occurred when more powerful states overcame weaker ones, and the proclamation of the Christian gospel was inextricably linked to the encounter.

Protestant and Catholic Competition in East Africa during the "Scramble" for Empire

Intensive European colonization of sub-Saharan Africa is relatively recent as compared to the Americas, apart chiefly from much earlier Portuguese efforts in Angola and Mozambique and the Dutch in South Africa. The "scramble for Africa," as the exploitative European competition to carve up the continent is often called, was essentially compressed into 25 years toward the end of the nineteenth century, following the Berlin Conference of 1885. Christian missionary efforts to convert Africans south of the Sahara had previously proceeded for much of the nineteenth century without strong European colonial support. It is surprising how much evangelizing work was done more or less spontaneously either by Protestant lay missionary societies from Great Britain, Germany, or elsewhere, especially under the influence of Pietism (see Chapter 19), or by newer Catholic religious orders founded after the French Revolution. At the same time, British missionary efforts doubtless shared a common "globalist" assumption that London was in some sense the world's intellectual and commercial capital. Eventually, this cultural self-confidence would lead to an unhappy convergence of commerce, imperialism, and the condescending sense that it was "the white man's burden" to bring Christianity and civilization to the dark-skinned peoples of Africa. On the more positive side, the missionary program also included strong opposition to slavery and to the slave trade. The advocates of mission work typically promoted self-governing churches and "native agency" as the ultimate goal, even though they sometimes found it hard to let go of actual control (see below on the **three-self principle**). Additionally, the missions themselves could become critics of colonialism. "Africa for the Africans" was a favorite slogan in some quarters, especially with missions that had taken root before the colonial "scramble" following the Conference of Berlin. Even so, they usually welcomed British colonial takeover as preferable to the threat posed by Arab and Portuguese slavers.

Here we look at what happened in the last quarter of the nineteenth century in the area north of Lake Victoria, in the kingdom of Buganda or what is now Uganda. There and in East Africa generally, Protestant Great Britain became the dominant colonial power, but Catholic missionaries from various nationalities also founded missions in competition with British Anglicans, Methodists, and Scottish Presbyterians. The area is interesting because of the depth of the roots that Christianity achieved there, because of the Catholic and Protestant interaction, and not least because of the rivalry with Islam.

Buganda offers what has been called the classic case of mass conversion. Protestant and Catholic theorists of conversion originally envisioned Africa becoming Christian in the same way they thought the Germanic kingdoms of early medieval Europe had become Christian, from the top down, via the creation of "little Christendoms" under newly converted native rulers. They eventually abandoned that vision. But it did almost happen in Buganda after missionaries arrived in the late 1870s—British Protestants from the Church Missionary Society in London, and the new Catholic religious order of the White Fathers, founded in 1868 by Cardinal Charles Lavigerie (1825–1892), Archbishop of Algiers, for ministry to Muslims in French-occupied North Africa (the White Fathers got their name from their Arab-style white robes). But the king or *kabaka* of the time, Mutesa (1837–1884), had little interest in committing himself prematurely and he shrewdly cultivated a Muslim presence at his court, including a mosque, as well as hosting Protestant and Catholic missionaries. A number of Baganda (as the people called themselves) had already become Muslim; Islam had the appeal of an inspired book, growing acceptance across central Africa, and polygamy, but the disadvantage of circumcision. The existence of a deeply rooted traditional polytheistic religion added to a very pluralistic and competitive environment. Christianity nevertheless quickly struck a chord among the young elite gathered around the court, and perhaps several hundred had been baptized by the time Mutesa died in 1884, to be succeeded by his son Mwanga. This large response, in a wholly non-colonial situation and on the part of the established classes (by contrast with the more common conversion of freed slaves or other marginal peoples), is almost without parallel.

These early converts formed groups, though Protestants and Catholics were in separate areas. They were very largely self-directed and very self-confident. Mwanga, the successor king, was unnerved by their independence. A princess named Nalumansi and also a daughter of Mutesa's, caused scandal when she burned charms of a tomb of which she was guardian, and cut up and discarded the umbilical cord presented to her by her mother as a symbol of her ancestral religion. A brutal but haphazard persecution began, in which 45 Christians—22 Catholic, 23 Anglican— were burned alive or otherwise killed from 1885 to 1887. Almost half of those died on June 3, 1886, including their spiritual leader Charles Lwang. In 1964, he and the other Catholics were canonized as the **Ugandan martyrs** by Pope Paul VI, who at the same time recognized the deaths of their fellow Anglican Christians. All of them are hailed as martyrs by the Anglican Communion as well.

The next four years saw Buganda descend into a confusing sequence of coups and civil and religious wars. In 1888, King Mwanga was deposed and a joint Christian and Muslim regime appointed as his successor another son of Mutesa. Just one month later, the Muslims staged a second coup, installed a Muslim *kabaka* (king), and tried to impose Islamization on the country. That provoked a violent Christian uprising, joined by the pagan traditionalists, which invited back the former persecutor Mwanga as legitimate king. After successfully expelling the Muslim regime, the Christians promptly turned to fighting one another, with Protestants and Catholics separating into different parts of the kingdom, and both groups excluding the pagan traditionalists from power.

The sequence of persecutions and wars, ending in civil and religious stalemate, made the arrival of true colonial British government in 1893 an inevitability, along with a denominational partition of the country, though not before another Catholic and Protestant civil war broke out in 1892. The Uganda Agreement of 1900 formalized relations between the British government, the king and the other chiefs, and the churches. The lasting legacy of the preceding turbulent years was the transformation of a Christianity of the elite into a genuinely national (if divided) mass Christianity. In the words of historian Adrian Hastings,

> a movement of religious conversion and political revolution had in no more than ten years provided for African Christianity as a whole a major new powerhouse, a new model of conversion, new saints to emulate. Nowhere else did such things ever happen so fast or so effectively.
>
> (Hastings 2004, 384)

The result today is a Uganda in which over 80 percent of the population is Christian, evenly divided between Catholic and Protestant, and another 12 percent is Muslim.

Lived Religion: Liturgy in Africa
Inculturation: Marriage

When missionaries brought Christianity to Africa in the nineteenth and twentieth centuries, they encountered cultural norms that conflicted with Christian belief and practice. One important issue was marriage. For centuries, Christianity has required words and actions that make a valid marriage. The couple must give free consent, accept that marriage is life-long, and they must promise to be faithful to each other. In Africa, Christian marriage ceremonies include these things, but sometimes traditional customs have been added.

In Africa, marriage is the union of the couple and of two families. Parents present their children for marriage, asking for grandchildren and God's blessing to ward off evil. Africans see marriage as a process that begins at the engagement and continues until the birth of the first child, not as one sacramental event. Ceremonies traditionally accompany each stage of the process, which now includes scripture readings, community prayer, and blessings. Customs include the giving of the dowry and the acceptance of the woman into the man's family. The dowry comes from the family who receives the woman, and is given to the family that allowed her to leave. Next is settling the couple in their home, an exchange of consent and a blessing in church. The birth of the first child is the occasion for a solemn vow of fidelity.

Each stage is accompanied by traditional gifts and symbols. In the church, the couple sits together on a mat in front of the altar to symbolize their unity. Parents may place a plant in the couple's hands to symbolize both fertility and their blessing, and a cup of wine may be passed from the bride to her father-in-law, and then to the priest to symbolize acceptance by the family and by God. In this way, the church is trying to include African tradition and still respect Christian belief.

THE CHRISTIAN GLOBE TILTS SOUTH

Sometime around the year 2000, Christianity reached a tipping point. The median Christian in the world was no longer of European descent, but more likely to be an economically poor woman living in a village in sub-Saharan Africa or an urban shantytown in Brazil. If Christianity had ever really been a "Western religion" with a necessary affinity toward Europe and North America, it no longer was. The Christian globe had been tilting southward for decades, but now the majority of Christians worldwide were living in the Global South. Having replaced earlier terms such as the "developing world" or the "Third World," the **Global South** refers to most countries in a broad band from Latin America to Africa to Asia. Vastly diverse in their cultures, what these countries share are historical, cultural, and economic legacies still shaped in the modern era by colonialism. By a slight but steadily growing margin, most Christians in the world now live in these places, and their challenges increasingly define the agenda of the worldwide Christian community. As historian Philip Jenkins has argued, far from dying out in the face of modern culture and scientific world-views, Christianity is quite alive worldwide and is even thriving, in what may be the most under-reported story of our time.

In 2011, the Pew Forum on Religion and Public Life published a report on the size and distribution of the world's Christian population, and how these had changed between 1910 and 2010. Their findings dramatically illustrate the tilting Christian globe:

- In 1910, two-thirds of all Christians lived in Europe. In 2010, only one-quarter of all Christians lived in Europe.
- By 2010, nearly one-quarter of all Christians lived in sub-Saharan Africa, compared to 1.4 percent in 1910.
- Although Indonesia is a Muslim-majority country, in 2010, it was also home to more Christians than all 20 Middle-Eastern and North-African countries, where Christianity began.
- Nigeria now has more Protestants than Germany, the birthplace of the Protestant Reformation.
- Brazil now has twice as many Catholics as Italy, the historic center of Roman Catholicism.

- The worldwide Christian population as a whole numbered 2.18 billion, making Christianity the largest single religion in the world.

For an American audience, in a book titled *The Future Church*, veteran Vatican journalist John L. Allen, Jr. added one more telling statistic about global Catholicism, with a comment that could apply to many other churches as well: North Americans comprise only 6 percent of the global Catholic population, he noted, "which means that 94 percent of the Catholics in the world are not necessarily like us. If anything the United States probably looms too large already on the global Catholic scene" (Allen 2009, 11).

Indeed, although journalists, academics, and ordinary Christians in the West are often preoccupied with their own debates and "culture wars," the tilting Christian globe is already proving to have profound theological, social, and political implications. For more than 1,000 years, the accidents of history may have confined Christianity more and more to Europe, and then the Americas, but does that make Christianity essentially Western or Northern? If not, Christians in an age of globalization have fresh reasons to

CHRISTIAN POPULATION BY REGION, 1910

REGIONS	ESTIMATED CHRISTIAN POPULATION	PERCENTAGE OF POPULATION THAT WAS CHRISTIAN	PERCENTAGE OF WORLD CHRISTIAN POPULATION
Americas	165,890,000	95.9	27.1
Europe	405,780,000	94.5	66.3
Sub-Saharan Africa	8,560,000	9.1	1.4
Asia-Pacific	27,510,000	2.7	4.5
Middle East and North Africa	4,070,000	9.5	0.7
WORLD TOTAL	**611,810,000**	**34.8**	**100.0**

CHRISTIAN POPULATION BY REGION, 2010

REGIONS	ESTIMATED CHRISTIAN POPULATION	PERCENTAGE OF POPULATION THAT WAS CHRISTIAN	PERCENTAGE OF WORLD CHRISTIAN POPULATION
Americas	804,070,000	86.0	36.8
Europe	565,560,000	76.2	25.9
Sub-Saharan Africa	516,470,000	62.7	23.6
Asia-Pacific	285,120,000	7.0	13.1
Middle East and North Africa	12,840,000	3.8	0.6
WORLD TOTAL	**2,184,030,000**	**31.7**	**100.0**

Source: Pew Forum analysis of data from the Center for the Study of Global Christianity. Pew Research Center's Forum on Religion & Public Life. *Global Christianity*, December 2011.

Note: Population estimates are rounded to the ten thousands. Percentages are calculated from unrounded numbers. Figures may not add exactly due to rounding.

Figure 21–3 Distribution of Christians by region around the world.

attend closely to the dynamics of **inculturation**—the process of expressing Christian faith in ways that are intelligible and appropriate within a given culture. The need and struggle to reach across cultures and peoples in order to form a new multicultural people has been intrinsic to Christianity from its beginnings, when the apostles navigated relationships between Jewish and Gentile believers. The challenge of inculturation is to welcome richly diverse expressions of Christian faith and worship while holding one another accountable to a common core that remains faithful to scripture and tradition.

Christianity as a Non-Western Religion

In his acclaimed 1958 novel, *Things Fall Apart*, Nigerian author Chinua Achebe (1930–2013) captured the alternately troubling and life-giving impact of Christianity on an African village in the late nineteenth century. As the British colonial government began reaching into the Nigerian hinterlands, Christian missionaries had followed in its wake. The missionaries Achebe portrayed dialogue respectfully with village elders to understand their religious world-view deeply, hoping to present the Christian gospel on authentically African terms. But they also call in colonial enforcers when crisis erupts. The novel's chief protagonist is Okonkwo, a proud but violent leader in his tribe, intent on preserving the customs of his people. He considers Christianity to be folly because it initially appeals most to those deemed worthless in his own community—the poor, marginalized, cursed. Yet Okonkwo's own son Nwoye has joined the small Christian church at the edge of the village, in part to escape Okonkwo's abuse. Nwoye finds in Christianity both consolation and a new sense of dignity. "It was not the mad logic of the Trinity that captivated him," writes Achebe.

> He did not understand it. It was the poetry of the new religion, something felt in the marrow. ... He felt a relief within as the hymn poured into his parched soul. The words of the hymn were like the drops of frozen rain melting on the dry palate of the panting earth.
>
> (Achebe 1994, 39)

To understand the spread, growth, and appeal of Christianity requires the honesty and nuance of someone like Achebe, a Christian convert who unlike many converts of his generation insisted on keeping his African name. As colonialism and technology were making the interior regions of all the world's continents more accessible to Westerners, a vibrant modern missionary movement fired the imagination especially of Protestants but also of Catholics from the late eighteenth century well into the twentieth century. Increasingly, the organizers of modern mission movements were not official churches aligned with colonizing nations but grass-roots "voluntary associations" of lay people. In many circles, the ultimate image of a heroic, dedicated Christian was one who sacrificed the comforts of home to travel dangerous routes, learn difficult languages, risk tropical diseases, and then live for decades in challenging conditions as they shared their faith, their know-how, and their resources with "the less fortunate." That phrase obviously hints at patronizing attitudes of Western superiority that sometimes sully this picture and raise questions about the real motives of missionaries. Too often their endeavor not only accompanied Western colonial rule, but continued to justify the colonialist project itself. Yet the faith, motivations, and heroism of many missionaries also rendered some of them the most culturally sensitive of all foreigners, and the first to resist exploitative colonialist policies.

In any case, although missionary work has certainly been one key factor in the coming of global Christianity, it is only one. Christianity has always spread through a variety of means. Throughout the centuries, migration, one-on-one sharing within social networks, and the witness of lay people have played at least as big of a role as conquest and colonization. Even when professional missionaries have first introduced the Christian faith, it has only taken hold and spread because ordinary Christians have believed themselves to be experiencing something worth sharing with family and friends.

In his survey of the southward shift in global Christianity, Philip Jenkins argues that since Christianity has never been exclusively or essentially Western, we should actually see current trends as a return to Christianity's roots (Jenkins 2011). The Christian faith is spreading in the Global South, suggests Jenkins, because it has an authentic appeal that does *not* depend on Western culture or imperialism to take root. Repeatedly throughout its 2,000 years Christianity has proven quite able to flourish as a minority religion, without state support. Even when it *has* spread in part through imperial or colonialist power, it has only taken root by meshing with local cultures in fresh ways—often as a counter-force against the powerful. An example familiar to many Catholics throughout the Americas is the apparition of the Virgin Mary to the Mexican Indian Juan Diego in 1532. Christianity had indeed been largely the religion of the Spanish conquerors until the account of Jesus' mother appearing as "the Virgin of Guadalupe" communicated dignity and hope. *La Guadalupeña* was dark-skinned and compassionate, drawing together the best qualities of a pre-Christian Aztec goddess. Only as devotion to her and other apparitions of the Virgin Mary spread throughout Latin America did Christianity take root. But perhaps Jenkins' most poignant argument against the assumption that Christianity is necessarily a Western religion comes from the record of martyrdom on all continents in subsequent centuries. It is "inconceivable" that so many missionaries "would have been prepared to lay down their lives for European commerce alone," he writes. But it is downright "ludicrous to claim that the new religion was solely for white people" when new believers have refused to renounce their faith in the face of persecution, as with the 22 Ugandan Christians who were burned alive on a single day in 1886.

Missionaries themselves have consistently been the first to recognize the need

Figure 21-4 The Virgin Mary is said to have appeared to Juan Diego in 1531 at Tepeyac, near Mexico City. The image he saw in his vision has come to be known as Our Lady of Guadalupe. Devotion to Mary under this title continues to be an important part of Spanish-American Catholicism. Eighteenth-century oil painting of the Virgin of Guadalupe in the former convent of San Agustin, Yuriria, Guanajuato.

for culturally appropriate expression of Christian faith and local leadership. Compare this to extractive industries mining gold in the past, or drilling for oil today. Industry executives at best have only a minimal need to understand local cultures and no great incentive to preserve them. In contrast, missionaries whose lifelong goal has been to leave behind a thriving local church that could study the Bible in its own language and worship in its own cultural idiom have had every need to do so. For many indigenous cultures, much of what we know about their history and religion survives because missionaries were the ones to document and preserve them. The arduous work of translating the Bible into thousands of local languages alone has probably done more than any other endeavor to give vulnerable cultures both written languages and the tools to preserve their cultural records in the face of globalization's more destructive forces.

The Challenge of Inculturation

Planting culturally authentic Christian communities has been the foundational goal of the modern Protestant missionary movement at least since the eighteenth century, when influential mission strategists Henry Venn and Rufus Anderson posited the **three-self principle**. According to this principle, new churches should become "self-governing," "self-supporting," and "self-propagating" (or "self-extending") as quickly as possible. The goal of *self-governing* churches required missionaries to prioritize the training of local leaders and aim to turn over leadership within a generation or two. The goal of *self-supporting* churches made it imperative to avoid indefinite financial dependency on foreign mission agencies. The goal of *self-propagating* churches recognized that local believers should quickly assume primary responsibility for evangelizing and spreading the Christian message. Together, these three principles constituted a clear recognition that the role of foreign missionaries should always be transitional and empowering, leading to actual transfers of power.

This vision of new churches coming into their own must take a somewhat different shape in Catholicism. Self-governance cannot mean cutting ties of accountability that lead back to Rome, since Catholic ecclesiology frankly centers ultimate decision-making in the pope. Yet developments at the Second Vatican Council in the early 1960s led prominent Catholic theologian Karl Rahner S.J. to foresee the coming of a truly global Church and point out ways that Catholicism has been pursuing its own vision for mature churches that fully embody the gospel according to their own cultural patterns. As Rahner noted, the number of bishops from the Global South at Vatican II may still have been small, but for the first time non-European church leaders representing every continent and skin color were present as full participants. The decrees that the council promulgated between 1962 and 1965 in turn gave them a new measure of independence, beginning with the signal change requiring celebration of the Mass in local languages. Other decrees demonstrated a widening global vision by reflecting a sense of pastoral responsibility for all humanity. The council also explicitly renounced using state-backed force in proclaiming the gospel. As Rahner noted, this began to de-link Catholicism officially from traditional church–state patterns in Europe, thus placing all churches on equal standing as "mission churches."

The entire premise of the Second Vatican Council, as Pope John XXIII explained when he launched it, was to express the abiding ancient faith in fresh ways that would be more comprehensible within modernity, the cultural context of the modern world (see Chapter 24). But modernity is not just science and technology; it also involves an increasing pluralism linking together the fate of cultures and peoples around the globe. Thus, Vatican II marked the church's growing recognition of the need to inculturate the gospel in *every* cultural setting. In 1975, when Pope Paul VI celebrated the ten-year anniversary of the council, he did so by publishing a guide to the process of proper inculturation. Churches of every region and culture, he wrote, are always founded not only by gathering in new people but by drawing upon their cultural heritages. To continue growing, churches "have the task of assimilating the essence of the Gospel message and of transposing it, without the slightest betrayal of its essential truth, into the language that these particular people understand, then of proclaiming it in this language." The question of how to hold in tension these twin imperatives—adapting to new cultures *even while* remaining faithful to the abiding core of Christianity—is often "a delicate one," he admitted. Yet, that very tension has been intrinsic to Christianity since its earliest decades. As the influential historian of Christian mission Andrew Walls has observed, "It is a feature of Christian faith that throughout its history it has spread through cross-cultural contact. ... Cross-cultural transmission is integral to Christian faith" (Walls 1987, 26). Inculturation is not simply an obligatory task, therefore—it is an opportunity.

African Initiated Churches: A Case Study

For Philip Jenkins, one more sign that Christianity is not by necessity a Western religion is this: Whatever the role of missionaries from Europe and North America in the coming of global Christianity, its numbers have actually surged most when foreigners have either left or begun to lose influence. Perhaps no phenomenon illustrates this better than the early twentieth-century explosion of **African Initiated Churches** (also known as African *Independent* Churches, African *Indigenous* Churches, African *Instituted* Churches, or simply AICs). One of the first and best documented of these is the Church of Jesus Christ on Earth through the Prophet Simon Kimbangu—or the Kimbanguists for short. Despite a vast diversity among AICs, the story of Kimbangu and the movement, then church, that his prophetic ministry inspired illustrates many dynamics common to AICs.

Simon Kimbangu was born in 1889 in Congo under Belgian colonial rule. He became a Christian as a youth, was educated by Baptists, and baptized in July 1915. Soon afterward, he had a dream in which he heard God's voice calling him to ministry and promising the power of the Holy Spirit in abundance. The Baptist Missionary Society rejected him, however, saying he was only "village trained" and did not read well. From 1918 to 1921, he experienced still more dreams reaffirming a call to "care for my flock" and convert many. Finally, in April 1921, he felt compelled to go to a neighboring village, lay hands on a sick woman, and pray for her healing in the name of Christ. Her recovery was the first of many healings, and his followers would later call the event the beginning of a new Pentecost—recalling the day when Jesus' earliest disciples first received the Holy Spirit. Colonialism had not only brought foreign rule, but also new contagious diseases that European medicine was powerless to stop. For Kimbanguists, healings and other miracles were God's gift, meeting immediate needs in a way that missionaries and their abstract doctrines did not.

Kimbangu had no intention of starting a new church, but as thousands joined his movement and abandoned missionary-led churches, Belgian authorities not only suspected otherwise, they accused him of inciting hatred of Europeans and rebellion against their rule. Despite his denunciation of witchcraft, European missionaries saw Kimbanguist practices of healing and prayer for other miracles as a return to witchcraft. Protestant theology considered the age of miracles long past, and Catholic piety saw miracles as the exceptional work of saints. So the phenomenon *was* in fact a rebellion of sorts—the assertion of a distinctively African Christianity attuned to the needs and sensibilities of Africans. Only five months into his ministry, in the face of orders for his arrest, Kimbangu presented himself freely to his persecutors after admonishing his followers to suffer courageously, without recourse to violence. Following a show trial, Kimbangu was sentenced to life imprisonment and died in prison 30 years later. But meanwhile, despite nearly 40 years of persecution, Kimbanguist congregations emerged throughout central Africa.

By now, Kimbanguism has developed into an established church denomination. Estimates of its size vary widely from 2 to 8 million adherents worldwide, including in Europe and North America. In 1969, after long negotiation, it became the first AIC to join the World Council of Churches, which brings together many Protestant and Eastern Orthodox denominations together for consultation. Negotiation dragged in part due to continuing theological suspicion on the part of European and American churches, whose representatives worried that Kimbanguist practices did not constitute inculturation so much as **syncretism**—the merging of Christianity with some other religious world-view in a way that threatens to undermine its Christian essence. Complicating such questions was the fact that experience rather than creeds had long defined the Kimbanguists' Christian faith, making doctrinal issues harder to pin down.

The Kimbanguist church is but one prominent example among thousands of AICs. Although AIC numbers have not overtaken those of churches founded by Protestant and Catholic missionaries to Africa, they illustrate the power of inculturation to impel the growth of Christianity in the Global South. They have also goaded traditional churches to Africanize in order to compete, thus accelerating their growth as well. Statistics are often difficult with AICs, but together they constitute 10 to 20 percent of Christians in sub-Saharan Africa—and in a few regions much more. In South Africa, some 40 percent of all blacks belonged to such churches by the mid-1990s, and in neighboring Botswana, fully two-thirds of all blacks belonged to AICs. Migration has now spread many AICs to metropolitan hubs of globalization not only in African countries but throughout the world.

Such a diverse and increasingly far-flung movement defies generalization, yet many common traits characterize African Initiated Churches. Their founding leaders were usually considered prophets, and they continue to welcome prophetic utterance and lively preaching. Those founders have often had at least some training from Western missionaries, only to grow dissatisfied with the doctrinal abstractions and formal worship styles of Western Christianity, turning instead to more African styles. Ambivalent if not vehemently opposed to what they consider to be evil and demonic forces at work in traditional African religion, they have often been more successful than Western missionaries at rooting out such practices from their communities. Instead of simply denouncing such practices, they replace them with Christian practices of healing, exorcism, and ecstatic utterance that meet similar needs and resonate with African sensibilities. Assuming the active role of spiritual forces in human affairs, they find in Christianity the promise that the power of the Holy Spirit will be victorious over the "principalities and powers" of which the New Testament speaks and other malignant spiritual forces that Western missionaries often dismissed as illusory and thus ignored.

Colonialist administrators who once suspected AICs as fronts for political revolt were not altogether wrong, for they have often constituted intuitive movements of resistance to colonialism and Western domination. Nowhere is their African cultural resonance more obvious than in styles of worship that incorporate dance, drumming, special worship attire such as white robes, and elaborate rituals inspired by Hebrew worship in the Old Testament, which often resonate with African sensibilities more than those of European Christians. When Western Christians object that AICs are insufficiently orthodox, AICs cite biblical precedents for all of these practices and ask whether secularized Western Christians are the ones who have distanced themselves from orthodox Christianity instead. Deeply attuned to spiritual realities, AICs if anything expect salvation to be all the more concrete and this-worldly—not just something awaiting them in heaven. For them, Jesus Christ is above all the one who brings healing and material well-being through his victory over the evil forces that hold the world in their grip.

The Spread of Global Pentecostalism

Although scholars debate where phenomena like African Initiated Churches end and **Pentecostalism** begins, Pentecostal theology need not expect clear lineage marking its beginning at a precise time and place. In the view of Pentecostals, their founder is Jesus at work through his Holy Spirit, and their origin is in God's promise to pour out the Spirit "on all flesh"—in other words, on all classes and races of people—"in the last days." Pentecostals find that promise in the second chapter of the Old Testament prophet Joel, which explains to them why miracles like healing, exorcism, **speaking in tongues**, and prophecy apparently ceased for so many centuries but now are being restored in their midst:

> O children of Zion, be glad
> and rejoice in the Lord your God;
> for he has given the early rain for your vindication,
> he has poured down for you abundant rain,
> the early and the later rain [*or in some translations, "the latter rain"*] ...
> Then afterward
> I will pour out my spirit on all flesh;
> your sons and your daughters shall prophesy,
> your old men shall dream dreams,
> and your young men shall see visions.
> Even on the male and female slaves,
> in those days, I will pour out my spirit.

(Joel 2:23, 28–29)

If the "early rain" was the first Pentecost and its first-century overflow, as recorded in the Acts of the Apostles, "the latter rain" has come in our own time, Pentecostals believe. In this view of history, totally independent accounts of "outpourings" on many continents, already in the nineteenth century but increasingly in the early twentieth century, are evidence of that "latter rain." The event that often marks the beginning of the movement took place on Azusa Street in Los Angeles, California, in 1906, when a racially integrated group of Christians under the leadership of the African-American preacher William J. Seymour experienced what they called **Baptism in the Holy Spirit**, marked by speaking in unknown tongues (*glossolalia*) and other forms of

Figure 21–5 Pentecostal Church Service, Kensington Temple, London.

ecstatic worship, as well as miraculous physical healings. Yet similar events had already taken place in India in the previous century, and the first decade of the twentieth century saw dramatic Pentecostal outpourings in Wales, China, Korea, more parts of India, and other locations in North America—either before Azusa or with little-to-no news about it soon after. With an estimated 600 million adherents worldwide as of 2010 and still continuing to spread worldwide, Pentecostalism is believed to be the fastest-growing segment of Christianity today.

Given its decentralized dynamic, flexibility of church structure, emphasis on experience, and global dispersion, Pentecostalism has evolved quickly with almost dizzying variations. Early Pentecostals believed that speaking in tongues was the most reliable sign of Baptism in the Holy Spirit, but today many groups with Pentecostal influences simply emphasize exuberant participation in worship. Pentecostal expectation that God is doing "new things" (Isaiah 42:9, 48:6) as the Spirit leads God's people in fresh ways allowed some groups to recognize women in leadership long before mainstream Protestant denominations. In their attitudes toward other Christians, Pentecostalism from its beginnings has been pulled in two quite opposite directions—sometimes seeing itself as a movement to renew and unify all Christians across traditions (an "ecumenical" pull), and sometimes considering themselves the only true Christians (a "sectarian" pull). Furthermore, as one historian has noted, "Pentecostalism started as a reaction against dogma and creeds, but was soon engaged in doctrinal haggling." Yet for all its diversity, Pentecostalism or its influence is clearly recognizable in a confidence that God intervenes directly in the life of believers, sometimes miraculously, often intimately, and always in ways that invite a vibrant response of praise and emotion. That thread has run through what historians generally agree are three major phases:

Phase 1: Classical Pentecostalism. Although the Azusa Street revival that began in Los Angeles in 1906 was not the first Pentecostal "outpouring" in the modern world, its interracial character during the very period of the United States' most vicious racial segregation, as well as its missionary zeal, illustrate Pentecostalism's impact. Although emerging Pentecostal denominations soon divided along racial lines, some Pentecostal theologians see the racial reconciliation at Azusa as itself a telling "miracle." Even without an explicit theology of social justice, wherever Pentecostalism has gone in the world, it has begun as a movement for and among the poor. In economically neglected rural villages or in sprawling urban shantytowns across the globe, Pentecostal churches rebuild community among people whom modernizing economic development has dislocated or left behind. So while Pentecostalism at first seemed like a fringe movement, those dynamics have made it a major force in global Christianity. Furthermore, Pentecostalism often displays a strong missionary impulse. Believing that the end times were fast approaching, leaders like those at Azusa Street interpreted their experience as God's way to energize a final wave of worldwide evangelism. Azusa Street quickly drew Christians seeking the Baptism of the Holy Spirit from as far away as Europe, and within two years that single church had sent missionaries to over 25 countries. Today, Latin America has the largest Pentecostal presence, though Asia may be catching up, and Africa's numbers trail only because Pentecostalism is often indistinguishable from African Initiated Churches.

Phase 2: The Charismatic Movement. The greatest impact of Pentecostalism may not be in the formation of specifically Pentecostal denominations, however, but on other traditions, both mainline Protestant and Catholic. Despite their initially fringe identity, a few visionary Pentecostal leaders sought relationships with other churches, and preachers in some Pentecostal ministries shared their message with other Christians without expecting them to leave their churches. By the 1950s, those efforts were growing, and in the 1960s, a movement taking Pentecostal teachings and practices into other churches seemed to explode into the news. This phenomenon came to be known as the **Charismatic Movement**. Thanks to the movement, a certain "Pentecostalization" has spread throughout much of Christianity. It continues to be evident in the "contemporary Christian" worship styles of many denominations in North America, and it is even more prominent around the world. If anything, the largest and most visible expression of the Charismatic Movement globally is now Catholic, with an estimated 120 million participants, or over 10 percent of Catholics worldwide as of 2012.

Phase 3: Neo-Pentecostalism. Individual Pentecostals and their families typically experience a certain upward mobility lifting them into the middle or even the upper class. Upward mobility may be the best way to identify the third wave of the Pentecostal-Charismatic movement, Neo-Pentecostalism. Initially used as a term for the Charismatic Movement itself, "Neo-Pentecostalism" now refers more often to new churches that have repackaged Pentecostal-Charismatic approaches to build large, media-savvy, institutionally impressive organizations. The most prominent of these are "megachurches" with attendees numbering in the thousands, or even tens of thousands. While worship services continue to appeal to emotion, they now do so through tightly choreographed multimedia productions led by professional musicians more than through contagiously ecstatic prayer. In continuity with classical Pentecostalism, Neo-Pentecostals offer the promise of healing, victory over demonic forces, and other "signs and wonders." "Come and claim your miracle" has been an appeal of Pentecostal-Charismatic churches for decades, but among Neo-Pentecostals the promise has coalesced into a controversial set of teachings known as the **Prosperity**

Doctrine, which equates God's blessings with material success. Critics argue that the Prosperity Doctrine has reinforced the consumer values of global capitalism and led to support for oppressive regimes that protect wealthy privilege.

The grass-roots flexibility of Pentecostal ecclesiology can certainly be a weakness as well as a strength. The decentralized dynamics of Pentecostalism in all its phases have been a major force in the coming of global Christianity. But with no magisterium or official teaching authority, and with its consistent emphasis on experience, Pentecostal teaching and practice can veer in wildly divergent directions. At its best, however, it has allowed for creative inculturation in diverse settings and offered a home to those displaced by the forces first of colonialism and then of globalization.

Figure 21–6 Jesus of the People, Janet McKenzie.

Late in 1999, just as calendars were about to mark a new millennium, a striking painting titled "Jesus of the People" won awards and drew controversy. To model the image of Jesus, artist Janet McKenzie had employed an African-American woman. To widen identification with Jesus still further, McKenzie had also incorporated prominent symbols from Asian and indigenous American cultures. To place Jesus among the marginalized, she had clothed him in a rough-hewn cloak suggesting working-class or peasant roots. A few critics objected to what felt like a challenge to their traditional image of an ethnically European Jesus, white and bearded with long flowing hair. Yet McKenzie's portrayal of Jesus was no more culturally skewed than thousands of classics hanging in museums and cathedrals around the world, which artists have created using styles they knew from their own times and places.

Everyone encounters Jesus Christ from within their culture, after all. To be good news, the Christian gospel must always, in some way, come clothed in the cultural garb of the recipient—it must be "inculturated." In any case, McKenzie was not claiming to do a historically realistic representation of the Semitic, Middle-Eastern, Jewish Jesus of Nazareth, yet her painting did reflect another telling historical datum quite accurately—not about the first-century "Jesus of the People" but about the twenty-first century *people of Jesus*. The median Christian in the world around the year 2000 actually looked a lot like the Jesus of her painting.

Global Challenges Today

When Cardinal Jorge Bergoglio of Argentina became Pope Francis in 2013, the elevation of the first leader of the Roman Catholic Church from the Global South signaled a new day. If some Catholics in Europe and North America found him speaking in a fresh accent, one reason was that his priorities were less those of the Global North and more those of the Global South. And the tilt is sure to continue. After all, the need for Christians to inculturate the gospel in diverse settings around the globe is not simply a matter of taste. Doing so creatively, while preserving a common confession of faith, requires both patience and accountability. That, in turn, presses questions about who holds power, makes decisions, and commands resources across the global Church, and not just for Catholics. Bitter theological disagreements may have divided Christians into competing traditions and denominations historically in the West, and bitter "culture wars" over social issues sometimes divide denominations today. But churches in the Global South often find other issues more pressing, or else respond in ways that defy the standard "left–right" political alignments common in the Global North. For this very reason, the need to demonstrate Christian solidarity across borders, cultures, ethnicities, and classes has never been clearer. How to be Church in a globalized world? As the Acts of the Apostles makes clear, the challenge of becoming a truly multicultural, multi-ethnic, transnational people has been key to the Christian story all along. Potentially, and by faith, the Christian Church has always been a global people. Now, globalization in the modern world is making this calling both obvious and urgent.

Key Terms

African Initiated
   Churches
Baptism in the Holy
   Spirit
Bartolomé de Las Casas
Charismatic Movement
encomienda

Global South
glossolalia
inculturation
Inter caetera
Neo-Pentecostalism
Pentecostalism
Prosperity Doctrine

Matteo Ricci
reductions
Rites controversy
speaking in tongues
syncretism
three-self principle
Ugandan Martyrs

Questions for Reading

1. What were some of the negative consequences, intended as well as unintended, of the spread of Christianity as a parallel phenomenon of European conquest and colonialization?

2. What justifications were offered in defense of the conquest and the enslavement of indigenous peoples?

3. Describe Las Casas' views on slavery. Why and how did he criticize it? Did he change his mind on slavery?

4. What was Las Casas' main goal in the mission he started in Guatemala in 1537, or, to put it another way, what was he trying to demonstrate?

5. What was the core issue that divided opinions about Jesuit methods in adapting to Confucianism in China?

6. What (if anything) was especially distinctive about the spread of Christianity in Buganda in the last half of the nineteenth century, especially the 1880s?

7. Historian Philip Jenkins argues against the widespread assumption that Christianity is essentially a "Western religion." What is some of his evidence?

8. How would you assess the role of Western missionaries in spreading Christianity?

9. What is "inculturation" and why do some theologians consider it essential to Christianity? How has it contributed to the coming of global Christianity?

10. Many observers believe that Pentecostalism and related movements constitute the fastest growing segment of global Christianity. What are some of the reasons for its appeal?

11. How might the southward shift in the global Christian population challenge and reshape the priorities of Christians in North America and Europe?

Works Consulted/Recommended Reading

Achebe, Chinua. 1994. *Things Fall Apart.* New York: Anchor Books.

Allen, John L., Jr. 2009. *The Future Church: How Ten Trends are Revolutionizing the Catholic Church.* New York: Doubleday.

Anderson, Allan Heaton. 2014. *An Introduction to Pentecostalism: Global Charismatic Christianity.* Cambridge: Cambridge University Press.

Brockey, Liam Matthew. 2007. *Journey to the East: The Jesuit Mission to China, 1579–1724.* Cambridge, MA: Harvard University Press.

Castro, Daniel. 2007. *Another Face of Empire: Bartolomé de las Casas, Indigenous Rights, and Ecclesiastical Imperialism.* Durham, NC: Duke University Press.

Cleary, Edward L. 2011. *The Rise of Charismatic Catholicism in Latin America.* Gainesville, FL: University Press of Florida.

Cox, Harvey. 1995. *Fire from Heaven: The Rise of Pentecostal Spirituality and the Reshaping of Religion in the Twenty-First Century.* Reading, MA: Addison-Wesley.

Davis, Kortright. 1992–1993. "'Sunshine Christopher': Bearer of Christ in Caribbean History." *Journal of Religious Thought* 7–24.

Ganson, Barbara. 2003. *The Guaraní under Spanish Rule in the Río de la Plata.* Stanford, CA: Stanford University Press.

Gornik, Mark R. 2011. *Word Made Global: Stories of African Christianity in New York City.* Foreword by Andrew F. Walls, with an Afterword by Emmanuel Katongole. Grand Rapids, MI: W.B. Eerdmans.

Hastings, Adrian. 2004. *The Church in Africa 1450–1950.* Oxford History of the Christian Church. Oxford: Clarendon Press.

Hollenweger, Walter J. 1997. *Pentecostalism: Origins and Developments Worldwide.* Peabody, MA: Hendrickson Publishers.

Hopkins, Donald P. 2002. *The Greatest Killer: Smallpox in History.* Chicago, IL: University of Chicago Press.

Hopkins, Dwight N. 1992–1993. "Columbus, the Church, and Slave Religion." *Journal of Religious Thought* 49: 25–35.

Jenkins, Philip. 2011. *The Next Christendom: The Coming of Global Christianity.* 3rd edn. Oxford: Oxford University Press.

Las Casas, Bartolomé de. 1992. *The Devastation of the Indies: A Brief Account.* Translated by Herma Briffault. Baltimore, MD: Johns Hopkins University Press.

Lynch, John. 2012. *New Worlds: A Religious History of Latin America.* New Haven, CT: Yale University Press.

Martin, Marie-Louise. 1976. *Kimbangu: An African Prophet and His Church.* With a Foreword by Bryan R. Wilson, trans. D.M. Moore. Grand Rapids: Eerdmans.

Miller, Donald E., and Tetsunao Yamamori. 2007. *Global Pentecostalism: The New Face of Christian Social Engagement.* Berkeley, CA: University of California Press.

Neill, Stephen. 1984. *A History of Christian Missions.* New York: Penguin Books.

New Catholic Encyclopedia. 2nd edn. 2003. Detroit, MI: Thomson/Gale; Washington, DC: Catholic University of America Press.

Paul VI, Pope. 1975. *Evangelii Nuntiandi [Evangelization in the Modern World].* Apostolic letter.

Pew Forum on Religion and Public Life. 2011. *Global Christianity: A Report on the Size and Distribution of the World's Christian Population.* Washington, DC: Pew Research Center. www.pewforum.org/files/2011/12/Christianity-fullreport-web.pdf.

Rahner, Karl. 1979. "Towards a Fundamental Theological Interpretation of Vatican II." *Theological Studies* 40, no. 4 (December): 716–727.

Robeck, Cecil M., and Amos Yong, eds. 2014. *The Cambridge Companion to Pentecostalism.* Cambridge Companions to Religion. New York: Cambridge University Press.

Wagner, Henry Raup, with Helen Rand Parish. 1967. *The Life and Writings of Bartolomé de las Casas.* Albuquerque, NM: University of New Mexico Press.

Walls, Andrew F. 1996. "The Gospel as Prisoner and Liberator of Culture." In *The Missionary Movement in Christian History: Studies in the Transmission of Faith,* 3–15. Maryknoll, NY: Orbis Books.

Walls, Andrew F. 1987. "The Old Age of the Missionary Movement." *International Review of Mission* 76, no. 301 (January): 26–32.

Chapter

CHRISTIANITY IN THE MODERN PERIOD

The modern period witnessed dramatic changes in Western societies, and we continue to live with the legacy of those cultural transformations. In fact, the sheer scope and pace of change during the modern period have led many to view it as a decisive break from previous eras. To be "modern" is do things in new ways, based on new understandings of the world, the human being, and God. Indeed, the high value placed on innovation during the modern period resulted in veritable *revolutions* (industrial, scientific, political, and philosophical). The spirit of the age audaciously insisted that modern persons can fashion the world anew, according to new standards.

These revolutionary ways of thinking presented the Christian theological tradition with unprecedented challenges. The modern period stands out as distinct from previous eras in a fundamental way: whereas past periods beheld debate about the nature of a God who was widely assumed to exist, during the modern period the very existence of God itself became a point in favor of which one had to argue. Similarly, although Christian claims about the Trinity and the divinity of Christ had remained relatively stable since their formulation in the fourth and fifth centuries (see Chapter 9), during the modern period these central Christian doctrines were questioned to their foundations. This penchant for thorough, relentless criticism of tradition is a major feature of modernity that continues to challenge Christian theology today.

With that said, one should not view the modern period as exclusively a time of loss. After all, modern ideas about individual freedom and the equality of all persons played major roles in the refashioning of Western societies. There was during this time a remarkably optimistic belief that human beings could develop new universal standards through which to reform Western culture. To many, a better society was on the horizon. In a number of ways, this hope remains in our world today, even if the so-called post-modern sensibility questions the prospects of agreement on universal standards (see Chapter 26).

Within the Christian tradition, too, modernity has had positive effects in spite of the difficulties it has presented to Christian theologians. To some, the modern criticisms of Christianity have ultimately *refined* Christian theology so as to make it more credible. According to this way of thinking, questionable elements of the Christian tradition have been eliminated during the modern period, and a more durable version of the Christian faith has been articulated. Indeed, modern challenges elicited remarkable creativity from Christian theologians, and they reached new heights of sophistication in their efforts at meeting those critiques. One can therefore claim that modern criticisms have ultimately served Christian theology well, as they have exposed key ambiguities and blind spots that would have otherwise endured.

This chapter will begin by organizing the *nova*, or "new things," of modernity around four interconnected themes, each of which has had profound effects on Christian theology: (1) a new role for reason; (2) a new understanding of the human being; (3) a new way to do history; and (4) a new degree of skepticism toward religion. The second half of the chapter will describe responses to the modern critiques advanced by Christian theologians.

A New Role for Reason, and the Rise of the Secular

Modernity is often thought to begin with the intellectual movement known as **the Enlightenment** (seventeenth–eighteenth centuries), which is also called the Age of Reason. Reason had certainly played a role in Christian theology during the patristic and medieval periods. However, during the Enlightenment, reason came to occupy a position of new importance. Specifically, many Enlightenment figures insisted that reason should be used as the only tool for knowing God and the world. To this way of thinking (often called **rationalism**), one does not need any other source (e.g., divine revelation) for such knowledge. During the course of the Enlightenment, reason eventually came to replace and even judge the claims made in revelation, such that all Christian doctrines had to submit to reason. Whereas theologians in previous eras regarded some claims as simply beyond human reason's capacities to evaluate (they were seen as "above" reason), in the modern period human reason itself became the measure of all things.

Reason rose to prominence during the Enlightenment as a result of two factors. First, seventeenth-century Europe was weary of religious conflict, and many saw reason as a key tool with which to prevent further violence. Religious wars had raged since the beginning of the Reformation, and by the mid-seventeenth century, the Thirty Years' War (1618–1648) had devastated much of Europe. In response, there were calls to abandon religion altogether, as it seemed to lead inescapably to conflict. However, many sought to base religion on reason in the hope of finding common ground among different Christians, thereby achieving peace. The Enlightenment has been vividly portrayed as built on a "pile of bones" because of the role that religious wars played in turning Enlightenment thinkers toward reason (Kramnick 1995, 119).

The discussions of reason that occurred during the Enlightenment, then, did not consist of abstract speculations unconnected from the real world. Instead, a rational version of religion was desperately needed in order to prevent the all-too-real violence that Europe had endured for well over a century. In the early modern period, European societies were torn apart because of religious conflict, and reason was asked to repair the breach. Many theologians, historians, and politicians in the present day continue the Enlightenment project of using reason to prevent religious violence.

Second, reason began to be used in new ways in academic inquiry, and the results were spectacular. The natural sciences, in particular, advanced by leaps and bounds during this time. As mentioned briefly above, the term "scientific revolution" is used to describe just how dramatically old ways of thinking were being overturned in the name of new scientific theories. In this regard, a particular form of reason was especially important: inductive reason, which begins with empirical observations about the world and derives its conclusions as the best explanation of the facts on the ground. Francis Bacon (1561–1626) was particularly influential in steering scientists toward the use of inductive reason, and this method endures in the present day in the natural sciences (e.g., biology, chemistry, and physics). Inductive reasoning strives to avoid committing to an idea or theory before empirical investigation begins; it is an open style of inquiry that allows itself to be driven by the evidence, wherever that might lead. If established theories are unable to make sense of new findings, they are discarded in the name of a superior explanatory model. Accordingly, the success of science in the seventeenth century depended on scientists' willingness to jettison old views when necessary. The tendency to regard previous learning as irrelevant had revolutionary consequences in the modern period, not just for Christian theology, but for many other areas of study as well.

Reason was used in a new way not only in the natural sciences, but also in philosophy. Most notably, **René Descartes** (1596–1650) used reason to found a new philosophical system that offered an unprecedented degree of certainty. Descartes began his philosophical explorations with an extreme skepticism that cast universal doubt on all claims for knowledge. He doubted everything, and resolved to accept as true *only* those claims that could be absolutely proved. In his *Discourse on Method* (1637), he records that his relentless doubt came to a halt when he realized that the one thing he could not doubt was his own existence. He expressed this breakthrough with his famous phrase "I think, therefore I am" (Descartes 1998, 18). In other words, because Descartes knew he was thinking (he observed himself doing it, so to speak), he knew that he must exist. From this indubitable foundation, Descartes thought he could further prove that God exists. Although he had *doubted* the existence of God at a new level, then, he also *proved* God's existence with a new degree of certitude (so he thought, at least), placing the affirmation of God's existence on an unprecedentedly firm foundation. Descartes is therefore often upheld as the founder of a way of thinking known as **foundationalism**, which holds that *only* those things that can be proved beyond a doubt are rational to believe. Although foundationalism has had an enormous influence on modern figures (it is indeed a quintessentially modern way of thinking), it comes under heavy criticism in the mid-twentieth century (see Chapter 26).

With an understanding of the factors that led to the rise of reason in place, we now offer some examples of the ways this new view of reason reshaped Christianity in the modern period. The works of **John Locke** (1632–1704) are highly significant in this connection, as Locke exhibits a clear desire to refashion Christianity so as to bring it into accord with reason. To Locke, revelation-based claims, such as Jesus being the Messiah or the eternal damnation of the unrighteous, need to be assessed by reason. In 1695, Locke published *The Reasonableness of Christianity*, in which he used reason to sift through various traditional Christian claims in order to arrive at an eminently reasonable version of the Christian faith. The existence of God and the belief in Jesus as the Messiah are supported by reason, but Locke deems some other claims, such as the eternal punishment of the unrighteous, to be irrational. After all, such condemnation would be inequitable, which would not be fitting for God's perfect justice.

Although Locke's efforts resulted in a substantial revision of the Christian faith, the upshot was that Christianity, which was at this time sharply criticized by some for its role in violence, was characterized as a *rational* religion. Christianity as a whole, then, did not need to be eliminated for the sake of political stability, even though, according to Locke's program, certain elements had to be discarded.

Locke maintained that divine revelation was still necessary, but his younger contemporaries John Toland (1670–1722) and Matthew Tindal (1655–1733) sought to redefine Christianity further so as to make it yet more reasonable, in their eyes. In so doing, they eliminated the need for revelation altogether. In this effort, they developed a view known as **deism**, which had originated in the writings of Edward Lord Herbert of Cherbury (1583–1648). Lord Herbert believed that "true religion" could be reduced to a small set of claims: God exists and requires ethical conduct and worship; people should repent of their sins; after death, there will be rewards for the good and punishments for the bad. These are frequently viewed as some of the central tenets of deism.

Tindal's *Christianity as Old as the Creation* (1730) is often seen as the text in which deism reaches its highest and clearest expression. Tindal explicitly claimed that the natural world is the *only* source necessary for knowledge of God. In keeping with the Enlightenment ideal of equality, Tindal insisted that true doctrines must be those to which *all* human beings have access through natural knowledge. Revelation, then, is completely unnecessary. It is bestowed on only a *part* of humanity (and is therefore suspiciously exclusive, to Tindal), and in any case, it simply repeats what can already be found in the creation itself.

In holding that creation offers evidence of God, Tindal and other deists drew from the physics of the day, especially those of Newton, who had likened the intricately ordered universe to a watch, with God cast as the watchmaker. Although Newton thought this analogy suggested that God would continually tinker with the creation to keep it running, many deists later insisted that the world must have been *perfectly* designed by a perfect creator. No interaction with the world was therefore necessary after God hit the universe's "on" switch, so to speak. In fact, many deists would hold that God *could not* intervene in the world once it was "started" at the moment of creation. This idea that God made the world like a gigantic machine became another central tenet of deism, and in fact it is the most well-known feature of deism to many today.

Deism, then, was often styled as the "freethinker's religion" during the Enlightenment. To deists, traditional Christianity led toward fanaticism, superstition, ignorance, and interminable conflicts, as had been displayed during the religious wars of the sixteenth and seventeenth centuries. Deism offered a much more rational, equitable, enlightening, and peaceful alternative.

Although this "religion of reason," as it is sometimes called, held out great promise in the middle of the eighteenth century, its remaining course demonstrates just how radically some of its advocates were willing to interpret its demands. In France, where citizens did not enjoy the religious protections offered to the English, the religion of reason took a more aggressively anti-church tone. In particular, a group of figures known as *philosophes* repackaged the (often plodding) arguments of English deists and made them into succinct, witty barbs with which they attacked the Catholic Church and the French monarchy. Foremost among the *philosophes* stood François Marie Arouet (1694–1778), known as Voltaire, who satirically lampooned traditional Christianity in many of his later writings. Voltaire famously directed the slogan *écrasez l'infâme* ("crush the infamous thing") toward traditional Christianity. He saw orthodox Christian belief as dangerously fanatical, and he suggested that eliminating the church would be the best course of action.

The attacks on the Catholic Church soon spread to criticism of the state. In the eyes of many, it was not only traditional Christianity but also the French monarchy that imperiled the well-being of French citizens. Beginning in 1789, revolutionaries in France took advantage of the heightened anti-monarchical and anti-ecclesial sentiment by overthrowing the monarchy and establishing a secular republic in its place. The French Revolution (1789–1799) triggered the toppling of monarchical rule across Europe and beyond, thus acting as a watershed for the emergence of democratic forms of government around the world. And yet, in their zeal to eliminate any remnant of the *ancien régime* (the "old regime"), revolutionaries executed thousands of French citizens; in many cases, the fates of those citizens were sealed by the fact that they espoused traditional Christian beliefs.

Eliminating traditional Christian beliefs (not by argument, but now by force) preoccupied those in power during the French Revolution, and a radical version of the religion of reason reached the height of its influence at this time. The authorities not only banned Catholicism in 1792; they went so far as to rededicate a number of Catholic churches throughout France as "Temples of Reason." In fact, on November 10, 1793, in the Cathedral of Notre Dame in Paris, a "Feast of Reason" took place during which an actress dressed in the revolutionary colors of red, white, and blue was enthroned on the altar of the cathedral as the Goddess of Liberty. Traditional Christianity had been forcibly expelled from its historic home in French churches.

LA FÊTE DE LA RAISON, DANS NOTRE-DAME DE PARIS, LE 10 NOVEMBRE 1793

Figure 22–1 The "Goddess of Reason" processes through the Cathedral of Notre Dame, Paris. Note the crucifix at her feet.

Other aspects of the religion of reason could certainly be highlighted, but the above account demonstrates that it was not only an intellectual movement that concerned an elite set of philosophers and theologians. Instead, the religion of reason affected all levels of European society, as it played a crucial role in the political and cultural upheavals witnessed toward the end of the eighteenth century. At its beginning, it appeared to be a means through which to achieve peace after decades of religious conflict. By the end of the eighteenth century, however, it had ironically become a key agent in fomenting violence.

Christian theologians, then, may have been open to the refining spirit of the Enlightenment at its beginning; however, by the middle of the eighteenth century, such individuals grew increasingly concerned that nothing would be left after the modern efforts at making a more reasonable religion had run their course.

Deism, in particular, had no place for traditional Christian ideas such as the Incarnation, the Resurrection, miracles, or even prophecy. Additionally, if as the deists claim, the world is an enormous machine that has been constructed by God, but God does not interact with the world after creating it, then the world is effectively evacuated of divine action and presence. God remains categorically *outside* of the world and cannot be found within it. Scholars today describe modernity as a period of "disenchantment," and deism has had a great deal to do with the loss of the supernatural and sacramental that accompanies modernity.

With the spread of deism, one sees the rise of the idea that there is a **secular**, religion-free aspect of reality. Once God has been removed from the world, what is left is purely natural, free from any supernatural influence, any religion at all. Although deism itself fell out of fashion toward the end of the eighteenth century, the notion of the secular remains, and indeed constitutes one of the most enduring legacies of modernity.

A New View of the Human Being: The Rise of the Autonomous Individual and the Rejection of Authority

If "reason" is one major watchword of the Enlightenment, "autonomy" (or freedom) is the other. During the Enlightenment, a new view of the human being emerges: the independent individual who does not submit to external authority, but instead knows things for him- or herself. In a certain sense, this emphasis on autonomy has its roots in the Reformation; Martin Luther (1483–1546) had asserted that his individual conscience should take precedence over the authority of the Catholic Church (see Chapter 18). Luther, however, retained a place for other sorts of authority (e.g., scripture), whereas the Enlightenment rejection of authority reaches much further. In his essay, "What is Enlightenment?" (1784), the philosopher **Immanuel Kant** (1724–1804) gives impeccable expression to this Enlightenment ideal: "Enlightenment is humankind's exit from its self-incurred immaturity. ... *Sapere aude!* Have courage to use your own reason!" (Schmidt 1996, 58, translation emended). To be enlightened is to rely on *oneself*, to be autonomous. The person who looks to *others* to know what to think stays dependent on them, and he or she remains immature.

Kant was particularly concerned about the misuse of religious authority, and he insisted that attempts by church leaders to prevent enlightenment "trample on the sacred rights" of human beings (Schmidt 1996, 62). According to this deeply modern way of thinking, one is perfectly within one's rights if one chooses to resist those who would use power to command assent. In other words, the Enlightenment ethos insists that one can reject authority purely on principle because it attempts to violate the freedom and rights of the individual.

The Enlightenment objection to authority rests on not only the idea of individual freedom and rights, but also on the inadequacy of traditional appeals to authority. Enlightenment figures regarded first-hand knowledge as highly preferable to blind adherence to another person's claims. In fact, some figures insist that simply believing what someone else declares to be true is not actually *knowing* at all. Another way to put this concern is to say that Enlightenment figures are preoccupied—if not obsessed—with *evidence*. (This concern reflects the dominance of the natural sciences at this historical moment; many Enlightenment figures sought to apply the experimental methods of the sciences to theology.) Belief should be proportioned to the evidence produced in support of the claim that is made. If there is insufficient evidence, assent to the claim should be withheld.

The Enlightenment focus on the human being, then, led to an entirely new approach to **epistemology**, or the study of knowledge. Unlike the epistemology of previous eras, this modern version focuses on the "subjective conditions" for knowledge. In other words, it centers on the human being rather than on God or the objective world. Descartes arguably began this turn by basing all knowledge on his awareness of his own existence, as described briefly above. To Descartes, claims such as "there is an outside world" and "God exists" rely on the prior assertion, "I exist." Kant, in his *Critique of Pure Reason* (1781), takes this human-centered epistemology further. He brings about the "turn to the subject" by arguing that all knowledge is conditioned by structures of the human mind. In other words, Kant claims that human beings' minds are built in such a way that they synthesize and make coherent the wide array of stimuli that our senses receive from the world. These stimuli would be utterly chaotic without the efforts of the mind. A key consequence follows: according to Kant, we have no *direct* access to the objective world, as every stimulus we receive is "filtered," so to speak, by the human subject. This epistemology has far-reaching implications; one of them is that any pronouncements from the church about the nature of God attempt to describe a realm about which *no one* can in fact have any knowledge. To Kant and his followers, then, many traditional Christian claims are not adequately supported.

Another key feature of Enlightenment anthropology concerns the extraordinary optimism about human beings espoused at this time. Indeed, a certain confidence in humanity is required in order to maintain with Kant that we are capable of knowing for ourselves, and this modern optimism stands in sharp contrast to the anthropology of previous eras. Much traditional Christian theology had viewed human beings as created good, yet deeply flawed by sin. Among the effects of sin is a darkened intellect, which hobbles our efforts at reasoning clearly. To many Christian theologians, if we are able to use our reason effectively, it is due to God's grace, not our own inherent abilities. During the Enlightenment, however, a much loftier assessment of human beings became dominant. Figures such as Jean-Jacques Rousseau (1712–1778) insisted that the doctrine of original sin is an unnecessarily pessimistic idea. Enlightenment figures held that human beings are morally and intellectually sound, and that we do not need any special intervention from God to do good and think well.

This widespread rejection of sin influenced the notion of progress afoot during this time. Rousseau saw the doctrine of original sin as stultifying human efforts at making the world a better place; other Enlightenment figures held that once European societies were free from the "shackles" of traditional Christianity, a new age would dawn. The Enlightenment, then, has not only given us a world in which individual rights and human dignity are affirmed. At a more fundamental level, it has given us the idea that human beings can change the world. Whereas those in earlier eras viewed the world as fixed in its order, modernity has brought with it a mind-set that the world can actually be altered so as to benefit more people in better ways. Optimism about the individual human being, then, contributes to the widespread belief that human societies as a whole are progressing toward a better future. What often accompanies this notion of progress is the idea that the goal or "telos" of human existence lies within *this* world, not the next.

No topic better captures the complex legacy of the Enlightenment than autonomy. On the one hand, the notions of individual freedom and inherent rights played a crucial role in forming the democratic governments that are deeply valued features of the world in which we live today. On the other hand, however, the rejection of authority presented enormous challenges to Christian theology. Any traditional Christian claim that could not be experientially demonstrated became suspect, and a human-centered version of religion emerged during this time. The human being became the measure of all things.

Issues in Moral Theology: Modernity and Human Rights

An important development in Christian moral thinking during the modern period has been the general acceptance of *human rights* as a fundamental aspect of morality. According to the notion of human rights, all people, regardless of gender, race, religion, social class, or nationality, have a set of legitimate moral claims on others (particularly their governments). Such a notion is not found in the Bible nor in any historical period before modernity.

Before the modern period, "rights" were understood to be legitimate claims that persons had based on their position or authority in society, whether as kings or priests, for example, or as owners of property, or as husbands and wives within marriage. Such rights claims generally were understood within the larger moral context of duty and responsibility. People had these rights because they were required to live certain types of lives given their social position.

The notion of rights has changed dramatically in the modern period. First, people are now said to have rights simply because they are human, regardless of their position in society. Second, these rights are now expressed primarily as freedoms—that is to say, they are seen as moral claims to do or to say things without the interference of others. Third, these rights have replaced duty or responsibility as the primary element of morality. The notion of human rights is foundational to democracy.

Neither the Bible nor Christian tradition can claim direct credit for this development. But there are biblical and Christian elements that are compatible with it. And it is within countries with a Christian history that these rights have been developed. Three theological ideas have come into play to justify and support the notion that all humans have rights: the *imago Dei* of Genesis 1; the Incarnation of Jesus Christ; and the universal destiny of humanity in God. That is to say, all human beings share a common origin in God, a common identity with Jesus, and a common end in God.

A New Way to Do History: "Scientific History" and the Challenge to Christian History

Both the Enlightenment emphasis on reason and its suspicion toward authority affect the way in which history has been approached during the modern period. Although this changing attitude toward history begins during the Enlightenment, it achieves greatest sophistication during the nineteenth century, after the Enlightenment itself had come to an end. The modern approach to history can be characterized as an effort in making it "scientific." That is, just as natural sciences such as physics, chemistry, and biology had insisted that evidence should be carefully weighed so as to make objective judgments about reality, modern historians began to require unbiased assessment of historical evidence so that the truth of "what actually happened" could be determined. Modern historians, then, worry that pre-modern historical accounts are biased and not actually based on the evidence. The new attitude to history can be summed up as follows: *use reason to get history right, rejecting previous views whenever necessary.*

Additionally, just as physicists, chemists, and biologists look for *natural* causes of the phenomena they investigate, historians in the modern period seek out natural causes of various events in Christian history. This attraction toward the natural instead of the supernatural had been to some extent set in motion by deism and the evacuation of God from the world, as described above, and it leads to a key principle of modern historical inquiry: *analogy.* **Ernst Troeltsch** (1865–1923) maintained that modern historians should conduct their investigations under the presumption that the past is analogous to the present. In other words, our experience of what is possible in the present should function as a tool with which to determine what could have been possible in the past. As historians seek to make sense of the past, then, present experience serves as their guiding principle. One sees the impact of this new way of doing history in treatments of the growth of Christianity in its first few decades. Whereas the book of Acts attributes the growth of the early church to the supernatural activity of the Holy Spirit, modern historians suggest instead that the church grew because of natural factors, such as the support that Christians offered to each other in their community life (see Chapter 8).

The new, scientific way of doing history profoundly affected modern understandings of the Bible. One sees the beginnings of this new approach to scripture in the works of **Johann Gottfried Herder** (1744–1803), who insisted that the Bible does not simply consist of God's "words that drop from heaven"; instead, the Bible reflects the values and thought-forms of ancient Near Eastern cultures (Livingston 1997, 77). Understanding the Bible, therefore, requires acquainting oneself with the time and place in which it was written.

Herder influenced a number of nineteenth-century figures who developed an approach to interpreting the Bible known as **historical criticism**. Advocates of this method sought to liberate biblical interpretation from the constraints of the church, and they insisted that the Bible should be subjected to the same kinds of critical questions that scholars had been applying to other texts. In particular, these figures were interested in the ways in which other cultures could have influenced the authors of biblical texts. For example, they found that the first chapters of Genesis are similar to a Babylonian creation story called the *Enuma Elish*, and they also observed that the *Epic of Gilgamesh* contains an ancient flood story (see Chapter 2). These non-biblical stories were composed before the first books of the Bible; therefore, scholars postulated that the authors of Genesis used them as sources for the biblical stories of creation and the flood. The content of the Bible was thus explained through natural causes (i.e., cultural influence) rather than supernatural causes (i.e., inspiration from God).

These new historical methods gave rise to a movement known as the **Quest for the Historical Jesus**, which operated under the presupposition that the New Testament is riddled with supernatural, mythological elements that need to be excised in order to find the true "Jesus of history." In this effort, scholars analyzed the Gospels in order to determine which one was written first; their operating assumption was that the earliest gospel would best capture who Jesus actually was. Their research developed the two-source hypothesis, which suggests that the Gospel of Mark was chronologically prior to the other Gospels. Mark's Gospel depicted the Jesus of history, according to these modern historians, and this understanding of Jesus differed enormously from the "Christ of faith," as found, for example, in John's Gospel. Scholars who conducted the Quest declared that Jesus was simply a moral teacher, not the Son of God.

The deepest challenge to Christian theology posed by modern historians has to do with their view of the very nature of history itself. Following **G.E. Lessing** (1729–1781) and others, modern figures came to view history as an arena within which purely *contingent events* occur. In other words, to Lessing, history contains one episode after another that could have unfolded differently from the way in which it happened. To Lessing, such contingent events cannot be used to support *necessary truths*, which are always the case; they are non-contingent. Or, to use different language to express the same idea, Lessing thought that history displayed simply *surface-level* events that could not say anything about the deeper truths of God. To use Lessing's example, it is one thing to claim that Jesus Christ raised a dead man to life, but this event does not provide adequate support for the additional claim that Jesus is the Son of God, who is "one in being" with God the Father. The latter claim refers to a sphere that is far beyond the reach of *any* historical event. Under the influence of Lessing, then, the historical events recorded in scripture are characterized as not providing sufficient support for central Christian doctrines such as the Incarnation and the Trinity.

The modern interest in scientific history dramatically rewrote the Christian story. Whereas Christian theologians had traditionally viewed the Bible as a record of God's direct communication with human beings, modern historians introduced other cultures as key influences on the biblical authors. As a result, the claim that the Bible is divinely inspired was deeply challenged during the modern period. According to some, the Bible's contents could be explained without recourse to divine inspiration at all. Instead, the Bible was seen as simply the product of cultural exchange among different human societies. One can account for its contents "horizontally," so to speak, without any intervention from God along a "vertical" axis. In addition to challenging notions of biblical inspiration, the modern way of doing history resulted in a radical revision of Christology. Scholars associated with the Quest for the Historical Jesus deeply questioned traditional claims for the divinity of Christ. At its deepest level, figures such as Lessing argued, history itself was not a useful or effective avenue through which to learn anything about God, who lives on a plane of existence that radically transcends anything that could take place within history.

A New Level of Skepticism toward Religion: The "Masters of Suspicion"

The final "new thing" that takes place in modernity concerns the era's unprecedented skepticism, which is directed not only at Christianity, but toward all religions. During the modern period, atheism became a viable option as never before. A group of figures known as the "masters of suspicion" began their multifaceted critique in the mid-nineteenth century, and although their arguments have been robustly challenged by modern theologians, their criticisms are very much a part of our world today.

The German philosopher **Ludwig Feuerbach** (1804–72) stands at the beginning of this development. He was a follower of G.W.F. Hegel (who will be treated below), and he is most well known for claiming that what we think of as God is in fact a "projection" that comes from human beings. To Feuerbach, human beings take their most cherished ideals and simply *imagine* a being who possesses them. The idea of God, then, originates from human beings themselves, not from some objective reality beyond them.

One might wonder why human beings would do this. Feuerbach holds that this projection arises from our "self-alienation." That is, according to Feuerbach, we have become disunited from our true selves. We mistakenly think that everything that is valuable (such as holiness, power, perfection, etc.) cannot possibly be a part of ourselves, so we concoct an imaginary being we call God, and we place all that is positive in it. As Feuerbach puts this point: "Religion is the disuniting of man from himself; he sets God before him as the antithesis of himself. … God is the absolutely positive, the sum of all realities; man the absolutely negative" (Feuerbach 1989, 33). Crucially, however, we think this only because we have lost touch with the positive aspects of ourselves. According to Feuerbach's analysis, the concept of God arises as the result of a profound underestimation, if not self-loathing, on the part of human beings. We think that we should not be valued, that there is no good in us, and that the only thing that could possibly be valued is something besides ourselves.

Feuerbach is often viewed as attempting to destroy the credibility of belief in God. However, some commentators hasten to make clear that he sought to build a new form of religion in which human beings would have a proper regard for their true nature. He envisioned a future in which human beings would overcome their self-alienation and cease projecting their ideals onto a being beyond themselves. They would achieve authentic self-realization, and they would see that the things they have given to God, so to speak, are in fact a part of themselves.

Feuerbach's unrelentingly negative view of Christianity and his lofty assessment of humanity are criticized by later figures. For now, we turn to someone who was powerfully affected by Feuerbach's thought: **Karl Marx** (1818–1883). Marx saw self-alienation as arising from a broader societal source—namely, the oppressive social conditions imposed upon the lower classes by their political and economic overlords. To Marx, human beings are inherently creative and productive, but capitalist societies allow their work to be taken from them and owned by another. This unpleasant state is remedied to some extent by religion, but to Marx religion only provides comfort like a drug that offers escape from reality. As Marx famously puts it, "Religion is the sigh of the oppressed creature, the heart of a heartless world … It is the opium of the people" (Marx 1994, 57). Marx is particularly critical of Christianity, which he sees as instructing human beings to be good rule-followers in this life so that their reward will be great in heaven. According to this way of thinking, Christianity is a powerful tool wielded by the ruling classes to maintain political and economic stability, which only means the continuation of the oppressive conditions under which most human beings live.

In response to this state of affairs, Marx advocated revolutionary change, and few figures have had such an enormous effect on the modern world. Marx held that if the unjust social conditions that give rise to religion can be eliminated, then religion will simply fade away. After all, religion is only a product of the alienation produced by oppression. An atheistic utopian vision, then, animates Marx's thought. To Marx, capitalism lies at the heart of the injustices of our world, and his withering indictment led to socialist and communist revolutions in the modern period, most famously the 1917 Bolshevik Revolution, which gave rise to the Soviet Union.

In a manner similar to Marx, **Friedrich Nietzsche** (1844–1900) saw Christianity as advocating an ethically objectionable outlook that has done tremendous harm to human beings. To Nietzsche, Christianity is the product of what he called a "slave morality," which begins within Judaism but culminates in Christianity. To Nietzsche, the Jews have known defeat all too well throughout their history. Out of resentment at being ruled over by worldly powers (e.g., Rome), they led a "slave revolt," not by taking up arms, but instead by pursuing the only option available to them: an attack on the *moral system* espoused by their conquerors (to Nietzsche, there is no objective morality; good and evil are culturally constructed ideas, as we will explore in Chapter 26). According to the slave morality, "the wretched alone are the good; the poor, impotent, lowly alone are the good … the powerful and noble, are on the contrary the evil" (Livingston 1997, 405). Rather than valuing strength, as Nietzsche thinks one should, the slave morality values weakness. Christianity picks up this idea and universalizes it, as found in Jesus' Sermon on the Mount, in which the meek and persecuted are blessed (Matthew 6).

One might ask what is wrong with the slave morality, as it seems to undergird countless social programs that many today would regard as good. To Nietzsche, not only does the slave morality contain an inherent resentment toward strength (i.e., it has anger at its heart), but it is also ultimately life-denying in its celebration of weakness. In a work titled *The Antichrist: A Curse on Christianity* (1888), Nietzsche insists that Christianity has resulted in "draining all blood, all love, all hope for life" (quoted in Livingston 1997, 408). He further maintains, "The Christian Church … is the highest of all conceivable corruptions … [It is] against health, beauty, whatever has turned out well, courage, spirit, *graciousness* of the soul, *against life itself*" (quoted in Livingston 1997, 408). In a contested reading of the Christian theological tradition that echoes Marx, Nietzsche holds that Christianity values only the next world (i.e., heaven), and in so doing evacuates this world of happiness, beauty, and meaning. In particular, Nietzsche holds that Christianity has a problematic view of the body; it sees the body as a source of sin, but he believes the body should be celebrated.

To Nietzsche, this culture shaped by the Christian "preachers of death" is near its end. In his "Parable of the Madman," Nietzsche describes a madman who goes about announcing, "God is dead." This phrase has been interpreted as meaning that modern European societies no longer refer to God as an agreed-upon reality. God has ceased being a part of the fabric of our culture. Instead, as the madman puts it, "*We have killed him*—you and I. All of us are his murderers" (quoted in Livingston 1997, 400). We are living in a world that has begun to see that God is an illusion, although we do not yet realize the full implications of that epoch-making insight. We will soon understand that the foundation of our values has disappeared, and we will enter into full-blown nihilism as a culture.

Although Nietzsche's prognosis for Western culture is bleak, to say the least, he was not utterly hopeless. He envisioned the possible rise of someone he called the

Übermensch (translated as either "Overman" or "Superman"), who would forge a new morality out of the ashes of Western civilization. This person would enact a "transvaluation of all values," as Nietzsche put it, a re-evaluation of morality that would say an emphatic "yes" to life. The *Übermensch* would not celebrate weakness, but neither would he or she be cruel. Through self-discipline this person would achieve self-mastery, and as a result not dominate others with his or her strength, but instead act tenderly toward lesser beings. Ultimately, the *Übermensch* would not conform to any familiar system of values, but he or she would approach existence in a deeply life-affirming manner. Importantly, too, this person would not need a transcendent realm (God) in which to ground his or her new values. The *Übermensch* would not look to anything beyond this world for meaning; even more, this person would not look to "eternalize" any moment, but instead would joyfully affirm that everything is in flux, ever becoming. This picture of the world ushered in by the *Übermensch* has been characterized as a "naturalistic religious vision" (Livingston 1997, 410). Although the changes that Nietzsche advocates would utterly overturn the value structures of Western societies, he regards them as ultimately therapeutic for a humanity that he views as oppressed and resentful.

Sigmund Freud (1856–1939) deepened the psychological aspects of Feuerbach's analysis, and his influence on Western civilization has been exceptionally far-reaching. Whereas previous figures in the history of philosophy and theology had viewed human beings as inherently *rational* creatures, to Freud that rationality is but a thin veneer atop a simmering cauldron of irrational impulses that lie beneath our conscious awareness. This "unconscious" or "subconscious," as Freud puts it, is in fact the main animator of our behavior and thought. Among the most powerful impulses within human beings are the need for protection and the desire to avoid death. After all, we find ourselves in a world in which we cannot control the forces of nature outside of us. We attempt to address these fears by projecting the idea of a father-like God who gives us protection and grants everlasting life. As Freud expresses his view in *The Future of an Illusion* (1927), "Religious ideas ... are illusions, fulfillments of the oldest, strongest, and most urgent wishes of mankind" (Freud 1961, 38). To Freud, then, religion is "wish-fulfillment." As such, it keeps human beings immature. We childishly hold out hope that something beyond ourselves will resolve our problems, never recognizing the illusory nature of our own creations.

Whereas some other modern critics chipped away at certain features of Christianity that one might see as peripheral, leaving something of a core behind, the masters of suspicion call the whole enterprise of religion into question. If they are right, religion is an illusion that has toxic effects on both the individual and society as a whole. With that said, these figures have not gone unchallenged. Both below and in later chapters in this book we will see some of the responses to them that Christian theologians offer.

THEOLOGICAL RESPONSES TO THE MODERN CRITIQUES OF RELIGION

One emerges from the modern criticisms of Christianity a bit dizzied by their virulence, but also wondering if the Christian tradition has been accurately represented by its detractors. The critics examined above often launch sweeping characterizations of Christianity in which thousands of years of theological reflection are summed up in a single idea or alleged ethos of Christianity as a whole.

This chapter cannot provide an exhaustive list of the wide range of responses to the modern critiques of religion offered by Christian theologians. It can, however, chart some of the general trends and most noteworthy figures (a task that continues in later chapters in this book). Broadly speaking, modern Christian theology pursued three different courses. The first of these was *accommodation*, which took the modern critiques so seriously that it simply ceased advocating Christian doctrines found to be irrational or otherwise objectionable to the modern mind. Put simply, this approach thought that modernity is right, and much of traditional Christianity is wrong (or at least outdated). The second option, *rejection*, flatly dismissed modernity as wrong-headed and instead reiterated traditional Christian beliefs. The opposite of accommodation, this approach held that traditional Christianity is right and modernity is wrong. The third option, *reformulation*, engaged in the much more complex task of transforming Christian views into new language in an effort at capturing the essence of traditional doctrines while remaining persuasive to the modern mind. This approach required a comprehensive grasp of the tradition and a willingness to reinterpret it (quite radically, in some cases) in order to appeal to the sensibilities of modern persons. It also included a range of theological positions, some of which came close to accommodation and others of which approached rejection. We briefly treat accommodation and rejection before discussing various reformulations below.

Accommodation was a common Christian response to modernity during the Enlightenment. At this point in time, it seemed to many that Christian theologians could make a few concessions to modern critics and still maintain a core set of essential claims. The position of John Locke, as described above, can be viewed as a version of accommodation; the eternal damnation of the unrighteous was eliminated because it was not in keeping with modern sensibilities, but the belief in the existence of God and in Jesus as the Messiah continued to be maintained because it was regarded as rational. The problem, of course, was that what was viewed as "rational" grew increasingly restrictive as the Enlightenment ran its course. As a result, Christian theologians seeking to accommodate modernity found themselves with fewer and fewer doctrines that they could uphold as reasonable. Deism, for instance, endorsed the existence of God, but it eliminated the Incarnation, Resurrection, miracles, and prophecy. A progressively thinner version of Christianity seemed inevitable as its advocates ceded more and more ground in the face of modern criticisms.

At the other end of the theological spectrum, a number of Christian theologians felt compelled during the modern period to reject modernity outright and boldly reassert what they saw as traditional Christian theology. One of the most extreme versions of rejection is Christian **fundamentalism**, which began during the late nineteenth century and continues to be especially prominent in the United States today. The movement acquires its name from the belief that there are certain non-negotiable "fundamentals" that form the basis of Christian theology. The Christian must not compromise on these basic claims in the face of modern criticism. In 1910, a five-point list of the essential beliefs was developed, and it is widely viewed as a creed of sorts for fundamentalists. The "fundamental" beliefs are as follows: (1) the "verbal, plenary inerrancy of scripture" (i.e., the belief that *all* of scripture is literally true and does not contain any type of error); (2) the virgin birth of Jesus Christ; (3) the belief that Christ's death on the cross atoned for human sin by bearing God's wrath for us (known as substitutionary atonement); (4) Christ's physical resurrection; and (5) the historical authenticity of Christ's miracles.

Christian theologians associated with fundamentalism were alarmed at the tendency for much modern theology to accommodate modernity and give up on central Christian beliefs. However, in its zeal to reaffirm traditional Christianity, fundamentalism ironically reinforced certain modern views. Most importantly, the belief that scripture is inerrant and literally true in every word fixates in an unbalanced way on only one of the many different "senses" or levels of meaning in scripture. Since Origen of Alexandria (*c.*184–*c.*253), Christian theologians have placed the literal meaning of scripture in a complex conversation with the allegorical, moral, and "anagogical" meanings of scripture (see Chapter 8). However, fundamentalists anachronistically insist that only the literal meaning is significant, thereby unwittingly adopting a highly *nontraditional* approach to the Bible. This "flattening" or simplification of the meaning of scripture is to some extent a product of modernity itself, which privileges scientific, literal, factual truth, and often views any allegorical or metaphorical understandings of truth as suspiciously non-rigorous. Rather than challenge this assumption, fundamentalism reinforces it, unintentionally ceding ground to modernity in its efforts at fighting against it.

Whereas accommodation runs the risk of losing everything traditional within Christian theology, outright rejection runs the risk of losing intellectual respectability and any ability to engage with the broader culture of which Christians are a part. The fundamentalist approach to scripture often requires believers to reject modern scientific views of the universe in favor of a literal, six-day creation. It also has significant difficulty explaining the many internal tensions or inconsistencies in the historical accounts described in the Bible. These tendencies have caused many to view fundamentalism as anti-intellectual, and a number of fundamentalists have actually embraced this understanding.

Having described theological responses to modernity from the two extremes, we now turn to the wide range of responses in the middle, which seek to reformulate Christian theology so as to meet the modern challenge, while retaining (to varying degrees) the vital message of the Christian faith.

Figure 22–2 Friedrich Schleiermacher (1768–1834).

Friedrich Schleiermacher: Using Experience to Reformulate Christian Theology

The task of reformulating Christian theology such that it could be compelling to the modern mind was taken up with extraordinary creativity by **Friedrich Schleiermacher** (1768–1834), who was a professor of theology at the University of Berlin and is often regarded as the "father of modern theology." His *On Religion: Speeches to Its Cultured Despisers* (1799) marks the beginning of a new era in Christian theology.

Schleiermacher was well aware of the skepticism of his age, but he insisted that Christianity's "cultured despisers" operated under a misconception of what religion is about in the first place. These skeptics had become preoccupied with the idea that religion concerns belief in a set of *doctrines*; Schleiermacher called his reader to penetrate beneath these "externals," and he held that religion begins with the innermost experience of the human being. Specifically, religion is grounded in "the immediate feeling of the Infinite and Eternal" (Schleiermacher 1994, 16). To Schleiermacher, human beings have a sense that they stand on the edge of a deeply mysterious reality that will always exceed their grasp. Religion springs from this astonishing experience of being exposed to an enormous realm that will remain perpetually beyond our understanding, despite our best efforts.

By rooting religion in feeling, Schleiermacher drew from the artistic and intellectual movement known as Romanticism, which reacted against the Enlightenment emphasis on reason. Romantic figures insisted that reason could not exhaustively describe reality, as Enlightenment philosophers had held. Romantic artists and literary figures such as Caspar David Friedrich (1774–1840) and William Wordsworth (1770–1850) appealed to feeling, intuition, and the imagination as deeper ways to engage with the world, insisting that focusing only on the rational misses an enormous portion of reality. Scholars often characterize Schleiermacher's theology as a part of this broader cultural movement.

In his later work *The Christian Faith* (1822), Schleiermacher creatively reinterpreted Christian theology with experience as his guiding principle. Christian theology begins with "the feeling of **absolute dependence**," as Schleiermacher puts it, which is "the consciousness that the whole of our ... activity comes from a source outside of us" (Schleiermacher 2016, 16). Schleiermacher highlights the fact that we do not ultimately determine our own reality, and he holds that we have an intuitive awareness that our existence is given to us by something beyond ourselves. He further claims that having consciousness of one's absolute dependence is the same thing as being in relationship with God. Schleiermacher, then, holds that relationship with God already lies hidden within our deepest experience of ourselves in the world.

Schleiermacher's experientially based reconstruction of Christianity continues in his Christology. To Schleiermacher, the essential thing to note about Jesus Christ is that he was completely receptive to the divine, and as a result he had a perfect "God-consciousness," or experiential awareness of God. Other human beings might have an experience of God at some level, but Jesus' experience of God was uniquely potent, so much so that his God-consciousness amounted to the very presence of God within him. In this formulation, Schleiermacher considerably revises the traditional view of the Incarnation; rather than maintain that the second person of the Trinity (the divine *logos*) entered into the world and joined with a human being, Schleiermacher claims that God has become incarnate through the *experience* of God that Jesus had.

With experience once again as his guide, Schleiermacher refashions Christian teaching about sin, which should not be understood as a biologically transmitted consequence of the original sin of Adam

Figure 22–3 *Wanderer above the Sea of Fog*, by Caspar David Friedrich (1774–1840).

and Eve. Instead, sin is viewed as any interruption of one's awareness of God. In this way of thinking, sin is the experience of losing sight of God's presence in one's life, or simply "God-forgetfulness," as Schleiermacher puts it.

How, then, would the Christian doctrine of redemption be understood in this reworked system of thought? To Schleiermacher, redemption is the revivifying of God-consciousness in one whose awareness of God has been dulled by sin. This increased experiential awareness of God is inspired by Christ. The work of Christ, then, is re-understood as follows: "The Redeemer assumes believers into the power of His God-consciousness, and this is His redemptive activity" (Schleiermacher 2016, 425). Christ's God-consciousness, therefore, was not just uniquely potent to himself, it also had a powerful effect on others such that it could elevate their awareness of God.

By rooting Christian theology in experience, Schleiermacher sought to make it relevant to modern persons. In one sense, he followed modern thought by beginning with the human being, as Kant had in his "turn to the subject." And yet, whereas much modern thought regards Christianity as failing to be sufficiently reasonable, Schleiermacher in an important sense protected Christian theology from key criticisms by insisting that it is not about reason at all, but instead *feeling* (or intuition). To Schleiermacher, Christian theology does not depend on reason; it is not about *knowing* in the sense in which most Enlightenment philosophers used the term. Although this approach accepted Kant's insistence that we cannot know God through reason, through his turn to feeling, Schleiermacher creatively found space within those Kantian confines to make Christianity attractive and credible to many in the modern age.

Figure 22–4 Georg Wilhelm Friedrich Hegel (1770–1832).

G.W.F. Hegel: Rethinking Christian Theology through a New View of Reason

The task of reformulating Christian theology took a markedly different route at the hands of the **Georg Wilhelm Friedrich Hegel** (1770–1832), who was a professor of philosophy at the University of Berlin and a rival to Schleiermacher. Hegel heaped scorn on Schleiermacher's turn to feeling and held instead that reason itself, when understood properly, could be used to draw out the philosophical truth that lies implicitly within historical Christianity.

Key to Hegel's system is a dynamic vision of how thought or reason works. Reason does not simply produce ready-made, static concepts, but instead is always testing the value and truth of those ideas, often by entertaining a claim that is the very opposite of the initial notion. In fact, Hegel held that any given idea actually *depends* on its opposite. In other words, we understand a particular thing only in relation to what that thing is *not*. The process of reasoning, then, moves from a first moment, in which the initial (incomplete, partial) idea is held, to a second moment, in which the idea's opposite is posited. From the tension between these two moments a superior, refined idea emerges. This refined idea takes into consideration the valuable aspects of both the initial idea and the negation of it. Or, to use the language that is often employed to describe this process in Hegel, he holds that thought proceeds from "thesis" to "antithesis," after which it arrives at a deeper, more all-encompassing "synthesis" that includes within itself both the idea and its negation (this is referred to as "Hegelian Dialectic"). Hegel writes in a notoriously abstract and difficult manner, but his view on this point can be encapsulated with the following simple formulation: understanding *progresses*. In other words, we understand things better at the *conclusion* of a process of thinking. Our initial view is incomplete, and we arrive at truth only at the end.

From this observation about how thought functions within the human mind, Hegel makes the much bolder claim that the universe as a whole manifests this process. Indeed, the very reason that thought progresses as it does within the human mind is that reality itself unfolds according to its logic. This much grander process begins with "Spirit" (in German, *Geist*), which is typically seen as Hegel's term for God. In God's initial state, God is undeveloped, not fully self-aware, in much the same way that the "thesis" moment described above remains incomplete. In order to achieve full self-awareness, the infinite, abstract God must first manifest God's self in a second moment as a concrete, finite "other" or "opposite." This is Hegel's highly inventive way of rearticulating the doctrines of creation and Incarnation. Creation is the "other" of God, produced as a necessary step in God's coming to full self-consciousness.

At this stage, however, God has only posited God's opposite, thus becoming alienated from God's self, without yet achieving "synthesis." For the third, final stage to take place, in the words of one commentator,

> the belonging-together of the Infinite Subject [God] and the finite world (their original identity) must be comprehended. For this to happen, human beings need to have the originating identity revealed to them. The implicit unity of divine and human must be made explicit (revealed).
>
> (McCormack 2012, 11)

In other words, although God and creation (including humans) were originally one, God has introduced division in order to arrive at self-understanding. For union to occur again, the original union must be made explicit. This occurs through Jesus, who is the very revelation of God, the union of the finite and the infinite made manifest in history. Jesus allows human beings to recognize *explicitly* their own original unity with God, and this increased human self-understanding actually brings God to full self-awareness. Put succinctly, God must go out of God's self in order to return to God's self with greater understanding, and human beings play a crucial role in this process.

According to this remarkably comprehensive system of thought, the history of the world is therefore the process through which God's self-consciousness develops. Whereas modern figures such as Lessing had viewed historical events as mere surface-level phenomena that could tell us nothing about the deep truths of God, Hegel's system claimed that history is the arena within which God has become concrete. Historical events, then, have an extraordinary significance, as they are steps in God's coming to self-awareness. God, too, is thoroughly *historicized* in Hegel's thought.

Whereas pre-modern theology had viewed God as a static, unchanging entity, God in Hegel's view never remains still, and is always *in process* toward greater self-awareness. God is *in* history like never before.

Hegel's understanding of God runs afoul of many traditional Christian views, not least in its introduction of both change and necessity into God (for traditional Christian theologians, God does not change, and God did not *need* to create the world in order to understand God's self). However, Hegel's grandiose, frequently heterodox system of thought offered some major advantages to Christian theologians. First, he reclaimed reason for Christian theology in his insistence that his system of thought was eminently *rational*. Whereas reason had during the Enlightenment resulted in a rather dried-up and dull theology that kept getting more and more timid, on Hegel's watch reason brought a bold and dynamic (if frequently problematic) understanding of God back to theology.

Additionally, whereas pre-modern Christian theologians faced a perennial challenge in explaining how a transcendent God could become incarnate in a human being, Hegel's system had incarnation built into it from the start. That is, for Hegel, the necessary movement of God from abstract to concrete in the process of self-realization makes the incarnation a perfectly normal step in the unfolding of Spirit. It is in the nature of God for God to become actualized through the incarnation.

Along similar lines, Hegel influenced modern theologians in that their understanding of revelation shifted from "information transfer" to "self-revelation." In other words, modern theologians drew from Hegel's idea that God's revelation to human beings does not consist of information *about* God; instead, God's revelation is nothing less than God's very self. This change would have far-reaching implications for Christian theology in the modern period, as we will see below.

Liberal Protestantism: A Practical Theology for Modern Societies

One cannot tell the story of Christian theology in the modern period without referring to Liberal Protestant theology. Schleiermacher provided this movement with its foundations by turning to experience as the source of Christian theology. Subsequent figures sought to reinterpret further the Christian tradition in accord with the broad outlines of Schleiermacher's reformulation, even if they disagreed with him on key issues. Most notably, the German historian and theologian **Albrecht Ritschl** (1822–1889) continued to root Christian theology in experience, but he thought that Schleiermacher's understanding of Christianity was both too individualistic and not sufficiently historical. Concerning the latter point, Ritschl charged Schleiermacher with simply arguing from an ideal vision of what Christ *should be like* to the historical person of Jesus Christ. According to Ritschl, Schleiermacher did not begin with actual historical investigation.

In his three-volume work, *The Christian Doctrine of Justification and Reconciliation* (1870–1874), Ritschl undertook a historical examination of the Christian tradition, and based on his efforts he argued that the central concern of Christian theology should be the moral effects of Christ on the community of his followers. To Ritschl, Christianity is about ethical action, not an introspective experience of the divine. He worried that Schleiermacher's view of the Christian life encouraged fleeing the world and its problems for the sake of an inner, mystical experience of God. To Ritschl, Jesus preached an extraordinary forgiveness of sins that reunites human beings with God, and this experience necessarily happens *in community*, not individualistically.

Those who have felt these effects are liberated from the necessity of nature and are enabled to be free, spiritual beings. They are then called to bring about reconciliation within Christian community such that it is permeated by "brotherly love."

This eminently practical view of Christianity regarded the "Kingdom of God" not as an otherworldly realm ushered in after a cataclysmic divine judgment, but instead as a this-worldly society in which a perfected love of God and neighbor will come to be realized. In this formulation, Ritschl not only extracted many of the dramatic supernatural elements from Christian eschatology, he also advocated a version of the Christian life in which following Jesus and doing God's will involved simply doing one's duty within one's society. Ritschl, then, did not see any significant contrast between the church and the world. As one commentator characterizes this feature of Ritschlian theology, "If one makes sound, reasonable value judgments, one must be Christian; and a reasonable world must be a Christian world" (Wilson 2007, 130). It is *not* the case, for example, that being Christian calls one to resist and critique the society of which one is a part. This indistinguishability between the church and the state would become one of the most infamous features of Ritschlian theology, as we will see below.

Adolf von Harnack (1851–1930) was Ritschl's most widely renowned student, and he continued his teacher's historical investigation of Christianity in his own work. Harnack, however, insisted more radically than Ritschl that significant portions of traditional Christian theology needed to be discarded. In his seven-volume *History of Dogma* (1886–1890), Harnack sought to liberate Christianity from traditional Christian theology, which he saw as distorting the original message of the primitive church. To Harnack, the earliest Christians preached about Jesus as a moral teacher who held out a vision of all human beings as brothers and sisters under the fatherhood of God. According to Harnack's historical investigations, Jesus did not actually claim to be divine. However, by the time the Gospel of John was written (roughly 100 C.E.), the church had been influenced by Greek philosophy, in particular its idea of the Logos (Word), which the author of John identified with Jesus (the prologue of John reads, "In the beginning was the Word [*Logos*], and the Word was with God, and the Word was God"). This "Logos Christology" views Jesus as the incarnation of God, but to Harnack it is inauthentic. It is part of the "husk" that must be discarded in an effort to arrive at the "kernel" of authentic Christianity. To Harnack, then, traditional Christian doctrines such as the Incarnation and the Trinity were later, false accretions; they were not part of the original, true message of the primitive church. Rather than focusing on these metaphysical abstractions, Harnack thought that Christian theology should continue the Ritschlian program of focusing on action in the world.

Liberal Protestantism may have begun with a bold reformulation of Christian theology at the hands of Schleiermacher, but 100 years later with Harnack it had become remarkably similar to the accommodation option outlined above. Within Liberal Protestant circles, Jesus was often regarded as simply a moral teacher, and all supernaturalism (miracles, incarnation, resurrection, etc.) was frequently discarded. Crucially for what was to come in the twentieth century, Liberal Protestant theology had difficulty articulating a way in which being a follower of Jesus differentiated one from being a moral person in one's society.

Karl Barth: The Otherness of God and the Turn to Revelation

The Swiss Protestant theologian **Karl Barth** (1886–1968) is often seen as the most significant figure in Protestantism since John Calvin. Although he was educated in

Figure 22–5 Karl Barth (1886–1968).

Liberal Protestant theology, he came to view its approach as deeply problematic. Barth saw Liberal Protestantism as a failed effort at starting theology "from below" (i.e., from within human experience), and he sought to set twentieth-century theology on an entirely new footing by beginning with God's revelation. His corrective to Liberal Protestant theology continues to be followed by many theologians today.

The initial impetus for this change came from an episode in Barth's life that occurred as Germany entered World War I. He recounts the key events as follows:

> Ninety-three German intellectuals issued a terrible manifesto, identifying themselves before all the world with the war policy of Kaiser Wilhelm II and Chancellor Bethmann-Holweg. … And, to my dismay, among the signatories I discovered the names of all my German teachers.
>
> (Livingston 2000, 62)

The support that Liberal Protestant theologians gave to the German government as it declared war in 1914 made it clear to Barth that something had gone terribly wrong with their theological method. In this moment, Barth saw the consequences of the Liberal Protestant identification of human societies with the Kingdom of God. He thought that Ritschl's approach to theology deprived the church of its prophetic voice, which was desperately needed in those moments when the state went in deeply troubling directions.

Barth issued a famous rebuke of Liberal Protestantism in his *Epistle to the Romans*. The second edition of the volume (published in 1921) is often credited with sparking a new theological movement known as "dialectical theology." This new approach insisted that there is a "dialectic," or contradiction, between God and human beings. To Barth, God *confronts* human beings and levels a sharp corrective on those who see continuity between human societies and God. Instead of being known to us in our innermost experience, or seen in our society's approximation of the Kingdom of God, Barth insisted that God is "Wholly Other," as he put it. In other words, there is an infinite distance between God and human beings. God is radically different from any idea that we might produce ourselves, and an unbridgeable chasm yawns between us and God. As Barth succinctly put this point, "There is no way from man to God."

Theology, then, cannot begin "from below," within human experience, but must instead rely entirely on God's revelation ("from above," as it were). Theologians should not craft ingenious systems of thought with which to try to understand the divine; instead, they should simply follow God as God has decided to reveal God's self. Theology is therefore a *response* to the way in which God makes God's self-known. Recalling our discussion of modern atheism above, we can view Barth's approach as a rejoinder to Feuerbach's claim that God is simply a projection that originates within the human being. To Barth, any such projection would not actually be capable of arriving at God. It might produce an illusion (or idol), but it would not generate a true idea of God.

Barth's return to revelation might appear to be an outright rejection of modernity and a naive reversion to pre-modern theological approaches. After all, Barth insisted that any human-derived academic discipline (including history and philosophy) cannot be used to judge the content of theology, which seems like a sharp reprimand of the Enlightenment emphasis on reason as the arbiter of all things. However, Barth's view of revelation was in fact deeply shaped by modernity. One sees this most vividly in his understanding of scripture as described in a portion of his 13-volume *Church Dogmatics*. In agreement with modern biblical scholars, Barth recognizes that the Bible is "a human document" (Barth 1963, 494). He holds that modern historical-critical examination of the Bible yields valuable insights, especially concerning the forms of literary expression in the Bible, and these findings should be carefully considered by theologians. "All relevant, historical questions must be put to the biblical texts, considered as witnesses in accordance with their literary form" (Barth 1963, 494).

With that said, Barth also holds that we must not *exclusively* focus on the original cultural setting in which various biblical texts were written, as if the meaning of the text lies only "behind" it or "beneath" it, in the ancient society that produced it. Instead, Barth maintained that the ultimate object of scripture is Jesus Christ, not ancient cultures. Scripture must be understood as bearing witness to the manner in which God has revealed God's self, even if it does so in a fragmentary and all-too-human way. In an effort at acknowledging the Bible as a human set of texts without allowing it to be reduced to *only* a description of human societies, Barth creatively applies to the Bible the church's claim that Jesus Christ is "truly God and truly man." He expresses his view as follows:

> Holy Scripture is like the unity of God and man in Jesus Christ. It is neither divine only nor human only. ... In its own way and degree it is truly God and truly man, i.e., a witness of revelation which itself belongs to revelation, and historically a very human literary document.
>
> (Barth 1963, 500, translation slightly emended)

Barth, then, sees God's revelation as first and foremost the Word of God, Jesus Christ himself. Scripture bears witness to the Word, but the Bible is not revelation itself. In this formulation, Barth shares some affinities with Hegel, who held that God manifests (or reveals) God's very self in God's relationship with the world. Revelation is not a transfer of information about God, but the disclosure of a *person*, Jesus Christ. Barth, however, rejects the way in which Hegel ascribes *necessity* to God's self-revelation. To Barth, God does not need to become manifest in order to reach self-understanding. Nevertheless, we can see Hegel's influence on modern theology through Barth's idea that revelation should be considered to be nothing less than Jesus Christ himself.

Barth used his revelation-centered theological approach to speak out against Hitler and the Nazis when they rose to power in Germany in 1933. The Nazi regime had co-opted many of the German churches; in so doing, they ensured that those churches would not offer resistance to the Third Reich. However, Barth led a handful of German theologians to found the Confessing Church, which boldly denounced the Nazi regime. Barth declared that Christians in Germany who supported Hitler put their hope in a false god, and that any church that followed the Nazis was heretical. In a somewhat controversial move, Barth insisted that the root of the problem was "natural theology," or the effort at making claims about God based on what human beings can attain "naturally," through their own investigation of the world. To Barth, such an approach was just another form of theology from below, based on human foundations, which could be corrupted all too easily.

Barth's theological approach is not without its difficulties (some modern persons simply will not begin with revelation, as he does), but it does some important work in expressing once again that God should be regarded as deeply mysterious and radically different from human beings. Barth thus issues a strong word of caution to those who would effectively reduce God to human categories, and his argument for theology beginning with God has been enthusiastically followed by many modern theologians.

Dietrich Bonhoeffer

One of the most influential twentieth-century theologians did not actually write great learned tomes but left his mark mainly through his personal witness and through shorter essays, an unfinished work called *Ethics*, and the letters he wrote from prison after being arrested as a resister against Adolf Hitler's Nazi dictatorship. Lutheran theologian **Dietrich Bonhoeffer** (1906–1945), born into the German academic elite, could have had a brilliant university career himself. Instead he chose to work actively to renew the Christian church and the proclamation of the Gospel in a world that in his experience was becoming ever more secular. He served first as a pioneer in the ecumenical movement for Christian reunion, then as a pacifist critic of German rearmament in the 1930s, and finally as an active member of the German resistance, which intended to end the dictatorship by assassination if necessary. Arrested in April 1943, he spent the last two years of World War II as a prisoner, before being executed—along with a brother and a brother-in-law—by Hitler's direct order weeks before the war ended. His prison letters to his close friend and former student Eberhard Bethge were published posthumously as *Letters and Papers from Prison*. They have had an enormous and ongoing impact for their bold and original reflections on what it meant to live as a believing Christian in "a world come of age," in which, he wrote, the Christian must imitate Jesus, "the man for others," who modeled the "weakness of God" (1 Corinthians 1:25) in the world by identifying with the marginal and the oppressed.

Wolfhart Pannenberg: Rethinking History to Argue for the Resurrection

Wolfhart Pannenberg (1928–2014) was a professor of theology at the University of Munich, and he is most well known for his treatment of history and the resurrection. In *Jesus—God and Man* (1964), he criticizes modern theologians who have given up on the resurrection of Jesus because they deem it too incredible for modern minds. Some theologians who espouse this modern way of thinking had developed the "subjective-vision hypothesis," which suggested that the disciples and others who claimed to see the resurrected Jesus experienced a vision *within their minds*. However, the hypothesis did not maintain that Jesus was physically resurrected. Although this view was perhaps an improvement over flat denial of the resurrection, to Pannenberg it still conceded too much to modern sensibilities.

Pannenberg argues that the physical resurrection of Jesus did most likely occur, and he makes his case first by questioning the method adopted by modern historians and theologians. He notes that, in these figures' attempts to understand the past, they *presume* that it is analogous to the present, as we saw in our treatment of Ernst Troeltsch above. Because modern historians do not observe miracles in the present, they assume that miracles could not have occurred in the past. To Pannenberg, this is a rather prejudiced view of history that rules out *ahead of time* the possibility of certain historical events. In other words, without even consulting the actual evidence, this approach has already decided that the resurrection did not occur, basing that conclusion on the presupposition that resurrection is simply impossible. What the modern historian does not allow for is the possibility that the past could be quite *unlike* the present. Pannenberg insists that the vantage point of the modern historian is in fact quite limited and that he or she is in no position to declare with such certainty what can and cannot happen.

Having carved out space for the *possibility* of the resurrection, Pannenberg next argues for its *high probability* by examining New Testament treatments of the topic. Pannenberg notes that the New Testament contains two separate traditions of reflection that pertain to this subject. In the first place, there is a stream in the New Testament that attests that the tomb in which Jesus was buried was empty shortly after he was placed there (e.g., Mark 16). In the second place, there is a stream that reports various appearances of the resurrected Jesus (e.g., 1 Corinthians 15). Pannenberg calls these the "grave tradition" and the "appearance tradition," respectively. After arguing at some length for the reliability of each narrative stream, he concludes his examination with the following:

> If the appearance tradition and the grave tradition came into existence independently, then by their mutually complementing each other they let the assertion of the reality of Jesus' resurrection ... appear as historically very probable, and that always means in historical inquiry that it is to be presupposed until contrary evidence appears.
>
> (Pannenberg 1977, 105)

In other words, from a historical viewpoint the resurrection has *corroborating evidence* that calls one to take the reports seriously unless evidence to the contrary can be produced. Pannenberg therefore holds that, if one can suspend one's modern prejudice against it, the resurrection can be shown to be highly plausible.

Pannenberg, then, insists that the modern historical approach imposes a foreign interpretive framework on the New Testament texts. That is, modern historians have taken their culturally specific set of interpretive tools and claimed that they have universal validity. In so doing, these modern historians have disregarded the values and meanings that lie within the ancient cultures they claim to investigate. Pannenberg holds that we must view the resurrection in the original context of its meaning to those who witnessed it and first proclaimed it. If one is attentive to this original setting, one sees that the framework in which Jewish tradition understands resurrection is that of the *general* resurrection of the dead, which occurs only at the eschaton, or end of history. As Pannenberg puts it, "If Jesus has been raised, then the end of the world has begun" (Pannenberg 1977, 67). The resurrection, then, is "proleptic." That is, it anticipates what is to come at the end of history; in fact, it even breaks into the present from the eschaton (or "end"). Pannenberg holds that the full meaning of the resurrection can be known only from the endpoint of all history, which should further give one pause in making any absolute judgments about its historicity.

Crucially, then, the resurrection is not simply an isolated event, and according to Pannenberg, it did not actually occur in the past, technically speaking. Instead, in the resurrection we behold the end and consummation of history. These claims lead to Pannenberg's assertion "If Jesus, having been raised from the dead, is ascended to God and if thereby the end of the world has begun, then God is ultimately revealed in Jesus" (Pannenberg 1977, 69). Whereas Lessing had insisted that no historical event could serve as an adequate warrant for claiming that Jesus is the Son of God, Pannenberg holds that it is precisely in the resurrection that Jesus is shown to be God's self-revelation. He is clear in insisting that this was not known before the resurrection, during Jesus' earthly ministry. As he puts this important point, "Only at the end of all events can God be revealed in his divinity" (Pannenberg 1977, 69).

Pannenberg, like Barth, may appear at first glance to reside firmly within a "rejection" model in his approach to modernity. However, he borrows tools from modern historical critics by focusing on the original context in which the resurrection was understood. Furthermore, in his thoroughly historicized view of God's revelation, Pannenberg shows affinities with Hegel. Pannenberg's notion that God is revealed only at the *end* of history reflects a deeply Hegelian view of the relationship between God and the world, even though Pannenberg is critical of Hegel on other points.

With these modern characteristics of Pannenberg's theology noted, we now make clear the ways in which he pushes back against modern figures. First, by rooting the resurrection in objective history, Pannenberg sought to respond to modern atheism, which since Feuerbach has regarded all claims about God as in fact simply projections that originate within human beings. The "subjective-vision hypothesis" of the resurrection easily fell into Feuerbach's critique, and it was often derided as merely a hallucination. However, in claiming that the resurrection was an objective event in history, Pannenberg saw himself as rising to the challenge laid down by Feuerbach.

Pannenberg, however, does not simply seek to go "outside" of the human being, so to speak, in his attempt at taking on Feuerbach and the masters of suspicion, and here we see a second arena within which he pushes back against modern figures. He thinks that modern theologians ignore the anthropology of modern atheism at their peril, and that one must not abandon this battleground, as Karl Barth has been seen to do in his turn to objectivity and revelation. In *Anthropology in Theological Perspective* (1985), Pannenberg explicitly engages with Feuerbach, Marx, Nietzsche, and Freud in an effort at reclaiming anthropology as a legitimate and trustworthy starting point for Christian theology. With Feuerbach's notion of projection as their foundation, other modern atheists viewed religion as a self-alienating, life-denying, and illusory form of thinking that does great harm to human beings (for Anne King's treatment of the repetition of many of these claims by the "New Atheists," see Chapter 26).

Pannenberg, however, begins his anthropology (unlike Freud) by maintaining that human beings are not simply determined by their instinctual drives, but can rise above them and (to a certain extent, at least) be free from them. Indeed, we resist succumbing to our biology all the time. Similarly, Pannenberg claims that human beings are not completely immersed in their environment, but instead can rise above themselves and observe themselves as objects. We have, in other words, a capacity for *self-transcendence* that distinguishes us from other animals; we are not wholly determined by the circumstances in which we find ourselves. To use the term that Pannenberg borrows from the German philosopher Helmut Plessner, we are "exocentric" creatures—that is, we are centered *outside of* ourselves. We are, therefore, *legitimately* oriented beyond ourselves. The "out there," then, beyond human beings, is an arena about which we have a rightful claim. We live there, so to speak, and our contact with objective reality can be viewed as trustworthy, not an inevitable projection, self-alienation, or illusion. In fact, if one were to ask where this capacity for self-transcendence ultimately comes from, Pannenberg would suggest that it arises from a "religious foundation" (Pannenberg 1999, 70).

Pannenberg, then, uses modern tools (the historical-critical method, a Hegelian conception of history) to criticize those modern attitudes that militate against key points made within traditional Christian theology. In so doing, he gives traditional Christian theology a robust set of resources for defending its viability in the modern world.

Roman Catholic Theology in the Modern Period

Modern Catholic theology is discussed in some detail in Chapter 24. However, we briefly situate three Catholic figures within the context described in this chapter, as these individuals have risen to the modern challenges to Christian theology in important ways.

Nineteenth-century Catholic theology is often characterized as a period of retrenchment and reaction against modernity, and there is truth in such a portrait. However, the English convert **John Henry Newman** (1801–1890) advanced seminal insights that would transform Catholic theology in the twentieth century. Most influentially, in his *Essay on the Development of Christian Doctrine* (1845), Newman provocatively argued that the teaching of the church has not in fact been always the same everywhere, as had been held in Catholic theology up to modern times. Instead, Newman insisted that doctrine *develops* over time, often in ways that cannot be known in advance because of the unpredictable situations in which the church finds itself as it marches its way through the centuries.

In claiming that doctrine develops, Newman acknowledged the important role of history in Christian theology, which was much discussed during the nineteenth century, as we have seen. However, unlike later figures such as Harnack, Newman maintained that Christian doctrine could change and still manifest *continuity* between the past and the present. In other words, the simple fact of change does not necessarily mean that falsehood has crept into Christian teachings. Change itself does not equal deviation. Newman certainly held that some doctrinal changes had gone in wrong directions (they were called heresies), but he also maintained that later teachings of the church could make explicit some ideas that were merely implicit in previous eras. The development of doctrine often proceeded in a fashion similar to the growth of an organism that in its maturity differs from its fledgling state, yet also manifests continuity and consistency in its development.

In the twentieth century, the German theologian **Karl Rahner** (1904–1984) developed an approach to Catholic theology that in some regards mirrors Schleiermacher's turn to experience. Rahner felt compelled to reformulate Christian theology in response to modernity, and to do so he analyzed experience by creatively combining modern philosophy and the thought of medieval theologian Thomas Aquinas (see Chapter 15). He undertook this project in an influential work, the

English translation of which has been published as *Spirit in the World* (1936). To Rahner, human beings experience God in the midst of seemingly mundane, everyday life. Specifically, whenever one identifies an object in the world, one is aware of the "horizon" or background against which that object stands. In other words, when one makes a judgment about a particular object (i.e., "that is a squirrel"), one distinguishes that object from everything else that exists. One, in effect, draws a line around the object and separates it from all other things. There is the object, and there is the horizon against which that object stands.

To Rahner, God is like that horizon, a limitless background that is required in order to know anything at all. God, then, is a "precondition" for knowledge. Although we might not have explicit awareness of God, we unavoidably presuppose the backdrop against which all things stand. If we did not, we would not be able to understand anything. To use one of Rahner's analogies, God is like light: we need light to see every particular thing, but we never actually see light itself. Similarly, God is in the midst of our everyday experience, always present, even if we might not recognize that fact.

Rahner, then, is interested in developing an anthropology that describes how it is that human beings can know God. In this respect, he follows Kant's "turn to the subject" and is a deeply modern thinker, even though he pushes modern theology to a different set of conclusions than Kant would have it follow. To Rahner, the fact that we are aware of God as the necessary backdrop for knowing all things tells us that, at a fundamental level, we are oriented toward God. Or as Rahner puts it, human beings are "absolutely opened upwards."

Whereas Rahner's starting point for modern theology is the human being, the Swiss theologian **Hans Urs von Balthasar** (1905–1988) begins his theology with revelation. In this respect, Balthasar's approach resembles that of Karl Barth. Balthasar thinks it is a mistake to follow Rahner by attempting to describe the structures of the human mind through which we know God. To Balthasar, God will always exhibit more grandeur, glory, and mystery than any human way of thinking could possibly imagine. Balthasar worries that theology following Kant's turn to the subject reduces God to the human level, thus ultimately falling prey to Feuerbach's critique. In his seven-volume work, *The Glory of the Lord* (1961–1969), Balthasar insists that the beauty of God was a key feature of ancient and medieval theology that should be reintegrated into modern theology. To Balthasar, our experiences of beauty are instructive for rethinking Christian theology in that they are moments when we encounter something that is beyond our control and understanding. To claim with Balthasar (and theologians such as Augustine, Pseudo-Dionysius, and Bonaventure) that God is absolute beauty is to say that God bursts open human structures of knowing while at the same time revealing something of God's glory to human beings. Balthasar's "theological aesthetics," as he calls this project, attempts to do justice to the awe-inspiring mystery that God is, thus reclaiming for the modern period a notion of theology that starts first and foremost with God.

Conclusion

In this chapter, we have seen that modernity presents Christian theologians with unprecedented challenges. The new use of reason, new view of the human being, new way of doing history, and new degree of skepticism all brought trenchant critiques to traditional Christian theology. The Christian tradition, however, was not bereft of resources in responding to those difficulties. Although some would simply accommodate modernity and others flatly reject it, a number of highly creative theologians reformulated the Christian faith so as to bring it into accord with certain modern sensibilities (while sometimes deeply challenging others). The task of addressing modernity is an unfinished project, and it continues to be discussed in the remaining chapters of this book.

Key Terms

absolute dependence	fundamentalism	Wolfhart Pannenberg
Hans Urs von Balthasar	Adolf von Harnack	Quest for the
Karl Barth	G.W.F. Hegel	Historical Jesus
Dietrich Bonhoeffer	Johann Gottfried Herder	Karl Rahner
deism	historical criticism	rationalism
René Descartes	Immanuel Kant	Albrecht Ritschl
the Enlightenment	G.E. Lessing	Friedrich Schleiermacher
epistemology	John Locke	secular
Ludwig Feuerbach	Karl Marx	Ernst Troeltsch
foundationalism	John Henry Newman	
Sigmund Freud	Friedrich Nietzsche	

Questions for Reading

1. What is the Enlightenment? What historical events are behind its rise, and why is it important for Christian theology?

2. Who are the main advocates of deism, and what did they believe about God and the world?

3. How did the Enlightenment emphases on reason and autonomy affect the manner in which history is conducted in the modern period?

4. Who are the "masters of suspicion," and why are they critical of Christianity?

5. How are the three basic theological responses to modernity characterized?

6. What is fundamentalism? Why is it not actually traditional?

7. How did Friedrich Schleiermacher reformulate Christian theology?

8. Why was G.W.F. Hegel attractive to Christian theologians?

9. What is Liberal Protestant theology?

10. Why did Karl Barth reject Liberal Protestant theology, and what did he offer as an alternative?

11. What is Ernst Troeltsch's view of history, and how does Wolfhart Pannenberg respond?

12. How do Catholic thinkers such as John Henry Newman, Karl Rahner, and Hans Urs von Balthasar respond to modernity?

Works Consulted/Recommended Reading

Balthasar, Hans Urs von. 1982–1989. *The Glory of the Lord: A Theological Aesthetics*. Translated by Erasmo Leiva-Merikakis et al. San Francisco, CA: Ignatius Press.

Barth, Karl. 1963. *Church Dogmatics* I/2: *The Doctrine of God*. Translated by G.T. Thompson. Edinburgh: T&T Clark.

Descartes, René. 1998. *Discourse on Method*. Translated by Donald A. Cress. Indianapolis, IN: Hackett.

Feuerbach, Ludwig. 1989. *The Essence of Christianity*. Translated by George Eliot. Amherst, NY: Prometheus Books.

Freud, Sigmund. 1961. *The Future of an Illusion*. Translated by James Strachey. New York: Norton.

Kramnick, Isaac. 1995. *The Portable Enlightenment Reader*. New York: Penguin.

Livingston, James C. 1997. *Modern Christian Thought*. Vol. 1. *The Enlightenment and the Nineteenth Century*. Upper Saddle River, NJ: Prentice Hall.

Livingston, James C., and Francis Schüssler Fiorenza. 2000. *Modern Christian Thought*. Vol. 2. *The Twentieth Century*. Upper Saddle River, NJ: Prentice Hall.

Locke, John. 1989. *The Reasonableness of Christianity*. Washington, DC: Regnery Gateway.

McCormack, Bruce L. 2012."Introduction: On 'Modernity' as a Theological Concept." In *Mapping Modern Theology: A Thematic and Historical Introduction*. Edited by Bruce L. McCormack and Kelly M. Kapic, 1–19. Grand Rapids, MI: Baker.

Marx, Karl. 1994. *Early Political Writings*. Cambridge: Cambridge University Press.

Newman, John Henry. 1989. *An Essay on the Development of Christian Doctrine*. Notre Dame, IN: University of Notre Dame Press.

Pannenberg, Wolfhart. 1977. *Jesus—God and Man*. Translated by Lewis L. Wilkins and Duane A. Priebe. Philadelphia, PA: Westminster Press.

Pannenberg, Wolfhart. 1999. *Anthropology in Theological Perspective*. Translated by Matthew J. O'Connell. Edinburgh: T&T Clark.

Rahner, Karl. 1968. *Spirit in the World*. Translated by William Dych. New York: Herder and Herder.

Schleiermacher, Friedrich. 1994. *On Religion: Speeches to Its Cultured Despisers*. Translated by John Oman. Louisville, KY: Westminster/John Knox Press.

Schleiermacher, Friedrich. 2017. *The Christian Faith*. London: Bloomsbury.

Schmidt, James, ed. 1996. *What Is Enlightenment? Eighteenth-Century Answers and Twentieth-Century Questions*. Berkeley, CA: University of California Press.

Wilson, John E. 2007. *Introduction to Modern Theology: Trajectories in the German Tradition*. Louisville, KY: Westminster John Knox Press.

Chapter 23

CHRISTIANITY IN THE UNITED STATES

INTRODUCTION: CHURCH AND STATE ACCORDING TO THE FIRST AMENDMENT

Christianity has left a deep imprint on the United States' laws, its politics, its moral values, its educational system, its social relations, its wars, and its foreign policy. That is true of the past and, despite increasing secularization and religious diversity, it remains true today, with 70.6 percent of Americans still identifying as Christians, according to the 2014 Pew Forum Religious Landscape Survey. That is down, however, from over 78.4 percent in the previous survey in 2007, while those reporting as "unaffiliated [i.e., none]" went from 16.1 percent to 22.8 percent. Among non-Christian faiths, the largest is still Jewish (1.9 percent), with Muslims increasing from 0.5 to 0.9 percent.

But the United States is also the first state in the Christian tradition to have effected a legal separation from Christianity, indeed, from any official national religion. According to the **First Amendment** to the Constitution, ratified in 1791, "Congress shall make no law respecting an establishment of religion, or prohibiting the free exercise thereof." Neither the Supreme Court nor legions of commentators have managed to agree on how those words should be understood. One school of thought, sometimes called *strict separationism*, holds that the First Amendment erected "a wall of separation between church and state," even though that phrase originated not in the Constitution but in a letter of Thomas Jefferson's. Government should therefore make no acknowledgment of religion, which must be kept out of the public square as much as possible and confined to a totally private and voluntary sphere. The Constitution never mentions God, and the only reference to religion is the stipulation in Article VI that "no religious test for office" shall be required of holders of office in the national government.

Others, however, argue that the Founders never intended such a thorough-going secularization of public life, and that strict separationism actually establishes *secularism* as the public religion ("the religion of no religion at all," as some would define secularism). Holders of this view note that the First Amendment only applied to the national government (it was not applied to the states for another century and a half). They point to such facts as the Constitutional Convention's passage of the Northwest Ordinance of 1787, Article 3 of which states: "Religion, morality, and knowledge, being necessary to good government and the happiness of mankind, schools and the means of education shall forever be encouraged." Therefore, they believe, government is free within certain limits to *accommodate* religious belief and practice, so long as one religion is not privileged over another. As Justice William O. Douglas wrote in a 1952 Supreme Court opinion defending the constitutionality of "released time" (releasing children from public school to receive religious education at a religiously affiliated institution), "We are a religious people whose institutions presuppose a Supreme Being..."

Regardless of which of these two interpretations is more correct, both of them recognize that the United States embarked on something decisively new, what Thomas Jefferson called a "fair experiment" on the question of whether religious freedom was compatible with good government and obedience to the laws. The new constitution was in fact reversing what had been two nearly universal assumptions going back to the fourth century, when Constantine converted to Christianity and the Roman Empire struck an alliance with the Christian Church: on the one hand, that the stability and well-being of a state required religious uniformity among its people; and on the other hand, that Christianity required and was best served by legal establishment.

This chapter consists of three parts: first, an overview of Protestant development in America, noting the diversity of new churches that have come into being here and the emergence of what has been called a "two-party system" among American Protestants; second, an account of how Catholicism, mainly a European transplant, has adapted itself to American conditions; and third, a description of how America itself has been understood in religious terms, and the implications this understanding has had for Christianity.

PROTESTANTISM IN AMERICA: FROM EVANGELICAL EMPIRE TO TWO-PARTY SYSTEM

The United States is not only historically Christian, it is mainly *Protestant* Christianity that has shaped American religious identity. Throughout the colonial period and for long afterwards, Protestants were by far the dominant religious grouping in the United States. Even after large-scale Catholic immigration began in the early nineteenth century, Protestants shared a common conviction that America was, despite the First Amendment to the Constitution, a virtual "evangelical empire." Since about 1900, however, Protestants have split into two broad camps on how they see their faith in relation to America as a whole.

Birthright Churches from the Colonial Period

In the colonial period, the original English colonies were dominated by churches from Great Britain. In New England were the Congregationalists (commonly called "Puritans"), whose Holy Commonwealths, as they styled them, were to be the model for reforming the Church of England back home. From Virginia southwards was the established Church of England or "Anglicans" (they renamed themselves "Episcopalians" after American independence made loyalty to King George III impossible), to whose control Maryland and New York later fell. The middle colonies claimed a variety of churches, notably William Penn's original experiment in religious liberty in his Quaker colony of Pennsylvania, where Baptists, Lutherans, Mennonites, Catholics, and Jews were also free to settle. Presbyterians (ecclesiastical cousins of the Congregationalists—see Chapter 19) were scattered from New York through the Shenandoah Valley of Virginia and into the south. Baptists also settled in Roger Williams' enclave of dissenters in tiny Rhode Island. Reformed (Calvinist) Christians in New York were reminders of that colony's Dutch origin as New Amsterdam. And once John Wesley's reforming movement withdrew from the Church of England in 1784, the Methodists too joined the spectrum as a distinct church.

For all their diversity, the British transplants to the colonies share a common sense of ownership or entitlement where America's spiritual identity and welfare are concerned. They are the original WASPs, "White Anglo-Saxon Protestants," though many were actually Scottish, Irish, or Welsh. These churches and their numerous American offspring have always shown a special sense of responsibility for American life as a whole. From their point of view, this is both a privilege of having been there at the conception and birthing of the new nation, and also a moral duty or obligation. In the past, they did not see this sense of a birthright as contradicting the First Amendment, because for them religious disestablishment did not entail total public secularization—America was still substantially a Christian, indeed Protestant nation. Throughout the nineteenth century, they shared a basic consensus about how to make America into a "righteous empire," a beacon to the world. Today, however, American Protestants are bitterly divided over how to exercise their historic custodial responsibility, and a kind of two-party system has emerged (see below).

The Denominational System: Democracy, Revivalism, and New Churches

The number of different Christian churches meant that the new United States of America would not have a national church, since no church could make a credible claim of majority support. There was also a widespread feeling that religion prospered more in conditions of religious freedom than of state establishment. As a result, even churches that were accustomed to state support gradually learned to survive without it. With the passage of the Bill of Rights, the federal government got out of the religion business—it "deregulated" religion, so to speak. The result, naturally, was new churches in an endless proliferation that shows no sign of stopping. Religious entrepreneurship was made all the more explosive by the democratic ethos that spread throughout America in the decades after the Revolution—Christianity itself became democratized as never before once ordinary people were told that every individual person should be "considered as possessing in himself or herself an original right to believe and speak as their own conscience, between themselves and God, may determine" (the words of a preacher in 1806, as cited in Wood 1997, 194–195). In short, every man (and eventually every woman) is his own interpreter of scripture.

The new religious configuration that resulted from this momentous change is called **denominationalism**. One definition of a *denomination* is "a voluntary association of like-minded and like-hearted individuals, who are united on the basis of common beliefs for the purpose of accomplishing tangible and defined objectives" (Mead 1963, 104). In a denominational system, the various churches accept the separation of church and state and the right of religious freedom. They agree to live and let live.

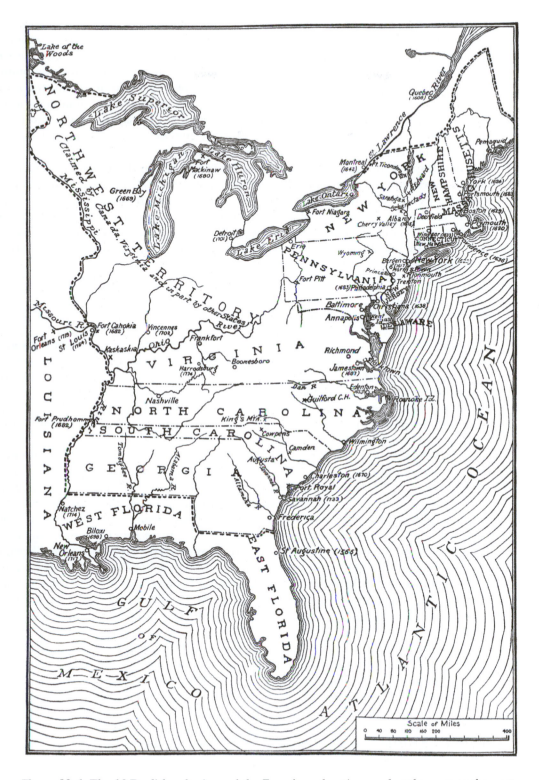

Figure 23–1 The 13 English colonies and the French explorations and settlements to the west.

The "denominations" are simply different—and, some would argue, equally valid—ways of being Christian and of naming Christian communities. In return for religious freedom, they agree to support democratic government and the basic goodness of the American way of life. Churches and movements that do not endorse denominationalism or that resist giving their support to mainstream American values tend to become marginalized, and sometimes condemned, as *sects*. Critics of denominationalism (and the democratic, voluntary principles underlying it) say it treats believers like consumers and the Christian faith like a product, muzzles true religious debate, and turns churches into conformist look-alikes. Defenders say it broadens personal choice and has ensured the vitality and adaptability of churches in the United States, where church attendance and involvement are much higher than in European countries with histories of religious establishment. "Megachurches," the huge, usually suburban churches founded by ambitious pastors and offering a rich menu of social services, activities, and entertainment, operate outside the traditional denominational structure. They are another outgrowth of the entrepreneurial spirit that marks American Christianity.

Methodism and its Revivalist Offspring

A further ingredient in the new denominational system was the spread of **revivalism** or "born-again" Christianity, which is based on the experience of a personal conversion to Jesus Christ as one's Lord and savior. American Protestants who today identify themselves as **evangelical** are likely to have had a born-again experience. In the nineteenth century, revivalism became almost generic in American Protestantism. Its ultimate origins are in the seventeenth-century European religious movement called **Pietism** (see Chapter 19).

In England, the chief impact of Pietism had been the reforming movement of John Wesley, the Anglican priest whose own conversion had occurred in 1738 while visiting a Pietist group called the Moravian Brethren. The experience led him to form a network of prayer fellowships to promote similar conversions—the beginning of what would come to be known as **Methodism**. Wesley sought to move Christians beyond justification to what he called "entire sanctification," meaning the restoration of original righteousness such as existed before the Fall. Christian perfection was therefore attainable in this life. Such a doctrine set Wesley's ideas apart from Lutheran and Reformed (Calvinist) theology. Despite Wesley's resistance to the formation of a separate church, Methodists in America finally withdrew from the Anglican Church in 1784 and organized the Methodist Episcopal Church.

In America, the Pietist impact was mediated through the Great Awakening, a religious revival movement that swept through the colonies in the 1740s. The Great Awakening created the template for all future revivalism in America. In the view of some historians, it may also have paved the way for the American Revolution. Gifted and tireless preachers like George Whitefield (1714–1770) traveled the length and breadth of the colonies to stir up religious zeal in a population that had gotten relaxed and comfortable amidst the economic opportunities of the New World. Large outdoor meetings provided a festive atmosphere removed from daily life, in which preachers discovered they could evoke spectacular emotional responses in their listeners. The great Puritan theologian Jonathan Edwards (1703–1758) provided a theological account and rationale for the movement.

Figure 23–2 This painting depicts a revival camp meeting, which included preaching and the singing of hymns. In the foreground, you can see the emotional responses people had to the preacher's call to conversion.

Lived Religion: Liturgy in Early America: Revival Camp Meeting

On the American frontier, people had few neighbors and even fewer churches. Before civilization began to move westward from states along the Atlantic coast, worship often consisted of a traveling preacher who would visit periodically, and people would travel from miles around for a camp meeting. Everyone looked forward to these events because they offered a chance to hear the Gospel preached, have children baptized, and couples married. They were also a time to catch up on news, trade for goods, and have a few days of rest from hard work.

When the preacher arrived, people gathered in an open area or under a tent, if possible. Many of the preachers were Methodists, who believed Baptism and Eucharist were important means of grace. They thought that faith should be "from the heart, rather than the head" and that people should reach out to the poor and needy.

The meeting began with preaching intended to move people to conversion and increase faith in those already converted. They were reminded that they were sinners and must seek forgiveness and a right relationship with God in order to attain salvation. The preaching could go on for hours or days, and people became very emotional, waving their arms, shouting and even crying or fainting. Some came forward for Baptism, but others simply found the experience entertaining.

When the preacher needed to rest, the community learned hymns, many of them written by John Wesley, the founder of Methodism. Those who chose Baptism were taught some basic prayers and received more education in scripture before being baptized in the nearest lake or river. The Methodists believed in lay leadership—even for women—and they often left a lay person in charge when they moved on. With luck, the tent revival would be the start of a new church.

Today revivalism's association with television evangelists, faith healing, and crusades against evolution can make it seem anti-intellectual and backward, at least in the eyes of its critics. But this was by no means true before the advent of fundamentalism (see fundamentalism section below). In the nineteenth century, revivalist Christians were in the forefront of reform movements of every kind: anti-slavery and abolitionism, temperance (the fight against alcohol and the social ills that accompanied it), prison reform, charitable work, and education—a large number of private colleges and universities owe their origin to educational energies unleashed by revivalism. Revivalism can thus claim much credit for the ongoing vitality and adaptability of American Protestantism, since it is well suited for a society in which religious commitment is *voluntary*. Today, the Protestant denominations that are growing fastest are those in which born-again Christianity dominates. Revivalism has also stimulated wave after wave of new church formations. In the early nineteenth century, a Second Great Awakening, this one on the western frontier at Cane Ridge, Kentucky, produced the "Restoration" movement of Alexander Campbell and Barton Stone. **Restorationism** claimed to end church division and return to a "predenominational" state by appealing to scripture alone. To symbolize the goal of restoring a lost original unity, the movement called itself simply "the Christian Church," and also the "Disciples of Christ." Despite its intention, the perhaps inevitable result was to create still more denominations—the movement eventually split three ways over the use of instruments in church services and the growing organizational structure.

Out of nineteenth-century Methodism came the **Holiness movement**. It began with worries among Methodists that Wesley's doctrine of Christian perfection was in danger of being ignored. Christians concerned with "full sanctification" held annual camp meetings, sponsored Bible conferences, founded urban missions, published newspapers, and, inevitably, became separate churches. Thus, the Holiness churches (such as the Free Methodist Church, Holiness Christian Church, Church of the Nazarene, and the Church of God) separated from the Methodist tradition to develop a lifestyle of personal holiness that reflected a stricter code of behavior than that held by their parent churches. As a response to what they called the second grace of God (the conversion made available to the Christian through the revivals), they developed an asceticism that rejected worldliness.

The Holiness movement in turn produced the intensely charismatic type of Christianity known as **Pentecostalism**. It takes its name from the Pentecost miracle recounted in the Acts of the Apostles 2:1–21, when the Holy Spirit was poured out on Jesus' followers and gave them the gift of "speaking in tongues" (sometimes called by its Greek name of *glossolalia*), a type of ecstatic group prayer mentioned in some of Paul's letters (e.g., 1 Corinthians 12:10). Pentecostalism's founder was Charles Parham (1873–1929), a Holiness preacher whose Sunday school students experienced "Spirit Baptism" and the gift of tongues in 1901. A related event was the famed

Azusa Street Revival in Los Angeles (1906–1909), led by African-American preacher William Seymour (1870–1922). Pentecostal churches now number in the hundreds, including large denominations like the Assemblies of God (to which prominent tele-vangelist Oral Roberts once belonged), the United Pentecostal Church International (UPCI), and the Church of God in Christ, the fastest growing African-American Pentecostal church. Some, such as the UPCI, are non-Trinitarian and practice Baptism in the name of Jesus only. Common to all is the belief that "Spirit Baptism" must be manifested as speaking in tongues, though other spiritual gifts such as faith healing and prophecy are also expected fruits of the Spirit. Despite their contemporary association with conservative political causes, Pentecostal churches have sometimes shown greater racial diversity and openness to women's leadership than more established churches: the International Church of the Four Square Gospel was started and led by Aimee Semple McPherson (1890–1944), whose flamboyant career made her a media celebrity. Pentecostal Christianity is marked by highly emotional prayer services, traditional codes of morality, biblical literalism, missionary zeal, and millennial expectations (the imminent Second Coming of Jesus). Worldwide Pentecostalism is growing faster than any other type of Christianity (see Chapter 21).

Millennialism and the Coming of Christ's Kingdom

Pentecostalism's millennial fervor represents yet another pervasive feature of revivalism: the hope for Christ's imminent return and earthly reign. Fresh outbursts of revivalist enthusiasm always rekindled hope that the great end-time drama described in the Bible was not far off, above all the promise of the millennial kingdom in the book of Revelation. According to Revelation 20:1–10, at the Second Coming of Jesus Christ, the bodies of the saints will be raised and the saints will reign with Christ for 1,000 years in an earthly kingdom. Christians have long debated whether these promises should be understood literally or symbolically. The dominant view, represented in early Christianity by St. Augustine, had seen the thousand years as a symbolic number (see Augustine's *On the City of God* 20.7–9). For Augustine and many others, the promise of the reign of Christ on earth was already fulfilled in the life of the church, the City of God on pilgrimage in this world. Among American Protestants, this interpretation came to be known as *postmillennialism* because Christ's Second Coming would take place *after* the symbolic millennium, when the gospel had been preached to the whole world, and human history was fully developed and ready for his return. Postmillenialism reflected an optimistic opinion of the progress of Christianity and of human development. Up to the end of the nineteenth century, it was the dominant viewpoint among American Protestants, no doubt reflecting their confident sense of their own pre-eminence in America, and of America's, and the gospel's, place in the world.

Other Protestants, however, held onto a more literal understanding of the millennial kingdom. For them, it was more natural to think that Christ's return would happen *before* the millennium promised in Revelation. This viewpoint is therefore called *premillennialism*. Combined with a scheme of biblical interpretation called *dispensationalism*, premillenialism would become a powerful force in modern Fundamentalist Christianity (see fundamentalism section below). Already in the nineteenth century, several very distinctive new churches came into being as a result of longings for the establishment of Christ's millennial kingdom: the Seventh Day Adventists, the Jehovah's Witnesses, and, most spectacularly, the Mormons.

The Seventh-Day Adventists originated with the prophecies of William Miller (1782–1849) concerning the end of the world, which he mistakenly predicted in 1843 and again in 1844. His movement survived the disappointment thanks to the leadership of James and Ellen White. Reorganized in 1860 as the "Seventh Day Adventists" (the name indicating their adoption of Saturday as the biblically ordained day of rest), they abandoned their expectation of an imminent Second Coming and today are known for their missionary zeal, their medical work, and their dedication to a healthy and simple way of life. Adventists give prophetic authority to Ellen White's voluminous writings, which grew out of the visionary experiences she enjoyed throughout her life.

The **Jehovah's Witnesses**, as they have been known since 1931, were founded by Charles Taze Russell (1852–1916). He prophesied that Christ would return secretly in 1874 and would begin his public reign in 1914. The Witnesses appear to deny the full divinity of Jesus Christ, although they have no systematic and fixed body of teaching. They have continued to be intensely focused on eschatology and on Christ's return. Their refusal to shed blood has led to their rejection of military service and of blood transfusions. Their allegiance to a theocratic kingdom (a kingdom ruled by God alone) prevents them from recognizing the legitimacy of any state or church. Their aggressive preaching of their faith has made them known far beyond their numbers.

The Church of Jesus Christ of **Latter-Day Saints** (LDS) was founded in 1830 in upstate New York. The *Mormons*, as they are commonly called, take their name from the Book of Mormon, which their founder Joseph Smith (1805–1844) claimed to have translated from golden plates revealed to him in 1827 by an angel named Moroni. Along with the Christian Bible and certain documents of the Mormon Church, the Book of Mormon is a basic component in the church's canon of inspired writings. The LDS church considers Joseph Smith (who was known to be disturbed by the variety and divisions among Christian denominations) to be a revealer and a prophet of the last days, and the church itself to be Christ's kingdom once again established on the earth, preparatory to Christ's second coming. Mormonism thus fits into a familiar nineteenth-century American restorationist and millennialist pattern. But its basic belief structure certainly takes it beyond what was conventional in American Christianity then or now.

The Book of Mormon purports to be the work of multiple long-dead authors, part of a migration of ancient peoples from biblical Israel around 600 B.C. who came to America long before Columbus. Joseph Smith's movement led a complex and turbulent history from its New York origins to its eventual destination in Utah, under the leadership of Brigham Young (1801–1877), who succeeded Smith after he was murdered by a mob in Illinois. The early Mormons inspired suspicion and fear, in part because of Smith's endorsement of plural marriage (polygamy), a practice that the church repudiated in 1890 when Utah was trying to gain admission to the Union as a state. From its base in Salt Lake City, home of the Mormon Temple, the religion has spread worldwide and continues to grow rapidly. The public face of Mormonism now looks typically denominational in its emphatic identification with the American way of life. Mormon teaching even regards the Constitution as an inspired document. It is doubtful, however, whether the church's doctrine is compatible with orthodox Christianity. Apart from specific theological questions, the Mormon claim to possess a new, canonical revelation (supplemented by further revelations to the prophet Joseph Smith and his successors) would seem to set Mormonism apart as a new religion altogether, despite its profession of faith in Jesus Christ. Mormonism thus seems to stand roughly in relation to Christianity as Christianity itself does in relation to Judaism.

Regardless of whether it is new or merely a creative restatement of Christianity, Mormonism has proven to be very adept at fitting into its American environment, as shown by its strong patriotism, its exuberant optimism about human potential, its emphasis on a strong family structure, and its high valuation of material prosperity. The tenth article of Joseph Smith's "Articles of Faith" proclaims:

> We believe in the literal gathering of Israel and in the restoration of the Ten Tribes; that Zion (the New Jerusalem) will be built upon the American continent; that Christ will reign personally upon the earth; and, that the earth will be renewed and receive its paradisiacal glory.

The expected millennial kingdom may not have arrived in its fullness, but Mormonism itself seems as at home in Zion as any other comfortably American church.

The Church as a Gathered Community Called out from the World

Quite different from the millennialist movements, though sharing their dissent from American denominationalism, is a small group of Christian churches sometimes called collectively the **Peace churches**. Primarily they include the Mennonites, Amish, Hutterites, and Church of the Brethren. The Quakers—or to call them by their proper name, the Society of Friends—are often grouped with the Peace churches, but they have a very different history and character owing to their origin as a "birthright" church. The "Peace churches" in the narrower sense are descended from the Anabaptists ("re-baptizers") of the Radical Reformation (see Chapter 19). They practice *believers' Baptism* (meaning adult Baptism, usually by full immersion) and a simple way of life intended to set them apart from the larger secular society. Traditionally, this often meant distinctive dress, separate schooling, and life in closed rural communities. The most controversial form of their dissent has been refusing to fight in wars, based on their reading of Jesus' call to discipleship in the Sermon on the Mount (Matthew 5–7). Although many of them are now somewhat modernized (e.g., by dress and participation in mainstream education), they still maintain their pacifist tradition. Their conscientious refusal to fight, along with that of the Quakers and also of the Jehovah's Witnesses, contributed to the American government's recognition of a right to a religiously based conscientious objection to military service (expanded in 1971 to a right to non-religiously based conscientious objection as well).

By far the most numerous Protestant grouping consists of the **Baptist churches**, the biggest of which is the Southern Baptist Convention (SBC). Two large African-American Baptist denominations are the American Baptist Churches U.S.A. and the National Baptist Convention U.S.A., Inc., second in size only to the SBC. Baptists' respect for congregational freedom has produced tremendous doctrinal and denominational diversity. Most Baptists, however, hold conservative views on the authority and inspiration of the Bible, and many are fundamentalists. As explained in Chapter 19, the original Baptists were English Puritans who wished to reform themselves independently and without waiting for the approval of the English government. While in exile in the Netherlands, some of them adopted "believers' Baptism" from Dutch Mennonites, because they concluded that adult Baptism was the logical corollary of separating from a state establishment. All American Baptists have maintained this original commitment to religious liberty and church independence. Nevertheless, they show their Puritan roots by their sense of birthright responsibility for the whole social order: they tend to be strongly patriotic and want to shape American law, government, and culture according to Christian standards. Baptists were prime movers in the resurgence of conservative Christian political activism that began in the late 1970s, when the Rev. Jerry Falwell (1933–2007) founded the Moral Majority (1978). It inspired numerous later conservative Christian political organizations such as Focus on the Family and the Family Research Council. His son, Jerry Falwell Jr. (1962–), is president of Liberty University in Lynchburg, VA, which calls itself the largest Christian university in the world.

Fundamentalism and Christian Protest against Modernity

The re-emergence of conservative Christian activism is only the latest phase in a cultural war within American Protestantism that began over a century ago and ended up destroying the broad Protestant consensus about a Christian America that had prevailed since the nation's founding. Ever since, Protestants have been divided about how to relate Christian faith to the modern world. "Fundamentalists" and "Modernists" disagreed, sometimes bitterly, over: how to deal with the intellectual challenges provoked by modern science, Darwinian evolution above all, and modern historical study of the Bible; the social changes produced by immigration and urbanization; and the cultural challenge provoked by the spread of a mass consumer culture. The **Fundamentalist movement** began as a militant and defensive reaction to these new developments, which conservative Protestants feared were eating away the supernatural basis of traditional Christian faith and corrupting American culture. The movement took its name from a series of pamphlets called "The Fundamentals," published in 1910–1915 by conservative Protestants. The pamphlets stressed that there were certain fundamental Christian beliefs that could not be changed or watered down. A list of these basic beliefs drafted by the Northern Presbyterian Church in 1910 contains five doctrines: biblical inerrancy; the deity and Virgin Birth of Christ; his substitutionary atonement (death on behalf of others); his bodily resurrection; and his miracles. In 1919, William B. Riley (1861–1947), a prominent Minnesota fundamentalist, anti-evolution crusader, and founder of the World's Christian Fundamentals Association, added the Second Coming of Christ to the list. Fundamentalism, then, in the narrow sense of the word, refers to the inerrancy of scripture, and in a broader sense, to a militant Christian opposition to particular aspects of modernity.

Fundamentalism allied itself with a new way of understanding the Bible called **dispensationalism**. This method of biblical interpretation divided the scriptural narrative of God's dealing with humanity into seven stages called "dispensations." Each stage moved God's plan for humanity forward. The idea itself is found already in the theology of the second-century bishop Irenaeus of Lyons (see Chapter 8). Modern dispensationalism is new, however, in the way it uses the stages as the key to unlock the Bible's prophetic message about the end of time, especially the setting up of Christ's millennial kingdom. *Dispensational premillennialism,* as the developed system of prophetic interpretation is known, holds that certain biblical prophecies, especially in Daniel and Revelation, must be literally fulfilled before Christ begins his earthly reign. These prophecies include God's promises to Israel. The restoration of Israel therefore plays a central role in this scheme. Dispensational premillennialists are strong supporters of the modern State of Israel, because they see the return of the Jews to their homeland as an outstanding clue that the prophetic end-time clock has begun ticking. Another distinctive feature of this interpretive system is the doctrine of "the Rapture," meaning the snatching up of true Christians (see 1 Thessalonians 4:17) to save them from the tribulations of the End. The contemporary series of apocalyptic novels called *Left Behind* is based on dispensationalist doctrines about the Rapture. Dispensational premillennialists are usually pessimistic about the moral and spiritual condition of America. They also tend to see mainstream Christian churches, both Protestant and Catholic, as apostate (fallen away) churches that have abandoned real faith in Christ. They are therefore often hostile to ecumenical movements for Christian reunion, and even to dialogue with other churches. Dispensational premillennialism was popularized by the hugely successful study Bible called the *Scofield Reference Bible*, first published in 1909 and still in print. Dispensational premillennialism remains a highly influential form of eschatology (end time teaching) among fundamentalist Christians.

African-American Christianity: From Slavery to Segregation to Civil Rights

Attention has already been drawn to several African-American denominations. The history of African-American Christianity in the U.S.A. is inextricably linked with the history of slavery and racial segregation. Both free and enslaved blacks were evangelized by Protestant churches, but when full participation was denied to them, separate black churches were organized as soon as America became independent. In 1787, Richard Allen (1760–1831) led a protest of Negro Methodists in Philadelphia against practices that excluded African Americans from full participation in the Methodist church. This protest community eventually became the African Methodist-Episcopal (A.M.E.) Church. In 1796, African Americans in New York who encountered similar resistance organized a similarly named A.M.E. church, which later added "Zion" to its name. Among A.M.E. Zion's members were prominent black abolitionists such as Frederick Douglass, Sojourner Truth, and Harriet Tubman. After emancipation, churches became one of the most vital social institutions everywhere that African Americans settled, and seedbeds of the Civil Rights Movement of the 1950s and 1960s (see below on Dr. Martin Luther King).

In states like Maryland and Louisiana that had Catholic owners of slaves, slaves were baptized as Catholics, a practice that came to public attention in 2017 when Georgetown, a Jesuit and Catholic university in Washington, DC, acknowledged that in 1838 the university had sold 272 slaves to plantations in Louisiana. Segregation of black and white Catholics was common, especially in the South, and the first publicly known African-American priest, Fr. Augustus Tolton, was not ordained until 1886. Today, there are about 3 million African-American Catholics, three-quarters of them in diverse or shared parishes, and a quarter of them in largely African-American parishes.

Figure 23–3 Frederick Douglass (1818–1895).

Especially since the 1986 publication of Albert Raboteau's epochal study *Slave Religion: The "Invisible Institution" in the Antebellum South*, historians have given increasing attention to the place Christianity played in African-American life first under slavery (e.g., what reciprocal influence was there between Christianity and beliefs and practices that slaves brought with them from Africa?), then after emancipation and under the regime of legal segregation and pervasive cultural and economic racism, and finally in the post-Civil-Rights era (for a separate theological assessment, see Chapter 27).

Here we comment only on the ambiguous role that Christianity and the Bible played in the era when slavery was legal. Among slaves themselves, historians debate whether Christianity mainly served to justify acceptance of slavery or to undermine its legitimacy. Albert Raboteau proposed cautiously that Christianity enabled a "pre-political solidarity" among slaves that offered partial resistance to chattel slavery's effectiveness. Anti-slavery arguments went from the extreme of rejecting all churches that did not demand abolition, and even the Bible itself if it were seen as justifying slavery, to reluctant admissions that while there were clear acceptances of slavery in both the Old and New Testaments, a deeper moral sense recognized that the true understanding of Jesus' message needed time to mature. Anti-slavery Christians emphasized the egalitarian implications of the love ethic of the Sermon on the Mount and of much of the New Testament, and minimized passages which legitimated patriarchal authority. They might also, especially among African Americans, exploit typological interpretation to read themselves into the Exodus story of Israel's liberation from slavery in Egypt (see Chapter 3)—or even see the book of Revelation as authorizing slave rebellion.

Pro-slavery arguments could simply repeat passages that accepted slavery as a given and told slaves to obey masters (e.g., Ephesians 6:5; Colossians 3:22; 1 Peter 2:18; 1 Timothy 6:1–5), including the traditional reading of Paul's letter to Philemon as endorsing the return of his runaway slave Onesimus. They could also appeal to crudely racist interpretation of a text like "the curse of Canaan" in Genesis 9:20–27 as a divine endorsement of African slavery. They had more difficulty with the powerful egalitarian impulse of the New Testament found in texts like Galatians 3:28, which said that in Christ there is neither slave nor free but all are one, or the Golden Rule of Matthew 7:12. Catholic reluctance to condemn slavery on principle (as opposed to the slave trade) derived as well from Catholic reliance on the philosophical argumentation of natural law, which in some forms accepted the legitimacy of slavery. Virtually the only churches not represented in the American Anti-Slavery Society were Catholics and Lutherans.

That biblical interpretation of issues of racial identity is still controversial was proven during the 2008 presidential campaign, when Barack Obama had to respond to criticism of the fierce anti-racist preaching of Rev. Jeremiah Wright, his pastor in Chicago. And Cornel West, the brilliant and forceful professor-activist, has long argued for racial justice on biblical grounds. In the current upsurge of a populist protest tinged with white identity anxiety, there is no doubt that Christianity's approach to racial harmony will continue to be contested ground between competing notions of who or what is truly American (see "America: National Destiny and Religious Reflection" in this chapter).

CATHOLICISM IN AMERICA

America has a Catholic past as well, with roots that go even deeper than those of the British Protestant "birthright" churches of the east coast. In much of the U.S.A., its visible evidence may be confined to familiar but very un-English place names like St. Louis, named by French explorer Louis Joliet in 1678 for King Louis XIV of France, as well as claiming the whole Mississippi valley for France under the name of "Louisiana." "Los Angeles" is shortened from *El Pueblo de Nuestra Señora la Reina de los Angeles de Porciúncula*, "The Town of Our Lady Queen of Angels of the Portiuncula," named by Spanish Franciscans on August 2, 1769, the day on which the Franciscan order celebrated the church in Italy where St. Francis of Assisi was buried (the "Portiuncula," "little plot of land").

We may distinguish several broad phases in American Catholic history:

1. *French and Spanish exploration and colonization (seventeenth–eighteenth centuries)*: Of the two, the Spanish experience in America left the more lasting imprint, because the French made fewer permanent settlements south of Quebec, New Orleans being the most prominent. In a great arc from Florida through Texas and the Southwest to San Francisco Bay, the Spanish established a chain of missions, military garrisons, and towns whose Catholic character survived American conquest and annexation in the nineteenth century. Thanks to that history and to surging immigration from Mexico, California, and the Southwest today are home to one-third of America's Catholic population. With colonization went conversion, as heroic French and Spanish missionaries risked their lives to bring Christianity to Native American peoples. Their efforts met with mixed success. Today there is intense debate about the mission enterprise and its effects on Native American culture. In California, the legacy of Fr. Junipero Serra (1713–1784), Franciscan friar and "Apostle of California," is contested territory in the wider debate over the effects of European conquest and Christian evangelization, especially since Pope John Paul II in 1985 promoted him to "Beatified" and Pope Francis canonized him as a saint in 2015. Fr. Serra's admirers praise his character, the mission system he built, his evangelization of California's Indians, and the economic progress that he pioneered. His critics condemn his use of coercive measures with the Indians and his role in the destruction of California's Indian cultures. He and the mission enterprise share responsibility for the unintended and disastrous demographic decline that accompanied Spanish settlement.

2. *British colonial and American Revolutionary era (1634–c.1820)*, when Catholics were a tiny minority in an overwhelmingly Protestant land. In Maryland, founded in 1634 as a proprietary colony by the Catholic family of the Calverts, Catholics for a time enjoyed political toleration. In general, Catholics in the colonies suffered from traditional English Protestant hatred and suspicion of their church. As a result, Catholics did not get their own American bishop until after the Revolution, when John Carroll was elected by his priests.

3. *Era of the immigrant church (c.1820–c.1950)*, when wave after wave of immigration, mainly from Europe, kept the Catholic Church busy constantly absorbing new arrivals: the major challenge was adjusting European habits and assumptions to American conditions, and the major question facing Catholics was "How do we fit in?" Catholic immigrants were resented by many Americans who saw them as religiously alien and potentially disloyal because of their allegiance to the pope. They were often scorned as socially and educationally backwards, and unfit for democracy because so many came from countries that were still monarchies. Partially to compensate for such suspicions, Catholics tried hard to prove their patriotism and loyalty to their new country, for example, by serving in America's

wars in numbers well beyond their percentage of the population. To ease the transition to America, the church developed its own subculture, complete with schools, professional associations, labor unions, insurance societies (the large lay organization called the Knights of Columbus began as an insurance society), religious societies, clubs, magazines, and newspapers. This was the era of "brick and mortar Catholicism," so called from the great churches that still dominate urban landscapes all over the northeast, the Midwest, and the Great Lakes region, and the sprawling parish complexes of rectory, convent, parochial school, and gymnasium. It was also an era of exceptional clerical dominance over the laity, whose energies were spent on establishing themselves and their families in a challenging new world. Historians of immigration have noted that the new immigrants often became *more* religious than they had been in the old country, as the churches played a vital supporting role in their adjustment to America. This deepened religious practice, in turn, was to bottom out somewhat in the fourth stage.

4. *Era of assimilation (c.1950 to the present)*: In the post-World War II period, many of the older obstacles to advancement withered away. John Kennedy's election in 1960 as the first Catholic president expressed a widespread sense that Catholics had finally "arrived." At the same time, however, what it meant to be Catholic became less certain throughout this period. Catholic identity was harder to take for granted once the dense ethnic solidarity of the big eastern and Great Lakes cities and Midwestern rural communities, where most Catholics lived, started to dissolve and the post-war exodus to the suburbs began. Increased education and greater prosperity had a similar diluting effect on religious identity. Another factor at work after the 1960s was the question of where America itself was heading in an age marked by the Civil Rights Movement, violent racial conflict, the Vietnam War, the cultural upheavals of the 1960s, and the women's liberation movement. To many Christians, a series of Supreme Court cases from the late 1940s to the landmark 1973 *Roe* v. *Wade* decision, which struck down state anti-abortion laws as unconstitutional, seemed bent on erasing every trace of America's Christian heritage from public life and law. The very definition of America seemed up for grabs. As a result, debates within the church about Catholic identity often reflected how Catholics felt about what was going on in the wider culture outside their church. Positions taken by Catholics in an emerging culture war in society at large tended to coincide with the positions they were also taking in the hostile and polarized climate that developed in the church after the Second Vatican Council (see Chapter 24).

5. A new and distinctive period is currently underway because of the rapid growth of Latino Catholics, who currently constitute about one-third of American Catholics, a proportion that is likely to grow and to change American Catholicism in ways as yet unknown.

The most important theological voice produced by American Catholicism was the Jesuit theologian John Courtney Murray (1904–1967). Murray's great achievement was his development of a Catholic understanding of the American system of religious freedom and non-establishment. For most of its history, the Catholic Church had enjoyed legal benefits and privileges from Christian states, privileges which it claimed by right as the true church of Jesus Christ. This traditional Catholic expectation of state sponsorship was re-emphasized by papal teaching after the French Revolution. In America, Catholics enjoyed the benefits of religious freedom and had

Figure 23–4 John Courtney Murray, S.J., with Clare Boothe Luce, wife of Henry Luce, publisher of *Time* magazine, holding the *Time* cover of December 12, 1960, a month after the election of John F. Kennedy as first Catholic president of the U.S.A.

no desire to make their church an established church. But they lacked any way to convince their fellow citizens of this, since nineteenth-century Catholic doctrine was so critical of religious freedom and of liberal democracy in general. Murray tried to demonstrate that religious freedom and the separation of church and state were positive goods, not just circumstances that Catholics had to tolerate because they were powerless to change them. America's historical experience appeared to prove that religious freedom could ensure both stabile government and religious flourishing: on the one hand, religious uniformity was not necessary for sound government, so long as the social order *outside* of the state—what Murray called "civil society"—possessed a healthy capacity for moral judgment; and on the other hand, American democracy permitted a great deal of practical freedom to all religions. Murray held that Catholicism had always recognized a certain dualism and independence of function in church and state. He saw American liberal democracy as a legitimate heir, in modern conditions, of the church–state dualism of the Catholic Middle Ages—the American version of liberalism had not exerted the kind of state control over the church that was typical of European liberal regimes.

Figure 23–5 Procession for cornerstone-laying of the first Mexican church in Chicago, Our Lady of Guadalupe, in steel mill district on the southeast side (Spring 1928).

Church authorities suspected that religious freedom implied that one religious choice was good as another, a relativist idea that nineteenth-century popes called "indifferentism." The endorsement of religious freedom also appeared to be a change from past papal teaching. For several years in the 1950s Murray was prohibited from publishing his work. Nevertheless, his ideas, as popularized in his book *We Hold These Truths: Catholic Reflections on the American Proposition* (1960), eventually received a practical vindication when Kennedy was elected president. The book played a role in reducing public anxiety at a Catholic in the White House, as *Time* magazine recognized by putting Murray on its cover the month after the election. In 1963, he received a belated vindication within the church when Cardinal Francis Spellman, archbishop of New York City, asked him to serve as his theological advisor at the Second Vatican Council, where he contributed to the drafting of Vatican II's *Declaration on Religious Liberty* (see Chapter 24).

The various crises of the 1960s and 1970s, above all the war in Vietnam, led some Catholics to subject Murray's ideas to a different kind of criticism. Because Murray had made a clear distinction between the secular and the religious spheres, with each having its appropriate degree of freedom, there was a danger that Catholics might defer too easily to the demands of the state. Catholics who became unquestioning supporters of everything that America did had failed to form their consciences first. Did religious freedom bring with it a risk of self-imposed moral handcuffs? Catholic critics of Murray pointed to such things as America's dependence on a massive nuclear deterrent during the tense years of the Cold War against the Soviet Union—it was impossible to reconcile the use of atomic weapons of mass destruction with the traditional criteria for fighting a just war, which forbid the targeting of noncombatants. During the Reagan administration, the American Catholic bishops published a pastoral letter titled *The Challenge of Peace* (1983), in which they expressed their concerns about America's reliance on nuclear weapons and advised Catholics on how to form their consciences.

One of the most radical critics of Catholic compromises with America was Dorothy Day (1897–1980), a journalist and social activist who converted from atheism to Catholicism in the 1920s. The **Catholic Worker Movement**, which she and Peter Maurin founded in 1933, continues to espouse her ideals of pacifism, anarchism, and direct service to the poor and outcast. In 2000, Pope John Paul II authorized the beginning of a process for her canonization.

A conservative critique of Murray's reconciliation of America and Catholicism has focused on his assumption that under democratic conditions civil society had matured sufficiently that "the people" could make responsible moral judgments about

Figure 23–6 Dorothy Day (1897–1980), founder of the Catholic Worker Movement.

the common good. That claim has been severely tested by *Roe* v. *Wade* and by subsequent judicial decisions, legislative actions, and popular referenda on controversial issues such as the legalization of same-sex marriage, physician assisted suicide, and stem cell research. If such developments are supported by a majority of the American people, that indicated to critics that Murray gave too much credit to the moral capacity of civil society. To take the example of abortion, which Catholic teaching forbids on the grounds that human life begins at conception and has an inalienable right to life: Catholic officeholders who defend legal access to abortion understand it as a religious issue and say they must keep their personal religious beliefs separate from their duties as the elected representatives of constituents who may disagree radically with Catholic teaching (in a similar way, Catholics who vote for pro-choice candidates may argue that criminalizing abortion in all circumstances would be bad law because it lacks popular support and may be unenforceable). In recent years, bishops appointed under Pope John Paul II have been less willing than their predecessors to tolerate what they see as equivocation and disobedience on the part of Catholic candidates and officeholders, and of Catholic voters as well. It is too soon to tell whether the bishops' stance on law and religion will shift under Pope Francis (see Chapter 24).

AMERICA: NATIONAL DESTINY AND RELIGIOUS REFLECTION

"God's New Israel": American Exceptionalism

"Consider that we shall be as a city upon a hill, the eyes of all nations will be upon us..." So spoke John Winthrop on board the Puritans' flagship the *Arbella*, as he and his co-religionists sailed to New England in 1630. Winthrop was alluding to the words of Jesus in the Sermon on the Mount:

> You are the light of the world. A city built on a hill cannot be hid. No one after lighting a lamp puts it under the bushel basket, but on the lampstand, and it gives light to all in the house. In the same way, let your light shine before others, so that they may see your good works...
>
> (Matthew 5:14–16)

The biblical image of the new community as a beacon that illuminates the world and that "all nations" look to as an inspiring example has exerted a powerful influence on America's self-understanding. Presidents have often exploited it in ceremonial speeches, such as Ronald Reagan's farewell address (January 11, 1989):

> I've spoken of the shining city all my political life, but I don't know if I ever quite communicated what I saw when I said it. But in my mind it was a tall proud city built on rocks stronger than oceans, wind-swept, God-blessed, and teeming with people of all kinds living in harmony and peace, a city with free ports that hummed with commerce and creativity, and if there had to be city walls, the walls had doors and the doors were open to anyone with the will and the heart to get here. That's how I saw it and see it still.
>
> (Reagan 1989)

Students are most likely to have encountered this national self-image in its secularized form as "Manifest Destiny," a phrase that first emerged in connection with American expansion at the time of the Mexican War (1846–1848). But the religiously framed version has been just as potent. Calling America "a city on a hill" says that America's experiment in democratic government is uniquely important to the rest of the world. Abraham Lincoln went so far as to call that experiment "the last, best hope of earth." Though never baptized or a member of any church, Lincoln could fairly be called America's greatest public theologian for his profound meditations on the meaning of the Civil War, above all, in his Second Inaugural Address. He spoke of Americans as "this almost chosen people," a phrase that suggests a providential national calling or destiny like the one possessed by Israel in the Bible. The trope of America as "God's new Israel" originated with the Puritans. But it was equally popular with Founders like Jefferson and Franklin, who otherwise were religious rationalists (see Chapter 22): for the Great Seal of the United States, Franklin proposed the defeat of Pharaoh and his army as recounted in the book of Exodus, and Jefferson suggested the people of Israel in the wilderness, led by the pillar of cloud and the pillar of fire.

Since its creation, then, and even more strongly since its emergence as a world power in the twentieth century, the United States has acted as though it has an exceptional status and role among the nations of the world. "American exceptionalism," as this sense of national mission has been called, can be a double-edged sword. On the one hand, it can mean that the nation is a law unto itself and need not answer to any standards but its own. Critics of American foreign policy ever since Woodrow Wilson's administration (1912–1920) argue that it has sometimes led to a self-righteous blindness that prevents America from seeing itself the way the rest of the world does. On the other hand, American exceptionalism can also express a set of ideals by which the nation is willing to be judged, and an awareness that its many advantages are given in a form of stewardship, for which an account is owed. This self-critical capacity too can be traced to America's origins, for it is rooted in the biblical idea of the *covenant*, according to which Israel was obliged to fulfill certain terms in its special relationship with God. To quote John Winthrop's shipboard sermon again:

> Thus stands the cause between God and us. We are entered into Covenant with him for this work, we have taken out a Commission, the Lord hath given us leave to draw our own Articles … Now if the Lord shall please to hear us, and bring us in peace to the place we desire, then hath he ratified this Covenant and sealed our Commission [and] will expect a strict performance of the Articles contained in it…
>
> (Cited in Cherry 1998, 40)

"A Nation With the Soul of a Church": The Civil Religion Question

As these biblical allusions demonstrate, America's sense of itself as a nation has often been expressed in religious terms. This has not ceased to be true, in spite of the First Amendment. In a famous essay published in 1967, the sociologist Robert Bellah proposed that, despite the free exercise and no establishment clauses, America still has something that looks very much like a national religion. Because it is distinctly political in its expression and cannot be identified with any existing church or religion, Bellah called it a **civil religion**. In his view, it was nevertheless rightly called a religion, as shown by its possession of belief in a deity ("the nation under God"), sacred texts (the Constitution and the Declaration of Independence), founders, martyrs (e.g., Lincoln and Martin Luther King), myths of creation and redemption (the Revolution and the Civil War), sacred shrines and sites, sacred times and commemorations, and sacred hymns and symbols (e.g., the flag). Its tenets and practices were specific enough to constitute a religion but broad enough to include most Christians and Jews and to minimize offense to those who professed no religion. Today, the concept of "Abrahamic faiths" may enable the inclusion of Islam into what has been a "Judeo-Christian" partnership.

This civil religion expressed and sanctioned the basic values that unified Americans as a distinct nation and tried to make the slogan on coins into a reality: *E pluribus unum* ("Out of Many, One"). While recognizing that America's civil religion could easily become idolatrous, Bellah argued that it had a powerful positive potential as well. He admired the way it could energize and inspire Americans to live up to the high ideals formulated in the nation's foundational documents. He saw the greatest example of this in the Civil Rights Movement, in which religious symbols and motivations served legal and political goals. No one perfected this religious and political synthesis more powerfully than Dr. Martin Luther King, Jr., a Baptist minister and the son of a Baptist minister. King's vision of racial justice drew both on core biblical sources and ideals, and on distinctively American values and traditions: from the Bible came the Exodus story of liberation from slavery, the prophets' demands for social justice, and the Sermon on the Mount's teaching on nonviolence; from America's founding came the democratic and egalitarian values of the Declaration of Independence. Dr. King's "Letter from a Birmingham Jail" (1963) and his "I Have a Dream" speech, delivered in 1963 from the steps of the Lincoln Memorial at the Civil Rights Movement's greatest rally, have become canonical documents in America's civil religion. The speech (ranked in a 1999 poll of scholars as the greatest American speech of the twentieth century) burns with the fiery rhetoric of a revivalist sermon, but the "call" (an integral feature of a revivalist sermon is the altar call, when those ready to declare themselves for Christ come down in front of the congregation) is a summons to legal equality and human brotherhood and dignity.

Not everyone has agreed with Bellah's thesis. Some deny that we have a civil religion at all, preferring instead to see our unifying national "myths" as technology, capitalism, or freedom, shorn of any religious halo or sanction. Others think that an American civil religion does exist but condemn it—either because they are secularists who oppose any connection between government and religion, or because they are believers who see it as a political distortion of genuine religion. Even if Bellah overstated the internal coherence and the pervasiveness of this unifying national symbol-system, it does seem to be true that in the United States the nation itself has taken on sacred dimensions. It is the *nation* that dwarfs any Christian church as a powerful locus of group identity and membership. Today, the resurgence of nationalism in the form of "populist" movements is once again demonstrating how strong—and problematic—that sense of special, shared identity can be. G.K. Chesterton, a British Catholic observer of the American scene, famously called the U.S.A. "a nation with the soul of a church."

Christianity and America

The modern nation-state and the ideology of nationalism have posed problems for Christians everywhere, including countries where Christianity still enjoys some degree of religious establishment. But the dilemma is especially acute in the United States, where the political and religious conditions referred to in the section of this chapter titled "Protestantism in America: From Evangelical Empire to Two-Party System" (voluntaryism, democracy, and revivalism) have created a fragmented denominational mosaic. The result is to make the nation look all the bigger and the churches all the smaller. Nationalism as a force promises to get even stronger in the future, as developed countries like the United States come under pressure from population movements caused by a globalized economy, climate change, and war. In the U.S.A. and in Europe, the fear of foreigners as threats to one's national identity is fueling a powerful populist reaction.

Given the global power of the United States, Christianity's universal claims lose credibility when American churches allow themselves and the gospel to be nationalized. Christianity resists being identified exclusively with any particular political or economic system. But the story told in this textbook shows that the enculturation of the gospel has sometimes led to political involvements that with hindsight look more like the capture of the gospel. Chapter 10 referred to St. Augustine's great apologetic work *On the City of God*, in which he had reminded Christians that the sack of Rome in 410 showed that God could use empires, even Christian empires, as he wished, and could discard them when they had served his purposes. According to the New Testament's Letter to the Hebrews, "we have here no lasting city, but we seek one which is to come" (Hebrews 13:14). In America, Christians have sometimes imagined they are already living in the heavenly Jerusalem (cf. Hebrews 12:22). Augustine would remind them that they are only pilgrims *in via*, on the way to it.

As was once true during the Cold War with Communism, and now again since the terrorist attacks of September 11, 2001, America's belief in its exceptional status has at times inspired an aggressive interventionism in other countries, especially in the Middle East and parts of Africa. Americans have at times imagined they can build walls against a threatening world. The rise of radical movements claiming to be inspired by Islam has created the possibility that a religiously based American exceptionalism could see Islam itself as an enemy. Those who hold such views run the risk of equating God's will with American policy. Reinhold Niebuhr (1892–1971), American Protestantism's greatest social ethicist, was keenly aware of this danger. Niebuhr ardently defended a special American role in the world because he believed the United States had an obligation to use its economic and military power to good ends. But he also shared Augustine's awareness of human fallibility and the danger of the sin of pride, as he showed in his many books and articles, notably in *Moral Man and Immoral Society* (1932) and *The Nature and Destiny of Man* (1941 and 1943). In an essay written during World War II, Niebuhr spoke about a special role for America and the temptation to self-righteousness that went with it:

> If we know that we have been chosen beyond our deserts, we must also begin to realize that we have not been chosen for our particular task in order that our own life may be aggrandized. We ought not to derive either special security or special advantage from our high historical mission. The real fact is that we are placed in a precarious moral and historical position by our special mission. It can be justified only if it results in good for the whole community of mankind. Woe unto us if we fail. For our failure will bring judgment upon us and the world. That is the meaning of the prophetic word, "Therefore will I visit you with your iniquities." This word must be translated by the church today into meanings relevant to our own history. If this is not done, we are bound to fail. For the natural pride of great nations is such that any special historical success quickly aggravates it until it becomes the source of moral and political confusion.
>
> ("Anglo-Saxon Destiny and Responsibility," reprinted in Cherry 1998, 299)

Key Terms

Baptist church
Catholic Worker
  Movement
civil religion
denominationalism
dispensationalism
evangelical

First Amendment
Fundamentalist
  movement
glossolalia
Holiness movement
Jehovah's Witnesses
Latter-Day Saints

Methodism
Peace churches
Pentecostalism
pietism
restorationism
revivalism

Questions for Reading

1. Cite the exact wording of the First Amendment's religion clauses. Describe two broadly different ways in which the religion clauses have been interpreted.

2. What is the special role in American society that the churches of the original English colonies believe is their responsibility?

3. Explain the main elements that contributed to the denominational system that came into being in the U.S.A. after independence. What are some of the pros and cons of that system?

4. Describe the various ways in which Pietism has contributed to the shaping of Christianity in America.

5. "Millennialism" is a prominent theme in American Protestant history. What are "millennial expectations," and how have they influenced the creation of new churches in America? Distinguish between the different ways in which "post-" and "pre-millennialism" view the direction of history.

6. List core Fundamentalist principles, and describe the central motivations of the Fundamentalist movement. How has dispensational pre-millennialism shaped Fundamentalist ways of understanding biblical prophecy?

7. What primarily distinguishes the third from the fourth phase of Catholic history in America? Answer in terms of how Catholics see themselves in relation to America.

8. How did John Courtney Murray defend, on Catholic grounds, the theological acceptability of religious freedom and democracy? What sorts of criticisms have his ideas received since Murray's death in 1967?

9. What are the religious sources of the common American sense that the nation has a special mission or destiny? How is it possible for that "exceptional" sense of mission to function in a *critical* way?

10. Explain what is meant by the term "civil religion," illustrating its possible relevance to understanding America's sense of itself as a nation. What are the challenges that an American civil religion would pose to actual Christian churches?

Works Consulted/Recommended Reading

Albanese, Catherine L. 1992. *America: Religion and Religions.* 2nd edn. Belmont, CA: Wadsworth Publishing Company (see especially: Chapter 13, "Civil Religion: Millennial Politics and History," 432–463).

Allitt, Patrick. 2003. *Religion in America since 1945: A History.* New York: Columbia University Press.

Bacevich, Andrew J. 2002. *American Empire: The Realities and the Consequences of U.S. Diplomacy.* Cambridge, MA: Harvard University Press.

Bellah, Robert. 1967. "Civil Religion in America." *Daedalus* 96, no. 1: 1–21.

Cherry, Conrad, ed. 1998. *God's New Israel: Religious Interpretations of American History.* Rev. edn. Chapel Hill, NC: University of North Carolina Press.

Cuddihy, John Murray. 1978. *No Offense: Civil Religion and Protestant Taste.* New York: Seabury Press.

Curry, Thomas J. 1986. *The First Freedoms: Church and State in America to the Passage of the First Amendment.* New York: Oxford University Press.

Day, Dorothy. 1997. *The Long Loneliness.* New York: HarperCollins.

Finkelman, Paul, ed. 2006. *The Encyclopedia of African American History, 1619–1895: From the Colonial Period to the Age of Frederick Douglass.* Oxford: Oxford University Press.

Finkelman, Paul, ed. 2009. *The Encyclopedia of African American History: 1896 to the Present.* Oxford: Oxford University Press.

Gaustad, Edwin S. 1993. *Faith of Our Fathers: Religion and the New Nation.* Grand Rapids, MI: Wm. B. Eerdmans.

Georgetown University Slave Archive. n.d. https://slaveryarchive.georgetown.edu/.

Gorski, Philip. 2017. *American Covenant: A History of Civil Religion from the Puritans to the Present.* Princeton, NJ: Princeton University Press.

Guelzo, Allen C. 1997. "God's Designs: The Literature of the Colonial Revivals of Religion, 1735–1760." In *New Directions in American Religious History.* Edited by Harry S. Stout and D.G. Hart, 141–172. New York: Oxford University Press.

Hackel, Steven W. 2005. "The Competing Legacies of Junipero Serra: Pioneer, Saint, Villain." *Common-place* 5:2 (January). www.common-place.org/vol-05/no-02/hackel/index.shtml.

Harrill, J. Albert. 2006. "The Use of the New Testament in the American Slave Controversy." In *Slaves in the New Testament: Literary, Social, and Moral Dimensions.* Minneapolis, MN: Fortress Press.

Hatch, Nathan O. 1989. *The Democratization of American Christianity.* New Haven, CT: Yale University Press.

Hennesey, James. 1983. *American Catholics: A History of the Roman Catholic Community in the United States.* New York: Oxford University Press.

Lipset, Seymour Martin. 1996. *American Exceptionalism: A Double-Edged Sword.* New York: W.W. Norton.

McGreevy, John T. 2003. *Catholics and American Freedom: A History.* New York: W.W. Norton.

MacIntyre, Alasdair. 1980. "America as an Idea." In *America and Ireland, 1776–1976.* Edited by David Noel Doyle and Owen Dudley Edwards, 57–68. Westport, CT: Greenwood Press.

Marsden, George. 2006. *Fundamentalism and American Culture 1875–1925.* 2nd edn. New York: Oxford University Press.

Marty, Martin E. 1970. *Righteous Empire: The Protestant Experience in America.* New York: The Dial Press.

Matovina, Timothy. 2011. *Latino Catholicism: Transformation in America's Largest Church.* Princeton, NJ: Princeton University Press.

Mead, Sidney E. 1963. *The Lively Experiment: The Shaping of Christianity in America.* New York: Harper and Row.

Murray, John Courtney. 1960. *We Hold These Truths: Catholic Reflections on the American Proposition.* New York: Sheed and Ward.

Niebuhr, Reinhold. 1943. "Anglo-Saxon Destiny and Responsibility." *Christianity and Crisis* (October 4). Reprinted in Conrad Cherry, ed., 1998. *God's New Israel: Religious Interpretations of American History.* Rev. edn. 296–300. Chapel Hill, NC: University of North Carolina Press.

Noll, Mark A. 2002. *America's God: From Jonathan Edwards to Abraham Lincoln.* New York: Oxford University Press.

Noll, Mark A. 2006. *The Civil War as a Theological Crisis.* Chapel Hill, NC: University of North Carolina Press.

Noonan, John T. 1998. *The Lustre of Our People: The American Experience of Religious Freedom.* Berkeley, CA: University of California Press.

Peterson, Merrill D., and Robert C. Vaughan, eds. 1988. *The Virginia Statute for Religious Freedom: Its Evolution and Consequences in American History.* Cambridge: University of Cambridge Press.

Pew Research Center. n.d. "Religious Landscape Study." www.pewforum.org/religious-landscape-study/.

Raboteau, Albert J. 2004. *Slave Religion: The "Invisible Institution" in the Antebellum South.* Updated edn. New York: Oxford University Press.

Reagan, Ronald. 1989. "Farewell Speech." Reagan Foundation. www.reaganfoundation.org/reagan/speeches/farewell.asp

Reid, Daniel G., et al., eds. 1990. *Dictionary of Christianity in America.* Downers Grove, IL: InterVarsity Press.

Sandos, James A. 1988. "Junipero Serra's Canonization and the Historical Record." *American Historical Review* 93: 1253–1269.

Shipps, Jan. 1985. *Mormonism: The Story of a New Religious Tradition.* Urbana, IL: University of Illinois Press.

Starr, Kevin. 2016. *Here from the Beginning: Roman Catholics in North America: The Colonial Experience.* San Francsico, CA: St. Ignatius Press.

Stout, Harry S. and D.G. Hart, eds. 1997. *New Directions in American Religious History.* New York: Oxford University Press.

Weber, Timothy P. 1987. *Living in the Shadow of the Second Coming: American Premillennialism, 1875–1982.* Chicago, IL: University of Chicago Press.

Weber, Timothy P. 2004. *On the Road to Armageddon: How American Evangelicals Became Israel's Best Friend.* Grand Rapids, MI: Baker Academic.

Wilentz, Sean. 1990. "American Exceptionalism." In *Encyclopedia of the American Left.* Edited by Mari Jo Buhle, Puhle, and Dan Georgakas, 20–22. New York: Garland.

Wilkerson, Isabel. 2010. *The Warmth of Other Suns: The Epic Story of America's Great Migration.* New York: Random House.

Witte, John. 2000. *Religion and the American Constitutional Experiment: Essential Rights and Liberties.* Boulder, CO: Westview Press.

Wood, Gordon S. 1997. "Religion and the American Revolution." In *New Directions in American Religious History.* Edited by Harry S. Stout and D.G. Hart, 173–205. New York: Oxford University Press.

Chapter

THE SECOND VATICAN COUNCIL IN CONTEXT

FROM THE FRENCH REVOLUTION TO VATICAN I

Following the French Revolution (1789–1799), the Catholic Church went into a reactionary mode that lasted into the twentieth century. The Revolution had been a traumatic experience for the church, first by nationalizing the French hierarchy as an arm of the state, then by executing the king, and finally by radically de-Christianizing France altogether. The Revolution was followed by Napoleon's dictatorship and his humiliating treatment of the popes and the Papal States. Nineteenth-century popes were therefore hostile to "the principles of 1789" ("Liberty, Equality, Fraternity") and thought the church's interests lay with an "alliance of throne and altar" as protection against the anticlericalism and atheism that seemed to be the natural fruit of democratic systems, whether liberal or socialist.

In the years after the Congress of Vienna (1814–1815), the papacy and Catholicism as a whole experienced a powerful rejuvenation. Intellectuals and artists who had misgivings about aspects of the Enlightenment or about modernity in general sometimes found Catholicism and its medieval heritage (architecture, art, music, social theories, etc.) an attractive alternative. New religious orders grew up to meet practical needs in education, health care, and missionary work, especially missions in parts of Africa that European states were just beginning to colonize. Traditional devotion to Mary as the Blessed Virgin and the Mother of God grew even stronger, nourished by numerous occurrences in which Mary was said to have appeared to believers. In 1854, Pope Pius IX proclaimed the dogma of the Immaculate Conception, which holds that Mary was conceived in the womb of her mother without inheriting original sin. Because this teaching is not attested in the Bible, the pope consulted with bishops around the world before declaring that it was a truth revealed in tradition even if it was not clearly stated in scripture. This belief in Mary's conception without original sin—not to be confused with the virginal conception of Jesus in Mary's womb—is not accepted by other Christian churches. Four years later, in the southern French town of Lourdes, a peasant girl named Bernadette Soubirous claimed that Mary had appeared to her and declared, "I am the Immaculate Conception." Lourdes became an immensely popular pilgrimage center and also the site of healing miracles. Other sites of modern Marian apparitions also became popular pilgrimage destinations:

Knock in Ireland in 1879; Fatima in Portugal in 1917, where Mary was said to advocate devotion to the rosary; and Medjugorje in 1981 in Bosnia. The most recent of these, the Medjugorje apparitions, have yet to receive official recognition from church authorities.

During this period, the pope became even more firmly established at the top of the clerical hierarchy. Devotion to the person of the pope, as distinct from the status conferred by his office, was something rather new. It began in sympathy for the suffering of Pope Pius VII (1800–1823) at the hands of Napoleon, who captured the pope and put him under virtual house arrest in France. It deepened with affection for the person of Pius IX (1846–1878), in whose pontificate papal infallibility was defined as a revealed dogma. In the twentieth century, the "personalization" of the papacy grew even more under strong, vigorous popes like Pius XI (1922–1939) and Pius XII (1939–1958). The moral and intellectual stature and powerful charisma of Pope John Paul II (1978–2005) brought it to an almost excessive extreme. Papal prestige was heightened by the trend toward canonizing popes as saints: Pius X (1903–1910), John XXIII (1958–1963), and John Paul II are all now venerated as saints. Four other recent popes are in various stages of the canonization process.

Loyalty to the pope was fostered by improved travel and communications, which made it easier for Catholics around the world to visit Rome and to keep informed about the pope. Photography made it possible for everyone to see what the pope looked like: his picture hung in schools, rectories, and convents. At the same time, the curia, the governing structure of the church, used such technical advances to make the universal governing authority of the papacy more effective all over the globe.

Another factor was the anticlerical policies of governments of many countries in which Catholics lived. Where it still enjoyed a measure of state establishment, the church resisted giving up control over spheres such as education, marriage, or censorship. These were areas that the church had always regarded as its special responsibility but which modern states were now seeking to control. Many of the church–state conflicts of the nineteenth and twentieth centuries focused on efforts to make marriage a civil contract and to legalize divorce. State control of ecclesiastical affairs was also an issue, such as clerical appointments, church property and funds, and church communications. Bishops who might once have valued distance from Rome came to appreciate papal authority when they needed external help against hostile governments. An example of such hostile state pressure in the 1870s was the *Kulturkampf* ("culture war"), German Chancellor Otto von Bismarck's campaign to subordinate the Catholic Church to the newly formed German Empire.

Many nineteenth-century Catholics were also eager to strengthen the pope's authority because his teaching office was seen as the last bastion against the intellectual challenges to Christianity surveyed in Chapter 22. Some Catholics saw the modern world in apocalyptic terms as a place crippled by doubt, uncertainty, and loss of faith. They believed that the church needed to present itself to human beings as the ultimate authority that could end argument and debate by delivering a final and irreversible judgment. For people who shared this pessimistic outlook, maximizing papal authority answered a need somewhat similar to the role that scriptural inerrancy played for fundamentalist Protestants (see Chapter 23).

The nineteenth-century tendency to exalt the authority of the papacy is called **ultramontanism**, "beyond the mountains," referring to Rome's location south of the Alps. Ultramontanism reached its high-water mark at the **First Vatican Council**

(1869–1870). An overture to that council was the *Syllabus of Errors* issued by Pope Pius IX in 1864. It consisted of 80 condemned propositions, some of which concerned basic religious liberties, such as no. 15 on freedom of religion and no. 55 on the separation of church and state. Several others concerned the temporal power of the pope as the ruler of his own state. The defiant spirit of the Syllabus is captured in the final one, no. 80, which condemned the proposition that "the Roman Pontiff can, and ought to, reconcile himself, and come to terms with, progress, liberalism and modern civilization."

The First Vatican Council, the first Catholic ecumenical council since the Council of Trent 300 years earlier, was intended in part to rally the Catholic world around the pope, who was threatened with losing the Papal States to the forced unification of the Italian peninsula as a single nation-state. Pope Pius IX convened the Council in the hope of saving the Papal States and establishing beyond all doubt the unique governing and teaching authority of the pope. Only two major documents or "constitutions" could be produced before the nationalist movement invaded Rome in August 1870 and forced the suspension of the Council. The constitution called *Pastor Aeternus* ("Eternal Pastor") declared that the pope had a primacy of jurisdiction (legal governing authority) over the whole Church that was universal, ordinary, and immediate (*Pastor Aeternus* §3.2), meaning that the pope was a bishop of the universal church, with a direct governing authority over all churches. The constitution stated that the pope's authority did not contradict the authority of individual bishops in their dioceses but did not explain how, a topic that would not be dealt with until the Second Vatican Council a century later.

Pastor Aeternus also declared that, under certain circumstances, the pope's teaching authority possessed a divinely granted protection against error:

> We teach and define that it is a dogma divinely revealed that when the Roman pontiff speaks *ex cathedra* ["from the chair" of Peter], that is when in the exercise of his office as shepherd and teacher of all Christians, in virtue of his supreme apostolic authority, he defines a doctrine regarding faith or morals to be held by the whole church, he possesses, by the divine assistance promised to him in blessed Peter, that infallibility which the divine Redeemer willed his church to enjoy in defining doctrine concerning faith or morals. Therefore, such definitions of the Roman pontiff are of themselves, and not by the consent of the church, irreformable.
>
> (*Pastor Aeternus* §4.9; Tanner, ed., *Decrees of the Ecumenical Councils*, 2: 816)

The definition carefully hedged the doctrine of **papal infallibility** with important conditions. The pope's infallibility was not his personal prerogative but the church's; it extended to subjects involving "faith and morals," not to any subject whatsoever; and it applied only when it was explicitly invoked. Infallibility also did not mean the capacity to produce new revelation—Catholic teaching has always held that public revelation ended with the death of the apostles. Apart from the dogma of the Immaculate Conception, which was proclaimed in 1854, the only subsequent occasion when a pope appealed to papal infallibility has been Pope Pius XII's declaration in 1950 of the dogma of the Assumption of Mary into heaven.

Infallible papal declarations were said to be "irreformable of themselves and not by the consent of the Church," meaning that there was no higher court of appeal. That finality was intended chiefly to eliminate the resistance popes had once faced from national hierarchies of bishops who chose in questions relating to the state to obey their governments rather than Rome, as for instance French bishops used to do before the Revolution. Vatican I sought to build a line of defense for the church's universality against potentially hostile modern governments, such as the current tensions between the Vatican and the People's Republic of China.

THEOLOGICAL TRENDS
BETWEEN VATICAN I AND VATICAN II

The Thomist Revival

During the century between Vatican I and Vatican II, Catholicism was confronted with numerous and fundamental challenges to its teaching. Its default response was to re-emphasize traditional ways of doing theology. That was officially recognized by Pope Leo XIII (1878–1903) in 1879 in his encyclical letter *Aeterni Patris* (Of the Eternal Father), which recommended the philosophy and theology of Thomas Aquinas as the outstanding instrument with which Catholic theologians should engage the modern world. Endorsing Aquinas meant endorsing Scholasticism, the method of argument perfected in the medieval schools, and also the philosophy of Aristotle, which had been Aquinas' and Scholasticism's chief intellectual resource. Because of the way in which Thomas' philosophy was taught—depending especially on later sixteenth- and seventeenth-century commentators on Thomas—it is customary to call this revival **Neo-Scholasticism**. The appeal of Neo-Scholasticism consisted in several things: its clarity, based on careful definitions and logical argumentation; its conception of truth as constant and unchanging; the objectivity of its truth claims, which claimed to be about an objective reality that transcended the consciousness and experience of the individual knower; and its rationality, since it rested on reason alone and did not depend on revelation.

More intense study of Thomas' philosophy in the early twentieth century led to some important developments that altered the dominance of Neo-Scholasticism. Scholars like Étienne Gilson (1884–1978), an expert on medieval philosophy in general and Thomas Aquinas in particular, recognized that there were significant differences among medieval philosophers, and that it was not possible to distill a single, tightly defined system of propositions that represented a single, Christian philosophy. Gilson held that all of the medieval philosophers were actually theologians, and that their Christian faith was the prerequisite for understanding their philosophy. He regarded Thomas as the outstanding example of the Christian philosopher. But he did not think that Thomas' philosophy could be detached, as it were, from his theology, and then put to use to deal with modern intellectual problems. By taking this viewpoint, Gilson in effect undercut the program of renewal that Pope

Leo XIII had outlined in 1879, since Leo had expected the recovery of St. Thomas to be the point of departure for new advances. Gilson certainly agreed that Thomas was the supreme practitioner of Christian philosophy, and, in Gilson's view, he has had no successor who might claim to be his superior. But Thomas had to be accepted and taken as he was—there was no way that his thought could be "adapted" to deal with new problems, as in the area of the natural sciences, where intellectual changes had rendered Aristotle's conception of natural science outmoded.

Despite Gilson's arguments, the Thomist revival inspired some impressive intellectual accomplishments. The most influential such effort was the long and productive career of the philosopher Jacques Maritain (1882–1973), a convert to Catholicism. Maritain's many books, such as *The Degrees of Knowledge,* covered strictly philosophical subjects. But he also applied Thomas' ideas to other dimensions of human culture as well: education, art, politics, science, etc., in a creative application of Thomas' ideas that has gained the name of *Neo-Thomism.*

John Henry Newman

There have been figures who never fit into the Neo-Scholastic mode at all, such as the English convert John Henry Newman (1801–1890), who became the most original Catholic thinker of the nineteenth century. Newman had been a prominent figure in the Oxford Movement in the Church of England (see Chapter 19), but his historical studies convinced him that Roman Catholicism preserved more of the historic core of patristic Christianity than had Anglicanism. His *Essay on the Development of Christian Doctrine* (original edition in 1845, while Newman was still an Anglican, reissued in 1878 after his conversion) defended elements in Roman Catholicism that appeared to depart from biblical precedent by arguing that later doctrines could be legitimate developments of earlier ones. This was a novel theory at a time when Catholics, and many other Christians as well, believed orthodox doctrine had never changed.

Newman's originality is preserved in several other fundamental works. *An Essay in Aid of a Grammar of Assent* presented a subtle psychological and conceptual account of how an individual person comes to adopt and hold religious convictions. His *Apologia pro Vita Sua* (Defense of His Life) is an intellectual and religious autobiography that has become a literary classic. *On Consulting the Faithful in Matters of Doctrine* offered a theological assessment of the place of the laity in the church that anticipated some of the ideas of the Second Vatican Council. A forceful and articulate defender of religious authority, which he saw threatened by individualistic liberalism, Newman nevertheless wrote a classic

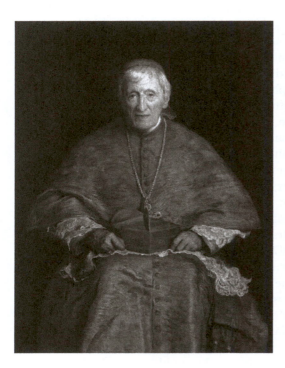

Figure 24–1 John Henry Newman (1801–1890). Portrait by John Everett Millais (1829–1896).

defense of the rights of conscience in the church, if that conscience was rightly formed. His *Letter to the Duke of Norfolk*, written in 1872, immediately following Vatican I's promulgation of papal infallibility, defended English Catholics against the charge of political disloyalty to Queen Victoria. As an Englishman and a convert, Newman was thus a bit of a theological oddity in the Catholic world. He did not depend on the kind of logical argumentation and metaphysical categories that were basic to Neo-Scholasticism. His thinking and writing drew more from history and literature, and from profound reflection on his own personal experience. Catholic Modernism (see Roman Catholic Modernism below) drew inspiration from him. In 2010, Pope Benedict XVI recognized Newman's contribution and his sanctity by beatifying him, the last step on the road to canonization as a saint.

Roman Catholic Modernism

In the period between the two Vatican councils, a more fundamental challenge to the dominance of Neo-Scholasticism was Roman Catholic **Modernism**. The "Modernists," as they came to be called in official Catholic condemnations, were not a unified movement but individual figures who shared a common desire to break free from what they saw as the conceptual rigidity, spiritual dryness, and unhistorical limitations of Neo-Scholasticism. They included the French priest and biblical scholar Alfred Loisy, the Irish priest George Tyrrell, the Italian priest Ernesto Buonaiuti, the English nun Maude Petre, and the Austrian-English layman and aristocrat Baron Friedrich von Hügel.

"Modernism" is difficult to define because those who were condemned for it did not share an explicit program. The term was first created and officially used as a broad abstraction in the encyclical *Pascendi dominici gregis* (Pasturing the Lord's Flock, 1907). In the bombastic style that was common for the time, Pope Pius X (r. 1903–1910) and his encyclical writers solemnly condemned Modernism as the "synthesis of all heresies." Along with *Lamentabili sane exitu* (With Truly Lamentable Results), its accompanying list of 65 condemned propositions, the encyclical attacked such errors as the reduction of dogmas to mere symbols, devoid of truth content, and open to indefinite change and adaptation; the naturalistic approach to the church as a merely social, this-worldly institution; and the separation of dogma and church authority from reason, understood as merely scientific reason. The official reaction against Modernism led to severe repression in the church in the form of denunciations, censorship, firings, and excommunications that were orchestrated by a secret society. An Anti-Modernist Oath was imposed on all Catholic clergy and seminary professors in 1910 and not lifted until 1967. To those who saw the supernatural substance of the Christian faith being destroyed from within, the repression seemed justified. But its excesses turned Catholics against Catholics, suppressed the normal process of church reform, discouraged historical research on the Bible, and stifled theological creativity for the next generation.

For the most part, the Modernists began as reform-minded ecclesiastical scholars who had heeded Pope Leo XIII's call for the renewal of the intellectual life of Catholicism. They were responding to new philosophical, historical, and social developments and, in some cases, to the individualism and subjective nature of religious experience found in Liberal Protestantism. They raised and discussed a broad range of theological issues, such as the corporate, sacramental, and mysterious nature of the church; the role of the laity and governance within the church; the recognition of the changing and developing character of doctrine; the use of historical-critical methods in scriptural studies and church history; and the significance of experience and tradition in the pursuit of truth. Many of these concerns would be recognized and adopted in some form by subsequent popes, formulated in the documents of the Second Vatican Council, and integrated into the framework and discourse of mainstream, orthodox contemporary Catholic theology. The rest of this section will review movements and individuals that nevertheless breathed new life into Catholicism and paved the way for the Second Vatican Council.

Biblical Studies

Marie-Joseph Lagrange, O.P., a true godfather of modern Catholic biblical studies, had founded in 1890 the École Biblique in Jerusalem as a center for scientific study of the Bible in the setting in which it originated. Lagrange escaped being condemned during the anti-Modernist repression, and his institute is now in its second century as a research center open to members of all faiths. In 1943, Pope Pius XII's encyclical *Divino Afflante Spiritu* (Inspired by the Divine Spirit) gave a cautious endorsement to the full use of all means available (linguistic, archaeological, literary, and historical) to uncover the intended meaning of the canonical texts. This included, significantly, the necessity of recognizing the literary genre or "forms of expression" (*Divino Afflante Spiritu* §36) used by the inspired writers. This cautious endorsement was ratified in Vatican II's statement on divine revelation (*Dei Verbum* §12; see section on Vatican II below). Since that time, Catholic biblical scholars have felt free to practice the same critical and historical methods used by scholars of other faiths and none.

Maurice Blondel and the Philosophy of Action

Another figure from the century between the two Vatican councils who influenced the renewal of Catholic thought was the French Catholic philosopher of religion Maurice Blondel (1861–1949). In 1893, Blondel published his philosophical treatise *Action (1893): Essay on a Critique of Life and a Science of Practice.* It was immediately praised as an innovative and important work for its argument that the phenomenon of human action disclosed traces of God's presence within human beings and society. Blondel's book spoke to the confident dynamism of late nineteenth-century European civilization and to the need to reconnect the supernatural and the natural in a comprehensive Christian vision of the world. *Action,* and *The Letter on Apologetics* (1896) published three years later, thus rediscovered the Catholic synthesis between nature and grace, faith and reason, and theology and history that seemed to have become separated in modern experience. The two works raised the issue that if faith is supernatural, we need to rethink how its inaccessible essence is made accessible through the senses and reason, and recognized in actual human life.

During the height of the Modernist crisis, Blondel wrote a series of articles called *History and Dogma* (1904), in which he applied his new philosophy of action to the pressing problem of theology's relation to history. Although tradition certainly included history and Christian teachings, Blondel maintained that tradition could not be reduced to a mere collection of historical facts, teachings, and customs preserved from the past. Tradition was a dynamic, living reality with the power to conserve the past and illuminate the future. As a living reality, it is capable of adopting cultural and intellectual means from any period of time to express the truths of faith.

Blondel's fullest impact was delayed until the 1940s, and it was felt among the French theologians who laid the groundwork for Vatican II and wrote many of its most important documents. That influence led to his being called "the Philosopher of Vatican II."

The "New Theology" and Its Return to the Sources

The disasters of two world wars and the Great Depression forced all Christian theologians to think again about their most basic assumptions. Among Protestant Christians, great figures like Karl Barth (1886–1968) in Germany and Switzerland, and Reinhold Niebuhr (1892–1971) in America went back to the Bible and to Reformation theologians like Luther and Calvin. Among Catholics, French theologians such as the Jesuits Henri de Lubac (1896–1991) and Jean Daniélou (1905–1974), and the Dominicans M.-D. Chenu (1895–1990) and Yves Congar (1904–1995) sought theological renewal by a "return to the sources" (*ressourcement* in French) of Christian faith in scripture and tradition, especially the patristic writers of the early Church, who were thought to be more attuned to the symbolic and spiritual meanings of the Bible than their later medieval successors. Their efforts were opposed by Neo-Scholastic critics who called it "the new theology" (*nouvelle théologie*), which was not meant as a compliment. At the heart of the *nouvelle théologie* was the belief that God had created the human person for a supernatural end or purpose, and that this supernatural end was not something added or tacked onto human nature arbitrarily, from "outside" so to speak. Rather, it grew from within and was inseparable from the rest of the life of the human person. The purpose of theological reflection was to reconnect ordinary human life with the human person's relationship with God. There was thus a deeply practical and pastoral incentive in this theological movement, a wish to reinvigorate the actual life of the church as a whole, not just in the classroom.

In this way, the *nouvelle théologie* was a direct forerunner of the Second Vatican Council, and its leading figures played major roles a decade later in drafting key documents at the Council. Yves Congar wrote path-breaking works on the concept of reform (at a time when nervous Church authorities would only associate "reform" with the Protestant Reformation), on the nature of tradition, and on the place of the laity in the church. His Dominican colleague M.-D. Chenu specialized in the study of Thomas Aquinas. One of his chief accomplishments was an innovative study of Aquinas' *Summa Theologiae* that aroused strong opposition among Neo-Scholastic theologians by its insistence that Thomas must be read first of all in terms of the historical context in which he wrote if we are to appreciate properly his value for today. Chenu is credited with having urged the Council to take a positive stance toward the modern world, an influence shown above all in Vatican II's Pastoral Constitution on the Church in the Modern World (*Gaudium et Spes*; see below). Henri de Lubac published several of the most important works of twentieth-century Catholic theology. His book *Catholicism: A Study of the Corporate Destiny of Mankind* (1946; English translation 1950) stressed the social dimensions of Catholicism as a way of answering the criticism that Catholics were taught to care only about individual salvation and not about their place in the this-worldly destiny of the human race. His most controversial book was titled *Surnaturel* ("Supernatural"; 1946). *Surnaturel's* discussion of the theological concepts of nature and grace sought to bring together again an understanding of the "natural" and "supernatural" orders that de Lubac thought Neo-Scholasticism had artificially separated.

Transcendental Thomism and Theological Aesthetics

The first half of the twentieth century also saw Catholic intellectuals engage various modern philosophical insights, stemming especially from the philosophy of Immanuel Kant. This development has been called "Transcendental Thomism." The name describes Thomistic thinkers who were impressed with Kant's analysis of the conditions of the possibility for the mind to understand what was mediated by the senses. Kant argued that the mind had a creative or shaping power that made sense perception intelligible (see Chapter 22). His critical attention to the knowing subject seemed to these Thomists to be a valuable corrective to what they saw as Neo-Scholasticism's overconfidence about the mind's grasp of objective reality. Two of the most creative twentieth-century Catholic theologians came out of this development. The Canadian Jesuit Bernard Lonergan (1904–1984) wrote a brilliant philosophical treatise called *Insight* (1957), which used the experience of understanding something to ground Thomistic metaphysics. His book *Method in Theology* (1972) was an ambitious proposal for reorganizing theological research to fit modern cognitional theory (how we know things). The German Jesuit Karl Rahner (1904–1984), perhaps the dominant Catholic theologian of the twentieth century, also adapted ideas of philosopher Martin Heidegger to portray the human person in his or her concrete existence as already under the action of God's grace, based on God's universal saving will (1 Timothy 2:4) (see Chapter 22).

Another important figure in Catholic theology during the first half of the twentieth century leading up to the Second Vatican Council was the Swiss theologian Hans Urs von Balthasar (1905–1988). Balthasar was prolific and the body of work he produced draws on and considers much of Western intellectual history from classical antiquity to contemporary European literature. His impact has been felt especially since the pontificate of Pope John Paul II (r. 1978–2005), in part because his theology seemed more respectful of the particularities of God's revelation to the world than had Rahner, whom some have criticized for appearing to dilute revelation. Perhaps the most fertile theological trend that Balthasar initiated has to do with the recovery of theological reflection on beauty. In his theological aesthetics, Balthasar suggested that while theology is always in pursuit of "truth" as it seeks to comprehend God's revelation to the world and the "good" as it discerns how to live in light of that revelation, modern theology must also attend to the encounter between God and the created world as it comes to expression through the category of "beauty."

Liturgical Renewal

A final important precursor to the Council involved research and reflection on Catholic worship. The renewal of the liturgy began already in the nineteenth century, when French Benedictines sought to recover medieval musical traditions as part of the monastic revival after the French Revolution. In the early twentieth century, the movement was centered in Benedictine monasteries in Germany, from where it was exported to the U.S.A., especially to St. John's Abbey in Minnesota. Liturgical renewal envisioned reforming the worship experience not just for monks but for ordinary laypeople as well. Advocates for renewal were most concerned about the Mass, which they thought was no longer at the center of Catholics' spiritual lives. It seemed to have become the exclusive business of the priest, who "said" the Mass in Latin, a language which people could no longer understand. During the course of the centuries, additional prayers and ceremonies had obscured the collective meaning that the Mass had once possessed when the liturgy was more truly "the work of the people," which is what "liturgy" literally means in Greek. If the overlays were peeled away—rather like restoring a painting to its original brilliant colors—perhaps a simplified and more understandable liturgy would remind Catholics that they were not just random individuals who happened to be in church to fulfill their individual Sunday obligation, but an actual community and the very body of Christ: Christ's body was not only the consecrated Eucharistic bread but the community constituted by their reception of the Eucharist. Recovering the sense of belonging to a community that was Christ's body in the world might also carry over to daily life outside the church, in a world that was becoming ever more secular. Liturgical reform was therefore not just about worship but about the way in which what was believed and expressed in worship was lived out as well. With these goals in mind, liturgical scholars labored over ancient and medieval texts in an effort to recover and return to what they thought were older and more authentic forms of worship than what had marked Catholic life in more recent centuries.

THE SECOND VATICAN COUNCIL

Pope John's Agenda

Within 100 days of taking office after the death of Pope Pius XII, Pope John XXIII (r. 1958–1963) surprised the Roman Catholic world by announcing his intention to convoke an Ecumenical Council and, as Bishop of Rome, a synod in Rome. His announcement came on January 25, 1959, the feast of the Conversion of St. Paul and the last Sunday of the Week of Prayer for Christian Unity, a fitting date, since the restoration of Christian unity would become one of the goals of the new council.

Figure 24–2 Pope John XXIII (1881–1963).

Three years later, in his opening address to the Council Fathers (so called because they were all ordained clergy), John gave them freedom to proceed but added some directions. The Pope encouraged the participants to employ "the methods of research and … the literary forms of modern thought," saying, "The substance of the ancient doctrine of the deposit of faith is one thing, and the way in which it is presented is another" (Abbott 1966, 715). The term *aggiornamento* ("renewal") was coined to describe the updating that Pope John encouraged in this opening address. He recommended "the medicine of mercy rather than that of severity. She [the Church] considers that she meets the needs of the present day by demonstrating the validity of her teaching rather than by condemnations" (Abbott 1966, 716). He also encouraged the council to consider the Roman Catholic Church's relationships with other Christians and with the followers of other world religions. His vision was of a "pastoral" council that would be ecumenical and would foster a spiritual renewal in the church. Those who expected doctrinal formulations such as were adopted at Trent or Vatican I were destined to be disappointed.

The bishops who received the Pope's invitation were not of one mind about what to expect from the new council. But there were many who shared his commitment to renewal and who proved it by rejecting the first draft they were sent of a document on the nature of the church itself. Bishop de Smedt of Bruges (Belgium) spoke for many when he said that the church could not let itself be reduced to the clergy and the hierarchy alone, nor could it limit itself to a merely juridical (legal) understanding of the church. The bishops voted to return the document to a reorganized drafting commission that was asked to prepare something more consistent with the *aggiornamento* for which Pope John had called the Council. By the time the Council closed on December 8, 1965, 16 documents had been accepted, now known collectively as "the Documents of Vatican II." This section of Chapter 24 reviews the four major documents called "Constitutions" and two short Declarations. In addition, ten Decrees on various subjects such as religious life, priestly life, the reunion of separated Christian churches, and Eastern Catholic churches were also adopted.

An Ecumenical Council

Vatican II is, according to Roman Catholic understanding, the 21st Ecumenical Council. The Eastern Orthodox Churches object to the term "Ecumenical," since they hold that only the first seven councils of the undivided Church are truly ecumenical (see Chapter 11). From their perspective, Vatican II looks more like a General Council of the Western Church. However, if ecumenical is understood in terms of the entire world, which is the meaning of the Greek word *oikumene*, from which "ecumenical" derives, then Vatican II was more genuinely ecumenical than any previous council of the universal church. Eighty percent of those eligible to participate in the Council did so. For the first time in history, there were participants from all five continents. At any one time during the four sessions of the Council, there were over 2,000 bishops in attendance, approximately ten times the number of participants at the Council of Trent and three times the number at Vatican I. Despite its multicultural attendance, the Council and its documents were still heavily influenced by theologians from the North Atlantic nations, though those from the Global South (especially of course heavily Catholic Latin America) were not silent at the Council.

Vatican II was also ecumenical in the sense of the twentieth-century movement for Christian reunion. Previously, the popes had resisted all invitations to join the movement, because of the Catholic conviction of being the one true Church of Jesus Christ, in comparison with which other Christians were either schismatic (separated) or heretical. There was understandable skepticism, then, when the Catholic Church invited Protestant and Orthodox observers to come to the Council. The ice began to thaw when Rome sent Official Observers to the New Delhi Assembly of the World Council of Churches in 1961. Once it became clear that Pope John did not conceive Vatican II simply as a reunion or "come home to Rome" council, acceptances began to flow in. In the end, among Protestants, only the Baptist World Federation declined to attend. By the end of the Council, about 186 Official Observers

Figure 24–3 The Second Vatican Council. St. Peter's Basilica, Rome.

had attended many, if not all the sessions and formed a real presence, though without voting privileges. At the Council, they were no longer called schismatics and heretics but welcomed as "separated brethren [*sic*]," a term they accepted as a modest improvement over the traditional hostile language. During the Council, the Observers met weekly with representatives from the Secretariat for Promoting Christian Unity. With this precedent, the Catholic Church made clear its readiness to become involved in a movement it had resisted, at least officially, for over 50 years. To those used to the ecumenical climate since Vatican II, it can be hard to appreciate what a change in mentality this entailed: the beginning of the closing of a distance that seemed unbridgeable.

The Four Constitutions of Vatican II

Constitution on the Sacred Liturgy—Sacrosanctum Concilium (December 4, 1963)

The pre-conciliar liturgical and biblical renewal movements bore fruit in the first document promulgated by the Council, **Sacrosanctum Concilium**. The document expressed the renewal movement's goal to return the liturgy to the center of the prayer life of the church. The phrase "active participation" of the laity in the liturgy became a refrain of the Constitution, which says, "Such participation by the Christian people as 'a chosen race, a royal priesthood, a holy nation, a redeemed people' (1 Peter 2:9; cf. 2:4–5), is their right and duty by reason of their baptism" (§14). This conscious and active participation, it was hoped, would restore the Eucharist to the center of a Catholic's life and make liturgy once more the "work of the people," which is what "liturgy" means in Greek. More private devotions were gently de-emphasized in favor of participation (§§13, 27). In addition, it was hoped liturgical reform would renew not just the internal life of the church but also Catholics' life in the world. Because Catholics had long been taught that the faith never changed, the constitution took care to note that elements of the liturgy that were not divinely insti-tuted were subject to change—and "not only could but ought to be changed," if they became less functional and their core meanings less clear (§21). At the same time, the constitution insisted on careful and authorized change that grew "organically from forms already existing" (§23). Most importantly, the partial use of the ver-nacular or spoken language of the people was permitted in place of the traditional Latin (§§36,63). The promulgation of *Sacrosanctum Concilium* encouraged a new gen-eration of artists from around the world to develop sacred music, church furnishings, sacred art and architecture that would facilitate greater participation in the Eucharist.

Lived Religion: Liturgy after Vatican II: Architecture, Church Design

The Second Vatican Council called for dramatic changes to worship in the document *Sacrosanctum Concilium*. While most people welcomed these changes, they were not universally accepted. Alterations often took place very quickly, and worship spaces that had stood for years, even centuries, now looked very different.

Parishes faced challenges because of the architectural changes mandated by the Council. Most churches had a beautiful altar built into the far wall of the sanctuary, which was replaced by a freestanding altar so the priest could face the people. Before, flowers and candlesticks could be placed on the altar. After the changes, those things could be next to the altar but not on it, the table being reserved only for consecrating the Eucharist. Small, side altars dedicated to Mary and the saints were also removed so there would be only one altar in the church, not several.

Other liturgical centers also received greater attention. Churches had a pulpit for preaching and a chair for the presider, but now the chair had to be "clearly visible" to everyone to emphasize that the priest is the leader of worship "for the whole community." Small baptismal fonts were replaced by a font large enough for adults to stand in, situated where everyone could participate by witness and prayer.

Perhaps the biggest changes were in the body of the church where the community gathers. To allow more people to be close to the altar, the pulpit, the font, and the presider, pews were replaced by movable chairs. This increased participation in prayer, responses, and singing. Altar rails, which separated the sanctuary from the community, were often removed. Liturgy was understood as something the priest does with the people, not for the people, and God's house was seen as the house of the people of God.

Dogmatic Constitution on the Church—Lumen Gentium (November 21, 1964)

Lumen Gentium (Light of Nations), the second Constitution promulgated at the Council, deals explicitly with the Church *ad intra*, in its inner life and understanding. It presents the Church as a "mystery," in the sense that the Church's reality cannot be fully expressed in human language and categories. By virtue of her connection with Christ, who is the Light of Nations, the Church is said to be "a kind of sacrament or sign of intimate union with God, and of the unity of all mankind" (§1). Since in Catholic understanding a sacrament is a sign that not only signifies but also causes what it signifies, that is a powerful mission statement.

Figure 24–4 The Roman Catholic Cathedral of Christ the King, Liverpool, UK. Note the centrally located altar and circular seating arrangement.

Lumen Gentium was intended to go beyond the traditional doctrine of the Church as "a perfect hierarchical society," which stressed the Church's institutional and clerical aspects, by building on pre-conciliar ideas of the Church as the "mystical body of Christ," to quote the title of Pope Pius XII's 1943 encyclical letter. *Lumen Gentium* highlighted the biblical and patristic idea of the Church as "the people of God" on pilgrimage through time. The "people of God" formulation stressed continuity with biblical Israel, recognized the essential place of the laity (which means "people" in Greek) in addition to the clergy, and seemed more open to dialogue with other Christians. The hierarchy of ordained clergy was said to have the special function of administering the sacraments, preserving the teaching of the apostles, and maintaining church discipline. Vatican I's assertion of the pope's primacy and infallibility was repeated (see especially §25). But *Lumen Gentium* completed unfinished business from Vatican I by asserting the "collegiality" of the bishops, who were not simply deputies or delegates of the pope, and who constituted a "college" with the pope as their head (§22). In embracing the notion of the Church as the people of God, Vatican II was actually returning to a more ancient conception of the Church and correcting exaggerated interpretations of Vatican I, which made it seem that the Holy Spirit spoke to the church only through the pope, who then told the rest of the Church what to believe. In fact, the Holy Spirit speaks through all the members of the Church.

That is made clear in a section devoted specifically to the laity (§§30–38). *Lumen Gentium* called lay men and women the Church's presence in the world: "A secular quality is proper and special to laypeople ... they can work for the sanctification of the world from within, in the manner of leaven" (§31). The document also asserted that, among laity and clergy, there was "no inequality" and "an equal privilege of faith," even though there were different roles and responsibilities (§32).

Lumen Gentium was careful in describing the Catholic Church's relationship to those outside the Church. It affirmed that: "the one Church of Christ ... subsists in the Catholic Church ... though many elements of sanctification and of truth can be found outside of her visible structure" (§8). It insisted on the Church's unique status as the means of salvation, while recognizing degrees of incorporation in the society of the Church (§14). It carefully described the relative standing of classes of outsiders, from Eastern Orthodox to Protestants to Jews to Muslims and even to those "who through no fault of their own do not know the gospel of Christ or of his Church" (§16; see Chapter 28).

Dogmatic Constitution on Divine Revelation—Dei Verbum (November 18, 1965)

Unlike the Council Fathers at Vatican I, the Council Fathers at Vatican II had the benefit of historical, biblical, and liturgical studies of the inter-conciliar period to assist them in writing the *Constitution on Divine Revelation*. The Protestant Reformation had set scripture over against tradition, saying that only scripture was a source of revelation. The Catholic tradition has tended to treat scripture and tradition as separate sources of revelation without officially defining them that way. Vatican II stated that scripture and tradition were intrinsically and mutually related and could not be separated one from the other:

> For both of them [scripture and tradition], flowing from the same divine wellspring, in a certain way merge into a unity and tend toward the same end ... Therefore both sacred tradition and sacred scripture are to be accepted and venerated with the same sense of loyalty and reverence.
>
> (§9)

Dei Verbum recognized that, while revelation cannot change, there is a "growth in the understanding of the realities that have been handed down," and that tradition therefore "develops in the Church with the help of the Holy Spirit" (§8). This emphasis on development and movement toward the fullness of divine truth was something new. The authors of the books of scripture were inspired by God, who used them "as true authors," so that they can be said to have written "without error that truth which God wanted put in the sacred writings for the sake of our salvation" (§11). Since the writers were true authors, they spoke in the language of their times, and *Dei Verbum* recognized that, to find out their intended meaning, regard for literary forms was necessary (§12). Deciding the authentic interpretation was ultimately the responsibility of "the living teaching office of the Church" (§10).

Dei Verbum encouraged "easy access to Sacred Scripture ... for all the Christian faithful," as well as ecumenical translations of the Bible. It especially recommended a more central place for scripture in the liturgy and in preaching, and in the study of theology itself (§§22–25).

Pastoral Constitution on the Church in the Modern World—Gaudium et Spes (December 7, 1965)

The opening words of **Gaudium et Spes** expressed not just the substance of this particular constitution but in a special way Pope John's intention for the Council as a whole:

> The joys and the hopes, the griefs and the anxieties of the men [*sic*] of this age, especially those who are poor or in any way afflicted, these are the joys and hopes, the griefs and anxieties of the followers of Christ. Indeed, nothing genuinely human fails to raise an echo in their hearts.

(§1)

Whereas documents regarding the Church *ad intra* (regarding its interior life as Church) had dominated the work of the Council's preparatory commission, this document, with its emphasis upon the Church *ad extra* (in relation to the world at large), had not received such attention. In a special way, *Gaudium et Spes* was thus a child of the Council itself. It spoke with unprecedented directness to all of humanity.

Gaudium et Spes was unique in other ways as well. Until the third session of the Council, Vatican II was a male-dominated session. The only women present were the wives of the Observers and the female cleaning staff. Thanks to interventions by both Cardinal Leo Suenens of Belgium and the Melkite priest (an Eastern Catholic church in the Middle East; see Chapter 11) Msgr. George Hakim, women were invited to attend the third and fourth sessions of the Council as auditors. Six of these women were assigned to various drafting sub-commissions of *Gaudium et Spes*: Dr. Pilar Bellosillo, Rosemary Goldie, Sr. Mary Luke Tobin, Suzanne Guillemin, Rie Vendrik, and Marie-Louise Monnet. Of these, Bellosillo, Goldie, and Tobin became part of the inner circle of drafters of *Gaudium et Spes*. Because they led international organizations of lay people, Pilar Bellosillo observed that they had a better understanding of both the world Church and the Church in the world than the bishops did at the time.

If active participation is a refrain in *Sacrosanctum Concilium*, then dialogue is a refrain in *Gaudium et Spes*. The people of God were encouraged to dialogue with atheists (§21), with those who think differently than we do (§28), with the world (§40), and with people of all shades of opinion (§43). They were also encouraged to foster dialogue between groups and nations (§56) and dialogue within the Church itself between the clergy and laity (§92). There is a marked rhetorical and substantive contrast with the hostile and oppositional language of official documents from the preconciliar period.

Gaudium et Spes stands in a trajectory of Catholic Social Teaching that began with Pope Leo XIII's encyclical letter *Rerum Novarum* (1891), on industrialization and its resulting class tensions, and had most recently been addressed by Pope John himself in his encyclicals *Mater et Magistra* (1961) and *Pacem in Terris* (1963), the first on the inequities caused by economic development, and the second on the international tensions of the Cold War. *Gaudium et Spes* sought seriously to "[scrutinize] the signs of the times and interpret them in the light of the Gospel" (§4), and did so especially in its second half, with detailed teaching on the family, on the civil order, on economics, on culture, and on international relations and war, especially nuclear war. The document repeated the teaching of recent popes in condemning "total war" and in particular the obliteration bombing of entire cities (§80), a tactic that, as all knew, had been practiced by the victorious Allies in World War II. The "so-called balance" underlying the strategy of nuclear deterrence was regarded with skepticism as a way of avoiding a nuclear holocaust (§81). The economist Barbara Ward (Lady Jackson) had been invited to speak to the Council on these issues. Her invitation was revoked, however, on the grounds that it was "premature" for a woman to address the Council. James Norris, one of the male auditors addressed the Council in her stead. Themes from his impassioned address regarding poverty, hunger, and global economic disparities were taken up by the bishops (see §§63–72, 83–90). Many of the Council Fathers, especially those from the Global South, wanted *Gaudium et Spes* to go much further than it did on these issues.

The lay auditors had also chosen Pilar Bellosillo to speak on their behalf in the Council regarding the role of the laity in the draft document. She was eminently qualified to do so especially because of her work on the draft, but she too was forbidden to speak and once again a male auditor spoke in her place. Professor Juan Vasquez, her proxy, memorably declared that the laity were the church and were also the world. Despite disappointments to some, *Gaudium et Spes* did provide inspiration after the Council for a multitude of "contextualized" theologies that would develop around the globe in its wake (see Chapter 27).

As a "pastoral" constitution, *Gaudium et Spes*, of all the sixteen documents, best reflected Pope John's vision for his pastoral council. This doesn't mean that it was not also a "teaching" document, but it was one that sought to teach in a pastoral way. *Gaudium et Spes* said its goal was "to explain to everyone how it conceives of the presence and activity of the Church in the world of today" (§2). It was the special role of lay people to carry out that work by penetrating the world with a Christian spirit, a world that was increasingly secular (§43).

Decrees and Declarations

Decree on Ecumenism (November 21, 1964), Declaration on the Relation of the Church to Non-Christian Religions (October 28, 1965), Declaration on Religious Freedom (December 7, 1965).

Three other documents need brief mention. The *Decree on Ecumenism*, the *Declaration on the Relation of the Church to Non-Christian Religions (**Nostra Aetate**)* and the *Declaration on Religious Freedom (**Dignitatis Humanae**)* were all written by the Secretariat for

Promoting Christian Unity (SPCU), a special body created by Pope John that reported directly to him. Its original mandate was "the promotion of Christian Unity." But it became clear during the Council that its autonomy could assist the Council in the writing of the short but controversial declarations *Nostra Aetate* and *Dignitatis Humanae*. The *Decree on Ecumenism* benefited from the contributions of the Observers and weekly meetings with the SPCU. The concept of an "ecclesiology of communion" between separated churches enabled the Roman Catholic Church to accept that there were *degrees* of communion in the relationships of different Christian communions, one to the other.

Nostra Aetate, the *Declaration on Non-Christian Religions*, began as an appendix to the *Decree on Ecumenism* dealing with Judaism and then became a separate declaration that addressed the Church's relationship not only with Judaism but with the world's other great religions, Hinduism, Buddhism, Islam, and Judaism (though references to indigenous religions are noticeably absent; see Chapter 27). In *Nostra Aetate*, the Council declared that:

> The Catholic Church rejects nothing that is true and holy in these religions. She regards with sincere reverence those ways of conduct and of life, those precepts and teachings which, though differing in many aspects from the ones she holds and sets forth, nonetheless often reflect a ray of that Truth which enlightens all men.
>
> (*Nostra Aetate* §2)

And in an attempt to overcome the contempt and denigration of Jews and Judaism that was commonly taught by Catholics, Protestants, and Orthodox Christians alike, the declaration stated unequivocally that "what happened in [Jesus'] passion cannot be charged against all the Jews, without distinction, then alive, nor against the Jews of today" (§4). This ended the teaching that the Jews were a cursed people whose historic sufferings were an inherited divine punishment for the death of Jesus. The declaration condemned "hatred, persecutions, displays of anti-Semitism, directed against Jews at any time and by anyone" (§4).

Dignitatis Humanae (Of Human Dignity), or the *Declaration on Religious Freedom*, began as a chapter in *Gaudium et Spes* and then developed into a separate declaration. It was the most bitterly contested of all the documents of the Council because it represented a dramatic shift in the Church's teaching on the civil order in relation to the Church. The declaration said that immunity from coercion in religious matters was a human and therefore a civil right (§2). Prior to the Council, the Church had maintained that the State had a positive duty to favor the Catholic Church because of its claim to be the one Church of Christ. Without retracting such a claim, the declaration announced it intended "to develop the doctrine of recent popes on the inviolable rights of the human person and on the constitutional order of society" (§1). The contrast, though, between the embrace of the right of religious freedom and the teaching, for example, of Pope Pius IX in the 1864 *Syllabus of Errors* (see From the French Revolution to Vatican I above), helps explain the resistance to the declaration. Its eventual acceptance freed the church from the charge that it expected religious freedom for itself when it was in a minority situation, but could deny it to others when it was the majority. The declaration was also a vindication of the work on religious freedom by the American Catholic theologian John Courtney Murray prior to the Council (see Chapter 23).

THE RECEPTION OF VATICAN II

Vatican II and post-Vatican II Overlap

Although the council ended over 50 years ago, the Catholic Church is still involved with understanding and incorporating it. Theologians call this ongoing process the **reception** of an ecumenical council. Vatican II's reception will continue for many more decades to come. It took the Council of Trent more than a century to have its full worldwide impact. Vatican II is the equivalent of the Council of Trent for the Catholic Church in dealing with modernity and post-modernity.

The major difference between the reception of Trent and the reception of Vatican II is the "global turn" of Catholicism. Vatican II took the Catholic Church's understanding of its universality to a deeper theological level. The Council's reception takes place in a Catholic Church that is no longer dominated culturally and theologically by its Euro-Mediterranean center. Vatican II thus offers an interesting and complex mix of trends: together with the globalization of Catholicism, the Council's reception is marked by a papacy that is much more visible than before on the global scene and within the Catholic Church. The reception of Vatican II is thus also a top-down process, a push coming from the papacy to implement Vatican II in the local churches.

"Reception" actually began even before the end of the Council on December 8, 1965. The constitution *Sacrosanctum Concilium* authorized a worldwide liturgical reform beginning with the new church year of 1964, while the Council was still underway. The liturgical reform was thus in a real sense also the beginning of the post-Vatican II period. It became the key to understanding the Council as a whole, and the gate through which the rest of the Council's reforms would go.

Institutional Reform and Cultural Changes

The years right after the Council showed immediately how difficult its reception would be. The Council had dealt not only with reform inside the church, but also with the church's response to huge changes in society and culture. The first dramatic test was Pope Paul VI's 1968 encyclical *Humanae Vitae* (Of Human Life, July 25, 1968). It repeated, with only minor changes but in the footsteps of the constitution *Gaudium et Spes* (1965), the teaching of Pope Pius XI's encyclical 1930 *Casti Connubii* (On Christian Marriage) against artificial contraception. For the church as an institution, this led to the most serious crisis of the authority of church teaching in modern times. Widespread and unprecedented public protest revealed how difficult it would be for Catholicism to cope with secularization, individualization, and the impact of the modern economy on family life. Advances in medical science, along with the need of the modern state to legislate on all aspects and moments of human life—a complex of trends sometimes called "biopolitics"—were changing the conditions of married life, at least in the Western world, much more than the Council fathers and their theological advisers could have imagined just a few years before.

These changes affected especially the Catholic churches of Europe and North America. In the rest of the world, the reception of Vatican II took the shape of a revitalization of local churches and local theological traditions, starting most dramatically with Latin America, where the 1968 meeting of the Conference of Latin American Bishops (CELAM, from the Spanish acronym) in Medellín, Columbia, marked a movement away from the clerical leadership's historic alliance with the social and economic elite, toward identification with the poor and the marginalized. The theology of liberation is rooted in that shift (see Chapter 27). Much of the theological interpretation of Vatican II could be called "liberationist": feminist theology (especially in North America and Europe); a new approach to the issue of race and of racism (especially in the Americas and Africa); the theology of religions for interreligious dialogue (especially in Asia); and a new consciousness of the relevance for Christians of concerns for world peace and for the environment (see Chapters 26, 27, and 28). All these post-conciliar theological streams are rooted in the Council, but even more in the post-Vatican II appropriation of the Council's call to dialogue with the modern world. The push came not only from the local churches, but also from the papacy. Paul VI's exhortation *Evangelii Nuntiandi* (On the Proclamation of the Gospel), published on December 8, 1975 following the 1974 Bishops' Synod held in the Vatican in 1974 on evangelization of the modern world, does not talk directly about theological **inculturation** of the Christian message, but the interaction of the church with modern culture and local cultures is at the center of the document— Pope Francis would later say that, for him, it was the most important pastoral document ever written.

Reception and Rejection of Vatican II

The reception of Vatican II has also meant in some quarters a rejection of the Council. The most famous Catholic group to denounce Vatican II as heretical is the Society of St. Pius X (SSPX), founded in 1970 by French Archbishop Marcel Lefebvre (1905–1991). (Lefebvre had been one of the 70 Council fathers—representing about 3 percent of the total—who voted against the *Declaration on Religious Freedom* on December 7, 1965. His later rejection of the Council was not a great surprise.) In 1988, his consecration of four priests in his society as bishops incurred his automatic excommunication. The schism of Marcel Lefebvre and of the SSPX shows the firm resolve of Paul VI in defending the reforms of Vatican II, beginning with the liturgical reform.

John Paul II: Global Papacy and Vatican II

A different way of defending Vatican II came to the papacy with the election in 1978 of John Paul II, Karol Wojtyła from then Communist-ruled Poland—the first non-Italian pope since the Dutch Adrian VI (r. 1522–1523). John Paul II saw clearly a need to reassess the legacy of Vatican II, and to do it from the perspective of the Vatican itself as the center of Catholicism. During the course of one of the longest pontificates in the history of the Catholic Church (1978–2005), he sought through many acts and documents, and the projection of his own charismatic personality on countless trips, to counteract the decentralizing impact of the Council, which to many seemed to fragment Catholicism's global unity. Key developments included: the new *Code of Canon Law* (1983), the Extraordinary Bishops' Synod of 1985 on the celebration, verification, and promotion of Vatican II; and the *Catechism of the Catholic Church* (1992). In 1989, the Congregation for the Doctrine of the Faith issued a new profession of faith and in 1998 John Paul II issued a *motu proprio* (a personal edict of the pope) in order "to protect the faith of the Catholic Church against errors arising from certain members of the Christian faithful, especially from among those dedicated to the various disciplines of sacred theology." The letter to the bishops about the "ecclesiology of communion" (*Communionis Notio*, May 28, 1992), and the "declaration on the unicity and salvific universality of Jesus Christ and the Church" about the relationship between Christ, the Church, and the non-Christian religions (*Dominus Iesus*, August 6, 2000; see Chapter 28) marked two other important steps in the Roman reception of Vatican II. The apostolic constitution *Apostolos Suos* (May 21, 1998), on the status and authority of episcopal conferences, reinforced the view of Cardinal Joseph Ratzinger, chair of the International Theological Commission and the future Pope Benedict XVI, of the need to scale back some aspects of the post-Vatican II decentralization and empowerment of national bishops' conferences.

In other acts consistent with this protective posture, John Paul II strengthened the traditional doctrine on priestly celibacy, ruled against the ordination of women, and warned against the theology of liberation in Latin America. On the other hand, John Paul II clearly innovated on some traditional issues because of his interpretation of Vatican II: a much stronger emphasis on the role of lay people in the church, on the role of families in the church, and on the theology of love and sexuality in marriage. John Paul II accelerated the Catholic Church's engagement in the ecumenical movement, and in a sense changed the ecumenical movement by putting the Catholic Church into the center of it, thanks to the global visibility of the papacy. His forceful projection of the papacy showed that religion was not going to be dismissed easily in a post-Communist world, as some European scholars of religion and theorists of secularization had speculated in the early 1970s. From John Paul II's visit to Mainz in Germany in 1980, to the encyclical *Ut Unum Sint* (That They May Be One) of 1995, to the *Joint Declaration on the Doctrine of Justification* with the Lutheran World Federation in 1999, the ecumenical engagement of the Catholic Church was built by John Paul II on the foundations of Vatican II, but also on a much stronger papacy. The role of the papacy was evident also in interreligious dialogue, ever more important in the world of the "comeback of God" in international affairs: from John Paul II's meeting with Muslim youth in Casablanca (Morocco) in 1985, to the first visit of a pope to the Jewish synagogue of Rome in 1986, to the visit to Syria in 2001, the Catholic Church of John Paul II became a key international actor for dialogue and peace among religions and for religious liberty. John Paul II saw, before many others, the need for this, as he demonstrated in 1986 when (over much internal opposition) he invited the world's religious leaders to gather in Assisi to pray together for world peace.

Benedict XVI's Reassessment of the Interpretation of Vatican II

The terrorist attacks of September 11, 2001, and the rise of international terrorism had an impact on the Catholic Church's reception of Vatican II. On the one hand, they made even clearer the necessity and the prophetic nature of Vatican II's teachings on ecumenism, on religious liberty and freedom of conscience, and on interreligious dialogue. On the other hand, the tensions within Islam that underlay the rise of terrorism gave some in the church reasons to reconsider critically Vatican II's promotion of dialogue as too naive and making the church vulnerable to those who would take advantage of it. In this sense, the election of Benedict XVI on April 19, 2005 was a continuation of some of the theological trajectories of John Paul II about Vatican II, but with a more cautious approach to ecumenism, interreligious dialogue, and dialogue with the modern world. One example was the Regensburg speech of September 12, 2006, which revealed Benedict XVI's understanding of the relationship of the Catholic Church with its Greek and European heritage. Benedict encouraged a growing re-Europeanization of the church by retreating somewhat from the theology of Vatican II as a Council of the global Catholic Church, especially of the non-European churches. The most important of Benedict XVI's statements on Vatican II was the speech of December 22, 2005, on the "two hermeneutics" of the Council, meaning two different ways in which the Council should be understood and received. He warned that a hermeneutic of "discontinuity and rupture" with tradition before the Council had to be countered with a hermeneutic of "continuity and reform." This speech should be interpreted in the context of Benedict XVI's major decisions concerning Vatican II. A Vatican document (released June 29, 2007) on the doctrine of the church in Vatican II's constitution *Lumen Gentium* tightened interpretation of a key passage in *Lumen Gentium* about the relationship between the Catholic Church and the true Church of Jesus Christ (according to *Lumen Gentium* §8, the true Church of Jesus Christ "subsists in" the Catholic Church). Benedict authorized freer use of the old, "Tridentine" (from the Council of Trent) rite of Mass in July 2007. And he opened a door to reconciliation with the schismatic Society of St. Pius X in January 2009. In his own way, Benedict XVI was a critical defender of Vatican II against what he saw as deviations from the texts and the intentions of the Council. But he was also capable of going beyond the texts and the intention of Vatican II in the most important decision of his pontificate: his dramatic decision to resign from the papal office (the first such resignation in six centuries), announced on February 11, 2013, and effective on February 28.

Pope Francis: Vatican II from the South of the World

The pontificate of Pope Francis means for the Catholic Church the first pope who was not at Vatican II. The Jesuit Jorge Mario Bergoglio was ordained a priest in 1969, in the first years of the Council's reception, in Argentina—hence also the first pope from the southern hemisphere.

From the very beginning of his pontificate, Francis showed a firm acceptance and reception of Vatican II in its core legacy: liturgy, ecclesiology, ecumenism, interreligious dialogue, and dialogue with the modern and secularized world. In the words addressed to the people in Saint Peter's Square after his election on March 13, 2013, Francis presented himself as the "bishop of Rome," thus stressing his bond with the local church. Meeting with journalists three days later, recalling words put to him by

Brazilian cardinal Claudio Hummes, Francis claimed to want "a poor Church and for the poor." His inaugural Mass on March 19 marked a visible difference in liturgical style from that of his predecessor: at the celebration was present, for the first time, the Ecumenical Patriarch Bartholomew of Constantinople, whom Francis would later meet several times during his pontificate. The following day, after hearing from the fraternal delegates from other churches and religions, Francis mentioned the Second Vatican Council for the first time, and in particular the declaration *Nostra Aetate* (1965) on non-Christian religions. His decision, just six months into his pontificate, to call a Bishops' Synod on the theme of family and marriage for 2014 and 2015, as well as his decision to celebrate the Extraordinary Jubilee of Mercy in 2016 (a "jubilee year" in Catholic terms is recognized every 25 years; Francis highlighted its import-ance by breaking that normal cycle), was intended to rediscover the courage of the church to go forth into the world, following the intention of Pope John XXIII when he first called Vatican II.

The words, symbols, and acts of the 2013 conclave and of the beginning of Francis' pontificate were clearly an echo of the 1958 conclave and of the beginning of John XXIII's pontificate. Francis' election has thus changed the landscape of the church and especially of the debate on Vatican II. Francis only infrequently mentions the Council by name. That does not mean a devaluing of the Council, but rather a recognition that Vatican II can now be taken for granted, that there is no nostalgic going back to the pre-Vatican II period. Ecumenism, interreligious dialogue, an understanding of the church "that goes forth," a Church of mercy and for the poor—these are all the theology of Vatican II in act.

Part of the reception process of Vatican II during Pope Francis' pontificate has been the re-opening of the sexual abuse crisis in the Catholic Church. Under Francis, the crisis has also become a global Catholic crisis in how Catholics perceive the Vatican itself. The abuse crisis has also revealed the pressure on an ecclesiological model that in the post-Vatican II period frustrated the theological role of the local and national levels of the Church. Francis' action on the sex abuse crisis has been a mix of necessary central impulses from the Vatican and of a new opening of spaces for collegiality and the conciliar and collective character of the Church. Such a mix reflects not only Francis' own ecclesiology, but also a wider awareness of the need for better coordination between the universal-central level and the local level in Roman Catholicism.

Francis' typical contribution to the reception of Vatican II is the perspective of a Latin American bishop who is more worried for the huge social and economic issues affecting the poor in the South of the world than with the "biopolitical" issues that seem to preoccupy the northern hemisphere. Vatican II took place more than 50 years ago. It was the Council of a Church that was still very European, with non-European churches still largely led by a European missionary episcopate. The church of today is more genuinely global, and Francis is its embodiment.

Key Terms

aggiornamento	inculturation	papal infallibility
Dei Verbum	*Lumen Gentium*	reception
Dignitatis Humanae	Modernism	*ressourcement*
First Vatican Council	Neo-Scholasticism	*Sacrosanctum Concilium*
Gaudium et Spes	*Nostra Aetate*	ultramontanism

Study Questions

1. When was the First Vatican Council called and what was its purpose? What was its most important teaching, and how was it to be understood?

2. Explain how the Modernist movement attempted to respond to what were seen as inadequate features of Neo-Scholasticism.

3. The Second Vatican Council was preceded by several renewal movements in Catholic theology. Did they have features in common or do they seem completely unrelated?

4. When was the Second Vatican Council called, and what were its purposes? Explain arguments for and against its "ecumenical" status.

5. What was a main goal of the reform of the liturgy in the constitution *Sacrosanctum Concilium?*

6. According to the constitution *Dei Verbum,* does the revelation of God change? Explain your answer.

7. How did the constitution *Lumen Gentium* try to compensate for an overemphasis on the clerical and hierarchical order of the Catholic Church?

8. How did the constitution *Gaudium et Spes* try to deal with the reality of secularization?

9. How did the teaching on the Jews in *Nostra Aetate* and the teaching on religious freedom represent changes in church teaching?

10. Discuss different ways in which Pope John Paul II's reception of Vatican II counterbalanced the decentralizing thrust of the council's doctrine.

11. How did Pope Benedict XVI's pontificate represent a cautionary approach to Vatican II's reception?

12. What may be Pope Francis' most typical contribution to the reception of Vatican II?

Bibliography and Recommended Reading

Abbott, Walter M., ed. 1966. *The Documents of Vatican II.* New York: Guild Press.

Alberigo, Giuseppe. 2006. *A Brief History of Vatican II.* Maryknoll, NY: Orbis Books.

Alberigo, Giuseppe, and Joseph A. Komonchak, eds. 1995. *History of Vatican II.* Maryknoll, NY: Orbis; and Leuven: Peeters.

Alberigo, Giuseppe, Jean-Pierre Jossua, and Joseph A. Komonchak, eds. 1987. *The Reception of Vatican II.* Washington, DC: Catholic University of America Press.

Bevans, Stephen B. and Jeffrey Gros. 2009. *Evangelization and Religious Freedom:* Ad Gentes, Dignitatis Humanae. New York: Paulist Press.

Bulman, Raymond F., and Frederick J. Parrella, eds. 2006. *From Trent to Vatican II: Historical and Theological Perspectives.* New York: Oxford University Press.

Cafardi, Nicholas P. 2008. *Before Dallas: The U.S. Bishops' Response to Clergy Sexual Abuse of Children.* Mahwah, NJ: Paulist Press.

Cassidy, Edward Idris. 2005. *Ecumenism and Interreligious Dialogue: Unitatis Redintegratio, Nostra Aetate.* New York: Paulist Press.

Clifford, Catherine E. 2014. *Decoding Vatican II: Interpretation and Ongoing Reception.* Madeleva Lecture in Spirituality, 2013. New York: Paulist Press.

Congar, Yves. 2012. *My Journal of the Council.* Hindmarsh: ATF Press.

Faggioli, Massimo. 2012. *Vatican II: The Battle for Meaning.* Mahwah, NJ: Paulist Press.

Faggioli, Massimo. 2015. *A Council for the Global Church. Receiving Vatican II in History.* Minneapolis, MN: Fortress Press.

Ferrone, Rita. 2007. *Liturgy: Sacrosanctum Concilium.* New York: Paulist Press.

Gaillardetz, Richard R. 2006. *The Church in the Making: Lumen Gentium, Christus Dominus, Orientalium Ecclesiarum.* New York: Paulist Press.

Howard, Thomas Albert. 2017. *The Pope and the Professor: Pius IX, Ignaz von Döllinger, and the Quandary of the Modern Age.* Oxford: Oxford University Press.

Kerr, Fergus. 2007. *Twentieth-Century Catholic Theologians.* Malden, MA, Oxford: Blackwell Publishing.

McEnroy, Carmel Elizabeth. 1996. *Guests in Their Own House: The Women of Vatican II.* New York: Crossroad Publishing.

Massa, Mark S. 2010. The *American Catholic Revolution: How the Sixties Changed the Church Forever.* New York: Oxford University Press.

Melloni, Alberto, Federico Ruozzi, Enrico Galavotti, and John XXIII Foundation for Religious Studies in Bologna. 2015. *Vatican II: The Complete History.* New York: Paulist Press.

O'Malley, John W. 2008. *What Happened at Vatican II.* Cambridge, MA: Belknap Press of Harvard University Press.

O'Malley, John W. 2018. *Vatican I: The Council and the Making of an Ultramontane Church.* Cambridge, MA: Harvard University Press.

Schatz, Klaus. 1996. *Papal Primacy: From its Origins to the Present.* Translated by John A. Otto and Linda M. Maloney. Collegeville, MN: Liturgical Press.

Schultenover, David G., ed. 2007. *Vatican II: Did Anything Happen?* New York: Continuum.

Tanner, Norman P. 2005. *The Church and the World: Gaudium et Spes, Inter Mirifica.* New York: Paulist Press.

Witherup, Ronald D. 2006. *Scripture: Dei Verbum.* New York: Paulist Press.

Chapter

25

CHRISTIANITY AND SCIENCE

For all their differences, Christianity and science share something basic—the quest for truth. Although truth can be defined in different ways, a definition that works for both religion and science is "contact with reality." Truth is thus a relationship between the human mind and the *reality* that it seeks to know and understand—whether it be the reality of the natural world or the reality of God.

From its inception, Christianity has been dedicated to truth. John the Baptist did not think that he was dying to protect a mythical fiction; Jesus did not get himself arrested, whipped, and tortured to death for the sake of falsehood. Stephen, the first Christian martyr, preferred death to discontinuing his public proclamation of truth. In fact, the original Greek term for martyr (*martus*) literally means "witness"—in the sense of witnessing to the truth. As Jesus said, "You will know the truth, and the truth will make you free" (John 8:32). Truth, including the truth that science has discovered, is food for Christian life and thought. Every authentic scientific discovery is thus a gift to Christianity, but incorporating the gift requires intelligent effort.

Confronting scientific discoveries is both a challenge for Christianity and an opportunity.

Scientific findings are challenges when they seem to question claims made by the Bible or by the church. These challenges arise when scientists address vital common concerns, like what the world and the universe are like, what we are like, and by implication, what the Creator is like—or if there is even a need for a Creator.

Science is also an opportunity for Christian faith, because it has strongly developed human *reason*; and like science, Christianity has an enormous stake in reason—which is one of main avenues of approaching and developing truth. Given the common interest in reason and in truth, Christianity benefits whenever scientific discoveries make new contacts with reality, new achievements of truth.

Since the eleventh century, St. Anselm's "faith seeking understanding" has been one of the great mottos of Christian theology. To understand requires reason, and when faith and reason are joined, they are mutually beneficial to all involved. A person who has both faith and reason is broader and more well balanced than a person who has only one of them. Working together as complements, faith and reason complete and protect each other: faith illuminates the scientific reason of our age by putting it in a meaningful context, by connecting it to a greater whole; scientific reason guards against fanaticism and narrowmindedness by disciplining and grounding thought in the material world.

If God is infinitely intelligent, infinitely good, and wanted to create a universe home for us, then all our endeavors, *science included,* are housed within a larger purpose—relationship with the Creator God. Apart from God and left to its own devices, reason can be a tool of either good or evil. It can be used to understand the world, ourselves, and God; or it can be used to exploit the world and to dominate other people. Reason, especially scientific reason, needs direction from something greater than reason. Without goodness, without a greater sense of purpose, reason can lose interest in truth and then become dangerous. But working in partnership, faith and scientific reason can unleash new forces for the betterment of human life.

FOUR MODELS OF INTERACTION

It is a popular misconception that science and Christianity have always been in conflict with each other. In fact, the historical and current relationship is far more nuanced. Ian Barbour, who was both a scientist and a theologian, recently introduced four models of interaction between science and religion: conflict, independence, dialogue, and integration (Barbour 1997). Even though some writers have suggested alternatives, Barbour's four models have become broadly recognized in the growing field that relates science and theology. The relationship between science and theology is complex; one size does not fit all.

Conflict

In the complex relationship between Christianity and science, conflict sometimes does occur. Conflict with science is generated from the religious side when the words of the Bible are taken literally, especially parts of the Bible that address issues studied by science. If the biblical account of a seven-day creation (Genesis 1), or a single day of creation (Genesis 2), is read literally, there will be conflict with current science. Likewise, there will be conflict if the order of the creation of sun, moon, stars, plants, animals, and human beings in Genesis is insisted upon. The 13.8-billion-year development of the cosmos that physics has demonstrated, and the 3.45-billion-year evolution of planetary life that almost all biologists accept, simply cannot be harmonized with biblical fundamentalism. An insistence on reading the Bible as a scientific authority means that most of modern science will have to be rejected.

Some scientists, as well as many non-scientists, generate conflict with Christianity when they insist that science is all that matters. However, this dogmatic insistence is actually not science; it is a *belief* that is more accurately called *scientism.* Like many "isms" it is an extreme position, one that is not very well thought out. Unfortunately, science is often confused with scientism. Unlike scientism, authentic science is very modest in recognizing its own limited purpose: to understand physical aspects of the universe, the earth, or things and people on the earth. Real science does not pretend to know why the universe exists, and it does not make pronouncements about the existence or non-existence of God. Scientists who make such pronouncements are no longer being scientific; whether affirming or denying God, they have entered the field of philosophy, metaphysics, or theology. Having scientific expertise is an admirable achievement and a good starting point, because authentic science trains people to respect reality. Like the rest of us, scientists are free to express their own views. However, scientific expertise does not of itself confer wisdom about the meaning of human life. Turning science into a questionable belief like scientism is bound to generate conflict with Christianity.

The philosophy used to justify scientism is called **naturalism**. Naturalism holds that nature is all that is real; therefore, all real knowledge must be directed to understanding nature. According to naturalism, since nature is the only reality, the scientific study of nature is the only real form of knowledge. From this perspective, religion is just a mass of irrelevant error, because religion attempts to tell us about something that may or may not exist, something that is probably not real. The presuppositions of naturalism ensure conflict with Christian belief, especially belief in divine creation.

Naturalism, however, is not belief-free. In spite of claims to be based solely on reason, naturalism places numerous beliefs in the physical universe itself. Naturalism attributes creative capacity to a non-knowing, non-feeling physical realm. According to naturalism, the universe somehow generates its own order and intelligibility, maintains itself in being, and somehow starts life, replicates life (DNA), and develops life from single-celled bacteria to *Homo sapiens*. In most of its variants, naturalism holds the material universe to be never-beginning and never-ending—which are rather god-like characteristics. But it is a god without consciousness. And yet this completely unconscious universe is believed to produce beings who do have consciousness. Advocates of naturalism have clearly not rid themselves of belief; they have only concentrated their belief onto the material universe. They are otherwise known as reductionists, because their position reduces everything to nature. This position pays an ironic compliment to the work of the Creator, whose personal existence is denied, but whose impersonal universe is believed to have such extensive and marvelous powers. The beliefs presupposed by naturalism generate conflict because they leave no room for the reality of a God who is above nature, that is, a *super*natural being, where "super" is understood in its original Latin sense of "above."

The Galileo Affair: An Historical Conflict

Perhaps the most famous historical example of conflict between science and Christianity is the Galileo affair. This conflict was a perfect storm of misunderstandings, unclear agreements, and hurt feelings between old friends. However, recent evidence has convincingly shown that the often-repeated charge that the church tortured and imprisoned Galileo is false (Finocchiaro 2009). Also untrue is the charge that the church of Galileo's day was opposed to science.

Galileo Galilei (1564–1642) was a renowned mathematician and scientist, a devout Catholic, and a good friend of Pope Urban VIII. In 1609, Galileo ran into trouble when he enthusiastically defended the heliocentric theory of Copernicus, the theory that the earth moves around the sun. It may be surprising to learn that Copernicus (1473–1543) had developed his theory in response to a request from Pope Leo X. The church wanted a more accurate way to date events like the resurrection of Christ, and Copernicus conceived his heliocentric theory to help the church. It may also be surprising to learn that the church maintained its own group of astronomers; some sided with Galileo and others opposed him. But because the church actually supported scientists, financially and through education, and because many of the best scientists were priests, the accusation that the church was against science is simply misinformed.

The conflict between Galileo and the church arose because Galileo contended that the earth is moving around an unmoving sun, a claim that contradicted the literal sense of some Old Testament passages. When Joshua and the Israelites needed more daylight to pursue their foes, "Joshua spoke to the LORD; and he said in the sight of Israel, 'Sun, stand still at Gibeon' ... And the sun stood still ... until the nation took vengeance on their enemies" (Joshua 10:12–13). Likewise, one of the Psalms appeared to support an unmoving earth: God "has established the world; it shall never be moved" (Psalms 93:1). Notice that a strictly *literal* reading of scripture is at the center of the conflict, even though St. Augustine had many centuries earlier warned against narrowly literal readings that conflict with the best science of the day. When Galileo offered his own interpretation of the offending passages, he unfortunately resembled the Protestants who had only recently separated from the Roman Catholic Church, a suspicion made worse when he seemed to argue that the Bible is not a scientific authority. In the conflict's historical context, the recent Protestant Reformation added tension and colored the controversy about how scientific claims fit with scripture.

In early 1616, Cardinal Robert Bellarmine apparently warned Galileo not to claim publicly that the earth moves. However, Galileo got permission from a different Catholic authority to publish his *Dialogue on the Two Great World Systems*, a book in which one of the characters did claim that the earth moves. Unfortunately, the character in Galileo's *Dialogue* whose argument looked the worst (it was the worst) just happened to be the view of Galileo's old friend, Pope Urban VIII. Once informed of the public slight, the friendship turned sour, thereby making a difficult matter even worse (Langford 1999, 111–113).

A common misconception is that Galileo *proved* that the earth moves and the allegedly anti-science church refused to allow his proof. The facts, however, are far more complicated. Galileo was mostly right in asserting that the sun is fixed and that the earth moves around the sun. But as is now known, the sun is not fixed; the sun also moves in an orbit around the center of our galaxy. More importantly, Galileo's "proof" was a complete failure: he incorrectly argued that the earth's orbital motion causes the ocean tides. However, as his German contemporary Johannes Kepler (1571–1630) showed, the tides are caused by the gravitational attraction of the moon. Galileo's incorrect argument about the tides is important, because the church had earlier asked him not to claim proof, but only to present the earth's movement as a hypothesis.

The evidence now available shows that Galileo did stand trial but was not tortured. In a significant dissent, three out of ten judges refused to sign the condemnation against him; nonetheless, Galileo was found guilty of an intermediate, but still serious, offense. At the time of the trial, Galileo was 69 years old and frail. Until recently, it was widely believed that Galileo was tortured and imprisoned; but actually, during the hearings, he stayed in the very comfortable palace of the grand Duke of Tuscany, where servants brought him his meals.

It is true that Galileo was threatened with torture, forced to recant what he believed to be true, forced to keep silent about the earth's alleged movement, and sentenced to house arrest for the duration of his life (his house was a very comfortable villa). However, Galileo was permitted to walk to church and also to visit his daughter, who was a nun in a nearby convent. In spite of the complications and extenuating circumstances, the church's treatment of Galileo was wrong; and in 1992, Pope John Paul II publicly acknowledged the church's error.

The Independence Model

The strength of the independence model for science and Christianity is almost self-evident, because some areas require independent inquiry. Theologians should not be in the business of telling chemists how to set up a laboratory experiment. Likewise, chemistry does not have anything to contribute to questions about the two natures of Christ, the Trinity, or whether God loves us. Yet, while conducting separate kinds of inquiry, the two disciplines remain united in the quest for truth.

In their separate quests for truth, each discipline may also share the discipline of submitting to the reality that is sought. These independent inquiries can thus offer similar character training—the preference for truth over one's own subjective fantasies. Even in their independence, success in both areas requires far more than the subjective, childish imposition of one's own will. Success requires the habit of *listening* to the reality that would be known. This habit is good for the one who develops it, and it is also the path to discovery, whether learning something new about chemistry or about God.

Some writers have stressed that science investigates *how* the physical universe works and theology seeks to understand *why* it works, or even why there is a universe in the first place. This distinction between *how* and *why* suggests that some areas of inquiry really must be independent.

Over the centuries, many Christian leaders have appreciated science without seeing it as vital to faith. Cardinal Cesare Baronius, a contemporary of Galileo, famously declared: "The Holy Ghost intended to teach us how to go to heaven, not how the heavens go" (Langford 1999, 65). Most scientific developments, for example, Isaac Newton's discovery of the law of gravity, simply do not impinge upon theology in any clearly significant ways.

However, there are certain dangers to seeing the independence model as dominant or exclusive. The chief problem is that areas of overlap between science and theology do in fact arise. And when faced with overlapping claims of science and theology, students may simply revert to a conflict interpretation; or, if unable to adjudicate what looks like conflict, students may simply compartmentalize both the particular issue and the big picture of the two disciplines. For example, many student-believers take biology classes that are based on evolution. Once such students come to realize the explanatory power of evolution, they may experience considerable conflict, that is, cognitive dissonance, between the truth of evolution and the truth that their church or theology classes may have taught them. Such students must then decide for evolution, decide for their church teaching, or compartmentalize the issue—keeping evolutionary biology in one compartment of their mind and faith in the other. Compartmentalizing is uncomfortable because it tries to avoid the big issues; it tries to keep what looks like conflicting ideas at the same time in the same mind. To an honest thinker, the failure to resolve how science and faith fit together is unsettling and unsatisfactory.

Another big issue that does not allow easy compartmentalization is how the universe began. Here again both science and theology make overlapping claims, and the overlap spills over the boundaries of the independence model. Can something as important as the origin of the universe be put into safe little compartments of the mind? Or is it possible that from physics, Big Bang cosmology, and theology, a doctrine of creation, can be fruitfully combined? Big Bang cosmology and the belief that God originated the universe have been combined, but joining them together takes us beyond the independence model.

Dialogue

In the large and in the small, science has accomplished a new picture of the cosmos. Its successes—its discoveries of new *truth*—have made possible a new conversation with Christian faith. Over the last few centuries, science has taught us things about the material universe that no human beings knew when the Bible was written. For example, advances in molecular biology have uncovered worlds within worlds tucked into spaces so tiny that, even 200 years ago, what are now proven facts of cellular activity would have been considered as unbelievable fantasy. And 200 years ago, who could have imagined that within these miniscule cells, there are organized, life-promoting activities rivaling the hustle and bustle of major cities? Similarly, advances in astronomy have uncovered a vast and expanding universe in which our sun, moon, and planet are merely pinpricks in the outskirts of the galactic immensity (Rolnick 2015, 3). As Pope John Paul II declared, "It is a duty for theologians to keep themselves regularly informed of scientific advances in order to examine if … there are reasons for taking them into account … or for introducing changes in their teaching (John Paul II, Allocution, para. 8). For Christianity, engaging scientific truth is serious, both a duty and an opportunity.

Dialogue with science is advantageous for theology, because science has proven to be a powerful partner in discovering truth. Almost every partnership includes disagreements and areas of independence, but good partnerships foster new magnitudes of strength. To date, most of the obvious advantages have been for theology, but in partnership with faith, science also benefits in less apparent ways. Unannounced and far less consciously than in our own day, theology has always been in a kind of dialogue with the science of its time.

When Hebrew priests wrote the first chapter of Genesis during the Babylonian Captivity (587–539 B.C.), they used the best Babylonian science of their day: "And God said, 'Let there be a dome in the midst of the waters, and let it separate the waters from the waters'" (Genesis 1:6). In this ancient view of the cosmos, a gigantic dome, much like a greatly expanded dome of a modern sports stadium, separated what were incorrectly believed to be heavenly waters from the earthly waters. The human author of Genesis 1 *used* the best science of that time, science which is no longer relevant. But in depicting divine creation, the inspiration of Genesis 1 remains highly relevant; its inspired vision of divine creation is vastly more important than its use of Babylonian science. The religious use of science is hardly new. But now, due to the impressive gains that science has made, a dialogue is more pressing and potentially more helpful than ever before. Science has given us new ways of seeing our universe home, new ways of appreciating the intricacies and beauty of creation.

The dialogue between science and theology is made more complicated, but also more interesting, by their different techniques, tendencies, and goals. In a good dialogue, everyone does not say the same thing in the same way. Long ago, Aristotle (384–322 B.C.) wisely recognized that different fields of knowledge require different methods: "One should not require precision in all pursuits alike, but in each field precision varies with the matter under discussion and should be required only to the extent to which it is appropriate to the investigation" (Aristotle 1962, 1098a). For science and theology, what are these different techniques, tendencies, and goals?

One major difference is that in science everything begins with human effort. By contrast, in many conceptions of theology and the Christian life, everything begins with revelation: God's activity in creation, in the coming of Christ, and in continuing guidance to the church and to individuals. Science tests its theories through observation, by asking quantitative questions about particular aspects of the physical universe. By contrast, Christianity asks questions about the Person believed to have created the universe. Christianity is interested in science's quantitative questions and discoveries, but it is even more interested in questions about quality—about the purpose of life and how to live it. Science is primarily about attaining knowledge; Christianity also seeks knowledge, but goes beyond knowledge in seeking wisdom. It is possible to understand a great deal of science and to live a foolish or even a wicked life. At times, when Christianity does not have much to contribute to a particular scientific inquiry, it still has a great deal to contribute to the scientist.

Another divergent tendency is the way the two disciplines look at the past. Current science looks at past science with little or no interest. What the Babylonians thought about cosmology, or what a great eighteenth-century scientist thought, holds little or no interest for current cosmologists, because the field has made so many dramatic improvements. Science has become a cumulative enterprise, in which the current state of knowledge builds upon the past, but is clearly more advanced than the past. Its focus is on current knowledge and current problems; science always has a certain restlessness; it keeps pushing the envelope toward the future, toward new development.

Christianity, however, has an ongoing link to the past that it never relinquishes. Like science, Christian thought develops over time, but this development tends to be more gradual. Rather than dismissing past achievements, Christianity develops by applying old principles to new problems. What Jesus said and did has as much value today as it did in the first century. Great insights from people both before and after Jesus remain valuable, because human nature remains basically the same over time. For instance, we confront the same problems of temptation, selfishness, and pride as did Jesus' Apostles. Hence, whenever and wherever anyone in the Christian tradition says or writes something worth hearing, the new insight is retained and becomes part of the cumulative treasure trove of Christian thought. As Christianity moves forward through time, continuity with the past tends to be practiced, not a radical departure from past beliefs.

The goals of science and Christianity are also different. For the most part, science investigates particular things, such as a particular kind of star, the behavior of electrons, or the mechanism of biological inheritance. As we have seen, if scientists move beyond the modest, particular goals of inquiry and make grandiose pronouncements about the big picture of life and its meaning (or meaninglessness), they are no longer doing science; they are instead doing philosophy or theology. Their pronouncements may be helpful or sophomoric, good or bad, but they are not scientific.

Unlike science, Christianity is deeply concerned with the meaning of the big picture. Christianity must ask why the universe is habitable for human persons; Christianity must ask (and answer) about the purpose of the universe and our purpose within it. The different focuses of science and theology give each partner something valuable to contribute to the conversation.

A fruitful dialogue between science and theology must begin by asking the right questions. To ask that God be empirically observable is like demanding that a meter be squeezed into a centimeter. Starting with impossible demands will prove nothing and can lead only to conflict. Each *level* of reality must be approached with a method suitable to its reality. When different levels of reality are recognized and respected, a real dialogue can take place.

Recognizing and respecting different levels of reality is the linchpin of the relationship between science and theology. Trying to flatten our understanding of reality, trying to reduce everything to components of physics and chemistry, has to generate conflict between science and theology. But such reductionism is both unnecessary and demonstrably false. When reading a book, it would be possible, but not very intelligent, to reduce everything to the chemistry that leaves black marks on the piece of paper. Moving up a level, it is possible to stop at the letters that the ink forms. But, of course, single letters lack meaning. Continuing an upward movement, we could arbitrarily stop at single words, single sentences, or single paragraphs. Or we could examine the meaning of the entirety, of the whole text that the author wrote (Haught 1995, 92). There is a kind of metaphysical silliness in insisting that everything be reduced to its lowest level components. There is nothing particularly rational or scientific about such reductionism. Once reductionism is exposed for the faulty belief that it is, the more human, more moderate, and more helpful dialogue between real science and real religion can emerge, a dialogue that acknowledges the meaningfulness of different levels of reality.

Starting and proceeding with the right questions are crucial to any inquiry, but especially to approaching a divine reality that infinitely exceeds human capability. Theologians have much to learn from the dialogue with science; but for their part, scientists must learn to ask the right questions when they step into a realm that is inherently beyond strict science.

Integration

In both science and theology, the achievement of truth never occurs in an all-at-once fashion. Every new act of learning or discovery is a prelude to further learning and discovery. As a result, integrating science and Christian thought is also an ongoing task. This task actually begins in conversation, where new ways of thinking stimulate new conversations, which may or may not lead to integration. Hence, movement between the last two models, dialogue and integration, can be highly fluid. The models are tools for contemplation; they are not meant to be airtight categories.

In science, new discoveries expand, deepen, or change understanding of the physical world. A new scientific discovery sometimes causes complete rejections of previous understandings, but more often, it revises and expands them. For example, Isaac Newton's understanding of gravity was dominant for about 200 years. It was highly accurate in its calculations and predictions. However, in the early twentieth century, Albert Einstein's Theory of General Relativity presented a new understanding of gravity that has expanded our ability to calculate and predict. Technologies like GPS are possible to develop under Einstein's theory, but not under Newton's. Newton's theory remains highly serviceable for most things most of the time. But Einstein's new and expanded understanding lets us do new things. And even now new discoveries and revisions are possible.

Science is very much a cumulative process. Once new discoveries are made, they become old by being incorporated into the scientific curriculum. However, only the durable discoveries are built upon, while others views that do not stand up to the test of time are discarded. There follows a period of stability during which the new understandings are taught to new generations, a stability which is eventually disrupted by even newer discoveries. As the latest discoveries are incorporated into what is taught, the cycle continues.

Just as science is always learning new things, there is always more to learn about God. How could finite beings ever know all there is to know about an infinite being? This differential, between an infinite, perfect being and finite imperfect beings, suggests the morality of growth. Such growth is suggested because God is something all at once that we must imitate by a process of becoming—by continually learning more and more. In our current age, this process includes engaging and integrating scientific discoveries of truth, because every authentic scientific discovery is revealing something about the universe that God has created. Advances in understanding creation can be a joint goal of science and a scientifically informed theology.

Science becomes the benefactor of theology if its discoveries are used to refresh and reinvigorate our understanding of creation. Likewise, as scientists incorporate a mature theological understanding, they can experience the beauty of what they are doing in new ways. Thus, Francis Collins, who was the head of the Human Genome Project, declared: "The God of the Bible is also the God of the genome. He can be worshipped in the cathedral or in the laboratory. His creation is majestic, awesome, intricate, and beautiful" (Collins 2006, 211). Collins had spent years as an atheist, but he became convinced of a moral law that exceeded science, and he then began to see the created world in a new way. Thinking is a vital part of Christianity, but so too is the way we live. Learning to appreciate how creation is "majestic, awesome, intricate, and beautiful" comes from thinking a certain way, and it also leads us to live a certain way—an integration of scientific reason and faith in the God who made a law-governed universe.

One of the difficulties in integrating science into Christianity is that science sometimes rapidly changes. Because Christian theology is a subject concerned with eternity—God's and ours—we must be very careful in incorporating scientific ideas that may be discarded 50 or 100 years from now. The changing nature of scientific understanding makes the task of integration more difficult, but it does not prevent scientific understanding being incorporated into Christian thought. For human beings, the acquisition of *any* knowledge is both orderly and messy—a lot like human life itself.

A History of Integration

Historically, the relationship of science and Christianity has had setbacks like the Galileo affair, but it has mostly had long and fruitful periods of integration. A brief outline of the history of some great scientists—Catholics, Protestants, and Eastern Orthodox—will show the historical cooperation and integration of science with the major expressions of Christian faith.

Selected Catholic Scientists

Robert Grosseteste (*c.*1168–1253) was bishop of Lincoln and founder of the Oxford School, which fostered the tradition of experimental physical science.

Thomas Bradwardine (1290–1349) was both Archbishop of Canterbury and one of the first to write an equation for physical processes.

Nicholas of Oresme (1323–1382) was a bishop who made important advances in both mathematics and physics. He showed how to combine exponents and used graphs to depict mathematical functions; showed how the rotation of the earth on its axis could explain what was then believed to be the movement of the sun; contributed to early accounts of acceleration; and probably influenced the later work of Galileo and Newton.

Nicolas of Cusa (1401–1464) was a philosopher and cardinal. He boldly suggested that all bodies are in motion, and that the universe was infinite and without a center.

Copernicus (1473–1543), as noted above, developed his heliocentric model in order to serve the church. Although never ordained a priest, Copernicus was a canon of the church, that is, an official church administrator. He was also responsible for reciting the prayers of the Daily Office.

Fr. Marin Mersenne (1588–1648) had a kind of prime number named after him and invented improvements in the telescope.

The Jesuits have had a long tradition of studying astronomy.

Fr. Christoph Scheiner (1573–1650) discovered new things about sunspots and the sun's rotation on its axis.

Fr. Francesco Grimaldi (1613–1653) was one of the first to map the moon and name its features. He published discoveries about the refraction of light, its diffraction, and destructive interference.

Fr. Giovanni Riccioli (1598–1671) discovered the first binary star.

Fr. Giuseppe Piazzi (1746–1826) directed the Palermo Observatory and in 1801 discovered Ceres, the first known asteroid.

Fr. Pietro Secchi (1818–1878), was a founder of astrophysics; developed the spectral classification of stars still used today; invented the meteorograph; and was the first to understand that nebulae were clouds of gas.

Fr. Lazzaro Spallanzani (1729–1799) was a leading biologist who first showed that digestion was a process of solution using gastric juices. He researched animal fertilization, respiration, regeneration, and the senses in bats. He contributed to early studies of vulcanology and meteorology.

Fr. Bernhard Bolzano (1781–1848) contributed to the mathematical subcategory of analysis and to understanding infinite quantities.

Gregor Mendel (1822–1884), was an Austrian monk who discovered the laws of heredity that have been so crucial to all subsequent biology.

Abbé Henri Breuil, S.J. (1877–1961) was an archaeologist, anthropologist, ethnologist, and geologist. He was known for his studies of cave art in France and around the world.

Fr. Julius Nieuwland (1878–1936) was chemistry professor at Notre Dame, who was a co-developer of neoprene, the first synthetic rubber-like compound.

Figure 25–1 Abbé Georges Lemaître (1894–1966), originator of the Big Bang theory. Pictured with Albert Einstein in 1932.

Abbé Georges Lemaître (1894–1966) was one of the originators of Big Bang theory and the first to publish a scholarly article defending the theory (Barr 2003, 9–10).

Selected Protestant Scientists

Johannes Kepler (1571–1630) discovered basic laws of planetary motion.

Robert Boyle (1627–1691) showed the inverse relation between pressure and volume of a gas in an enclosed space (Boyle's Law).

Isaac Newton (1642–1727) formulated laws of motion, the law of gravity, and calculus. He also wrote numerous biblical commentaries and works of theology.

Joseph Priestley (1733–1804) discovered the element oxygen.

Michael Faraday (1791–1867) discovered essential features of electromagnetism.

William Thomson Kelvin (1824–1907) devised a mathematical analysis of electricity; the 1st and 2nd Laws of Thermodynamics; and the lower limit of temperature.

Max Planck (1858–1947) discovered quantum reality.

Rev. John Polkinghorne (1930–) was physics chair at Cambridge and became an Anglican priest. Polkinghorne specialized in quantum physics, and he has written numerous books on the relation of science and theology.

Francis Collins (1950–) was head of the Human Genome Project and is an evangelical Christian.

Werner Arber (1929–) is a Swiss molecular biologist, Nobel Prize Laureate, and President of the Pontifical Academy of Sciences, which first existed over 400 years ago. Arber is the first non-Catholic to be its President.

Selected Orthodox Scientists

Alexander Friedmann (1888–1925) did the mathematical work that lent credence to what became Big Bang cosmology. His mathematical analyses overcame Einstein's objections and showed that Einstein's equations could imply an expanding universe. Friedmann was a baptized member of the Russian Orthodox Church.

Theodore Dobzhansky (1900–1975) was a great evolutionary biologist and geneticist and also a member of the Eastern Orthodox Church. He did valuable work in synthesizing

Darwin's evolutionary theory with genetics. Having emigrated from Ukraine to the United States, Dobzhansky received the United States National Medal of Science in 1964.

Sergei Khoruzhy (1941–) is a Russian physicist and mathematician who has also done important work in philosophy and theology.

This long list of celebrated scientists who were also Catholics, Protestants, or Eastern Orthodox should at the very least dispel the erroneous idea that science and Christianity have long been at war. Although conflicts have arisen, as with Galileo and with some Christian thinkers after Darwin, the overall history has been one of dialogue and integration.

Currently, there are 80 men and women who are academic members of the Pontifical Academy of Sciences, originally founded in 1603. In 1610, Galileo became a member of this organization, a fact that, in spite of his conflict with the church, points to the historical integration of science and faith. Recently revitalized, this Pontifical Academy of Sciences encourages its members to explore a broad range of sciences. Among other things, its website states its mission as "to promote the progress of the mathematical, physical and natural sciences and the study of epistemological problems relating thereto."

Another group seeking integration of science and Christianity is the American Scientific Association (ASA), founded in 1941. According to its website, the American Scientific Affiliation believes:

> that God is both the creator of our vast universe and is the source of our ability to pursue knowledge—also, that honest and open studies of both scripture and nature are mutually beneficial in developing a full understanding of human identity and our environment.

The diverse, international membership is committed to the ethical pursuit of mainstream science and to "belief in orthodox Christianity, as defined by the Apostles' and Nicene creeds."

Yet another group seeking integration is BioLogos, founded in 2007. Its website describes its mission: "BioLogos invites the church and the world to see the harmony between science and biblical faith as we present an evolutionary understanding of God's creation." The emphasis on evolutionary biology stems from its founder, Francis Collins.

Integration of science and Christian theology is a lofty goal that requires a lot of effort. It begins, like a great deal of learning, with a good conversation—where both disciplines are carefully listening to the other in the joint search for truth.

THREE TEST CASES FOR THE RELATIONSHIP: BIG BANG, FINE-TUNING, AND EVOLUTION

Big Bang Theory

The evidential confirmation of Big Bang theory came as a shock to many physicists, especially to naturalists. According to Big Bang theory, the universe began from a *singularity*, an episode of infinite pressure, heat, and density in zero space from which all matter, energy, space, and time originate. Just as an explosion makes things fly apart, the big bang singularity caused the unimaginably hot and inconceivably tiny universe rapidly to expand. The term "big bang" originated as a term of abuse, a shorthand mockery that captured the seemingly outlandish character of a universe with a datable beginning.

However, strong evidence has been found confirming that our universe began in a hot big bang 13.8 billion years ago. In a major discovery in 1929, Edwin Hubble telescopically observed that the universe is expanding—an observation that strongly supported Big Bang theory. But for opponents of Big Bang theory, the final blow came in 1965, with the discovery of **cosmic microwave background radiation** (CMB). This cosmic radiation, found everywhere in interstellar space, clinched the game for Big Bang theory. If the physical universe began in a stupendously hot big bang, over time the universe would have expanded and cooled; and when the universe was sufficiently cool, stable atoms could form and photons would be released everywhere—the origin of the CMB. Since the discovery of CMB, additional evidence has pointed to a big bang beginning. In fact, few scientific theories have enjoyed so much evidential verification. The big bang is so strongly confirmed that, in spite of its theological implications, it is the consensus among cosmologists—virtually a unanimous consensus.

Discourse about the origin of the universe is now shared turf between science and theology. Except for those who insist on a six-day creation, having a scientific date for a beginning certainly looks consonant with belief in creation, even creation *ex nihilo*. Big Bang theory has led scientists to think what Christians, Jews, and Muslims have long believed—that the universe had an origin, that it is not **past-eternal**. Nonetheless, it would be rash to think that the big bang *proves* that God created the universe. Christianity does not need proof from science, only compatibility. And Big Bang cosmology is highly compatible with Christian faith in creation.

The success of Big Bang theory greatly perturbed the naturalistic bent of many mid-twentieth century scientists. Some eminent scientists at first refused to believe it. German chemist Walter Nernst declared: "To deny the infinite duration of time would be to betray the very foundation of science." Likewise, American astronomer Allan Sandage said of big bang: "It is such a strange conclusion ... it cannot really be true" (Jastrow 1978, 112–113). Scientists who want to explain everything scientifically are understandably upset by discovering that the universe has a beginning that escapes their explanations. Walter Jastrow, a Dartmouth physics professor who also worked with NASA, humorously addressed Big Bang's success: "This is an exceedingly strange development, unexpected by all but the theologians" (Jastrow 1978, 115). Jastrow drew a comic picture of the unexpected development:

> For the scientist who has lived by his faith in the power of reason, the story ends like a bad dream. He has scaled the mountains of ignorance; he is about to conquer the highest peak; as he pulls himself over the final rock, he is greeted by a band of theologians who have been sitting there for centuries.
>
> (Jastrow 1978, 116)

Big Bang theory has been what physicist Stephen Barr called a "plot twist" in the relation of science and theology (Barr 2003, 22).

However, while virtually everyone agrees that the big bang was the origin of *our* universe, many astrophysicists continue to seek a breakthrough, to seek a way past the big bang and into a larger universe that would be both infinite and past-eternal. Many alternatives to big bang have been proposed and, if the assumptions of infinite time and space are granted, their mathematics becomes at least plausible. But to date, proposals for a so-called multiverse are entirely speculative; there is no supporting evidence. If evidence of a multiverse ever were discovered, a new conversation would be initiated; a multiverse would not require giving up belief in divine creation. But for now, the scientific consensus, restless though it may be, is that the one universe we know about began 13.8 billion years ago with the big bang. Recent cosmology is quite harmonious with Christian theology.

Fine-Tuning

Just as Big Bang cosmology has been highly compatible with Christian faith, so too has the discovery that the universe is finely tuned to support life. As physicists discovered more and more about the universe's origin and development, they also found how the odds of forming a life-supporting universe were overwhelmingly bad. Looking at the physics alone, our existence, our planet, and our current universe are extremely improbable. There are *numerous* relations among basic physical forces where changing any one of the related items—in either direction—would result in a cosmic wasteland. The evidence indicates that we should not be here.

Fine-tuning is exemplified in the relation of gravity and the explosive outward force of the big bang. These two forces are exquisitely balanced in precisely the right way to form a universe with galaxies and planets. Gravity and the explosive force work in opposite ways: gravity pulls things together; the explosive force drives things apart. If the gravitational force were slightly stronger than it actually is, gravity would stop the expansion of the universe, pulling all matter and energy back into the infinitely dense and uninhabitable starting point. If the explosive force were slightly stronger, then the universe would have expanded so rapidly that no important structural interactions could occur. Both scenarios would have been calamitous; there would be no habitable universe. Instead, the balance between the two opposing forces is astonishing. Physicist Paul Davies calculates that almost immediately (10^{-43} seconds) after the big bang, the opposing forces are balanced to one part in 10^{60}. A change of just $1/10^{60}$ in either direction would mean no developed universe and no life. This remarkable balancing act demonstrates the essence of fine-tuning, and there are many other instances of fine-tuning that are equally astonishing.

That fine-tuning has occurred is clear; how to interpret fine-tuning is controversial. For religious believers, the discovery of fine-tuning is another fulfillment of their religious expectation. If the universe was created by an infinitely intelligent Creator, then we should expect to find something as remarkable as fine-tuning, another scientific uncovering of the depth of intelligible law imprinted in the fabric of reality. If we begin in faith and seek to understand, we do not find scientific proof of God, but we do find scientific compatibility.

On the other side, naturalists have proposed various strategies that would discount the evidence of fine-tuning. Again appealing to a possible multiverse, they argue that the numerical improbabilities disappear when given infinite time for the universe to run through infinite possibilities; one or more of these infinite practice runs will eventually work. Moreover, our current knowledge is limited. There could be hidden factors necessitating what looks like fine-tuning to us.

While the debate about how to interpret fine-tuning continues, the discovery that the universe is finely tuned is highly compatible with belief in divine creation.

Natural Selection

The third test case for integrating science and Christian faith appears at first sight to be the toughest. Natural selection was arguably Darwin's most important contribution. He described it as follows:

> Can we doubt (remembering that many more individuals are born than can possibly survive) that individuals having any advantage, however slight, over others, would have the best chance of surviving and of procreating their kind? On the other hand, we may feel sure that any variation in the least degree injurious would be rigidly destroyed. This preservation of favourable variations and the rejection of injurious variations, I call Natural Selection.
>
> (Darwin 1979, 130–131)

In combination with mutations and vast stretches of time, natural selection is the driving force of the evolutionary process. Over time, random mutations generate novelty, while natural selection coldly judges novel attempts with life-or-death consequences. As natural selection judges new developments, it lets most of them perish (along with the creatures in which they occur), and lets only a small minority survive and establish a new standard. Mutations make the evolutionary process dynamic; natural selection makes it stable. Through natural selection, advantages are preserved, disadvantages eliminated. Mutations are either "selected for" or "selected against." Selection language is offensive to social sensibilities, but it is the reality of the evolutionary world, and a challenge to understanding God as love (1 John 4:8).

Every biological development is subject to the judgment of natural selection: fit or unfit. The "judgment" is entirely impersonal, blind, and automatic. Actually, there is no judge and no judgment; there is only success or failure. If a new variation works well, it tends to spread through its species. If it does not work well, its bearer normally dies without reproducing. An insect may have the ability to leap or fly, but those that also have camouflage have a distinct advantage in avoiding predators. A grasshopper with a gene for camouflage is more likely to survive and bear camouflaged offspring that can also survive. By contrast, insects without camouflage are more likely to become extinct. In evolution, every advantage contributes to the long-term survival of the species. By adjudicating new developments as fit or unfit, natural selection keeps living things strong and competitive. Like a ghost, natural selection has no substance or location; like an "invisible hand" it sorts interactions in the marketplace of life.

In concert with mutations and vast swathes of geologic time, natural selection keeps the biosphere vibrant. Removing unworkable features, it preserves advantageous features, both old and new, thus both maintaining stability and fostering a controlled development of novelty and diversity. These are no small accomplishments, but if they are purely naturalistic, then any role for divine design and activity looks superfluous (Rolnick 2015, Ch. 3). For many, natural selection has been the best argument for naturalism.

Beyond the issue of divine design, natural selection raises a moral issue: Can an evolutionary world governed by natural selection be created by a God of love?

Every organism alive at this moment is descended from a long line of evolutionary winners. Minimally, the ancestors of current organisms had to survive long enough and to compete well enough to reproduce. But untold trillions of organisms and most historical species did not survive. While natural selection is clearly effective, what does its heartlessness, its regime of winners and losers, say about the Creator?

Further exacerbating this challenge, natural selection intrudes into areas we hold dear, such as the human brain and motherly love. The brain is a powerful evolutionary feature, but it is biologically expensive. Although big brains are selected for, they require a lot of energy. The chimpanzee brain uses 8 percent of the basal metabolic rate; the human brain uses about 22 percent, which then necessitates better nourishment. Larger brains not only need better food, they also need larger heads. Meeting these needs is a feat of evolutionary ingenuity.

A seemingly unsurpassable limit for brain size was the size of a woman's birth canal. If the birth canal were too large, normal movement would be impeded and therefore selected against. The evolutionary solution is ingenious: let human babies' brains grow in size for 12 months after birth. Essentially, the human baby is born 12 months premature, a situation that demands an intense and lengthy period of mother–child nurture. To get the evolutionary advantage of larger brains, natural selection, by means of selected-for mutations, found a workaround of the birth-canal problem. But the troubling implication is that large brains and human motherly love are only by-products and servants of biological adaptation. To think that our brains and mother-love are no more than stratagems of natural selection is disturbing.

Furthermore, when necessary, natural selection can do the opposite and turn a mother against offspring. As Darwin observed,

> It may be difficult, but we ought to admire the savage instinctive hatred of the queen-bee, which urges her instantly to destroy the young queens her daughters as soon as born, or to perish herself in the combat; for undoubtedly this is for the good of the community; and maternal love or maternal hatred, though the latter fortunately is most rare, is all the same to the inexorable principle of natural selection.
>
> (Darwin 1979, 230)

This mother–daughter combat, even though among insects, is still unsettling. We seem to be ensconced in an evolutionary realm wherein natural selection is invisibly manipulating behavior toward one ultimate goal: biological survival. This heartless manipulation and the ongoing extermination of countless evolutionary losers do not seem compatible with a God of love.

The theological challenge of natural selection is deepened when we consider that struggle, pain, and death are biologically universal. The universality of struggle, pain, and death call into question the goodness of creation—and thereby the goodness of the Creator.

By the early nineteenth century, excavations had made it clear that a great number of entire *species* had died. At some point, every human child learns to deal with death, but the fact that entire species perish, over 99 percent of those that have ever lived, forces a reconsideration of the natural world. The fossil record indicates that most mammalian species last for about 2 million years; marine invertebrates about 3.4 million; and insects about 3.6 million. We can only speculate about how long the human race will persist. Both collectively and individually, we are involved in a biological arms race. To struggle and experience pain are the high prices that natural selection demands and, since all biological beings die, the rewards are decidedly temporary.

Pondering this evolutionary reality, a naturalist can simply say, that's the way things are. But for those who believe in the goodness of creation, the harshness of natural selection is a challenge that requires response.

At first sight, natural selection and a God of love seem incompatible. But in spite of its harshness, natural selection not only serves indispensable biological purposes, but also prepares human beings for something greater than the biosphere. Natural selection has produced a diverse biosphere of strength, complexity, adaptability, and beauty, and *Homo sapiens* is very much part of this evolutionary development. By providing humanity with a difficult initial setting, an evolutionary creation is part of the training ground that human persons need to develop character fit for eternity.

Natural selection forces us to stop dreaming of a perfect earth filled with creature comforts for all. Instead, it points us toward a principal purpose of creation: to let humanity freely participate in its own growth in biology, culture, and, most importantly, toward God. Seen in this light, natural selection and divine love are in no way incompatible: "Do not despise the Lord's discipline, and do not resent his rebuke, because the Lord disciplines those he loves, as a father the son he delights in" (Proverbs 3:11–12, capitalization altered). Apart from discipline, imperfect and immature beings like us are unlikely to advance in our engagement of nature, culture, God, and one another. We are multileveled creatures and for us, on the levels of nature, culture, and spirit, discipline is part of love.

Admittedly, natural selection has played a key role in the evolution of the human brain and the correlated mother–child nurture. Bigger brains are indeed selected for greater survival, but they are also prerequisites of the higher-level activities of seeking truth, goodness, and beauty, and these higher-level activities go well beyond evolutionary demands.

Naturalism would build an interpretative wall around natural phenomena, focusing solely on the lower level of what happens and what causes what. But natural phenomena can also be construed as servants of supernatural purposes. From this perspective, the selective pressures leading to mother–child attachment are only the beginning of the story. Beyond biology, receiving a mother's love and nurture introduces a child to interpersonal affection and orients it toward future acts of affection and kindness. Without this parental introduction into a realm of love, it may be difficult if not impossible for the child to love others, let alone to follow Jesus' call to love all people, even enemies (cf. Matthew 5:43–46; Luke 10:25–37). By promoting the biological attachment of mother and child, natural selection also supports the higher possibilities of a life of love.

In Darwin's example of a queen bee attacking its own offspring, the behavior is unquestionably vicious and unsettling to us. The takeaway point is not that insects can be cruel (they can); rather, it is that within the evolutionary biosphere there is a species that cares about cruelty—even when that cruelty is perpetrated within a distant species. Living within nature, humanity has spiritual capacities that exceed nature.

It is possible but not necessary to interpret natural selection solely through the lens of naturalism. Natural selection is nature's form of winning and losing. During 3.45 billion years of evolution, competition for limited resources has prompted the biosphere's tremendous development. The struggle of the parts, including our struggles, has benefited the whole. Like gravity, there is something unyielding and completely impersonal about natural selection and the price that it has exacted. But in spite of the cost, it is difficult even to conceive a biosphere where losing had no effect and where being weak and ineffectual did not matter. Natural selection teaches us to face reality as it is, and not as we would have it to be. In and of itself, the natural world cannot be called ethical, but it could be called pre-ethical.

Even in Jesus' parable of the talents we encounter winners and losers. Two servants develop their given talents and are strongly rewarded. A third servant buries his one talent in the ground and is severely punished (Matthew 25:14–30). It is an unfortunately common illusion that the material world is difficult and the spiritual realm is easy. On all levels of reality—in nature, in culture, and with the Spirit of God— human persons and communities must learn to overcome difficulties. It is easy to fail; continued success over time requires character.

Winning and losing are part of the natural world; more tamely, with fewer life-and-death consequences, they are part of human civilization; and greatly transformed, they are part of Jesus' gospel. Darwin's natural selection is about winning in the biological world; Jesus' teaching is ultimately about the greatest possible victory, about entering into "the fellowship of eternal happiness" (Rolnick 2015, Chs. 4–5).

These three test cases, Big Bang, fine-tuning, and the natural selection of evolution, show that contemporary science and contemporary faith can be compatible. In each case, scientific discovery provides material that, rightly interpreted, can nourish and stimulate Christian thought.

Logos: The Divine Source and Possibility of Science

From the perspective of faith, science can be seen as a quest to understand the details of creation. Far from being a cause of concern, discoveries of microcosmic and macrocosmic splendor have opened new paths into the love of creation. Science has progressively uncovered an intricate order and profound intelligibility in the natural world, order and intelligibility so beautiful that they point beyond science—to something that has made science possible.

These pointers are signs of transcendence discovered in the material world. They conjure up a basic religious intuition, leading us to ask: what is it that makes an orderly, intelligible, and inhabitable universe possible? Thus, Nobel physicist Eugene Wigner famously wondered why mathematics so neatly corresponds to the actual patterns of the physical world, why mathematics has such "unreasonable effectiveness" (Wigner 1960). And Albert Einstein declared: "The only incomprehensible thing about the universe is that it is comprehensible" (cited in Polkinghorne 1993, 235). But if the universe is created by God, mathematical effectiveness should be expected, and the human ability to comprehend the universe is right on schedule. There is a reason that there is reason; a cause of all causality; and an initiating purpose that makes all subsequent purpose possible (Rolnick 2015, 150).

From the perspective of faith, the universe can be scientifically explored only because it originates in a Creator of infinite intelligence. Scientific reason is thus not a lucky accident; nor is it a flicker of virtuosity played out on an ultimately meaningless universe stage. Instead, science is a rational activity rationally applied to a universe imbued with its own rational laws. Science is a human response to what the ancient Greeks—and the biblical Prologue of John—called *Logos*—the reason that there is reason.

This foundational reason, cause, and purpose is in the very roots of created reality. In the original Greek language New Testament, *Logos* had several important meanings, the most currently well known being "Word." But equally well known to the ancient Greeks was reason—reason in the deepest sense, even the ground and source of all reason. For almost 600 years before its biblical use, Logos had been used in Greek philosophical and religious writing, mostly to indicate the divine, rational principle that had caused the ordered, law-like structure of the cosmos.

Drawing upon yet moving beyond these historical precedents, the opening of the Gospel of John salutes the role of the Logos in creation. Repeating the first phrase of the creation story in Genesis, "In the beginning," John's Gospel then elaborates—by stipulating that all of creation comes forth from the divine Person identified as the Logos:

> In the beginning was the Logos, and the Logos was with God, and the Logos was God. He was in the beginning with God. All things came into being through him, and without him not one thing came into being.
>
> (John 1:1–3)

Since all things come into being through the Logos, the reason or the mind of God, all of creation is imprinted with a share of divine reason. Thus, all created things act according to principles of reason, principles that can be scientifically discovered. Given the centrality of the Logos in the Gospel of John, scientific development should be seen as the fulfillment of an expectation, the expectation that an infinitely intelligent Creator, the Logos, has imbued the creation, and especially the human mind, with its own logos. Science is possible because, in the beginning, all things came into being through the Logos—the divine source of reason.

Concluding Reflections

The relationship between science and theology in many ways depends on how reason is interpreted. In naturalism, scientific (and other) reason is believed to be an outgrowth of evolutionary pressure to use bigger brains for better rates of survival in a perennially tough neighborhood. In this reductionist view, reason is encircled by absurdity, because our appearance, like the appearance of galactic structures to support human life, is believed to be accidental, unintended, and temporary. If naturalism accurately describes the way things are, it would not be good news, not even for those who hold the view. But if scientific reason is seen as a logos derived from the original Logos of the Creator, then human reason is not an anomaly, but rather, a sign of transcendence and a bestowed capacity for pursuing meaningful purpose.

In spite of its claims, naturalism is, like Christianity, a belief. Belief of some kind or another simply cannot be avoided. The naturalist, reductionist belief prevents meaningful dialogue, let alone integration, with Christian faith. Moreover, because this naturalist belief places science and all human effort in an ultimately meaningless and purposeless universe, it contributes to the eventual weakening of science. Why pursue scientific reason in a universe that has no purpose and where death will have the final word? The naturalist belief is really a form of betting against oneself.

But when science is partnered with faith, science can recognize the debt that it owes before its inquiries begin: a universe home that is not only habitable, but also capable of being studied. It is entirely reasonable to ask why the universe is so well ordered and why it functions everywhere according to intelligent law. And it is also reasonable to believe that in the beginning was the Logos—the divine source of reason and the ground and possibility of science.

That God created has long been a belief of Christians and other monotheists, but if prodded and poked, this belief is too often revealed as somewhat flimsy. For many believers creation is something so distant and vague that it is ineffective in shaping life performance. The good news is, recent scientific discoveries like the Big Bang, fine-tuning, and even natural selection have revealed details about the cosmos that can give belief in creation a new solidity, an understanding that more fully grasps the intricacy and beauty of our universe home.

In the sixth century B.C., the Hebrew priests provided an inspired view of the origin, development, and purpose of the cosmos. But the science of our age lets us see a universe even more beautiful, with discoverable laws displaying awe-inspiring rationality. Joining faith with scientific understanding, allowing scientific discovery to foster a broader and deeper love of creation, is a difficult task, but also one of the great opportunities of our age.

Key Terms

Big Bang theory	fine-tuning	natural selection
cosmic microwave background radiation	Galileo Galilei	past-eternal
	naturalism	

Questions for Reading

1. What are the four models for the interaction between Christian theology and science described by Ian Barbour?

2. How have contemporary scholars corrected previous histories of the Galileo affair?

3. What is the significance of the Big Bang for Christian theology? Why do some theologians regard the Big Bang as good news for Christian claims about the creation?

4. What is meant by the term "fine-tuning," and why is it important for Christian theology?

5. What does natural selection tell us about the evolutionary process that is theologically significant?

Works Consulted/Recommended Reading

Aristotle. 1962. *Nicomachean Ethics*. Translated by Martin Oswald. Indianapolis, IN: Bobbs-Merrill.

Barbour, Ian G. 1997 (1990). *Religion and Science: Historical and Contemporary Issues*. Revised and expanded edition of *Religion in an Age of Science*. New York: HarperSanFrancisco.

Barr, Stephen M. 2003. *Modern Physics and Ancient Faith*. Notre Dame, IN: University of Notre Dame Press.

Collins, Francis. 2006. *The Language of God: A Scientist Presents Evidence for Belief*. New York: Simon and Schuster.

Darwin, Charles. 1979. *The Origin of Species*. Foreword by Patricia Horan. New York: Gramercy Books.

Finocchiaro, Maurice A. 2009. "Myth 8: That Galileo Was Imprisoned and Tortured for Advocating Copernicanism." In *Galileo Goes to Jail and Other Myths about Science and Religion*. Edited by Ronald L. Numbers, 68–78. Cambridge, MA: Harvard University Press.

Haught, John F. 1995. *Religion and Science: From Conflict to Conversation*. New York: Paulist Press.

Jastrow, Robert. 1978. *God and the Astronomers*. New York: W.W. Norton & Co.

John Paul II, Pope. 1992. "Allocution to the Pontifical Academy of Sciences." http://bertie.ccsu.edu/naturesci/Cosmology/GalileoPope.html, accessed January 17, 2018.

Langford, Jerome J. 1999. *Galileo, Science, and the Church.* 3rd edn. Ann Arbor, MI: University of Michigan Press.

Polkinghorne, John. 1993. "More to the World Than Meets the Eye." *Religion and the Natural Sciences: The Range of Engagement.* Edited by James E. Huchingson. Fort Worth, TX: Harcourt Brace Jovanovich.

Rolnick, Philip A. 2015. *Origins: God, Evolution, and the Question of the Cosmos.* Waco, TX: Baylor University Press.

Wigner. Eugene. 1960. "The Unreasonable Effectiveness of Mathematics in the Natural Sciences." *Communications on Pure and Applied Mathematics* 13, no. 1: 1–14.

Chapter

CHRISTIANITY IN THE CONTEMPORARY SITUATION

In Chapter 22, we saw that modern thinkers highly value the use of reason in discovering truth. However, in our contemporary situation one encounters the idea that there are multiple truths that can all be supported for different reasons that are equally valid. This way of thinking is distinct from that found in modernity, and it has been called **post-modern** in an effort at capturing the new historical moment in which we find ourselves today. Modern thinkers certainly knew that multiple views could be held on a topic. However, they typically maintained that through discussion and debate a single viewpoint could be determined to be *correct*, and the others could be determined to be *incorrect*. By contrast, post-modern thinkers tend to see difference of opinion as insurmountable. To be post-modern is to acknowledge and value *diversity*.

Another feature of post-modernity follows from this characterization. If a diversity of viewpoints ever is actually overcome, and only one position is held on a topic, the post-modern thinker worries that this has occurred simply through an exertion of *power*, not because of truth triumphing over error. That is, post-modern figures are acutely aware of the ways in which those in positions of power have used their influence to silence dissenting voices. Such efforts might produce a veneer of unanimity that makes it seem as if a single truth has been achieved, but post-modern thinkers attempt to uncover alternative viewpoints (i.e., other truths) from those whose voices have been suppressed. The well-known saying "History is written by the victors" captures this sentiment. Those who *win* get to determine what stories will be told. Post-modern thinkers view criticizing so-called master narratives (i.e., those histories that are written by the victors) as one of their most important duties. They contend that such histories have been successfully advanced only through the use of force. There are always other stories that have been pushed to the margins by those in positions of authority. Recovering insights from the marginalized constitutes a major preoccupation of the post-modern approach.

One more characteristic of post-modernity will complete this opening outline. Whereas many modern thinkers view their intellectual efforts as attaining a neutral, objective understanding of the object of their study, post-modern figures emphasize the ways in which everyone is in fact biased, so much so that objectivity can never actually be achieved. There simply is no neutral ground from which to make objective judgments. We are all committed to one degree or another to the various topics we investigate, and such commitments inevitably influence our viewpoints.

In these regards, then, post-modernity represents a decided break from modernity, and even a repudiation of it. However, certain features of the post-modern condition can be viewed as extreme versions of modern sensibilities. For instance, the value placed on the autonomy of the individual human being, outlined in Chapter 22, arguably finds its *completion* in post-modernism. As we have seen, modern thinkers regard independent, first-hand knowledge as superior to any submission to authority. Left unchecked, this mind-set can lead to the idea that the individual gets to determine what is true for him- or herself, without needing to justify his or her views to any "authority" (i.e., anyone else) at all. In other words, autonomy can lead quite easily to hyper-individualization and subjectivism.

The other way in which some see the post-modern sensibility as a continuation of modernity concerns the role of history, which we discussed in Chapter 22. The modern person's awareness of the ways in which ideas *develop* over time leads to a "historical consciousness," or the understanding that the ways we think have not been constant throughout history. Instead, those ways of thinking change quite drastically depending on the particular time period in which we live. Left unchecked, this awareness can cause one to question the extent to which those at any point in history have a grasp of truth; after all, other people at other historical moments no doubt thought they had things right, yet many of their viewpoints now seem definitively outdated.

In a nutshell, this is the post-modern condition. Now, our question: Is it good or bad for Christian theology? Two points should be made. First, post-modernity presents a profound set of difficulties to Christian theology, many of which are even more vexing than the challenges posed in the modern period. The most potent problem is that proclaiming any kind of single, authoritative, unbiased truth will be met with suspicion in a post-modern setting. As a result, Christian truth claims will be exceedingly difficult to advance in such an environment (as will any other truth claims, for that matter).

Second, however, post-modernity offers opportunities for Christian theology that might not initially be obvious. A number of theologians today hold that post-modernity loosens the stifling grip that Enlightenment reason had on the modern mind, and that Christian theology now has space to breathe, if you will, in the cracks that have opened up. In other words, the post-modern critique of modernity claims that *any* allegedly comprehensive way of thinking is in fact only a partial view from a particular vantage point, and certainly not a universally valid way of thinking. Post-modernity demotes every "totalizing discourse" to a lower status as a merely fragmentary description of reality. Those modern systems of thought that have precluded Christian theological claims (such as Enlightenment rationalism) are therefore defanged by the post-modern critique. Simply put, post-modernity takes reason down a notch.

This sense of opportunity for Christian theology increases as we turn to another feature of our contemporary situation: **post-secularism**. As discussed in the Introduction to this book, the so-called secularization thesis held sway among prominent intellectuals in the mid-twentieth century. Peter Berger was particularly influential as one of the foremost advocates of the theory in the 1960s. The secularization thesis held that the world would become increasingly secular as the central ideas of modernity spread and religion would gradually disappear. This view owed a great deal to Karl Marx, who as we saw in Chapter 22 held that religion is simply a human response to oppression, and that religion will vanish as oppressive conditions are eliminated. As the twentieth century progressed, many waited for the demise of religion, only to find that it never came. Finally, in the last year of the twentieth century, Peter Berger himself proclaimed the following,

> The world today, with some exceptions … is as furiously religious as it ever was, and in some places more so than ever. This means that a whole body of literature by historians and social scientists loosely labeled "secularization theory" is essentially mistaken.
>
> (Berger 1999, 2)

What once seemed inevitable strikes many now as highly unlikely. With the failure of the secularization thesis come new openings for religion in general and Christianity in particular.

This chapter will outline some of the most important figures and schools of Christian thought that have tended to see post-modernity as an opportunity, despite the difficulties it raises. These figures have proposed forms of theology that are distinct from the modern theological projects described in previous chapters. Broadly speaking, whereas the response of many Christian theologians during the modern period was to insist that Christianity can be reformulated so as to appeal to modern sensibilities, during the post-modern period Christian theologians frequently insist that Christianity is a separate discourse with its own rules that cannot be infringed upon by non-Christians. These are Christian theologies in a new mode of operation, and they are rightly seen as *post*-modern.

This treatment of post-modernity will also aid the reader in understanding the material in Chapter 27 on theologies of liberation. Liberation theology concerns itself with those who speak from the margins, those who have been on the receiving end of power and historically have had no voice. Major strands of liberation theology insist not only that such persons deserve to be heard, but also that God seeks to liberate them from their oppression. This interest in the margins and attentiveness to power are entirely consonant with the post-modern sensibility described above. This book's final chapter, on Christianity and interreligious dialogue, also does its work within a post-modern world that respects differences among various religious traditions.

Although post-modernism describes a great deal of our contemporary situation, it does not encompass every single feature of today's world. One important contemporary movement that does not fit easily into the post-modern framework is the "New Atheism," which Anne King describes in the final section of this chapter. As will become clear, the New Atheism is best viewed as a continuation of modernity rather than as a post-modern way of thinking.

HOW DID WE GET HERE? A BRIEF HISTORY OF POST-MODERNISM

Although the precise date at which post-modernism begins is a matter of some debate, it is widely agreed that by the 1970s it was in full swing in Western European and North American societies. With that said, one sees foreshadowings of post-modernism as early as the mid-nineteenth century; both **Søren Kierkegaard** (1813–1855) and **Friedrich Nietzsche** (1844–1900) are often regarded as "prophets" of post-modernity. These figures anticipated the post-modern critique of modernity long before it became culturally widespread. Whereas Nietzsche presents a nihilistic form of post-modern thought, Kierkegaard intriguingly shows a way in which Christian faith can actually thrive in such a setting. We presently turn to Nietzsche, and we will examine Kierkegaard in the next section.

Nietzsche was a powerful critic of Christianity, as we saw in Chapter 22. He also ruthlessly questions the entire Enlightenment project of relying on reason to arrive at truth. Nietzsche thinks that reason is a deeply flawed tool for learning about reality. He holds that, although we might think of ourselves as using reason to develop concepts that describe the world, those concepts are in fact arbitrary inventions that do not grant any actual contact with reality. To use Nietzsche's example, in response to witnessing a wide variety of leaves in the world, we develop the single concept "leaf." Although we regard this concept as describing reality, each individual leaf actually *differs* from all other leaves, and we arrive at the concept "leaf" only if we look past these differences. The move, then, to assert *sameness* instead of paying attention to *difference* ignores the complexity of the actual state of affairs, which is that there is a tremendous diversity of individual leaves, none of which is adequately captured by the concept "leaf."

Although the consequences of Nietzsche's critique might seem trivial when foliage is the issue in question, he insists that *all* of our attempts to know things work in the same way. The concepts we develop do give us a set of ideas that we can comprehend, but they are all ultimately false inventions that bear no relation to reality itself.

To Nietzsche, the problem is even deeper, and here one sees a second aspect of his criticism of Enlightenment reason. Nietzsche holds that our use of reason is tied up with our *interests*, with what we want to be the case about the world. The various concepts we develop through reason, then, are not dispassionately formed, but instead confer advantages on those who create them. In other words, we regard as true those ideas that give us *power*.

In a third blow to the notion that our ideas reflect the way things objectively are, Nietzsche notes that our ideas have changed over time. He does this especially with our sense of values. He suggests that studying history reveals that the things we regard as good are arbitrarily determined by the historical moment in which we happen to live. The genre of writing that does this work is the "genealogy," as it comes to be called, or historical tracing of an idea. In Chapter 22, we saw one such genealogy in Nietzsche's treatment of the emergence of the "slave morality." Nietzsche suggests that caring for the weak is not an inherently good action that reflects a timeless truth about how the world should be. Instead, according to Nietzsche, that deeply held value developed because of a historically contingent situation; it arose because of something that did not have to occur. The people who created the slave morality were themselves weak and looked for a way to improve their situation, but things most certainly would have been different if they had been in a position of dominance in their culture.

In these three ways, then, Nietzsche undermined the Enlightenment project of using reason to discover truth and sowed the seeds of post-modern thought. Although it would take some time for his views to become widely known, we now turn to a figure who played a significant role in spreading Nietzsche's ideas in the twentieth century: the French philosopher and historian **Michel Foucault** (1926–1984), who has been called "Nietzsche's truest disciple."

Foucault amplifies Nietzsche's three criticisms from above and follows Nietzsche's arguments through to some extraordinarily far-reaching conclusions. Concerning the first point, Foucault holds with Nietzsche that our concepts impose arbitrary mental constructions onto the world, and that we have no actual knowledge of reality. Perhaps more than Nietzsche, Foucault emphasizes that the *otherness* of individual entities (such as leaves) is violated when an all-encompassing concept is used to speak about all of those discrete things as if they could be unified under a single idea. To Foucault, individual things have an integrity of sorts that is infringed upon when one asserts sameness about things that are in fact different.

Foucault's attention to the violation of otherness leads to the second manner in which he amplifies an aspect of his Nietzschean inheritance. Nietzsche had exposed the way in which our efforts at knowing are not dispassionately undertaken, but instead involve the interests of those who pursue knowledge. Foucault goes one step further (or perhaps makes something explicit that had only been implicit in Nietzsche himself) in claiming that all knowledge is *violence*. As he vividly states this claim, "Knowledge is not made for understanding; it is for cutting" (Foucault 1977, 154).

This striking point can be explained by reference to Foucault's idea of "discourse." Foucault holds that what we ordinarily think of as "knowledge" is better understood as "discourse." In other words, we become accustomed to ways of speaking or conducting discourse with one another, but these ways in which we use language have themselves been shaped by various interests and institutions that influence us to think of certain things as true and other things as false. They are *regulated* forms of speech that preclude certain possibilities and allow for others. (The political arena provides countless examples of this phenomenon.) As Foucault puts it, what we think of as truth is in fact "a system of ordered procedures for the production, regulation, distribution, circulation, and operation of statements" (quoted in Grenz 1996, 133). We accept as authoritative those experts and institutions that tell us how to use language and construct knowledge. Truth, however, is ultimately an invention that serves those in power and does a disservice—even violence—to all the rest.

In response to this, Foucault applies Nietzsche's method of historical investigation to a much broader range of topics than Nietzsche himself examined. Foucault writes a number of genealogies through which he exposes how some of the dominant discourses of Western societies have arisen. In tellingly titled works such as *Madness and Civilization: A History of Insanity in an Age of Reason*, *Discipline and Punish: The Birth of the Prison*, and *A History of Sexuality*, Foucault investigates the ways in which Western culture has constructed our views of insanity, criminality, and sexuality, respectively. He does this work in order to present a "counter-memory" that will disrupt the existing order by exposing the arbitrary way in which it has been constructed. His writings are often interpreted as creating new discourses that will legitimate those who have been pushed to the margins by the dominant narratives within Western societies. This attention to the "Other" is very much a part of our world today, and it is often regarded as one of the most ethically significant aspects of post-modern thought.

This final aspect of Foucault's work leads to another thinker, Jean-François Lyotard (1924–1988), who was actually the first to use the term "postmodern" in his classic *The Postmodern Condition: A Report on Knowledge*. To Lyotard, post-modernity can be succinctly characterized as "incredulity toward metanarratives" (Lyotard 1984, xxiv). In other words, the post-modern person is aware that metanarratives, or sweeping explanations that claim to be all-encompassing, tell their stories from a particular perspective with a particular set of goals in mind. As such, they reflect the interests of those who write them. Lyotard suggests that the savvy post-modern person simply does not believe that these histories are as comprehensive as they have been made out to be, and that suppressed views lie in the margins of those metanarratives.

To gain a sense of how far Lyotard's critique reaches, it will be helpful to know that his primary concern is an Enlightenment-based notion of science as commanding universal authority. Lyotard seeks to expose the way in which even modern science does not actually produce *truth*, but instead is just another form of discourse that arises in an attempt at exerting power.

The post-modern condition, then, is one of fragmentation in which universal claims do not have credibility. In this setting, all attempts at asserting truth are viewed as in fact exertions of power. Figures such as Nietzsche insist that modern ideas about reason and the knowledge that it can produce are deeply flawed, and that we should acknowledge just how *uncertain* we are about the world in which we live.

Of course, not everyone agrees with the ways of thinking described above, and post-modernism has no shortage of virulent critics. Some argue that unacceptable ethical implications follow from the idea that there is no objective idea of truth or goodness in the world. These critics maintain that post-modernism has produced an environment in which relativism has flowered, allowing a defense of deeply troubling behaviors and beliefs through the claim that they are good or true "for me."

Others point out that post-modern thinkers do in fact make truth claims despite their opposition to them. These critics assert that figures such as Nietzsche do actually hold that something is true about how our concepts relate to the world, even if it is only that our concepts have no relation to the world at all. In other words, even the negative claim made by Nietzsche is a truth claim; it is a claim about how things actually are.

Sympathetic critics of post-modern thought point out that, although difference is important to acknowledge, claiming radical incommensurability among different things (be they leaves or more important things) fails to recognize that *similarity* sometimes accurately describes relationships among things. Although post-modern thinkers are right to hold that previous uses of reason objectionably glossed over difference in developing overarching concepts, some will say that the pendulum has swung too far in the other direction, such that only difference is emphasized now, thus glossing over similarity when it is appropriate to maintain it.

In spite of these criticisms and the reassessment of post-modernity that they have sparked in recent years, one cannot deny that post-modernity has powerfully shaped our contemporary setting. Although the average person on the street might not be familiar with the complex terminology described above, post-modern ideas saturate daily life in our world. For instance, the value placed on diversity on college campuses and in the workplace has arisen directly from the intellectual movements outlined in this section. Similarly, the contemporary emphasis on respecting different religious traditions is often based on the notion that no single religion has a claim on truth, which is a deeply post-modern idea. Additionally, the concern with ensuring that marginalized perspectives are heard and acknowledged has become prevalent as a result of post-modern thought. Post-modernity, then, certainly consists of attitudes that many find deeply worrying, but it also animates ethical stances that are often regarded as the most admirable features of our contemporary world.

With this sketch of the post-modern condition in place, we now offer a number of theological responses to it. As mentioned above, we will see that these post-modern theological options differ from modern theologies in that they respond to a distinct set of criticisms in a different cultural context.

EXISTENTIALIST THEOLOGY: EMBRACING SUBJECTIVITY IN THE NAME OF AUTHENTICITY

If, as post-modern thinkers hold, there is no truth "out there," objectively in the world, but instead only what it true *for me*, then one response is to embrace this state of affairs and pursue one's own truth with utmost vigor. Although the movement known as existentialism is sometimes characterized as a modern phenomenon (it precedes the beginnings of post-modernity by a few decades), it offers considerable resources to those who, in post-modern fashion, see the search for objective truth as a misguided quest.

The Danish religious thinker Søren Kierkegaard (1813–1855) is often regarded as both a prophet of post-modernity and the father of existentialism. As such, his writings exhibit both a relentless critique of rationalism (or the over-reliance on reason in the effort to attain objective truth) and a passionate search for authenticity. Kierkegaard was a sharp critic of G.W.F. Hegel (see Chapter 22), and through a number of pseudonymous works, he inveighed against Hegel by insisting that reason is a woefully insufficient tool for understanding human existence. The human being is first and foremost an *individual*, a particular being in a concrete situation who cannot be comprehensively described through general categories. The individual person is not simply a particular instance of a broader category ("millennial," "American," "Democrat," "Republican"), as if the category alone could capture who that person is. The unique characteristics of the existing individual cannot be understood through general concepts. In a manner similar to Nietzsche's concern about concepts obscuring differences among individual things, to Kierkegaard the individual is inassimilable and in an important sense unknown to abstract reason.

Additionally, Hegel used reason to develop an all-encompassing system that promised a comprehensive account of reality, but Kierkegaard's writings insist that concretely existing human beings have only a fragmentary glimpse of things. We are perpetually confronted with *uncertainty*. The proper response to this intractable state of affairs is not to pretend that we can attain certain, objective truth concerning the most important questions about human existence, such as the meaning of our lives and the ultimate destiny of our souls. Instead, the proper response is to understand anew what truth means in the first place. In *Concluding Unscientific Postscript* (1846), for which Kierkegaard intriguingly creates the pseudonymous author "Johannes Climacus," the author famously claims that *truth is subjectivity*. That is, attaining truth is not about seeking what is the case objectively. The desire to attain objective truth too frequently involves putting off any real *decision*

Figure 26–1 Søren Kierkegaard (1813–1855).

about what one thinks. The scholar conducting research in his or her field may get closer and closer to certainty about a specific topic, but his or her investigations yield only *probability*, never certainty, and the theories developed in many fields are always revisable; they are never fixed, once and for all. Therefore, they cannot claim absolute certainty.

Only in subjective "appropriation," only in *committing* to an idea unreservedly and saying that it is true *for me* can one find truth. Truth, then, is redefined as follows in the *Postscript*: "An objective uncertainty, held fast through appropriation with the most passionate inwardness, is the truth, the highest truth there is for an existing person" (Kierkegaard 1992, 203). In other words, in the most important human endeavors, we simply cannot attain objective certainty; it might be available to God, but it is not available to us. The "existing person," then, attains truth by devoting himself or herself to an idea with infinite passion; finding truth is about *committing*, even in the face of uncertainty.

It is important to understand that Kierkegaard's writings do not claim that there is no objective truth at all; they do not celebrate subjectivism, as do some twentieth century post-modern thinkers. However, his work does hold that we, in all of our limitations, will never be able to reach objective truth ourselves on those matters of utmost importance to us for understanding our existence. In the face of this difficulty, we should focus on our inner attitude, not on an exterior, objective state of affairs.

This rather difficult idea will become clearer if we use an example near to Kierkegaard's heart—namely, the subjective appropriation of Christianity by the individual Christian. Kierkegaard regarded his life's work as an effort at making Christians in the midst of Christendom. In other words, he worried that a Christian society produces people who unreflectively, automatically become part of the church without truly thinking about Christianity and owning it for themselves. He was concerned about phony Christians who proudly wear the name without understanding what it means or living the life it involves. To Kierkegaard, being Christian is not about checking boxes on a list of those doctrines with which one agrees; it is instead about allowing the Christian faith to affect *who one is*. A parrot can recite the Nicene Creed, but a parrot is not a Christian. Why? Because the parrot has not *appropriated* the Christian faith. A well-known portion of *Concluding Unscientific Postscript* makes this point with controversial force:

> If someone who lives in the midst of Christianity enters, with knowledge of the true idea of God, and prays, but prays in untruth, and if someone lives in an idolatrous land but prays with all the passion of infinity, although his eyes are resting upon the image of an idol—where, then is there more truth? The one prays in truth to God although he is worshipping an idol; the other prays in untruth to the true God and is therefore in truth worshipping an idol.
>
> (Kierkegaard 1992, 201)

To worship with utmost intensity is more important than simply having knowledge about God—even if that knowledge is correct. As the author puts it a few lines later in the text, *how* one worships is ultimately more important than *what* one worships. To be clear, the text here does not endorse idolatry; it merely says that passionate devotion is more important than having a correct idea about God that does not actually affect one's life.

Another way to put this point is to say that the question for the individual Christian is not "Does God exist?," nor is it "Is Jesus Christ the incarnation of God?" One can never establish an objective rationale with which to respond to these questions, and even if one could say yes to both, those affirmative answers alone would not address the central issue. The question for the individual Christian is, "Am I in relationship with God?," or, perhaps better, "Have I committed to God despite the fact that I remain uncertain?" Nothing is demanded of the person who simply assents to claims that have been demonstrably proved. By contrast, character is formed precisely in those moments when one does not know, yet commits. Finding truth involves *risk*.

This approach fundamentally differs from the modern theological effort of making Christianity reasonable through one apologetic strategy or another. Kierkegaard's writings insist again and again on a radical transcendence of God that will always far surpass human understanding. There is an "infinite qualitative distinction" between God and human beings. In other words, the difference between God and humans is not one of quantity, according to which God would be placed at a "10" on a scale of sorts, with human beings ranking at a "1" or "2." Instead, God is *qualitatively* different, meaning that God is not even on the same plane of existence as human beings.

To Kierkegaard, precisely because God differs so completely from human beings, the entrance of the eternal, infinite God into history (i.e., the Incarnation) can be viewed only as an "Absolute Paradox." It is something that must strike us as utterly absurd. It cannot be proved or demonstrated; it is far beyond the capacity of objective, scientific inquiry to ascertain. Instead, it can be known only in faith, which is a leap into the absurd made by the individual. In a sharp rebuke of modern apologetics, Kierkegaard's works insist that Christian faith is not supported by any "reason" whatsoever. Quite the opposite, in fact: the Incarnation is an *offense* to reason, and any effort at diminishing that offense waters down Christianity by attempting to domesticate the radically transcendent God. One does not believe because one has through reason established that Christianity is true. As one commentator helpfully puts it,

> If I believe what God has revealed only because I myself have independently investigated matters and found that the doctrines revealed are true, then my belief does not stem from trust in God and thus does not count as genuine faith.
>
> (Evans 2009, 144)

In this regard Kierkegaard resembles Martin Luther, who famously characterized faith as trust.

Kierkegaard's writings have stirred considerable controversy, not least because the view of faith they endorse strikes many as objectionably irrational and fideistic. However, they offer formidable resources to the contemporary Christian mired in post-modern uncertainty. Kierkegaard's works unflinchingly address the most profound difficulties human beings face, and he provides no facile answers in response to these challenges. Most intriguingly, the notion of faith developed in Kierkegaard's writings is undaunted by the post-modern condition, as it actually *thrives* in an environment of uncertainty. In fact, the points for which Kierkegaard had to argue so forcefully in his own time (concerning our fragmented view of reality and the failures of objective reason) are taken as givens by many in our contemporary society. Postmodernity, then, is a boon for Kierkegaardian faith, as it makes the first step in his project for him.

Although Kierkegaard did not have much impact on nineteenth-century religious thought, his influence in the twentieth and twenty-first centuries has been profound and enduring. The German Protestant theologian **Paul Tillich** (1886–1965) continued the project of developing Christian theology along existentialist lines. Tillich insisted that Christianity is not simply a set of doctrines, but instead must be appropriated by the individual as having meaning for him or her. However, whereas Kierkegaard presented a highly traditional theology to his reader, Tillich sought to rethink Christianity rather substantially in accord with existentialist concerns. In this effort, he employed a **method of correlation**, as he called it. He insisted that the Christian faith provides answers to human beings' most urgent existential questions, but he also held that the Christian message needs to be "correlated" to the contemporary situation. In other words, Christianity needs to be reframed so as to make clear the way in which it speaks to contemporary human beings.

In this regard, Tillich continues the project that began with Schleiermacher (see Chapter 22)—namely, reformulating Christian theology in an idiom that will be comprehensible and compelling to Christians today. The difference between Tillich and Schleiermacher consists of what "today" means in each case. Whereas Schleiermacher had a modern world as the backdrop against which his theology did its work, the world occupied by Tillich's Christian can be characterized as post-modern in certain key respects, as described below.

Tillich begins his theological approach with the existential situation of human beings, which he, like Kierkegaard and many post-modern figures, sees as permeated by uncertainty, fragmentation, and anxiety. Or, to use the language Tillich most often employs, human beings are confronted with *finitude*. In other words, we are aware that we are finite, limited creatures who do not determine our own existence and who will ultimately experience death. In response to this realization, we seek an ultimate ground for our existence; we want something that can support our fragile, contingent being. Such a search is our "**ultimate concern**." There is no pursuit that could be more important for us. This, to Tillich, is what faith is about: the quest for relationship with the ultimate ground or support of our existence.

The problem, to Tillich, is that human beings too often place ultimate concern on an object that cannot bear the weight, so to speak, of ultimacy. In other words, we seek ultimate, lasting reassurance through things that are unable to handle the most profound difficulties we face. We look to money, status, success, or the state to offer us security, but these things can provide at best only a temporary relief from our existential anxiety. They are idols that we end up worshipping by being ultimately concerned about them instead of God. To Tillich, whatever we care about most is, in effect, our God. Worship of some sort is therefore inescapable, even for the atheist. We must be highly discerning as we determine where our ultimate concern will land.

Only God, then, offers us an adequate support in response to our finitude. Crucially, however, we cannot think of God as a being among other beings. If we did, we would place God within the realm of other finite beings and subject God to the same rules, so to speak. As Tillich puts this point, "If God is *a* being, he is subject to the categories of finitude ... Even if he is called the 'highest being' this situation has not changed" (Tillich 1951, 146). Echoing Thomas Aquinas (see Chapter 15), Tillich calls his reader to view God as "being itself," as the ground and support of all beings, undergirding everything that is. Only such a conception of God sufficiently responds to our plight as finite creatures.

This point can be put in a slightly different way. In becoming aware of our finitude, we become cognizant not only that we are finite and contingent, but that everything else we encounter in the world is finite and contingent as well. If there is to be a support for this world of finite things, it must come from *outside* the entire system, which is inherently unstable and in need of grounding. That support cannot be another being among beings. To Tillich, all finite things must face "non-being," or not existing. Only God as being itself has the power to resist and overcome non-being.

Where does Jesus Christ fit in Tillich's existential theology? To Tillich, the above view of God as being itself remains mere speculation, only a possibility and not a reality, without God being *revealed* to human beings. Christ, then, is the vehicle through which the power to resist non-being is shown to humanity. In other words, because of Christ, God as being itself does not simply *remain* outside the system, ultimately inaccessible to human beings. Instead, through Christ, God becomes known *within* the world, in space and time. Christ, then, is the "New Being," as Tillich puts it, who brings about a new way of existing that triumphs over anxiety and despair by offering human beings ultimate consolation in response to their finitude. As one commentator puts it,

> The new being is the power from beyond man that heals his existential conflicts and overcomes his sin, understood as his estrangement from himself, from others, and from his ground. Thus the new being manifested in Christ answers man's ultimate concern and his quest for the ground of being.
>
> (Macquarrie 1963, 369)

CHRISTIAN THEOLOGY AS ITS OWN "LANGUAGE GAME": THE WITTGENSTEINIAN APPROACH

If the post-modern condition is one of fragmentation and a lack of universals, one response is to insist that Christian theology consists of its own internal meanings, which do not need to justify themselves to the outside observer. The modern philosopher **Ludwig Wittgenstein** (1889–1951) has inspired a number of contemporary theologians and philosophers along these lines. These Christian thinkers take post-modernism seriously, and they in fact think it presents an opportunity to Christian theology.

Although Wittgenstein's own religious views are difficult to determine, his idea of **language games** has become highly useful for Christian theologians and philosophers since the mid-twentieth century. In *Philosophical Investigations* (1953), Wittgenstein explains that the meanings of words can be understood only from within a "game" of sorts that determines the rules according to which the words must be used. For example, the meaning of a touchdown can be comprehended only from within the rules of football. If one is going to understand what a touchdown is and why it matters, one must enter into the rules of the game. Outside of the game, a touchdown is meaningless. Its meaning is derived, then, from a web of connections with other words and concepts *within* the game of football.

In Wittgenstein's view, we make a mistake when we try to understand the meaning of a word by imposing criteria on it that are foreign to its native language game. For instance, Wittgenstein objects to the approach of the anthropologist James Frazer (1854–1941), who attempted to explain the religious rituals of ancient societies by using modern social-scientific tools. To Wittgenstein, "Frazer's account of the magical and religious notions of men is unsatisfactory: it makes these views look like *errors*" (Wittgenstein 1993, 119). In other words, as far as Wittgenstein is concerned, Frazer is in no position to comment on whether those ancient people are acting and believing correctly or incorrectly, as he has not entered into the language game (i.e., the culture) in which their words have meaning. To continue the example used above, it is as if Frazer is an umpire who knows only the rules of baseball, yet he is trying to determine whether a touchdown has taken place in a football game. He simply is not qualified to issue a judgment, and any attempt to do so will necessarily be unhelpful and even inappropriate.

Among Christian theologians and philosophers who have applied Wittgenstein's writings to contemporary Christian thought, D.Z. Phillips (1934–2006) stands out as the most influential. Phillips insists that Christian beliefs can make sense only within the language game of Christian faith. If one is to understand what Christians mean when they talk about "God," "Christ," "sin," or "salvation," one must enter into the web of interconnected ideas used by Christians in their own understanding of faith. One implication of this approach is that any atheistic attempt at denying God's existence is fundamentally off track because it does not actually understand what the term "God" means to Christians in the first place. Phillips expresses this idea as follows:

> Philosophers who do not believe in God can no longer think of their rejection as the denial of something *with which they are familiar.* Discovering that there is a God is not like establishing that something is the case within a universe of discourse with which we are already familiar. On the contrary, it is to discover that there is a universe of discourse we had been unaware of.
>
> (quoted in Livingston 2000, 516)

According to this approach to Christian theology in the post-modern situation, Christian belief cannot be evaluated by anything external to the "game" in which it is played, such as foreign philosophical criteria about how reasonable it is.

As powerful as this point is, Phillips has been criticized for seemingly giving license to any sort of belief whatsoever. Indeed, it would seem that the holder of any view at all can simply retreat to his or her language game and cry foul if another person attempts to interfere by criticizing from outside. Although some have indeed used the Wittgensteinian line of thinking for such purposes, Phillips himself is not saying that Christians should be allowed to hold on to their beliefs, no matter how archaic and simplistic they are. Instead, he actually suggests that Christian belief in God is in fact more sophisticated than many outside observers expect:

> Coming to see that there is a God is not like coming to see that an additional being exists. ... Coming to see that there is a God involves seeing a new meaning in one's life, and being given a new understanding. The Hebrew-Christian conception of God is not a conception of a being among beings.
>
> (quoted in Livingston 2000, 516)

Phillips suggests here that language games are not free-for-alls in which anything goes. Instead, there are rules within language games according to which meaning is regulated and determined. To revisit once again the example from above: to play football is not to do whatever one likes just because it has different rules from other sports. Instead, playing football involves entering into a world in which one follows certain rules, even if they are internal to the game itself. Similarly, although Phillips would not think of an *outsider* as having the right to say what is meant by the term God, he does suggest that Christians have the capability and the right to determine *among themselves* which uses of the term are proper and which are improper. The idea of God can and should be refined, then, but the implication of Phillips' position is that only Christians themselves can do it.

With that said, some critics are still unhappy with the way in which this approach to post-modern theology tends to cordon off Christian communities and suggest that there is no overlap between Christian language games and other uses of language that one finds in the contemporary setting. For two approaches that are similarly inspired by post-modern thought, yet emphasize rationality to a greater degree than Phillips does, we turn to Reformed epistemology and Post-Liberal theology.

Lived Religion: Liturgy in the Post-Modern Era: Non-Denominational Worship

The late twentieth century saw a huge increase in Christian denominations that regard themselves as non-denominational. The worship in these churches is often far simpler than the services found in pre-Reformation and early post-Reformation denominations.

The worship space in these churches often seats well over 1,000 people. The room is simple, painted in pale colors with no religious images. At the front is a stage for the worship band that leads praise and worship music at the start of every service. The rest of the space is taken up with comfortable, theater-style chairs, since most of the service consists of a message by a pastor. Sermons are often part of a series on a theme, with examples drawn from the Bible and projected on screens. Pastors do not wear vestments, but instead preach in the same kind of casual attire worn by the congregation, since people are encouraged to come as they are.

Like the worship space, beliefs are also simple. The church believes in a Trinitarian God, and that Jesus came to save everyone who believes in Him. The Bible is the inspired, often inerrant Word of God, and is the final authority for Christian belief and practice. There are two sacraments: Baptism and Communion. Baptism is a public declaration of faith, given only to those able to make a personal faith commitment. Communion, a memorial of the Last Supper, occurs periodically throughout the year. The church generally welcomes anyone to receive, but some communities limit reception to those who consider themselves professed Christians.

An important value in the church is fellowship. To encourage relationships, the church offers a wide variety of ministries and activities, including Bible studies, groups for women, men, families, singles, teens, children, and many service opportunities. By encouraging its members to participate in these groups, the church aims to grow the community and serve others.

REFORMED EPISTEMOLOGY: BELIEF IN GOD AS "PROPERLY BASIC"

The movement known as **Reformed Epistemology** draws inspiration from Reformed Christianity, especially John Calvin (see Chapter 19), and its advocates hold that the post-modern condition presents Christian theology with an opportunity. Figures such as Alvin Plantinga (b. 1932) and William Alston (1921–2009) agree with post-modern philosophers who argue that modern "foundationalism" has failed. As we saw in Chapter 22, modern philosophers such as René Descartes sought clear, indubitable *foundations* on which knowledge can stand. These foundations were supposedly not derived from other beliefs; instead, they were thought of as "basic." In other words, foundational beliefs are simply evident to our senses, such as the belief that there is an external world, or they are self-evident based on logic, such as Descartes' "I think, therefore I am" (Descartes knew he existed because he noticed himself thinking; logically speaking, in order to think, one must first exist). According to foundationalists, knowledge can be built on this firm foundation of beliefs that are either self-evident or evident to the senses, giving us an extraordinary degree of certainty. However, foundationalism has had a negative impact on Christian theology, as foundationalist philosophers have insisted that belief in God is not adequately supported and is therefore irrational. To them, belief in God is not self-evident, evident to the senses, or derived from those two types of foundational beliefs.

In a positive turn for Christian theology, post-modern figures criticize foundationalism, and Reformed epistemologists join them in this regard. Plantinga holds that certain beliefs regarded as basic by foundationalists do not in fact meet their own standards as self-evident or evident to the senses. For instance, Plantinga maintains that foundationalists *assume* things like "other minds exist" and "there is a past," but such claims are not adequately supported by the rigorous standards that foundationalists themselves develop; they cannot be determined with absolute certainty. If foundationalists were to adhere closely to their own strict rules, they should think of such beliefs as irrational. To be clear, Plantinga himself thinks that such beliefs are rational; his point is that we need to relax the standards for determining whether they are reasonable beliefs, as we will never reach the high bar for truth that modernity has bequeathed to us since Descartes. To Plantinga, there might not be firm, indubitable foundations for such claims, but they are *warranted* nonetheless.

After making this critique of foundationalism, Plantinga moves to the constructive portion of his argument, which involves his claim that belief in God resembles the kinds of beliefs upheld as basic by foundationalists, and that it therefore is rational. Drawing from the thought of the Protestant reformer John Calvin (1509–1564), Plantinga holds that human beings believe in God naturally and spontaneously, without prompting or extensive demonstrations. Calvin had asserted that implanted within us is a *sensus divinitatis*, a "sense" or awareness of God. Plantinga uses this idea and puts it in more contemporary terms by saying that belief in God is "properly basic." That is, such a belief does not depend on any prior beliefs, but instead is "hardwired" in us, so to speak. This belief might not be absolutely *certain* (in post-modern, "non-foundationalist" fashion Plantinga insists that little if anything is absolutely certain), but it is nevertheless reliably formed and warranted, and therefore rational.

William Alston, like Plantinga, conducts his academic work in the context of post-modern non-foundationalism. In *Perceiving God* (1991), he seeks to establish that belief in God is justified based on the perception of God, which mystics have described throughout the Christian tradition. To Alston, just as ordinary sense perception can be used to justify beliefs about the world, "mystical perception," as Alston calls it, can be used to justify beliefs about God. Thanks to the post-modern, non-foundational condition in which contemporary persons find themselves, Alston holds that such mystical perception can be successfully defended against those who would criticize it. Mystical perception, like ordinary sense perception, involves a situation in which something *appears* to the human being. This occurs when the appearing thing is not the result of the mind generating the experience, and it happens in ordinary sense perception all the time. Things appear to us, and we learn how to determine which sense perceptions are reliable and which are unreliable.

Alston holds that the Christian tradition gives those who report perceiving God similar tools with which to determine which perceptions are reliable and which are not. Many monastic communities, for instance, educate their novices in how to discern which of their various perceptions of God are valid. Although these practices might take some time to develop because of their complexity, there are criteria that can be used to falsify certain perceptions. Some experiences that initially seem like the perception of God are determined to be simply the result of one's feelings, or even dreams. However, if those criteria are met, Alston holds that the perception of God should be viewed as justified, and the beliefs that result should be upheld as rational.

In classic post-modern fashion, Alston insists that, although mystical perception is analogous to ordinary sense perception, the standards used to assess sense perception must not be imposed on mystical perception. Mystical perception does not often offer the same kind of obvious evidence that ordinary sense perception does, and different rules should therefore be followed within each set of practices. One must not be an "imperialist" and insist that criteria foreign to the proper assessment of mystical perception should be employed in evaluating it.

Looking at Reformed Epistemology as a whole, we can see similarities between it and the Wittgensteinian trajectory described above. Both approaches insist that there are no universal standards that can be applied to Christian beliefs from outside of Christian communities. However, Reformed Epistemology more aggressively criticizes non-Christian claims for knowledge by insisting that they do not rest on a certain foundation, as they are sometimes thought to do. In this state of affairs, in which little to no knowledge is absolutely certain, figures such as Plantinga and Alston characterize Christian belief in God as acceptably warranted or justified.

POST-LIBERAL THEOLOGY: INVITING NON-CHRISTIANS TO JOIN THE CHRISTIAN STORY

In a manner similar to Reformed Epistemology and the Wittgensteinian approach described above, the theological movement known as **Post-Liberal theology** focuses on the internal meanings generated within Christian communities rather than submitting Christian claims to external criteria concerning their credibility. And, like the other two approaches mentioned above, Post-Liberal theology has this opportunity because of the post-modern condition, which insists that universal standards to which all claims must adhere simply do not exist.

What distinguishes the Post-Liberal approach from the other two post-modern theologies mentioned above is that it looks to the biblical narrative as its primary source for meaning. The German-born theologian Hans Frei (1922–1988) is typically viewed as a key founding figure of Post-Liberal theology. Frei immigrated to the United States in 1938, and he studied the theology of Karl Barth, with a particular focus on Barth's break from Liberal Protestant theology in the early twentieth century. In *The Eclipse of Biblical Narrative* (1974), Frei laments the "great reversal" that took place during the modern period with the rise of historical criticism of the Bible. During the modern period, the exercise of understanding the Bible turned into "a matter of fitting the biblical story into another world [i.e., the modern world] ... rather than incorporating that world into the biblical story" (Frei 1974, 130). In other words, Frei calls his reader's attention to the fact that in previous eras the Bible was regarded as an extraordinary chronicle of human beings in relationship with God, and the reader would incorporate his or her own personal story into this deeply compelling narrative. However, during the modern period, interpreters have presumed that the story put forward in the Bible needs to be reworked and fit into contemporary categories. Frei seeks to reassert an interpretive approach that uses the biblical narrative as the primary lens through which the rest of life is viewed.

The American theologian George Lindbeck (1923–2018) continued the Post-Liberal project by focusing on the role played by narrative in Christian theology. In works such as *The Nature of Doctrine* (1984), Lindbeck insisted that being Christian is a matter of grafting oneself onto the Christian narrative: "To become a Christian involves learning the story of Israel and of Jesus well enough to interpret and experience oneself and one's world in its terms" (Lindbeck 1984, 34). In this effort, one should interpret the Bible not in the interest of justifying it to a secular reader, but on its own terms. Lindbeck notes the manner in which great works of literature are read, and he views this approach as instructive for interpreting the Bible:

> Masterpieces such as *Oedipus Rex* and *War and Peace*, for example, evoke their own domains of meaning. They do so by what they themselves say about the events and personages of which they tell. In order to understand them in their own terms, there is no need for extraneous references to, for example, Freud's theories or historical treatments of the Napoleonic wars.
>
> (Lindbeck 1984, 116)

Just as one can understand great literature through the world it creates, the Bible should be interpreted on its own terms, "*intra*-textually."

Figure 26–2 George Lindbeck (1923–2018).

Further reflection on this approach will drive home just how deeply it differs from the liberal theology that preceded it. Broadly speaking, as we saw in Chapter 22, Liberal Protestant theology sought to translate Christian ideas into an idiom that could be understood and appreciated by modern secular persons. It did this in the hope that the Christian and the non-Christian could find some common ground through the rearticulation of traditional doctrines in new, modern language. It proceeded on the assumption that there were universally shared human experiences, values, and concepts that could be mined for their theological relevance.

However, Post-Liberal theologians insist that everything has changed in the post-modern situation. Specifically, post-modernity questions deeply whether there are in fact universally shared experiences, values, and concepts, and instead it celebrates difference among various peoples and systems of belief. The search for common ground, then, is a fruitless endeavor, according to the post-modern sensibility. This might be good news in that no outsider has the authority to tell a Christian reader of the Bible that he or she is incorrectly interpreting the text, but it risks turning Christianity into an inwardly focused storytelling exercise with no ability to reach out to the non-Christian. Lindbeck takes this challenge seriously: "If there are no such universals, then how can one make the faith credible, not only to those outside the church but to the half-believers within it and, not least, to theologians" (Lindbeck 1984, 129)? The problem is worsened by the fact that, in its rejection of universal standards, Post-Liberalism seems at times to have no place for reason.

In response to these challenges, Lindbeck creatively develops a new definition of what rationality consists of in the first place. As he puts the central point, "The reasonableness of a religion is largely a function of its assimilative powers, of its ability to provide an intelligible interpretation in its own terms of the varied situations and realities adherents encounter" (Lindbeck 1984, 131). In other words, Christianity can be judged to be rational if it offers its adherents a way of making their lives comprehensible, if it can assimilate a wide range of experiences into its world-view and shed light on them. Christianity reaches out to the non-Christian, then, by offering him or her an entire world of meaning in which he or she can participate. Lindbeck acknowledges just how non-modern this view is. He likens his approach to the ancient process of bringing new members into the church:

> Pagan converts to the catholic mainstream did not, for the most part, first understand the faith and then decide to become Christians; rather, the process was reversed: they first decided and then they understood. More precisely, they were first attracted by the Christian community and form of life.
>
> (Lindbeck 1984, 132)

To Lindbeck, if the non-Christian is to understand Christianity, he or she cannot stand outside of it hoping that it will eventually make sense, or that it will be made palatable enough for the skeptic. Instead, one must first commit to the faith in the hope that by seeing it from the inside one will come to comprehend its teachings. Post-Liberal theologians call Christianity to regain its confidence by reminding Christians and non-Christians alike just what a striking vision of life with God it offers. In one sense, then, the Post-Liberal approach refuses to meet contemporary persons where they are, if doing so means that Christianity would have to compromise its distinctive elements in the interest of connecting with secular individuals. However, the Post-Liberal approach does eagerly invite non-Christians to enter into the Christian story in the hope that such persons will find meaning and renewal of life with God there.

Issues in Moral Theology: Bioethics

Until the mid-twentieth century, ethical issues raised by advances in the life sciences and medicine were largely handled internally, that is, within the scientific societies and medical profession themselves, and usually by reference to the customs and codes of the professional organizations to which the majority of life scientists and physicians belonged. The best-known of such codes is the Oath of Hippocrates (fifth century B.C.E.), which enjoins practitioners to "do no harm" and to seek the good of patients above all, and which explicitly prohibits, among other things, abortion, euthanasia, and sexual relations with patients.

As important as such codes were and still are, they were unable to provide sufficient guidance to researchers, physicians, and, significantly, an increasingly concerned public, especially as the pace of research and the scope of technological innovation began to increase in the early twentieth century. Advances in genetics and life-prolonging interventions (e.g., antibiotics, organ transplants) are particularly noteworthy here. A tipping point occurred at mid-century, when disclosures of unethical scientific research by "Nazi doctors" in the 1930s and 1940s—much of it in genetics—led to the formulation of the first major code of medical ethics, the "Nuremberg Code," in 1947. The "Declaration of Helsinki" by the World Medical Association followed in 1964. However, it was not until the mid-1970s, at least in the United States, that the protection of research subjects called for by these codes was incorporated into statutory law.

By then, the term "bioethics" had been coined (1972), in recognition of the growing public discourse around the multiple ethical questions being raised, not only by the persistence of unethical conduct by scientific and medical researchers, including the government itself (e.g., the Tuskegee syphilis study), but also by the continued progress in saving and prolonging human life, both in its earliest beginnings and end stages, through pharmaceutical, surgical, and other sophisticated mechanical interventions. Further interest was stoked by the advent of assisted reproductive technologies in the 1980s, and the successful mapping of the human genome at the turn of the millennium.

What came to be the dominant approach to these ethical questions was first articulated by a group of theologically trained scholars working on two government commissions in the 1970s. Their work, published in 1978 as *The Belmont Report*, identified three (later expanded to four) fundamental ethical principles intended to help scientific researchers and medical practitioners navigate the complex questions their work was raising: (1) respect for individual self-determination (autonomy); (2) a commitment to seek the well-being of persons (beneficence); and (3) a determination that the benefits of scientific and medical research be fairly distributed (justice).

While theologians no longer play as central a role in the formulation of bioethical law and policy as they once did, they still participate in significant ways in the "cultural" sphere of contemporary bioethics, and will continue to do so, because ongoing progress in our ability to create life, forestall death, and much else, inevitably raises questions too important to be left to scientists and medical professionals alone: where did we come from, who are we, and where are we going?

THE "NEW ATHEISM"

Although post-modernism describes much of our contemporary situation, some current developments do not easily fit within a post-modern mold. The "New Atheism" is one such phenomenon, and it is most accurately seen as a continuation of modernity rather than a post-modern way of thinking, as will be demonstrated below.

The twenty-first century has witnessed a development in atheism such that it has become aggressively opposed to theism in a new way. The New Atheist movement is represented by thinkers such as Richard Dawkins (b. 1941), Sam Harris (b. 1967), and Christopher Hitchens (1949–2011). The popularity of these figures is reflected in the sales of their books, which have been widely read, discussed, and reviewed as bestsellers in the United States and the United Kingdom. It is this mass appeal through their books (and subsequently their websites) that has made them a cultural phenomenon of considerable force.

Although they have some common attitudes, each of these authors has a different way of presenting his claims. First, let us consider what they have in common. The New Atheists as a whole seek to promote radical secularism. They do so often from a viewpoint of **scientism** (or the claim that the only valid method of knowing is science, and that what cannot be known by science does not exist), especially evolutionary biology, genetics, and cognitive sciences. Although New Atheism is only one among a number of nonreligious movements and groups, it is distinguished by its militant "anti-theism," which rejects religious faith entirely. In this respect, it does *not* adopt a post-modern attitude that values a diversity of viewpoints. It sees religion and religious institutions as responsible for a whole host of social ills and problems, including child abuse, sexual repression, terrorism, and violence. As a result, they hold that religion should be eradicated in its entirety. In particular, the New Atheists reject the "Religions of the Book" (Judaism, Christianity, and Islam) in a way that is deliberately confrontational, with a rhetoric that is intolerant and meant to shock.

Whether or not they are actually "new" in their attitudes continues to be a matter for debate; in many ways, they simply re-present the arguments of Enlightenment figures and the nineteenth-century "masters of suspicion" covered in Chapter 22.

However, they reach a far more popular audience than many other atheists have managed to do up to this point. Additionally, in a manner unlike their predecessors, they focus their efforts on "liberating" atheists from the supposedly negative repercussions of "coming out" publicly as an atheist in today's world. They insist that theism and religion have made them a marginalized and oppressed group. This claim is questionable in the countries of the West, where atheism has been a viable option for some time.

How, then, do Dawkins, Harris, and Hitchens differ among themselves in their approach to eradicating religion, faith, and theism? The key points are found in their varying styles and the premises with which they begin their arguments.

Richard Dawkins

Richard Dawkins (b. 1941), with a degree in zoology from Oxford, is one of the most vocal of the New Atheists. His book *The God Delusion* (2008) is widely read and quoted. The book centers on the plausibility of what he calls the "God Hypothesis," which he then sets out to demolish. In making his arguments, he relies on his scientific background, and his use of scientific language tends to persuade the reader that in all cases his claims are scientifically based. However, Dawkins often makes claims that are not in fact conclusions derived from rigorous scientific inquiry. For instance, he supports **methodological naturalism**, which is a *philosophy* holding that only natural elements and forces have value. According to naturalism, all phenomena can be covered by the laws of science, and the spiritual and supernatural are illusions. Dawkins believes that *everything* can be accounted for by science (specifically, by evolutionary biology), which is a starting assumption, not a scientific conclusion. As we saw in Chapter 25, any number of influential scientists believe that there is a realm beyond the natural. Dawkins' thesis and central argument reflect his approach:

> I shall define the God Hypothesis more defensibly: *there exists a superhuman, supernatural intelligence who deliberately designed and created the universe and everything in it, including us.* This book will advocate an alternative view: *any creative intelligence, of sufficient complexity to design anything, comes into existence only as the end product of an extended process of gradual evolution.* Creative intelligences, being evolved, necessarily arrive late in the universe, and therefore cannot be responsible for designing it. God, in the sense defined, is a delusion; and, as later chapters will show, a pernicious delusion.
>
> (Dawkins 2008, 52)

By making God "a hypothesis," Dawkins makes his work appealing to those who want to reject the existence of God (or gods) and religion in favor of science as the basis for meaning in life. He opposes any "argument from design," and he opts instead for evolution as the ultimate explanation of all life.

However, his approach leaves more than enough room for refutation of his claims. Most importantly, he must establish that his thesis as stated above is a correct use of hypothesis in the scientific method. To use it correctly, he would have to allow for it to be disproved in some way and then corrected or refined in response to the evidence he finds. He is unwilling to do this, and he instead discards the God hypothesis at the earliest opportunity without actually giving it a chance to succeed. It is not a hypothesis in the proper sense of the word.

At a deeper level, one can argue that it is not appropriate to subject theology to the methodology of the natural sciences in the first place. Theology, after all, has its own method, as do other academic disciplines such as philosophy and English literature. Theology certainly involves *in part* the empirical investigation of our world, but this enterprise is accompanied by a much broader and deeper set of considerations that are collectively used to determine theological views. By insisting that theology should submit to the method used by natural science, Dawkins demonstrates a rather narrow—even closed-minded—understanding of academic inquiry.

Dawkins, then, benefits from the credit given to scientists in our contemporary culture, but he reaches beyond his expertise as he ranges into theological subject matter. He convinces many who are not scientists at all that his investigations are rigorous and scientifically based. However, many scientists who share his atheism do not actually agree with the way he makes his arguments.

We can say little about the New Atheists unless we have a sense of the way they write; here is typical Dawkins, probably the most quoted passage from *The God Delusion*:

> The God of the Old Testament is arguably the most unpleasant character in all fiction: jealous and proud of it; a petty, unjust, unforgiving control-freak; a vindictive, bloodthirsty ethnic cleanser; a misogynistic, homophobic, racist, infanticidal, genocidal, filicidal, pestilential, megalomaniacal, sadomasochistic, capriciously malevolent bully.
>
> (Dawkins 2008, 51)

This quotation makes evident the level of hostility to God and to religious faith mentioned above. Dawkins uses charged rhetoric to browbeat his reader into agreement, and he goes on elsewhere in his book to accuse God and religion of causing all of society's ills.

To call this confrontational is an understatement. Dawkins, like most of the New Atheists, wants to evoke an emotional response to his claims (which stands in some tension with his supposedly scientific approach), and he does so by ridiculing his targets. One way in which he achieves his objectives is through a literalist interpretation of scripture—Dawkins seems neither to know nor to care that religious scriptures were read on a variety of levels. In an important sense, this is "atheist proof-texting"; passages are taken out of context from scripture and used to prove a point of view that easily serves the atheist's argument. For this reason, Dawkins and other New Atheists have been criticized as "fundamentalist" in their attitudes toward the Western religions.

Sam Harris

Sam Harris (b. 1967) has written various books, but the one that concerns us is his first, *The End of Faith: Religion, Terror, and the Future of Reason* (2004). Unlike Dawkins, Harris concentrates on the harmful effects of all religious faith, not just Christianity. Like Dawkins, Harris insists that he is coming from a scientific position, although he frequently has said in interviews that the book was catalyzed by the events of 9/11. His concern with religious violence is demonstrated in the first chapter:

> A glance at history, or at the pages of any newspaper, reveals that ideas which divide one group of human beings from another, only to unite them in slaughter, generally have their roots in religion. It seems that if our species ever eradicates itself through war, it will not be because it was written in the stars but because it was written in our books; it is what we do with words like "God" and "paradise" and "sin" in the present that will determine our future.
>
> (Harris 2004, 12)

His basic thesis is that religious faith must be eradicated by reason in order for us to survive as a species. In this regard, his work can be seen as a continuation of the Enlightenment project of replacing religion with reason in order to avoid violence (see Chapter 22). Harris' style is to sound quite reasonable at the outset of his argument, and then launch into attacks on religious faith that are deliberately belligerent to those who adhere to it. Although much of his rhetoric in the book is concerned with terrorism and extremism, he regards religious tolerance and religious moderation as dangerous, as it "colludes" with the growth of dangerous extremism and allows people to wallow in superstition. His attitude in his book and in his debates is very much on the offensive, in both senses of the word. He is geared up for a fight against the forces of faith, which he considers irrational and dangerous; he is typically abrasive and given to hyperbole, as seen in the following passage:

> Jesus Christ—who, as it turns out, was born of a virgin, cheated death, and rose bodily into the heavens—can now be eaten in the form of a cracker. A few Latin words spoken over your favorite Burgundy, and you can drink his blood as well.
>
> (Harris 2004, 73)

Disturbingly, much of the book offends in this manner. Islam comes in for harsher treatment than the other two Religions of the Book. It is likely that this aversion comes not only from 9/11 itself, but also from Harris' appraisal of Islam as dangerous because the "only future devout Muslims can envisage—as Muslims—is the one in which all infidels have been converted to Islam, subjugated, or killed" (Harris 2004, 110). This worry about Islam culminates in a deeply unsettling statement, placed within a previous narrative about the importance of reason for human flourishing and progress:

> What will we do if an Islamist regime, which grows dewy-eyed at the mere mention of paradise, ever acquires long-range nuclear weapons? If history is any guide, we will not be sure about where the offending warheads are or what the state of their readiness is, and we will be unable to rely on targeted, conventional weapons to destroy them. In such a situation, the only thing likely to ensure our survival may be a nuclear first strike of our own. Needless to say, this would be an unthinkable crime—as it would kill tens of millions of innocent civilians in a single day—but it may be the only course of action available to us, given what Islamists believe.
>
> (Harris 2004, 129)

Harris is able to make such a devastating claim only because of his conviction that religious faith, especially Islam, is the most destructive force in the world. It consistently stands in the way of progress, reason, and happiness, and it does not contribute positively to human societies. To Harris, religious faith is sheer ignorance (Harris 2004, 66–67), and does not give *reasons*—commitment to faith is categorically irrational.

Christopher Hitchens

Of the three New Atheists examined here, Christopher Hitchens (1949–2011) is the one who had a public profile before publishing his book on atheism; he was a journalist, an essayist, and a writer, voted one of the top public intellectuals by the British media at one point in time. Hitchens' book, *God Is Not Great: How Religion Poisons*

Everything (2007), is a passionate first-person account of his own sense of outrage against religion in general, and the Religions of the Book in particular. It is difficult to summarize this work, as it is a set of experiences and reflections on religious faith and religion, and so lacks a central argument. Nevertheless, some key assertions in the book make his attitude toward religion clear.

Hitchens believes that "religion kills," as he titles a chapter, and his central target is organized religion and its practices. Throughout the book, he provides examples of why religion is poisonous: it is man-made, often invented by illiterates and corrupt leaders; it has no reliable evidence or method of transmission; and it creates itself out of the raw material of other religions. This corruption leads to unsatisfactory explanations of the beliefs of each group, which rely upon their leaders for clarification. Religion thus involves embracing ignorance, according to him. This leads to other ethical flaws, such as a form of racism claiming that dark-skinned people have been punished by God (Hitchens 2007, 167). He maintains throughout that we cannot forgive religion's poison, because religion is itself against the welfare of humanity.

Echoing the criticisms of religion offered by modern figures beginning in the seventeenth century (see Chapter 22), Hitchens sees religion as a disease, and he strongly endorses Enlightenment values (especially reason and autonomy) as an alternative. Although he seems at many points to hope that our society will transcend religion, he recognizes that religion is firmly entrenched in human beings. As he puts this point, "Religious faith ... will never die out, or at least not until we get over our fear of death, and of the dark, and of the unknown, and of each other" (Hitchens 2007, 12). Similarly, later in his book, he declares the following:

> Only the most naïve utopian can believe that this new humane civilization will develop, like some dream of "progress," in a straight line. We first have to transcend our pre-history, and escape the gnarled hands which reach out to drag us back to the catacombs and the reeking altars and the guilty pleasures of subjection and abjection.
>
> (Hitchens 2007, 276)

This is a theme to which Hitchens will devote the last chapter of the book, where he unambiguously calls for a "renewed Enlightenment," which recognizes the futility of religion and studies its proper subject, which is humanity itself (Hitchens 2007, 283).

According to this way of thinking (which has its roots not only in the Enlightenment, but also in Feuerbach, Marx, and Freud), human beings have religious faith because it eases unpleasant aspects of the human condition. If those unpleasant experiences can be eliminated, if we can get over our fears, then religion will die out. This position shows Hitchens' adherence to the secularization theory examined previously in this chapter; he has not come to grips with the relinquishment of this theory that has taken place in recent years.

Because Hitchens writes compellingly, it is possible to miss the places in which he makes outright mistakes of fact or decides to gloss over questionable points. For instance, he claims that Martin Luther King was really a "profound humanist" and only a "nominal Christian," despite the evidence to the contrary. He also somewhat curiously maintains that the Christian church was ultimately responsible for the atrocities committed by totalitarian regimes (such as that of Stalin), even though they are typically seen as atheistic. Additionally, he oddly claims that Christ never died at all on the cross (which is widely thought to be historically established) and that the witnesses were inconsistent and unreliable, and so we should "disbelieve the whole thing."

Assessing the New Atheism

How do the New Atheists show us where we are in the twenty-first century when it comes to religious faith? Their popularity indicates that there is considerable interest in this topic today, and in particular it shows that producing books on atheism for mass consumption is a profitable enterprise. And yet, in their efforts to achieve popularity, the New Atheists indulge in an approach that is overtly hostile, intentionally outrageous, and often offensive. They are convinced that this will shake people up, and it does, but it also lowers the level of discourse and demonstrates their willful misunderstanding of religion, especially Christianity. Those who object to the New Atheists are often characterized as closed off to the hard truth about their faith, yet the New Atheists demonstrate breathtaking ignorance of the topics they purport to understand.

In the first place, they characterize religion as categorically opposed to progress, reason, and science. To them, religion stifles humanity. This charge began among seventeenth-century Enlightenment figures, as we saw in Chapter 22, and is now hundreds of years old, so it is not particularly new. More importantly, it is simply inaccurate in its sweeping characterization of religion as a whole. Although it might apply in select (often non-representative) cases, many religious traditions have been intimately involved in advancing our understanding of the world and improving the human condition. For instance, as we saw in Chapter 25, the history of Christianity and science reveals that some of the most important scientists of the modern period were themselves committed Christians. Those figures saw no incompatibility between Christianity and science, and some historians have claimed that their Christian worldview (according to which the creator gave order to the cosmos) actually *aided* their scientific investigations. The New Atheists, then, play on the common assumption that religion and science are opposed to each other without actually examining that history.

Along similar lines, the New Atheists insist that an enormous number of social ills and injustices stem directly from religious faith in God, including child abuse, racism, terrorism, and authoritarianism. One cannot deny that certain religious views have played a role in some of these disturbing developments and that they present a danger to our world today, but they are typically seen as *distortions* of those religions, not their true essence. It is not as if there is a single way of thinking that is "religious," which is intent on oppressing as many people as possible, and there is another way of thinking that is "secular," which seeks to liberate humankind. Instead, resistance to religious violence arises organically from *within* the religions of the world; it does not need to be imposed from the outside, and religion as a whole does not need to be eradicated for the sake of some peace that would supposedly emerge from those efforts. By ignoring the admirable aspects of religious traditions, the New Atheists do a particular disservice to Liberation Theology, which as we will see in Chapter 27 understands liberation from oppression to be the foremost concern of the Christian God.

The above points indicate that the New Atheists' view of the scriptures and traditions of religious groups is highly literalistic, as mentioned briefly above, and there is little attempt to nuance this. Concerning the Bible, the New Atheists seem to grasp only its surface-level meaning, and they refuse to see the larger context of the short quotations they use. Traditional tools for interpretation are studiously ignored, even though those traditions have grappled for centuries with the material that the New Atheists quote and could provide a tremendous resource for understanding troubling portions of scripture. The New Atheists also show a dismissive attitude toward theology and religious philosophies, whether or not they are informed on these subjects, especially on the arguments for God's existence. Dawkins enters into this terrain more than the other New Atheists, yet he seems to know very little about the history of those arguments. As a whole, the New Atheists seem unaware of the fact that theologians have been responding to modernity for some 400 years now, in many cases meeting the challenges imposed by modern ways of thinking with bold reformulations of Christianity for the contemporary world. The picture of an old-fashioned, unyielding, closed-minded Christianity might appeal to certain modern stereotypes, but it simply does not reflect the current state of Christian theology.

Somewhat ironically, it is the New Atheists themselves who appear old-fashioned to those acquainted with the history of the modern period. They owe a great debt to the classical atheist figures of previous centuries, yet aside from the New Atheists' newly strident tone, they do not add much substance to the views of their predecessors. They seem not to know the works of Feuerbach, Marx, Nietzsche, and Freud very well; as a result, they leave themselves open to critiques that could have been foreseen with better knowledge of modern philosophy and theology. In particular, they evade Nietzsche's profound challenge to atheism: Nietzsche saw, in his "Parable of the Madman" as well as other works, the emptiness of atheism when it depends upon the structures that religious faith built up. That is, Nietzsche saw Christianity as responsible for the compassion for the disadvantaged found throughout Western societies, and he sought to replace Christianity with a culture that would *not* care for the weak (interestingly, to Nietzsche Christianity is not objectionable because it sponsors violence, as the New Atheists maintain; instead it is objectionable precisely because it does the opposite—namely, it fosters kindness toward human frailty). If you get rid of that God, you get rid of that foundation of compassion. The New Atheists, however, seek to maintain much of the Christian ethic while disposing of the Christian God. In this regard, they are seen as rather naïve from a Nietzschean point of view.

In failing to meet the critiques of the past, and many of those of the present, the New Atheists succeed only in arousing the emotions and reinforcing the assumptions of the previous centuries. By playing on the fears of their readers (at one point, Hitchens ominously warns that religious people are "planning your and my destruction" [Hitchens 2007, 13]), the New Atheists do not so much advance understanding as perpetuate damaging stereotypes of religion and religious faith. Their heated rhetoric and religious illiteracy all but guarantee that efforts at mutual understanding between religious individuals and their atheistic counterparts will be hindered, not helped, by their works.

CONCLUSION

This chapter has claimed that our contemporary situation is profoundly shaped by post-modern thought, and it has presented some of the most influential responses to the post-modern challenges to Christian theology. Those post-modern difficulties are distinct from the modern challenges described previously in this book; as such, they require a different sort of theological response. With that said, features of our contemporary setting such as the New Atheism do not fit within post-modernity, and instead continue the modern effort of using reason to refine and even replace religion, often in the name of avoiding violence.

In the chapters to come, we will see continued responses to the post-modern condition. Next up is a treatment of theologies of liberation, which rely on the post-modern idea that one should attend carefully to the margins of society in order to take note of those whose voices have been suppressed. The final chapter of this book will examine Christian theology in the context of other world religions.

Key Terms

Michel Foucault	Friedrich Nietzsche	Paul Tillich
Søren Kierkegaard	Post-Liberal theology	ultimate concern
language game	post-modernism	Ludwig Wittgenstein
method of correlation	post-secularism	
methodological naturalism	Reformed Epistemology scientism	

Questions for Reading

1. How do scholars often characterize post-modernism? In what ways does it break from modernism, and in what ways is it a continuation of modernity?

2. In what ways is post-modernism viewed as a threat to Christian theology? In what ways could it be seen as an opportunity?

3. Broadly speaking, how does post-modern Christian theology differ from its modern counterparts?

4. In what ways does Michel Foucault extend the claims made by Friedrich Nietzsche?

5. How does Søren Kierkegaard embrace the post-modern condition and yet still espouse Christian views?

6. What does Paul Tillich mean by "ultimate concern," and how is it relevant to his theology?

7. What does it mean to say that Christian theology is its own language game, and why does such a formulation matter?

8. How do Reformed epistemologists critique foundationalism, and why is their criticism helpful to Christian theology?

9. How do Post-Liberal theologians such as Hans Frei and George Lindbeck criticize modern biblical interpretation, and what do they propose as an alternative?

10. In what respects is the "New Atheism" actually new, and in what ways is it familiar (even old) to modern theologians and philosophers?

11. How do the New Atheists get religion (in particular, Christianity) wrong, according to their critics?

Works Consulted/Recommended Reading

Alston, William. 1991. *Perceiving God: The Epistemology of Religious Experience.* Ithaca, NY: Cornell University Press.

Berger, Peter. 1999. "The Desecularization of the World: A Global Overview." In *The Desecularization of the World: Resurgent Religion and World Politics.* Edited by Peter Berger, 1–18. Washington, DC: Ethics and Public Policy Center; Grand Rapids, MI: Eerdmans.

Dawkins, Richard. 2008. *The God Delusion.* Boston, MA: Houghton Mifflin.

Evans, C. Stephen. 2009. *Kierkegaard: An Introduction.* Cambridge: Cambridge University Press.

Foucault, Michel. 1977. "Nietzsche, Genealogy, History." Translated by Donald Bouchard and Sherry Simon. In *Language, Counter-Memory, Practice: Selected Essays and Interviews.* Edited by Donald Bouchard, 139–164. Ithaca, NY: Cornell University Press.

Frei, Hans. 1974. *The Eclipse of Biblical Narrative.* New Haven, CT: Yale University Press.

Grenz, Stanley. 1996. *A Primer on Postmodernism.* Grand Rapids, MI: Eerdmans.

Harris, Sam. 2004. *The End of Faith: Religion, Terror, and the Future of Reason.* New York: Norton.

Hart, David Bentley. 2009. *Atheist Delusions: The Christian Revolution and Its Fashionable Enemies.* New Haven, CT: Yale University Press.

Hitchens, Christopher. 2007. *God Is Not Great: How Religion Poisons Everything.* New York: Twelve.

Kierkegaard, Søren. 1992. *Concluding Unscientific Postscript to Philosophical Fragments.* Vol. 1. Translated by Howard V. Hong and Edna H. Hong. Princeton, NJ: Princeton University Press.

Lindbeck, George. 1984. *The Nature of Doctrine: Religion and Theology in a Postliberal Age.* Philadelphia, PA: Westminster Press.

Livingston, James C. 1997. *Modern Christian Thought.* Vol. 1. *The Enlightenment and the Nineteenth Century.* Upper Saddle River, NJ: Prentice Hall.

Livingston, James C., and Francis Schüssler Fiorenza. 2000. *Modern Christian Thought.* Vol. 2. *The Twentieth Century.* Upper Saddle River, NJ: Prentice Hall.

Lyotard, Jean-François. 1984. *The Postmodern Condition: A Report on Knowledge.* Translated by Geoff Bennington and Brian Massumi. Minneapolis, MN: University of Minnesota Press.

McGrath, Alister E. 2007. *The Dawkins Delusion? Atheist Fundamentalism and the Denial of the Divine.* London: IVP Books.

Macquarrie, John. 1963. *Twentieth Century Religious Thought: The Frontiers of Philosophy and Theology, 1900–1960.* New York: Harper and Row.

Plantinga, Alvin. 1993. *Warrant and Proper Function.* New York: Oxford University Press.

Plantinga, Alvin. 2000. *Warranted Christian Belief.* New York: Oxford University Press.

Tillich, Paul. 1951. *Systematic Theology.* Vol. 1. Chicago, IL: University of Chicago Press.

Wittgenstein, Ludwig. 1953. *Philosophical Investigations.* Translated by G.E.M. Anscombe. New York: Macmillan.

Wittgenstein, Ludwig. 1993. *Philosophical Occasions: 1912–1951.* Edited by James C. Klagge and Alfred Nordman. Indianapolis, IN: Hackett Publishing Company.

Chapter

THEOLOGIES OF LIBERATION

TIMELINE

1441	The first group of Africans were forcibly taken from the West African coast and the first slave auction was held in Portugal.
1619	The first group of Africans were forcibly taken to the North American colony of Jamestown, Virginia.
1800	A slave revolt in Richmond led by Gabriel Prosser.
1822	A slave revolt led in Charleston by Denmark Vesey.
1831	A slave revolt in Southampton, Virginia led by Nat Turner.
1830–1860	The rise of the abolitionist movement led by Frederick Douglass, among many others.
1853	Afrikaners establish the *volkskerk*, or people's church, of South Africa.
1859	The *Gereformeerde Kerk* breaks away from the *volkskerk* in South Africa.
1863	Emancipation; slavery was legally abolished in the United States because of the black struggle for freedom.
1865–1877	Reconstruction Era.
1877–1950	The period of "lynch law" in which 4,000 black people were publicly tortured and hanged on trees across the United States as a mechanism intended to intimidate, terrorize, and suppress the ongoing black struggle for freedom in the wake of Emancipation.
1896	The Supreme Court established the doctrine of "separate but equal" in *Plessy* v. *Ferguson*.

1900	Ida B. Wells delivers her speech, "Lynch Law in America."
1912	The African National Congress (ANC) is founded as a political party to secure the rights of black and mixed-race South Africans.
1939	American jazz musician and singer Billie Holiday performs "Strange Fruit."
1948	The National Party of the Afrikaners wins the general election in South Africa and begins to implement apartheid.
1952	Heavy smog in London kills approximately 12,000 people and sickens another 100,000.
1955–1968	American Civil Rights Movement.
1956	The Parliament of the United Kingdom passes the first in a series of Clean Air Acts.
1960	The Sharpeville Massacre occurs in South Africa, and 69 black South Africans are killed.
1962	Rachel Carson publishes *Silent Spring*, documenting the effects of harmful pesticides such as DDT.
1962–1965	Brazilian Catholic bishops begin to promote Christian base communities, based on pilot projects in the late 1950s.
1966	The emergence of the Black Power movement.
1967	Pope Paul VI issues the encyclical *Populorum progressio* (The Development of Peoples) on the need to counter global inequities.
1968	The assassination of Rev. Dr. Martin Luther King, Jr.
1968	Gathered in Medellín, Colombia, the Latin American Conference of Bishops call for reorienting church priorities according to a "preferential option for the poor."
1969	James Cone publishes *Black Theology and Black Power*.
1970	United States Environmental Protection Agency founded.
1971	Pope Paul VI mentions the threat of environmental degradation in his encyclical *Octogesima Adveniens*.
1973	Gustavo Gutiérrez's book *A Theology of Liberation* is published in English.
1977–1980	Óscar Romero serves as archbishop of El Salvador, but is assassinated on March 24, 1980.
1979	Pope John Paul II visits Mexico to meet with the Latin American Conference of Bishops meeting in Puebla. Encountering living conditions in Latin America seems to temper his suspicion of liberation theology, and the bishops reaffirm the urgency of work for social justice.

1979	Jacquelyn Grant publishes *Black Theology and the Black Woman*.
1983	The World Council of Churches initiates their "Justice, Peace, and the Integrity of Creation" process.
1983	Alice Walker publishes *In Search of Our Mothers' Gardens*.
1984	The Anglican Consultative Council includes care for creation as one of the central marks of mission for the Worldwide Anglican Communion.
1987	The United Church of Christ releases "Toxic Wastes and Race," a landmark study documenting the siting of toxic waste sources near poor communities and communities of color in the United States.
1987	Delores Williams publishes "Womanist Theology: Black Women's Voices."
1990	Pope John Paul II dedicates his message on World Day of Peace to addressing the ecological crisis.
1990	Nelson Mandela is released from prison in South Africa after 27 years of confinement.
1992	United Nations Conference on Environment and Development (UNCED) summit in Rio de Janeiro; World Council of Churches participates.
1993	The National Religious Partnership for the Environment founded (United States).
1994	Nelson Mandela is elected President of South Africa.
2008	Under Pope Benedict XVI, the Vatican installs over 2,000 solar panels on one of its main buildings, cutting its carbon emissions by more than 200 tons per year.
2011	In a church-wide encyclical, Ecumenical Patriarch Bartholomew I of Constantinople calls the destruction of the environment a sin.
2015	Pope Francis welcomes liberation theologian Fr. Gustavo Gutiérrez to the Vatican and accelerates the process for recognizing slain Archbishop Óscar Romero as a saint.
2015	Pope Francis promulgates his major ecological encyclical, *Laudato Si': On Care for our Common Home*.

This chapter examines "theologies of liberation," which can be characterized broadly as Christian theologies that insist that God desires deliverance for those who are oppressed in our world today. In this concern for the downtrodden, liberation theology continues the post-modern concern for those who have been marginalized by structures of power in their societies (see Chapter 26). As do many post-modern thinkers, liberation theologians seek to recover the perspectives of those whose stories have been lost. However, liberation theologians add to this post-modern sensibility the claim that God is centrally concerned with the fate of the oppressed, and that God seeks liberation for God's people.

Additionally, liberation theology can be seen as a response to Karl Marx's critique of Christianity, as examined in Chapter 22. Marx held that Christianity is a tool used by those in power to keep their subjects docile and easily controlled. Certain versions of Christianity would seem to support this characterization, especially those that encourage subjugated peoples simply to endure their unfortunate situation in this life (and not agitate with the goal of changing their societies) because their reward will be great in heaven. Liberation theologians, however, appeal to aspects of scripture and tradition to present a picture of Christianity different from that which Marx upheld. Looking at the Exodus narrative, among other sources, liberation theologians insist that God desires liberation for God's people *here and now*, in this life, not exclusively in the next life. As a result, one can work for societal change and remain squarely within Christian teaching.

Although the above characterization applies to liberation theology as a whole, the movement takes a number of different forms around the world today in which different emphases can be observed. This chapter examines four different varieties of liberation theology: Latin American liberation theology, South African liberation theology, African American liberation theology, and feminist theology. The chapter concludes with a treatment of the ways in which Christian theological concern for the environment aligns with theologies of liberation.

LATIN AMERICAN LIBERATION THEOLOGY

In February 1977, in the midst of a brutal civil war in the Central American country of El Salvador, a quiet traditionalist bishop of an outlying region was appointed archbishop of the nation's capital. **Óscar Romero** seemed to most observers a safe choice who would keep the church out of politics. No one expected him to challenge the U.S.-backed military government aligned with the wealthy ruling classes that owned so much of El Salvador's land. Yet soon he was using his weekly radio addresses to denounce the sufferings of the poor and persecution of the church for defending the poor. On March 23, 1980, he appealed directly to his "brothers" in the military:

> No soldier is obliged to obey an order that is contrary to the will of God. In the name of God, then, and in the name of this suffering people, I ask you, I beg you, I order you: stop the repression!

The next day, as Archbishop Romero was celebrating Mass, an assassin from one of El Salvador's notorious paramilitary "death squads" shot him dead. In 2015, Pope Francis officially recognized Romero as a martyr for the Catholic faith—not simply for a political stance—thus paving the way for the church to name him a saint.

Romero's story of transformation reflects the story of liberation theology in Latin America. Christians who were often quite theologically conservative found the grinding poverty and brutal inequalities of their societies forcing them to ask how the

Figure 27–1 Óscar Romero (1917–1980).

gospel speaks to those conditions. Priests and bishops responded with community organizing projects that they considered basic charitable work, but that ruling elites saw as politically threatening. Government repression of even basic development efforts served to radicalize those with a growing thirst for justice. In exceptional cases, some political movements turned into guerrilla movements seeking to ignite insurrection against ruling regimes. In many more cases, work for *development* turned into calls for *liberation*. Amid the ferment, many Christians who turned to their faith for guidance also had to re-examine their faith. Their conclusion: faithful theology must draw them deeper into action for justice and advocacy of human rights. Other Christians, though, found such theology threatening and accused its practitioners of politicizing Christianity. Or they attacked it—quite literally and violently. The fact that it took the Vatican nearly 25 years to recognize an assassinated archbishop as a martyr and likely saint is a sign of the controversy that liberation theology prompted, but also its transformative power.

Reading the Signs of the Times

Liberation theology in Latin America was in part a response to the call of the Second Vatican Council for Christians to "read the signs of the times" in order to proclaim and practice their ancient faith in contemporary contexts. The church is to accompany humanity amid its struggles and journey through history, the council had insisted. The guidance it offers is to be that of a pastor, or shepherd. As the first Latin American pope, Francis, would explain decades later, true shepherds must live close enough to their flocks that they "smell like the sheep."

What did all this mean in a continent where vast majorities of the people lived in grinding poverty, while the wealthy owned most land and productive resources, with strongman rulers or military dictatorships intent on keeping things that way? Latin America was supposed to be the most Catholic region of the world. But having brought Christianity to that region on the heels of Spanish and Portuguese conquest—and then been part of the power structure for centuries—the Catholic Church itself bore some responsibility for Latin America's structures of inequality and violence. For believers who took seriously Jesus' promise that his message was "good news to the poor," the glaring gap between Christian faith and practice was a scandal that called for radical conversion. And that required fresh scrutiny of both the church's pastoral priorities and the very task of theology.

Across the globe, the 1950s through the 1970s brought pressing questions of human dignity and economic development for peoples. Two world wars in the first half of the twentieth century had broken up a global system in which the "great powers" of Europe competed for prestige and resources through imperial control of far-flung colonies. The uneasy system that took its place was the "Cold War"—a stand-off between "Western" allies with capitalist systems and democratic ideals, and an "Eastern" bloc of socialist systems and communist ideals. Caught between these rivals was the so-called Third World of poorer nations. Many were newly independent former colonies trying to jump-start economic development even as they sought to forge stable political cultures. Latin American countries had gained independence from Spain and Portugal already in previous centuries. But they shared both the drive for economic and social development, and vulnerability to manipulation amid the Cold War. When development projects faltered or military dictators repressed grass-roots change, pastors and theologians alike began to ask whether more was needed—namely, "liberation."

"Give a man a fish and he'll eat for a day," goes a well-known proverb; "teach a man to fish and he will eat for a lifetime." But what if a mining company upstream is poisoning the river? What if commercial fishing trawlers are depleting sacred waters that once sustained indigenous communities? Acts of basic charity, which Catholics have traditionally called the **works of mercy**, may then prompt recognition that sin and evil are not just personal matters. Rather, the power configurations of society turn individual sins into larger systems of **structural evil**.

To liberation theologians, Christian love of neighbor is what demands work for justice and political struggle. In many ways, liberation theology is simply a radicalized outworking of official Catholic social teaching. Liberation theologians insist that the radically degrading social conditions of Latin America are what have done the radicalizing, not a political ideology such as Marxist communism. If some of them *have* turned to Marxism to make sense of their historical reality—and drawn suspicion thereby—their claim has been that it simply offered analytical tools, and that is has not been their core motivation.

For the first Latin American liberation theologians that motivation was pastoral. Although Latin America was overwhelmingly Catholic, rural villages might only receive a visit from a priest once or twice a year. Meanwhile, the urban shantytowns in metropolitan areas could be just as distant from the experience of priests and bishops born into upper-class families. Over the centuries, the church had focused on educating the elites, assuming that they would then guide society according to Christian values. In the late 1950s (prior to Vatican II), some clergy began to re-evaluate their strategies. In Brazil, a few priests experimented with a more grass-roots approach to Christian education known as "popular catechesis." They formed small neighborhood groups, trained lay people to lead them, and invited open-ended reflection on how

Figure 27–2 Christian base community. Bolivians in the traditional dress of the Quechua Native Americans making music and singing together.

the gospel might address their lives. Such groups soon became known as **Christian base communities** or base ecclesial communities because they functioned at the grass-roots or "base" of society and church. Even as Catholic bishops from across the globe were meeting in Rome for the Second Vatican Council, Brazil's bishops were incorporating such models into nationwide pastoral plans aimed at redirecting church resources toward grass-roots education and lay participation.

In 1968, bishops from across Latin America met together in Medellín, Colombia, to agree on how to follow through on Vatican II in their own context. Reflecting a reorientation of the church's priorities from elites to grassroots, they committed themselves to the **preferential option for the poor**. This principle requires individuals, churches, and societies alike to guide their actions and test their policies according to the impact they will have on the poor and most vulnerable. For the bishops at Medellín, grass-roots initiatives from Brazil provided a template. By the 1970s, the number of Christian base communities were estimated in the hundreds of thousands. That meant hundreds of thousands of places throughout the hemisphere where the church was—often for the first time—encouraging ordinary Catholics to ask hard questions about how the gospel spoke to their own living conditions. When they concluded that grinding poverty was not God's will for them, but that Christ had come to empower them to help build a new world according to the Kingdom of God, the implications could easily threaten the status quo—and prove dangerous for anyone who acted on them.

Figure 27–3 Gustavo Gutiérrez (b. 1928).

Engagement, Hard Questions, Fresh Retrieval

Many refer to the Peruvian parish priest and theologian **Gustavo Gutiérrez** as the "father of liberation theology," yet the label reflects a misunderstanding. The very 1973 book that prompted this label, *A Theology of Liberation*, takes pains to place its origin elsewhere—in "the gospel and the experiences of men and women committed to the process of liberation in the oppressed and exploited land of Latin America." Theologians like himself were not inventing liberation theology, in other words. They were simply reflecting on shared Christian engagement in the struggle of the poor in which they were already immersed. If anything, Gutiérrez argued, what they had rediscovered was the interplay between lived faith and theological reflection that had characterized ancient Christianity. Liberation theologians call that interplay **praxis**—simultaneously reflecting upon one's actions while acting upon one's deepening reflection. Gutiérrez's book simply sought to bring this reflection into conversation with the "universal Christian community," while demonstrating to academic theologians that liberation theology was legitimate.

Reading through the eyes of the poor could liberate the Bible itself, as well as other ancient Christian authorities, in a way. Did God not take sides in the Exodus by hearing the anguished cry of Abraham's descendants and liberating them from slavery in Egypt? Why have Christians spiritualized the revolutionary hymn of the peasant girl Mary when she proclaimed that God was pulling down the thrones of the powerful and raising up the lowly, giving food to the hungry, and sending the rich away empty (Luke 2:46–55, also known as the *Magnificat*)? Indeed, Jesus had inaugurated his ministry by citing the prophet Isaiah's promise of a day when the poor would hear good news, captives would find release, and the oppressed would go free (Luke 4:18–19); he had warned the nations that they would be judged by whether they recognized and served him in the hungry, thirsty, immigrant, sick, and imprisoned (Matthew 25:31–46). Christian tradition includes many saints who had made their own "preferential option for the poor" and renowned doctors of the faith who could sometimes sound as radical as any Marxist. In the fourth century, for example, both Ambrose in the Latin West and John Chrysostom in the Greek East insisted that to accumulate excess wealth was actually to steal from the poor, while gifts to the poor merely returned what was theirs, for God's gift of creation belongs equally to all.

Elaborating on the dynamics of *praxis*, theologian Juan Luis Segundo described this entire process as a **hermeneutical circle**. The term **hermeneutics** is standard for the science of interpreting texts. Liberation theologians insist that to read the Bible and church tradition well, one must also interpret one's historical moment well. Liberation theologians have presented various versions of the hermeneutical circle, but the basic dynamic is this: Since their own transformation often began amid the struggles of the poor, the hermeneutical circle begins with (1) *engaging reality at the grassroots* of society. When suffering and injustice then shake up one's world-view, the next step comes by (2) *accepting hard but authentic questions*, especially about the theologies and biblical interpretations that have rationalized oppression. For the Christian believer, the experience can actually be life-giving insofar as it prompts (3) *fresh reflection on the gospel*— bringing new insights into the Bible and the liberating promise of the Christian message. Still, unless someone *acts* on knowledge—liberation theologians insist—one does not really know it. So all of this must also issue in (4) a *deeper practice of faith in action*. Such action continues the circle through renewed commitment to the poor and deepened engagement with one's historical reality at the grassroots.

The Hermeneutical Circle

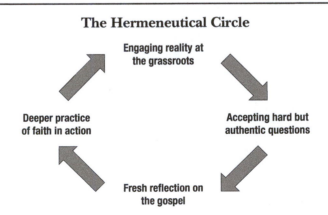

Liberation theologians have presented various versions of what they call the "hermeneutical circle." What all versions seek to explain is the need for theological reflection and social action to proceed in a dynamic relationship with each other known as "praxis." The hermeneutical circle also expresses confidence that Christians will recover fuller insights into the Bible and church tradition when they are living in authentic relationship with the poor and reading both texts and reality through their eyes.

Struggle for Legitimacy

Born amid struggles for justice, liberation theology has always anticipated conflict. To insist that God takes the side of the oppressed is bound to provoke a reaction from those who are invested in the status quo—especially when liberation theologians call upon Christians to join in the struggle. Such a message need not exclude good news to the rich and the privileged. Liberation theologians insist that true liberation embraces even oppressors by offering freedom from self-centered lives that are dedicated to false and dehumanizing values. But the Christian message always requires some kind of conversion, with no promise that it will be easy. It is hardly a surprise that liberation theology has elicited controversy not only within Latin American society but within the church itself.

If the global context of Cold War animated the development of liberation theology, it also complicated it. Latin America was not emerging from colonial rule in the second half of the twentieth century in the same way as the rest of the "Third World." Instead, it contended with a subtler "neocolonialist" reality—geopolitical domination by the United States. To be sure, the U.S.A. has regularly promised support for democracy and economic development to its Latin American neighbors. Announcing his Alliance for Progress in 1961, President John F. Kennedy even warned Latin American despots and ruling classes that "Those who make peaceful revolution impossible will make violent revolution inevitable." But when peaceful revolution through democratic and economic reform has required redistribution of land or stricter enforcement of labor rights, Latin American military dictatorships have sometimes made revolutionary movements "inevitable" indeed by clamping down on peaceful social movements for reform. In the end, U.S. administrations have consistently backed them, as fear of communism and a preference for stability have won out over the risks of change. Amid both local and geopolitical pressures, practitioners of liberation theology have had to make hard choices. Christian motivations have hardly exempted them from denunciation and outright repression. As the charismatic Catholic archbishop of Recife, Brazil, **Dom Hélder Câmara**, once remarked, "When I give food to the poor, they call me a saint; when I ask why the poor have no food, they call me a communist." Under some regimes, merely that accusation has been a death sentence.

Popes and Vatican officials have sometimes seemed to join in criticism of liberation theology. Although Pope Paul VI, writing on *The Development of Peoples* (*Populorum progressio*) in 1967, had sought not only to guide but also to inspire liberation theology, his successor Pope John Paul II was more suspicious. As archbishop of Krakow, Poland, Karol Wojtyła had spent decades resisting Soviet domination of his homeland and the Marxist ideology that claimed to justify its dehumanizing policies. When he actually made papal visits to Latin America, the living conditions there seemed to temper his suspicion of liberation theology as he reaffirmed Christian involvement in struggles for social justice. Nonetheless, he continued to warn sternly lest Marxist analysis of Latin American social conditions distort what was distinctively Christian about liberation theology, thus pitting class against class in violent revolution and encouraging atheist ideologies. Many bishops in the Latin American Catholic hierarchy interpreted this as a mandate for suppressing the very movement that their predecessors had once helped to inspire.

Liberation theologians have responded in various ways. In a small but widely influential book called *Spiral of Violence*, Archbishop Câmara analyzed the way that "violence attracts violence." The "counter-violence" of revolts and guerrilla movements is a reaction to the pre-existing "established violence" of poverty, indifference, and exploitation, he argued. When violence becomes institutionalized into a cultural and economic system, it may look superficially like peace, but is a false peace—"the peace of a swamp with rotten matter fermenting in its depths." Archbishop Câmara was a passionate advocate for strategies of active nonviolence. Yet Catholicism has long allowed for the possibility of "just wars" in the face of exceptionally dire threats, including tyrants, so he could not dismiss the reasoning that was leading some Christians in Latin America to take up arms. Still, his hope was in what he called the "Abrahamic minorities" within every religion and human community who, like Abraham of old, were willing to "hope against hope" and begin organizing to work in their neighborhoods and workplaces for a more just and equitable world. Indeed, while Christian participation in movements like the Sandinista revolution that came to power in Nicaragua in 1979 has often garnered the most attention, the overwhelming majority of practitioners throughout Latin America have dedicated themselves to exactly the kind of nonviolent grass-roots organizing that Câmara championed.

To answer charges from within the church itself, liberation theologians have not only returned repeatedly to the biblical mandates to "do justice" and bring "good news to the poor," but have insisted on the essential orthodoxy of their thought. Already in his groundbreaking book *A Theology of Liberation*, in the early 1970s, Gustavo Gutiérrez noted one of the movement's distinctions. Unlike European Christians who had become involved in previous political movements for social change, liberation theologians had not passed through Enlightenment philosophy with its secularizing tendencies in order to get there, and felt no need to question basic church doctrines or sacramental realities that they believed to ground their thought. Having written that book in part to demonstrate that liberation theology was faithful to the wider Christian tradition, Gutiérrez later wrote a more pastoral account of liberation theology, *We Drink from Our Own Wells: The Spiritual Journey of a People*. Written to show the authentic heart of liberation theology, the book draws on biblical and classic themes of discipleship, conversion, mysticism, pilgrimage, grace, and sharing in both the suffering of Jesus' cross and the hope of his resurrection.

The "Hermeneutical Circle" Continues

Latin American liberation theology has arguably been the continent's way of carrying out Catholic social teaching in the Vatican II era—radicalized at times mainly because social conditions and violent repression were so radical. If liberation theology is no longer breaking news in the twenty-first century, that is because it has flowed back into the church's official teaching and programmatic work around the world. Pastoral letters from bishops on all continents, as well as papal encyclicals addressing the global church, regularly cite key themes from liberation theology—the preferential option for the poor, the call to solidarity, the concept of structural sin, and the need to extend traditional Catholic "works of mercy" beyond personal charity into work for social justice on behalf of the common good. Pope Francis has rehabilitated the movement by inviting theologians like Gutiérrez to the Vatican, accelerating the process to recognize Óscar Romero as a saint, and reinstating priests who had once been suspended from ministry for taking political roles in progressive Latin American governments. If anything, Francis himself has extended liberation theology in his 2015 encyclical *Laudato Si'* on environmental issues and care of creation. In it, he critiqued the compulsive consumerism of modern culture and called for "liberation from the dominant technocratic paradigm" that seeks to assert "unlimited human power" over the natural world and "accepts every advance in technology with a view to profit, without concern for its potentially negative impact on human beings." "Everything is connected," he observed; the same "throwaway culture" that fails to protect the unborn and exploits the poor is endangering the future of our planet.

Indeed, since liberation theology requires Christians to "read the signs of the times" and engage the concrete historical situations in which they find themselves rather than attempt to do timeless theology, its practitioners can never stop moving around its "hermeneutical circle." While developed most prominently in Catholic contexts, liberation theology has long since moved into Protestant, Evangelical, and even some Pentecostal circles. There are now Asian, African, Palestinian, and many other versions, as well as the Black theology, feminist theology, and specifically South African liberation theology surveyed in the next section of this chapter. In a way, there can be no one "liberation theology" in the singular, but only "liberation theologies" in the plural. After all, praxis requires that Christians always begin by engaging their realities directly, at the grassroots, in the time and place where God asks them to follow the one who lived out the promise of good news to the poor.

CONTEXTUAL THEOLOGY IN SOUTH AFRICA

In 1972, James Matthews, a dissident poet in South Africa, published a collection of poems under the title, *Cry Rage*. Due to content that his government considered to be treasonous because of its capacity to incite a revolt, the book was banned a year later. In the collection's first poem, Matthews lamented that whereas other poets write of beauty, flowers, and love, the same was not true for him. "I cannot join in their merriment," he wrote, "my heart drowned in bitterness/with the agony of what/white man's law has done" (Matthews 1972). For penning such words, Matthews was arrested and served a sentence of six months in prison, some of them in solitary confinement. An authoritarian state had come to power in South Africa, and it tolerated no resistance—artistic or otherwise. The state arrested, tortured, raped, and killed political prisoners who were perceived to threaten law and order. Once the apartheid state fell, more than 27,000 cases of gross human rights abuses were investigated. Theology played an influential role in South African politics, for the apartheid system was established, in part, on theological principles. The situation also gave rise to a distinctly South African form of black liberation theology. The role of theologians in establishing as well as in dismantling apartheid will be the focus of this chapter.

The Historical Context: Afrikaner Nationalism

The apartheid system of government that would control South Africa from 1948 to 1994 was rooted in Afrikaner nationalism—a pride in **Afrikaner** cultural and linguistic identity. Afrikaners are descendants of immigrants from the Netherlands who settled on South African soil initially in the seventeenth century because of trade through the Dutch Indian Trading Company. They became, for the most part, farmers or **boers** in their new land. In 1853, Afrikaners trekked into the interior of the country to establish a homeland independent from the British, and it was there that they formed the *volkskerk*, or "people's church," of South Africa. A few years later, in 1859, the *Gereformeerde Kerk* broke away from the *volkskerk*. This was the church that would lay the foundation for Afrikaner nationalist policy rooted in a form of neo-Calvinism.

576

Pride in Afrikaner identity only increased after skirmishes with the British. The British were colonizing South Africa, having arrived in great numbers after the discovery of gold and diamonds. The most consequential of these conflicts was the Second Boer War (1899–1902). When Afrikaners lost, the British put them into concentration camps. As many as 27,000 Afrikaners died, mainly women and children, giving rise to an Afrikaner form of nationalism that soared among them. The Union of South Africa, intended to represent both British and Afrikaners, was created after the defeat of the Boers in 1902. After it held its first parliament in 1910, laws were quickly enacted severely restricting black South Africans from self-determination.

The National Party of the Afrikaners was launched in 1914 in opposition to the attempt at a unified government. By 1918, the **Broederbond**, an Afrikaner secret society, was active. Its ultimate aim was to overthrow British rule, an aspiration realized in 1948 when it won the general election. It had campaigned on the promise to implement a system of **apartheid**, an Afrikaans word which means "hoods" that are kept "apart" from one another. Apartheid would legalize the segregation of South African society not only in terms of housing, but also in terms of education, health care, criminal justice, and so on, thereby structuring access to opportunities for meaningful work and financial independence—all on the basis of skin color. The notorious regime maintained its power through brutal control for almost 50 years (1948–1994).

Among the architects of apartheid were theologians who were constructing the religious foundations for apartheid law from their respective theology departments and seminaries in Potchefstroom, Stellenbosch, and Pretoria. In fact, the first three prime ministers under apartheid were all pastors in the Dutch Reformed Church. The third of these was **Hendrik Verwoerd** (1901–1966), often called "the architect of apartheid" for his role in developing the policies that would be implemented for the next half century. In particular, nationalist interpretations of the Tower of Babel, the Pentecost, and the Kingdom of God enabled the National Party to provide theological rationalizations for apartheid law. They believed that the Tower of Babel proved God wanted them to live separately, divided not by race but by language. They argued that the Holy Spirit did not abolish linguistic differences when communicating "in the Spirit" at Pentecost, which proved to them that God wanted linguistic differences to be protected by separate development. And they believed that, when Paul wrote "There is neither Jew nor Greek, there is neither bond nor free, there is neither male nor female: for ye are all one in Christ Jesus" (Galatians 3:28), Paul referred to an eschatological age whereas, in the here and now, humans were meant to be divided on the basis of linguistic, cultural, and ethnic differences.

The Struggle: South African Liberation Theology

These examples show how thoroughly biblical interpretation was being manipulated for the purposes of reinforcing the political agenda of those who defended apartheid, and indicate the need for theological challenge. The origins of liberation theology in South Africa can be traced to 1912 when the **African National Congress** (ANC) was founded as a political party to secure the rights of black and mixed-race citizens. The earliest leaders of the ANC were clergymen who were inspired by the Christian ideals of equality and justice. James Dube, the first president of the ANC, was a Congregational minister as was Albert Luthuli, who would one day receive a Nobel Prize for his nonviolent leadership; Zacheus Mahabana, who served as president of the Cape Congress of the ANC, was a Methodist minister as was Robert Sobukwe, who would later break away from the ANC to form the **Pan Africanist Congress** (PAC); and Fr. James Calata, who served as the General Secretary of the ANC, was an Anglican priest, as was Zachariah Matthews, who has been called the continent's most distinguished African intellectual of the time period. Despite their efforts, apartheid was enacted, and soon the apartheid government would ban the activities of the ANC, which went underground from 1960 to 1990.

After the **Sharpeville Massacre**, during which 69 black South Africans were shot and killed by the police in 1960 for protesting pass laws, the World Council of Churches called the **Cottesloe Consultation**, which urged churches to take a strong and active role in challenging the injustices of apartheid. Although individual theologians such as Fr. Trevor Huddleston, an Anglican monk, and Beyers Naudé, a minister in the Dutch Reformed Church, staunchly opposed the apartheid regime, the mainline Christian churches of South Africa did not directly or decisively use their prominence to challenge the government's racial policies.

Theologians such as Desmond Tutu, Allan Boesak, Manas Buthelezi, and Sabelo Ntswassa nevertheless went on to lay the theological foundations for **Black Theology**, a distinctly South African form of liberation theology that was less Marxist in orientation than its Latin American counterparts and more biblically grounded than African-American versions of the same, though it was indebted to each. Grounded in principles of black empowerment as articulated in South Africa by activist and socialist **Steve Biko**, who taught that "Black is Beautiful," and rooted in the idea that all are equal in the eyes of God and thus all are wonderfully made for freedom, black theology speaks of the necessity of black self-love. Instead of internalizing white theology's message that to be white is to be truly human and that to be black is to be intrinsically inferior, black theology encourages Christians in black and mixed-race communities to recognize their own inherent dignity and loveworthiness, and to resist the oppression that threatens them with annihilation.

Theologians who are oriented to the framework of black liberation thought approach their task as a recovery of the central message of the prophets and of Jesus, and as a disentanglement of that message from the racist presuppositions that had enabled white theologians to justify the enactment of apartheid. Black theology stresses right practice, or **praxis**, and seeks not only to liberate the poor and oppressed—but also to liberate their oppressors by drawing white Christians into an understanding of a God of radical justice, hospitality, and mercy.

Desmond Tutu (b. 1931) is one of South Africa's most prominent practitioners of South African liberation theology. He served as the General Secretary of the South African Council of Churches from 1978 until 1985 when he became the Bishop of Johannesburg, and then was elevated a year later to the Archbishopric of Cape Town. Through his activism, he especially drew international attention to two principles of black liberation thought: forgiveness and reconciliation.

Informed by patterns of **restorative justice**, the ancient African practice of aggrieved parties meeting with a community elder to find "justice under a tree" (i.e., coming together to find solutions to conflict that are satisfactory to both parties),

Figure 27–4 Desmond Tutu (b. 1931).

Tutu believed that God's justice *is* merciful, and that God desires the healing of relationships more than God desires punishment for a wrongdoer. Tutu advocated for a theology further rooted in a South African understanding of **ubuntu**, a philosophy of interdependence that recognizes "I am because you are." In such a world-view of radical interdependence, when conflict arises, nothing matters more than the restoration of a broken relationship.

For Tutu, forgiveness and reconciliation are two entirely distinct movements on the path to a restored relationship. Forgiveness, or the practice of "letting go" of resentment against a wrongdoer, is in the power of the violated one. As such, it does not require an apology. For those raised in churches imbued with African sensibilities and the *ubuntu*-inspired philosophical principles upon which they are based, this understanding of forgiveness is radically paradoxical. Forgiveness is extended not for the benefit of the wrongdoer, but for the empowerment of the violated one. Because the violator's wrongdoing is an expression of coercive power—a way of overpowering and controlling a target—Tutu believed that to withhold forgiveness until one hears an apology is to yield power over again into the hand of the perpetrator. For him, to grant forgiveness is a means of ending the abusive cycle. Forgiveness is a means of saying: I am taking my power back. I will not allow you to control me. I am letting go of vengeance. I am letting go of hatred. I forgive, because I refuse to become what you are. In the act of forgiving, power is reclaimed by the one against whom a violation has occurred.

Reconciliation, by contrast, is sometimes a long and arduous process to restore mutual trust once a violation has occurred. Reconciliation, unlike forgiveness, *will* require an apology—an acknowledgment of wrongdoing, something that an offer of forgiveness can sometimes elicit. It will also require hard work on the relationship to heal what was broken. To put it mathematically, forgiveness plus reconciliation equals restoration of relationship in Desmond Tutu's theology of liberation.

The Situation: The End of Apartheid and South Africa Today

There was a quickening of a critical theological response to apartheid and the demise of the regime when, in 1982, the World Alliance of Reformed Churches (WARC) met in Ottawa, Canada, for a conference on "Racism and South Africa." The General Council adopted the **WARC Declaration**, a document that reads, in part,

> We declare with black Reformed Christians of South Africa that apartheid ("separate development") is a sin, and that the moral and theological justification of it is a travesty of the Gospel and, in its persistent disobedience to the Word of God, a theological heresy.

The move to declare apartheid a heresy was a controversial one, but the declaration's drafters believed the error in the political ideology of apartheid which had been constructed theologically needed an equally strong theological response in order to be deconstructed—and thus, the alliance succeeded in declaring apartheid to be heretical. It is important to note, however, that the *Gereformeerde Kerk* was not a member of the alliance.

Three years later, on July 21, 1985, the apartheid government issued a "state of emergency," which gave the police the power to detain prisoners, impose curfews, and control the media, leading to the death of almost 600 people with more than half killed by the police. In response, an anonymous group of predominantly black South African theologians in Soweto believed to have been led by a black Pentecostal cleric, **Frank Chikane**, issued the **Kairos Document**. The Greek word "kairos" means "special moment," and speaks to time from God's vantage point breaking into chronological time as experienced by humankind. Thus, "kairos" moments are thought to be times when God speaks in a special way to a particular situation. The authors referred to theirs as "the moment of truth," insisting on theological grounds that the Christian churches must oppose the racist minority government and defend the black majority population. The authors offered a scathing critique of the "state theology" that used Paul's letter to the Romans to insist on submission to governing authorities, since "[t]he authorities that exist have been established by God" (Romans 13:7). Moreover, the authors of the Kairos Document argued that it was wrong for Christians to submit to unjust laws and regimes, and they called on Christians to wage an active nonviolent struggle against the structural injustice that had been inflicted by the state. Eventually signed by more than 150 members of the clergy, this theological statement condemned the quietism of the Christian churches in response to the atrocious brutality of the apartheid government, and offered an alternative **prophetic theology** that found in the Bible evidence that God opposed injustice, worked for liberation, and turned despair into hope.

The WARC Declaration and the Kairos Document showed how unstable the theological foundations were upon which the apartheid state was constructed. By opposing apartheid on theological grounds, and by declaring it a dangerous heresy, cracks in apartheid's infrastructure were widened to huge fissures when domestic social protests and armed resistance movements combined with a worldwide anti-apartheid movement to demand economic divestment from South Africa. Together, these forces would eventually coalesce to force the collapse of the brutal regime. After spending 27 years in prison, Nelson Mandela was released in 1990. He began working with colleagues to write the constitution for the new government, over which he was elected to be President when South Africa held its first democratic elections in 1994. Archbishop Desmond Tutu declared South Africa to be the rainbow people of God, and the new government initiated efforts to redress the wrongdoings of the past. Although there are many issues that South Africa faces, including ongoing racial tension, disparities in health care and education, not to mention poverty, crime, HIV/AIDS, violence against women, and governmental corruption, no one disputes how remarkable it was that South Africa was able to transition to democracy without descending into civil war.

BLACK THEOLOGY

The publication of James H. Cone's *Black Theology and Black Power* in 1969 is widely regarded as the first academic treatment of **Black Theology** in the United States. Published two years prior to the Peruvian theologian, Gustavo Gutiérrez's 1971 *A Theology of Liberation: History, Politics, and Salvation*, Cone's *Black Theology and Black Power* may also be regarded as the beginning of the theological movement known as Liberation Theology. Together with Cone's 1970 systematic theology, *A Black Theology of Liberation, Black Theology and Black Power* marks one of the most significant turning points in twentieth-century Christian theology.

As is the case with all intellectual movements, Black Theology did not emerge in a vacuum. Black Theology should be understood against the backdrop of the centuries-long struggle of black people to resist white supremacy and systemic anti-black racist oppression. Black Theology is, in part, a response to the more than 500-year history of white oppression, which has included more than 200 years of chattel slavery in which black people were bought and sold as commodities, lynching, legal segregation, racist laws and policies, discriminatory policing, mass incarceration, and economic disempowerment. In a sense, then, Black Theology had its origins not in 1969, but in 1441, when the first group of Africans were taken from the West African coast to what became the Christian land of Portugal, where the first slave auction was held in 1441. However, that is not to say that Black Theology is merely a reaction to white oppression. On the contrary, Black Theology draws inspiration from the manifold traditions originating from black communities of faith, traditional African religions, spirituality, culture, and politics, as well as from black preachers, philosophers, activists, musicians, poets, and artists.

From the time of the earliest colonial expeditions into North America, European settlers appealed to the Bible, early modern science, and philosophy to justify their enslavement of African people, genocidal wars against Native American people, and the theft of land. White Christian theologians and preachers maintained that African people were descendants of an inferior race and ordained by God to be the slaves of European peoples (specifically subject to those classified as "Anglo-Saxon"). From the beginning, black people countered arguments for their enslavement and inferiority with different interpretations of scripture and different understandings of

God, insisting on God's affirmation of blackness and on the history of God's liberating activity on the behalf of the oppressed. For example, in the eighteenth century, black ministers like Bishop Richard Allen argued against the institution of slavery on theological and biblical grounds, and in the nineteenth century, figures such as Nat Turner, Denmark Vessey, and Gabriel Prosser organized slave rebellions in the name of God. Drawing on African spirituality, the Exodus narrative, and the prophetic and apocalyptic traditions of scripture, in the early nineteenth century, Robert Alexander Young and David Walker wrote anti-slavery theological pamphlets criticizing the racism of white people by appealing to the coming judgment and justice of God.

During the period of slavery, and even after Emancipation in 1863, black women in particular were subject to some of the harshest forms of physical, psychological, and sexual violence at the hands of white slaveholders. In response, figures such as Mary Prince, Maria Stewart, and Sojourner Truth developed what A. Elaine Brown Crawford has called a "counter-cultural theology" of resistance, empowered by a persistent spirit of hope. For example, the abolitionist Sojourner Truth contrasted the "religion of Jesus" with the "religion of America," challenging the pretentions of the white man who, Truth maintained, falsely thought of himself as equal to God and superior to black people. The abolition of slavery was enlivened, in no small part, by the communal theological imagination of black women who resisted and rebelled against the violence of the slaveholding religion of America and persisted in the struggle for freedom.

Racial discrimination toward black people did not end after the legal abolition of the institution of slavery in the United States. The **theo-ideology** of white supremacy persisted and the discrimination of black people continued. According to Kelly Brown-Douglas (2015), the theo-ideological legitimation of racism is the combination of natural law theory with the **myth of Anglo-Saxon superiority**. In a 1861 address, the vice-president of the Confederacy, Alexander H. Stephens, expressed this theo-ideology in his "Cornerstone Address." Drawing on the Bible and natural law, Stephens argued that a cornerstone of the Confederacy rested on the idea that: "the negro is not equal to the white man; that slavery, subordination to the superior race, is his natural and moral condition." Stephens maintained,

> The negro by nature, or by the Curse against Canaan ... is fitted for that condition which he occupies in our system. ... It is best, not only for the superior but for the inferior race, that it should be so. It is, indeed, in conformity with the Creator. It is not for us to inquire into the wisdom of His ordinances or to question them. For His own purposes He has made one race to differ from another, as He has made one star to differ from another in glory.
>
> (Stephens 1861)

In this quotation one can see how racist claims about the laws of nature combined with biblical claims about the "ordinances" and "purposes" of God served to theologically legitimate the ideology of Anglo-Saxon superiority and the supposedly "natural" character of the subordination of African-American people. In this way, a particular theology came to ideologically legitimate and even sanctify the idea that black people were destined to be chattel slaves. In this framework, to suggest otherwise, would be to not only challenge the laws of nature, but also to challenge the very purposes of God the Creator.

The theo-ideology that legitimated white supremacy persisted after the abolition of slavery. The extrajudicial murder in the form of **lynching**, in which black people were publicly tortured and hanged on trees across the United States, rose dramatically in the decades following the emancipation of slaves. Between 1877 and 1950, nearly 4,000 African-American men and women were victims of lynching across the North and the South of the United States. In 1939, the African-American jazz musician and singer, Billie Holiday, famously performed and recorded the song, "Strange Fruit," which linked the fruit of a tree with the victims of lynching.

Ida B. Wells was one of the most vocal opponents of lynching. In her 1900 speech, "Lynch Law in America," she said,

> Our country's national crime is lynching. It is not the creature of an hour, the sudden outburst of uncontrolled fury, or the unspeakable brutality of an insane mob. It represents the cool, calculating deliberation of intelligent people who openly avow that there is an "unwritten law" that justifies them in putting human beings to death without complaint under oath, without trial by jury, without opportunity to make defense, and without right of appeal.

(Wells 1990)

According to Wells, "Lynch Law" was not only a national crime but an "unwritten law" in the United States that functioned to intimidate, terrorize, and suppress black people who had been struggling for full emancipation in the wake of slavery, fighting for economic, social, and civil rights in the aftermath of slavery. In recent years, James Cone has sought to interpret the theological significance of the cross in light of the lynching tree in order to highlight the history of lynching as well as the ongoing reality of anti-black racism in America.

Two movements provide the immediate backdrop to contemporary Black Theology. First, out of the **Civil Rights Movement**, spanning from the early 1950s to the late 1960s, came the widely influential theological voice of the Rev. Dr. Martin Luther King, Jr. Drawing on the history of the black struggle for freedom, the social gospel of liberal Protestant theology, and the nonviolent resistance led by Mahatma Ghandi, King famously articulated a moral, theological, and political vision for black civil rights, the end of racial segregation, and Jim Crow segregation which had denied black people basic human rights, and the hope for the eventual reconciliation of blacks and whites. Along with many other civil rights organizers, King led the Montgomery bus boycott in 1955, helped organize the March on Washington in 1963, and Selma to Montgomery marches in 1965. While King strongly criticized racial segregation and white moderates who called for gradual change, some black leaders believed that his commitment to nonviolence, Civil Rights, desegregation, and reconciliation with whites did not yet go far enough to address the ongoing violence of white oppression.

Second, the emergence of the Black Power movement in the spring of 1966, which appeared in the wake of the assassination of Malcolm X a year earlier, demanded a more radical vision of black emancipation in America. Drawing on what Cedric Robinson has called the Black Radical tradition, consisting of voices such as Richard Wright, C.L.R. James, Frantz Fanon, and W.E.B. DuBois, the Black Power movement criticized Western social, political, and economic structures as fundamentally racist at their foundation. As such, these figures argued that the Civil Rights Movement and desegregation in America, while undoubtedly important, did not yet go far enough to challenge the systemic nature of anti-black racism. In response to the growing Black Power movement in America and to the surprise of white church leaders who had been calling for black church leadership to denounce Black Power as unchristian, a group of black clergy published a full-page declaration in the *New York Times* on July 31, 1966 titled, "Black Power," which claimed that God-talk was inseparable from black self-determination and black power.

Black Theology as a discipline developed in the wake of the Civil Rights and Black Power movements. Wrestling with the legacies of King and Malcolm X, James Cone, a young professor at Union Theological Seminary in New York City, maintained that Black Power is "Christ's central message to twentieth-century America" (1970, 1). Against white theologians and church leaders, Cone maintained that Black Power is an authentic and faithful expression of Christian faith in twentieth-century America. Cone argued that the meaning of the Gospel of Jesus Christ is liberation. Cone defined Black Theology as the analysis of "black [people's] condition in the light of God's revelation in Jesus Christ with the purpose of creating a new understanding of black dignity among black people, and providing the necessary soul in that people to destroy white racism" (Cone 1970, 117).

For Cone, **Black Power** means the radical affirmation of freedom and self-determination for black people and the "complete emancipation of black people from white oppression by whatever means black people deem necessary" (Cone 1969, 6). In contrast to white liberals and some black moderates, Cone insisted that Black Power does not primarily seek out "reconciliation" and "integration" with whites, but conflict and opposition. For Cone, peace and reconciliation can only be achieved on the basis of complete black liberation, which involved a critique of the white status quo in the church and society. Such a theological vision caused unrest among many white theologians. However, it was met with approval among key black church leaders. James Forman's presentation of the "Black Manifesto" on May 4, 1969 at Riverside Church in New York City and the National Committee of Black Churchmen's public statement on "Black Theology" on June 13, 1969, endorsed Cone's understanding of Black Theology as a theology of liberation. In 1970, Cone released *A Black Theology of Liberation*, which further developed the theological vision already implicit in his earlier work.

Since the publication of Cone's two early books, Black Theology has developed in a number of important ways. In conversation with Cone, J. Deotis Roberts challenged key elements of Cone's black theology of liberation. Roberts worried that Cone downplayed the centrality of the Gospel message of reconciliation. While Roberts agreed with Cone that liberation must precede reconciliation, he nevertheless argued that the Gospel is the news that "all are 'one in Christ Jesus,'" which means that "all slave–master, servant–boss, inferior–superior frames of reference between blacks and whites have been abolished" (Roberts 1971, 72). For Roberts, Christian love demands that one "hold up at all times the possibility for black–white interracial fellowship and cooperation" (Roberts 1971, 72). While both theologians agree that Black Theology is a theology of liberation, their disagreements serve to highlight the important differences among black theologians on issues that touch on a number of significant theological and political questions. What is the contemporary meaning of the Gospel's call of freedom in relation to the black struggle against racism? Is Civil Rights, reconciliation, and "integration" an adequate way of framing the freedom of the Gospel elicited by the black church tradition? Or is reconciliation primarily an eschatological (the doctrine of the last things) category? If white racism is America's "original sin," what does soteriology (the doctrine of salvation) mean for black people? How do biblical themes of God's liberating activity on the behalf of the oppressed relate to Jesus' command to "love your enemy?" What is the nature of God's affirmation of black people and God's judgment on white people?

Womanist Theology is arguably the most important theological development that has emerged in the wake of these debates within Black Theology. Drawing on the past and present of black women's intellectual thought and activism, Womanist theology seeks to combine a theological analysis of race, gender, and class. Womanist Theology emerged in critical relation to both Black Theology and White feminist theology. Already in 1979, Jacquelyn Grant challenged the male-dominated discourse of Black Theology, claiming that black women are "invisible in black theology" (Grant 1989, 326). While affirming the critiques of white racism in Black Theology and the critiques of patriarchy in White feminist theology (see the next section, on feminist theology), Womanist theologians maintain that both discourses have failed to account for the particularities of the lived experiences of black women.

In her 1983 book, *In Search of Our Mothers' Gardens*, Alice Walker defined womanism in the following way:

1. From womanish (opp. of "girlish," i.e., frivolous, irresponsible, not serious). A Black feminist or feminist of color. From the Black folk expression of mothers to female children, "You acting womanish," i.e., like a woman. Usually referring to outrageous, audacious, courageous, or willful behavior. Wanting to know more and in greater depth than is considered "good" for one. Acting grown up. Being grown up. Interchangeable with another Black folk expression: "You trying to be grown." Responsible. In charge. Serious.

2. Also: A woman who loves other women, sexually and/or nonsexually. Appreciates and prefers women's culture, women's emotional flexibility (values tears as natural and counterbalance of laughter), and women's strength. Sometimes loves individual men, sexually and/or nonsexually. Committed to survival and wholeness of the entire people, male and female. Not a separatist, except periodically, for health. Traditionally universalist, as in: "Mama why are we brown, pink, and yellow, and our cousins are white, beige, and black? Ans.: "Well, you know the colored race is just like a flower garden, with every color flower represented." Traditionally capable, as in: "Mama, I'm walking to Canada and I'm taking you and a bunch of slaves with me." Reply: "It wouldn't be the first time."

3. Loves music. Loves dance. Loves the moon. Loves the Spirit. Loves love and food and roundness. Loves the struggle. Loves the Folk. Loves herself. Regardless.

4. Womanist is to feminist as purple is to lavender.

The work of Katie Cannon, Jacquelyn Grant, Delores Williams, and Kelly Brown-Douglas, all of whom are graduates of Union Theological Seminary, have paved the way for fresh articulations of a distinctively womanist or "black feminist" theological perspective. Williams' landmark work, *Sisters in the Wilderness: The Challenge of Womanist God-Talk* (1993), challenges the centrality of the motif of liberation in much of Black Theology. Williams privileges the theme of survival in the wilderness in a womanist theological perspective, and calls into question the uses of the Exodus narrative and the cross in male-dominated Black Theology. Reading the biblical narrative in light of the experiences of black women in the United States, Williams discerns a "non-liberative thread running through the Bible" (Williams 1993, 128). While God is consistently described as the liberator of the Israelite slaves in scripture, where is God in relation to non-Hebrew female slaves ("the oppressed of the oppressed"), such as the figure of Hagar in the Genesis narrative? Why does God not condemn slavery outright in the Exodus narrative? As it regards the cross, Williams challenges Western theories of atonement that tend to ascribe a kind of "sacred aura" to the cross, interpreting Jesus as "the ultimate surrogate figure" whose suffering brings redemption to humanity. In light of the surrogate experiences of black women who were sexually exploited during slavery, Williams wonders whether such interpretations of the cross end up supporting and reinforcing the exploitation of black women. As Williams puts it, "If black women accept this idea of redemption, can they not also passively accept the exploitation that surrogacy brings?" (1993, 143). As an alternative, Williams develops a Christology (doctrine of Christ) and soteriology that emphasizes the life-giving power of the "perfect *ministerial* vision" of Jesus whose life and death is best characterized as a form of resistance against death-dealing powers. Williams interprets the resurrection of Jesus as the affirmation of Jesus' ministry of healing, exorcism, prayer, faith, compassion, and love.

While Black Theology is most often associated with theologies that have emerged in Protestant black churches, it is important to note that several notable contributions in Black Theology have come from Black Catholic theologians. The work of Cyprian Davis, Toinette Eugene, the Dominican Sister Jamie Phelps, Edward Braxton, and more recently, Diana L. Hayes, M. Shawn Copeland, and Bryan Massingale have done much to develop theologies that address African-American Catholic history, theology, and practice that attend to issues of black self-determination and self-definition on matters related to pastoral care, education, and racial justice in the church and society.

Black Theology continues to grow and develop in new ways in the twenty-first century. In dialogue with emerging voices in Critical Race Theory and Black Studies, black theologians continue to analyze the multiple dimensions of racism and its various expressions in church and society. With the rise of the Black Lives Matter movement and a new consciousness about how the persistence of police violence and mass incarceration disproportionately affect people of color, particularly African-American people, black theologians continue to wrestle with what it might mean to affirm God's solidarity with black people in their struggle for liberation from white racism.

FEMINIST THEOLOGY

During the latter half of the twentieth century, feminist theology developed in many religious traditions, including Christianity. This theology recognizes that normative and authoritative theology has been done primarily, if not exclusively, by men. For much of Christian history, women have been denied access to formal education and excluded from positions of leadership in the church. Women have still experienced God and reflected on the meaning of that experience, but for the most part they have been denied the right to make public and authoritative theological statements. Feminist theology responds to this history of exclusion by asserting that the experience and ideas of women are as valuable as those of men and should also be regarded as a source for theological reflection.

Given the diversity of women's experiences, feminist theology is rich and multifaceted; indeed, it would be more accurate to speak of feminist theologies. These varied feminist theologies recognize the importance of intersectionality: the understanding that gender intersects with other sources of identity and discrimination for women, including race, class, and sexual orientation (among others). Thus, for example, women have developed feminist theologies that reflect their own racial or ethnic identities such as *Womanist* theologies by African-American women and *Mujerista* theologies by Latina women.

Sin and Salvation

These varied feminist theologies have some commitments and contributions in common, however. They all analyze the oppression of women and are committed to working toward the equality and inclusion of women in church and society. Many feminist theologians build on the insights of liberation theology, particularly its identification of poverty as structural sin, to analyze the structural sin of sexism. Sexism is sin because it leads to broken and unjust relationships between humans. While not denying individual sin, these theologians explore the ways in which sin is built into the very structures and institutions of society, including the church. For example, many of the early Church Fathers (theologians of the first centuries of the church)

587

identified all women with Eve and interpreted Eve (and therefore all women) as the source of sin. In his treatise "On the Apparel of Women," Tertullian wrote:

> And do you not know that you are (each) an Eve? The sentence of God on this sex of yours lives in this age: the guilt must of necessity live too. *You* are the devil's gateway: *you* are the unsealer of that (forbidden) tree: *you* are the first deserter of the divine law: *you* are she who persuaded him whom the devil was not valiant enough to attack. *You* destroyed so easily God's image, man. On account of *your* desert—that is, death—even the Son of God had to die.
>
> (Tertullian I.1)

Women were defined as weaker and more susceptible to temptation, in part because men were identified with reason and the spirit while women were identified with emotion and the body. Just as reason should control emotion and spirit should rule over the body, so men were called to control women. The ideal Christian woman therefore was defined as silent, obedient, and submissive. As Augustine wrote in *The Literal Meaning of Genesis*: "For we must believe that even before her sin woman had been made to be ruled by her husband and to be submissive and subject to him" (Augustine XI, 37), Christian feminist theology seeks to counter this history of sexism by looking to scripture and tradition for insights and examples that empower and liberate women. The creation of woman in the image of God (Genesis 1:26–27) is a key text for supporting the dignity and equality of women.

This concern for justice and equality is rooted in feminist theology's understanding of salvation. While defined in a variety of ways, salvation is often understood in terms of liberation or healing (its primary meaning in Latin). Feminist theologians look to the bible for this understanding of salvation, pointing to God's liberation of the Israelite slaves in the Exodus and the Israelite prophets who called for justice and *shalom* (wholeness and peace) in society and all of creation. They also look to Jesus' proclamation of the kingdom (or reign) of God, the triumph of good over evil, which he brought about by not only forgiving sins but also healing diseases, reaching out to the poor and marginalized, and criticizing unjust religious and political systems. Salvation as healing and liberation is therefore the overcoming of the brokenness of sin that is found in individuals and in society. It involves a loving and just relationship with God, with other people, and with all of creation. Ecofeminism has pointed out the ways in which Western culture has identified men with civilization and women with nature in an effort to justify the subjugation of women as well as the exploitation of nature. Therefore, women (and men) cannot be truly liberated until we live in harmonious and respectful relationship with nature as well as other humans and God.

Biblical Interpretation

Feminist theologians and biblical scholars bring this understanding of sin and salvation to their study of the bible. They note that women do not appear in the biblical texts as often as men and when they do appear, they are often not named and their perspective is not represented. Recognizing that the Bible and other texts central to the church's tradition have been produced by and for men, feminist theologians approach those texts with a "hermeneutics of suspicion." Hermeneutics refers to principles of interpretation. It seeks to identify the values, convictions, and biases people bring to a text and to articulate the principles they should use to best interpret it. While not denying that biblical texts have been inspired by God, Christian feminists argue that they also reflect the culture, experiences, and biases of the men who produced them. In doing so, feminist theologians are reflecting a view of inspiration consistent with Roman Catholic, Orthodox, and mainline Protestant traditions. Feminists analyze the patriarchal nature of the societies that produced the Bible and the ways in which sexism is embedded in biblical texts. The goal of interpretation is, whenever possible, to liberate these texts from their sexist bias and to find the liberating possibilities within them. This might involve recovering neglected texts, asking different questions of the text, or offering an interpretation of the text that leads to justice and liberation for women.

For example, many feminist biblical scholars point out that Paul's letters (the earliest texts of the New Testament) reveal an ambiguous attitude toward women. He assumes a patriarchal attitude when he tells the Corinthians that "the husband is the head of his wife" but in this same passage he emphasizes their mutual relationship when he declares that: "Nevertheless, in the Lord woman is not independent of man *or man independent of woman*" (I Corinthians 11:3 and 11:11; emphasis added). In his letter to the Romans, he mentions several women involved in the early Christian community, including a couple in leadership roles: Phoebe, who is identified as a "deacon" or "minister," and Junia, who is "prominent among the apostles" (Romans 16:1 and 16:7).

The Gospels also portray a complicated and diverse picture of women in early Christianity, particularly since each Gospel has its own distinctive character. While men appear much more often in these texts, women are also represented as followers of Jesus. For example, in Luke's Gospel, Jesus approves of Mary sitting at his feet as a disciple (Luke 10:38–42). In John's Gospel, Jesus has an extended theological discussion with a most unlikely individual, a Samaritan woman, who then goes out to evangelize her village (John 4:1–42). Throughout the Gospels, women, many of whom are unnamed, are presented as exemplars of faith: the hemorrhaging woman who was healed by Jesus (Mark 5:25–34), the penitent woman (Luke 7:36–50), and the Syrophoenician woman who asks Jesus to heal her daughter (Mark 7:24–30; Matthew 15:21–28). The descriptions of the resurrection vary, but in all four Gospels Mary Magdalene is named as one of the women who discovered the empty tomb. In the Gospel of John, Jesus himself tells her to witness to his resurrection, thus earning her the title of "apostle to the apostles" in the early church (John 20:1–18).

Figure 27–5 Portrait of Prof. Elisabeth Schüssler Fiorenza, December 15, 1987.

In the later texts of the New Testament, there are more restrictions on women. For example, wives are told that they must be subject to their husbands in Ephesians 5:22 and Colossians 3:18. Women are told that they may not teach or have authority over a man and are enjoined to be silent and submissive in 1 Timothy 2:11–12. In her classic study, *In Memory of Her: A Feminist Theological Reconstruction of Christian Origins* (1994), Elisabeth Schüssler Fiorenza describes these texts as the "patriarchalization" of the church and interprets them as the result of its efforts to conform to the larger Greco-Roman society by adopting more restrictive gender roles for women.

Language for God

Feminist theologians note that language and images for God are often male, in particular, a ruling and powerful male: God as Father, Son, Lord, and King. They argue that this reflects the cultures in which these images developed, namely, patriarchal societies in which elite men held economic, social, political, and religious power. Feminist theologians contend that using *exclusively* male language for God helps to perpetuate the idea, even if only subconsciously, that God is in fact male. This is problematic because the Christian tradition affirms that God is Spirit and therefore not literally or biologically male. In fact, the Bible affirms that both male and female are created in the image of God (Genesis 1:26–27). The solution proposed by most Christian feminists is not to abandon masculine terms for God but to include a wide variety of words and images for God, including the feminine. Some of these terms are found in the Bible, while others are drawn from the tradition or women's experience. The theologian Sallie McFague, for example, explores images of God as mother, lover, and friend in her book *Models of God* (1987). In doing so, she and other feminist theologians point out that the Judeo-Christian tradition has insisted that theological language is not literal but analogical or metaphorical. It reflects something of who God is by comparison to human experience but it is not a full or complete description of God because that is beyond human ability to either conceive or communicate. By using many words and images for God, the mystery of God is preserved and idolatry (the worship of an image of God) is avoided.

Role of Women in the Church

During the twentieth century, the role of women in the church, particularly in terms of ordination to ministry, became a major issue. Protestant and Catholic views on the ordination of women focus on different sources of authority and emphasize different ministerial roles. For Protestants, the primary authority for this question is the Bible and the central issue is often whether or not women should preach. For Catholics, the primary authority for this question is tradition and the central issue is whether or not women can celebrate the Eucharist. The debate among Protestants is tied to different understandings of the inspiration and inerrancy of the Bible. Conservative Protestant denominations (such as the Lutheran Church-Missouri Synod, Wisconsin Evangelical Lutheran Synod, and Southern Baptist Convention) have a fundamentalist view of scripture which contends that God directly inspired every word of the Bible. These denominations continue to deny ordination to women on the basis of a literal reading of biblical passages which support the subordination and silencing of women, some of which were discussed above. However, most Protestant denominations (such as the Evangelical Lutheran Church in America, Presbyterian Church [U.S.A.], United Methodist Church, Episcopal Church, and United Church of Christ) have a view of biblical inspiration which affirms God's role in inspiring the text but assumes that humans were also involved in the process. In this view, the Bible reflects the cultures and times in which it was written. These denominations ordain women by interpreting passages which advocate their silence and subordination as reflective of the patriarchal cultures of the Bible. They also point to biblical texts that support preaching and leadership roles for women, such as the gospel accounts which describe women as the first ones to witness and proclaim the resurrection of Jesus.

For the Catholic Church, tradition as well as scripture is authoritative and revealed by God. Although the Catholic Church agrees with the view of biblical inspiration that acknowledges human participation in the writing of the Bible, it denies ordination to women on the basis of tradition. It points to apostolic succession, the understanding that the authority of the apostles was transmitted to the succession (or series) of bishops who followed them. The magisterium (teaching authority) of the Catholic Church states that it is bound by the example of Jesus, who entrusted the foundation and leadership of the church to 12 male apostles, who then passed it on to male bishops. The Catholic Church also declares that the priest must be male because he represents Jesus in the exercise of his ministry and this representation requires a "natural resemblance" between Jesus and the priest, especially when celebrating the Eucharist (*Inter Insigniores* and *Ordinatio Sacerdotalis*).

Some Catholics who support the ordination of women respond to the claim that Jesus chose 12 male apostles by attributing his choice to his historical context and the limited role of women in that time. Others argue that the definition of apostle (one chosen by Jesus to preach the gospel) should include Mary Magdalene, recognized as "the apostle to the apostles" and Junia, described by Paul as "prominent among the apostles" (Romans 16:7). They respond to the idea that the priest must bear a natural (or physical) resemblance to Jesus by asking why gender should be the deciding factor. Should we not also demand that the priest be Jewish, as Jesus was? Supporters of women's ordination argue that spiritual rather than physical similarity to Jesus (i.e., similarity in love) is what really matters.

Christian feminists are not only concerned about the roles of women in the church but the nature of the church itself. Many seek to redefine the church by stressing relationships of mutuality and partnership over relationships of hierarchy and dominance. They often do so by reference to the "priesthood of all believers" or the church as the people of God and they look to models of church that encourage participation by all members of the community. Some feminist theologians reject ordination to ministry completely by arguing that it only sustains an existing patriarchal structure and encourages clericalism or an emphasis on the power of the clergy over lay people. Others believe that churches can be transformed from within by ordaining women to leadership roles. In both cases, Christian feminists advocate for a greater role for women within the church and a recognition of their gifts in ministry, worship, education, and service. They believe the church should be a community that advocates for justice for all humans and the care of all creation.

CHRISTIANITY AND ENVIRONMENTAL SUSTAINABILITY

Perhaps the biggest challenge to contemporary Christianity is one shared by every person on earth: human activity threatens the ecological systems that support human life. The pre-modern world occasionally experienced collapses of local habitats due to overgrazing, overfishing, groundwater depletion, and the like. But only in the wake of the Industrial Revolution in the nineteenth century have humans been able to disrupt the environment on a global scale.

Scientists regularly inform us about air and water pollution, soil contamination, water scarcity and soil depletion, species extinction and loss of biodiversity, overpopulation, and an increase in natural disasters such as severe hurricanes, floods, droughts, and wildfires. The dynamics of the crisis are complex, but a common thread running through most of these events is **anthropogenic climate change**: an overall rapid change in planetary temperature, precipitation, and wind patterns caused by human activity. The worldwide scientific community has reached an overwhelming consensus (97 percent of actively publishing climate scientists) that these changes, with their accompanying impacts, are real and human-caused. The impact of human activity on earth systems is so profound that geologists have given this period in Earth's history a new name: the **Anthropocene** period.

Christianity's awareness of environmental destruction has been gradual, but a wake-up call came in 1967 with the publication of an article in the journal *Science* by historian Lynn White, titled "The Historical Roots of our Ecologic Crisis." White argued that Western Christian tradition has taught people to devalue non-human life. According to White, the belief that we are authorized by God to heedlessly exploit the natural world can be traced back to the dual emphasis on God's transcendence and human **dominion** found in Genesis. He called for a thorough overhaul of Western Christian attitudes:

> What we do about ecology depends on our ideas of the man[*sic*]–nature relationship. More science and more technology are not going to get us out of the present ecologic crisis until we find a new religion, or rethink our old one.
>
> (White 2004, 1206)

Christians responded to White's charge in a number of ways: some nuanced his claims, noting that his characterization of Christian beliefs was overly simplistic and that other factors beyond religion played a role in bringing civilization to this predicament. But Christians also took White's criticism to heart and began to critically evaluate Christianity's role in the ecological crisis. In recent decades, theologians have discerned ways that Christianity has contributed to ecological destruction, and also how it can be a source of ecological renewal. Theologians are now critically retrieving ancient Christian teachings about creation and constructing new theologies in light of environmental questions.

As an example of critical retrieval, one of the first questions theologians ask is whether Christianity's **anthropocentric** world-view necessarily leads to abuse of the natural world. If humans alone are made in the "image of God" to exercise "dominion" or rule over the rest of creation, as Genesis 1 describes, do human needs and desires pre-empt all consideration of the natural world? Does the rest of creation only have **instrumental value**—does its goodness lie solely in its usefulness to us? Or does it also have **intrinsic value**—is it good and worthwhile in itself? When scholars revisit biblical accounts as well as patristic sources with an eye to ecological questions, new insights emerge about the value of creation and humanity's role in it.

First, Christianity's anthropocentrism is tempered by perhaps an even more pervasive theocentrism: the belief that all of creation belongs to God, is created to glorify God, and will be renewed and transformed by God at the end of time. Human beings are just one voice in the chorus of creatures, which includes even inanimate elements; as Basil of Caesaraea wrote in the fourth century, "the deeps sing in their language a harmonious hymn to the glory of the Creator" (*Hexaemeron*, Homily 3.9). Humans must respect the ultimate purpose of each creature's existence—it exists for God. As biblical scholar Christopher Wright explains,

> To love God ... means to value what God values. Conversely, therefore, to contribute to, or collude in, the abuse, pollution and destruction of the natural order is to trample on the goodness of God reflected in creation. It is to devalue what God values, to mute God's praise and to diminish God's glory.

> (Wright 2004, 116)

Because God values the whole creation and deems it very good (Genesis 1:31), people are called to act accordingly. This links to a second insight found in biblical teaching that moderates Christian anthropocentrism: while humans have unique value in God's creation, we are also uniquely responsible for creation. Humankind may exercise dominion, but we must "till and tend" (Genesis 2:15) rather than exploit and abuse.

New and constructive environmental theologies emerge as theologians place classic Christian teachings in dialogue with specific areas of ecological concern. For example, mundane activities such as eating have environmental, ethical, and spiritual significance. American farmer, poet, and essayist Wendell Berry inspired a generation of theological reflection on the way we eat and what it says about our relationships to plants, animals, the soil, the people who produce our food, and ultimately to God. In his famous essay, "The Pleasures of Eating," he concludes,

> Eating with the fullest pleasure—pleasure, that is, that does not depend on ignorance—is perhaps the profoundest enactment of our connection with the world. In this pleasure we experience and celebrate our dependence and our gratitude, for we are living from mystery, from creatures we did not make and powers we cannot comprehend.

> (Berry 1990, 54)

Subsequent developments in Christian **ecotheology** explore the rich spiritual signifi-cance of food and how it can inform Christians' eating habits to be more ecologically sustainable and socially just. A relatively new but growing question in this area involves the ethics of eating meat. Lutheran theologian Kristin Johnston Largen presents a "Christian Rationale for Vegetarianism," addressed specifically to well-off Christians who have the freedom to choose their diet. She reflects on the human person as made in the image of God, which means we are subjects (not objects), we are relational, and we are called to solidarity with all other creatures.

> The concept of solidarity encourages us to recognize that human well-being is intimately linked to animal well-being. We see this in a variety of ways. Humans cannot be well when our destructive manipulation of animal populations dramatically increases pollution and environmental destruction. Humans cannot be well when our societies do not take cruelty to animals seriously. Humans cannot be well when restaurants are constantly on the lookout for the next "exotic meat" to serve on their menus, and when hunters can, for a price, kill even the most critically endangered animal species for sport. Christian solidarity calls us to stand against these and all oppressive practices.
>
> (Largen 2009, 154)

Largen invokes the intrinsic goodness of animals and argues that humans are called to love animals not for how they might be enjoyable to us, but as fellow creatures who are valuable to God.

Ecofeminism is another constructive theological approach that integrates ecolo-gical healing with liberation from injustice. In the words of one prominent Catholic ecofeminist, Rosemary Radford Ruether, ecofeminism "examines the interconnec-tion between the domination of women and the domination of nature. It aims at strategies and world-views to liberate or heal these interconnected dominations" (Hessel and Reuther 2000, 97). Ruether describes how unjust relationships between men and women, rich and poor, whites and other races are inextricably intertwined with humanity's unjust relationship to the earth. In each case, the fundamental sin is to "distort the original harmony [of creation] by usurping power over others." In Ruether's theology, Christ heals and restores the original cosmic harmony; "redemp-tion means not just a promise of spiritual equality in heaven, but a social struggle to overcome unjust domination of men over women, masters over slaves, here on Earth," (Hessel and Reuther 2000, 104). Alongside many other theologians, she criti-cizes the Genesis image of humans ruling over earth. Instead, she draws on biblical and patristic traditions to suggest that the proper role for humanity is to contemplate creation, understand it, and work to harmonize human life with all other beings.

Christian responses to the environmental threat extend from thought into policy and action. Nearly every branch of Christianity has published declarations calling the faithful to prevent further environmental harm, to relieve the suffering of the people most affected by environmental collapse, and to praise God for the good-ness and beauty of the non-human world.

Prominent Christian leaders have made the environment a religious priority: the spiritual leader of Eastern Orthodox Christians, Patriarch Bartholomew I of Constanti-nople, earned the nickname "the Green Patriarch" for his outspoken statements on the environment. In 2011, he made news headlines for a strongly worded encyclical in which he called environmental destruction a sin, and for nearly two decades, he has brought together scientists and theologians to consult on environmental issues.

The most recent three popes of the Roman Catholic Church have given environmental sustainability an increasingly prominent place in their teachings and actions. Pope Saint John Paul II dedicated his New Year's Day address for the World Day of Peace in 1990 entirely to the need to care for creation, and together with Patriarch Bartholomew issued a Common Declaration on Environmental Ethics in 2002. Pope Benedict XVI was dubbed the "Green Pope" both for his teachings on the environment and for actions such as installing more than 2,000 solar panels in Vatican City, significantly cutting the papal state's carbon emissions.

Pope Francis is the first Roman pontiff to write an environmental encyclical, titled *Laudato Si': On Care for our Common Home*. Addressing his letter to the entire human family and drawing on the tradition of Catholic Social Teaching, Francis surveys the manifold problems associated with environmental collapse and offers a nuanced analysis of the philosophical, political, economic, technological, social, and spiritual aspects of the crisis. Perhaps the greatest achievement of *Laudato Si'* is that it inextricably links the suffering of poor and marginalized people with the suffering of the earth. Francis calls for an "integral ecology" that addresses the needs of both human and non-human creation.

> We are faced not with two separate crises, one environmental and the other social, but rather with one complex crisis which is both social and environmental. Strategies for a solution demand an integrated approach to combating poverty, restoring dignity to the excluded, and at the same time protecting nature.
>
> (*Laudato Si'*, para. 139)

The promotion of ecological sustainability has brought Christian churches together in shared efforts like the work produced by Pope Benedict XVI and Patriarch Bartholomew I. The World Council of Churches (WCC), a worldwide inter-church organization that collectively represents almost 600 million Christians in over 130 churches, is another major body that has been instrumental in promoting Christian ecological sustainability. Since 1983, it has coordinated environmental conversations and efforts of its members around the globe. It addresses pressing issues such as safe drinking water, climate change, and ecological inequities between richer and poorer countries. In the United States, the WCC assisted in the formation of the National Religious Partnership for the Environment, an alliance of the U.S. Conference of Catholic Bishops, the National Council of Churches, the Coalition on the Environment and Jewish Life, and the Evangelical Environmental Network. Nor have ordinary Christians waited for their leaders to take up environmental causes. Many thousands of Christian groups have grown up from the grassroots as local churches and nonprofit organizations have engaged some aspect of God's call to care for creation and all people.

A notable example of a local Christian community making a difference on a national environmental issue comes from the United Church of Christ (USA). In the early 1980s, the state of North Carolina sited a toxic waste dump in a poor, mostly African-American community. The United Church of Christ Commission for Racial Justice (CRJ) assisted the community in its struggle against the state by supporting a campaign of nonviolent resistance. As a result of this experience, the Commission for Racial Justice completed a study to investigate what seemed to be "an intentional placement of hazardous waste sites, landfills, incinerators, and polluting industries in communities inhabited mainly by African Americans, Hispanics, Native Americans, Asians and Pacific Islanders, farm workers and the working poor" (United Church of Christ 2017). Issued in 1987, under the title "Toxic Wastes and Race," the investigation's report provided convincing statistical evidence that poor communities and communities of color were far more likely to host toxic waste sites than wealthier white communities.

"Toxic Wastes and Race" caught the attention of media and lawmakers, and the concept of **environmental racism** gained currency. As a result of this landmark study, President Bill Clinton issued an executive order in 1994 directing all federal agencies to "make achieving environmental justice part of its mission by identifying and addressing, as appropriate, disproportionately high and adverse human health or environmental effects of its programs, policies, and activities on minority populations and low-income populations" (Huang 2017). It was the first major federal action on ecological justice in the United States.

Christianity has experienced remarkable change in its ecological consciousness in the last 50 years. Even so, the level of ecological awareness and commitment varies widely among different communities and individual Christians. Relatively few pastors in the U.S.A. are willing to preach ecological sustainability as part of Christian faith, for fear of alienating a portion of their congregations. The reasons for Christian apathy on the environment are the same as for people everywhere: lack of information, feelings of powerlessness or lack of control over events, entrenched social customs, and distraction by more immediate concerns, all of which conspire to maintain the status quo. All of these barriers, however, have an antidote in the strength of Christian community. Churches have become centers of environmental teaching, effective group organization, social influence, and prayerful focus. As organizations with both spiritual and social power, Christian churches can help make life-changing improvements in our ecological situation.

Key Terms

Afrikaner
African National Congress
Anthropocene
anthropocentric
Anthropogenic climate change
apartheid
Steve Biko
Black Power
Black Theology
Boers
Broederbond
Dom Hélder Câmara
Frank Chikane
Christian base communities (or ecclesial base communities)

Civil Rights Movement
Cottesloe Consultation
dominion
ecofeminism
ecotheology
environmental racism
Feminist theologies
Gustavo Gutiérrez
hermeneutical circle
hermeneutics of suspicion
instrumental value
intersectionality
intrinsic value
Kairos Document
Laudato Si'
lynching
myth of Anglo-Saxon superiority

Pan Africanist Congress
Populorum progression
praxis
preferential option for the poor
prophetic theology
restorative justice
Óscar Romero
Sharpeville Massacre
structural evil, structural sin
theocentric
theo-ideology
Desmond Tutu
ubuntu
Hendrik Verwoerd
WARC Declaration
Womanist Theology
works of mercy

Questions for Reading

1. How does the trajectory of Archbishop Óscar Romero illustrate the development of Latin American liberation theology?

2. Have you ever gone through a learning process similar to the "hermeneutical circle?" Be prepared to explain.

3. In what ways is Latin American liberation theology a radical development? In what ways is it orthodox—that is, faithful to the Christian theological tradition?

4. What would it look like for you to do liberation theology in your own "concrete historical situation?" How would you begin?

5. How does black theology in South Africa differ from black liberation theology in the United States?

6. What role did theological statements like those issued from the Cottesloe Consultation and the Kairos Document play in the political dismantling of apartheid law?

7. Archbishop Desmond Tutu understood "forgiveness" differently from the way in which European theologians have typically defined it. Describe points of distinction between African and Western understandings of the concept of forgiveness.

8. How did white Christian theologians and preachers justify their enslavement of black people? How did black people resist these theological justifications?

9. In what ways did white racism persist after the abolition of slavery? What is the theo-ideology of white supremacy and the myth of Anglo-Saxon superiority?

10. What are some of the theological differences between James Cone and J. Deotis Roberts? How do their differences relate to questions raised by the Civil Rights and Black Power movements?

11. Reflect and summarize the key characteristics of Alice Walker's definition of "womanism." What is Womanist Theology? What are the similarities and differences between Womanist Theology and White feminism and male-dominated forms of Black Theology?

12. What is Delores Williams' concern about Western theories of atonement that focus on the saving significance of the cross? What does Williams propose as an alternative understanding of Jesus' life, ministry, and death?

13. Describe the major characteristics of feminist theology and the issues it seeks to address. Why are there multiple feminist theologies?

14. How do feminist theologians influenced by liberation theology redefine sin and salvation? How would you evaluate the strengths and weaknesses of this view?

15. Describe the method and goals of feminist biblical interpretation. Give examples of how feminist theologians might interpret specific biblical texts.

16. Why do many feminist theologians call for multiple images of God (including feminine images)? What effect would this have on a person's experience and understanding of God?

17. Describe the issue of women's ordination in Protestant and Catholic churches today. How is it different for Protestants and for Catholics? How would you evaluate the biblical and theological positions behind this issue?

18. What elements of Christian thought did historian Lynn White find particularly harmful for environmental sustainability? To what extent do you agree with his criticism?

19. What is theocentrism, and how does it help moderate anthropocentrism?

20. What is intrinsic and instrumental value? Do you think that creatures have one, or the other, or both kinds of value?

21. Some Christians feel resistance to environmental theology because it represents a change in Christian teaching. Do you think this kind of change is legitimate, or should Christianity try to remain the same as it always was? Where do you think the emphasis in Christian theology should lie—on retrieval of church teachings, or on new, constructive ecotheology?

22. Many Christian thinkers see connections between social injustice and environmental harm. What other real-life examples can you think of in which vulnerable people suffer along with plants, animals, air, water, etc.?

Works Consulted/Recommended Reading

Alexander, Torin. 2017. "World/Creation in African American Theology." *Oxford Handbooks Online*. May 25.

Anonymous. 1985. "Challenge to the Church: A Theological Comment on the Political Crisis in South Africa: The Kairos Document", September 25. www.sahistory.org.za/archive/challenge-church-theological-comment-political-crisis-south-africa-kairos-document-1985, accessed October 1, 2017.

Augustine of Hippo. 1982. *The Literal Meaning of Genesis*. Translated and Annotated by John Hammond Taylor. Mahwah, NJ: Newman Press.

Bell, Colin, ed. 2016. *Creation Care and the Gospel: Reconsidering the Mission of the Church*. Peabody, MA: Hendrickson.

Berry, Wendell. 1990. "The Pleasures of Eating." *East West*, December.

Boesak, Allan Aubrey. 1977. *Farewell to Innocence: A Socio-Ethical Study on Black Theology and Power*. Maryknoll, NY: Orbis Books.

Boesak, Allan Aubrey. 2015. *Kairos, Crisis, and Global Apartheid: The Challenge to Prophetic Witness*. New York: Palgrave Macmillan.

Boff, Leonardo, and Clodovis Boff. 1987. *Introducing Liberation Theology*. Translated by Paul Burns. Maryknoll, NY: Orbis Books.

Brown, Robert McAfee. 1984. *Unexpected News: Reading the Bible with Third World Eyes*. Philadelphia, PA: The Westminster Press.

Brown-Douglas, Kelly. 2015. *Stand Your Ground: Black Bodies and the Justice of God*. Maryknoll, NY: Orbis Books.

Câmara, Hélder. 1971. *Spiral of Violence*. Translated by Della Couling. London: Sheed and Ward.

Câmara, Hélder. 2009. *Dom Helder Camara: Essential Writings*. Selected with an Introduction by Francis McDonagh. Modern Spiritual Masters Series. Maryknoll, NY: Orbis Books.

Chryssavgis, John, and Bruce V. Foltz, eds. 2013. *Toward an Ecology of Transfiguration: Orthodox Christian Perspectives on Environment, Nature, and Creation*. New York: Fordham University Press.

Cone, James. 1969. *Black Theology and Black Power*. Maryknoll, NY: Orbis Books.

Cone, James. 1970. *A Black Theology of Liberation*. Maryknoll, NY: Orbis Books.

Cone, James. 2011. *The Cross and the Lynching Tree*. Maryknoll, NY: Orbis Books.

Cone, James, and Gayraud S. Wilmore, eds. 1993a. *Black Theology: A Documentary History, 1966–1979*. Maryknoll, NY: Orbis Books.

Cone, James, and Gayraud S. Wilmore, eds. 1993b. *Black Theology: A Documentary History, 1980–1992.* Maryknoll, NY: Orbis Books.

Copeland, M. Shawn. 2009. *Enfleshing Freedom: Body, Race, and Being.* Minneapolis, MN: Fortress Press.

Crawford, A. Elaine Brown. 2002. *Hope in the Holler: A Womanist Theology.* Louisville, KY: Westminster John Knox.

Fiorenza, Elisabeth Schüssler. 1994. *In Memory of Her: A Feminist Theological Reconstruction of Christian Origins.* New York: Crossroad.

Garrard-Burnett, Virginia, ed. 1999. *On Earth as It Is in Heaven: Religion in Modern Latin America.* Wilmington, DE: Scholarly Resources.

Gobodo-Madikizela, Pumla. 2004. *A Human Being Died That Night: A South African Woman Confronts the Legacy of Apartheid.* Boston, MA: Mariner Books.

Gottlieb, Roger S., and Jacob K. Olupona. 2006. *The Oxford Handbook of Religion and Ecology.* Oxford: Oxford University Press.

Grant, Jacqueline. 1989. *White Women's Christ and Black Women's Jesus: Feminist Christology and Womanist Response.* Atlanta, GA: Scholar's Press.

de Gruchy, John, with Steve de Gruchy. 2004. *The Church Struggle in South Africa: 25th Anniversary Edition.* Minneapolis, MN: Fortress Press.

de Gruchy, John, and Charles Villa-Vicencio, eds. 1983. *Apartheid is a Heresy.* Grand Rapids, MI: Eerdmans.

Gutiérrez, Gustavo. 1973 (1971). *A Theology of Liberation: History, Politics and Salvation.* Translated and edited by Sister Caridad Inda and John Eagleson. Maryknoll, NY: Orbis.

Gutiérrez, Gustavo. 2003 (1984) *We Drink from Our Own Wells: The Spiritual Journey of a People.* 20th Anniversary Edition. Translated by Matthew J. O'Connell. Maryknoll, NY: Orbis Books.

Hessel, Dieter T. and Rosemary Radford Ruether, eds. 2000. *Christianity and Ecology: Seeking the Well-Being of Earth and Humans.* Cambridge, MA: Harvard University Press for the Harvard University Center for the Study of World Religions.

Hopkins, Dwight. 1999. *Introducing Black Theology of Liberation.* Maryknoll, NY: Orbis Books.

Hopkins, Dwight, and Edward P. Antonio, eds. 2012. *The Cambridge Companion to Black Theology.* Cambridge: Cambridge University Press.

Huang, Albert. 2017. "The 20th Anniversary of President Clinton's Executive Order 12898 on Environmental Justice." NRDC.org., May 26.

Hyun-Kyung, Chung. 1990. *Struggle to Be the Sun Again: Introducing Asian Women's Theology.* Maryknoll, NY: Orbis Books.

Isasi-Díaz, Ada María. 1993. *En la Lucha: A Hispanic Women's Liberation Theology.* Minneapolis, MN: Fortress Press.

Isherwood, Lisa, and Dorothea McEwan. 1993. *Introducing Feminist Theology.* Sheffield: Sheffield Academic Press.

Japinga, Lynn. 1999. *Feminism and Christianity: An Essential Guide.* Nashville, TN: Abingdon Press.

Johnson, Elizabeth A. 1992. *She Who Is: The Mystery of God in Feminist Theological Discourse.* New York: Crossroad.

LaCugna, Catherine Mowry, ed. 1993. *Freeing Theology: The Essentials of Theology in Feminist Perspective.* San Francisco, CA: HarperOne.

Largen, Kristin Johnston. 2009. "A Christian Rationale for Vegetarianism." *Dialog: A Journal of Theology* 48: 147–157.

Lernoux, Penny. 1982. *Cry of the People: The Struggle for Human Rights in Latin America—the Catholic Church in Conflict with U.S. Policy.* New York: Penguin Books.

Lothes Biviano, Erin. 2016. *Inspired Sustainability: Planting Seeds for Action.* Maryknoll, NY: Orbis Books.

McFague, Sallie. 1987. *Models of God: Theology for an Ecological Nuclear Age.* Minneapolis, MN: Fortress Press.

Mandela, Nelson. 1994. *Long Walk to Freedom.* New York: Back Bay Books.

Massingale, Bryan. 2010. *Racial Justice and the Catholic Church.* Maryknoll, NY: Orbis Books.

Matthews, James. 1972. *Cry Rage.* Johannesburg: Spro-cas Publications.

Matthews, James. 2005. *Cry Rage: Odyssey of a Dissident Poet.* Athlone: Realities.

National Aeronautics and Space Administration (NASA). 2017. "Climate Change: Scientific Consensus." September 20.

Naude, Beyers. 1963. *My Decision.* Johannesburg: Christian Institute.

Paul VI, Pope. 1967. *Populorum progressio [On the Development of Peoples].* Encyclical letter.

Roberts, J. Deotis. 1971. *Liberation and Reconciliation: A Black Theology.* Philadelphia, PA: Westminster Press.

Ruether, Rosemary Radford. 1983. *Sexism and God-Talk: Toward a Feminist Theology.* Boston, MA: Beacon Press.

Russell, Letty M., ed. 1988. *Inheriting Our Mothers' Gardens: Feminist Theology in Third World Perspective.* Philadelphia, PA: Westminster Press.

Russell, Letty M., and J. Shannon Clarkson, eds. 1996. *Dictionary of Feminist Theologies.* Louisville, KY: Westminster John Knox Press.

Schaefer, Jame. 2009. *Theological Foundations for Environmental Ethics: Reconstructing Patristic and Medieval Concepts.* Washington, DC: Georgetown University Press.

Schut, Michael. 2009. *Food & Faith: Justice, Joy and Daily Bread.* New York: Morehouse Publishing.

Segundo, Juan Luis. 1979. *Liberation of Theology.* Translated by John Drury. 1975. Maryknoll, NY: Orbis Books.

Slee, Nicola. 2003. *Faith and Feminism: An Introduction to Christian Feminist Theology.* London: Darton, Longman, and Todd.

Sobrino, Jon. 1978. *Christology at the Crossroads.* Translated by John Drury. 1976. Maryknoll, NY: Orbis Books.

Tertullian. n.d. "On the Apparel of Women." www.newadvent.org/fathers/0402.htm.

Tutu, Desmond. 1999. *No Future Without Forgiveness.* New York: Doubleday.

United Church of Christ. 2017. "Environmental Racism." UCC.org., May 26.

Walker, Alice. 1983. *In Search of Our Mothers' Gardens: Womanist Prose.* New York: Hartcourt Brace Jovanovich.

Watson, Natalie K. 2003. *Feminist Theology.* Grand Rapids, MI: William B. Eerdmans.

White, Lynn. 1967. "The Historical Roots of Our Ecologic Crisis." *Science* 155, no. 3767: 1203–1207.

Williams, Delores. 1993. *Sisters in the Wilderness: The Challenge of Womanist God-Talk.* Maryknoll, NY: Orbis Books.

Wilmore, Gayraud. 1998. *Black Religion and Black Radicalism: An Interpretation of the Religious History of African Americans.* Maryknoll, NY: Orbis Books.

Winright, Tobias L., ed. 2011. *Green Discipleship: Catholic Theological Ethics and the Environment.* Winona, MN: Anselm Academic.

Wright, Christopher J.H. 2004. *Old Testament Ethics for the People of God.* Downers Grove, IL: Inter-Varsity Press.

Chapter

CHRISTIANITY AND INTERRELIGIOUS DIALOGUE

In the present millennium, dialogue among the world's religions is becoming ever more unavoidable and urgent. Dialogue has become more *unavoidable* because globalization is bringing the world's religions into regular contact with one another, whether they like it or not. Factors leading to this are the speed and expansiveness of communication, the increase and ease of travel, and the expansion of world trade. Further, the migration of peoples forced to become refugees means an increased level of exposure among peoples who are different from each other. For many Americans, contact with members of non-Christian religions is becoming commonplace due to immigration from Asia and the Middle East.

Dialogue is not only unavoidable but also *urgent* because we live in an age marked by explosive conflict in which religion is often involved. Sometimes religion is a cause, and sometimes religion is simply an identifying "marker" of the parties at odds with one another. In the latter case, members of the two religions may be fighting with each other, not over religion, but over some other issue. All the same, dialogue is crucial for resolving conflict.

This chapter will give a historical survey of negative and positive approaches to other religions during 2,000 years of Christian history. It will place special emphasis on theological developments in the nineteenth and twentieth centuries. The final section will explore some negative reactions to some of the positive evaluations that have emerged. That section will put special emphasis on the prominent twentieth-century theologian, Karl Barth, who argued that all religions, Christianity included, are idolatrous efforts to control God.

EARLY CHURCH

The apostles of Christ and many of his other followers believed that through him they had experienced an unprecedented reconciliation with God and with their neighbors. Hence, they traveled across the countryside, even across the Mediterranean Sea, spreading the news of his death and resurrection. A new, tight-knit community developed through these efforts. St. Paul believed that this community, to which he referred as the *ekklesia* or "assembly," often translated as "church," was the true Israel and the true body of Christ:

> As a body is one though it has many parts, and all the parts of the body, though many, are one body, so also Christ. For in one Spirit we were all baptized into one body, whether Jews or Greeks, slaves or free persons, and we were all given to drink of one Spirit.
>
> (1 Corinthians 12:12–13, New American Bible)

In the first centuries of the Christian era, the belief in the church as the body of Christ gradually developed into a negative judgment on those outside it. This did not begin as a condemnation of non-Christians, but rather as a warning against those who endangered the unity of the church. As discussed in earlier chapters, there was a wide range of schisms in the early church over belief and practice. To counter these divisions, leaders like Bishop Ignatius of Antioch (died *c.*108) quoted St. Paul's warning against schism, saying, "'Make no mistake, my brothers,' anyone who follows a maker of schism 'will not inherit the Kingdom of God' [1 Corinthians 6:9–10]" (*Letter to the Philadelphians* 3.3, trans. M.J. Hollerich). In the third century, Cyprian, bishop of Carthage, denied that heretical baptism could be valid, "since there is no salvation outside the Church" (*Letter* 73.21.2, trans. M.J. Hollerich). To those who would withdraw from the Church because they thought it was corrupt, he wrote,

> whoever separates from the Church and is joined to an adulteress [*by which Cyprian means a false church*] is separated from the promises of the Church, nor will one who leaves the Church of Christ arrive at Christ's rewards. That person is a foreigner, someone profane, an enemy. Whoever does not have the Church as mother cannot have God as father.
>
> (*On the Unity of the Catholic Church* 6, trans. M.J. Hollerich)

In the fourth century, the dictum "no salvation outside the church" came to be applied not only to those who endangered its unity but also to those Jews and pagans who did not accept Christian faith. Christianity grew even more rapidly after the conversion of Constantine, and by the end of the fourth century, it was the official religion of the Roman Empire. Hence, it was argued that there was no longer a reason for any sincere seeker after truth not to consider Christianity and to realize that it held the truth. As St. **John Chrysostom** wrote,

> You will find that such a one [*a pagan*] has not really been diligent in seeking the truth, since what concerns the truth is now clearer than the sun. How shall they obtain pardon who, when they see the doctrine of truth spread before them, make no effort to come to know it? For now the name of God is proclaimed to all, what the prophets predicted has come true, and the religion of the pagans has been proved false.
>
> (Cited in Dupuis 2001, 89)

There was a darker aspect to Chrysostom's thought. He criticized the non-Christian world as a whole, but had special scorn for the Jews. The common links between Judaism and Christianity were grounds for criticism of Judaism rather than appreciation. The Law of Moses and the Prophets, he argued, had been preparing the Jews for thousands of years for the coming of Jesus. However, when he came, the Jews as a whole did not accept Jesus. In contrast, former worshippers of Greek and Roman gods were flooding into the church in the fourth century. Chrysostom's conclusion was that the Jews must be a horrible people, for they were prepared by God to accept Christ but did not, whereas the pagans, who did not have the benefit of the Law and the Prophets, were accepting Christ in vast numbers. Chrysostom concluded that since the Jews did not accept Christ, and since Christ is God, that "no Jew adores God!" (*Discourses* 1.3.2). Rather, "Demons dwell in the synagogue, not only in the place itself but also in the souls of the Jews" (*Discourses* 1.6.6). One finds similar ideas in the writings of the other church fathers, but generally not as extreme as this.

Although the Church Fathers took a hard stance against the non-Christian world, that is not the entire picture. For instance, there is evidence that Jews and Christians freely intermingled with each other into the fourth century, and that hard and fast distinctions between the two religions developed only over several centuries. Also, converts from non-biblical religions often carried aspects of their prior identities with them into the church. The most evident example of this fact is that many of the Church Fathers, like St. Augustine, were deep admirers of Greek philosophy and relied on it in their theological writings. Justin Martyr regarded Socrates and Plato as great wise men who had gained glimpses of the *logos* or divine word that later became flesh as Jesus Christ. This respect for Greek philosophy continued into the Middle Ages, when **Thomas Aquinas** relied on the writings of Aristotle and the Greek and Jewish commentators on him.

Constructive interactions between Christianity and non-Christian culture were not limited to the intellectual life of the church. The liturgical year, for instance, was partially shaped by the religious festivals of pre-Christian Europe. The church commemorates the communion of saints on November 1, All Saint's Day, a celebration that coincides with Samhain, the earlier Celtic festival when the souls of the dead were believed to return to their earthly homes. Certain customs of Christmas, such as the lighting of the Christmas tree, are believed to have originated in earlier customs that celebrated the return of light on the shortest day of the year, the winter solstice. At the Easter vigil, the Paschal candle, representing Christ, is lit in the darkened church. Lighting the candle, and the practice of hunting for Easter eggs may have originated with spring rituals attempting to ensure a fertile harvest and celebrating the rebirth of nature. Further, when Christianity was legalized in the fourth century, it borrowed much of the ritual, architecture, and structural organization of the Roman world. It thereby transformed itself from a confederation of communities meeting in homes to a highly organized, imperial religion which held elaborate rituals in ornate basilicas. Hence, in many ways, pre-Christian beliefs and practices were the fabric out of which Christianity grew and developed. Although there were these constructive interactions between the Christian and non-Christian realms, the idea that salvation is impossible outside the Catholic Church became commonplace.

LATER DEVELOPMENTS

The negative trends discussed above became increasingly institutionalized in the church during the second millennium. For instance, in 1215, the Fourth Lateran Council had mandated that that Jews and Muslims distinguish themselves in dress from Christians, and that they not appear in public during Passion Sunday and the final three days of Holy Week. It also stated that Jews must not hold public office, "Since it is absurd that a blasphemer of Christ exercise authority over Christians" (*Disciplinary Decrees* §69). Later, in 1442, the Council of Florence explicitly condemned Jews and pagans in its "Decree for the Copts." The council's goal was to reunite the Catholic Church and the separated Eastern churches (see Chapter 11).

Summarizing the essentials of Catholic belief in order to share them with the Coptic Orthodox Church, the document stated that the church

> firmly believes, professes and preaches that "no one remaining outside the Catholic Church, not only pagans," but also Jews, heretics and schismatics, can become partakers of eternal life; but they will go to the "eternal fire prepared for the devil and its angels."
>
> (Cited in Dupuis 2001, 95)

In the 1500s, the Protestant Reformation took place, and the Protestants were, generally speaking, not any more positive than the Catholics on these issues. They, like the Catholics, believed that there is no salvation outside the church. The difference in viewpoint was in terms of what that church is. The Catholics believed there was no salvation outside of membership in the Catholic Church, whereas the Protestants spoke of the "true church" and tended to avoid considering any particular denomination as the true church. Rather, they tended to hold that the "true church" was invisible and known to God alone, though it had existed since the coming of Christ and was composed of all those who have genuine faith in him. The reformers adopted their stance in reaction to the corruption in the Catholic Church.

Further, the Protestant reformers stressed that salvation is not through works but solely through faith in Christ. This excludes Jews, Muslims, and the Catholics or "Papists," the followers of the Pope, all of whom stress that works play a role in our salvation. To the contemporary mind, it might seem overly negative and narrow to say that good deeds will not save one, that it is solely a matter of believing in Jesus. However, the main concern was to stress the glory, power, and grace of God. We are too sinful before God for our good deeds to procure our salvation. Rather, salvation comes solely from what Christ did for us by dying on the cross.

Although both Catholics and Protestants believed there is no salvation outside the church, there is a long history of considering possible exceptions to the general rule. One of the earliest ideas is found in Thomas Aquinas' *Summa Theologica*. He considered the case of a catechumen, one who has been preparing to enter the church, but whose life was cut short before he or she was able to be baptized and join the church. Aquinas argued that it is possible for such a person to be saved. Aquinas argued that whereas one normally becomes a member of the church through Baptism, God can act independently of this ritual to save one (*Summa Theologica* III.68.2). The notion that the catechumen whose life is cut short may be saved is often referred to as the "Baptism of desire." By virtue of his or her desire to enter the church, he or she may be saved. Over the coming centuries, the notion of the Baptism of desire would undergo considerable expansion. In the 1500s, the Age of Discovery was well underway, and Western Europeans were realizing how incredibly vast the world is, and that at that time only a small portion of the world's population was Christian. Could it be that those vast, countless numbers of people were condemned simply because they had not heard of Christ?

A variety of different theologians argued that it is possible for someone who had never heard of Christ to be saved. **Domingo Soto**, who, like Aquinas, belonged to the Order of Preachers, argued that God might grant an interior illumination to those who, ignorant of Christ, strive to follow objective standards of moral rightness. Through this interior illumination, Christ might save such a one, although he or she is ignorant of the Christian religion. Thus, whereas Aquinas had earlier argued that the catechumen whose life has been cut short might be saved, Soto argued the same for someone who had never heard of Christ.

In the 1600s, going beyond Aquinas and Soto, **Juan de Lugo** considered the cases of the Jew and the Muslim. Both know of Christ, but neither accepts him as the savior. Contemporary Americans are sometimes skeptical that Jews and Muslims of that time knew of Christ. However, most Jews were living in Christian lands, and many suffered prejudice from Christians. Knowing of Christianity through personal experience, they knew of Christ. In terms of Muslims, there is significant overlap between the contents of the Qur'an and the Bible, and the Qur'an teaches that Jesus was the second greatest of prophets, Muhammad having been the first. Both the Jew and the Muslim know of Christ, but both believe it compromises the transcendence and unity of God to consider a human being as God; it is a reversion to polytheism and idolatry.

De Lugo argued that because the Jew and the Muslim were taught to think in those distinct ways, it is not necessarily their faults that they do not accept Christ as the savior. Furthermore, he argued that through their respective sacred books, the Tanakh and the Qur'an, that the saving grace of God might be available to them. The Tanakh is implicitly accepted as divine revelation by Christians since its contents are included in what Christians call the "Old Testament." Further, many historians believe the Qur'an was influenced by the Bible, and by virtue of that connection, Lugo believed that Muslims can be saved. One might expect Lugo to have been ostracized because of these stances. In fact, he was one of the most highly regarded theologians of the time and was made a cardinal by the pope.

In the 1800s, these developing ideas would impact formal church teaching. By this time, the Catholic Church had lost its hegemony over Western society and culture due to the Protestant Reformation, the rise of modern nations, and many other factors. To reaffirm that the Catholic Church is the vehicle of salvation, and not any other religious body, **Pius IX** issued *Quanto Conficiamur Moerore* in 1863. Therein, he restated the doctrine that there is no salvation outside the Catholic Church. However, he qualified this with the Baptism of desire. Non-Catholics who observe "the natural law and its precepts inscribed by God on all hearts and ready to obey God" may be "able to attain eternal life by the efficacious virtue of divine light and grace" (*Quanto Conficiamur Moerore* §7). The pope added,

> God forbid that the children of the Catholic Church should even in any way be unfriendly to those who are not at all united to us by the same bonds of faith and love. On the contrary, let them be eager always to attend to their needs with all the kind services of Christian charity, whether they are poor or sick or suffering any other kind of visitation.
>
> (*Quanto Conficiamur Moerore* §9)

Pius IX probably endorsed the Baptism of desire as a response to Enlightenment critiques of traditional Christianity. Although they believed in God, Enlightenment thinkers argued that the notion that only one religious body is the route to salvation implies that God is a cruel tyrant since that leaves most of the rest of humanity to burn in hell. A few years later, after issuing *Quanto Conficiamur Moerore*, Pius IX convened the First Vatican Council, and the Council reaffirmed the doctrine of the Baptism of desire (however, in his *Syllabus of Errors*, Pius IX condemned the idea that one can be optimistic about the salvation of those outside the church; in spite of the Baptism of desire, he believed one has to take a pessimistic approach). In the following century, although not explicitly stating that one could be either pessimistic or optimistic about the salvation of those outside the church, the Second Vatican Council, in *Lumen Gentium* §16, taught a modified and more developed version of the Baptism of desire.

There were developments in the Protestant world as well. Key in that regard was the founder of Methodism, the eighteenth-century figure, **John Wesley** (see Chapter 19). He believed, like other Protestants, that through faith in Christ, the Christian could be certain of his or her salvation. However, he did not believe it was the place of the Christian to judge the Jew or the Muslim, and to say that he or she is necessarily damned. God, he stated, "is the God of the Heathens as well as the Christians," and that he "hateth nothing that he hath made" (*Works* 7:353). Wesley believed that God had, through ways other than Christ, made himself known in other times and places. He cited biblical passages that suggest this, stating, that

> God never, in any age or nation, "left himself" quite "without a witness" in the hearts of men; but while he "gave them rain and fruitful seasons," imparted some imperfect knowledge of the Giver. "He is the true Light that" still, in some degree, "enlighteneth every man that cometh into the world."
>
> (*Works* 7:258)

THE TWENTIETH CENTURY

At the outset of the twentieth century, there was a highly significant theological development in the Protestant world. However, to grasp this development, one needs to look to the prior two centuries. In the late 1700s, a new wave of religious enthusiasm began, a wave which later included America's famous "Great Awakening." This wave of enthusiasm involved the belief that the entire world could be converted to Christianity and that when that would happen, God's final, definitive reign on earth would begin. Thus, Protestant missionaries from Europe and North America fanned out across the world.

Ironically, this missionary enthusiasm resulted in a certain appreciation of the non-Christian world. Kenneth Cracknell explains that some of these missionaries "were voracious in their reading and had remarkable academic learning at their disposal," but

> their chief source of information about Hinduism or Buddhism or any other tradition was through personal encounter with living adherents to these traditions. They knew the faith of other men and women at first hand, through friendship and through "participant observation." Above all they knew the language of the people they worked among.
>
> (Cracknell 1995, 107)

These experiences made the missionaries "new people, with a new spirituality and a new perception of the world" (Cracknell 1995, 107).

A key example of this new, emerging perspective was the view of **J.N. Farquhar** (1861–1929), who was a missionary in India and a scholar of Hinduism. On the one hand, he remained convinced throughout his life that Jesus Christ is the sole way to God and that non-Christian religions must give way to Christianity. On the other hand, he also came to believe, through his study and experiences, that Hinduism has many admirable aspects. He bridged his convictions about Jesus with his conclusions about Hinduism with an evolutionary approach. He considered Christ to be the fulfillment of Hinduism, just as Christians have traditionally viewed Christ as the fulfillment of the Hebrew Bible:

The greater books of Hinduism will form a sort of second Old Testament. ... Every Hindu belief, rite and institution will be seen to have been a germ, an adumbration, the full-blown flower and reality of which came with Christ. ... Is He not the crown of Hinduism?

(Farquhar 1910, 68)

This was one example of a new openness among some Christians, an approach known as "fulfillment theology." The theology of fulfillment regards Christ as supreme, but recognizes positive aspects of other religions, which find completeness or fulfillment in Christ. Another Christian who took this type of approach was C.F. Andrews, an Anglican missionary and a close friend of Mahatma Gandhi.

Later in the twentieth century, the theology of fulfillment would be adopted by the Catholic world. In the 1940s, the cardinal, theologian, and church historian, **Jean Daniélou** (1905–1974) articulated this perspective. In 1951, Pope Pius XII expressed this perspective in the encyclical, *Evangelii Praecones*. In the 1960s, the major theologian **Hans Urs von Balthasar** (1905–1988) also adopted a theology of fulfillment. Most significantly, the Second Vatican Council took this approach in *Nostra Aetate*, also known as the *Declaration on the Relation of the Church to Non-Christian Religions*. The idea is that the positive strivings in other religions find fulfillment in Christianity.

Pope John XXIII called the Second Vatican Council in 1962 (see Chapter 24). Recognizing that the church had by that time become a truly global church, he felt it was time to call all the bishops of the Catholic Church to Rome to discuss affairs in their countries and dioceses, and see if there was anything that needed updating in the church. The three most central documents that came out of the Council were *Sacrosanctum Concilium* (Constitution on the Sacred Liturgy), *Dei Verbum* (Dogmatic Constitution on Divine Revelation, and *Lumen Gentium* (Dogmatic Constitution on the Church). In addition to the general goal of updating, John XXIII had several specific goals for the Council. One of these concerned the Jews. In the 1940s, when John XXIII was Cardinal Angelo Roncalli, he served as the Vatican ambassador to Turkey. From 1942 to 1944, he helped thousands of Jews escape Europe into Israel. Thereby, he became "sensitive to the atrocities of the Holocaust and to the complicity of many Catholics in them" (O'Malley 2008, 219). He was profoundly disturbed by anti-Jewish stances in Christianity, and resolved to put an end to them in the Catholic Church.

Early drafts of *Nostra Aetate* addressed Judaism alone, but the final version addressed the non-Christian religions as a whole. The time of the Council, the first half of the 1960s, was a time of extremely high tension between Israel and the Arab nations. Hence, the bishops thought it wise to couch the discussion of Judaism in a larger discussion of the religions of the world. It discussed the religions of the world, as a whole, by adopting a theology of fulfillment. It recognized that there are areas of overlap between Christianity and other religions, and it stated that the Christian should value "those ways of conduct and of life, those rules and teachings which, though differing in many particulars from what she holds and sets forth, nevertheless often reflect a ray of that Truth which enlightens all men" (*Nostra Aetate* §2; Abbott 1966, 662). Furthermore, somewhat like Pius IX in the nineteenth century, it stated that

we cannot in truthfulness call upon that God who is the Father of all if we refuse to act in a brotherly way toward certain men ... the Church rejects, as foreign to the mind of Christ, any discrimination against men or harassment of them because of their race, color, condition of life, or religion ... this sacred Synod ardently implores the Christian faithful to "maintain good fellowship among the nations" (1 Peter 2:12).

(*Nostra Aetate* §5; Abbott 1966, 667–668)

The document pointed out areas of overlap between Christianity and non-Christian religions. To begin, Judaism and Christianity share much in common since

> the Church, ... received the revelation of the Old Testament through the people with whom God ... deigned to establish the Ancient Covenant. Nor can she forget that she draws sustenance from the root of that good olive tree onto which have been grafted the wild olive branches of the Gentiles ... the spiritual patrimony common to Christians and Jews is thus so great.
>
> (*Nostra Aetate* §4; Abbott 1966, 664–665)

Islam, like Christianity, teaches that God is "one, ... living and enduring, merciful and all-powerful, Maker of heaven and earth" (*Nostra Aetate* §3; Abbott 1966, 663). Furthermore, many of the figures of the Bible appear in the Qur'an, and Muslims revere Abraham, Mary, and Jesus.

With regard to Hinduism, it differs from Christianity and Islam in that it has multiple deities. However, many Hindus believe in a supreme god above all others; some consider the many deities as simply different names of one deity, and some believe there is a unitary reality that underlies the multiplicity of gods and humans. Thus, *Nostra Aetate* points out that through stories and philosophy, Hindus have deeply explored the mystery of the divine and have admirable traditions of asceticism and religious devotion (*Nostra Aetate* §2; Abbott 1966, 661–662). Buddhism might seem to have less in common with Christianity since it does not teach the existence of a supreme, personal, creator god. However, there is at least one highly significant area of overlap. That overlap is the diagnosis of the condition of the world. Buddhism teaches, like Christianity, that there is no lasting happiness or satisfaction to be found in this world, that true joy lies elsewhere. The two religions offer different solutions, the extinction of desire in one case and Christ in the other, but their diagnoses of the world are, in broad terms, similar: "Buddhism in its multiple forms acknowledges the radical insufficiency of this shifting world" (*Nostra Aetate* §2; Abbott 1966, 662).

Although *Nostra Aetate* addressed the religions of the world in general, the inspiration behind the document was combating anti-Judaism in the church. Writing in the fourth century, St. John Chrysostom severely condemned the Jews for not accepting Christ. However, the committee that developed *Nostra Aetate* relied on the earlier teaching of St. Paul in the Bible, in his Letter to the Romans. St. Paul, like other early Christians, was shocked and surprised that the Jewish people, as a whole, did not accept Christ. However, instead of arguing, like Chrysostom later did, that the Jews were essentially devil worshippers because of their refusal to accept Christ as God, he argued that the Jewish refusal to accept Christ was a part of God's plan. He compared the family of Abraham to a tree and argued that the Jews were being removed from the tree in order to make room for new branches to be grafted on. These new branches were the Gentiles, incorporated into the family through their faith in Christ (Romans 11:1–32). Later, the Jews will be grafted back in, and Abraham's family will consist of both Gentiles and Jews (Romans 11:23).

Nostra Aetate was a watershed in Catholic history, transforming a closed stance to a much more positive one. For instance, since then the popes have become promoters of interreligious dialogue. Among many other highly symbolic acts are the annual World Day of Prayer for Peace events. Pope Paul VI established this event in 1967, and in 1986, John Paul II called leaders of the world's religions together at Assisi to pray for peace. This has been the standard practice since then. John Paul II wrote on interreligious dialogue and performed many other symbolic acts. Benedict XVI was

Figure 28–1 Pope John Paul II and participants of World Day of Peace at Assisi, Italy, in 1986. Pope John Paul II was intensely involved in interreligious dialogue throughout his long reign as pope.

more reserved about interreligious dialogue in general, but strongly promoted Jewish–Christian dialogue. Pope Francis wrote on dialogue in *Evangelii Gaudium,* or *The Joy of the Gospel.* He, too, performed many symbolic actions, such as, in his 2015 trip to Sri Lanka, visiting the tomb of two disciples of the Buddha. Other major Christian bodies composed statements similar to *Nostra Aetate.* For instance, the World Council of Churches, an association of a broad range of major Christian denominations, issued in 1948 "The Christian Approach to the Jews." It affirmed that Christ should be proclaimed to all peoples, including Jews, but it also stated,

> We [Christians] have failed to fight with all our strength the age-old disorder of man which anti-Semitism represents. The churches in the past have helped to foster an image of the Jews as the sole enemies of Christ, which has contributed to anti-Semitism in the secular world. In many lands virulent anti-Semitism still threatens and in other lands the Jews are subjected to many indignities. We call upon all the churches we represent to denounce anti-Semitism, no matter what its origin, as absolutely irreconcilable with the profession and practice of the Christian faith. Anti-Semitism is sin against God and man.
>
> (World Council of Churches 1948, §3)

Likewise, in 1994, the Evangelical Lutheran Church of America issued the "Declaration of the Evangelical Lutheran Church in America to Jewish Community," which addressed the vindictive words of Martin Luther, who during the Reformation had written about the Jews. Among other things it stated,

> Grieving the complicity of our own tradition within this history of hatred, moreover, we express our urgent desire to live out our faith in Jesus Christ with love and respect for the Jewish people. We recognize in anti-Semitism a contradiction and an affront to the Gospel, a violation of our hope and calling, and we pledge this church to oppose the deadly working of such bigotry, both within our own circles and in the society around us.
>
> (Evangelical Lutheran Church of America 1994)

There are also formal, institutional statements regarding interreligious dialogue in general. The World Council of Churches has a history of issuing documents on dialogue. One of the earliest available is the 1970 "Communiqué from WCC and CID," which is a joint product of the World Council of Churches and the Centre for Inter-Religious Dialogue of the Islamic Culture and Relations Organization in Tehran. Among other things, the document stated,

> Dialogue is the best means of overcoming misunderstandings and fostering mutual appreciation and peaceful coexistence between the adherents of different religions in today's multicultural world … effective dialogue can constitute a significant means to counteract the words and actions of those who incite religious hatred or seek deliberately to dishonour what is sacred to others. … We encourage inter-religious dialogue in all sectors of society with the aim of involving all in ensuring justice, equality, non-violence, welfare, friendship and compassion in society.
>
> (World Council of Churches and Centre for Inter-Religious Dialogue 1970)

For some Christians, simply expressing respect for other religions and arguing that the non-Christian can be saved were not enough. These theologians wanted to argue that the non-Christian religions themselves could be gateways to salvation. More specifically, they wanted to argue that the saving grace of Christ can be mediated by the non-Christian religions, a position which is known as **inclusivism**. The key example of an inclusivist is the influential Catholic theologian **Karl Rahner** (1904–1984).

As a Christian, Rahner believed that grace comes to humanity through the death and resurrection of Jesus Christ. He argued that the fullness of this grace is present only in that religion historically bound with the life and death of Christ—the Catholic Church. Additionally, he argued that the Holy Spirit carries this grace to all times and places, making it available in non-Christian religions. Insofar as these religions are not opposed to the Christian message but are conformed to a message of love and self-surrender, they mediate the grace of Christ. Non-Christians who lead lives of love and commitment to other people may receive grace and may therefore be known as "anonymous Christians," even though they do not explicitly know Christ or profess him as the savior.

Figure 28–2 Karl Rahner (1904–1984), Roman Catholic theologian and Jesuit priest.

Writing in the 1950s, Rahner built upon the idea of a Baptism of desire. While agreeing with the fundamental idea, the doctrine as it was then formulated seemed very barren to him, for it did not explain *how* the grace of Christ came to be transmitted to the non-Christian. A fundamental belief of the Catholic tradition is that the grace of Christ is received through the rituals and community of the church. To be saved independently from contact with a living tradition fundamentally violates the Catholic vision. Rahner thus argued that the communities, rituals, and ethical codes of non-Christian religions might *themselves* be channels of the grace of Christ. However, this participation is limited in nature—the fullness of grace is present only in Christianity.

Rahner is often held out as the key example of an inclusivist, but there are many other examples of inclusivist arguments. For example, the 1990 "Baar Statement" of the World Council of Churches advocates an inclusivist stance. On the one hand, the "Baar Statement" affirms, "The saving presence of God's activity ... comes to its focal point in the event of Christ." On the other hand, it states that "we have seen and experienced goodness, truth and holiness among followers of other paths and ways" (§3). Further, it points out that portions of the Bible make it clear that God is concerned with the salvation of all peoples. The document bridges the idea that Christ is the focal point of salvation with God's will to save all peoples with the resurrection. It states that although "the saving power of the reign of God made present in Jesus during His earthly ministry was in some sense limited (cf. Matt. 10.23), through the event of His death and resurrection, the paschal mystery itself, these limits were transcended" (§3). Hence, the "saving mystery" of Christ

> may be available to those outside the fold of Christ (Jn. 10.16) in ways we cannot understand, as they live faithful and truthful lives in their concrete circumstances and in the framework of the religious traditions which guide and inspire them.
>
> (§3)

Rahner's ideas were a controversial development, but in the view of many people, he did not go far enough. **Pluralism**, as opposed to exclusivism and inclusivism, designates the position that any religion may be a direct route to God. One of the most prominent pluralists, the philosopher John Hick (1922–2012), began arguing in the 1970s that ideas of men such as Aquinas, Soto, Lugo, and Rahner are like the epicycles of the ancient astronomers. The ancients believed that the stars and planets rotate around the earth, but detailed observation of the heavenly bodies did not fit the predictions of a geocentric system. Attempting to preserve a geocentric solar system from these discrepancies, the astronomers posited that the planets each have their own, secondary centers of orbit in addition to that of the earth. However, in the 1500s, Copernicus posited the heliocentric system, which matched observation well and eliminated the complexities of epicycles. Hick argued that theories like those of Lugo and Rahner are efforts to explain the existence of truth and goodness outside of Christianity while retaining Christianity at the center, just as epicycles were attempts to retain the earth at the center of the solar system. Hick argued that Christians should drop their "ecclesiocentrism" and "christocentrism," beliefs that the church and Christ are the center of salvation, in favor of "theocentrism," a view that God is the center of salvation and that he directly saves non-Christians through their religions, not through the intervention of the church or of Christ.

Although teaching that all religions may lead directly to God, Hick is aware of the many contradictions in belief and practice between them. He resolves this issue by appealing to the traditional teaching, present in some form or other in many religions, that the ultimate reality is beyond human description. He argues that beliefs and practices are ultimately human constructs, and that the divine reality is beyond all of them. Religions should simply be regarded as pathways to the divine, not as ultimate in themselves.

The twentieth century closed with a broad range of reflection on interreligious issues, but little overall consensus among theologians. For instance, Hick's approach may seem to be the most tolerant and open, but many argue that it is actually very closed and narrow. If no religious beliefs of any religion have ultimate validity, then why bother to dialogue and to share them? Instead of interacting, the religions will become closed and narrow worlds, just as they can be with the exclusivist approach. Yet, if the religions are not considered as equally valid, as they are in Hick's approach, can there be a genuine dialogue among their members? In light of these and other bewildering problems, many scholars, like James Fredericks and **Francis Clooney**, who are Catholic theologians and scholars of Asian religions, argue that it is best for the Christian, at present, to focus on actual dialogue and comparison, rather than on theories about non-Christian religions (in 2017, Clooney received a major award, the John Courtney Murray Award of the Catholic Theological Society of America).

A COUNTER-REACTION

The twentieth century was a time of rapid development in terms of a positive, Christian evaluation of non-Christian religions. However, this was accompanied by a history of reaction. For instance, in 1910 and 1928, there were the International Missionary Conferences, which were gatherings of a wide variety of Christians for the sake of discussing the progress of their mission work. The meetings of 1910 and 1928 gave some consideration of positive aspects of non-Christian religions, but at the 1938 Conference there was a counter-reaction. In preparation for the Council, the theologian and scholar of Islam, Hendrik Kraemer, wrote *Christian Message in a Non-Christian World*, in which he sharply distinguished Christian revelation from all non-Christian religious experience. Kraemer emphasized that the proclamation of Jesus Christ as lord and savior must be at the forefront of all missionary activity, and must not take second place to dialogue or social service activities. Later, just as there was a reaction to the International Missionary Conferences of 1910 and 1928, so there was a reaction to the emphasis on dialogue by the World Council of Churches. This resulted in the Lausanne Movement, a large and influential confederation of evangelical Christians, first organized in 1974 by the well-known American preacher, Billy Graham. This continues to be a very active organization today, with a fervor for spreading Christianity throughout the world.

There are reactions, too, in the Catholic world to the new, twentieth-century rapprochement with the non-Christian world. One of the most significant examples was the papacy of Benedict XVI and his earlier role as the prefect of the Congregation for the Doctrine of the Faith. Although a strong supporter of Jewish–Christian dialogue, he was less enthusiastic about dialogue with other religions. He was deeply concerned that in today's world the particularities of Catholic belief and practice were disappearing into an amorphous, interreligious spirituality. Benedict XVI hence stressed that although non-Christians might receive saving grace, non-Christian religions are "gravely deficient" in comparison with the Catholic Church (*Dominus Iesus* §22). Furthermore, though very different from Kraemer in the specifics of Christian belief and practice, like Kraemer he underscored that evangelization must assume a central place in Christian life:

The Church, guided by charity and respect for freedom, must be primarily committed to proclaiming to all people the truth definitively revealed by the Lord, and to announcing the necessity of conversion to Jesus Christ and of adherence to the Church through Baptism and the other sacraments, in order to participate fully in communion with God.

(*Dominus Iesus* §22)

A specific reaction against some of the trends that emerged in the nineteenth and twentieth centuries is the exclusivist position. It denies the inclusivist and pluralist positions that non-Christian religions can be routes to God. **Exclusivism** might appear to be a narrow-minded, regressive stance. However, there are some important considerations behind the exclusivist position, one of these being a concern that the distinctiveness of Christianity not be lost; another is that having faith in Christ and being regenerated by him brings something fundamentally new to the world.

Some scholars consider the Swiss theologian **Karl Barth** (1886–1968), who is highly regarded among both Protestant and Catholic theologians, as a key example of an exclusivist. For him, the concern that Christianity not be contaminated by outside influences was especially critical. His exclusivism stemmed not from a mere unwillingness to consider other religions but from a great disillusionment with the modern world. The core of Barth's ideas took shape after World War I as a protest against the Liberal Protestantism that had dominated pre-war Germany (see Chapter 22). Liberal Protestantism thought that Christianity needed to be reshaped in order to be compatible with modern intellectual and cultural advances. In Germany, this emphasis on compatibility with modern trends assumed a strongly patriotic and nationalistic stance and gave an uncritical endorsement to Germany's participation in World War I. When Adolf Hitler and his Nazi party came to power in 1933, many Christians thought they could see the hand of God at work in a dynamic movement that, after its humiliating defeat in World War I, would make Germany great again. Some Christians even saw in the Third Reich an instance of divine revelation.

The conjunction of Nazism and Christianity might seem absurd. However, it was only as World War II progressed that worldwide condemnation of Nazism developed. Initially, there was support for Nazism across the world. For instance, prominent Americans like Henry Ford and Charles Lindbergh were Nazi sympathizers. Many people in the Western world considered National Socialism to be a bulwark against Communism and its atheism. Further, in Germany, Nazism brought jobs to people and restored to Germans a sense of pride after the chaos and humiliation that had followed World War I. Last, to many Germans, Nazism connoted moral purity, tradition, and austerity.

The conjunction of Nazism and Christianity horrified Barth. Further, he believed

Figure 28–3 Karl Barth (1886–1968).

that theologies of fulfillment, which emphasize points of contact between Christianity and the non-Christian world, allow the Christian message to be contaminated and ruined. Points of contact that are stressed become entryways into the Christian tradition of things that are essentially opposed to it. Barth therefore rejected any conjunction of Christianity and Nazism, regarding it as sheer idolatry. Instead of theologies of fulfillment, Barth was drawn to the more pessimistic view of human nature and the uncompromising belief in God's sovereignty as taught by the original Reformers like Martin Luther and John Calvin.

In 1934, Protestants who shared Barth's views met at the German town of Barmen and organized a dissenting movement within the official Protestant church. It became known as the "Confessing Church" because of its confession of faith, the celebrated Barmen Declaration, the first article of which proclaimed:

> We reject the false doctrine as though the Church could and would have to acknowledge as a source of its proclamation, apart from and besides this one Word of God, still other events and powers, figures and truths, as God's revelation.
>
> (Confessing Church 1934)

Given Barth's theology of revelation and his experience of the dismaying German Christian sellout to Nazi ideology, it should not surprise us that he refused to see knowledge of God anywhere but in the Bible. He regarded all religions, including Christianity, as idolatrous and sinful expressions of humanity. The critical difference, however, between Christianity and other religions is that Christ extends his saving grace to Christianity in spite of its corruption. Hence, like the Christian herself, Christianity is at once corrupt and redeemed. Other religions are simply corrupt.

At first glance, Barth's theology appears wholly negative about other religions, and equally negative about the place of other human beings in God's redemptive plan. The first assertion seems true enough, but not necessarily the second. Surprising as it may seem, Barth is known to have speculated about the possibility of universal salvation, even of those who did not profess or even know of Jesus Christ. He thought universal salvation might be justified on the basis of God's sovereign will, and on Jesus Christ as both the subject *and the object* of God's election. Paul says in his letter to the Romans that just as God had condemned all in Adam, so he really and truly elected all in Jesus Christ (see Romans 5:12–21). Barth took this to mean that Christ absorbed in himself the entire salvation history of the human race, not just as its culmination but as its very substance: what Christ did and what happened to him truly is the fate of all. However, these ideas do not mean that he was an inclusivist rather than an exclusivist, for the inclusivist affirms the value of non-Christian religions, but Barth did not. If non-Christians are saved, it is through God's will, not through the religions. Also, though he never denied it, Barth never explicitly endorsed the idea of universal salvation.

Key Terms

Thomas Aquinas	Exclusivism	Pluralism
Hans Urs von Balthasar	J.N. Farquhar	Karl Rahner
Karl Barth	John Hick	Domingo Soto
John Chrysostom	Inclusivism	Theology of fulfillment
Francis Clooney	Juan de Lugo	John Wesley
Jean Daniélou	Pius IX	

Questions for Reading

1. Describe how negative views of the non-Christian world developed in the early church.

2. Describe examples of constructive interactions between Christianity and the non-Christian world in the early church.

3. Explain the ways the teaching "outside the church there is no salvation" has been understood during the course of the Christian tradition.

4. What was John Wesley's stance on the salvation of non-Christians?

5. Choose one theologian of the twentieth century and describe his positive views on non-Christian religions.

6. Choose an institutional statement by a major Christian body and describe its position.

7. What are some of the concerns of those who have reacted against these newer, positive considerations of non-Christian religions?

8. Concerning the relationship of Christianity and other religions, describe the view of Karl Barth, paying particular attention to Barth's understanding of religion and also of election.

Works Consulted/Recommended Reading

Abbott, Walter M., ed. 1966. *The Documents of Vatican II.* Translated by Joseph Gallagher. Angelus Books. New York: Herder & Herder.

Confessing Church. 1934. "The Barmen Declaration." Evangelische Kirche in Deutschland Website. www.ekd.de/en/The-Barmen-Declaration-133.htm.

Congregation of the Doctrine of the Faith [Benedict XVI]. 2000. *Declaration: "Dominus Iesus": On the Unicity and Salvific Universality of Jesus Christ and the Church.* The Holy See Website. www.vatican.va/roman_curia/congregations/cfaith/documents/rc_con_cfaith_doc_20000806_dominus-iesus_en.html.

Cracknell, Kenneth. 1995. *Justice, Courtesy and Love: Theologians and Missionaries Encountering World Religions, 1846–1914.* London: Epworth Press.

Dupuis, Jacques. 2001. *Toward a Christian Theology of Religious Pluralism.* Maryknoll, NY: Orbis.

Evangelical Lutheran Church of America. 1994. "Declaration of the Evangelical Lutheran Church in America to the Jewish Community." www.jewishvirtuallibrary.org/declaration-of-the-evangelical-lutheran-church-in-america-to-the-jewish-community.

Farquhar, J.N. 1910. "The Crown of Hinduism." *Contemporary Review* 535 (July): 56–68.

Gillingham, Richard. n.d. "Is Barth's Theology Necessarily Exclusivist?" *Quodlibet Journal.* www.quodlibet.net/gillingham-barth.shtml.

John Chrysostom. 1979. *Discourses against Judaizing Christians.* Translated by Paul W. Harkins. Washington, DC: Catholic University of America Press.

Knitter, Paul F. 2002. *Introducing Theologies of Religions.* Maryknoll, NY: Orbis Books.

O'Malley, John W. 2008. *What Happened at Vatican II.* Cambridge, MA: Belknap Press of Harvard University Press.

Pius IX. 1863. *On Promotion of False Doctrines: Quanto Conficiamur Moerore.* Papal Encyclicals Online Website. www.papalencyclicals.net/Pius09/p9quanto.htm.

Sanders, John. 2001. *No Other Name: An Investigation into the Destiny of the Unevangelized.* Eugene, OR: Wipf and Stock.

Schroeder, H.J. 1937. *Disciplinary Decrees of the General Councils: Text, Translation, and Commentary.* St. Louis, MO: B. Herder.

Sullivan, Francis A. 1992. *Salvation Outside the Church? Tracing the History of the Catholic Response.* New York: Paulist Press.

Wesley, John. 1984. *The Works of John Wesley.* Peabody, MA: Hendrickson Publishers.

World Council of Churches. 1948. "The Christian Approach to the Jews." The World Council of Churches Website. www.ccjr.us/dialogika-resources/documents-and-statements/ecumenical-christian/737-wcc1948.

World Council of Churches. 1990. "Baar Statement: Theological Perspectives on Plurality." The World Council of Churches Website. www.oikoumene.org/en/resources/documents/wcc-programmes/interreligious-dialogue-and-cooperation/christian-identity-in-pluralistic-societies/baar-statement-theological-perspectives-on-plurality.

World Council of Churches and Centre for Inter-Religious Dialogue of the Islamic Culture and Relations Organization. 1970. "Comminiqué from WCC and CID Inter-Religious Dialogue Meeting." The World Council of Churches Website. www.oikoumene.org/en/resources/documents/wcc-programmes/interreligious-dialogue-and-cooperation/interreligious-trust-and-respect/communique-from-wcc-and-cid-inter-religious-dialogue-meeting.

Glossary

Aaron—according to the Exodus story, Moses' brother and assistant.

abbot—the spiritual leader who governs an organized community of monks.

Abelard, Peter (1079–1142)—medieval theologian and philosopher known for his work *Sic et Non* (*Yes and No*), in which he examines seeming inconsistencies among ancient theologians in an effort at achieving consistency and coherence in Christian theology. Key figure for scholasticism.

Abraham—the first patriarch of the Israelite people (lived mid-nineteenth to mid-eighteenth century B.C.E.), with whom God formed an everlasting covenant; claimed as an ancestor by Jews, Christians, and Muslims.

absolute dependence—in Friedrich Schleiermacher's theology, the idea that human beings have an experiential awareness that they are not self-sufficient, and that they instead are dependent on something else for their existence.

absolution—forgiveness for the guilt associated with sin.

Adeodatus—meaning "Gift of God," the son of Augustine of Hippo (A.D. 354–430), born of his relationship with a concubine whose name we do not know.

ad fontes—Latin metaphor meaning "Back to the wellsprings!" that imagines the historical transmission of knowledge as a river that flows down into the present from its wellsprings in the ancient past. During the Renaissance, painters, sculptors, poets, and scholars exhorted each other to go back to the river's pure and undiluted source—the artists, philosophers, and historians of classical Greece and Rome—and drink directly from their works.

Adoptionism—an early Christology that claimed that Jesus was adopted by God when he was chosen to be the messiah, typically at his Baptism. Adoptionism was seen as a heresy in the early church.

Aeterni Patris—the papal encyclical issued by Pope Leo XIII in 1879 that endorsed Neo-Thomism and sparked a strong campaign within the Catholic Church to develop and spread the teachings of Thomas Aquinas.

African Initiated Churches—churches founded and led by Africans with little or no direct influence from Western missionaries. They share common features with Pentecostal churches, such as founders and leaders who have often been prophets, healers, and exorcists, while their worship styles incorporate African cultural practices.

African National Congress (ANC)—the political party founded in 1912 to give voting rights to black and mixed-race Africans; after the establishment of apartheid, it was the party that sought to end legalized racial segregation. It was the party of Nelson Mandela, and was banned from 1940–1990. At the national level, it has been the ruling party of post-apartheid South Africa.

Afrikaner—the group identity of Afrikaans-speaking persons in South Africa who are descended from Dutch and Huguenot settlers

617

agent of God—drawn from the analogy of a king and his messenger, this phrase is used by biblical scholars to describe how first-century people might have understood the relationship between God and Jesus, who acts on God's behalf in the world.

aggiornamento—meaning "a bringing up to date." This term describes the spirit of the Second Vatican Council as it attempted to reinterpret the church's doctrine and reform its practice in a way that was suitable for the present.

agnostic—someone who is unsure about the existence of God or gods.

Albert the Great (*c.*A.D. 1200–1280)—Scholastic theologian and interpreter of Aristotle famous in part for having been a teacher of Thomas Aquinas.

Albigensians—see *Cathars.*

Alexander of Alexandria—a fourth-century bishop of Alexandria who excommunicated Arius as a heretic. Alexander taught that the Father and Son were co-eternal on account the Father's eternal generation of the Son.

alienation of property—during the early medieval period, the practice of deeding church goods as the private inheritance of bishops' or priests' children.

Alighieri, Dante—see Dante Alighieri.

'**Ali ibn Abi Talib** (d. A.D. 661)—The Prophet Muhammad's first cousin and the husband of his daughter Fatima. 'Ali's supporters (the *shi'a* or Shiites) thought he should be Muhammad's immediate successor (i.e., "caliph") as head of the Muslim community, but he is regarded by Sunnis as the fourth caliph.

Allah—the Muslim name for God; the one and only God.

allegorical—a method of interpreting scripture that looks for a hidden spiritual meaning beneath the bare literal or historical meaning of the biblical text.

al-Quds—Arabic name for the city of Jerusalem. Literally, "the Holy."

Ambrose of Milan (*c.*A.D. 339–397)—bishop and former provincial governor whose sermons inspired the young Augustine to take Christianity seriously.

Amos—an eighth-century B.C.E. prophet who condemned the social injustice of the Northern Kingdom of Israel and foresaw its destruction by the Assyrians.

analogy—a likeness or similarity of meaning between language as applied to God on the one hand and to created things on the other. Thomas Aquinas locates the use of analogical language between univocation (or the use of a single term or phrase in the same way in more than one context) and equivocation (or the use of a single term or phrase in different ways in different contexts).

anchorite/anchoress—a hermit who pledges his or her life to prayer and contemplation. During the Middle Ages, they lived in small enclosed rooms attached to a church, where they could be spiritual counselors for the people of the area.

Anglican Communion—the worldwide body of 44 different churches in the tradition of the Church of England. The Episcopal Church is the American component of the Anglican Communion.

animism—worship of the forces of nature.

Anselm of Canterbury (A.D. 1033–1109)—Benedictine monk and archbishop of Canterbury, Anselm is known for his "debt satisfaction" theory of atonement and for his ontological argument for the existence of God.

Anthropocene—the name geologists apply to the current era of Earth's history, acknowledging that human beings are the dominant natural force influencing global climate and the environment.

anthropocentric—human-centered.

Anthropogenic climate change—the overall rapid change in Earth's temperature, precipitation, and wind patterns caused by human activity.

anthropology—the study of human beings or a particular view about the nature of human beings, based on various philosophical, cultural, and scientific methods; theological explanations concerning humanity's relationship to God, the human condition, and the promise or potential of a renewed humanity.

anthropomorphism—attributing human-like characteristics to God.

anticlericalism—antagonism toward priests and clergy.

Antony of Egypt (A.D. 251–356)—the father of Christian monasticism. Antony felt that Christ's teachings called him to sell all of his possessions and devote himself completely to following the gospel through a life of prayer in isolation from the world. Many Christians—early, medieval, and modern—have been inspired to follow his example.

apartheid—the system of legalized racial segregation (affecting housing, health care, education, criminal justice, political engagement, and economic access) instituted by South African law from 1948–1994.

apocalyptic—from a Greek word meaning "to reveal" or "to uncover," referring to revelations of the heavenly realms or the destiny of this world. It can also be used to describe a person, group, or text that expresses the beliefs that the present world is evil and that God will soon bring an end to it, destroying the evildoers and rescuing the righteous.

Apocrypha—name given to the seven books that are included in the Old Testament by Catholics and Orthodox Christians but excluded from the scriptures by Protestants and Jews. The term is also used more broadly to refer to certain Jewish and Christian religious texts written during the same time as or somewhat later than the biblical books and considered inspired by some, but not included in the Bible itself.

Apollinaris of Laodicaea (d. A.D. 390)—a Christian theologian who solved the problem of the dual nature of Christ (human and divine) by saying that Christ had a human body but not a human soul. His views came to be regarded as heretical.

Apologist—meaning "defender." The Apologists of the early church attempted to respond to pagan criticisms of Christianity by explaining what Christians believed and how they lived their lives in terms that made sense to outsiders.

apophatic theology—refers to the use of "negation" (*apophasis* in Greek) in talking about God, based on the belief that God surpasses everything in creation and that human understanding of God is limited. Examples of such negations include "God is invisible, immutable, unknowable," and so on.

apostasy—falling away from the faith or renunciation of the faith under threat of persecution.

apostle—from the Greek word *apostello*, which means "to send out." It is used by Christians to refer to "one who is sent out by Jesus to preach the word about him."

apostolic tradition—the witness of the apostles and early disciples of Jesus; according to Irenaeus of Lyons, it is preserved by the bishops as successors of the apostles.

Aquinas, Thomas (A.D. 1224/5–1274)—Catholic theologian and saint; author of the *Summa Theologiae*, a comprehensive overview of Christian theology; best known for his

integration of the philosophy of Aristotle into Christian faith, his view of the compatibility of reason and revelation, and his "proofs" for God's existence.

Aristotle—Greek philosopher and scientist of the fourth century B.C.E.; his ideas were seen as a challenge to religions like Christianity because—without any access to divine revelation—he had developed an account of reality that seemed more complete, more sophisticated, and more coherent than that of Christianity. He had a major influence on Scholastic theologians, especially Thomas Aquinas, who refer to Aristotle as "the Philosopher."

Arius (*c.*A.D. 250/56–336)—a fourth-century priest in Alexandria, who taught that only God the Father was God in the true sense; the Son (Jesus Christ), though also divine, was created by the Father and therefore less than him. His teaching was rejected at the Council of Nicaea (A.D. 325) and the Council of Constantinople (A.D. 381).

Ark of the Covenant—A wooden box, overlaid with gold, which represented the presence of God for the Israelites. It also contained the Ten Commandments and other relics of the Exodus. It was kept in the Holiest Place in the Temple.

article—the basic unit of many medieval theological works, such as the *Summa Theologiae* of Thomas Aquinas. Each article considers one question and contains the following elements: a statement of the question, a review of the arguments for and against the proposition, the author's own view on the question, and finally a reply to the arguments with which the author ultimately disagreed.

asceticism—the training or discipline of the passions and the appetites (e.g., abstaining from food and sexual activity, denying the body comfort). In the case of hermits and monks, the practice was designed to foster spiritual development.

Ashkenazim—the term given to Jewish immigrants to the Americas from northern Europe.

Assyria—A civilization in Mesopotamia (modern-day Iraq) that dominated the region in the eighth century. They destroyed the Northern Kingdom of Israel.

Athanasius of Alexandria—(d. A.D. 373) bishop of Alexandria who was a staunch defender of the Nicene Creed. Athanasius emphasized the "genetic" understanding of "Father–Son" language, in which God the Father, like any father, begets a Son that is of the same nature. Also wrote the *Life of Antony*, contributing much to the spread of monastic ideals.

atheist—someone who disbelieves or denies that God or gods exist.

Augsburg Confession—a statement of faith drafted by Philip Melanchthon, representing the Lutheran position, at the Diet of Augsburg (A.D. 1530). The diet, which was called to resolve differences between Protestants and Catholics, failed, but Lutherans signed Melanchthon's statement, making it one of the most important documents of Lutheran doctrine even today.

Augustine of Hippo (A.D. 354–430)—theologian and bishop of Hippo; his conversion is described in the autobiographical work *Confessions*; best known for his opposition to Donatism and Pelagianism, his theological doctrines of grace, original sin, and predestination, and his solution to the problem of evil.

Averroes (A.D. 1126–1198)—medieval Muslim scholar known for his learned commentaries on the works of Aristotle.

Avicenna (A.D. 980–1037)—medieval Muslim scholar noted for medical commentaries on the classical Greek physician-scholars Galen and Hippocrates, mathematical commentaries on the classical Greek mathematician Euclid, and philosophical commentaries on Aristotle.

Avignon Papacy (A.D. 1309–1377)—referring to a period in the Late Middle Ages when the pope moved his court to Avignon, France. Before the papacy returned to Rome, the church leadership would be involved in an even greater struggle for power called the Great Schism.

Babylon—A civilization in Mesopotamia (modern-day Iraq) that dominated the region in the sixth century. They destroyed the southern kingdom of Judah, tore down and looted the temple that Solomon built.

Babylonian Exile—the period during the sixth century B.C.E. when the Judeans were held captive in Babylon by the Babylonians.

Balthasar, Hans Urs von (A.D. 1905–1988)—Swiss theologian and Jesuit priest, he is perhaps best known for his research on the topic of revelation and his theological reflections on beauty.

Baptism—a Christian rite of initiation, which brings about the forgiveness of sins, makes the person a member of the Christian community, and confers the Holy Spirit on the person. To baptize means "to plunge." Immersion into the water symbolizes entry into Jesus' death from which one is raised to new life.

Baptism, believer's—see *believer's Baptism*.

Baptism in the Holy Spirit—the ecstatic experience of God's presence that Pentecostals and Charismatics believe necessary to live a full and spiritually empowered Christian life, often with the expectation that the recipient will speak in an unknown language (*glossolalia*) or receive some other gift of the Holy Spirit. These experiences are believed to replicate those of first-century Christians as recorded in the Acts of the Apostles, and to be a sign of the restoration of New Testament Christianity. Also known as Baptism *of* or *with* the Holy Spirit, as well as *Spirit Baptism*. See also *glossolalia*.

Baptist churches—a family of Christian churches that have their roots in the Puritan movement in England. They were also influenced by the Dutch Mennonites and millennialist movements who looked to the books of Daniel and Revelation, seeking "signs of the times" and a proper way of life for Christian believers. They hold conservative views on the authority and inspiration of the Bible, but otherwise they are committed to religious liberty and church independence.

baptistery—in the early church, a Christian building used for Baptism; later, a place in the church set aside for Baptism. The baptisteries of the early church had a centered design, and the focus was on the baptismal font into which the candidate stepped.

baroque—an ornate style of art and architecture that was especially popular in Roman Catholic churches and among Roman Catholic artists during the Catholic Reformation. The baroque style was designed to dramatically illustrate the truths of Catholic orthodoxy but also to involve the viewer in the experience of faith by appealing to their emotions and overwhelming them with a sense of awe.

Barth, Karl (A.D. 1886–1968)—leading twentieth-century Protestant theologian who criticized Liberal Protestantism and placed modern theology on a new footing by claiming that it should begin with divine revelation, not human experience.

Basil of Caesarea—one of the Cappadocian Fathers instrumental in the articulation of pro-Nicene Trinitarian doctrine. Also instrumental to the development of monasticism in Eastern Christianity.

basilica—a style of Christian church architecture, distinguished from other churches by its adaptation of the standard rectangular layout of royal audience halls and public buildings in Roman cities.

beatitude—meaning "blessed" or "happy," a statement of blessing to be conferred on a person (e.g., "Blessed are you…").

Beguines—independent communities of lay-women that first emerged in Europe in the High Middle Ages. They had no rule or permanent religious vows, but they shared a form of common life and engaged in contemplative prayer or ministries of caring for the sick and poor.

believer's Baptism—the idea, popularized by the churches of the Radical Reformation, that since Baptism involves entering into a covenant with God, it requires an act of conscious, active belief on the part of the person being baptized. Since only adults are old enough to formulate such belief and make such a decision, infant Baptism is ruled out.

Benedict of Nursia (A.D. 480–547)—founder of the Benedictine monastery at Monte Cassino and author of the *Rule for Monasteries*, which eventually became the primary rule of monasticism in the West.

benevolence—good will.

Berger, Peter (A.D. 1929–2017)—sociologist of religion who championed the "secularization thesis" in the mid-twentieth century, yet ultimately concluded in the late twentieth century that the world was not in fact becoming more secular.

Bernard of Clairvaux (A.D. 1090–1153)—a Cistercian monk who wrote and preached extensively on the spiritual life.

Bible—meaning "the books," Christianity's sacred and inspired literature.

Big Bang theory—the view that the universe began from a *singularity*, an episode of infinite pressure, heat, and density in zero space from which all matter, energy, space, and time originate. The current theory is that the universe began approximately 13.8 billion years ago.

Biko, Steve (A.D. 1946–1977)—a South African anti-apartheid activist who was at the forefront of the Black Consciousness Movement in the 1960s and 1970s, and who was arrested and beaten to death by state security officers in prison in 1977.

bishop—meaning "overseer." In early Christianity, bishops were overseers of local churches, chiefly responsible for teaching and presiding at the Eucharist. Later, the bishop is an overseer of a group of churches known as a diocese.

Black Power—a diverse set of ideas that emphasize black self-determination, black liberation, and black pride. Advocates often seek to push for more than legal civil rights for black people, criticizing Western social, political, and economic structures as fundamentally racist at their foundation.

Black Theology—(1) inspired by the manifold religious, spiritual, and cultural traditions originating from black communities of faith and by the history of resistance to anti-black racism. It is a form of theology that interprets the Bible and the Christian tradition in the light of black experience and the struggle for liberation. (2) a distinctly South African form of liberation theology grounded in principles of black empowerment; less Marxist in orientation than its Latin American counterparts and more biblically grounded than African-American versions of the same, Black Theology emphasized the need for black self-love.

boers—the Afrikaans word for "farmer," the term designates Afrikaans-speaking descendants of the Dutch settlers of South Africa. Contemporary usage of the term is complicated. Some Afrikaans-speaking citizens of the new democracy of South Africa prefer to be called "boers," while some consider it to be a pejorative term.

Boniface VIII (r. A.D. 1294–1303)—the pope who published *Unam Sanctam*, perhaps the most famous medieval statement on church and state, which asserts the authority of the papacy over the emerging nation kingdoms of that time.

Bonhoeffer, Dietrich (1906–1945)—Lutheran theologian and pastor whose involvement in the conspiracy to overthrow Hitler ended in two years of imprisonment and execution on April 9, 1945. His writings, especially his letters and papers from prison, have influenced and inspired believers and unbelievers alike with their reflections on following Christ in "a world come of age."

breviary—a prayer book containing the Liturgy of the Hours, the official prayer of the church, regularly prayed by priests, monks, and religious sisters. It is composed of psalms and readings from the Bible and other religious literature.

Broederbond—"Afrikaner Brotherhood," the Calvinist, white supremacist secret society established in the 1920s to advance racist Afrikaner interests in government, especially to undermine self-determination for African tribes.

Bronze age—the age when copper/bronze was the prevailing technology. It corresponds to the early periods of Israelite history up to the time of King David (1000 B.C.E.).

bull, papal—see *papal bull.*

Byzantium—see *Constantinople.*

Caesaro-papism—term applied by some Western writers to the Byzantine political theory, which held that the civil ruler ("Caesar") also served as head of the church ("pope").

caliph—meaning "successor," that is, of Muhammad. This title was given to a succession of leaders of the young Muslim movement after the death of Muhammad in A.D. 632. In theory, there was only one, though competing ruling dynasties claimed it at various times; defunct since abolished by the Republic of Turkey in 1924.

Calvin, John (A.D. 1509–1564)—the French reformer and theologian who led the Swiss city of Geneva through the Reformation. Calvin is known especially for the doctrines of the sovereignty of God and double predestination and for grappling with the problem of church authority after the Protestant rejection of the authority of Rome. His teachings are most influential in the Christian Reformed Church and the Presbyterian Church.

Câmara, Dom Hélder (1909–1999)—Catholic bishop of Recife, Brazil from 1964 to 1985. Câmara was a charismatic advocate of liberation theology and social justice especially on behalf of developing nations in the "Third World" or Global South.

Canaan—the land that the Israelites settled, subsequently called "Israel," and then "Israel and Judah."

canon—(1) the collection of authoritative writings of a particular religious group; (2) the "rule" or norm of religious truth in the Christian tradition; (3) church law as defined by councils or other church authorities.

canonization—a process by which the church designates certain persons as saints and therefore models of the Christian life; also the process by which the canon of the Bible took shape.

Cappadocian Fathers—a group of Christian priests, including Basil of Caesarea (A.D. 330–379), his brother Gregory of Nyssa (c.A.D. 335–after 394), and Basil's friend Gregory of Nazianzus (c.A.D. 330–390), whose theological advances and appropriation of Greek philosophical thought are reflected in the clarifications of the Nicene Creed adopted at the Council of Constantinople (A.D. 381).

Capuchins—a reform branch of the Franciscan movement, this religious order was officially recognized in 1528 during the Catholic Reformation. They got their name from the unique four-pointed hood that they wore with their brown habit.

cataphatic theology—refers to the use of "affirmation" (*kataphasis* in Greek) in talking about God, either based on human speculation or revelation. Examples of such affirmations include "God is love," "God is merciful," "God is a judge," and so on.

catechism—from a Greek word meaning "to instruct." A catechism is a manual of Christian doctrine used to instruct believers in the Christian faith. They were especially popular in the sixteenth century among both Protestant and Catholic reformers, because of the emphasis on religious instruction for ministers as well as laity.

catechumen—a candidate for Baptism who is undergoing instruction in the Christian religion.

Cathars—meaning "pure ones," this anticlerical, Christian reform movement emerged in the twelfth century A.D., teaching that the world and the flesh were the work of an evil god. Thus they practiced severe asceticism. Catharism was widespread in southern France, where they came to be known as the Albigensians.

cathedral—a bishop's church. It gets its name from the bishop's chair, his *cathedra*, which is the symbol of his teaching authority.

Catherine of Siena (c.A.D. 1347–1380)—a mystic of the late medieval period, she was a Dominican tertiary and influential in bringing an end to the Avignon Papacy, only to see it fall into the situation of the Great Schism. Catherine's prayer life had led her into a vision of mystical marriage to Christ. Her visions often were of the nourishing and cleansing blood of the sacrifice of Christ on the cross.

catholic (or **catholicity**)—meaning "universal." The term Catholic is also used in a restrictive sense to refer to a tradition within Christianity, namely, the Roman Catholic Church or to describe those churches that claim a continuity of leadership that goes back to the early Christian churches (e.g., Eastern Orthodox, Oriental Orthodox, Anglicans, and Episcopalians).

Catholic Reformation—a term given to the efforts of those Roman Catholics who wanted to bring about the internal rebirth of Catholic sensibility—in theology, spirituality, religious piety, and morality—in the sixteenth century, during the time of the Protestant Reformation.

Catholic Worker Movement—begun in 1933 by Dorothy Day and Peter Maurin as a radical newspaper called *The Catholic Worker*, the Catholic Worker Movement soon created "houses of hospitality" to serve the poor directly. The movement practices voluntary poverty, nonviolence, and "the works of mercy," in some 228 houses of hospitality in the U.S.A and around the world.

cenobitic monasticism—a form of monasticism in which monks live together in a community, rather than as hermits.

Chalcedon—see *Council of Chalcedon.*

Charismatic Movement—a movement for Christian renewal that took Pentecostal teachings and practices of prayer for healing, speaking in tongues, other "gifts of the Holy Spirit," and ecstatic worship into mainline Christian churches, including Roman Catholicism, beginning in the late 1960s. See *Pentecostalism; Baptism in the Holy Spirit; glossolalia.*

Charlemagne—(Charles the Great), Frankish king (r. 768–814) and crowned Roman emperor by Pope Leo III in 800. He enabled a rebirth of learning and culture in Western Europe known as the Carolingian Renaissance, named for his dynasty.

Chikane, Frank (A.D. 1347–1380)—a South African anti-apartheid activist and Pentecostal theologian from Soweto especially known for his leadership in issuing the Kairos Document, a Christian denunciation of apartheid.

Christ—from a Greek word meaning "anointed one," or *messiah* in Hebrew. Christians use it to refer to Jesus as God's anointed, the fulfillment of the prophecy made to David concerning an heir who would be an eternal king (2 Samuel 7).

Christ, cosmic—a term used in theologies of world religions to describe how Christ, who is present throughout the universe, can be present in non-Christian religions.

Christendom—a term that modern historians have given to the thorough merging of Christianity and culture, which took place in Europe during the twelfth and thirteenth centuries, also known as the High Middle Ages.

Christian base communities—small groups of poor and disenfranchised people and/or their advocates, who meet together to study the Bible, discuss issues of common concern, and strategize about how to remedy or respond to social injustices. These groups are often associated with liberation theology. They are also known as *ecclesial base communities* or CEBs for their Spanish and Portuguese acronym.

Christocentric—an approach to theology and ethics that maintains a central focus on the person and work of Jesus Christ in matters of belief and practice.

Christology—meaning "words or teaching about the Christ." A study concerned with who Jesus is as the Christ (Messiah) and what his role is in God's relationship with humanity.

Chrysostom, John (*c.*A.D. 349–407)—prominent early Christian theologian known for his eloquent preaching. The "Divine Liturgy of St. John Chrysostom," the most frequently celebrated liturgy in Eastern Orthodox Christianity, is attributed in part to him. Also known for his anti-Jewish sermons.

Churchly Pietism—a branch of Pietism whose members sought to remain within the church as they reformed it.

Church of Jesus Christ of Latter-Day Saints—also known as the Mormons, who take their name from the Book of Mormon, which their founder Joseph Smith (1805–1844) claimed to have translated from golden plates revealed to him in 1827 by an angel named Moroni. This American church was founded in 1830.

Cicero (106–43 B.C.)—orator, scholar, and politician during the waning years of the Roman republic, his Latin prose style, defense of republican politics, and valorization of the *studia humanitatis* (the study of the humanities or liberal arts) as essential to living a free human life were major sources of inspiration for the fourteenth-century Renaissance.

Cistercians—a group of monks who, in the twelfth century A.D., sought religious reform by returning to the primitive Benedictine life in wilderness areas. They are named for their first house at Cîteaux in France.

civil religion—a theory derived from the sociology of religion which holds that for societies to cohere, they produce a unifying symbol system that acts as a virtual religion. It has been applied to the United States despite its rejection of an official religion.

Civil Rights Movement—a term that encompasses the social movements that fought for black civil rights spanning from the early 1950s to the late 1960s, which called for an end to racial segregation and discrimination against African Americans and for protection of their rights under the Constitution and federal law.

clean/unclean—These are ritual terms given to various things that can either be brought into the Temple (clean) or must be kept outside of the Temple (unclean). For example, clean animals are those that can be sacrificed to God. Sometimes the terms pure/impure are used for these same categories.

Clooney, Francis (b. A.D. 1950)—comparative theologian who focuses on dialogue and comparison between Christianity and other religions of the world.

College of Cardinals—"cardinal" is an honorific office, not an ordained office such as a deacon, priest, or bishop. Originally the cardinals were local Roman clergy who assisted the pope in his work as bishop of Rome. In the Middle Ages, they gained exclusive responsibility for electing the pope and for advising him on matters pertaining to the governance of the Roman Catholic Church. Today they come from all over the world and represent, along with the college of bishops, the universality of the church.

communion of saints—the ancient belief, enshrined in the creeds, that deceased holy ones share a relationship with the living members of the church.

comparative theology—comparison of the views of various religious traditions on theological themes like revelation, the nature of God, sin and salvation.

conciliarism—a theory of church authority advanced by certain theologians and bishops of the Roman Catholic Church intended to resolve the Great Schism of the papacy (A.D. 1378–1417). According to this theory, the bishops, when they were gathered together in an official council in time of crisis, had the right to make binding decisions independent of the pope.

concubinage—during the early medieval period, the practice among some clergy of maintaining concubines in a relationship something like marriage.

concupiscence—meaning desire or lust; Augustine of Hippo saw inordinate desire, especially sexual desire, as a chief mark of the disorder introduced into the soul after the Fall.

confessional approach—also called a theological or committed approach, an examination of topics within Christian theology from the perspective of an insider, or one who holds the beliefs he or she examines for him or herself. Contrasts with a "religious-studies approach."

confessors—in early Christianity, those who were arrested during persecution and stood firm in their faith but who were not put to death. Confessors enjoyed great prestige in the churches, and some claimed the right to forgive sins.

congregationalist—a model of church organization based upon the style of the earliest Christian communities. Its leaders are part of the local community and their authority comes from within the local community.

consistory—the governing council of the Calvinist Geneva, consisting of members from the city government, the church leadership, and the laity.

Constantine (r. A.D. 306–337)—the first Christian emperor of Rome. He paved the way for the establishment of Christianity as the sole legal religion in the Roman Empire and began the practice of calling ecumenical councils to resolve urgent issues affecting the whole church.

Constantinople—a major city in what is modern-day Turkey; formerly the capital of the Eastern Roman Empire, founded by Constantine c.330 on the site of the ancient city of Byzantium; historically, one of five patriarchal sees (along with Rome, Alexandria, Antioch, and Jerusalem) from which Christianity was governed; today, the seat of the foremost of the four patriarchs (along with the bishops of Alexandria, Antioch, and Jerusalem) who govern the Eastern Orthodox Church. See also *Council of Constantinople*.

contrition—sorrow for sin.

conventicles—small groups for prayer, bible study, and the sharing of religious experiences organized by Pietists and intended to bring about both individual renewal and church reform.

Copernicus, Nicholas (A.D. 1473–1543)—Polish astronomer who proposed that the earth and other planets revolved around the sun.

cosmic microwave background radiation—electromagnetic radiation that permeates the universe. CMB, as it is sometimes called, is the oldest electromagnetic radiation in the universe and gives important evidence for the Big Bang theory.

cosmology—the study of the nature and structure of the universe; a particular model ("picture") of the structure of the universe.

Cottesloe Consultation—a conference sponsored by the World Council of Churches in December 1960 in Cottesloe, a suburb of Johannesburg, providing the churches with an opportunity to respond to the Sharpeville Massacre; those assembled encouraged the churches to take a strong and active role in challenging the injustices of apartheid.

Council of Chalcedon—an ecumenical council held in A.D. 451, which considered the question of Christ's human and divine natures and taught that the incarnate Jesus Christ possessed a complete human nature and a complete divine nature united in one person.

Council of Constantinople—an ecumenical council held in A.D. 381 that affirmed the Nicene Creed and added clauses about the co-equal divinity of the Holy Spirit.

Council of Ephesus—an ecumenical council held in A.D. 431 that taught that Mary, the mother of Jesus, should be venerated as *Theotokos* ("Mother of God"). This safeguards the unity of Jesus Christ as one human–divine person.

Council of Nicaea—an ecumenical council held in A.D. 325, which maintained the true divinity of the Son (Jesus Christ) against the teaching of Arius.

Council of Trent—declared by Roman Catholics to be an ecumenical council, this church council met over a period of 18 years (1545–1563) to address doctrinal and practical issues of reform, both within the Catholic Church and in response to the Protestant Reformation.

Counter-Reformation—a term given to the efforts of those who, during the Protestant Reformation, were loyal to the pope and supportive of the customary practices of the Roman Catholic Church in order to counter (go against) the teachings and practices of the Protestant reformers.

covenant—an agreement between two individuals or parties that usually includes promises, obligations, and curses if the covenant is broken. God's interactions with Israelite leaders often take the form of a covenant.

Cranmer, Thomas (A.D. 1489–1556)—archbishop of Canterbury for most of the early years of the English Reformation. He is recognized for his contributions to the *Articles of Religion*, which sets out the views of the Church of England, and the 1549 and 1552 versions of *The Book of Common Prayer*, a hugely popular and influential liturgical document.

creed—a short summary of belief; the earliest creeds originated as teaching instruments to prepare catechumens for Baptism; they later became formal instruments by which churches defined themselves.

crusades—began as armed, penitential pilgrimage; in the narrow sense, a series of military campaigns from Christian Europe, between A.D. 1095 and 1291, aimed at recapturing the Holy Land (Palestine and Syria) and protecting the Eastern Byzantine Empire from Turkish Muslim encroachment. From the eleventh to the seventeenth centuries, crusades were also directed against other internal and external enemies of Christendom.

curia—the pope's court staffed by the College of Cardinals, a papal advisory team of bishops, and clergy.

Daniel—book in the Hebrew Bible known for its apocalypticism, especially its account of the general resurrection of the dead and its description of a "Son of Man," a heavenly emissary who will purge the world of evil and rescue the righteous.

Daniélou, Jean (A.D. 1905–1974)—French theologian and Jesuit priest, he is best known for his research and writing on the early church Fathers.

Dante Alighieri (A.D. 1265–1321)—Florentine poet, scholar, and early humanist whose inimitable poem *The Comedy* inaugurates the central themes of Renaissance culture and theology and synthesizes the prior achievements of medieval Scholasticism.

dar al-Islam—literally, "the abode of submission [to God]" or "the abode of Islam," meaning the geographic territory where Muslims rule in accordance with God's will for peace and justice among people.

Darwin, Charles (A.D. 1809–1882)—an English scientist who developed the theory of evolution and the principle of natural selection.

David (r. 1000–961 B.C.E.)—The second king of united Israel. He defeated the Philistines and established an extensive empire and sphere of influence. His dynasty lasted for 400 years, until Jerusalem, his capital, was destroyed. The tradition regards him as the greatest of the kings of Israel, known for his military genius, musical abilities, love of God, and his occasional moral failures.

Dead Sea Scrolls—The large collection of scrolls found in 1947 in eleven caves near the northwestern edge of the Dead Sea at the ancient site of Qumran, a home of the Essene movement. They are religious writings from the third century B.C.E. to the second century C.E. Mostly in Hebrew with some in Aramaic and a few in Greek, they consist both of writings now in the Hebrew Bible and of many others that are non-biblical.

deconstruction—applied first to philosophical texts and later to other literature, including religious writings, this approach to reading reveals how the text might not mean what it appears to mean and ultimately how its central message will always elude the reader.

Deism—a view popular during the Enlightenment that God created the world but does not thereafter intervene in its operation. According to this view, the world is like a watch or clock that runs on its own without the help of the watchmaker, God.

Dei verbum—"Word of God": Vatican II's dogmatic constitution on divine revelation, seeing written scripture and tradition as in continuity from a common source; recognized necessity of interpreting scripture in the literary categories in which it was written.

de Las Casas, Bartolomé (A.D. 1474–1566)—the Spanish Dominican friar and bishop whose advocacy and writing on behalf of indigenous peoples in the Americas became a landmark in the history of human rights.

denomination—sociological term for a particular church within the Christian faith, having its own tradition, a common doctrine, and a specific organizational structure.

denominationalism—according to this principle, the individual Christian churches, with their particular forms of worship and their unique organizational structures, are understood to be denominations of the one true church, which is Christianity, and not separate churches; in America, it became the classic way Christianity adapted to the separation of church and state.

Descartes, René (A.D. 1596–1650)—French philosopher, known for his skepticism about the value of tradition. He began his philosophical method by doubting every-

thing he had been taught—all tradition—and by believing only what could be shown by reason to be absolutely certain.

desire, implicit—see *implicit desire.*

deuterocanonical—meaning "second canon," the term refers to certain Old Testament books and parts of books whose canonical status has been disputed over time. Christians who do not accept them as canonical call them *apocryphal.*

Deuteronomic Historian—author(s) of a series of books of the Old Testament/Hebrew Bible, whose agenda was to show how Israel's fortunes were correlated to her obedience to the terms of the covenant with God.

Deuteronomc History—name given to a series of books of the Old Testament written by the Deuteronomic Historian, books that emphasized the necessity of Israel adhering strictly to its covenant with God.

Deuteronomisit tradition—according to the Documentary Hypothesis, the third of four sources that make up the Pentateuch; it dates to the seventh and sixth centuries B.C.E.

Diaspora—the dispersion of Jewish people outside the traditional Jewish homeland in Palestine.

Didache—meaning "teaching," the term refers to the title of a very early church document, *The Teaching of the Twelve Apostles.* It is a church order, that is, a document describing how the Christian ought to live and how the sacraments ought to be celebrated.

diet—a governmental assembly or meeting, such as the imperial congresses or parliaments of the Holy Roman Empire.

Dignitatis Humanae—*Of Human Dignity* or Declaration on Religious Freedom, is the last of the documents of Vatican II; it recognized for the first time that freedom from religious coercion was a human and therefore also a civil right, thereby reversing much nineteenth-century papal teaching.

Discalced Carmelites—a reform branch of the Carmelite order founded by Teresa of Avila and John of the Cross. It became a separate order in A.D. 1593. The term discalced means "unshod," referring to the spiritual practice of going barefoot in order to fulfill Jesus' mandate to provide themselves with nothing for the journey, not even sandals for their feet (Matthew 10:9–10).

disciple—a learner or a follower. Christians use the term to refer to those who followed Jesus.

dispensationalism—a method of interpreting biblical prophecy; it divides the scriptural narrative of God's dealings with humanity into seven stages called "dispensations." Each stage moved God's plan for humanity forward toward its completion. Especially important interpretive method in modern fundamentalism.

divine simplicity—God's characteristic of being free from any metaphysical composition, that is, God's quality of not being made up of parts. Thomas Aquinas defines divine simplicity in reliance on Aristotle's philosophy of being.

docetism—from a Greek word meaning "to seem" or "to appear to be." The belief of some early Christians that Jesus Christ did not really become flesh but only seemed to have a body. In reality, he was a spiritual being who could not suffer or die.

Doctor of the Church—an honor reserved for those whose teaching and scholarship have reflected Catholic Christian beliefs and been important in the lives and faith of others.

doctrine—the official teachings or principles of a religion.

Documentary Hypothesis—the theory that the Pentateuch was produced by combining four strands of tradition (the Yahwist, the Elohist, the Deuteronomist, and the Priestly tradition) over a long period of time (ninth–fifth centuries B.C.E.).

dogma—doctrines or teachings that have been proclaimed authoritatively by a given religion or church.

Dominicans—an order of beggar friars founded by Dominic Guzman, also called the "Order of Preachers." Known for their radical understanding of the vow of poverty, their primary vocation was to preach and hear confessions.

Dominic Guzman (d. A.D. 1221)—founder of the Dominican order of mendicants, also called the "Order of Preachers."

dominion—literally means "rule"; most often a reference to God's command in Genesis 1:28, giving humanity special responsibility to care for creation, safeguard it from abuse, and use it wisely for the good of all creatures.

Donatists—a group of Christians (primarily in North Africa) that split from the main body of the church in the fourth century A.D. in a dispute over whether priests or bishops who collaborated with Roman persecutors of Christianity could retain their offices or administer the sacraments. Donatists maintained that clergy needed to be free from any serious sin to administer the sacraments validly. They were vigorously opposed by Augustine.

double predestination—the Calvinist idea that God has not only chosen some people for salvation (the Elect) but also others for damnation (the reprobate). It emphasizes God's sovereignty (rule) over human free will.

dualism—(1) in Gnosticism and Manicheism, a way of looking at reality as divided between two hostile divine powers, one representing good and the other evil; (2) a way of looking at reality in terms of polar opposites (belief/unbelief; darkness/light; truth/falsehood; spiritual/material).

ecofeminism—combination of the words ecology and feminism. It is a theological approach that examines the interconnection between the domination of women and the domination of nature, and proposes strategies and world-views to address these problems.

ecotheology—ecological theology, or theology that addresses ecological questions and problems.

ecumenical—meaning "worldwide"; (1) term applied to a general council or synod of church leaders in theory attended by representatives of Christians throughout the world; (2) term applied to efforts designed to bring unity and cooperation between divided Christian churches or between Christians and non-Christians.

ecumenical council (or **general council**)—a universal (or worldwide) gathering of Christian bishops called to resolve urgent issues affecting the whole church.

Edict of Worms (A.D. 1521)—the statement issued by the emperor of the Holy Roman Empire of the German nation that declared Martin Luther an outlaw and a heretic.

Edwards, Jonathan (A.D. 1703–1758)—a Calvinist minister who was one of the more famous revival preachers of the Great Awakening, an eighteenth-century spiritual renewal movement in the English colonies.

Elect—meaning "chosen." Although the term is used widely in Judaism and Christianity, the Manichees used it to refer specifically to their leaders.

election—the biblical idea, emphasized most strongly by John Calvin, that God mysteriously chooses to enter into special relationship with some persons and groups, but not with others.

Elizabeth I (A.D. 1533–1603)—the queen of England beginning in 1558, Elizabeth guided England through a tumultuous period during which it achieved religious and political stability.

Elohist—according to the Documentary Hypothesis, the second earliest of the four sources that make up the Pentateuch; it dates to the eighth century B.C.E.

encomienda—the system of granting the indigenous peoples of the Americas to Spanish conquerors and settlers as forced labor, in return for their care and education in the Catholic faith. Opposed by critics like the Dominican friar Bartolomé de Las Casas and others.

enculturation—a term used to describe the process by which an individual learns to live and act within a particular culture in such a way that the culture's particular pattern of actions and thought becomes second nature to the person.

Enlightenment, the—an intellectual movement of the seventeenth and eighteenth centuries which emphasized reason, science, the goodness and rights of humanity, religious toleration, progress, and human freedom.

environmental racism—discrimination that systematically excludes marginalized races from decisions about the environment, while exposing them to greater environmental hazards and risks.

Ephesus—see *Council of Ephesus.*

episcopacy—government by bishops. The adjectival form of the word is episcopal (e.g., episcopal authority is the authority of the bishop).

Episcopal Church—the American branch of the Anglican Communion, meaning those churches that trace their roots to the Church of England and regard episcopacy as a biblically mandated ministry of the church.

epistemology—the study of knowledge, especially the ways in which things are known and the nature of knowledge itself. From the Greek, *epistēmē*, meaning "knowledge."

equivocation—the use of a single term or phrase in different ways in different contexts, as opposed to univocation.

Erasmus, Desiderius (*c.*A.D. 1466–1536)—a scholar of the Renaissance period, learned in the writings of both the Latin and Greek early church writers. His reconstruction of the New Testament text became the basis for many subsequent translations into the vernacular (language of the people).

Essenes—a Jewish group of the first century B.C.E. and first century C.E., who withdrew into the desert, perhaps in protest of the activities of the Jerusalem Temple leadership. They shared an apocalyptic worldview, awaiting the end of the world. They were probably the community whose library at Qumran near the Dead Sea was discovered in 1947.

Eucharist—meaning "to give thanks," the Christian ritual reenactment of Jesus' Last Supper with his disciples. According to Catholic doctrine, when the bread and wine is consecrated, it becomes the body and blood of Jesus Christ.

Eusebius of Caesarea (*c.*A.D. 260–339)—bishop of Caesarea in Palestine and early Christian historian, Apologist, and biographer of Constantine, whose *Ecclesiastical History* preserved for later generations excerpts from a number of ancient Christian documents no longer available to us.

Evagrius of Pontus (A.D. 345–339)—a monk who lived among the desert fathers of Egypt. His systematization of their teachings is the most influential conceptual presentation of the monastic life.

evangelical—having to do with the gospel or the Bible; sometimes used as a synonym for *Protestant.* In the fundamentalist-modernist controversy of the early twentieth century, it describes some of the more traditional forms of Protestant Christianity, especially those that stress the importance of personal conversion or being "born again."

evangelist—one who preached the "good news." This term is also used to refer to the gospel writers.

evil, structural—see *structural evil, structural sin.*

evolution—a theory advocated by Charles Darwin about the development of species. The theory of evolution claims that species emerge by natural processes alone (e.g., natural selection) rather than by the miraculous creation of God.

exclusivism—an attitude or disposition of exclusion; in theologies of world religions, the belief that truth resides only in Christianity and that there are no meaningful similarities between Christianity and other religions.

Exile, Babylonian—see *Babylonian Exile.*

Exodus—(1) the second book of the Hebrew Bible/Old Testament; (2) the mass departure of the Israelites from slavery in Egypt through the saving action of God.

Ezekiel—the sixth-century B.C.E. prophet who counseled the Judeans who were in exile in Babylon that, with renewed faithfulness to the covenant, God would allow them to return to their land.

faith—(1) a relationship of trust in God; (2) personal insight or knowledge-in-action about God; (3) belief in a set of propositions about God, humanity, and the created order that carry a claim to be true.

Fall, the—the theological doctrine that holds that human beings were originally created in a state of perfection but lost that state when they sinned against God.

Farquhar, J.N. (A.D. 1861–1929)—scholar of Hinduism and Christian missionary who developed a "theology of fulfillment," according to which Christ is the supreme fulfillment of the search for God expressed in other religions.

Feminist theologies—theologies that analyze the oppression of women and are committed to working toward the equality and inclusion of women in church and society.

Fertile Crescent—the arc of arable land reaching from the Nile in Egypt, northwards along the Mediterranean coast in Palestine and Syria, and eastwards to Iraq and the Tigris and Euphrates Rivers, to the Persian Gulf.

feudal system—in the early medieval period, the organization of society on the basis of bonds of personal loyalty between a lord and his vassal ("feudal" is from Latin *foedus*, meaning treaty or agreement), based on mutual duties and benefits. Feudalism provided protection at a time when central political authority was weak. Wealthy landlords deeded large tracts of land to vassals who, in return, agreed to provide certain services like military assistance for the landlords. The vassals, in turn, required serfs or peasants to work the land.

Feuerbach, Ludwig (A.D. 1804–1872)—modern German philosopher known for his claim that ideas about God are simply projections generated by human beings, not descriptions of objective reality.

Ficino, Marsilio (A.D. 1433–1499)—Florentine priest, medical doctor, and scholar of Greek who published editions and translations of the works of Plato, Plotinus, and other classical and Christian Greek texts during the Renaissance.

filioque—meaning "and from the Son," the term refers to a phrase which Western Christians centuries later added to the Nicene Creed without the approval of Eastern Christians: "We believe in the Holy Spirit who proceeds from the Father and the Son." Orthodox Christians opposed the addition because they believe that the Father is the sole source of being in the Trinity, and because the Creed was amended without their consent.

fine-tuning—in contemporary discussions of religion and science, the view that the universe has been finely tuned for the emergence and ongoing support of life.

First Vatican Council (A.D. 1869–1870)—the first Catholic ecumenical council since the Council of Trent was convened to rally the Catholic world around Pope Pius IX, when the Papal States were threatened by the formation of the new Kingdom of Italy. The council declared that the pope had a universal primacy of jurisdiction (legal governing authority) and under certain conditions possessed the divine protection of infallibility in teaching on matters of faith and morals.

Five pillars of Islam—the most basic obligations of Islam: profession of faith, prayer, fasting, almsgiving, and pilgrimage to Mecca.

Five Ways, the—Thomas Aquinas' five proofs for the existence of God as presented in his *Summa theologiae.*

Former Prophets—also known as Deuteronomistic History; the biblical books of Joshua, Judges, 1–2 Samuel, and 1–2 Kings, which tell the stories of legendary early prophets like Samuel, Nathan, Elijah, and Elisha.

Foucault, Michel (A.D. 1926–1984)—post-modern French philosopher known as "Nietzsche's truest disciple" for his emphasis on the role of power in making truth claims and his genealogies, which detailed the historical development of concepts of criminality, sanity, and sexuality.

foundationalism—a modern philosophy that holds that all claims for knowledge should rest on indubitable foundations, or beliefs that are either self-evident or evident to the senses. To foundationalists, any claims that do not meet these criteria should be seen as irrational.

Fourth Crusade (A.D. 1204)—Western crusade that was diverted to the capture and sack of Constantinople and imposition of a Latin emperor and a Latin patriarch; it resulted in weakening the Byzantine Empire, and a lasting resentment of Orthodox Christians for Western Christians.

Fourth Lateran Council (A.D. 1215)—urged reform of the clergy and defined the dogma of transubstantiation, concerning the real presence of Christ in the Eucharist.

Franciscans—the community founded by Francis of Assisi, also known as the Friars Minor ("the lesser brothers"). Known for their radical understanding of the vow of poverty, their primary vocation was to preach the gospel and to witness to it in action.

Francis of Assisi (*c.*A.D. 1182–1226)—founder of the Franciscan order of friars.

Francis Xavier (A.D. 1506–1552)—a companion of Ignatius of Loyola, the founder of the Jesuit order, and the leader of the Catholic mission to India, Japan, and China.

Francke, August Hermann (1663–1727)— German Lutheran pastor and professor who established an important Pietist center at the University of Halle.

Freud, Sigmund (A.D. 1856–1939)—founder of psychoanalysis, a branch of psychiatry, known especially for his investigations into the unconscious aspects of the human mind. Freud was a critic of religion, believing that religious ideas (like God) were fictitious projections of child-like wishes. The scientific value of his theories has met severe criticism.

friar—from a Latin word meaning "brother," the term refers to a person who belongs to a mendicant order.

fulfillment, theology of—used to explain how human (non-Christian) customs and beliefs that do not explicitly contradict Christ and Christian belief can be brought to a greater level of perfection through Christ.

Fundamentalist movement—a movement that began in America as a militant reaction to Liberal Protestantism and to developments in modern science and the historical study of the Bible. The name comes from a series of pamphlets called "The Fundamentals" published in 1910–1915 by conservative Protestants, which stressed that there were certain fundamental Christian beliefs that could not be changed or watered down. The term has since been applied to anti-modernist movements in religions other than Christianity.

Galilei, Galileo (A.D. 1564–1642)—astronomer and scientist who attempted to prove the Copernican theory that the earth revolves around the sun. He was disciplined by the church for advocating views that were contrary to the Bible and church teaching.

Gaudium et Spes—"*Joy and Hope*" is the "pastoral" constitution of Vatican II that sought to open up dialogue between the Catholic Church and the modern world by emphasizing what Catholics shared with all human beings of goodwill and by calling Catholics to work in common for human development.

general council—see ecumenical council.

Gentiles—from the Latin *gentilis* meaning having to do with "family" or "nation," and in the Bible referring to all peoples other than Jews.

Global South—countries of Latin America, Africa, and Asia that were often subject to colonial rule by Western powers and that have continued to struggle for economic development since gaining independence in the nineteenth and twentieth centuries. This term has increasingly replaced earlier ones such as "the developing world" or "the Third World."

glossolalia—a Greek term meaning "speaking in tongues," one of the gifts of the Holy Spirit.

Gnosticism—from the Greek word *gnosis*, meaning "knowledge." Gnostics claimed to have access to a special kind of knowledge known to them alone and by which they could be saved. They divided God into a higher and a lower divinity: the higher divinity was perfect and good and was unknown until Jesus came to reveal him; the lower divinity was at best merely just or actually evil and, as the creator of the evil physical universe equated with the God of the Old Testament. Gnostics believed that they belonged to the divine realm and their goal was to return there unharmed by this physical world.

God-fearers—from the Acts of the Apostles: people who were attracted to Judaism but uncertain whether to become fully Jewish (perhaps because of other Jewish requirements, such as circumcision and the dietary restrictions). Biblical scholars believe that some of the early Jesus followers came from among these people.

gospel—meaning "good message" or "good news"; (1) a written account of the life of Jesus Christ; (2) a proclamation of the Christian message.

grace—free, unmerited assistance given to human beings by God for their salvation. It is participation in the life of God.

grace, order of—or the supernatural order, the arrangement of created things and their relationships to God insofar as they are elevated beyond their innate characteristics and possibilities to a greater likeness to or closer intimacy with God.

Great Awakening—a great religious renewal that swept the American colonies in the 1740s. Marked by powerful preaching and intense emotional experiences, the movement sought to awaken people whose faith was spiritually dead or who had no faith at all.

Great Schism—this may refer to two different events: (1) the severing of relationships in A.D. 1054 between the pope and the patriarch of Constantinople; and (2) the split *within* the Roman Catholic Church from A.D. 1378 to 1417, when European Catholicism was evenly divided between the competing claims of two different popes (and from 1409 to 1414 of a third pope). The schism of 1054 has never been healed. The split within the papacy was resolved by the Council of Constance (1414–1418).

Gregorian chant—a repertoire of music consisting of chants used in the city of Rome together with the native chants of the Frankish churches, mandated by Charlemagne to be used as church music throughout the empire.

Gregorian Reform—The eleventh-century papal and monastic movement to free the church (now equated especially with the clergy) from control of laypeople. It targeted simony, concubinae, and lay investiture. Named for Pope Gregory VII, though it preceded his pontificate.

Gregory I (r. A.D. 590–604)—also known as "Gregory the Great." Statesman, theologian, and prodigious writer, his wise and pastoral leadership made him a model for subsequent popes. Among his accomplishments was his decision to sponsor a mission to convert the Anglo-Saxons in England.

Gregory VII (r. A.D. 1073–1085)—a reform pope, he attacked abuses such as simony, alienation of property, and lay investiture. He also declared the pope to be the supreme judge under God, holding the absolute powers of absolution and excommunication.

Gregory of Nazianzus (c.A.D. 330–390)—one of the Cappadocian fathers; a bishop and theologian who helped define Trinitarian doctrine and joined Greek rhetoric and philosophy with faith; for his achievement, simply "the Theologian" among Eastern Orthodox Christians.

Gregory of Nyssa (c.335–after 394)—youngest of the Cappadocian fathers and a brother of Basil the Great; though married, also a bishop of Nyssa; author of influential treatises on asceticism, exegesis, and theology.

Gregory Palamas (A.D. 1296–1359)—an Orthodox Christian monk of Mount Athos in Greece whose work, *The Triads*, defended the hesychast spirituality and used the distinction between God's essence and God's energies to explain how people participate through grace in a union of love with the divine.

Guadalupe, Our Lady of—see *Our Lady of Guadalupe*.

Gutiérrez, Gustavo (b. 1928)—a Peruvian parish priest and theologian, Gutiérrez became a leading spokesperson for liberation theology in the early 1970s with the publication of *A Theology of Liberation: History, Politics and Salvation.*

hadith—reports concerning the sayings and deeds of Muhammad, six major collections of which were compiled during the first 300 years of Islamic history. Their status and authority is second only to the Qur'an.

Hagia Sophia—the great "Church of Holy Wisdom" in Constantinople, where the patriarch of Constantinople held services and the Byzantine emperors were crowned, until A.D. 1453, when the city of Constantinople was conquered by the Muslims and the church became a mosque.

hajj—pilgrimage to Mecca. The fifth pillar of Islam is the obligation for Muslims, whose resources and personal circumstances allow, to perform pilgrimage to Mecca.

Hanukkah—the Jewish holiday celebrating the rededication of the Jerusalem Temple following the victory over Antiochus IV in the Maccabean Revolt (167–164 B.C.E).

Harnack, Adolf von (A.D. 1851–1930)—Liberal Protestant German theologian and historian who claimed that traditional church teachings concerning Jesus Christ and the Trinity are late developments under the influence of Greek philosophy that deviated from the view of the original church.

Hearers—the name given to the members of the Manichees who did not have leadership roles. Augustine was a Hearer for a time prior to his conversion to Christianity.

Hebrews—referring to the ethnic group to which Abraham belonged, the term is sometimes used interchangeably with the terms *Israelites* and *Jews.*

Hegel, G.W.F. (A.D. 1770–1832)—highly influential modern German philosopher known for his creative rethinking of the relationship between God and the world, and also for Hegelian Dialectic, according to which thesis and antithesis are resolved in synthesis.

heliocentrism—the "sun-centered" system of sun and planets, first proposed by Nicolaus Copernicus in 1543 and popularized and partially verified by Galileo; it replaced the older, geocentric (earth-centered) model attributed to the second-century B.C.E. mathematician and astronomer Ptolemy.

hellenization—in the wake of the conquests of Alexander the Great, the spread of Greek language, cultural ideals, and political institutions throughout the ancient Near East.

Henry VIII (A.D. 1491–1547)—the king of England who led his country through the Reformation. At first a supporter of Catholicism against the reformers, Henry eventually broke with the pope and the Catholic Church and established the Church of England with himself at its head, at least in part in a dispute with Rome over Henry's desire to divorce his wife.

Herder, Johann Gottfried (A.D. 1744–1803)—modern German historian often credited with giving the historical-critical method important tools. Herder held that the words of the Bible did not come directly from God, and he emphasized that human cultures played an important role in forming the biblical text.

heresy—false teaching, or teaching that goes against orthodoxy (correct teaching) in the eyes of the church.

hermeneutical circle—a concept used to summarize the methodology of liberation theology, which insists that Christian theology should be rooted in the concrete historical situations of engagement with the poor and their struggles for justice. Such questions can lead to fresh insight into the gospel, which in turn require action and fresh engagement in the struggles of the poor, thus continuing the circle. See also *praxis*.

hermeneutics—principles of interpretation, especially of the Bible and other literary texts. By extension, the term sometimes applies to the interpretation of social reality.

hermeneutics of suspicion—process of interpretation that recognizes the influence of the oppressive cultures in which a text was written and interpreted.

hesychia—meaning "inner stillness" or "silence of the heart," the term is used by Eastern Orthodox Christians to describe this state of deep meditation.

Hick, John (A.D. 1922–2012)—modern philosopher and theologian known for his pluralistic views, according to which the different religions of the world can all lead to the same God.

hijra—an Arabic term meaning "migration," referring to the migration in 622 C.E. of Muhammad and the early Muslim community of Mecca to the city of Yathrib, which became known as Medina. This *hijra* marks the beginning of the Islamic "*hijri*" calendar.

historical criticism—(1) a development of the Renaissance movement, the use of historical knowledge to evaluate ancient writings, as well as existing traditions and institutions; (2) a modern approach to the study of the Bible, whereby the Bible is subjected to scientific scrutiny and the critic attempts to discover the historical circumstances of the biblical text and the intended meaning of its author.

historical theology—a study of the development of the Christian faith in the various periods of history after the biblical era.

Holiness movement—a family of Protestant churches who seek perfection in the world by developing a lifestyle of personal holiness and following a rigid code of behavior. It includes the Free Methodist Church, the Church of God, the Holiness Christian Church, and the Church of the Nazarene.

Holy of Holies—the innermost part of the Temple in Jerusalem, where God's presence is believed to have dwelled. Entrance was restricted to once per year by the high priest.

Holy Roman Empire—The recreation of the Roman Empire in the West by the papacy, when the Frankish king Charlemagne was crowned "emperor of the Romans" in Rome on Christmas Day, A.D. 800.

homoousios—meaning "same-in-substance," this term was used in the Nicene Creed to affirm that the Son shared the same divine substance as the Father, in opposition to the heresy of Arius.

Hosea—an eighth-century B.C.E. prophet of Israel who used the imagery of marital infidelity to characterize Israel's relationship with Yahweh.

humanism—in general, a mentality or outlook which puts supreme value on human beings. There are both secular humanisms, which can be hostile or indifferent to religion, and religious humanisms, which are grounded in faith. "Renaissance humanism" was a fifteenth- and sixteenth-century cultural movement to recover Latin and Greek standards of literature, history, oratory, beauty, and ethics, and an educational program shaped around them.

Hus, Jan (A.D. 1372–1415)—a reformer of the late medieval period. Like his contemporary, John Wycliffe, he preached against abuses in the church and challenged some of the church's doctrines. He was eventually executed as a heretic.

icon—a painted image of Christ, his mother, angels, or saints (tempera on wood). This religious art form is usually associated with Eastern Christianity.

iconoclasm—meaning "image breaking." Hostility to images derives from the biblical condemnation of idolatry (Exodus 20:4–5). Two major iconoclastic episodes: (1) the efforts of Eastern Orthodox opponents of images to abolish devotion to icons thrust the Byzantine Empire into intermittent turmoil from *c.*725 to 843; (2) during the Protestant Reformation, some reformers forcibly entered churches and removed or destroyed statues, stained glass, and paintings containing images.

iconoclast—one who is opposed to the veneration of icons.

iconodule—one who supports the veneration of icons.

iconostasis—meaning "icon screen," a wall bearing icons arranged in a prescribed order, which divides sanctuary from nave in Orthodox Christian churches.

Ignatius of Loyola (A.D. 1491/95–1556)—founder of the Society of Jesus, also known as the Jesuits. A Spaniard, Ignatius was trained as a knight, but he took up a life dedicated to the church after reading devotional books, including a life of Christ and lives of the saints, during a long convalescence.

imam—a leader of an Islamic community; an Islamic scholar; in Shi'ism, the *imam* is the successor and direct descendant of Muhammad or 'Ali, a number suspended at 12 for "Twelver" Shi'ism.

imperial cult—in the Roman world, a partly political and partly religious ceremony in honor of the emperor who was recognized as a superhuman or divine figure.

Incarnation—meaning "enfleshment"; the Christian doctrine that asserts that God became human, specifically, that the divinity called "the Word" (or *Logos* or the Son) became human, or took on flesh, in the person of Jesus of Nazareth.

inclusivism—an attitude or disposition of inclusion; in theologies of world religions, the

belief that Christ fulfills the longings and aspirations of other religions and that the good qualities in those religions are included within the scope of Christianity.

inculturation—a term used to describe the process by which a religion "learns" to live and act within a culture different from the one in which it began, and which leads to reciprocal influence between religion and culture. In Christian theology and missionary strategy, inculturation is sometimes spoken of as an imperative, in order for the Christian message to be accessible to people of every culture, and embodied in culturally authentic ways by the Christian communities made up by those who respond to that message. See also *syncretism*.

indigenization—the church policy that the native people of a country in which missionary work is being done should eventually take charge of the church in that country.

indulgences—a practice popular in the medieval church in which the church would cancel all or part of the penance (punishment) due to an individual who had sinned, when the individual had completed certain devotions, acts of charity, or services for the church, as substitutes.

inerrancy—the belief that the Bible is "without error." For faith communities who accept the verbal inspiration of the Bible, this means that the Bible is completely accurate in all respects and contains no mistakes whatsoever. For other faith traditions, it means that the Bible is a trustworthy guide to salvation.

infancy narratives—stories about the birth and early childhood of an important personality. The Gospels of Matthew and Luke contain infancy narratives concerning Jesus.

Innocent III (r. A.D. 1198–1216)—pope of the Roman Catholic Church, perhaps best known for his political involvements. The Fourth Lateran Council took place during his reign.

inquisition—a legal body set up to investigate and punish heretics. Although the inquisition itself was usually under the jurisdiction of church officials, civil leaders were often called upon to execute whatever punishments were assigned.

inspiration—in Christian theology, the belief that the Bible was written under the influence of the Holy Spirit and that it contains the Word of God. Christian churches have differing understandings about how inspiration took place.

inspiration, verbal—the theory that God (or the Holy Spirit) directed the biblical authors to write what is contained in the Bible without any input from the human author.

Institutes of the Christian Religion—John Calvin's major work which was first published in 1536 and revised throughout his life until the definitive editions in Latin (1559) and French (1560). It was intended to provide clear instruction in the Christian faith and inspire devotion and piety.

instrumental value—the worth of a thing due to its usefulness to human beings.

Inter caetera—in 1493, Pope Alexander VI's bull *Inter caetera* ("Among other [works]") established a dividing line in the Atlantic, from the North Pole to the South Pole, that granted Portugal ownership of newly discovered lands to the east of the line and to Spain lands to the west of it.

interdict—a kind of "strike" in which the church shuts down the sacramental system (Eucharist, Baptism, Penance, etc.). It was used in the medieval period by popes who wished to discipline civil leaders (kings, princes, etc.).

intersectionality—the interaction of multiple systems of oppression or discrimination based on gender, race, class, sexual orientation, etc.

intrinsic value—the goodness and worth of a person or thing in and of itself, even if it is not important or useful to human beings.

Irenaeus of Lyons—a late second-century bishop of the church at Lyons, he wrote *Against Heresies*, primarily in response to Gnosticism.

Iron Age—the age that followed the Bronze Age. Iron was harder and more durable than bronze, but more difficult to work. The Philistines' advanced use of iron gave them an advantage over Israelites.

Isaac—son of Abraham (by his wife Sarah) and patriarch of the Israelite people, with whom the covenant with the Israelites is continued and through whom the promises to Abraham are fulfilled.

Isaiah—an eighth-century B.C.E. prophet, who reassured the people of Judah that a Davidic king and possession of the Temple would protect them from harm.

Isaiah, Second—see *Second Isaiah*.

Ishmael—son of Abraham by his wife's maid Hagar, who was sent away into the desert but rescued by God; claimed by the Muslim tradition as the son of Abraham whom Abraham was asked to sacrifice.

Islam—meaning "submission" to the one God. One of the three major religions that trace their roots back to Abraham. A person who practices Islam is called a Muslim, that is, one who has submitted to God.

Israel—(1) the Israelite people, so named after their common ancestor Jacob, who was renamed Israel by God; (2) the country in which the Israelites dwelled; (3) the name of the Northern Kingdom of the Israelites, from 922 B.C.E. until it was conquered by the Assyrians in 721 B.C.E.; (4) the modern Jewish state, founded in 1948.

Israelite—the people who claimed Jacob, also known as Israel, as their ancestor. The term is sometimes used interchangeably with the terms Hebrew and Jew.

Istanbul—see *Constantinople*.

Jacob—son of Isaac and patriarch of the Israelite people, renamed "Israel" by God. Jacob migrated from Canaan to Egypt with his 12 sons.

jahiliyya—The pre-Islamic period in Arabian history, referred to as the age of "ignorance," which is the literal meaning of the term.

Jehovah's Witnesses—an American Christian church that has its origins in the International Bible Students Association founded by Charles Taze Russell (1852–1916). The church is intensely focused on eschatology and on the immanent return of Christ in the end time.

Jeremiah—a sixth-century B.C.E. prophet who warned the people of Judah of their coming destruction by the Babylonians and counseled them to rely on faith and justice rather than on their possession of the Temple and a Davidic king.

Jerusalem—the capital of united Israel. It was founded by David, who conquered and subjugated its previous inhabitants. Solomon, David's son and heir, built a grand temple in Jerusalem. The Babylonians destroyed the city in 587 B.C.E.

Jerusalem Conference—a meeting of Christian leaders held in Jerusalem in 49 or 50 C.E. According to the Acts of the Apostles, it was attended by Paul and Barnabas and the leaders of the Jerusalem church, and its purpose was to determine whether Gentile converts to Christianity needed to follow all of the requirements of Judaism.

Jesuits—see *Society of Jesus*.

Jesus Prayer—a brief meditation prayer, usually "Lord Jesus Christ, Son of the living God, have mercy on me, a sinner," which a person repeats again and again in order to enter into a state of deep meditation or stillness.

Jew—the term originated with the return of the people of Judah from the Babylonian Exile in the latter part of the sixth century B.C.E. It is sometimes used interchangeably with the term Israelite.

jihad—considered by some Muslims to be a sixth pillar of the faith, it involves inner striving to purify oneself of the forces of evil and to follow the way of Allah. A *jihad* might also consist of corporate attempts to purify the Islamic community of anti-Islamic features or warfare to defend Islamic land or spread Islamic territorial jurisdiction.

John Cassian (A.D. 360–435)—known as the "father of Western monasticism," he sought to establish a standardized form of monasticism for the Western Roman Empire based upon the ideals of Eastern monasticism.

John of the Cross (A.D. 1542–1591)—a follower of Teresa of Avila, the cofounder of the Discalced Carmelites, a reform branch of the Carmelite order, and a Spanish mystic. His writings include the *Ascent of Mount Carmel* and the *Dark Night of the Soul.*

John of Damascus (d. A.D. 749)—Arab Christian monk and theologian notable for his formative contributions to Eastern Orthodox theology and his Christian theological interpretation of Muslims as heretics.

Joint Declaration on the Doctrine of Justification—document issued by the Catholic Church's Pontifical Council for Promoting Christian Unity and the Lutheran World Federation in 1999; it affirmed a common understanding of justification while acknowledging they had not resolved everything that either church teaches about this doctrine.

Joseph—favorite son of Jacob and founder of one of the 12 tribes of Israel, he was sold into slavery in Egypt but eventually ascended to become a high government official.

Joshua—the successor to Moses, who led the Israelites into the promised land of Canaan and conquered the peoples who dwelled there.

Judah—the name of the Southern Kingdom of the Israelites, from 922 B.C.E. until it was conquered by the Babylonians in 597 B.C.E.

judge (Hebrew *shofet*)—in ancient Israel, a military and political leader who was chosen by God to rescue the Israelites from oppression brought about by their sin.

Julian of Norwich (*c.*A.D. 1342–after 1417)—an English mystic of the Late Middle Ages; author of *Showings*, which includes a series of visions she received during a brief illness and her theological reflections on those mystical experiences. She also reflects on the motherhood of Christ, the meaning of sin, and the question of why God allows sin and evil to exist.

justification—(1) generally, making straight that which is crooked or ragged; (2) in theology, being set in right relationship with God. Justification is closely related to the notion of sin as a severing of humanity's relationship with God.

justification by faith—the belief that humans cannot achieve right relationship with God through their own actions but that humanity is justified by God as a free gift to those who trust in Jesus Christ.

justification by works—the belief that right relationship with God can be achieved by avoiding sin and atoning for any transgressions with good deeds. In Paul's writings, the phrase is shorthand for *justification through observance of works of the Law.*

Justinian (A.D. 527–565)—the Byzantine emperor best known for compiling the *Codex Juris Civilis* (Code of Civil Law) and for rebuilding the great Church of Holy Wisdom (or Hagia Sophia) in Constantinople.

Ka'ba—a pilgrimage site located at Mecca. Muslims are encouraged to make a pilgrimage or *hajj* to the *Ka'ba* once during their lifetime (health and finances permitting) to commemorate the key events from the founding era of Islam and from the time of Abraham.

Kairos Document—an 11,000 word, five-chapter theological statement issued in 1985 that was signed by more than 150 church leaders and theologians in South Africa criticizing the silence of the churches in the face of apartheid and challenging the churches to engage in the struggle against apartheid.

Kant, Immanuel (A.D. 1724–1804)—modern philosopher known for insisting that human beings should rely on themselves for knowledge, and not external authorities. In epistemology, Kant effected the "turn to the subject" (or the human being), according to which all knowledge is conditioned by the structures of the human mind.

Khadija bint Khuwaylid—A wealthy merchant who was the Prophet Muhammad's first wife, to whom he was married monogamously for

25 years until her death. She was the mother of Fatima, who married 'Ali ibn Abi Talib.

Kierkegaard, Søren (A.D. 1813–1855)—modern Danish philosopher and religious thinker known as both the father of existentialism and a prophet of post-modernity. Kierkegaard insisted on authenticity in the Christian life and on committing to Christianity in spite of uncertainty.

King, Martin Luther, Jr. (A.D. 1929–1968)—leader of the Civil Rights Movement and American Baptist minister. He was awarded the Nobel Peace Prize in 1964 for his leadership of nonviolent resistance movements protesting racial inequality in the United States.

Kingdom of God—the reign of God, which is manifested in the coming of Jesus Christ, in the Spirit's continued presence in the world, and in the conviction that God will triumph over the forces of evil.

kosher—in Judaism, the special dietary restrictions required by the Torah, whereby certain foods are prohibited (e.g., pork) and other foods must be prepared according to certain guidelines.

language game—associated with the philosophy of Ludwig Wittgenstein, the idea that language only has meaning within a game of sorts that determines the possibilities for its use.

Latter-Day Saints—the Church of Jesus Christ of Latter-Day Saints, more commonly called the Mormon church; founded by Joseph Smith in 1830 in New York, on the basis of a written revelation called the Book of Mormon, and claiming to be the restoration in America of the true church of Jesus Christ.

Latter Prophets—comprised of the Major Prophets (Isaiah, Jeremiah, and Ezekiel) and the Minor Prophets (Hosea, Joel, Amos, Obadiah, Johan, Micah, Nahum, Habakkuk, Zephaniah, Haggai, Zechariah, and Malachi), also called The Book of the Twelve.

Laudato Si'—Encyclical by Pope Francis promulgated in 2015 and addressed to all people, on the topic of care for creation and just, sustainable economic development.

Law, the—(1) the first five books of the Hebrew Bible, also known as the Pentateuch or Torah; (2) the first major grouping of books in the Hebrew Bible or Old Testament, the other groupings being the Prophets and the Writings; (3) the Israelites' obligation to the Mosaic covenant.

lay investiture—during the early medieval period, secular rulers (emperors, kings, and nobility) took upon themselves the right to appoint bishops, abbots, and other church officials; the right of appointment was expressed ritually in the ceremony in which the secular ruler "invested" the official with the spiritual symbols of his office.

legalism—rigid adherence to the letter of the law, without allowing for exceptions or special circumstances.

Lent—a period of 40 weekdays in which Christians fast and do penance in anticipation of the feast of Easter, commemorating the resurrection of Jesus Christ.

Leo I (r. 440–461)—eventually recognized as Leo the Great, Pope Leo shaped understanding of the pope as a successor of Peter, promoted papal primacy in the West, and contributed to defining the dogma of the Incarnation at the Council of Chalcedon.

Lessing, G.E. (A.D. 1729–1781)—modern German philosopher known for "Lessing's ditch," which claimed that the contingent events of history could not serve as a foundation for claims about the eternal truths of God.

Locke, John (A.D. 1632–1704)—modern English philosopher and religious thinker known for his claim that Christianity, when its objectionable components are eliminated, can be understood as a reasonable religion.

Logos—a Greek word meaning "word" or "reason." John's Gospel uses this term to describe Jesus as the revelation of God.

Lollards—a group of anticlerical reformers in the Late Middle Ages who attempted to put into practice the ideals of John Wycliffe. They were active in several social uprisings, and as a result many were put to death for their heretical ideas and their radical political actions.

Lombard, Peter (*c.*A.D. 1095–1160)—author of the *Four Books of Sentences*, which gathered together statements from scripture and the Church Fathers according to various theological topics and sought to reconcile them. Lombard's *Sentences* became a standard text in medieval Scholasticism.

de Lugo, Juan (A.D. 1583–1660)—Roman Catholic theologian who pioneered interreligious dialogue by suggesting that some non-Christians could be saved.

Lumen gentium—Vatican II's dogmatic constitution on the Church, which recognized the Church as the People of God, in an effort to do justice to the integral role of the laity in the Church; also recognized the collegiality of the bishops.

lynching—the name for the history of public torture and execution of black people at the hands of white people in the United States, in the decades following the emancipation of slaves. Between 1877 and 1950, nearly 4,000 African-American men and women were victims of lynching across the North and the South of the United States.

Maccabees—the family who led the revolt by the Jews against Antiochus IV in the second century B.C.E.

madrasa—literally, "a place of study." A traditional Muslim school of advanced study of the Qur'an and other subjects.

magisterium—the teaching office of the Roman Catholic Church, made up of the pope and the bishops.

Maimonides, Moses (A.D. 1135–1204)—medieval Jewish scholar; author of the *Guide of the Perplexed*, in which he synthesized rabbinic Judaism and the Muslim form of Aristotelian philosophy. He also wrote some influential works on medicine and Jewish Law.

Malcolm X (d. A.D. 1965)—African-American Muslim civil rights activist assassinated in New York City.

Manicheism—a strongly dualistic religion deriving its name from Mani, a third-century A.D. prophet and visionary. Like the Gnostics before them, they believed in a dualism of evil matter and good spirit, a kingdom of Darkness and a Kingdom of Light, in perpetual conflict. They taught that people could liberate spirit from matter through the strict practice of asceticism.

Manifest Destiny—a term used to describe the Pilgrims' belief that their call to come to the New World was a divinely granted second chance for the human race, and that God was making a new covenant with them.

Marburg Colloquy—a meeting organized by Philip of Hesse in 1529 to unite the Swiss and German reformers in a military alliance against the Holy Roman Empire. This required coming to an agreement on articles of faith and led to a debate between Martin Luther and Ulrich Zwingli on the meaning of the Eucharist. Although the reformers eventually agreed on 14 of 15 articles of faith, they were unable to come to a consensus on the Eucharist.

martyr—from the Greek term meaning "witness," someone who, under persecution, dies rather than give up his or her faith.

Marx, Karl (A.D. 1818–1883)—modern German philosopher and economist, who advocated the socialist economic system, and on whose ideas Communism is built. Marx was an outspoken critic of religion, calling it the "opium of the people," since he believed that it was like a drug which kept the lower classes passive and resigned in their economic oppression.

materialism—a philosophy that views only matter as real, and which regards any seemingly immaterial or "spiritual" realities (e.g., mind) as in fact products of matter.

Mecca—one of the most holy cities in Islam. It is the location of the *Ka'ba* or pilgrimage site where Muslims go to commemorate the key events from the founding era of Islam and from the time of Abraham. It is also revered as the birthplace of Muhammad and, according to Muslim tradition, the site of Ishmael's rescue.

Medina—the city in which Muhammad founded the first Islamic community in A.D. 622.

memoria—a type of church building built to honor the tomb of a saint or martyr, or a holy site. *Memoriae* had a centered design, focusing attention on the place of honor.

mendicants—from a Latin word for "begging," a type of religious order that emerged in High Middle Ages. Unlike monks, mendicants lived in towns and cities, begged for their livelihood, and performed whatever ministry needed to be done.

merit, treasury of—see *treasury of merit*.

messiah—meaning "anointed one"; a term used in Judaism and Christianity for the one "anointed" by God to rescue or save God's people.

Messianic Secret—a term used to describe the apparent commands to silence concerning the identity of Jesus contained in the Gospel of Mark.

method of correlation—pioneered by modern German theologian Paul Tillich, an approach to theology that seeks to correlate the Christian message to contemporary persons in an effort at demonstrating the relevance of Christianity in the contemporary world.

Methodism/Methodist Church—an independent Protestant church founded by John Wesley, which began as a reform movement within the Church of England. It differed from the Church of England in its greater emphasis on personal spirituality, Bible study, evangelistic preaching, and lively services.

methodological naturalism—see naturalism.

midrash—Refers to a wide variety of Jewish biblical interpretations, especially in the premodern period. It comes from the Hebrew verb meaning "seek," as in seeking the meaning of the text.

Modernism—an early twentieth-century reform movement in the Roman Catholic church that challenged the Neo-Scholastic approach to theology on a broad range of theological issues from the use of historical-critical methods in the study of scripture and church history, emphasizing the corporate and sacramental nature of the church to the role of the laity in church governance.

monasticism—from the Greek word *monos*, meaning "one," "unique," "solitary," or "alone." A rule and way of life for Christian men or women dedicated to holiness by separating from existing society, either by withdrawing into unpopulated areas or by living within a cloister (walled enclosure).

Monica—mother of Augustine of Hippo (A.D. 354–430). Augustine writes about her in his *Confessions*.

monk—from the Greek word *monachos*, meaning a single or a solitary person, the word monk was coined in the fourth century A.D. as a name for Christians who had begun to withdraw to secluded desert regions to lead lives of prayer and spiritual discipline. Later it would come to refer to any person who abandoned life in the everyday world to devote themselves completely to their religion.

monophysite—from the Greek words for "of one nature"; one who holds that Jesus did not have two natures—one human and one divine—but only one. Eutyches, for example, believed that the humanity of Christ had been absorbed into his single divine nature. Dissenters against the "two-natures" definition of the Council of Chalcedon went into schism as separate Christian churches in Armenia, Syria, Egypt, and Ethiopia; though unfairly stigmatized as "monophysite," they held and still hold that Jesus Christ was fully human, while rejecting Chalcedon's two-natures terminology.

Monotheism/monotheistic—belief in only one God.

moral theology—a study of the values arising from Christian beliefs and the behaviors that are congruent or incongruent with these values.

Moravians—members of the Moravian Church or *Unitas Fratrum* (Unity of Brethren) who began as followers of John Hus in the fifteenth century. The church was renewed under the patronage of the Pietist Count von Zinzendorf in the eighteenth century.

Mormons—see *Church of Jesus Christ of Latter-Day Saints*.

mortal sin—sin that is committed willfully and deliberately and with the understanding that it is serious wrongdoing which separates the soul from God.

Moses—the greatest prophet of Israel, who led the Israelites out of slavery in Egypt and into the promised land of Canaan, and who received from God on Mount Sinai the Law on which the Israelite covenant with God is based.

mosque—Arabic term meaning "place of prostration" or "place of prayer." Ordinarily, mosques have an open space where the daily prayer is performed. On one wall is a niche that indicates the direction of Mecca. It also contains a pulpit with a staircase from which the *imam* (the leader of prayer) presents the sermon at Friday noon prayers.

Muhammad (A.D. 570–632)—the first leader and greatest prophet of Islam. According to Muslim tradition, the one god Allah sent the angel Gabriel to deliver messages to Muhammad to be recited aloud as guidance to the followers. The revelations were later collected and recorded in the Islamic scriptures known as the Qur'an.

Muslims—followers of the Islamic faith.

mystery religions—in the Greek and Roman religious world, secret cults that conducted ritual initiations into the mysteries of a particular god or goddess. Their celebrations usually involved purification rituals and sacred meals.

mysticism—a spiritual phenomenon that expresses itself in direct, intense experiences of union and oneness with God. Generally, the mystical journey consists of three phases: purgation (cleansing from sin); illumination (an attraction to all the things of God); and union (the state of oneness with God).

myth—a story that articulates, in symbolic words and images, a people's most profound sense of themselves and their world, their destiny, and their relationship to the deity.

myth of Anglo-Saxon superiority—the racist myth propagated by Anglo-Saxons on the basis of theology, philosophy, and science primarily serving to justify their inherent superiority over all people in the world and their enslavement of African people.

Nathan—King David's court prophet. Nathan confronted David when he murdered Bathsheba's husband to cover up a pregnancy.

naturalism—a view that regards only nature as real. According to naturalists, there are no supernatural causes. The natural realm alone accounts for everything that exists. Closely allied with materialism.

natural selection—a principle of the theory of evolution, which holds that individuals in a species who have characteristics that are advantageous for survival in their environment will survive, while individuals without these characteristics will perish. Gradually, this transformation of the character of individuals in a species will lead to the development of new species.

nature, order of—or the "natural order," the arrangement of created things and their relationships to God according to their innate characteristics and possibilities, as opposed to the order of grace.

negative theological language—language that asserts not what God is, but rather what God is not, in contrast to positive or affirmative theological language.

Neo-Pentecostalism—following upon classical Pentecostalism and then the Charismatic Movement, this third wave of Pentecostalism continues to emphasize God's power to do miraculous healing, deliver people from demonic forces at work in the world, and bring them prosperity, through their ministries in large, well-organized "megachurches" that offer high-tech worship experiences. See *Charismatic Movement; Pentecostalism; Prosperity Doctrine.*

Neo-Scholasticism—a renewal of Catholic theology that took place between the First Vatican Council and the Second Vatican Council. It involved an endorsement of Thomas Aquinas' philosophy and theology—and the Scholasticism that attended his writings—as the way in which Catholic theologians should engage the modern world.

Neo-Thomism—also sometimes called Neo-Scholasticism, the revival of Thomism spanning primarily from the nineteenth century until the Second Vatican Council, Neo-Thomism sought to counter modern Western philosophy.

nepotism—the practice of allowing dispensations from church law for the advancement of one's relatives.

Nestorian—one who accepts the Christology promoted by Nestorius, who held that Jesus had two separate natures (one the perfect man without sin who is son of Mary in the flesh, the other the divine word of God or *Logos* settled within him); a term sometimes applied to the Ancient Assyrian Church of the East.

Nestorius (*c.*A.D. 386–451)—a fifth-century A.D. patriarch of Constantinople, who taught that it was inappropriate to call Mary the Mother of God, on the grounds that God could not be said to have been born; at best, she was only the Mother of Christ, the man. His views were condemned at the Council of Ephesus in 431, on the grounds that he divided Christ into two separate persons.

Newman, John Henry (A.D. 1801–1890)—one of the leaders of the Oxford Movement, which fostered a revival of the Catholic elements of English (Anglican) Christianity. He later converted to Roman Catholicism and eventually was named a cardinal. Known especially for his work on the historical development of Christian doctrine.

Newton, Isaac (A.D. 1642–1727)—mathematician and scientist who was able to explain the motion of the planets by means of natural laws (e.g., the law of gravity) rather than the will of God, and hence was a major contributor in the development of the "mechanistic" view of the universe.

Nicaea—see *Council of Nicaea.*

Nicene Creed—adopted at the Council of Nicaea in 325 to assert that the Son of God was of the same divine substance as the Father; recited today in the expanded form adopted at the Council of Constantinople in 381.

Nietzsche, Friedrich (A.D. 1844–1900)—modern German philosopher known for his relentless critiques of Christianity and for heralding the beginning of post-modern thought.

nihilism—the belief that there is no objective basis for truth and that human values are worthless.

nominalism—a late medieval philosophical movement that addresses issues of human knowledge. It argues that knowledge can be derived only from the experience of individual things. Universals such as "humanity" or "truth" do not really exist.

nonconformity—the belief of that conformity (or obedience) to Christ means nonconformity (or disobedience) to what the New Testament writers call "the world."

"nones"—term coined for those who do not identify with any religion; the religiously unaffiliated; those who rarely or never attend religious services.

Nostra Aetate—"*In our age*" is Vatican II's Declaration on non-Christian Religions; it stresses that the church accepts everything in other religions that is good and holy; most importantly, it rejected the doctrine that the Jews have inherited guilt for the death of Jesus, thus taking a great first step toward rolling back Christian anti-semitism.

omnipotent—all-powerful.

omniscient—all-knowing.

ontological, ontology—having to do with being, the study of being.

option for the poor—see "preferential option for the poor."

oracles—pronouncements that come from God and are delivered through the voice of prophets.

oratory—a society of Roman Catholic priests who live in community but do not take vows.

Order of Preachers—an order of beggar friars founded by Dominic Guzman, also called the "Dominicans." Known for their radical understanding of the vow of poverty, their primary vocation was to preach and hear confessions.

Orientalism—refers to the European project of studying the languages, literature, cultures, and art of the "Orient," which encompassed many Muslim peoples; Edward Said's book *Orientalism* treated the term as an ideological construct for Western control and domination of "the Orient."

Origen of Alexandria (*c.*A.D. 185–*c.*253)—leading early Christian theologian who left a lasting impact on Christian theology, spirituality, and exegesis, despite posthumous condemnations for heresy in 543 and 553. Important works include *Against Celsus*, the most significant Greek Christian response to pagan critiques of Christianity, and *On First Principles*, an exposition of Christian doctrine that went beyond defined apostolic tradition.

original sin—the idea that human nature is wounded and deprived of original holiness and right relationship with God because of the sin of Adam and Eve. As a result of original sin, human nature is subject to suffering and has an inclination to sin. Western Christianity traditionally holds that all human beings also inherit the guilt as well as the consequences of the sin of Adam and Eve.

Orthodox—as a proper adjective, it is claimed as a name for Eastern Christian churches that are in communion with the Patriarch of Constantinople, and also by Eastern Christian churches that do not accept the Council of Chalcedon and are therefore not in communion with Constantinople.

orthodoxy—meaning "right teaching" or "right opinion." The term is often used to describe doctrine or teaching that is declared by the church (or any religious authority) to be correct and binding for believers; it is contrasted with heresy.

Our Lady of Guadalupe—(1) title given to Mary, the mother of Jesus, based on her miraculous appearance to Juan Diego at Tepeyac, Mexico in A.D. 1531; (2) a painted image of the appearance of Mary to Juan Diego.

Oxford Movement—a nineteenth-century group of teachers in Oxford who argued for continuity between the Roman Catholic Church and the Church of England. John Henry Newman was one of its leaders.

Pachomius—a Egyptian monk instrumental in the evolution of cenobitic monasticism.

pagan—a term used (especially in Roman times) to describe those persons who are neither Christians nor Jews.

Pan Africanist Congress (PAC)—the "Africanist" political party that broke off from the ANC (African National Congress) in 1959 and was founded by Robert Sobukwe, among others, that advocated for an African government established for Africans by Africans.

Pannenberg, Wolfhart (A.D. 1928–2014)—modern Protestant German theologian known for both using and criticizing modern historical tools in his defense of the historicity of the resurrection of Christ.

papacy—referring to the office of the bishop of Rome as head of the entire Catholic Church.

papal bull—a formal document issued by the pope, from the container (Latin *bulla*) in which the document was held.

papal infallibility—the Roman Catholic dogma defined at the First Vatican Council in 1870 that holds the pope is protected from error when he teaches on matters of faith and morals, and says that he is doing so.

papal primacy—referring to the pope's status as first among the other bishops. In Roman Catholic teaching, as defined at the First Vatican Council, the pope's primacy gives him jurisdiction (legal authority) over the universal church. In Eastern Orthodox teaching his primacy is only honorary and not jurisdictional.

parousia—meaning "coming" or "presence"; the term is used of the second coming of Christ at the end time.

passion narrative—a term used to describe the gospel stories of the arrest, trial, crucifixion, and death of Jesus.

passive or alien righteousness—Martin Luther (A.D. 1483–1546) used this phrase to explain that God is the one who justifies people. Salvation does not depend on a person's own goodness or righteousness, but on God's righteousness, which is imputed or credited to believers because of the merits of Christ's atoning death.

Passover—the Jewish holiday that celebrates the event when God rescued the Israelites from captivity in Egypt by killing the firstborn sons of the Egyptians but "passing over" the houses of the Israelites (c.1250 B.C.E.).

past-eternal—in contemporary cosmology, the view that the universe does not have a beginning, and that it has always existed.

pastoral theology—education and formation for people who minister to communities of faith through activities like preaching, teaching, spiritual direction, and counseling and advocacy for persons in need.

patriarch—(1) in the Pentateuch, the Patriarchs are the fathers of the people of Israel, normally identified as Abraham, Isaac, Jacob, and Jacob's 12 sons; some scholars also refer to the "Matriarchs" of the Pentateuch, the wives and mothers of the Patriarchs; (2) in Christian ecclesiastical terminology, an honorific term given by the fourth and fifth centuries to the bishops of Rome, Constantinople, Alexandria, Antioch, and Jerusalem. The title has since been extended to bishops of other important churches as well.

patriarchal sees—the "head or leading seats" of early Christianity, originally five in number (see *patriarch*); the word "see" comes via the Latin word *sedes* for "chair," since the bishop's chair symbolized his authority to teach.

patristic—an adjective describing a period in Christian history, roughly the second century to the fifth or sixth century A.D. in the West, though the East traditionally extends it as far as the ninth century. The period is so named because the major writers of the time are known as the "fathers" (*patres* in Latin) of the church.

Paul—a first-century C.E. Jew who embraced belief in Jesus Christ after a visionary experience on the way to Damascus. He became a missionary for the Christian way, establishing churches throughout Asia Minor. Several of his letters are preserved in the New Testament.

Peace churches—descended from the Anabaptists ("re-baptizers") of the Radical Reformation, these churches practice believer's Baptism and live a simple way of life intended to set them apart from the larger secular society. They include the Mennonites, Amish, Hutterites, and Church of the Brethren.

Pelagius—a Christian monk (mid-fourth to early fifth century A.D.) who introduced the "Pelagian" notion that original sin did not seriously damage the human capacity to do good, that human nature remained essentially good, and that human beings could lead holy lives, if they exerted sufficient effort; these notions were opposed by Augustine and eventually condemned as heretical by the Catholic Church.

penance—(1) actions that show repentance for sin (e.g., praying, fasting, giving alms, or making a pilgrimage); (2) the sacrament of forgiveness of sin, which consists of the penitent's acts of repentance, confession of sin, the intention to make reparation, and the priest's absolution of sin.

penitent—a person who is denied Communion because of serious sin such as murder, adultery, or apostasy, and who is doing penance (a penalty) for that sin.

Pentateuch—the first five books of the Hebrew Bible or Old Testament, also known as the Torah or the Law: Genesis, Exodus, Leviticus, Numbers, and Deuteronomy.

Pentecost—(1) a Jewish harvest festival that came to mark the 50 days separating the Israelites' escape from Egypt and God's gift of the Law on Mt. Sinai; (2) a Christian feast celebrated 50 days after Easter, commemorating the day in which the Holy Spirit came down upon Jesus' disciples when they were in hiding after his death and resurrection. According to the Acts of the Apostles, this happened during the Jewish feast of Pentecost; thus, the gift of the Spirit is intended to parallel and transcend the gift of the Law.

Pentecostalism—a family of Protestant churches whose members demonstrate their Christian faith through the gifts of the Holy Spirit, in particular, healing, wisdom to discern spirits, prophecy, and speaking in tongues (*glossolalia*). It includes the Assemblies of God, the Church of God, the Pentecostal Holiness Church, the Apostolic Faith Church, the Church of God in Christ, and the Full Gospel Fellowship. See also *Charismatic Movement; Neo-Pentecostalism.*

People of the Land—in ancient Judaism, the poor and uneducated peasant farmers who comprised the majority of the Jewish population.

Pericope—used primarily to designate a section of the biblical text that is being read or interpreted

Peter the Venerable (d. A.D. 1156)—Abbot of the Benedictine monastery of Cluny (in France) who commissioned the first Latin translation of the Qur'an and reflected theologically on Islam.

Pharisees—Jewish religious leaders and scholars of the Torah (second century B.C.E through the first century C.E.) who were experts on the written Law and its interpretation.

Philistines—enemies of ancient Israel, who used their monopoly on iron weapons to defeat the Israelites prior to the reign of King David.

philosophical theology—a form of reflection on God that primarily uses reason rather than other sources for Christian theology, such as scripture.

pietà—artistic representations of Mary holding the dead body of her son Jesus after he had been taken down from the cross. These were especially popular in the late medieval period.

Pietists/Pietism—a family of Protestant churches that were established out of a Bible-centered revivalism and a desire to fight against religious indifference by focusing on sharing the experience of God in their lives. It includes the Methodists, Scandinavian evangelical churches, and Moravian Christians.

pilgrimage—a journey undertaken for religious reasons, usually to a sacred site such as Jerusalem or the tomb of a saint. Christians undertake pilgrimages for penance, out of devotion to God and the saints, and for the love of travel.

Pilgrims—the English Puritan settlers who arrived on the Mayflower in A.D. 1620 to establish the Massachusetts Bay colony. The name "pilgrim" (a reference to Hebrews 11:13–14) was given to these founders a decade later and was formally adopted in 1798.

Pius XII (r. A.D. 1939–1958)—head of the Roman Catholic Church during World War II and the first decade of the Cold War, he wrote several encyclicals for which he is well known, including *Mystici Corporis Christi* (The Mystical Body of Christ) and *Divino Afflante Spiritu*, which opened the way for Catholic scholars to use modern biblical critical methods in the study of scripture.

pluralism—the view that different religions are of equal value and that they all offer paths to God. Also the presence of different religious or cultural groups within a single society.

polyglot Bible—a single Bible in which the text was presented in several languages. Polyglot Bibles were especially popular in the sixteenth and seventeenth centuries A.D.

polytheism/polytheistic—belief in many gods.

pope—the bishop of the church in Rome and the head of the Roman Catholic Church.

Populorum progressio—"The Development of Peoples," encyclical of Pope Paul VI issued in 1967, it expresses concern for the disadvantaged and seeks to guide and inspire liberation theology.

positive theological language—or affirmative theological language, language that declares something true or definitive about God, in contrast to negative theological language.

Post-Liberal theology—a contemporary movement in Christian theology that relinquishes the liberal project of attempting to make Christianity palatable to modern persons by revising it in accord with modern ideas. Post-Liberal theology focuses on the internal meanings generated within Christian communities rather than submitting Christian claims to external criteria concerning their credibility.

postmillennialism—the eschatological (end-time) doctrine that Christ's second coming would not take place until after the gospel had been preached to the whole world and human history was fully developed and ready for his return; in this view the promised millennial (thousand year) reign of Christ (see Revelation 20:1–10) tends to be interpreted symbolically and optimistically as the progressive improvement of the world or the universal spread of the church.

post-modernism—a cultural and intellectual movement that emerged out of modernism and therefore builds upon or provides a corrective to modernism. Whereas modernism is characterized by reliance on reason and scientific methodology as the measure of human progress, post-modernism calls attention to the limits of reason and offers a critique of the assumption that scientific methodology and reason, by themselves, can produce certitude.

post-secularism—the view that secularism has reached an end in certain respects, and that religion will endure as a feature of contemporary societies.

practical theology—an examination of the relationships between abstract theological concepts and particular concrete situations encountered by individuals and communities of faith through a process of theological reflection.

praxis—reflective action; in other words, to simultaneously reflect upon one's course of action while consciously acting upon one's reflections. The concept is prominent among liberation theologians, who use it to summarize their methodology and argue that Christian faith should never remain abstract, but must express itself in ethical action in solidarity with the poor and oppressed. See also *hermeneutical circle*.

predestination—the idea that God has decided in advance that certain events will come to pass (e.g., God has chosen some people to be saved).

predestination, double—see *double predestination*.

preferential option for the poor—the principle that church and society should always prioritize the needs of the poor and vulnerable in their actions, programs, and policies. Advocated by liberation theologians, the principle became prominent when Catholic bishops endorsed it in Medellín, Colombia in 1968, and has since found a prominent place in Catholic social teaching worldwide.

premillennialism—the eschatological (end-time) doctrine that Christ's return would happen *before* the millennial (thousand year) reign of Christ promised in Revelation 20:1–10 would take place. Premillenial eschatology tends to be pessimistic about the state of the world and of the church. Allied with *dispensationalist* biblical interpretation, it has been a powerful force in modern fundamentalism.

priesthood of the laity—a position advocated by many Protestant Reformers, and especially by Radical Reformers, insisting that every baptized Christian, not only those ordained by the church, is a minister of the gospel.

Priestly tradition (Priestly writer)—according to the Documentary Hypothesis, the latest of the four sources that were combined to form the Pentateuch, written around the fifth century B.C.E. or later.

priests—(1) in ancient Judaism, people who were specialists in conducting sacrifices; (2) in Christianity, ordained clergy, meaning a group set apart from the laity (the rest of the baptized community) by the ritual of the laying on of hands (ordination). Only Catholic, Orthodox, and Anglican forms of Christianity have priests (the word comes from Greek *presbyteros*, "elder") in the biblical sense of the word—someone whose duty is the offering of sacrifice—because Protestant Christianity generally rejected sacrificial understandings of the liturgy.

Promised Land—Because God's covenant with Abraham promises him land, some people refer to the land of Israel as the "Promised Land." While this phrase has fallen out of use because of its problematic nature in contemporary world politics, theological discourse still sometimes retains the phrase.

prophet—from a Greek word meaning "one who speaks in place of [someone else]." A spokesperson for God, chosen by God to reveal his will to people. Biblical prophecy arose in ancient Israel in response to the increasing power of the king. Prophets represented YHWH in the kings' counsel. Often they confronted and challenged the various kings.

prophetic theology—a theological methodology of hope articulated in South Africa in opposition to the official theology of the state, and enunciated above all in the Kairos Document, which involves critical social analysis especially of unjust social structures and biblical interpretation rooted in the prophetic stance against injustice.

Prophets, Former—see *Former Prophets*.

Prophets, Latter—see *Latter Prophets*.

Prosperity Doctrine—a controversial teaching often associated with Neo-Pentecostalism that equates God's blessing with material success and upward mobility. See *Neo-Pentecostalism*.

Protestant—a term used to describe members of the churches that trace their ultimate origin to the Reformation of the sixteenth century A.D. It derives from an incident in the early period of the Reformation in which six German princes protested a declaration of the Second Diet of Speyer (1529) designed to suppress Lutheranism.

Protestant Reformation—a term given to the sixteenth-century A.D. reform efforts initiated by Martin Luther, it eventually led to the separation between Roman Catholics and Protestants.

Pseudo-Dionysius the Areopagite—the pseudonym of an anonymous Syrian monk of the early sixth century A.D., who authored several important and influential theological works. He is perhaps most famous for his *via negativa* ("negative approach") in which all affirmations concerning God must be denied since the divine reality so far supersedes any word that can be said about it.

pseudonymity—the practice of writing a document with a false name attached to it. Pseudonymous writings were quite common in the ancient world, in part as a way of honoring famous people in a particular culture or religious tradition and in part as a way of increasing the authority of the document.

purgatory—a place or state following death in which sinners destined for heaven undergo the punishment still remaining for forgiven sins and thereby are "purged" or made ready for heaven.

Q—representing the German word *Quelle*, meaning "source." A hypothetical written document or documents, mostly containing parables and sayings of Jesus, used as a source for the Gospels of Matthew and Luke.

Quest for the Historical Jesus—an area of modern scholarly research that seeks to uncover what can be known about the actual historical person, Jesus of Nazareth, and to reconstruct his story based upon verifiable historical and scientific evidence.

Qur'an—the sacred writings of Islam. The Qur'an consists of the revelations that the angel Gabriel delivered to Muhammad from the one god *Allah* for the guidance of the followers.

rabbis—(1) in ancient Judaism, teachers (especially of the Torah); (2) in modern Judaism, the leader of a Jewish synagogue or a scholar qualified to interpret Jewish law.

Radical Pietism—a branch of Pietism whose members decided that reform of the church was only possible by separating from it and establishing their own communities.

Rahner, Karl (A.D. 1904–1984)—A Roman Catholic theologian and Jesuit priest, he authored numerous books and articles on topics of systematic theology. Although he believed that the fullness of grace was available only within Christianity, he argued that the Holy Spirit carries grace to all people in every time, including those in non-Christian religions.

rationalism—the belief that reason alone can provide us with a knowledge of all reality. It is opposed to the belief that there are some dimensions of reality (e.g., God) that are beyond reason and that can only be known through revelation.

recapitulation—a doctrine about redemption taught by Irenaeus of Lyons, who said that the redemption effected by Jesus Christ was a "doing over again" of all that had gone wrong in human history.

reception—a theological concept for the process by which an ecumenical council is gradually understood and incorporated into the actual life of the church; reception may take quite a long time but is crucial for understanding a council's real impact and weight.

redemption—having been bought back for God and thus ransomed from our sinfulness.

reductions—name given to the planned communities set up by Jesuits in Paraguay and nearby areas, to protect the indigenous peoples from Spanish and Portuguese enslavement and exploitation.

Reformation, Catholic—see *Catholic Reformation*.

Reformation, Protestant—see *Protestant Reformation*.

Reformed Christianity—a form of Protestant Christianity associated with John Calvin and Ulrich Zwingli, Reformed Christianity began in modern-day Switzerland but quickly spread to other parts of Europe, including especially the Netherlands and Scotland. Reformed Christianity is distinct from Lutheran Christianity in several ways.

Reformed Epistemology—movement in contemporary philosophy and theology. Reformed Epistemology maintains that belief in God is warranted and reliably formed even though the existence of God cannot be proved without a doubt. Key exponents include Alvin Plantinga and William Alston.

relativism—the view that all theological positions are equally valid and that truth or moral goodness is not absolute but is relative to individuals' experiences.

relics—originally the bodily remains of martyrs or other saints; eventually extended to physical objects thought to have been in touch with the bodies of saints.

religion—a comprehensive world-view that involves belief in some god or power beyond human existence, together with actions or teachings that support that belief (ritual, stories, doctrine, organizational structure, and ethical conduct).

religious studies—an "umbrella" term that encompasses a variety of social-scientific and philosophical approaches to questions concerning humanity's engagement with religion and religious phenomena.

religious-studies approach—an approach to examining religious topics that does so as an outsider, using social-scientific tools to examine religious systems of belief and practice. Contrasts with a "confessional approach."

Renaissance—meaning "rebirth," a cultural movement that began in Italy approximately A.D. 1350 and spread to other European countries by the time it came to a close in 1600. It involved a renewed interest in the Latin and Greek classics, a focus on the individual person and the natural world, and a more scientific approach to history and literature. It was accompanied by a burst of creative activity in art and architecture.

repentance—a change of thinking with regard to one's past behavior, characterized by genuine remorse, acknowledgment of wrongdoing, a commitment to behave differently in the future, and an attempt to set things right with those one has wronged.

ressourcement—meaning "going back to the origin," a French term that was used to describe a common desire of several theological renewal movements of the late nineteenth and early twentieth centuries to rejuvenate theology by recovering older sources in scripture and tradition.

restorationism—the idea that the way to reform and renew Christianity was to "restore" the church to the original structures, beliefs, and practices that prevailed during the time of Jesus and the apostles. The Radical Reformers of the sixteenth century held this belief. In early nineteenth-century America, the Second Great Awakening (religious revival) inspired new restorationist churches that called themselves simply "the Christian Church" and also the "Disciples of Christ."

restorative justice—often defined in opposition to retributive forms of justice, an approach to criminal justice that attempts to rehabilitate perpetrators by reaching a restitution or reconciliatory agreement that is agreeable to both victims and offenders as a means of restoring broken relationships between persons and within communities.

revelation—(1) God's act of disclosing God's self to believers; (2) that which has been revealed by God through nature and human conscience, but also through the Bible, mystical experience, and worship, about God and God's relationship to creation.

revival—a religious meeting designed to awaken in people an awareness of their sin and their need for forgiveness. Revival meetings were part of the Great Awakening, an eighteenth-century A.D. spiritual renewal movement in the English colonies.

revivalism—an American Christian movement sometimes described as born-again Christianity, which is based on the experience of a personal conversion to Jesus Christ as one's Lord and savior.

Ricci, Matteo (A.D. 1552–1610)—an Italian Jesuit known for his successful missionary work in China, especially his efforts to make Catholic Christianity intelligible in Chinese cultural terms.

righteousness, passive or alien—see *passive or alien righteousness*.

Rites controversy—sometimes called the "Chinese rites" controversy because it involved adaptations made by Jesuit missionaries in China to certain Confucian rituals. The issue turned on whether the rituals were seen as truly religious or merely civil. After over a century of debate, the papacy finally condemned the rituals in 1742, effectively ending Catholic missionary work in China. The decision was effectively overturned two centuries later by Pope Pius XII.

Ritschl, Albrecht (A.D. 1822–1889)—Liberal Protestant German theologian influenced by Friedrich Schleiermacher, but who found Schleiermacher too individualistic and not sufficiently historical. Ritschl emphasized the need for historical investigation of the Christian tradition, and the communal dimension of its teachings, especially concerning reconciliation and forgiveness.

Romanesque architecture—the style of buildings developed during the Carolingian and Ottonian dynasties of early medieval Europe. The structures featured stone vaulted ceilings, heavy walls and piers, and small openings for light, creating a fortress-like impression.

Roman Rite—the primary form of liturgy for the Roman Catholic Church, which was standardized by Charlemagne in the second half of the eighth century. Some of its prayers are thought to have been composed by Pope Gregory I.

Romero, Óscar (1917–1980)—archbishop of El Salvador, in Central America, from 1977 until his assignation by a right-wing paramilitary "death squad" associated with the U.S.-backed military government on May 24, 1980. Though once known for his conservative Catholic theology, his outspoken denunciation of repression and injustice turned him into a well-known prophet of liberation theology. He was beatified in May 2015.

Sabbath—From the Hebrew verb meaning "to rest." The weekly observance of rest is the only ritual obligation mentioned in the Ten Commandments. In Exodus, the day commemorates God's rest on the seventh day of creation, while in Deuteronomy it reminds the Israelites that God had delivered them from slavery, when they could not rest. It begins at sundown on Friday evening, and ends at sundown on Saturday.

Sacra doctrina—"sacred doctrine" or "holy teaching," Thomas Aquinas' term for what is today called "theology," but whose meaning also includes scripture, the writings of the Church Fathers, and authoritative Church pronouncements.

sacrament—a symbolic ritual consisting of words and visible gestures or material substances (bread, wine, water, oil, etc.) which, when properly performed for a recipient disposed to its action, becomes the means of transmitting the grace of God. Traditionally, it has been defined as an outward sign instituted by Christ to give grace. Christians do not agree on the number, the precise meaning, or the effectiveness of the sacraments.

sacramentals—a term used to describe certain religious practices and objects that are similar to sacraments in that they have tangible qualities (water, oil, rosary, etc.), but differ from sacraments in that they are not publicly celebrated and are not considered to be instituted by Christ.

sacramental theology—the study of Christian worship; also called liturgical theology.

sacramentary—a book containing the prayers needed by a priest to celebrate the Eucharist and (sometimes) other sacraments.

sacrifice—referring to the practice of offering gifts (animals, grains, etc.) to God or the gods as a way to make a request of the deity or to give thanks for favors received.

sacrificial atonement—making up for one's sins with a sacrificial offering; in Christianity, the doctrine that our sins are forgiven through the death of Jesus Christ on the cross.

Sacrosanctum concilium—the first of Vatican II's four constitutions, dealing with the reform of the Catholic liturgy; it sought to restore the Eucharistic liturgy to the center of the church's common life.

Sadducees—members of the Jewish aristocracy, consisting mostly of the priests who ran the Jerusalem Temple (second century B.C.E. through first century C.E.)

salaf—the Companions of the Prophet Muhammad. Certain modern fundamentalist Muslims are called "*salafi*s," since they consider themselves to be carefully imitating these Companions.

salah—The second pillar of Islam, "prayer," which obliges Muslims to perform a series of ritual actions five times in each 24-hour period, namely, at dawn, noon, afternoon, sunset, and nightfall.

salvation—a theological term referring to the process of being saved or rescued from harm.

salvation history—The story that Christians trace through the Bible of God's plan to save or rescue all people from sin, and to heal humans' relationship with God, with other people, and with the world.

Samaritans—Israelites who were left behind in the Northern Kingdom, when Israel was taken over by the Assyrians in the eighth century B.C.E.

Samuel—an Israelite prophet and last of the judges, he appointed Saul as king of Israel (r. 1020–1000 B.C.E.).

sanctification—the idea of someone or something being made holy for God.

sanctuary—the principle that all who take refuge from civil authority in a church or on church land cannot be removed without the permission of the abbot or bishop; a holy place within a church or temple.

Sanhedrin—a Hebrew adaptation of Greek *synedrion*, meaning "council" or "court"; in the Roman period, the body in Jerusalem, composed of chief priests and non-priests, that oversaw judicial and legal matters and was the political link with the Roman governor.

Saracens—A term of uncertain origin used by Europeans in the medieval period and afterwards to refer to Muslims.

satisfaction, vicarious—see *vicarious satisfaction*.

satisfaction, works of—see *works of satisfaction*.

Saul (r. 1020–1000 B.C.E.)—the first king of Israel who was replaced by David when God found him unworthy to be king.

sawm—the third pillar of Islam, "fasting," which requires Muslims who are healthy and of age to abstain from all food and drink from sunrise to sunset during the holy month of Ramadan.

Schleiermacher, Friedrich (A.D. 1768–1834)— Liberal Protestant German theologian often called the "father of modern theology." Schleiermacher is known for reformulating Christian theology dramatically, using experience as his guide for doing so.

Scholasticism—medieval theology that took the truths uncovered by philosophers like Aristotle and showed how they were compatible with Christianity. In general, Scholastic theology, so-called because of its setting in medieval schools and the new universities, tried to harmonize faith with reason.

scientism—the claim that the only valid method of knowing is science, and that what cannot be known by science does not exist.

scribes—(1) in ancient Judaism, the class of people who could read and write and who made their living from these skills. They are portrayed in the Gospels as enemies of Jesus and associates of the Pharisees; (2) in the ancient and medieval world, people whose occupation involved the copying of manuscripts.

scriptures—sacred writings or texts.

Second Isaiah—a sixth-century B.C.E. prophet and the author of Chapters 40–55 of the book of Isaiah, who foretold the Jews' return from exile.

Second Temple—the Temple in Jerusalem that was built following the destruction of Solomon's Temple by the Babylonians; destroyed by the Romans in 70 C.E.

Second Vatican Council (A.D. 1962–1965)—a gathering of Catholic bishops, abbots, and theological experts called by Pope John XXIII to renew the religious life of the church and to bring it into the modern world.

secularism—from Latin *saeculum,* meaning "world" or "age"; the belief that religion has no place in the public or political realm; sometimes criticized as "the religion of no religion at all," though its defenders argue that a neutral public space is the only alternative to some form of religious preference or establishment.

secularization thesis—twentieth-century theory that holds that the world is becoming increasingly secular, and that religion will eventually disappear as the world becomes more and more modern. The secularization thesis was abandoned by some of its foremost advocates in the late twentieth century, most notably Peter Berger.

seminary—a school of theology especially designed for the training of priests. The Council of Trent (A.D. 1545–1563) ordered that every Roman Catholic diocese establish a seminary for the training of its priest candidates. Many dioceses still retain their own seminaries today.

separationism, strict—see *strict separationism.*

Sephardim—the term given to Spanish and Portuguese Jewish immigrants to the Americas.

Septuagint—a Greek version of the Hebrew scriptures, created in the centuries before Christ by Greek-speaking Jews, but differing from the Hebrew Bible in the order of the books and in its inclusion of the Apocrypha or deuterocanonical books; appropriated by Greek-speaking Christian Jews, it became the dominant version of the Christian Bible for hundreds of years, and remains so for Orthodox Christians.

Seventh-Day Adventists—an American church that emerged out of the millennial expectation that accompanied the second Great Awakening, a spiritual renewal that spread across the United States and its territories toward the beginning of the nineteenth century A.D. They observe Saturday as the proper day for worship and view a literal reading of the Bible as the only rule of faith.

shahada—the first pillar of Islam, the profession of faith: "There is no god but God and Muhammad is the Prophet of God."

Shari'a—the Islamic law code that is based upon the Qur'an and the *sunna,* or way of the prophet, together with human reason and community consensus.

Sharpeville Massacre—an incident in which more than 5,000 people gathered at a police station in Sharpeville, Transvaal, on March 21, 1960, for protesting pass laws; police opened fire on the crowd. Official records indicate that 69 South Africans were shot and killed by the police though some place the death count much higher.

Shenoute of Atripe (*c.*348–*c.*464)—Abbot of the White Monastery in Egypt, his influence went far beyond the monastic enclosure.

Shi'a—meaning "partisans of 'Ali," Muhammad's cousin and son-in-law. This Muslim group arose soon after the death of Muhammad, as a consequence of a dispute over how the position of caliph (Muslim ruler) ought to be filled. Today, it continues to be a minority group within Islam as a whole, but the dominant form of Islam in Iran since the sixteenth century.

shofet—the Hebrew term for a judge, a military, and political leader who was chosen by God to rescue the Israelites from oppression brought about by their sin.

simony—the buying and selling of spiritual things, including church leadership positions.

sin, mortal—see *mortal sin.*

sin, structural—see *structural evil, structural sin.*

Social Gospel—the solution of the White Anglo-Saxon Protestant society (WASP) to social problems of the late nineteenth and early twentieth century A.D. Inspired by the writings of Walter Rauschenbush (1861–1918), the Social Gospel movement said that the church should be seen as the vehicle for spreading God's kingdom on earth and therefore should be primarily concerned about social justice. They hoped to "Christianize" the United States by changing the social structure of the nation.

Society of Jesus—also known as the Jesuits, this religious order was founded by Ignatius of Loyola in A.D. 1540. Dedicated to the service of the pope, they played an important role in the Catholic Reformation both as missionaries and teachers. Today, they are the largest Catholic religious order, with a large and respected system of high schools, colleges, and universities.

Solomon (r. 961–922 B.C.E.)—successor to his father David as king of Israel, known for his wisdom, excessive wealth, and the building of the Temple in Jerusalem.

soteriology—the study of, or teachings about salvation. Christian soteriology is primarily concerned with the saving work of Jesus Christ.

Sovereignty of God—God's supreme power and authority, particularly the ability to rule and govern all of creation.

speaking in tongues—see *glossolalia.*

Spener, Philipp Jakob (1635–1705)—German Luther pastor considered the founder of churchly Pietism.

Spiritual Exercises—developed by Ignatius of Loyola, this month-long spiritual examination allows the individual to participate in the drama of sin and salvation, leading to a turning over of everything, especially the will, to obedience to one's religious superior, to the teachings of the church and its traditions, for the spread of the faith.

spirituality—describes various forms of prayer and religious practice that orient persons toward God (or the divine) and that direct the way they live in the world.

strict separationism—the view that the First Amendment of the U.S. Constitution erects "a wall of separation between church and state" and requires total religious neutrality on the part of the state.

structural evil; structural sin—the notion that sin and evil become embedded into institutions, cultures, and norms in a way that has unjust and dehumanizing consequences independent of the weakness or willful intention of individuals.

studia humanitatis—important Latin phrase from Cicero's oration *Pro Archia* meaning "humane studies" or liberal arts, including Latin and Greek literature, history, rhetoric, and ethics. In studying these subjects, students learned to read, write, reason, and speak well—skills that were especially necessary for civic leaders and scholars.

Suffering Servant—a figure in the book of Isaiah who suffers on behalf of the whole people and wins forgiveness for their sins (see Isaiah 52:13–53:12).

Sufism—a movement within Islam that stresses the way of the heart. It originated in the late ninth and early tenth centuries as a reaction against the legalism and intellectual rationalism of Shari'a.

sultan—meaning "holder of power," the Turkish tribe known as the *Seljuks* used this title for their leaders.

Summa contra gentiles—the "Summary against the Gentiles," fully titled *Book on the Truth of the Catholic Faith Against the Errors of Unbelievers,* one of Thomas Aquinas' major writings, likely intended for missionaries planning to engage Jews, Muslims, and other non-Christians.

Summa theologiae—the "Summary of Theology," Thomas Aquinas' most famous and comprehensive work, probably intended for the training of young Dominicans in preaching and hearing confessions.

sunna—the "way of the prophet"; sayings of the Prophet Muhammad and reports of his deeds, as recorded in the *hadith.*

Sunnis—meaning "those who followed the example or custom of Muhammad." In the dispute concerning who was qualified to assume the position of leader of the Muslim community, this group argued that it should be someone who best exemplified Muhammad's thought and way of life, rather than someone who was related to

Muhammad by blood. Today, it is the main body of the Islamic faith, comprising approximately 85 percent of Muslims worldwide.

sura—an individual chapter of the Qur'an.

Syllabus of Errors—a document issued by Pope Pius IX in 1864 consisting of 80 condemned propositions concerning topics like freedom of religion, separation of church and state, and the temporal power of the pope. It provided an overture for the First Vatican Council.

Symeon the New Theologian (A.D. 942–1022)—an Eastern Christian mystic and theologian, representative of the spirituality and theology of the early medieval period.

synagogue—a Jewish place of worship where the Torah is read and interpreted.

syncretism—the fusion of formerly distinct religions or world-views. While cultural anthropologists and other social scientists use the term as a value-neutral descriptor, Christian theological discourse tends to use the term negatively to describe the merging of Christianity with some other religious world-view in a way that threatens to undermine the essence of the Christian faith, in contrast to a more positive process of inculturation. See *inculturation*.

synoptic—literally "seeing together." The term is usually used with reference to the Gospels of Matthew, Mark, and Luke, which tell the same general story of the life and teaching of Jesus.

synoptic problem—the question concerning the literary relationship among the Gospels of Matthew, Mark, and Luke, which are so similar that it is almost universally believed that one or more of their authors used another gospel as a source.

systematic theology—a study of the basic formulations of Christian belief (called "dogmas" or "doctrines") and their relationship to one another.

Tanakh—an acronym for Torah (Law), Nevi'im (Prophets), and Khetubim (Writings); a term used to refer to the Jewish scriptures.

temple—(1) any building dedicated to the worship of a god or gods, at which sacrifices are usually performed; (2) the building in Jerusalem in which Israelites performed sacrifices and where God was said to dwell; first built by Solomon in the tenth century B.C.E., destroyed by the Babylonians in 587 B.C.E., rebuilt later in the sixth century B.C.E. after the return from the Exile, refurbished by King Herod in the first century B.C.E., and then destroyed by the Romans in 70 C.E.

Teresa of Avila (A.D. 1515–1582)—a Spanish mystic and founder of the Discalced Carmelites. Her writings include the *Life*, an autobiographical account of her life, and the *Interior Castle*, a description of her method of prayer.

tertiary—referring to a layperson who follows an adapted rule of a founder of a monastery or a friar movement and the ideals or charisms of that group, but does so outside of the convent or monastery. Examples include the third order Dominicans and the third order Franciscans.

testament—a synonym for covenant, this term is applied by Christians to the two major collections of books of the Bible.

theocentric—God-centered.

theocracy—literally "the rule of God," a system of government which has as its world-view a common set of beliefs about God and God's relationship with their community, whose civil laws are governed by its religious agenda, and in which religious authorities have the ultimate power to govern.

Theodosius I (r. A.D. 379–395)—emperor of Rome who established Christianity as the sole legal religion in the Roman Empire and who affirmed the Nicene Creed as the benchmark of orthodox Christian faith.

theo-ideology—the combination of appeals to divine revelation and natural law theory to justify an ideology of racial discrimination.

theology—an intellectual discipline that explores (religious) reality from a particular perspective, namely, God as ultimate ground and goal of all reality; in the words of Anselm, it is "faith seeking understanding."

Thomism—a school of thought in philosophy or theology dependent largely on or inspired directly by Thomas Aquinas.

Theotokos—Greek for "one who gives birth to God"; applied to Mary in the Eastern Orthodox tradition and the equivalent of "Mother of God" in the West.

three-self principle—posited by missionary strategists in the Protestant mission movement in late 1800s, this principle sets the goal that new churches should become "self-governing," "self-supporting," and "self-propagating" (or "self-extending") as quickly as possible. Protestant churches that are officially registered with the Chinese communist government are called Three-Self Patriotic churches, but the three-self principle has an older and wider application that should not be assumed to justify nationalistic cooperation with authoritarian governments.

Tillich, Paul (A.D. 1886–1965)—modern German theologian who integrated existentialist ideas into his theology. Tillich is known for his method of correlation, which sought to correlate the Christian message to contemporary persons so as to make it relevant.

Torah—Hebrew term for the first five books of the Old Testament or the Pentateuch. The word itself, although often translated as "law" actually means "teaching" and captures the Jewish sense that the Law provides guidance for their lives.

tradition—the accumulated wisdom of the church and its leaders, whereby the faith derived from the scriptures, contained in the creeds, and expressed in the liturgy is interpreted for contemporary believers.

tradition, apostolic—see *apostolic tradition.*

transubstantiation—a teaching about how the bread and wine of the Eucharist become the body and blood of Jesus Christ: after consecration (blessing) by a validly ordained priest, the accidents (physical appearance) remain as bread and wine, but the substance (or essence) changes and becomes the body and blood of Jesus Christ.

treasury of merit—in the late medieval period, a treasury of surplus good works of the saints and of Christ. The pope could draw from this treasury and transfer excess merits to a repentant sinner in the form of an indulgence.

Trent, Council of—see *Council of Trent.*

Trinity—a theological term used to describe the relationship of the three "persons" of Father, Son, and Holy Spirit in one Godhead; as defined at the fourth-century ecumenical councils of Nicaea and Constantinople, the dogma of the Trinity affirms that the three persons are co-eternal and share equally in the same divine nature.

Troeltsch, Ernst (A.D. 1865–1923)—German modern historian who held that historical inquiry should be conducted according to the principle of analogy, which holds that the past is analogous to the present, and that present experience can therefore serve as a guide for determining which reports about past events are credible, and which are not credible.

Tutu, Desmond (A.D. 1931–)—a South African cleric and Anglican theologian who served as General Secretary of the South African Council of Churches from 1978 until 1985, when he became the Bishop of Johannesburg and then Archbishop in 1986. He is known for his activism for human rights and against apartheid.

Two-Source Hypothesis—a theory that explains the literary relationship among the synoptic gospels by suggesting that the writers of the Gospels of Matthew and Luke used the Gospel of Mark and a hypothetical source Q (a written document or documents mostly containing parables and sayings of Jesus) as sources for their Gospels.

Tyndale, William (*c.*A.D. 1494–1536)—an admirer of Martin Luther, he was the first to publish an English translation of major parts of the Bible.

ubuntu—a humanist philosophy rooted in the idea that "a person is a person through other people," and the idea that "I am because you are" that was popularized in South Africa under the leadership of Nelson Mandela and Desmond Tutu.

Ugandan martyrs—group of 45 Catholic and Anglican Christians killed between 1885 and 1887 in present-day Uganda, among them Charles Lwang.

ulama—"those who are learned," referring to the Sunni class of religious and legal scholars trained in the great mosque-colleges or madrasas.

ultimate concern—concept associated with modern German theologian Paul Tillich that views faith in God as the issue about which one is most fundamentally concerned in one's life.

ultramontanism—a nineteenth-century tendency to exalt the authority of the papacy "beyond the mountains," referring to Rome's location south of the Alps.

ummah—an Arabic term referring to the community of Muslims; the Islamic community.

university—originally the "guild" or association of teachers and students united in the "craft" of teaching and learning. By the thirteenth century, universities began to develop into institutions of higher learning with permanent faculties that offered basic degrees in the "arts" and more advanced degrees in theology, civil and canon law, and medicine.

univocation—the use of a single term or phrase in the same way in more than one context, as opposed to equivocation.

vernacular—language of the common people.

Verwoerd, Hendrik (A.D. 1901–1966)—a South African politician who is infamously known as "the architect of apartheid"; he was prime minister from 1958 until his assassination in 1966.

vicarious satisfaction—the possibility that someone could pay the debt of another person's sin.

voluntary discipleship—becoming a Christian or a follower of Christ requires an active decision of faith. Radical Reformers insisted that discipleship must be *freely* chosen by the individual as a response to God's grace and call.

Vulgate—a Latin translation of the Bible, containing also the books of the Apocrypha, widely used in the West at least from the sixth century A.D. and declared by the Council of Trent to be the only authoritative translation of the Bible.

Waldensians—named for their founder Valdes, these twelfth-century A.D. "Poor Men of Lyons" sought to return to the apostolic life of the early church. Their hostility toward the clergy (because of clerical abuses) eventually led to their condemnation by the Council of Verona in 1184.

WARC Declaration—the World Alliance of Reformed Churches (WARC) met in Ottawa, Canada, in 1982, adopting a declaration that proclaimed apartheid in South Africa to be a theological heresy.

Wesley, John (A.D. 1703–1791)—an English theologian and reformer, Wesley was originally a member of the Church of England. He and his followers eventually broke away to form the Methodist Church.

Whitefield, George (A.D. 1714–1770)—a Methodist minister who was one of the more famous revival preachers of the Great Awakening, an eighteenth-century spiritual renewal movement in the English colonies.

Wittgenstein, Ludwig (A.D. 1889–1951)—modern philosopher known for his idea of "language games," according to which words only have meaning within a game of sorts that determines the possibilities for their use.

Womanist Theology—arguably the most important theological development that has emerged in the wake of the earliest advocates of Black Theology. Drawing on the past and present of black women's intellectual thought and activism, it seeks to combine a theological analysis race, gender, and class that account for the particularities of the lived experiences of black women.

works of mercy—inspired in part by Jesus' anticipation of a day of judgment on which people and nations will be sorted into "sheep" and "goats" based on their treatment of the poor and needy. The Catholic Church has traditionally recognized two lists of seven. The "spiritual" works of mercy are to instruct the ignorant, counsel the doubtful, admonish the sinners, bear patiently those who wrong us, forgive offenses, comfort the afflicted, and pray for the living and the dead. The "corporal" or bodily works of mercy are to feed the hungry, give water to the thirsty, clothe the naked, shelter the homeless, visit the sick, visit the imprisoned or ransom the captive, and bury the dead.

works of satisfaction—prayers, fasting, pilgrimages, or works of piety assigned to a person in the sacrament of penance to remove the penalties or consequences of sin.

Wycliffe, John (A.D. 1330–1384)—a reformer of the late medieval period. He preached against abuses in the church and challenged some of the church's doctrines. He also advocated the translation of the Bible into English, the language of the people.

Yahwist—according to the Documentary Hypothesis, the earliest of the four sources that make up the Pentateuch; it dates to the ninth century B.C.E.

YHWH (Yahweh)—the name for God that is most commonly used in the Hebrew Bible/Old Testament (Exodus 3:14). It is derived from the verb meaning "to be," and depending on how it is vocalized, means either "the one who is" or "the one who creates." Traditionally, never pronounced except by the high priest on Yom Kippur, the Day of Atonement. "Adonai" (Lord) is used as a euphemistic substitute.

Yom Kippur—the "Day of Atonement," a Jewish holiday in which people reflect upon their sins. In ancient Judaism, this was the only day of the year in which the high priest would enter the Holy of Holies to offer a sacrifice.

zakat—the fourth pillar of Islam, almsgiving, which obliges Muslims to give of their wealth, whether it be great or small, to sustain those in need

Zealots—a Jewish group of the first century C.E., who advocated the violent overthrow of the Romans and were major players in the disastrous revolt of 66–70 C.E.

Zinzendorf, Nikolaus Ludwig von (A.D. 1700–1760)—German Pietist and leader of the Moravian church.

Zwingli, Ulrich (A.D. 1484–1531)—Swiss reformer and theologian, known especially for his emphasis on justification by grace alone, his "spiritual" understanding of the Eucharist, his exclusive reliance on the Bible rather than church traditions and proclamations, and his opposition to priestly celibacy and the use of images in worship. Zwingli was killed defending Zurich, the city he led through the Reformation, against attack by Catholics.

Index

Page numbers in *italics* denote figures.